To Agnes, Grace, and James

Brief Contents

GLOBAL BUSINESS

Fourth Edition

Mike W. Peng, Ph.D.

Jindal Chair of Global Business Strategy

University of Texas at Dallas

Fellow, Academy of International Business (2012)

Decade Award Winner, *Journal of International Business Studies* (2015)

The Only International Business Textbook Author Listed in

The World's Most Influential Scientific Minds (2015)

Australia • Brazil • Canada • Mexico • Singapore • United Kingdom • United States

Global Business, Fourth Edition
Mike W. Peng

Vice President, General Manager, Social Science & Qualitative Business: Erin Joyner

Product Director: Jason Fremder

Senior Product Manager: Mike Roche

Content Developer: John Sarantakis

Product Assistant: Jamie Mack

Marketing Director: Kristen Hurd

Marketing Manager: Emily Horowitz

Marketing Coordinator: Christopher Walz

Senior Content Project Manager: Kim Kusnerak

Manufacturing Planner: Ron Montgomery

Production Service: MPS Limited

Senior Art Director: Linda May

Cover/Internal Designer: Tippy McIntosh

Cover Image: Matvienko Vladimir/ShutterStock.com

Intellectual Property

    Analyst: Diane Garrity

    Project Manager: Sarah Shainwald

© 2017, 2014 Cengage Learning, Inc.

WCN: 01-100-101

ALL RIGHTS RESERVED. No part of this work covered by the copyright herein may be reproduced, transmitted, stored, or used in any form or by any means graphic, electronic, or mechanical, including but not limited to photocopying, recording, scanning, digitizing, taping, Web distribution, information networks, or information storage and retrieval systems, except as permitted under Section 107 or 108 of the 1976 United States Copyright Act, without the prior written permission of the publisher.

For product information and technology assistance, contact us at
Cengage Customer & Sales Support, 1-800-354-9706

For permission to use material from this text or product,
submit all requests online at **www.cengage.com/permissions**
Further permissions questions can be emailed to
permissionrequest@cengage.com

Unless otherwise noted all items © Cengage.

Library of Congress Control Number: 2015951129

ISBN: 978-1-305-50089-1

ISBN: 978-1-305-64246-1

Cengage
200 Pier 4 Boulevard
Boston, MA 02210
USA

Cengage is a leading provider of customized learning solutions with employees residing in nearly 40 different countries and sales in more than 125 countries around the world. Find your local representative at **www.cengage.com**.

To learn more about Cengage platforms and services, register or access your online learning solution, or purchase materials for your course, visit **www.cengage.com**.

Printed in the United States of America
6 7 8 9 10 11 25 24 23 22 21

Table of Contents

Preface

The first three editions of *Global Business* aspired to set a new standard for international business (IB) textbooks. They have been widely used in Australia, Austria, Brazil, Britain, Canada, China, Denmark, Egypt, France, Hong Kong, India, Indonesia, Ireland, Israel, Lithuania, Macau, Malaysia, Mexico, the Netherlands, Netherlands Antilles, New Zealand, Puerto Rico, Russia, Slovenia, South Africa, South Korea, Spain, Sweden, Switzerland, Taiwan, Thailand, and the United States. Based on the enthusiastic support from more than 30 countries, the first three editions achieved unprecedented success. Available in Chinese and Spanish, *Global Business* has also launched a European adaptation (with Klaus Meyer) and an Indian adaptation (with Deepak Srivastava). In short, *Global Business* is global.

The fourth edition endeavors to achieve even more. It continues the market-winning framework centered on one big question and two core perspectives, and has been thoroughly updated to capture the rapidly moving recent research and events. Written for undergraduate and MBA students around the world, the fourth edition will continue to make IB teaching and learning (1) more engaging, (2) more comprehensive, (3) more fun, and (4) more relevant.

More Engaging

As an innovation in IB textbooks, a unified framework integrates all chapters. Given the wide range of topics in IB, most textbooks present the discipline in a fashion that "Today is Tuesday, it must be Luxembourg." Very rarely do authors address: "*Why* Luxembourg today?" More important, why IB? What is the big question in IB? Our unified framework suggests that the discipline can be united by one big question and two core perspectives. The big question is: What determines the success and failure of firms around the globe? To address this question, *Global Business* introduces two core perspectives—(1) the institution-based view and (2) the resource-based view—in *all*

chapters.[1] It is this relentless focus on our big question and core perspectives that enables this book to engage a variety of topics in an integrated fashion. This provides unparalleled continuity in the learning process.

Global Business further engages readers through an *evidence-based* approach. I have endeavored to draw on the latest research, as opposed to the latest fads. As an active researcher myself, I have developed the unified framework not because it just popped up in my head when I wrote the book. Rather, this is an extension of my own research that consistently takes on the big question and leverages the two core perspectives.[2]

Another vehicle to engage students is debates. Most textbooks present knowledge "as is" and ignore debates. But, obviously, our field has no shortage of debates. It is the responsibility of textbook authors to engage students by introducing cutting-edge debates. Thus, I have written a beefy "Debates and Extensions" section for *every* chapter.

More Comprehensive

Global Business offers the most comprehensive and innovative coverage of IB topics available on the market. Unique chapters not found in other IB textbooks are: Chapter 9 (entrepreneurship and small firms' internationalization), Chapter 11 (global competitive dynamics), and Chapter 16 (corporate finance and governance).

The most comprehensive topical coverage is made possible by drawing on the latest and most comprehensive range of the research literature. I have accelerated my own

---

[1] On the integration of these two perspectives, see K. Meyer, S. Estrin, S. Bhaumik, & M. W. Peng, 2009, Institutions, resources, and entry strategies in emerging economies, *Strategic Management Journal*, 30(1): 61–80; D. Zoogah, M. W. Peng, & H. Woldu, 2015, Institutions, resources, and organizational effectiveness in Africa, *Academy of Management Perspectives*, 29(1): 7–31.

[2] For the big question, see M. W. Peng, 2004, Identifying the big question in international business research, *Journal of International Business Studies*, 35(2): 99–108. For the institution-based view, see M. W. Peng, D. Wang, and Y. Jiang, 2008, An institution-based view of international business strategy: A focus on emerging economies, *Journal of International Business Studies*, 39(5): 920–936. For the resource-based view, see M. W. Peng, 2001, The resource-based view and international business, *Journal of Management*, 27(6): 803–829.

research, publishing a total of 30 articles after I finished the third edition.[3] Some of these recent articles appear in top-tier outlets in IB, such as the *Academy of Management Journal* (2012), *Journal of International Business Studies* (2014 and 2016), *Journal of Management Studies* (2012, 2013, and 2015), *Journal of World Business* (2012, 2014, and 2015), and *Strategic Management Journal* (2013, 2015, and 2016). Writing *Global Business* has also enabled me to broaden the scope of my research, publishing recently in top-tier journals in operations (*Journal of Operations Management*), ethics (*Journal of Business Ethics*), entrepreneurship (*Journal of Business Venturing* and *Entrepreneurship Theory and Practice*), and human resources (*International Journal of Human Resource Management*). In addition to my own work, I have also drawn on the latest research of numerous colleagues. The end result is the unparalleled, most comprehensive set of evidence-based insights on the IB market. While citing every article is not possible, I am confident that I have left no major streams of research untouched. Feel free to check the Name Index to verify this claim. (Unfortunately, a number of older references have to be deleted to make room for more recent research.)

Finally, the fourth edition of *Global Business* continues to have a global set of cases contributed by scholars around the world—an innovation on the IB market. Virtually all other IB textbooks have cases written by book authors. In comparison, this book has been blessed by a global community of case contributors who are based in Australia, Austria, Canada, China, Mexico, and the United States. Many are experts who are located in or are from the countries in which the cases take place. For example, we now have a Mexico case penned by two Mexico-based authors (see Integrative Case on Farmacias Similares), and a China case written by a China-based author (see Integrative Case on Ostnor). This edition also features a Russia case contributed by the world's top two leading experts on Russian management (see Integrative Case on Wikimart).

More Fun

If you fear this book must be boring because it draws so heavily on latest research, you are wrong. I have used a clear, engaging, conversational style to tell the "story." Relative to rival books, my chapters are shorter and more lively. Some earlier users commented that reading *Global Business* is like reading a "good magazine." A large number of interesting anecdotes have been woven

into the text. Non-traditional ("outside-the-box") examples range from ancient Chinese military writings to mutually assured destruction (MAD) strategy during the Cold War, from LEGO toys to Tolstoy's *Anna Karenina*. Check out the following fun-filled features that spice up the book:

The rebirth of the East India Company (Chapter 1 Opening Case)

Testing the Dell theory of peace in East Asia (Emerging Markets 2.2)

LEGO's secrets (Chapter 4 Opening Case)

ANA: Refreshing the parts other airlines cannot reach (In Focus 4.1)

Why are US exports so competitive? (Chapter 5 Closing Case)

One multinational versus many national companies (In Focus 6.1)

Sriracha spices up American food (Chapter 9 Opening Case)

Mickey goes to Shanghai (Chapter 10 Closing Case)

Patent wars and shark attacks (Chapter 11 Opening Case)

Is a diamond (cartel) forever? (In Focus 11.1)

Can mergers of equals work? (In Focus 12.2)

Marketing Aflac in the United States and Japan (Chapter 14 Opening Case)

Dallas versus Delhi (Chapter 15 Closing Case)

High drama at Hewlett-Packard (HP) (Chapter 16 Opening Case)

Professor Michael Jensen as an outside director (In Focus 16.2)

Global warming and Arctic boom (In Focus 17.1)

Finally, the PengAtlas allows you to conduct IB research using informative maps and other geographic tools to enhance your learning. In addition, a series of new videos enhance the multi-media, fun aspects of learning (see below).

More Relevant

So what? Most textbooks leave students to figure out the crucial "so what?" question for themselves. In contrast, I conclude every chapter with an action-packed section titled "Management Savvy." Each section has at least one table (or slide) to summarize key learning points from a *practical* standpoint. No other IB book is so savvy and so relevant.

As a theme, ethics cuts through the book, with at least one "Ethical Dilemma" feature and a series of Critical

---

[3] All my articles are listed at www.mikepeng.com and www.utdallas.edu/~mikepeng. Go to "Journal Articles."

Discussion Questions on ethics in each chapter. Finally, many chapters offer *career* advice for students. For example, Chapter 4 develops a resource-based view of the individual—that is, about you, the student. The upshot? You want to make yourself into an "untouchable," someone who adds valuable, rare, and hard-to-imitate capabilities indispensable to an organization. In other words, you want to make sure your job cannot be outsourced.

What's New in the Fourth Edition?

In addition to the completely updated content, the fourth edition has (1) created a new video package, (2) dedicated more space to emerging economies, (3) enhanced the quantity and variety of cases, and (4) drawn directly on the author's consulting experience.

First, a new video package has been created that is tightly coupled with the content of the Opening and Closing Cases for *every* chapter. Instructors can ask students to watch such videos before class and answer questions online, or to watch videos as a way to open or close class sessions. In short, students can "watch TV" and gain knowledge.

Second, this edition builds on *Global Business'* previous strengths by more prominently highlighting emerging economies. At least one Emerging Markets feature is launched in every chapter. Many of the Integrative Cases deal with emerging economies, such as Brazil, China, Cuba, Mexico, Russia, Slovakia, Thailand, and Turkey. Numerous in-chapter features (Opening/Closing Cases, In Focus, and Emerging Markets) deal with emerging economies other than those mentioned previously, such as the Czech Republic, Greenland, Guinea, India, Kenya, Liberia, Nigeria, Poland, Senegal, Sierra Leone, South Africa, Taiwan, Tanzania, and the United Arab Emirates.

Third, in response to students' and instructors' enthusiasm about the wide-ranging and globally relevant cases in previous editions, the fourth edition has further enhanced the quantity and variety of cases. The variety has also been enhanced not only in terms of the geographic diversity noted above, but also in terms of the mix of longer cases and shorter cases. In addition, I have pushed myself to more actively participate in case writing. Finally, users of the online MindTap version of the product will have access to Media Cases that pair the Opening and Closing chapter cases with news articles from sources such as the *New York Times, The Economist,*

and other leading publications, as well as videos from sources such as the BBC and CBS and access to additional information from *Business Insights*. More information on the MindTap product is discussed later in this Preface.

Finally, I have directly drawn on my recent consulting experience to inject new insights. Chapter 1 Closing Case ("Two Scenarios of the Global Economy in 2050") is adapted from a major consulting engagement I completed for the UK Government Office for Science as part of its two-year Future of Manufacturing project. Integrative Case 2.2 ("Twelve Recommendations to Enhance UK Export Competitiveness") is a direct excerpt from the final report submitted (coauthored with Klaus Meyer). Table 3.4 ("Texas Instruments Guidelines on Gifts in China," which is in the public domain) is shared with me by a consulting client at TI. Overall, I am confident that students can directly benefit from such new insights gained from my consulting engagements with multinationals and governments.

MindTap

Online resources are transforming many aspects of everyday life and learning is not immune to the impact of technology. Rather than simply take the book pages of *Global Business* and place them on a screen to be accessed via a PC, tablet, or smartphone, we have reset the content and have adapted it to fully utilize the potential that the medium allows. Students can highlight passages, take notes in the MindTap content, and compile their notes for review in the EverNotes app. We have embedded assessments for each chapter as well as provide Flash Cards for all of the key terms that provide feedback to students and provide guidance so that they can address gaps in the course requirements. Faculty can use the results from the quizzes as well as using the Media Cases for assignments (see above) and utilize the assigned student work outside the classroom to benefit from a "flipped learning" approach that can result in more favorable outcomes and more rewarding experiences for students and faculty. Additional apps such as ConnectYard allow faculty to integrate social media capabilities into their course and are especially useful in online and hybrid course delivery.

As part of the MindTap product, we are not limited to the page length limitation of a physical book. Students certainly don't enjoy carrying 1,000-page volumes, and are also frustrated when material included in the book is not assigned by the instructor. Since we are not limited by length online, faculty will also have access to numerous additional cases that they can select and add to their course. We have also included additional homework assessments and unique pre- and postcourse Global Literacy assessments that can be used to demonstrate student awareness of global business knowledge. We want to thank Anne Magi of the University of Illinois at Chicago for her work on the homework and Global Literacy assessments.

Finally, users of MindTap will also have access to *Business Insights: Global* from Gale, which provides a rich online research tool.

Support Materials

A full set of support materials is available for students and adopting instructors:

- Product Support Website
- Instructor's Manual
- Test Bank
- PowerPoint Slides
- MindTap (see above)
- Peng DVD

Acknowledgments

As *Global Business* celebrates the launch of its fourth edition, I first want to thank all the customers—instructors and students around the world who have made the book's success possible. A special thank you goes to Klaus Meyer (China Europe International Business School, China) and Deepak Srivastava (Nirma University, India), who respectively spearheaded the adaptation of the European, Middle Eastern, and African (EMEA) edition and the Indian edition. In China, a big thanks goes to Liu Yi (Shanghai Jiao Tong University), Xie En and Wang Longwei (Xi'an Jiaotong University), and Yi Jingtao (Renmin University of China). In Mexico, my heart-felt appreciation goes to two groups of colleagues: (1) professional translators Ma. del Pilar Carril Villarreal and Magda Elizabeth Treviño Rosales and (2) faculty colleagues who engaged in some technical revisions Claudia P. Gutiérrez Rojas (Tecnológico de Monterrey, Campus Estado de México), Mercedes Muñoz (Tecnológico de Monterrey, Campus Santa Fe y Estado de México), and Enrique Benjamín Franklin Fincowski (Facultad de Contaduría y Administración, Universidad Nacional Autónoma de México). They loved the book so much that they were willing to endure the pain of translating it into Chinese and Spanish. My

kudos to these colleagues who have made *Global Business* more global.

At the Jindal School at UT Dallas, I appreciate Naveen Jindal's generous support to fund the Jindal Chair. I thank my colleagues Shawn Carraher, Larry Chasteen, Emily Choi, Tev Dalgic, Van Dam, Greg Dess, Dave Ford, Richard Harrison, Maria Hasenhuttl, Charlie Hazzard, Jeff Hicks, Shalonda Hill, Seung-Hyun Lee, Sheen Levin, John Lin, Ginny Lopez-Kidwell, Livia Markóczy, Toyah Miller, Joe Picken, Orlando Richard, Jane Salk, Rajiv Shah, Eric Tsang, Habte Woldu, and Jun Xia—as well as Hasan Pirkul (dean) and Varghese Jacob (associate dean). I also thank my PhD students (Sergey Lebedev, Canan Mutlu, and Cristina Vlas) for their assistance. One colleague (Charlie Hazzard), three PhD students (Pawinee Changphao, Sergey Lebedev, and Canan Mutlu), and an EMBA student (Nagaraj Savithri) contributed excellent case materials.

At Cengage Learning, I thank the "Peng team" that not only publishes *Global Business*, but also *Global Strategy*: Erin Joyner, Vice President, Social Sciences and Qualitative Business; Jason Fremder, Product Director; Mike Roche, Senior Product Manager; John Sarantakis, Content and Media Developer; Kristen Hurd, Marketing Director; Emily Horowitz, Marketing Manager; Chris Walz, Marketing Coordinator; Kim Kusnerak, Senior Content Production Manager.

In the academic community, I appreciate the meticulous and excellent comments from the reviewers and many colleagues and students who provided informal feedback to me on the book. It is especially gratifying to receive unsolicited correspondence from students. Space constraints force me to only acknowledge those who wrote me since the third edition, since those who wrote me earlier were thanked in earlier editions. (If you wrote me but I failed to mention your name here, my apologies—blame this on the volume of such emails.)

Rosemary Bernal (Del Mar College, USA)
Santanu Borah (University of North Alabama, USA)
Thierry Brusselle (Chaffey Community College, USA)
Lauren Carey (University of Miami, USA)
Limin Chen (Wuhan University, China)
John Clarry (Rutgers University, USA)
Ping Deng (Cleveland State University, USA)
Robert Eberhart (Santa Clara University, USA)
Gwyneth Edwards (HEC Montréal, Canada)
Felipe Fiuza (Florida Gulf Coast University, USA)
Kenneth Fox (The Citadel, USA)

Mike Geringer (Ohio University, USA)

C. Gopinath (O. P. Jindal Global University, India)

Steve Hurst (Mount Hood Community College, USA)

Anisul Islam (University of Houston, USA)

Michael Jacobsen (Copenhagen Business School, Denmark)

Sajal Kabiraj (Dongbei University of Finance and Economics, China)

Ann Langlois (Palm Beach Atlantic University, USA)

Yumei Li (Southwest University, China)

Lianlian Lin (California State Polytechnic University, USA)

Leonid Lisenco (University of Southern Denmark, Denmark)

Dong Liu (Georgia Institute of Technology, USA)

David Liu (George Fox University, USA)

Donna Lubrano (Newbury College, USA)

David Lucero (Yantai University, China)

Charles Mambula (Langston University, USA)

Asmat Nizam (Universiti Utara, Malaysia)

Eydis Olsen (Drexel University, USA)

Jung-Min Park (University of Ulsan, South Korea)

Gongming Qian (Chinese University of Hong Kong, China)

Surekha Rao (Indiana University Northwest, USA)

Pradeep Ray (University of New South Wales, Australia)

Daniel Rottig (Florida Gulf Coast University, USA)

Henryk Sterniczuk (University of New Brunswick, Canada)

David Stiles (University of Canterbury, New Zealand)

Anne Smith (University of Tennessee, USA)

Clyde Stoltenberg (Wichita State University, USA)

Steve Strombeck (Azusa Pacific University, USA)

Vas Taras (University of North Carolina at Greensboro, USA)

Rajaram Veliyath (Kennesaw State University, USA)

Jose Vargas-Hernandez (Universidad de Guadalajara, Mexico)

Loren Vickery (Western Oregon University, USA)

George White (University of Michigan at Flint, USA)

Phil Wilton (University of Liverpool, UK)

Xiaohua Yang (University of San Francisco, USA)

Andrcy Yukhanaev (Northumbria University, UK)

Wu Zhan (University of Sydney, Australia)

Man Zhang (Bowling Green State University, USA)

For the fourth edition, my gratitude goes to 23 colleagues who graciously contributed excellent case materials:

Ruth Ann Althaus (Ohio University, USA)

Dirk Michael Boehe (University of Adelaide, Australia)

Charles Byles (Virginia Commonwealth University, USA)

Mauricio Cervantes (Tecnológico de Monterrey, Mexico)

Pawinee Changphao (University of Texas at Dallas, USA)

Zhu Chen (SIA Energy, China)

Charles Hazzard (University of Texas at Dallas, USA)

Sergey Lebedev (University of Texas at Dallas, USA)

Daniel McCarthy (Northeastern University, USA)

Klaus Meyer (China Europe International Business School, China)—*two cases*

Miguel Montoya (Tecnológico de Monterrey, Mexico)

Canan Mutlu (Kennesaw State University, USA)

Sheila Puffer (Northeastern University, USA)

Alfred Rosenbloom (Dominican University, USA)

Nagaraj Savithri (University of Texas at Dallas, USA)

Arnold Schuh (Vienna University of Economics and Business, Austria)

Weilei (Stone) Shi (Baruch College, City University of New York, USA)

Pek-Hooi Soh (Simon Fraser University, Canada)

Sunny Li Sun (University of Missouri at Kansas City, USA)

Hao Tan (University of Newcastle, Australia)

Yanli Zhang (Montclair State University, USA)

Yanmei Zhu (Tongji University, China)

David Zoogah (Morgan State University, USA)

Last, but by no means least, I thank my wife Agnes, my daughter Grace, and my son James—to whom this book is dedicated. When the first edition was conceived, Grace was three and James one. Now my 13-year-old Grace is already a voracious reader and a prolific writer of young-adult novels, and my 11-year-old James can beat me in chess. Both are competitive swimmers and world travelers, having been to more than 30 countries. As a third-generation professor in my family, I can't help but wonder whether one (or both) of them will become a fourth-generation professor. To all of you, my thanks and my love.

About the Author

courtesy of Mike Peng

Mike W. Peng is the Jindal Chair of Global Business Strategy at the Jindal School of Management, University of Texas at Dallas. He is also a National Science Foundation (NSF) CAREER Award winner and a Fellow of the Academy of International Business (AIB). At UT Dallas, he has been the number-one contributor to the list of 45 top journals tracked by *Financial Times*, which consistently ranks UT Dallas as a top 20 school in research worldwide.

Professor Peng holds a bachelor's degree from Winona State University, Minnesota, and a PhD degree from the University of Washington, Seattle. He had previously served on the faculty at the Ohio State University, University of Hawaii, and Chinese University of Hong Kong. He has taught in five states in the United States (Hawaii, Ohio, Tennessee, Texas, and Washington), as well as in China, Hong Kong, and Vietnam. He has also held visiting or courtesy appointments in Australia, Britain, China, Denmark, Hong Kong, and the United States, and lectured around the world.

Professor Peng is one of the most-prolific and most-influential scholars in international business (IB). Both the United Nations and the World Bank have cited his work. During the decade 1996–2006, he was the top seven contributor to IB's number-one premier outlet: *Journal of International Business Studies*. In 2015, he received the *Journal of International Business Studies* Decade Award. A *Journal of Management* article found him to be among the top 65 most widely cited management scholars, and an *Academy of Management Perspectives* study reported that he is the fourth most-influential management scholar among professors who obtained their PhD since 1991. Overall, Professor Peng has published more than 120 articles in leading journals, more than 30 pieces in nonrefereed outlets, and five books. Since the launch of *Global Business*' third edition, he has not only published in top IB journals, such as the *Academy of Management Journal, Journal of International Business Studies, Journal of World Business*, and *Strategic Management Journal*, but also in leading outlets in entrepreneurship (*Entrepreneurship Theory and Practice*), ethics (*Journal of Business Ethics*), and human resources (*International Journal of Human Resource Management*).

Used in more than 30 countries, Professor Peng's best-selling textbooks, *Global Business, Global Strategy*, and *GLOBAL*, are global market leaders that have been translated into Chinese, Portuguese, and Spanish. A European adaptation (with Klaus Meyer) and an Indian adaptation (with Deepak Srivastava) have been successfully launched.

Truly global in scope, Professor Peng's research has investigated firm strategies in Africa, Asia Pacific, Central and Eastern Europe, and North America. He is best known for his development of the institution-based view of strategy and his insights about the rise of emerging economies such as China in global business. With more than 18,000 Google citations and an H-index of 57, he is listed among *The World's Most Influential Scientific Minds* (compiled by Thomson Reuters based on citations covering 21 fields)—in the field of economics and business, he is one of the only 95 world-class scholars listed and the *only* IB textbook author listed.

Professor Peng is active in leadership positions. He has served on the editorial boards of the *AMJ, AMP, AMR, JIBS, JMS, JWB*, and *SMJ*; and guest-edited a special issue for the *JMS*. At AIB, he co-chaired the AIB/JIBS Frontiers Conference in San Diego (2006), guest-edited a *JIBS* special issue (2010), chaired the Emerging and Transition Economies track for the Nagoya conference (2011), and chaired the Richard Farmer Best Dissertation Award Committee for the Washington conference (2012). At the Strategic Management Society (SMS), he was elected to be the Global Strategy Interest Group Chair (2008). He also co-chaired the SMS Special

Conferences in Shanghai (2007) and in Sydney (2014). He served one term as Editor-in-Chief of the *Asia Pacific Journal of Management*. He managed the successful bid to enter the Social Sciences Citation Index (SSCI), which reported *APJM*'s first citation impact to be 3.4 and rated it as the top 18 among 140 management journals (by citation impact factor) for 2010. In recognition of his significant contributions, *APJM* has named its best paper award the Mike Peng Best Paper Award. Currently, he is a Senior Editor at the *Journal of World Business*.

Professor Peng is also an active consultant, trainer, and keynote speaker. He has provided on-the-job training to more than 400 professors. He has consulted and been a keynote speaker for multinational enterprises (such as AstraZeneca, Berlitz, Nationwide, SAFRAN, and Texas Instruments), nonprofit organizations (such as World Affairs Council of Dallas-Fort Worth), educational and funding organizations (such as Canada Research Chair, Harvard Kennedy School of Government, National Science Foundation of the United States, and Natural Science Foundation of China), and national and international organizations (such as the UK Government Office for Science, US-China Business Council, US Navy, and World Bank).

Professor Peng has received numerous honors, including an NSF CAREER Grant ($423,000), a US Small Business Administration Best Paper Award, a *JIBS* Decade Award, a (lifetime) Distinguished Scholar Award from the Southwestern Academy of Management, a (lifetime) Scholarly Contribution Award from the International Association for Chinese Management Research (IACMR), and a Best Paper Award named after him. He has been quoted by *The Economist, Newsweek, Dallas Morning News, Smart Business Dallas, Atlanta Journal-Constitution, The Exporter Magazine, The World Journal, Business Times* (Singapore), *CEO-CIO* (Beijing), *Sing Tao Daily* (Vancouver), and *Brasil Econômico* (São Paulo), as well as on the Voice of America.

© Lonely/Shutterstock.com

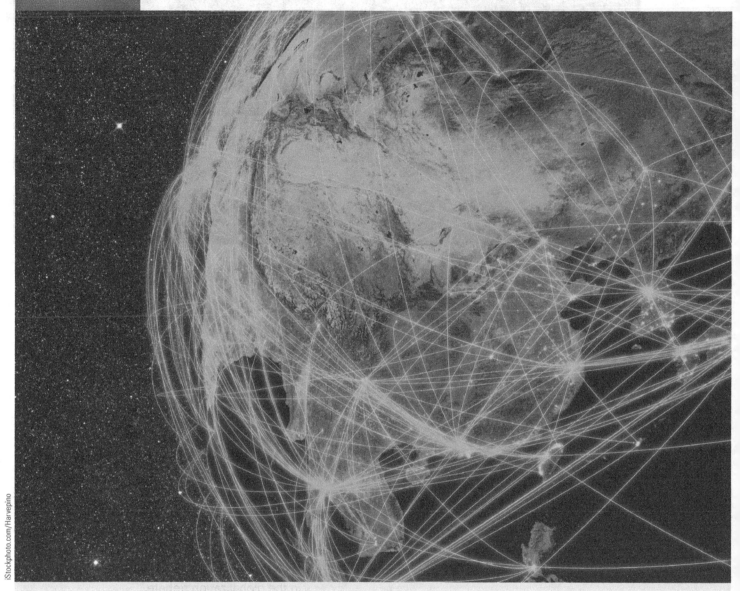

iStockphoto.com/Harvepino

PART 1 Laying Foundations

Chapters

The East India Company Limited

CHAPTER 1

IN THE NEWS

Lulu Group Invests in The East India Company

The East India Company Launches in the UAE

Limited Edition Sachin Tendulkar Coins Launched by The East India Company

READ MORE

FINE FOODS WEBSITE | GOLD WEBSITE | PRESS | CONTACT US | LEGAL

COPYRIGHT © 2014 THE EAST INDIA COMPANY LTD. ALL RIGHTS RESERVED

Learning Objectives

After studying this chapter, you should be able to

- explain the concepts of international business and global business, with a focus on emerging economies.

- give three reasons why it is important to study global business.

- articulate one fundamental question and two core perspectives in the study of global business.

- identify three ways of understanding what globalization is.

- state the size of the global economy and its broad trends, and understand your likely bias in the globalization debate.

Globalizing Business

EMERGING MARKETS: The Rebirth of the East India Company

Before picking up this book, the majority of readers are likely to have already heard of the East India Company. Yes, we are talking about *the* East India Company, the colonial trading company that created British India, founded Hong Kong and Singapore, and introduced tea, coffee, and chocolate to Britain and large parts of the world. Wait a minute—as you scratch your head over your rusty memory from history books—wasn't the company dead? Yes, it was dead—or, technically, dissolved or nationalized in 1874 by the British government. But, no, it was not dead.

After a hiatus of more than 130 years, the East India Company was reborn and relaunched in 2005 by a visionary and entrepreneurial Indian businessman, Sanjiv Mehta. With permissions granted by the UK Treasury for an undisclosed sum of money, Mumbai-born Mehta became the sole owner, chairman, and CEO of the *new* East India Company, with the rights to use the name and original trademarks. His goals were to unlock and strengthen the potential value of the world's first multinational and the world's first global brand. In 2010, with much fanfare, the East India Company launched its first luxury fine foods store in the prestigious Mayfair district of London. In 2014, the East India Company set up a new boutique inside London's most prestigious department store, Harrods—a format called "store in store." The initial products included premium coffees and teas, artisan sweet and savory biscuits, an exquisite range of chocolates, and gourmet salts and sugars. While the old company obviously never had a website, the new one proudly announced on its website:

We see our role as bringing together the best the world has to offer; to create unique goods that help people to explore and experience what's out there. Products that help people see their world in a different and better light. Products that have the power to amaze and astonish . . . The East India Company made a wide range of elusive, exclusive, and exotic ingredients familiar, affordable, and available to the world; ingredients which today form part of our daily and national cuisines. Today we continue to develop and market unique and innovative products that breathe life into the history of the Company. We trade foods crafted by artisans and specialists from around the world, with carefully sourced ingredients, unique recipes, and distinguished provenances.

Just like the old East India Company, the new company is a "born global" enterprise, which immediately declared its intention to expand globally upon its launch. By 2014, it had expanded throughout Europe (Austria, Finland, France, Germany, the Netherlands, Norway, and Spain), Asia Pacific (Australia, China,

Hong Kong, Japan, Malaysia, and South Korea), and the Middle East (Kuwait and Qatar). Its online store can deliver anywhere worldwide. Overall, in the first five years since 2005, the East India Company spent US$15 million to develop its new business. In 2011, the Mahindra Group, one of India's most respected business houses, acquired a minority stake in the East India Company. After receiving capital injection from Mahindra, the East India Company announced that it would invest US$100 million in the next five years to grow the iconic brand.

What had made the (old) East India Company such a household name? Obviously, the products it traded had to deliver value to be appreciated by customers around the world. At its peak, the company employed a third of the British labor force, controlled half of the world's trade, issued its own coins, managed an army of 200,000, and ruled 90 million Indians. Its organizational capabilities were awesome. Equally important were its political abilities to leverage and control the rules of the game around the world, ranging from managing politicians back home in the UK to manipulating political intrigues in

India. Granted a royal charter by Queen Elizabeth I in 1600, the old East India Company certainly benefitted from formal backing of the state. Informally, the brand still resonates with the 2.5 billion people in the British Commonwealth, especially Indians. Mehta was tremendously moved by the more than 14,000 e-mails from Indians all over the world wishing him well when he announced the acquisition. In his own words: "I have not created the brand, history has created it. I am just the curator of it."

Blending continuity and change, the saga of the East India Company continues. Mehta said he believed the East India Company was the Google of its time. But one reporter suggested, "Google is in fact the East India Company of its modern era. Let's see if Google is still around and having the same impact in 400 years' time."

Sources: Based on (1) *Arabian Business*, 2014, The empire strikes back, October 4, www.arabianbusiness.com; (2) East India Company, 2014, EIC today, www.theeastindiacompany.com; (3) East India Company, 2014, History, www.theeastindiacompany.com; (4) East India Company, 2014, Press, www.theeastindiacompany.com; (5) East India Company, 2014, History of fine foods, www.eicfinefoods.com; (6) *Economist*, 2011, The Company that ruled the waves, December 17; (7) *Economist*, 2014, Hidden gems, April 12.

How do firms such as the old and the new East India Company compete around the world? How do they deal with the various rules of the game? What capabilities do they have? How do they enter new markets? What determines their success and failure? This book will address these and other important questions.

Learning Objective
Explain the concepts of international business and global business, with a focus on emerging economies.

International business (IB)
(1) A business (firm) that engages in international (cross-border) economic activities, and/or (2) the action of doing business abroad.

Multinational enterprise (MNE)
A firm that engages in foreign direct investment.

Foreign direct investment (FDI)
Investment in, controlling, and managing value-added activities in other countries.

1-1 What Is Global Business?

1-1a Defining International Business and Global Business

Traditionally, international business (IB) is defined as a business (firm) that engages in international (cross-border) economic activities. It can also refer to the action of doing business abroad. The previous generation of IB textbooks almost always takes the foreign entrant's perspective. Consequently, such books deal with issues such as how to enter foreign markets and how to select alliance partners. The most frequently discussed foreign entrant is the multinational enterprise (MNE), defined as a firm that engages in foreign direct investment (FDI) by directly investing in, controlling, and managing value-added activities in other countries.[1] Of course, MNEs and their cross-border activities are important. But they only cover one aspect of IB—the foreign side. Students educated by these books often come away with the impression that the other aspect of IB—namely, domestic firms—does not exist. Obviously, this is not true. Domestic firms do not just sit around in the face of foreign entrants. They often actively compete and/or collaborate with foreign entrants in their markets.

Sometimes, strong domestic firms have also gone overseas themselves. Overall, focusing on the foreign entrant side captures only one side of the coin at best.[2]

There are *two* key words in IB: international (I) and business (B).[3] However, many previous textbooks focus on the international aspect (the foreign entrant) to such an extent that the business part (which also includes domestic business) almost disappears. This is unfortunate, because IB is fundamentally about B (business) in addition to being I. To put it differently, the IB course in the undergraduate and MBA curricula at numerous business schools is probably the *only* one with the word "business" in its title. All other courses are labeled management, marketing, finance, and so on, representing one functional area but not the overall picture of business. Does it matter? Of course! It means that your IB course is an *integrative* course that can provide you with an overall business perspective (rather than a functional view) grounded in a global environment. Therefore, it makes sense that your textbook should give you both the I and B parts, not just the I part.

To cover both the I and the B parts, global business is defined in this book as business around the globe—thus, the title of this book is *Global Business* (not IB). In other words, global business includes both (1) international (cross-border) business activities covered by traditional IB books *and* (2) domestic business activities. Such deliberate blurring of the traditional boundaries separating international and domestic business is increasingly important today, because many previously domestic markets are now globalized.

Consider the competition in college textbooks, such as this *Global Business* book you are studying now. Not long ago, competition among college business textbook publishers was primarily on a nation-by-nation basis. The Big Three—Cengage Learning (our publisher, which is the biggest in the college business textbook market), Prentice Hall, and McGraw-Hill—primarily competed in the United States. A different set of publishers competed in other countries. As a result, most textbooks studied by British students would be authored by British professors and published by British publishers, most textbooks studied by Brazilian students would be authored by Brazilian professors and published by Brazilian publishers, and so on. Now Cengage Learning (under British and Canadian ownership), Pearson Prentice Hall (under British ownership), and McGraw-Hill (under US ownership) have significantly globalized their competition, thanks to the rising demand for high-quality business textbooks in English. Around the globe, they are competing against each other in many markets, publishing in multiple languages and versions. For instance, *Global Business* and its sister books, *Global Strategy, Global* (paperback), and *International Business* (an adaptation for the European market), are published by different subsidiaries in Chinese, Spanish, and Portuguese in addition to English, reaching customers in more than 30 countries. Despite such worldwide spread of competition, in each market—down to each school—textbook publishers have to compete locally. Since no professor teaches globally and all students study locally, this means *Global Business* has to win adoption every class, every semester. Overall, it becomes difficult to tell in this competition what is international and what is domestic. Thus, "global" seems to be a better word to capture the essence of this competition.

1-1b Global Business and Emerging Economies

Global Business also differs from other books on IB because most of them focus on competition in developed economies. Here, by contrast, we devote extensive space to competitive battles waged throughout emerging economies, a term that

Global business

Business around the globe.

Emerging economy

A term that has gradually replaced the term "developing country" since the 1990s.

Emerging market

A term that is often used interchangeably with "emerging economy."

Purchasing power parity (PPP)

A conversion that determines the equivalent amount of goods and services that different currencies can purchase.

has gradually replaced the term "developing countries" since the 1990s. Another commonly used term is emerging markets (see PengAtlas Map 1). How important are emerging economies? Collectively, they command 48% of world trade, attract 60% of FDI inflows, and generate 40% FDI outflows. Overall, emerging economies contribute approximately 50% of the global gross domestic product (GDP).[4] In 1990, they accounted for less than one-third of a much smaller world GDP. Note that this percentage is adjusted for purchasing power parity (PPP), which is an adjustment to reflect the differences in cost of living (see In Focus 1.1). Using official (nominal) exchange rates without adjusting for PPP, emerging economies contribute about 30% of the global GDP. Why is there such a huge difference

IN FOCUS 1.1

SETTING THE TERMS STRAIGHT

GDP, GNP, GNI, PPP—there is a bewildering variety of acronyms that are used to measure economic development. It is useful to set these terms straight before proceeding. **Gross domestic product (GDP)** is measured as the sum of value added by *resident* firms, households, and governments operating in an economy. For example, the value added by foreign-owned firms operating in Mexico would be counted as part of Mexico's GDP. However, the earnings of *non-resident* sources that are sent back to Mexico (such as earnings of Mexicans who do not live and work in Mexico, and dividends received by Mexicans who own non-Mexican stocks) are not included in Mexico's GDP. One measure that captures this is **gross national product (GNP)**. Recently, the World Bank and other international organizations have used a new term, **gross national income (GNI)**, to supersede GNP. Conceptually, there is no difference between GNI and GNP. What exactly is GNI/GNP? It comprises GDP plus income from non-resident sources abroad.

While GDP, GNP, and now GNI are often used as yardsticks of economic development, differences in cost of living make such a direct comparison less meaningful. A dollar of spending in Thailand can buy a lot more than in Japan. Therefore, conversion based on purchasing power parity (PPP) is often necessary. The PPP between two countries is the rate at which the currency of one country needs to be converted into that of a second country to ensure that a given amount of the first country's currency will purchase the same volume of goods and services in the second country

(see Chapter 7 for details). According to the International Monetary Fund (IMF), the Swiss per capita GDP is US$81,276 based on official (nominal) exchange rates—*a lot higher* than the official US per capita GDP of US$53,001. However, everything is more expensive in Switzerland. A Big Mac costs US$6.83 in Switzerland versus US$4.80 in the United States. Thus, Switzerland's per capita GDP based on PPP shrinks to US$53,977—only slightly higher than the US per capita GDP based on PPP of US$53,001 (the IMF uses the United States as a benchmark in PPP calculation, which does not change from the nominal number).

One of the most recent and probably most important debates concerns the size of the Chinese GDP. Calculations based on the nominal exchange rates would find China's GDP to be 47% of the US GDP. But new calculations based on PPP released by the World Bank in 2014 reported China's GDP to be 87% as large as the US GDP. Given that the Chinese economy grows a lot more quickly than the US economy, some experts believe that China may become the world's largest economy by the time you read this book—as opposed to in the next decade or so (see the Closing Case). Overall, when you read statistics about GDP, GNP, and GNI, always pay attention to whether these numbers are based on official exchange rates or PPP, which can make a huge difference.

Sources: Based on (1) *Bloomberg Businessweek*, 2014, Recognizing China's clout, May 12: 14; (2) *Economist*, 2014, Calculating European GDP, August 23: 68–69; (3) *Economist*, 2014, The dragon takes wing, May 3: 65; (3) *Economist*, 2014, The Big Mac index, July 26: 61; (4) International Monetary Fund, 2014, *Report for Selected Countries and Subjects (PPP Valuation of Country GDP)*, October, Washington, DC.

between the two measures? Because the cost of living (such as housing and haircuts) in emerging economies tends to be lower than that in developed economies. For instance, US$1 spent in Mexico can buy a lot more than US$1 spent in the United States.

Of many emerging economies, Brazil, Russia, India, and China—commonly referred to as BRIC—command more attention. With the addition of South Africa, BRIC becomes BRICS. As a group, BRICS countries have 40% of the world's population, cover a quarter of the world's land area, and contribute more than 25% of global GDP (on a PPP basis). In addition to BRICS, other interesting terms include BRICM (BRIC + Mexico), BRICET (BRIC + Eastern Europe and Turkey), and Next Eleven (N-11—consisting of Bangladesh, Egypt, Indonesia, Iran, Korea, Mexico, Nigeria, Pakistan, the Philippines, Turkey, and Vietnam).

Does it make sense to group together as "emerging economies" so many countries with tremendous diversity in terms of history, geography, politics, and economics? As compared to developed economies, the label of "emerging economies," rightly or wrongly, has emphasized the presumably homogenous nature of so many different countries. While this single label has been useful, more recent research has endeavored to enrich it. Specifically, the two dimensions illustrated in Figure 1.1 can help us differentiate various emerging economies.[5] Vertically, the development of market-supporting political, legal, and economic institutions has been noted as a crucial dimension of institutional transitions. Horizontally, the development of infrastructure and factor markets is also crucial.

Traditional (or stereotypical) emerging economies suffer from both the lack of institutional development and the lack of infrastructure and factor market development. Most emerging economies 20 years ago would have fit this description. Today, some emerging economies still have made relatively little progress along these two dimensions (such as Belarus and Zimbabwe).

However, much has changed. A great deal of institutional development and infrastructure and factor market development has taken place. Such wide-ranging development has resulted in the emergence of a class of *mid-range* emerging economies

Figure 1.1 **A Typology of Emerging Economies**

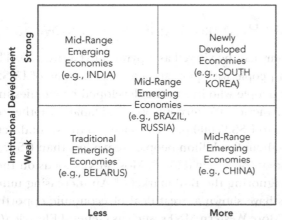

Source: Adapted from R. Hoskisson, M. Wright, I. Filatotchev, & M. W. Peng, 2013, Emerging multinationals from mid-range economies: The influence of institutions and factor markets (p. 1297), *Journal of Management Studies*, 50: 1295–1321.

Gross domestic product (GDP)

The sum of value added by resident firms, households, and governments operating in an economy.

Gross national product (GNP)

GDP plus income from non-resident sources abroad.

Gross national income (GNI)

GDP plus income from non-resident sources abroad. GNI is the term used by the World Bank and other international organizations to supersede the term GNP.

BRIC

Brazil, Russia, India, and China.

BRICS

Brazil, Russia, India, China, and South Africa.

that differ from both traditional emerging economies and developed economies. For example, the top-down approach to government found in China has facilitated infrastructure and factor market development. But China's political and market institutions tend to be underdeveloped relative to physical infrastructure. Alternatively, India has strong political institutions supporting market institutions. While Indian government policy reforms have facilitated better market institutions and associated economic development, world-class physical infrastructure is lacking. In the middle area of Figure 1.1, Brazil and Russia are examples, with democratic political institutions and some infrastructure and factor market development. Finally, some economies have clearly graduated from the "emerging" phase and become what we call "newly developed economies." South Korea is such an exemplar country.

Overall, the Great Transformation of the global economy is embodied by the tremendous shift in economic weight and engines of growth toward emerging economies in general and BRIC(S) in particular.[6] Led by BRIC(S), emerging economies accomplished "the biggest economic transformation in modern economy," according to the *Economist*.[7] In China, per capita income doubled in about ten years, an achievement that took Britain 150 years and the United States 50 years as they industrialized.[8] Throughout emerging economies, China is not alone. While groupings such as BRIC(S) and N-11 are always arbitrary, they serve a useful purpose—namely, highlighting the economic and demographic scale and trajectory that enable them to challenge developed economies in terms of weight and influence in the global economy.

Of course, the Great Transformation is not a linear story of endless and uniform high-speed growth. All BRIC(S) countries and most emerging economies have experienced some significant slowdown recently.[9] It is possible that they may not be able to repeat their extraordinary growth sprints of the decade between 1998 (the Asian economic crisis) and 2008 (the global financial crisis). For example, in 2007, Brazil accomplished an annual economic growth of 6%, Russia 8%, India 10%, and China 14%. In 2017, they would be lucky to achieve half of these enviable growth rates. However, it seems that emerging economies *as a group* are destined to grow both their absolute GDP and their percentage of world GDP relative to developed economies. The debate centers on how much and how quickly (or slowly) such growth will be in the future (see the Closing Case).

1-1c Base of the Pyramid and Reverse Innovation

The global economy can be viewed as a pyramid (Figure 1.2). The top consists of about one billion people with per capita annual income of US$20,000 or higher. These are mostly people who live in the developed economies in the Triad, which consists of North America, Western Europe, and Japan. Another one billion people earning US$2,000 to US$20,000 per year make up the second tier. The vast majority of humanity—about five billion people—earn less than US$2,000 per year and comprise the base of the pyramid (BoP). Most MNEs focus on the top and second tiers and end up ignoring the BoP markets.[10] An increasing number of such low-income countries have shown a great deal of economic opportunities as income levels have risen. More Western MNEs, such as General Electric (GE), are investing aggressively in the BoP and leveraging their investment to tackle markets in both emerging and developed economies.

Great Transformation
Transformation of the global economy that is embodied by the tremendous shift in economic weight and engines of growth toward emerging economies in general and BRIC(S) in particular.

Triad
North America, Western Europe, and Japan.

Base of the pyramid (BoP)
Economies where people make less than US$2,000 per capita per year.

Figure 1.2   **The Global Economic Pyramid**

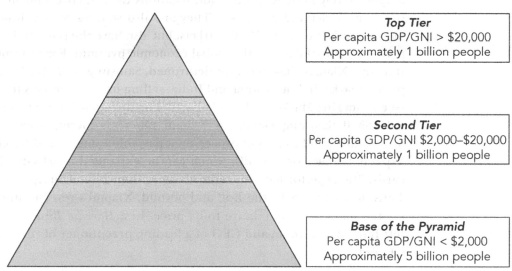

Top Tier
Per capita GDP/GNI > $20,000
Approximately 1 billion people

Second Tier
Per capita GDP/GNI $2,000–$20,000
Approximately 1 billion people

Base of the Pyramid
Per capita GDP/GNI < $2,000
Approximately 5 billion people

Sources: Adapted from (1) C. K. Prahalad & S. Hart, 2002, The fortune at the bottom of the pyramid, *Strategy+Business*, 26: 54–67; (2) S. Hart, 2005, *Capitalism at the Crossroads*, Philadelphia: Wharton School Publishing, 111.

One interesting recent development out of emerging economies is reverse innovation—an innovation that is adopted first in emerging economies and then diffused around the world.[11] Traditionally, innovations are generated by Triad-based multinationals, with the needs and wants of rich customers at the top of the pyramid in mind. When such multinationals entered lower-income economies, they tended to simplify the product features and lower prices. In other words, the innovation flow is *top-down*. However, as Deere & Company found out in India, its large-horsepower tractors designed for American farmers were a poor fit for the different needs and wants of Indian farmers. Despite Deere's efforts to simplify the product and reduce the price, the price was still too high in India. Instead, Mahindra & Mahindra brought its widely popular small-horsepower tractors that were developed in India to the United States and carved out a growing niche that eventually propelled it to be the world's *largest* tractor maker by units sold.[12] (Mahindra & Mahindra is now so committed to the United States that it sponsors bull-riding tournaments in Texas.) In response, Deere abandoned its US tractor designs and "went native" in India, by launching a local design team charged with developing something from scratch—with the needs and wants of farmers in India (or, more broadly, in emerging economies) in mind. The result was a 35-horsepower tractor that was competitive with Mahindra & Mahindra not only in India, but also in the United States and elsewhere. In both cases, the origin of new innovations is from the BoP. The flow of innovation is bottom-up—in other words, reverse innovation.

Reverse innovation

An innovation that is adopted first in emerging economies and is then diffused around the world.

India Pictures RM/Dinodia Photos/Alamy Limited

Does this Mahindra & Mahindra tractor developed from a BoP market have potential elsewhere?

The reverse innovation movement suggests that emerging economies are no longer merely low-cost production locations or attractive new markets (hence the term "emerging markets"). They are also sources of new innovations that may not only grow out of BoP markets, but also have the potential to go uphill to penetrate into the top of the global economic pyramid. For example, a Chinese start-up, Xiaomi, has recently dethroned Samsung and Apple in the smartphone market in both China and India, selling its smartphones for only US$100 (see Emerging Markets 1.1). Relative to a feature-rich US$600 Apple iPhone or a US$500 Samsung Galaxy, a Xiaomi phone is merely good enough. It is 3G-capable and has a solid processor, a passable camera, and barely decent but expandable memory (8 GB), which can be expanded to 64 GB with cheap SD cards. But its performance is certainly more than 20% of an Apple or a Samsung. Thus, to customers in the BoP and beyond, Xiaomi's reverse innovation delivers tremendous value relative to its price. In a *Harvard Business Review* article, Jeff Immelt, chairman and CEO of a leading practitioner of reverse innovation, GE, noted:

> To be honest, the company is also embracing reverse innovation for defensive reasons. If GE doesn't come up with innovations in poor countries and take them global, new competitors from the developing world—like Mindray, Suzlon, Goldwind, and Haier—will . . . GE has tremendous respect for traditional rivals like Siemens, Philips, and Rolls-Royce. But it knows how to compete with them; they will never destroy GE. By introducing products that create a new price-performance paradigm, however, the emerging giants very well could. Reverse innovation isn't optional; it is oxygen.[13]

As advised by GE's Immelt, today's students—and tomorrow's business leaders—will ignore the opportunities and challenges at the BoP at their own peril. This book will help ensure that *you* will not ignore these opportunities and challenges.

Learning Objective
Give three reasons why it is important to study global business.

1-2 Why Study Global Business?

Global business (or IB) is one of the most exciting, most challenging, and most relevant subjects offered by business schools. Why study it? Table 1.1 outlines three compelling reasons.

First, you don't want to be a loser. Mastering global business knowledge helps advance your employability and career in an increasingly competitive global economy. Take a look at the Opening Day Quiz in Table 1.2. Can you answer all the questions correctly? If not, you will definitely benefit from studying global business.

The answer to Question 1 is empirical—that is, based on data. You should guess first and then look at the label of your shirt yourself or ask a friend to help you. The key here is international trade. Do you wear a shirt made in your own country or another country? Why?

Table 1.1   Why Study Global Business?

- Enhance your employability and advance your career in the global economy
- Better preparation for possible expatriate assignments abroad
- Stronger competence in interacting with foreign suppliers, partners, and competitors, and in working for foreign-owned employers in your own country

Table 1.2	Opening Day Quiz

1. Which country made the shirt you are wearing?

(A) China   (D) Romania

(B) Malaysia   (E) US

(C) Mexico

2. Which country made your mobile device?

(A) China   (D) Taiwan

(B) Germany   (E) US

(C) Singapore

3. How many member countries does the G-20 have?

(A) 20   (D) 19

(B) 21   (E) 18

(C) 22

4. Which city has the largest number of *Fortune* Global 500 company headquarters? (operational headquarters where top executives go to work, not place of registration)

(A) Beijing   (D) New York

(B) Hong Kong   (E) Tokyo

(C) London

5. A 2,000-employee manufacturing plant is closing in a developed economy, and production is moving to an emerging economy. How many of the 2,000 jobs will the company keep?

(A) 0   (D) 20–30

(B) 5–10   (E) 30–50

(C) 10–20

In Question 2, smart students typically ask whether the mobile device (such as a smartphone or an iPad) means the motherboard or the components. My answer is: "I mean the whole device, all the production that went into making the machine." Then some students respond: "But they could be made in different countries!" My point exactly. Specifically, the point here is to appreciate the complexity of a global value chain, with different countries making different components and handling different tasks. It is likely the tiny components inside your mobile device have crossed borders a dozen or more times. Such a value chain is typically managed by an MNE—such as Apple, Dell, Foxconn, HP, Lenovo, or Samsung. The capabilities necessary to organize a global supply chain hints at the importance of resources and capabilities—one of the two key themes of this book.

Question 3 is deceptively simple. Unfortunately, 100% of my own students—ranging from undergraduates to PhDs—*miss* it. Surprise! The Group of 20 (G-20) only has 19 member countries. The 20th member is the European Union (EU)—a regional bloc, not a single country. Ideally, why the G-20 is formed in such an interesting way will make you more curious about how the rules of the game are made around the world. In this case, why are 19 countries in, but numerous others out? What is special about the EU? Why are other regional blocs not included in the G-20? A focus on the rules of the game—more technically, institutions—is another key theme of the book.

Question 4 is interesting. Most of my own students pick New York, which has the *third*-largest number of headquarters of *Fortune* Global 500 companies (measured by sales). Beijing now has 52 *Fortune* Global 500 headquarters, followed by 41 in Tokyo, which until recently dethroned by Beijing had had the largest cluster of *Fortune*

Group of 20 (G-20)

The group of 19 major countries plus the EU whose leaders meet on a biannual basis to solve global economic problems.

Do you know Beijing now has the world's largest number of *Fortune* Global 500 headquarters?

Global 500 headquarters. In comparison, New York has 20 such headquarters (17 in New York City and three outside the city).[14] The rise of Beijing is indicative of the changing global economic winds, which have propelled China to become the world's second-largest economy in the years between the second and third editions of this book. To gain a better understanding of global economy, you need to pay more attention to companies based in Beijing (and in China and other emerging economies).

Question 5 will really frighten you. Some students typically clarify: "Do you mean the few security guards looking after the closed plant?" "Not necessarily," I point out. "The question is: How many jobs will be kept by the *company*?" Students eventually get it: even adding a few jobs as security guards at the closed plant, the most optimistic estimates are that only 30 to 50 jobs may be kept. Yes, you guessed it: these jobs typically are high-level positions such as the CEO, CFO, CIO, factory director, and chief engineer. These managers will be sent by the MNE to start up operations in an emerging economy. You need to realize that in a 2,000-employee plant, even if you may be the 51st-highest-ranked employee, your fate may be the same as the 2,000th employee. You really need to work hard and work smart to position yourself as one of the top 50 (preferably one of the top 30). Doing well in this class and mastering global business knowledge may help make that happen.

In addition to the first reason to equip you with relevant knowledge, the second compelling reason why you should study global business is related to Question 5. Because many ambitious students aspire to join the top ranks of large firms, expertise in global business is often a prerequisite. Today, it is increasingly difficult, if not impossible, to find top managers at large firms without significant global competence. Of course, eventually, hands-on experience, not merely knowledge acquired from this course, will be required. However, mastery of the knowledge of, and demonstration of interest in, global business during your education will set you apart as a more ideal candidate to be selected as an expatriate manager ("expat")—a manager who works abroad—to gain such an experience (see Chapter 15 for details).

Thanks to globalization, low-level jobs not only command lower salaries, but are also more vulnerable.[15] However, high-level jobs, especially those held by expats, are both financially rewarding and relatively secure. Expats often command a significant international premium in compensation—a significant pay raise when working overseas. In US firms, an expat's total compensation package is approximately US$250,000 to US$300,000 (including perks and benefits; not all is take-home pay). When they return to the United States after a tour of duty (usually two to three years), a firm that does not provide attractive career opportunities to experienced expats often finds them to be lured away by competitor firms. Competitor firms also want to globalize their business, and tapping into the expertise and experience of these former expats makes such expansion more likely to succeed. And yes, to hire away these internationally experienced managers, competitor firms have to pay an even larger premium. This indeed is a virtuous cycle. This hypothetical example is designed to motivate you to study hard so that, someday, you may become one of these sought-after globetrotting managers. But even if you

Expatriate manager (expat)
A manager who works abroad.

International premium
A significant pay raise when working overseas.

Figure 1.3 **Jobs Outsourced**

Source: *Harvard Business Review*, April 2012: 34.

don't want to be an expat, you really don't want to join the army of the unemployed due to factory closings and business failures (see Figure 1.3).

Lastly, even if you do not aspire to compete for the top job at a large company and instead work at a small firm or are self-employed, you may find yourself dealing with foreign-owned suppliers and buyers, competing with foreign-invested firms in your home market, or perhaps even selling and investing overseas. Alternatively, you may find yourself working for a foreign-owned firm, your domestic employer acquired by a foreign player, or your unit ordered to shut down for global consolidation. Understanding how global business decisions are made may facilitate your own career in such firms. If there is a strategic rationale to downsize your unit, you want to be prepared and start polishing your résumé right away. In other words, it is your career that is at stake. Don't be the last in the know!

1-3 A Unified Framework

Global business is a vast subject area. It is one of the few courses that will make you appreciate why your university requires you to take a number of seemingly unrelated courses in general education. We will draw on major social sciences, such as economics, geography, history, political science, psychology, and sociology. We will also draw on a number of business disciplines, such as strategy, finance, and marketing. The study of global business is, thus, quite interdisciplinary. It is easy to lose sight of the "forest" while scrutinizing various "trees" or even "branches." The subject is not difficult, and most students find it to be fun. The number-one student complaint (based on previous student feedback) is that there is an overwhelming amount of information. Honestly, this is also *my* number-one complaint as your author. You may have to read and learn this material, but I have to bring it all together in a way that makes sense and in a (relatively) compact book that does not go on and on and on for 990 pages.

To make your learning more focused, more manageable, and (hopefully) more fun, in this section—and throughout the book—we will develop a unified

Learning Objective
Articulate one fundamental question and two core perspectives in the study of global business.

Figure 1.4   **A Unified Framework for Global Business**

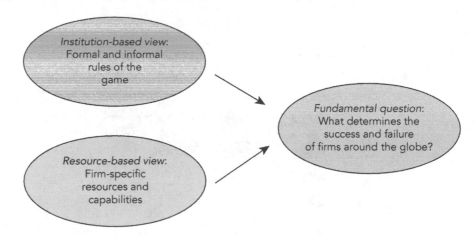

framework (shown in Figure 1.4). This will provide great continuity to facilitate your learning. Specifically, we will discipline ourselves by focusing only on one most fundamental question and two core perspectives. A fundamental question acts to define a field and to orient the attention of students, practitioners, and scholars in a certain direction. Our "big question" is: *What determines the success and failure of firms around the globe?*[16] To answer this question, we will introduce only two core perspectives throughout this book: (1) an institution-based view and (2) a resource-based view.[17] The remainder of this section outlines this framework.

1-3a One Fundamental Question

What is it that we do in global business? Why is it so important that practically all students in business schools around the world are either required or recommended to take this course? While there are certainly many questions to raise, a relentless interest in what determines the success and failure of firms around the globe serves to focus the energy of our field. Global business is fundamentally about not limiting yourself to your home country. It is about treating the global economy as your potential playground (or battlefield). Some firms may be successful domestically but fail miserably overseas. Other firms successfully translate their strengths from their home markets to other countries. If you were expected to lead your firm's efforts to enter a particular foreign market, wouldn't you want to find out what drives the success and failure of other firms in that market?

Overall, the focus on firm performance around the globe defines the field of global business (or IB) more than anything else. Numerous other questions all relate in one way or another to this most fundamental question. Therefore, all chapters in this book will be centered on this consistent theme: What determines the success and failure of firms around the globe?

1-3b First Core Perspective: An Institution-Based View[18]

An institution-based view suggests that the success and failure of firms are enabled and constrained by institutions. By institutions, we mean the rules of the game. Doing business around the globe requires intimate knowledge about both formal rules (such as laws) and informal rules (such as values) that govern competition in various countries. Firms that do not do their homework and thus remain ignorant of the rules of the game in a certain country are not likely to emerge as winners.

Formal institutions include laws, regulations, and rules. For example, Hong Kong's laws are well known for treating all entrants, whether from neighboring mainland China (whose firms are still technically regarded as "non-domestic") or far-away Chile, the same as they treat indigenous Hong Kong firms. Such equal treatment enhances the potential odds for foreign firms' success. Thus, it is not surprising that Hong Kong attracts numerous outside firms. Other rules of the game discriminate against foreign firms and undermine their chances for success. India's recent attraction as a site for FDI was only possible after its regulations changed from confrontational to accommodating. Prior to 1991, India's rules severely discriminated against foreign firms. For example, in the 1970s, the Indian government demanded that Coca-Cola either hand over the recipe for its secret syrup, which it does not even share with the US government, or get out of India. Painfully, Coca-Cola chose to leave India. Its return to India since the 1990s speaks volumes about how much the rules of the game have changed in India.

Informal institutions include cultures, ethics, and norms. They also play an important part in shaping the success and failure of firms around the globe (see the Opening Case). For example, individualistic societies, particularly the English-speaking countries, such as Australia, Britain, and the United States, tend to have a relatively higher level of entrepreneurship, as reflected in the number of business start-ups. Why? Because the act of founding a new firm is a widely accepted practice in individualistic societies. Conversely, collectivistic societies, such as Japan, often have a hard time fostering entrepreneurship. Most people there refuse to stick their neck out to found new businesses, because it is contrary to the norm.

Overall, an institution-based view suggests that institutions shed a great deal of light on what drives firm performance around the globe. Next, we turn to our second core perspective.

1-3c Second Core Perspective: A Resource-Based View[19]

The institution-based view suggests that the success and failure of firms around the globe are largely determined by their environments. This is certainly correct. Because of their institutions (or specifically, institutional imperfections), India did not attract much FDI prior to 1991 and Japan does not nurture a lot of internationally competitive start-ups. However, insightful as this perspective is, there is a major drawback. If we push this view to its logical extreme, then firm performance around the globe would be *entirely* determined by environments. The validity of this extreme version is certainly questionable.

The resource-based view helps overcome this drawback. While the institution-based view primarily deals with the *external* environment, the resource-based view focuses on a firm's *internal* resources and capabilities. It starts with a simple observation: In harsh, unattractive environments, most firms either suffer or exit. However, against all odds, a few superstars thrive in these environments. For instance, despite the former Soviet Union's obvious hostility toward the United States during the Cold War, PepsiCo began successfully operating in the former Soviet Union in the 1970s (!). In another example, airlines often lose money. But a small number of players, such as Southwest in the United States, Ryanair in Ireland, Hainan in China, and IndiGo in India, have been raking in profits year after year. In the fiercely competitive fashion industry, Zara has been defying gravity. How can these firms succeed in such challenging environments? What is special about them? A short answer is that PepsiCo, Southwest, Ryanair, Hainan, IndiGo, and Zara must have certain valuable and unique *firm-specific* resources and capabilities that are not shared by competitors in the same environments.

Doing business outside one's home country is challenging. Foreign firms have to overcome a liability of foreignness, which is the *inherent* disadvantage that foreign firms experience in host countries because of their non-native status.[20] Just think about all the differences in regulations, languages, cultures, and norms. Think about the odds against Mahindra & Mahindra when it tried to eat some of John Deere's lunch in the American heartland. Against such significant odds, the primary weapons that foreign firms such as Mahindra & Mahindra employ are *overwhelming* resources and capabilities that can offset their liability of foreignness (Figure 1.5). Today, many of us take it for granted that the best-selling car in the United States rotates between the Toyota Camry and the Honda Civic, that Coca-Cola is the best-selling soft drink in Mexico, and that Microsoft Word is the world's number-one word processing software. We really shouldn't. Why? Because it is *not* natural for these foreign firms to dominate nonnative markets. These firms must possess some very rare and powerful firm-specific resources and capabilities that drive these remarkable success stories. This is a key theme of the resource-based view, which focuses on how winning firms acquire and develop such unique and enviable resources and capabilities, and how competitor firms imitate and then innovate in an effort to outcompete the winning firms.

Figure 1.5 **In Every Country, Multinationals Possess Better Management Capabilities Than Do Local Firms**

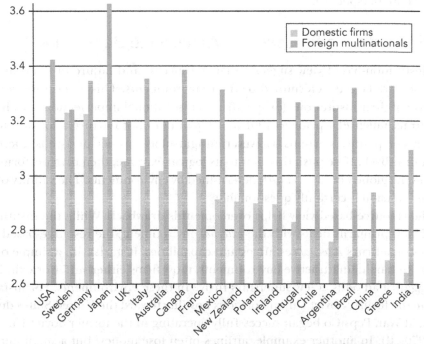

Average management scores range from 1 (worst practice) to 5 (best practice)

Liability of foreignness

The inherent disadvantage that foreign firms experience in host countries because of their non-native status.

Source: Adapted from N. Bloom, C. Genakos, R. Sadun, & J. Van Reenen, 2012, Management practices across firms and countries (p. 23), *Academy of Management Perspectives*, February: 12–33. Sample of 7,262 manufacturing and 661 retail firms, of which 5,441 are purely domestic and 2,482 are foreign multinationals. Domestic multinationals (such as the domestic subsidiaries of Toyota in Japan) are excluded.

1-3d A Consistent Theme

Given our focus on the fundamental question of what determines the success and failure of firms around the globe, we will develop a unified framework by organizing the material in *every* chapter according to the two core perspectives, namely, the institution-based and resource-based views (see Emerging Markets 1.1). With our unified framework—an innovation in IB textbooks—we will not only explore the global business "trees," but also see the global business "forest."

EMERGING MARKETS 1.1

Fighting In and Out of the Chinese Smartphone Industry

Commanding one-third of worldwide sales, China is now the largest smartphone market in the world. Not surprisingly, global leaders Samsung and Apple (in that order) sell a lot in China, which absorbs approximately 20% of their output. What is interesting is that six of the top eight vendors are Chinese firms, and that neither Samsung nor Apple is the volume leader. Competing intensely among themselves, the "Gang of Six" consists of computer king Lenovo, telecom equipment giants Huawei and ZTE, consumer electronics firms TCL and Coolpad, and red-hot start-up Xiaomi.

Which firm is the market leader by volume in China? Surprise: it is Xiaomi (pronounced "shee-owl-mee," meaning "Little Rice"). In the second quarter of 2014, Xiaomi, which only sells online, dethroned Samsung to be the market champion by volume, with a 14% market share. Xiaomi's secrets? From a resource-based view, plenty. Fast prototyping, with very short "launch-test-improve" cycles. Offering special software not available in other Android devices. Undercutting rivals with rock-bottom prices—US$100 for most Xiaomi models vis-à-vis Samsung's high-end Galaxy smartphones that retail for US$500. Imitating leading brands—Xiaomi's founder, Lei Jun, is famous for wearing Steve Jobs-style black T-shirts and jeans when showing off new models on stage. Overall, Xiaomi grew 240% in the second quarter of 2014, compared with the second quarter of 2013. Its extraordinary performance propelled it to become the fifth-largest smartphone player in the world—behind Samsung, Apple, Huawei, and Lenovo (in that order).

Chinese smartphone makers are naturally salivating about global markets. Xiaomi only sells 3% of its smartphones outside of China, Lenovo 16%, and Huawei 41%. They are likely to drive smartphones' commoditization—a process of competition through which unique products that command high prices and high margins are no longer able to do so, thus becoming commodities. Just as in China, Xiaomi at US$98 apiece has rapidly become the market leader in India. But here is a catch from an institution-based view. As they increasingly venture outside China, similarities in design between Chinese brands and global leaders—and potential intellectual property (IP) infringement inside the devices—are likely to incur the wrath of Apple and Samsung. IP disputes, of course, are nothing unusual among smartphone giants. Apple and Samsung themselves fought nasty court battles for years. Xiaomi and other Chinese smartphone makers have armed themselves with Google executives and Silicon Valley lawyers seasoned at navigating the perilous waters between war and peace in IP. While the last page of Chinese smartphone makers' story is not likely to be written any time soon, their performance will ultimately be driven by a combination of their technological and marketing capabilities and their institutional and legal savvy.

Sources: Based on (1) *Bloomberg Businessweek*, 2014, Samsung's China problems come to India, October 27: 44–45; (2) *Economist*, 2014, Smartening up their act, October 25; (3) *Forbes*, 2014, China's Xiaomi becomes world's 5th largest smartphone maker, July 31; (4) T. Hout & D. Michael, 2014, A Chinese approach to management, *Harvard Business Review*, September; (5) *South China Morning Post*, 2014, Chinese companies drive commoditization of smartphone market, August 18; (6) *Wall Street Journal*, 2014, Xiaomi overtakes Samsung in China smartphone market, August 4; (7) P. Williamson & E. Yin, 2014, Accelerated innovation, *MIT Sloan Management Review*, summer.

Learning Objective
Identify three ways of
understanding what
globalization is.

1-4 What Is Globalization?

Globalization, generally speaking, is the close integration of countries and peoples of the world. This abstract five-syllable word is now frequently heard and debated. Those who approve of globalization count its contributions to include greater economic growth, higher standards of living, increased technology sharing, and more extensive cultural integration. Critics argue that globalization undermines wages in rich countries, exploits workers in poor countries, grants MNEs too much power, destroys the environment, and promotes inequality. So, what exactly is globalization? This section outlines three views on globalization, recommends the pendulum view, and introduces the idea of semiglobalization.

1-4a Three Views on Globalization

Depending on what sources you read, globalization could be

- a new force sweeping through the world in recent times
- a long-run historical evolution since the dawn of human history
- a pendulum that swings from one extreme to another from time to time

An understanding of these views helps put into perspective the debate about globalization. First, opponents of globalization suggest that it is a new phenomenon beginning in the late 20th century, driven by recent technological innovations and a Western ideology focused on exploiting and dominating the world through MNEs. The arguments against globalization focus on environmental stress, social injustice, and sweatshop labor, but present few clear alternatives to the present economic order. Nevertheless, anti-globalization advocates and protesters often argue that globalization needs to be slowed down if not stopped.[21]

A second view contends that globalization has always been part and parcel of human history. Historians debate whether globalization started 2,000 or 8,000 years ago. The earliest traces of MNEs have been discovered in Assyrian, Phoenician, and Roman times.[22] International competition from low-cost countries is nothing new. In the first century A.D., the Roman emperor Tiberius was so concerned about the massive quantity of low-cost Chinese silk imports that he imposed the world's first known import quota of textiles.[23] Today's most successful MNEs do not come close to wielding the historical clout of some MNEs, such as the (old) East India Company during colonial times (see the Opening Case). In a nutshell, globalization is nothing new and will probably always exist.

A third view suggests that globalization is the "closer integration of the countries and peoples of the world which has been brought about by the enormous reduction of the costs of transportation and communication, and the breaking down of artificial barriers to the flows of goods, services, capital, knowledge, and (to a lesser extent) people across borders."[24] Globalization is neither recent nor one-directional. It is, more accurately, a process similar to the bi-directional swing of a pendulum.

1-4b The Pendulum View on Globalization

Globalization
The close integration of
countries and peoples of the
world.

The pendulum view probably makes the most sense because it can help us understand the ups and downs of globalization. The current era of globalization originated in the aftermath of World War II, when major Western countries committed to global trade and investment. However, between the 1950s and the 1970s, this view was not widely shared. Communist countries, such as China and the Soviet Union, sought to develop self-sufficiency. Many noncommunist developing countries, such as Brazil, India, and Mexico, focused on fostering and protecting domestic industries. But refusing to participate in global trade and investment ended up breeding uncompetitive industries. In contrast, four developing economies in Asia—Hong Kong, Singapore, South Korea, and Taiwan—earned their stripes as the "Four Tigers" by participating in the global economy. They became the *only* economies once recognized as less developed (low-income) by the World Bank to have subsequently achieved developed (high-income) status.

Inspired by the Four Tigers, more countries and regions—such as China in the late 1970s, Latin America in the mid-1980s, Central and Eastern Europe in the late 1980s, and India in the 1990s—realized that joining the global economy was a must. As these countries started to emerge as new players in the global economy, they became collectively known as "emerging economies." As a result, globalization rapidly accelerated.

However, globalization, like a pendulum, is unable to keep going in one direction. Rapid globalization in the 1990s and the 2000s saw some significant backlash. First, the rapid growth of globalization led to the historically inaccurate view that globalization is new. Second, it created fear among many people in developed economies that they would lose jobs. Emerging economies not only seem to attract many low-end jobs away from developed economies, but they also increasingly appear to threaten some high-end jobs. Finally, some factions in emerging economies complained against the onslaught of MNEs, alleging that they destroy local companies as well as local cultures, values, and environments.

The December 1999 anti-globalization protests in Seattle and the September 2001 terrorist attacks in New York and Washington were undoubtedly some of the most visible and most extreme acts of anti-globalization forces at work. As a result, international travel was curtailed, and global trade and investment flows slowed in the early 2000s. Then in the mid-2000s, however, worldwide GDP, cross-border trade, and per capita GDP all soared to historically high levels. It was during that period that "BRIC" became a buzzword (discussed earlier).

Unfortunately, the party suddenly ended in 2008. The 2008–2009 global economic crisis was unlike anything the world had seen since the Great Depression (1929–1933). The crisis showed, for better or worse, how interconnected the global economy has become. Deteriorating housing markets in the United States, fueled by unsustainable subprime lending practices, led to massive government bailouts of failed firms. The crisis quickly spread around the world, forcing numerous governments to bail out their own troubled banks. Global output, trade, and investment plummeted, while unemployment skyrocketed. The 2008–2009 crisis became known as the Great Recession. Many people blamed globalization for the Great Recession.

After unprecedented government intervention in developed economies, confidence was growing that the global economy had turned the corner and that the recession was ending.[25] However, starting in 2010, the Greek debt crisis and then the broader PIGS debt crisis erupted. ("PIGS" refers to Portugal, Ireland or Italy, Greece, and Spain). The already-slow recovery in Europe thus became slower, and unemployment hovered at very high levels (see Chapter 8).

The Great Recession reminds all firms and managers of the importance of risk management—the identification and assessment of risks and the preparation to minimize the impact of high-risk, unfortunate events.[26] As a technique to prepare and plan for multiple scenarios (either high risk or low risk), scenario planning is now used extensively around the world.[27] The recovery has seen more protectionist measures, since the stimulus packages and job-creation schemes of various governments often emphasize "buy national" (such as "buy American") and "hire locals." In short, the pendulum is swinging back. The Closing Case shows a pendulum consisting of two polar scenarios—continued globalization and de-globalization—with a view toward 2050.

Like the proverbial elephant, globalization is seen by everyone, yet rarely comprehended. The sudden ferocity of the 2008–2009 crisis surprised everybody—ranging from central bankers to academic experts. Remember, all of us felt sorry when we read the story of a bunch of blind men trying to figure out the shape and form of the elephant. We really shouldn't have. Although we are not blind, our task is more challenging than the blind men who study a standing animal. Our beast—globalization—does not stand still and often rapidly moves, back and forth (!). Yet, we try to live with it, avoid being crushed by it, and even attempt to profit from it. Overall, relative to the other two views, the view of globalization as a bi-directional pendulum is more balanced and more realistic. In other words, globalization has both rosy and dark sides, and these change over time.

1-4c Semiglobalization

Despite the debate over it, globalization is not complete. Do we really live in a globalized world? Are selling and investing abroad just as easy as at home? Obviously not. Most measures of market integration, such as trade and FDI, have recently scaled new heights, but still fall far short of pointing to a single, globally integrated market. In other words, what we have may be labeled semiglobalization, which is more complex than extremes of total isolation and total globalization. Semiglobalization suggests that barriers to market integration at borders are high, but not high enough to insulate countries from each other completely.[28]

Semiglobalization calls for more than one way of doing business around the globe. Total isolation on a nation-state basis would suggest localization—a strategy of treating each country as a unique market. So an MNE marketing products to 100 countries will need to come up with 100 versions of local cars or drinks. This approach is clearly too costly. Total globalization, on the other hand, would lead to standardization—a strategy of treating the entire world as one market. The MNE in our previous example can just market one version of "world car" or "world drink." But the world obviously is not that simple. Between total isolation and total globalization, semiglobalization has no single correct strategy, resulting in a wide variety of experimentations (see Emerging Markets 1.2). Overall, (semi)globalization is neither to be opposed as a menace nor to be celebrated as a panacea; it is to be *engaged*.

Risk management

The identification and assessment of risks and the preparation to minimize the impact of high-risk, unfortunate events.

Scenario planning

A technique to prepare and plan for multiple scenarios (either high- or low-risk).

Semiglobalization

A perspective that suggests that barriers to market integration at borders are high, but not high enough to insulate countries from each other completely.

EMERGING MARKETS 1.2

Coca-Cola's Deep Dive in Africa

Founded in 1892, Coca-Cola first entered Africa in 1929. While Africa had always been viewed as a "backwater," it has recently emerged as a major growth market commanding strategic attention. Of the US$27 billion that Coca-Cola would invest in emerging economies between 2010 and 2020, US$12 billion will be used to beef up the plants and distribution facilities in Africa. Why does Coca-Cola show such a strong interest in a "deep dive" in Africa? Both the push and pull effects are at work.

The push comes from the necessity to find new sources of growth for this mature firm, which has promised investors of 7% to 9% earnings growth. In 1998, its stock reached a high-water mark at US$88. But it dropped to US$37 in 2003. Since 2004, the share price has rallied again, rising from US$43 to a new peak of US$90 in November 2014 (adjusted for a 2:1 share split in 2012). Can Coca-Cola's stock reach higher?

Its home markets are unlikely to help. Between 2006 and 2011, US sales declined for five consecutive years. Further, health advocates accused Coca-Cola of contributing to an epidemic of obesity in the United States and proposed to tax soft drinks to pay for health care. While Coca-Cola defeated the tax initiative, it is fair to say that the room for growth at home is limited. In Europe and Japan, sales are similarly flat. Elsewhere, in China, strong local rivals have made it tough for Coca-Cola to break out. Its acquisition of a leading local fruit juice firm was blocked by the government, which did not seem to bless Coca-Cola's further growth. In India, Pepsi is so popular that "Pepsi" has become the Hindi shorthand for all bottled soft drinks (including Coke!). In Latin America, sales are encouraging, but growth may be limited. Mexicans, on average, are already guzzling 665 servings of Coca-Cola products every year, the highest in the world. There is only so much sugary water one can drink every day.

In contrast, Coca-Cola is pulled by Africa, where it has a commanding 29% market share versus Pepsi's 15%. With 65,000 employees and 160 plants, Coca-Cola is Africa's largest private-sector employer. Yet, annual per capita consumption of Coca-Cola products is only 39 servings in Kenya. For the continent as a whole, disposable income is growing. In 2014, 100 million Africans earned at least US$5,000 per person. While Africa indeed has some of the poorest countries in the world, 12 African countries (with a combined population of 100 million) have a GDP per capita that is greater than China's. Coca-Cola is hoping to capitalize on Africa's improved political stability and physical infrastructure. Countries not fighting civil wars make Coke's operations less disruptive, and new roads penetrating the jungle can obviously elevate sales.

Coca-Cola is already in all African countries. The challenge now, according to chairman and CEO Muhtar Kent, will be to *deep dive* into "every town, every village, every township." This will not be easy. War, poverty, and poor infrastructure make it extremely difficult to distribute and market products in hard-to-access regions. Undaunted, Coca-Cola is in a street-by-street campaign to increase awareness and consumption of its products. The crowds and the poor roads dictate that some of the deliveries have to be done manually on pushcarts or trolleys. Throughout the continent, Coca-Cola has set up 3,000 Manual Distribution Centers. Taking a page from its playbook in Latin America, especially Mexico, Coca-Cola has aggressively courted small corner stores. Coca-Cola and its bottlers offer small corner store owners delivery, credit, and direct coaching—ranging from the tip not to ice down the Cokes until the midday rush to save electricity, to helping on how to buy a house after vendors make enough money.

In Africa, US-style accusations of Coca-Cola's alleged contribution to the obesity problem are unlikely. After all, the primary concern in many communities is too few available calories of any kind. However, this does not mean Africa is Coca-Cola's marketing Shangri-La, free from any criticisms. It has to defend itself from critics who accuse it of depleting fresh water, encouraging expensive and environmentally harmful refrigeration, and hurting local competitors who hawk beverages. In response, Coca-Cola often points out the benefits it has brought. In addition to the 65,000 jobs it has directly created, one million local jobs are indirectly created by its vast system of distribution, which moves beverages from bottling plants deep into the slums and the bush a few crates at a time.

Sources: Based on (1) M. Blanding, 2010, *The Coke Machine*, New York: Avery; (2) *Bloomberg Businessweek*, 2010, Coke's last round, November 1: 54–61; (3) *Bloomberg Businessweek*, 2010, For India's consumers, Pepsi is the real thing, September 20: 26–27; (4) *Bloomberg Businessweek*, 2011, Can Coke surpass its record high of $88 a share? June 6: 49–50; (5) D. Zoogah, M. W. Peng, & H. Woldu, 2015, Institutions, resources, and organizational effectiveness in Africa, *Academy of Management Perspectives*, 29(1): 7–31.

Learning Objective
State the size of the global economy and its broad trends, and understand your likely bias in the globalization debate.

1-5 Global Business and Globalization at a Crossroads

Twenty-first-century business leaders face enormous challenges. This book helps overcome these challenges. As a backdrop for the remainder of this book, this section makes two points. First, a basic understanding of the global economy is necessary. Second, it is important to critically examine your own personal views and biases regarding globalization.

1-5a A Glance at the Global Economy

The global economy in 2013 was an approximately US$75 trillion economy (total global GDP calculated at official, nominal exchange rates—US$100 trillion on PPP basis).[29] While there is no need to memorize a lot of statistics, it is useful to remember this US$75 trillion (or US$100 trillion) figure to put things in perspective.

One frequent observation in the globalization debate is the enormous size of MNEs. Take a look at the largest MNE within one sizeable country: Volkswagen's worldwide sales would represent 10% of German GDP, Samsung's sales 17% of South Korean GDP, and BP's sales 26% of British GDP.[30] Table 1.3 shows the most recent top ten firms. The top three largest MNEs—measured by sales—happened to be headquartered in North America, Europe, and Asia. If the largest MNE, Wal-Mart, were an independent country, it would be the 27th largest economy—its sales are smaller than Belgium's GDP but larger than Venezuela's. The sales of the largest EU-based MNE, Royal Dutch Shell, were larger than the GDP of each of the following EU member countries: Austria, Denmark, Finland, Portugal, and Ireland. The sales of the largest Asia-based MNE, SINOPEC, were larger than the GDP of each of the following Asian economies: Thailand, Malaysia, Hong Kong, Singapore, and the Philippines. Today, more than 82,000 MNEs manage at least 810,000 subsidiaries overseas.[31] Total annual sales for the largest 500 MNEs exceed US$31 trillion (about one-third of global output).[32]

Table 1.4 documents the change in the makeup of the 500 largest MNEs. While MNEs from the Triad (North America, Europe, and Japan) dominate the list, their share has been shrinking—thanks to the Great Transformation (discussed earlier). Among MNEs from emerging economies, those from BRIC contribute 118 firms to the *Fortune* Global 500 list. In particular, MNEs from China have come on strong.[33]

Table 1.3	Top Ten Largest Firms in the World (Measured by Sales in US$)		
	Corporate name	**Home country**	**Revenues**
1	Wal-Mart Stores	USA	$476 billion
2	Royal Dutch Shell	Netherlands	$460 billion
3	SINOPEC Group	China	$457 billion
4	China National Petroleum Corporation	China	$432 billion
5	ExxonMobil	USA	$408 billion
6	BP	UK	$396 billion
7	State Grid	China	$333 billion
8	Volkswagen	Germany	$261 billion
9	Toyota Motor	Japan	$256 billion
10	Glencore	Switzerland	$233 billion

Source: Adapted from *Fortune*, 2014, Global 500, July 21: F–1. Data refer to 2013.

Table 1.4	Recent Changes in the *Fortune* Global 500		
	2005	**2010**	**2014**
Developed economies			
United States	170	133	128
European Union	165	149	128
Japan	70	68	57
Switzerland	12	15	13
Canada	14	11	10
Australia	8	8	8
Emerging economies			
China	20	61	95
India	6	8	8
Brazil	4	7	7
Russia	5	7	8
BRIC	35	83	118

Sources: Adapted from various *Fortune* issues. The most recent *Fortune* Global 500 list (for 2014) was published in *Fortune,* July 21, 2014.

Beijing is now headquarters to 52 *Fortune* Global 500 firms, more than New York's 20—remember Question 4 in Opening Day Quiz. Clearly, Western rivals cannot afford to ignore these emerging multinationals, and students studying this book need to pay attention to these emerging multinationals.[34]

1-5b The Globalization Debate and You

As a future business leader, you are not a detached reader. The globalization debate directly affects *your* future.[35] Therefore, it is imperative that you participate

© Shalunts/Shutterstock.com

Why do protestors like these object to globalization?

Nongovernmental organization (NGO)

An organization that is not affiliated with governments.

in the globalization debate instead of letting other people make decisions on globalization that will significantly affect your career, your consumption, and your country. It is important to know your own biases when joining the debate. By the very act of taking an IB course and reading this book, you probably already have some pro-globalization biases, compared to non-business majors elsewhere on campus and the general public in your country.

You are not alone. In the last several decades, most executives, policy makers, and scholars in both developed and emerging economies, who are generally held to be the elite in these societies, are biased toward acknowledging the benefits of globalization. However, many other members of the society do not necessarily share the same views. Unfortunately, many of the elite fail to understand the limits of their beliefs and mistakenly assume that the rest of the world thinks like them. To the extent that powerful economic and political institutions are largely controlled by the elite in almost every country, it is not surprising that some anti-globalization groups, feeling powerless, end up resorting to unconventional tactics, such as mass protests, to make their point.

Many of the opponents of globalization are nongovernmental organizations (NGOs), such as environmentalists, human rights activists, and consumer groups. Ignoring them will be a grave failure when doing business around the globe. Instead of viewing NGOs as opponents, many firms view them as partners. NGOs do raise a valid point when they insist that firms, especially MNEs, should have a broader concern for the various stakeholders affected by the actions of MNEs actions around the world. At present, this view is increasingly moving from the peripheral to the mainstream (see Chapters 3 and 17).

It is certainly interesting, and perhaps alarming, to note that as would-be business leaders who will shape the global economy in the future, current business school students already exhibit values and beliefs in favor of globalization similar to those held by executives, policy makers, and scholars and different from those held by the general public. Shown in Table 1.5, US business students have significantly more positive (almost one-sided) views toward globalization than does the general public. My lectures around the world suggest that most business students—regardless of their nationality—seem to share such positive views on globalization. This is not surprising. Both self-selection to study business and socialization within the curriculum, in which free trade is widely regarded as positive, may lead to certain attitudes in favor of globalization. Consequently, business students tend to focus more on the economic gains of globalization and to be less concerned with its darker sides.

Current and would-be business leaders must be aware of their own biases embodied in such one-sided views toward globalization. Since business schools aspire to train future business leaders by indoctrinating students with the dominant values

Table 1.5	**Views on Globalization: General Public versus Business Students**	
Percentage answering "good" for the question: Overall, do you think globalization is *good* or *bad* for	**General public[1] (N = 1,024)**	**Business students[2] (N = 494)**
US consumers like you	68%	96%
US companies	63%	77%
The US economy	64%	88%
Strengthening poor countries' economies	75%	82%

Sources: Based on (1) A. Bernstein, 2000, Backlash against globalization, *BusinessWeek,* April 24: 43; (2) M. W. Peng & H. Shin, 2008, How do future business leaders view globalization? *Thunderbird International Business Review,* 50 (3): 175–182. All differences are statistically significant.

that managers hold, business schools may have largely succeeded in this mission. However, to the extent that current managers (and professors) have some strategic blind spots, these findings are potentially alarming. They reveal that business students already share these blind spots. Despite possible self-selection in choosing to major in business, there is no denying that student values are shaped, at least in part, by the educational experience that business schools provide. Knowing such limitations, business school professors and students need to work especially hard to break out of this mental straitjacket.

In order to combat the widespread tendency to have one-sided, rosy views, a significant portion of this book is devoted to the numerous debates that surround globalization.[36] Debates are systematically introduced in *every* chapter to provoke more critical thinking—a hallmark for high-level university training. Virtually all textbooks uncritically present knowledge "as is" and ignore the fact that the field is alive with numerous debates. No doubt, debates drive practice and research forward. Therefore, it is imperative that you be exposed to cutting-edge debates and encouraged to form your own views. In addition, business ethics are emphasized throughout the book. A featured Ethical Dilemma can be found in every chapter. Two whole chapters are devoted to ethics, norms, and cultures (Chapter 3) and corporate social responsibility (Chapter 17).

1-6 Organization of the Content

This book has four parts. Part I is *foundations*. Following this chapter, Chapters 2, 3, and 4 address the two leading perspectives—namely, institution-based and resource-based views. Part II covers *tools*, focusing on trade (Chapter 5), foreign investment (Chapter 6), foreign exchange (Chapter 7), and global and regional integration (Chapter 8). Part III sheds light on *strategy*. We start with the internationalization of small, entrepreneurial firms (Chapter 9), followed by ways to enter foreign markets (Chapter 10), to manage competitive dynamics (Chapter 11), to make alliances and acquisitions work (Chapter 12), and to strategize, structure, and learn (Chapter 13). Finally, Part IV builds *excellence in different functional areas*: marketing and supply chain (Chapter 14), human resource management (Chapter 15), finance and corporate governance (Chapter 16), and corporate social responsibility (Chapter 17).

CHAPTER SUMMARY/LEARNING OBJECTIVES

1-1 Explain the concepts of international business and global business, with a focus on emerging economies.

- IB is typically defined as (1) a business (firm) that engages in international (cross-border) economic activities, and/or (2) the action of doing business abroad.
- Global business is defined in this book as business around the globe.
- This book has gone beyond competition in developed economies by devoting extensive space to competitive battles waged in emerging economies and the base of the global economic pyramid.
- An interesting recent development out of emerging economies is reverse innovation.

1-2 Give three reasons why it is important to study global business.

- Enhance your employability and advance your career in the global economy by equipping yourself with global business knowledge.
- Better preparation for possible expatriate assignments abroad.
- Stronger competence in interacting with foreign suppliers, partners, and competitors, and in working for foreign-owned employers in your own country.

1-3 Articulate one fundamental question and two core perspectives in the study of global business.

- IB's most fundamental question is: What determines the success and failure of firms around the globe?
- The two core perspectives are (1) the institution-based view and (2) the resource-based view.
- We develop a unified framework by organizing materials in *every* chapter according to the two perspectives guided by the fundamental question.

1-4 Identify three ways of understanding what globalization is.

- Some view globalization as a recent phenomenon, and others believe that it has been a one-directional evolution since the dawn of human history.
- We suggest that globalization is best viewed as a process similar to the bi-directional swing of a pendulum.

1-5 State the size of the global economy and its broad trends, and understand your likely bias in the globalization debate.

- MNEs, especially large ones from developed economies, are sizable economic entities.
- Current and would-be business leaders need to be aware of their own hidden pro-globalization bias.

KEY TERMS

Base of the pyramid (BoP), 8	Emerging market, 6	Global business, 5
BRIC, 7	Expatriate manager (expat), 12	Globalization, 18
BRICS, 7	Foreign direct investment (FDI), 4	Great Transformation, 8
Emerging economy, 5		Gross domestic product (GDP), 6

Gross national income
(GNI), 6

Gross national product
(GNP), 6

Group of 20 (G-20), 11

International business
(IB), 4

International premium, 12

Liability of foreignness, 16

Multinational enterprise
(MNE), 4

Nongovernmental
organization
(NGO), 24

Purchasing power parity
(PPP), 6

Reverse innovation, 9

Risk management, 20

Scenario planning, 20

Semiglobalization, 20

Triad, 8

REVIEW QUESTIONS

1. What is the traditional definition of IB? How is global business defined in this book?

2. Compare PengAtlas Maps 2.1 (Top Merchandise Importers and Exporters), 2.2 (Top Service Importers and Exporters), and 2.3 (FDI Inflows and Outflows) and note that the United States is number one in all categories except one. What is it? Many people feel that is a big problem—do you? In your opinion, what—if anything—should be done about that?

3. Compare PengAtlas Maps 2.1 (Top Merchandise Importers and Exporters), 2.2 (Top Service Importers and Exporters), and 2.3 (FDI Inflows and Outflows) once again and note the BRIC countries that are referenced in this chapter. Which of the BRIC countries is most often among the categories in those maps? Do you think that the long-term trend will be for that country to continue to become more important and perhaps surpass the United States, or do you think that it may decline, and one of the other BRIC countries will become more important? Why?

4. *ON CULTURE:* Not all people in your country support globalization, and some feel that globalization is an economic threat. However, to what extent could it be they may also feel that it is a threat to their culture?

5. Discuss the importance of emerging economies in the global economy. Use current news.

6. What is your interest in studying global business? How do you think it may help you succeed in the future?

7. If you were to work as an expatriate manager, where would you like to go? Why?

8. How would you describe an institution-based view of global business?

9. How would you describe a resource-based view of global business?

10. After comparing the three views of globalization, which seems the most sensible to you and why?

11. What is semiglobalization? What factors contribute to it?

12. Do those who protest against globalization make any valid point(s) that all people, whether for or against globalization, should consider?

13. You may view yourself as objective and neutral regarding globalization, but do you sense any bias that you may have, one way or the other? What bias most likely exists on the part of other students taking this course?

14. Given the size of the global economy and the size of some of the large corporations, do you think it is possible to carve out a niche that you can exploit as a small businessperson? Or do you feel that the most practical way to participate in the global economy is to do so as an employee or manager in a global corporation?

CRITICAL DISCUSSION QUESTIONS

1. A classmate says: "Global business is relevant for top executives, such as CEOs, in large companies. I am just a lowly student who will struggle to gain an entry-level job, probably in a small domestic company. Why should I care about it?" How do you convince her that global business is something to care about?

2. *ON CULTURE:* Thomas Friedman, in his book *The World is Flat* (2005), suggests that the world is flattening—meaning that it is increasingly interconnected by new technology, such as the Internet. On the other hand, this presents significant challenges for developed economies, whose employees may feel threatened by competition from low-cost countries. How does this flattening world affect you?

3. *ON ETHICS:* What are some of the darker sides (in other words, costs) associated with globalization? How can business leaders make sure that the benefits of their various actions outweigh their costs?

4. *ON ETHICS:* Some argue that aggressively investing in emerging economies is not only economically beneficial but also highly ethical, because it could lift many people out of poverty. However, others caution that in the absence of decent profits, rushing to emerging economies is reckless. What do you think?

BUSINESS INSIGHTS GLOBAL

GLOBAL ACTION

1. Chemical companies are among the largest firms worldwide. Two approaches to evaluating their operations are by capital spending and by research and development (R&D) spending. Access a resource that provides this information about top global chemical producers. Then compare the top five capital-spending and R&D-spending chemical companies. Are any companies found on both lists? What insights does this information provide?

2. One important aspect of globalization is the fundamental stability of the global economic order currently in place. Thus, FDI intentions can be influenced by its perceived sustainability to some degree. Identify the three most important issues related to global economic stability over the next 20 years.

CLOSING CASE

EMERGING MARKETS: Two Scenarios of the Global Economy in 2050

In the perilous exercise of predicting the future of the global economy, two scenarios have emerged with a view toward 2050. Known as "continued globalization," the first scenario is the rosy one that has been widely known. Spearheaded by Goldman Sachs, whose chairman of its Asset Management Division, Jim O'Neil, coined the term "BRIC" more than a decade ago, this scenario suggests that—in descending order—China, the United States, India, Brazil, and Russia will become the largest economies by 2050 (Figure 1.6). BRIC countries together may overtake the US by 2015 and the G-7 by 2032, and China may individually dethrone the US by 2026. In PPP terms, BRIC's share of global GDP, which rose from 18% in 2001 to 25% currently, may reach 40% by 2050. In addition, by 2050, the N-11 as a group may become significantly larger than the US and almost twice the size of the Euro area.

Broadening our thinking beyond a focus on acronyms such as BRIC and N-11, one interesting way is to identify the *larger* emerging markets (defined as exceeding 1% of global GDP by 2050). Nine of the N-11 may exceed the 1% of global GDP threshold by 2050. In addition, a number of other relatively *smaller* emerging markets (defined as not exceeding 1% of

global GDP by 2050) will exhibit strong growth dynamism and potential (Figure 1.7). The upshot? While BRIC growth rates will slow down, emerging economies *as a group*—consisting of BRIC, N-11, and other "larger" and "smaller" emerging markets—will continue to drive global growth.

Goldman Sachs's predictions have been largely supported by other influential forecasting studies. For example, Organization for Economic Cooperation and Development (OECD) predicted that by 2060, China, India, and the US will become the top three economies. The combined GDP of China and India will be larger than that of the entire OECD area (Figure 1.8). In 2011, China and India accounted for less than one-half of GDP of the seven major (G-7) OECD economies. By 2060, the combined GDP of China and India may be 1.5 times larger than the G-7. India's GDP will be a bit larger than the US's, and China's a lot larger.

Despite such dramatic changes, one interesting constant is the relative rankings of income per capita. Goldman Sachs predicted that by 2050, the G-7 countries will still be the richest, led by the US, Canada, and the UK (Figure 1.9). Ranked eighth globally (US$63,486—all dollar figures in this paragraph refer to 2010 US dollars), Russia may top the

Figure 1.6 **BRIC and the US Will Become the Largest Economies by 2050**

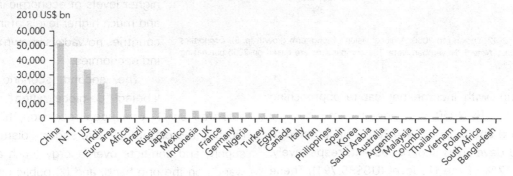

Source: Goldman Sachs, 2012, An update on the long-term outlook for the BRICs and beyond (p. 3), *Monthly Insights from the Office of the Chairman, Goldman Sachs Asset Management*, January. "N-11" refers to the Next Eleven identified by Goldman Sachs: Bangladesh, Egypt, Indonesia, Iran, Korea, Mexico, Nigeria, Pakistan, the Philippines, Turkey, and Vietnam.

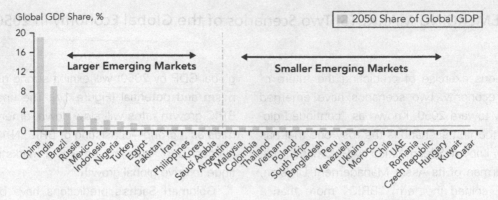

Figure 1.7   Larger (> 1% Global GDP) and Smaller (< 1% Global GDP) Emerging Markets by 2050

Source: Adapted from Goldman Sachs, 2012, An update on the long-term outlook for the BRICs and beyond (p. 3), *Monthly Insights from the Office of the Chairman, Goldman Sachs Asset Management*, January. In the original publication, "larger emerging markets" are labeled "growth markets," and "smaller emerging markets" are labeled "emerging markets." To avoid confusion, we label all of them "emerging markets," which are differentiated by size. The orange line is 1% global GDP.

Figure 1.8   The Percentages of Global GDP, 2011 and 2060

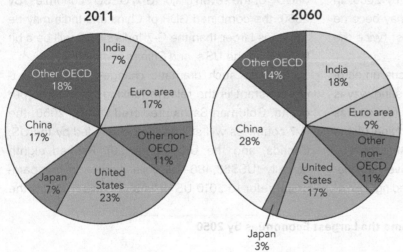

Source: OECD, 2012, Looking to 2060: A global vision of long-term growth (p. 8), *Economics Department Policy Note* 5, November. Note: The comparisons are based on 2005 purchasing power parity (PPP).

BRIC group, with income per capita approaching that of Korea. By 2050, per capita income in China (US$40,614) and India (US$14,766) will continue to lag behind developed economies—at, respectively, 47% and 17% of the US level (US$85,791). These predictions were supported by OECD, which noted that by 2060, Chinese and Indian per capita income would only reach 59% and 27% of the US level, respectively.

Underpinning this scenario of "continued globalization" are three assumptions: (1) emerging economies as a group will maintain strong (albeit gradually reduced) growth; (2) geopolitical events and natural disasters (such as climate changes) will not create significant disruption; and (3) regional, international, and supranational institutions continue to function reasonably. This scenario envisions a path of growth that is perhaps more volatile than that of the past 20 years, but ultimately leads to considerably higher levels of economic integration and much higher levels of incomes in countries nowadays known as emerging economies.

The second scenario can be labeled "de-globalization." It is characterized by (1) prolonged recession, high unemployment, droughts, climate shocks, disrupted food supply, and conflicts over energy (such as "water wars") on the one hand; and (2) public unrest, protectionist policies, and the unraveling of certain institutions that we take for granted (such as the EU) on the other hand. As protectionism rises, global economic integration suffers.

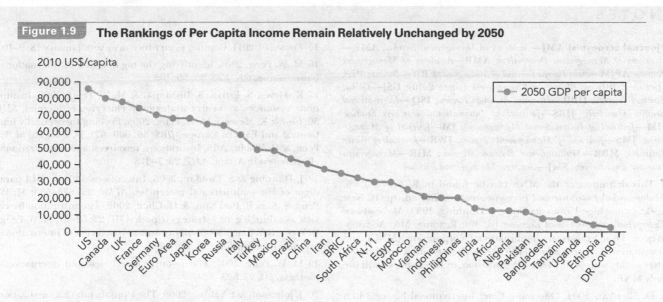

Figure 1.9   **The Rankings of Per Capita Income Remain Relatively Unchanged by 2050**

Source: Goldman Sachs, 2012, An update on the long-term outlook for the BRICs and beyond (p. 4), *Monthly Insights from the Office of the Chairman, Goldman Sachs Asset Management*, January. See footnote to Figure 1.6 for N-11.

The upshot? Weak economic growth around the world. While global de-integration would harm economies worldwide, regional de-integration would harm countries of Europe, especially those outside a likely residual core of the EU. Unable to keep growing sustainably, BRIC may become "broken bricks" and may fail to reach their much-hyped potential. For example, in the 1950s and 1960s, Russian economic growth was also very impressive, fueling Soviet geopolitical ambitions that eventually turned out to be unsupportable. In the late 1960s, Burma (now Myanmar), the Philippines, and Sri Lanka were widely anticipated to become the next Asian Tigers, only to falter badly. Over the long course of history, it is rare to sustain strong growth in a large number of countries over more than a decade. It is true that the first decade of the 21st century—prior to the Great Depression—witnessed some spectacular growth in BRIC and many other emerging economies. A key question concerns how unique the current times are. Historically, "failure to sustain growth has been the general rule," according to a pessimistic expert.

In both scenarios, one common prediction is that global competition will heat up. Competition under the "de-globalization" scenario would be especially intense since the total size of the "pie" will not be growing sufficiently (if not negatively). At the same time, firms would operate in partially protected markets, which result in additional costs for market penetration. Competition under the "continued globalization" scenario would also be intense, but in different ways. The hope is that a rising "tide" may be able to lift "all boats."

CASE DISCUSSION QUESTIONS

1. Which of the two scenarios is more plausible for the global economy in 2050? Why? How does that affect *you* as a consumer, as a professional, and as a citizen of your country?

2. From a resource-based view, what should firms do to better prepare for the two scenarios?

3. ***ON ETHICS:*** From an institution-based view, what should firms do to better prepare for the two scenarios? (HINT: For example, if they believe in "continued globalization," they may be more interested in lobbying for reduced trade barriers. But if they believe in "de-globalization," they may lobby for higher trade barriers.)

Sources: Based on (1) Foresight Horizon Scanning Centre, 2009, *World Trade: Possible Futures*, London: UK Government Office for Science; (2) Goldman Sachs, 2012, An update on the long-term outlook for the BRICs and beyond, *Monthly Insights from the Office of the Chairman, Goldman Sachs Asset Management*, January; (3) OECD, 2012, Looking to 2060: A global vision of long-term growth, *Economics Department Policy Note* 5, November; (4) M. W. Peng & K. Meyer, 2013, Winning the future markets for UK manufacturing output, *Future of Manufacturing Project Evidence Paper* 25, London: UK Government Office for Science; (5) R. Sharma, 2012, Broken BRICS: Why the rest stopped growing, *Foreign Affairs*, November: 2–7.

NOTES

[**Journal acronyms**] **AMJ**—*Academy of Management Journal;* **AMP**—*Academy of Management Perspectives;* **AMR**—*Academy of Management Review;* **APJM**—*Asia Pacific Journal of Management;* **BW**—*BusinessWeek* (before 2010) or *Bloomberg Businessweek* (since 2010); **GSJ**—*Global Strategy Journal;* **HBR**—*Harvard Business Review;* **ISQ**—*International Studies Quarterly;* **JIBS**—*Journal of International Business Studies;* **JIM**—*Journal of International Management;* **JM**—*Journal of Management;* **JMS**—*Journal of Management Studies;* **JWB**—*Journal of World Business;* **MBR**—*Multinational Business Review;* **MIR**—*Management International Review;* **SMJ**—*Strategic Management Journal*

1 This definition of the MNE can be found in R. Caves, 1996, *Multinational Enterprise and Economic Analysis,* 2nd ed. (p. 1), New York: Cambridge University Press; J. Dunning, 1993, *Multinational Enterprises and the Global Economy* (p. 30), Reading, MA: Addison-Wesley. Other terms are multinational corporation (MNC) and transnational corporation (TNC), which are often used interchangeably with MNE. To avoid confusion, in this book, we will use only MNE.

2 O. Shenkar, 2004, One more time: International business in a global economy (p. 165), *JIBS,* 35: 161–171. See also J. Boddewyn, B. Toyne, & Z. Martinez, 2004, The meanings of "international management," *MIR,* 44: 195–215; J.-F. Hennart, 2009, Down with MNE-centric models! *JIBS,* 40: 1432–1454.

3 C. Pitellis, 2009, IB at 50, *AIB Insights,* 9 (1): 2–8.

4 United Nations, 2014, *World Investment Report 2014* (p. ix), New York and Geneva: UN.

5 R. Hoskisson, M. Wright, I. Filatotchev, & M. W. Peng, 2013, Emerging multinationals from mid-range economies, *JMS,* 50: 1295–1321.

6 C. Layne, 2012, This time it's real: The end of unipolarity and the *Pax Americana, ISQ,* 56: 203–213; J. Nye, 2012, The twenty-first century will not be a "post-American" world, *ISQ,* 56: 215–217; F. Zakaria, 2008, *The Post-American World,* New York: Norton.

7 *Economist,* 2013, When giants slow down, July 27: 20.

8 McKinsey Global Institute, 2012, *Manufacturing the Future* (p. 9), November.

9 *BW,* 2013, Why emerging markets are getting crushed, August 5: 10–11; *Economist,* 2014, Emerge, splurge, purge, March 8: 65–68; *Economist,* 2014, Submerging hopes, March 8: 12.

10 S. Ansari, K. Munir, & T. Gregg, 2012, Impact at the "bottom of the pyramid," *JMS,* 49: 813–842; J. Hall, S. Matos, L. Sheehan, & B. Silvestre, 2012, Entrepreneurship and innovation at the base of the pyramid, *JMS,* 49: 787–812; G. Kistruck, C. Sutter, R. Lount, & B. Smith, 2013, Mitigating principal-agent problems in base-of-the-pyramid markets, *AMJ,* 56: 659–682; T. London, 2009, Making better investments at the base of the pyramid, *HBR,* May: 106–113; C. K. Prahalad, 2005, *The Fortune at the Bottom of the Pyramid,* Philadelphia: Wharton School Publishing.

11 V. Govindarajan & C. Trimble, 2012, *Reverse Innovation* (p. 4), Boston: Harvard Business Review Press. See also S. Bradley, J. McMullen, K. Artz, & E. Smimiyu, 2012, Capital is not enough, *JMS,* 49: 684–717.

12 *Economist,* 2013, Mahindra & Mahindra: SUVival of the fittest, November 2: 67–68.

13 J. Immelt, V. Govindarajan, & C. Trimble, 2009, How GE is disrupting itself, *HBR,* October: 56–65.

14 These numbers come from *Fortune,* 2014, Global 500, July 21. They change every year.

15 *Economist,* 2014, Coming to an office near you, January 18: 9–10.

16 M. W. Peng, 2004, Identifying the big question in international business research, *JIBS,* 35: 99–108.

17 K. Meyer, S. Estrin, S. Bhaumik, & M. W. Peng, 2009, Institutions, resources, and entry strategies in emerging economies, *SMJ,* 30: 61–80; K. Meyer & M. W. Peng, 2005, Probing theoretically into Central and Eastern Europe, *JIBS,* 36: 600–621; D. Zoogah, M. W. Peng, & H. Woldu, 2015, Institutions, resources, and organizational effectiveness in Africa, *AMP,* 29: 7–31.

18 J. Dunning & S. Lundan, 2008, Institutions and the OLI paradigm of the multinational enterprise, *APJM,* 25: 573–593; M. W. Peng, S. Sun, B. Pinkham, & H. Chen, 2009, The institution-based view as a third leg for a strategy tripod, *AMP,* 23: 63–81; M. W. Peng, D. Wang, & Y. Jiang, 2008, An institution-based view of international business strategy, *JIBS,* 39: 920–936.

19 M. W. Peng, 2001, The resource-based view and international business, *JM,* 27: 803–829.

20 J. Johanson & J. Vahlne, 2009, The Uppsala internationalization process model revisited: From liability of foreignness to liability of outsidership, *JIBS,* 40: 1411–1431.

21 *BW,* 2006, Free trade can be too free, July 3: 102–104; H. Chang, 2008, *Bad Samaritans,* New York: Bloomsbury.

22 K. Moore & D. Lewis, 2009, *The Origins of Globalization,* New York: Routledge.

23 D. Yergin & J. Stanislaw, 2002, *The Commanding Heights* (p. 385), New York: Simon & Schuster.

24 J. Stiglitz, 2002, *Globalization and Its Discontents* (p. 9), New York: Norton.

25 M. W. Peng, R. Bhagat, & S. Chang, 2010, Asia and global business, *JIBS,* 41: 373–376.

26 L. Purda, 2008, Risk perception and the financial system, *JIBS,* 39: 1178–1196; M. Sharfman & C. Fernando, 2008, Environment risk management and the cost of capital, *SMJ,* 29: 569–592.

27 S. Lee & M. Makhija, 2009, The effect of domestic uncertainty on the real options value of international investments, *JIBS,* 40: 405–420.

28 P. Ghemawat, 2003, Semiglobalization and international business strategy, *JIBS,* 34: 138–152.

29 The nominal GDP figures are from the World Bank, 2014, GDP (current US$), World Development Database, Washington. The PPP GDP figures are from the International Monetary Fund (IMF), 2014, *Report for Selected Countries and Subjects (PPP Valuation of Country GDP),* October, Washington.

30 *BW,* 2013, Supersized national champs, April 8: 14.

31 United Nations (UN), 2010, *World Investment Report 2010* (p. 10), New York and Geneva: UN.

32 *Fortune,* 2014, Global 500, July 21: 53.

33 M. W. Peng, 2012, The global strategy of emerging multinationals from China, *GSJ,* 2: 97–107.

34 A. Cuervo-Cazurra & M. Genc, 2011, Obligating, pressuring, and supporting dimensions of the environment and the non-market advantages of developing-country multinational companies, *JMS,* 48: 441–455; L. Cui & F. Jiang, 2010, Behind ownership decision of Chinese outward FDI, *APJM,* 27: 751–774; P. Deng, 2009, Why do Chinese firms tend to acquire strategic assets in international

expansion? *JWB*, 44: 74–84; P. Gammeltoft, H. Barnard, & A. Madhok, 2010, Emerging multinationals, emerging theory, *JIM*, 16: 95–101; G. Gao, J. Murray, M. Kotabe, & J. Lu, 2010, A "strategy tripod" perspective on export behaviors, *JIBS*, 41: 377–396; S. Gubbi, P. Aulakh, S. Ray, M. Sarkar, & R. Chittoor, 2010, Do international acquisitions by emerging-economy firms create shareholder value? *JIBS*, 41: 387–418.

35 T. Friedman, 2005, *The World is Flat,* New York: Farrar, Straus, & Giroux; R. Rajan, 2010, *Fautlines*, Princeton, NJ: Princeton University Press.

36 M. W. Peng, S. Sun, & D. Blevins, 2011, The social responsibility of international business scholars, *MBR,* 19: 106–119; D. Rodrik, 2011, *The Globalization Paradox,* New York: Norton.

© Netkoff/Shutterstock.com

Learning Objectives

After studying this chapter, you should be able to

- explain the concept of institutions and their key role in reducing uncertainty.

- articulate the two core propositions underpinning an institution-based view of global business.

- identify the basic differences between democracy and totalitarianism.

- outline the differences among civil law, common law, and theocratic law.

- understand the importance of property rights and intellectual property rights.

- appreciate the differences among market economy, command economy, and mixed economy.

- participate in two leading debates concerning politics, laws, and economics.

- draw implications for action.

Understanding Formal Institutions: Politics, Laws, and Economics

EMERGING MARKETS: The Peril and Promise of Russia

Russia is not the Soviet Union. But what is it? Despite the extraordinary transitions moving from a centrally planned economy to a market economy and from a totalitarian regime to a democracy, most of the news we read (in the West) on Russia is negative. Corruption is widespread (Russia ranks 146th out of 180 countries, according to Transparency International). In 2004, Russia was downgraded from "Partly Free" to "Not Free"—on a 1 to 3 scale of "Free," "Partly Free," and "Not Free"—by Freedom House, a leading nongovernmental organization (NGO) promoting democracy. In 2012, Vladimir Putin was reelected as president (after he served as president for two terms between 2000 and 2008, and as prime minister between 2008 and 2012). The election was largely symbolic, as all viable candidates were not allowed to run against him. In 2014, Russia successfully staged the winter Olympics in Sochi. Then Russia quickly showed its aggressive side, swallowing Crimea and destabilizing Ukraine. Even before the geopolitical events in 2014, some commentators bearish on Russia had suggested kicking Russia out of the BRIC group, given its alleged lack of dynamism, and to focus more business attention on China, India, and Brazil. After Russia became deeply involved in the mess of Ukrainian politics, the United States, the European Union, Norway, Australia, Canada, and Japan imposed a series of sanctions to "punish" and "isolate" Russia.

Is Russia really that bad? The answer is: Of course not! Russia is simply being Russia. While Russia's gross domestic product (GDP) is smaller than that of China and Brazil, it is larger than that of India. Russia's per capita GDP, approximately US$16,000 (at purchasing power parity), is one-third higher than that of Brazil, three times that of China, and five times that of India. Russia has the second-largest automobile market in Europe (behind Germany), and it has more college graduates (as a percentage of population) than any other country. Simply put, Russia is too big and too rich to ignore. None of the high-tech giants (such as Cisco, HP, and Intel) and industrial and consumer goods firms (such as Carrefour, Danone, IKEA, Nestlé, PepsiCo, and Unilever) has announced plans to quit Russia. Russia's economic growth may not be as fast as China's or India's, but it will certainly be higher than US or EU growth. Russia exports more than 30% of its GDP, in contrast to 26% for China, 25% for India, and 13% for Brazil.

Because Russia is so large and complex, how to "read" Russia has remained a constant debate. The debate centers on political, economic, and legal dimensions. Politically, Russia has indeed become less democratic. Certain segments of the population (especially the better educated) are disappointed by the return of Putin. But a more relevant question is: Is Russia better off under Putin's more authoritarian rule since 2000, compared with Boris Yeltsin's more democratic (and more chaotic) rule in the 1990s? Russia under Putin between 2000 and 2008 grew 7% annually, whereas Russia under Yeltsin during the 1990s experienced a catastrophic economic decline.

Economically, the Russian economy indeed has great room for development. It is overly dependent on oil and gas exports, contributing 70% of its US$515 billion exports. In the World Economic Forum's *Global Competitiveness Report*, Russia ranks only 51st in innovation (out of 133 countries), behind China (26th) and India (30th). Dmitry Medvedev, who served as president between 2008 and 2012 (while Putin was prime minister), published an article in 2009 titled "Russia Forward!" He asked a provocative question: "Should we drag a primitive economy based on raw materials and endemic corruption into the future?"

Legally, establishing the rule of law that respects private property is important. In a society where nobody had any significant private property until recently, how a small number of individuals became super-rich oligarchs (tycoons) almost overnight is intriguing. By the 2000s, the top ten families or groups owned 60% of Russia's total market capitalization. The government thus faced a dilemma: Redistributing wealth by confiscating assets from the oligarchs creates more uncertainty, whereas respecting and protecting the property rights of the oligarchs results in more resentment among the population. Thus far, the government largely sided with the oligarchs, as long as the oligarchs played by Putin's rules: (1) mind your own business—do not get involved in politics, and (2) pay taxes.

Internationally, the sanctions were designed to target Putin's inner circle first. They soon spilled over to the financial, energy, and defense industries. In retaliation, Russia banned agricultural imports from any country that imposed sanctions. As a result, US$6.5 billion worth of EU agricultural products that normally would have gone to Russia ended up being dumped in the EU. Since Russia accounted for one-third of the EU's fruit and vegetable exports and one-quarter of EU's beef exports, the Russian ban caused prices for Dutch beef, Finnish dairy products, Latvian cabbage, and Spanish peaches to *collapse*. Dealing with the more abundant and cheaper food, the German agriculture minister urged Germans to eat fruits at least five (!) times a day. While governments butted heads, European farmers could not sustain their losses. In August 2014, European taxpayers had to cough up US$200 million in new subsidies to farmers. Firms withdrawing from Russia due to its peril obviously cannot benefit from its promise, and can only salivate over rivals that can tap into the promise of Russia. Since Russians had to eat, Chinese farmers happily started to fill the market vacated by EU farmers. Likewise, as European demand for Russian gas declined, in 2014 China National Petroleum Corporation (CNPC) signed an unprecedented US$300 billion deal with Gazprom, unlocking the vast promise of Russia's underground wealth.

Sources: Based on (1) *Bloomberg Businessweek*, 2014, Putin's paradox, September 1: 12–13; (2) *Bloomberg Businessweek*, 2014, This apple was once headed to Russia, not anymore, September 15: 13–15; (3) *Economist*, 2012, Moscow doesn't believe in tears, March 10: 62–63; (4) *Economist*, 2012, Moscow spring, February 11: 12; (5) *Economist*, 2014, The long game, September 6: 15; (6) S. Michailova, S. Puffer, & D. McCarthy, 2013, Russia: As solid as a BRIC? *Critical Perspectives on International Business*, 9: 5–18; (7) www.freedomhouse.org.

Institutional transition

Fundamental and comprehensive changes introduced to the formal and informal rules of the game that affect firms as players.

Why is Western news reporting on Russia so negative? Does Russia really have a democracy? Does it matter? Is democracy the best political system to develop Russia's economy? Does Russia have the rule of law? If your firm is currently doing business in Russia, should it consider withdrawing from Russia? As the Opening Case illustrates, answers to these questions boil down to institutions, popularly known as the "rules of the game." As economic players, firms play by these rules. However, institutions are not static, and they may change, resulting in institutional transitions— "fundamental and comprehensive changes introduced to the formal and informal rules of the game that affect firms as players."[1] Examples of institutional transitions include Russia's transitions from a communist totalitarian state to a market economy with regular elections (never mind the imperfections).

Overall, the success and failure of a firm around the globe are, to a large extent, determined by its ability to understand and take advantage of the different rules of the game. In other words, how firms play the game and win (or lose), at least in part, depends on how the rules are made, enforced, and changed. This calls for firms to constantly monitor, decode, and adapt to the changing rules of the game in order to survive and prosper. As a result, such an institution-based view has emerged as a leading perspective on global business.[2] This chapter first introduces the institution-based view. Then, it focuses on *formal* institutions (such as political, legal, and economic systems). *Informal* institutions (such as cultures, ethics, and norms) will be discussed in Chapter 3.

2-1 Understanding Institutions

Building on the "rules of the game" metaphor, Douglass North, a Nobel laureate in economics, more formally defines institutions as "the humanly devised constraints that structure human interaction."[3] An institutional framework is made up of formal and informal institutions governing individual and firm behavior. These institutions are supported by three "pillars" identified by Richard Scott, a leading sociologist. They are the (1) regulatory, (2) normative, and (3) cognitive pillars.[4]

Shown in Table 2.1, formal institutions include laws, regulations, and rules. Their primary supportive pillar, the regulatory pillar, is the coercive power of governments. For example, while many individuals and companies may pay taxes out of their patriotic duty, a larger number of them do so in fear of the coercive power of the government if they are caught not paying.

On the other hand, informal institutions include norms, cultures, and ethics. The two main supportive pillars are normative and cognitive. The normative pillar refers to how the values, beliefs, and actions of other relevant players—collectively known as norms—influence the behavior of focal individuals and firms.[5] The recent norms centered on rushing to invest in China and India have prompted many Western firms to imitate each other without a clear understanding of how to make such moves work. Cautious managers resisting such "herding" are often confronted by board members and investors: "Why are we not in China and India?" In other words, "Why don't we follow the norm?"

Also supporting informal institutions, the cognitive pillar refers to the internalized, taken-for-granted values and beliefs that guide behavior.[6] For example, what triggered whistleblowers to report Enron's wrongdoing was their belief in what was right and wrong. While most employees may not feel comfortable with organizational wrongdoing, the norm is to shut up and not to "rock the boat." Essentially,

Table 2.1 Dimensions of Institutions

Degree of formality	Examples	Supportive pillars
Formal institutions	• Laws • Regulations • Rules	• Regulatory (coercive)
Informal institutions	• Norms • Cultures • Ethics	• Normative • Cognitive

Learning Objective

Explain the concept of institutions and their key role in reducing uncertainty.

Institution-based view

A leading perspective in global business that suggests that the success and failure of firms are enabled and constrained by institutions.

Institution

Formal and informal rules of the game.

Institutional framework

Formal and informal institutions that govern individual and firm behavior.

Formal institution

Institution represented by laws, regulations, and rules.

Regulatory pillar

The coercive power of governments.

Informal institution

Institution represented by cultures, ethics, and norms.

Normative pillar

The mechanism through which norms influence individual and firm behavior.

Norms

Values, beliefs, and actions of relevant players that influence the focal individuals and firms.

Cognitive pillar

The internalized (or taken-for-granted) values and beliefs that guide individual and firm behavior.

IN FOCUS 2.1
CALIFORNIA VERSUS TEXAS

As the two largest states by land area, population, GDP, and exports, California and Texas compete along a variety of dimensions (Table 2.2). For a long time, the Golden State was winning. The home of Silicon Valley and Hollywood, according to the *Economist*, has been the "brainier, sexier, and trendier of the two." The Lone Star State has often been known as the "Cowboy" state. In the old American adage, "Go west, young man," the West typically means California, not necessarily Texas. Generations of people flocking to California have made its population and its GDP the largest in the nation.

However, fortunes change. Today, a net 100,000 people leave California every year, and many rush to Texas—your author knows quite a few of them. Texas now attracts a net inflow of 150,000 people every year. The cost to rent a self-drive, small moving truck for household goods for a one-way journey from Los Angeles to Houston is *three* times more than the other way around—there are that many more people to move from California to Texas.

So, what happened? In short, the Golden State has lost some of its shine, and the Lone Star State has risen. In the harsher words of the *Economist*, California

Table 2.2	California versus Texas		
Rankings in the United States		**California**	**Texas**
Land area*		2	1
Population		1	2
GDP		1	2
Exports		2	1

*The rankings are based on the 48 contiguous United States. If Alaska (the largest state by land area) is included, Texas and California are, respectively, the second and third largest states by area.

whistleblowers choose to follow their internalized personal beliefs on what is right by overcoming the norm that encourages silence.

How do these three forms of supportive pillars *combine* to shape individual and firm behavior? Let us use two examples—one at the individual level and another at the firm level (In Focus 2.1 provides another example). First, a speed limit formally defines how fast drivers can go. However, many drivers adjust their speed depending on the speed of *other* vehicles—a form of normative pillar. When some drivers are ticketed by police because they drive above the legal speed limit, they protest: "We are barely keeping up with traffic!" This statement indicates that they do not have a clear cognitive pillar regarding what is the right speed (never mind the posted speed limit signs). They often let other drivers define what is the right speed. Second, in 2008, a year during which Wall Street had to be bailed out by trillions of taxpayer dollars, Wall Street executives paid themselves US$18 billion in bonuses. The resulting public outcry was understandable. However, by paying themselves so handsomely, these executives did not commit any crime. Therefore, the regulatory pillar had little teeth. Rather, this was a case of major clashes between normative pillar and cognitive pillar held by these executives. In the minds of these executives, supported by their own cognitive pillar, they deserved such bonuses. What they failed to read was the normative pressure coming from an angry public.

has become "an inhospitable place plagued by over-regulation, mindless bureaucracy, and high taxes." In 2014, *Chief Executive* magazine named California America's *worst* state for business and Texas the *best* state for business—for the *tenth* year in a row.

The byzantine layers of regulations in the Golden State seem insurmountable. It takes two years to open a new restaurant in California. In Texas? Six to eight weeks. Between 2007 and 2011, some 2,500 businesses with three or more employees—with over 100,000 jobs—left California.

In sharp contrast to California's high-tax, big-government, big-spending model, Texas operates on a low-tax, small-government, small-spending basis. Phenomenally business friendly, Texas has neither state income tax nor capital gains tax. It is business friendly and immigrant tolerant. Since 2006, more than half a million new jobs have been created in Texas, resulting in an unemployment rate of 7%, two points below the national average. At 11%, California's unemployment has been hovering above the national average.

The rivalry between California and Texas is not just domestic. It has global ramifications. In 2014, Toyota moved its North America headquarters with 4,000 jobs from Torrance in southern California to Plano, a Dallas suburb in north Texas. For half a century, Japanese firms such as Toyota clustered in southern California because California offered the best location to launch and operate US operations and to manage their logistics flows to and from Japan. This logic of being headquartered in California is now breaking down under the push-and-pull effects of the outsized penalties of doing business in California and the lucrative incentives offered by Texas (US$40 million in cash). The average salaries for the 4,000 new jobs in Plano would be in the six figures, far more than manufacturing wages. Given that Japanese firms tend to follow the norm set by leaders such as Toyota, the spillover benefits to Texas of possibly attracting other Japanese firms—as well as multinationals from elsewhere—are tremendous.

Sources: Based on (1) the author's interviews; (2) *Chief Executive*, 2014, 2014 Best and worst states for business, May 8, www.chiefexecutive .net; (3) *Economist*, 2009, America's future, July 9, www.economist .com; (4) *Economist*, 2009, Lone Star rising, July 9, www.economist .com; (5) *Forbes*, 2014, It makes sense for Toyota to leave California for Texas, April 27, www.forbes.com; (6) *Forbes*, 2014, It's not about incentives, April 29, www.forbes.com.

2-2 What Do Institutions Do?

While institutions do many things, their key role, in two words, is to *reduce uncertainty*.[7] By signaling which conduct is legitimate and which is not, institutions constrain the range of acceptable actions. In short, institutions reduce uncertainty, which can be potentially devastating.[8] Political uncertainty, such as terrorist attacks and ethnic riots, may render long-range planning obsolete. Political deadlocks in Washington have made the US government "less stable, less effective, and less predictable," which led Standard & Poor's to downgrade its AAA crediting rating to AA+.[9] Economic uncertainty, such as failure to carry out contractual obligations, may result in economic losses. During the Great Recession of 2008–2009, a number of firms, such as Dow Chemical and Trump Holdings, argued that the "unprecedented economic crisis" should let them off the hook.[10] *Force majeure* is a long-standing legal doctrine that excuses firms from living up to the terms of a deal in the event of natural disasters or other calamities. But was the economic crisis a *force majeure*? If the argument prevails, critics contend, then every debtor in a country suffering economic crisis can avoid paying debts. While these arguments are debated in court battles, a great deal of economic uncertainty looms on the horizon.

Uncertainty surrounding economic transactions can lead to transaction costs, which are defined as costs associated with economic transactions—or, more broadly,

Transaction cost

The cost associated with economic transactions or, more broadly, the costs of doing business.

costs of doing business. Nobel laureate Oliver Williamson refers to frictions in mechanical systems: "Do the gears mesh, are the parts lubricated, is there needless slippage or other loss of energy?" He goes on to suggest that transaction costs can be regarded as "the economic counterpart of frictions: Do the parties to exchange operate harmoniously, or are there frequent misunderstandings and conflicts?"[11]

One important source of transaction costs is opportunism, defined as self-interest seeking with guile. Examples include misleading, cheating, and confusing other parties in transactions that will increase transaction costs. Attempting to reduce such transaction costs, institutional frameworks increase certainty by spelling out the rules of the game so that violations (such as failure to fulfill a contract) can be mitigated with relative ease (such as through formal arbitration and courts).

Without stable institutional frameworks, transaction costs may become prohibitively high, to the extent that certain transactions simply would not take place. For example, in the absence of credible institutional frameworks that protect investors, domestic investors may choose to put their money abroad. Although Africa is starving for capital, rich people in Africa put a striking 39% of their assets outside of Africa.[12]

Institutions are not static. Institutional transitions are widespread in the world. Institutional transitions in some emerging economies, particularly those moving from central planning to market competition (such as China, Poland, Russia, and Vietnam), are so pervasive that these countries are simply called transition economies (a *subset* of emerging economies). Institutional transitions in countries such as China, Cuba, India, Russia (see the Opening Case), and South Africa create both huge challenges and tremendous opportunities for domestic and international firms.[13]

Having outlined the definitions of various institutions and their supportive pillars as well as their key role in uncertainty reduction, next we introduce the first core perspective on global business—an institution-based view.

Learning Objective
Articulate the two core propositions underpinning an institution-based view of global business.

2-3 An Institution-Based View of Global Business

Shown in Figure 2.1, an institution-based view focuses on the dynamic interaction between institutions and firms, and considers firm behaviors as the outcome of such an interaction.[14] Specifically, firm behaviors are often a reflection of the

Opportunism
The act of seeking self-interest with guile.

Transition economies
A subset of emerging economies, particularly those moving from central planning to market competition (such as China, Poland, Russia, and Vietnam).

| Figure 2.1 | **Institutions, Firms, and Firm Behaviors** |

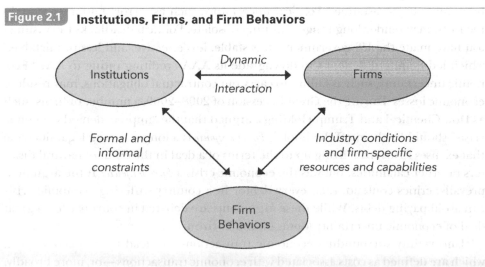

Table 2.3	Two Core Propositions of the Institution-Based View
Proposition 1	Managers and firms *rationally* pursue their interests and make choices within the formal and informal constraints in a given institutional framework
Proposition 2	While formal and informal institutions combine to govern firm behavior, in situations where formal constraints are unclear or fail, informal constraints will play a *larger* role in reducing uncertainty and providing constancy to managers and firms

formal and informal constraints of a particular institutional framework.[15] In short, institutions matter.

How do institutions matter? The institution-based view suggests two core propositions (Table 2.3). First, managers and firms *rationally* pursue their interests and make choices within institutional constraints. In Brazil, the infamous *custo Brasil* (Brazil cost) is legendary (Emerging Markets 2.1). Contributing to the sky-high cost of doing business in Brazil are taxes, which reach 35% of GDP, much higher than Mexico's 18% and China's 16%. Not surprisingly, the gray market in Brazil accounts for a much higher percentage of the economy than in Mexico and China.[16] Likewise, in the United States, the Obama administration's proposal to tax the overseas earnings of US-based multinationals, which are currently exempt from US taxes, met fierce resistance from the business community. Having already paid overseas taxes, US-based multinationals naturally resented having to pay US$190 billion in extra US taxes, when their global competitors pay lower taxes. "Doesn't the Obama administration recognize that most big US companies are multinationals that happen to be headquartered in the United States?" asked Duncan Niederauer, CEO of NYSE Euronext in a *BusinessWeek* interview.[17] One case in point is Seagate Technology, a formerly Silicon Valley-based disk-drive maker that incorporated in the Cayman Islands a few years ago.[18] Avoidance of such a financial hit was one of the reasons behind Seagate's move, and more US-based multinationals are likely to follow Seagate. Both Brazilian firms' migration to the gray market and US firms' interest in migrating overseas are rational responses when they pursue their interests within formal institutional constraints in these countries.

Obviously, nobody has perfect rationality—possessing all the knowledge under all circumstances. Proposition 1 specifically concerns bounded rationality, which refers to the necessity of making rational decisions in the absence of complete information.[19] Without prior experience, many managers from emerging multinationals getting their feet wet overseas, and numerous individuals getting involved in counterfeiting do not know exactly what they are getting into. So, emerging multinationals often burn cash overseas, and counterfeiters sometimes land in jail, which are indicative of their *bounded* rationality.

The second proposition is that while formal and informal institutions combine to govern individual and firm behavior, in situations where formal constraints are unclear or fail, informal constraints play a *larger* role in reducing uncertainty and providing constancy to managers and firms. For example, in Kinshasa (population ten million people), capital of the Democratic Republic of Congo (formerly Zaire), "where metrics like per capita nutrition levels and water quality would suggest a near-death state of being," the city is "all too alive."[20] "This is a city of frenzied

Bounded rationality

The necessity of making rational decisions in the absence of complete information.

EMERGING MARKETS 2.1

The Brazil Cost

In São Paulo, a cheese pizza costs US$30. In Rio de Janeiro, a three-star hotel room costs more than US$200 a night and an iPhone 5s more than US$1,000 (see Table 2.4). While these may be extreme examples in two of the largest and most expensive cities, prices in the rest of Brazil are no better. Large domestic appliances and cars cost at least 50% more than in most other countries. While first-time visitors to Brazil are often shocked by the high price of everything, locals are used to it. They simply call it the *custo Brasil* (Brazil cost)—the exorbitant cost of living and doing business in Brazil.

The Brazil cost is jacked up by high taxes and rising wages. Government tax revenues at all levels reach 35% of GDP, which is much higher than Mexico's 18% and China's 16%. At 58% of salary, payroll taxes scare away a lot of would-be entrepreneurs and job takers. As a result, the informal economy is thriving, which puts even more pressures on individuals with formal jobs and taxable wages. Consumption is also heavily taxed. While sky-high import tariffs and taxes can explain why a made-in-China Apple iPhone 5s costs nearly US$1,100, it is harder to believe that a made-in-Brazil car costs up to 45% *more* in Brazil itself than in Mexico.

In the decade after 2003, labor costs doubled, while inflation "only" grew 67%. Top-notch office rents in Rio are now the most expensive in the Americas, north or south. Brazilian top executives are among the world's highest paid. Executives at subsidiaries of Western multinationals often command a salary higher than what their bosses in New York or London make. Manpower, a leading global employment agency, has complained that Brazil is the second hardest place for firms to fill high-level jobs, behind only aging Japan. Overall, operating costs in Brazil are now higher than in many developed economies. One expert noted:

> If you were to take a factory by helicopters from Germany to Brazil, your costs would jump 48% as soon as you touched down. Those of us producing in Brazil are doomed to be uncompetitive.

The government does want to help by protecting uncompetitive industries. In this respect, President Dilma Rousseff has not deviated from her days as a graduate student studying developmental economics with some of Brazil's most left-wing professors. Since taking power in 2011, she has imposed tariffs on shoes, textiles, chemicals, and even Barbie dolls. Brazil also threatens to tear up an agreement with Mexico that allows free trade in cars, because Brazil—thanks to its uncompetitive automobile industry—suffers from an embarrassing trade deficit in cars.

Individuals and firms cope with a variety of strategies. A lot of Brazilian firms hide in the informal sector. Many foreign firms simply shy away. Individuals, to the extent they can, shop overseas. Brazilian tourists spent a record US$22 billion abroad in 2014. So many of them flock the malls and outlets in Miami that Portuguese-speaking staff are often hired to cater to such customers. TAM, a Brazilian airline, reports that the home-bound legs of its Miami–São Paulo and Miami–Rio flights burn much more fuel compared with the Miami-bound leg, because of the extraordinary amount of excess baggage that its passengers haul back home.

Sources: Based on (1) the author's interviews; (2) *Bloomberg Businessweek*, 2012, Look who's bringing up the rear, March 26: 9–10; (3) *Economist*, 2012, Two ways to make a car, March 10: 48–49; (4) *Economist*, 2013, The price is wrong, September 28 (special report): 5; (5) *Economist*, 2014, One phone, many countries, March 8: 39–40.

Table 2.4 The Cost of a 16GB Apple iPhone 5s in the Americas (US$)

Argentina	Brazil	Chile	Colombia	Mexico	Peru	United States
$1,014	$1,076	$842	$750	$798	$1,039	$700

Source: Extracted from data from *Economist*, 2014, One phone, many countries, March 8: 39.

entrepreneurship, where everyone is a salesman of whatever merchandise comes along." Outsiders who are used to a functioning state with market-supporting formal institutions are likely to view the city as total chaos—"a marvel of dysfunction," according to a Western reporter. "For me," according to an entrepreneur, "it is not chaos at all. We've developed an informal system. And within this informal system, there's an organization."

Many observers have the impression that relying on informal connections is only relevant to firms in emerging economies and that firms in developed economies only pursue "market-based" strategies. This is far from the truth. Even in developed economies, formal rules only make up a small (although

What govern market transactions in a city such as Kinshasa, Democratic Republic of the Congo?

important) part of institutional constraints, and informal constraints are pervasive. Just as firms compete in product markets, they also fiercely compete in the political marketplace, characterized by informal relationships.[21] Basically, if a firm cannot be a market leader, it may still beat the competition on another ground—namely, the nonmarket, political environment.[22] In September 2008, a rapidly falling Merrill Lynch was able to sell itself to Bank of America for a hefty US$50 billion. Supported by US government officials, this mega deal was arranged over 48 hours (shorter than the time most people take to buy a car), and the negotiations took place *inside* the Federal Reserve building in New York. In contrast, Lehman Brothers failed to secure government support and had to drop dead by filing for bankruptcy. Overall, the skillful use of a country's institutional frameworks to acquire advantage is at the heart of the institution-based view (see Figure 2.2).

While there are numerous formal and informal institutions, in this chapter we focus on *formal* institutions (informal institutions will be covered in Chapter 3). Chief among formal institutions are (1) political systems, (2) legal systems, and (3) economic systems. Each is briefly introduced next.

Figure 2.2   **Bank of America CEO Brian Moynihan (left) and Goldman Sachs CEO Lloyd Blankfein (right) Walk Out of a Happy Meeting at the White House**

Source: *Bloomberg Businessweek*, 2013, CEOs can't get enough of the capital, October 20.

Learning Objective
Identify the basic differences
between democracy and
totalitarianism.

2-4 Political Systems

A political system refers to the rules of the game on how a country is governed politically. At the broadest level, there are two primary political systems: (1) democracy and (2) totalitarianism. This section first outlines these two systems and then discusses their ramifications for political risk.

2-4a Democracy

Democracy is a political system in which citizens elect representatives to govern the country on their behalf. Democracy was pioneered by Athens in ancient Greece. In today's world, Britain has the longest experience of running a democracy (since the founding of its Parliament in the 1200s), and India has the largest democracy (by population).

One fundamental aspect of democracy that is relevant to global business is an individual's right to freedom of expression and organization. For example, starting up a firm is an act of economic expression, essentially telling the rest of the world: "I want to be my own boss! And I want to make some money!" In most modern democracies, this right to organize economically has been extended not only to domestic individuals and firms, but also to *foreign* individuals and firms that come to do business. While those of us fortunate enough to be brought up in a democracy take for granted the right to found a firm, we should be reminded that this may not necessarily be the case under other political systems. Before the 1980s, if someone had dared to formally found a firm in the former Soviet Union, he or she would have been arrested and *shot* by the authorities.

2-4b Totalitarianism

The opposite end of democracy is totalitarianism (also known as dictatorship), which is defined as a political system in which one person or party exercises absolute political control over the population. There are four major types of totalitarianism.

- **Communist totalitarianism** centers on a communist party. This system had been embraced throughout Central and Eastern Europe and the former Soviet Union until the late 1980s. It is still practiced in China, Cuba, Laos, North Korea, and Vietnam.
- **Right-wing totalitarianism** is characterized by its intense hatred against communism. One party, typically backed by the military, restricts political freedom, arguing that such freedom would lead to communism. In postwar decades, Argentina, Brazil, Chile, the Philippines, South Africa, South Korea, and Taiwan practiced right-wing totalitarianism. Most of these countries have recently become democracies.
- **Theocratic totalitarianism** refers to the monopolization of political power in the hands of one religious party or group. Iran and Saudi Arabia are leading examples.
- **Tribal totalitarianism** refers to one tribe or ethnic group (which may or may not be the majority of the population) monopolizing political power and oppressing other tribes or ethnic groups. Rwanda's bloodbath in the 1990s was due to some of the most brutal practices of tribal totalitarianism.

Political system

The rules of the game on how a country is governed politically.

Democracy

A political system in which citizens elect representatives to govern the country on their behalf.

Totalitarianism (dictatorship)

A political system in which one person or party exercises absolute political control over the population.

2-4c Political Risk

While the degree of hostility toward business varies among different types of totalitarianism (some can be more pro-business than others), totalitarianism in general is not as good for business as is democracy. Totalitarian countries often experience wars, riots, protests, chaos, and breakdowns, which result in higher political risk—risk associated with political changes that may negatively impact domestic and foreign firms (see Emerging Markets 2.2).[23] The most extreme political risk may lead to nationalization (expropriation) of foreign assets. This happened in many totalitarian countries from the 1950s through the 1970s. It has not become a thing of the past. Recently, Argentina expropriated the assets of YPF—the subsidiary of Spanish oil firm Repsol. Zimbabwe demanded that foreign mining companies cede 51% of their equity without compensation.[24] It is hardly surprising that foreign firms are sick and tired of such expropriation and would rather go to "greener pastures" elsewhere.

Firms operating in democracies also confront political risk. However, such risk is qualitatively lower than that in totalitarian countries. For example, Scotland's potential independence from the rest of the UK created some political risk.[25]

Political risk

Risk associated with political changes that may negatively impact domestic and foreign firms.

EMERGING MARKETS 2.2

Testing the Dell Theory of Peace in East Asia

Ethical Dilemma

Thomas Friedman, a *New York Times* columnist, suggested in his 2005 bestseller *The World Is Flat* a Dell theory of peace: No two countries that are both part of a major global supply chain, like Dell's, will ever fight a war against each other as long as they are both part of the same global supply chain. Countries involved in major global supply chains focus on just-in-time deliveries of goods and services, which raise standards of living. In the case of Dell, the following countries are involved: China, Costa Rica, Germany, Israel, Japan, Malaysia, the Philippines, South Korea, Taiwan, Thailand, and the United States.

East Asia is both a manufacturing hub for IT giants such as Dell and a hot neighborhood for territorial disputes. In 2012, the Japanese government ignored warnings from China and purchased from a right-wing politician five barren rocks in the East China Sea, which the Chinese call Diaoyu and the Japanese call Senkaku. (For compositional simplicity, we will call them the Diaoyu/Senkaku islands in the rest of the case.) Totaling less than three square miles, the uninhabited islands have long been disputed. In 1972, China and Japan agreed to shelve the issue indefinitely. Fast forward to 2012, the Japanese government nationalized the islands, in fear of a right-wing politician whose plans for the islands would certainly have provoked China. But an assertive China argued that even the Japanese government's purchase was an unacceptable change in the status quo. Anti-Japanese riots and boycotts erupted in some Chinese cities in August and September 2012, vandalizing stores selling Japanese products, burning Japanese-branded cars, and setting a Panasonic factory on fire. Sales of Toyota, Honda, Nissan, and Mazda cars in China plummeted in the remainder of 2012. Chinese business and tourist visitors also cancelled visits and vacations, hurting hotels, resorts, and restaurants in Japan—All Nippon Airlines (ANA) alone suffered 46,000 seat cancellations. In all, between 0.5% and 1% of Japanese GDP was shaved off—all for a bunch of barren rocks.

Since then, Chinese and Japanese ships and aircraft routinely face off each other in the disputed waters and airspace surrounding the Diaoyu/Senkaku islands. Will such a new cold war turn hot? Most experts believe this to be *unlikely*, simply because China needs Japanese products as much as Japan needs to sell them. Japan provides some of the most critical components for made-in-China exports—think of the Sharp LCD screens and Toshiba flash memory drives that power the Apple iPhones assembled in China. Japan is also one of the largest foreign direct investors in China, employing approximately 1.5 million

Chinese workers in 4,600 factories throughout the country. One-tenth of Japan's foreign direct investment (FDI) stock is in China. Because the two economies are complementary, there is a great deal of economic integration characterized by dense trade, investment, and personnel flows. Neither side risks disrupting these flows through conflicts without crippling its own economy—or both. While there is no guarantee that cooler heads would always prevail in Beijing and Tokyo, Thomas Friedman and peace lovers of the world—a group that presumably includes all readers of *this* book—would certainly hope that the Dell theory of peace would continue to be supported in East Asia and beyond.

Sources: Based on (1) *Bloomberg Businessweek*, 2012, Japan, China, and a pile of rocks, October 22: 20–21; (2) *Bloomberg Businessweek*, 2013, Battered in China, Japan Inc. seeks refuge, February 11: 11–12; (3) *Bloomberg Businessweek*, 2014, Anti-China riots scare Taiwan, May 26: 18–19; (4) *Economist*, 2014, Hot oil on troubled waters, May 17: 38; (5) *Foreign Affairs*, 2013, Beijing's brand ambassador, July: 10–17; (6) *Foreign Affairs*, 2013, Japan is back, July: 2–8; (7) T. Friedman, 2005, *The World Is Flat*, New York: Farrar, Straus, and Giroux; (8) R. Katz, 2013, Mutual assured production: Why trade will limit conflict between China and Japan, *Foreign Affairs*, July: 18–24.

Colin McPherson/Alamy

Would political risk to firms operating in the UK become too high if Scotland became independent?

Although firms highly exposed to Scotland experienced some drop in their stock prices, there was no general collapse of stock prices in the UK or flight of capital out of the country.[26] Investors are confident that should Scotland become independent at some time in the future, the British democracy is mature enough to manage the break-up process in a relatively non-disruptive way.

Obviously, when two countries are at each other's throats, we can forget about doing business between them (perhaps other than smuggling).[27] Reportedly, no two democracies have gone to war with each other. Thus, the recent advance of democracy and retreat of totalitarianism is highly beneficial for global business. It is not a coincidence that globalization took off in the 1990s, a period during which both communist and right-wing totalitarianism significantly lost their power and democracy expanded around the world.

2-5 Legal Systems

A legal system refers to the formal rules of the game on how a country's laws are enacted and enforced. By specifying the do's and don'ts, a legal system reduces transaction costs by minimizing uncertainty and combating opportunism. This section first introduces the three legal traditions and then discusses crucial issues associated with property rights and intellectual property.

Legal system

The rules of the game on how a country's laws are enacted and enforced.

2-5a Civil Law, Common Law, and Theocratic Law

Learning Objective
Outline the differences among civil law, common law, and theocratic law.

Laws in different countries typically are not enacted from scratch, but are often transplanted—voluntarily or otherwise—from three legal traditions (or legal families): (1) civil law, (2) common law, and (3) theocratic law (Table 2.5). Each is briefly introduced here.

Civil law was derived from Roman law and strengthened by Napoleon's France. It is "the oldest, the most influential, and the most widely distributed around the world."[28] It uses comprehensive statutes and codes as a primary means to form legal judgments. More than 80 countries practice civil law. Common law, which is English in origin, is shaped by precedents and traditions from previous judicial decisions. Common law has spread to all English-speaking countries and their (former) colonies.

Relative to civil law, common law has more flexibility, because judges have to resolve specific disputes based on their *interpretation* of the law, and such interpretation may give new meaning to the law, which will shape future cases. Civil law has less flexibility, because judges only have the power to *apply* the law. On the other hand, civil law is less confrontational, because comprehensive statutes and codes serve to guide judges. You may have seen common law in action in Hollywood movies such as *A Few Good Men, Devil's Advocate,* and *Legally Blond.* Common law is more confrontational, because plaintiffs and defendants, through their lawyers, must argue and help judges to favorably interpret the law, largely based on precedents. This confrontation is great material for movies. In contrast, you probably have rarely seen a civil law court in action in a movie—you have not missed much, because civil law lacks the drama and its proceedings tend to be boring. In addition, contracts in common law countries tend to be long and detailed to cover all possible contingencies, because common law tends to be relatively underdefined. In contrast, contracts in civil law countries are usually shorter and less specific, because many issues typically articulated in common law contracts are already covered in comprehensive civil law codes.

The third legal family is theocratic law, a legal system based on religious teachings. Examples include Jewish law and Islamic law. Although Jewish law is followed by some elements of the Israeli population, it is *not* formally embraced by the Israeli government. Islamic law is the only surviving example of a theocratic legal system that is formally practiced by some governments, such as those in Iran and Saudi Arabia. Despite the widespread characterization that Islam is anti-business, it is

Table 2.5	**Three Legal Traditions**[1]	
Civil law countries	**Common law countries**	**Theocratic law countries**
Argentina, Austria, Belgium, Brazil, Chile, China, Egypt, France, Germany, Greece, Indonesia, Italy, Japan, Mexico, Netherlands, Russia, South Korea, Sweden, Switzerland, Taiwan	Australia, Canada, Hong Kong, India, Ireland, Israel, Kenya, Malaysia, New Zealand, Nigeria, Singapore, South Africa, Sri Lanka, United Kingdom, United States, Zimbabwe	Iran, Saudi Arabia, United Arab Emirates[2]

[1] The countries are examples and do not exhaustively represent all countries practicing a particular legal system.
[2] Certain parts of Dubai (an emirate within the UAE), such as the Dubai International Finance Center, practice common law.

Civil law
A legal tradition that uses comprehensive statutes and codes as a primary means to form legal judgments.

Common law
A legal tradition that is shaped by precedents and traditions from previous judicial decisions.

Theocratic law
A legal system based on religious teachings.

important to note that Mohammed was a merchant trader and that the tenants of Islam are pro-business in general. However, the holy book of Islam, the Koran, advises against *certain* business practices. In Saudi Arabia, McDonald's operates "ladies only" restaurants to be in compliance with the Koran's ban on direct, face-to-face contact between men and women (who often wear a veil) in public. Banks have to maintain two retail branches: One for male customers staffed by men, and another for female customers staffed by women. This requirement obviously increases the property, overhead, and personnel costs. To reduce costs, some foreign banks, such as HSBC, staff their back office operations with both male and female employees who work side by side.[29]

Overall, as an important component of the first, regulatory pillar, legal systems are a crucial component of the institutional framework. They directly impose do's and don'ts on businesses around the globe. Overall, under the broad scope of a legal system, there are numerous components. Two of these, property rights and intellectual property, are discussed next.

2-5b Property Rights

Learning Objective

Understand the importance of property rights and intellectual property rights.

Regardless of which legal family a country's legal system belongs to, one of the most fundamental economic functions that a legal system serves is to protect property rights—the legal rights to use an economic property (resource) and to derive income and other benefits from it. Examples of property include homes, offices, and factories. (Intellectual property will be discussed in the next section.)

What difference do property rights supported by a functioning legal system make? A lot. Why did developed economies become developed (remember, for example, the United States was a "developing" or "emerging" economy 100 years ago)? While there are many answers, a leading answer, which is most forcefully put forward by Hernando de Soto, a Peruvian economist, focuses on the role played by formal institutions, particularly the protection of property rights afforded by a functioning legal system.[30] In Africa, only approximately 1% of land is formally registered.[31] In developed economies, every parcel of land, every building, and every trademark is represented in a property document that entitles the owner to derive income and other benefits from it, and prosecute violators through legal means. Because of the stability and predictability of such a legal system, tangible property can lead to an invisible, parallel life alongside its material existence. It can be used as collateral for credit. For example, the single most important source of funds for new start-ups in the United States is the mortgage of entrepreneurs' houses.

However, if you live in a house but cannot produce a title document specifying that you are the legal owner of the house (which is a very common situation throughout the developing world, especially in shanty towns), no bank in the world will allow you to use your house as collateral for credit. To start up a new firm, you must borrow funds from family members, friends, and other acquaintances through *informal* means. But funds through informal means are almost certainly more limited than funds that could have been provided formally by banks. As a result, in the aggregate, because of such under-funding, the average firm size in the developing world is smaller than that in the developed world. Such insecure property rights also result in using technologies that employ little fixed capital ("cash and carry" is the best) and do not entail long-term investment (such as R&D). These characteristics do not bode well in global competition, where leading firms reap benefits from economies of scale, capital-intensive technologies, and sustained investment

Property right

The legal right to use an economic property (resource) and to derive income and benefits from it.

in R&D. What the developing world lacks, and desperately needs, is formal protection of property rights in order to facilitate economic growth.

2-5c Intellectual Property Rights

While the term "property" traditionally refers to *tangible* pieces of property (such as land), intellectual property (IP) specifically refers to *intangible* property that is the result of intellectual activity (such as books, videos, and websites). Intellectual property rights (IPR) are rights associated with the ownership of intellectual property. They primarily include rights associated with (1) patents, (2) copyrights, and (3) trademarks.

- Patents are legal rights awarded by government authorities to inventors of new products or processes, who are given exclusive (monopoly) rights to derive income from such inventions through activities such as manufacturing, licensing, or selling.
- Copyrights are the exclusive legal rights of authors and publishers to publish and disseminate their works (such as this book).
- Trademarks are the exclusive legal rights of firms to use specific names, brands, and designs to differentiate their products from others.

Because IPR are usually asserted and protected on a country-by-country basis, one pressing issue arises internationally: How can IPR be protected when countries have uneven levels of enforcement? The Paris Convention for the Protection of Industrial Property is the "gold standard" for a higher level of IPR protection. Adopting the Paris Convention is required in order to become a signatory country to the WTO's Agreement on Trade-Related Aspects of Intellectual Property Rights (TRIPS) (see Chapter 8). Given the global differences in the formal rules, much stricter IPR protection is provided by TRIPS. Once countries join TRIPS, firms are often forced to pay more attention to innovation.

IPR need to be asserted and enforced through a *formal* system, which is designed to provide an incentive for people and firms to innovate and to punish violators. However, the intangible nature of IPR makes their protection difficult.[32] Around the world, piracy—unauthorized use of intellectual property—is widespread, ranging from unauthorized sharing of music files to deliberate counterfeiting of branded products.

Overall, an institution-based view suggests that the key to understanding IPR violation is to realize that IP violators are not amoral monsters, but ordinary people and firms. Given an institutional environment of weak IPR protection, violators have made a rational decision by investing in skills and knowledge in this business (Proposition 1 in Table 2.3). When filling out a survey that asks, "What is your dream career?" no high-school graduate will answer, "My dream career is counterfeiting." Nevertheless, thousands of individuals and firms *voluntarily* choose to be involved in this business worldwide.[33] Stronger IPR protection may reduce their incentive to do so. For example, counterfeiters

Intellectual property (IP)

Intangible property that is the result of intellectual activity.

Intellectual property right (IPR)

Right associated with the ownership of intellectual property.

Patent

Exclusive legal rights of inventors of new products or processes to derive income from such inventions.

Copyright

Exclusive legal rights of authors and publishers to publish and disseminate their work.

Trademark

Exclusive legal rights of firms to use specific names, brands, and designs to differentiate their products from others.

Piracy

Unauthorized use of intellectual property.

Lynnette Peizer/Alamy

What other examples of pirated intellectual property can you think of?

in China will be criminally prosecuted only if their profits exceed approximately US$10,000. No counterfeiters are dumb enough to keep records showing they make that much money. If they are caught and are found to make less than US$10,000, they can usually get away with a US$1,000 fine, which is widely regarded as a (small) cost of doing business. However, IP reforms to criminalize *all* counterfeiting activities regardless of the amount of profits, which have been discussed in China, may significantly reduce counterfeiters' incentive.

2-6 Economic Systems

Learning Objective
Appreciate the differences among market economy, command economy, and mixed economy.

An economic system refers to the rules of the game on how a country is governed economically. At the two ends of a spectrum, we can find (1) a market economy and (2) a command economy. In between, there is a mixed economy.

A pure market economy is characterized by the "invisible hand" of market forces first noted by Adam Smith in *The Wealth of Nations* in 1776. The government takes a hands-off approach known as *laissez faire*. Specifically, all factors of production should be privately owned. The government should only perform functions that the private sector cannot perform (such as providing roads and defense).

A pure command economy is defined by a government taking, in the words of Lenin, the "commanding height" in the economy. All factors of production should be government-owned or state-owned, and all supply, demand, and pricing are planned by the government. During the heydays of communism, the former Soviet Union and China approached such an ideal.

A mixed economy, by definition, has elements of both a market economy and a command economy. It boils down to the relative distribution of market forces versus command forces. In practice, no country has ever completely embraced Adam Smith's ideal *laissez faire*. Here is a quiz: Which economy has the highest degree of economic freedom (the lowest degree of government intervention in the economy)? Hint: Given extensive government intervention since 2008, it is obviously *not* the United States. A series of surveys report that it is Hong Kong.[34] (The post-1997 handover to Chinese sovereignty does not make a difference.) The crucial point here is that even in Hong Kong, there is still some noticeable government intervention in the economy. During the aftermath of the 1997 economic crisis, when the share prices of all Hong Kong listed firms took a nosedive, the Hong Kong government took a highly controversial action. It used government funds to purchase 10% of the shares of all the "blue chip" firms listed under the Hang Seng Index. This action did slow down the sliding of share prices and stabilized the economy, but it turned all the "blue chip" firms into state-owned enterprises (SOEs)—at least 10% owned by the state. At the height of the global financial crisis in 2008 and 2009, most governments in developed economies took similar action by bailing out their banks and turning them into SOEs.

Likewise, no country has ever practiced a complete command economy, despite the efforts of communist zealots throughout the Eastern bloc during the Cold War. Poland never nationalized its agriculture. Hungarians were known to have second (and private!) jobs while all of them theoretically only worked for the state. While the former Soviet Union and Central and Eastern European countries threw away communism, all ongoing practitioners of communism, such as China, Cuba, and Vietnam, have embraced market reforms. Even North Korea is now interested in attracting foreign investment.

Economic system
Rules of the game on how a country is governed economically.

Market economy
An economy that is characterized by the "invisible hand" of market forces.

Command economy
An economy that is characterized by government ownership and control of factors of production.

Mixed economy
An economy that has elements of both a market economy and a command economy.

State-owned enterprise (SOE)
A firm owned and controlled by the state (government).

The economic system of most countries is a mixed economy. When we say a country has a "market economy," it is really a shorthand version for a country that organizes its economy *mostly* (but not completely) by market forces and that still has certain elements of a command economy. China, Russia, Sweden, and the United States all claim to have a "market economy," but the meaning is different in each case. In short, "free markets" are not "free." It boils down to a matter of degree. Overall, it may be prudent to drop the "F" word ("free") from the term "free market economy." Instead, it makes sense to acknowledge that there is a variety of capitalism, with each version of "market economy" differing in some ways.[35]

2-7 Debates and Extensions

Learning Objective
Participate in two leading debates on politics, laws, and economics.

As some of the most important forces affecting global business, formal institutions such as political, legal, and economic systems provoke some significant debates. In this section, we focus on two major debates: (1) drivers of economic development and (2) private ownership versus state ownership.

2-7a Drivers of Economic Development: Culture, Geography, or Institutions?

The differences in economic development around the globe are striking. The highest and lowest per capita income countries are Norway (US$76,450) and Burundi (US$110), respectively. Why are some countries such as Norway so developed (rich), and some African countries such as Burundi so underdeveloped (poor)? More generally, what drives economic development in different countries?

Scholars and policy makers have debated this important question since Adam Smith's time.[36] Various debate points boil down to three explanations: (1) culture, (2) geography, and (3) institutions. The culture side argues that rich countries tend to have smarter and harder-working populations driven by a stronger motivation for economic success (such as the Protestant work ethic identified by Max Weber—see Chapter 3). However, it is difficult to imagine that on average, Norwegians are *700 times* smarter and harder at work than Burundians. This line of thinking, bordering on racism, is no longer acceptable in the 21st century.

The geography school of thought suggests that rich countries (such as the United States)—thanks to their lucky geographic locations—tend to be well endowed with natural resources. However, one can easily point out that some poor countries (such as the Democratic Republic of Congo [Zaire]) also possess rich natural resources, and that some rich countries (such as Denmark and Japan) are very poor in natural resources. In addition, some countries are believed to be cursed by their poor geographic locations, which may be landlocked (such as Malawi) and/or located near the hot equator zone infested with tropical diseases (such as Burundi). This argument is not convincing either, because some landlocked countries are phenomenally well developed (such as Switzerland), and some countries near the equator have accomplished enviable growth (such as Singapore). Geography is important, but it is not destiny.

Finally, institutional scholars argue that institutions are "the basic determinants of the performance of an economy."[37] Because institutions provide the incentive structure of a society, formal political, legal, and economic systems have a significant impact on economic development by affecting the incentives and the costs of doing business.[38] In short, rich countries are rich because they have developed better market-supporting institutional frameworks. Specifically, several points can be made:

- It is economically advantageous for individuals and firms to grow and specialize in order to capture the gains from trade. This is the "division of labor" thesis first advanced by Adam Smith (see Chapter 5).

- A lack of strong formal, market-supporting institutions forces individuals to trade on an informal basis with a small neighboring group and forces firms to remain small, thus foregoing the gains from a sharper division of labor by trading on a large scale with distant partners. For example, most of the transactions in Africa are local in nature, and most firms are small. Over 40% of Africa's economy is reportedly informal, the highest proportion in the world.[39]

- Emergence of formal, market-supporting institutions encourages individuals to specialize and firms to grow in size to capture the gains from complicated long-distance trade (such as transactions with distant, foreign countries). As China's market institutions progress, many Chinese firms have grown their size. In 2014, 91 Chinese firms were among the *Fortune* Global 500 largest firms in the world (measured by sales). In 1984, there were none.

- When formal, market-supporting institutions protect property rights, they will fuel more innovation, entrepreneurship, and, thus, economic growth. While spontaneous innovation existed throughout history, why has its pace accelerated significantly since the Industrial Revolution starting in the 1700s? In no small measure, this was because of the Statute of Monopolies enacted in Great Britain in 1624, which was the world's first patent law to formally protect the IPR of inventors and make innovation financially lucrative.[40] This law has been imitated around the world. Its impact is still felt today, as we now expect *continuous* innovation to be the norm. This would not have happened had there not been a system of strong protection of IPR. Why do we now routinely expect IT products to double their computing power roughly every two years? The answer is certainly not because humans (or even IT geniuses) are two times smarter every two years—the key is institutions affording better and stronger IP protection that fuels such relentless (and, yes, routine!) innovation.[41]

These arguments, of course, are the backbone of the institution-based view of global business. Championed by Douglass North, the Nobel laureate quoted earlier, this side has clearly won the debate on the drivers of economic development. However, the debate does not end, because it is still unclear *exactly* what kind of political system facilitates economic development. For example, whether democracy is good for economic development has been subject to a fierce debate (see the Closing Case).

2-7b Private Ownership versus State Ownership[42]

Private ownership is good. State ownership is bad. Although crude, these two statements fairly accurately summarize the intellectual and political reasoning behind three decades of privatization around the world between 1980 and 2008. Table 2.6 outlines the key differences between private ownership and state ownership. As providers of capital, private owners are otherwise known as capitalists, and their

Table 2.6	**Private Ownership versus State Ownership**	
	Private ownership	**State ownership**
Objective of the firm	Maximize profits for private owners who are capitalists (and maximize shareholder value for public shareholders if the firm is publicly listed).	Optimal balance for a "fair" deal for all stakeholders. Maximizing profits is not the sole objective of the firm. Protecting jobs and minimizing social unrest are legitimate goals.
Establishment of the firm	Entry is determined by entrepreneurs, owners, and investors.	Entry is determined by government officials and bureaucrats.
Financing of the firm	Financing is from private sources (and public shareholders if the firm is publicly traded).	Financing is from state sources (such as direct subsidiaries or banks owned or controlled by governments).
Liquidation of the firm	Exit is forced by competition. A firm has to declare bankruptcy or be acquired if it becomes financially insolvent.	Exit is determined by government officials and bureaucrats. Firms deemed "too big to fail" may be supported by taxpayer dollars indefinitely.
Appointment and dismissal of management	Management appointments are made by owners and investors, largely based on merit.	Management appointments are made by government officials and bureaucrats who may also use non-economic criteria.
Compensation of management	Managers' compensation is determined by competitive market forces. Managers tend to be paid more under private ownership.	Managers' compensation is determined politically with some consideration given to a sense of fairness and legitimacy in the eyes of the public. Managers tend to be paid less under state ownership.

Sources: Extracted from text in (1) M. W. Peng, 2000, *Business Strategies in Transition Economies* (p. 19), Thousand Oaks, CA: Sage; (2) M. W. Peng, G. Bruton, & C. Stan, 2014, Theories of the (state-owned) firm, Working paper, Jindal School of Management, University of Texas at Dallas.

central role in the economic system gives birth to the term "capitalism." State ownership emphasizes the social and public nature of economic ownership, and leads to the coinage of the term "socialism." Obviously, both forms of ownership have their own pros and cons. The debate is about which form of ownership is better—whether the pros outweigh the cons.

The debate on private versus state ownership has underpinned much of the global economic evolution since the early 20th century. The Great Depression (1929–1933) was seen as a failure of capitalism and led numerous elites in developing countries and a nontrivial number of scholars in developed economies to favor the Soviet-style socialism centered on state ownership. As a result, the postwar decades saw a rise of state ownership. State ownership was not only extensive throughout the former Eastern bloc (the former Soviet Union, Central and Eastern Europe, China, and Vietnam), but was also widely embraced throughout developed economies in Western Europe. By the early 1980s, close to half of the GDP in major Western European countries, such as Britain, France, and Italy, was contributed by SOEs.

Experience throughout the former Eastern bloc and Western Europe indicated that SOEs typically suffer from a lack of accountability and a lack of economic efficiency. SOEs were known to feature relatively equal pay between the managers and the rank and file. Since extra work did not translate into extra pay, employees had little incentive to improve the quality and efficiency of their work. Given the generally low pay and the nondemanding work environment, formerly Soviet SOE employees summed it up well: "They pretend to pay us, and we pretend to work."

Would the income of these automobile manufacturing workers in China increase if their state-owned employer were privatized?

Britain's former prime minister Margaret Thatcher privatized a majority of British SOEs in the 1980s. SOEs throughout Central and Eastern Europe soon followed suit. After the former Soviet Union collapsed, the new Russian government unleashed some of the most aggressive privatization schemes in the 1990s. Eventually, the privatization movement became global. In no small part, such a global movement was championed by the Washington Consensus, spearheaded by the US government and two Washington-based international organizations: the International Monetary Fund (IMF) and the World Bank. One core value of the Washington Consensus is the unquestioned belief in the superiority of private ownership over state ownership. The widespread privatization movement suggested that the Washington Consensus clearly won the day—or it seemed.

But in 2008, the pendulum suddenly swung back. During the Great Recession (2008–2009), many governments in developed economies bailed out numerous failing private firms using public funds, effectively turning them into SOEs. As a result, the arguments in favor of private ownership and "free market" capitalism collapsed. Since SOEs had such a dreadful reputation (essentially a "dirty word"), the US government has refused to acknowledge that it has SOEs. Instead, it admits that the United States has "government-sponsored enterprises" (GSEs), such as General Motors (nicknamed "Government Motors") and Citigroup (nicknamed "Citigovernment").

Conceptually, what are the differences between SOEs and GSEs? Hardly any! The right column in Table 2.6 is based on my own research on the "classical" SOEs in pre-reform China and Russia published more than a decade ago. This column also accurately summarizes what is happening in developed economies featuring GSEs now. For example, protecting jobs is one of the stated goals behind bailouts. Entry and exit are determined by government officials, and some firms that have been clearly run into the ground, such as AIG and GM, are deemed "too big to fail" and are bailed out with taxpayer dollars. The US government has forced the exit of GM's former chairman and CEO, and is now directly involved in the appointment of executives at GM and other GSEs. Not surprisingly, the US government is now drafting rules to regulate executive compensation.

One crucial concern is that despite noble goals to rescue the economy, protect jobs, and fight recession, government bailouts may encourage moral hazard—recklessness when people and organizations (including firms and governments) do not have to face the full consequences of their actions.[43] In other words, capitalism without the risk of failure becomes socialism. It is long known that managers in SOEs face a "soft budget constraint," in that they can always dip into state coffers to cover their losses.[44] When managers in private firms who make risky decisions to "bet the farm" find out when these decisions turn sour, but their firms do not go under—thanks to generous bailouts—they are likely to embrace more risk in the future. In other words, bailouts foster the kind of thinking among managers regarding state coffers and taxpayer dollars: "Heads I win, tails you lose." Per Proposition 1 (Table 2.3), these managers are being

Washington Consensus

A view centered on the unquestioned belief in the superiority of private ownership over state ownership in economic policy making, which is often spearheaded by the US government and two Washington-based international organizations: the IMF and the World Bank.

Moral hazard

Recklessness when people and organizations (including firms and governments) do not have to face the full consequences of their actions.

Table 2.7	How Many of the Top Ten Largest and Top Ten Most Profitable Firms in the World Are SOEs?		
	Top ten largest firms measured by sales		**Top ten firms with the largest profits**
1	Wal-Mart Stores (USA)	1	Vodafone Group (UK)
2	Royal Dutch Shell (Netherlands)	2	Fannie Mae (USA)—SOE
3	SINOPEC Group (China)—SOE	3	Freddie Mac (USA)—SOE
4	China National Petroleum Corporation (China)—SOE	4	Industrial & Commercial Bank of China (China)—SOE
5	ExxonMobil (USA)	5	Apple (USA)
6	BP (UK)	6	Gazprom (Russia)—SOE
7	State Grid (China)—SOE	7	China Construction Bank (China)—SOE
8	Volkswagen (Germany)—SOE	8	ExxonMobil (USA)
9	Toyota Motor (Japan)	9	Samsung Electronics (South Korea)
10	Glencore (Switzerland)	10	Agricultural Bank of China (China)—SOE

Source: Adapted from Fortune, 2014, Global 500, July 21: F-1 and F-13.

perfectly rational: Taking on risks, if successful, will enrich their private firms, their owners (shareholders), and themselves; if unsuccessful, the government will come to the rescue.

Far from being swept to the dustbin of history, SOEs as an organizational form have shown some amazing longevity.[45] Today, SOEs represent approximately 10% of the global GDP. Even in developed (OECD member) countries, they command 5% of the GDP.[46] From the ashes of the Washington Consensus emerged a Beijing Consensus, which centers on state ownership and government intervention. Anchored by SOEs, China over the past 30 years has grown its GDP by 9.5% per year and its international trade volume by 18% per year. SOEs represent 80% of China's stock market capitalization. But China is not alone. In Russia, the figure is 62%, in Brazil 38%, and in Norway 38%.[47] Overall, SOEs not only occupy four spots among the top ten largest firms worldwide (measured by sales), but also represent six of the top ten most *profitable* firms globally (measured by amount of profits) (see Table 2.7). While some SOEs have become large and profitable, the majority of them have continued to be inefficient. Despite the hoopla about the alleged "muscle" of Chinese SOEs, as a group their return on assets (ROA) since 2008 has been barely 3%.[48] In summary, some SOEs do well, most muddle through, but they are unlikely to disappear any time soon.

2-8 Management Savvy

Focusing on *formal* institutions, this chapter has sketched the contours of an institution-based view of global business. (Chapter 3 will reinforce this view with a focus on *informal* institutions.) How does the institution-based view help us answer the fundamental question that is of utmost managerial concern around the globe: What determines the success and failure of firms around the globe? In a nutshell, this chapter suggests that firm performance is, at least

Learning Objective
Draw implications for action.

Beijing Consensus
A view that questions Washington Consensus's belief in the superiority of private ownership over state ownership in economic policy making, which is often associated with the position held by the Chinese government.

Table 2.8	**Implications for Action**

- When entering a new country, do your homework by having a thorough understanding of the formal institutions governing firm behavior.

- When doing business in countries with a strong propensity for informal relational exchanges, insisting on formalizing the contract right away may backfire.

in part, determined by the institutional frameworks governing firm behavior. It is the growth of the firm that, in the aggregate, leads to the growth of the economy. Not surprisingly, most developed economies are supported by strong, effective, and market-supporting formal institutions, and most underdeveloped economies are pulled back by weak, ineffective, and market-distorting formal institutions. In other words, when markets work smoothly in developed economies, formal market-supporting institutions are almost invisible and taken for granted. However, when markets work poorly, the absence of strong formal institutions may become conspicuous.

For managers doing business around the globe, this chapter suggests two broad implications for action (Table 2.8). First, managerial choices are made rationally within the constraints of a given institutional framework. Therefore, when entering a new country, managers need to do their homework by having a thorough understanding of the formal institutions affecting their business.[49] The rules for doing business in a democratic market economy are certainly different from the rules in a totalitarian command economy. In short, "when in Rome, do as the Romans do." While this is a good start, managers also need to understand *why* "Romans" do things in a certain way, by studying the formal and informal institutions governing "Roman" behavior.

Second, while this chapter has focused on the role of formal institutions, managers should follow the advice of the second proposition of the institution-based view: In situations where formal constraints are unclear or fail, informal constraints (such as relationship norms) will play a *larger* role in reducing uncertainty. This means that when doing business in countries with a strong propensity for informal, relational exchanges, insisting on formalizing the contract right away may backfire.[50] Because these countries often have relatively weak legal systems, personal relationship building is often used to substitute for the lack of strong legal protection.[51] Attitudes such as "business first, relationship afterwards" (have a drink *after* the negotiation) may clash with the norm the other way around (lavish entertainment first, talk about business later). For example, we often hear that because of their culture, the Chinese prefer to cultivate personal relationships (*guanxi*) first. This is *not* entirely true, because in the absence of a strong legal and regulatory regime in China, investing in personal relationships up front may simply be the initial cost one has to pay if interested in eventually doing business together. Such investment in personal relationships is a must in countries ranging from Argentina to Zimbabwe. The broad range of these countries with different cultural traditions suggests that the interest in cultivating what the Chinese call *guanxi*, which is a word found in almost every culture (such as *blat* or *sistema* in Russia and *guan he* in Vietnam), is not likely to be driven by culture alone, but more significantly by common institutional characteristics—in particular, the lack of formal market-supporting institutions.

CHAPTER SUMMARY/LEARNING OBJECTIVES

2-1 Explain the concept of institutions and their key role in reducing uncertainty.

- Institutions are commonly defined as the rules of the game.
- Institutions have formal and informal components, each with different supportive pillars.
- Their key function is to reduce uncertainty, curtail transaction costs, and combat opportunism.

2-2 Articulate the two core propositions underpinning an institution-based view of global business.

- Proposition 1: Managers and firms *rationally* pursue their interests and make choices within formal and informal institutional constraints in a given institutional framework.
- Proposition 2: When formal constraints are unclear or fail, informal constraints will play a *larger* role.

2-3 Identify the basic differences between democracy and totalitarianism.

- Democracy is a political system in which citizens elect representatives to govern the country.
- Totalitarianism is a political system in which one person or party exercises absolute political control.

2-4 Outline the differences among civil law, common law, and theocratic law.

- Civil law uses comprehensive statutes and codes as a primary means to form legal judgments.
- Common law is shaped by precedents and traditions from previous judicial decisions.
- Theocratic law is a legal system based on religious teachings.

2-5 Understand the importance of property rights and intellectual property rights.

- Property rights are legal rights to use an economic resource and to derive income and other benefits from it.
- Intellectual property refers to intangible property that is the result of intellectual activity.

2-6 Appreciate the differences among market economy, command economy, and mixed economy.

- A pure market economy is characterized by *laissez faire* and total control by market forces.
- A pure command economy is defined by government ownership and control of all means of production.
- Most countries operate mixed economies, with a different emphasis on market versus command forces.

2-7 Participate in two leading debates concerning politics, laws, and economics.

- (1) What drives economic development: Culture, geography, or institutions? (2) Private ownership versus state ownership

2-8 Draw managerial implications for action.

- Have a thorough understanding of the formal institutions before entering a country.
- Insisting on formalizing the contract in initial negotiations may backfire in some countries.

KEY TERMS

REVIEW QUESTIONS

1. *ON CULTURE:* **Is there any relationship between the culture of a given country and the extent to which it will likely have a dynamic, growing economy? Are there cultures that would be more likely to limit economic growth and even result in poverty? Defend your answer.**

2. **Compare PengAtlas Maps 1.1 (Developed Economies and Emerging Economies) and Map 1.2 (Political Freedom Around the World). To what extent do developed economies tend to have a high level of political freedom—or is there any relationship? If there is any relationship, is it causal or coincidental? Explain.**

3. **Compare PengAtlas Map 1.3 (Legal Systems Around the World) and Map 1.1. In your opinion, what stands out to you regarding each category of legal system? Are there any relationships? If so, are they causal or coincidental? Defend your answer.**

4. **How can the "rules of the game" reduce uncertainty?**

5. **Do "rules of the game" promote or prevent opportunism?**

6. **Do you agree that managers and firms really pursue their interests? Why or why not?**

7. **What are examples of informal constraints that affect global business firms?**

8. **What are the pros and cons of expanding into a democratic country?**

9. **What are the pros and cons of expanding into a totalitarian country?**

10. **Would you rather do business in a country that uses civil law or common law? Why?**

11. **What are some of the issues to consider before doing business in a theocracy?**

12. **What is the relationship between property rights and economic development?**

13. **Why is it important to protect IPR?**

14. **Under what circumstances would it be easier to do business in a command economy than a market economy?**

15. Many view the United States as a mixed economy. In your opinion, is the mix changing? If so, how? Is it shifting more to a command economy or a market economy?

16. In your opinion, which is most important to economic development—culture, geography, or institutions?

17. Given whatever plans you have for the future, do you feel you would have the greatest likelihood of success under private ownership or under state ownership? Why?

18. Why is it important to understand formal institutions before entering a country? Explain by using an example.

19. *ON CULTURE:* Why is understanding of human relations within a culture sometimes more important than legal expertise?

CRITICAL DISCUSSION QUESTIONS

1. How do you explain your country's economic success (or failure)?

2. What is your view on the debate between private ownership and state ownership?

3. *ON ETHICS:* As manager, you discover that your firm's products are counterfeited by small family firms that employ child labor in rural Bangladesh. You are aware of the corporate plan to phase out the products soon. You also realize that once you report to the authorities, these firms will be shut down, employees will be out of work, and families and children will be starving. How do you proceed?

4. *ON ETHICS:* Your multinational is the largest foreign investor and enjoys good profits in (1) Sudan, where government forces are reportedly cracking down on rebels and killing civilians; and (2) Vietnam, where religious leaders are reportedly being persecuted. As country manager, you understand that your firm is pressured by activists to exit these countries. The alleged government actions, which you personally find distasteful, are not directly related to your operations. How would you proceed?

GLOBAL ACTION

BUSINESS
INSIGHTS
GLOBAL

1. Evaluating political risk is an important element of country risk analysis. In fact, your personal interest relates to countries in the Middle East and North Africa region that have a high political risk. Provide a brief overview of the region and the reasoning behind assessing these countries that have been assessed with high political risk. From this list, which country has the highest overall country risk?

2. Since you work for a diversified multinational corporation, economic risk across different sectors of the world economy is an integral part of analysis as it indicates the future business prospects for specific industries. Evaluate the risk assessment of three industry sectors that are available to analyze. Prepare a report, and provide a recommendation concerning which industry and region would be most beneficial to your company.

CLOSING CASE

Ethical Dilemma

EMERGING MARKETS: Is Democracy Good for Economic Development?

© Kenishirotie/Shutterstock.com

Democracy is good. Dictatorship is bad. Although crude, these two statements fairly accurately summarize the political sentiments in many parts of the world. It is not hard to understand why. Compared with dictatorships, on average, democracies are richer, less corrupt, and less likely to go to war. Beyond such nontrivial benefits, deep down, democracies allow people to make their own political choices. In the second half of the 20th century, the march of democracy was impressive. This powerful idea took root in some of the most difficult terrains, such as Germany (where Nazism had to be defeated militarily), India (which had the world's largest population of poor people), Japan (where emperor worship had to be curtailed and military adventurism destroyed), and South Africa (which had practiced apartheid for decades). Throughout Asia and Africa, decolonization gave birth to a number of new democracies. A series of autocratic governments gave themselves up to democracy: Spain (1975), Argentina (1983), Brazil (1985), South Korea (1987), Taiwan (1988), and Chile (1989). The collapse of the Soviet Union (1991) resulted in the proliferation of young democracies throughout Central and Eastern Europe as well as Central Asia. Recently, the Arab Spring expanded democracy to North Africa: Algeria (2011), Egypt (2011), and Libya (2011). Overall, there is no doubt that democracy has spread around the world: from 69 countries in the 1980s to 120 in the 2000s.

However, according to the *Economist*, democracy is "going through a difficult time." In new democracies such as Egypt, Iraq, Libya, Thailand, and Ukraine, an unenviable pattern emerges: It seems easier to get rid of the old regime than to establish a functioning democratic government. The new regime fumbles, the economy suffers, jobs disappear, and people find their conditions to be as bad as they were before. Civil disturbance broke out in Iraq and Libya, military coups smashed democracy in Egypt and Thailand, and foreign intervention (from Russia) pushed Ukraine's vulnerable democracy to its limits. At the same time, established democracies have not been good role models lately. The United States has become a joke for dysfunctional politics—with partisan politicians shutting down the federal government once (2013) and threatening to default on its debt twice (2011 and 2013). The European Union is hardly a paradise for democracy either. The fateful decision to introduce the euro in 1999 was largely dictated to the public. In the only two EU countries that held a democratic referendum on whether to adopt the euro—Denmark and Sweden—voters in both of them said "No." Not surprisingly, many ordinary people in Europe who had to cough up higher taxes to plug the hole of the recent euro mess were mad. Far from marching to dominate the world, democracy seems to have lost its forward momentum lately.

One of the litmus tests is: Is democracy good for economic development? While champions of democracy shout, "Yes," the fastest-growing major economy in the last three decades, China, remains totalitarian. The growth rate of India, the world's largest democracy, in the same period is only about half of China's. With little democracy, Hong Kong has achieved enviably higher per capita income than its old colonial master, Britain, which enjoys the world's oldest democracy—US$52,000 versus US$37,000, according to the World Bank based on purchasing power parity. In another example, Russia grew faster under Putin's more authoritarian rule during the 2000s, compared with the 1990s, when Russia was presumably more democratic under Yeltsin. In contrast, the economies of most established democracies have been stagnant or declining—the Great Recession of 2008–2009 can serve as Exhibit A here. Many Westerners have been tremendously disillusioned by their governments' actions to use taxpayer dollars and euros to bail out banks—without much democratic consultation with the taxpayers.

Many Chinese willingly put up with the dictatorship that governs China if the regime delivers jobs, wealth, and economic growth. Of course, they do not have a choice anyway. But tellingly, the 2013 Pew Survey of Global Attitudes found that 85% of Chinese were "very satisfied" with their country's direction, compared with only 31% of Americans, 30% of British, and 20% of Japanese. Some Chinese elites argue that their model is more efficient than democracy in delivering growth. Just witness the new skyscrapers, highways, and airports that are thrown up in an amazingly short period of time. In two years, China implemented pension coverage to an additional 240 million rural residents—a process that would take decades in a democracy. Despite the regime's heavy hand in control (ranging from jailing dissidents to censoring the Internet), paradoxically such obsession with control forces it to pay close attention to public opinion, which serves as meaningful constraints on the regime's behavior. Conceptualized as the Beijing Consensus, the Chinese model has increasingly gained credibility in the developing world.

Despite democracies' unenviable scorecard on economic development lately, no one outside China has seriously argued for totalitarianism in order to facilitate economic development. In an influential paper concerned about the decline of US competitiveness and the rise of Chinese competitiveness, strategy guru Michael Porter nevertheless wrote, "We do not want to copy China, whose speed comes partly from a political system unacceptable to Americans." If democracy in the 21st century aspires to be as successful as it was in the 20th century, faith in democracy will need to be translated into strengths in economic development. So stay tuned.

CASE DISCUSSION QUESTIONS

1. Why does democracy have such broad appeal as a political system around the world?

2. How does democracy suffer from severe setbacks in some countries lately?

3. How does the Chinese experience answer the question: "Is democracy good for economic development?"?

4. **ON ETHICS:** The military governments in Egypt and Thailand have invited your firm to do business there. As CEO, you appreciate the lucrative offers. But you are also concerned that your firm may be labeled "devil's advocate" or "accomplice" by democracy activists around the world. How would you proceed?

Sources: Based on (1) *Bloomberg Businessweek*, 2014, Welcome to Thailand, land of coups, June 2: 17; (2) *Economist*, 2013, Has the Arab Spring failed? July 13: 11; (3) *Economist*, 2013, The battle for Egypt, August 17: 11; (4) *Economist*, 2014, What's wrong with democracy, March 1: 47–52; (5) Economist, 2014, When will the rainbow end? May 3: 41–43; (6) M. Porter & J. Rivkin, 2012, Choosing the United States, *Harvard Business Review*, March: 80–93.

NOTES

[**Journal acronyms**] **AER**—*American Economic Review;* **AME**—*Academy of Management Executive;* **AMJ**—*Academy of Management Journal;* **AMP**—*Academy of Management Perspectives;* **AMR**—*Academy of Management Review;* **AP**—*American Psychologist;* **APJM**—*Asia Pacific Journal of Management;* **BH**—*Business Horizons;* **GSJ**—*Global Strategy Journal;* **HBR**—*Harvard Business Review;* **JBV**—*Journal of Business Venturing;* **JEL**—*Journal of Economic Literature;* **JEP**—*Journal of Economic Perspectives;* **JIBS**—*Journal of International Business Studies;* **JM**—*Journal of Management;* **JMS**—*Journal of Management Studies;* **JPE**—*Journal of Political Economy;* **JWB**—*Journal of World Business;* **MBR**—*Multinational Business Review;* **NG**—*National Geographic;* **SMJ**—*Strategic Management Journal;* **SO**—*Strategic Organization;* **WSJ**—*Wall Street Journal*

1 M. W. Peng, 2003, Institutional transitions and strategic choices (p. 275), *AMR*, 28: 275–296.

2 M. W. Peng, S. Sun, B. Pinkham, & H. Chen, 2009, The institution-based view as a third leg for a strategy tripod, *AMP*, 23: 63–81; M. W. Peng, D. Wang, & Y. Jiang, 2008, An institution-based view of international business strategy, *JIBS*, 39: 920–936.

3 D. North, 1990, *Institutions, Institutional Change, and Economic Performance* (p. 3), New York: Norton.

4 W. R. Scott, 1995, *Institutions and Organizations*, Thousand Oaks, CA: Sage.

5 D. Philippe & R. Durand, 2011, The impact of norm-conforming behaviors on firm reputation, *SMJ*, 32: 969–993.

6 S. Hannah, B. Avolio, & D. May, 2011, Moral maturation and moral conation, *AMR*, 36: 663–685.

7 M. W. Peng, 2000, *Business Strategies in Transition Economies* (pp. 42–44), Thousand Oaks, CA: Sage.

8 O. Branzai & S. Abdelnour, 2010, Another day, another dollar, *JIBS*, 41: 804–825; M. Czinkota, G. Knight, P. Liesch, & J. Steen, 2010, Terrorism and international business, *JIBS*, 41: 826–843; L. Weber & K. Mayer, 2014, Transaction cost economics and the cognitive perspective, *AMR*, 39: 344–363.

9 *Economist*, 2011, Looking for someone to blame, August 13: 25–26.

10 *BW*, 2009, The financial crisis excuse, February 23: 32.

11 O. Williamson, 1985, *The Economic Institutions of Capitalism* (pp. 1–2), New York: Free Press.

12 P. Collier & J. Gunning, 1999, Explaining African economic performance, *JEL*, 37: 64–111.

13 R. Corredoira & G. McDermott, 2014, Adaptation, bridging, and firm upgrading, *JIBS*, 45: 699–672; A. Cuervo-Cazurra & L. Dau, 2009, Promarket reforms and firm profitability in developing countries, *AMJ*, 52: 1348–1368; L. Dau, 2013, Learning across geographic space, *JIBS*, 44: 235–262; R. Hoskisson, M. Wright, I. Filatotchev, & M. W. Peng, 2013, Emerging multinationals from mid-range economies, *JMS*, 50: 1295–1321.

14 M. W. Peng, 2002, Towards an institution-based view of business strategy, *APJM*, 19: 251–267. See also J. Battilana & T. Casciaro, 2012, Change agents, networks, and institutions, *AMJ*, 55: 381–398; H. Berry, M. Guillen, & N. Zhou, 2010, An institutional approach to cross-national distance, *JIBS*, 41: 1460–1480; M. Besharov & W. Smith, 2014, Multiple institutional logics in organizations, *AMR*, 39: 364–381; J. Doh & R. Lucea, 2013, So close yet so far, *GSJ*, 3: 171–194; J. Lepoutre & M. Valente, 2012, Fools breaking out, *AMJ*, 55: 285–313; C. Stevens & J. Cooper, 2010, A behavioral theory of governments' ability to make credible commitments to firms, *APJM*, 27: 587–610; W. Helms, C. Oliver, & K. Webb, 2012, Antecedents of settlement on a new institutional practice, *AMJ*, 55: 1120–1145.

15 M. Abdi & P. Aulakh, 2012, Do country-level institutional frameworks and interfirm governance arrangements substitute or complement in international business relationships? *JIBS*, 43: 477–497; A. Chacar, W. Newburry, & B. Vissa, 2010, Bringing institutions into performance persistence research, *JIBS*, 41: 1119–1140; T. Kostova, K. Roth, & M. T. Dacin, 2008, Institutional theory in the study of multinational corporations, *AMR*, 33: 994–1006; K. Meyer & H. Thein, 2014, Business under adverse home country institutions, *JWB*, 49: 156–171; R. Salomon & Z. Wu, 2012, Institutional distance and local isomorphism strategy, *JIBS*, 43: 343–367; G. Shinkle & A. Kriauciunas, 2010, Institutions, size, and age in transition economies, *JIBS*, 41: 267–286; T. Tong, T. Alessandri, J. Reuer, & A. Chintakananda, 2008, How much does country matter? *JIBS*, 39: 387–405.

16 *Economist*, 2007, Heavy going (p. 5), April 14: 5–7.

17 *BW*, 2009, NYSE chief Duncan Niederauer on Obama and business (p. 15), June 8: 15–16.

18 *BW*, 2009, The overseas tax squeeze, May 18: 18–20.

19 D. Ariely, 2009, The end of rational economics, *HBR*, July: 78–84; D. Kahneman, 2003, A perspective on judgment and choice, *AP*, 58: 697–720; P. Rosenzweig, 2010, Robert S. McNamara and the evolution of modern management, *HBR*, December: 87–93.

20 All the quotes in this paragraph are from R. Draper, 2013, Kinshasa, urban pulse of the Congo (pp. 106–109), *NG*, September: 100–123.

21 M. Hadani & D. Schuler, 2013, In search of El Dorado, *SMJ*, 34: 165–181; S. Lux, T. Crook, & D. Woehr, 2011, Mixing business with politics, *JM*, 37: 223–247; C. Oliver & I. Holzinger, 2008, The effectiveness of strategic political management, *AMR*, 33: 496–520.

22 Y. Li, M. W. Peng, & C. Macaulay, 2013, Market-political ambidexterity during institutional transitions, *SO*, 11: 205–213.

23 L. Dai, L. Eden, & P. Beamish, 2013, Place, space, and geographical exposure, *JIBS*, 44: 554–578; W. Henisz, E. Mansfield, & M. von Glinow, 2010, Conflict, security, and political risk, *JIBS*, 41: 759–764; J. Oetzel & K. Getz, 2012, Why and how might firms respond strategically to violent conflict? *JIBS*, 43: 166–186.

24 *Economist*, 2012, Wish you were mine, February 11: 51–52.

25 S. Young, D. Ross, & B. MacKay, 2014, Inward foreign direct investment and constitutional change in Scotland, *MBR*, 22: 118–138.

26 *Economist*, 2014, Don't leave us this way, July 12: 11; *Economist*, 2014, Scottish finance, September 6: 58.

27 I. Arikan & O. Shenkar, 2014, National animosity and cross-border alliances, *AMJ*, 56: 1516–1544; R. Click & R. Weiner, 2010, Resource nationalism meets the market, *JIBS*, 41: 783–803; Q. Li & T. Vashchilko, 2010, Dyadic military conflict, security alliances, and bilateral FDI flows, *JIBS*, 41: 765–782.

28 R. La Porta, F. Lopez-de-Silanes, A. Shleifer, & R. Vishny, 1998, Law and finance (p. 1118), *JPE*, 106: 1113–1155.

29 The author's interview, Middle East Women's Delegation visiting the University of Texas at Dallas, January 23, 2006.

30 H. de Soto, 2000, *The Mystery of Capital*, New York: Basic Books.

31 W. Easterly, 2008, Institutions: Top down or bottom up? *AER*, 98: 95–99.

32 P. Chaudhry & A. Zimmerman, 2009, *The Economics of Counterfeit Trade*, Berlin: Springer; C. Hill, 2007, Digital piracy, *APJM*, 24: 9–25.

33 M. W. Peng, 2013, An institution-based view of IPR protection, *BH*, 56: 135–139.

34 Heritage Foundation, www.heritage.org.

35 M. Carney, E. Gedajlovic, & X. Yang, 2009, Varieties of Asian capitalism, *APJM*, 26: 361–380; P. Hall & D. Soskice, 2001, *Varieties of Capitalism*, Oxford, UK: Oxford University Press; W. Judge, S. Fainshmidt, & J. Brown, 2014, Which model of capitalism best delivers both wealth and equality? *JIBS*, 45: 363–386.

36 A. Deaton, 2010, Understanding the mechanisms of economic development, *JEP*, 24: 3–16; D. Ray, 2010, Uneven growth, *JEP*, 24: 45–60; D. Radrik, 2010, Diagnostics before prescription, *JEP*, 24: 33–44.

37 D. North, 2005, *Understanding the Process of Economic Change* (p. 48), Princeton, NJ: Princeton University Press.

38 D. Acemoglu & J. Robinson, 2012, *Why Nations Fail*, New York: Crown; R. Barro & X. Sala-i-Martin, 2003, *Economic Growth*, Cambridge, MA: MIT Press.

39 *Economist*, 2005, Doing business in Africa, July 2: 61.

40 D. North, 1981, *Structure and Change in Economic History* (p. 164), New York: Norton.

41 Y. Lu, E. Tsang, & M. W. Peng, 2008, Knowledge management and innovation in the Asia Pacific (p. 359), *APJM*, 25: 361–374.

42 State ownership is also often referred to as "public ownership." However, since a lot of privately owned firms are publicly listed and traded, this label can cause confusion, I have decided to use "state ownership" here to minimize confusion.

43 P. Bernstein, 2009, The moral hazard economy, *HBR*, July–August: 101–102; S. Harrington, 2009, Moral hazard and the meltdown, *WSJ*, May 23, online.wsj.com.

44 J. Kornai, 1992, *The Socialist System*, Princeton, NJ: Princeton University Press.

45 G. Bruton, M. W. Peng, D. Ahlstrom, C. Stan, & K. Xu, 2015, State-owned enterprises around the world as hybrid organizations, *AMP*, 29: 92–114.

46 M. W. Peng, G. Bruton, & C. Stan, 2014, Theories of the (state-owned) firm, Working paper, Jindal School of Management, University of Texas at Dallas.

47 *Economist*, 2012, The rise of state capitalism, January 21: 11.

48 A. Batson, 2013, The SOE irritant in US–China relations, *WSJ*, July 8: 13.

49 C. Stevens, E. Xie, & M. W. Peng, 2015, Toward a legitimacy-based view of political risk, *SMJ* (in press).

50 B. Gunia, J. Brett, & A. Nandkeolyar, 2012, In global negotiations, it's all about trust, *HBR*, December: 26; D. Malhotra, 2009, When contracts destroy trust, *HBR*, May: 25.

51 C. Su, Z. Yang, G. Zhuang, N. Zhou, & W. Dou, 2009, Interpersonal influence as an alternative channel behavior in emerging markets, *JIBS*, 40: 668–689.

© imtmphoto/Shutterstock.com

Learning Objectives

After studying this chapter, you should be able to

- define culture and articulate its four main manifestations: language, religion, social structure, and education.

- discuss how cultures systematically differ from each other.

- understand the importance of ethics and ways to combat corruption.

- identify norms associated with strategic responses when firms deal with ethical challenges.

- participate in three leading debates concerning cultures, ethics, and norms.

- draw implications for action.

Emphasizing Informal Institutions: Cultures, Ethics, and Norms

Cut Salaries or Cut Jobs?

As a Japanese expatriate in charge of US operations of Yamakawa Corporation, you scratch your head when confronting a difficult decision: Cut salaries across the board or cut jobs when dealing with a horrific economic downturn with major losses? Headquarters in Osaka has advised that earnings at home are bad, and that you cannot expect headquarters to bail out your operations. Too bad, US government bailouts are only good for US-owned firms and are thus irrelevant for your unit, which is 100% owned by the Japanese parent company.

As a person brought up in a collectivistic culture, you instinctively feel compelled to suggest across-the-board pay cuts for all 1,000 employees in the United States. Personally, as the highest-paid US-based employee, you are willing to take the *highest* percentage of a pay cut (you are thinking of 25%). If implemented, this plan would call for other executives, who are mostly Americans, to take a 20% to 25% pay cut, mid-level managers and professionals a 15% to 20% pay cut, and all the rank-and-file employees a 10% to 15% pay cut. Indeed, in your previous experience at Yamakawa in Japan, you did this with positive results among all affected Japanese employees. This time, most executive colleagues in Japan are doing the same. However, since you are now managing US operations, headquarters in Osaka (being more globally

minded and sensitive) does not want to impose any uniform solutions around the world and asks you to make the call.

As a conscientious executive, you have studied all the books—in both Japanese and English—that you can get your hands on for this tough decision. While you understand that US executives routinely undertake reduction in force (RIF), which is a euphemism for mass layoffs, you have also noticed that in the recent recession, even some *bona fide* US firms, such as AMD, FedEx, HP, and *New York Times*, have trimmed the base pay for all employees. If there is a time to change the norm moving toward more across-the-board pay cuts in an effort to preserve jobs and avoid RIF, this time may be it, according to some US executives quoted in the media.

At the same time, you have also read that some experts note that across-the-board pay cuts are *anathema* to a performance culture enshrined in the United States. "The last thing you want is for your A players—or people in key strategic positions delivering the most value—to leave because you have mismanaged your compensation system," said Mark Husclid, a Rutgers University professor and a leading expert on human resource management, in a media interview. You have also read in a *Harvard Business Review* survey that 20% of high-potential players in US firms voluntarily jumped ship during the 2008–2009 recession, in search of greener pastures elsewhere. Naturally, you are worried that should you decide to implement the across-the-board pay cuts you have envisioned, you may end up losing a lot of American star performers and end up with a bunch of mediocre players who cannot go elsewhere—and you may be stuck with the mediocre folks for a long time, even after the economy recovers.

After spending two days reading all the materials you have gathered, you still do not have a clear picture. How would you proceed?

Sources: This case is fictitious. It was inspired by (1) M. Brannen, 2008, Global talent management and learning for the future: Pressing concerns for Japanese multinationals, *AIB Insights*, 8: 8–12; (2) *BusinessWeek*, 2009, Cutting salaries instead of jobs, June 8: 46–48; (3) *BusinessWeek*, 2009, Pay cuts made palatable, May 4: 67; (4) N. Carter & C. Silva, 2009, High potentials in the downturn: Sharing the pain? *Harvard Business Review*, September: 25.

Why does the Japanese executive in the Opening Case, who was brought up in a collectivistic culture, feel uncomfortable about mass layoffs? Why do US executives who have grown up in an individualistic culture routinely undertake mass layoffs when their firms run into difficulties? What is the right (ethical) thing to do? What action would you recommend to this Japanese executive? More fundamentally, how do informal institutions govern individual and firm behavior in different countries?

This chapter continues our coverage of the institution-based view, which began with formal institutions in Chapter 2. Here we focus on informal institutions represented by cultures, ethics, and norms, which play an important part in shaping the success and failure of firms around the globe. Remember that the institution-based view suggests two propositions. First, managers and firms rationally pursue their interests within a given institutional framework. Second, in situations where formal institutions are unclear or fail, informal institutions play a larger role in reducing uncertainty. The first proposition deals with both formal and informal institutions. The second proposition hinges on the informal institutions we are about to discuss. As the Opening Case shows, informal institutions are about more than just how to wine and dine properly. Informal institutions on the do's and don'ts can make or break operations, which is why they deserve a great deal of our attention.

3-1 Where Do Informal Institutions Come From?

Recall that any institutional framework consists of formal and informal institutions. While formal institutions such as politics, laws, and economics (see Chapter 2) are important, they make up a small (although important) part of the "rules of the game" that govern individual and firm behavior. As pervasive features of every economy, informal institutions can be found almost everywhere.

Where do informal institutions come from? They come from socially transmitted information and are a part of the heritage that we call cultures, ethics, and norms. Those within a society tend to perceive their own culture, ethics, and norms as "natural, rational, and morally right."[1] This self-centered mentality is known as ethnocentrism. For example, many Americans believe in "American exceptionalism"—that is, the United States is exceptionally well endowed to lead the world. But they are not alone in their self-identified "exceptionalism." The Chinese call China *zhong guo*, which literally means "country in the middle" or "middle kingdom." Ancient Scandinavians called their country by a similar name: *Midgaard*.

Recall from Chapter 2 that informal institutions are underpinned by the two normative and cognitive pillars, while formal institutions are supported by the

Informal institution

Institution represented by cultures, ethics, and norms.

Ethnocentrism

A self-centered mentality by a group of people who perceive their own culture, ethics, and norms as natural, rational, and morally right.

regulatory pillar. While the regulatory pillar clearly specifies the do's and don'ts, informal institutions, by definition, are more elusive. Yet, they are no less important. Thus, it is imperative that we pay attention to the three major aspects of informal institutions highlighted in this chapter: culture, ethics, and norms.

3-2 Culture

Learning Objective
Define culture and articulate its four main manifestations: language, religion, social structure, and education.

Out of many informal institutions, culture probably is most frequently discussed. This section first defines culture, and then highlights four major components.

3-2a Definition of Culture

Among hundreds of definitions of culture available, we will use the definition proposed by the world's foremost cross-cultural expert, Geert Hofstede, a Dutch professor. He defines culture as "the collective programming of the mind which distinguishes the members of one group or category of people from another."[2] Before proceeding, it is important to clarify two points to minimize confusion. First, although it is customary to talk about the American culture, there is no strict one-to-one correspondence between cultures and nation-states. Many subcultures exist within many multiethnic countries, such as Australia, Belgium, Brazil, Britain, Canada, China, India, Indonesia, Russia, South Africa, Switzerland, and the United States (see In Focus 3.1). Second, within a firm one may find a specific organizational culture (such as the IKEA culture). Having acknowledged the validity of these two points, we will follow Hofstede by using the term "culture" when discussing *national* culture—unless otherwise noted. This is not only a matter of expediency, but also a reflection of the institutional realities of the world with about 200 nation-states.

Each one of us is a walking encyclopedia of our own culture. Due to space constraints, we only highlight four major components of culture: (1) language, (2) religion, (3) social structure, and (4) education.

3-2b Language

Among approximately 6,000 languages in the world, Chinese is the largest in terms of the number of native speakers (20% of the world population).[3] English is a distant second (8%), followed closely by Spanish (7%) and Hindi (6%). Yet, the dominance of English as a global business language, known as the *lingua franca*, is unmistakable.[4] This is driven by two factors. First, English-speaking countries contribute the largest share (about one-third) of global output. Such economic dominance not only drives trade and investment ties between English-speaking countries and the rest of the world, but also generates a constant stream of products and services marketed in English—think about the ubiquitous Hollywood movies and *Economist* magazines. In the online world, the dominance of English is more extraordinary: one in three people logs on in English.

Second, recent globalization has called for the use of one common language.[5] Countries sharing a common language obviously will find it easier and cheaper to trade with each other. Interestingly, countries that do not share a common language—as long as they share a common *foreign* language—may still benefit from increased trade and investment.[6] In European countries where English is not an official language, the ability to speak English fluently helps significantly facilitate bilateral trade. Hypothetically, if English proficiency in all European countries were to increase by

Culture
The collective programming of the mind that distinguishes the members of one group or category of people from another.

Lingua franca
A global business language.

IN FOCUS 3.1
MARKETING TO HISPANICS IN THE UNITED STATES

According to the US Census Bureau definition, Hispanics refer to individuals of Latin American descent living in the United States who may be of any race or ethnic group (such as white or black). Now approximately 52 million people (15% of the US population), Hispanics represent the largest minority group in the United States. To put things in perspective, the US Hispanic population is larger than the population of Australia, Denmark, Finland, Norway, and Sweden *combined*. Their buying power has jumped from US$1 trillion in 2010 to US$1.5 trillion by 2015. The print media advertising revenues for the US Hispanic market, US$1.5 billion, have now surpassed the advertising revenues for the entire UK magazine market.

How to effectively market products and services to this sizable group of customers is a leading challenge among many marketers. Although most US Hispanics speak some English, Spanish is likely to remain their language of preference. Approximately 38% of Hispanics surveyed report English-language ads to be less effective than Spanish-language ads in terms of recall. Half of US Hispanics who watch TV during prime time watch Spanish language programming. Calling itself the "Hispanic heart of America," the Spanish-language TV network Univision is now the fifth-largest TV network in the United States, behind ABC, CBS, Fox, and NBC.

The typical debate in *international* marketing, standardization versus localization, is relevant here *within* a country. Direct translation of English-language campaigns is often ineffective, because it tends to miss the emotional and cultural nuances. Savvy marketers thus call for "transcreation." For instance, Taco Bell's tagline "Think outside the bun" evolved into a Hispanic adaption: "*No solo de pan vive el hombre*"

("A man does not live by bread alone"). Volkswagen completely changed its "Drivers Wanted" English slogan, and marketed to US Hispanics with a new slogan, "*Agarra Calle*" ("Hit the Road"), with a specific, Spanish-language website agarracalle.com. When marketing its minivans on TV, Chrysler showed a grandfather figure engaged in a puppet show at a child's birthday party—a traditional way for Hispanics to entertain children.

Interestingly, although about 60% of the US Hispanic population can trace their roots to Mexican heritage, direct importation of ads used in Mexico may not necessarily be successful either. The reasons are twofold. First, the US Hispanic culture, with influences from numerous other Latin American countries, is much more diverse than the Mexican culture. Second, mainstream (Anglo) media in the United States has asserted substantial influence on US Hispanics. A case in point is that 40% of Spanish-dominant Hispanics regularly watch English-language TV. Univision has started English-language programming to capture its younger, US-born viewers.

Overall, US Hispanics possess a distinctive cultural identity that is neither mainstream (Anglo) American nor pure Mexican. One size does not fit all. Any firm interested in marketing products and services to the "US market" needs to use both caution and creativity when marketing to Hispanics.

Sources: Based on (1) *Bloomberg Businessweek*, 2012, Where pizza gets some Latin spice, October 8: 26–27; (2) *Bloomberg Businessweek*, 2013, Won in translation, September 5: 53–57; (3) N. Kumar & J. Steenkamp, 2013, Diaspora marketing, *Harvard Business Review*, October: 127–131; (4) N. Singh & B. Bartikowski, 2009, A cross-cultural analysis of print advertising targeted to Hispanic and non-Hispanic American consumers, *Thunderbird International Business Review*, 51: 151–164; (5) US Census Bureau, 2015, Hispanics in the United States, www.census.gov.

10% (while keeping UK and Irish proficiency levels constant), intra-Europe trade would grow by 15%. Bringing up the English proficiency of all Europeans to the level of the Dutch (which is very high) may boost intra-Europe trade by 70%.[7]

Around the world, nonnative speakers of English who can master English, such as the Taiwanese-born Hollywood director Ang Lee, Hong Kongese-born kung-fu master Jackie Chan, Austrian-born actor and politician Arnold Schwarzenegger, and Colombian-born pop star Shakira, increasingly command a premium in jobs and compensation. This fuels the rising interest in English. The European Union (EU) insists that documents be translated into all other official languages. The 24 official languages for 28 member countries make this requirement almost impossible to satisfy. For example, nobody can fluently translate Estonian into Portuguese. An Estonian document needs to be translated into English, which then can be translated into Portuguese. Translators well versed in English, thus, are in much greater demand.

On the other hand, the dominance of English, which does give native speakers of English a great deal of advantage in global business, may also lead to a disadvantage.[8] An expatriate manager not knowing the local language misses a lot of cultural subtleties and can only interact with locals fluent in English. Weak (or lacking) ability in foreign languages makes it difficult (or impossible) to detect translation errors, which may result in embarrassments. For example, Coors Beer translated its slogan "Turn it loose!" into Spanish as "Drink Coors and get diarrhea!" Electrolux advertised its powerful vacuum machines in the United States with a slogan: "Nothing sucks like an Electrolux!" To avoid such embarrassments, you will be better off if you can pick up at least one foreign language during your university studies.[9]

Ethan Miller/Getty Images

Would Shakira be so famous worldwide if she only sang in Spanish?

3-2c Religion

Religion is another major manifestation of culture. Approximately 85% of the world's population reportedly possesses some religious belief. The four leading religions are (1) Christianity (approximately 1.7 billion adherents), (2) Islam (1.6 billion), (3) Hinduism (1 billion), and (4) Buddhism (500 million). Of course, not everybody claiming to be an adherent actively practices a religion. For instance, some Christians may go to church only *once* every year—during Christmas.

Because religious differences have led to numerous challenges, knowledge about religions is crucial even for *non*-religious managers. For example, in Christian countries, the Christmas season represents the peak in shopping and consumption. In the United States, half of the toys purchased in an entire year are sold in one month before Christmas. Because (spoiled) kids in America consume half of the world's toys and virtually all toys are made outside the United States (mostly in Asia), this means that 25% of the world toy output is sold in one country in one month, thus creating severe production, distribution, and coordination challenges. For toy makers and stores, missing the boat from Asia, whose transit time is at least two weeks, can literally devastate an entire season (and probably the entire year).

Managers and firms ignorant of religious differences may end up with embarrassments and, worse, disasters. For example, a US firm blundered in Saudi Arabia by sending a meticulously prepared proposal bound with an expensive pigskin leather cover, hoping to impress the clients. The proposal was never read and soon rejected, because Muslims avoid pig products. The hope is that religiously sensitive managers and firms will avoid such blunders in the future.

3-2d Social Structure

Social structure refers to the way a society broadly organizes its members—with rigidity or flexibility. There are two key terms associated with social structure. Social stratification is the hierarchical arrangement of individuals into social categories (strata), such as classes, castes, and divisions, within a society. Social mobility refers to the degree to which members from a lower social category can achieve a higher status. In general, highly stratified societies have a low degree of social mobility. For example, India is well known for its caste system, in which individuals born into the lowest caste have very little chance of breaking into the social circles and jobs occupied by members of the highest caste. Britain historically had a rigid class system with low social mobility. Only in newer environments, such as Australia, Canada, and the United States, could upwardly mobile but lower-class British individuals have greater chances of advancing socially and economically. It was this relatively looser social structure and higher social mobility in the newly founded English-speaking colonies and countries that attracted waves of British immigrants from the lower social strata in the last several centuries.

Social structure is the outcome of a society's formal and informal rules of the game that give birth to its norms and values. In China, pronounced social stratification can be found along the urban–rural divide. While urban dwellers around the world often informally look down on rural residents (by calling them "rednecks" or "country bumpkins"), in China such discrimination is formalized by the official residence (*hukou*) system. Approximately 70% of Chinese citizens whose identification (ID) cards specify their official residence to be in rural areas have little (or no) health insurance, cannot compete for high-class urban jobs at state-owned firms, and cannot send their children to urban schools—all of which are privileges enjoyed by urban dwellers. As migrant workers, many rural residents travel to urban areas to find low-end jobs and live in shanty towns. Although they may be unofficially living in urban areas, they have very little hope of achieving social mobility in the cities.

Multinational enterprises (MNEs) operating in highly socially stratified countries need to be sensitive to local norms. The most suitable person for a job may not necessarily be the most technically qualified individual. Hiring managers from traditionally lower socioeconomic strata to supervise employees from more prestigious socioeconomic backgrounds may torpedo workplace morale and create hard feelings.

At the same time, it is important to note that all societies evolve. Even socially rigid societies such as India, Britain, and China have recently experienced institutional transitions that have facilitated social mobility. In India, the caste system has been legally banned (although it is still widely practiced informally). In the last two decades, Britain has made moves toward a relatively "classless" society similar to that of the United States. Likewise, the last three decades of economic reforms in China have made a large number of entrepreneurs with rural backgrounds very affluent. Owning companies and properties and creating jobs in urban areas, they can hardly care less about their lack of urban ID cards. While these entrepreneurs are clearly exceptions rather than the rule, they do help break down barriers for social mobility during China's institutional transitions.[10]

3-2e Education

Education is an important component of any culture. From an early age, schools teach children the mainstream values and norms and foster a sense of cultural identity. In collectivistic societies, schools often foster collectivistic values and

Social structure

The way a society broadly organizes its members.

Social stratification

The hierarchical arrangement of individuals into social categories (strata) such as classes, castes, and divisions within a society.

Social mobility

The degree to which members from a lower social category can rise to a higher status.

emphasize the "right" answers in learning. In individualistic societies, schools emphasize individual initiatives and encourage more independent thinking with a lot of questions with "no right or wrong answers"—think of all the debates introduced in *this* book.

In socially rigid societies, education—especially access to a small number of elite schools and universities—is one of the primary means to maintaining social stratification. In an effort to limit access, Cambridge and Oxford Universities, until recently, guaranteed a certain percentage of entry positions for graduates from prestigious private schools (such as Eton). Here is a quiz: Which is the most selective university in the world? The answer is the Indian Institute of Management (IIM). Every year, its seven campuses accept only 1,500 students out of approximately 300,000 applicants—a 0.5% acceptance ratio (!). Such limited access to higher education opportunities fosters social stratification.

On the other hand, in socially mobile societies, education is typically one of the leading forces to break down social barriers. In Britain, the number of universities expanded from 46 to 84 in the 1990s and then to 115 in the 2000s, resulting in significantly broader access to higher education by more members of the society. Britain is not alone in this regard. Overall, the dramatic expansion of higher education around the world in postwar decades has facilitated more social mobility.

iStockphoto.com/Chris Schmidt

How is higher education related to social stratification and culture?

In addition to language, religion, social structure, and education, there are numerous other manifestations of culture. However, if we keep going with these differences, this chapter—in fact, this book—may never end, given the tremendous differences around the world. Readers will be frustrated with a seemingly random collection of the "rules of the game": Do this in Muslims countries, don't do that in Catholic countries, and so on. While all these are interesting "trees," let us not forget that we are more interested in the "forest." The point about seeing the "forest" is to understand how cultures are *systematically* different. We address this next.

3-3 Cultural Differences

Learning Objective
Discuss how cultures systematically differ from each other.

Before reading this chapter, every reader already knew that cultures are different. There is no controversy in stating that the Indian culture is different from the Indonesian culture. But how are the Indian and Indonesian cultures *systematically* different? This section first outlines three ways to understand cultural differences: (1) context, (2) cluster, and (3) dimension approaches. Then, culture is linked with different firm behavior.

3-3a The Context Approach

Of the three main approaches probing into cultural differences, the context approach is the most straightforward. It focuses on a single dimension: context.[11] **Context** is the underlying background upon which social interaction takes place. Figure 3.1 outlines the spectrum of countries along the dimension of low context

Context
The underlying background upon which social interaction takes place.

Figure 3.1   **High-Context versus Low-Context Cultures**

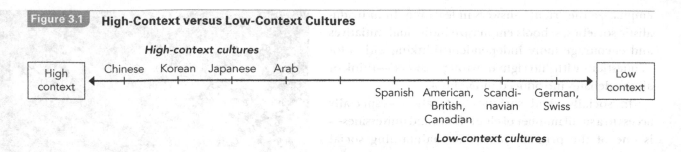

versus high context. In low-context cultures (such as North American and Western European countries), communication is usually taken at face value without much reliance on unspoken context. In other words, "no" means "no." In contrast, in high-context cultures (such as Arab and Asian countries), communication relies a lot on the underlying unspoken context, which is as important as the words used. For example, "No" does not necessarily mean "No."

Why is context important? Because failure to understand the differences in interaction styles may lead to misunderstanding. For instance, in Japan, a high-context culture, negotiators prefer not to flatly say "No" to a request. They will say something like "We will study it," or "We will get back to you later." Their negotiation partners are supposed to understand the context of these responses that lack enthusiasm and figure out that these responses essentially mean "No" (although "No" is never mentioned). In the United States, a low-context culture, lawyers often participate in negotiations by essentially attempting to remove the "context"—a contract should be as straightforward as possible, and parties are not supposed to "read between the lines." Because of this reason, negotiators from high-context countries (such as China) often prefer *not* to involve lawyers until the very last phase of contract drafting. In high-context countries, initial rounds of negotiations are supposed to create the "context" for mutual trust and friendship. For individuals brought up in high-context cultures, decoding the context and acting accordingly are second nature. But, straightforward communication and confrontation, typical in low-context cultures, often baffle them.

3-3b The Cluster Approach

The cluster approach groups countries that share similar cultures together as one cluster. There are three influential sets of clusters (Table 3.1). The first is the Ronen and Shenkar clusters, proposed by management professors Simcha Ronen and Oded Shenkar.[12] In alphabetical order, these clusters are: (1) Anglo, (2) Arab, (3) Eastern Europe, (4) Far East, (5) Germanic, (6) Latin America, (7) Latin Europe, (8) Near East, (9) Nordic, and (10) Sub-Saharan Africa.

The second set of clusters is called the GLOBE clusters, named after the Global Leadership and Organizational Behavior Effectiveness project led by management professor Robert House.[13] The GLOBE project identifies 10 clusters, five of which use identical labels as the Ronen and Shenkar clusters: (1) Anglo, (2) Eastern Europe, (3) Germanic Europe, (4) Latin America, (5) Latin Europe, (6) Nordic Europe, and (7) Sub-Saharan Africa. In addition, GLOBE has (8) Confucian Asia, (9) Middle East, and (10) Southern Asia, which roughly correspond with the respective Ronen and Shenkar clusters.

Low-context culture

A culture in which communication is usually taken at face value without much reliance on unspoken context.

High-context culture

A culture in which communication relies a lot on the underlying unspoken context, which is as important as the words used.

Cluster

Countries that share similar cultures.

Table 3.1	Cultural Clusters[1]

Ronen and Shenkar Clusters	GLOBE Clusters[2]	Huntington Civilizations
Anglo	Anglo	Western (1)[3]
Arab	Middle East	Islamic
Eastern Europe	Eastern Europe	Slavic-Orthodox
Far East	Confucian Asia	Confucian (Sinic)
Germanic	Germanic Europe	Western (2)
Latin America	Latin America	Latin American
Latin Europe	Latin Europe	Western (3)
Near East	Southern Asia	Hindu
Nordic	Nordic Europe	Western (4)
Sub-Saharan Africa	Sub-Saharan Africa	African
Independents: Brazil, India, Israel, Japan		Japanese

[1] This table is the *first* time these three major systems of cultural clusters have been compiled side by side. Viewing them together can allow us to see their similarities. However, there are also differences. Across the three systems (columns), even though clusters sometimes share the same labels, there are still differences. For example, Ronen and Shenkar's Latin America cluster does not include Brazil (which is regarded as an "independent"), whereas GLOBE and Huntington's Latin America includes Brazil.

[2] GLOBE includes ten clusters, covering 62 countries.

[3] Huntington includes eight civilizations, in theory covering *every* country. For the Western civilization, he does not use such labels as Western 1, 2, 3, and 4 as in the table. They are added by the present author to establish some rough correspondence with the respective Ronen and Shenkar and GLOBE clusters.

Sources: Based on (1) S. Huntington, 1996, *The Clash of Civilizations and the Remaking of World Order*, New York: Simon & Schuster; (2) R. House, P. Hanges, M. Javidan, P. Dorfman, & V. Gupta (eds.), 2004, *Culture, Leadership, and Organizations: The GLOBE Study of 62 Societies*, Thousand Oaks, CA: Sage; (3) S. Ronen & O. Shenkar, 1985, Clustering countries on attitudinal dimension, *Academy of Management Review*, 10: 435–454; (4) S. Ronen & O. Shenkar, 2013, Mapping world cultures, *Journal of International Business Studies*, 44: 867–897.

The third set of clusters is the Huntington civilizations, popularized by political scientist Samuel Huntington. A civilization is "the highest cultural grouping of people and the broadest level of cultural identity people have."[14] Shown in Table 3.1, Huntington divides the world into eight civilizations: (1) African, (2) Confucian (Sinic), (3) Hindu, (4) Islamic, (5) Japanese, (6) Latin American, (7) Slavic-Orthodox, and (8) Western. While this classification shares a number of similarities with the Ronen and Shenkar and GLOBE clusters, Huntington's "Western" civilization is a very broad cluster that is further subdivided by Ronen and Shenkar and by GLOBE into Anglo, Germanic, Latin Europe, and Nordic clusters. In addition to such an uncontroversial classification scheme, Huntington has advanced a highly controversial idea that the Western civilization will clash with the Islamic and Confucian civilizations in the years to come.

For our purposes, we do not need to debate the validity of Huntington's provocative thesis of the "clash of civilizations"—we will leave that debate to your political science or international relations classes. However, we do need to appreciate the underlying idea that people and firms are more comfortable doing business with other countries within the same cluster/civilization. Having a common language, history, religion, and customs reduces the liability of foreignness when operating in another country but within the same cluster/civilization. For example, Hollywood movies are more likely to succeed in English-speaking countries. Most foreign investors in China are from

Civilization

The highest cultural grouping of people and the broadest level of cultural identity people have.

Hong Kong and Taiwan—in other words, they are not "very foreign." Brazilian firms enjoy doing business in Africa's Angola and Mozambique, which are also Portuguese-speaking countries.

3-3c The Dimension Approach

While both the context and cluster approaches are interesting, the dimension approach is more influential. The reasons for such influence are probably twofold. First, insightful as the context approach is, context only represents one dimension. What about other dimensions? Second, the cluster approach has relatively little to offer regarding differences of countries *within* one cluster. For example, what are the differences between Argentina and Chile, both of which belong to the same Latin America cluster, according to Ronen and Shenkar and GLOBE? By focusing on multiple dimensions of cultural differences both within and across clusters, the dimension approach has endeavored to overcome these limitations. While there are several competing frameworks,[15] Hofstede's work is by far the most influential, and thus is our focus.

Hofstede and his colleagues have proposed five dimensions (Figure 3.2). Power distance is the extent to which less powerful members within a country expect and

Power distance

The extent to which less powerful members within a country expect and accept that power is distributed unequally.

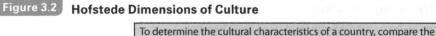

Figure 3.2   **Hofstede Dimensions of Culture**

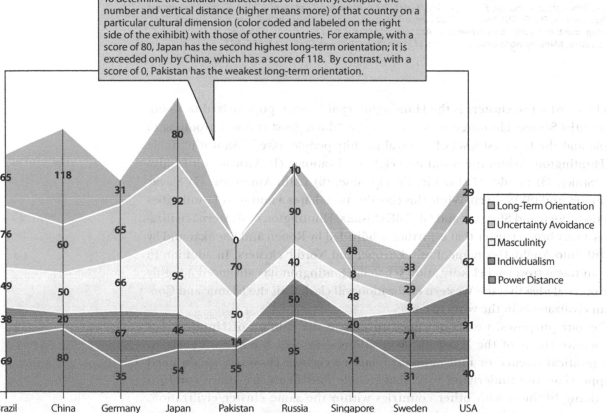

Sources: Based on (1) G. Hofstede, 1993, Cultural constraints in management theories, *Academy of Management Executive*, 7: 81–94; (2) G. Hosftede, 1997, *Cultures and Organizations: Software of the Mind* (pp. 25, 26, 53, 84, 113, 166), New York: McGraw-Hill. For newest updates, see www.geerthofstede.com.

accept that power is distributed unequally. In high power distance Brazil, the richest 10% of the population pockets approximately 50% of the national income, and everybody accepts this as "the way it is." In low power distance Sweden, the richest 10% only obtains 22% of the national income. Even within the same cluster, there are major differences. For example, in the United States, subordinates often address their bosses on a first-name basis, a reflection of a relatively low power distance. While this boss, whom you call Mary or Joe, still has the power to fire you, the distance appears to be shorter than if you had to address this person as Mrs. Y or Dr. Z. In low power distance American universities, all faculty members, including the lowest-ranked assistant professors, are commonly addressed as "Professor A." In high power distance British universities, only full professors are allowed to be called "Professor B." (Everybody else is called "Dr. C" or "Mr. D," if D does not have a PhD). German universities are perhaps most extreme: Full professors with PhDs must be honored as "Prof. Dr. X"—your author would be "Prof. Dr. Peng" if I were to work at a German university.

Individualism refers to the perspective that the identity of an individual is fundamentally his or her own, whereas collectivism refers to the idea that the identity of an individual is primarily based on the identity of his or her collective group (such as family, village, or company).[16] In individualistic societies (led by the United States), ties between individuals are relatively loose and individual achievement and freedom are highly valued. In contrast, in collectivist societies (such as many countries in Africa, Asia, and Latin America), ties between individuals are relatively close and collective accomplishments are often sought. In Chinese restaurants, most dishes are served "family style" to be shared by all the people around the table. In American restaurants, most dishes are served "individual style" to be only enjoyed by specific persons who order them. Shown in our Opening Case, in Japan when facing an economic downturn, the norm is to impose across-the-board pay cuts. In the United States, expect mass layoffs so that people who keep their jobs will not suffer from pay cuts.

The masculinity versus femininity dimension refers to sex role *differentiation*. In every traditional society, men tend to have occupations that reward assertiveness, such as politicians, soldiers, and executives. Women, on the other hand, usually work in caring professions, such as teachers and nurses, in addition to being homemakers. High masculinity societies (led by Japan) continue to maintain such a sharp role differentiation along gender lines. In low masculinity societies (led by Sweden), women increasingly become politicians, scientists, and soldiers, and men frequently assume the role of nurses, teachers, and *househusbands*.

Uncertainty avoidance refers to the extent to which members in different cultures accept ambiguous situations and tolerate uncertainty. Members of high uncertainty avoidance cultures (led by Greece) place a premium on job security and retirement benefits. They also tend to resist change, which, by definition, is uncertain. Low uncertainty avoidance cultures (led by Singapore) are characterized by a greater willingness to take risk and less resistance to change.

Long-term orientation emphasizes perseverance and savings for future betterment. China, which has the world's longest continuous written history of approximately 4,000 years and the highest contemporary savings rate, leads the pack. On the other hand, members of short-term orientation societies (led by Pakistan) prefer quick results and instant gratification.

Individualism

The idea that an individual's identity is fundamentally his or her own.

Collectivism

The idea that an individual's identity is fundamentally tied to the identity of his or her collective group.

Masculinity

A relatively strong form of societal-level sex role differentiation whereby men tend to have occupations that reward assertiveness and women tend to work in caring professions.

Femininity

A relatively weak form of societal-level sex role differentiation whereby more women occupy positions that reward assertiveness and more men work in caring professions.

Uncertainty avoidance

The extent to which members in a culture accept or avoid ambiguous situations and uncertainty.

Long-term orientation

Dimension of how much emphasis is placed on perseverance and savings for future betterment.

Overall, Hofstede's dimensions are interesting and informative. However, it is important to note that Hofstede's work is not perfect and has attracted some criticisms. The criticisms center on four points:[17]

1. Cultural boundaries are not the same as national boundaries.
2. Although Hofstede was careful to remove some of his own cultural biases, "the Dutch software" of his mind, as he acknowledged, "will remain evident to the careful reader." Being more familiar with Western cultures, Hofstede might inevitably be more familiar with dimensions relevant to Westerners. Thus, crucial dimensions relevant to Easterners (Asians) could be missed.
3. Hofstede's initial research was based on surveys of more than 116,000 IBM employees working at 72 national subsidiaries from 1967 to 1973. This study had both pros and cons. On the positive side, it took place not only in the same industry, but also in the same company. Otherwise, it would have been difficult to determine whether findings were due to differences in national cultures or industry or organizational cultures. However, because of such a single firm/single industry design, it was possible that Hofstede's findings captured what was unique to that industry or to IBM. Given anti-American sentiments in some countries, some individuals might refuse to work for an American employer. Thus, it was difficult to ascertain whether employees working for IBM were true representatives of their respective national cultures.
4. Because the original data are now more than 40 years old, critics contend that Hofstede's framework would simply fail to capture aspects of recent cultural change.

Hofstede has responded to all four criticisms.[18] First, he acknowledges that his focus on national culture is a matter of expediency with all its trappings. Second, since the 1980s, Hofstede and colleagues have relied on a questionnaire derived from cultural dimensions most relevant to the Chinese, and then translated it from Chinese to multiple languages. That is how he has uncovered the fifth dimension, long-term orientation (originally labeled "Confucian dynamism"). In response to the third and fourth criticisms, Hofstede points out a large number of more recent studies conducted by other scholars, using a variety of countries, industries, and firms. Most results are supportive of his findings. Overall, while Hofstede's work is not perfect, on balance, its value seems to outweigh its drawbacks.

3-3d Culture and Global Business

A great deal of global business activities are consistent with the context, cluster, and dimension approaches on cultural differences. For example, the average length of contracts is longer in low-context countries (such as Germany) than in high-context countries (such as Vietnam). This is because in high-context countries, a lot of agreements are unspoken and not necessarily put in a legal contract.

Also, as pointed out by the cluster approach, firms are a lot more serious in preparation when doing business with countries in other clusters, compared with how they deal with fellow countries within the same cluster. Recently, countless new books have been published on "how to do business in China." Two decades ago, gurus wrote about "how to do business in Japan." However, has anyone ever seen a book in English on "how to do business in Canada"?

Hofstede's dimension approach is also often supported in the real world. For example, managers in high-power distance countries, such as France and Italy, have a greater penchant for centralized authority. Solicitation of subordinate feedback and participation, widely practiced in low-power distance Western countries (known as empowerment), is often regarded as a sign of weak leadership and low integrity in high-power distance countries, such as Egypt, Russia, and Turkey.[19]

Individualism and collectivism also affect business activities. Individualist US firms may often try to differentiate themselves from competitors, whereas collectivist Japanese firms tend to follow each other. Because entrepreneurs "stick their neck out" by founding new firms, individualistic societies tend to foster a relatively higher level of entrepreneurship.

Likewise, masculinity and femininity affect managerial behavior. The stereotypical manager in high-masculinity societies is "assertive, decisive, and 'aggressive' (only in masculine societies does this word carry a positive connotation)," whereas the stylized manager in high-femininity societies is "less visible, intuitive rather than decisive, and accustomed to seeking consensus."[20]

Managers in low-uncertainty avoidance countries (such as Britain) rely more on experience and training, whereas managers in high-uncertainty avoidance countries (such as China) rely more on rules. In addition, cultures with a long-term orientation are likely to nurture firms with long horizons. In comparison, Western firms often focus on relatively short-term profits (often on a *quarterly* basis).

Overall, there is strong evidence pointing out the importance of culture. Sensitivity to cultural differences does not guarantee success, but can at least avoid blunders (Table 3.2).

Table 3.2	**Some Cross-Cultural Blunders**

- Electrolux, a major European home appliance maker, advertised its powerful vacuum machines in the United States using the slogan "Nothing sucks like an Electrolux!"

- A Japanese subsidiary CEO in New York, at a staff meeting consisting of all American employees, informed everyone of the firm's grave financial losses and passed on a request from headquarters in Japan that everyone redouble efforts. The staff immediately redoubled their efforts—by sending their resumes out to other employers.

- In Malaysia, an American expatriate was introduced to an important potential client he thought was named "Roger." He proceeded to call this person "Rog." Unfortunately, this person was a "Rajah," which is an important title of nobility in high-power distance Malaysia. Upset, the Rajah walked away from the deal.

- In the United States, some Brazilian and Japanese expatriates treated American secretaries as personal servants, insisting that they serve coffee. Shortly after arrival, a British expatriate angered minority employees by firing several black middle managers (including the head of the affirmative action program). They were all sued by employees.

Sources: Based on text in (1) P. Dowling & D. Welch, 2005, *International Human Resource Management*, 4th ed., Cincinnati: Cengage Learning; (2) M. Gannon, 2008, *Paradoxes of Culture and Globalization*, Thousand Oaks, CA: Sage; (3) D. Ricks, 1999, *Blunders in International Business*, 3rd ed., Oxford, UK: Blackwell.

IN FOCUS 3.2
BANK SCANDALS: BAD APPLES VERSUS BAD BARRELS

Ethical Dilemma

It is tough to be a banker after the Great Recession of 2008–2009. It seems that not a day goes by without a new scandal being unearthed and punished. Since 2009, Barclays, ING, and Lloyds have all paid big settlements related to allegations that they moved money for people or companies that were on the US sanctions list. In July 2012, HSBC paid a huge US$1.9 billion fine to settle US government charges that it had facilitated money laundering for rogue states (such as Cuba, North Korea, Sudan) and groups (such as Hamas, Mexican drug lords, Syrian terrorists, and the Taliban). Since 2010, six major Wall Street banks—Bank of America, Citigroup, Goldman Sachs, JPMorgan Chase, Morgan Stanley, and Wells Fargo—have agreed to pay a combined US$80 billion in settlements and penalties related to the financial crisis. For example, in 2013, JPMorgan Chase agreed

to pay an astronomical US$13 billion fine in connection with mortgage-backed securities that were illegally sold by itself as well as by Washington Mutual and Bear Stearns, two banks that JPMorgan Chase took over during the financial crisis. In 2014, Credit Suisse pleaded guilty to a criminal charge of helping its clients dodge American taxes. The upshot? A US$2.8 billion fine.

What is the root cause of such large-scale unethical and often illegal business behavior? It is difficult to imagine such wrong-doing is due to just a few "bad apples." Yet, few people have lost their jobs, and no one has been criminally charged. The top brass at Credit Suisse, for example, argued that it played no role in the actions for which the bank was prosecuted. Its board discussed firing some top executives, but concluded that the benefits would not outweigh the

---

Learning Objective

Understand the importance of ethics and ways to combat corruption.

3-4 Ethics

Cross-cultural differences can be interesting, but they can also be unethical, all depending on the institutional frameworks in which firms are embedded (see the Opening Case).

3-4a Definition and Impact of Ethics

Ethics refers to the principles, standards, and norms of conduct governing individual and firm behavior. Ethics is not only an important part of informal institutions, but is also deeply reflected in formal laws and regulations. To the extent that laws reflect a society's minimum standards of conduct, there is a substantial overlap between what is ethical and legal, and between what is unethical and illegal. However, there is a gray area because what is legal may be unethical (see the Closing Case).

Recent scandals (In Focus 3.2) have pushed ethics to the forefront of global business discussions.[21] Numerous firms have introduced a code of conduct—a set of guidelines for making ethical decisions. There is a debate on firms' ethical motivations.

Ethics

The principles, standards, and norms of conduct that govern individual and firm behavior.

Code of conduct

A set of guidelines for making ethical decisions.

- A negative view suggests that firms may simply jump onto the ethics "bandwagon" under social pressures to appear more legitimate without necessarily becoming better.
- A positive view maintains that some firms may be self-motivated to "do it right" regardless of pressures.
- An instrumental view believes that good ethics may simply be a useful instrument to help make money.

upheaval such firing would introduce. After coughing up the record US$13 billion fine that would cripple the finances of many firms and a nontrivial number of countries, JPMorgan Chase chairman and CEO Jamie Dimon managed to keep his dual titles—never mind shareholder uproar. In short, the banks argue that a small number of "bad apples" have caused all the trouble.

By naming, shaming, and fining the banks (not individuals), the government begs to differ. All are treated as "bad barrels" that need to be cleaned up. All the "bad barrels" named above have promised to enhance compliance and behave better. How much credibility do such statements deserve? One argument suggests that people may have ethical or unethical predispositions *before* joining firms. Another side of the debate argues that while there are indeed some opportunistic "bad apples," many times people commit unethical behavior not because they are "bad apples," but because they are spoiled by "bad

barrels." Some firms not only condone but may even expect unethical behavior.

The debate on "bad apples" versus "bad barrels" is an extension of the broader debate on "nature versus nurture." Are we who we are because of our genes (nature) or our environment (nurture)? Most studies report that human behavior is the result of both nature *and* nurture. Although individuals and firms do have some ethical or unethical predispositions that influence their behavior, the institutional environment (such as organizational norms and cultures) can also have a profound impact. In a nutshell, even "good apples" may turn bad in "bad barrels." Therefore, despite the record number of fines and settlements, future bank scandals remain to be unearthed.

Sources: Based on (1) *Bloomberg Businessweek*, 2013, Hell to pay, November 4: 47–48; (2) *Bloomberg Businessweek*, 2013, Too big to cry, October 28: 14–15; (3) *Bloomberg Businessweek*, 2013, Wall Street's guilt moment, October 28: 33–34; (4) *Economist*, 2012, HSBC's grilling, July 21: 61–62; (5) *Economist*, 2014, Credit Suisse in court, May 24: 65–66; (6) *Economist*, 2014, The criminalization of American business, August 30: 9.

Perhaps the best way to appreciate the value of ethics is to examine what happens after a crisis. As a "reservoir of goodwill," the value of an ethical reputation is *magnified* during a time of crisis. After the 2008 terrorist attacks on the Taj Mahal Palace Hotel in Mumbai, India, that killed 31 people (including 20 guests), the hotel received only praise. Why? The surviving guests were overwhelmed by employees' dedication to duty and their desire to protect guests in the face of terrorist attacks. Eleven employees laid down their lives while helping between 1,200 and 1,500 guests safely escape (see Emerging Markets 4.1). Paradoxically, catastrophes may allow more ethical firms such as the Taj, which are renowned for their integrity and customer service, to shine.[22] Shown in Figure 3.3, the upshot seems to be that ethics pays.

3-4b Managing Ethics Overseas

Shown in the Opening Case, managing ethics overseas is challenging, because what is ethical in one country may be unethical elsewhere.[23] Facing such differences, how can managers cope? Two schools of thought exist.[24] First, ethical relativism refers to an extension of the cliché, "When in Rome, do as the Romans do." If women in Muslim countries are discriminated against, so what? Likewise, if rivals in Mexico can fix prices, who cares? Isn't that what "Romans" do in "Rome"? Second, ethical imperialism refers to the absolute belief, "There is only one set of Ethics (with the big E), and we have it." Americans are especially renowned for believing that their ethical values should be applied universally. For example, since sexual discrimination and price fixing are wrong

Ethical relativism

A perspective that suggests that all ethical standards are relative.

Ethical imperialism

A perspective that suggests that "there is one set of Ethics (with a capital E) and we have it."

Figure 3.3 **Integrity Can Command a Premium**

"Jenny, can we charge the client extra because of our reputation for integrity?"

Source: Reprinted with permission from Nick Hobart.

in the United States, they must be wrong everywhere else. However, neither of these schools of thought is realistic in practice. At the extreme, ethical relativism would accept any local practice, whereas ethical imperialism may cause resentment and backlash among locals.

Three "middle-of-the-road" guiding principles have been proposed by Thomas Donaldson, a business ethicist (Table 3.3). First, respect for human dignity and basic rights (such as those concerning health, safety, and the needs for education instead of working at a young age) should determine the absolute minimal ethical thresholds for *all* operations around the world.

Second, respect for local traditions suggests cultural sensitivity. If gifts are banned, foreign firms can forget about doing business in China and Japan. Whereas hiring employees' children and relatives instead of more qualified applicants is illegal according to US equal opportunity laws, Indian companies routinely practice such nepotism, which would strengthen employee loyalty. What should US companies setting up subsidiaries in India do? Donaldson advises that such nepotism is not necessarily wrong—at least in India.

Finally, respect for institutional context calls for a careful understanding of local institutions. Codes of conduct banning bribery are not very useful unless accompanied by guidelines for the scale of appropriate gift-giving or -receiving (see Table 3.4). Citigroup allows employees to accept noncash gifts with nominal

Table 3.3 **Managing Ethics Overseas: Three "Middle-of-the-Road" Approaches**

- Respect for human dignity and basic rights
- Respect for local traditions
- Respect for institutional context

Sources: Based on text in (1) T. Donaldson, 1996, Values in tension: Ethics away from home, *Harvard Business Review*, September-October: 4–11; (2) J. Weiss, 2006, *Business Ethics*, 4th ed., Cincinnati: Cengage Learning.

Table 3.4	**Texas Instruments (TI) Guidelines on Gifts in China**

- These China-specific Guidelines are based on TI's *Global Standard Guidelines*, taking into consideration China's local business climates, legal requirements, customs, and cultures as appropriate. Employees of TI entities in China ("TIers") should comply with both these China-specific Guidelines and Global Standard Guidelines. In any event of conflict, the stricter standard will apply.

- Acceptable gifts include calendars, coffee cups, appointment books, notepads, small pocket calculators, and ballpoint pens.

- Gifts with excessive value refer to those that are worth more than RMB 200 yuan (approximately US$32), and need approval from Asia Finance Director.

- If you are not sure when you can accept or offer any gift, the following two Quick Tests are recommended:

  a. "Reciprocity" Test. Ask this question: Based on your knowledge of TI's policy and culture, would TI under similar circumstances allow you to provide a TI business partner a gift of an equivalent nature? If the answer is no, then politely refuse the offer.

  b. "Raise Eyebrow" or "Embarrassments" Test. Ask those questions: Would you "raise eyebrows" or feel uncomfortable in giving or receiving the gift in the presence of others in a work area? Would you feel comfortable in openly displaying the gift you are offering or receiving? Would you feel embarrassed if it were seen by other TI business partners or by your colleagues/supervisor?

- No cash or cash equivalent gift cards may be given. Gift cards that are redeemable only for a specific item (and not cash) with a fixed RMB value, such as a Moon Cake card,* are permitted as long as the gift is otherwise consistent with these Guidelines.

Source: Adapted from Texas Instruments, *Comprehensive Guidelines on Gifts, Entertainment, and Travel in China* (2014).

* Moon Cake is a special dissert for the Mid-Autumn Festival, which is a major holiday for family reunion in September.

value of less than US$100. The *Economist* lets its journalists accept any noncash gift that can be consumed in a single day—thus, a bottle of wine is acceptable, but a *case* of wine is not. Overall, these three principles, although far from perfect, can help managers improve the quality of their decisions.

3-4c Ethics and Corruption

Ethics helps to combat corruption, often defined as the abuse of public power for private benefits, usually in the form of bribery (in cash or in kind).[25] Corruption distorts the basis for competition that should be based on products and services, thus causing misallocation of resources and slowing economic development.[26] Therefore, corruption discourages foreign direct investment (FDI). If the level of corruption in Singapore (very low) were to increase to the level in Mexico (in the midrange), it reportedly would have the same negative impact on FDI inflows as raising the tax rate by 50%.[27]

In the global fight against corruption, the Foreign Corrupt Practices Act (FCPA) was enacted in 1977. It bans bribery to foreign officials. Many US firms complain that the act has unfairly restricted them. They also point out that overseas bribery expenses were often tax-deductible (!) in many EU countries, such as Austria, France, Germany, and the Netherlands—at least until the late 1990s. However, even with the FCPA, there is no evidence that US firms are inherently more ethical than others. The FCPA itself was triggered by investigations of many corrupt US firms in the 1970s. Even the FCPA makes exceptions for small "grease" payments to get goods through customs abroad. Most alarmingly, a World Bank study reports that despite more than three decades of FCPA enforcement, US firms actually "exhibit systematically *higher* levels of corruption" than other OECD firms (original italics).[28]

Overall, the FCPA can be regarded as an institutional weapon in the fight against corruption.[29] Recall that every institution has three supportive pillars: regulatory,

Corruption

The abuse of public power for private benefits, usually in the form of bribery.

Foreign Corrupt Practices Act (FCPA)

A US law enacted in 1977 that bans bribery of foreign officials.

normative, and cognitive (Table 2.1). Despite the FCPA's formal *regulatory* "teeth," for a long time there was neither a *normative* pillar nor a *cognitive* pillar. The norms among other OECD firms used to be to pay bribes first and get a tax deduction later (!)—a clear sign of ethical relativism. Only in 1997 did the OECD Convention on Combating Bribery of Foreign Public Officials commit all member countries (essentially all developed economies) to criminalize bribery. It went into force in 1999. A more ambitious campaign is the UN Convention Against Corruption, signed by 106 countries in 2003 and activated in 2005. If every country criminalizes bribery and every firm resists corruption, then their combined power will eradicate it. However, this will not happen unless FCPA-type legislation is institutionalized *and* enforced in every country.

Learning Objective

Identify norms associated with strategic responses when firms deal with ethical challenges.

3-5 Norms and Ethical Challenges

As an important informal institution, norms are the prevailing practices of relevant players—the proverbial "everybody else"—that affect the focal individuals and firms. How firms strategically respond to ethical challenges is often driven, at least in part, by norms. Four broad strategic responses are: (1) reactive, (2) defensive, (3) accommodative, and (4) proactive strategies (see Table 3.5).

A reactive strategy is passive. When problems arise, denial is usually the first line of defense. In the absence of formal regulation, the need to take necessary action is neither internalized through cognitive beliefs nor becoming any norm in practice. For example, as early as in 2005, General Motors (GM) had been aware that the ignition switch of some of its cars could accidentally shut off the engine. Yet, it refused to take any actions and proceeded to produce and sell the cars for a decade. Sure enough, accidents happened and people were killed and injured due to the faulty switches. Only when victims' families sued and Congressional pressures increased did GM belatedly recall millions of cars in 2014.[30]

A defensive strategy focuses on regulatory compliance. In the absence of regulatory pressures, firms often fight informal pressures coming from the media and activists. In the 1990s, Nike was charged with running "sweatshops," though these incidents took place in its contractors' factories in Indonesia and Vietnam. Although Nike did not own or manage those factories, its initial statement, "We don't make shoes," failed to convey any ethical responsibility. Only when several US senators began to suggest legislative solutions did Nike become more serious.

An accommodative strategy features emerging organizational norms to accept responsibility and a set of increasingly internalized cognitive beliefs and values toward making certain changes. In 2000, when Ford Explorer vehicles equipped with Firestone tires had a large number of fatal roll-over accidents, Ford evidently took the painful lesson from its Pinto fire fiasco. In the 1970s, Ford marketed the Pinto car

Table 3.5 **Strategic Responses to Ethical Challenges**

Strategic Responses	Strategic Behaviors	Examples in the Text
Reactive	Deny responsibility, do less than required	GM (the 2000s)
Defensive	Admit responsibility but fight it, do the least that is required	Nike (the early 1990s)
Accommodative	Accept responsibility, do all that is required	Ford (the 2000s)
Proactive	Anticipate responsibility, do more than is required	BMW (the 1990s)

despite being aware of a design flaw that could make the car susceptible to exploding in real-end collisions. Similar to GM's recent scandal, Ford had not recalled the Pinto until Congressional, consumer, and media pressures heated up. In 2000, Ford aggressively initiated a speedy recall, launched a media campaign featuring its CEO, and discontinued its 100-year-old relationship with Firestone. While critics argue that Ford's accommodative strategy was to place blame squarely on Firestone, the institution-based view (especially Proposition 1 in Chapter 2) suggests that such highly rational actions are to be expected. Even if Ford's public relations campaign was only "window dressing," publicizing a set of ethical criteria against which it could be judged opened doors for more scrutiny by concerned stakeholders. It is probably fair to say that Ford became a better corporate citizen in 2000 than it was in 1975.

Finally, proactive firms anticipate institutional changes and do more than is required. For example, BMW anticipated its emerging responsibility associated with the German government's proposed "take-back" policy, requiring automakers to design cars whose components can be taken back by the same manufacturers for recycling. BMW not only designed easier-to-disassemble cars, but also signed up the few high-quality dismantler firms as part of an exclusive recycling infrastructure. Further, BMW actively participated in public discussions and succeeded in establishing its approach as the German national standard for automobile disassembly. Other automakers were thus required to follow BMW's lead. But they had to fight over lower-quality dismantlers or develop in-house dismantling infrastructure from scratch. Through such a proactive strategy, BMW set a new industry standard, facilitating the emergence of new environmentally friendly norms.

3-6 Debates and Extensions

Learning Objective

Participate in three leading debates concerning cultures, ethics, and norms.

In this section, we focus on three debates: (1) Western values versus Eastern values, (2) cultural convergence versus divergence, and (3) opportunism versus individualism/collectivism.

3-6a Drivers of Economic Development: Western Values versus Eastern Values

Western values versus Eastern values is another component of the debate on the drivers of economic development first discussed in Chapter 2. Here our focus is on the role of informal cultural values. About 100 years ago, at the apex of Western power (which ruled the majority of Africans and Asians in colonies), German sociologist Max Weber argued that it was the Protestant work ethic that led to the "spirit of capitalism" and strong economic development. As a branch of Christianity (the other two branches are Catholic and Orthodox), Protestantism is widely practiced in English-speaking countries, Germany, the Netherlands, and Scandinavia. This is where the Industrial Revolution (and modern capitalism) took off. Weber suggested that the Protestant emphasis on hard work and frugality was necessary for capital accumulation—hence the term "capitalism." Adherents of other religious beliefs, including

Is this fast-food restaurant an example of Western values, Eastern values, or a blending of the two?

Catholicism, were believed to lack such traits. At that time, Weber's view was widely accepted.

Such belief in the superiority of Western values has recently been challenged by two sets of Eastern values: (1) Islam and (2) Asian (Confucian). Islamic fundamentalism, rightly or wrongly, argues that it is Western dominance that *causes* the lackluster economic performance of Muslim countries. Aggressive marketing of Western products in these countries is seen as a cultural invasion. Islamic fundamentalists prefer to go "back to the roots" by moving away from Western influence.

A second challenge comes from East Asia, whose values center on Confucianism that is based on the teachings of Confucius, an ancient Chinese scholar who lived more than 2,000 years ago. Confucianism is not a religion, but rather is a set of moral codes guiding interpersonal relationships, which emphasize respect, loyalty, and reciprocity. More than 100 years ago, Weber criticized Confucianism as a leading cause of Asian backwardness. However, winds shift. In postwar decades, while Western economic growth has been stagnant, it is Confucian Asia—first led by Japan in the 1960s, then by the four tigers (Hong Kong, Singapore, South Korea, and Taiwan) in the 1970s, and most recently by China since the 1980s—that has generated the fastest economic growth in the world and for the longest time. Interestingly, the same Confucianism, trashed by Weber, has been widely viewed by many (including authors of an influential World Bank report) as the engine behind such an "Asian economic miracle."[31]

While Islamic fundamentalists prefer to drop out of the game of economic development, Asian value proponents claim to have beaten the West at its own game. However, any declaration of winning the game needs to be viewed with caution. By 1997, much of Asia was suddenly engulfed in a financial crisis. Then—guess what?—Confucianism was blamed, by both Asians and non-Asians, for having *caused* such hardship (!). Respect, loyalty, and reciprocity become inertia, nepotism, and cronyism. Fast-forward to 2010: Asia had not only recovered from the 1997 crisis, but had also quickly rebounded from the 2008–2009 recession.[32] With the emergence of Confucian China as a global economic powerhouse, the Asian value gurus again are practicing their craft—although with a lower voice this time.

As we can see from this wide-ranging debate, our understanding of the connection between cultural values and economic development is superficial. To advocate certain cultural values as key to economic development may not be justified. A new generation of students and managers must be more sophisticated and guard against such ethnocentric thinking. One speculation is that if there will ever be an African economic takeoff, there will be no shortage of gurus pontificating on how the African cultural values provide such a booster behind this yet-to-happen African economic takeoff.

3-6b Cultural Change: Convergence versus Divergence

Every culture evolves. A great debate thus erupts on the *direction* of cultural change. In this age of globalization, one side of the debate points out a great deal of convergence, especially toward more "modern," Western values, such as individualism and consumerism. As evidence, gurus point to the global interest in Western products, such as Levi's Jeans, iPhones, Kindle, and Facebook, especially among the youth.

However, another side argues that Westernization in consumption does not necessarily mean Westernization in values. In a most extreme example, on the night of September 10, 2001, terrorists enjoyed some American soft drinks, pizzas, and movies, and then went on to kill thousands of Americans the next day.[33] In another example, the increasing popularity of Asian foods (such as sushi) and games (such as Pokémon and Bakugan) in the West does not necessarily mean that Westerners are converging toward "Asian values." In short, the world may continue to be characterized by cultural divergence.

A "middle-of-the-road" group makes two points. First, the end of the Cold War, the rise of the Internet, and the ascendance of English all offer evidence of some cultural convergence—at least on the surface and among the youth. For example, relative to the average citizens in their countries, younger Chinese, Japanese, and Russian managers are becoming more individualistic and less collectivistic. Second, deep down, cultural divergence may continue to be the norm.[34] Therefore, perhaps a better term is "crossvergence" that acknowledges the validity of both sides of the debate. This idea suggests that when marketing products and services to younger customers around the world, a more "global" approach (featuring uniform content and image) may work, whereas when dealing with older, more tradition-bound consumers, local adaptation may be a must.

3-6c Opportunism versus Individualism/Collectivism[35]

As noted in Chapter 2, opportunism is a major source of uncertainty that adds to transaction costs; and transaction cost theorists maintain that institutions emerge to combat opportunism.[36] However, critics argue that emphasizing opportunism as "human nature" may backfire. If A insists on specifying minute details in a contract in order to prevent B from behaving opportunistically *in the future*, A is likely to be regarded by B as being not trustworthy and being opportunistic *now*. This may especially be the case if B is from a high-context (or collectivist) society. Thus, A's attempts to combat opportunism may beget opportunism.

Transaction cost theorists acknowledge that opportunists are a minority in any population. However, theorists contend that because of the difficulty in identifying such a minority of opportunists *before* they cause any damage, it is imperative to place safeguards that, unfortunately, treat everybody as a potential opportunist. For example, thanks to the work of only 19 terrorists, millions of air travelers around the world since September 11, 2001, now have to endure heightened airport security. Everybody hates it, but nobody argues that it is unnecessary. This debate, therefore, seems deadlocked.

One cultural dimension, individualism/collectivism, may hold the key to an improved understanding of opportunism. A common stereotype is that players from collectivist societies (such as China) are more collaborative and trustworthy, and that those from individualist societies (such as the United States) are more competitive and opportunistic.[37] However, this superficial understanding is not necessarily the truth. Collectivists are more collaborative *only* when dealing with in-group members—individuals and firms regarded as a part of their own collective. The flip side is that collectivists discriminate more harshly against out-group members—individuals and firms not regarded as a part of "us."[38] On the other hand, individualists, who believe that every person (firm) is on his/her (its) own,

In-group

Individuals and firms regarded as a part of "us."

Out-group

Individuals and firms not regarded as a part of "us."

make less distinction between in-group and out-group members. Therefore, while individualists may indeed be more opportunistic than collectivists when dealing with in-group members (this fits the stereotype), collectivists may be *more* opportunistic when dealing with out-group members. This can be seen at the street level. In China, drivers do not yield to pedestrians and often get mad by honking the horn when pedestrians cross the street in front of their cars. In the United States, drivers often yield to pedestrians and wave to let them cross the street first. To drivers, pedestrians by definition are out-group members. As collectivists, the same Chinese drivers who are rude to pedestrians often demonstrate impeccable courtesy when dealing with their in-group members. As individualists, American drivers typically show little distinction when dealing with in-group and out-group members (pedestrians).

Thus, on balance, the average Chinese is not inherently more trustworthy than the average American. The Chinese motto regarding out-group members is, "Watch out for strangers. They will screw you!" Or, "Watch out for cars when crossing the street. They will smash you!" This helps explain why the United States, the leading individualist country, is among societies with a higher level of spontaneous trust, whereas there is greater interpersonal and interfirm *distrust* in the large society in China.[39] This also explains why it is so important to establish *guanxi* (relationship) in China; otherwise, life can be very hard in a sea of strangers.

While this insight is not likely to help improve airport security screening, it can help managers and firms better deal with one another. Only through repeated social interactions can collectivists assess whether to accept newcomers as in-group members. If foreigners who, by definition, are from an out-group refuse to show any interest in joining the in-group, then it is fair to take advantage of them. This is why many cross-culturally naïve Western managers and firms often bemoan being taken advantage of in collectivist societies—they are simply being treated as "deserving" out-group members.

Learning Objective
Draw implications for action.

3-7 Management Savvy

One leading contribution of the institution-based view is to emphasize the importance of informal institutions—cultures, ethics, and norms—as the bedrock propelling or constraining business around the globe. How does this perspective answer our fundamental question: What determines the success and failure of firms around the globe? The institution-based view argues that firm performance is, at least in part, determined by the informal cultures, ethics, and norms governing firm behavior.

For savvy managers around the globe, this emphasis on informal institutions suggests two broad implications. First, it is necessary to enhance cultural intelligence, defined as an individual's ability to understand and adjust to new cultures.[40] Acquisition of cultural intelligence passes through three phases: (1) awareness, (2) knowledge, and (3) skills.[41] *Awareness* refers to the recognition of both the pros and cons of your "mental software" and the appreciation of people from other cultures. *Knowledge* refers to the ability to identify the symbols, rituals, and taboos in other cultures—also known as *cross-cultural literacy*. Finally, *skills* are based on awareness and knowledge, plus good practice (Table 3.6). Of course, culture is not everything. It is advisable not to read too much into culture, which is one of many variables affecting global business.[42] However, it is imprudent to ignore culture.

Cultural intelligence
An individual's ability to understand and adjust to new cultures.

Table 3.6	Implications for Action: Six Rules of Thumb When Venturing Overseas

- Be prepared

- Slow down

- Establish trust

- Understand the importance of language

- Respect cultural differences

- Understand that no culture is inherently superior in all aspects

While cultural knowledge can be taught, the most effective way to understand a culture is total immersion within that foreign culture. Even for gifted individuals, learning a new language and culture to function well at a managerial level will take at least several months of full-time studies. Most employers do not give their expatriates that much time to learn before sending them abroad. Thus, most expatriates are inadequately prepared, and the costs for firms, individuals, and families are tremendous (see Chapter 15). This means that you, a student studying this book, are advised to invest in your own career by picking up at least one foreign language, spending one semester (or year) abroad, and reaching out to make some international friends who are taking classes with you (and perhaps sitting next to you). Such an investment will make you stand out among the crowd and propel your future career to new heights.

Second, managers need to be aware of the prevailing norms and their transitions globally. The norms around the globe in the 21st century are more culturally sensitive and ethically demanding than in, say, the 1970s (see the Closing Case). This is not to suggest that every local norm must be followed. However, failing to understand and adapt to the changing norms by "sticking one's neck out" in an insensitive and unethical way may lead to disastrous results (Emerging Markets 3.1).

EMERGING MARKETS 3.1

GSK's Bribery Scandal in China

Since 2012, thanks to its bribery scandal, GlaxoSmith-Kline (GSK) has been on the hot spot in China. The case has unfolded in a sensational way. In December 2012, one of GSK's China leadership team members was dismissed. In the following month, emails were sent to GSK's global headquarters in the UK alleging bribery with sexually embarrassing materials featuring China chief officer Mark Reilly attached. In July 2013, police detained four GSK employees in China (including Reilly) as a result of a broad investigation by the Chinese government into GSK's sales practices. In June 2014, Chinese authorities accused Reilly of ordering employees to offer bribes and overseeing a large bribery network internally. According to the accusation, GSK employees were involved in passing a total of US$484 million to bribe doctors, hospital administrators, government officials, and medical associations. Channeled through 700 third-party travel agencies, the money—in the form of cash and hiring of prostitutes—was aimed at expanding and boosting drug sales in China. The scandal has created profound repercussions. Following the accusation, GSK has reported that sales in the fast-growing Chinese market dropped by 61% since July 2013. Despite the huge losses of its China business, GSK's CEO Andrew Witty has insisted that the pharmaceutical giant will remain firm in China.

The GSK bribery case represents a microcosm of China's growing anti-corruption programs that President Xi Jinping has set in motion since taking office. Between 2012 and 2014, 11 provincial-level leaders and numerous state-owned enterprise (SOE) executives have been charged for corruption. Under the backdrop of a determined anti-corruption campaign, the GSK case is a high-profile example.

The GSK scandal can also be viewed from another perspective: the weak foundation of China's healthcare system. Specifically, except for a few star doctors, most doctors are paid poorly (the average pay ranges from US$10,000 to US$40,000 annually) and are chronically over-worked compared with professions in other industries, such as IT, education, and finance. On average, doctors in China only spend 5 minutes for each patient and they need to see more than 100 patients on a daily base. Under these pressures, doctors are unlikely to provide excellent service to patients. It is also no surprise that doctors usually find alternative ways to earn more income. For one, doctors are often directly paid by patients through "red envelopes" containing cash. This will ensure patients get proper and timely care, but at the same time generates stronger resentment from other patients who feel unfair treatment due to their lack of access to doctors. In addition, doctors supplement their pay through the sort of bribes unearthed by the GSK scandal case. Because Chinese hospitals operate their own pharmacies, doctors are usually paid by the quantity of drugs that they prescribe to patients. To push more drug sales, GSK offered doctors kick-backs. Such kick-backs could be in a variety of forms, such as cash, sponsored travels, all expenses-paid conferences, and research grants. After the scandal, GSK has changed its incentive system. Sales reps are no longer evaluated based on the volume of drugs they sell, but on the training of the product knowledge they receive. This new practice has generated an immediate and disastrous response from doctors. During an informal conversation, one of the doctors openly told the author: "Since GSK now totally ignores China's unique situation, we will absolutely not prescribe GSK's products any more."

Other aspects of the "unique situation" in China include the "lethal" combination of (1) hospitals' incentives for doctors to prescribe unnecessary drugs, tests, and surgical procedures; and (2) the demanding China sales targets set up by headquarters of GSK in an effort to profit from China's ongoing healthcare reform. Bribery is widely believed to be endemic in China, and particularly in the pharmaceutical sector. Many global pharmaceutical giants have strict global policies regarding how to interact with external stakeholders, such as doctors, hospital administrators, government officials, and university scientists. However, the majority of these policies are symbolic in nature in China. If one company does not bribe doctors, competitors are likely to do it anyway. Although GSK, after paying a fine of US$490 million (3 billion yuan), has promised to clean up, delivering on this promise remains a huge challenge.

Sources: This case was written by Professor **Weilei (Stone) Shi** (Baruch College, City University of New York). It was based on (1) the author's interviews; (2) BBC News, 2014, July 3, www.bbc.com/news/world-asia-china-28142118; (3) *Economist*, 2013, Bitter pill, July 20: 56–57; (4) *Forbes*, 2013, September 4, www.forbes.com/sites/benjaminshobert/2013/09/04/three-ways-to-understand-gsks-china-scandal; (5) Reuters, 2014, China hands drugmaker GSK record fine, September 19.

The best managers expect norms to shift over time by constantly deciphering the changes in the informal "rules of the game" and by taking advantage of new opportunities.[43] How BMW managers proactively shaped the automobile recycling norms serves as a case in point. Firms that fail to realize the passing of old norms and adapt accordingly are likely to fall behind or even go out of business.

CHAPTER SUMMARY/LEARNING OBJECTIVES

3-1 Define what culture is and articulate its four major components: language, religion, social structure, and education.

- Culture is the collective programming of the mind, which distinguishes one group from another.
- Managers and firms ignorant of foreign languages and religious traditions may end up with embarrassments and, worse, disasters when doing business around the globe.
- Highly stratified societies have a low degree of social mobility, and vice versa.
- Education fosters a sense of cultural identity by teaching children the mainstream values and norms.

3-2 Discuss how cultures systematically differ from each other.

- The context approach differentiates cultures based on the high-context versus low-context dimension.
- The cluster approach groups similar cultures together as clusters and civilizations.
- Hofstede and colleagues have identified five cultural dimensions: (1) power distance, (2) individualism/collectivism, (3) masculinity/femininity, (4) uncertainty avoidance, and (5) long-term orientation.

3-3 Understand the importance of ethics and ways to combat corruption.

- When managing ethics overseas, two schools of thought are ethical relativism and ethical imperialism.
- Three "middle-of-the-road" principles help guide managers make ethical decisions.
- The fight against corruption around the world is a long-term, global battle.

3-4 Identify norms associated with strategic responses when firms deal with ethical challenges.

- When confronting ethical challenges, individual firms have four strategic choices: (1) reactive, (2) defensive, (3) accommodative, and (4) proactive strategies.

3-5 Participate in three leading debates concerning cultures, ethics, and norms.

- (1) Western values versus Eastern values, (2) cultural convergence versus divergence, and (3) opportunism versus individualism/collectivism.

3-6 Draw implications for action.

- It is important to enhance cultural intelligence, leading to cross-cultural literacy.
- It is crucial to understand and adapt to the changing norms globally.

KEY TERMS

Civilization, 73	Context, 71	Ethical imperialism, 79
Cluster, 72	Corruption, 81	Ethical relativism, 79
Code of conduct, 78	Cultural intelligence, 86	Ethics, 78
Collectivism, 75	Culture, 67	Ethnocentrism, 66

REVIEW QUESTIONS

1. *ON CULTURE:* As you review how cultures differ from one another, imagine that you want to develop a flexible and mobile work force that is not controlled by a given culture, but which could easily relocate to countries with a variety of different cultures. You want people who can easily and effectively fit in so as to be accepted by employees and customers. In your opinion, what are some of the barriers or issues that you would encounter, and how might you achieve your objective?

2. Compare PengAtlas Map 1.4 (Religious Heritage) and Map 1.5 (Education Levels Around the World). Which do you think has a more powerful effect in both the cultural and economic realm? Why? If your answer is "Both of the above," is one of the two a bit more powerful in creating a unified culture, and one more powerful in creating a dynamic economy? Explain your answer.

3. Compare PengAtlas Map 3.2 (Top Reformers) with Maps 1.4 and 1.5. Are there any relationships between reformers and religious heritage? Why or why not? If there are any relationships, are they causal or coincidental? Any relationship between reformers and educational level? Why or why not? If there are any relationships, are they causal or coincidental? Defend your answer.

4. *ON CULTURE:* Suppose the education system of a given country teaches values that can make it very difficult to do business profitably in the country. Is that an impossible barrier, or is there anything that can be done to change that or cope with it? Defend your answer.

5. Non-verbal communication (e.g., tone of voice, gestures, facial expressions) can be important in all cultures, but would it be more important in a high-context or low-context culture? Why?

6. What are the pros and cons of doing business in a culture characterized as individualistic?

7. What are the pros and cons of doing business in a culture characterized as collectivist?

8. Some countries have a long tradition of bribery for public officials. Is it "ethical imperialism" to prohibit companies headquartered in one's own country from engaging in bribery when doing business in countries with such traditions?

9. Why is the fight against corruption a long-term battle?

10. Does corruption always only involve money? If not, what else may be involved?

11. Although a proactive strategy may always seem most desirable in dealing with ethical challenges, are there any circumstances under which a reactive strategy may be the best strategy or even the only strategy? Explain.

12. In dealing with changing global norms, does that mean that you should reject your own values and go along with whatever now seems to be in vogue? Defend your answer.

CRITICAL DISCUSSION QUESTIONS

1. *ON CULTURE:* When you take an airline flight, the passenger sitting next to you tries to have a conversation with you. He or she asks, "What do you do?" You would like to be nice, but don't want to give too much information about yourself (such as your name). How would you answer this question? A typical US manager may say: "I am a marketing manager"—without mentioning the employer. A typical Japanese manager may say: "I work for Honda." Why are there such differences? How would you answer this question?

2. *ON ETHICS:* Suppose you work for a New Zealand company exporting a container of kiwi fruit to Haiti or Iraq. The customs official informs you that there is a delay in clearing your container through customs, and the delay may last a month. However, if you are willing to pay an "expediting fee" of US$200, he will try to make it happen in one day. What are you going to do?

3. *ON ETHICS:* Most developed economies have some illegal immigrants. The United States has the largest number of illegal immigrants in the country: approximately 10 to 11 million. Without legal US identification documents, they cannot open bank accounts or buy houses. Many US firms have targeted this population, accepting their ID issued by their native countries and selling them products and services. Some Americans are furious with these business practices. Other Americans suggest that illegal immigrants represent a growth engine in an economy with relatively little growth elsewhere. How would you participate in this debate?

GLOBAL ACTION

BUSINESS INSIGHTS GLOBAL

1. *ON CULTURE:* Religion is an integral component of your company's operations because it manufacturers food products according to Islam's *Halal* requirements. Top management wants information concerning the largest populations of Islam worldwide in order to develop the company's distribution capabilities. Provide a report with any information relevant to this company-wide initiative. What are your recommendations?

2. One approach to understanding corruption perceptions is to compare information across a variety of countries. Your company has had operations in South America for some time. However, there has not been an internal evaluation of perceived regional corruption to date. Therefore, you have been asked to provide insight on this topic for each country in South America. Based on an annual corruption perceptions index, develop a brief report and recommendations for the entire company.

CLOSING CASE

EMERGING MARKETS: Monetizing the Maasai Tribal Name

Thomas Concordia/Getty Images

Karl Prouse/Catwalking/Getty Images

Living in Kenya and Tanzania, the Maasai with their recognizable red attire represent one of the most iconic tribes in Africa. As (semi-)nomadic pastoralists, the Maasai have been raising cattle and hunting with some small-scale agriculture near Africa's finest game parks, such as Serengeti, for ages. Known as fierce warriors, the Maasai have won the respect of rival tribes, colonial authorities, and modern governments of Kenya and Tanzania. Together with lions, giraffes, and zebras, a Maasai village is among the "must-see" places for a typical African safari trip.

For those of you who cannot travel so far to visit Africa, you can still get a piece of the colorful Maasai culture. Jaguar Land Rover marketed a limited-edition version of its Freelander 4 × 4 named Maasai. Louis Vuitton developed a line of menswear and womenswear fashion inspired by the Maasai dress. Diane von Furstenberg hawked a red pillow and cushion line simply called Maasai. The Switzerland-based Maasai Barefoot Technology (MBT) developed a line of round-bottom shoes to simulate the challenge of Maasai walking barefoot on soft earth. An Italian penmaker, Delta, named its high-end red-capped fountain pen Maasai. A single pen retails at US$600, "which is like three or four good cows," according to a Maasai tribesman. These are just high-profile examples. Experts estimate that perhaps 10,000 firms around the world use the Maasai name, selling everything from hats to legal services.

All this sounds fascinating, except one catch. While these firms made millions, neither a single Maasai individual nor the tribe has ever received a penny. This is where a huge ethical and legal debate has erupted. Legally, the Maasai case is weak. The tribe has never made any formal effort to enforce any intellectual property rights (IPR) of its culture and identity. With approximately two million tribe members spread between Kenya and Tanzania, just who can officially represent the Maasai is up in the air. An expert laughed at this idea, by saying, "Look, if it could work, the French budget deficit would be gone by demanding royalties on French fries."

However, from an ethical standpoint, all the firms named above claim to be interested in corporate social responsibility (CSR). If they indeed are interested in the high road to business ethics, expropriating—or, if you may, "ripping off" or "stealing"—the Maasai name without compensation has obviously become a huge embarrassment.

Although steeped in tradition, the Maasai are also constantly in touch with the modern world. Their frequent interactions with tourists have made them aware how much value there is in the Maasai name. But they are frustrated by their lack of knowledge about the rules of the game concerning IPR. Fortunately, they have been helped by Ron Layton, a New Zealander who is a former diplomat and now runs a nonprofit Light Years IP advising groups in the developing world such as the Maasai. Layton previously helped the Ethiopian government wage a legal battle with Starbucks, which marketed Harrar, Sidamo, and Yirgacheffe coffee lines from different regions of Ethiopia without compensation. Although Starbucks projects an image of being very serious about CSR, it initially fought these efforts but eventually agreed to recognize Ethiopia's claims.

Sven Torfinn/Panos

(left to right) Isaac ole Tiabolo, Ron Layton, and a staff member with MIPI

Source: *Bloomberg Businessweek*, 2013, Maasai™, October 24: 88.

Emboldened by the success in fighting Starbucks, Layton worked with Maasai elders such as Issac ole Tialolo to establish a nonprofit registered in Tanzania called Maasai Intellectual Property Initiative (MIPI). They crafted MIPI bylaws that would reflect traditional Maasai cultural values and that would satisfy the requirements of Western courts—in preparation for an eventual legal showdown. Layton himself made no money from MIPI, and his only income was the salary from his own nonprofit Light Years IP. A US$1.25 million grant from the US Patent and Trademark Office (USPTO) helped to defray some of the expenses. The challenge now is to have more tribal leaders and elders to sign up with MIPI so that MIPI would be viewed both externally and internally as the legitimate representative of the Maasai tribe. How the tribe can monetize its name remains to be seen in the future.

CASE DISCUSSION QUESTIONS

1. ***ON ETHICS:*** Assuming you can afford (and are interested in) some of the "Maasai" products, would you like to pay more for these products if royalties are paid to the Maasai?

2. ***ON ETHICS:*** As CEO of one of the firms mentioned, how are you going to respond?

3. ***ON ETHICS:*** If you were a judge in the home country of any of these firms named, how would you proceed with the legal dispute (assuming MIPI can eventually represent the tribe and press legal charges)?

Sources: Based on (1) *Bloomberg Businessweek*, 2013, Maasai™, October 24: 84–88; (2) ca.mbt.com; (3) V. Kaster, 2014, Maasai tribe wants control over commercial uses of its name, March 6, www.iplegalfreebies.wordpress.com; (4) www.dvf.com; (5) www.louisvuitton.com; (6) www.jaguarlandrover.com; (7) www.penggallery.com.

NOTES

[**Journal acronyms**] **AMJ**—*Academy of Management Journal*; **AMLE**—*Academy of Management Learning and Education*; **AMR**—*Academy of Management Review*; **APJM**—*Asia Pacific Journal of Management*; **HBR**—*Harvard Business Review*; **JIBS**—*Journal of International Business Studies*; **JM**—*Journal of Management*; **JMS**—*Journal of Management Studies*; **JWB**—*Journal of World Business*; **MIR**—*Management International Review*; **PR**—*Personnel Review*; **RES**—*Review of Economics and Statistics*; **SMJ**—*Strategic Management Journal*.

1 G. Hofstede, 1997, *Cultures and Organizations* (p. xii), New York: McGraw-Hill.

2 Hofstede, 1997, *Cultures and Organizations* (p. 5).

3 D. Graddol, 2004, The future of language, *Science*, 303: 1329–1331.

4 R. McCrum, 2010, *Globish: How the English Language Became the World's Language*, New York: Norton; T. Neeley, 2012, Global business speaks English, *HBR*, May: 117–124.

5 W. Barner-Rasmussen, M. Ehrnrooth, A. Koveshnikov, & K. Makela, 2014, Cultural and language skills as resources for boundary spanning within the MNC, *JIBS*, 45: 886–905; M. Brannen, R. Piekkari, & S. Tietze, 2014, The multifaceted role of language in international business, *JIBS*, 45: 495–507; J. Heikkila & A. Smale, 2011, The effects of language standardization on the acceptance and use of e-HRM systems in foreign subsidiaries, *JWB*, 46: 305–313; N. Holden & S. Michailova, 2014, A more expansive perspective on translation in IB research, *JIBS*, 45: 906–918; V. Peltokorpi & E. Vaara, 2012, Language policies and practices in wholly owned foreign subsidiaries, *JIBS*, 43: 808–833; H. Tenzer, M. Pudelko, & A. Harzing, 2014, The impact of language barriers on trust formation in multinational teams, *JIBS*, 45: 508–535; J. Usunier, 2011, Language as a resource to access cross-cultural equivalence in quantitative management research, *JWB*, 46: 314–319.

6 *Economist*, 2014, The English empire, February 15: 61; *Economist*, 2014, The Globish-speaking union, May 24: 50.

7 J. Fidrmuc & J. Fidrmuc, 2009, Foreign languages and trade, working paper, Uxbridge, UK: Brunel University.

8 S. Volk, T. Kohler, & M. Pudelko, 2014, Brain drain, *JIBS*, 45: 862–885.

9 A. Chidlow, E. Plakoyiannaki, & C. Welch, 2014, Translation in cross-language international business research, *JIBS*, 45: 562–582;

M. Janssens & C. Steyaert, 2014, Re-considering language within a cosmopolitan understanding, *JIBS*, 45: 623–639; P. Hinds, T. Neeley, & C. Cramton, 2014, Language as a lightning rod, *JIBS*, 45: 536–561.

10 *Economist*, 2014, China's cities: The great transition, March 22: 17.

11 E. Hall & M. Hall, 1987, *Hidden Differences*, Garden City, NY: Doubleday.

12 S. Ronen & O. Shenkar, 1985, Clustering countries on attitudinal dimension, *AMR*, 10: 435–454; S. Ronen & O. Shenkar, 2013, Mapping world cultures, *JIBS*, 44: 867–897.

13 R. House, P. Hanges, M. Javidan, P. Dorfman, & V. Gupta (eds.), 2004, *Culture, Leadership, and Organizations: The GLOBE Study of 62 Societies*, Thousand Oaks, CA: Sage.

14 S. Huntington, 1996, *The Clash of Civilizations and the Remaking of World Order* (p. 43), New York: Simon & Schuster.

15 S. Schwartz, 1994, Cultural dimensions of values, in U. Kim et al. (eds.), *Individualism and Collectivism* (pp. 85–119), Thousand Oaks, CA: Sage; F. Trompenaars, 1993, *Riding the Waves of Culture*, Chicago: Irwin.

16 E. Ravlin, Y. Liao, D. Morrell, K. Au, & D. Thomas, 2012, Collectivist orientation and the psychological contract, *JIBS*, 43: 772–782; L. Yang et al., 2012, Individualism-collectivism as a moderator of the work demands-strains relationship, *JIBS*, 43: 424–443; X. Zheng, S. Ghoul, O. Guedhami, & C. Kwok, 2013, Collectivism and corruption in bank lending, *JIBS*, 44: 363–390.

17 T. Fang, 2010, Asian management research needs more self-confidence, *APJM*, 27: 155–170; B. Kirkman, K. Lowe, & C. Gibson, 2006, A quarter century of *Culture's Consequences*, *JIBS*, 37: 285–320.

18 G. Hofstede, 2006, What did GLOBE really measure? *JIBS*, 37: 882–896; G. Hofstede, 2007, Asian management in the 21st century, *APJM*, 24: 411–420;

19 G. Hirst, P. Budhwar, B. Cooper, M. West, C. Long, C. Xu, & H. Shipton, 2008, Cross-cultural variations in climate for autonomy, stress, and organizational productivity relationships, *JIBS*, 39: 1343–1358.

20 Hofstede, 1997, *Cultures and Organizations* (p. 94).

21 M. Bazerman, 2014, Becoming a first-class notice, *HBR*, July: 116–119; D. Welsh & L. Ordonez, 2014, Conscience without cognition, *AMJ*, 57: 723–742.

22 R. Deshpande & A. Raina, 2011, The ordinary heroes of the Taj, *HBR*, December: 119–123.

23 D. McCarthy & S. Puffer, 2008, Interpreting the ethicality of corporate governance decisions in Russia, *AMR*, 33: 11–31.

24 This section draws heavily from T. Donaldson, 1996, Values in tension, *HBR*, September–October: 4–11.

25 N. Jensen, Q. Li, & A. Rahman, 2010, Understanding corruption and firm responses in cross-national firm-level surveys, *JIBS*, 41: 1481–1504; I. Montiel, B. Husted, & P. Christmann, 2012, Using private management standard certification to reduce information asymmetries in corrupt environments, *SMJ*, 33: 1103–1113; J. Spencer & C. Gomez, 2011, MNEs and corruption, *SMJ*, 32: 280–300;

26 S. Lee & S. Hong, 2012, Corruption and subsidiary profitability, *APJM*, 29: 949–964; S. Lee & D. Weng, 2013, Does bribery in the home country promote or dampen firm exports? *SMJ*, 34:

1472–1487; J. Zhou & M. W. Peng, 2012, Does bribery help or hurt firm growth around the world? *APJM*, 29: 907–921.

27 S. Wei, 2000, How taxing is corruption on international investors? *RES*, 82: 1–11.

28 J. Hellman, G. Jones, & D. Kaufmann, 2002, Far from home: Do foreign investors import higher standards of governance in transition economies (p. 20), Working paper, Washington: World Bank (www.worldbank.org).

29 A. Cuervo-Cazzura, 2008, The effectiveness of laws against bribery abroad, *JIBS*, 39: 634–651.

30 *BW*, 2014, If only GM had listened ... June 23: 49–53.

31 World Bank, 1993, *The East Asian Miracle*, Washington: World Bank.

32 M. W. Peng, R. Bhagat, & S. Chang, 2010, Asia and global business, *JIBS*, 41: 373–376.

33 National Commission on Terrorist Attacks on the United States, 2004, *The 9/11 Report* (p. 364), New York: St. Martin's.

34 H. Berry, M. Guillen, & A. Hendi, 2014, Is there convergence across countries? *JIBS*, 45: 387–404.

35 This section draws heavily from C. Chen, M. W. Peng, & P. Saparito, 2002, Individualism, collectivism, and opportunism: A cultural perspective on transaction cost economics, *JM*, 28: 567–583.

36 O. Williamson, 1985, *The Economic Institutions of Capitalism*, New York: Free Press.

37 J. Cullen, K. Parboteeah, & M. Hoegl, 2004, Cross-national differences in managers' willingness to justify ethically suspect behaviors, *AMJ*, 47: 411–421.

38 M. Muethel & M. Bond, 2013, National context and individual employees' trust of the out-group, *JIBS*, 2013: 312–333.

39 F. Fukuyama, 1995, *Trust*, New York: Free Press; G. Redding, 1993, *The Spirit of Chinese Capitalism*, New York: Gruyter.

40 Y. Kandogan, 2011, Determinants of individuals' preference for cross-cultural literacy, *JWB*, 46: 328–336; V. Peltokorpi & E. Vaara, 2014, Knowledge transfer in multinational corporations, *JIBS*, 45: 600–622.

41 G. Lucke, T. Kostova, & K. Roth, 2014, Multiculturalism from a cognitive perspective, *JIBS*, 45: 169–190; M. Mendenhall, A. Arnardottir, G. Oddou, & L. Burke, 2013, Developing cross-cultural competencies in management education via cognitive-behavior therapy, *AMLE*, 12: 436–451; A. Molinsky, 2013, The psychological processes of cultural retooling, *AMJ*, 56: 683–710; S. B. Szkudlarek, J. McNett, L. Romani, & H. Lane, 2013, The past, present, and future of cross-cultural management education, *AMLE*, 12: 477–493; O. Varela & R. Gatlin-Watts, 2014, The development of the global manager, *AMLE*, 13: 187–207; N. Yagi & J. Kleinberg, 2011, Boundary work, *JIBS*, 42: 629–653.

42 S. Lee, O. Shenkar, & J. Li, 2008, Culture distance, investment flow, and control in cross-border cooperation, *JIBS*, 29: 1117–1125; O. Shenkar, 2012, Beyond cultural distance, *JIBS*, 43: 12–17; S. Zaheer, M. Shomaker, & L. Nachum, 2012, Distance without direction, *JIBS*, 43: 18–27.

43 A. Kuznetsov & O. Kuznetsova, 2014, Building professional discourse in emerging markets, *JIBS*, 45: 583–599; A. Zavyalova, M. Pfarrer, R. Reger, & D. Shapiro, 2012, Managing the message, *AMJ*, 55: 1079–1101.

© Lonely/Shutterstock.com

Chris Ratcliffe/Bloomberg/Getty Images

Learning Objectives

After studying this chapter, you should be able to

- define resources and capabilities.

- explain how value is created from a firm's resources and capabilities.

- articulate the difference between keeping an activity in-house and outsourcing it.

- explain what a VRIO framework is.

- participate in two leading debates concerning leveraging resources and capabilities.

- draw implications for action.

CHAPTER 4

Leveraging Resources and Capabilities

LEGO's Secrets

LEGO is everywhere—toys, games, books, magazines, competitions, retail stores, theme parks, and now movies. If all of the approximately 400 billion colorful interlocking bricks ever produced by LEGO were to be divided equally among the world's population, each person would have 86 bricks (!). *Fortune* magazine half-joked that "at least ten billion are under sofa cushions and three billion are inside vacuum cleaners." By itself, a single plastic brick is lifeless. But snap two of these inorganic blocks together, suddenly they take on a life of their own, and a world of nearly infinite possibilities opens up. Igniting the imagination of millions of children and adults around the world, the little LEGO brick has become a universal building block for fostering creativity. Nicknames such as "the toy of the (20th) century" and "the most popular toy of all time" are routine. Nearly everyone seems to love LEGO. Around the world, LEGO fan clubs abound, often with their own conferences and competitions. "With the possible exception of Apple, arguably no brand sparks as much cult-like devotion as LEGO," noted an expert. What are LEGO's secrets?

Relentless innovation and experimentation are one of the foremost characteristics of LEGO. Derived from the Danish phase *leg godt* ("play well"), LEGO was founded in 1932 by Ole Kirk Christiansen, a carpenter from Billund, Denmark, a rural town three hours away from Copenhagen. (Today, LEGO Group is still headquartered in Billund.) As a firm self-styled "to stimulate children's imagination and creativity" and "to nurture the child in each of us," LEGO is known for being willing to entertain numerous experiments in order to capture the hearts and minds of its fickle primary customers—boys aged seven to 16—as well as the wallets of their parents. LEGO started with wooden toys. In 1947, it became the first Danish toymaker to experiment with plastics, even though trade magazines at that time predicted that plastics would never replace wooden toys. The now-ubiquitous brick was not LEGO's original invention. It was based on "Self-Locking Bricks" patented in the UK in 1939 and released to the public domain in 1947. LEGO tinkered with the brick, and initial efforts were not successful. The bricks snapped together, but could not be separated easily. LEGO continued to experiment, eventually hitting a stud-and-tube coupling design that was patented in Copenhagen in 1958. When a child snapped two bricks together, they would stick with a click. The two bricks would stay together until the child separated them with an easy tug. Because such bricks would not come apart, kids could build from the ground up, leveraging what LEGO continues to call "clutch power." While the brick proved to be one of the toy industry's greatest innovations, LEGO's experiment marched on, with numerous hits and also numerous misses in the last five decades since the finalization of the basic design of the brick.

Another LEGO hallmark is insisting on excellence. Coming from the founder, "only the best is good enough" is a company motto engraved on a plaque that graces the entrance to LEGO Group headquarters' cafeteria even today. The seemingly simple tight fit of two bricks—and their easy separation—calls for extremely precise manufacturing. Since the size of each brick is so tiny, misalignment in the range of a few millimeters can easily create misfit when bricks are stacked together. Competitors can produce LEGO-look-alikes that tolerate higher levels of variations, but kids often quickly figure out LEGO is the best after playing with competing products for a short while. This is not to say LEGO's quality is perfect. It is not, as on average 18 out of one million bricks produced fail to meet LEGO's quality standards and have to be tossed. In addition to tight fit and easy separation, LEGO is also known for its strength that is legendarily indestructible. More than half a million people (mostly parents) have "liked" the Facebook page "For those who have experienced the pain caused by stepping on LEGO" (!).

LEGO is also world famous for generating a system, not merely a product. Long before the days when computer programs were supposed to be backward compatible (a new version of Windows must allow users to open old files), LEGO made its bricks backward compatible—new bricks would click with old bricks of the 1950s vintage. As a result, kids (and adults) can mix and match old and new sets and the LEGO universe can grow exponentially. Likewise, the bewildering array of new LEGO gadgets and experiences—such as board games, online games, competitions, books, magazines, theme parks, retail stores, and movies—unleash a powerful and mutually reinforcing ecosystem (or a product family) centered on the brick.

Of course, numerous other secrets reside within LEGO, each contributing to its success. Dozens of books and hundreds of articles have been written, slicing and dicing LEGO in a variety of ways in order to probe its secrets. In the end, what exactly is *it* remains elusive.

Sources: Based on (1) the author's interviews of LEGO customers (especially James Peng) and LEGO store personnel in Copenhagen and Dallas; (2) *Economist*, 2013, Lego in Asia, November 16: 72; (3) *Economist*, 2014, Unpacking Lego, March 8: 71; (4) D. C. Robertson, 2013, *Brick by Brick: How LEGO Rewrote the Rules of Innovation and Conquered the Global Toy Industry*, New York: Crown Business.

Why is LEGO so popular and successful? Why do competitors have a hard time chipping away its market? The answer must be that certain resources and capabilities specific to a winning firm such as LEGO are not shared by competitors. This insight has been developed into a resource-based view, which has emerged as one of the two core perspectives on global business.[1]

One leading tool in global business is SWOT analysis. A SWOT analysis determines a firm's strengths (S), weaknesses (W), opportunities (O), and threats (T). In global business, the institution-based view deals with the *external* O and T, enabled and constrained by formal and informal rules of the game (see Chapters 2 and 3). The resource-based view builds on the SWOT analysis,[2] and concentrates on the *internal* S and W to identify and leverage sustainable competitive advantage.[3] In this chapter, we first define resources and capabilities and then discuss the value chain analysis, concentrating on the decision to keep an activity in-house or outsource it. We then focus on the VRIO framework: value (V), rarity (R), imitability (I), and organization (O). Debates and extensions follow.

Learning Objective
Define resources and capabilities.

SWOT analysis
A tool for determining a firm's strengths (S), weaknesses (W), opportunities (O), and threats (T).

Resource
The tangible and intangible assets a firm uses to choose and implement its strategies.

4-1 Understanding Resources and Capabilities

One basic proposition of the resource-based view is that a firm consists of a bundle of productive resources and capabilities.[4] Resources are defined as "the tangible and intangible assets a firm uses to choose and implement its strategies."[5] There is some debate regarding the definition of capabilities. Some scholars define them as "a firm's capacity to dynamically deploy resources," suggesting a "dynamic capabilities" view that emphasizes a crucial distinction between resources and capabilities.[6]

While scholars may debate the fine distinctions between resources and capabilities, these distinctions are likely to "become badly blurred" in practice.[7] Is LEGO's R&D prowess a resource or capability? How about its abilities in precision manufacturing? For current and would-be managers, the key is to understand how these attributes help improve firm performance, not to figure out whether they should be defined as resources or capabilities. Therefore, in this book, we will use the terms "resources" and "capabilities" *interchangeably* and often in *parallel*. In other words, capabilities are defined here the same as resources.

All firms, even the smallest ones, possess a variety of resources and capabilities. How do we meaningfully classify such diversity? One useful way is to separate the resources and capabilities into two categories: tangible and intangible (Table 4.1). Tangible resources and capabilities are assets that are observable and easily quantified. They can be broadly organized in four categories: financial, physical, technological, and organizational resources and capabilities.

By definition, intangible resources and capabilities are harder to observe and more difficult (or even impossible) to quantify (see Table 4.1). Yet, it is widely acknowledged that they must be there, because no firm is likely to generate competitive advantage by relying on tangible resources and capabilities alone. Examples of intangible assets include human, innovation, and reputational resources and capabilities. Emerging Markets 4.1 illustrates how extraordinary human resources (HR) can be during crisis.

Table 4.1   Examples of Resources and Capabilities

Tangible resources and capabilities	Examples
Financial	Ability to generate internal funds Ability to raise external capital
Physical	Location of plants, offices, and equipment Access to raw materials and distribution channels
Technological	Possession of patents, trademarks, copyrights, and trade secrets
Organizational	Formal planning, command, and control systems Integrated management information systems

Intangible resources and capabilities	Examples
Human	Managerial talents Organizational culture
Innovation	Research and development capabilities Capacities for organizational innovation and change
Reputational	Perceptions of product quality, durability, and reliability Reputation as a good employer Reputation as a socially responsible corporate citizen

Sources: Adapted from (1) J. Barney, 1991, Firm resources and sustained competitive advantage, *Journal of Management*, 17: 101; (2) R. Hall, 1992, The strategic analysis of intangible resources, *Strategic Management Journal*, 13: 135–144.

Capability
The tangible and intangible assets a firm uses to choose and implement its strategies.

Tangible resource and capability
Assets that are observable and easily quantified.

Intangible resource and capability
Assets that are hard to observe and difficult (if not impossible) to quantify.

EMERGING MARKETS 4.1

The Ordinary Heroes at the Taj

On November 26, 2008, Unilever hosted a dinner at the Taj Mahal Palace Hotel in Mumbai. Unilever's directors, senior executives, and their spouses were bidding farewell to a departing CEO and welcoming a new CEO. About 35 Taj employees, led by a 24-year-old banquet manager, Mallika Jagad, were assigned to manage the event in a second-floor banquet room. Around 9:30 p.m., as they served the main course, they heard what they thought were fireworks at a nearby wedding. In reality, these were the first gunshots from terrorists who were storming the Taj.

The staff quickly realized something was wrong. Jagad had the doors locked and the lights turned off. She asked everyone to lie down quietly under tables and refrain from using cell phones. She insisted that husbands and wives separate to reduce the risk to families. The group stayed there all night, listening to the terrorists rampaging through the hotel, hurling grenades, firing automatic weapons, and tearing the palace apart. The Taj staff kept calm, and constantly went around offering water and asking people if they needed anything else. Early the next morning, a fire started in the hallway outside, forcing the group to try to climb out the windows. A fire crew spotted them and, with its ladders, helped the trapped people escape quickly. The staff evacuated the guests first, and no casualties resulted.

Elsewhere in the hotel, the upscale Japanese restaurant Wasabi was busy by 9:30 p.m. A warning call from a hotel operator alerted the staff that terrorists had entered the building and were heading toward the restaurants. Thomas Varghese, the 48-year-old senior waiter, immediately instructed his 50-odd guests to crouch under tables, and he directed employees to form a human cordon around them. Four hours later, security forces asked Varghese if he could get the guests out of the hotel. He decided to use a spiral staircase near the restaurant to evacuate the customers first and then the staff. The 30-year Taj veteran insisted that he would be the last man to leave, but he never did get out. The terrorists gunned him down as he exited.

When Karambir Singh Kang, the Taj's general manager, heard about the attacks, he immediately left the conference he was attending offsite. He took charge at the Taj the moment he arrived, supervising the evacuation of guests and coordinating the efforts of firefighters amid the chaos. His wife and two young children were in a sixth-floor suite, where the general manager traditionally lives. When he realized that the terrorists were on the upper floors, he tried to get to his family. It was impossible. By midnight, the sixth floor was in flames, and there was no hope of anyone surviving there. Kang led the rescue efforts until noon the next day. Only then did he call his parents to tell them that the terrorists had killed his wife and children. His father, a retired general, told him, "Son, do your duty, do not desert your post." Kang replied, "If the hotel goes down, I will be the last man out."

During the onslaught on the Taj, 31 people died and 28 were hurt, but the hotel received only praise the day after. Its guests were overwhelmed by employees' dedication to duty, their desire to protect guests with little regard to their own personal safety, and their quick thinking. As many as 11 Taj employees—a third of the hotel's casualties—laid down their lives while helping between 1,200 and 1,500 guests escape.

At some level, that isn't surprising. One of the world's top hotels, the Taj is ranked number 20 by *Condé Nast Traveler*. The hotel is known for the highest levels of quality, its ability to go many extra miles to delight customers, and its staff of highly trained employees. It is a well-oiled machine, where every employee knows his or her job, has encyclopedic knowledge about regular guests, and is comfortable taking orders. Even so, the Taj employees gave customer service a whole new meaning during the terrorist strike.

Source: Excerpted from R. Deshpandé & A. Raina, 2011, The ordinary heroes of the Taj, *Harvard Business Review*, December: 119–123.

Note that all resources and capabilities discussed here are merely *examples*. They do not represent an exhaustive list. Firms will forge ahead to discover and leverage new resources and capabilities.

4-2/4-3 Resources, Capabilities, and the Value Chain

Learning Objective
Explain how value is created from a firm's resources and capabilities.

If a firm is a bundle of resources and capabilities, how do they come together to add value? A value chain analysis allows us to answer this question. Shown in Panel A of Figure 4.1, most goods and services are produced through a chain of vertical activities (from upstream to downstream) that add value—in short, a value chain. The value chain typically consists of two areas: primary activities and support activities.[8]

Each activity requires a number of resources and capabilities. Value chain analysis forces managers to think about firm resources and capabilities at a very micro, activity-based level.[9] Given that no firm is likely to be good at all primary and support activities, the key is to examine whether the firm has resources and

Figure 4.1   **The Value Chain**

Panel A. An Example of Value Chain with Firm Boundaries

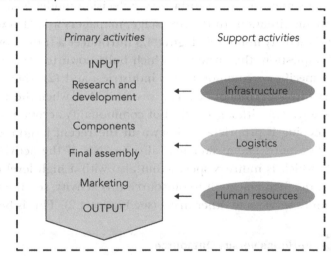

Panel B. An Example of Value Chain with Some Outsourcing

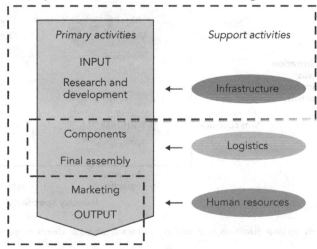

Note: Dotted lines represent firm boundaries.

Value chain

A stream of activities from upstream to downstream that add value.

Figure 4.2   **A Two-Stage Decision Model in Value Chain Analysis**

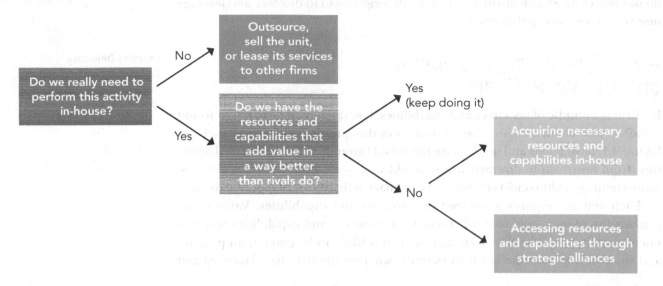

capabilities to perform a *particular* activity in a manner superior to competitors—a process known as benchmarking in SWOT analysis. If managers find that their firm's particular activity is unsatisfactory, a decision model (shown in Figure 4.2) can remedy the situation. In the first stage, managers ask, "Do we really need to perform this activity in-house?" Figure 4.3 introduces a framework to take a hard look at this question, the answer to which boils down to (1) whether an activity is industry-specific or common across industries, and (2) whether this activity is proprietary (firm-specific) or not. The answer is "No" when the activity is found in Cell 2 in Figure 4.3 with a great deal of commonality across industries and little need for keeping it proprietary—known in the recent jargon as a high degree of commoditization. The answer may also be "No" if the activity is in Cell 1 in Figure 4.3, which is industry-specific but also with a high level of commoditization. Then, the firm may want to outsource this activity, sell the unit involved, or lease the unit's services to other firms (see Figure 4.2). This is because operating

Figure 4.3   **In-House versus Outsource**

Benchmarking

Examining whether a firm has resources and capabilities to perform a particular activity in a manner superior to competitors.

Commoditization

A process of market competition through which unique products that command high prices and high margins gradually lose their ability to do so, thus becoming commodities.

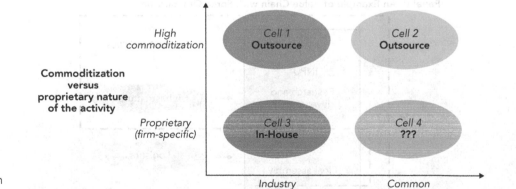

Note: At present, no clear guidelines exist for Cell 4, where firms either choose to perform activities in-house or outsource.

multiple stages of uncompetitive activities in the value chain may be cumbersome and costly.

Think about steel, definitely a crucial component for automobiles. But the question for automakers is: "Do we need to make steel by ourselves?" The requirements for steel are common across end-user industries—that is, the steel for automakers is essentially the same for construction, defense, and other steel-consuming end-users (ignoring minor technical differences for the sake of our discussion). For automakers, while it is imperative to keep the automaking activity (especially engine and final assembly) proprietary (Cell 3 in Figure 4.3), there is no need to keep steelmaking in-house. Therefore, although many automakers, such as Ford and GM, historically were involved in steelmaking, none of them does it now. In other words, steelmaking is outsourced and steel commoditized.

Outsourcing is defined as turning over an activity to an outside supplier that will perform the activity on behalf of the focal firm.[10] For example, many consumer products companies (such as Nike and Apple), which possess strong capabilities in upstream activities (such as design) and downstream activities (such as marketing), have outsourced manufacturing to suppliers in low-cost countries. A total of 70% of the value of Boeing's new 787 Dreamliner is provided by outside suppliers. This compares with 51% for existing Boeing aircraft.[11] Recently, not only is manufacturing often outsourced, but a number of service activities, such as IT, HR, and logistics, are also outsourced. The driving force is that many firms, which used to view certain activities as a very special part of their industries (such as airline reservations and bank call centers), now believe that these activities have relatively generic attributes that can be shared across industries. Of course, this changing mentality is fueled by the rise of service providers, such as IBM and Infosys in IT, Manpower in HR, Foxconn in contract manufacturing, and DHL in logistics. These specialist firms argue that such activities can be broken off from the various client firms (just as steelmaking was broken off from automakers decades ago) and leveraged to serve multiple clients with greater economies of scale.[12] Such outsourcing enables client firms to become "leaner and meaner" organizations, which can better focus on their core activities (see Figure 4.1 Panel B).

© Christian Mueller/Shutterstock.com

How can specialist firms such as DHL in logistics facilitate outsourcing?

If the answer to the question, "Do we really need to perform this activity in-house?" is "Yes" (Cell 3 in Figure 4.3), but the firm's current resources and capabilities are not up to the task, then there are two choices (see Figure 4.2). First, the firm may want to acquire and develop capabilities in-house so that it can perform this particular activity better.[13] Second, if a firm does not have enough skills to develop these capabilities in-house, it may want to access them through alliances.

Conspicuously lacking in both Figures 4.2 and 4.3 is the *geographic* dimension— domestic versus foreign locations.[14] Because the two terms "outsourcing" and "offshoring" have emerged rather recently, there is a great deal of confusion, especially among some journalists, who often casually equate them. So, to minimize

Learning Objective

Articulate the difference between keeping an activity in-house and outsourcing it.

Outsourcing

Turning over an activity to an outside supplier that will perform it on behalf of the focal firm.

| Figure 4.4 | **Location, Location, Location** |

Mode of activity

	In-House	Outsourcing	
Location of activity	*Cell 1* Captive sourcing/FDI	*Cell 2* Offshoring	*Foreign location*
	Cell 3 Domestic in-house	*Cell 4* Onshoring	*Domestic location*

Note: "Captive sourcing" is a new term, which is conceptually identical to "foreign direct investment" (FDI), a term widely used in global business. See Chapter 6 for details.

confusion, we go from two terms to four terms in Figure 4.4, based on locations and modes (in-house versus outsource):[15]

- Offshoring—international/foreign outsourcing
- Onshoring—domestic outsourcing
- Captive sourcing—setting up subsidiaries to perform in-house work in foreign locations
- Domestic in-house activity

Outsourcing—especially offshoring—has no shortage of controversies and debates (see the Debates and Extensions section). Despite this set of new labels, we need to be aware that "captive sourcing" is conceptually identical to foreign direct investment (FDI), which is nothing new in the world of global business (see Chapters 1 and 6 and PengAtlas Map 2.3 for details). We also need to be aware that "offshoring" and "onshoring" are simply international and domestic variants of outsourcing, respectively. While offshoring low-cost IT work to India, the Philippines, and other emerging economies has been widely practiced, interestingly, eastern Germany, northern France, and the Appalachian, Great Plains, and southern regions of the United States have emerged as new hotbeds for onshoring.[16] In job-starved regions such as Michigan, high-quality IT workers may accept 35% lower wages than at headquarters in Silicon Valley.

One interesting lesson we can take away from Figure 4.4 is that even for a single firm, value-adding activities may be geographically dispersed around the world, taking advantage of the best locations and modes to perform certain activities. For instance, a Dell laptop may be designed in the United States (domestic in-house activity), its components may be produced in Taiwan (offshoring) as well as the United States (onshoring), and its final assembly may be done in China (captive sourcing/FDI). When customers call for help, the call center may be in India, Ireland, Jamaica, or the Philippines, manned by an outside service provider—Dell may have outsourced the service activities through offshoring.

Overall, a value chain analysis engages managers to ascertain a firm's strengths and weaknesses on an activity-by-activity basis, *relative to rivals*, in a SWOT analysis. The recent proliferation of new labels is intimidating, causing some gurus to claim, "21st-century offshoring really is different."[17] In reality, it is not. Under the skin of the new vocabulary, we still see the time-honored SWOT analysis at work. The next section introduces the VRIO framework on how to do this.

Offshoring

Outsourcing to an international or foreign firm.

Onshoring

Outsourcing to a domestic firm.

Captive sourcing

Setting up subsidiaries abroad so that the work done is in-house but the location is foreign. Also known as foreign direct investment (FDI).

4-4 From SWOT to VRIO[18]

Recent progress in the resource-based view has gone beyond the traditional SWOT analysis. The new work focuses on the value (V), rarity (R), imitability (I), and organizational (O) aspects of resources and capabilities, leading to a VRIO framework. Summarized in Table 4.2, addressing these four important questions has a number of ramifications for competitive advantage.

Learning Objective
Explain what a VRIO framework is.

4-4a Value

Do firm resources and capabilities add value? The preceding value chain analysis suggests that this is the most fundamental question to start with.[19] Only value-adding resources can lead to competitive advantage, whereas non-value-adding capabilities may lead to competitive *disadvantage*. The evolution of IBM is another case in point. IBM historically excelled in making hardware, including tabulating machines in the 1930s, mainframes in the 1960s, and PCs in the 1980s. However, as competition heated up, IBM's capabilities in hardware not only added little value, but also increasingly stood in the way for it to move into new areas. Since the 1990s, IBM has been transformed into focusing on more lucrative software and services, where it has developed new value-adding capabilities, aiming to become an on-demand computing *service* provider for corporations. As part of this new strategy, in 2002 IBM purchased PricewaterhouseCoopers (PwC), a leading technology consulting firm. In 2004, IBM sold its PC division to Lenovo. In 2011, IBM proudly celebrated its 100th anniversary.

The relationship between valuable resources and capabilities and firm performance is straightforward. Instead of becoming strengths, non-value-adding resources and capabilities, such as IBM's historical expertise in hardware, may become weaknesses. If firms are unable to get rid of non-value-adding assets, they are likely to suffer below-average performance.[20] In the worst case, they may become extinct, a fate IBM narrowly skirted during the early 1990s. According to IBM's CEO Ginni Rometty:

> Whatever business you're in, it's going to commoditize over time, so you have to keep moving it to a higher value and change.[21]

VRIO framework

The resource-based framework that focuses on the value (V), rarity (R), imitability (I), and organizational (O) aspects of resources and capabilities.

Table 4.2 **The VRIO Framework: Is a Resource or Capability . . .**

Valuable?	Rare?	Costly to imitate?	Exploited by organization?	Competitive implications	Firm performance
No	—	—	No	Competitive disadvantage	Below average
Yes	No	—	Yes	Competitive parity	Average
Yes	Yes	No	Yes	Temporary competitive advantage	Above average
Yes	Yes	Yes	Yes	Sustained competitive advantage	Persistently above average

Sources: Adapted from (1) J. Barney, 2002, *Gaining and Sustaining Competitive Advantage*, 2nd ed. (p. 173), Upper Saddle River, NJ: Prentice Hall; (2) R. Hoskisson, M. Hitt, & R.D. Ireland, 2004, *Competing for Advantage* (p. 118), Cincinnati: Cengage Learning.

4-4b Rarity

Possessing valuable resources and capabilities may not be enough. The next question is: "How rare are valuable resources and capabilities?"[22] At best, valuable but common resources and capabilities will lead to competitive parity but not an advantage. Consider the (nearly) identical aircraft made by Boeing and Airbus used by numerous airlines. They are certainly valuable, yet it is difficult to derive competitive advantage from these aircraft alone. Airlines work hard on how to use these same aircraft *differently* (see In Focus 4.1).

IN FOCUS 4.1

ANA: REFRESHING THE PARTS OTHER AIRLINES CANNOT REACH

Delivered first in 2011, the new Boeing 787 Dreamliner is the first plane to introduce a game-changing technology—lightweight plastic composites. As a result, this widebody long-haul jet is regarded as a technological wonder that is 20% more fuel efficient and 30% less costly to maintain than similar-sized planes. Not surprisingly, airlines around the world love it. In the seven years (2004–2011) before the 787 entered service, it became the fastest selling airliner in history, winning more than 800 orders. Its launch customer is All Nippon Airways (ANA), Japan's number one airline, which has ordered 55.

Despite the initial bugs that resulted in the grounding of the 787 fleet for several months in 2013, the Dreamliner is certainly valuable to the first airline to fly it. However, its novelty will soon disappear, as more than 800 planes will follow ANA's first 55 to enter service. In other words, the Dreamliner is valuable, not necessarily rare, and relatively easy to imitate—Boeing is happy to sell a copy to any airline that is willing to cough up US$170 million. In fact, ANA's archrival Japan Airlines is the world's second airlines that flies the Dreamliner, having launched its service in 2012.

What is ANA's response to hold on to its competitive advantage associated with the 787? It has asked Boeing to install bidet-toilets (washlets) that offer a variety of buttons controlling warm-water sprays and flushes for "the ultimate hygienic experience." This is an innovative but also desperate bid to attract more fastidious passengers from Japan where the washlet is common. Approximately 70% of Japanese households have a bidet. As service providers, airlines naturally brag about their efforts to make passengers "feel at home." Made by the top producer Toto, the bidet on board the Dreamliner, according to ANA, adds "another touch of home for Japanese passengers and a gentle introduction to Japanese domestic technology for those traveling to the country." In short, packing the mighty Dreamliner with the tiny washlet enhances the rarity and inimitability of ANA's passenger service.

In July 2007, when the Dreamliner was first unveiled at Boeing's plant in Everett, Washington, ANA chief executive Mineo Yamamoto proudly announced at the ceremony that the washlets onboard the 787 would be a key source of differentiation by "refreshing the parts other airlines cannot reach."

Sources: Based on (1) *Bloomberg Businessweek*, 2011, ANA: First in class, businessweek.com/adsections, (2) *Bloomberg Businessweek*, 2013, Don't dream it's over, January 28: 4–5; (3) *South China Morning Post*, 2007, Boeing unveils new, green 787 jetliner, July 10: A8; (4) All Nippon Airways, 2014, www.ana.co.jp/787.

Lisa Werner/Alamy

Only valuable and rare resources and capabilities have the potential to provide some temporary competitive advantage. Overall, the question of rarity is a reminder of the cliché: If everyone has it, you can't make money from it. For example, the quality of the Big Three automakers in the United States is now comparable with the best Asian and European rivals. However, even in their home country, the Big Three's quality improvements have not translated into stronger sales. Embarrassingly, in 2009, both GM and Chrysler, despite the decent quality of their cars, had to declare bankruptcy and be bailed out by the US government (and also by the Canadian government). The point is simple: Flawless high quality is now expected, is no longer rare, and, thus, provides no advantage.

4-4c Imitability

Valuable and rare resources and capabilities can be a source of competitive advantage only if competitors have a difficult time imitating them. While it is relatively easier to imitate a firm's *tangible* resources (such as plants), it is a lot more challenging and often impossible to imitate *intangible* capabilities (such as tacit knowledge, superior motivation, and managerial talents).

Imitation is difficult. Why? Two words: causal ambiguity, which refers to the difficulty of identifying the causal determinants of successful firm performance.[23] What exactly has caused LEGO to be such an enduring and continuously relevant company (see the Opening Case)? LEGO has no shortage of competitors and imitators. One natural question is: "How does LEGO do it?" Usually, a number of resources and capabilities will be nominated, such as an innovative culture, a commitment to precision manufacturing, a willingness to change, a strong leadership team, and a multinational presence. While all of these resources and capabilities are plausible, what *exactly* is it? This truly is a million-dollar (or billion-dollar) question, because knowing the answer is not only intriguing to scholars and students, but it can also be hugely profitable for LEGO's rivals. Unfortunately, outsiders usually have a hard time understanding what a firm does inside its boundaries. We can try, as many rivals have, to identify LEGO's recipe for success by drawing up a long list of possible reasons, labeled as "resources and capabilities" in our classroom discussion. But in the final analysis, as outsiders we are not sure.[24]

What is even more fascinating for scholars and students, and more frustrating for rivals, is that often managers of a focal firm such as LEGO do not know exactly what contributes to their firm's success. When interviewed, they can usually generate a long list of their contributing factors. To make matters worse, different managers within the same firm may have a different list. When probed as to which resource or capability is "it," they often suggest that it is all of the above in *combination*. This is probably one of the most interesting and paradoxical aspects of the resource-based view: If insiders have a hard time figuring out what unambiguously contributes to their firm's performance, it is not surprising that outsiders' efforts in understanding and imitating these capabilities are usually flawed and often fail.

Overall, valuable and rare, but imitable, resources and capabilities may give firms some temporary competitive advantage, leading to above-average performance for some period of time. However, such advantage is not likely to be sustainable. Shown by the example of LEGO, only valuable, rare, and *hard-to-imitate* resources and capabilities may potentially lead to sustained competitive advantage.

Causal ambiguity
The difficulty of identifying the actual cause of a firm's successful performance.

4-4d Organization

Even valuable, rare, and hard-to-imitate resources and capabilities may not give a firm a sustained competitive advantage if it is not properly organized.[25] Although movie stars represent some of the most valuable, rare, and hard-to-imitate (as well as highest-paid) resources, *most* movies flop. More generally, the question of organization asks: "How can a firm (such as a movie studio) be organized to develop and leverage the full potential of its resources and capabilities?"

Numerous components within a firm are relevant to the question of organization.[26] In a movie studio, these components include talents in "smelling" good ideas, photography crews, musicians, singers, makeup artists, animation specialists, and managers on the business side. These components are often called complementary assets,[27] because by themselves they cannot generate box office hits. For the favorite movie you saw most recently, do you still remember the names of its makeup artists? Of course not—you probably only remember the stars. However, stars alone cannot generate hit movies, either. It is the *combination* of star resources and complementary assets that create hit movies. "It may be that not just a few resources and capabilities enable a firm to gain a competitive advantage but that literally thousands of these organizational attributes, bundled together, generate such advantage."[28]

Another idea is social complexity, which refers to the socially complex ways of organizing that are typical of many firms. Many multinational firms consist of thousands of people scattered in many different countries. How they overcome cultural differences and organize as one corporate entity to achieve corporate goals is profoundly complex. Oftentimes, it is their invisible relationships that add value. Such organizationally embedded capabilities are thus very difficult for rivals to imitate. This emphasis on social complexity *refutes* what is half-jokingly called the "LEGO" view of the firm, in which a firm can be assembled (and disassembled) from modules of technology and people (a là LEGO toy blocks). By treating employees as identical and replaceable blocks, the "LEGO" view fails to realize that social capital associated with complex relationships and knowledge permeating many firms can be a source of competitive advantage.

Overall, only valuable, rare, and hard-to-imitate capabilities that are organizationally embedded and exploited can possibly lead to sustained competitive advantage and persistently above-average performance.[29] Because capabilities cannot be evaluated in isolation, the VRIO framework presents four interconnected and increasingly difficult hurdles for them to become a source of sustainable competitive advantage (Table 4.2). In other words, these four aspects come together as one "package" (see In Focus 4.2).

4-5 Debates and Extensions

Learning Objective
Participate in two leading debates concerning leveraging resources and capabilities.

Complementary asset
The combination of numerous resources and assets that enable a firm to gain a competitive advantage.

Social complexity
The socially intricate and interdependent ways firms are typically organized.

Like the institution-based viewed outlined in Chapters 2 and 3, the resource-based view has its fair share of controversies and debates. Here, we introduce two leading debates: (1) domestic resources versus international (cross-border) capabilities, and (2) offshoring versus not offshoring.

4-5a Domestic Resources versus International (Cross-Border) Capabilities

Do firms that are successful domestically have what it takes to win internationally? Some domestically successful firms continue to succeed overseas—think of LEGO

IN FOCUS 4.2

ENHANCING VRIO AT BURBERRY

Asked to name an iconic British luxury brand, most people would probably nominate Burberry. Founded in 1856, Burberry grew to become a leading global fashion house with £3.5 billion revenue in 2012. Most famous for its trench coats worn by soldiers in the trenches during World War I, Burberry became such a part of British culture that it earned a royal warrant as an official supplier to the royal family.

However, by the mid-2000s, Burberry had lost its focus. It had 23 licensees in a variety of products and locations around the world, each doing something different, ranging from dog cover-ups and leashes to kilts. In luxury, ubiquity by definition is the killer of exclusivity. Among numerous Burberry products, outerwear exemplified by the "boring old trench coat" only represented 20% of its global revenue. While luxury sales were growing globally, Burberry seemed to be losing out, with a lackluster growth rate of only 2% per year by 2006. Each of Burberry's two leading global rivals (LVMH and Gucci) had more than ten times Burberry's revenue and much higher growth. How could Burberry, which became a "David," grow against such "Goliaths"?

In 2006, with the arrival of the new CEO Angela Ahrendts, significant soul searching took place at Burberry. Deploying the classic resource-based logic (especially the VRIO framework), the firm realized that its greatest assets lay in its *Britishness*, more specifically its trench coat roots—hence the highest value it could deliver. Further, such a focus on Britain's positive country-of-origin image would be rare in a world largely populated by French and Italian luxury brands. It would also be difficult (or sometimes impossible) to imitate if this heritage were emphasized and strengthened.

With this powerful insight, Burberry adopted a new strategy centered on the iconic trench coat—its first social media platform was named www.artofthetrench.com. Before the transformation, Burberry sold just a few styles of trench coats and almost all were beige with the signature check lining. Now with centralized and consistent design (a significant intangible capability), it sells more than 300 products in a wide variety of styles and colors related to trench coats. By 2012, 60% of its revenue came from apparel, and outerwear made up more than half of that. Many of its stylish trench coats are priced over US$1,000. Further, instead of outsourcing, Burberry has concentrated its trench coat production at the Castleford factory in the north of England, adding more than 1,000 jobs in the UK in the last two years alone (of a global labor force of 9,000). In summary, a Burberry trench coat designed and manufactured in the UK is valuable, rare, and impossible to imitate by rivals.

The upshot? Burberry has been rewarded handsomely by the market. In five years (2007–2012), its revenue and operating income doubled. In 2011, Interbrand named it the fourth fastest-growing global brand (behind Apple, Google, and Amazon) and the fastest-growing luxury brand. So impressed was Apple that in 2013 it poached Ahrendts, who quit Burberry and became Apple's senior vice president in charge of retail and online operations.

Sources: Based on (1) A. Ahrendts, 2013, Burberry's CEO on turning an aging British icon into a global luxury brand, *Harvard Business Review*, January–February: 39–42; (2) *Daily Mail*, 2013, Burberry share price plummets after CEO Angela Ahrents quits fashion house to take key role at Apple, October 13: www.dailymail.co.uk; (3) M. W. Peng, 2014, High fashion fights recession, in M. W. Peng, *Global Strategy*, 3rd ed. (57–59), Cincinnati: Cengage Learning; (4) www.artofthetrench.com; (5) www.burberry.com.

(see the Opening Case). IKEA has found that its Scandinavian-style furniture, combined with do-it-yourself flat packaging, is popular around the globe. Thus, IKEA has become a global cult brand. The young generation in Russia is now known as the "IKEA Generation."

However, many other firms that are formidable domestically are burned badly overseas. Wal-Mart withdrew from Germany, India, and South Korea. Similarly, its leading global rival, Carrefour, had to exit the Czech Republic, Japan, Mexico, and South Korea. In electronics, Best Buy found it was the "worst buy" in China and had to quit the country. Similarly, Media Markt of Germany had to leave China in tears.

Are domestic resources and cross-border capabilities essentially the same? The answer can be either "Yes" or "No." This debate is an extension of the larger debate on whether international business (IB) is different from domestic business. The argument that IB is different is precisely the argument for having stand-alone IB courses in business schools. If the two are essentially the same, then it is possible to argue that IB fundamentally is about "business," which is well covered by strategy, finance, and other courses. (Most textbooks in these areas have at least one chapter on "international topics.") This question is obviously very important for companies and business schools. However, there is no right or wrong answer.

4-5b Offshoring versus Not Offshoring

As noted earlier, offshoring—or, more specifically, international (offshore) outsourcing—has emerged as a leading corporate movement in the 21st century.[30] Outsourcing low-end manufacturing to countries such as China and Mexico is now widely practiced. But increased outsourcing of high-end services, particularly IT and other business process outsourcing (BPO) services, to countries such as India is controversial. Because digitization and commoditization of service work are enabled only by the recent rise of the Internet and the reduction of international communication costs, it is debatable whether such offshoring proves to be a long-term benefit or hindrance to Western firms and economies.

Proponents argue that offshoring creates enormous value for firms and economies.[31] Western firms are able to tap into low-cost yet high-quality labor, translating into significant cost savings. Firms can also focus on their core capabilities, which may add more value than noncore (and often uncompetitive) activities. In turn, offshoring service providers, such as Infosys and Wipro, develop *their* core competencies in IT/BPO. A McKinsey study reports that for every dollar spent by US firms' offshoring in India, the US firms save 58 cents (see Table 4.3). Overall, US$1.46 of new wealth is created, of which the US economy captures US$1.13, through cost savings and increased exports to India, which buys Made-in-USA equipment, software, and services. India captures the other 33 cents through profits, wages, and taxes.[32] While acknowledging that some US employees may regrettably lose

Business process outsourcing (BPO)

Outsourcing business processes to third-party providers.

Table 4.3   Benefit of US$1 US Spending on Offshoring to India

Benefit to the United States	US$	Benefit to India	US$
Savings accruing to US investors/customers	0.58	Labor	0.10
Exports of US goods/services to providers in India	0.05	Profits retained in India	0.10
Profit transfer by US-owned operations in India back to the US	0.04	Suppliers	0.09
Net direct benefit retained in the United States	*0.67*	Central government taxes	0.03
Value from US labor reemployed	0.46	State government taxes	0.01
Net benefit to the United States	*1.13*	*Net benefit to India*	*0.33*

Source: Based on text in D. Farrell, 2005, Offshoring: Value creation through economic change, *Journal of Management Studies*, 42: 675–683. Farrell is director of the McKinsey Global Institute, and she refers to a McKinsey study.

their jobs, offshoring proponents suggest that, on balance, offshoring is a win-win solution for both US and Indian firms and economies. In other words, offshoring can be conceptualized as the latest incarnation of international trade (in tradable services), which theoretically will bring mutual gains to all involved countries (see Chapter 5).

Critics of offshoring make three points on strategic, economic, and political grounds. Strategically, according to some outsourcing gurus, if "even core functions like engineering, R&D, manufacturing, and marketing can—and often should—be moved outside,"[33] what is left of the firm? In manufacturing, US firms have gone down this path before, with disastrous results. In the 1960s, Radio Corporation of America (RCA) invented the color TV and then outsourced its production to Japan, a *low*-cost country at that time. Fast-forward to 2010: the United States no longer has any US-owned color TV producers left. The nationality of RCA itself, after being bought and sold several times, is now *Chinese* (France's Thomson sold RCA to China's TCL in 2003). Critics argue that offshoring nurtures rivals.[34] Why are Indian IT/BPO firms now emerging as strong global rivals to Western firms such as IBM? It is in part because they built up their capabilities doing work for IBM in the 1990s to fix the "millennium bug" (Y2K) problem.

In manufacturing, many Asian firms, which used to be original equipment manufacturers (OEMs) executing design blueprints provided by Western firms, now want to have a piece of the action in design by becoming original design manufacturers (ODMs) (see Figure 4.5). Having mastered low-cost and high-quality manufacturing, Asian firms such as BenQ, Compal, Flextronics, Hon Hai/Foxconn, and Huawei are indeed capable of capturing some design function from Western firms such as Dell, HP, Kodak, and Nokia. Therefore, increasing outsourcing of design work by Western firms may accelerate their own long-run demise. A number of Asian OEMs (such as Taiwan's HTC), now quickly becoming ODMs, have openly announced that their real ambition is to become original brand manufacturers (OBMs). Thus, according to critics of offshoring, isn't the writing already on the wall?

Economically, critics contend that they are not sure whether developed economies, on the whole, actually gain more. While shareholders and corporate high-flyers embrace offshoring (see Chapter 1), offshoring increasingly results in job

---

Figure 4.5 **From Original *Equipment* Manufacturer (OEM) to Original *Design* Manufacturer (ODM)**

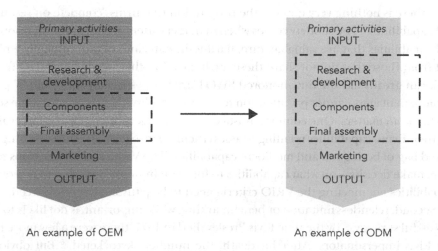

An example of OEM   An example of ODM

Note: Dotted lines represent organizational boundaries. One further extension is to become an original *brand* manufacturer (OBM), which would incorporate brand ownership and management in the marketing area. For graphic simplicity, it is not shown here.

Original equipment manufacturer (OEM)

Firm that executes design blueprints provided by Western firms and manufactures such products.

Original design manufacturer (ODM)

Firm that both designs and manufactures products.

Original brand manufacturer (OBM)

Firm that designs, manufactures, and markets branded products.

losses in high-end areas such as design, R&D, and IT/BPO. While white-collar individuals who lose jobs will naturally hate it, the net impact (consolidating all economic gains and losses including job losses) on developed economies may still be negative.

Finally, critics make the political argument that many large US firms claim that they are global companies and, consequently, that they should neither represent nor be bound by American values any more. According to this view, all that these firms are interested in is the cheapest and most exploitable labor. Not only is work commoditized, people (such as IT programmers) are degraded as tradable commodities that can be jettisoned. As a result, large firms that outsource work to emerging economies are often accused of being unethical, destroying jobs at home, ignoring corporate social responsibility, violating customer privacy (for example, by sending medical records, tax returns, and credit card numbers to be processed overseas), and in some cases undermining national security. Not surprisingly, the debate often becomes political, emotional, and explosive when such accusations are made. More recently, as the cost of producing in China rises because of rising labor cost and unreliable quality, some Western firms have brought back the work back to their home countries—a process known as reshoring.

It is important to note that this debate takes place primarily in developed economies. There is little debate in emerging economies, because they stand to gain from such offshoring to them. Taking a page from the Indian playbook, the Philippines, with numerous English-speaking professionals, is trying to eat some of India's lunch. Northeast China, where Japanese is widely taught, is positioning itself as an ideal location for call centers for Japan. Central and Eastern Europe gravitates towards serving Western Europe. Central and South American firms want to grab call center contracts for the large Hispanic market in the United States.

Learning Objective
Draw implications for action.

4-6 Management Savvy

How does the resource-based view answer the big question in global business: "What determines the success and failure of firms around the globe?" The answer is straightforward. Fundamentally, some firms outperform others because the winners possess some valuable, rare, hard-to-imitate, and organizationally embedded resources and capabilities that competitors do not have.

The resource-based view thus suggests four implications for action (see Table 4.4). First, there is nothing very novel in the proposition that firms "compete on resources and capabilities." The subtlety comes when managers attempt to distinguish resources and capabilities that are valuable, rare, hard-to-imitate, and organizationally embedded from those that do not share these attributes. In other words, the VRIO framework can greatly aid the time-honored SWOT analysis, especially the S and W parts. Because managers cannot pay attention to every capability, they must have some sense of what *really* matters. One common mistake that managers often make when evaluating their firms' capabilities is failing to assess them relative to rivals', thus resulting in a mixed bag of both good and mediocre capabilities. The VRIO framework helps managers make decisions on what capabilities to focus on in-house and what to outsource. Capabilities not meeting the VRIO criteria need to be jettisoned or outsourced.

Second, relentless imitation or benchmarking, while important, is not likely to be a successful strategy.[35] By the time Elvis Presley died in 1977, there were a few more than 100 Elvis impersonators. After his death, the number skyrocketed.[36] But obviously none of these imitators achieved any fame remotely close to the star status attained by the King of Rock 'n' Roll. Imitators have a tendency to mimic the most visible, the

Reshoring
Moving formerly offshored activities back to the home country of the focal firm.

Table 4.4	Implications for action

- Managers need to build firm strengths based on the VRIO framework.

- Relentless imitation or benchmarking, while important, is not likely to be a successful strategy.

- Managers need to build up resources and capabilities for future competition.

- Students need to make themselves into "untouchables" whose job cannot be easily outsourced.

most obvious, and, consequently, the *least* important practices of winning firms (and musicians). At best, follower firms that meticulously replicate every resource possessed by winning firms can hope to attain competitive parity. Firms so well endowed with resources to imitate others may be better off by developing their own unique and innovative capabilities—as Natura has done in Brazil (see the Closing Case).

Third, a competitive advantage that is sustained does not imply that it will last forever, which is not realistic in today's global competition. The failure of managers to appreciate this insight can run an otherwise highly capable firm to the ground. In fact, competitive advantage has become shorter in duration.[37] All a firm can hope for is a competitive advantage that can be sustained for as long as possible. Over time, all advantages erode.[38] Each of IBM's product-related advantages associated with tabulating machines, mainframes, and PCs was sustained for a period of time. But, eventually, these advantages disappeared. Even IBM's newer focus on software and servers is severely challenges by cloud computing heavyweights such as Amazon.[39] The lesson for all firms, including current market leaders, is to develop strategic *foresight*—"over-the-horizon radar" is a good metaphor. Such strategic foresight enables firms to anticipate future needs and move early to identify and develop resources and capabilities for future competition.

Finally, here is a very personal and relevant implication for action. As a student who is probably studying this book in a developed (read: high-wage and, thus, high-cost!) country such as the United States, you may be wondering: What do I get out of this? How do I cope with the frightening future of global competition? There are two lessons you can draw. First, the whole debate on offshoring—a part of the larger debate on globalization—is relevant and directly affects your future as a manager, a consumer, and a citizen. So, don't be a coach potato! You should be active, get involved, and be prepared, because it is not only "their" debate, but it is *yours* as well. Second, be very serious about the VRIO framework of the resource-based view. While the resource-based view has been developed to advise firms, there is no reason you cannot develop that into a resource-based view of the *individual*. In other words, you can use the VRIO framework to make yourself into an "untouchable"—a person whose job cannot be outsourced, as Thomas Friedman defines it in *The World Is Flat* (2005). An untouchable individual's job cannot be outsourced, because he or she possesses valuable, rare, and hard-to-imitate capabilities indispensable to an organization. This won't be easy. But you really don't want to be mediocre. A generation ago, American parents told their kids, "Eat your food—kids in China and India are starving." Now, Friedman would advise you, "Study this book and leverage your education—students in China and India are starving for your job."[40]

CHAPTER SUMMARY/LEARNING OBJECTIVES

4-1 Define resources and capabilities.

- "Resources" and "capabilities" are tangible and intangible assets a firm uses to choose and implement its strategies.

4-2 Explain how value is created from a firm's resources and capabilities.

- A value chain consists a stream of activities from upstream to downstream that add value.
- A SWOT analysis engages managers to ascertain a firm's strengths and weaknesses on an activity-by-activity basis relative to rivals.

4-3 Articulate the difference between keeping an activity in-house and outsourcing it.

- Outsourcing is defined as turning over all or part of an organizational activity to an outside supplier.
- An activity with a high degree of industry commonality and a high degree of commoditization can be outsourced, and an industry-specific and firm-specific (proprietary) activity is better performed in-house.
- On any given activity, the four choices for managers in terms of modes and locations are (1) offshoring, (2) onshoring, (3) captive sourcing/FDI, and (4) domestic in-house activity.

4-4 Explain what a VRIO framework is.

- A VRIO framework suggests that only resources and capabilities that are valuable (V), rare (R), inimitable (I), and organizationally (O) embedded will generate sustainable competitive advantage.

4-5 Participate in two leading debates concerning resources and capabilities.

- (1) Domestic resources versus international capabilities and (2) offshoring versus not offshoring.

4-6 Draw implications for action.

- Managers need to build firm strengths based on the VRIO framework.
- Relentless imitation or benchmarking, while important, is not likely to be a successful strategy.
- Managers need to build up resources and capabilities for future competition.
- Students are advised to make themselves into "untouchables" whose jobs cannot be outsourced.

KEY TERMS

Benchmarking, 102

Business process outsourcing (BPO), 110

Capability, 99

Captive sourcing, 104

Causal ambiguity, 107

Commoditization, 102

Complementary asset, 108

Intangible resource and capability, 99

Offshoring, 104

Onshoring, 104

Original brand manufacturer (OBM), 111

Original design manufacturer (ODM), 111

Original equipment manufacturer (OEM), 111

Outsourcing, 103

Reshoring, 112

Resource, 98

Social complexity, 108

SWOT analysis, 98

Tangible resource and capability, 99

Value chain, 101

VRIO framework, 105

REVIEW QUESTIONS

1. Describe at least three types of tangible and intangible resources and capabilities.

2. In the text, are human resources used as an example of tangible or intangible resources? Do you agree with that classification? Why or why not?

3. What is meant by "commoditization"?

4. When analyzing a value chain with a VRIO framework, what is the most important question to begin with and why?

5. Show how the rarity of capabilities is an advantage for both a firm and a job seeker.

6. What is the difference between outsourcing and captive sourcing?

7. How can SWOT analysis be used in value chain analysis? Use an example to support your answer.

8. Which is more difficult: imitating a rival's tangible resources or its intangible resources?

9. How do complementary assets and social complexity influence a firm's organization?

10. If a firm is successful domestically, is it likely to be successful internationally? Why or why not?

11. After reviewing the arguments for and against offshoring, state your opinion on this issue.

12. *ON CULTURE:* How can differences in values and traditions affect the success of offshoring?

13. Identify a developed country on PengAtlas Map 1.1, and explain why it may be the location of offshoring from a firm in an emerging economy.

14. What is one common mistake that managers often make when evaluating their firm's capabilities?

15. What is the likely result of relentless imitation or benchmarking?

16. Why is it a good idea for the VRIO framework to focus on future competition?

17. Check Map 1.1, and imagine that your firm is headquartered in a developed country. Pick an emerging economy that your firm may enter. Explain what resources and capabilities your firm has that may enable it to succeed in this new market.

CRITICAL DISCUSSION QUESTIONS

1. Pick any pair of rivals (such as Samsung/Apple, Boeing/Airbus, and LEGO/Hasbro), and explain why one outperforms another.

2. Rank your business school relative to the top three rival schools in terms of the following six dimensions. If you were the dean with a limited budget, from a VRIO standpoint, where would you invest precious financial resources to make your school number one among rivals. Why?

	Your school	Competitor 1	Competitor 2	Competitor 3
Perceived reputation				
Faculty strength				
Student quality				
Administrative efficiency				
Information systems				
Building maintenance				

3. *ON ETHICS:* **Since firms read information posted on competitors' websites, is it ethical to provide false information on resources and capabilities on corporate websites? Do the benefits outweigh the costs?**

BUSINESS INSIGHTS GLOBAL

GLOBAL ACTION

1. **Currently, your firm has manufacturing and logistics units in the Russian cities of Moscow and Saint Petersburg, which provide access to Russia's vast countrywide market. However, recent business regulations have discouraged growth in specific regions of the country. As such, you have been asked to reconfigure your firm's strategy in Russia. Identify the location(s) where you should move operations. Provide detailed and compelling rationale to support your decision.**

2. **The technology company that you work for wants to enter a foreign market for the first time. The objective is for the firm to make a sustainable international investment that can create long-term competitive advantages and allow it to be recognized as important in the industry. Evaluate the opportunities available to your company by assessing the national conditions among leading emerging economies.**

CLOSING CASE

EMERGING MARKETS: Natura Makes Brazil Look Beautiful

Most people in the world, including many who have never been to Brazil, would agree that Brazil is beautiful. Likewise, Brazilians are widely known to be beautiful. However, beauty has to be maintained. Brazilian women's spending on beauty products is legendary. Although Brazil has the fifth-largest population (with 200 million people) and the seventh-largest economy in the world, it has become the second-largest market for beauty products—only behind the United States. Beauty products spending per woman in Brazil matches that in Britain, which has a much higher income. While Brazil is obviously the attractive B in BRIC, beauty products are among Brazil's most attractive consumer markets, with multinationals such as Avon, Estée Lauder, L'Oreal, P&G, Shiseido, and Unilever salivating over a share of the growing spoils. Emerging as the leading foreign player, Avon, in fact, now sells more cosmetics in Brazil than in the

United States. Yet, the queen of Brazil's highly attractive and competitive market is its home-grown Natura. It is everywhere in Brazil. Its cosmetics, perfume, and hygiene products are in 60% of all households and it leads the market with a 14% share in terms of sales (a total of US$3 billion). Founded in 1969 and listed on the São Paulo Stock Exchange since 2004, Natura is already the world's 20th most valuable cosmetics brand. But since 90% of its sales are in Brazil and almost 100% of its sales are in Latin America, few people outside the region have heard about it.

What is Natura's recipe for dominating such a large and diverse market? Its recipe has at least two ingredients. First, by definition, Natura is green. About 70% of its products are plant-based (by dry weight) and approximately 10% come from the Amazon region, where it purchases from village co-operatives and indigenous tribes. Natura is also among the first cosmetics firms in the world to pay attention to the specific hair-care needs of black women, which tend to be ignored by mainstream firms.

Second, Natura relies on a small army of 1.2 million direct sales ladies, who work like the legendary Avon Ladies and since 2006 have been beating the Avon Ladies—Natura's number-one foreign rival in the country. With US$3 billion sales, Natura's total number of employees is only 6,200. In comparison, Avon worldwide has US$10 billion sales but has 37,000 employees (and 6.4 million Avon Ladies). Thanks to Brazil's sky-high labor costs and tax rates, Natura has deliberately kept its employee base small in order to save cost. Since 1974, its marketing has been relying on direct sales, leveraging hard-working women who go the extra mile (sometimes literally penetrating into the jungles of the Amazon) to deliver products. Direct sales thus give Natura a cost advantage relative to its number-one domestic rival, O Boticário, which relies on a traditional retail format. An additional beauty of direct sales is that Natura's sales force is directly in touch with end-users, whose needs, wants, and aspirations can be conveyed back to corporate headquarters for new product development.

Facing the onslaught of multinational cosmetics giants, Natura has realized that the best defense is offense. In 2005, Natura opened its first boutique in Paris, announcing its arrival in the cosmetics capital of the world. While progress has been slow overseas (in part thanks to the hot growth back home, which dominates executive attention and capital allocation), Natura is indeed committed in making a big push globally. While around the world Brazil is famous for commodity exports such as coffee and soy beans and for one high-tech firm (Embraer, which is renowned for its regional jets), no Brazilian consumer products have made a big splash overseas. Can Natura leverage Brazil's positive country-of-origin effect of being beautiful? In addition to soccer and beaches, most people associate Brazil with the rainforest and biodiversity, which seems to be an obvious advantage for a firm that calls itself Natura using a heavy dose of ingredients from the Amazon. So stay tuned . . .

CASE DISCUSSION QUESTIONS

1. In most countries around the world, the beauty products industry is dominated by a small set of multinational giants named in the case. Why in Brazil none of them has emerged as a market leader?

2. From a VRIO standpoint, what is behind Natura's enviable performance?

3. Beyond Latin America, which foreign markets should Natura first enter? Will it be successful there?

Sources: Based on (1) J. Chelekis & S. M. Mudambi, 2010, MNCs and micro-entrepreneurship in emerging economies: The case of Avon in the Amazon, *Journal of International Management*, 16: 412–424; (2) J. Chelekis & S. M. Mudambi, 2014, Direct selling at the base of the pyramid, in M. W. Peng, *Global Business*, 3rd ed. (pp. 28–30), Cincinnati: Cengage Learning; (3) *Economist*, 2013, Consumer goods: Looks good, September 28 (special report): 14–15.

NOTES

[**Journal acronyms**] **AME**—*Academy of Management Executive;* **AMJ**—*Academy of Management Journal;* **AMR**—*Academy of Management Review;* **BW**—*BusinessWeek* (before 2010) or *Bloomberg Businessweek* (since 2010); **CMR**—*California Management Review;* **GSJ**—*Global Strategy Journal;* **HBR**—*Harvard Business Review;* **JIBS**—*Journal of International Business Studies;* **JIM**—*Journal of International Management;* **JM**—*Journal of Management;* **JMS**—*Journal of Management Studies;* **JWB**—*Journal of World Business;* **MIR**—*Management International Review;* **OSc**—*Organization Science;* **SMJ**—*Strategic Management Journal*

1 J. Barney, 1991, Firm resources and sustained competitive advantage, *JM*, 17: 99–120; M. W. Peng, 2001, The resource-based view and international business, *JM*, 27: 803–829.

2 A. Cuervo-Cazurra & L. Dau, 2009, Promarket reforms and firm profitability in developing countries, *AMJ*, 52: 1348–1368; G. Gao, J. Murray, M. Kotabe, & J. Lu, 2010, A "strategy tripod" perspective on export behaviors, *JIBS*, 41: 377–396; D. Sirmon, M. Hitt, J. Arregle, & J. Campbell, 2010, The dynamic interplay of capability strengths and weaknesses, *SMJ*, 31: 1386–1409.

3 J. A. Adegbesan, 2009, On the origins of competitive advantage, *AMR*, 34: 463–475; M. Sun & E. Tse, 2009, The resource-based view of competitive advantage in two-sided markets, *JMS*, 46: 45–64.

4 M. W. Peng & P. Heath, 1996, The growth of the firm in planned economies in transition, *AMR*, 21: 492–528. See also W. Egelhoff & E. Frese, 2009, Understanding managers' preferences for internal markets versus business planning, *JIM*, 15: 77–91; A. Goerzen & P. Beamish, 2007, The Penrose effect, *MIR*, 47: 221–239; H. Greve, 2008, A behavioral theory of firm growth, *AMJ*, 51: 476–494; M. Huesch, 2013, Are there always synergies between productive resources and resource deployment capabilities? *SMJ*, 34: 1288–1313; T. Reus, A. Ranft, B. Lamont, & G. Adams, 2009, An interpretive systems view of knowledge investments, *AMR*, 34: 382–400; S. Sonenshein, 2014, How organization foster the creative use of resources, *AMJ*, 57: 814–848.

5 J. Barney, 2001, Is the resource-based view a useful perspective for strategic management research? (p. 54) *AMR*, 26: 41–56.

6 J. Denrell, C. Fang, & Z. Zhao, 2013, Inferring superior capabilities from sustained superior performance, *SMJ*, 34: 182–196; Y. Kor & A. Mesko, 2013, Dynamic managerial capabilities, *SMJ*, 34: 233–244; G. Lee, 2008, Relevance of organizational capabilities and its dynamics, *SMJ*, 29: 1257–1280; D. Teece, 2007, Explicating dynamic capabilities, *SMJ*, 28: 1319–1350.

7 J. Barney, 2002, *Gaining and Sustaining Competitive Advantage*, 2nd ed. (p. 157), Upper Saddle River, NJ: Prentice Hall.

8 M. Porter, 1985, *Competitive Advantage*, New York: Free Press.

9 A. Parmigiani, 2007, Why do firms both make and buy? *SMJ*, 28: 285–311; M. W. Peng, Y. Zhou, & A. York, 2006, Behind make or buy decisions in export strategy, *JWB*, 41: 289–300.

10 S. Beugelsdijk, T. Pedersen, & B. Petersen, 2009, Is there a trend toward global value chain specialization? *JIM*, 15: 126–141; K. Coucke & L. Sleuwaegen, 2008, Offshoring as a survival strategy, *JIBS*, 39: 1261–1277; J. Hatonen & T. Eriksson, 2009, 30+ years of research and practice of outsourcing, *JIM*, 15: 142–155; P. Jensen, 2009, A learning perspective on the offshoring of advanced services, *JIM*, 15: 181–193; J. Kedia & D. Mukherjee, 2009, Understanding offshoring, *JWB*, 44: 250–261; K. Kumar, P. van Fenema, & M. von Glinow, 2009, Offshoring and the global distribution of work, *JIBS*, 40: 642–667; Q. Li, P. Maggitti, K. Smith, P. Tesluk, & R. Katila, 2013, Top management attention to innovation, *AMJ*, 56: 893–916; S. Mudambi & S. Tallman, 2010, Make, buy, or ally? *JMS*, 47: 1434–1456; P. Puranam, R. Gulati, & S. Bhattacharya, 2013, How much

to make and how much to buy? *SMJ*, 34: 1145–1161; G. Trautmann, L. Bals, & E. Hartmann, 2009, Global sourcing in integrated network structures, *JIM*, 15: 194–208; C. Weigelt & M. Sarkar, 2012, Performance implications of outsourcing for technological innovations, *SMJ*, 33: 189–216.

11 S. Kotha & K. Srikanth, 2013, Managing a global partnership model, *GSJ*, 3: 41–66.

12 S. Lahiri, B. Kedia, & D. Mukherjee, 2012, The impact of management capability on the resource-performance linkage, *JWB*, 47: 145–155; R. Mudambi & M. Venzin, 2010, The strategic nexus of offshoring and outsourcing decisions, *JMS*, 47: 1510–1533; H. Safizadeh, J. Field, & L. Ritzman, 2008, Sourcing practices and boundaries of the firm in the financial services industry, *SMJ*, 29: 79–91; C. Weigelt, 2013, Leveraging supplier capabilities, *SMJ*, 34: 1–21.

13 D. Gregorio, M. Musteen, & D. Thomas, 2009, Offshore outsourcing as a source of international competitiveness of SMEs, *JIBS*, 40: 969–988; D. Griffith, N. Harmancioglu, & C. Droge, 2009, Governance decisions for the offshore outsourcing of new product development in technology intensive markets, *JWB*, 44: 217–224; C. Grimpe & U. Kaiser, 2010, Balancing internal and external knowledge acquisition, *JMS*, 47: 1483–1509; M. Kenney, S. Massini, & T. Murtha, 2009, Offshoring administrative and technical work, *JIBS*, 40: 887–900; A. Lewin, S. Massini, & C. Peeters, 2009, Why are companies offshoring innovation? *JIBS*, 40: 901–925; Y. Li, Z. Wei, & Y. Liu, 2010, Strategic orientation, knowledge acquisition and firm performance, *JMS* 47: 1457–1482.

14 J. Doh, K. Bunyaratavej, & E. Hahn, 2009, Separable but not equal, *JIBS*, 40: 926–943; J. Hatonen, 2009, Making the locational choice, *JIM*, 15: 61–76; R. Liu, D. Fails, & B. Scholnick, 2011, Why are different services outsourced to different countries? *JIBS*, 42: 558–571; M. Demirbag & K. Glaister, 2010, Factors determining offshore location choice for R&D projects, *JMS*, 47: 1534–1560; S. Zaheer, A. Lamin, & M. Subramani, 2009, Cluster capabilities or ethnic ties? *JIBS*, 40: 944–968.

15 F. Contractor, V. Kuma, S. Kundu, & T. Pedersen, 2010, Reconceptualizing the firm in a world of outsourcing and offshoring, *JMS*, 47: 1417–1433.

16 A. Pande, 2011, How to make onshoring work, *HBR*, March: 30.

17 D. Levy, 2005, Offshoring in the new global political economy (p. 687), *JMS*, 42: 685–693.

18 Barney, 2002, *Gaining and Sustaining Competitive Advantage* (pp. 159–174).

19 R. Adner & R. Kapoor, 2010, Value creation innovation ecosystems, *SMJ*, 31: 306–333; F. Bridoux, R. Coeurderoy, & R. Durand, 2011, Heterogenous motives and the collective creation of value, *AMR*, 36: 711–730; O. Chatain & P. Zemsky, 2011, Value creation and value capture with frictions, *SMJ*, 32: 1206–1231; J. Grahovac & D. Miller, 2009, Competitive advantage and performance, *SMJ*, 30: 1192–1212; T. Holcomb, M. Holmes, & B. Connelly, 2009, Making the most of what you have, *SMJ*, 30: 457–485; M. Kunc & J. Morecroft, 2010, Managerial decision making and firm performance under a resource-based paradigm, *SMJ*, 31: 1164–1182; V. La, P. Patterson, & C. Styles, 2009, Client-perceived performance and value in professional B2B services, *JIBS*, 40: 274–300.

20 D. Sirmon, S. Gove, & M. Hitt, 2008, Resource management in dyadic competitive rivalry, *AMJ*, 51: 919–935.

21 *BW*, 2011, Can this IBMer keep Big Blue's edge? October 31: 31–32.

22 F. Aime, S. Johnson, J. Ridge, & A. Hill, 2010, The routine may be stable but the advantage is not, *SMJ*, 31: 75–87; D. Tzabbar, 2009,

When does scientist recruitment affect technological repositioning? *AMJ*, 52: 873–896; T. Zenger, 2013, Strategy: The uniqueness challenge, *HBR*, November: 52–58.

23 A. King, 2007, Disentangling interfirm and intrafirm casual ambiguity, *AMR*, 32: 156–178.

24 S. Jonsson & P. Regner, 2009, Normative barriers to imitation, *SMJ*, 30: 517–536; F. Polidoro & P. Toh, 2011, Letting rivals come close or warding them off? *AMJ*, 54: 369–392; H. Posen, J. Lee, & S. Yi, 2013, The power of imperfect imitation, *SMJ*, 34: 149–164.

25 I. Kastalli, B. Van Looy, & A. Neely, 2013, Steering manufacturing firms towards service business model innovation, *CMR*, 56: 100–123; M. Kownatzki, J. Walter, S. Floyd, & C. Lechner, 2013, Corporate control and the speed of strategic business unit decision making, *AMJ*, 56: 1295–1324; A. Krzeminska, G. Hoetker, & T. Mellewigt, 2013, Reconceptualizing plural sourcing, *SMJ*, 34: 1614–1627; P. Liesch, P. Buckley, B. Simonin, & G. Knight, 2012, Organizing the modern firm in the worldwide market for market transactions, *MIR*, 52: 3–21; Y. Luo, S. Wang, Q. Zheng, & V. Jayaraman, 2012, Task attributes and process integraton in business process offshoring, *JIBS*, 43: 498–524.

26 G. Carnabuci & E. Operti, 2013, Where do firms' recombinant capabilities come from? *SMJ*, 34: 1591–1613; S. Ethiraj, N. Ramasubbu, & M. Krishnan, 2012, Does complexity deter customer-focus? *SMJ*, 33: 137–161; M. Gruber, F. Heinemann, M. Brettel, & S. Hungeling, 2010, Configurations of resources and capabilities and their performance implications, *SMJ*, 31: 1337–1356; R. Ployhart, C. Van Iddekinge, & W. Mackenzie, 2011, Acquiring and developing human capital in service contexts, *AMJ*, 54: 353–368; R. Sinha & C. Noble, 2008, The adoption of radical manufacturing technologies and firm survival, *SMJ*, 29: 943–962; K. Srikanth & P. Puranam, 2011, Integrating distributed work, *SMJ*, 32: 849–875.

27 T. Chi & A. Seth, 2009, A dynamic model of the choice of mode for exploiting complementary capabilities, *JIBS*, 40: 365–387; A. Hess & F. Rothaermel, 2011, When are assets complementary? *SMJ*, 32: 895–909.

28 J. Barney, 1997, *Gaining and Sustaining Competitive Advantage* (p. 155), Reading, MA: Addison-Wesley.

29 G. Ray, L. Xue, & J. Barney, 2013, Impact of information technology capital on firm scope and performance, *AMJ*, 56: 1125–1147.

30 F. Ceci & A. Prencipe, 2013, Does distance hinder coordination? *JIM*, 19: 324–332; J. Chen, R. McQueen, & P. Sun, 2013, Knowledge transfer and knowledge building at offshored technical support centers, *JIM*, 19: 362–376; P. Jensen, M. Larsen, & T. Pedersen, 2013, The organizational design of offshoring, *JIM*, 19: 315–323; R. Raman, D. Chadee, B. Roxas, & S. Michailova, 2013, Effects of partnership quality, talent management, and global mindset on performance of offshore IT service providers in India, *JIM*, 19: 333–346; A. Soderberg, S. Krishna, & P. Bjorn, 2013, Global software development, *JIM*, 19: 347–361;

31 D. Mukherjee, A. Gaur, & A. Dutta, 2013, Creating value through offshore outsourcing, *JIM*, 19: 377–389.

32 D. Farrell, 2005, Offshoring, *JMS*, 42: 675–683.

33 M. Gottfredson, R. Puryear, & S. Phillips, 2005, Strategic sourcing (p. 132), *HBR*, February: 132–139.

34 C. Rossetti & T. Choi, 2005, On the dark side of strategic sourcing, *AME*, 19: 46–60.

35 K. Kim & W. Tsai, 2012, Social comparison among competing firms, *SMJ*, 33: 115–136.

36 D. Burrus, 2011, *Flash Foresight* (p. 11), New York: HarperCollins.

37 M. Chari & P. David, 2012, Sustaining superior performance in an emerging economy, *SMJ*, 33: 217–229; R. D'Aveni, G. Dagnino, & K. Smith, 2010, The age of temporary advantage, *SMJ*, 31: 1371–1385; D. Souder & P. Bromiley, 2012, Explaining temporal orientation, *SMJ*, 33: 550–569.

38 G. Pacheco-de-Almeida, 2010, Erosion, time compression, and self-displacement of leaders in hypercompetitive environments, *SMJ*, 31: 1498–1526.

39 *BW*, 2014, It's not us, it's you: Why customers are breaking up with IBM, May 26: 58–63.

40 The author's paraphrase based on T. Friedman, 2005, *The World Is Flat* (p. 237), New York: Farrar, Straus, & Giroux.

Map 1.1 Developed Economies, Emerging Economies, and the Group of 20 (G-20)

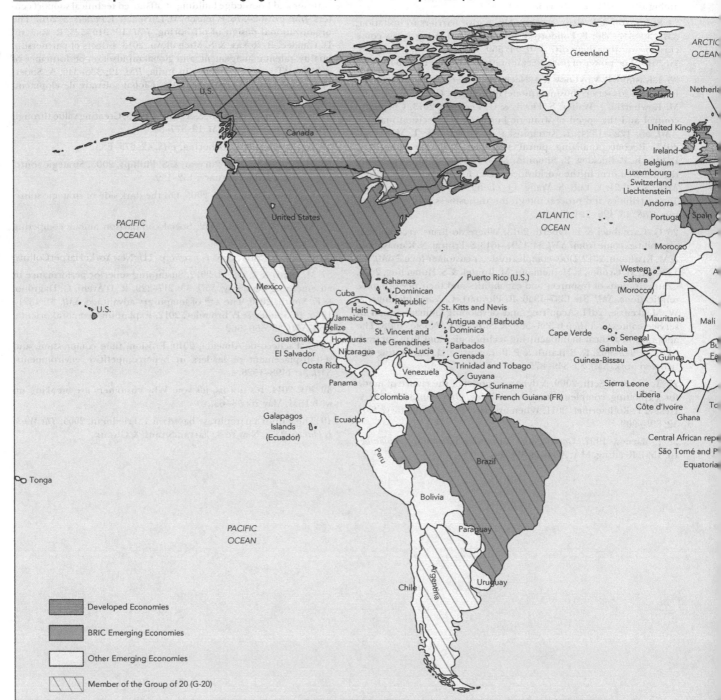

Developed Economies

BRIC Emerging Economies

Other Emerging Economies

Member of the Group of 20 (G-20)

* The G-20 includes 19 individual countries—Argentina, Australia, Brazil, Canada, China, France, Germany, India, Indonesia, Italy, Japan, Mexico, Russia, Saudi Arabia, South Africa, South Korea, Turkey, the United Kingdom, and the United States—along with the European Union (EU).

Sources: IMF, www.imf.org; US Census Bureau, International Database, *World Factbook*, 2014. The IMF recognizes 182 countries and economies. It labels developed economies "advanced economies", and labels emerging economies "emerging and developing economies".

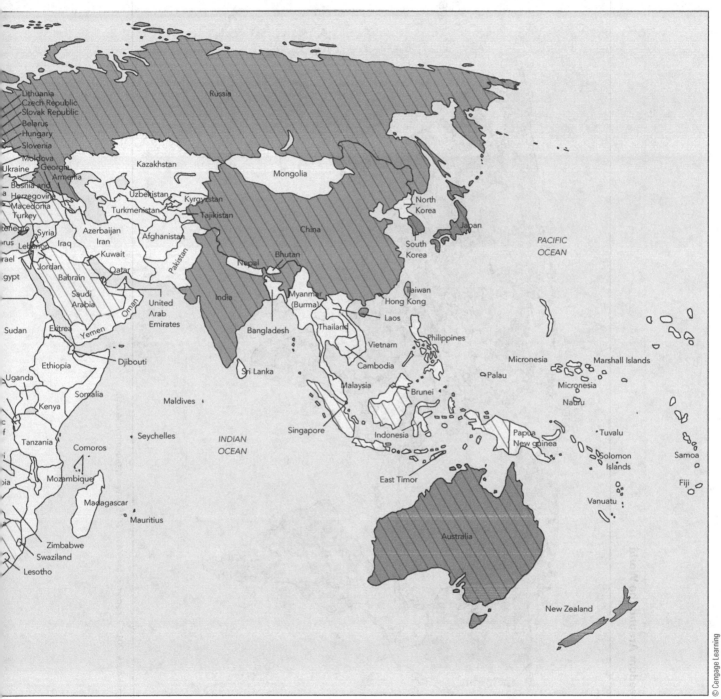

Lithuania
Czech Republic
Slovak Republic
Belarus
Hungary
Slovenia
Moldova
Ukraine Georgia
Bosnia and Armenia
a Herzegovina
Macedonia
Turkey
enegro
Syria Azerbaijan
us Iraq Iran
Lebanon Kuwait
Jordan Qatar
rael
gypt Bahrain
Saudi
Arabia Oman
Sudan Eritrea Yemen
Ethiopia Djibouti
Uganda
Somalia
Kenya Maldives
Seychelles
Tanzania Comoros
Mozambique
Madagascar
Mauritius
Zimbabwe
Swaziland
Lesotho

Russia

Kazakhstan

Mongolia

Uzbekistan Kyrgyzstan

Turkmenistan Tajikistan

Afghanistan

China

North
Korea

Japan

South
Korea

PACIFIC
OCEAN

Pakistan

Nepal Bhutan

Myanmar
(Burma)

Taiwan

Hong Kong

United
Arab
Emirates

India

Laos

Bangladesh

Thailand

Vietnam

Cambodia

Philippines

Sri Lanka

Malaysia

Micronesia

Marshall Islands

Palau

Micronesia

Brunei

Nauru

Singapore

Indonesia

INDIAN
OCEAN

Papua
New guinea

Tuvalu

Solomon
Islands

Samoa

East Timor

Vanuatu

Fiji

Australia

New Zealand

© Cengage Learning

Map 1.2   Political Freedom Around the World

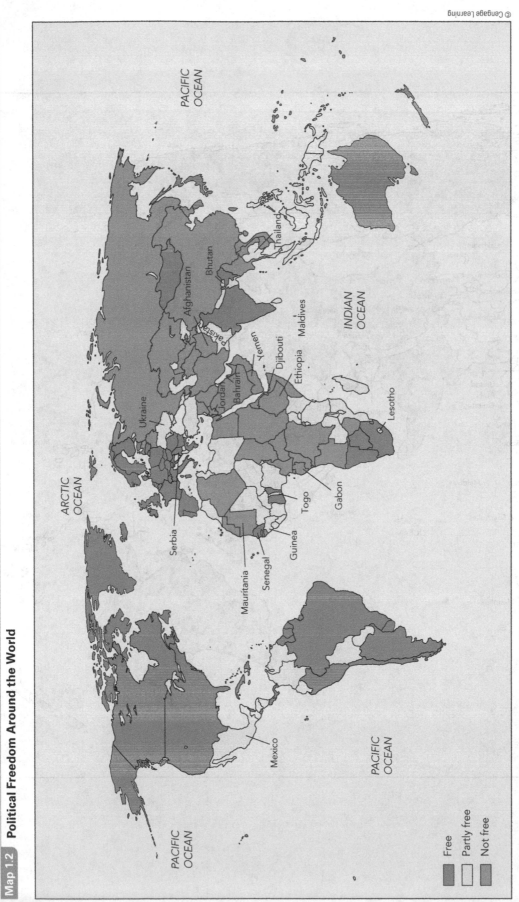

Free
Partly free
Not free

Source: Adapted from Freedom House, 2015, *Freedom in the World 2015*, www.freedomhouse.org.

© Cengage Learning

© Cengage Learning

Map 1.3 **Examples of Legal Systems Around the World**

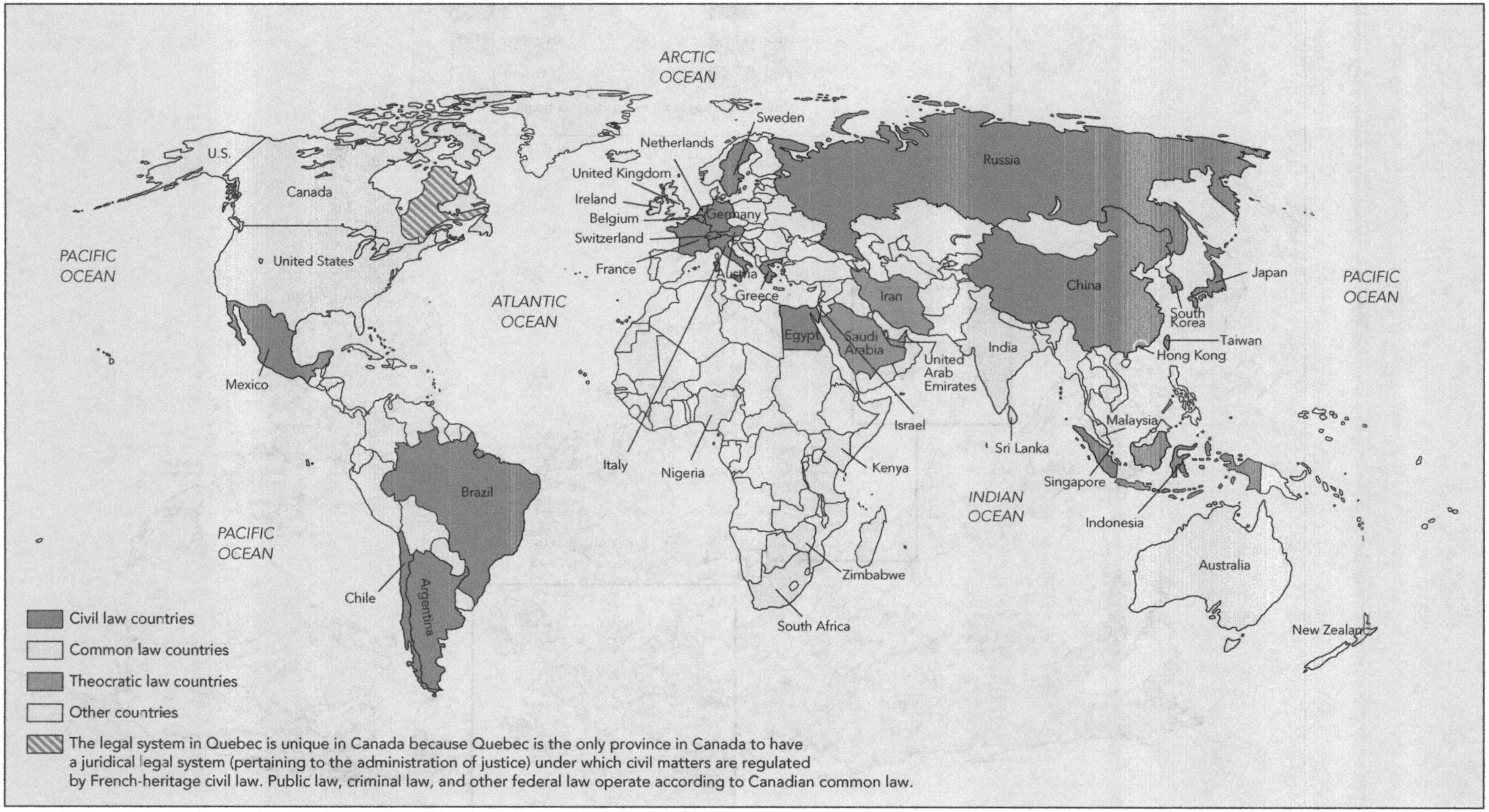

PACIFIC OCEAN

Japan
South Korea
Taiwan
Hong Kong

Russia

China

Malaysia
Singapore
Indonesia

India
Sri Lanka

United Arab Emirates

Iran
Saudi Arabia
Egypt

Israel
Kenya

INDIAN OCEAN

Zimbabwe
South Africa

Sweden
Germany
Austria
Greece

Nigeria

Netherlands
United Kingdom
Ireland
Belgium
Switzerland
France

Italy

ARCTIC OCEAN

Australia

New Zealand

ATLANTIC OCEAN

Canada
United States
U.S.

Mexico

PACIFIC OCEAN

Brazil
Argentina
Chile

PACIFIC OCEAN

Civil law countries
Common law countries
Theocratic law countries
Other countries

The legal system in Quebec is unique in Canada because Quebec is the only province in Canada to have a juridical legal system (pertaining to the administration of justice) under which civil matters are regulated by French-heritage civil law. Public law, criminal law, and other federal law operate according to Canadian common law.

© Cengage Learning

Map 1.4 Religious Heritage Around the World

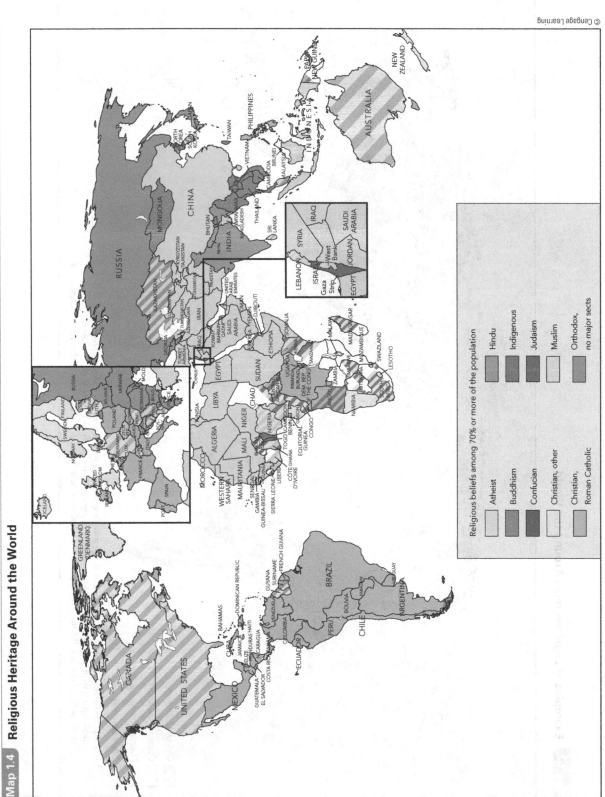

Religious beliefs among 70% or more of the population

- Atheist
- Buddhism
- Confucian
- Christian, other
- Christian, Roman Catholic
- Hindu
- Indigenous
- Judaism
- Muslim
- Orthodox, no major sects

Source: *World Factbook*, 2000. Note that Confucianism, strictly speaking, is not a religion but a set of moral codes guiding interpersonal relationships.

© Cengage Learning

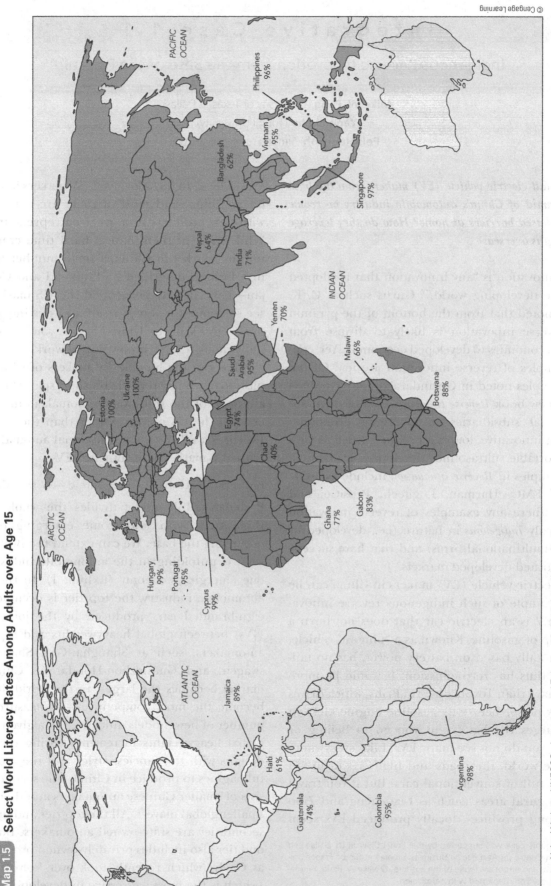

Map 1.5   Select World Literacy Rates Among Adults over Age 15

Source: United Nations, UNESCO, data accessed February 12, 2015. http://data.uis.unesco.org/

Integrative Case 1.1

Indigenous Reverse Innovation from the Base of the Pyramid[1]

Mike W. Peng (University of Texas at Dallas)
Yanmei Zhu (Tongji University)
Pek-Hooi Soh (Simon Fraser University)

How do small electric vehicle (EV) makers from the base of the pyramid of China's automobile industry overcome institution-based barriers at home? How do they leverage their strengths overseas?

Reverse innovation is "any innovation that is adopted first in the developing world."[2] Gurus such as C. K. Prahalad noted that from the bottom of the pyramid (BoP), reverse innovation is likely to diffuse from emerging economies to developed economies. Yet, concrete examples of reverse innovation are few. Of the list of examples noted in Govindarajan and Trimble's excellent new book *Reverse Innovation*, *all* of them are multinational subsidiaries in emerging economies developing innovative, low cost products (such as GE's storied portable ultrasound developed in China). Other examples in *Reverse Innovation* include Deere & Company, EMC, Harman, Logitech, PepsiCo, and P&G. Are there any examples of reverse innovation that are truly *indigenous* in nature (i.e., developed by local/non-multinational firms) and that have successfully penetrated developed markets?

The electric vehicle (EV) makers in China can be a great example of such indigenous reverse innovation. An EV is an electric car that does not burn a single drop of gasoline. Known as a "plug-in" vehicle, an EV is totally based on battery power, has no tailpipe, and thus has zero emission. It would be more revolutionary than Toyota's hybrid Prius, which drives on battery power before its gasoline engine kicks in and recharges the battery. If you go to Beijing or Shanghai, you do not see many EVs. Like everywhere else in the world, the roads and highways in urban China are full of conventional cars. But if you travel to certain rural areas (such as Liaocheng and Zibo in Shandong province), locally produced EVs seem

everywhere. In fact, dozens of EV makers have popped up in China, and most of them are experimenting with new products in a great entrepreneurial drive. While most of them have a hard time cracking the top tier market in China, a small number of them—in a fashion described by Prahalad and Govindarajan—have already penetrated the US market. If you see someone (or you yourself are) driving a Wheego or CODA EV in the United States, you are witnessing indigenous reverse innovation at work.

How can the humble EV makers of China accomplish so much in a remarkably short span of time? After all, none of the traditional automakers in China has cracked the US market. Other than the Nissan Leaf (which is a full EV), few traditional automakers active in the US market have launched EVs.

From the Bottom of the Pyramid—Within China

Prahalad's BoP model divides the whole world in three tiers, with low-income emerging economies occupying the base. We can extend the BoP model to what is unfolding in the automobile industry *within* one emerging economy (Exhibit 1). In the Chinese automobile industry, the top tier is occupied by foreign-branded cars produced by the joint ventures (JVs) between global heavyweights and top Chinese automakers, such as Shanghai-GM, Shanghai-Volkswagen, and Guangzhou-Honda. As China's auto market becomes the largest in the world, it has also become the most competitive—as measured by the number of new models unleashed in a given year. The global heavyweights increasingly bring their newest designs with the fanciest styles and the most powerful engines to produce in China. The second tier consists of smaller Chinese automakers and their JVs with smaller global players. All the top-tier and most of the second-tier are state-owned automakers. But the second tier also includes privately-owned producers such as Geely (which recently took over Volvo) and BYD (which is the most aggressive in developing EVs powered by lithium-ion battery technology). Overall, the

1) Research on this case was supported by the Jindal Chair at UT Dallas and the Jack Austin Centre for Asia Pacific Business Studies at Simon Fraser University. All views and errors are those of the authors. © Mike W. Peng, Yanmei Zhu, and Pek-Hooi Soh. Reprinted with permission.
2) V. Govindarajan & C. Trimble, 2012, *Reverse Innovation* (p. 4), Boston: Harvard Business Review Press.

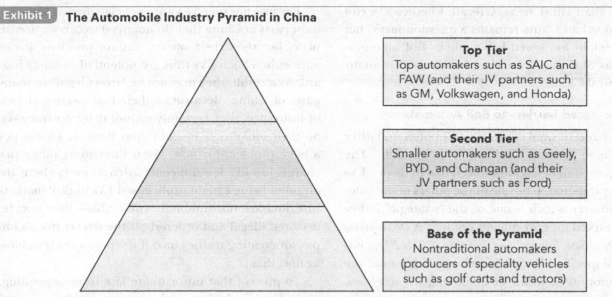

Exhibit 1   The Automobile Industry Pyramid in China

Top Tier
Top automakers such as SAIC and FAW (and their JV partners such as GM, Volkswagen, and Honda)

Second Tier
Smaller automakers such as Geely, BYD, and Changan (and their JV partners such as Ford)

Base of the Pyramid
Nontraditional automakers (producers of specialty vehicles such as golf carts and tractors)

second tier players' capabilities and aspirations are similar to those of the top tier.

The BoP in China's automobile industry consists of nontraditional producers of specialty vehicles—some of which are not necessarily "automakers" if you define automakers as the Toyotas, Fords, and Fiats of the world or the SAICs, FAWs, and Dongfengs of China. The BoP producers in China can typically trace their roots to agricultural vehicles (such as tractors and small pickups), recreational vehicles (such as golf carts), and/or electric motorcycles (such as mopads). They tend to be much smaller than the top-tier and second-tier automakers in China, have little influence or brand awareness outside their own regions, and thus are outside the radar screens of the global heavyweights. While larger automakers in China (and their foreign JV partners) are still embracing a largely "wait-and-see" attitude regarding EVs, BoP automakers in China, being smaller and more entrepreneurial, have rushed in. While dozens of them have entered, a few leading ones have emerged as winners. For example, Shandong-based Shifeng has sold more than 10,000 EVs, and has built an EV plant with a maximum capacity of producing 200,000 vehicles a year.

So far, the EVs in China are technically known as *low-speed* EVs, because their maximum speed is typically only 40–80 kilometers (25–50 miles) per hour. They typically have a range of 80–100 kilometers (50–65 miles). Instead of using the more advanced lithium-ion battery, they often use off-the-shelf lead acid battery. While primitive by conventional standards, these EVs are meeting a great deal of demand

in rural China. In such a BoP market within China, road conditions are not great (so high speed is not necessary), income levels are low, but people's needs to travel longer distances are increasing. Marketed at about 30,000 yuan (about $4,400), these cars are not as inexpensive as Tata's storied Nano (priced at $2,000–$3,000 in India). With the rising income levels, EVs become increasingly affordable to the rural population in China. For the same distance traveled, electricity is only 25% the cost of gasoline. Last but not the least, with zero emission, EVs offer unparalleled environmental benefits—potentially a great solution to China's pollution problems.

A total of 70% of China's population live in small towns and rural areas—that is a huge market of about 900 million (three times the total size of the US population). Few of the rural folks commute more than 20 kilometers (12.5 miles) a day. Travel speed rarely exceeds 60 kilometers (37.5 miles) per hour. Moreover, from an infrastructure standpoint, EVs have a huge *advantage* in rural areas because of the low population density and more spacious housing—typically with a yard or a driveway where EVs can be plugged in and charged with little need to build additional and costly charging stations. In contrast, widespread development of EVs in urban China has to overcome significant infrastructure challenges: population density is high and housing tight (high-rises everywhere). Few can afford single-family dwellings that would allow for convenient charging in the yard or on the driveway. Therefore, wide spread investment in and construction of charging stations is a must, but urban land is much more expensive than rural areas. Overall, whether EVs can take off in urban China remains a question mark, but EVs—especially low-speed EVs made by BoP automakers such as Shifeng—have already taken off in many parts of rural China.

Institution-Based Barriers to BoP Automakers

One of the recent (and controversial) policy initiatives in China is to promote "indigenous innovation." The Chinese government has announced that in theory, EVs are being promoted to be one of the pillars of the automobile industry, which is one of the "strategic" industries earmarked for government support. A *Development Plan for the "New Energy" Car Industry (2011–2020)* has listed nine specific EV models on its catalog for nationwide promotion in terms of qualifying for subsidies. While many foreign firms and governments naturally worry that the promotion of "indigenous innovation" would shut them out and some have complained to the Chinese government, not a single foreign automaker has complained. The reason is very simple: instead of being promoted by the government, BoP automakers are being *discriminated* against by institution-based barriers in China. Foreign automakers simply have no need to worry about any preferential treatment of the BoP automakers.

Instead, BoP EVs are technically not even defined as "cars" (or "passenger vehicles") by existing Chinese standards. Only *high-speed* EVs are classified as "cars" in China. But of the nine (high-speed) EV models on the catalog for the *Development Plan for the "New Energy" Car Industry (2011–2020)* that are eligible for subsidies, only one high speed EV—the BYD F3DM with a maximum speed of 150 kilometers (95 miles) per hour and a maximum range of 100 kilometers (62.5 miles)—has entered mass market. But the BYD F3DM is a Prius-like hybrid and not a pure EV. Despite the subsidies, its high price and low performance have not attracted many customers. On the other hand, none of the dozens of BoP EV models appears on the government's catalog for subsidies.

Despite the proclamation to promote "green cars," the omission of BoP EVs on the government promotion catalogue is not an oversight. It is *intentional*. This is because the government promotion catalogue is influenced by China's top-tier and second-tier automakers (and their foreign JV partners). Although these incumbents themselves are not too enthusiastic to introduce EVs, they do not wish to legitimate BoP EVs.

Because low speed EVs are not classified as "cars," in most parts of China they do not need to carry a license plate, but then their owners cannot purchase insurance either. Such EVs thus are potentially a safety hazard. As a result, they may not be "street legal" in many parts of China. Because of their low speed and lack of insurance, they certainly cannot drive on freeways. So their mobility is by definition limited. This is not a huge problem for now, given their short range per charge. Just like few unlicensed drivers everywhere are afraid of being caught, unlicensed EVs in BoP markets in China are institutionally vulnerable—they may be declared illegal and ordered off the streets (for example, for creating traffic jams) if the political winds blow against them.

To prevent that unfortunate fate from happening, some local and provincial governments have passed city, county, and provincial regulations to legalize and protect the BoP EV producers and owners. This localized rule-making has typically taken place in regions that house such BoP automakers, such as Liaocheng and Zibo in Shandong province, Dafeng in Jiangsu province, and Fuyang in Anhui province. To facilitate further development of the EV industry, Shandong has become the first province to explicitly legalize low-speed EVs and allow them to hit the roads.

In the community of Chinese policymakers, executives, and scholars, supporters of low-speed BoP EVs have urged for tolerance and nurturing given these vehicles' upside potential and environmental attractiveness. Critics argue that with little regulation, safety features, and insurance protection, low-speed EVs are likely to proliferate to create more traffic jams and safety hazards. Critics claim that local rules protecting locally produced EVs are "unconstitutional" because they violate the central government's power in making and enforcing nationwide traffic and vehicle registration laws. While debates continue to rage, one thing for sure is that such indigenous reverse innovation has a hard time breaking into the top tier, urban market in its own home country.

Go Global from BoP Markets

Since going from the BOP to the top tier market in their own country is so tough, a number of Chinese EV makers have gone global. At least two of them have cracked the US market.

In 2007, Hebei-based Shuanghuan Auto developed its first EV, the two-door, two-passenger Noble.

Unfortunately, the Noble was not allowed to be marketed as a "car" in China (as noted earlier). In 2009, Shuanghuan Auto joined hands with Wheego, an Atlanta-based start-up specializing in all-electric cars. After considerable modification and enhancement in terms of control and safety features undertaken in Ontario, California, the Noble was marketed as the Wheego Whip EV in the United States starting in December 2009. With a top speed of 40–55 kilometers (25–35 miles) per hour, a range of 65 kilometer (40 miles), and 10 hours to fully charge its engine, the Wheego Whip retailed at $18,995. After adding options and taxes and then applying a $2,500 federal tax credit, the net price was $17,995.

After a year, a significantly improved Noble became the Wheego Life. With a top speed of 105 kilometers (65 miles) per hour, Wheego Life was fully highway capable (and "street legal") in the United States. It had a range of 160 kilometers (100 miles) and only needed five hours to fully charge its engine. The Wheego Life retailed at $32,995. After adding options and taxes and then applying a $7,500 federal tax credit, the net price was $26,495. In addition, some US state and local tax credit can further bring down the price tag. For example, in California, the Wheego Life appeared on the state's list of approved "green cars" for state subsidies—this is no small accomplishment, considering that the Noble (and all BoP EVs in China) *failed* to appear on China's *Development Plan for the "New Energy" Car Industry (2011–2020)* that would make them eligible for subsidies. As a result, Wheego Life owners in California could enjoy an additional $2,000 off. In addition, Arizona, California, Florida, Georgia, Hawaii, Maryland, New Jersey, New York, North Carolina, Tennessee, Utah,

and Virginia allowed EVs such as the Wheego Life to enjoy the privilege of using high-occupancy vehicle (HOV) lanes.

Another example is Hebei-based Great Wall Motors. In 2011, Great Wall signed an alliance agreement with Los Angeles-based CODA Automotive, which would export EVs to the United States. With a top speed of 136 kilometers (85 miles) per hour, the four-door, five-passenger CODA car was also fully "street legal" in the United States. It had a range of 240 kilometers (150 miles) and needed six hours to fully charge. It retailed at $44,900. After applying a $7,500 federal tax credit, the net price was $37,400.

As of this writing, 25 dealers in 18 states as well as Japan and the Cayman Islands signed up with Wheego. Five dealers in Southern California signed up with CODA. The diffusion of such indigenous reverse innovation is likely to proliferate.

Case Discussion Questions

1. **From a resource-based view, what are some of the outstanding capabilities that EV producers in China have? Why their larger competitors (incumbents) in China do not have such capabilities?**

2. **From an institution-based view, what are domestic incumbents in China—in collaboration with global heavyweights—interested in leveraging their influence on the Chinese government to heighten entry barriers for EV producers?**

3. **Given that some EV producers from China's BoP can penetrate the US market, what are some of the lessons from indigenous reverse innovation in the era of globalization?**

Integrative Case 1.2

The Future of Cuba[1]

Mike W. Peng (University of Texas at Dallas)

As Cuba gradually opens up its economy to market competition, private sector, and foreign investment, what does its future hold?

Cuba is the only practitioner of communism in the Western Hemisphere. Five decades of communism have delivered some accomplishments. Life expectancy (at 79 years) is on par with that of the United States, and Cuba has more doctors per 100,000 persons than Britain and France. Social benefits cover everyone from cradle to grave, providing free world-class health care and education in addition to free pensions and funerals. However, people are poor and income is low. The average monthly wage is only $19. Food is often in shortage, forcing the government to ration supply. Cuba's 11 million people enjoy only 600,000 cars, with an average age of 15 years. Half of them belong to the state. Many 1950s vintage cars are still workhorses in the streets.

Raúl Castro, the younger brother of the 88-year-old leader Fidel Castro, took over as Cuba's president in 2008 and as first secretary of the Communist Party in 2011. (For compositional simplicity, this case will refer to each Castro brother by his first name.) Raúl has been busy, transferring a substantial chunk of the state-owned enterprises (SOEs) to private hands, freeing political prisoners, and signing the UN Convention on Human Rights, something that Fidel had refused to do. While change seems to be in the air, there are limits—after all, Raúl is also a Castro. Neither "reform" nor "transition" is allowed to be mentioned. These words immediately bring back the painful memory of the collapse of the Soviet Union, which overnight withdrew subsidies and traumatized Cuba's leaders. Instead, the changes are labeled "updating," in which "nonstate actors" and "cooperatives" will be tolerated. "But," noted the *Economist*, "whatever the language, this means an emerging private sector."

Thanks to the Soviet collapse, the Cuban economy shrank by a painful 35% between 1989 and 1993. In desperation, Fidel declared a national emergency, opened Cuba for foreign direct investment (FDI) and mass tourism, and legalized small family businesses and the use of the US dollar. He also found a new benefactor, Venezuela president Hugo Chávez, who (prior to his death in 2013) provided Cuba with cheap oil. In exchange, Fidel sent 20,000 doctors and professionals to work in Venezuela. Thus, the regime's widely predicted demise did not materialize. After surviving the emergency, Fidel went back to the old ways. Many family businesses and foreign ventures were shut down, and the US dollar ceased to be legal tender in 2004.

This time, Raúl has proclaimed that changes are here to stay. While Fidel has a massive ego and is famously ideological, Raúl is more modest and more pragmatic. Raúl seems to realize that Cuban communism lives on borrowed time. The economy is terribly unproductive. Cuba has a legendary agricultural past—think of its world-famous cigars and sugar. However, state ownership of farms has been disastrous. Output per head of sugar in 2012 has dropped to an eighth of its level in 1958. State farms control 75% of arable land, but 45% of this lies idle. Raúl has allowed private farmers and co-ops to lease idle state land. Yet, private farmers have a hard time scraping a living off land. This is not because the land is not fertile; it is. It is because of the grip of Acopio, the state-owned monopoly supplier of seeds, fertilizer, and equipment as well as the monopoly purchaser of farm produce. There is hardly a market to motivate farmers to try harder.

In manufacturing and services, SOEs are also notorious for shoddy quality and low pay. But there is one advantage in working for SOEs: plenty of opportunities to pilfer (steal) supplies from the workplace. Employees' justification goes like this: The SOE belongs to the state, which belongs to the people—that is, us. Since our wages are so low, we should feel free to take home the stuff that, after all, belongs to us anyway (!). Experimenting on a limited scale, Raúl has allowed private entrepreneurs to own and operate small shops, such as barber shops, beauty parlors, and restaurants, as well as private taxis. Although by global standards these

1) This research was supported by the Jindal Chair at the Jindal School of Management, University of Texas at Dallas. All views and errors are those of the author. © Mike W. Peng. Reprinted with permission.

entrepreneurial opportunities are extremely limited, they nevertheless have attracted well-educated (but starving) professionals, such as teachers, doctors, and accountants. For example, a doctor who used to make $23 per month can now take home $40 in an improvised craft shop.

Slowly but surely, outside influence has arrived. While (until recently) US firms cannot do business in Cuba, multinationals from Brazil, Canada, China, and Spain have no such institution-based barriers. In 2013, 2.7 million tourists (a record) flocked to Cuba. While the US embargo is still technically in effect, from Miami, eight flights—technically labeled "charter" (not regularly scheduled) flights—go to Havana every day. In 2014, the parliament approved the Foreign Investment Law, which for the first time allows Cubans living abroad to invest in Cuba (unless, according to the foreign minister, they are part of the "Miami terrorist mafia"—otherwise known as the Cuban American community in Miami). Such investors are exempt from profit taxes for eight years, after which, instead of paying tax at the normal 30%, a 15% rate will apply. *Havana Reporter* calls this new law "game changing."

Although still healthy, Raúl is already 84. Given the inescapable "biological factor" (a Cuban euphemism referring to the eventual death of the Castro brothers), the days of the Castros running the show in Cuba are clearly numbered. In December 2014, President Barack Obama announced plans to gradually lift sanctions. Both Obama and Raúl—separately in Washington and Havana—declared interests to restore commercial and diplomatic relations. What does the future hold for Cuba?

Case Discussion Questions

1. **Why has state ownership of farms resulted in a disaster in Cuban farming?**

2. ***ON ETHICS:* What are the norms governing employee behavior in Cuban SOEs? Are these norms right or wrong?**

3. **The *Economist* predicted that "whatever the intentions of Cuba's communist leaders, they will find it impossible to prevent the island from moving to some form of capitalism." Do you agree or disagree?**

4. **Should foreign firms be interested in entering Cuba?**

5. **As US sanctions are gradually lifted, what will happen to Cuban politics and economy?**

Sources: Based on (1) *Economist*, 2012, Edging toward capitalism, March 24: 7–9; (2) *Economist*, 2012, Revolution in retreat, March 24: 3–4; (3) *Economist*, 2012, The deal's off, March 24: 5–7; (4) *Economist*, 2012, The Miami mirror, March 24: 10–11; (5) *Economist*, 2013, Cuba's economy, July 20: 33–34; (6) *Economist*, 2015, The new normal, January 3: 11–12; (7) *Havana Reporter*, 2014, Growing interest in Cuban investment opportunities, May 6: 14; (8) J. Sweig & M. Bustamante, 2013, Cuba after communism, *Foreign Affairs*, July: 101–114.

Integrative Case 1.3

Political Risk of Doing Business in Thailand[1]

Pawinee Changphao (University of Texas at Dallas)

Thailand has experienced a series of military coups that toppled democratically elected governments. Should companies in Thailand and those interested in doing business with it be concerned about political risk?

Thailand, the second-largest economy in Southeast Asia, is a constitutional monarchy headed by King Bhumibol Adulyadej, Rama IX, with a parliamentary government. Since the coup d'état of May 22, 2014 (the 13th successful coup out of 22 attempts since the first written Constitution was issued in 1932),[2] the 2007 Constitution was revoked, except for the second chapter, relating to the monarchy.[3] As of this writing, Thailand has been under the rule of the military organization called National Council for Peace and Order (NCPO), led by the coup leader and prime minister General Prayuth Chan-ocha.

Thailand's Economy

Thailand's economy is heavily export dependent, with exports accounting for more than two-thirds of its gross domestic product (GDP). Its main products exported are computers, rubber, delivery trucks, refined petroleum, and gold. Thailand once experienced the world's highest growth rate during the period of 1986–1995. However, the 1997 Asian Financial Crisis led Thailand to sharply devaluate the baht against the US dollar and to seek over US$17.2 billion loans from the International Monetary Fund (IMF).[4] The collapse of the Southeast Asian economic boom in 1997 led to public disillusion with free-market policies and encouraged the rise of populist Prime Minister Thaksin Shinawatra, a leader of then Thai Rak Thai Party. He was condemned by the urban elites and royalists, but enjoyed widespread support among the poor, particularly those in rural areas.

Thaksin and the 2006 Coup

Thaksin won a landslide victory in the 2001 general election. During Thaksin's first term (2001–2005), Thailand's economy regained momentum and the country paid off its IMF debt by July 2003 (two years ahead of schedule)—partly thanks to economic reforms continued from the previous government led by the Democrat Party. Thaksin's party won another landslide victory over the Democrat Party in the 2005 general election. His popularity largely derived from his populist policies aimed at Thailand's rural people, who made up the majority of his votes. The policies included, for instance, the 30-baht health scheme, which guarantees universal healthcare coverage for just 30 baht (about US$0.75) a visit at state hospitals; a four-year debt moratorium for farmers; a rice-subsidy scheme; one-million baht locally managed development funds for all Thai villages; and over US$500 billion invested in public infrastructure (including the new Bangkok International Airport).

However, Thaksin failed to serve his second term (2005–2009) in full. In 2006, in the midst of continuing violent unrest in the south and anti-Thaksin ("yellow shirt") street protests (the largest public rallies since 1992), a bloodless coup d'état led by General Sonthi Boonyaratglin ousted Thaksin and later a military junta led by General Surayud Chulanont ruled the country. Thaksin was accused of many sins, ranging from corruption and nepotism to gross incompetence in his management of the fight against Muslim insurgents. He was also accused of violating Article 112 of the Thai Criminal Code, which states that whoever "defames, insults or threatens the king, the queen, the heir-apparent or the regent" will be punished with up to 15 years in prison.[5] Thaksin was also lambasted for his dominance of the airwaves through his communications group, Shin-Corp.—and then attacked for hugely enriching himself by selling it to Temasek Holdings, an investment company owned by the Government of Singapore.[6]

---

1) This case was written by Pawinee Changphao (University of Texas at Dallas) under the supervision of Professor Mike Peng. All information used is from the public domain. © Pawinee Changphao. Reprinted with permission.

2) *Economist Intelligence Unit.* 2014. Thailand: Country fact sheet. December 17.

3) *Economist Intelligence Unit.* 2014. Thailand: Country fact sheet. December 17.

4) International Monetary Fund. 2000. *Recovery from the Asian Crisis and the Role of the IMF.* www.imf.org/external/np/exr/ib/2000/062300.htm#box1, accessed December 17, 2014.

5) *BBC News*, 2014, Thailand's lèse majesté laws explained, December 1, www.bbc.com/news/world-asia-29628191, accessed January 7, 2015.

6) *Economist*, 2006, Thailand's dangerous coup: Soldiers in power, September 23: 12.

During his two terms, Thaksin promoted international business by following a privatization agenda. His government liberalized investment laws, which previously had severely restricted foreign ownership of strategic national assets, including those in the broadband communications industry. The new laws permitted up to 50% foreign ownership.[7] He signed free trade agreements (FTA) with Australia, China, India, New Zealand, and the United Arab Emirates, leading to an increase in trade volumes with the partners, especially in the energy-related industry and the broadband telecommunications industry.[8]

Yingluck and the 2014 Coup

Although Thaksin lived in self-imposed exile in various countries since the 2006 coup d'état, his political influence remained strong through his proxies winning all the following general elections in 2007 and 2008. In 2011, Thaksin's sister, Yingluck Shinawatra, the leader of Thaksin-backed Pheu Thai Party, won elections by a landslide and became Thailand's first female prime minister. During her term, Yingluck not only continued her brother's populist policies, but also forcefully attempted to pass a bill granting Thaksin amnesty from convictions for corruption and abuse of power. These political moves fueled mass street protests, leading to the shutting down of key areas of the capital and the debilitating confrontation between the northern "red shirts" (Thaksin's supporters) and "yellow shirts" (a royalist establishment) that control much of the capital and the southern provinces. In 2014, after nearly three years of the Yingluck government, another bloodless coup d'état took over the country, aiming to not only resolve the political conflicts, but also erase the influence of Thaksin. Thus, the military junta appointed establishment figures to write a new constitution, containing ideally "fairness and wisdom" contents to accomplish their initial motivation of the bloodless army coup.[9]

The Generals' Challenge

The 2014 coup seems to be different from the 2006 coup, since the generals leading the 2014 coup were eager to carry on running Thailand under martial law,

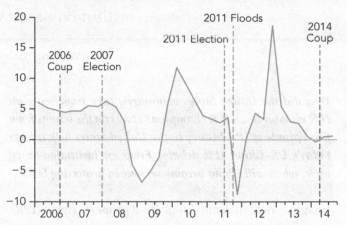

Exhibit 1   The Generals' Challenge: Thailand's Annual GDP Change (%)

Source: *Economist*, 2014, Thai politics: Delaying the day of reckoning (p. 45), December 6: 45.

whereas those leading the 2006 coup were not. However, it could be a challenge for the coup leader and prime minister, General Prayuth Chan-ocha, to keep control of the country as well as to revive the economy when its economic growth was much less than that in 2013 (see Exhibit 1).[10] Despite economic policy confusion and uncertainties, Prayuth Chanocha repeatedly told foreign investors that Thailand was open for business. As a piece of evidence, in early November 2014, he dusted off plans to restrict foreign ownership and control of companies. This could be good news for foreign investors—at least for now. For companies in Thailand and those interested in doing business with Thailand, the question is: How can they cope with the political risk in the country?

Case Discussion Questions

1. **Does Thailand have a democracy?**

2. **As CEO of a multinational that has already invested in and been successfully producing in Thailand (for both Thailand and overseas markets), when you heard the news about the 2006 and 2014 coup that toppled democratically elected governments, should you be concerned?**

3. **As CEO of a company that is ready to export to Thailand or that is ready to source from Thailand, would you be concerned about the political risk in Thailand? Would you proceed as planned or look for alternative export markets or alternative countries from which to source products?**

7) K. Rowley, 2006, *The Downfall of Thaksin Shinawatra's CEO-State*, APSNet Policy Forum, http://nautilus.org/apsnet/0634a-rowley-html/, accessed December 20, 2014.

8) S. W. Crispin, 2001, Power politics trump reform, *Far Eastern Economic Review*, September 27, 2001. www.globalpolicy.org/component/content/article/213/45712.html, accessed January 7, 2015.

9) *Economist*, 2014, Thai politics: Delaying the day of reckoning, December 6: 45.

10) *Economist*, 2014, Thai politics: Delaying the day of reckoning, December 6: 45.

Integrative Case 1.4

An Institution-Based View of IPR Protection[1]

Mike W. Peng (University of Texas at Dallas)

Why did the United States voluntarily turn from being an IPR violator to an IPR champion? How can the lessons from this episode of IPR history in the United States help inform today's US–China IPR debate? From an institution-based view, when will China become serious in protecting IPR?

Imagine some difficult intellectual property rights (IPR) negotiations between a superpower and an emerging economy. Negotiators from the superpower demanded that its IPR be respected. Their counterparts from the emerging economy shrugged: "Well, we are still a developing country, but we need to promote education and facilitate learning." In other words, IPR piracy had to go on in the emerging economy—never mind the protests from the superpower.

Which two countries are involved? If you think this scenario describes the challenging negotiations between the United States and China recently, you would only be given "partial credit" in my class. This scenario also describes the tough negotiations between Great Britain (the superpower at that time) and the United States (the emerging economy of the day) in most of the 19th century. Between the founding of the United States and 1891 when the Chace Act was passed, pirating British publications was the widely accepted norm for American book publishers, newspapers, and magazines. There was no shortage of frustrated British authors (such as Charles Dickens) and officials who sought to change Americans' behavior—and then became more frustrated by Americans' lack of willingness to honor and protect IPR.

In today's discussion about IPR, few have bothered to draw lessons from the earlier history of IPR disputes between Great Britain and the United States (although this history is well documented). Without

drawing lessons from *this particular episode* of history, the future outlook for better IPR protection around the world is not encouraging, and the future outlook for better IPR protection in China—widely noted as the leading violator of IPR of our time—is very depressing. Zimmerman's (2013) paper in *Business Horizons* is indicative of such thinking, which is widely shared by many authors. Zimmerman's lessons drawn from Chinese cultural history, economic development, and political development seem to suggest that Chinese are culturally and politically conditioned to engage in a high level of IPR violation. If we push this line of thinking further, then it is virtually hopeless to envision better IPR protection in China in the absence of significant changes to Chinese culture and politics.

I beg to differ from this pessimistic view. I argue that the history of IPR development in the United States—from a leading violator to a leading advocate of IPR—offers a great deal of hope regarding the future of IPR development in China and numerous other countries implicated by the United States Trade Representative (USTR) and the Oragnization for Economic Co-operation and Development (OECD), such as Argentina, Brazil, Chile, Egypt, India, Israel, Lebanon, Mexico, Paraguay, Russia, Thailand, Turkey, Ukraine, and Venezuela. The key does not lie in culture or politics, which are enduring features of a country's institutional framework that cannot be changed quickly. Numerous British critics in the 19th century wrote extensively (and quite persuasively at that time) that Americans were culturally and politically conditioned to engage in a high level of IPR violation. Charles Dickens must be turning in his grave if he heard that the leading pirating nation of his time, the United States, would become the leading *advocate* for IPR in the late 20th and early 21st century. The key, in my view, lies in institutions, which are known as the "rules of the game" (see Chapter 2). While culture and politics can be regarded as informal institutions that change relatively slowly, formal institutions, especially laws, rules, and regulations as well as their enforcement mechanisms, can be enacted very quickly—literally with the stroke of a pen if there is sufficient determination. More specifically,

1) Excerpted from an article originally published as M. W. Peng, 2013, An institution-based view of IPR protection, *Business Horizons*, 56(2): 135–139. © Kelley School of Business, Indiana University. Reprinted with permission. I thank Peggy Chaudhry for her able guidance and Alan Zimmerman for his helpful discussion. Discussion questions are added by M. W. Peng. Going above and beyond this case, a longer article with more fully developed arguments can be found in M. W. Peng, D. Ahlstrom, S. Carraher, & W. Shi, 2014, How history can inform the debate over intellectual property, working paper, Jindal School of Management, University of Texas at Dallas.

what made Americans decide to change their IPR institutions by 1891? What are the lessons of this particular episode of history for today's discussion of (and frustration with) IPR protection in China and elsewhere? The goal of this article is to leverage this widely known but rarely appreciated historical episode of IPR development in the United States to advance an institution-based view of IPR protection.

The Depressing Outlook

Focusing on contemporary antipiracy efforts, Chaudhry and Zimmerman's (2009) excellent book *The Economics of Counterfeit Trade* has exhaustively reviewed governments' and firms' responses to IPR violations around the world. Chaudhry and Zimmerman's (2009) book concludes:

> The price-performance ratio of technology continues to decline, meaning pirates can get the production and communications equipment they need at ever-lower costs. Trade barriers continue to fall . . . Consumers do not see much harm in purchasing counterfeit product. Advertising attempting to change this perception is judged relatively ineffective by managers involved in fighting the counterfeit problem . . . Many consumers will not be able to afford to purchase a legitimate product. This will also be a force for the continued increase in sales of counterfeit goods. Managers surveyed by the authors generally do not see international bodies as particularly effective in slowing down the growth of pirated product. In addition, enforcement of local laws is uneven at best. Since other considerations often are far more important in multilateral negotiations, the enforcement of IPR rights in many countries will probably not improve much (p. 175).

Depressing, isn't it?! It seems that the more efforts and resources expended on IPR protection, the worse the scale and scope of IPR violation around the world. Continuing this line of research, Zimmerman (2013) dives deeper into Chinese history and politics, and reaches essentially the same but more pointed conclusion regarding the depressing outlook of IPR protection in China.

As leading scholars, Chaudhry and Zimmerman (2009) obviously are well aware of the history of IPR development in the United States. They do offer a glimmer of hope:

> Judging by US history, it is possible that indigenous manufacturers will demand improved enforcement of IPR laws in these newly emerging markets and that could significantly slow local pirate activities (p. 175).

In other words, the outlook does not necessarily need to be so depressing if we can draw more optimistic lessons from the development of IPR in the United States. Yet, Chaudhry and Zimmerman have not expanded on this intriguing point. This is an important missing point that the next section endeavors to fill, culminating in an institution-based view of IPR protection.

The United States as a Leading IPR Violator

From its founding, the United States had a conceptualization of IPR and a formal system of IPR protection—starting from the Copyright Act of 1790 and Patent Act of 1793. However, US IPR protection would only protect US-based inventors and authors. By definition, the IPR of foreign inventors and authors was up for grabs. In his first tour of the United States in 1842, Charles Dickens was appalled by the widespread pirating of his work and called for better protection of IPR. Instead, the US media, which made a living (and a killing) by using pirated British content to fill a sizeable portion of their pages, argued that Dickens should be grateful for his popularity and that he was greedy to complain about his work being pirated.

Calls for Americans to become more ethical and to be respectful of foreign authors and inventors' IPO issued by luminaries such as Dickens generally went nowhere. Until his death in 1870, Dickens had not collected a single dollar of royalties from US sales. There was no shortage of British critics, such as Dickens, who believed that Americans were culturally and politically hopeless in improving IPR protection. Threats by British negotiators to impose sanctions on the United States were met by Americans negotiators' more provocative challenge: "Invade us?" Unfortunately, the last time the British were able to gather their strengths to invade the United States was in 1812. After that, the British had neither the guts nor the resources to seriously contemplate such an invasion. Fast forward to today's IPR negotiations between the United States and China. To it put bluntly, the Chinese negotiators essentially said to frustrated American negotiators: "Invade us?" Of course, the United States today cannot seriously contemplate such an invasion. So the IPR negotiations between the UK and the US in the mid-19th century and between the US and China in the late 20th and early 21st century typically went nowhere, despite some diplomatic proclamation of some "progress and improvement based on a frank exchange of views."

Proposition 1 in the Institution-Based View

To the pleasant surprise of British critics, the United States *voluntarily* changed its IPR laws in 1891 with the passing of the International Copyright Act (popularly known as the Chace Act after Senator Jonathan Chace of Rhode Island, who sponsored the bill). The Chace Act protected the IPR of foreign works. What happened? Clearly, the US government was deaf to both moral pleas called for by foreign authors and toothless threats made by foreign governments. It was not foreign pressures that led to this sea change. Instead, it was pressures from indigenous authors, inventors, and firms within the United States that led to such transformation.

Proposition 1 in the institution-based view of global business states that governments, firms, and managers *rationally* pursue their interests and make choices (see Chapter 2). By refusing to protect the IPR of foreign inventors and authors until 1891, the US government had been perfectly rational. Given the low level of literary and economic development, protecting foreign IPR would simply benefit foreign authors, inventors, and firms (such as publishers) at the expense of domestic consumers who had to shoulder higher costs for books, media products, and innovative products.

However, toward the end of the 19th century, rapid economic development in the United States turned it from a net consumer of IP to a net producer. As more Americans started to write books and more American publishers started to publish and market them overseas (a leading market was the UK), they demanded better protection from foreign governments. However, foreign governments would not grant US authors copyright protection if the United States did not reciprocate.

Further, as the United States nurtured more authors, inventors, and publishers, their IP was pirated *elsewhere*—notably in Canada in the late 19th century. Taking a page from the US playbook, the Canadians did not offer IPR protection to foreign (technically non-British Commonwealth, essentially American) authors and inventors. Therefore, unauthorized piracies of US-authored books were widespread in Canada, causing an uproar among American writers, such as Mark Twain.[2]

Given these changing winds, it is perfectly rational for the US government—via the Chace Act of 1891—to start offering IPR protection in the United States to foreign authors and inventors. Only by doing that would American authors and inventors have any hope of having their IPR protected overseas.

In summary, only when the US economy became sufficiently developed and the US IP production became more competitive overseas did IPR protection improve in the United States. As the United States became the new superpower with more of its GDP (and export earnings) driven by IPR, not surprisingly it took the banner from Great Britain in the 20th century to become the most vocal advocate of IPR. Any argument that Americans were culturally and politically predisposed to engage in a high level of IPR violation would collapse when being confronted by the 180-degree change of IPR protection in the United States circa 1891. Is culture important? Of course. Is politics crucial? Yes. But what matters more in this case? None of the above! It is institutions. Proposition 1 of the institution-based view regarding players' rationality indeed offers a great deal of insights into how institutions matter in IPR protection.

Neither American Exceptionalism nor Chinese Exceptionalism

How generalizable is the American experience in the 19th century to today's IPR debate concerning China (and other counterfeiting nations)? If one believes in American exceptionalism, then this discussion is not relevant to China's current and future IPR protection. Likewise, if one believes in Chinese exceptionalism, then this episode of US history is not relevant either.

I believe in none of the above. As great as the United States and China are, they belong to the global family of nations. The international exchange and diffusion of ideas and practices have scaled new heights recently. Neither of these two countries—nor any other country for that matter—can evolve its own IPR system in total isolation. If we embrace a longer and more global view of history, we see that IPR violation started at least during the Roman times. In the 1500s, the Netherlands (an emerging economy at that time) were busy making counterfeit Chinese porcelain. In the 19th century, Americans improved their literacy level by feasting on pirated British works. In the 1960s, Japan was the global leader for counterfeits. In the 1970s, Hong Kong grabbed this dubious distinction. In the 1980s, South Korea and Taiwan led the world. Now it is China's turn.

---

2) For example, Mark Twain had to establish residency in Canada in order to protect his novel *The Prince and the Pauper*, which would then be registered as a Canadian resident's work that would have copyright protection in Canada. Given the tremendous costs involved, few authors could entertain establishing multiple residencies around the world.

An institution-based view of IPR suggests a clearly discernable pattern: as these economies developed, indigenous industries grew, and IPR protection was enhanced—such development was rational and made sense. Anyone believing that Chinese are culturally and politically conditioned to engage in a high level of IPR violation will need to confront the evidence that during the Beijing Olympics (2008), *not* a single case of IPR violation of Olympic logos and mascots was reported. Perhaps the counterfeiters became more patriotic—although not a focus here, informal norms are another often-researched area in the institution-based view. Perhaps IPR enforcement was beefed up. More likely the answer was "all of the above." The usual Chinese negotiators' defense when facing foreign pressures that Chinese IPR enforcement capabilities were weak simply does not hold water in the face of shining accomplishments of zero (reported) IPR violation during the Beijing Olympics. When there is a will, there is a way. Currently, there is little will on the part of the Chinese government to satisfy US IPR demands, because foreign (and primarily US) IPR holders would benefit more from such enhanced protection. If history around the world is any guide, someday China and other leading counterfeiting nations will hopefully follow the same path by offering better IPR protection.

How long do we have to wait until this "someday" comes? In 1870, Dickens died at the age of 58, knowing that his IPR would not be protected in the United States in his lifetime. But had he lived another 21 years, he would have seen the arrival of that "someday." Given the rapid development of the Chinese economy, I think (and I certainly hope!) most readers of this article will see the arrival of that "someday" for better IPR protection in China before we die. Specifically, when will China be serious in offering better IPR protection to foreign authors, inventors, and firms? My prediction from the institution-based view of IPR protection is that the day will come when Chinese IPR are widely pirated by *foreign* violators outside of China.

Case Discussion Questions

1. **Why did the United States voluntarily turn from being an IPR violator to an IPR champion?**

2. **How can the lessons from this episode of IPR history in the United States help inform today's US–China IPR debate?**

3. **From an institution-based view, when will China become serious in protecting IPR?**

Sources: Based on (1) P. Chaudhry & A. Zimmerman, 2009, *The Economics of Counterfeit Trade*, Heidelberg, Germany: Springer; (2) W. Fisher, 1999, The growth of intellectual property: A history of the ownership of ideas in the United States, working paper, Harvard Law School, cyber.law.harvard.edu; (3) C. Hill, 2007, Digital piracy: Causes, consequences, and strategic responses, *Asia Pacific Journal of Management*, 24: 9–25; (4) S. Lohr, 2002, The intellectual property debate take a page from 19th-century America, *New York Times*, October 14, www.nytimes.com; (5) C. Tomalin, 2011, *Charles Dickens: A Life*, New York: Viking; (6) A. Zimmerman, 2013, Contending with Chinese counterfeits: Culture, growth, and management responses, *Business Horizons*, 51(2): 141–148; (7) A. Zimmerman & P. Chaudhry, 2014, Fighting counterfeit motion pictures, in M. W. Peng, *Global Business*: 128–130. Cincinnati: Cengage Learning.

Integrative Case 1.5

Bank Scandals: Bad Apples versus Bad Barrels[1]

Mike W. Peng (University of Texas at Dallas)

Banks have been fined left and rights for misconduct since the Great Recession of 2008–2009. Are they "bad barrels" or they just happen to have a few "bad apples"?

It is tough to be a banker after the Great Recession of 2008–2009. It seems that not a day goes by without any new scandal being unearthed and punished. Since 2009, Barclays, ING, and Lloyds have all paid big settlements related to allegations that they moved money for people or companies that were on the US sanctions list. In 2012, HSBC paid a huge $1.9 billion fine to settle US government charges that it had facilitated money laundering for rogue states and groups such as Cuba, North Korea, Sudan, as well as Hamas, Mexican drug lords, Syrian terrorists, and the Taliban. Since 2010, six major Wall Street banks—Bank of America, Citigroup, Goldman Sachs, JPMorgan Chase, Morgan Stanley, and Wells Fargo—agreed to pay a combined $80 billion in settlements and penalties related to the financial crisis. For example, in 2013, JPMorgan Chase agreed to pay another $13 billion fine in connection with mortgage-backed securities that it missold as well as securities sold by Washington Mutual and Bear Stearns, two banks that JPMorgan Chase took over during the financial crisis. In 2014, Credit Suisse pleaded guilty to a criminal charge of helping its clients dodge American taxes. The upshot? An enormous $2.8 billion fine.

What is the root cause of such large-scale unethical and often-illegal business behavior? It is difficult to imagine such wrongdoing is due to just a few "bad apples." Yet, few people have lost their jobs, and none has been criminally charged. The top brass at Credit Suisse, for example, argued that it played no role in the actions for which the bank was prosecuted. Its board discussed firing some top executives, but concluded that the benefits would not outweigh the upheaval such firing would introduce. After coughing up the record $13 billion fine that would cripple the finances of many firms and a nontrivial number of countries, JPMorgan Chase chairman and CEO Jamie Dimon managed to keep his dual titles—never mind shareholder uproar. In short, the banks argue that a small number of "bad apples" have caused all the trouble.

By naming, shaming, and fining the banks (but not individuals), the government begs to differ. All are treated as "bad barrels" that need to be cleaned up. As part of the settlement, all the "bad barrels" named above promised to enhance compliance and behave better. How much credibility do such statements have? One argument suggests that people may have ethical or unethical predispositions *before* joining firms. Another side of the debate argues that while there are indeed some opportunistic "bad apples," many times people commit unethical behavior not because they are "bad apples," but because they are spoiled by "bad barrels." Some firms not only condone, but may even expect unethical behavior.

The debate on "bad apples" versus "bad barrels" is an extension of the broader debate on "nature versus nurture." Are we who we are because of our genes (nature) or our environments (nurture)? Most studies report that human behavior is the result of both nature *and* nurture. Although individuals and firms do have some ethical or unethical predispositions that influence their behavior, the institutional environment (such as organizational norms and cultures) can also have a profound impact. In a nutshell, even "good apples" may turn bad in "bad barrels." Therefore, despite the record number of fines and settlements, future bank scandals remain to be unearthed. Stay tuned for the raging debate on "bad apples" versus "bad barrels" in the banking industry and beyond.

Case Discussion Questions

1. *ON ETHICS:* **Concerning the banks implicated above, are some of their employees "bad apples" or are these banks "bad barrels"?**

1) This research was supported by the Jindal Chair at the Jindal School of Management, University of Texas at Dallas. All views and errors are those of the author. © Mike W. Peng. Reprinted with permission.

2. *ON ETHICS:* As a new CEO for one of these banks, how are you going to clean up the mess and restore reputation?

3. *ON ETHICS:* As a regulator, what would be your response to deter the next wave of scandals?

Sources: Based on (1) *Bloomberg Businessweek*, 2013, Hell to pay, November 4: 47–48; (2) *Bloomberg Businessweek*, 2013, Too big to cry, October 28: 14–15; (3) *Bloomberg Businessweek*, 2013, Wall Street's guilt moment, October 28: 33–34; (4) *Economist*, 2012, HSBC's grilling, July 21: 61–62; (5) *Economist*, 2014, Credit Suisse in court, May 24: 65–66; (6) *Economist*, 2014, The criminalization of American business, August 30: 9.

Integrative Case 1.6

Occidental Petroleum (Oxy): From Also-Ran to Segment Leader[1]

Charles F. Hazzard (University of Texas at Dallas)

How does Oxy grow from poor profitability to a consistent #1 ranking on both Fortune's "Most Admired" and "Business Sector Ranking" lists?

In 1956, when Armand Hammer took over as CEO of a small company, Occidental Petroleum (Oxy), he had a vision for the future that involved multiple businesses and dramatic growth. By the early 1980s, Hammer had achieved the growth but *not* the profitability that should have gone with it. His search for someone to turn around his company had led him to fire seven presidents over the prior ten years: actions not seen before or since.

Finally in 1983, Hammer asked Dr. Ray R. Irani to come in and make Oxy profitable. Irani was highly regarded in the chemical industry, having graduated from the University of Southern California with a PhD in chemistry at the age of 20. He had developed 150 US patents over his career. He had been president of Olin Corporation, a smaller, $2 billion chemical conglomerate, when Hammer's headhunters called.

Attracting Irani to a company that Fortune had ranked #1 out of the Five "Worst Managed" Companies in the Top 500 in 1982 was a major effort by Hammer and, ultimately, saved his company (NYSE: OXY). In the early 1980s when Irani joined as Executive Vice President, Oxy, and Chairman and CEO, OxyChem (a division within Oxy), Oxy was a $14 billion firm that was a struggling also-ran in the oil industry. By 2013, when Irani retired as CEO, Oxy was consistently ranked number one on *Fortune's* "Most Admired" Mining & Crude Oil Production Companies list. What happened?

Starting Small

In 1983, Irani, and his team of three executives who he hand picked from Olin, came into Oxy. They were put in charge of Occidental Chemical Corporation (OxyChem), which was Oxy's smallest and least profitable division. While, in most companies, profit improvement programs are immediately launched in dire situations, OxyChem had no profits to improve.

1) The author thanks Professor Mike Peng for helpful discussions and editorial assistance. © Charles F. Hazzard. Reprinted with permission.

Shown in Exhibit 1, OxyChem was, in fact, in a negative profitability situation. When there are no profits, look for cash flow. In a commodity business, find cash flow and become the low cost producer. That in fact was Irani's plan for OxyChem.

By 1986, OxyChem had purchased Diamond Shamrock Chemical from Maxxus Energy. Maxxus needed cash. OxyChem wanted to double its chlorine capacity. The deal was *good for both sides*. This is a key point: what we all learned from Irani through deals large and small was that those who made deals with him saw what was the positive for them as well as for Oxy. Through asset sales, cash flow improvements, and profits, OxyChem made back the cost of that purchase within 18 months.

By 1988, OxyChem was making a much larger deal to buy Cain Chemical, an ethelyne leveraged buyout (LBO) worth roughly $2.2 billion. Ethelyne was an essentially cyclical chemical but highly profitable in predictable cycles. In this case, OxyChem was competing with a much larger company to make the deal to purchase Cain. To purchase Cain, Oxy quickly dipped into an $8 billion credit line and offered $2.2 billion first. In this case, Oxy was able to leverage its agility as a smaller company. In comparison, the larger company had to go through a capital review committee,

Exhibit 1 Turning Around OxyChem

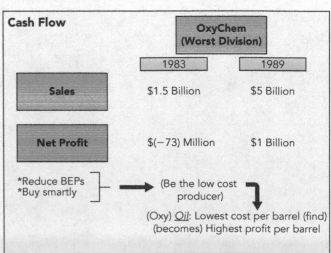

which was more time consuming. OxyChem's net profit from that deal the following year was $1 billion. *Fortune* ranked the deal in its Top 30 Business Deals for 1988.

Saving the Parent Company

Less than two years into Irani's tenure at OxyChem, Hammer asked him to come to Oxy's Los Angeles head-quarters to save the rest of the company. For any big deals that OxyChem made (such as Cain Chemical), Irani led the discussions. But Hammer was satisfied with the game plan and the quality of the management in place at OxyChem.

Between 1985 and 1990, Irani worked hard to improve Oxy's profitability while waiting until he took over as CEO in 1990 to change the overall mix of businesses for the company. For example, Iowa Beef was the largest operating division (by sales) of Oxy. It had very low profit margins. *Fortune* categorized companies by whatever product category their largest operating division occupied. This made Oxy a "food company." Explaining that to security analysts and investors was problematic.

By 1990, Hammer had passed away and Irani had become CEO. His first moves were to divest divisions that did not make sense for an oil company (such as Iowa Beef) and to look forward to Oxy's future as an oil company (Exhibit 2).

Among Oxy's strengths was to have had the best oil finders in the world. Irani's emphasis was to harness that and spend capital on finds that would eventually enable Oxy to become the lower or lowest cost producer (see Exhibit 1).

As Oil prices languished in the late 1990s ($11 to $14 per barrel), Oxy had invested in aging oil fields in Texas and California, which was consistent with its goal to get cost per barrel as low as possible. Oxy's

expertise at enhanced oil recovery (EOR) positioned Oxy to maximize these opportunities.

As the century turned, oil prices began to rise again and, by 2005, Oxy was the world's most profitable oil company with an impressive $20-per-barrel profit (Exhibit 3), tops in the industry.

Argentina and Agility

Security analysts preach about and respect "quality of earnings" concerns. While the term wears many hats, dependability of earnings or earnings growth fits most situations. A case in point is Oxy's withdrawal from Argentina and re-investment in its home country.

Reproduced in Exhibit 4, Oxy's December 2010 board presentation was entitled: "Divestment of Argentine Assets, Purchase of New US Assets, Dividend Increase." In a refreshingly short set of slides, Oxy advocated monetizing the value of its Argentine oil for cash ($2.5 billion) and investing that cash into shale oil plays in Texas and North Dakota. In this case Oxy wanted out of Argentina where its assets could be nationalized at any time. Oxy approached a Chinese oil giant Sinopec, which was charged with acquiring oil as a priority for the Chinese government. In 2010, 15% of foreign direct investment (FDI) in South America was China's investment in oil, copper, and soy.[2] The strong implication here is that Argentina would be less inclined to nationalize the oil assets of a Chinese company, as opposed to those of an American company.

Just getting the value of Oxy's oil assets out of Argentina was an improvement in the quality of its earnings because it removed a "threat" of loss stemming from very real political risk. The withdrawal from Argentina (and sale to Sinopec) was also good timing, because in 2012, Argentina nationalized the oil company YPF by expropriating 51% of the shares belonging to its majority owner Repsol from Spain.

The agility that Oxy showed in finding the right buyer (Sinopec) and reinvesting the sale proceeds back into the United States was another improvement in earnings quality, because the investment back home had a high potential for growth.

Oxy Today

Few CEOs of top 500 companies stay in their positions for 20 years or more. Irani was one of them. Thanks to a massive effort to divest non-core assets when he took over in 1990 and an emphasis on capital spending to find oil and gas throughout the decade of the 1990s,

---

Exhibit 2   **A 20-Year Strategy to Turn Around Oxy**

A 20 Year Strategy

- **1990s**
  - Dr. Irani takes over as Oxy CEO: 1990
    - Garage Sale
    - All cash goes to search for oil
    - Oil price languishes through 1999 ($11 to $14 pb)
- **2000s**
  - Oxy cements its place as low cost producer
  - Oil prices begin to rise
  - By 2005 Oxy had highest profit per barrel of oil

2) Ian James, Associated Press, June 6, 2011

Exhibit 3   **Oxy was Ranked 6th by the *Businessweek* 50 Ranking**

Ann Summa/Getty Images

Ray R. Irani, 71
CEO since 1990

Company Info	
2005 RANK	6
GET MORE COMPANY INFO	OXY
MARKET VALUE $ MILLION	36,809.9
TOTAL RETURN $ MILLION	(1-YR.) 32.4 (3-YR.) 227.6
2005 SALES $ BILLION	15.2
SALES GROWTH $ MILLION	(1-YR.) 34 (3-YR.) 26.9
LONG-TERM GROWTH EST. %	10.0
NET INCOME $ MILLION	5,272.0
NET INCOME GROWTH $ MILLION	(1-YR.) 102 (3-YR.) 65.3
NET MARGIN (%)*	34.7
RETURN ON INV. CAPITAL (%)*	28.9
SHARE PRICE 12-MO. HI/LO	98/64
P/E RATIO	7
INDUSTRY	ENERGY

6 Occidental Petroleum

BACK IN THE LATE 1990s, when oil prices were low, Occidental's CEO placed two big bets, spending just over $7 billion to snap up aging oil fields in Texas and California. Today, with near record prices for crude, those wells have turned Oxy into the world's most profitable oil company. In 2004 the Los Angeles outfit managed an impressive $20-per-barrel profit, tops in the industry, according to Deutsche Bank Securities Inc. Lebanese-born Irani is still on the hunt. In 2004 he pounced on Tulsa's Vintage Petroleum for $3.8 billion and built up the biggest acreage position in Libya, newly open to American companies after years of sanctions. That nation was the site of Oxy's largest discoveries back in the day when industry legend Armand Hammer ruled the roost. Irani figures that new projects and acquisitions could boost production to nearly 1 million barrels a day by 2010, a sizable jump from the current 590,000. No doubt old man Hammer would be proud of the way his hand-picked successor is managing things.

Oxy was positioned to reap record profits as the new century began and oil prices went back up.

Over the five year period between 2001 and 2005, Oxy's total debt decreased 53% while oil and gas production increased 23%. During that same period, the value of Oxy's common stock appreciated by $20.6 billion with Oxy paying $2.0 billion in dividends to stockholders for a total increase in shareholder value of $22.6 billion.[3]

Oxy has paid dividends every year since 1975 and, with a current quarterly dividend of $0.72 per share, yielding 3.0% to its investors.[4] Oxy is one of only five stocks that increased dividends more than 15% during 2013: Oxy (18%), Kinder Morgan (18%), Sherwin Williams (17.9%), Freeport-McMo Run (17.6%), and Xerox (17.6%). Through 2013, Oxy had had a 5-year dividend growth rate of 17.2% and had increased its dividend for 11 consecutive years.

3) Oxy proxy 2006.

4) *Seeking Alpha*, The Value Investor, 2014, Occidental Petroleum: As investors applaud the restructuring, how much is the core business valued at? May

Exhibit 4 **A Slide from Oxy's Presentation to the Board in December 2010 Discussing the Impact of Assets in Argentina on the Quality of Earnings**

Impact of Transactions

- These new acquisitions and the sale of Argentina will:*
  - be immediately accretive to our earnings, ROCE and cash flow after capital;
  - provide greater certainty in achieving both our short-term and long-term average annual production growth outlook of 5 to 8%;
  - increase the domestic weighting of our oil and gas operations;
  - not materially alter the mix between our oil and natural gas reserves or production.

- These properties, combined with acquisitions completed earlier this year, will more than replace the production from the sale of Argentina

- We expect that each of these new acquisitions together with future drilling, potential exploration and consolidation opportunities in these areas, over time, will grow to 50+ mboe/d

*NY Times, "DealBook," December 2010, Andrew Ross Sorkin.

The Oxy turnaround and growth strategy between 1985 and 2010 evolved into a next phase under a new CEO. How Oxy competes into the future is a function of world oil markets and Oxy's strengths. As of fall 2013, security analysts estimated that Oxy would buy back up to 10% of its outstanding shares while increasing its dividend in anticipation of a spinoff of assets into as many as three different companies.

By early 2014, Oxy announced the separation of its California gas assets into a separately traded company. The new company would have 8,000 workers and would own 2.3 million net acres in the state for a business that reported $1.5 billion in operating earnings in 2013.[5] Oxy continues to be the number one gas producer in California. Simultaneously, Oxy announced that it would be moving its corporate headquarters from Los Angeles to Houston, Texas, where the company is the number one producer of oil in that state.

In closing, it is interesting to quote a leading investment source regarding the future outlook of Oxy:

The company has an excellent balance sheet with a healthy cash flow to support the dividend. Oxy is likely to make additional acquisitions in the future that should keep both top and bottom lines growing nicely. The company is a technology leader in retrieving deposits from *hard-to-reach reserves* and *mature fields*. This is a big plus since both

areas should provide huge potential in coming years. The appreciation rate is well ahead of 12% average annual ROI projections. A reasonable five year price target would be $136 per share.[6]

Appendix: Armand Hammer, Oxy, and Doing Business in Russia

Few companies had the relationship with Russia that Oxy did for the last 50 years of the 20th century. That is because Armand Hammer was there at the beginning of the Soviet Union with Vladimir Lenin. Born in 1898 in New York to Russian immigrant parents, Hammer had developed a strong interest in the land of his father's birth. Immediately after the 1917 Russian Revolution, he was one of the first American businessman who entered Soviet Russia. He was declared by Lenin one of the first "Heroes" of the Soviet Union in 1921, when he had developed a way to alleviate suffering and starvation in the Ural mountains through a business deal that swapped American grain for Russian precious metals and furs.*

Hammer had gone into Russia for humanitarian reasons, but continued his relationship with the country until the 1930s because of his personal relationship with Lenin and subsequent business opportunities. Between 1931 and 1961, Hammer had no dealings with Russia because those were the Stalin years and business was not possible.*

During World War II, Hammer has extensive dealings with President Franklin D. Roosevelt (FDR) and later in his career reflected on the similarities of Lenin and Roosevelt (Exhibit 5). Few, if any, people in the 20th century even had the opportunity for such a

Exhibit 5 **Hammer on Lenin and FDR**

Hammer on Lenin and FDR

Shared Many Qualities:

1. Both "approachable".

2. Non-intimidating men who did not for a moment stand on the dignity of their office.

3. Non half-baked idea, no vagueness could be risked with either man: they would detect it instantly and dismiss it.

Like FDR, Lenin was Capable of Dazzling Intellectual Flexibility

Source: A. Hammer (with N. Lyndon), 1987, *Hammer*, New York: G. P. Putnam's Sons.

5) *Seeking Alpha*, Ibid.

6) Seeking Alpha, 2013, The dividend investor's guide: Part II–Integrated oil 2013 review, by M. Bern, October 20.

comparison based on direct experience dealing with these two leading politicians.

By 1955, Hammer was approaching 60 years of age. He went to California with his third wife to "retire." He and his wife each put $50,000 into two wells that a small company called Occidental Petroleum wanted to drill. Both wells successfully produced oil. By 1957, Hammer became president and CEO of the rapidly growing Oxy.*

Russia was more a part of Hammer's "DNA" than Oxy's. When Hammer took over Oxy in 1957, he brought "Russia" with him. Hammer's relationship with Russia was reinforced in 1961 when President John F. Kennedy asked him to do something to help improve the relationship between himself and Soviet Premier Nikita Khrushchev. This was because during the heydays of the Cold War, Khrushchev had very vocal disrespect for Kennedy.*

Aside from the fact that Hammer was one of the original "Heroes of the Soviet Union" conferred by Lenin, the founding father of the Soviet Union, Hammer had cultivated relationships with subsequent Soviet Premiers by giving them "trinkets" that Lenin had given him. While a small thing in the US culture, these historic items were a big thing to Soviet Premiers. It worked. Hammer was perceived as a credible go-between between the two superpowers. Therefore, in a nontrivial way, his visits reduced the tension between the two superpowers at that time (Exhibit 6).

When Mikhail Gorbachev came to power as the new Soviet Premier in 1985, he had concluded that he was presiding over a sinking economic ship. In 1988, Gorbachev asked Hammer if he could send an Oxy executive over to Moscow in order to present to key members of his senior finance/economic staff some of the essence of how a company such as Oxy would work within a capitalistic system. Hammer asked Irani to send an executive, and Irani recommended your case author, who was Oxy's Senior Vice President, Administration (OxyChem) at that time. The presentations in Moscow were well received. But the economy had too much negative momentum at that point to reverse itself. Gorbachev ended up losing power, and the Soviet Union was dissolved in 1991.

During the 1990s, Russia slipped into economic chaos, depression, and what some have called a "kleptocracy." Since 2000, Vladimir Putin has coalesced power around a unidimensional economy centered on oil and gas. Corruption has been rampant. In 2009, a Russian Ministry of the Interior Survey established that the average bribe in the country was $1,000 (27,000 rubles).[†]

Large integrated oil companies such as Exxon continue to do business in Russia because there are large oil and gas reserves in Siberia. Exxon signed a joint venture (JV) agreement with Rosneft and was proceeding with it. Exxon spent more money but pumped less oil and natural gas, leading to a 27% drop in profit for 2013. In 2014, Exxon was forced by the US government to stop its joint work in the Kara Sea with Rosneft when sanctions were imposed on Russia due to its intervention in Ukraine.

Oxy stopped doing business in Russia in 2007.

Case Discussion Questions

1. **What were unique about Oxy's resources and capabilities that enabled it to reap the highest profit per barrel of oil in this industry?**

2. **How effective did Oxy deal with the recent turmoil in the industry?**

3. **Drawing on Oxy's experience in Russia and Argentina, comment on how it managed political risk.**

| Exhibit 6 | **Hammer Met Khrushchev in 1961** |

Bettmann/Corbis

* A. Hammer (with N. Lyndon), 1987, *Hammer*, New York: G. P. Putnam's Sons.

† *Wall Street Journal*, August 22, 2009.

Integrative Case 1.7

Ostnor's Offshoring and Reshoring[1]

Klaus E. Meyer (China Europe International Business School)

Sweden's Ostnor searches for the best locations for its business.

In Mora, Sweden, a small town four hours north of Stockholm, there was a company named Ostnor making bathroom armatures and mixers for households and businesses (see Exhibit 1). Faced with German and Swiss competitors challenging Ostnor's market leadership in Sweden, Ostnor decided in 2003 to follow the trend of offshoring and outsourced its production to partners in China. However, business did not develop well: lead times for new product introduction became longer, capital employed increased because of the need to hold more stock in the warehouses, and quality control consumed substantial resources. In short, the re-location of production to China turned into a nightmare.

In 2010, a new CEO, Claes Seldeby, came in and decided to turn back the time. The new vision was reshoring to bring back the business to its hometown of Mora. Moreover, the "made in Sweden" identity would become an increasingly valuable brand feature as consumers were skeptical of the reliability of products imported from the Far East. Swedish craftsmen from the local community were again to make the armatures using high technology and local inputs. Since these armatures were produced in modest volumes, the process required substantial skilled labor. Yet, this reshoring was not easy. Young people in the local area were looking for job opportunities, yet they needed to be trained—and manufacturing jobs were not so popular in the Internet generation. In response, Ostnor invited school classes to visit its factories for them to see the high tech nature of the work and to attract future apprentices. Another challenge was finding suppliers for manufactured components in the Nordic and East European area. Chinese suppliers were neither interested nor able to deliver the relatively small volumes to Sweden.

Ostnor managed two brands with very distinct design characteristics: Mora Armatura and F.M. Mattson. Both brands had their origins in the same family firm. But in the 1920s two brothers disagreed on how to manage the company and one of them left to set up his own business. The brothers' rivalry stimulated both of them to produce ever better products, and some 80 years later they were re-integrated. Yet, they had developed distinct organizational cultures and brand identities, which still occasionally led to tensions.

Ostnor emphasized innovation and introduced new product lines about every 18 months. Seldeby modernized the innovation process to stay in close touch with consumer preferences. For example, the R&D team was almost all male when he arrived, yet in Sweden 82% of purchasing decisions on bathroom and kitchen equipment were made by women. So, he brought in new people, especially some women, into the R&D team who would not only understand the technologies, but also the consumers.

In 2014, Ostnor acquired a Danish competitor, Damixa (see Exhibit 2). Together they became number one or two in all five Nordic countries (Denmark,

---

Exhibit 1 Basic Data for 2013/2014

- 570 employees (including Damixa)
- SEK 824 M turnover (89 M euro) in 2013 slightly down from previous years.
- 164 shareholders
- Ca 60% of equity in the family, 30% externals (including financial investors), less than 10% management team (IPO was envisioned for the future)
- Sales by region: Sweden 76%, other Nordics 17%, rest of the World 7%.

---

1) The author thanks Mike Peng for helpful discussion. All views and errors are those of the author. © Klaus E. Meyer. Reprinted with permission. Discussion questions were added by M. Peng.

Exhibit 2 Timeline

- 2003 offshore
- 2010 new CEO
- 2011 reshore
- 2014 Damixa acquisition

Finland, Iceland, Norway, and Sweden). Ostnor also had its own sales subsidiaries in Belgium, China, Germany, the Netherlands, and Singapore, and sold via distributors to Australia, the Baltic countries, Britain, France, and Russia.

By 2014, Ostnor faced three new challenges.

1. With the acquisition of Damixa, Ostnor now had three brands. The CEO proposed to position Mura Armatura at the top end, F.M. Mattson in the middle, and Damixa as an economy brand. This however raised operational challenges. First, employees at Damixa were not pleased to become the lower end brand compared to the Swedish brands. Second, if Ostnor wanted to develop a brand for the economy segment, then offshoring some parts of the operations again was on the agenda for discussion.

2. With the company's growth, Ostnor hit the limits of what could be achieved in the community of Mora. It was difficult to attract skilled workers to the area, and the board's need to travel internationally made the four -hour car journey (if there was no snow) from Mora to Stockholm Arlanda Airport rather cumbersome. Therefore, Ostnor decided to relocate its headquarters and some operations to Stockholm, and Seldeby and his family moved back to Stockholm after four years in Mora.

3. Ostnor took initiatives to enter the Chinese market, where its designs would only be able to serve a small niche market. Yet, a small niche in China can quickly outgrow total sales in the Nordic region because China's population is so big. Hence, Ostnor in 2013 established a sales office in Hong Kong and participated in trade shows in China to develop sales in the Greater China area. In fact, it had to investigate the necessary regulations and certifications, Chinese consumers design preferences, and decision making processes. Ostnor quickly learned that "hand made" was not a good way to advertise—in China a "machine made" product was supposed to be highly reliable. It also found that putting a Swedish flag on the packaging to emphasize "made in Sweden" helped creating a premium image.

Case Discussion Questions

1. **What motivated Ostnor's offshoring?**
2. **What motivated Ostnor's reshoring?**
3. **From a resource-based view, what are the lessons from Ostnor's offshoring and reshoring?**
4. **Which area should the firm focus on in 2015?**

Sources: Based on the CEO's presentation and company documents.

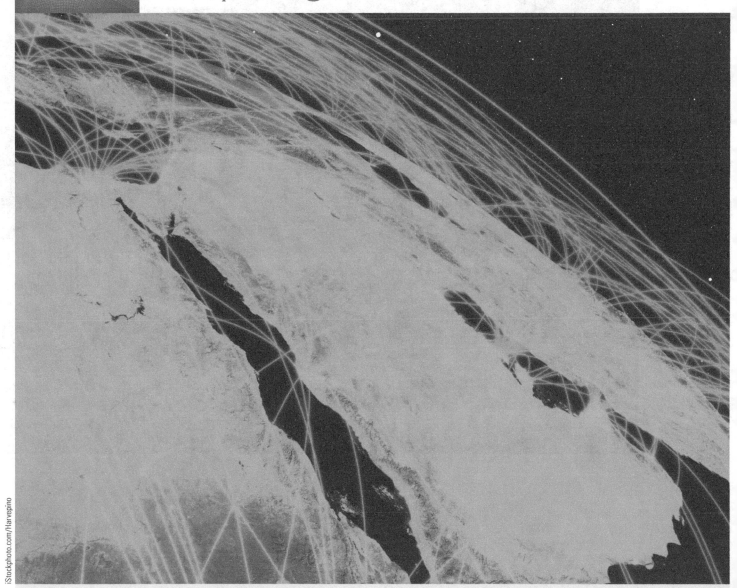

PART 2 Acquiring Tools

iStockphoto.com/Harvepino

Chapters

Stefan Hofecker/Alamy

CHAPTER

5

Learning Objectives

After studying this chapter, you should be able to

- use the resource-based and institution-based views to answer why nations trade.

- understand classical and modern theories of international trade.

- realize the importance of political realities governing international trade.

- participate in two leading debates concerning international trade.

- draw implications for action.

Trading Internationally

OPENING CASE

EMERGING MARKETS: Is China the Largest Trading Nation of the World?

International trade has two directions: export and import. It has two components: merchandise (goods) and services. The ratio between merchandise and service trade is generally 4:1. Is China now the world's largest trading nation?

The ubiquitous Made-in-China products around the world are the most visible evidence of the rise of China as a trading nation. Between the publication of *Global Business*'s second edition (with 2008 data) and third edition (with 2011 data), China dethroned Germany to become the world's champion merchandise exporter—a distinction it has maintained in this (fourth) edition (with 2013 data). Why does the rest of the world buy so many Made-in-China products? Without getting into details, we can safely say—from a resource-based view—that Chinese exports win markets because they deliver value, are rare, and possess hard-to-imitate attributes. Such products range from low-tech shoes and toys to high-tech smartphones (made by Lenovo and Xiaomi) and telecom equipment (made by Huawei and ZTE). With 33% of GDP coming from manufacturing (the world's highest), China's manufacturing capabilities have not only propelled its export growth, but have also underpinned its rise as the world's second-largest economy.

From an institution-based view, China's accession to the World Trade Organization (WTO) in 2001 has certainly contributed to its rise as a trading nation. In addition, it has free trade agreements (FTAs) with the Association of Southeast Asian Nations (ASEAN—with ten member countries), Chile, Costa Rica, New Zealand, Pakistan, Peru, and Singapore. China is also negotiating FTAs with Australia, Iceland, Japan, Norway, and South Korea as well as two regional bodies: the (Persian) Gulf Cooperation Council (GCC) and Southern Africa Customs Union (SACU).

While China's merchandise exports often attract attention, less visible but equally important is China's voracious appetite for merchandise imports. Between the third and fourth editions of *Global Business*, China displaced Germany as the second-largest merchandise importer—only behind the United States. The majority of Chinese imports consists of raw materials (such as Australian coal, Chilean copper, and Russian oil) and industrial supplies (such as Toshiba electronic components and Texas Instruments semiconductors). A curious feature of Chinese exports is that most of them are produced by non-Chinese firms operating in China. These firms source a lot of components from around the world to be assembled in China. Meticulous research on "Designed in California, Assembled in China" Apple iPhones and iPads finds that that 60% to 70% of their value comes from imports from economies such as Germany, Japan, South Korea, Taiwan, and the United States. The real value-added in China is about 10%—Apple captures the rest. Given that iPhones and iPads are made in China by Taiwan-based Foxconn, which repatriates some of its earnings to Taiwan, the real value-added that stays in China due to all that hard work to assemble and export iPhones and iPads is significantly less than 10%. While iPhones and iPads may be extreme cases, overall China only adds 67% of the value of its exports. In comparison, the United States adds 89% of the value to its exports (see the Closing Case).

China does enjoy the world's second-largest merchandise trade surplus (US$259 billion)—behind Germany's slightly larger merchandise surplus (US$264 billion). At the same time, China suffers from the world's biggest deficit in service trade (US$124 billion). As an active trader of services, China is fifth in service exports (behind the United States, Britain, Germany, and France) and second in service imports (behind the United States). Its leading contributor to service trade deficit is tourism. As the largest group of international tourists, one out of every ten international tourists is now Chinese. As a group, they spend more and focus more on shopping. In 2013, they spent US$129 billion, followed by American tourists who spent US$86 billion. The average Chinese tourist indulges him/herself with US$1,130 tax-free purchases vis-à-vis US$494 by the average Russian tourist.

With US$4.2 trillion in merchandise trade, China is the world's largest merchandise trader. However, adding all the merchandise exports and imports as well as service exports and imports (see Table 5.1), China, whose total trade volume is US$4.7 trillion, is *not* the largest trading nation. It is the second-largest trading nation. With a total trade volume of US$5 trillion, the United States is the world's trade champion. In percentage terms, a substantially higher percentage (53%) of Chinese GDP is traded vis-à-vis a lower 30% of US GDP that is traded. In the next decade, as the overall size of the Chinese economy becomes larger than the US economy, it is likely that China will dethrone the United States to become the largest trading nation. While examining the total volume of trade is interesting, on a per capita basis, China only ranks 99th in the world given its huge population of 1.34 billion.

Sources: Based on (1) *Bloomberg Businessweek*, 2014, Taiwan's protests point to a deeper crisis, April 17: 17–18; (2) *Economist*, 2014, A number of great import, February 15: 40; (3) *Economist*, 2014, Coming to a beach near you, April 19: 53–54; (4) *Economist*, 2014, Picking the world champion of trade, January 18: 72–73; (5) *Economist*, 2014, Trading places, April 5: 49; (6) M. W. Peng & K. Meyer, 2013, Winning the future markets for UK manufacturing output, *Future of Manufacturing Project Evidence Paper* 25, London: UK Government Office for Science; (7) World Trade Organization, 2014, *World Trade Report 2014*, Geneva: WTO.

Why are Chinese merchandise exports so competitive in the world? Why does China's service trade suffer a huge deficit? More generally, how does international trade contribute to a nation's economic growth and prosperity? International trade is the oldest and still the most important building block of international business. It has never failed to generate debates. Debates on international trade tend to be very ferocious, because so much is at stake. We begin by addressing a crucial question: Why do nations trade? Then we outline how the two core perspectives introduced in earlier chapters—namely, resource-based and institution-based views—can help answer this question. The remainder of the chapter deals with the theories and realities of international trade. As before, debates and implications for action follow.

Learning Objective

Use the resource-based and institution-based views to answer why nations trade.

Export

Selling abroad.

Import

Buying from abroad.

Merchandise (goods)

Tangible products being traded.

Services

Intangible services being traded.

5-1 Why Do Nations Trade?

Internationally, trade means export (sell abroad) and import (buy from abroad). Table 5.1 provides a snapshot of the top 10 exporting and importing nations in the two main sectors: merchandise (goods) and services. In merchandise exports, China, the United States, and Germany are the top three. In merchandise imports, the top three are the United States, China, and Germany. In services, the United States is both the largest exporter and the largest importer. Britain and Germany

Table 5.1 **Leading Trading Nations**

	Top 10 *merchandise* exporters	Value (US$ billion)	World share (%)	Annual change (%)		Top 10 *merchandise* importers	Value (US$ billion)	World share (%)	Annual change (%)
1	China	2,209	11.7%	8%	1	United States	2,329	12.3%	0%
2	United States	1,580	8.4%	2%	2	China	1,950	10.3%	7%
3	Germany	1,453	7.7%	3%	3	Germany	1,189	6.3%	2%
4	Japan	715	3.8%	−10%	4	Japan	833	4.4%	−6%
5	Netherlands	672	3.6%	3%	5	France	681	3.6%	1%
6	France	580	3.1%	2%	6	United Kingdom	655	3.5%	−5%
7	South Korea	562	3.0%	2%	7	Hong Kong, China	622	3.3%	12%
8	United Kingdom	542	2.9%	15%	8	Netherlands	590	3.1%	0%
9	Hong Kong, China	536	2.8%	9%	9	South Korea	516	2.7%	−1%
10	Russia	523	2.8%	−1%	10	Italy	477	2.5%	−2%
	World total	**18,816**	**100%**	**2%**		**World total**	**18,890**	**100%**	**2%**
	Top 10 *service* exporters	Value (US$ billion)	World share (%)	Annual change (%)		Top 10 *service* importers	Value (US$ billion)	World share (%)	Annual change (%)
1	United States	662	14.3%	5%	1	United States	432	9.8%	4%
2	United Kingdom	293	6.3%	2%	2	China	329	7.5%	18%
3	Germany	286	6.2%	8%	3	Germany	317	7.2%	8%
4	France	236	5.1%	10%	4	France	189	4.3%	8%
5	China	205	4.4%	7%	5	United Kingdom	174	4%	−1%
6	India	151	3.2%	4%	6	Japan	162	3.7%	−7%
7	Netherlands	147	3.2%	12%	7	Singapore	128	2.9%	4%
8	Japan	145	3.1%	2%	8	Netherlands	127	2.9%	7%
9	Spain	145	3.1%	6%	9	India	125	2.8%	−3%
10	Hong Kong, China	133	2.9%	6%	10	Russia	123	2.8%	18
	World total	**4,644**	**100%**	**6%**		**World total**	**4,381**	**100%**	**11%**

Source: Adapted from World Trade Organization, 2014, *Word Trade Report 2014*, Appendix Tables 3 and 5, Geneva: WTO (www.wto.org). All data are for 2013.

are the top two and three service exporters, respectively. China and Germany are the top two and three service importers, respectively.

Why do nations trade?[1] Without getting into details, we can safely say that there must be economic gains from trade (see PengAtlas Map 2.1 and 2.2). More importantly, both sides must share such gains—otherwise, there will be no willing exporters and importers. In other words, international trade is a *win-win* deal. Figure 5.1 shows that world trade growth (averaging more than 5% between 1993 and 2013) generally outpaces GDP growth (averaging nearly 3% during the same period). However, in 2012 and 2013, world trade grew at roughly the same rate as world GDP growth.

Why are there gains from trade?[2] How do nations benefit from such gains? The remainder of the chapter will answer these questions. Before proceeding, it is important to clarify that "nations trade" is a misleading statement. A more accurate expression should be: "Firms from different nations trade."[3] Unless different

Figure 5.1 **Growth in World Trade Generally Outpaces Growth in World GDP (Annual % Change)**

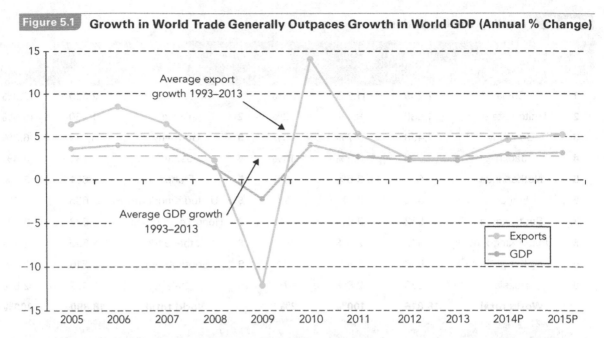

Source: World Trade Organization, 2014, Modest trade growth anticipated for 2014 and 2015 following two-year slump, press release, April 14, Geneva: WTO (www.wto.org). The figure refers to merchandise (goods) exports.

governments directly buy and sell from each other (such as arms sales), the majority of trade is conducted by firms, which pay little attention to country-level ramifications. For example, Wal-Mart imports a lot into the United States and does not export much. Wal-Mart thus directly contributes to the US trade deficit (a nation imports more than it exports), which is something the US government does not like. However, in most countries, governments cannot tell firms, such as Wal-Mart, what to do (and not to do) unless firms engage in illegal activities. Therefore, when we ask, "Why do nations trade?" we are really asking, "Why do *firms* from different nations trade?" When discussing the US–China trade whereby China runs a trade surplus (a nation exports more than it imports), we are really referring to thousands of US firms buying from and selling to China, which also has thousands of firms buying from and selling to the United States. The aggregation of such buying (importing) and selling (exporting) by both sides leads to the country-level balance of trade—namely, whether a country has a trade surplus or deficit.

Having acknowledged the limitations of the expression that "nations trade," we will still use it. Why? Because it is commonly used and serves as a short-hand version of the more-accurate but more-cumbersome expression that "firms from different nations trade." This clarification does enable us to use the two *firm-level* perspectives introduced earlier—namely, the resource-based and institution-based views—to shed light on why nations trade.

Recall from Chapter 4 that it is valuable, rare, inimitable, and organizationally derived (VRIO) products that determine the competitive advantage of a firm. Applying this insight, we can suggest that VRIO products generated by organizationally strong firms in one nation can lead to the competitive advantage of its exports (see the Opening and Closing Cases).[4] Further, recall from Chapters 2 and 3 that numerous politically and culturally derived rules of the game (known as institutions) constrain and facilitate individual and firm behavior. For example, although American movies are the best in the world, Canada, France, and

Trade deficit

An economic condition in which a nation imports more than it exports.

Trade surplus

An economic condition in which a nation exports more than it imports.

Balance of trade

The aggregation of importing and exporting that leads to the country-level trade surplus or deficit.

IN FOCUS 5.1
STILL MADE IN JAPAN

On March 11, 2011, Japan suffered from a triple disaster—a 9.0 earthquake (its worst in recorded history), a huge tsunami, and a nuclear power plant accident. From a global standpoint, a lot of non-Japanese firms that relied on Made-in-Japan products were ill prepared for such a sudden catastrophic event. Despite the widely noted migration of manufacturing jobs to low-cost countries such as China and Malaysia, Japan has remained an export powerhouse. In 2010, it was the world's fourth-largest merchandise (goods) exporter (after China, Germany, and the United States), with US$765 billion exports. For example, Japan produces approximately one-fifth of the world's semiconductors and 40% of electronic components. While low-end products tend to be made overseas, "Japan has higher and higher market share of specialty materials as you go up the value chain," noted one expert. For example, Boeing outsourced 35% of the work on

its newest 787 Dreamliner to Japanese manufacturers. Among them, Mitsubishi Heavy Industries built the 787's wings, and no one else in the world could do the job—Boeing had no plan B. On March 17, 2011, General Motors closed two US-based factories for a week, due to a lack of components arriving from Japan. For planes, cars, laptops, and phones assembled outside of Japan, the Made-in-Japan components may represent a relatively small amount, but they tend to be *mission-critical*. "If the Japanese cannot supply," noted another expert, "then no one is going to get their iPad" because no smart factory can build an iPad with only 97% of parts.

Sources: Based on (1) *Bloomberg Businessweek*, 2011, Downsides of just-in-time inventory, March 28: 17–18; (2) *Bloomberg Businessweek*, 2011, Facing up to nuclear risk, March 21: 13–14; (3) *Bloomberg Businessweek*, 2011, Now, a weak link in the global supply chain, March 21: 18–19; (4) *Bloomberg BusinessWeek*, 2011, The cataclysm this time, March 21: 11–13.

South Korea limit the market share of American movies. Thus, various regulations create trade barriers around the world. On the other hand, we also see the rise of rules that facilitate trade, such as those advocated by the World Trade Organization (WTO) (see Chapter 8).

Overall, why are there economic gains from international trade? According to the resource-based view, this is because some firms in one nation generate exports that are valuable, unique, and hard-to-imitate that firms from other nations find it beneficial to import (see In Focus 5.1). How do nations benefit from such gains? According to the institution-based view, different rules governing trade are designed to share (or not to share) such gains.[5] The remainder of this chapter expands on these two perspectives.

5-2 Theories of International Trade

Theories of international trade provide one of the oldest, richest, and most influential bodies of economics, whose founding is usually associated with the publication of British economist Adam Smith's *The Wealth of Nations* in 1776. Theories of international trade predate Adam Smith. In fact, Adam Smith wrote *The Wealth of Nations* to challenge an earlier theory: mercantilism. In this section, we introduce major theories of international trade: (1) mercantilism, (2) absolute advantage, (3) comparative advantage, (4) product life cycle, (5) strategic trade, and (6) national competitive advantage. The first three are often regarded as classical trade theories, and the last three are viewed as modern trade theories.

Learning Objective

Understand classical and modern theories of international trade.

Classical trade theories

The major theories of international trade that were advanced before the 20th century, which consist of (1) mercantilism, (2) absolute advantage, and (3) comparative advantage.

Modern trade theories

The major theories of international trade that were advanced in the 20th century, which consist of (1) product life cycle, (2) strategic trade, and (3) national competitive advantage of industries.

5-2a Mercantilism

Widely practiced between the 1600s and the 1700s, the theory of mercantilism viewed international trade as a zero-sum game. Its theorists, led by French statesman Jean-Baptiste Colbert, believed that the wealth of the world (measured in gold and silver at that time) was fixed. A nation that exported more and imported less would enjoy the net inflows of gold and silver and, thus, become richer. On the other hand, a nation experiencing a trade deficit would see its gold and silver flowing out and, consequently, would become poorer. The upshot? Self-sufficiency would be best.

Although mercantilism is the oldest theory in international trade, it is not an extinct dinosaur. Very much alive, mercantilism is the direct intellectual ancestor of modern-day protectionism, which is the idea that governments should actively protect domestic industries from imports and vigorously promote exports. Many modern governments may still be mercantilist at heart. Thank about all these export assistance programs run by many governments (see the Closing Case). Has anyone seen an *import* assistance program?

5-2b Absolute Advantage

The theory of absolute advantage, advocated by Adam Smith in 1776, opened the floodgates of the free trade movement that is still going on today. Smith argued that in the aggregate, the "invisible hand" of markets, rather than governments, should determine the scale and scope of economic activities. This is known as *laissez faire* (see Chapter 2). By trying to be self-sufficient and (inefficiently) produce a wide range of goods, mercantilist policies *reduce* the wealth of a nation in the long run. Smith thus argued for free trade, which is the idea that free market forces should determine how much to trade with little government intervention.

Specifically, Smith proposed a theory of absolute advantage: With free trade, each nation gains by specializing in economic activities in which it has absolute advantage. What is absolute advantage? It is the economic advantage one nation enjoys that is absolutely superior to other nations. For example, Smith argued that because of better soil, water, and weather, Portugal enjoyed an absolute advantage over England in the production of grapes and wines. Likewise, England had an absolute advantage over Portugal in the production of sheep and wool. England could grow grapes at a greater cost and with much lower quality—has anyone heard of any world-famous English wines? Smith suggested (1) that England should specialize in sheep and wool, (2) that Portugal should specialize in grapes and wines, and (3) that they should trade with each other. Here are two of Smith's greatest insights. First, by specializing in the production of goods for which each has an absolute advantage, both can produce more. Second, by trading, both can benefit more. By specializing, England produces more wool than it can use, and Portugal produces more wine than it can drink. When both nations trade, England gets more (and better) wine and Portugal more (and better) wool than either country could produce on its own. In other words, international trade is not a zero-sum game as suggested by mercantilism. It is a *win-win* game.

How can this be? Let us use an example with hypothetical numbers (Figure 5.2 and Table 5.2). For the sake of simplicity, assume there are only two nations in the world: China and the United States. They only perform two economic activities: growing wheat and making aircraft. Production of wheat or aircraft, naturally, requires resources such as labor, land, and technology. Assume that both

Theory of mercantilism
A theory that suggests that the wealth of the world is fixed and that a nation that exports more and imports less will be richer.

Protectionism
The idea that governments should actively protect domestic industries from imports and vigorously promote exports.

Free trade
The idea that free market forces should determine how much to trade with little or no government intervention.

Theory of absolute advantage
A theory that suggests that under free trade, a nation gains by specializing in economic activities in which it has an absolute advantage.

Absolute advantage
The economic advantage one nation enjoys that is absolutely superior to other nations.

Figure 5.2 Absolute Advantage

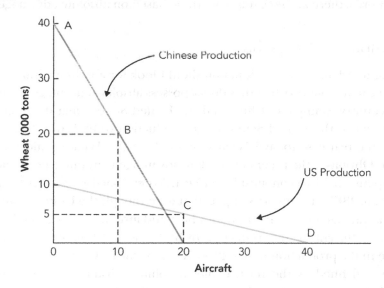

Table 5.2 Absolute Advantage

Total units of resources = 800 for each country		Wheat	Aircraft
(1) Resources required to produce 1,000 tons of wheat and 1 aircraft.	China	20 resources	40 resources
	US	80 resources	20 resources
(2) Production and consumption with no specialization and without trade (each country devotes *half* of its resources to each activity).	China (point B)	20,000 tons	10 aircraft
	US (point C)	5,000 tons	20 aircraft
	Total production	*25,000 tons*	*30 aircraft*
(3) Production with specialization (China specializes in wheat and produces no aircraft, and the United States specializes in aircraft and produces no wheat).	China (point A)	40,000 tons	0
	US (point D)	0	40 aircraft
	Total production	*40,000 tons*	*40 aircraft*
(4) Consumption after each country trades one-quarter of its output while producing at points A and D, respectively (Scenario #3).	China	30,000 tons	10 aircraft
	US	10,000 tons	30 aircraft
	Total consumption	*40,000 tons*	*40 aircraft*
(5) *Gains* from trade: Increase in consumption as a result of specialization and trade (Scenario #4 versus #2).	China	+10,000 tons	0
	US	+5,000 tons	+10 aircraft

are equally endowed with 800 units of resources. Between the two activities, the United States has an absolute advantage in the production of aircraft—it takes 20 resources to produce an aircraft (for which China needs 40 resources), and the total US capacity is 40 aircraft if it does not produce wheat (point D in Figure 5.2). China has an absolute advantage in the production of wheat—it takes 20 resources to produce 1,000 tons of wheat (for which the United States needs 80 resources) and the total Chinese capacity is 40,000 tons of wheat if it does not make aircraft (point A). It is important to note that the United States can grow wheat and that China can make aircraft, albeit inefficiently. Since both nations need wheat and aircraft, without trade, they produce both by spending half of their resources on each—China at point B (20,000 tons of wheat and 10 aircraft) and the United States at point C (5,000 tons of wheat and 20 aircraft). Interestingly, if they stay at points A and D, respectively, and trade one-quarter of their output with each other (10,000 tons of Chinese wheat with 10 American aircraft), these two countries, and by implication the global economy, both produce more and consume more (Table 5.2). In other words, there are *net* gains from trade based on absolute advantage.

5-2c Comparative Advantage

According to Adam Smith, each nation should look for absolute advantage. However, what can nations do when they do *not* possess absolute advantage? Continuing our two-country example of China and the United States, what if China is absolutely inferior to the United States in the production of both wheat and aircraft (which is the real case today)? What should China do? What should the United States do? Obviously, the theory of absolute advantage runs into a dead end.

In response, British economist David Ricardo developed a theory of comparative advantage in 1817. This theory suggests that even though the United States has an absolute advantage over China in both wheat and aircraft, as long as China is not equally less efficient in the production of both goods, China can still choose to specialize in the production of one good (such as wheat) where it has comparative advantage—defined as the relative (not absolute) advantage in one economic activity that one nation enjoys in comparison with other nations. Figure 5.3 and Table 5.3 show that China's comparative advantage lies in its *relatively less inefficient* production of wheat: If China devotes all resources to wheat, it can produce 10,000 tons, which is four-fifths of the 12,500 tons the United States can produce. However, at a maximum, China can only produce 20 aircraft, which is merely half of the 40 aircraft the United States can make. By letting China specialize in the production of wheat and importing some wheat from China, the United States is able to leverage its strengths by devoting its resources to aircraft. For example, if (1) the United States devotes four-fifths of its resources to aircraft and one-fifth to wheat (Point C in Figure 5.3), (2) China concentrates 100% of its resources on wheat (Point E), and (3) they trade with each other, both countries produce and consume more than what they would produce and consume if they inefficiently devote half of their resources to each activity.

Again, there are *net* gains from trade, this time from comparative advantage. One crucial concept here is opportunity cost—given the alternatives (other opportunities),

Theory of comparative advantage

A theory that focuses on the relative (not absolute) advantage in one economic activity that one nation enjoys in comparison with other nations.

Comparative advantage

Relative (not absolute) advantage in one economic activity that one nation enjoys in comparison with other nations.

Opportunity cost

Cost of pursuing one activity at the expense of another activity, given the alternatives (other opportunities).

Figure 5.3   **Comparative Advantage**

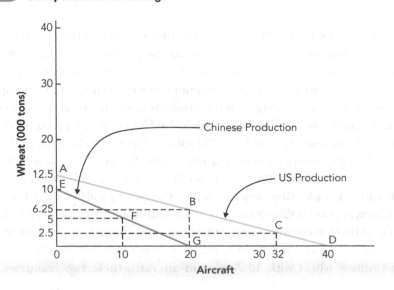

Table 5.3	**Comparative Advantage**			
Total units of resources = 800 for each country			**Wheat**	**Aircraft**
(1) Resources required to produce 1,000 tons of wheat and 1 aircraft.	China		80 resources	40 resources
	US		64 resources	20 resources
(2) Production and consumption with no specialization and without trade (each country devotes *half* of its resources to each activity).	China (point F)		5,000 tons	10 aircraft
	US (point B)		6,250 tons	20 aircraft
	Total production		*11,250 tons*	*30 aircraft*
(3) Production with specialization (China devotes all resources to wheat, and the United States devotes one-fifth of its resources to wheat and four-fifths of its resources to aircraft)	China (point E)		10,000 tons	0
	US (point C)		2,500 tons	32 aircraft
	Total production		*12,500 tons*	*32 aircraft*
(4) Consumption after China trades 4,000 tons of wheat for 11 US aircraft while producing at points E and C, respectively (Scenario #3).	China		6,000 tons	11 aircraft
	US		6,500 tons	21 aircraft
	Total consumption		12,500 *tons*	*32 aircraft*
(5) *Gains* from trade: Increase in consumption as a result of specialization and trade (Scenario #4 versus #2).	China		+1,000 tons	+1 aircraft
	US		+250 tons	+1 aircraft

the cost of pursuing one activity at the expense of another activity. For the United States, the opportunity cost of concentrating on wheat at point A in Figure 5.3 is tremendous relative to producing aircraft at point D, because it is only 25% more productive in wheat than China, but is 100% more productive in aircraft.

Relative to absolute advantage, the theory of comparative advantage seems counterintuitive. However, this theory is far more realistic and useful in the real world. This is because, while it is easy to identify an absolute advantage in a highly simplified, two-country world as in Figure 5.2, how can each nation decide what to specialize in when there are more than 200 nations in the world? It is simply too challenging to ascertain that one nation is absolutely better than all others in one activity. Is the United States *absolutely* better than not only China, but also all other 200 nations in aircraft production? European nations that produce Airbus obviously beg to differ. The theory of comparative advantage suggests that even without an absolute advantage, the United States can still profitably specialize in aircraft as long as it is relatively more efficient than others. This insight thus has greatly lowered the threshold for specialization.

Where do absolute and comparative advantages come from? In one word, productivity. Smith looked at *absolute* productivity differences, and Ricardo emphasized *relative* productivity differences—in this sense, absolute advantage is really a special case of comparative advantage. But what leads to such productivity differences? In the early 20th century, Swedish economists Eli Heckscher and Bertil Ohlin argued that absolute and comparative advantages stem from different factor endowments, namely, the extent to which different countries possess various factors, such as labor, land, and technology. This factor endowment theory (or Heckscher-Ohlin theory) proposed that nations will develop comparative advantage based on their *locally abundant* factors. Numerous examples support the theories of comparative advantage and factor endowments. For example, Brazil is blessed by an abundant supply of sunshine, soil, and water, which make it a world-class player in agricultural products. When Nissan makes cars in Japan, it uses a lot of robots. But Nissan in India relies more heavily on labor to make cars. In another example, when Indian firms set up call centers to service Western clients, they use human labor, a factor that is abundant in India, to replace some automation functions when answering the phone—telephone automation technology has been developed in the West

Factor endowment

The extent to which different countries possess various factors of production such as labor, land, and technology.

Factor endowment theory (Heckscher-Ohlin theory)

A theory that suggests that nations will develop comparative advantages based on their locally abundant factors.

because of labor shortage. Western clients are happier, because they can actually talk to a live person instead of talking to or dialing to a machine (dial 1 for this, dial 2 for that).

In summary, *classical* theories—(1) mercantilism, (2) absolute advantage, and (3) comparative advantage (which includes factor endowments)—had evolved from approximately 300 to 400 years ago to the beginning of the 20th century. More recently, three *modern* theories, outlined next, emerged.

5-2d Product Life Cycle

Up to this point, classical theories all paint a *static* picture: If England has an absolute or comparative advantage in textiles (thanks to its favorable weather and soil), it should keep producing textiles. However, this assumption of no change in factor endowments and trade patterns does not always hold true in the real world. While Adam Smith's England, more than 200 years ago, was a major exporter of textiles, today England's textile industry is insignificant. So, what happened? While one may argue that in England weather has changed and soil has become less fertile, it is difficult to believe that weather and soil have changed so much in 200 years, which is a relatively short period for long-run climatic changes. In another example, since the 1980s, the United States turned from being a net exporter to a net importer of personal computers (PCs), while Malaysia transformed itself from being a net importer to a net exporter of PCs—and this change has nothing to do with weather or soil change. Why do patterns of trade in PCs change over time? Classical theories have difficulty answering this intriguing question.

In 1966, American economist Raymond Vernon developed the product life cycle theory, which is the first *dynamic* theory to account for changes in the patterns of trade over time.[6] Vernon divided the world into three categories: (1) lead innovation nation (which, according to him, is typically the United States), (2) other developed nations, and (3) developing nations. Further, every product has three life cycle stages: new, maturing, and standardized. Shown in Figure 5.4, in the first stage, production of a new product (such as a TV) that commands a price premium will concentrate in the United States, which exports to other developed nations. In the second, maturing stage, demand and ability to produce grow in other developed nations (such as Australia and Italy), so it is now worthwhile to produce there. In the third stage, the previously new product is standardized (or commoditized). Thus, much production will now move to low-cost developing nations, which export to developed nations. In other words, comparative advantage may change over time.

While this theory was first proposed in the 1960s, some later events (such as the migration of PC production) have supported its prediction. However, this theory has been criticized on two accounts. First, it assumes that the United States will always be the lead innovation nation for new products. This may be increasingly invalid. For example, the fanciest cell (mobile) phones are now routinely pioneered in Asia and Europe. Second, this theory assumes a stage-by-stage migration of production, taking at least several years (if not decades). In reality, however, an increasing number of firms now *simultaneously* launch new products (such as iPads) around the globe.

Product life cycle theory

A theory that accounts for changes in the patterns of trade over time by focusing on product life cycles.

5-2e Strategic Trade

Except mercantilism, none of the theories above has anything to say about the role of governments. Since the days of Adam Smith, government intervention has

Figure 5.4   **Theory of Product Life Cycles**

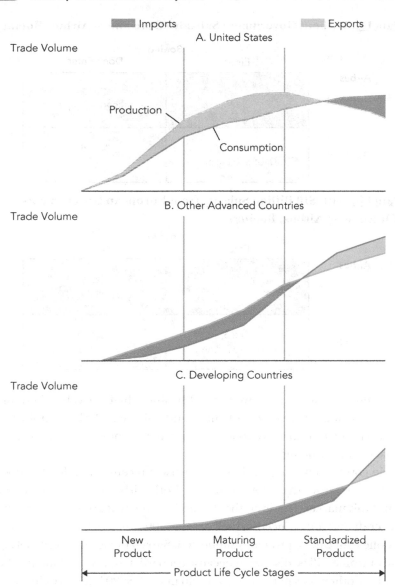

usually been regarded as undesirable. However, government intervention is extensive and is not going away. Can government intervention actually add value? Since the 1970s, a new theory, strategic trade theory, has addressed this question.[7]

Strategic trade theory suggests that strategic intervention by governments in certain industries can enhance their odds for international success. What are these industries? They tend to be high capital-intensity, high entry-barrier industries in which domestic firms may have little chance without government assistance. These industries also feature substantial first-mover advantages—namely, advantages that first entrants enjoy and do not share with late entrants. One leading example is the commercial aircraft industry. Founded in 1915 and strengthened by large military orders during World War II, Boeing has long dominated this industry. In the jumbo jet segment, Boeing's first-mover advantages associated with its 400-seat 747, first launched in the late 1960s, are still significant today. Alarmed by such US dominance, in the late 1960s, British, French, German, and Spanish governments realized that if they did not intervene in this industry, individual European aerospace

Strategic trade theory

A theory that suggests that strategic intervention by governments in certain industries can enhance their odds for international success.

First-mover advantage

Benefit that accrues to firms that enter the market first and that late entrants do not enjoy.

| Figure 5.5 | Entering the Very Large, Super-Jumbo Market? |

Panel A. Without Government Subsidy (Outcome = Airbus, Boeing)

		Boeing	
		Enter	Don't Enter
Airbus	Enter	(Cell 1) –US$5 billion, –US$5 billion	(Cell 2) US$20 billion, 0
	Don't Enter	(Cell 3) 0, US$20 billion	(Cell 4) 0, 0

Panel B. With $10 Billion Subsidy from European Governments
(Outcome = Airbus, Boeing)

		Boeing	
		Enter	Don't Enter
Airbus	Enter	(Cell 1) US$5 billion, –US$5 billion	(Cell 2) US$30 billion, 0
	Don't Enter	(Cell 3) 0, US$20 billion	(Cell 4) 0, 0

firms on their own might be driven out of business by US rivals. Therefore, these European governments agreed to launch and subsidize Airbus. In four decades, Airbus has risen from nowhere to a position where it now has a 50–50 split of the global market with Boeing.

How do governments help Airbus? Let us use a recent example: the super-jumbo aircraft, which is larger than the Boeing 747. Both Airbus and Boeing are interested in entering this market. However, the demand in the next 20 years is only about 400 to 500 aircraft and a firm needs to sell at least 300 just to break even, which means that only one firm can be profitably supported. Shown in Figure 5.5 (Panel A), if both enter, the outcome will be disastrous because each will lose US$5 billion (Cell 1). If one enters and the other does not, the entrant will make US$20 billion (Cells 2 and 3). It is possible that both will enter and clash. If a number of European governments promise Airbus a subsidiary of, say, US$10 billion if it enters, then the picture changes to Panel B. Regardless of what Boeing does, Airbus will find it lucrative to enter. In Cell 1, if Boeing enters, it will lose US$5 billion as before, whereas Airbus will make US$5 billion (US$10 billion subsidy minus US$5 billion loss). So, Boeing has no incentive to enter. Therefore, the more likely outcome is Cell 2, where Airbus enters and enjoys a profit of US$30 billion. Therefore, the subsidy has given Airbus a *strategic* advantage, and the policy to assist Airbus is known as a strategic trade policy.[8] This has indeed been the case, as the 550-seat A380 has recently entered service.

Strategic trade theorists do not advocate a mercantilist policy to promote all industries. They only propose to help a few strategically important industries. However, this theory has been criticized on two accounts.

Strategic trade policy

Government policy that provides companies a strategic advantage in international trade through subsidies and other supports.

How would strategic trade theory explain Airbus' decision to launch this aircraft?

© Olga Besnard/Shutterstock.com

Ideologically, many scholars and policy makers are uncomfortable. What if governments are not sophisticated and objective enough to do this job? Practically, a lot of industries claim that they are strategically important. Overall, where to hold the line between strategic and nonstrategic industries is tricky.

5-2f National Competitive Advantage of Industries

The most recent theory is known as the theory of national competitive advantage of industries. This is popularly known as the "diamond" theory because its principal architect, Harvard strategy professor Michael Porter, presents it in a diamond shaped diagram (Figure 5.6).[9] This theory focuses on why certain *industries* (but not other industries) within a nation are competitive internationally. For example, while the Japanese automobile industry is a global winner, the Japanese service industry is notoriously inefficient. Porter is interested in finding out why.

Porter argues that the competitive advantage of certain industries in different nations depends on four aspects that form a "diamond." First, he starts with factor endowments, which refer to the natural and human resource repertoires noted by the Heckscher-Ohlin theory. Some countries (such as Saudi Arabia) are rich in natural resources but short on population, and others (such as Singapore) have a well-educated population but few natural resources. Not surprisingly, Saudi Arabia exports oil, and Singapore exports semiconductors (which need abundant skilled labor). While building on these insights from previous theories, Porter argues that factor endowments are not enough.

Second, tough domestic demand propels firms to scale new heights.[10] Why are American movies so competitive worldwide? One reason is that American moviegoers demand the very best "sex and violence" (two themes that sell universally if artfully

---

Figure 5.6   **National Competitive Advantage of Industries: The Porter Diamond**

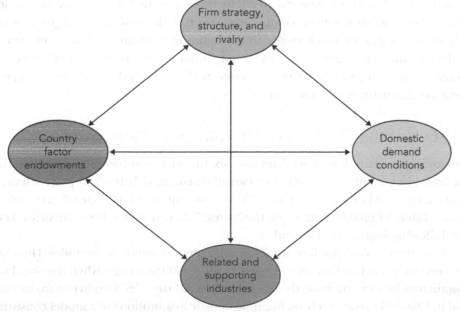

Theory of national competitive advantage of industries

A theory that suggests that the competitive advantage of certain industries in different nations depends on four aspects that form a "diamond."

"Diamond" theory

A theory that suggests that the competitive advantage of certain industries in different nations depends on four aspects that form a "diamond."

Source: M. Porter, 1990, The competitive advantage of nations (p. 77), *Harvard Business Review*, March–April: 73–93. Reprinted with permission.

packaged). Endeavoring to satisfy such domestic demand, movie studios unleash *High School Musical 3* after *High School Musical* and *High School Musical 2,* and *Spider-Man 3* after *Spider-Man* and *Spider-Man 2*—each time packing more excitement. In another example, strong domestic demand to care for an aging and shrinking population in Japan motivates firms to innovate with new technology that can better take care of the elderly. Panasonic is testing a bed that can be converted into a wheel chair for the permanently bedridden. Overall, abilities to satisfy a tough domestic crowd may make it possible to successfully deal with less-demanding overseas customers.

Third, domestic firm strategy, structure, and rivalry in one industry play a huge role behind its international success or failure. One reason that a number of Chinese manufacturing industries are so competitive globally—coining the term the "China Price"—is because their *domestic* rivalry is probably the most intense in the world (see the Opening Case). Think of appliances, cell phones, furniture, and pianos. The price wars keep everyone lean, and most firms struggle to make a profit. However, the few top firms (such as Xiaomi in smartphones and Pearl River in pianos) that win the tough competition domestically may have a relatively easier time when venturing abroad because overseas competition is less demanding.

Finally, related and supporting industries provide the foundation upon which key industries can excel. In the absence of strong related and supporting industries, such as engines, avionics, and materials, a key industry such as aerospace cannot become globally competitive. Each of these related and supporting industries requires years (and often decades) of hard work. For instance, emboldened by the Airbus experience, Chinese, Korean, and Japanese governments poured money into their own aerospace industry. Eventually, they all realized that Europe's long history and excellence in a series of crucial related and supporting industries made it possible for Airbus to succeed. A lack of such related and supporting industries made it unrealistic for an aerospace industry to take off.

Overall, Porter argues that the dynamic interaction of these four aspects explains what is behind the competitive advantage of leading industries in different nations. This theory is the first *multilevel* theory to realistically connect firms, industries, and nations, whereas previous theories only work on one or two levels. However, it has not been comprehensively tested. Some critics argue that the "diamond" places too much emphasis on domestic conditions.[11] The recent rise of India's IT industry suggests that its international success is not entirely driven by domestic demand, which is tiny compared with overseas demand—it is overseas demand that matters a lot more in this case.

5-2g Evaluating Theories of International Trade

In case you are tired after studying the six theories, you have to appreciate that we have just gone through over 300 years of research, debates, and policy changes around the world in about ten pages (!). As a student, that is not a small accomplishment. Table 5.4 enables you to see the "forest." As you review these theories, keep the following four points in mind.

First, the classical pro-free trade theories seem common sense today. However, we need to appreciate that they were *revolutionary* 200 years ago, when the world was dominated by mercantilistic thinking. Second, all theories simplify to make their point. Classical theories rely on highly simplistic assumptions of a model consisting of only two nations and two goods. Third, the theories also assume perfect resource mobility—the assumption that one resource removed from wheat production can

Resource mobility

Assumption that a resource used in producing a product for one industry can be shifted and put to use in another industry.

Table 5.4   Theories of International Trade: A Summary

Classical theories	Main points	Strengths and influences	Weaknesses and debates
Mercantilism (Colbert, 1600s–1700s)	• International trade is a zero-sum game—trade deficit is dangerous. • Governments should protect domestic industries and promote exports.	• Forerunner of modern-day protectionism.	• Inefficient allocation of resources. • Reduces the wealth of the nation in the long run.
Absolute advantage (Smith, 1776)	• Nations should specialize in economic activities in which they have an absolute advantage and trade with others. • By specializing and trading, each nation produces more and consumes more. • The wealth of all trading nations, and the world, increases.	• Birth of modern economics. • Forerunner of the free trade movement. • Defeats mercantilism, at least intellectually.	• When one nation is absolutely inferior than another, the theory is unable to provide any advice. • When there are many nations, it may be difficult to find an absolute advantage.
Comparative advantage (Ricardo, 1817; Heckscher, 1919; Ohlin, 1933)	• Nations should specialize in economic activities in which they have a comparative advantage and trade with others. • Even if one nation is absolutely inferior to another, the two nations can still gainfully trade. • Factor endowments underpin comparative advantage.	• More realistic guidance to nations (and their firms) interested in trade but having no absolute advantage. • Explains patterns of trade based on factor endowments.	• Relatively static, assuming that comparative advantage and factor endowments do not change over time.
Modern theories			
Product life cycle (Vernon, 1966)	• Comparative advantage first resides in the lead innovation nation, which exports to other nations. • Production migrates to other advanced nations and then developing nations in different product life cycle stages.	• First theory to incorporate dynamic changes in patterns of trade. • More realistic with trade in industrial products in the 20th century.	• The United States may not always be the lead innovation nation. • Many new products are now launched simultaneously around the world.
Strategic trade (Brander, Spencer, Krugman, 1980s)	• Strategic intervention by governments may help domestic firms reap first-mover advantages in certain industries. • First-mover firms, aided by governments, may have better odds at winning internationally.	• More realistic and positively incorporates the role of governments in trade. • Provides direct policy advice.	• Ideological resistance from many "free trade" scholars and policy makers. • Invites all kinds of industries to claim they are strategic.
National competitive advantage of industries (Porter, 1990)	• Competitive advantage of different industries in different nations depends on the four interacting aspects of a "diamond." • The "diamond" consists of (1) factor endowments, (2) domestic demand, (3) firm strategy, structure, and rivalry, and (4) related and supporting industries.	• Most recent, most complex, and most realistic among various theories. • As a multilevel theory, it directly connects firms, industries, and nations.	• Has not been comprehensively tested. • Overseas (not only domestic) demand may stimulate the competitiveness of certain industries.

be moved to make aircraft. In reality, farm hands will have a hard time assembling modern aircraft. Finally, classical theories assume no foreign exchange complications and zero transportation costs.

So, in the real word of many countries, numerous goods, imperfect resource mobility, fluctuating exchange rates, high transportation costs, and product life cycle changes, is free trade still beneficial as Smith and Ricardo suggested? The answer is still "Yes!" as worldwide data support the *basic* arguments of free traders such as Smith and Ricardo.[12] (See "Debates and Extensions" for disagreements.)

Instead of relying on simple factor analysis, modern theories rely on more-realistic product life cycles, first-mover advantages, and the "diamond" to explain and predict patterns of trade. Overall, classical and modern theories have significantly contributed to today's ever-deepening trade links. Yet, the victory of classic and modern pro-free trade theories is not complete. The political realities governing international trade, outlined next, indicate that mercantilism is alive and well.

Learning Objective
Realize the importance of political realities governing international trade.

5-3 Realities of International Trade

The political realities of the world suggest that as "rules of the game," plenty of trade barriers exist. Although some are being dismantled (see In Focus 5.2), many remain. Let us examine why this is the case. To do so, we will first discuss the two broad types of trade barriers: tariff barriers and nontariff barriers.

5-3a Tariff Barriers

Tariff barrier
Trade barrier that relies on tariffs to discourage imports.

Import tariff
A tax imposed on imports.

Deadweight cost
Net losses that occur in an economy as a result of tariffs.

A tariff barrier is a means of discouraging imports by placing a tariff (tax) on imported goods. As a major tariff barrier, an import tariff is a tax imposed on a good brought in from another country. Figure 5.7 uses rice tariffs in Japan to show that there are *unambiguously* net losses—known as deadweight costs.

- Panel A: In the absence of international trade, the domestic price is P_1 and domestic rice farmers produce Q_1, determined by the intersection of domestic supply and demand curves.

IN FOCUS 5.2

CANADA DIVERSIFIES ITS TRADE

Canada has the 11th-largest economy (measured by nominal GDP) or the 14th-largest (measured by PPP) in the world. The bilateral trading relationship between Canada and the United States is the world's largest, with approximately US$600 billion in volume. The two-way traffic that crosses the Ambassador Bridge between Windsor, Ontario, and Detroit, Michigan, alone equals all US trade with Japan. Approximately three-fourths of Canadian exports go to the United States, which also provide half of Canadian imports. While enjoying a US$32 billion surplus in trading with the United States, Canadians have been frustrated by the occasional disputes, such as salmon runs, magazine content, softwood lumber, and food labeling (for some details, see the first three editions of *Global Business*).

While disputes are resolved in bilateral negotiations or through NAFTA or WTO forums, Canadians have also sought to diversify their trading relationship away from too much reliance on the United States. They have focused on two areas. The first is to cultivate trade ties with major Asian economies, such as China and Japan.

As Canada's second-largest trading partner, China now absorbs 5% of Canadian exports and contributes 10% of Canadian imports. The second area is to negotiate more free trade agreements (FTAs) beyond NAFTA. Canada has FTAs with Chile, Colombia, Costa Rica, Israel, Jordan, and Panama. While Canada is negotiating with a number of other countries, one of the major breakthroughs is the Comprehensive Economic and Trade Agreement (CETA) with the European Union (EU) announced in 2013. As a bloc, the EU is the largest economy in the world. CETA would not only eliminate 99% of tariffs on both sides, but would also open competition for large government contracts in Canada to European firms and contracts in the EU to Canadian firms. CETA is likely to boost the Canada–EU bilateral trade by 23%, thus reducing Canada's reliance on the United States, whose share has decreased but still remained dominant.

Sources: Based on (1) *Economist*, 2011, Canada and the United States, December 19: 41; (2) *Economist*, 2013, Canada doesn't get any sexier than this, October 26: 18; (3) *Economist*, 2013, The Canada–EU trade deal, October 26: 44: (4) *Globe and Mail*, 2009, Canada turns to WTO over US label law, October 8: B7.

Figure 5.7   **Tariff on Rice Imports in Japan**

Panel A. No international trade

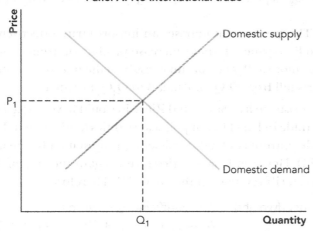

Panel B. Imports with no tariff

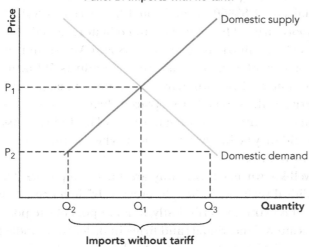

Panel C. Imports with tariff

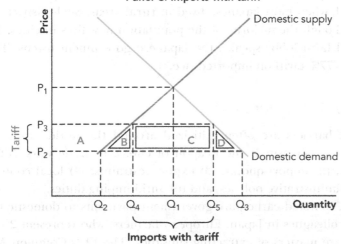

- Panel B: Because Japanese rice price P_1 is higher than world price P_2, foreign farmers export to Japan. In the absence of tariffs, Japanese farmers reduce output to Q_2. Japanese consumers enjoy more rice at Q_3 at a much lower price, P_2.
- Panel C: The government imposes an import tariff, effectively raising price from P_2 to P_3. Japanese farmers increase production from Q_2 to Q_4, and consumers pay more at P_3 and consume less by reducing consumption from Q_3 to Q_5. Imports fall from Q_2Q_3 in Panel B to Q_4Q_5 in Panel C.

Classical theorists such as Smith and Ricardo would have advised Japan to enjoy the gains from trade in Panel B. But political realities land Japan in Panel C, which, by limiting trade, introduces total inefficiency, represented by the area consisting of A, B, C, and D. However, Japanese rice farmers gain the area of A and the government pockets tariff revenues in the area of C. Therefore:

$$
\begin{aligned}
\text{Net losses (deadweight)} &= \text{Total inefficiency} - \text{net gain} \\
&= \text{Area (A + B + C + D)} - \text{Area (A + C)} \\
&= \text{Area (B + D)}
\end{aligned}
$$

The net losses (areas B and D) represent unambiguous economic inefficiency to the nation as a whole.[13] Japan is not alone in this regard. A Microsoft Xbox 360 console that retails for US$360 in the United States costs US$1,000 (!) in Brazil, after adding import tariffs.[14] In 2009, the United States slapped a 35% import tariff on tires made in China. Brazilian Xbox gamers and American tire buyers have to pay more, and some may be unable to afford the products. While not being able to get your arms around an Xbox will have no tangible damage, some economically struggling US drivers who should have replaced their worn-out tires may be forced to delay replacing their tires. According to the US Tire Industry Association, some may be *killed* should they be involved in accidents before they are able to afford the now-more-expensive tires.[15]

Given the well-known net losses, why are tariffs imposed? The answer boils down to the political realities. Although "everybody" in a country suffers because of higher prices, it is extraordinarily costly, if not impossible, to politically organize geographically scattered individuals and firms in order to promote free trade. On the other hand, special interest groups tend to be geographically concentrated and skillfully organized to advance their interests. In Japan, although farmers represent less than 1% of the population, they represent disproportionate votes in the Diet (Japanese parliament). Why? Diet districts were drawn up in the aftermath of World War II, when most Japanese lived in rural areas. Such districts were never re-zoned, although the majority of the population now lives in cities. Thus, when the powerful farm lobby speaks, the Japanese government listens. The upshot? A whopping 777% tariff on imported rice.[16]

5-3b Nontariff Barriers (NTBs)

Nontariff barrier (NTB)
Trade barriers that rely on nontariff means to discourage imports.

Subsidy
Government payments to domestic firms.

Today, tariff barriers are often criticized around the world. Nontariff barriers (NTBs) are now increasingly the weapon of choice in trade wars. NTBs include (1) subsidies, (2) import quotas, (3) export restraints, (4) local content requirements, (5) administrative policies, and (6) antidumping duties.

Subsidies, as noted earlier, are government payments to domestic firms. Similar to their colleagues in Japan, European farmers, who represent 2% of the EU population, are masters of extracting subsidies. The EU's Common Agricultural

Policy (CAP) costs European taxpayers US$150 billion per year, eating up 40% of the EU budget. European consumers do not like the CAP, and governments and farmers in developing countries eager to export their foodstuffs to the EU hate it.

Import quotas are restrictions on the quantity of imports. They are worse than tariffs, because foreign goods can still be imported if tariffs are paid. Quotas are thus the most straightforward denial of absolute or comparative advantage. For example, between 2003 and 2009, Australia annually exported 770,000 head of live cattle to Indonesia, to the delight of Indonesian beef lovers. However, since 2009, import permits suddenly became harder to obtain. A quota of only 500,000 head of imported cattle was set for 2011.[17] For Indonesia, a densely populated island nation, importing beef from a sparsely populated cattle country next door would tap into Australia's comparative advantage and would be win-win for both countries. But with the shrinking quota, Aussie cattle exporters are devastated, and Indonesian beef lovers have to put up with skyrocketing prices—and some of them may have to simply quit eating beef.

How do import quotas affect businesses and consumers in both the importing and exporting countries?

Because import quotas are protectionist pure and simple, countries have to shoulder political costs in today's largely pro-free trade environment. In response, voluntary export restraints (VERs) have been developed to show that on the surface, exporting countries *voluntarily* agree to restrict their exports. VERs, in essence, are export quotas. One of the most (in)famous examples is the VERs that the Japanese government agreed in the 1980s to restrict US-bound automobile exports. This, of course, was a euphemism because the Japanese did not volunteer to restrict their exports. Only when faced with concrete protectionist threats did the Japanese reluctantly agree.

Another NTB is local content requirements, which require a certain proportion of the value of the goods made in one country to originate from that country. The Japanese automobile VERs are again a case in point here. Starting in the 1980s, because of VERs, Japanese automakers switched to producing cars in the United States through foreign direct investment (FDI—see Chapter 6 for details). However, such factories initially were "screw driver plants," because a majority of components were imported from Japan and only the proverbial "screw drivers" were needed to tighten the bolts. To deal with this issue, many countries impose local content requirements, mandating that a "domestically produced" product will still be treated as an "import" subject to tariffs and NTBs unless a certain fraction of its value (such as 51% specified by the Buy America Act) is produced locally.

Administrative policies refer to bureaucratic rules that make it harder to import foreign goods. India recently banned Chinese toys, citing safety concerns. Argentina has recently ordered importers of foreign cars to find export buyers of Argentine wines; otherwise, port authorities would not release imported cars. Foreign print publications, including time-sensitive newspapers and magazines, are held at the Buenos Aires airport unless subscribers go there to pay an additional fee.

Finally, the arsenal of trade warriors also includes antidumping duties. Chapter 11 will expand the discussion on dumping (selling below cost) and antidumping duties in much greater detail.

Import quota

Restrictions on the quantity of imports.

Voluntary export restraint (VER)

International agreement that shows that exporting countries voluntarily agree to restrict their exports.

Local content requirement

Requirement stipulating that a certain proportion of the value of the goods made in one country must originate from that country.

Administrative policy

Bureaucratic rules that make it harder to import foreign goods.

Antidumping duty

Tariff levied on imports that have been "dumped" (selling below costs to "unfairly" drive domestic firms out of business).

Taken together, trade barriers reduce or eliminate international trade. While certain domestic industries and firms benefit, the entire country—or at least a majority of its consumers—tends to suffer. Given these well-known negative aspects, why do people make arguments against free trade? The next two sections outline economic and political arguments against free trade.

5-3c Economic Arguments Against Free Trade

Two prominent economic arguments against free trade are: (1) the need to protect domestic industries and (2) the necessity to shield infant industries. The oldest economic argument against free trade is the urge to protect domestic industries, firms, and jobs from "unfair" foreign competition—in short, protectionism. The following excerpt is from an 1845 petition of the French candle makers to the French government:

> We are subject to the intolerable competition of a foreign rival, who enjoys such superior capabilities for the production of light, that he is flooding the domestic market at an incredibly low price. From the moment he appears, our sales cease, all consumers turn to him, and a branch of French industry whose ramifications are innumerable is at once reduced to complete stagnation. This rival is nothing other than the sun. We ask you to be so kind as to pass a law requiring the closing of all windows, skylights, shutters, curtains, and blinds—in short, all openings and holes through which sunlight penetrates.[18]

Although this was a hypothetical satire written by a French free trade advocate Fredric Bastiat 170 years ago, these points are often heard today. Such calls for protection are not limited to commodity producers like candle makers. Highly talented individuals, such as American mathematicians and Japanese sumo wrestlers, have also called for protection. Foreign math PhDs grab 40% of US math jobs, and recent US math PhDs face a jobless rate of 11%. Thus, many American math PhDs have called for protection of their jobs. Similarly, Japanese sumo wrestlers insist that foreign sumo wrestlers should not be allowed to throw their weight around in Japan.

Another argument is the infant industry argument. If domestic firms are as young as "infants," in the absence of government intervention they stand no chance of surviving and will be crushed by mature foreign rivals. Thus, it is imperative that governments level the "playing field" by assisting infant industries. While this argument is sometimes legitimate, governments and firms have a tendency to abuse it. Some protected infant industries may never grow up—why bother? When Airbus was a true "infant" in the 1960s, it no doubt deserved some subsidies. However, by the 2000s, Airbus had become a giant that could take on Boeing. In some years, Airbus *outsells* Boeing. Nevertheless, Airbus continues to ask for subsidies, which European governments continue to provide.

5-3d Political Arguments against Free Trade

Political arguments against free trade advance a nation's political, social, and environmental agenda, regardless of possible economic gains from trade. These arguments include (1) national security, (2) consumer protection, (3) foreign policy, and (4) environmental and social responsibility.

National security concerns are often invoked to protect defense-related industries. Many nations fear that if they rely on arms imports, their national security may be compromised if there are political or diplomatic disagreements between

Infant industry argument

The argument that if domestic firms are as young as "infants," in the absence of government intervention, they stand no chances of surviving and will be crushed by mature foreign rivals.

them and the arms-producing nation. France has always insisted on maintaining an independent defense industry to produce nuclear weapons, aircraft carriers, and combat jets. While the French can purchase such weapons at much lower costs from the United States that is eager to sell them, the French answer has usually been: "No, thanks!"

Consumer protection has frequently been used as an argument for nations to erect trade barriers. Several years ago, the United States implemented the Mandatory Country of Origin Labeling (COOL) legislation, requiring US firms to track and notify consumers of the country of origin of meat. Many young Canadian pigs were exported to the United States, and were raised with indigenous US pigs for fattening. After several months, separating the (immigrant) Canadian pigs from the (native-born) US pigs was next to impossible. As a result, major US pork producers simply stopped buying hogs from Canada. Such a seemingly innocent move in the name of protecting consumers provoked fierce protests from the Canadian government, which eventually sued the US government at the WTO.[19]

Foreign policy objectives are often sought through trade intervention. Trade embargos are politically motivated trade sanctions against foreign countries to signal displeasure (see Emerging Markets 5.1). Many Arab countries maintain embargoes

Trade embargo
Politically motivated trade sanction against foreign countries to signal displeasure.

EMERGING MARKETS 5.1

Expanding UK Exports in Russia

Ethical Dilemma

Russia is the richest emerging economy (by per capita income) within BRIC group of nations. Among its BRIC peers, Russia is also the geographically closest country from the UK. Therefore, it would make sense for the UK to have relatively higher export sales in Russia. Yet, among BRIC, UK exports (or, viewed from Russia, UK imports) command a very low market share (Figure 5.8). The total value of UK manufacturing imports in Russia in 2011 was US$7.2 billion, which accounted for just 2% of Russia's merchandise imports. The UK, thus, was not only behind its usual global rivals (such as China, Germany, and the United States) and Russia's "near abroad" (post-Soviet) neighbors (such as Ukraine and Belarus) that naturally trade a lot with Russia, but it was also behind Korea, Poland, and Turkey. However, Russia is one of the fastest growing markets for UK exports. UK exports to Russia in 2011 increased by 39% from 2010. Since 2001, UK–Russia trade has been growing by an average of 21% year-on-year rate.

Clearly, the room for growth is tremendous. For example, the Russian government is committed to developing its automotive industry and car sales went up 15% in 2011–2012. For UK firms that tap into this market, such as industrial measurement (metrology) equipment producer Renishaw, the opportunities already turned into profits. In Russia, Renishaw enjoyed a 20%–30% growth in sales between 2010 and 2011, and further double-digit growth was predicted. Russia belonged to a core group of emerging markets with high growth that the firm hoped to balance against big traditional markets in the West with low growth.

If there is British technology not yet developed or sold within Russia, Rydian Pountney, general manager of rest of the world (ROW) sales at Renishaw and board member on UK Trade and Investment's Advanced Engineering Sector group, recommended that UK firms enter to fill the gap. It is important to note that Russia is *not* among the most price-sensitive markets. Quality means a lot to Russians, who tend to look at the technical aspects of a product more than the cost and are willing to pay for a better product.

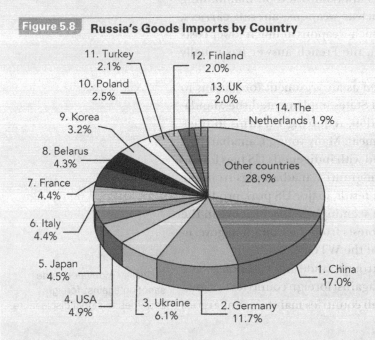

Figure 5.8 **Russia's Goods Imports by Country**

Sources: Goskomstat, www.gks.ru; www.ved.gov.ru/exportcountries/gb/gb_ru _relations/gb_ru_trade. Data refer to 2010.

Renishaw was able to maintain its margins in Russia as customers were willing to pay for quality not just at the point of sale, however throughout the life of a product. Therefore, selling on price is generally not advised. Tariff reductions associated with Russia's WTO membership, effective August 2012, would typically bring down the price of manufacturing imports by 10%, making them more affordable to Russian customers.

However, since 2014, trade sanctions imposed by the UK government—in collaboration with other Western allies in protest of Russian annexation of Crimea and Russian intervention in the turmoil in Ukraine—have introduced significant stress and dilemma to UK firms, such as Renishaw, which are eager to expand their business in Russia. While sanctions are designed to hurt the Russian government, they also hurt consumers in Russia as well as jobs back home in the UK, which is desperate to grow the manufacturing sector. If Renishaw executives such as Pountney have a chance to lobby the UK government, what would they say?

Sources: This case was written by **Sergey Lebedev** (University of Texas at Dallas, under the supervision of Professor Mike Peng). It was based on (1) *Bloomberg Businessweek*, 2014, This apple was once headed to Russia, not anymore. September 15: 13–15; (2) *Manufacturer*, 2012, Russian opportunities as it finally joins WTO, August 22, www.themanufacturer.com; (3) *Manufacturer*, 2012, To Russia, with love, May 4, www.themanufacturer.com; (4) M. W. Peng & K. Meyer, 2013, Winning the future markets for UK manufacturing output, *Future of Manufacturing Project Evidence Paper* 25, London: UK Government Office for Science; (6) UK Trade and Investment, 2015, Russia, www.ukti.gov.uk.

against Israel. The United States has embargoed against Cuba, Iran, North Korea, Russia, Sudan, and Syria. In 2009, DHL paid a record fine of US$9.4 million because it had violated US embargoes and sent shipments to Iran, Sudan, and Syria. According to a US Treasury Department statement, DHL "may have conferred a significant economic benefit to these sanctioned countries that potentially created extraordinarily adverse harm." What are such dangerous shipments? Condoms, jewelry, and radar detectors for cars, according to the same Treasury Department statement.[20]

Environmental and social responsibility can be used as political arguments to initiate trade intervention against certain countries. In a "shrimp–turtle" case, the United States banned shrimp imports from India, Malaysia, Pakistan, and Thailand. This was because shrimp were caught in their waters using a technique that also accidentally trapped sea turtles, an endangered species protected by the United States. These nations were upset and brought the case to the WTO, alleging that the United States invoked an environmental law as a trade barrier. The WTO sided with those nations and demanded that the US ban be lifted.

5-4 Debates and Extensions

Learning Objective
Participate in two leading debates concerning international trade.

International trade has substantial mismatch between theories and realities. This section highlights two leading debates: (1) trade deficit versus surplus and (2) classical theories versus new realities.

5-4a Trade Deficit versus Trade Surplus

Smith and Ricardo would probably turn in their graves if they heard that one of today's hottest trade debates still echoes the old debate between mercantilists and free traders 200 years ago. Nowhere is the debate more ferocious than in the United States, which runs the world's largest trade deficit (combining the US deficit in merchandise trade with its surplus in service trade). In 2006, it reached a record-breaking US$760 billion (6% of GDP). Thanks to reduced US (import) consumption due to the Great Recession and beefed-up export efforts (see the Closing Case), the US trade deficit was "only" US$519 billion (3% of GDP) in 2013. Should this level of trade deficit be of concern?

Armed with classical theories, free traders argue that this is not a grave concern. They argue that the United States and its trading partners mutually benefit by developing a deeper division of labor based on comparative advantage. Former Secretary of the Treasury Paul O'Neill went so far as to say that trade deficit was "an antiquated theoretical construct."[21] Paul Krugman, the 2008 Nobel laureate in economics, argued:

> International trade is not about competition, it is about mutually beneficial exchange. . . . Imports, not exports, are the purpose of trade. That is, what a country gains from trade is the ability to import things it wants. Exports are not an objective in and of themselves: the need to export is a burden that a country must bear because its import suppliers are crass enough to demand payment.[22]

Critics strongly disagree. They argue that international trade *is* about competition—about markets, jobs, and incomes. Highlighting the importance of exports, Boeing CEO Jim McNerney said: "Every time a Boeing 777 lands in China, it lands with about 4 million parts reflecting the workmanship of some 11,000 small, medium, and large suppliers."[23] Trade deficit has always been blamed on a particular country with which the United States runs the largest deficit, such as Japan in the 1980s. Because the US trade deficit with China reached US$318 billion in 2013 (two-thirds of the total deficit), the recent trade deficit debate is otherwise known as the China trade debate (Table 5.5). While the United States runs trade deficits with all of its major trading partners—Canada, the EU, Japan, and Mexico—and is in trade disputes with them most of the time, the China trade debate is by far the most emotionally charged and politically explosive.

5-4b Classical Theories versus New Realities

While the first debate (mostly on China) is primarily about *merchandise* trade and unskilled manufacturing jobs that classical theories talk about, the second debate (mostly on India) is about *service* trade and high-skill jobs in high technology, such as IT. Typically dealing with wheat from Australia to Britain on a slow boat, classical theorists certainly could not have dreamed about using the Internet to send *this* manuscript to India to be typeset and counted as India's service exports. In addition to the traditional label of "trade in services,"[24] a new jargon is "trade in tasks."[25]

Table 5.5 **Debate on the US Trade Deficit with China**

US trade deficit with China is a huge problem	US trade deficit with China is not a huge problem
Naïve trader versus unfair protectionist (in China) • The United States is a "naïve" trader with open markets. China has "unfairly" protected its markets.	*Market reformer versus unfair protectionist (in the US)* • China's markets are already unusually open. Its trade volume (merchandise and services) is 53% of GDP, whereas the US volume is only 30%.
Greedy exporters • Unscrupulous Chinese exporters are eager to gut US manufacturing jobs and drive US rivals out of business.	*Eager foreign investors* • Two-thirds of Chinese exports are generated by foreign-invested firms in China, and numerous US firms have invested in and benefited from such operations in China.
The demon who has caused deflation • Cheap imports sold at "the China price" push down prices and cause deflation.	*Thank China (and Wal-Mart) for low prices* • Every consumer benefits from cheap prices brought from China by US firms such as Wal-Mart.
Intellectual property (IP) violator • China is a major violator of IP rights, and US firms lose billions of dollars every year.	*Inevitable step in development* • True, but (1) the US did that in the 19th century (to the British), and (2) IP protection has been improving in China.
Currency manipulator • The yuan is severely undervalued, giving Chinese exports an "unfair" advantage in being priced at an artificially low level.	*Currency issue is not relevant* • The yuan is somewhat undervalued, but (1) US and other foreign firms producing in China benefit, and (2) the US also manipulates its own currency via quantitative easing.
Trade deficit will make the United States poorer • Since imports have to be paid, the United States borrows against its future with disastrous outcomes.	*Trade deficit does not cause a fall in the US standard of living* • As long as the Chinese are willing to invest in the US economy (such as Treasury bills), what's the worry?
Something has to be done • If the Chinese don't do it "our way," the United States should introduce drastic measures (such as slapping 20%–30% tariffs on all Chinese imports).	*Remember the gains from trade argued by classic theories?* • Tariffs will not bring back US jobs, which will simply go to Mexico or Malaysia, and will lead to retaliation from China, a major *importer* of US goods and services.

Sources: Based on (1) *BusinessWeek*, 2009, Free trade in the slow lane, September 21: 50; (2) *China Business Review*, 2008, US exports to China hit new high, September-October: 36–39; (3) *Economist*, 2005, From T-shirts to T-bonds, July 30: 61–63; (4) *Economist*, 2014, A number of great import, February 15: 40; (5) *Economist*, 2014, Picking the world champion of trade, January 18: 72–73; (6) *Economist*, 2014, Trading places, April 5: 49; (7) G. Locke, 2011, A message from the US Ambassador to China, *China Business Review*, October: 16; (8) M. W. Peng, D. Ahlstrom, S. Carraher, & W. Shi, 2014, How history can inform the debate over intellectual property, Working paper, Jindal School of Management, University of Texas at Dallas; (9) O. Shenkar, 2005, *The Chinese Century*, Philadelphia: Wharton School Publishing.

We already discussed a part of this debate in Chapter 4 when focusing on outsourcing. That debate deals with *firm*-level capabilities. Here, let us examine *country*-level and *individual*-level ramifications. Classical theorists and their modern-day disciples argue that the United States and India trade by tapping into each other's comparative advantage. India leverages its abundant, high-skill, and low-wage labor. Americans will channel their energy and resources to higher-skill, higher-paying jobs. While, regrettably, certain Americans will lose jobs, the nation as a whole benefits, so the theory goes.

But, not so fast!—argued retired MIT economics professor Paul Samuelson. In an influential paper, Samuelson suggested that in a more realistic world, India can innovate in areas where the United States traditionally enjoys comparative advantage, such as IT.[26] Indian innovation can reduce the price of US software exports and curtail the wage of American IT workers. Despite the availability of cheaper goods (which is a plus), the net effect may be that the United States is *worse* off as a whole. Samuelson is not an anti-globalization ideologue. Instead, he won a Nobel Prize for his penetrating research on the gains from international trade, and his mainstream economics textbook has trained generations of students (including your author). Now, even Samuelson is not so sure about one of the founding pillars of modern economics, comparative advantage.

Jagdish Bhagwati, a Columbia University trade expert, and his colleagues quickly countered Samuelson by arguing that classical pro-free trade theories still hold.[27] They argued:

> Imagine that you are exporting aircraft, and new producers of aircraft emerge abroad. That will lower the price of your aircraft, and your gains from trade will diminish. You have to be naïve to believe that this can never happen. But you have to be even more naïve to think that the policy response to the reduced gains from trade is to give up the remaining gains as well. The critical policy question we must address is: When external developments, such as the growth of skills in China and India, for instance, do diminish the gains from trade to the US, is the harm to the US going to be reduced or increased if the US turns into Fortress America? The answer is: The US will only increase its anguish if it closes its markets.[28]

In any case, according to Bhagwati and colleagues, the "threat" posed by Indian innovation is vastly exaggerated and offshoring is too small to matter much. They argue that newer and higher-level jobs will replace those lost to offshoring. One question is: Will there be enough of such jobs in the United States?

5-5 Management Savvy

Learning Objective
Draw implications for action.

How does this chapter answer the big question in global business, adapted for the context of international trade: What determines the success and failure of firms' exports around the globe? The two core perspectives lead to two answers. Fundamentally, the various economic theories underpin the resource-based view, suggesting that successful exports are valuable, unique, and hard-to-imitate products generated by certain firms from a nation (see the Opening and Closing Cases). However, the political realities stress the explanatory and predictive power of the institution-based view: As rules of the game, institutions—such as laws and regulations promoted by various special interest groups—can protect certain domestic industries, firms, and individuals; erect trade barriers; and make the nation as a whole worse off.

Three implications for action emerge (Table 5.6). First, location, location, location! In international trade, the savvy manager's number-one job is to leverage comparative advantage of world-class locations. Shown in the Opening Case, one crucial reason behind China's rise as the world's top merchandise exporting nation is that many non-Chinese managers at non-Chinese firms have discovered China's comparative advantage as a low-cost production location. As a result, they set up factories and export from China—*two-thirds* of the value-added of Chinese exports is generated by such foreign-invested firms.

Table 5.6	Implications for Action

- Discover and leverage comparative advantage of world-class locations.
- Monitor and nurture the current comparative advantage of certain locations, and take advantage of new locations.
- Be politically active to demonstrate, safeguard, and advance the gains from international trade.

Second, comparative advantage is not fixed. Managers must constantly monitor and nurture the current comparative advantage of a location and take advantage of new promising locations. Managers who fail to realize the departure of comparative advantage from certain locations are likely to fall behind. For example, numerous German managers have moved production elsewhere, citing Germany's relatively reduced comparative advantage in basic manufacturing. However, they still concentrate top-notch, high-end manufacturing in Germany, leveraging its excellence in engineering.

Third, managers need to be politically active if they appreciate the gains from trade. In times of economic difficulties, governments are often under pressure to adopt protectionist policies. While managers at many uncompetitive firms have long mastered the game of twisting politicians' arms for more protection, managers at competitive firms, who tend to be pro-free trade, have a tendency to shy away from "politics." They often fail to realize that free trade is *not* free—it requires constant efforts and sacrifices to demonstrate, safeguard, and advance the gains from such trade. For example, the US–China Business Council, a pro-free trade (in particular, pro-China trade) group consisting of 250 large US firms that are active in China (such as Coca-Cola and GE), has stood up and spoken out against various "China bashers."

CHAPTER SUMMARY/LEARNING OBJECTIVES

5-1 Use the resource-based and institution-based views to answer why nations trade.

- The resource-based view suggests that nations trade, because some firms in one nation generate valuable, unique, and hard-to-imitate exports that firms in other nations find it beneficial to import.
- The institution-based view argues that as rules of the game, different laws and regulations governing international trade aim to share gains from trade.

5-2 Understand classical and modern theories of international trade.

- Classical theories include (1) mercantilism, (2) absolute advantage, and (3) comparative advantage.
- Modern theories include (1) product life cycles, (2) strategic trade, and (3) "diamond."

5-3 Realize the importance of political realities governing international trade.

- The net impact of various tariffs and NTBs is that the whole nation is worse off while certain special interest groups (such as certain industries, firms, and regions) benefit.
- Economic arguments against free trade center on (1) protectionism and (2) infant industries.
- Political arguments against free trade focus on (1) national security, (2) consumer protection, (3) foreign policy, and (4) environmental and social responsibility.

5-4 Participate in two leading debates concerning international trade.

- (1) Trade deficit versus trade surplus and (2) classical theories versus new realities.

5-5 Draw implications for action.

- Be accurately aware of the comparative advantage of certain locations and leverage their potential.

- Monitor and nurture the current comparative advantage and take advantage of new locations.
- Be politically active to demonstrate, safeguard, and advance the gains from international trade.

KEY TERMS

Absolute advantage, 154	Import, 150	Strategic trade theory, 159
Administrative policy, 167	Import quota, 167	Subsidy, 166
Import tariff, 164	Tariff barrier, 164
Antidumping duty, 167	Infant industry argument, 168	Theory of absolute advantage, 154
Balance of trade, 152
Classical trade theories, 153	Local content requirement, 167	Theory of comparative advantage, 156
Comparative advantage, 156	Merchandise (goods), 150	Theory of mercantilism, 154
Modern trade theories, 153
Deadweight cost, 164	Theory of national competitive advantage of industries, 161
"Diamond" theory, 161	Nontariff barrier (NTB), 166
Export, 150
Factor endowment, 157	Opportunity cost, 156	Trade deficit, 152
Factor endowment theory (Heckscher-Ohlin theory), 157	Product life cycle theory, 158	Trade embargo, 169
Trade surplus, 152
Protectionism, 154	Voluntary export restraint (VER), 167
First-mover advantage, 159	Resource mobility, 162
Services, 150
Free trade, 154	Strategic trade policy, 160

REVIEW QUESTIONS

1. **Look at PengAtlas Maps 2.1 (Top Merchandise Importers and Exporters) and 2.2 (Top Service Importers and Exporters). Compare the global position of the United States in merchandise versus service imports and exports.**

   a. **Does the United States have an advantage globally in either merchandise or services? Does it have an advantage in both? If it has any type of advantage, is it absolute or comparative? Or does it have a disadvantage in both? Explain your answers.**

   b. **Imagine that you were asked to give reasons why you think it is good, from the US perspective, to have its position among the countries of the world as the top importer in both merchandise and services. What reasons would you mention?**

2. **Looking at PengAtlas Maps 2.1 and 2.2, given the size of US exports, why does the United States import so much? Why not use resources in the US to produce the things the US currently imports instead of using them to produce exports?**

3. *ON CULTURE:* **Mercantilism involved a relatively significant amount of government control over both domestic and international activity, whereas Smith's concept of absolute advantage focused on relative economic freedom**

and minimal government controls over domestic and international economic activity. Do you think that the values prevalent in American culture today are more in line with those of the mercantilists or those of Smith? If there is some combination of Smith and mercantilism, which tends to be dominant?

4. The rules of the game for international trading can be quite complex, so why do nations routinely engage in this activity?

5. Name and describe the two key components of a balance of trade.

6. Compare and contrast the six theories of international trade.

7. What are two primary economic arguments that critics use against free trade?

8. Summarize four political arguments against free trade.

9. Is a persistent trade deficit a matter of grave concern? Why or why not?

10. Will the service trade benefit or hurt rich countries?

11. What are some of the factors that managers need to consider when assessing the comparative advantage of various locations around the world?

12. Why is it necessary for business people to monitor political activity concerning international trade?

CRITICAL DISCUSSION QUESTIONS

1. Is the trade policy of your country's government protectionist? Why?

2. What is the ratio of merchandise international trade (exports + imports) to GDP in your country? How about the ratio for Brazil, China, the EU, Egypt, India, Japan, Russia, Singapore, Turkey, and the US? Why are there such differences?

3. *ON ETHICS:* As a foreign policy tool, trade embargoes, such as US embargoes against Cuba, Iraq (until 2003), and North Korea, are meant to discourage foreign governments. But they also cause a great deal of misery among the population (such as shortages of medicine and food). Are embargoes ethical?

4. *ON ETHICS:* While the nation as a whole may gain from free trade, there is no doubt that certain regions, industries, firms, and individuals may lose their jobs and livelihood due to foreign competition. How can the rest of the nation help the unfortunate ones cope with the impact of international trade?

BUSINESS
INSIGHTS
GLOBAL

GLOBAL ACTION

1. Cities worldwide differ considerably along many dimensions. However, one facet of trading internationally is to identify global cities to base a network of operations. Choose one dimension on which to measure different cities. Then, develop a report that discusses your findings in detail.

2. At times, corporate tax rates in specific locations can be considered a trade barrier to business development. As a result, locations that have lower tax rates may encourage corporations to conduct operations or relocate headquarters there. Find a list of tax rates for a variety of locations. If you were part of a company seeking to relocate its operations, which location(s) would you recommend and why?

CLOSING CASE

Why Are US Exports So Competitive?

© James BO Insogna/Shutterstock.com

Since the launch of the first edition of *Global Business*, the rise of China as the leading exporter has been widely reported (see the Opening Case). Yet, what has been little reported by the media is that the United States also rocketed ahead of Germany and is now the world's second-largest exporter.* Never mind all that talk about the decline of US competitiveness. An important part of your university education is to foster a critical thinking mindset by relying on data and forming evidence-based judgments, as opposed to being excessively influenced by media fads. Shown in Table 5.7, the data suggest a story that is different from that typically portrayed by the media.

In 2013, the United States exported a record US$1.58 trillion, with an enviable 8.4% annual increase. Of China's US$2.21 trillion exports, only about two-thirds of the value-added was contributed by China. The United States contributed approximately 89% of the value-added of its exports. Do your math: the real value-added of US exports (US$1.41 trillion) was almost the same as the real value-added of Chinese exports (US$1.48 trillion).

In addition, the United States again outsold the long-time export champion, Germany, which exported US$1.45 trillion, and the previously (and still) formidable Japan, which exported US$715 billion. Don't forget: The United States accomplished such enviable export success during the very difficult aftermath of the Great Recession, in which every nation was eager to export its way out of recession. What were the top US export categories? Refined petroleum products, civilian aircraft, semiconductors, passenger cars, and telecom equipment. The top five export states were Texas (which exported one-sixth of the nation's total exports), California, Illinois, Louisiana, and New York. The US Department of Commerce proudly noted, "fueling our economic recovery, exports are a bright spot in the US economy."

Why are US exports so competitive? What is unique about US exports? What has been driving their recent rise in a bleak global economic environment? On top of the Great Recession, one can add more recent catastrophes such as the Japanese earthquake,

Table 5.7 | **Top Five Merchandise (Goods) Exporting Nations**

	2006	2008	2011	2013
1	Germany	Germany	China	China
2	United States	China	United States	United States
3	China	United States	Germany	Germany
4	Japan	Japan	Japan	Japan
5	France	Netherlands	Netherlands	Netherlands

Sources: The first three columns are adapted from M. W. Peng, 2009, 2011, 2014, *Global Business*, 1st, 2nd, and 3rd ed., Cincinnati: Cengage Learning. 2013 data are from the World Trade Organization, 2014, *World Trade Report 2014*, Geneva: WTO.

* This case only deals with *merchandise* (*goods*) exports. In *service* exports, the United States is even more competitive—it is the world champion (see Table 5.1).

the Thai floods, the euro zone crisis, the Middle East turmoil, the Russian sanctions, and the Ebola crisis. To make a long story short, first, US exports have to deliver *value*. Consider civilian aircraft. One crucial reason that the new Boeing 787 Dreamliner became the hottest-selling airliner prior to its launch is its ability to reduce fuel consumption by 15%—music to the ears of airline executives who suffer from high oil prices. Second, US exports also have to be *rare* and *hard to imitate*. There is no shortage of global rivals tearing apart US products and trying to reverse-engineer them. European, Russian, and Chinese aerospace firms are doing this at this moment by trying to out-Boeing Boeing. While Airbus has been quite successful, neither Russian nor Chinese civilian aircraft makers have much presence in export markets. Finally, US exporters have to *organize* themselves in a more productive and efficient manner relative to their global rivals. It is hard enough to design and manufacture world-class aircraft, but it is no less challenging to operate service, training, and maintenance networks for airlines that cannot afford any equipment breakdown for a long period—on a worldwide basis and for 20 to 30 years after the initial sale.

While the products themselves have to be strong and competitive, Uncle Sam has also helped. At least ten federal agencies offer export assistance: the Departments of Commerce, State, Treasury, Energy, and Agriculture as well as the Office of US Trade Representative (USTR), Export-Import Bank (Ex-Im Bank), US Agency for International Development (USAID), Overseas Private Investment Corporation (OPIC), and Small Business Administration (SBA). Since only approximately 1% of all US firms export and 58% of them export to just one country, clearly more assistance will be helpful if more firms are interested in joining the export game.

Going beyond routine export assistance, new initiatives focus on negotiating free trade agreements (FTAs) with trading partners. As of this writing, the United States has 12 FTAs in force with 18 countries: Australia, Bahrain, Chile, DR-CAFTA (Dominican Republic–Central America FTA, which covers Costa Rica, Dominican Republic, El Salvador, Guatemala, Honduras, and Nicaragua), Israel, Jordan, Morocco, NAFTA (which covers Canada and Mexico), Oman, Peru, Singapore, and South Korea. In addition, two FTAs with Panama and Colombia were negotiated, but they are still pending Congressional approval. FTAs typically reduce trade barriers to US exports and create a more stable and transparent trading environment. In the first FTA with an East Asian country, the South Korea–US FTA (also known as KORUS), South Korea agreed to phase out a 40% tariff on US beef imports, and the United States agreed to waive a 2.5% tariff on Korean auto imports.

In addition to FTAs, the US government often negotiates with other foreign governments for better market access and terms of trade for US exporters. The push to get the Chinese to let the yuan appreciate, so that the dollar can be cheaper and US exports can be more competitive, is a case in point. Despite an allegedly "artificially" low yuan and a government eager to promote China's own exports, China rose from being the ninth-largest US export market in 2001 to the third-largest in 2011 (behind Canada and Mexico). During that period, US exports to China jumped more than 400%, while US exports to the rest of the world only grew 55%. Given the still huge US trade deficit (of which the US–China trade deficit is the largest component), clearly there is more room to push US exports.

In addition to formal institutions, informal norms and values—both at home and abroad—play a role behind US exports. At home, all the talk about the virtue and necessity of energy conservation and going green evidently has slowly become a part of the American cultural norm. One piece of evidence is that US oil consumption has declined since 2006. This helps explain why refined petroleum products (such as gasoline, diesel, and jet fuel) recently shot ahead of civilian aircraft to become the number-one export category. This is partly because much of the refining capacity the United States added in the past decade is now geared toward exports. While gurus write about the decline of US influence, the informal norms of consuming and appreciating US products seem to proliferate overseas. In Paris metro (underground) stations, almost every other poster seems to be about a Hollywood blockbuster. In Accra, the middle class flock into Ghana's first KFC and lick their fingers greased by grown-in-USA chicken. If you are studying *this* book outside the United States, then you are a US export customer too. Enjoy!

CASE DISCUSSION QUESTIONS:

1. ***ON ETHICS:*** Prior to taking this class and studying this case, have you often heard or read about the decline of US export competitiveness? What are the social and ethical implications of such excessive (one-sided) negative reporting? Does this case change your mind? Why?

2. From a resource-based view, explain why US exports are so competitive?

3. From an institution-based view, explain why US exports are so competitive?

Sources: This case draws on a long line of my own research on US export strategy, starting with my PhD dissertation (cited as 6 below) and more recently with an interview with the *Dallas Morning News* on Texas export competitiveness (cited as 3 below). This case is based on (1) *Bloomberg Businessweek*, 2012, Yum's big game of chicken, March 29: 64–69; (2) *Bloomberg Businessweek*, 2011, The real way a trade deal gets done, October 24: 30–32; (3) *Dallas Morning News*, 2012, Texas exports spike higher on energy goods, February 23; (4) *Economist*, 2010, Go sell, March 13: 32; (5) *Economist*, 2014, Picking the world champion of trade, January 18: 72–73; (6) M. W. Peng, 1998, *Behind the Success and Failure of US Export Intermediaries*, Westport, CT: Quorum; (7) US Commercial Service, 2012, export.gov.

NOTES

[**Journal acronyms**] **AER**—*American Economic Review;* **BW**—*Business-Week* (prior to 2010) or *Bloomberg Businessweek* (since 2010); **JEL**—*Journal of Economic Literature;* **JEP**—*Journal of Economic Perspectives;* **JIE**—*Journal of International Economics;* **JIBS**—*Journal of International Business Studies;* **JM**—*Journal of Management;* **JMS**—*Journal of Management Studies;* **QJE**—*Quarterly Journal of Economics;* **RES**—*Review of Economics and Statistics*

1 E. Helpman, M. Melitz, & Y. Rubinstein, 2008, Estimating trade flows, *QJE*, 123: 441–487; D. Jacks, C. Meissner, & D. Novy, 2008, Trade costs, 1870–2000, *AER*, 98: 529–534; R. Kali & J. Reyes, 2007, The architecture of globalization, *JIBS*, 38: 595–620.

2 M. Amiti & J. Konings, 2007, Trade liberalization, intermediate inputs, and productivity, *AER*, 97: 1611–1638; C. Arkolakis, S. Demidova, P. Kelnow, & A. Rodriguez-Clare, 2008, Endogenous variety and the gains from trade, *AER*, 98: 444–450; A. Smith, 2014, Follow me to the innovation frontier? *JIBS*, 45: 248–274.

3 J. Baggs & J. Brander, 2006, Trade liberalization, profitability, and financial leverage, *JIBS*, 37: 196–211.

4 M. W. Peng, 2001, The resource-based view and international business, *JM*, 27: 803–829.

5 J. Ederington, 2002, International coordination of trade and domestic policies, *AER*, 91: 1580–1593; G. Maggi & A. Rodriguez-Calre, 2007, A political-economy theory of trade agreements, *AER*, 97: 1374–1406.

6 R. Vernon, 1966, International investments and international trade in product life cycle, *QJE*, May: 190–207.

7 This theory is sometimes referred to as "new trade theory." However, it is now nearly 30 years old and no longer that new. Therefore, to avoid confusion, we label this "strategic trade theory." See J. Brander & B. Spencer, 1985, Export subsidies and international market share rivalry, *JIE*, 18: 83–100; P. Krugman (ed.), 1986, *Strategic Trade Policy and the New International Economics*, Cambridge, MA: MIT Press.

8 P. Krugman, 1994, *Peddling Prosperity* (p. 238), New York: Norton.

9 M. Porter, 1990, *Competitive Advantage of Nations*, New York: Free Press.

10 M. Sakakibara & M. Porter, 2001, Competing at home to win abroad, *RES*, 83: 310–322.

11 H. Davies & P. Ellis, 2001, Porter's *Competitive Advantage of Nations*: Time for the final judgment? *JMS*, 37: 1189–1215.

12 D. Bernhofen & J. Brown, 2005, An empirical assessment of the comparative advantage gains from trade, *AER*, 95: 208–225.

13 S. Tokarick, 2008, Dispelling some misconceptions about agricultural trade liberalization, *JEP*, 22: 199–216.

14 *BW*, 2009, Seeking the next billion gamers, July 6: 54.

15 Tire Industry Association (TIA), 2009, Tire Industry Association expresses disappointment with President's decision concerning Chinese tire tariff, September 14, Bowie, MD: TIA, www.tireindustry.org.

16 *BW*, 2014, Japan's micro farms face extinction, January 6: 14–15; *Economist*, 2013, Field work, April 13: 43–44.

17 *Economist*, 2011, A row over cows, February 17: www.economist.com.

18 F. Bastiat, 1964, *Economic Sophisms*, edited and translated by A. Goddard, New York: Van Norstrand.

19 M. W. Peng, 2014, Canada and the United States fight over pigs, in M. W. Peng, *Global Business*, 3rd ed. (pp. 270–271), Cincinnati: Cengage Learning.

20 *USA Today*, 2009, DHL will pay US$9.4M fine to settle shipping dispute, August 7: 2A.

21 *BW*, 2005, America's trade deficit, October 3: 31.

22 P. Krugman, 1993, What do undergrads need to know about trade? (p. 24), *AER*, 83: 23–26.

23 *Fortune*, 2010, Why free trade matters to companies like Caterpillar, July 26: 40.

24 J. Boddewyn, M. Halbrich, & A. Perry, 1986, Service multinationals, *JIBS*, 17: 41–57; J. Francois & B. Hoekman, 2010, Services trade and policy, *JEL*, 48: 642–692.

25 G. Grossman & E. Rossi-Hansberg, 2008, Trading tasks, *AER*, 98: 1978–1997.

26 P. Samuelson, 2004, Where Ricardo and Mill rebut and confirm arguments of mainstream economists supporting globalization, *JEP*, 18(3): 135–146.

27 J. Bhagwati, A. Panagariya, & T. Sribivasan, 2004, The muddles over outsourcing, *JEP*, 18(4): 93–114.

28 J. Bhagwati & A. Panagariya, 2004, Trading opinions about free trade (p. 20), *BW*, December 27: 20.

© ruskpp/Shutterstock.com

Learning Objectives

After studying this chapter, you should be able to

- use the resource-based and institution-based views to answer why foreign direct investment (FDI) takes place.

- understand how FDI results in ownership, location, and internalization (OLI) advantages.

- identify different political views on FDI based on an understanding of its benefits and costs to host and home countries.

- participate in two leading debates concerning FDI.

- draw implications for action.

Investing Abroad Directly

EMERGING MARKETS: Indian FDI in Britain

Britain has been a favored destination of foreign direct investment (FDI) from India since economic reforms were launched in the early 1990s. According to a UK Trade and Investment (UKTI) report, Indian FDI helped create as many as 7,255 jobs in Britain in 2012 alone. From a recent Ernst and Young report, 49% of India's outward FDI goes to Britain, and India has been among the top five countries undertaking FDI in Britain. Among the Brazil, Russia, India, China and South Africa (BRICS) countries, India ranks first in terms of FDI in Britain. The Tata Group alone employs more than 50,000 employees in 19 companies operating in the UK. It is now the largest private-sector employer in the UK. In total, more than 100,000 jobs are created by Indian FDI in Britain.

The 2008 acquisition of Land Rover and Jaguar from Ford by Tata for more than US$2.3 billion was a significant milestone of Indian FDI in Britain. Turning around the initial losses and tripling revenues have become a new success story of profitable acquisitions by multinationals from a developing country. In a Grant Thornton report, the top 41 fastest-growing Indian companies in Britain contribute more than US$30 billion in revenue. Automotive, service, technology, and telecommunication sectors dominate the largest contributors.

The Indian government's continued reforms in FDI policies and the booming entrepreneurial culture in India further aid the overall outward FDI from India. The inflows of dividends from overseas investments in joint ventures and wholly owned subsidiaries enjoy a 50% reduction in the tax rate. There are also some tax benefits and incentives for businesses created with FDI outflow. With the election of Narendra Modi as the prime minister in the elections of May 2014, there is increased optimism in economic growth, which may further aid FDI initiatives.

In 2011, India overtook Ireland in the number of non-UK-born residents in Britain, although Ireland is so much closer geographically. Hundreds of years of cultural links, an increasing Indian diaspora in Britain, and the growing stature of India are significant contributors behind the increase of Indian FDI in Britain. While the manufacturing export segment in the UK is weak, increase of FDI from emerging economies, such as India, would help boost the manufacturing segment and propel exports from Britain (such as Made-in-UK Jaguar and Land Rover) to emerging economies.

However, not all is rosy. While not specific to Britain, Indian outward FDI growth has potential risks. A key risk is foreign currency exchange fluctuations. Purchase of foreign exchange in India is one of the common methods of funding overseas investments, while swapping of shares of an Indian entity with those of an overseas entity and capitalization of foreign currency proceeds received for trade is also often used. With India's heavy exposure to oil imports and current account deficit, Indian investors must be extremely careful about foreign exchange fluctuations. In a span of two months between July and August 2013, the Indian rupee (INR) devalued by more than 15%. Indian overseas investors could be heavily exposed to such currency fluctuations. Such steep fluctuations prompted the Reserve Bank of India to institute several measures, including limiting the amount of FDI outflows—thus putting projects on hold. Although these restrictive measures have been subsequently relaxed, they show a critical weakness associated with Indian outward FDI in general.

Although India and Britain share a special and long relationship hailed as a "relationship of choice," shifting dynamics in the global economy, according to the *Economist*, makes India and Britain an "odd couple." Simply put, they do not trade a lot. Global trade statistics show that India is ranked 18th on the list of Britain's export destinations and 17th as a supplier of imports. China's trade volume with India is four times that of Britain. In September 2014,

China and India signed deals worth more than US$20 billion and trade winds are blowing differently than before.

In addition, although the September 2014 referendum for Scotland independence was rejected by a 55-45 vote, the underlying currents create uncertainty in the minds of Indian executives entertaining FDI in Britain, when many other opportunities exist elsewhere in the world. India's political winds are also uncertain and can change for populist schemes for electoral gains. Given these risks and uncertainties in the global economy, multinationals from India and their partners in Britain would have to be persistent in order to sustain the momentum and realize the growth potential.

Sources: This case was written by **Dr. Nagaraj Savithri** (UT Dallas Global Leadership Executive MBA, Class of 2014, under the supervision of Professor Mike Peng). It was based on: (1) *Economist*, 2013, Britain and India, The odd couple, September 28; (2) Ernst and Young, 2014, *UK Attractiveness Survey;* (3) Grant Thornton, 2013, *India Meets Britain: Tracking the UK's Top Indian Companies;* (4) H. R. Khan, 2012, *Outward Indian FDI— Recent Trends and Emerging Issues*, Mumbai: Reserve Bank of India; (5) N. Robins, 2006, *The Corporation that Changed the World: How the East India Company Shaped the Modern Multinational*, London: Pluto; (6) M. W. Peng & K. Meyer, 2013, Winning the future markets for UK manufacturing output, *Future of Manufacturing Project: Evidence Paper 25*, London: UK Government Office for Science; (7) Tata Group, 2014, *Corporate Sustainability in the UK;* (8) UK Trade and Investment (UKTI), 2013, *2012/13 Inward Investment Annual Report.*

Why are many Indian firms increasingly interested in outward foreign direct investment (FDI)? Why are they interested in Britain in particular? Why do some of them succeed and others struggle? Recall from Chapter 1 that FDI is defined as directly investing in activities that control and manage value creation in other countries.[1] Also recall from Chapter 1 that firms that engage in FDI are known as multinational enterprises (MNEs). In 2014, while most developed economies slowly recovered from the Great Recession of 2008–2009, emerging economies as a group attracted approximately 60% of the FDI inflows. Firms from emerging economies, such as those from India discussed in the Opening Case, generated approximately 40% of FDI outflows worldwide.[2]

This chapter starts by first clarifying the FDI terms. Then we address a crucial question: Why do firms engage in FDI? We outline how the two core perspectives introduced earlier—namely, resource-based and institution-based views—can help answer this question.[3] Debates and implications for action follow.

Learning Objective
Use the resource-based and institution-based views to answer why FDI takes place.

6-1 Understanding the FDI Vocabulary

Part of FDI's complexity is associated with the vocabulary. We will try to reduce this complexity by setting the terms straight in this section.

6-1a The Key Word Is D

International investment can be made primarily in two ways: FDI and foreign portfolio investment (FPI). FPI refers to investment in a portfolio of foreign securities, such as stocks and bonds, that do not entail the active management of foreign assets. Essentially, FPI is "foreign *indirect* investment." In contrast, the key word in FDI is *D* (*direct*)—the direct hands-on management of foreign assets. While reading this book, some of you may have some FPI at the same time—that is, you own some foreign stocks and bonds. However, as a student taking this course, it is by definition impossible that you are also engaging in FDI at the same time, which requires you to be a manager getting your feet "wet" by actively managing foreign operations.

For statistical purposes, the United Nations defines FDI as an equity stake of 10% or more in a foreign-based enterprise.[4] Without a sufficiently large equity, it is difficult to exercise management control rights—namely, the rights to appoint key managers and establish control mechanisms. Many firms invest abroad for the explicit purpose of managing foreign operations, and they need a large equity (sometimes up to 100%) to be able to do that.

6-1b Horizontal and Vertical FDI

FDI can be horizontal or vertical. Recall the value chain from Chapter 4, whereby firms perform value-adding activities stage-by-stage in a vertical fashion, from upstream to downstream. When a firm *duplicates* its home country-based activities at the same value-chain stage in a host country through FDI, we call this horizontal FDI (see Figure 6.1). For example, BMW makes cars in Germany. Through horizontal FDI, it does the same thing in the United States. Overall, horizontal FDI refers to producing the same products or offering the same services in a host country as firms do at home.

If a firm through FDI moves upstream or downstream in different value-chain stages in a host country, we label this vertical FDI (Figure 6.2). For instance, if BMW (hypothetically) only assembles cars and does not manufacture components in Germany, but in Indonesia it enters into components manufacturing through FDI (an upstream activity), this would be upstream vertical FDI. Likewise, if BMW does not engage in car distribution in Germany but invests in car dealerships in Egypt (a downstream activity), it would be downstream vertical FDI.

Foreign portfolio investment (FPI)
Investment in a portfolio of foreign securities such as stocks and bonds.

Management control right
The right to appoint key managers and establish control mechanisms.

Horizontal FDI
A type of FDI in which a firm duplicates its home country-based activities at the same value chain stage in a host country.

Vertical FDI
A type of FDI in which a firm moves upstream or downstream at different value chain stages in a host country.

Upstream vertical FDI
A type of vertical FDI in which a firm engages in an upstream stage of the value chain in a host country.

Downstream vertical FDI
A type of vertical FDI in which a firm engages in a downstream stage of the value chain in a host country.

Figure 6.1	**Horizontal FDI**

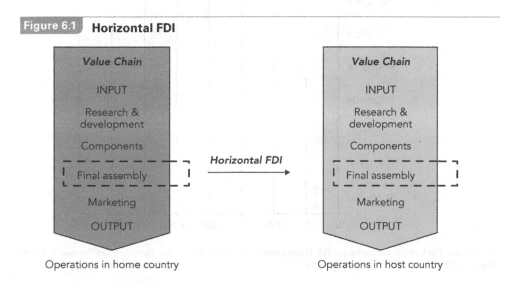

Operations in home country   Operations in host country

Figure 6.2   Vertical FDI

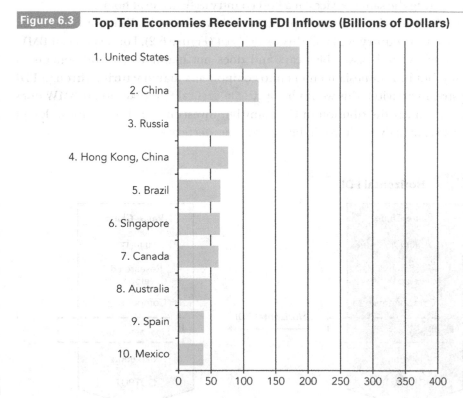

Value Chain		Value Chain
INPUT		INPUT
Research & development		Research & development
Components		Components
Final assembly	Upstream vertical FDI	Final assembly
Marketing	Downstream vertical FDI	Marketing
OUTPUT		OUTPUT

Operations in home country   Operations in host country

6-1c FDI Flow and Stock

Another pair of words often used is flow and stock. FDI flow is the amount of FDI moving in a given period (usually a year) in a certain direction. FDI inflow usually refers to inbound FDI moving into a country in a year, and FDI outflow typically refers to outbound FDI moving out of a country in a year. Figures 6.3 and 6.4 illustrate the top ten economies receiving inflows and generating outflows. FDI stock is the total accumulation of inbound FDI in a country or outbound FDI from a country. Hypothetically, between two countries A and B, if firms from A undertake US$10 billion of FDI in B in Year 1 and another US$10 billion in Year 2, then we

Figure 6.3   Top Ten Economies Receiving FDI Inflows (Billions of Dollars)

1. United States	
2. China	
3. Russia	
4. Hong Kong, China	
5. Brazil	
6. Singapore	
7. Canada	
8. Australia	
9. Spain	
10. Mexico	

0   50   100   150   200   250   300   350   400

Source: Adapted from United Nations, 2014, *World Investment Report 2014* (p. xv), New York and Geneva: UN. Data refer to 2013.

FDI flow

The amount of FDI moving in a given period (usually a year) in a certain direction.

FDI inflow

Inbound FDI moving into a country in a year.

FDI outflow

Outbound FDI moving out of a country in a year.

FDI stock

Total accumulation of inbound FDI in a country or outbound FDI from a country across a given period (usually several years).

can say that in each of these two years, B receives annual FDI *inflows* of US$10 billion and, correspondingly, A generates annual FDI *outflows* of US$10 billion. If we assume that firms from no other countries undertake FDI in country B and prior to Year 1 no FDI was possible, then the total *stock* of FDI in B, by the end of Year 2, is US$20 billion. Essentially, flow is a snapshot of a given point in time, and stock represents cumulating volume.

6-1d MNE versus non-MNE

An MNE, by definition, is a firm that engages in FDI when doing business abroad.[5] An MNE is sometimes called a multinational corporation (MNC) or a transnational corporation (TNC). To avoid confusion, we will stick with the term "MNE" throughout the book. Note that non-MNE firms can also do business abroad, by (1) exporting and importing, (2) licensing and franchising, (3) outsourcing, (4) engaging in FPI, or other means. What sets MNEs apart from non-MNEs is FDI. An exporter has to undertake FDI in order to become an MNE. In other words, BMW would not be an MNE if it made all its cars in Germany and exported them around the world. BMW became an MNE only when it started to directly invest abroad.

Although a lot of people believe that MNEs are a new organizational form that emerged recently, that is not true. MNEs have existed for at least 2,000 years, with some of the earliest traces discovered in the Assyrian, Phoenician, and Roman times.[6] In 1903 when Ford Motor Company was founded, it exported its sixth car. Ford almost immediately engaged in FDI by having a factory in Canada that produced its first output in 1904.[7] It is true that MNEs have experienced significant

---

Figure 6.4 | **Top Ten Economies Generating FDI Outflows (Billions of Dollars)**

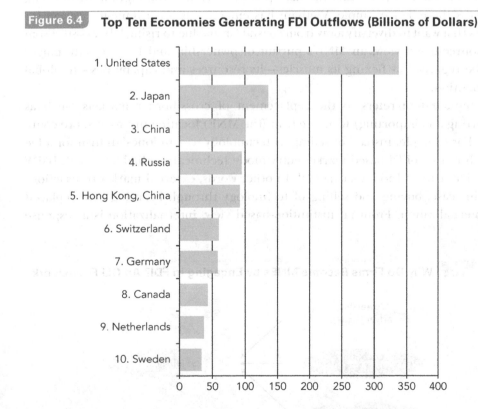

Source: Adapted from United Nations, 2014, *World Investment Report 2014* (p. xv), New York and Geneva: UN. Data refer to 2013.

growth since World War II. In 1970, there were approximately 7,000 MNEs world-wide. By 2010, more than 82,000 MNEs managed approximately 810,000 foreign affiliates.[8] Clearly, there is a proliferation of MNEs lately.

Learning Objective
Understand how FDI results in OLI advantages.

6-2 Why Do Firms Become MNEs by Engaging in FDI?

Having set the terms straight, we need to address a fundamental question: Why do so many firms—ranging from those in the ancient world to today's GE and Tata—become MNEs by engaging in FDI? Without getting into details, we can safely say that there must be economic gains from FDI. More importantly, given the tremendous complexities, such gains must significantly outweigh the costs. What are the sources of such gains? The answer, as suggested by British scholar John Dunning and illustrated in Figure 6.5, boils down to firms' quest for ownership (O) advantages, location (L) advantages, and internalization (I) advantages—collectively known as the OLI advantages.[9] The two core perspectives introduced earlier, resource-based and institution-based views, enable us to probe into the heart of this question.

In the context of FDI, ownership refers to MNEs' possession and leveraging of certain valuable, rare, hard-to-imitate, and organizationally embedded (VRIO) assets overseas. Owning proprietary technology and management know-how that goes into making a BMW helps ensure that the MNE can beat rivals abroad.

Location advantages are those enjoyed by firms because they do business in a certain place. Features unique to a place, such as its natural or labor resources or its location near particular markets, provide certain advantages to firms doing business there. For example, Vietnam has emerged as a convenient location for MNEs that want to diversify away from coastal China due to rising labor costs. From a resource-based view, an MNE's pursuit of ownership and location advantages can be regarded as flexing its muscles—its resources and capabilities—in global competition.

Internalization refers to the replacement of cross-border markets (such as exporting and importing) with one firm (the MNE) locating in two or more countries. For example, instead of selling its technology to a Indonesian firm for a fee (which is a non-FDI-based market entry mode technically called licensing), BMW assembles cars in Indonesia via FDI. In other words, external market transactions (in this case, buying and selling of technology through licensing) are replaced by internalization. From an institution-based view, internalization is a response

OLI advantage

A firm's quest for ownership (O) advantages, location (L) advantages, and internalization (I) advantages via FDI.

Ownership

An MNE's possession and leveraging of certain valuable, rare, hard-to-imitate, and organizationally embedded (VRIO) assets overseas in the context of FDI.

Location

Advantages enjoyed by firms operating in a certain location.

Internalization

The replacement of cross-border markets (such as exporting and importing) with one firm (the MNE) locating and operating in two or more countries.

Licensing

Firm A's agreement to give Firm B the rights to use A's proprietary technology (such as a patent) or trademark (such as a corporate logo) for a royalty fee paid to A by B. This is typically done in manufacturing industries.

Figure 6.5 **Why Do Firms Become MNEs by Engaging in FDI? An OLI Framework**

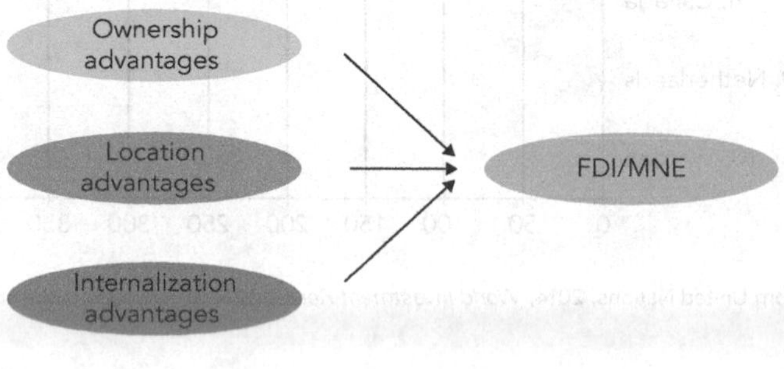

to the imperfect rules governing international transactions—known as market imperfections (or market failure). Evidently, Indonesian regulations governing the protection of intellectual property such as BMW's proprietary technology do not give BMW sufficient confidence that its rights will be protected. Therefore, internalization is a must.

Overall, firms become MNEs because FDI provides the three-pronged OLI advantages that they otherwise would not obtain. The next three sections outline why this is the case. In addition, MNEs also enjoy some other advantages, such as being able to reduce tax payments by tapping into favorable rules of the game around the world (In Focus 6.1).

Market imperfection (market failure)

The imperfect rules governing international transactions.

IN FOCUS 6.1

ONE MULTINATIONAL VERSUS MANY NATIONAL COMPANIES

We often treat each multinational enterprise (MNE) as one firm, regardless of how many countries it operates in. However, from an institution-based standpoint, one can argue that a "multinational" enterprise may be a total fiction that does not exist. This is because, legally, incorporation is only possible under national law, every so-called MNE is essentially a bunch of national companies (subsidiaries) registered in various countries. A generation ago, such firms were often labeled "multi-national companies" with a hyphen. Although some pundits argue that globalization is undermining the power of national governments, there is little evidence that the modern nation-state system, in existence since the 1648 Treaty of Westphalia, is retreating.

This debate is not just academic hair-splitting fighting over a hyphen. It is very relevant and stakes are high. In 2010, Zhejiang Geely Holding Group (in short, "Geely") of China acquired Volvo Car Corporation (Volvo Personvagnar AB in Swedish—in short, "Volvo Cars" in English) from Ford Motor Company of the United States for US$1.8 billion. Volvo Cars thus became a wholly owned subsidiary of Geely. Everybody in the world, including Geely's owner Li Shufu, thought Volvo Cars was "Chinese"—except the Chinese government. Refusing to acknowledge the existence of any "multinational," the Chinese government maintained that Volvo Cars, registered in Sweden and headquartered in Gothenburg, Sweden, was Swedish. When Li sought to produce Volvo vehicles in Chengdu, Daqing, and Zhangjiakou in China, the government advised that he set up a new joint venture (JV) between Volvo Cars

(a Swedish firm) and Geely (a Chinese firm). Since Li was chairman of the board for Volvo Cars and chairman of the board for Geely, he ended up signing *both* sides of the JV contract. In other words, one individual represented both the Swedish firm and the Chinese firm (!). In 2013, the Chinese government approved this new international JV, in which the Swedish side (Volvo Cars) owned 30% equity.

If Li signing his name twice on a JV contract is funny, a more serious case in point concerns tax avoidance. Legally, Google Ireland is not a branch of the US-based Google Corporation. Although 100% owned by Google Corporation, Google Ireland is a separate, legally independent corporation registered in Ireland. While Google Corporation intentionally lets Google Ireland earn a lot of profits, the US Internal Revenue Service (IRS) cannot tax a dime Google Ireland makes, unless it sends back (repatriates) the profits to Google Corporation. Google Corporation does not have just one subsidiary. It has many around the world. Overall, 54% of Google's profits are parked overseas and are not taxable by the IRS. Google is not alone. The list of leading US firms that have left a majority of their profits overseas includes Chevron, Cisco, Citigroup, ExxonMobil, GE, HP, IBM, Johnson & Johnson, Microsoft, P&G, PepsiCo, and Pfizer. Running huge budget deficits, Congress is understandably furious.

Sources: Based on (1) *21st Century Business Insights*, 2012, Geely-Volvo JV to push Volvo brand and new energy cars, April 1: 27; (2) S. Kobrin, 2009, Sovereignty@bay, in A. Rugman (ed.), *The Oxford Handbook of International Business* (pp. 183–204), New York: Oxford University Press; (3) C. Needham, 2013, Corporate tax avoidance by multinational firms, Library of the European Parliament; (4) www.volvocars.com.

6-3 Ownership Advantages

All investments, including both FDI and FPI, entail ownership of assets. So, what is unique about FDI? This section (1) highlights the benefits of direct ownership, and (2) compares FDI to licensing when entertaining market entries abroad.

6-3a The Benefits of Direct Ownership

Remember the key word of FDI is D (direct) and it requires a significant equity ownership position. The benefits of ownership lie in the *combination* of equity ownership rights and management control rights. Specifically, it is significant ownership rights that provide much needed management control rights. In contrast, FPI represents essentially insignificant ownership rights but no management control rights. To compete successfully, firms must deploy overwhelming resources and capabilities to overcome their liabilities of foreignness (see Chapters 1 and 4). FDI provides one of the best ways to facilitate such extension of firm-specific resources and capabilities abroad.

6-3b FDI versus Licensing

When entering foreign markets, basic entry choices include (1) exporting, (2) licensing, and (3) FDI. Successful exporting may provoke protectionist responses from host countries, thus forcing firms to choose between licensing and FDI (see Chapters 5 and 10). Between licensing and FDI, which is better? Three reasons may compel firms to prefer FDI to licensing (Table 6.1).

First, FDI affords a high degree of direct management control that reduces the risk of firm-specific resources and capabilities being opportunistically taken advantage of. One of the leading risks abroad is dissemination risks, defined as the possibility of unauthorized diffusion of firm-specific know-how. If a foreign company grants a license to a local firm to manufacture or market a product, the licensee (or an employee of the licensee) may disseminate the know-how by using it against the wishes of the foreign company. For instance, Pizza Hut found out that its long-time licensee in Thailand disseminated its know-how and established a direct competitor, simply called The Pizza Company, which controlled 70% of the market in Thailand.[10] While owning and managing proprietary assets through FDI does not completely shield firms from dissemination risks (after all, their employees can quit and join competitors), FDI is better than licensing that provides no management control at all. Understandably, FDI is extensively used in knowledge-intensive, high-tech industries, such as automobiles, electronics, chemicals, and IT.

Second, FDI provides more direct and tighter control over foreign operations. Even when licensees (and their employees) harbor no opportunistic intention to take away "secrets," they may not follow the wishes of the foreign firm that provides

Dissemination risk

Risk associated with unauthorized diffusion of firm-specific know-how.

Table 6.1　**Why Firms Prefer FDI to Licensing**
• FDI reduces dissemination risks
• FDI provides tight control over foreign operations
• FDI facilitates the transfer of tacit knowledge through "learning by doing"

the know-how. Without FDI, the foreign firm cannot order or control its licensee to move ahead. For example, Starbucks entered South Korea by licensing its format to ESCO. Although ESCO soon opened ten stores, Starbucks felt that ESCO was not aggressive enough. But there was very little Starbucks could do. Eventually, Starbucks switched from licensing to FDI, which allowed Starbucks to directly call "the shots" and promote the aggressive growth of the chain in South Korea.

Finally, certain knowledge (or know-how) calls for FDI, as opposed to licensing. Even if there is no opportunism on the part of licensees and if they are willing to follow the wishes of the foreign firm, certain know-how may be simply too difficult to transfer to licensees without FDI. Knowledge has two basic categories: (1) explicit and (2) tacit. Explicit knowledge is codifiable (i.e., it can be written down and transferred without losing much of its richness). Tacit knowledge, on the other hand, is non-codifiable and its acquisition and transfer requires hands-on practice. For instance, a driving manual represents a body of explicit knowledge. However, mastering this manual without any road practice does not make you a good driver. Tacit knowledge is evidently more important and harder to transfer and learn—it can only be acquired through learning by doing (in this case, driving practice supervised by an experienced driver). Likewise, operating a Wal-Mart store entails a great deal of knowledge, some explicit (often captured in an operational manual) and some tacit. However, simply giving foreign licensees a copy of the Wal-Mart operational manual will not be enough. Foreign employees will need to learn from experienced Wal-Mart personnel side-by-side (learning by doing).

From a resource-based standpoint, it is Wal-Mart's tacit knowledge that gives it competitive advantage (see Chapter 4). Wal-Mart owns such crucial tacit knowledge, and has no incentive to give it away to licensees without having some management control over how such tacit knowledge is used. Therefore, properly transferring and controlling tacit knowledge calls for FDI. Overall, ownership advantages enable the firm, now becoming an MNE, to more effectively extend, transfer, and leverage firm-specific capabilities abroad.[11] Next, we discuss location advantages.

6-4 Location Advantages

The second key word in FDI is F, referring to a *foreign* location. Given the well-known liability of foreignness, foreign locations must offer compelling advantages.[12] This section (1) highlights the sources of location advantages and (2) outlines ways to acquire and neutralize location advantages.

6-4a Location, Location, Location

Certain locations possess geographical features that are difficult to match by others. We may regard the continuous expansion of international business (IB), such as FDI, as an unending saga in search of location advantages.[13] For example, although Austria politically and culturally belongs to the West, the country is geographically located in the heart of Central and Eastern Europe (CEE). In fact, Austria's capital Vienna is actually *east* of Prague, the Czech Republic, and Ljubljana, Slovenia. Not surprisingly, Vienna attracts significant FDI from MNEs to set up regional headquarters for CEE. Due to its proximity to the United States, Mexico attracts numerous automakers to set up production there. Thanks to such FDI, 64% of Mexico's vehicle production is exported to the United States (see the Closing Case).

Beyond natural geographical advantages, location advantages also arise from the clustering of economic activities in certain locations—referred to as agglomeration. For instance, the Netherlands grows and exports two-thirds of the world's exported cut flowers. Dallas attracts all of the world's major telecom equipment makers and many telecom service providers, making it the Telecom Corridor. Denmark enjoys the clustering of the world's leading wind turbine makers and suppliers (In Focus 6.2). Overall, agglomeration advantages stem from:

- Knowledge spillovers (knowledge being diffused from one firm to others) among closely located firms that attempt to hire individuals from competitors.[14]
- Industry demand that creates a skilled labor force whose members may work for different firms without having to move out of the region.
- Industry demand that facilitates a pool of specialized suppliers and buyers also located in the region.[15]

6-4b Acquiring and Neutralizing Location Advantages

Note that from a resource-based view, location advantages do *not* entirely overlap with country-level advantages such as factor endowments discussed in Chapter 5. Location advantages refer to the advantages one firm obtains when operating in

What advantages did Volkswagen enjoy as one of the first foreign entrants into China's auto market?

one location due to its *firm-specific* capabilities. In 1982, General Motors (GM) ran its Fremont, California, plant to the ground and had to close it. Reopening the same plant, Toyota in 1984 initiated its first FDI project in the United States (in a joint venture [JV] with GM). Since then, Toyota (together with GM) has leveraged this plant's location advantages by producing award-winning cars that American customers particularly like, the Toyota Corolla and Tacoma. The point is: it is Toyota's unique capabilities, applied to the California location, that literally saved this plant from its demise. The California location in itself does not provide location advantages per se, as shown by GM's inability to make it work prior to 1982.

Agglomeration

Clustering of economic activities in certain locations.

Knowledge spillover

Knowledge diffused from one firm to others among closely located firms.

Oligopoly

Industry dominated by a small number of players.

Firms do not operate in a vacuum. When one firm enters a foreign country through FDI, its rivals are likely to follow by undertaking additional FDI in a host country to either (1) acquire location advantages themselves or (2) at least neutralize the first mover's location advantages. These actions to follow competitors are especially likely in industries characterized by oligopoly—industries populated by a small number of players (such as aerospace and semiconductors).[16] The automobile industry is a typical oligopolistic industry. In China, Volkswagen was the first foreign entrant, starting production in 1985 and enjoying a market share of 60% in the 1990s. Now, every self-respecting global automaker has entered China trying to eat some of Volkswagen's lunch. Overall, competitive rivalry and imitation, especially in oligopolistic industries, underscores the importance to acquire and neutralize location advantages around the world.

IN FOCUS 6.2

AGGLOMERATION OF WIND TURBINE PRODUCERS IN DENMARK

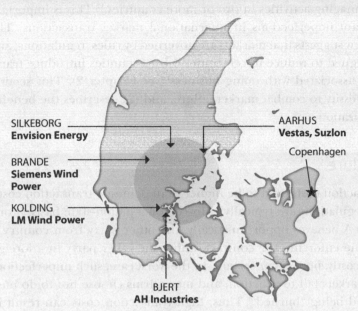

SILKEBORG
Envision Energy

BRANDE
Siemens Wind Power

KOLDING
LM Wind Power

AARHUS
Vestas, Suzlon

Copenhagen

BJERT
AH Industries

Source: © Danish Ministry of Foreign Affairs.

On a clear day, passengers with window seats on planes taking off and landing at Copenhagen airport can clearly see dozens of huge wind turbines offshore in Oresund (the straight that separates Denmark and Sweden). Chances are that these wind turbines are also developed and made in Denmark. Thanks to visionary government policies that offer generous subsidies, Denmark is a first mover, and now a world leader, in the wind turbine industry. At present, *one-third* of Danish energy consumption comes from wind. No other country comes close. Denmark's goal is to become the first country in the world to meet 50% of energy needs with wind power by 2020 and 100% by 2050. Underpinning these achievements and ambitions is a cluster of wind turbine manufacturers and suppliers in one part of Denmark—Jutland, the peninsula in western Denmark that is attached to the European mainland (Copenhagen is located in the easternmost part of the country on the island of Zealand).

Based in Aarhus (Denmark's second largest city), Vestas is the world leader in terms of installed turbines (60 GW), accounting for nearly one-fifth of the total capacity of all the installed turbines in the

world. Founded in 1979, Vestas employs 15,000 people, including 4,000 in Denmark. About 80 kilometers west of Aarhus, in the small town of Brande, Siemens Wind Power is headquartered. Founded in 2004 following the acquisition of Bonus Energy, which was established in 1979, Siemens Wind Power (a division of Siemens) is another giant in this industry. It has 23 GW installed turbines and 11,000 employees worldwide (of which 5,500 are in Denmark). In addition, major Danish-owned suppliers LM Wind Power and AH Industries are also nearby.

Attracted by the greatest agglomeration of know-how in this specialized but rapidly expanding industry, a number of international wind turbine manufacturers, such as India's Suzlon and China's Envision Energy, have also undertaken foreign direct investment (FDI) in this region of Denmark. With an investment of US$400 million, Japan's Mitsubishi Heavy Industries (MHI) has recently established a 50-50 joint venture with Vestas named MHI Vestas Offshore Wind that focuses on the huge 8.0 MW turbines. Anders Rebsdorf, director of Envision Energy (Denmark) located in Silkeborg, a town almost equidistant between the global headquarters of the two giants Vestas and Siemens Wind Power, articulated the firm's location choice:

> Our choice of Denmark is directly related to the country's strong cluster of know-how in the area of turbine design. It is also important that there are manufacturers of turbine components and experts in turbine service. The entire value chain is represented to a degree that is not found anywhere else . . . If we are to earn the right to join the battle for international orders, then we must be visible where the competition is fierce.

Sources: Based on (1) *Focus Denmark*, 2014, A wind energy hub, summer-autumn: 24; (2) *Focus Denmark*, 2014, Titans of wind energy arm for battle, summer-autumn: 18–23; (3) Vestas, 2014, MHI Vestas Offshore Wind now operational, announcement, April 1; (4) *Wall Street Journal*, 2013, Vestas, Mitsubishi form offshore joint venture, September 27, online.wsj.com.

6-5 Internalization Advantages

Known as internalization, another great advantage associated with FDI is the ability to replace the external market relationship with one firm (the MNE) owning, controlling, and managing activities in two or more countries.[17] This is important because of significant imperfections in international market transactions. The institution-based view suggests that markets are governed by rules, regulations, and norms that are designed to reduce uncertainties.[18] Uncertainties introduce transaction costs—costs associated with doing business (see Chapter 2). This section (1) outlines the necessity to combat market failure, and (2) describes the benefits brought by internalization.

6-5a Market Failure

International transaction costs tend to be higher than domestic transaction costs. Because laws and regulations are typically enforced on a nation-state basis, if one party from country A behaves opportunistically, the other party from country B will have a hard time enforcing the contract. Suing the other party in a foreign country is not only costly, but also uncertain. In the worst case, such imperfections are so grave that markets fail to function, and many firms choose not to do business abroad to avoid being "burned." Thus, high transaction costs can result in market failure—the imperfections of the market mechanisms that make transactions prohibitively costly and sometimes make transactions unable to take place. However, recall from Chapter 5 that there are gains from trade. In response, MNEs emerge to overcome and combat such market failure through FDI.

6-5b Overcoming Market Failure Through FDI

How do MNEs combat market failure through internalization? Let us use a simple example: An oil importer, BP in Britain, and an oil exporter, Nigerian National Petroleum Corporation (NNPC) in Nigeria. For the sake of our discussion, assume that BP does all its business in Britain and NNPC does all its business in Nigeria—in other words, none of them is an MNE for the time being. BP and NNPC negotiate a contract that specifies that NNPC will export from Nigeria a certain amount of crude oil to BP's oil refinery facilities in Britain for a certain amount of money. Shown in Figure 6.6, this is both an export contract (from NNPC's perspective) and an import contract (from BP's standpoint) between two firms.

However, this international market transaction between an importer and an exporter may suffer from high transaction costs. What is especially costly is the potential opportunism on both sides. For example, NNPC may demand a higher-than-agreed-upon price, citing a variety of reasons, such as inflation, natural disasters, or simply rising oil price, after the deal is signed. BP thus has to either (1) pay more than the agreed-upon price or (2) refuse to pay and suffer from the huge costs of keeping expensive refinery facilities idle. In other words, NNPC's opportunistic behavior can cause a lot of BP's losses.

Opportunistic behavior can go both ways in a market transaction. In this particular example, BP can also be opportunistic. For instance, BP may refuse to accept a shipment after its arrival from Nigeria, citing unsatisfactory quality, but the real reason could be BP's inability to sell refined oil downstream because gasoline demand is going down (in a recession, the jobless do not need to commute to work).

Figure 6.6 **An International Market Transaction between Two Companies in Two Countries**

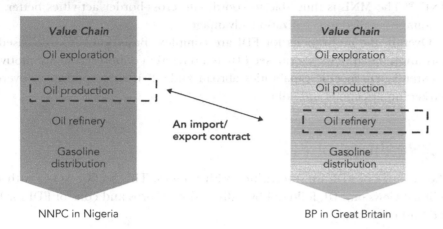

NNPC is thus forced to find a new buyer for a huge tanker load of crude oil on a last-minute, "fire sale" basis with a deep discount, losing a lot of money.

Overall, in a market (export/import) transaction, once one side behaves opportunistically, the other side will not be happy and will threaten or initiate lawsuits. Because the legal and regulatory frameworks governing such international transactions are generally not as effective as those governing domestic transactions, the injured party will generally be frustrated, whereas the opportunistic party can often get away. All these are examples of transaction costs that increase international market inefficiencies and imperfections, ultimately resulting in market failure.

In response, FDI combats such market failure through internalization. The MNE reduces cross-border transaction costs and increases efficiencies by replacing an external market relationship with a single organization spanning both countries—in a process called internalization (transforming the external market with in-house links).[19] In theory, there can be two possibilities: (1) BP undertakes *upstream* vertical FDI by owning oil production assets in Nigeria, or (2) NNPC undertakes *downstream* vertical FDI by owning oil refinery assets in Britain (Figure 6.7). FDI essentially

Figure 6.7 **Combating Market Failure Through FDI: One Company (MNE) in Two Countries[1]**

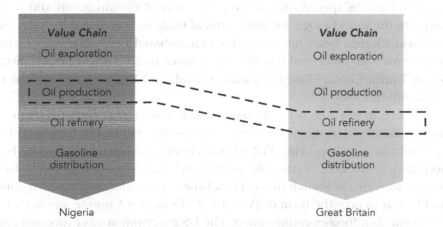

1. In theory, there can be two possibilities: (1) BP undertakes *upstream* vertical FDI by owning oil production assets in Nigeria, or (2) NNPC undertakes *downstream* vertical FDI by owning oil refinery assets in Great Britain. In reality, the first scenario is more likely.

transforms the international trade between two independent firms in two countries to intrafirm trade between two subsidiaries in two countries controlled by the same MNE. [20] The MNE is thus able to coordinate cross-border activities better. Such advantage is called internalization advantage.

Overall, the motivations for FDI are complex. Based on resource-based and institution-based views, we can see FDI as a reflection of both (1) firms' motivation to extend firm-specific capabilities abroad and (2) their responses to overcome market imperfections and failures.

6-6 Realities of FDI

Learning Objective

Identify different political views on FDI based on an understanding of its benefits and costs to host and home countries.

The realities of FDI are intertwined with politics. This section starts with three political views on FDI, followed by a discussion of pros and cons of FDI for home and host countries.

Why have some countries welcomed FDI, like US-based Ford's plan to build this manufacturing plant in China?

6-6a Political Views on FDI

There are three primary political views on FDI. First, the radical view is hostile to FDI. Tracing its roots to Marxism, the radical view treats FDI as an instrument of imperialism and as a vehicle for exploitation of domestic resources by foreign capitalists and firms. Governments embracing the radical view often nationalize MNE assets, or simply ban (or discourage) inbound MNEs. Between the 1950s and the early 1980s, the radical view was influential throughout Africa, Asia, Eastern Europe, and Latin America.[21] However, the popularity of this view is in decline worldwide, because (1) economic development in these countries was poor in the absence of FDI, and (2) the few developing countries (such as Singapore) that embraced FDI attained enviable growth (see Chapter 1).

On the other hand, the free market view suggests that FDI, unrestricted by government intervention, will enable countries to tap into their absolute or comparative advantages by specializing in the production of certain goods and services. Similar to the win-win logic for international trade as articulated by Adam Smith and David Ricardo (see Chapter 5), free market-based FDI will lead to a win-win situation for both home and host countries. Since the 1980s, a series of countries, such as Brazil, China, Hungary, India, Ireland, and Russia, have adopted more FDI-friendly policies.

However, in practice, a totally free market view on FDI does not really exist. Most countries practice pragmatic nationalism—viewing FDI as having both pros and cons and only approving FDI when its benefits outweigh costs. The French government, invoking "economic patriotism," has torpedoed several foreign takeover attempts of French firms. The Chinese government insists that automobile FDI has to take the form of JVs with MNEs so that Chinese automakers can learn from their foreign counterparts. The US government has expressed alleged "national security concerns" over the FDI made by Chinese telecom equipment makers Huawei and ZTE.[22]

Intrafirm trade

International transactions between two subsidiaries in two countries controlled by the same MNE.

Radical view

A political view that is hostile to FDI.

Free market view

A political view that suggests that FDI unrestricted by government intervention is the best.

Pragmatic nationalism

A political view that only approves FDI when its benefits outweigh its costs.

More countries in recent years have changed their policies to be more favorable to FDI. Even hardcore countries that practiced the radical view on FDI, such as Cuba and North Korea, are now experimenting with some opening to FDI, which is indicative of the emerging pragmatic nationalism in their new thinking. However, there is some creeping increase of restrictions in the form of policies discouraging inbound FDI in some countries. For example, France and Russia have recently issued decrees reinforcing control for FDI in the interest of public security or national defense.

6-6b Benefits and Costs of FDI to Host Countries

Underpinning pragmatic nationalism is the need to assess the various benefits and costs of FDI to host (recipient) countries and home (source) countries (see the Closing Case). In a nutshell, Figure 6.8 outlines these considerations. This section focuses on host countries, and the next section deals with home countries.

Cell 1 in Figure 6.8 shows four primary benefits to host countries:[23]

- Capital inflow can help improve a host country's balance of payments. (See Chapter 7 for more coverage on balance of payments.)
- Technology, especially more advanced technology from abroad, can create technology spillovers that benefit domestic firms and industries.[24] Local rivals, after observing such technology, may recognize its feasibility and strive to imitate it. This is known as the demonstration effect—sometimes also called the contagion (or imitation) effect.[25] It underscores the important role that MNEs play in stimulating competition in host countries.[26]
- Advanced management know-how may be highly valued. It is often difficult for indigenous development of management know-how to reach a world-class level in the absence of FDI (see the Closing Case).
- FDI creates a total of 80 million jobs, which represent approximately 4% of the global workforce.[27] FDI creates jobs both directly and indirectly. Direct benefits arise when MNEs employ individuals locally. In Ireland, more than 50% of the manufacturing employees work for MNEs.[28] In the UK, the largest private sector employer is an MNE: India's Tata has 50,000 employees in the UK (see the Opening Case).[29] Indirect benefits include jobs created when local suppliers increase hiring and when MNE employees spend money locally resulting in more jobs.

Figure 6.8 **Effects of FDI on Host and Home Countries**

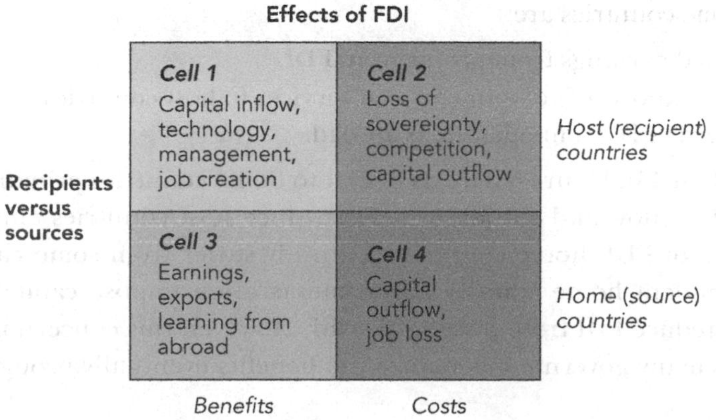

Effects of FDI

	Benefits	Costs
Recipients versus sources — Host (recipient) countries	**Cell 1** Capital inflow, technology, management, job creation	**Cell 2** Loss of sovereignty, competition, capital outflow
Home (source) countries	**Cell 3** Earnings, exports, learning from abroad	**Cell 4** Capital outflow, job loss

Technology spillover

Technology diffused from foreign firms to domestic firms.

Demonstration effect

The reaction of local firms to rise to the challenge demonstrated by MNEs through learning and imitation.

Contagion (imitation) effect

The reaction of local firms to rise to the challenge demonstrated by MNEs through learning and imitation.

Cell 2 in Figure 6.8 outlines three primary costs of FDI to host countries: (1) loss of sovereignty, (2) adverse effects on competition, and (3) capital outflow. The first concern is the loss of some (but not all) economic sovereignty associated with FDI. Because of FDI, decisions to invest, produce, and market products and/or to close plants and lay off workers in a host country are being made by foreigners—or if locals serve as heads of MNE subsidiaries, they represent the interest of foreign firms. Will foreigners and foreign firms make decisions in the best interest of host countries? This is truly a "million dollar" question. According to the radical view, the answer is "No!" because foreigners and foreign firms are likely to maximize their own profits by exploiting people and resources in host countries. Such deep suspicion of MNEs leads to policies that discourage or even ban FDI. On the other hand, countries embracing free market and pragmatic nationalism views agree that despite some acknowledged differences between foreign and host country interests, there is a sufficient overlap of interests between MNEs and host countries. Thus, host countries are willing to live with some loss of sovereignty.

A second concern is associated with the negative effects on local competition. While we have just discussed the positive effects of MNEs on local competition, it is possible that MNEs may drive some domestic firms out of business. Having driven domestic firms out of business, MNEs, in theory, may be able to monopolize local markets. While this is a relatively minor concern in developed economies, this is a legitimate concern for less-developed economies, where MNEs are of such a magnitude in size and strength and local firms tend to be significantly weaker. For example, as Coca-Cola and PepsiCo extend their "cola wars" from the United States around the world, they have almost "accidentally" wiped out much of the world's indigenous beverages companies, which are—or were—much smaller.

A third concern is associated with capital outflow. When MNEs make profits in host countries and repatriate (send back) such earnings to headquarters in home countries, host countries experience a net outflow in the capital account in their balance of payments. As a result, some countries have restricted the ability of MNEs to repatriate funds. Another issue arises when MNE subsidiaries spend a lot of money to import components and services abroad, which also results in outflows of capital and reduction of tax revenue (see In Focus 6.1).

6-6c Benefits and Costs of FDI to Home Countries

As exporters of capital, technology, management, and (in some cases) jobs, home (source) countries often reap benefits and endure costs associated with FDI that are *opposite* to those experienced by host countries. In Cell 3 of Figure 6.8, three benefits to home countries are:

- Repatriated earnings from profits from FDI.
- Increased exports of components and services to host countries.
- Learning via FDI from operations abroad.

Shown in Cell 4 in Figure 6.8, costs of FDI to home countries primarily center on (1) capital outflow and (2) job loss. First, since host countries enjoy capital inflow because of FDI, home countries naturally suffer from some capital outflow. Less-confident home country governments often impose capital controls to prevent or reduce FDI from flowing abroad. However, this concern is now less significant, as many governments realize the benefits eventually brought by FDI outflows.

The second concern is now more prominent: job loss. Many MNEs simultaneously invest abroad by adding employment overseas and curtail domestic production by laying off employees. It is not surprising that restrictions on FDI outflows have been increasingly vocal, called for by politicians, union members, journalists, and activists in many developed economies.

6-7 How MNES and Host Governments Bargain

MNEs react to various policies by bargaining with host governments. The outcome of MNE-host government relationship, namely, the scale and scope of FDI in a host country, is a function of the relative bargaining power of both sides—the ability to extract favorable outcome from negotiations due to one party's strengths. MNEs typically prefer to minimize the intervention from host governments and maximize the incentives provided by host governments. Host governments usually want to ensure a certain degree of control and minimize the incentives provided to MNEs. Sometimes, host governments "must coerce or cajole the multinationals into undertaking roles that they would otherwise abdicate."[30] However, host governments have to "induce, rather than command," because MNEs have options elsewhere.[31] Different countries, in effect, are competing with each other for precious FDI dollars.

Shown in Figure 6.9, FDI is not a zero-sum game. The negotiations are characterized by the "three Cs": common interests, conflicting interests, and compromises.[32] The upshot is that despite conflicts, the interests of both sides may converge on an outcome that makes each side better off.[33]

Typically, FDI bargaining is not one round only. After the initial FDI entry, both sides may continue to exercise bargaining power. A well-known phenomenon is the obsolescing bargain, referring to the deal struck by MNEs and host governments, which change their requirements *after* the initial FDI entry. It typically unfolds in three rounds:

- In Round One, the MNE and the government negotiate a deal. The MNE usually is not willing to enter in the absence of some government assurance of property rights and incentives (such as tax holidays).
- In Round Two, the MNE enters and, if all goes well, earns profits that may become visible.
- In Round Three, the government, often pressured by domestic political groups, may demand renegotiations of the deal that seems to yield "excessive"

Figure 6.9 **How MNEs Negotiate with Host Governments: The Three Cs**

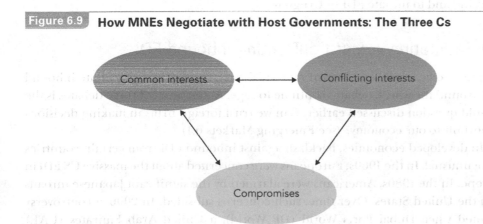

Bargaining power

Ability to extract favorable outcome from negotiations due to one party's strengths.

Obsolescing bargain

The deal struck by MNEs and host governments, which change their requirements after the initial FDI entry.

profits to the foreign firm (which, of course, regards these as "fair" and "normal" profits). The previous deal, thus, becomes obsolete. The government's tactics include removing incentives, demanding more profits and taxes, and even expropriation (confiscating foreign assets).

At this time, the MNE has already invested substantial sums of resources (called sunk costs) and often has to accommodate some new demands. Otherwise, it may face expropriation or exit at a huge loss. Not surprisingly, MNEs do not appreciate the risk associated with such obsolescing bargains. Unfortunately, recent actions in Argentina, Bolivia, Ecuador, and Venezuela suggest that obsolescing bargains have not necessarily become obsolete (see the next section for some details).

Learning Objective

Participate in two leading debates concerning FDI.

6-8 Debates and Extensions

As an embodiment of globalization, FDI has stimulated many debates. This section highlights two: (1) FDI versus outsourcing and (2) facilitating versus confronting inbound FDI.

6-8a FDI versus Outsourcing

While this chapter has focused on FDI, we need to be aware that FDI is *not* the only mode of foreign market entry (see Chapter 10). Especially when undertaking a value chain analysis regarding specific activities (see Chapter 4), a decision to undertake FDI will have to be assessed relative to the benefits and costs of outsourcing. Recall from Chapter 4 that in a foreign location, overseas outsourcing becomes "offshoring," whereas FDI—that is, performing an activity in-house at an overseas location—has been recently labeled "captive sourcing" by some authors (see Figure 4.4). A strategic debate is whether FDI (captive sourcing) or outsourcing will serve firms' purposes better.

The answer boils down to (1) how critical the activity being considered to perform abroad is to the core mission of the firm, (2) how common the activity is being undertaken by multiple end-user industries, and (3) how readily available the overseas talents to perform this activity are. If the activity is marginal, is common (or similar) across multiple end-user industries, and is able to be provided by proven talents overseas, then outsourcing is called for. Otherwise, FDI is often necessary. For instance, when Travelocity outsourced its call center operations to India, its rival Sabre carefully considered its options. Sabre eventually decided to avoid outsourcing and to initiate FDI in Uruguay.

Expropriation

Government's confiscation of foreign assets.

Sunk cost

Cost that a firm has to endure even when its investment turns out to be unsatisfactory.

Sovereign wealth fund (SWF)

A state-owned investment fund composed of financial assets such as stocks, bonds, real estate, or other financial instruments funded by foreign exchange assets.

6-8b Facilitating versus Confronting Inbound FDI

Despite the general trend toward more FDI-friendly policies to facilitate inbound FDI around the world, debates continue to rage. At the heart of these debates is the age-old question discussed earlier: Can we trust foreign firms in making decisions important to our economy? (see Emerging Markets 6.1)

In developed economies, backlash against inbound FDI from certain countries is not unusual. In the 1960s, Europeans were concerned about the massive US FDI in Europe. In the 1980s, Americans were alarmed by the significant Japanese inroads into the United States. Over time, such concerns subsided. In 2006, a controversy erupted when Dubai Ports World (DP World), a United Arab Emirates (UAE)

EMERGING MARKETS 6.1

Welcoming versus Restricting Sovereign Wealth Fund Investments

A sovereign wealth fund (SWF) is a state-owned investment fund composed of financial assets such as stocks, bonds, real estate, or other financial instruments funded by foreign exchange assets. Although the term "SWF" was only coined in 2005 by Andrew Rozanov, a senior manager at State Street Global Advisors, outside the United States investment funds that we now call SWFs were first created in 1953 by Kuwait. Both the United States and Canada have had their own SWFs—at least at the state and provincial level, such as the Alaska Permanent Fund and Alberta Heritage Fund. In the United States, Texas Permanent School Fund was established in 1854.

In the recent global financial crisis, SWFs came to the rescue. For example, in 2007, the Abu Dhabi Investment Authority injected US$7.5 billion (4.9% of equity) into Citigroup. In 2008, China Investment Corporation (CIC) invested US$5 billion for a 10% equity stake in Morgan Stanley.

Such large-scale investments have ignited the debate on SWFs. On the one hand, SWFs have brought much-needed cash to rescue desperate Western firms. On the other hand, concerns are raised by host countries, which are typically developed economies. One primary concern is national security in that SWFs may be politically (as opposed to commercially) motivated. Another concern is SWFs' inadequate transparency. Governments in several developed economies, in fear of the "threats" from SWFs, have been erecting anti-SWF measures to defend their companies.

Foreign investment certainly has both benefits and costs to host countries. However, in the absence of any evidence that the costs outweigh benefits, the rush to erect anti-SWF barriers is indicative of protectionist (or, some may argue, even racist) sentiments. For executives at hard-pressed Western firms, it would not seem sensible to ask for government bailouts on the one hand, and to reject cash from SWFs on the other hand. Most SWF investment is essentially free cash with few strings attached. For example, CIC, which now holds 10% of Morgan Stanley equity, did not demand a board seat or a management role. For Western policymakers, it makes little sense to spend taxpayers' dollars to bail out failed firms, run huge budget deficits, and then turn away SWFs. Commenting on inbound Chinese investment in the United States (including SWF investment), then-Secretary of the Treasury Henry Paulson argued in *Foreign Affairs*:

> These concerns [on Chinese investment] are misplaced ... the United States would do well to encourage such investment from anywhere in the world—including China—because it represents a vote of confidence in the US economy and it promotes growth, jobs, and productivity in the United States.

Lastly, thanks to the financial crisis in 2008-2009, recent SWF investment in developed economies suffered major losses. Such a "double whammy"—both the political backlash and the economic losses—has severely discouraged SWFs. Some SWFs, especially those from the Gulf, are increasingly investing in their domestic public services (such as healthcare, education, and infrastructure). As a result, the competition for funds puts a premium on maintaining a welcoming climate. As part of the efforts to foster such a welcoming climate in times of great political and economic anxiety, the US-China Strategic and Economic Dialogue (S&ED) in July 2009 confirmed:

> The United States confirms that the Committee on Foreign Investment in the United States (CFIUS) process ensures the consistent and fair treatment of all foreign investment without prejudice to the place of origin. The United States welcomes sovereign wealth fund investment, including that from China.

In September 2008, major SWFs of the world at a summit in Santiago, Chile, agreed to a voluntary code of conduct known as the Santiago Principles. These principles are designed to alleviate some of the concerns for host countries of SWF investment and to enhance the transparency of such investment. These principles represent an important milestone of SWFs' evolution. Since then SWF assets have grown faster than the assets of any other institutional investor group, including private equity and hedge funds. Today more than 70 major SWFs manage approximately US$6.4 trillion assets. In the EU, between 15% and 25% of listed firms have SWF shareholders. Norway's Government Pension Fund Global, the world's largest SWF, owns an average of 2.5% every European listed firm and 1% of all the equities in the world.

Sources: Based on (1) *Economist*, 2013, More money than Thor, September 14: 73; (2) D. Drezner, 2008, Sovereign wealth funds and the (in)security of global finance, *Journal of International Affairs*, 62: 115–130; (3) V. Fotak & W. Megginson, 2009, Are SWFs welcome now? *Columbia FDI Perspectives*, No. 9, July 21, www.vcc.columbia.edu; (4) H. Paulson, 2008, The right way to engage China. *Foreign Affairs*, September/October, www.foreignaffairs.org; (5) A. Rozanov, 2005, Who holds the wealth of nations? *Central Banking Journal*, May; (6) Sovereign Wealth Fund Institute, 2015, About sovereign wealth fund, www.swfinstitute.org; (7) United Nations (UN), 2014, *World Investment Report 2014* (pp. 19–20), New York and Geneva: UN; (6) US Department of the Treasury, 2009, *The First US-China Strategic and Economic Dialogue Economic Track Joint Fact Sheet*, July 28, Washington.

government-owned company, purchased US ports from another *foreign* firm, Britain's P&O. This entry gave DP World control over terminal operations at the ports of New York/New Jersey, Philadelphia, Baltimore, Miami, and New Orleans. Although the UAE has been a US ally for three decades, many politicians, journalists, and activists opposed such FDI. In this "largest political storm over US ports since the Boston Tea Party,"[34] DP World eventually withdrew. Similarly, Chinese firm CNOOC's bid for US firm Unocal and another Chinese firm Chinalco's bid for Australia's Rio Tinto were torpedoed by a politicized process. Recent media sensation often focuses on China's rise as an active foreign investor.[35]

In some parts of the developing world, tension over foreign ownership can heat up. There were numerous incidents of nationalization and expropriation against MNE assets throughout the developing world between the 1950s and the 1970s. Given the recent worldwide trend toward more FDI-friendly policies, many people thought that such actions were a thing of the past. During 2006, individuals holding such a view had a rude awakening. In 2006, Venezuelan President Hugo Chavez ordered Chevron, ENI, Royal Dutch, Total, and other oil and gas MNEs to convert their operations in the country into forced JVs with state-owned Venezuelan firm PDVSA, with PDVSA holding at least 60% of the equity. When France's Total and Italy's ENI rejected such terms, the government promptly seized their fields.[36] Also in 2006, Bolivia seized control of MNEs' oil fields.[37] Soon after, Ecuador expropriated the oil fields run by America's Occidental Petroleum. More recently, in 2012 Argentina nationalized YPF, which was owned by Spain's Repsol.[38]

It is important to note that the anti-MNE actions in Latin America were not sudden impulsive policy changes. The politicians leading these actions were all democratically elected. These actions were the result of lengthy political debates concerning FDI in the region, and such takeovers were popular among the public. Until the 1970s, Latin American governments had often harshly confronted MNEs. Only in the 1990s when these countries became democratic did they open their oil industry to inbound FDI.

Why did Argentina's government led by President Cristina Fernandez de Kirchner, take over YPF in 2012?

ITAR-TASS Photo Agency/Alamy

Therefore, the 180-degree policy reversal is both surprising (considering how recently these governments welcomed MNEs to arrive) and not surprising (considering the history of how MNEs were dealt with in the region). Some argue that these actions represent the swing of a "pendulum" toward more confrontation (see Chapter 1 on the "pendulum" view on globalization).

6-9 Management Savvy

Learning Objective
Draw implications for action.

The big question in global business, adapted to the context of FDI, is: What determines the success and failure of FDI around the globe? The answer boils down to two components. First, from a resource-based view, why some firms are very good at FDI is because they leverage OLI advantages in a way that is valuable, unique, and hard-to-imitate by rival firms. Second, from an institution-based view, the political realities either enable or constrain FDI from reaching its full economic potential (see Emerging Markets 6.1). Therefore, the success and failure of FDI also significantly depends on institutions governing FDI as "rules of the game" (see the Closing Case).

As a result, three implications for action emerge (Table 6.2). First, carefully assess whether FDI is justified, in light of other possibilities, such as outsourcing and licensing. This exercise must be conducted on an activity-by-activity basis as part of the value-chain analysis (see Chapter 4). If ownership and internalization advantages are deemed not crucial, then FDI is not recommended.

Second, once a decision to undertake FDI is made, pay attention to the old adage: "Location, location, location!" The quest for location advantages has to create a fit with the firm's strategic goals. For example, if a firm is searching for the best "hot spots" for innovations, certain low cost locations that do not generate sufficient innovations will not become very attractive (see Chapters 10 and 13). High-cost locations, such as Denmark, would be ideal for wind turbine makers in search of cutting-edge innovations (In Focus 6.2).

Finally, given the political realities around the world, be aware of the institutional constraints. Savvy MNE managers should not take FDI-friendly policies for granted. Setbacks are likely. The global economic slowdown has made many developed economies less attractive to invest in, and the credit crunch means that firms are less able to invest abroad. Attitudes toward certain forms of FDI (such as sovereign wealth funds [SWF] discussed in Emerging Markets 6.1) are changing, which may lead to FDI policies to become more protectionist. In the long run, the interests of MNEs in host countries can be best safeguarded if MNEs accommodate, rather than neglect or dominate, the interests of host countries. In practical terms, contributions to local employment, job training, education, innovation, and pollution control will tangibly demonstrate the commitment of MNEs to host countries (see the Closing Case).[39]

Table 6.2 | **Implications for Action**

- Carefully assess whether FDI is justified, in light of other foreign entry modes such as outsourcing and licensing

- Pay careful attention to the location advantages in combination with the firm's strategic goals

- Be aware of the institutional constraints and enablers governing FDI and enhance legitimacy in host countries

---

CHAPTER SUMMARY/LEARNING OBJECTIVES

6-1 Use the resource-based and institution-based views to answer why FDI takes place.

- The resource-based view suggests that the key word of FDI is D (direct), which reflects firms' interest in directly managing, developing, and leveraging their firm-specific resources and capabilities abroad.
- The institution-based view argues that recent expansion of FDI is indicative of generally more friendly policies, norms, and values associated with FDI (despite some setbacks).

6-2 Understand how FDI results in OLI advantages.

- Ownership refers to MNEs' possession and leveraging of certain valuable, rare, hard-to-imitate, and organizationally embedded (VRIO) assets overseas.
- Location refers to certain locations' advantages that can help MNEs attain strategic goals.
- Internalization refers to the replacement of cross-border market relationship with one firm (the MNE) locating in two or more countries. Internalization helps combat market imperfections and failures.

6-3 Identify different political views on FDI based on an understanding of FDI's benefits and costs.

- The radical view is hostile to FDI, and the free market view calls for minimum intervention in FDI.
- Most countries practice pragmatic nationalism, weighing the benefits and costs of FDI.
- FDI brings a different (and often opposing) set of benefits and costs to host and home countries.

6-4 Participate in two leading debates concerning FDI.

- (1) FDI versus outsourcing, and (2) facilitating versus confronting inbound FDI.

6-5 Draw implications for action.

- Carefully assess whether FDI is justified, in light of other options such as outsourcing and licensing.
- Pay careful attention to the location advantages in combination with the firm's strategic goals.
- Be aware of the institutional constraints governing FDI and enhance legitimacy in host countries.

KEY TERMS

Agglomeration, 190

Bargaining power, 197

Contagion (imitation) effect, 195

Demonstration effect, 195

Dissemination risk, 188

Downstream vertical FDI, 183

Expropriation, 198

FDI flow, 184

FDI inflow, 184

FDI outflow, 184

FDI stock, 184

Foreign portfolio investment (FPI), 183

Free market view, 194

Horizontal FDI, 183

Knowledge spillover, 190

Internalization, 186

Intrafirm trade, 194

Licensing, 186

Location, 186

Management control rights, 183

REVIEW QUESTIONS

1. What is the primary difference between FDI and FPI?

2. Why does the resource-based view suggest that the key word of FDI is direct?

3. How does horizontal FDI compare to vertical FDI?

4. How does internationalization help combat market imperfections and failures?

5. Briefly summarize each of the three OLI advantages.

6. Discuss the pros and cons of FDI versus licensing.

7. Identify your own example of agglomeration that demonstrates your understanding of the concept.

8. Compare and contrast the three political views of FDI.

9. Describe two benefits and two costs to a host country of FDI and to a home country of FDI.

10. Given that outsourcing is a viable alternative to FDI, what issues should be considered before a firm decides between the two?

11. *ON CULTURE:* Many people in the United States are opposed to both outsourcing and FDI. Would it be easier to get such people to accept one of these alternatives, and if so, which one? Why or why not?

12. Why do some countries object to inbound FDI?

13. In the United States, many states and cities deliberately seek investment in their states and communities by firms from other parts of the country. Why are some of those who seek investment from elsewhere in the US worried about investment from overseas?

14. What issues should a savvy manager consider when evaluating a particular location for FDI?

15. Some Americans feel that US-based firms should not undertake FDI in other countries because it results in expanding business opportunities in those countries and does not benefit the United States. How may the data on PengAtlas Map 2.3 be used to refute that view?

16. Consider PengAtlas Map 2.3 showing US FDI, and then look at PengAtlas Maps 2.1 and 2.2. Given the possibility that some US imports are from operations in which US firms have made FDI, how does that affect your view of the US trade deficit? Does it make the deficit seem like less of a problem or greater? Explain your answer.

17. In Questions 12, 13, and 15, we have noted controversies regarding FDI in terms of both inflows and outflows. Regarding PengAtlas Map 2.3, public concern about FDI often focuses on the FDI of US-based companies, and some argue that investment going overseas may otherwise have occurred within the US.

However, the map also shows that the US is a major recipient of such investment from overseas—but some who oppose FDI outflows also oppose FDI inflows. They fear that the United States is losing control over its economy as a result of such inflows. Do you think the two views are compatible? Why or why not?

CRITICAL DISCUSSION QUESTIONS

1. Identify the top five (or ten) *source* countries of FDI into your country. Then identify the top ten (or 20) foreign MNEs that have undertaken inbound FDI in your country. Why do these countries and companies provide the bulk of FDI into your country?

2. Identify the top five (or ten) *recipient* countries of FDI from your country. Then identify the top ten (or 20) MNEs headquartered in your country that have made outbound FDI elsewhere. Why do these countries attract FDI from the top MNEs from your country?

3. *ON ETHICS:* Undertaking FDI, by definition, means not investing in the MNE's home country. What are the ethical dilemmas here? What are your recommendations, as (1) MNE executives, (2) labor union leaders of your domestic (home country) labor forces, (3) host country officials?

BUSINESS
INSIGHTS
GLOBAL

GLOBAL ACTION

1. Your MNE is looking to evaluate the industrial capability of various locations worldwide. Based on readily available data concerning the potential and performance of different countries, the information you provide will drive future investment by your company. Choose a country from Asia, Europe, North America, and South America, and summarize your findings about each. Of the four countries from four continents, how would you rank them? Why?

2. The main premise for development at your company in the coming years is to shift its offshore services to Africa. You have been asked to develop a report that evaluates which African countries have increased the possibility of creating a long-term advantage for your company. Also, be sure to include the African countries that have *decreased* their capacity to create a long-term advantage. Can you generate a top-five list and a bottom-five list from Africa for this purpose?

CLOSING CASE

EMERGING MARKETS: Automobile FDI in Brazil and Mexico

Brazil and Mexico are, respectively, the top one and two largest economies in Latin America in terms of GDP. Globally, Brazil and Mexico are, respectively, the seventh- and eighth-largest car producers and the fourth- and 16th-largest automobile markets. Almost all of their production is undertaken by global automakers via foreign direct investment (FDI). Audi, Fiat, Ford, General Motors (GM), Honda, Nissan, Renault,

Toyota, and Volkswagen (VW) have assembly factories in both countries. In addition, Hyundai, MAN, and Mercedes-Benz produce in Brazil; and BMW, Chrysler, Isuzu, Kia, and Mitsubishi operate assembly plants in Mexico. For multinationals striving for ownership, location, and internalization (OLI) advantages, their efforts in leveraging O and I advantages are similar in both countries. However, these two countries have pursued location (L) advantages in different ways.

Viviane Moos/Corbis News/Corbis

Brazil attracts FDI primarily due to its largest domestic market, while Mexico pulls in FDI due to its proximity to the United States. As a result, only 13% of Brazil's vehicle production is exported (67% of such exports go to its neighbors in Mercosur—a customs union with Argentina, Paraguay, Uruguay, and Venezuela). In contrast, 64% of Mexico's vehicle production is exported to the United States, and all together 82% of its output is exported. Brazil maintains high import tariffs on cars and auto components (except when 65% of the value is imported from one of the Mercosur partners or from Mexico—with which Brazil had a bilateral free trade deal in cars and auto components). As a result, only 21% of the content of Brazil's exports is imported. This ratio of imported content among exports is 47% for Mexico, indicating a much more open and less protectionist environment in which automakers can import a great deal more components tariff-free and duty-free.

The differences in the production, export, and import patterns, of course, are not only shaped by the resources and capabilities of multinationals, but also by government policies in both host countries of FDI. Whether Brazil or Mexico gains more is subject to intense debates in these two countries and beyond. One side of the argument posits that Mexico is only leveraging its low-cost labor and has not fostered a lot of domestic suppliers. Indeed, most first-tier suppliers in Mexico are foreign owned and they import a great deal of components to be assembled into final products. As a result, most final assembly plants are *maquiladora* type, otherwise known as "screw driver plants." With little technology spillovers to local suppliers, the innovation ability of the Mexican automobile industry is thus limited.

Brazil, on the other hand, has pushed automakers to work closely with domestically owned suppliers or with foreign-owned suppliers that have to source locally. With a domestic focus, Brazilian subsidiaries of multinational automakers, aided by suppliers, have endeavored to search for solutions to meet unique local demand, such as ethanol fuel. Brazil is a world leader in ethanol—a sustainable biofuel based on sugarcane. By law, no light vehicles in Brazil are allowed to run on pure gasoline. Led by Volkswagen's Gol 1.6 Total Flex in 2003, the Brazilian automobile industry has introduced flexible-fuel vehicles that can run any combination of ethanol and gasoline. All the multinational automakers producing in Brazil have eagerly participated in the flex movement. Starting with 22% of car sales in 2004, flex cars reached a record 94% by 2010. By 2012, the cumulative production of flex cars and light vehicles reached 15 million units. Advocates of Brazil's policy argue that such success has generated opportunities to involve locally owned component producers, local research institutions, and smaller suppliers, which have specific knowledge not available elsewhere in the world.

The other side of the debate points out Mexico's shining accomplishments as an export hub with a more open trade and investment regime. Mexico has successfully leveraged its NAFTA membership and its free trade agreements with more than 40 countries. While such institution-based boosters are helpful, at the end of the day, Made-in-Mexico vehicles—from a resource-based standpoint—have to be valuable, rare, and hard-to-beat on performance and price in export markets. This is largely attributed to Mexico's persistent efforts to keep its wage levels low, its labor skills upgraded, and its infrastructure modernized.

Brazil, on the other hand, suffers from the legendary (and notorious) *custo Brasil* (Brazil cost)—the exorbitant cost of living and doing business in Brazil (see Emerging Markets 2.1). Since President Dilma Rousseff took office in 2011, she has imposed new tariffs on shoes, textiles, chemicals, and even Barbie dolls. In the absence of protectionism, the Brazilian automobile industry, according to critics, simply cannot stand on its own. Brazil even threatened to tear up the agreement with Mexico that allowed free trade in cars and components, because Brazil—thanks to its uncompetitive automobile industry—suffered from an embarrassing trade deficit. In 2012, Brazil renegotiated the deal with Mexico, imposing import quotas on Made-in-Mexico cars and components. More recently, the Brazilian government has introduced *Inovar Autos*, a new automotive regime for 2013–2017, which is intended to encourage firms to hit specific targets in localization of production and R&D incentivized by additional tax benefits. Critics argue that this is just one more round of protectionism and government meddling that is ultimately counter-productive.

CASE DISCUSSION QUESTIONS:

1. What are the costs and benefits of FDI inflows for a host country such as Brazil and Mexico?

2. If you were an executive working for an emerging automaker from China or India, assuming your firm only has the ability to enter one Latin American country for the time being, which country would you recommend: Brazil or Mexico?

3. The automobile industry in both Brazil and Mexico is thriving. If you were a government official from an African country (such as Morocco, Nigeria, or South Africa) who has visited both countries and has been very impressed, which approach would you recommend to your own government interested in attracting FDI from global automakers: the Brazilian approach or the Mexican approach? Why

Sources: Based on (1) *Economist*, 2012, Two ways to make a car, March 10: 48–49; (2) *Economist*, 2013, The price is wrong, September 28 (special report): 5; (3) P. Figueiredo, 2011, The role of dual embeddedness in the innovative performance of MNE subsidiaries: Evidence from Brazil, *Journal of Management Studies*, 48: 417–440; (4) M. Kotabe, R. Parente, & J. Murray, 2007, Antecedents and outcomes of modular production in the Brazilian automobile industry, *Journal of International Business Studies*, 38: 84–106; (5) R. Quadros & F. Consoni, 2009, Innovation capabilities in the Brazilian automobile industry, *International Journal of Technological Learning, Innovation, and Development*, 2: 53–75; (6) T. Sturgeon & J. van Biesebroek, 2010, Effects of the crisis on the automotive industry in developing countries, Policy Research Working Paper 5330, Washington, DC: World Bank; (7) United Nations, 2014, *World Investment Report 2014* (pp. 65–69), New York & Geneva: United Nations.

NOTES

[**Journal acronyms**] **AMJ**—*Academy of Management Journal;* **AMR**—*Academy of Management Review;* **BW**—*BusinessWeek* (before 2010) or *Bloomberg Businessweek* (since 2010); **CFDIP**—*Columbia Foreign Direct Investment Perspectives;* **EJ**—*Economic Journal;* **FEER**—*Far Eastern Economic Review;* **GSJ**—*Global Strategy Journal;* **IBR**—*International Business Review;* **JMS**—*Journal of Management Studies;* **JIBS**—*Journal of International Business Studies;* **JIM**—*Journal of International Management;* **JWB**—*Journal of World Business;* **MBR**—*Multinational Business Review;* **MIR**—*Management International Review;* **SMJ**—*Strategic Management Journal.*

1 R. Caves, 1996, *Multinational Enterprise and Economic Analysis,* 2nd ed. (p. 1), New York: Cambridge University Press.

2 United Nations, 2014, *World Investment Report 2014* (p. ix), New York and Geneva: United Nations.

3 T. Khoury & M. W. Peng, 2011, Does institutional reform of intellectual property rights lead to more inbound FDI? Evidence from Latin America and the Caribbean, *JWB*, 46: 337–345; S. Sun, M. W. Peng, R. Lee, & W. Tan, 2015, Institutional open access at home and outward internationalization, *JWB*, 50: 234–246.

4 United Nations, 2005, *World Investment Report 2005* (p. 4), New York and Geneva: United Nations.

5 R. Aggarwal, J. Berrill, E. Hutson, & C. Kearney, 2011, What is a multinational corporation? *IBR*, 20: 557–577.

6 K. Moore & D. Lewis, 2009, *The Origins of Globalization,* New York: Routledge.

7 M. Wilkins, 2001, The history of MNE (p. 13), in A. Rugman & T. Brewer (eds.), *The Oxford Handbook of International Business,* 3–35, New York: Oxford University Press.

8 United Nations, 2009, *World Investment Report 2009* (p. xxi), New York and Geneva: UN.

9 J. Dunning, 1993, *Multinational Enterprises and the Global Economy,* Reading, MA: Addison-Wesley. See also C. Pitelis, 2007, Edith Penrose and a learning-based perspective on the MNE and OLI, *MIR*, 47: 207–219.

10 *FEER*, 2002, Pepperoni power, November 14: 59–60.

11 B. Elango & C. Pattnaik, 2007, Building capabilities for international operations through networks, *JIBS*, 38: 541–555; D. Yiu, C. M. Lau, & G. Bruton, 2007, International venturing by emerging economy firms, *JIBS*, 38: 519–540;

12 J. Galan, J. Gonzalez-Benito, & J. Zuniga-Vicente, 2007, Factors determining the location decisions of Spanish MNEs, *JIBS*, 38: 975–997.

13 J. Alcacer, C. Dezso, & M. Zhao, 2013, Firm rivalry, knowledge accumulation, and MNE location choices, *JIBS*, 44: 504–520; L. Alcantara & H. Mitsuhashi, 2012, Make-or-break decisions in choosing foreign direct investment locations, *JIM*, 18: 335–351; S. Beugelsdijk &

R. Mudambi, 2013, MNEs as border-crossing multi-location enterprises, *JIBS*, 44: 413–426; K. Boeh & P. Beamish, 2012, Travel time and the liability of distance in foreign direct investment, *JIBS*, 43: 525–535; J. Dunning, 2009, Location and the MNE, *JIBS*, 40: 5–19; A. Schotter & P. Beamish, 2013, The hassle factor, *JIBS*, 44: 521–544.

14 N. Driffield & J. Love, 2007, Linking FDI motivation and host economy productivity effects, *JIBS*, 38: 460–473; P. Ghauri & P. Rao, 2009, Intellectual property, pharmaceutical MNEs, and the developing world, *JWB*, 44: 206–215; M. Hansem, T. Pedersen, & B. Petersen, 2009, MNC strategies and linkage effects in developing countries, *JWB*, 44: 121–130; F. Hatani, 2009, The logic of spillover inception, *JWB*, 44: 158–166; G. Santangelo, 2009. MNCs and linkages creation, *JWB*, 44: 192–205.

15 J. Scott-Kennel, 2007, FDI and local linkages, *MIR*, 47: 51–77; J. Singh, 2007, Asymmetry of knowledge spillovers between MNCs and host country firms, *JIBS*, 38: 764–786.

16 F. Knickerbocker, 1973, *Oligopolistic Reaction and Multinational Enterprise*, Boston: Harvard Business School Press.

17 S. Feinberg & A. Gupta, 2009, MNC subsidiaries and country risk, *AMJ*, 52: 381–399.

18 L. Allen, S. Chakraborty, & W. Watanabe, 2011, FDI and regulatory remedies for banking crises, *JIBS*, 42: 875–893; C. Peinhardt & T. Allee, 2012, Different investment treaties, different effects, *CFDIP*, 61: 1–3.

19 P. Buckley & M. Casson, 1976, *The Future of the Multinational Enterprise*, London: Macmillan; S. Chen, 2010, A general TCE model of international business institutions, *JIBS*, 41: 935–959.

20 I. Filatotchev, R. Strange, J. Piesse, & Y. Lien, 2007, FDI by firms from new industrialized economies in emerging markets, *JIBS*, 38: 556–572.

21 R. Vernon, 1977, *Storm over the Multinationals*, Cambridge, MA: Harvard University Press.

22 US Congress, 2012, *Investigative Report on the US National Security Issues Posed by Chinese Telecommunications Companies Huawei and ZTE*, Washington, DC: House of Representatives.

23 P. Dimitratos, I. Liouka, & S. Young, 2009, Regional location of MNC subsidiaries and economic development contribution, *JWB*, 44: 180–191; J. Oetzel & J. Doh, 2009, MNEs and development, *JWB*, 44: 108–120; M. Yamin & R. Sinkovics, 2009, Infrastructure or FDI? *JWB*, 44: 155–157.

24 B. Jindra, A. Giroud, & J. Scott-Kennel, 2009, Subsidiary roles, vertical linkages, and economic development, *JWB*, 44: 167–179; X. Liu, C. Wang, & Y. Wei, 2009, Do local manufacturing firms benefit from transaction linkages with MNEs in China? *JIBS*, 40: 1113–1130; K. Meyer & E. Sinani, 2009, When and where does FDI generate positive spillovers? *JIBS*, 40: 1075–1094; Y. Zhang, Y. Li, & H. Li, 2014, FDI spillovers over time in an emerging market, *AMJ*, 57: 698–722.

25 C. Altomonte & E. Pennings, 2009, Domestic plant productivity and incremental spillovers from FDI, *JIBS*, 40: 1131–1148.

26 G. Blalock & D. Simon, 2009, Do all firms benefit equally from downstream FDI? *JIBS*, 40: 1095–1112.

27 United Nations, 2010, *World Investment Report 2010* (p. 17), New York and Geneva: UN.

28 F. Barry & C. Kearney, 2006, MNEs and industrial structure in host countries, *JIBS*, 37: 392–406.

29 *Economist*, 2011, Tata for now, September 10: 61–62.

30 P. Evans, 1979, *Dependent Development* (p. 44), Princeton, NJ: Princeton University Press.

31 C. Lindblom, 1977, *Politics and Markets* (p. 173), New York: Basic Books.

32 T. Agmon, 2003, Who gets what, *JIBS*, 34: 416–427.

33 M. W. Peng, 2000, Controlling the foreign agent, *MIR*, 40: 141–165.

34 *Economist*, 2006, Trouble on the waterfront, February 25: 33–34.

35 M. W. Peng, 2011, The social responsibility of international business scholars: The case of China, *AIB Insights*, 11(4): 8–10; M. W. Peng, 2012, The global strategy of emerging multinationals from China, *GSJ*, 2: 97–107; M. W. Peng, S. Sun, & D. Blevins, 2011, The social responsibility of international business scholars, *MBR*, 19: 106–119.

36 *BW*, 2006, Venezuela: You are working for Chavez now, May 15: 76–78.

37 *Economist*, 2006, Bolivia: Now it's the people's gas, May 6: 37–38.

38 *BW*, 2012, Argentina goes rogue again, April 23: 16–17.

39 M. Zhao, S. Park, & N. Zhou, 2014, MNC strategy and social adaptation in emerging markets, *JIBS*, 45: 842–861.

© Nils Versemann/Shutterstock.com

CHAPTER
7

Learning Objectives

After studying this chapter, you should be able to

- understand the determinants of foreign exchange rates.

- track the evolution of the international monetary system.

- identify firms' strategic responses to deal with foreign exchange movements.

- participate in three leading debates concerning foreign exchange movements.

- draw implications for action.

Dealing with Foreign Exchange

OPENING CASE

Toyota's Yen Advantage

Thanks to an obsessive emphasis on quality, Toyota Motor grew from a tiny spinoff of a Japanese loom manufacturer in the 1930s into the world's largest automaker. Chief executive officer Akio Toyoda has nothing more virtuous than Japan's weakening currency for a recent assist in his quest for even greater market-share dominance. The yen has fallen 16% against the dollar since October 31, 2012. That gives Toyota and other Japanese carmakers a financial gain on every car, which they can use to cut prices, boost advertising, or improve their vehicles in ways not open to US rivals.

Morgan Stanley estimates the currency boost to operating profits at about US$1,500 per car, while Detroit carmakers put the figure closer to US$5,700. "We're concerned about what the long-term ramifications are," says Joe Hinrichs, Ford Motor's Americas chief. Sergio Marchionne, CEO of Chrysler Group and Fiat, also frets about the impact. "We didn't need this, to put it bluntly," he told Bloomberg TV on March 5, 2013. "It's going to make life tougher."

Toyota in February 2013 raised its profit forecast by 10% for the fiscal year ending March 31, 2013, to 860 billion yen (US$9 billion), a five-year high. That would more than double the previous year's profit and signal a convincing comeback from the global recalls and 2011 Japanese earthquake that shook Toyota's standing as a leader in earnings, sales, and quality.

Detroit automakers are watchful for a replay of the 1990s and 2000s, when a weak yen allowed Japanese automakers to offer American buyers cars loaded with extra features at prices US companies could not match. It took government-backed bankruptcies at General Motors (GM) and Chrysler in 2009 and a wrenching restructuring at Ford to get their costs in line with Toyota's. Those gains are being eroded by the currency shift, says Morgan Stanley auto analyst Adam Jonas. "This is, without a doubt, the biggest change affecting the global auto industry," Jonas says. "The dollar versus the weak yen will make the Japanese automakers richer, and they can use those profits to target more aggressive growth. Ford and GM are in their bull's-eye. This is a real threat."

Toyota enjoys a special edge because it exports more than two million vehicles from Japan annually, according to a recent analysis by Deutsche Bank. About 27% of the models Toyota sells in the US are imported, compared with 10% of those sold by Honda Motor, Deutsche Bank says. "We see Toyota as having the most to gain from a weaker yen with improved profits on exports," write Deutsche Bank analysts Jochen Gehrke and Kurt Sanger. They see Toyota's net profit margin topping 6% next year, up from 1.5% in the year ended March 31, 2012.

Just as Toyota was cautious of not trumpeting its toppling of GM from the global No. 1 automaker title in 2012—a sensitive issue in the US—it has been similarly restrained about any benefits from the weak yen. Toyota spokesman Steve Curtis says the automaker is working to build more models in North America, which would reduce the impact of currency swings. "We do our best to reduce currency fluctuations by localizing" production, Curtis says. "Whether it's a greenfield plant that came online a year and a half ago in Mississippi or the expansion of our component plants or the expansion of capacity for Highlander [built in Princeton, Indiana], across the operations in North America, that's the way we've approached this."

Yet even Toyota's North American production benefits from a weak yen, according to Deutsche Bank. Citing data from the National Highway Traffic Safety Administration, Deutsche Bank says 15%–35% of the parts in Toyota's North American-built models actually come from Japan, providing another advantage US makers do not have.

Morgan Stanley's Jonas says Toyota typically does not discount as deeply as Detroit automakers, so rather than waging a price war, Toyota may use its yen-effect benefits elsewhere. The carmaker is replacing 60% of its lineup by 2014 and now can afford to appoint those models with more lavish interiors and high-tech features that would be costly for US carmakers to match, Jonas says. The result: "We could see the Japanese gaining a couple points of [market] share in the US," he says.

Source: *Bloomberg Businessweek*, 2013, Toyota's awesome yen advantage, March 25: 21–22. © XXXX.

Why is the value of currencies so important to the global automobile industry? What determines foreign exchange rates? How do foreign exchange rates affect trade and investment undertaken by firms such as Toyota as well as Chrysler, Fiat, Ford, GM, and Honda? How can firms respond strategically? This chapter addresses these crucial questions. At the heart of our discussion lie the two core perspectives introduced earlier: the institution-based and resource-based views. Essentially, the institution-based view suggests that domestic and international institutions influence foreign exchange rates and affect capital movements. In turn, the resource-based view sheds light on how firms can profit from favorable foreign exchange movements or avoid being crushed by unfavorable movements by developing their own firm-specific resources and capabilities.

We start with a basic question: What determines foreign exchange rates? Then, we track the evolution of the international monetary system, and continue with firms' strategic responses.

Learning Objective
Understand the determinants of foreign exchange rates.

Foreign exchange rate
The price of one currency in terms of another.

Appreciation
An increase in the value of the currency.

Depreciation
A loss in the value of the currency.

7-1 What Determines Foreign Exchange Rates?

A foreign exchange rate is the price of one currency, such as the dollar, in terms of another, such as the euro. Table 7.1 provides some examples. An appreciation is an increase in the value of the currency, and a depreciation is a loss in the value of the currency. This section addresses a key question: What determines foreign exchange rates?

7-1a Basic Supply and Demand

The concept of an exchange rate as the price of a commodity—one country's currency—helps us understand its determinants. Basic economic theory suggests that the price of a commodity is most fundamentally determined by its supply and demand. Strong demand will lead to price hikes, and over-supply will result in price drops. Of course, we are dealing with a most unusual commodity here, money, but

Table 7.1	Examples of Key Currency Exchange Rates						
	US Dollar (US$)	Euro (€)	UK Pound (£)	Swiss Franc (SFr)	Mexican Peso (Mex$)	Japanese Yen (¥)	Canadian Dollar (C$)
Canadian Dollar (C$)	1.10	1.41	1.79	1.16	0.08	0.010	—
Japanese Yen (¥)	109.05	139.90	177.61	115.89	8.25	—	99.49
Mexican Peso (Mex$)	13.21	16.95	21.52	14.04	—	0.121	12.05
Swiss Franc (SFr)	0.94	1.21	1.53	—	0.07	0.009	0.859
UK Pound (£)	0.61	0.79	—	0.65	0.05	0.006	0.56
Euro (€)	0.78	—	1.27	0.83	0.06	0.007	0.71
US Dollar (US$)	—	1.28	1.63	1.06	0.08	0.009	0.91

Source: Adapted from *Wall Street Journal*, 2014, Key currency cross rates, September 19 (online.wsj.com). Reading *vertically*, the first column means US$1 = C$1.10 = ¥109.05 = Mex$13.21 = SFr0.94 = £0.61 = €0.78. Reading *horizontally*, the last row means €1 = US$1.28; £1 = US$1.63; SFr1 = US$1.06; Mex$1 = US$0.08; ¥1 = US$0.009; C$1 = US$0.91. The official code for Mexican Peso is MXN. The official code for Swiss Franc is CHF.

the basic underlying principles still apply. When the United States sells products to China, US exporters often demand that they be paid in US dollars—the Chinese yuan is useless (technically, nonconvertible) in the United States. Chinese importers of US products must somehow generate US dollars in order to pay for US imports. The easiest way to generate US dollars is to *export* to the United States, whose buyers will pay in US dollars. In this example, the dollar is the common transaction currency involving both US imports and US exports. As a result, the demand for dollars is much stronger than the demand for yuan (while holding the supply constant). Worldwide, a wide variety of users outside the United States, such as Chinese exporters, Swiss bankers, and Russian mafia members, prefer to hold and transact in US dollars, thus fueling the demand for dollars. Such a strong demand explains why the US dollar is the most sought-after currency in postwar decades (see Figure 7.1). At present, more than 80% of the world's foreign exchange transactions are in dollars. Approximately 65% of the world's foreign exchange holdings is in US dollars, followed by 26% in euros, 4% in British pounds, and 3% in yens.[1]

| Figure 7.1 | US Dollar's Share of World Total (%) |

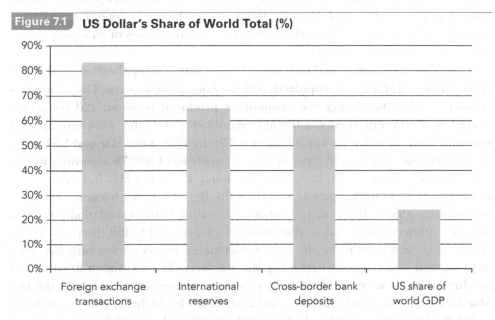

Source: Based on data in *Economist*, 2010, Beyond Bretton Woods 2 (p. 85), November 6: 85–87.

Figure 7.2   **What Determines Foreign Exchange Rates?**

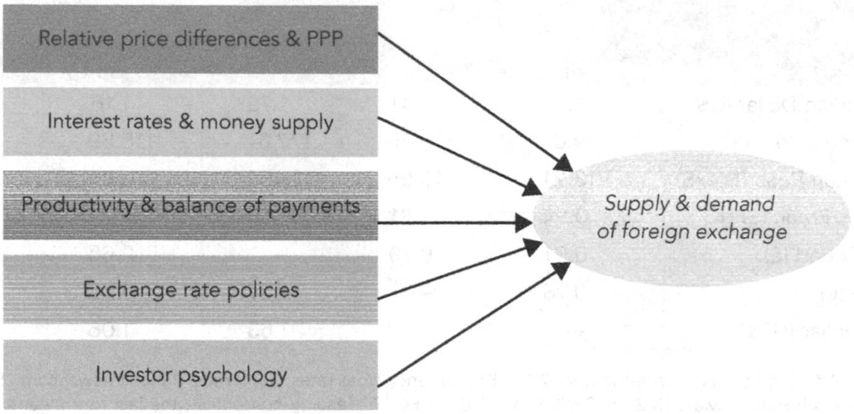

Because foreign exchange is such a unique commodity, its markets are influenced not only by economic factors, but also by numerous political and psychological factors. The next question is: What determines the supply and demand of foreign exchange? Figure 7.2 sketches the five underlying building blocks: (1) relative price differences, (2) interest rates and monetary supply, (3) productivity and balance of payments, (4) exchange rate policies, and (5) investor psychology.

7-1b Relative Price Differences and Purchasing Power Parity

Some countries (such as Switzerland) are famously expensive, and others (such as the Philippines) are known to have cheap prices. How do these price differences affect exchange rates? An answer is provided by the theory of purchasing power parity (PPP), which is essentially the "law of one price." The theory suggests that in the absence of trade barriers (such as tariffs), the price for identical products sold in different countries must be the same. Otherwise, traders (or arbitragers) may "buy low" and "sell high," eventually driving prices for identical products to the same level around the world. The PPP theory argues that in the long run, exchange rates should move toward levels that would equalize the prices of an identical basket of goods in any two countries.[2]

One of the most influential and certainly most fun-filled applications of the PPP theory is the Big Mac index, popularized by the *Economist* magazine. The *Economist's* "basket" is McDonald's Big Mac hamburger produced in about 120 countries. According to the PPP theory, a Big Mac should cost the same anywhere around the world. In reality, it does not (see Figure 7.3). In 2014, a Big Mac cost US$4.8 in the United States and 16.76 yuan in China, which was US$2.73 according to the nominal exchange rate of 6.14 yuan to the dollar. If the Big Mac indeed cost the same, the de facto exchange rate based on the Big Mac index became 3.49 yuan to the dollar (that is, 16.76 yuan/US$4.80). According to this calculation, the yuan was 43% "undervalued" against the dollar ([6.14–3.49]/6.14). But the yuan, which several years ago used to be the most undervalued currency, was only the 12th most-undervalued currency in the Big Mac universe. The Ukrainian hryvnia and the Indian rupee were the most undervalued currencies. In other words, the Big Mac in Ukraine and the chicken-based Maharaja Mac in India (where the beef-based Big Mac is not available) had the best "value" in the world, based on official exchange rates. They only cost US$1.63 and US$1.75, respectively.[3]

Figure 7.3 **The Big Mac Index**

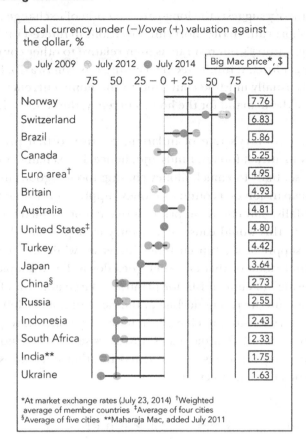

Source: *Economist*, 2014, The Big Mac index: A basket of sliders, July 26: 61. © The Economist Newspaper Limited. Reproduced by permission.

Overall, four observations emerge:

- The Big Max index confirms that prices in some European countries are very expensive. A Big Mac in Norway was the most expensive in the world, costing US$7.76.

- Excluding the special case of Ukraine (which was engulfed in a conflict), a Big Mac in South Africa and Indonesia and a Maharaja Mac in India are cheap in dollar terms. This makes sense, because a Big Mac is a product with both traded and non-traded inputs. To simplify our discussion, let us assume that the costs for traded inputs (such as flour for the bun) are the same. It is obvious that non-traded inputs (such as labor and real estate) are cheaper in emerging economies.

- The Big Mac is not a traded product. No large number of American hamburger lovers would travel to South Africa simply to get the best deal on the Big Mac, and then somehow take with them large quantities of the Made-in-South Africa Big Mac (perhaps in portable freezers). If they did that, the Big Mac price in South Africa would be driven up and the price in the United States would be pushed down—remember supply and demand?

- After having a laugh, we shouldn't read too much into this index. PPP signals where exchange rates may move in the *long run*. But it does not suggest that the yuan should appreciate by 43% or the Norwegian kroner should depreciate by 62% next year. According to the *Economist*, anyone interested in the PPP theory "would be unwise to exclude the Big Mac index from their diet, but Super Size servings (of this index) would equally be a mistake."[4]

7-1c Interest Rates and Money Supply

While the PPP theory suggests the long-run direction of exchange rate movement, what about the short run? In the short run, variations in interest rates have a powerful effect. If one country's interest rate is high relative to other countries, then the country will attract foreign funds (see the Closing Case on Brazil). Because inflows of foreign funds usually must be converted to the home currency, a high interest rate will increase the demand for the home currency, thus enhancing its exchange value.

In addition, a country's rate of inflation, relative to that prevailing abroad, affects its ability to attract foreign funds and, hence, its exchange rate. A high level of inflation is essentially too much money chasing too few goods in an economy—technically, an expansion of a country's money supply. A government, when facing budgetary shortfalls, may choose to print more currency, which tends to stimulate inflation. In turn, this would cause its currency to depreciate. This makes sense because as the supply of a given currency increases while the demand stays the same, the per-unit value of that currency goes down. For example, the policy of "quantitative easing" (a euphemism for printing a large amount of money) is one of the reasons behind the recent decline of the value of the US dollar. In short, the exchange rate is very sensitive to changes in monetary policy. It responds swiftly to changes in money supply. To avoid losses, investors sell assets denominated in the depreciating currency for assets denominated in other currencies. Such massive sell-offs often worsen the depreciation.

7-1d Productivity and Balance of Payments

In international trade, the rise of a country's productivity, relative to other that of countries, will improve its competitive position—this is the basic proposition of the theories of absolute and comparative advantage (see Chapter 5). More foreign direct investment (FDI) will be attracted to the country, fueling demand for its home currency. One recent example is China. Most of the China-bound FDI inflows in dollars, euros, and pounds must be converted to local currency, boosting the demand for the yuan and, hence, its value.

Recall from Chapter 5 that changes in productivity will change a country's balance of trade. A country highly productive in manufacturing may generate a merchandise trade surplus, whereas a country less productive in manufacturing may end up with a merchandise trade deficit. These have ramifications for the balance of payments (BOP)—officially known as a country's international transaction statement, including merchandise (goods) trade, service trade, and capital movement. Table 7.2 shows that the United States had a merchandise trade deficit of US$702 billion and a service trade surplus of US$226 billion in 2013. In addition to merchandise and service trade, we add receipts on US assets abroad (such as repatriated earning from US multinational enterprises [MNEs] in Ireland and dividends paid by Japanese firms to American shareholders), subtract payments on US-based foreign assets (such as repatriated earnings from Canadian MNEs in the United States to Canada and dividends paid by US firms to Dutch shareholders), and government grants and private remittances (such as US foreign aid thrown at Iraq and the money that Mexican farm hands in America sent home). After doing all of the math, we can see that the United States ran a US$405 billion current account deficit. Technically, the current account balance consists of exports minus

Balance of payment (BOP)

A country's international transaction statement, which includes merchandise trade, service trade, and capital movement.

Table 7.2	The US Balance of Payments (Billion US Dollars)		
I. Current Account			
1. Exports of goods (merchandise)		1,592	
2. Imports of goods (merchandise)		−2,294	
3. Balance on goods (merchandise trade—lines 1 + 2)			**−702**
4. Exports of services		682	
5. Imports of services		−456	
6. Balance on services (service trade—lines 4 + 5)			**226**
7. Balance on goods and services (trade deficit/surplus—lines 3 + 6)			**−476**
8. Income receipts on US-owned assets abroad		767	
9. Income payments on foreign-owned assets in the US		−558	
10. Government grants and private remittances		−137	
11. Balance on current account (current account deficit/surplus—lines 7 + 8 + 9 + 10)			**−405**
II. Financial Account			
12. US-owned private assets abroad (increase/financial outflow = − [negative sign])		−586	
13. Foreign-owned private assets in the US		959	
14. Balance on financial account (lines 12 + 13)			**373**
15. Overall balance of payments (Official reserve transactions balance—lines 11 + 14)			**−32**

Source: This is a simplified table adapted from US Department of Commerce, Bureau of Economic Analysis, 2014, *US International Transactions: Fourth Quarter and Year 2013*, Table 2, Washington: BEA (www.bea.gov [accessed September 21, 2014]). This table refers to 2013. The official table has 109 lines. Numbers may not add due to rounding.

imports of merchandise and services, plus income on a country's assets abroad minus payments on foreign assets in the focal country, plus government transfers and private remittances.

A current account deficit has to be financed by financial account—consisting of purchases and sales of assets. This is because a country needs to balance its accounts in much the same way as a family deals with its finances. Any deficit in a family budget must be financed by spending from savings or by borrowing.[5] In a similar fashion, the overall US deficit of US$32 billion was financed by spending from savings and borrowing (selling US government securities such as Treasury bonds to foreign central banks, such as the People's Bank of China).

To make a long story short, a country experiencing a current account surplus will see its currency appreciate. Conversely, a country experiencing a current account deficit will see its currency depreciate. This may not happen overnight, but will happen in a span of years and decades. The current movement between the yuan (appreciating) and the dollar (depreciating) is but one example. Going back to the 1950s and the 1960s, the rise of the dollar was accompanied by a sizeable US surplus on merchandise trade. By the 1970s and the 1980s, the surplus gradually turned into a deficit. By the 1990s and the 2000s, the US current account deficit became ever increasing, forcing the dollar to depreciate relative to other currencies in developed economies such as the euro, the Canadian dollar, the Australian dollar (see In Focus 7.1), and the Swiss franc, as well as currencies in emerging economies, such as the yuan and the Brazilian real. Broadly

IN FOCUS 7.1

AUSTRALIAN WINE: MADE FROM THE GRAPES OF CURRENCY WRATH

SUETONE Emilio/hemis/AGE Fotostock

Why do the Australian wines become more expensive overseas?

Cellebrations, a wine shop in the inner Sydney suburb of Newtown, sells Moët & Chandon Burt Impérial, a popular French Champaign produced by LVMH Moët Hennesy Louis Vuitton, for A$49.99 (US$52.61) a bottle. Wine House, a Melbourne-based online store, is selling LVMH's Chandon Green Point Cuvée 1995, a sparkling wine produced in Australia's Yarra Valley, for A$52. Much to the dismay of Australia's wine industry, its days of offering lower-priced alternatives to French vintages are fading.

With the Australian dollar at record levels against the euro, Aussie vintners are caught in a double-bind: Exports have been slammed as the cost of Australian wine has risen overseas, while oenophiles back home

are embracing European bottles that suddenly are bargains. Imported wine has rarely been more affordable, with prices for some labels dropping 30%. "It's absolutely fantastic," says Jeremy Oliver, a Melbourne-based wine critic. "If you have A$100 (US$105) in your pocket, that will get you a top bottle of Australian cabernet or shiraz. Today it also buys you a pretty serious Bordeaux, a very good Italian from any region, or a sensational Spanish red."

Australia, the world's largest wine exporter by volume outside of Europe, saw the value of its exports decline to the lowest level in a decade in 2011, falling 10% from a year earlier, to A$1.89 billion. At Melbourne-based Treasury Wine Estates, the world's second-biggest publicly traded vintner and owner of the Lindeman's and Penfolds brands, sales in the US, its largest market, fell 15%, to A$803 million, in the year through June 2011. The currency hit is more pronounced in Europe, where the euro fell 8.9% over the last three months (in 2011) to make it the worst-performing major currency against the Australian dollar, compared with a 2.2% decline for the US dollar.

That is quite a turnabout. Driven by signature brands such as Yellow Tail and Jacob's Creek and support from influential critics such as Robert Parker, Australia's exports rose more than four-fold in the ten years to 2007, when they peaked at 786 million liters. Australia overtook France as Britain's top supplier of imported wine in 2005 and for a brief time in 2008 was the front-runner in the United States.

Then things turned. Competition had for years been increasing from other emerging wine areas such as Argentina, Chile, and South Africa, when a domestic glut in Australia put too much low-quality product on the market. In 2009, bush fires swept through the wine country of Victoria state, incinerating vineyards and tainting grapes with smoke. Exports have dropped 11% in the past four years, to 703 million liters in 2011.

The high price of labor and land and the small-scale nature of middle-market wineries in Australia also make it hard to compete with imports, says Oliver. "You can get seriously interesting, diverse wineries from Europe, South America, and South Africa for A$25 a blow retail," he says. "In Australia today, the small guys trying to do the equivalent are finding it very hard to get anything in the bottle for under A$45."

Since 2005, Australia's wine import volumes have risen 95%. French wine imports have risen 58%. Every six weeks, for instance, importer John Baker ships in a refrigerated container carrying about 10,800 bottles of French wine to his 270-square-meter

(2,900-square-foot) refrigerated warehouse in the Sydney suburb of Artarmon. That's double the import volume of five years before at his business, Bordeaux Shippers. The Aussie dollar is worth €0.81 now, compared with €0.54 when he started in 2003. "I've been selling a 2001 vintage Château tour du Haut Moulin, that's a 10-year-old wine from Bordeaux, and it's A$39 retail; that wine really should be A$80," he says.

Source: Excerpted from *Bloomberg Businessweek*, 2012, The grapes of currency wrath, January 30: 22–23.

speaking, the value of a country's currency is an embodiment of its economic strengths, as reflected in its productivity and balance of payments positions. Overall, the recent pressure for the US dollar to depreciate is indicative of the relative (not absolute) decline of the US economic strengths, compared with its major trading partners.

7-1e Exchange Rate Policies

There are two major exchange rate policies: (1) floating rate and (2) fixed rate. Governments adopting the floating (or flexible) exchange rate policy tend to be free market believers, willing to let the demand-and-supply conditions determine exchange rates—usually on a daily basis via the foreign exchange market. However, few countries adopt a clean (or free) float, which would be a pure market solution. Most countries practice a dirty (or managed) float, with selective government interventions. Of the major currencies, the US, Canadian, and Australian dollars, the yen, and the pound have been under managed float since the 1970s (after the collapse of the Bretton Woods system—see next section). Since the 1990s, several emerging economies, such as Brazil, Mexico, and South Korea, have also joined the managed float regime. Despite complaints from the US government, China currently does *not* fix its currency. Since 2005, China has been allowing the yuan to float—from 8.3 yuan to the dollar in 2005 to 6.14 yuan to the dollar in 2014 (a 26% appreciation).

The severity of intervention is a matter of degree. Heavier intervention moves the country closer to a fixed exchange rate policy, and less intervention enables a country to approach the free float ideal. The main objective for intervention is to prevent the emergence of erratic fluctuations that may trigger macroeconomic turbulence.[6] Some countries do not adhere to any particular rates. Others choose target exchange rates—known as crawling bands or more vividly "snake in a tube" (intervention will only occur when the "snake" craws out of a tube's upper or lower bounds).

Another major exchange rate policy is the fixed exchange rate policy—countries fix the exchange rate of their currencies relative to other currencies. Both political and economic rationales may be at play. During the German reunification in 1990,

Floating (flexible) exchange rate policy

A government policy to let supply-and-demand conditions determine exchange rates.

Clean (free) float

A pure market solution to determine exchange rates.

Dirty (managed) float

Using selective government intervention to determine exchange rates.

Fixed exchange rate policy

A government policy to set the exchange rate of a currency relative to other currencies.

Target exchange rate (crawling band)

Specified upper or lower bounds within which an exchange rate is allowed to fluctuate.

the West German government, for political considerations, fixed the exchange rate between West and East German mark as 1:1. Economically, the East German mark was not worth that much. Politically, this exchange rate reduced the feeling of alienation and resentment among East Germans, thus facilitating a smoother unification process. Of course, West Germans ended up paying more for the costs of unification.

Economically, many developing countries peg their currencies to a key currency (often the US dollar). There are two benefits for a peg policy. First, a peg stabilizes the import and export prices for developing countries. Second, many countries with high inflation have pegged their currencies to the dollar in order to restrain domestic inflation. (See Debates and Extensions for more discussion.)

7-1f Investor Psychology

While theories on price differences (PPP), interest rates and money supply, balance of payments, and exchange rate policies predict long-run movements of exchange rates, they often fall short of predicting short-run movements. It is investor psychology, some of which is fickle and thus very hard to predict, that largely determines short-run movements. Professor Richards Lyons at the University of California, Berkeley, is an expert on exchange rate theories. However, he was baffled when he was invited by a friend, a currency trader, to observe currency trading firsthand:

> As I sat there, my friend traded furiously all day long, racking up over US$1 billion in trades each day. This was a world where the standard trade was US$10 million, and a US$1 million trade was a "skinny one." Despite my belief that exchange rates depend on macroeconomics, only rarely was news of this type his primary concern. Most of the time he was reading tea leaves that were, at least to me, not so clear . . . It was clear my understanding was incomplete when he looked over, in the midst of his fury, and asked me: "What should I do?" I laughed. Nervously.[7]

Investors—currency traders (such as the one Lyons observed), foreign portfolio investors, and average citizens—may move as a "herd" at the same time in the same direction, resulting in a bandwagon effect. The bandwagon effect seemed to be at play in August 2014, when the Argentinean peso plunged against key currencies such as the US dollar, the euro, and the pound sterling. Essentially, a large number of individuals and firms exchanged the peso for the key foreign currencies in order to minimize their exposure to Argentina's sovereign default (its second since 2001)—a phenomenon known as capital flight. This would push down the demand for, and thus the value of, the domestic currency. Then, more individuals and companies joined the "herd," further depressing the exchange rate and worsening an economic crisis.

Overall, economics, politics, and psychology are all at play. The stakes are high, yet consensus is rare regarding the determinants of foreign exchange rates. As a result, predicting the direction of currency movements remains an art or, at best, a highly imprecise science.

Peg

A stabilizing policy of linking a developing contry's currency to a key currency.

Bandwagon effect

The effect of investors moving in the same direction at the same time, like a herd.

Capital flight

A phenomenon in which a large number of individuals and companies exchange domestic currency for a foreign currency.

NORBERTO DUARTE/Getty Images

What happened to the Argentinean peso when Argentina defaulted on its sovereign debt?

7-2 Evolution of the International Monetary System

Learning Objective
Track the evolution of the international monetary system.

Having outlined the basic determinants of exchange rates, let us undertake an historic excursion to trace the three eras of the evolution of the international monetary system: (1) the gold standard, (2) the Bretton Woods system, and (3) the post-Bretton Woods system.

7-2a The Gold Standard (1870–1914)

The gold standard was a system in place between 1870 and 1914, when the value of most major currencies was maintained by fixing their prices in terms of gold. Gold was used as the common denominator for all currencies. This was essentially a global peg system, with little volatility and every bit of predictability and stability. To be able to redeem its currency in gold at a fixed price, every central bank needed to maintain gold reserves. The system provided powerful incentives for countries to run current account surpluses, resulting in net inflows of gold.

7-2b The Bretton Woods System (1944–1973)

The gold standard was abandoned first in 1914 when World War I (WW I) broke out and several combatant countries printed excessive amounts of currency to finance their war efforts. After WW I, especially during the Great Depression (1929–1933), countries engaged in competitive devaluations in an effort to boost exports at the expense of trading partners. But no country could win such a "race to the bottom," and the gold standard had to be jettisoned.

Toward the end of World War II (WW II), at an allied conference in Bretton Woods, New Hampshire, 44 countries agreed on a new system—known simply as the Bretton Woods system. The Bretton Woods system was centered on the US dollar as the new common denominator. All currencies were pegged at a fixed rate to the dollar. Only the dollar, as the official reserve currency, was convertible into gold at US$35 per ounce. Other currencies were not required to be gold convertible.

It was the Bretton Woods system that propelled the dollar to the commanding heights of the global economy (see Figure 7.1). This was also a reflection of the higher US productivity level and the large US trade surplus with the rest of the world in the first two postwar decades. This was not surprising, because the US economy contributed approximately 70% of the global GDP at the end of WW II and was the export engine of the world.

7-2c The Post-Bretton Woods System (1973-present)

By the late 1960s and early 1970s, a combination of rising productivity elsewhere and US inflationary policies led to the demise of the Bretton Woods system. First, (West) Germany and other countries caught up in productivity and exported more, and the United States ran its first post-1945 trade deficit in 1971. This pushed the (West) German mark to appreciate and the dollar to depreciate—a situation very similar to the yen–dollar relationship in the 1980s and the yuan–dollar relationship in the 2000s. Second, in the 1960s, in order to finance both the Vietnam War and Great Society welfare programs, President Lyndon Johnson increased government

Gold standard

A system in which the value of most major currencies was maintained by fixing their prices in terms of gold.

Common denominator

A currency or commodity to which the value of all currencies are pegged.

Bretton Woods system

A system in which all currencies were pegged at a fixed rate to the US dollar.

spending, not by additional taxation, but by increasing money supply. These actions led to rising inflation levels and strong pressures for the dollar to depreciate.

As currency traders bought more German marks, Germany's central bank, the Bundesbank, had to buy billions of dollars in order to maintain the dollar/mark exchange rate fixed by Bretton Woods. Being stuck with massive amounts of the dollar that was worth less now, Germany unilaterally allowed its currency to float in May 1971.

The Bretton Woods system also became a pain in the neck for the United States, because the exchange rate of the dollar was not allowed to unilaterally change. Per Bretton Woods agreements, the US Treasury was obligated to dispense one once of gold for every US$35 brought by a foreign central bank, such as the Bundesbank. Consequently, there was a hemorrhage of US gold flowing into the coffers of foreign central banks. In August 1971, in order to stop such hemorrhage, President Richard Nixon unilaterally announced that the dollar was no longer convertible into gold. After tense negotiations, major countries collectively agreed to hammer the coffin nails of the Bretton Woods system, by allowing their currencies to float in 1973. In retrospect, the Bretton Woods system had been built on two conditions: (1) the US inflation rate had to be low and (2) the US could not run a trade deficit. When both these conditions were violated, the demise of the system was inevitable.

As a result, today we live in the post-Bretton Woods system. The strengths lie in its flexibility and diversity of exchange rate regimes (ranging from various schemes of floating systems to various ways of fixed rates). Its drawback is turbulence and uncertainty (see In Focus 7.1 and the Closing Case). Since the 1970s, the US dollar has no longer been the official reserve currency. However, it has retained a significant amount of "soft power" as a key currency (see Figure 7.1).

7-2d The International Monetary Fund (IMF)

Although the Bretton Woods system is no longer with us, one of its most enduring legacies is the International Monetary Fund (IMF), founded in 1944 as a "Bretton Woods institution." (The World Bank is the other Bretton Woods institution.) The IMF's mandate is to promote international monetary cooperation, exchange stability, and orderly exchange arrangements.

Lending is a core responsibility of the IMF, which provides loans to countries suffering from balance-of-payments problems. The IMF can be viewed as a lender of last resort to help member countries out of financial difficulty. Where does the IMF get its funds? The answer boils down to the same principle on how insurance companies obtain their funds to pay for insurance coverage. For the same reason that insurance companies obtain their funds from insurance subscribers who pay a premium, the IMF collects funds from member countries. Each member country is assigned a quota, which determines its financial contribution to the IMF, its capacity to borrow from the IMF, and its voting power.

By definition, the IMF's lending refers to loans, not free grants. IMF loans must be repaid in one to five years. Although payments have been extended in some cases, no member country has defaulted. An ideal IMF loan scenario would be a balance-of-payments crisis that threatens to severely disrupt a country's financial stability, such as when it imports more than it exports and cannot pay for imports.

While an IMF loan provides short-term financial resources, it also comes with strings attached. These strings are long-term policy reforms that recipient countries must undertake as conditions of receiving the loan. These conditions usually entail belt-tightening, pushing governments to embark on reforms that they otherwise probably would not have undertaken. For instance, when the IMF (together with the

Post-Bretton Woods system

A system of flexible exchange rate regimes with no official common denominator.

International Monetary Fund (IMF)

An international organization that was established to promote international monetary cooperation, exchange stability, and orderly exchange arrangements.

Quota

The weight a member country carries within the IMF, which determines the amount of its financial contribution (technically known as its "subscription"), its capacity to borrow from the IMF, and its voting power.

[European Union (EU)]) provided a loan to Greece in 2010, the Greek government had to agree to cut wages and pensions by 15% to 20% in order to pay for government debt. Since the 1990s, the IMF has helped Mexico (1994), Russia (1996 and 1998), Asia (Indonesia, South Korea, and Thailand, 1997), Turkey (2001), Brazil (2002), Iceland (2008), Ukraine (2008), Hungary (2008), Greece (2010), and several others.

While the IMF has noble goals, its actions are not without criticisms. A new alternative international organization, which is simply called the New Development Bank (NDB), has recently been set up by the BRICS countries (see In Focus 7.2).

IN FOCUS 7.2

Ethical Dilemma

INTERNATIONAL MONETARY FUND VERSUS NEW DEVELOPMENT BANK

The complexity of the IMF's actions means that it cannot please everyone. Debates about the IMF rage throughout the world. First, critics argue that the IMF's lending may *facilitate* moral hazard, which means recklessness when people and organizations (including governments) do not have to face the full consequences of their actions. Moral hazard is inherent in all insurance arrangements, including the IMF. Basically, knowing that the IMF would come to the rescue, certain governments may behave more recklessly. For example, between 1958 and 2001, Turkey was rescued by 18 (!) IMF loans.

A second criticism centers on the IMF's lack of accountability. Although the IMF can dictate terms over a host country that is being rescued and receiving loans, none of the IMF officials is democratically elected and most of them do not have deep knowledge of the host country. Consequently, they sometimes make disastrous decisions. For example, in 1997–1998, the IMF forced the Indonesian government to drastically cut back on food subsidies for the poor. Riots exploded the next day. Hundreds of people were killed and property damaged. Then, the IMF reversed its position by restoring food subsidies. However, in some quarters, the bitterness was all the greater. A lot of protesters argued: If food subsidies could have been continued, why were they taken away in the first place?

A third and perhaps most challenging criticism is that the IMF's "one-size-fits-all" strategy—otherwise known as the "bitter medicine"—may be inappropriate. Since the 1930s, in order to maintain more employment, most Western governments have abandoned the idea to balance the budget. Deficit spending has been used as a major policy weapon to pull a country out of an economic crisis. Yet, the IMF often demands governments in more vulnerable developing countries, in the midst of a major crisis, to balance their budgets by slashing spending (such as cutting food subsidies). These actions often make the crisis far worse than it needs to be. After the IMF came to "rescue" countries affected by the 1997 Asian financial crisis, unemployment rate was up threefold in Thailand, fourfold in South Korea, and tenfold in Indonesia.

However, the momentum of the criticisms, the severity of the global crisis, and the desire to better serve the international community have facilitated a series of IMF reforms since 2009. Some of these reforms represent a total (180 degrees) change from its previous directions, resulting in an "IMF 2.0" dubbed by *Time*. For example, the IMF now starts to promote more fiscal spending in order to stimulate the economy and to ease money supply and reduce interest rates, given the primary concern for the global economy now is deflation and recession, but not inflation. Obviously, the IMF's change of heart is affected by the tremendous stimulus packages unleashed by developed economies since 2008, which result in skyrocketing budget deficits. If the developed economies can (hopefully) use greater fiscal spending and budget deficits to pull themselves out a crisis, the IMF simply cannot lecture developing economies that receive its loans to balance their budgets in the middle of a crisis. Further, given the stigma of receiving IMF loans and listening and then implementing IMF lectures, many countries avoid the IMF until they run out of options. In response, in April 2009, the IMF unleashed a new Flexible Credit Line (FCL), which would be particularly useful for crisis *prevention* by providing the flexibility to draw on it at any time, with no strings attached—a

IN FOCUS 7.2 (continued)

radical contrast to its earlier requirement. Mexico, Colombia, and Poland have used the FCL so far.

Further, the IMF 2.0 has become three times bigger—leaders in the G20 Summit in London in 2009 agreed to enhance the IMF's funding from US$250 billion to US$750 billion. Of the US$500 billion new funding (technically Special Drawing Rights [SDRs]), the US, the EU, and Japan each was expected to contribute US$100 billion. China signed up for US$40 billion. Request for injection of substantial funding from emerging economies resulted in the calls for better representation of these countries. However, enhancing voting rights for emerging economies would lead to reduced shares for developed economies. As a result, progress is slow. Even with the new changes, Brazil, with 1.72% of the votes (up from the previous 1.38%), still carries less weight than Belgium (1.86%, down from the previous 2.09%). Despite having the world's second-largest economy, China has failed to be admitted as one of the top five IMF shareholders— with 3.81% of the votes, it has become the sixth largest, behind the United States (16.75%), Japan (6.23%), Germany (5.81%), France (4.29%), and the UK (4.29%). Overall, Western countries, which have been over-represented at the IMF, have refused to make room at the table for emerging economies.

In July 2014, at the sixth BRICS summit in Fortaleza, Brazil, BRICS countries—consisting of Brazil, Russia, India, China, and South Africa—launched a New Development Bank (NDB) as an alternative to the IMF. To be headquartered in Shanghai, the NDB, previously known as the BRICS Development Bank, represents a significant block of countries that have 2.8 billion people (40% of the world's population), cover a quarter of the world's land area, and account for more than 25% of global GDP. Unlike the IMF, which assigns votes to member countries differently, the NDB assigns each of the five participating countries one vote (each country contributing US$10 billion initial paid-in capital for a total of US$50 billion). While the NDB will focus on infrastructure and sustainable development projects, BRICS have also set up a US$100 billion Contingency Reserve Arrangement (CRA), with China contributing US$41 billion, Brazil,

Why did Brazil, Russia, India, China, and South Africa set up the New Development Bank in 2014?

Russia, and India each US$18 billion, and South Africa US$5 billion. Designed to provide protection against global liquidity pressures, the CRA is a precautionary instrument in response to actual or potential short-term balance of payments problems.

The NDB and the CRA have been set up due to BRICS' frustration with the IMF, which together they only wield about 11% of the votes (after recent IMF reforms). Further, they are set up in response to the IMF's enforcement of conditions on countries seeking emergency loans. The founding statement signed by BRICS leaders has stated: "International governance structures designed within a different power configuration show increasingly evident signs of losing legitimacy and effectiveness." In a couple of decades and with expanding membership, the NDB and the CRA may indeed become a rival of the IMF. However, in the short run, how to coordinate the divergent interests—and paper over disagreements—among BRICS remains to be seen.

Sources: Based on (1) R. Desai & J. Vreeland, 2014, What the new bank of BRICS is all about, *Washington Post*, July 17, www.washingtonpost. com; (2) *Economist*, 2009, New fund, old fundamentals, May 2: 78; (3) *Economist*, 2010, Beyond Bretton Woods 2, November 6: 85–87; (4) *Economist*, 2014, The 70-year itch, July 5: 12; (5) R. Fuller, 2014, Refusing to share: How the West created BRICS New Development Bank, www.rt.com; (6) A. Ghosh, M. Chamon, C. Crowe, J. Kim, & J. Ostry, 2009, Coping with the crisis: Policy options for emerging market countries, IMF staff position paper, Washington: IMF; (7) C. Lagarde, 2013, I try to spark new ideas, *Harvard Business Review*, November: 111–114; (8) R. Rajan, 2008, The future of the IMF and the World Bank, *American Economic Review*, 98: 110–115; (9) J. Stiglitz, 2002, *Globalization and Its Discontents*, New York: Norton; (10) *Time*, 2009, International Monetary Fund 2.0, April 20.

7-3 Strategic Responses to Foreign Exchange Movements

Learning Objective
Identify firms' strategic responses to deal with foreign exchange movements.

From an institution-based view, knowledge about foreign exchange rates and international monetary system (including the role of the IMF and the NDB) helps paint a broad picture of the rules of the game that govern financial transactions around the world.[8] Armed with this knowledge, savvy managers need to develop firm-specific resources and capabilities to rise to the challenge—or at least to avoid their firms from being crushed by unfavorable currency movements (see the Closing Case). This section outlines the strategic responses of two types of firms: financial and nonfinancial companies.

7-3a Strategies for Financial Companies

One of the leading strategic goals for financial companies is to profit from the foreign exchange market. The foreign exchange market is a market where individuals, firms, governments, and banks buy and sell foreign currencies. Unlike a stock exchange, the foreign exchange market has no central, physical location. This market is truly global and transparent. Buyers and sellers are geographically dispersed but constantly linked (quoted prices change as often as 20 times a *minute*).[9] The market opens on Monday first in Tokyo and then Hong Kong and Singapore, when it is still Sunday evening in New York. Gradually, Frankfurt, Zurich, London, New York, Chicago, and San Francisco wake up and come online.

Operating on a 24/7 basis, the foreign exchange market is the largest and most active market in the world. On average, the worldwide volume averages US$5.3 trillion a *day*.[10] To put this mind-boggling number in perspective, the amount of one single *day* of foreign exchange transactions is more than three times the amount of entire worldwide FDI inflows in one *year* (US$1.45 trillion in 2013),[11] and more than one-third of worldwide merchandise exports in one *year* (US$18.4 trillion in 2013).[12] Specifically, the foreign exchange market has two functions: (1) to service the needs of trade and FDI, and (2) to trade in its own commodity—namely, foreign exchange.

There are three primary types of foreign exchange transactions: (1) spot transactions, (2) forward transactions, and (3) swaps. Spot transactions are the classic single-shot exchange of one currency for another. For example, Canadian tourists buying several thousand euros in Italy with Canadian dollars will get their euros from a bank right away.

Forward transactions allow participants to buy and sell currencies now for future delivery, typically in 30, 90, or 180 days, after the date of the transaction. The primary benefit of forward transactions is to protect traders and investors from being exposed to the fluctuations of the spot rate, an act known as currency hedging. Currency hedging is a way to minimize the foreign exchange risk inherent in all non-spot transactions, which characterize most trade and FDI deals.[13] Traders and investors expecting to make or receive payments in a foreign currency in the future are concerned whether they will have to make a greater payment or receive less in terms of the domestic currency, should the spot rate changes. For example, if the forward rate of the euro (€/US$) is exactly the same as the spot rate, the euro is "flat." If the forward rate of the euro per dollar is *higher* than the spot rate, the euro has a forward discount. If the forward rate of the euro per dollar is *lower* than the spot rate, the euro then has a forward premium.

Hypothetically, assume that (1) today's exchange rate of €/US$ is 1, (2) a US firm expects to be paid €1 million six months later, and (3) the euro is at a 180-day forward

Foreign exchange market
The market where individuals, firms, governments, and banks buy and sell foreign currencies.

Spot transaction
The classic single-shot exchange of one currency for another.

Forward transaction
A foreign exchange transaction in which participants buy and sell currencies now for future delivery.

Currency hedging
A transaction that protects traders and investors from exposure to the fluctuations of the spot rate.

Forward discount
A condition under which the forward rate of one currency relative to another currency is higher than the spot rate.

Forward premium
A condition under which the forward rate of one currency relative to another currency is lower than the spot rate.

discount of 1.1. The US firm may take out a forward contract now and convert euro earnings into a dollar revenue of US$909,091 (€1 million/1.1) after six months. Does such a move make sense? There can be two answers. "Yes," if the firm knew in advance that the future spot rate would be 1.25. With the forward contract, the US firm would make US$909,091 instead of US$800,000 (€1 million/1.25)—the difference is US$109,091 (14% of US$800,000). However, the answer would be "No" if the spot rate after six months were actually below 1.1. If the spot rate remained at 1, the firm could have earned US$1 million, *without* the forward contract, instead of only US$909,091. This simple example suggests a powerful observation: Currency hedging *requires* firms to have expectations or forecasts of future spot rates relative to forward rates.

A third major type of foreign exchange transactions is swap. A currency swap is the conversion of one currency into another in Time 1, with an agreement to revert it back to the original currency at a specific Time 2 in the future. Deutsche Bank may have an excess balance of British pounds but need dollars. At the same time, Union Bank of Switzerland (UBS) may have more dollars than it needs at the moment but is looking for more British pounds. They can negotiate a swap agreement in which Deutsche Bank agrees to exchange with UBS pounds for dollars today and dollars for pounds at a specific point in the future.

The primary participants of the foreign exchange market are large international banks, such as Citigroup, Deutsche Bank, and UBS, which trade among themselves. How do these banks make money by trading money? They make money by capturing the difference between their offer rate (the price to sell) and bid rate (the price to buy)—the bid rate is *always* lower than the offer rate. The difference of this "buy low, sell high" strategy is technically called the spread. For example, Citigroup may quote offer and bid rates for the Swiss franc at US$1.0877 and US$1.0874, respectively, and the spread is US$0.0003. That is, Citigroup is willing to sell 1 million francs for US$1,087,700 and buy 1 million francs for US$1,087,400. If Citigroup can simultaneously buy and sell 1 million francs, it can make US$300 (the spread of US$0.0003 × 1 million francs). Given the instantaneous and transparent nature of the electronically linked foreign exchange market around the globe (one new quote in London can reach New York before you finish reading *this* sentence), the opportunities for trading, or arbitrage, can come and go very quickly. The globally integrated nature of this market leads to three outcomes:

- Razor-thin spread.
- Quick (often literally split-second) decisions on buying and selling (remember Professor Lyon's observation earlier).
- Ever increasing volume in order to make more profits (recall the *daily* volume of over US$5 trillion). In the example above, US$300 is obviously just a few "peanuts" for Citigroup. Do a little math: How much trading in Swiss francs does Citigroup have to do in order to make US$1 million profits for itself?

7-3b Strategies for Nonfinancial Companies

How do nonfinancial companies cope with the fluctuations of the foreign exchange market—broadly known as currency risks? There are three primary strategies: (1) invoicing in their own currencies, (2) currency hedging (as discussed earlier), and (3) strategic hedging.[14] The most basic way is to invoice customers in your own currency. By invoicing in dollars, many US firms have enjoyed such protection from unfavorable foreign exchange movements.

Currency swap

A foreign exchange transaction between two firms in which one currency is converted into another at Time 1, with an agreement to revert it to the original currency at a specified Time 2 in the future.

Offer rate

The price to sell a currency.

Bid rate

The price to buy a currency.

Spread

The difference between the offer rate and the bid rate.

Currency risk

The potential for loss associated with fluctuations in the foreign exchange market.

Currency hedging is risky in case of wrong bets of currency movements. For example, most airlines in the world engage in currency hedging to manage fuel cost fluctuations, and most suffered losses in 2009. In 2008, oil price was at a record high, US$147 per barrel. Some airlines entered 180-day forward transactions with foreign exchange traders, say, at US$100 per barrel. This looked like a fantastic deal, representing 32% savings. However, by 2009, oil was only trading at US$41 per barrel. But some airlines were bound by the contract to purchase oil at US$100 per barrel, they were thus paying 144% (!) higher than the market.

Strategic hedging means spreading out activities in different currency zones in order to offset the currency losses in certain regions through gains in other regions.[15] Therefore, strategic hedging can be considered as currency diversification. It reduces exposure to unfavorable foreign exchange movements (see the Opening Case). Strategic hedging is conceptually different from currency hedging. Currency hedging focuses on using forward contracts and swaps to contain currency risks, a financial management activity that can be performed by in-house financial specialists or outside experts (such as currency traders) (see the Closing Case). Strategic hedging refers to geographically dispersing operations—through sourcing or FDI—in multiple currency zones. By definition, this is more strategic, involving managers from many functional areas (such as production, marketing, and sourcing) in addition to those from finance.

Overall, the importance of foreign exchange management cannot be overstressed for firms of all stripes interested in doing business abroad. Firms whose performance is otherwise stellar can be devastated by unfavorable currency movements. For instance, the Australian wine makers had a hard time competing with cheap imports (see In Focus 7.1). On the other hand, thanks to crises in countries such as Greece, Ireland, Portugal, and Spain, the euro depreciated sharply against the dollar and the Swiss franc during the same period. While euro zone exporters such as Daimler-Benz (maker of Mercedes cars) and EADS (manufacturer of Airbus jets) could not be happier, Swiss exporters struggled.

From a resource-based view, it seems imperative that firms develop resources and capabilities that can combat currency risks, in addition to striving for excellence in, for example, operations and marketing.[16] Developing such expertise is no small accomplishment because, as noted earlier, prediction of currency movements remains an art or a highly imprecise science. Precisely because of such challenges, firms able to profit from (or at least avoid being crushed by) unfavorable currency movements will possess some valuable, rare, and hard-to-imitate capabilities that are the envy of rivals.

7-4 Debates and Extensions

Learning Objective
Participate in three leading debates concerning foreign exchange movements.

In the highly uncertain world of foreign exchange movements, debates are numerous. We review three major debates here: (1) fixed versus floating exchange rates, (2) a strong dollar versus a weak dollar, and (3) hedging versus not hedging.

7-4a Fixed versus Floating Exchange Rates[17]

Since the collapse of the Bretton Woods system in the early 1970s, debate has never ended on whether fixed or floating exchange rates are better.[18] Proponents of fixed exchange rates argue that fixed exchange rates impose monetary discipline by

Strategic hedging
Spreading out activities in a number of countries in different currency zones to offset any currency losses in one region through gains in other regions.

preventing governments from engaging in inflationary monetary policies (essentially, printing more money). Proponents also suggest that fixed exchange rates reduce uncertainty and, thus, encourage trade and FDI, not only benefiting the particular economy but also helping the global economy.

Proponents of floating exchange rates believe that market forces should take care of supply, demand, and, thus, the price of any currency. Floating exchange rates may avoid large balance-of-payments deficits, surprises, and even crises. In other words, flexible exchange rates may help avoid the crises that occur under fixed exchange rates when expectations of an impending devaluation arise. For example, Thailand probably would not have been devastated so suddenly in July 1997 (generally regarded as the triggering event for the 1997 Asian financial crisis) had it operated a floating exchange rate system. In addition, floating exchange rates allow each country to make its own monetary policy. A major problem associated with the Bretton Woods system was that other countries were not happy about pegging their currencies to the currency of the United States, which practiced inflationary monetary policies in the late 1960s.

There is no doubt that floating exchange rates are more volatile than fixed rates. Many countries have no stomach for such volatility. The most extreme fixed rate policy is through a currency board, which is a monetary authority that issues notes and coins convertible into a key foreign currency at a *fixed* exchange rate. Usually, the fixed exchange rate is set by law, making changes to the exchange rate politically very costly for governments. To honor its commitment, a currency board must back the domestic currency with 100% of equivalent foreign exchange. In the case of Hong Kong's currency board, every HK$7.8 in circulation is backed by US$1. By design, a currency board is passive. When more US dollars flow in, the board issues more Hong Kong dollars and interest rates fall. When more US dollars flow out, the board reduces money supply and interest rates rise. The Hong Kong currency board has been jokingly described as an Asian outpost of the US Federal Reserve. This is technically accurate, because interest rates in Hong Kong are essentially determined by the US Federal Reserve. While the Hong Kong currency board has been a successful bulwark against speculative attacks on the Hong Kong dollar in 1997-1998, it has been dragged down by the weakening US dollar recently.[19]

7-4b A Strong Dollar versus a Weak Dollar

In recent years, the debate on the value of the dollar is closely related to the debate on the value of the yuan.[20] The value of the US dollar is a trillion-dollar question. At present, 65% of the world's foreign exchange holdings are in dollars, while the US share of global GDP is only 24% (see Figure 7.1). The recent economic turmoil has intensified the global debate on the proper value of the dollar (see Table 7.3). In terms of international trade competitiveness, a strong dollar may make it harder for US firms to export and to compete on price when combating imports (see the Opening Case). Conversely, a weak dollar may facilitate more US exports and stem import growth. Since the Plaza Accord of 1985, after which the dollar declined sharply against the Japanese yen, the United States has been pursuing a "cheap dollar" policy in order to facilitate more exports and reduce trade deficits. Unfortunately, the policy has backfired. While US merchandise exports did rise (from US$1 trillion in 2007 to over US$1.5 trillion in 2012), US trade deficits remained consistently high. In part this was due to China's (pre-2005) policy to peg its yuan

Currency board

A monetary authority that issues notes and coins convertible into a key foreign currency at a fixed exchange rate.

| Table 7.3 | A Strong Dollar versus a Weak Dollar |

Panel A. A Strong (Appreciating) Dollar	
Advantages	**Disadvantages**
• US consumers benefit from low prices on imports.	• US exporters have a hard time to compete on price abroad.
• Lower prices on foreign goods help keep US price level and inflation level low.	• US firms in import-competing industries have a hard time competing with low-cost imports.
• US tourists enjoy lower prices abroad.	• Foreign tourists find it more expensive when visiting the US.
• US firms find it easier to acquire foreign targets.	

Panel B. A Weak (Depreciating) Dollar	
Advantages	**Disadvantages**
• US exporters find it easier to compete on price abroad.	• US consumers face higher prices on imports.
• US firms face less competitive pressure to keep prices low.	• Higher prices on imports contribute to higher price level and inflation level in the US.
• Foreign tourists enjoy lower prices in the US.	• US tourists find it more expensive when traveling abroad.
• Foreign firms find it easier to acquire US targets.	• Governments, firms, and individuals outside the US holding dollar-denominated assets suffer from value loss of their assets.
• The US can print more dollars (quantitative easing) to export its problems to the rest of the world.	

to the dollar, which made the yuan also cheap. Since 2005, the United States has complained that China did not let its yuan appreciate enough. However, the yuan has appreciated 26% against the dollar between 2005 and 2014.

In addition to debating what the "fair" value of the dollar is, a new voice is now calling for *abandoning* the dollar as a *de facto* reserve currency (since the demise of the Bretton Woods system in the 1970s, the US dollar is no longer the official reserve currency, but it has retained some characteristics of a reserve currency due to its "soft power"). Leading this new global movement is China. China is America's number one creditor country that holds about US$2.2 trillion in foreign exchange reserves, two-thirds of which are denominated in dollars. Since the yuan is not internationally accepted (technically nonconvertible), China does not suggest that the yuan be used to replace the dollar. Instead, China has proposed to use Special Drawing Rights (SDRs), already created by the IMF, to replace the dollar as a global reserve currency. While this proposal is made in the name of promoting global stability, China is not totally altruistic. Since the US budget deficit has exploded and the US Federal Reserve has been printing a ton of new money to fund stimulus packages (with the euphemism "quantitative easing"), China is deeply worried that a cheapening dollar will be a nasty hit to Chinese holdings of US Treasury bonds. There is some fundamental soul-searching among Beijing's economic mandarins. Their policy of keeping the yuan low versus the dollar to promote exports and then to recycle export earnings to buy US Treasury bonds has backfired. Even the typically timid, state-controlled media in China is now full of criticisms of the Chinese government's "irresponsible" investment policy, which ends up investing hard-earned dollars from a developing economy to subsidize a very rich economy. China's proposal to dethrone the dollar as a dominant currency, although clearly a long shot, quickly garnered support from Brazil, Russia, India, and other emerging economies.

How are you personally affected by fluctuations in currency exchange rates?

The United States, on the other hand, has every interest to keep the dollar's status quo as a (*de facto*) reserve currency around the world so that China and other surplus countries will keep buying US Treasury bonds—for lack of a better alternative. While China has continued to buy new US Treasury bonds, it has taken two concrete steps. First, the People's Bank of China, the central bank, made yuan available to pay for exports to Argentina, Belarus, Indonesia, Malaysia, and South Korea if they are short on dollars. Second, some Chinese exporters started to settle certain transactions in Hong Kong and in Africa with yuan (see Emerging Markets 7.1)—the first step for the yuan's eventual international convertibility.

EMERGING MARKETS 7.1

Chinese Exporters Cope with Currency Fluctuation in Africa

In 2000, trade between China and Africa was only US$10 billion. In 2010, the volume rocketed ahead to reach US$127 billion. While China has become Africa's number-one trading partner, the downside of such intense trading is the complications of having to deal with currency fluctuation. The vast majority of the trade deals between China and Africa are conducted in US dollars, which have fluctuated substantially. Since the dollar is likely to depreciate and the yuan is likely to correspondingly appreciate further, Chinese exporters with costs in yuan and payments in dollars stand to lose. While currency hedging is an obvious coping strategy, many small exporters cannot afford the expenses. In addition, currency hedging is not risk free. Wrong bets may end up burning firms big time.

To better cope with currency fluctuation, one straightforward mechanism for Chinese exporters is to insist on payment in yuan. The question is: Why would African importers agree to pay in yuan? Two compelling reasons emerge. First, Chinese

exporters can save approximately 7% to 10% of their costs if they are paid in yuan. If they can share some of these gains with their African trading partners with lower prices, the new deal to use yuan as the common transaction currency becomes a win-win solution for both sides. Second, an increasing number of Chinese firms have engaged in foreign direct investment (FDI) in Africa. Their subsidiaries in Africa would be comfortable to use yuan to buy supplies, components, and manufactured products from home.

Johannesburg, South Africa-based Standard Bank, which is the largest bank in Africa, has estimated that by 2015, 40% of the China-Africa trade (worth US$100 billion) may be settled in yuan. This would significantly eliminate the headache of currency fluctuation for Chinese exporters. By 2014, approximately 18% of China's foreign trade has already been settled in yuan. Little by little, China's currency is gaining ground in Africa and elsewhere. However, adding all international payments together, the yuan in 2014 only ranks

14th in the world, behind Russia's ruble and Thailand's baht, according to SWIFT, a company that specializes in transfer of funds between banks (most readers of this book have probably used "SWIFT code" for your banks when sending or receiving funds). Therefore, the rise of the "redback" as a major currency for international trade in Africa and beyond still has a long way to go.

Sources: Based on (1) *21st Century Business Insights*, 2011, Renminbi is popular in Africa, September 16: 26: (2) G. Allard, 2012, Chinese OFDI in Africa, in I. Alon, M. Fetscherin, & P. Gugler (eds.), *Chinese International Investments* (pp. 279–299), New York: Palgrave; (3) *Economist*, 2013, Yuan for the money, February 9: 14–15; (4) *Economist*, 2014, The red and the green, April 26: 44; (5) www.standardbank.com.

7-4c Currency Hedging versus Not Hedging

Given the unpredictable nature of foreign exchange rates, it seems natural that firms that deal with foreign transactions—both financial and nonfinancial types, both large and small firms—may want to engage in currency hedging. Firms that fail to hedge are at the mercy of the spot market.

Yet, many firms do not bother. Some euro zone exporters simply insist on payment in euro and some Chinese exporters have started to insist on payment in yuan (see In Focus 7.3). Among the largest US firms, only approximately one-third hedge. The standard argument for currency hedging is increased stability of cash flows and earnings. In essence, currency hedging may be regarded as a form of insurance, whose cost may be outweighed by the protection it provides. However, many large firms, such as 3M, John Deere, and ExxonMobil, do not care about such insurance. Managers argue that currency hedging eats into profits. A simple forward contract may cost up to half a percentage point per year of the revenue being hedged. More complicated transactions may cost more. As a result, many firms believe that the ups and downs of various currencies even out in the long run. Some, such as IBM, focus on strategic hedging (geographically dispersing activities) while refraining from currency hedging. Whether such a "no currency hedging" strategy outperforms a currency hedging strategy remains to be seen.

7-5 Management Savvy

Learning Objective
Draw implications for action.

The big question in global business, adapted to the context of foreign exchange movements, is: What determines the success and failure of currency management around the globe? The answer boils down to two components. First, from an institution-based standpoint, the "rules of the game"—economic, political, and psychological—enable or constrain firms. For example, Swiss exporters' frustration with the appreciation of the Swiss franc relative to the euro stems from the centuries-old policy of Switzerland to maintain its political and economic independence. While all of Switzerland's neighbors have joined the EU and adopted the euro, Switzerland will not. Second, from a resource-based perspective, how firms develop valuable, unique, and hard-to-imitate capabilities in currency management may make or break them. While Swiss multinationals such as ABB and Nestlé can reduce their exposure to the Swiss franc by engaging in strategic hedging to produce outside of Switzerland (and often outside of the euro zone), many smaller Swiss firms do not have such capabilities

As a result, three implications for action emerge (Table 7.4). First, foreign exchange literacy must be fostered. Savvy managers need to not only pay attention

Table 7.4	**Implications for Action**

- Fostering foreign exchange literacy is a must.
- Risk analysis of any country must include an analysis of its currency risks.
- A currency risk management strategy is necessary—via currency hedging, strategic hedging, or both.

to the broad long-run movements informed by PPP, productivity changes, and balance of payments, but also to the fickle short-run fluctuations triggered by interest rate changes and investor mood swings.

Second, risk analysis of any country must include its currency risks. Previous chapters have advised managers to pay attention to political, regulatory, and cultural risks of various countries. Here, a crucial currency risk dimension is added. An otherwise attractive country may suffer from high inflation, resulting in devaluation of its currency on the horizon. For example, prior to 2008, foreign and domestic banks in emerging European countries such as Hungary, Latvia, and Poland let numerous home buyers to take out mortgage loans denominated in the euro, while a majority of these customers' assets and incomes were in local currencies. Unfortunately, local currencies in these countries were severely devaluated in the 2008–2009 crisis, making many homebuyers unable to come up with the higher mortgage payments. Both domestic and foreign banks in the region also suffered from severe losses.[21]

Finally, a country's high currency risks do not necessarily suggest that this country needs to be totally avoided. Instead, they call for a prudent currency risk management strategy—via currency hedging, strategic hedging, or both. Not every firm has the stomach or capabilities to do both. Smaller, internationally inexperienced firms may outsource currency hedging to specialists such as currency traders. Strategic hedging may be unrealistic for such smaller, inexperienced firms. On the other hand, many larger, internationally experienced firms (such as 3M) choose not to touch currency hedging, citing its unpredictability. Instead, they focus on strategic hedging. Although there is no fixed formula, firms not having a well-thought-out currency management strategy will be caught off guard when currency movements take a nasty turn.

CHAPTER SUMMARY/LEARNING OBJECTIVES

7-1 Understand the determinants of foreign exchange rates.

- A foreign exchange rate is the price of one currency expressed in another.
- Basic determinants of foreign exchange rates include: (1) relative price differences and PPP, (2) interest rates, (3) productivity and balance of payments, (4) exchange rate policies, and (5) investor psychology.

7-2 Track the evolution of the international monetary system.

- The international monetary system evolved from the gold standard (1870–1914), to the Bretton Woods system (1944-73), and eventually to the current post-Bretton Woods system (1973–present).
- The IMF serves as a lender of last resort to help member countries fight balance-of-payments problems.
- In response to the criticisms, the IMF has initiated major reforms recently.

7-3 Identify firms' strategic responses to deal with foreign exchange movements.

- Three foreign exchange transactions are: (1) spot transactions, (2) forward transactions, and (3) swaps.
- Firms' strategic responses include: (1) invoicing in their own currencies, (2) currency hedging, and (3) strategic hedging.

7-4 Participate in three leading debates concerning foreign exchange movements.

- (1) Fixed versus floating exchange rates, (2) a strong dollar versus a weak dollar, and (3) hedging versus not hedging.

7-5 Draw implications for action.

- Fostering foreign exchange literacy is a must.
- Risk analysis of any country must include an analysis of its currency risks.
- A currency risk management strategy is necessary—via currency hedging, strategic hedging, or both.

KEY TERMS

REVIEW QUESTIONS

1. *ON CULTURE:* **Suppose that in country X, the culture is one that avoids risk and frowns on gambling. Suppose the country uses the US dollar in its international transactions, and a firm in X buys a product from Europe, which it will take delivery of in 60 days and for which it will have to pay 100,000 euros at that time. The firm does not know how many dollars will be needed in order to obtain those 100,000 euros 60 days from now. One way to know that would be to enter into a contract for the future delivery of that currency with a speculator who would guarantee that the firm will be able to obtain those euros for a specific dollar value. The firm would thus avoid the risk of having to pay too much for those euros 60 days from now by transferring the risk at the present time to a speculator. The speculator takes the risk, because he or she is expecting that the actual costs of those euros (in terms of dollars) will be less 60 days from now than what the speculator promises to the firm. As a result, the speculator profits from the price differential. Some in country X**

view contracts for the future delivery of a currency (forward contracts) as risk avoidance, but others view it as gambling. What do you think?

2. Do an online search regarding current challenges to the dollar, euro, and yen, and then refer to PengAtlas Maps 2.1 (Top Merchandise Importers and Exporters) and 2.2 (Top Service Importers and Exporters). To what extent do the users of these three currencies tend to dominate world trade?

3. Refer to PengAtlas Map 2.3 (FDI Inflows and Outflows), and compare to what you learned from Question 2 above. To what extent do the users of the three currencies dominate? In your opinion, will the rise of the BRIC countries ultimately reduce the dominance of those currencies?

4. What are foreign exchange rates?

5. How are foreign exchange rates affected by differences in the interest rates prevailing in various countries?

6. What happened toward the end of WW II that lifted the dollar to the commanding heights of the global economy?

7. What is the IMF, and how does it help countries?

8. In foreign exchange, what are spot and forward transactions? How do they differ?

9. What is the difference between currency hedging and strategic hedging?

10. What is the role of currency boards regarding fixed exchange rates? Discuss at least one problem that such boards may have in maintaining fixed rates.

11. Why a strong dollar is not always desirable to the United States, while it may be to other countries?

12. Why should a savvy manager become literate about foreign exchange?

13. What is one example that illustrates why risk analysis of a country should include its currency risks?

CRITICAL DISCUSSION QUESTIONS

1. Suppose US$1 = €0.7809 in New York and US$1 = €0.7793 in Paris, how can foreign exchange traders profit from these exchange rates? What actions they take may result in the same dollar/euro exchange rate in both New York and Paris?

2. Identify the currencies of the top three trading partners of your country in the last ten years. Find the exchange rates of these currencies, relative to your country's currency, ten years ago and now. Explain the changes. Then predict the movement of these exchange rates ten years from now.

3. As a manager, you are choosing to do business in two countries: one has a fixed exchange rate and another a floating rate. Which country would you prefer? Why?

4. *ON ETHICS:* You are an IMF official going to a country whose export earnings are not able to pay for imports. The government has requested a loan. Which areas would you recommend the government to cut: (1) education, (2) salaries for officials, (3) food subsidies, and/or (4) tax rebates for exporters?

GLOBAL ACTION

BUSINESS
INSIGHTS
GLOBAL

1. **Based in the United States, your firm trades extensively with European countries that have adopted the euro. You have been asked to evaluate the impact of currency fluctuations on sales in this region over the past month. The first step in this process is to develop an exchange rate table for daily exchange rates over the past month between the US dollar and the euro. Once this has been accomplished, what general trends do you notice? How could these trends impact your firm's sales in countries that use the euro?**

2. **Your company is examining possible market opportunities in the Asia Pacific region. As a part of this possible strategic shift, the benchmark currencies of the region must be identified to diversify currency risk for future operations. Using a resource that examines foreign exchange, determine which predominant currencies are likely candidates for your analysis.**

CLOSING CASE

EMERGING MARKETS: Jobek Do Brasil's Foreign Exchange Challenges

Jobek do Brasil is an outdoor furniture and hammock manufacturer and exporter based in Brazil. Focusing on European markets, it had to constantly deal with foreign exchange challenges. In 2008, sales went down by more than 60%, thanks to the global financial crisis. The existing business model—based on in-house manufacturing in Brazil's northeast and an administrative, purchasing, quality assurance and sales unit in Germany—was no longer viable. Fixed costs were substantial and manufacturing inputs had already been purchased. Sitting on debt and running short of working capital, Barny, the owner, shut down Jobek's plant in 2010; outsourced production to Reed Isaac, a former local partner; closed down the German unit; and signed a long term supply contract with Stern GmbH in Germany. In addition, Jobek temporarily discontinued the already-low sales outside Europe as well as the insignificant domestic sales in Brazil. The measures were necessary to refocus the business and ride down costs.

BRAZIL'S FOREIGN EXCHANGE POLICY
After more than a decade of high inflation, low growth, debt default, and failed stabilization policies, the Brazilian government introduced a new currency, the real (R$), in 1994. The new currency, valued at R$1 per US$1 in 1994, was pegged to the US dollar and could oscillate within an adjustable band until 1999. At that time, the effects of the Asian and the Russian crises also increased pressures on Brazil that still suffered from repetitive trade deficits and current account deficits. In 1998, Brazil earned only around US$51 billion from exports, corresponding to 6.5% of GDP. Then, subject to central bank interventions, the real depreciated rapidly and reached R$2.25 per dollar in January 2002. When it became increasingly likely that José Ignácio Lula da Silva would be elected Brazil's new president, hot money quickly left Brazil and the real dropped to R$3.83 per dollar in October 2002. The euro was roughly at parity with the US dollar at that time, and the R$/euro exchange rate was similar (see Figure 7.4). Contrary to initial expectations, Lula's government gained the confidence of international financial markets. Brazil's monetary policy aimed to quickly reduce inflationary pressures by raising real interest rates. During the 2003 crisis, for instance, the central bank's reference nominal interest rates topped 26%. Even at the beginning of 2012, nominal interest rates

| Figure 7.4 | **Brazilian Real to Euro Exchange Rate** |

Source: www.indexmundi.com/xrates/graph.aspx?c1=BRL&c2=EUR&days=3650

were around 10% and real interest rates were close to 5%, the highest worldwide. Brazil's conservative fiscal and monetary policy quickly showed positive results. After paying back its last IMF loan in 2005, the country obtained the investment grade rating in 2008. The international financial markets honored that and billions of US dollars poured into the country over the last few years. In addition, higher export sales, partly triggered by record commodity prices, led to a high level of foreign exchange reserves of US$356 billion in March 2012. However, the long expected and well-received macroeconomic stabilization came at a cost: the R$ had been appreciating since 2004 and about 2,700 (12%) exporters quit international markets between 2004 and 2011.

COUNTER MEASURES

Over the last 20 years, Jobek do Brasil built up a strong premium brand, especially in the German market. The branding strategy successfully associated Jobek's products with the Latin American life style. In addition, Jobek managed to link its brand with environmental friendliness by using Forest Stewardship Council (FSC) certified wood for accessories and with social responsibility by treating employees fairly and by sponsoring community projects. In addition, the Jobek brand was associated with high quality. Selling this brand asset to Stern GmbH

was a hard decision. Now, Stern GmbH owned the rights of the Jobek brand for Europe while Barny maintained the rights for the rest of the world. In exchange, Stern committed to buying all products it sold under the Jobek brand from Barny for the next ten years.

In addition, Barny also approached Jobek's account managers at Banco do Brasil, Brazil's largest and partly state-owned bank, and asked them to make an offer for a swap contract over R$1 million. After six months, Barny still did not receive the contract and grumbled that "here in the northeast of Brazil, they are 20 years back in some areas." Indeed, hedging the exposure to the euro is sometimes a problem in a country where, according to a financial risk consultant, "the US dollar is still a synonym for foreign exchange."

GETTING SQUEEZED

As if the past turbulence was not yet enough, more dark clouds moved across the horizon and tapped the usually strong sunshine in Brazil's northeast. With the euro in its deepest crisis since its introduction in 2002, many feared that quantitative easing might be used to get rid of the euro zone's mounting debt. Barny recently read one article in *Valor Econômico*: "Dilma Roussef [the new Brazilian president] sent a message to Mrs. Merkel [the German chancellor] complaining about 'the monetary *tsunami*' that is threatening to flood Brazil and other emerging economies with cheap money made available by the European Central Bank." In fact, Brazil was attracting foreign money as never before and received a record amount of foreign direct investment (FDI) of US$66 billion in 2011.

Barny complained, "with the resulting real appreciation, our clients are not very happy." He noted: "On November 29, 2011, Stern placed an order based on an exchange rate of R$2.49 per euro. Today, March 2, 2012, the euro dropped to R$2.28, that's an appreciation of about 10% in a very short period. The only way we can sell our products is because we have a strong brand name."

The telephone ringing interrupted Barny's thoughts. It was João Gonçalves, the boss at Reed Isaac, shouting through the handset: "You know, I am very concerned with the high minimum wage increases that Mrs. Dilma Roussef has pushed through congress, not to mention the ever-increasing tax charges. We can hardly survive at such costs and I am sorry but I need to talk to you about a price adjustment." Although disappointed, Barny politely asked João if he would like to have lunch together. Then Barny scratched his head on how he would respond to João's request over lunch.

CASE DISCUSSION QUESTIONS:

1. How do you evaluate Jobek's situation from the resource-based and institution-based views? Why have resources and institutions hindered Barny to cope with the foreign exchange situation, but simultaneously helped him to turn his company around?

2. How do you evaluate Jobek's strategic response to foreign exchange risks?

3. What would you do if you were Barny? Why?

Sources: This case was written by Dr. **Dirk Michael Boehe** (University of Adelaide). It is based on (1) the author's interviews; (2) internal information provided by Jobek do Brasil, www.jobek.com.br; (3) Brazilian Central Bank, www.bacen.gov.br; (4) Brazilian Ministry of Economic Development, www.mdic.gov.br; (5) Exchange rate converter, www.oanda.com; (6) *Forbes*, 2011. BRIC worker: A look at labor costs in the big EMs, March 11, www.forbes.com/sites/kenrapoza/2011/03/11/bric-worker-a-look-at-labor-costs-in-the-big-ems/; (6) Doing Business 2012 – Paying taxes, World Bank, www.doingbusiness.org/ data/exploretopics/paying-taxes; (7) *Valor Econômico*, 2012, Dilma: países ricos estão inundando o mundo com um "tsunami monetário," March 1; (8) *Economist*, 2011, Latin America's economies: Waging the currency war, January 13, www.economist.com /node/17906027.

NOTES

[**Journal acronyms**] **AER**—*American Economic Review;* **BW**—*BusinessWeek* (before 2010) or *Bloomberg Businessweek* (since 2010); **JEL**—*Journal of Economic Literature;* **JEP**—*Journal of Economic Perspectives;* **JIBS**—*Journal of International Business Studies;* **SMJ**—*Strategic Management Journal;* **WSJ**—*Wall Street Journal.*

1 *Economist*, 2009, Yuan small step, July 11: 71–72.

2 A. Taylor & M. Taylor, 2004, The purchasing power parity debate, *JEP*, 18: 135–158.

3 *Economist*, 2014, The Big Mac index: A basket of sliders, July 26: 61.

4 *Economist*, 2006, McCurrencies, May 27: 74.

5 M. Kreinin, 2006, *International Economics* (p. 183), Cincinnati: Cengage Learning.

6 L. Sarno & M. Taylor, 2001, Official intervention in the foreign exchange market, *JEL*, 39: 839–868.

7 R. Lyons, 2001, *The Microstructure Approach to Exchange Rates* (p. 1), Cambridge, MA: MIT Press.

8 P. Lane & G. Milesi-Ferretti, 2008, The drivers of financial globalization, *AER*, 98: 327–332.

9 R. Carbaugh, 2007, *International Economics*, 11th ed. (p. 360), Cincinnati: Cengage Learning.

10 *Economist*, 2013, Global foreign-exchange turnover, September 14: 97.

11 United Nations, 2014, *World Investment Report 2014* (p. ix), New York & Geneva: UN.

12 World Trade Organization, 2014, *World Trade 2013*, Geneva: WTO (www.wto.org).

13 E. Hutson & S. Stevenson, 2010, Openness, hedging incentives, and foreign exchange exposure, *JIBS*, 41: 105–122.

14 F. Carrieri & B. Majerbi, 2006, The pricing of exchange risk in emerging stock markets, *JIBS*, 37: 372–391.

15 S. Lee & M. Makhija, 2009, Flexibility in internationalization, *SMJ*, 30: 537–555; C. Pantzalis, B. Simkins, & P. Laux, 2001, Operational hedges and the foreign exchange exposure of US multinational corporations, *JIBS*, 32: 793–812.

16 R. Faff & A. Marshall, 2005, International evidence on the determinants of foreign exchange rate exposure of multinational corporations, *JIBS*, 36: 539–558; R. Weiner, 2005, Speculation in international crises, *JIBS*, 36: 576–587.

17 This section draws heavily from B. Yarbrough & R. Yarbrough, 2006, *The World Economy*, 7th ed. (p. 683), Cincinnati: Cengage Learning.

18 P. Henry, 2007, Capital account liberalization, *JEL*, 45: 887–935.

19 *BW*, 2011, Hong Kong's currency inflicts plenty of pain, October 3: 21–22.

20 *BW*, 2009, China's doubts about the dollar, June 8: 20; *Economist*, 2009, Time for a Beijing bargain, May 30: 15–16; *Economist*, 2009, Yuan small step, July 11: 71–72; *WSJ*, 2009, Geithner is exactly wrong on China trade, January 26.

21 M. W. Peng & K. E. Meyer, 2011, *International Business* (pp. 200–202), London: Cengage Learning EMEA.

HO Marketwire Photos/Newscom

Learning Objectives

After studying this chapter, you should be able to

- make the case for global economic integration.

- understand the evolution of the GATT and the WTO, including current challenges.

- make the case for regional economic integration.

- understand regional economic integration efforts in Europe, the Americas, the Asia Pacific, and Africa.

- participate in two leading debates concerning global and regional economic integration.

- draw implications for action.

Capitalizing on Global and Regional Integration

OPENING CASE

EMERGING MARKETS: Launching the Learjet 85: A NAFTA Collaboration

The North American Free Trade Agreement (NAFTA) celebrated its 20th anniversary in 2014. Founded in 1994, NAFTA was designed to make rules more market friendly to facilitate more trade and investment among its three member countries. In response, smart companies have taken advantage of the changed rules of the game to build expanded supply chains across NAFTA in an effort to enhance their global competitiveness.

While the maiden flight of the Learjet 85 in April 2014 was a coincidence, how Canada's Bombardier took advantage of NAFTA and tapped into the comparative advantage of the three member countries is a shining new example of how high NAFTA can soar. In 1990, Montreal-based Bombardier acquired Wichita, Kansas-based Learjet. Although in the aerospace industry Bombardier is the world's third largest player, it is dwarfed by the two giants Boeing and Airbus. In the business aviation market, Bombardier competes intensely with Beech Hawker, Cessna, and Gulfstream from the United States, Dassault Falcon from France, and Embraer from Brazil. Boeing and Airbus have also elbowed their way into this market for smaller airplanes by dressing up the smallest of their large jets (such as Boeing 737 and A320) as business jets. Honda has jumped in with HondaJet. Although business aviation seems glamorous, its customers are the most demanding ones in the world. Evidenced by the fate of

European rivals such as de Havilland, Fokker, and Short Brothers, crash landings (bankruptcies) are frequent. Firms need strong muscle to survive the brutal skies.

In 2007, Bombardier launched an innovative new eight-seat model, the Learjet 85. In 2010, it opened a US$250-million Learjet 85 aircraft component manufacturing facility in Querétaro, Mexico, which was inaugurated by President Felipe Calderón. The state-of-the-art factory makes the cockpit, fuselage, and tail sections of the Learjet 85. Instead of oily smells and noisy sound of welding, the factory is amazingly quiet. Technicians wear facial masks to work in a dust-free room. Instead of metal, the airplane uses carbon fiber, which is cut by laser. The carbon fiber is then baked in a giant oven to make a seamless combined section for the cockpit and the fuselage.

Except some parts of the wing made by another Bombardier unit in Belfast, Northern Ireland, UK, the Learjet 85 represents the fruit of NAFTA collaboration. The engine is designed by Pratt & Whitney in the United States, and is made in Canada. Made-in-Mexico airframes are shipped to Wichita, Kansas, where Learjet's headquarters is located, for final assembly and testing prior to being delivered to customers. In short, the Learjet 85 is a high-flying example of a successful NAFTA endeavor. Such trinational collaboration would not have taken place in the absence of NAFTA.

When the US$250 million investment in Mexico was first announced, Bombardier employees in Montreal and Wichita, where the Learjet would have been made had NAFTA not been around, complained. However, given the bankruptcies of a number of old European rivals and the emergence of new entrants from China, Japan, Russia, and South Korea, Canadian and American employees came to appreciate that if outsourcing some manufacturing to Mexico reduces cost and helps ensure Bombardier's future, it would help safeguard their jobs in the long run.

Sources: Based on (1) *BusinessWeek*, 2003, Happy birthday, NAFTA, December 22; (2) *Economist*, 2014, Deeper, better, NAFTA, January 4: 8; (2) *Economist*, 2014, Ready to take off again? January 4: 23–25; (3) *Economist*, 2014, Three countries or one continent? October 4: 44.

North American Free Trade Agreement (NAFTA)

A free trade agreement among Canada, Mexico, and the United States.

Regional economic integration

Efforts to reduce trade and investment barriers within one region.

Global economic integration

Efforts to reduce trade and investment barriers around the globe.

Why did Bombardier deliberately tap into the three member countries in the North American Free Trade Agreement (NAFTA), instead of concentrating its work in one country? In addition to NAFTA, why did it also manufacture some parts of the new Learjet 85 in Europe? In two words, the answer is: economic integration—both regionally and globally. Regional economic integration refers to efforts to reduce trade and investment barriers within one region, such as NAFTA. Global economic integration, in turn, refers to efforts to reduce trade and investment barriers around the globe.

Most fundamentally, this chapter is about how the two core perspectives in global business interact. Specifically, how do changes in the rules of the game via global and regional economic integration (as emphasized by the institution-based view) lead firms to better develop and leverage their capabilities (as highlighted by the resource-based view)? In other words, how do firms around the world capitalize on global and regional economic integration? We start with a description of global economic integration. Next, we introduce regional economic integration. Debates and extensions follow.

Learning Objective
Make the case for global economic integration.

8-1 Global Economic Integration

Current frameworks of regional and global economic integration date back to the end of World War II (WWII). The world community was mindful of the mercantilist trade wars in the 1930s, which worsened the Great Depression and eventually led to WWII. Two new developments after the war were initiated to prevent a repeat of these circumstances. Globally, the General Agreement on Tariffs and Trade (GATT) was created in 1948. In Europe, regional integration started in 1951. Both developments proved so successful that they are now considerably expanded: one became the World Trade Organization (WTO) and the other the European Union (EU).

General Agreement on Tariffs and Trade (GATT)

A multilateral agreement governing the international trade of goods (merchandise).

World Trade Organization (WTO)

The official title of the multilateral trading system and the organization underpinning this system since 1995.

European Union (EU)

The official title of European economic integration since 1993.

8-1a Political Benefits for Global Economic Integration

Recall from Chapters 5 and 6 that theoretically, there are economic gains when firms from different countries can freely trade and engage in foreign direct investment (FDI). However, until the end of WWII, most governments had not accepted these insights. In the late 1920s and the early 1930s, virtually all governments tried to protect domestic industries by imposing protectionist policies through tariffs and quotas. Collectively, these beggar-thy-neighbor policies triggered retaliation that further restricted trade (Figure 8.1). Eventually, trade wars turned into WWII.

The postwar urge for global economic integration grew out of the painful lessons of the 1920s and the 1930s. While emphasizing economic benefits, global

Figure 8.1   **Down the Tube: Contraction of World Trade during the Great Depression 1929–1933, millions US$)**

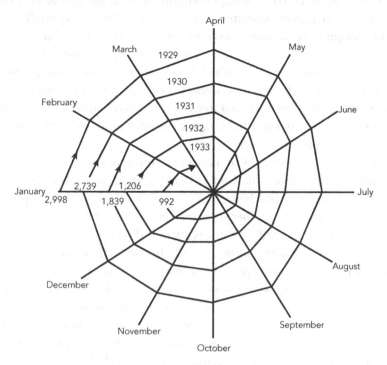

Source: C. Kindleberger, 1973, *The World in Depression* (p. 170), Berkeley: University of California Press.

economic integration is *political* in nature. Its most fundamental goal is to promote peace (Table 8.1). Simply put, buyers and sellers are usually reluctant to fight or kill each other. On the other hand, in 1941, when the United States cut off oil sales to Japan (in protest of its aggression in China), Japan attacked Pearl Harbor. Global economic integration seeks to build confidence. The trade wars in the 1930s were triggered by a lack of confidence. Confidence building is key to avoiding the tragedies of the 1930s. Governments, if they are confident that other countries will not raise trade barriers, will not be tempted to do the same.

Recently, as the global economy endeavors to recover from the worst economic crisis (now called the Great Recession) since the Great Depression, there is a grave danger of rising protectionism around the globe. Hopefully, leaders of the 21st century will be smarter and wiser than leaders of the 1920s and the 1930s. While protectionism may lead to short-term gains at the expense of trading partners, the world as a whole "has been there, done that"—with disastrous outcomes and tremendous wartime losses.

Table 8.1   **Benefits of Global Economic Integration**

Political benefits
- Promote peace by promoting trade and investment.
- Build confidence in a multilateral trading system.

Economic benefits
- Disputes are handled constructively.
- Rules make life easier and discrimination impossible for all participating countries.
- Free trade and investment raise incomes and stimulate economic growth.

8-1b Economic Benefits for Global Economic Integration

There are at least three compelling economic reasons for global economic integration. One is to handle disputes constructively. This is especially evident in the WTO's dispute resolution mechanisms (discussed later in this chapter). Although there is an escalation in the number of disputes brought to the WTO, such an increase, according to the WTO, "does not reflect increasing tension in the world. Rather, it reflects the closer economic ties throughout the world, the WTO's expanding membership, and the fact that countries have faith in the system to solve their differences."[1] In other words, bringing disputes to the WTO is so much better than declaring war on each other.

Another benefit is that global economic integration makes life easier for all participants. Officially, the GATT/WTO system is called the multilateral trading system—the key word being *multilateral* (involving all participating countries) as opposed to *bilateral* (between two countries). One crucial principle is non-discrimination. Specifically, a country cannot discriminate between its trading partners. Every time a country lowers a trade barrier, it has to do the same for *all* WTO member countries (except when giving preference to regional partners—discussed later). Such nondiscrimination makes life easier for all members.

Finally, global economic integration raises incomes, generates jobs, and stimulates economic growth. The WTO estimates that cutting global trade barriers by a third may raise worldwide income by approximately US$600 billion—equivalent to contributing an economy the size of Canada to the world.[2] While countries benefit, individuals also benefit because more and better jobs are created.

Of course, global economic integration has its share of problems. Critics may be unhappy with the environmental impact and distribution of the fruits from more trade and investment among the haves and have-nots in the world. However, when weighing all the pros and cons, most governments and people agree that global economic integration generates enormous benefits, ranging from preserving peace to generating jobs.[3] Next, let us examine its two principal mechanisms: the GATT and WTO.

Learning Objective
Understand the evolution of the GATT and the WTO, including current challenges.

Multilateral trading system
The global system that governs international trade among countries—otherwise known as the GATT/WTO system.

Non-discrimination
A principle that a country cannot discriminate among its trading partners.

8-2 Organizing World Trade

8-2a General Agreement on Tariffs and Trade (GATT): 1948–1994

Created in 1948, the GATT was technically an agreement but *not* an organization. Its major contribution was to reduce the level of tariffs by sponsoring rounds of multilateral negotiations. As a result, the average tariff in developed economies dropped from 40% in 1948 to 3% in 2005. Between 1950 and 1995 (when the GATT was phased out to become the WTO), while world GDP grew about fivefold, world merchandise exports grew about 100 times(!). During the GATT era, trade growth consistently outpaced GDP growth.

Despite the GATT's phenomenal success in bringing down tariff barriers, it was clear by the mid-1980s, when the Uruguay Round was launched, that reforms would be necessary. Such reforms were triggered by three concerns. First, because of the GATT's declared focus on merchandise trade, neither trade in services nor intellectual property (IP) protection was covered. Both of these areas were becoming more important. Second, in merchandise trade, there were a lot of loopholes that called for reforms. One of the most (in)famous loopholes was the Multifibre Arrangement (MFA) designed to *limit* free trade in textiles, which was a direct violation of the letter and spirit of the GATT. Finally, the GATT's success in reducing tariffs, combined with the global recessions in the 1970s and the 1980s, led many governments to invoke nontariff barriers (NTBs), such as subsidies and local content requirements. Unlike tariff barriers that were relatively easy to verify and challenge, NTBs were more subtle but more pervasive, thus triggering a growing number of trade disputes. The GATT, however, lacked effective dispute resolution mechanisms. Thus, at the end of the Uruguay Round, participating countries agreed in 1994 to upgrade the GATT and launch the WTO.

8-2b World Trade Organization (WTO): 1995–Present

Established on January 1, 1995, the WTO is the GATT's successor. This transformation turned the GATT from a provisional treaty serviced by an ad hoc secretariat to a full-fledged international organization, headquartered in Geneva, Switzerland. An interesting question is: What happened to the GATT? Did it "die"? Not really, because the GATT is still in existence as part of the WTO. But this is confusing. One straightforward way to distinguish the "new" GATT (as part of the WTO) from the original GATT is to identify the new one as "GATT 1994" and the old one as "GATT 1947." Significantly broader than the GATT, the WTO has six main areas (Figure 8.2):

- An umbrella agreement, simply called the Agreement Establishing the WTO.
- An agreement governing the international trade of goods, still using the old title as the General Agreement on Tariffs and Trade (GATT)—technically, as noted earlier, it is "GATT 1994."
- An agreement governing the international trade of services, the General Agreement on Trade in Services (GATS).
- An agreement governing IP rights, the Trade-Related Aspects of Intellectual Property Rights (TRIPS).
- Trade dispute settlement mechanisms, which allow for the WTO to adjudicate trade disputes among countries in a more effective and less time-consuming way (discussed next).
- Trade policy reviews, which enable other members to "peer review" a country's trade policy.

Overall, the WTO has a far wider scope, bringing into the multilateral trading system—for the first time—trade in services, IP, dispute settlement, and peer review of policy.[4] The next two sections outline two of its major initiatives: dispute settlement and the Doha Round.

Figure 8.2 | **Six Main Areas of the WTO**

Umbrella	Agreement Establishing the WTO		
Three main areas	Goods (GATT)	Services (GATS)	Intellectual Property (TRIPS)
Dispute settlement	Dispute Settlement Mechanisms		
Transparency	Trade Policy Reviews		

Source: Adapted from World Trade Organization, 2003, *Understanding the WTO* (p. 22), Geneva: WTO.

General Agreement on Trade in Services (GATS)

A WTO agreement governing the international trade of services.

Trade-Related Aspects of Intellectual Property Rights (TRIPS)

A WTO agreement governing intellectual property rights.

8-2c Trade Dispute Settlement

One of the main objectives for establishing the WTO was to strengthen the trade dispute settlement mechanisms. The old GATT mechanisms experienced (1) long delays, (2) blocking by accused countries, and (3) inadequate enforcement. The WTO addresses all three of these problems. First, it sets time limits for a peer review panel, consisting of three neutral countries as peers, to reach a judgment. Second, it removes the power of the accused countries to block any unfavorable decision. WTO decisions will be final. Third, in terms of enforcement, although the WTO has earned the nickname of "the world's supreme court in trade," it does *not* have real enforcement capability. The WTO simply recommends the losing country to change its laws or practices, and authorizes the winning country to use tariff retaliation to compel the offending country to comply with the WTO ruling.

Understandably, enforcement of the WTO ruling is controversial, because the losing country experiences some loss of sovereignty. It is important to note that fundamentally, the WTO ruling is a *recommendation* but not an order—no higher-level entity can order a sovereign government to do anything against its wishes. Because the WTO has no real enforcement "teeth," a country that has lost a dispute case can choose one of two options: (1) change its laws or practices to be in compliance; or (2) defy the ruling by doing nothing and suffer trade retaliation by the winning country, known as "punitive duties." Most of the WTO's trade dispute rulings, however, are resolved without resorting to trade retaliation. This supports the first proposition in the institution-based view (see Chapter 2): most offending countries have made a *rational* decision to respect the rules of the game, believing that the benefits of being in compliance with the rulings unfavorable to them outweigh the costs of "rocking the boat."

8-2d The Doha Round—"The Doha Development Agenda"

The Doha Round was the only round of trade negotiations sponsored by the WTO. In 1999, a WTO meeting in Seattle intended to start a new round of trade talks was not only devastated by the appearance of 30,000 protesters, but was also derailed by significant differences between developed and developing countries. Undeterred by the backlash, WTO member countries went ahead to launch a new round of negotiations in Doha, Qatar, in November 2001.

The Doha Round was significant for two reasons. First, it was launched in the aftermath of the "9/11" attacks. Members had a strong resolve to make free trade work around the globe in order to defeat the terrorist agenda to divide and terrorize the world. Second, this was the first round in the history of GATT/WTO to specifically aim at promoting economic development in developing countries. Consequently, the official title of the Doha Round was the "Doha Development Agenda." The agenda was ambitious: Doha would (1) reduce agricultural subsidies in developed countries to facilitate exports from developing countries; (2) slash tariffs, especially in industries that developing countries might benefit (especially textiles); (3) free up trade in services; and (4) strengthen IP protection. Note that in the Doha Round, *not* all meetings were held in Doha. Subsequent meetings took place in locations such as Bali, Indonesia; Cancun, Mexico; Geneva, Switzerland; and Hong Kong, China.

Unfortunately, numerous countries failed to deliver on promises made in Doha. The "hot potato" turned out to be agriculture. Australia, Argentina, and

Doha Round

A round of WTO negotiations to reduce agricultural subsidies, slash tariffs, and strengthen intellectual property protection that started in Doha, Qatar, in 2001. Officially known as the "Doha Development Agenda," it was suspended in 2006 due to disagreements.

most developing countries demanded that Japan, the EU, and the US reduce farm subsidies. Japan rejected any proposal to cut rice tariffs. The EU refused to significantly reduce farm subsidies. The US actually increased farm subsidies. On the other hand, many developing countries, led by India, refused to tighten IP protection, citing their needs for cheap generic drugs to combat deceases such as HIV/AIDS. Overall, developing countries refused to offer concessions in IP and service trade in part because of the failure of Japan, the EU, and the US to reduce farm subsidies.

Eventually, at the Geneva meeting in 2006, it was evident that member countries could not talk any more, because they were still miles apart. The Doha Round was thus officially suspended, and hopes of lifting millions out of poverty through free trade derailed. Labeled "the biggest threat to the postwar [multilateral] trading system" by the *Economist*,[5] the fiasco disappointed almost every country involved. Naturally, finger-pointing started immediately. To be fair, no country was totally responsible for the collapse of the Doha Round, and all members collectively were culpable. The sheer complexity of reaching an agreement on "everything" among 153 member countries (in 2006) was simply mind boggling.

What happens next? Officially, Doha was "suspended" but not "terminated" or "dead." In 2008, members tried but failed again in another meeting in Geneva. Efforts again emerged in 2011. Most recently in December 2013 in Bali, Indonesia, 159 members struck a trade facilitation agreement (TFA)—a pledge to cut red tape at customs posts in all countries. Although the TFA was far narrower and less ambitious than the sweeping deal envisioned when Doha was first launched, it was viewed as the first big win of the Doha Round. Unfortunately in July 2014, the TFA collapsed (see Figure 8.3). This was because India withdrew its support. The "hot potato" again turned out to be food subsidies (see Emerging Markets 8.1).

Multilateral trade negotiations are notoriously challenging.[6] In 1990, the Uruguay Round of the GATT was similarly suspended, only to rise again in 1994 with a far-reaching agreement that launched the WTO. Whether history will repeat itself remains to be seen. On the other hand, although global deals may be hard to do, regional deals are moving "at twice the speed and with half the fuss."[7] The upshot is stagnation of multilateralism and acceleration of regionalism—a topic we turn to next.

Figure 8.3   **Doha Makes No Progress**

Source: *Economist*, November 30, 2013, p. 8.

EMERGING MARKETS 8.1

Food versus Trade

In December 2013 in Bali, Indonesia, 159 members of the WTO struck a trade facilitation agreement (TFA)—a pledge to cut red tape at customs posts around the world. This would be the only tangible achievement of the Doha Round, which was launched in 2001. Limited in scope, the deal would simplify customs red tape rather than tackling the far-thornier problem of agricultural subsidies and intellectual property. Still, it would add up to US$400 billion a year to a struggling global economy.

Unfortunately, in July 2014, the TFA collapsed. This was because India withdrew its support. The "hot potato" again turned out to be food subsidies. India, like many developing countries, strengthened "food security" policies (a euphemism for agricultural subsidies) in response to recent swings in food prices. Such subsidies would soon grow large enough to violate WTO rules, which dictate that no developing country could subsidize more than 10% of the total value of harvests to farmers. Already spending US$19 billion (1% of GDP) on such subsidiaries, India is likely to exceed the 10% limit in the near future. When

that happens, India could be subject to a WTO challenge. While the Bali deal was signed by a previous government, the new Narendra Modi administration, elected into power in May 2014, insisted that it would not sacrifice food security on the altar of global trade. Even the WTO's efforts to let India to have four extra years (until 2017) of immunity from challenge were not viewed to be good enough. In other words, India would not trade food for trade.

India is hardly the only protectionist country when it comes to agricultural subsidies. According to the *Economist*, "the rich countries are the worst culprits." Japanese rice and sugar tariffs are, respectively, 778% and 328%. The EU dishes out 40% of its budget to farmers. But, by giving up the gains from more smooth trade, India is also hurting itself. Its massive food subsidies lead to huge stockpiles of unwanted, rotting produce and fan corruption. In the end, the biggest loser seems to be the WTO. With Doha dead and Bali (a subset of Doha) scuttled, the WTO had no concrete deal to show when it celebrated its 20th anniversary in 2015.

Sources: Based on (1) *Economist*, 2013, The Indian problem, November 23: 17; (2) *Economist*, 2013, Unaccustomed victory, December 14: 78; (3) *Economist*, 2014, Bailing out from Bali, August 9: 58–59; (4) *Economist*, 2014, No more grand bargains, August 9: 10.

Learning Objective
Make the case for regional economic integration.

8-3 Regional Economic Integration

There is now a proliferation of regional trade deals. This section first introduces the benefits for regional economic integration, followed by a discussion of its major types.

8-3a The Pros and Cons for Regional Economic Integration

Similar to global economic integration, the benefits for regional economic integration center on both political and economic dimensions (see Table 8.1). Politically, regional economic integration promotes peace by fostering closer economic ties and building confidence. Only in the last six decades did the Europeans break away from their deadly habit of war and violence against one another dating back hundreds of years. One leading cause of this dramatic behavioral change is economic integration. In addition, regional integration enhances the collective political weight of a region. Postwar European integration has been fueled by such a desire when dealing with superpowers such as the United States.

Economically, the three benefits associated with regional economic integration are similar to those associated with global economic integration: (1) disputes are handled constructively; (2) consistent rules make life easier, and discrimination impossible, for participating countries within one region; and (3) free trade and investment raise incomes and stimulate economic growth (see Table 8.1). Moreover, regional economic integration may bring additional benefits, such as a larger market, simpler standards, and economies of scale.

However, not everything is rosy in regional integration. A case can be made *against* it. Politically, regional integration, centered on preferential treatments for firms within a region, discriminates against firms outside a region, thus undermining global integration. Of course, in practice, global deals (such as the Doha Round) are challenging to accomplish, and regional deals emerge as realistic alternatives. Economically, regional integration may result in some loss of sovereignty. The 18 EU members adopting the euro can no longer implement independent monetary policies (see the Closing Case).

The simultaneous existence of both pros and cons means that countries are often cautious in joining regional economic integration. Norway and Switzerland chose not to join the EU. Even when countries are part of a regional deal, they sometimes choose to stay out of certain areas. For example, EU members Britain, Denmark, and Sweden refused to adopt the euro. Overall, different levels of enthusiasm call for different types of regional economic integration, which are outlined next.

8-3b Types of Regional Economic Integration

Figure 8.4 shows five main types of regional economic integration.

- A free trade area (FTA) is a group of countries that remove trade barriers among themselves. One of the newest examples is the Eurasian Union consisting of Belarus, Kazakhstan, and Russia, which was created in 2014. In an FTA, each member still maintains different external policies regarding

---

Figure 8.4   **Types of Regional Economic Integration**

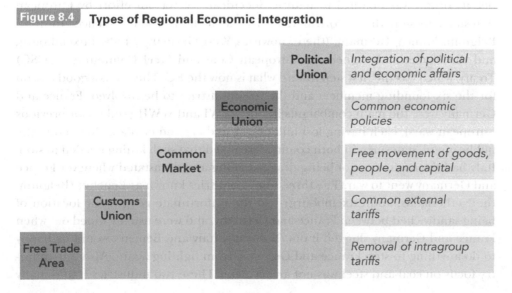

Free trade area (FTA)

A group of countries that remove trade barriers among themselves.

non-members. For example, three NAFTA members have each pursued *different* FTA agreements with the EU.

- A customs union is one step beyond an FTA. In addition to all the arrangements of an FTA, a customs union imposes common external policies on non-participants in order to combat trade diversion. One example is the Andean Community in South America.

- A common market combines everything a customs union has. In addition, a common market permits the free movement of goods and people. Today's EU used to be a common market.

- An economic union combines all the features of a common market. Members also coordinate and harmonize economic policies (for example, monetary, fiscal, and taxation) in order to blend their economies into a single economic entity. Today's EU is an economic union. One possible dimension of an economic union is to establish a monetary union, which has been accomplished by 18 EU members through the adoption of the euro (see next section).

- A political union is the integration of political and economic affairs of a region. The United States and the former Soviet Union are two examples. Whether the EU will eventually turn into a political union is subject to debate. At present, the EU is not a political union.

Overall, these five major types feature an intensification of the level of regional economic integration. Next, we tour the world to visit concrete examples of these arrangements.

8-4 Regional Economic Integration in Europe

At present, the most ambitious economic integration takes place in Europe. This section (1) outlines its origin and evolution, (2) introduces its current structure, and (3) discusses its challenges.

8-4a Origin and Evolution

Although European economic integration is now often noted for its economic benefits, its origin was political in nature. Specifically, it was an effort by European statesmen to stop the historical vicious cycle of hatred and violence. In 1951, Belgium, France, Germany (then known as West Germany), Italy, Luxembourg, and the Netherlands signed the European Coal and Steel Community (ECSC) Treaty, which was the first step toward what is now the EU. There was a good reason for the six founding members and the two industries to be involved. France and Germany were the main combatants in both WWI and WWII (and major previous European wars), each having lost millions of soldiers and civilians. Reflecting the public mood, statesmen in both countries realized that such killing needed to stop. Italy had the misfortune of being dragged along and devastated whenever France and Germany went to war. The three small countries known as Benelux (Belgium, the Netherlands, and Luxembourg) had the unfortunate geographic location of being sandwiched between France and Germany, and were usually wiped out when France and Germany slugged it out. Naturally, Italy and Benelux would be happy to do anything to stop France and Germany from fighting again. Also, the industry focus on coal and steel was not an accident. These two industries traditionally

Learning Objective
Understand regional economic integration efforts in Europe, the Americas, the Asia Pacific, and Africa.

Customs union
One step beyond a free trade area (FTA), a customs union imposes common external policies on nonparticipating countries.

Common market
Combining everything a customs union has, a common market, in addition, permits the free movement of goods and people.

Economic union
Having all the features of a common market, members also coordinate and harmonize economic policies (in areas such as monetary, fiscal, and taxation) to blend their economies into a single economic entity.

Monetary union
A group of countries that use a common currency.

Political union
The integration of political and economic affairs of a region.

supplied the raw materials for war. Integrating them might help prevent future hostilities from breaking out.

In 1957, six member countries of ECSC signed the Treaty of Rome, which launched the European Economic Community (EEC)—later known as the European Community (EC). Starting as an FTA, the EEC/EC progressed to become a customs union and eventually a common market. In 1991, 12 member countries signed the Treaty on European Union in Maastricht, the Netherlands (in short, the "Maastricht Treaty") to complete the single market and establish an economic union. The title the "European Union" (EU) was officially adopted in 1993 when the Maastricht Treaty went into effect. Recently, the Lisbon Treaty, signed in 2007 and enacted in 2009, amended the Maastricht Treaty that served as a constitutional basis for the EU.

8-4b The EU Today

Headquartered in Brussels, Belgium, today's EU (see PengAtlas Map 2.4) has 28 member countries, 500 million citizens, and US$18 trillion GDP. Contributing about 26% of the world's GDP, the EU is the world's largest economy, the largest exporter and importer of goods and services, and the largest trading partner with large economies, such as the United States, China, and India. Here is how the EU describes itself in an official publication:

> The European Union is not a federation like the United States. Nor is it simply an organization for cooperation between governments, like the United Nations. Neither is it a state intended to replace existing states, but it is much more than any other organization. The EU is, in fact, unique. Never before have countries voluntarily agreed to set up common institutions to which they delegate some of their sovereignty so that decisions on specific matters of joint interest can be made democratically at a higher, in this case European, level. This pooling of sovereignty is called "European integration."[8]

The EU today is an economic union. Internal trade barriers have been mostly removed. In aviation, the EU now has a single market, which means all European carriers compete on equal terms across the EU (including domestic routes in a foreign country). US airlines are not allowed to fly between pairs of cities within Germany. However, non-German, EU airlines (such as Ireland's Ryanair) can fly between any pair of cities within Germany. On the ground, it used to take Spanish truck drivers 24 hours to cross the border into France, due to paperwork requirements and checks. Since 1992, passport and customs control within most (but not all) member countries of the EU has been disbanded, and checkpoints at border crossings are no longer manned (see In Focus 8.1). The area covered by EU countries became known as the Schengen passport-free travel zone, named after Schengen, Luxembourg, where the agreement was signed in 1985. Now, Spanish trucks can move from Spain to France non-stop, similar to how American trucks go from Texas to Oklahoma. At present, 22 of the 28 EU member countries are in the Schengen zone. Six other members are not yet in: Britain and Ireland chose to opt out, and four new members—Bulgaria, Cyprus, Romania, and Slovenia—have yet to meet requirements. (Interestingly, three non-EU member countries—Iceland, Norway, and Switzerland—are also in the Schengen area.)

As an economic union, one of the EU's proudest accomplishments—but also one of its most significant headaches—is the introduction of a common currency, the euro, initially in 12 of the EU 15 countries. Since then, six more countries have

Schengen

A passport-free travel zone within the EU.

Euro

The currency currently used in 18 EU countries.

IN FOCUS 8.1
A DAY IN EUROPEAN BUSINESS

Axel Schmies/imagebroker/Alamy

It is Tuesday morning at five o'clock, and a nearly empty freeway lies ahead of Marcus as he heads for the airport in Munich, Germany. Traveling and engaging with other cultures is part of Marcus's daily job as a manager with European responsibilities.

Marcus is Vice President Northern Europe of an entrepreneurial software company that provides computer-aided design (CAD) software for use in organizations, such as large architectural firms, municipalities, automotive suppliers, aerospace manufacturers, and media and entertainment designers. His responsibilities include defining strategies for the region, budgeting for several European countries, negotiating with new potential business partners, and conducting business reviews with his own local teams, suppliers, and partners.

After parking the car and writing down the exact location (important!), Marcus heads for International Departures. In early morning, departure times are quite reliable. His flight departs on time: two hours to read the morning news, to get an update on worldwide financials, and to enjoy a cup of tea or two and an unspectacular sandwich.

When Marcus arrives at the Warsaw airport, he finds there is less border security than in the past. Since Poland became a member of the EU and the Schengen Agreement, there are no longer any passport controls. Business travelers try to avoid checking luggage to save time, and ten minutes later Marcus is greeted by his local country manager. Unfortunately, Marcus cannot take advantage of the EU's monetary union and still has to use five different wallets. In addition to his "euro wallet" for Germany and other countries that use the euro, he needs one for Swedish krones, one for Romanian leu, one for British pounds, and finally one for Polish zloty, which is what

he is carrying today. It is quite a challenge to grab the right one when leaving home at 4:30 in the morning.

While an experienced driver takes Marcus and his country manager through Warsaw's rush-hour traffic, they discuss the latest development at the Polish office. Since joining the EU, the level of professionalism has significantly increased at all levels of management in Poland, and English has become the norm for conversations with local staff. This was not the case when Marcus started doing business in Poland in 2001. Initially, he would only communicate with the country manager directly in English. For the first year, all employees were enrolled in English-language training every Friday afternoon. Now this training has paid off, and Marcus can easily talk to everyone in the office directly.

This time, Marcus's first appointment is with a major supplier in the center of Warsaw to discuss opportunities for the coming months. After three hours of PowerPoint presentations, financial reports, and marketing reviews, he is invited for a quick business lunch. Another two hours in the car on the way to his company's Polish office in Łodz are followed by an internal staff meeting with updates by all business unit managers.

Marcus's visits to a country office typically take three days, packed with meetings and events to justify the expenses of the journey. Modern technology allows high-quality video conferencing, yet it cannot replace the extremely important human factor in business negotiations. Marcus prefers face-to-face discussions where recognizing subtle expressions on the other's face can make a difference between closing a deal and coming home empty handed.

When doing business in different European countries, Marcus faces differences in bureaucracy at almost every step. In Poland, for example, it seems that everything needs to be filed in several copies, stamped, and signed. Notaries hold the "license to print money," because more or less everything related to the administration of a company needs to be signed in the presence of a notary. One of the easiest (and most depressing) ways to discover this is by having a dinner and requesting a receipt. If you ask a waiter for receipt, after ten minutes he may come back with a huge document (three pages) that needs to be filled with the company's long tax-ID number, signed several times, and finally stamped by the restaurant. Back home in Germany, Marcus would just take his credit card receipt—that's it.

After a long day, it is time to check in at one of the business hotels. Besides the construction of highways and roads, this is an area where the progress of economic transition and development of Poland is most visible. In 2001, business travelers in Łodz had the choice of one hotel. Today, international hotel chains such as Ibis and Radisson provide facilities at very good standards. It is past ten o'clock at night when Marcus returns from his business dinner to the hotel, and he will have to prepare for another busy day in European business.

Source: This case is fictitious. It was adapted from M. W. Peng & K. E. Meyer, 2011, *International Business* (pp. 228–229), London: Cengage Learning EMEA.

joined the euro zone, resulting in a total of 18 member countries. Today's euro zone accounts for approximately 330 million people and 21% of world GDP (relative to 24% for the United States). The euro was introduced in two phases. First, it became available in 1999 as "virtual money" only used for financial transactions but not in circulation. Second, in 2002, the euro was introduced as banknotes and coins. The EU printed 14.25 billion banknotes and minted 56 billion coins—with a total value of €660 billion (US$558 billion). The new banknotes would cover the distance between the earth and the moon *five* times (!).[9] Overall, the introduction of the euro was a great success.

Adopting the euro has three great benefits (Table 8.2). First, it reduces currency conversion costs. Travelers and businesses no longer need to pay processing fees to convert currencies for tourist activities or hedging purposes (see Chapter 7). Remember the five wallets stuffed with different currencies that Marcus had to carry in In Focus 8.1? Second, direct and transparent price comparison is now possible, thus channeling more resources toward more competitive firms. Third, adopting the euro imposes strong macroeconomic discipline on participating governments. Prior to adopting the euro, different governments independently determined exchange rates. Italy, for example, sharply devalued its lira in 1992 and 1995. While Italian exports became cheaper and more competitive overseas, other EU members (especially France) were furious. But Italy can no longer devalue its currency, although it has been engulfed in an economic crisis. Also, when confronting recessions, governments often printed more currency and increased spending. Such actions cause inflation, which may spill over to neighboring countries.

Table 8.2 Benefits and Costs of Adopting the Euro

Benefits	Costs
• Reduce currency conversion costs. • Facilitate direct price comparison. • Impose monetary discipline on governments.	• Unable to implement independent monetary policy. • Limit the flexibility in fiscal policy (in areas such as deficit spending).

Euro zone

The 18 EU countries that currently use the euro as the official currency.

By adopting the euro, euro zone countries agreed to abolish monetary policy (such as manipulating exchange rates and printing more currency) as a tool to solve macroeconomic problems. These efforts provide much-needed macroeconomic stability. Overall, the euro has boosted intra-EU trade by about 10%. Commanding a quarter of global foreign currency reserves, the euro has quickly established itself as the only credible rival to the dollar.

However, there are also significant costs involved. The first, noted above, is the loss of ability to implement independent monetary policy. Especially since 2008, economic life for many EU countries without the option of devaluation is tough. The possibility of leaving the euro zone has surfaced in public discussion in some countries.[10] The second cost is the lack of flexibility in implementing fiscal policy in areas such as deficit spending. When a country runs into fiscal difficulties, it may be faced with inflation, high interest rates, and a run on its currency. When a number of countries share a common currency, the risks are spread. But some countries can become "free riders," because they may not need to fix their own fiscal problems—other, more responsible members will have to shoulder the burden (see the Closing Case).

8-4c The EU's Challenges

Politically, the EU and its predecessors—the ECSC, the EEC, and the EC—have delivered more than half a century of peace and prosperity, and have turned some Cold War enemies into members. Although some people complain about the EU's huge expenses and bureaucratic meetings, they need to be reminded that one day spent on meetings is one day member countries are not shooting at one another. Given that most European countries, until WWII, had been involved in wars as their primary conflict resolution mechanism, negotiating to resolve differences via EU platforms is not only cheaper but also far more peaceful. For this extraordinary accomplishment, the EU—in the middle of a major economic crisis—received the Nobel *Peace* Prize in 2012.

Economically, the EU has launched a single currency and has built a single market in which people, goods, services, and capital can move freely—known as the "four freedoms of movement"—within the core Schengen area (although not throughout the entire EU). While the accomplishments are enviable in the eyes of other regional organizations, the EU has been engulfed in a midlife crisis.[11] Significant challenges lie ahead, especially in terms of (1) internal divisions and (2) enlargement concerns.

Internally, there is a significant debate on whether the EU should be an economic and political union, or just an economic union. One school of thought, led by France, argues that an economic union should inevitably evolve toward a political union, through which Europe speaks as "one voice." Proponents of this view frequently invoke the famous term enshrined in the 1957 Treaty of Rome, "ever closer union."[12] Another school of thought, led by Britain, views the EU as primarily an economic union, which should focus on free trade, pure and simple.

The 2010–2012 bailouts to rescue Greece (and Ireland and Portugal) have intensified this debate. While Germany reluctantly agreed to lead bailout efforts, Germany demanded that the EU-wide "economic governance" be strengthened, and that insolvent countries have to lose some of their economic sovereignty by having their budgets approved (or vetoed) by the EU. While this is viewed as a step toward closer political union, Germany does not share France's political motivation for an "ever closer union." In fact, the German media has called for Germany to withdraw from the euro zone in order to avoid the burden of paying for other countries' problems. However, abandoning the euro is not realistic for Germany. Germany ends up being a "reluctant hegemon" (see the Closing Case).

Britain, on the other hand, has seen its influence reduced. In 2011, Britain vetoed a new treaty supported by 26 EU members to enhance the "economic governance" for the euro zone. All EU treaties had to be signed off by all members—in this case, for a treaty on the euro zone governance, even members that did not use the euro (such as Britain) had to sign off. Therefore, Britain's veto torpedoed the whole treaty. Other EU members were forced to seek a separate pact to enforce greater fiscal discipline, which could be done despite the British veto. In 2013, British Prime Minister David Cameron announced that he would put the UK membership in the EU for a referendum by 2017. While his "bulldog spirit" won praise from the British Eurosceptics crowd, he was "gambling with his country's future."[13] Other EU leaders were infuriated, because Cameron was reigniting old debates settled through compromise a long time ago—in the 1970s, Britain's decision to join the EEC was itself the result of a referendum. France seems to emerge as a real winner. This is because France can now secure "a long-cherished French ambition: an agreement on holding frequent summits of EU leaders from an inner core of countries, excluding Britain."[14] Britain then finds it may have little influence or leverage in further deliberations within the EU.

There are also significant concerns associated with enlargement. The EU's largest expansion took place in 2004, with ten new members. Eight of them—the Czech Republic, Estonia, Hungary, Latvia, Lithuania, Poland, Slovakia, and Slovenia—were former eastern bloc Central and Eastern Europe (CEE) countries. Three of these—Estonia, Latvia, and Lithuania—had previously been part of the Soviet Union. While taking on ten new members was a political triumph, it was also an economic burden. The ten new members constituted 20% of the overall population, but contributed only 9% to GDP and had an average GDP per capita that was 46% of the average for the (pre-2004) EU 15.[15] In 2007, Bulgaria and Romania joined the EU and brought the average down further. In 2013, Croatia joined. With low economic growth and high unemployment throughout the EU and severe economic crisis in the so-called PIGS (Portugal, Ireland/Italy, Greece, and Spain) countries, many EU citizens are sick and tired of taking on additional burdens to absorb new members. Many EU 15 countries have restricted immigration from these new members.

Another major debate regarding enlargement is Turkey, whose average income is even lower. In addition, its large Muslim population is also a concern for a predominantly Christian EU. If Turkey were to join, its population of 73 million would make it the second-most populous EU country behind only Germany, whose population is 83 million now (but is declining). The weight of EU countries in voting is based (mostly) on population. Given the current demographic trends (high birth rates in Turkey and low birth rates in the EU), if Turkey were to join the EU, by 2020 it would become the most populous and thus the most powerful member by commanding most significant voting power. Turkey's combination of low incomes, high birthrates relative to current EU members, and Muslim majority visibly concern current member countries, especially given the history of Christian–Muslim tension in Europe.

Since 2008, the EU's challenges were magnified. A total of eight members were engulfed in embarrassing financial crises that had to be bailed out by other members (and the International Monetary Fund [IMF]): Hungary (2008), Lativia (2008), Romania (2009), Greece (2010), Ireland (2010), Portugal (2011), Cyprus

(2011), and Spain (2012). Not surprisingly, Germany and other relatively well-off EU countries, in the middle of their own Great Recession, were reluctant to foot the bill to bail out other countries (see the Closing Case). While each crisis was painful in its own ways, the Greek crisis was particularly gut-wrenching, resulting in calls for Greece to exit or to be expelled (a "Grexit" scenario). By 2014, the worst seemed to be over and any exit scenario was no longer entertained. Then in 2014, with Russia's intervention in Ukraine, the EU felt compelled to join the US-led sanctions on Russia, inflicting economic wounds on itself by abandoning hard-to-win markets in Russia (see Chapter 2 Opening Case).

Overall, we can view the EU enlargement as a miniature version of globalization, and the "enlargement fatigue" as part of the recent backlash against globalization (see Chapter 1). Given the accomplishments and challenges, what does the future of the EU hold? One possible scenario is that there will be an "EU à la carte," where different members pick and choose certain mechanisms to join and other mechanisms to opt out of. Seeking consensus among 28 members during negotiations may be simply impractical. If every country's representative were to spend ten minutes on opening remarks, *nearly five hours* would be gone before discussions even begin. The translation and interpretation among the 23 official languages now cost the EU €1.1 billion (US$1.4 billion) per year.[16] Since not every country needs to take part in everything, ad hoc groupings of member countries with similar interests are increasingly common, and discussions are more efficient.

Learning Objective
Understand regional economic integration efforts in Europe, the Americas, the Asia Pacific, and Africa.

8-5 Regional Economic Integration in the Americas

Two sets of regional economic integration efforts in the Americas have taken place: one in North America and the other in South America.

8-5a North America: North American Free Trade Agreement (NAFTA)

NAFTA is an FTA among Canada, Mexico, and the United States. Launched in 1994, NAFTA has no shortage of hyperbole and controversy. Because of the very different levels of economic development, NAFTA was labeled "one of the most radical free trade experiments in history."[17] Politically, the Mexican government was interested in cementing market liberalization reforms by demonstrating its commitment to free trade. Economically, Mexico was interested in securing preferential treatment for 80% of its exports. Consequently, by the stroke of a pen, Mexico declared itself a *North* American country. Many Americans, on the other hand, thought it was not the best time to open the borders, as the US unemployment rate was 7% at that time. Texas billionaire H. Ross Perot, a presidential candidate in 1992, described NAFTA's potential destruction of thousands of US jobs as a "giant sucking sound."

As NAFTA celebrated its 20th anniversary in 2014, NAFTA's supporters largely won the argument. In two decades, trilateral merchandise trade grew from US$289 billion in 1993 to US$1.1 trillion—a nearly fourfold increase. Approximately US$1.8 billion goods and service cross the border every day—US$1.2 million every *minute*.[18] US trade with Canada tripled and US trade with Mexico increased by 506%—while US trade with the rest of the world grew 279%. In two decades, Mexico's GDP per capita rose almost tripled to US$10,650 (ranked 64th in the world, based on nominal GDP)—more than 40% higher than China's US$7,000.

While many Americans and Canadians think of Mexicans as "poor" and "infested with crimes"—thanks to the negative (and typically one-sided) media—Mexico is the second-largest importer of US goods (next only to Canada), imports more US goods than China, and absorbs more US imports than Britain, France, and Germany combined.[19] Running the 14th largest economy in the world with a number of advanced manufacturing industries, such as automobile, pharmaceuticals, and aerospace (see the Opening Case), Mexico, according to the *Economist,* has been "NAFTA's biggest beneficiary."[20]

What about jobs? In brief, job destruction on a large scale never materialized. *Maquiladora* (export assembly) factories blossomed under NAFTA, with jobs peaking at 1.3 million in 2000. Yet, no "giant sucking sound" was heard. Approximately 300,000 US jobs were lost due to NAFTA, but about 100,000 jobs were added. The net loss was small, since the US economy generated 20 million new jobs during the first decade of NAFTA. NAFTA's impact on job destruction versus creation in the United States was essentially a wash.[21] But a hard count on jobs misses another subtle, but important, benefit. NAFTA has allowed US firms to *preserve* more US jobs, because 40% of the value of US imports from Mexico and 25% from Canada is actually made in USA—in comparison, only 10% of the value of US imports from China is made in USA. Without NAFTA, entire industries might be lost, rather than just the labor-intensive portions.

As NAFTA celebrated its 20th anniversary, not all was rosy. Opponents of globalization in both Canada and the United States no longer focus on the negative impact of competition from Mexico, but rather on China and India. Despite the impressive gains in their country, many Mexicans feel betrayed by NAFTA. Thanks to Chinese competition, many US, Canadian, European, and Japanese multinationals have shifted some of their factory work to China, which has now replaced Mexico as the second largest exporter to the United States (after Canada).[22] About 1,000 *maquiladora* factories have closed down since 2000. But rising wages in China and high fuel costs have recently led some multinationals to re-locate back to Mexico.

8-5b South America: Andean Community, Mercosur, USAN/UNASUR, and CAFTA

Despite NAFTA's imperfections, it is much more effective than the two customs unions in South America: Andean Community and Mercosur. Members of Andean Community (launched in 1969) and Mercosur (launched in 1991) are mostly countries on the *western* (Pacific-facing) and *eastern* (Atlantic-facing) sides of the Andean mountains, respectively (see PengAtlas Map 2.5). There is much mutual suspicion and rivalry between both organizations as well as within each of them.[23] Mercosur is relatively more protectionist and suspicious of the United States, whereas Andean Community is more pro-free trade.

Neither regional initiative has been effective, in part because only about 5%–20% of members' trade is within the Andean Community and Mercosur, respectively. Their largest trading partner, the United States, lies outside the region. An FTA with the United States, not among themselves, would generate the most significant benefits. For this reason, Chile, Colombia, Panama, and Peru signed bilateral FTAs with the United States, and reaped the benefits of higher economic growth than other countries.[24]

In 2008, Andean Community and Mercosur countries agreed to form the Union of South American Nations (USAN, more commonly known by its Spanish acronym, UNASUR, which refers to *Unión de Naciones Suramericanas*). Inspired by the EU,

Andean Community

A customs union in South America that was launched in 1969.

Mercosur

A customs union in South America that was launched in 1991.

Union of South American States (USAN/UNASUR)

A regional integration mechanism integrating two existing customs unions (Andean Community and Mercosur) in South America.

USAN/UNASUR announced its intention to eventually adopt a common currency, parliament, and passport. However, progress has been slow.

One regional accomplishment is the United States–Dominican Republic–Central America Free Trade Agreement (CAFTA), which took effect in 2005. Modeled after NAFTA, CAFTA is between "a whale and six minnows" (five Central American countries—Costa Rica, El Salvador, Guatemala, Honduras, and Nicaragua—plus the Dominican Republic). Although small, the six CAFTA countries collectively represent the second-largest US export market in Latin America (behind only Mexico). Globally, CAFTA is the tenth largest US export market, importing more than Russia, India, and Indonesia *combined.*[25]

Learning Objective

Understand regional economic integration efforts in Europe, the Americas, the Asia Pacific, and Africa.

8-6 Regional Economic Integration in the Asia Pacific

This section introduces regional integration efforts (1) between Australia and New Zealand, (2) in Southeast Asia, and (3) throughout the Asia Pacific. Their scale and scope differ tremendously.

8-6a Australia–New Zealand Closer Economic Relations Trade Agreement (ANZCERTA or CER)

The Australia–New Zealand Closer Economics Relations Trade Agreement (ANZCERTA or CER), launched in 1983, turned the historical rivalry between Australia and New Zealand into a partnership. As an FTA, the CER removed tariffs and NTBs over time. For example, both countries agreed not to charge exporters from another country for "dumping." Citizens from both countries can also freely work and reside in the other country. Mostly due to the relatively high level of geographic proximity and cultural homogeneity, CER has been regarded as a very successful FTA.

8-6b Association of Southeast Asian Nations (ASEAN)

Founded in 1967, the Association of Southeast Asian Nations (ASEAN) was inspired by the EU's success. In 1992, the ASEAN Free Trade Area (AFTA) was set up. ASEAN suffers from a similar problem that Latin American countries face: ASEAN's main trading partners—the US, the EU, Japan, and China—are outside the region. Intra-ASEAN trade usually accounts for less than a quarter of total trade. The benefits of AFTA, thus, may be limited. In response, ASEAN in 2002 signed an ASEAN-China Free Trade Agreement (ACFTA), which was launched in 2010. Given the increasingly strong competition in terms of Chinese exports and China-bound FDI that could have come to ASEAN, ACFTA hopes to turn such rivalry into a partnership. ACFTA is estimated to boost ASEAN's exports to China by 48% and China's exports to ASEAN by 55%, thus raising ASEAN's GDP by 0.9% and China's by 0.3%.[26]

United States-Dominican Republic-Central America Free Trade Agreement (CAFTA)

A free trade agreement between the United States and five Central American countries and the Dominican Republic.

Australia–New Zealand Closer Economic Relations Trade Agreement (ANZCERTA or CER)

A free trade agreement between Australia and New Zealand.

Association of Southeast Asian Nations (ASEAN)

The organization underpinning regional economic integration in Southeast Asia.

8-6c Asia-Pacific Economic Cooperation (APEC) and Trans-Pacific Partnership (TPP)

While ASEAN was deepening its integration, Australia was afraid that it might be left out and suggested in 1989 that ASEAN and CER countries form the

Asia-Pacific Economic Cooperation (APEC). Given the lack of a global heavyweight in both ASEAN and CER, Japan was invited. While the Japanese happily agreed to join, ASEAN and CER countries also feared that Japan might dominate the group and create a de facto "yen bloc." During WWII, Japan invaded most countries, bombed Darwin and attacked Sydney harbor in Australia (see the movie *Australia*). Bitter memories of Japanese wartime atrocities seemed to die hard. At that time, China was far less significant economically than it is now, and thus could hardly counterbalance Japan.

Then the United States requested to join APEC, citing its long West Coast that would qualify it as a Pacific country. Economically, the United States did not want to be left out of the most dynamically growing region in the world. Politically, the United States was interested in containing Japanese influence in any Asian regional deals. While the United States could certainly serve as a counterweight for Japan, the US membership would also change the character of APEC, which had been centered on ASEAN and CER. To make its APEC membership less odd, the United States brought on board two of its NAFTA partners, Canada and Mexico. Canada and Mexico were equally interested in the economic benefits but probably cared less about the US political motives. Once the floodgates for membership were open, Chile, Peru, and Russia all eventually got in, each citing their long Pacific coastlines.

Today, APEC's 21 member economies (shown in PengAtlas Map 2.6) span four continents, are home to 2.6 billion people, contribute 46% of world trade, and command 54% of world GDP, making it the largest regional integration grouping by geographic area. While it is nice to include "everyone," APEC may be too big. Essentially as a talking shop, APEC (nicknamed "a perfect excuse to chat") provides a forum for members to make commitments that are largely rhetorical (Figure 8.5). In part because APEC is too big and too difficult to get anything meaningful done, a newer and smaller Trans-Pacific Partnership (TPP) has been developing (see In Focus 8.2).

Figure 8.5   **US and Chinese Presidents Meet at the APEC Summit, Beijing, November 2014**

Source: *Economist*, 2014, Bridge over troubled water, November 15: 15.

Asia-Pacific Economic Cooperation (APEC)

The official title for regional economic integration involving 21 member economies around the Pacific.

Trans-Pacific Partnership (TPP)

A multilateral free trade agreement being negotiated by 12 Asia Pacific countries.

IN FOCUS 8.2

DOES THE TPP HAVE A FUTURE?

Launched by four small APEC members (Brunei, Chile, New Zealand, and Singapore) in 2005, the Trans-Pacific Partnership (TPP) is a multilateral free trade agreement (FTA). A number of additional APEC members—Australia, Canada, Malaysia, Mexico Peru, Japan, the United States, and Vietnam—are negotiating to join the group. Although smaller and less complex than APEC (and certainly simpler than the WTO), the TPP talks have run into a similar bunch of problems: (1) agriculture, (2) intellectual property (IP), (3) investor-state dispute settlement (ISDS), and (4) domestic politics.

As ever, the United States and Japan fight over agricultural subsidies, especially in beef and pork— a small problem in the larger scheme of things. In the United States, less than 1% of GDP comes from beef and pork production. In Japan, a country with 46 million households, only 100,000 households are involved in the beef and pork sectors. But in October 2014, the bilateral talks collapsed. The Japanese trade minister stormed out of a working lunch, leaving only his sandwiches on the table. Ironically, on many larger issues, both countries agree with each other.

In IP, the United States has sought the TPP to agree with tighter IP protection that would go *beyond* TRIPS. This makes sense from a US standpoint. In 2010, 40% of worldwide payments made to IP rights holders—nearly US$100 billion—went to Americans and American firms. These sums matched the profits from the export of aircraft, grain, and business services, the three leading US export sectors. Unfortunately, other countries are not so interested. Weaker IP protection enables faster diffusion of innovation (such as generic drugs) to less-developed countries—a US practice for about 100 years in the 19th century when the United States was a developing country itself.

Designed to deter governments from expropriating foreign assets, ISDS allows foreign firms to launch arbitration to sue governments that allegedly deny their rights under an FTA. For example, Philip Morris sued the Australian government for its requirements for nasty pictures of lung cancer victims on cigarette packages. Lone Pine, a US firm, sued the Canadian province of Quebec for its ban on fracking. Taking the painful lesson, Australia opposes having ISDS in the TPP. In comparison, the WTO only allows national governments, not private firms, to launch such cases.

Domestic politics is messy in every country. Lacking the "fast track authority" (formally known as trade promotion authority) since 2007, Presidents George W. Bush and Barack Obama cannot negotiate FTAs and then ask Congress to vote "go or no go" without the ability to amend any negotiated deals. Congressional intervention can, thus, be meticulous. For example, in July 2014, 140 members of the House of Representatives—107 Republicans and 33 Democrats—signed a letter demanding that Japan drop all farm tariffs; otherwise, forget about the TPP. Other countries understandably do not take US negotiators very seriously, since regardless of how the deal is reached, Congress is likely to tear it apart.

In an effort to aim for a "grand bargain," the TPP runs the risk of becoming another Doha, with endless negotiations that never reach agreement. Even if the TPP can be concluded, since all members are APEC members, what is the relationship between APEC and TPP remains to be seen. Finally, by deliberately excluding China (the second-largest economy in APEC and in the world), how meaningful the TPP will become is also a huge question mark. In Otober 2014, at the APEC summit meeting in Beijing with Obama in attendance, Chinese President Xi Jingping openly called for the establishmenr of a Free Trade Area of the Asia-Pacific (FTAAP) consisting all 21 members of APEC. Stay tuned . . .

Sources: Based on (1) *Economist*, 2012, Trading winds, May 19: 50; (2) *Economist*, 2014, Stalemate, October 4: 47; (3) *Economist*, 2014, Bridge over troubled water, November 15: 15; (4) *Economist*, 2014, The Pacific age, November 15: Special Report; (5) B. Gordon, 2012, Trading up in Asia, *Foreign Affairs*, July: 17–22; (6) R. Katz, 2014, The Trans-Pacific Partnership: Lessons from negotiations, *NBR Analysis Brief*, September, Seattle: National Bureau of Asian Research; (7) M. W. Peng, D. Ahlstrom, S. Carraher, & W. Shi, 2014, How history can inform the debate over intellectual property, working paper, Jindal School of Management, University of Texas at Dallas; (8) US Trade Representative, 2015, Trans-Pacific Partnership, www.ustr.gov.

Figure 8.6 **Regional Economic Integration in Africa**

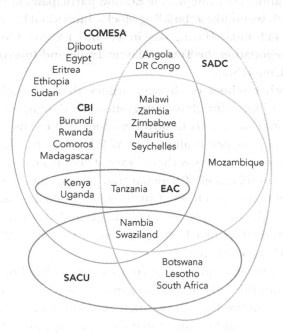

Source: J. Bhagwati, 2002, *Free Trade Today* (p. 115), Princeton, NJ: Princeton University Press. CBI—Cross Border Initiative; COMESA—Common Market for Eastern and Southern Africa; EAC—Commission for East Africa Co-operation; SADC—Southern African Development Community; SACU—Southern African Customs Union.

8-7 Regional Economic Integration in Africa

Regional integration initiatives in Africa are both numerous and ineffective. Because one country often has memberships in multiple regional deals, a map using one color to indicate one country's membership in one regional deal will be difficult to draw. Consequently, Figure 8.6 draws a "spaghetti bowl" to (hopefully) more clearly capture the various African regional deals—this (hopelessly) complicated diagram also suggests that no sane professor will want to quiz students on the membership of these different deals on your exam (!). While various African countries are interested in reaping the benefits from regional economic integration, there is relatively little trade within Africa (amounting to less than 10% of the continent's total trade) whereby protectionism often prevails. Frustration with a current regional deal often leads to a new deal, often with a different set of countries, eventually leading to a messy "spaghetti bowl" in Figure 8.5.

8-8 Debates and Extensions

In addition to some debates discussed earlier (such as what caused Doha to collapse and how Greece can be rescued), this section outlines two additional major debates: (1) building blocks versus stumbling blocks, and (2) impact of the WTO.

8-8a Building Blocks versus Stumbling Blocks

In the absence of global economic integration, regional economic integration is often regarded as the next best thing to facilitate free trade—at least within a region.

Learning Objective
Understand regional economic integration efforts in Europe, the Americas, the Asia Pacific, and Africa.

Learning Objective
Participate in two leading debates concerning global and regional economic integration.

Some may even argue that regional integration represents building blocks for eventual global integration. For example, the EU now participates in WTO negotiations as one entity, which seems like a "building block." Individual EU member countries no longer enter such talks. Having concluded an FTA with Canada in 2013, the EU is currently negotiating the Trans-Atlantic Trade and Investment Partnership (TTIP) with the United States.

However, another school of thought argues that regional integration has become stumbling blocks for global integration. By design, regional integration provides preferential treatments to members and, at the same time, *discriminates* against non-members (which is allowed by WTO rules). It is still a form of protectionism centered on "us versus them," except "us" is now an expanded group of countries. The proliferation of regional trade deals, thus, may be alarming. In the first few decades after WWII, the United States avoided regional deals. In part alarmed by the EU, the United States, with Canada and Mexico, launched NAFTA. Likewise, China signed its first FTA agreement (ACFTA) in 2002 with ASEAN. Clearly, the trend is accelerating.

Of course, all countries that are party to some regional deals participate in WTO talks, arguing that they are walking on two legs: regional and global. Yet, "instead of walking on two legs," critics such as Columbia professor Jagdish Bhagwati argue, "we have wound up on all fours"—crawling with slow progress.[27] This sorry state is triggered by the pursuit of individual countries' interest in a globally uncoordinated fashion. As regional deals proliferate, non-members feel that they are squeezed out, and begin plotting their own regional deals (see Figure 8.6). Very soon, we end up having a global "spaghetti bowl."

8-8b Does the WTO Really Matter?

China's experience since it acceded to WTO membership offers a resounding "Yes" to this question. After 15 years of long and arduous negotiations, China joined the WTO in 2001. Since then, it joined the "ranks of the world's trading superheavyweights," in the words of the US Ambassador to China.[28] Between 2001 and 2010, China dethroned Germany to become the world's champion merchandise exporter and became the world's third-largest merchandise importer (behind the United States and Germany) (see Chapter 5 Opening Case). In the crucial US–China trade, between 2001 and 2010, China's exports to the US (which the US counted as US imports) grew by 260%, and China became the second-largest exporter to the US (behind Canada). China's imports from the US (which the US counted as US exports) jumped more than 400%—in the same period, US exports to the rest of the world only grew 55%. In 2001, China was the ninth-largest US export market. In 2010, it became the third-largest US export market (behind Canada and Mexico).

In short, from an institution-based view, China's experience offers a compelling case that the WTO matters. However, globally, this point is being debated. Frustration associated with the collapse of Doha and other WTO initiatives hinges on a crucial assumption that the WTO actually matters. But this assumption itself is now subject to debate. Academic research has failed to find any compelling evidence that the WTO (and the GATT) has a significantly positive effect on trade.

True, trade has blossomed since the GATT was established in 1948. But Andrew Rose, a professor at the University of California, Berkeley, reports that trade has blossomed for the GATT/WTO members and nonmembers alike. Therefore, it is difficult to find that the GATT/WTO membership *caused* more trade.[29] An *Economist* article thus commented that "the 'hoopla' and 'hype' that surrounds the WTO's successes, failures, and admissions of new members are just that: hoopla and hype."[30] Another *Economist* article asked: "Can the WTO save itself from irrelevance?"[31]

Defenders of the WTO point out Rose's methodological imperfections.[32] Beyond such methodological hair-splitting, in the real world, the collapse of Doha has not caused any noticeable collapse of global trade (although the onslaught of the 2008–2009 Great Recession did severe damage). So, perhaps the WTO does not matter much? This debate is much more than just academic. Inspired by China's experience, Russia recently joined the WTO in 2012—after a record-breaking 19 years of arduous accession negotiations. Assuming governments in 160 WTO member countries are rational (Proposition 1 in the institution-based view), one has to believe that there must be some benefits associated with WTO membership.

8-9 Management Savvy

Learning Objective
Draw implications for action.

Of the two major perspectives on global business (institution-based and resource-based views), this chapter has focused on the institution-based view. In order to address the question, "What determines the success and failure around the globe?" the entire chapter has been devoted to an introduction of the rules of the game as institutions governing global and regional economic integration. How does this knowledge help managers? Shown in the Opening Case, managers such as those managing Bombardier's launch of the Learjet 85 need to combine the insights from the institution-based view with those from the resource-based view to come up with strategies and solutions on how their firms can capitalize on opportunities presented by global and regional economic integration. Two broad implications for action emerge (Table 8.3).

First, given the slowdown of multilateralism and the acceleration of regionalism, managers are advised to focus their attention more at regional than global levels.[33] To a large extent, they are already doing that. The majority of multinational enterprises (MNEs) generate most of their revenues in their home region (such as within the EU or NAFTA). The largest MNEs may have a presence all over the world, but their center of gravity (measured by revenues) is often still their home region. Thus, they are not really very "global." Regional strategies make sense, because most countries within a region share some cultural, economic, and geographic similarities.[34] From a resource-based standpoint, most firms are better prepared to compete on regional rather than global levels. Despite the hoopla associated with "global strategies," managers, in short, must think local and downplay global (while not necessarily abandoning global).

Table 8.3	Implications for Action

- Think regional, downplay global.
- Understand the rules of the game and their transitions, at both global and regional levels.

Second, managers must also understand the rules of the game and their transitions, both at global and regional levels. While the MFA was phased out in 2005, numerous managers at textile firms who had become comfortable under the MFA's protection cried out loud for their lack of preparation. In fact, they had 30 *years* to prepare for such eventuality. When the MFA was signed in 1974, it was agreed that it would be phased out by 2005. The typical attitude that "We don't care about (trade) politics" can lead to a failure in due diligence. The best managers expect their firm strategies to shift over time, by constantly deciphering the changes in the "big picture" and being willing to take advantage of new opportunities brought by global and regional trade deals.

CHAPTER SUMMARY/LEARNING OBJECTIVES

8-1 Make the case for global economic integration.

- There are both political and economic benefits for global economic integration.

8-2 Understand the evolution of the GATT and the WTO, including current challenges.

- The GATT (1948–1994) significantly reduced tariff rates on merchandise trade.
- The WTO (1995–present) was set up not only to incorporate the GATT, but also to cover trade in services, intellectual property, trade dispute settlement, and peer review of trade policy.
- The Doha Round to promote more trade and development has failed to accomplish its goals thus far.

8-3 Make the case for regional economic integration.

- Political and economic benefits for regional integration are similar to those for global integration.
- Regional integration may undermine global integration and lead to some loss of countries' sovereignty.

8-4 Understand regional economic integration efforts in Europe, the Americas, the Asia Pacific, and Africa.

- The EU has delivered more than half a century of peace and prosperity, launched a single currency, and constructed a single market. Its challenges include internal divisions and enlargement concerns.
- Despite problems, NAFTA has significantly boosted trade and investment among members.
- Regional integration in the Asia Pacific centers on CER, ASEAN, APEC, and TPP.
- Regional integration deals in Africa are both numerous and ineffective.

8-5 Participate in two leading debates concerning global and regional economic integration.

- (1) Building blocks versus stumbling blocks, and (2) the impact of the WTO.

8-6 Draw implications for action.

- Think regional, downplay global.
- Understand the rules of the game and their transitions, at both global and regional levels.

KEY TERMS

Andean Community, 253

Asia-Pacific Economic Cooperation (APEC), 255

Association of Southeast Asian Nations (ASEAN), 254

Australia-New Zealand Closer Economic Relations Trade Agreement (ANZCERTA or CER), 254

Common market, 246

Customs union, 246

Doha Round, 242

Economic union, 246

Euro, 247

Euro zone, 249

European Union (EU), 238

Free trade area (FTA), 245

General Agreement on Tariffs and Trade (GATT), 238

General Agreement on Trade in Services (GATS), 241

Global economic integration, 238

Mercosur, 253

Monetary union, 246

Multilateral trading system, 240

Non-discrimination, 240

North American Free Trade Agreement (NAFTA), 238

Political union, 246

Regional economic integration, 238

Schengen, 247

Trade-Related Aspects of Intellectual Property Rights (TRIPS), 241

Trans-Pacific Partnership (TPP), 255

Union of South American States (USAN/ UNASUR), 253

United States-Dominican Republic-Central America Free Trade Agreement (CAFTA), 254

World Trade Organization (WTO), 238

REVIEW QUESTIONS

1. *ON CULTURE:* Suppose the people of a given country place a very high value on their economic independence and control over their economic destiny. However, suppose the leaders of that country wish to join the EU and also use the euro instead of their own currency. What objections are leaders likely to encounter from their citizens? Do you agree with those objections? Why or why not? What would you recommend that the leaders use as a response to their citizens in order to persuade them to join?

2. Refer to PengAtlas Map 2.4 (European Union) and note those EU members that use the euro. Note also PengAtlas Map 3.4 (Top 10 and Bottom 10 Countries by GDP) and compare it to Map 2.4. Which country that is part of the top 10 in GDP and is also part of the EU does not use the euro? What are the pros and cons of it having its own currency? In your opinion, if it were to adopt the euro, which would gain more—that country or those countries that currently use the euro?

3. Refer to PengAtlas Maps 2.5 (Regional Economic Integration in South America) and 2.6 (Regional Integration in the Asia Pacific). Why have these examples of economic integration not been as successful as the EU and NAFTA? In your opinion, what do you see as the future for economic integration outside the EU and NAFTA?

4. How can economic integration produce the type of political benefits covered in this chapter?

5. How has the GATT/WTO played a role facilitating global economic integration?

6. What institutional arrangements exist for trade dispute settlement?

7. In what ways are the benefits of global and regional integration similar?

8. How may regional integration have a negative effect on global trade and global integration?

9. What do you personally believe about the value of the WTO? Explain why you feel the way you do.

10. Why do some believe that one should think regional and downplay global? Do you agree? Why?

11. What do you recommend that managers do in order to be prepared for changes in the rules of the game?

CRITICAL DISCUSSION QUESTIONS:

1. The Doha Round collapsed because many countries believed that no deal was better than a bad deal. Do you agree or disagree with this approach? Why?

2. Will Turkey become a full-fledged member of the EU? Why or why not?

3. *ON ETHICS:* Critics argue that the WTO single-mindedly promotes trade at the expense of the environment. Therefore, trade—or more broadly, globalization—needs to slow down. What is your view on the relationship between trade and the environment?

4. *ON ETHICS:* For the €750 billion European Stability Mechanism, even Sweden and Poland (EU members that do not use the euro) felt they had enough at stake to contribute. But Britain (another EU member that does not use the euro) decided not to contribute any funds. As a British official, how do you defend this decision?

BUSINESS
INSIGHTS
GLOBAL

GLOBAL ACTION

1. The WTO membership is viewed by some as a signal of a country's ability to guarantee and protect trade among companies in stable macroeconomic conditions. Since your company is looking to expand internationally for the first time since 1999, a list of countries that have been admitted to the WTO since 2000 is required. This will update your company's market-entry initiative so that it can review the international opportunities more thoroughly.

2. Your firm is considering developing business in South America. Many in your company are aware that there is considerable economic cooperation currently underway in the region. Identify at least one regional trade agreement and its member countries in South America. Then discuss the pros and cons of expanding to member countries of this regional trade agreement vis-a-vis non-member countries.

CLOSING CASE

The German Question in the European Union

© Santiago Cornejo/Shutterstock.com

Since the German unification in 1871, the German Question has never ceased to provoke debate in Germany and beyond. The question is about the proper role of Germany, which may be too big for Europe but too small for the world—as former US secretary of state Henry Kissinger famously put it. With the fourth-largest economy in the world and the largest in Europe, today's Germany accounts for one-fifth of all EU GDP, generates a quarter of all EU exports, and possesses an enviably balanced budget. In 2013, Germany was the third-largest merchandise exporter with US$1.45 trillion exported, and enjoyed a record-breaking surplus (US$270 billion—the highest ever in world history by any country). Strong, united, and rich, Germany is the beacon of hope for EU member countries, such as Greece and Cyprus, infested with unsustainable debt loads. Mean, bossy, and selfish, Germany also provokes a ton of resentment from the very countries that it has rescued. Prime Minister Angela Merkel has been portrayed as a Nazi with Hitler-style moustache in street protests and the press in Greece, Cyprus, and elsewhere. Of course, if Germany chooses not to bail out certain member countries in trouble, it would have been resented even more.

Labeled the "reluctant hegemon" by the *Economist*, Germany is reluctant to play an active leadership role. But without German leadership, practically nothing gets done in the EU. This dilemma stems from two sources. First, in terms of "do's and don'ts," German history is full of lessons of "don'ts." Even the German word for leader, *Führer*, brings up terrible memories of Nazism. Being aware of the year 2014 being the 100th anniversary of the outbreak of WWI and the 25th anniversary of the fall of the Berlin Wall, many Germans prefer their country to be a larger Switzerland: economically thriving, politically modest, and geopolitically enjoying splendid isolation.

Second, Germans, who themselves have suffered from the Great Recession since 2008, do not feel compelled to bail out others. Germany itself "bit the bullet" in the early 2000s by holding wage levels down. Since German labor costs only rose by 5% in one decade (2004–2014), the country was able to largely resist offshoring and to enhance its export competitiveness. Southern Europeans, according to the Germans, got everything wrong.

Exhibit A: Greece. What led to its mess? Consumer demand increase and government spending binge fueled by the 2002 adoption of the euro and the 2004 Olympics. Excessive borrowing, budget deficits (15% of GDP), and crushing national debt (€300 billion—115% of GDP) with unserviceable payments. Widespread corruption and tax evasion. The shadow (informal) economy was estimated to be between 20% and 30% of GDP. In 2010, the Greek government had to ask for help from the EU and the International Monetary Fund (IMF). "The best way to think of it is to think of Greece as a teenager," noted one expert, who continued:

> Many Greeks view the state with a combination of a sense of entitlement, mistrust, and dislike similar to that of teenagers vis-à-vis their parents. They expect to be funded without contributing; they often act irresponsibly without care about consequences and expect to be bailed out by the state—but that only increases their sense of dependency, which only increases their feeling of dislike for the state. And, of course, they refuse to grow up. But, like every teenager, they will.

While these comments describe the relationship between Greek citizens and the state, they also provide a great deal of insight into the relationship between Greece and the EU—in particular, Germany. But the metaphor can only go so far. At the end of the day, Germany is not Greece's parent. Although both countries belong to the "euro family," Germans are naturally furious as to why they have to foot the largest bill to bail out the profligate Greeks.

In 2010, Germany led the EU (and the IMF) rescue efforts by putting together for Greece the biggest bailout package in EU history: a €110 billion bailout loan. But in 2011, Greece came back being more broke. A larger €173 billion package was put together in 2012. Every time, the harsh medicine associated with the rescue dictated that the Greek government unleash sweeping reforms to put its financial house in order. Public sector pensions and wages were cut and value-added and excise taxes raised. Unemployment rose from 8% in 2008 to a record high of 25% in 2014, while youth unemployment rose from 22% to 48%. Such shock therapy generated widespread misery and protests. There were only so many austerity measures that a frustrated and largely unemployed public (especially the youth) could take. The same drama of the Greek government begging for help, of EU governments debating what to do (with all eyes fixed on Merkel), and of the Greek public protesting in the streets unfolded again and again.

While Greece was an extreme example, it was not the only EU member requesting bailouts. Bailouts had to be dished out to Hungary (2008), Latvia (2008), Romania (2009), Ireland (2010), Portugal (2011), Cyprus (2011), and Spain (2012). The lion's share of the bailout funds always came from Germany.

The tragedy was not only Greece's or Germany's, but also the EU's. It severely tested the logic of the euro, whose member countries are not only unequal economically, but also different in their spending and saving habits. Dumping the euro by individual countries was no longer unthinkable, but was increasingly discussed, especially in 2012. Leaving the euro zone—known as "Grexit"—would allow Greece to depreciate its own currency, which would enhance its export competiveness. Dumping the euro would also relieve Germany's responsibility to honor an almost open-ended commitment to troubled countries. But here is the catch: a revived Deutsche mark would certainly appreciate and undermine export competitiveness. In the end, a reluctant Germany—and a reluctant EU—had little alternative.

In addition to individual bailouts, the EU in 2012 set up a €750 billion euro zone stabilization fund (including €250 billion from the IMF), which is called European Stability Mechanism (ESM). Germany, which pledged €220 billion, demanded stronger fiscal discipline in the name of better "economic governance" from all members, and threatened sanctions (such as being fined and losing voting rights) if certain members failed to apply a "debt brake." But Germany refused to let the EU to assume all sovereign debts. "Solidarity," which in EU-speak means "German cash," plays a role, but primarily as a means of buying time and encouraging reforms—not a means to encourage moral hazard (see Chapter 2). But by imposing reforms centered on spending cuts, debt reduction, and balancing budgets, Greek GDP shrank 30% since 2010 and growth was excruciatingly slow. Critics argued that such measures would prolong the recession. In 2014, the entire euro zone suffered from *deflation* where prices fell and growth became more challenging.

In 2015, a frustrated Greek public elected a new prime minister. His campaign platform was to break away from the previous governments' promises to the EU to embrace austerity. In other words, the new Greek government would challenge the EU—read "Germany"—by demanding that a large chunk of its debts be forgiven; that its citizens, especially the youth and the pensioners, be able to live in less misery; and that German (and other EU) taxpayers' euros be evaporated. Otherwise, the danger of a "Grexit" would be more likely than that in 2012. Emboldened by Greece, anti-austerity backlash in other PIGS countries is likely to challenge Germany- (and EU-) imposed austerity measures.

A physicist by training, Merkel is good at using data to make her point. She is fond of saying "7, 25, and 50." These numbers mean that the EU has 7% of the world's population, generates 25% of GDP, but consumes 50% of social spending. Clearly by spending beyond its means, according to Merkel, the legendary European welfare state cannot sustain itself in the long run. In other words, unless the EU shapes up (and becomes like Germany), the Greek tragedy (and other tragedies) will have a bitter ending. Overall, how the German Question is answered will to a large part depend on what role Germany chooses to play in such European drama as the Greek tragedy.

CASE DISCUSSION QUESTIONS

1. Why is Germany a "reluctant hegemon" in the EU?

2. Why does Germany have to be assertive in the EU?

3. What are the benefits and costs of using a common currency for Germany, Greece, and the EU?

4. ***ON ETHICS:*** While Greece needs help, the German economy has also suffered a major recession itself. How would you advise the chancellor: to bail out or to kick out Greece? As a German taxpayer, are you willing to pay higher taxes to help Greece? (Bear in mind, after Greece, there will be numerous other countries.)

Sources: Based on (1) *Bloomberg Businessweek*, 2010, A more perfect union? December 6: 11–12; (2) *Economist*, 2011, Bite the bullet, January 15: 77–78; (3) *Economist*, 2011, Time for Plan B, January 15: 10; (4) *Economist*, 2012, Currency disunion, April 7: 65; (5) *Economist*, 2012, Flaming February, February 18: 53; (6) *Economist*, 2012, Still sickly, March 31: 64; (7) *Economist*, 2012, Tempted, Angela? August 11: 9; (8) *Economist*, 2013, Don't make us *Führer*, April 13: 53–54; (9) *Economist*, 2013, Europe's reluctant hegemon, June 15: special report; (10) *Economist*, 2014, Back to reality, October 25: 73–74; (11) *Economist*, 2014, That sinking feeling, August 30: 10; (12) *Economist*, 2014, The treasures of darkness, October 11: 83; (13) *Economist*, 2014, The world's biggest economic problem, October 25: 15; (14) *Economist*, 2014, Three illusions, September 27: 50; (15) *Economist*, 2014, Twenty-five years on, November 8: 54–55; (15) *Economist*, 2015, Go ahead, Angela, make my day, January 31: 9.

NOTES

[Journal acronyms] **AER**—*American Economic Review*; **BW**—*BusinessWeek (before 2010)* or *Bloomberg Businessweek (since 2010)*; **CBR**—*China Business Review*; **FA**—*Foreign Affairs*; **JIBS**—*Journal of International Business Studies*; **JIE**—*Journal of International Economics*; **JWB**—*Journal of World Business*; **RIE**—*Review of International Economics*; **SMJ**—*Strategic Management Journal*.

1 World Trade Organization, 2005, *10 Benefits of the WTO Trading System* (p. 3), Geneva: WTO.

2 *10 Benefits of the WTO Trading System* (p. 8).

3 S. Jandhyala & R. Weiner, 2014, Institutions *sans frontiers*, *JIBS*, 45: 649–669.

4 A. Verdorff & R. Stern, 2002, What you should know about globalization and the World Trade Organization, *RIE*, 10: 404–423.

5 *Economist*, 2006, The future of globalization (p. 11), July 29: 11.

6 *Economist*, 2014, WTO: No more grand bargains, August 9: 10.

7 *Economist*, 2006, In the twilight of Doha (p. 63), July 29: 63–64.

8 Delegation of the European Commission to the USA, 2005, *The European Union: A Guide for Americans* (p. 2), Washington: Delegation of the European Commission to the USA.

9 G. Zestos, 2006, *European Monetary Integration: The Euro* (p. 64), Cincinnati: Cengage Learning.

10 *Economist*, 2010, No easy exit, December 7: 87–88; *Economist*, 2012, Tempted, Angela? August 11: 9.

11 *Economist*, 2007, Europe's mid-life crisis, March 17: 13; M. Feldstein, 2012, The failure of the euro, *FA*, January: 105–116.

12 N. Berggruen & N. Gardels, 2013, The next Europe, *FA*, July: 134–142.

13 M. Matthijs, 2013, David Cameron's dangerous game (p. 10), *FA*, September: 10–16.

14 *Economist*, 2011, How Britain could leave Europe, December 17: 104.

15 *Economist*, 2004, A club in need of a new vision, May 1: 26.

16 *Economist*, 2006, Babelling on, December 16: 50.

17 *BW*, 2003, Mexico: Was NAFTA worth it? December 22.

18 Foreign Affairs, Trade, and Development Canada, 2014, January 1 marks 20th anniversary of North American Free Trade Agreement, press release, January 1, www.international.gc.ca.

19 *BW*, 2013, The stranger next door, May 6: 8–9.

20 *Economist*, 2014, Deeper, better NAFTA, January 4: 8.

21 J. Garten, 2003, At 10, NAFTA is ready for an overhaul, *BW*, December 22.

22 J. Sargent & L. Matthews, 2006, The drivers of evolution/upgrading in Mexico's *maquiladoras*, *JWB*, 41: 233–246.

23 *Economist*, 2012, Mercosur RIP? July 14: 31–32.

24 *BW*, 2014, Latin America's great divide, June 9: 18–20.

25 US Trade Representative, 2005, *The Case for CAFTA*, February, www.ustr.gov.

26 ASEAN Secretariat, 2002, *Southeast Asia: A Free Trade Area*, Jakarta: ASEAN Secretariat, www.asean.org.

27 J. Bhagwati, 2002, *Free Trade Today* (p. 119), Princeton, NJ: Princeton University Press.

28 G. Locke, 2011, A message from the US Ambassador to China, *CBR*, October: 16.

29 A. Rose, 2004, Do we really know that the WTO increases trade? *AER*, 94: 98–114.

30 *Economist*, 2005, Is there any point to the WTO? August 6: 62.

31 *Economist*, 2013, The other conclave, March 16: 74.

32 A. Subramanian & S. Wei, 2007, The WTO promotes trade, strongly but unevenly, *JIE*, 72: 151–175; M. Tomz, J. Goldstein, & D. Rivers, 2007, Do we really know that the WTO increases trade? Comment, *AER*, 97: 2005–2018.

33 R. Flores, R. Aguilera, A. Mahdian, & P. Vaaler, 2013, How well do supranational regional group schemes fit international business research models? *JIBS*, 44: 451–474; M. Fratianni & C. Oh, 2009, Expanding RTAs, trade flows, and the multinational enterprise, *JIBS*, 40: 1206–1277; A. Rugman, 2005, *The Regional Multinationals*, Cambridge, UK: Cambridge University Press.

34 G. Qian, T. Khoury, M. W. Peng, & Z. Qian, 2010, The performance implications of intra- and inter-regional geographic diversification, *SMJ*, 31: 1018–1030.

pengatlas

© Cengage Learning

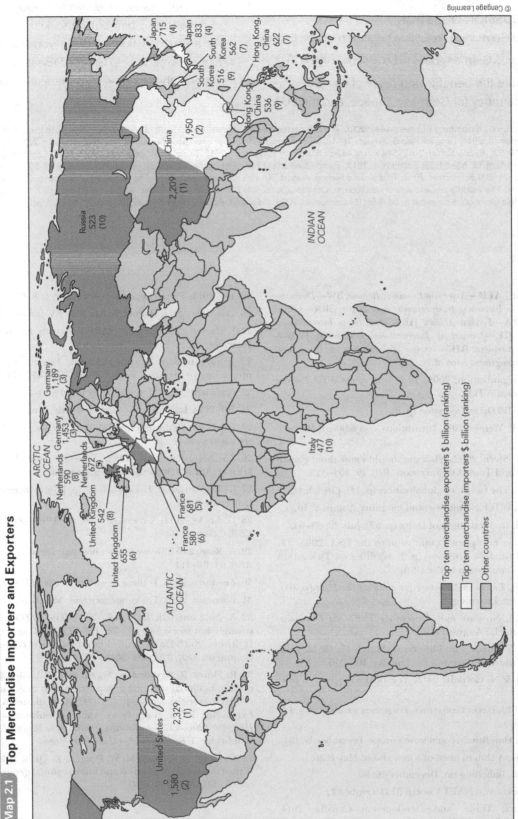

Map 2.1   Top Merchandise Importers and Exporters

United States
2,329
(1)

United States
1,580
(2)

ARCTIC OCEAN

ATLANTIC OCEAN

Germany
1,189
(3)

Germany
1,453
(3)

Netherlands
590
(8)

Netherlands
672
(5)

United Kingdom
542
(8)

United Kingdom
655
(6)

France
581
(5)

France
580
(6)

Italy
477
(10)

Russia
523
(10)

China
1,950
(2)

China
2,209
(1)

Japan
715
(4)

Japan
833
(4)

South Korea
516
(9)

South Korea
562
(7)

Hong Kong, China
536
(9)

Hong Kong, China
622
(7)

INDIAN OCEAN

Top ten merchandise exporters $ billion (ranking)

Top ten merchandise importers $ billion (ranking)

Other countries

Source: Adapted from World Trade Organization, 2014, *World Trade Report 2014*, Appendix Tables 3 and 5, Geneva: WTO (www.wto.org). All data are for 2013.

Map 2.2 Top Service Importers and Exporters

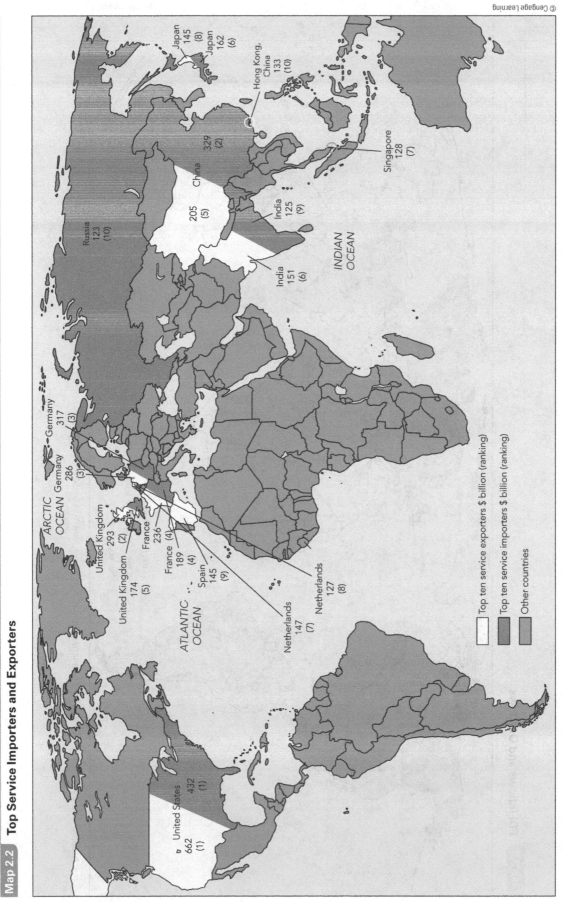

Japan 145 (8)
Japan 162 (6)
Hong Kong, China 133 (10)
Singapore 128 (7)
China 329 (2)
Russia 123 (10)
China 205 (5)
India 125 (9)
India 151 (6)
INDIAN OCEAN
Germany 317 (3)
ARCTIC OCEAN
Germany 286 (3)
United Kingdom 293 (2)
France 236 (4)
United Kingdom 174 (5)
France 189 (4)
Spain 145 (9)
ATLANTIC OCEAN
Netherlands 147 (7)
Netherlands 127 (8)
United States 432 (1)
United States 662 (1)

Top ten service exporters $ billion (ranking)
Top ten service importers $ billion (ranking)
Other countries

© Cengage Learning

Source: Adapted from World Trade Organization, 2014, *Word Trade Report 2014*, Appendix Tables 3 and 5, Geneva: WTO (www.wto.org). All data are for 2013.

© Cengage Learning

Map 2.3 FDI Inflows and Outflows

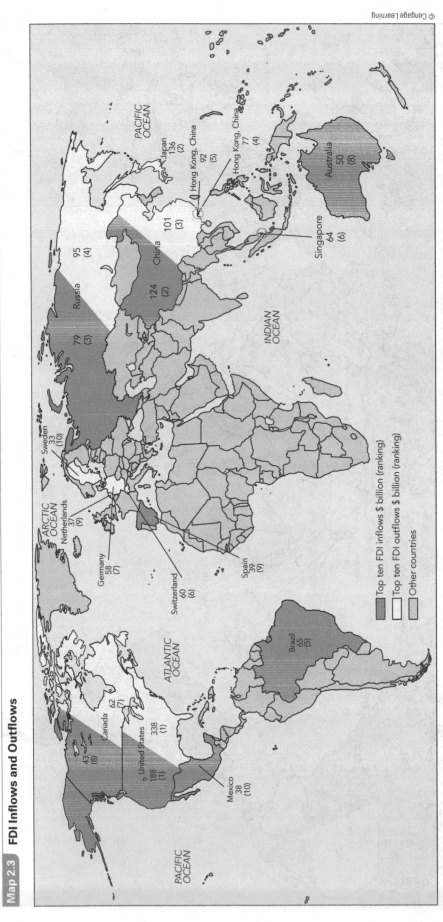

Source: Adapted from United Nations, 2014, *World Investment Report 2014* (p. xvi), New York and Geneva: UN. Data refer to 2013.

Map 2.4   **The European Union**

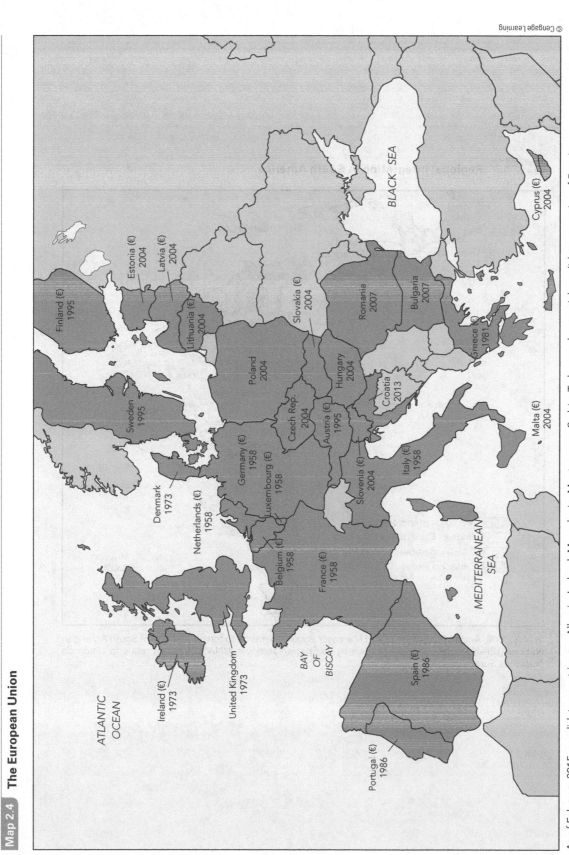

As of February 2015, candidate countries are Albania, Iceland, Macedonia, Montenegro, Serbia, Turkey, and potential candidate countries of Bosnia and Herzegovina, and Kosovo.

Source: Adapted from http://europa.eu

© Cengage Learning

Map 2.5 **Regional Integration in South America**

In May 2008, Andean Community and Mercosur agreed to merge to form the Union of South American Nations (USAN, more commonly known by its Spanish acronym, UNASUR, which refers to *Unión de Naciones Suramericanas*).

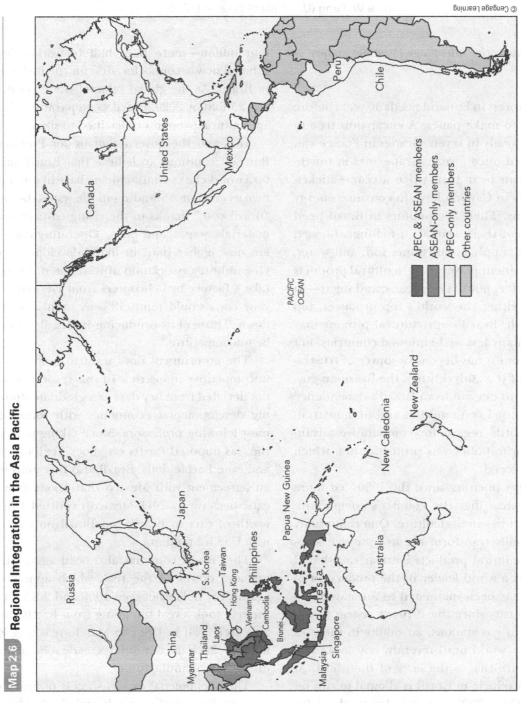

Map 2.6   **Regional Integration in the Asia Pacific**

In 2005, four APEC members—Brunei, Chile, New Zealand, and Singapore—established Trans-Pacific Partnership (TPP). As of this writing, eight additional APEC members—Australia, Canada, Malaysia, Mexico, Peru, Japan. the United States, and Vietnam—are negotiating to join TPP.

© Cengage Learning

Integrative Case 2.1

Brazil's Quest for Comparative Advantage[1]

Mike W. Peng (University of Texas at Dallas)

Does Brazil's comparative advantage lie in agriculture or manufacturing?

A pine tree in a forest in Finland needs 50 years before it can be felled to make paper. A eucalyptus tree in coastal Brazil is ready in seven. Grapes in France can only be harvested once a year. Grapevines in northeastern Brazil can bear fruit twice a year. Chicken and hog farmers in Canada have to consume energy to heat the barns. Their competitors in Brazil need no energy to heat their animals' dwellings. Blessed by an abundant supply of sunshine, soil, and water, Brazil is a preeminent player in agricultural products such as beef, coffee, poultry, soybeans, and sugar—in which Brazil is either the world's top producer, top exporter, or both. Brazil's agricultural prowess may be the envy of many less well-endowed countries, but in Brazil this prowess has become a source of frustration. For much of the 20th century, the Brazilian government sought to deviate from Brazil's dependence on agriculture-based commodities and to industrialize, often with little regard for comparative advantage. Their favorite policy was protectionism, which often did not succeed.

Brazil's market opening since the 1990s led more Brazilians to realize that the country's comparative advantage indeed lies in agriculture. One commodity that can potentially transform the low prestige associated with agricultural products is sugar cane-based ethanol. Brazil is a world leader in the production of ethanol, which has been mandated as an additive to gasoline used in cars since the 1970s. A system to distribute ethanol to gas stations, an oddity in the eyes of the rest of the world until recently, now looks like a national treasure that is the envy of the world. At present, no light vehicle in Brazil is allowed to run on pure gasoline. Since 2007, the mandatory blend for car fuels is at least 25% ethanol. Brazil currently produces 18 billion liters of ethanol, of which it exports four billion—more than half of worldwide exports. Ethanol now accounts for 40% for the fuel used by cars in Brazil. As the global ethanol trade is estimated to rise 25-fold by 2020, Brazil's comparative advantage in agricultural products is destined to shine.

However, the government under President Dilma Rousseff continues to believe that Brazil has to build up a world-class manufacturing base in order to modernize its economy. Standing in the way is the (in)famous "Brazil cost," thanks to the rising costs of energy, raw materials, wages, and taxes. Operating costs in Brazil are now higher than in many developed economies. One industry association official noted: "If you were to take a factory by helicopters from Germany to Brazil, your costs would jump 48% as soon as you touched down. Those of us producing in Brazil are doomed to be uncompetitive."

The government does want to help by protecting uncompetitive industries. In this respect, Rousseff has not deviated from her days as a graduate student studying developmental economics with some of Brazil's most left-wing professors. Since taking power in 2011, she has imposed tariffs on shoes, textiles, chemicals, and even Barbie dolls. Brazil also threatens to tear up an agreement with Mexico that allows free trade in cars, because in 2011 Mexico exported US$2 billion worth of cars to Brazil, but Brazil only reciprocated with US$372 million.

The "Brazil cost" has also been aggravated by the ups and downs of the real, which appreciated 38% against the dollar between 2009 and 2013. But in 2015 the real took a real hit, going from R$2.08 to US$1 in 2012 to R$2.31 to US$1 in March, reaching R$2.94 by midyear. Such fluctuation has made solid planning very difficult for manufacturers.

The phenomenal export success of Brazil's agricultural products and minerals and the lackluster condition of its manufacturing industries can force Brazil to reassess its comparative advantage. One expert noted: "The economy needs to redirect resources to where it is competitive. That is actually a healthy process." The catch, of course, is only if there is sufficient political will.

1) This research was supported by the Jindal Chair at the Jindal School of Management, University of Texas at Dallas. All views and errors are those of the author. © Mike W. Peng. Reprinted with permission.

Case Discussion Questions:

1. Why is Brazil's agriculture so competitive? Why do its manufacturing industries lack competitiveness?

2. Why have Brazil's governments in both the 20th and 21st centuries been eager to develop world-class manufacturing?

3. How can Brazil shift some of its resources from uncompetitive industries to competitive industries?

4. *ON ETHICS:* While President Rousseff's critics accuse her of ignoring Brazil's lack of comparative advantage in manufacturing, her supporters argue that her policies force Brazil to reduce its dependence on foreign-made manufacturing goods. If you were to participate in this debate, which side would you be on?

Sources: Based on (1) the author's interviews in Sao Paulo, Rio de Janeiro, and Iguassu Falls, Brazil; (2) *Bloomberg Businessweek*, 2012, Look who's bringing up the rear, March 26: 9–10; (3) *Economist*, 2007, The economy of heat, April 14: 8–9; (4) *Economist*, 2012, Two ways to make a car, March 10: 48–49; (5) L. F. Monteiro, 2011, Is God Brazilian? presentation at the Strategic Management Society Conference on Latin America, Rio de Janeiro, March 11; (6) World Bank, 2008, Biofuels: The promise and the risks, in *World Development Report 2008* (pp. 70–71), Washington: World Bank.

Integrative Case 2.2

Twelve Recommendations to Enhance UK Export Competitiveness[1]

Mike W. Peng (University of Texas at Dallas)
Klaus E. Meyer (China Europe International Business School)

Drawing from the resource-based and institution-based views, two consultants engaged by the UK government make 12 recommendations to managers and government policymakers on how to enhance the competitiveness of Made-in-UK exports.

Because manufacturing drives exports, innovation, and productivity, it matters a great deal by ultimately impacting standards of living and economic performance. We offer 12 recommendations to firm managers and government policymakers, which are organized according to the resource-based and institution-based views (Exhibit 1).[2]

Three Recommendations for Firm Managers

Recommendation 1: Build organizational strengths based on the resource-based framework by focusing on the value, rarity, and inimitability (VRI) of resources and capabilities

There is nothing novel on the proposition that firms "compete on resources and capabilities." The subtlety comes when managers attempt to distinguish firm-specific resources and capabilities that are valuable, rare, and hard to imitate, and build organizational strengths (such as dynamic capabilities) to continuously generate new resources and capabilities. Resources and capabilities not meeting the VRI criteria will need to be discontinued and/or outsourced unless they have critical linkages to firms' core value adding activity. Think of the Burberry dog cover-ups and leashes, which contributed to sales but not corporate strengths. A rigorous resource-based analysis helped managers (re)discover that it is *Britishness*—more specifically Burberry trench coats designed and made in the UK—that would meet the VRI criteria, thus deserving to be the center of gravity around which organizational strengths should be built (see In Focus 4.2).

Recommendation 2: Find and leverage unique, know-ledge-based, deep niches

To be competitive over the broad range of segments within any given industry is increasingly challenging. A focus on unique, deep niches by leveraging specialized knowledge is the way to go. German *Mittelstand* firms such as Krones (beverage bottling and packaging systems), Heidenhain (encoders for manufacturing equipment), and Dorma (moveable walls) may not be household names, but they hold up to 90% worldwide market share in their deep niches. *Mittelstand* firms as a group collectively contribute 40% of German exports. For UK firms, such niches exist in manufacturing industries using traditional technologies such as equestrian goods and textile threads, and may exist in emerging industries such as additive manufacturing, smart grid, and tidal and wave energy system. Ideally, such niches will focus on the high end, leveraging UK strengths in design, creativity, and R&D.

Recommendation 3: Look for value-adding ways to combine manufacturing with services

Manufacturing per se is often relatively easy to imitate. Smart combination of manufacturing and services will make it harder for rivals to imitate. A well-known success story is Rolls-Royce's transformation from an engine producer to a service provider for airlines. Similar examples galore where complex appliances (such as lifts, commericial vehicles, and power stations) are manufactured for use over long periods, especially by corporate customers. In the future, it is possible to envision UK leisure marine firms such as Fairline Boats (a world leader in the 38-80 ft powerboat segment) to both export Made-in-UK boats and provide 3-D printers that can "print" out spare parts on-site for export clients around the world—an interesting example of smart combination of manufacturing and services.

---

[1] This case is an excerpt from a consulting report commissoned by the UK Government Office for Science as part of the two-year (2011–2013) Foresight Project "The Future of Manufacturing." The report was published as M. W. Peng & K. E. Meyer, 2013, Winning the future markets for UK manufacturing output, *Future of Manufacturing Project Evidence Paper* 25, London: Foresight, Government Office for Science. It is in the public domain at www.bis.gov.uk/foresight. © Crown copyright. The views expressed are those of the authors and do not represent the policy of any government or organization. Discussion questions were added by M. W. Peng.

[2] Because we have offered some advice to managers in earlier sections of the report, our emphasis in this case is on policy recommendations.

| Exhibit 1 | Twelve Recommendations Based on the Resource-Based and Institution-Based Views |

	Recommendations for firm managers	Recommendations for government policymakers
Resource-based view	1. Build organizational strengths based on the resource-based framework by focusing on the value, rarity, and inimitability (VRI) of resources and capabilities 2. Find and leverage unique, knowledge-based, deep niches 3. Look for value-adding ways to combine manufacturing with services	4. Support pre-competitive manufacturing capabilities and future technology platforms 5. Push firms to reach for the high end and do not support competition on low cost for the sake of jobs 6. Strengthen human capital to enable advanced manufacturing
Institution-based view		7. Remove uncertainty by clarifying the UK's commitment to stay in the EU 8. Enhance certainty by negotiating more free Trade Agreements (FTAs) 9. Create a tax regime that is competitive, stable, and fair 10. Attract more inward FDI and promote more outward FDI 11. Facilitate the mobility of highly qualified individuals into and out of the UK 12. Lead efforts to lift regulatory trade barriers such as the EU arms embargo on China

Source: M. W. Peng & K. E. Meyer, 2013, Winning the future markets for UK manufacturing output (p. 42), *Future of Manufacturing Project Evidence Paper* 25, London: Foresight, Government Office for Science, www.bis.gov.uk/foresight. © Crown copyright.

Nine Recommendations for Government Policymakers

Recommendation 4: Support pre-competitive manufacturing capabilities and future technology platforms

The UK government, like all EU governments, is restricted in the ability to provide direct subsidies to firms. In global competition, this may place UK (and EU) firms at a disadvantage relative to their rivals in the US and Asia, which can benefit from more direct government support. However, there are ways for the UK government to be more active. For example, Technology Strategy Board (2012) announced its funding of at least £50 million a year to support pre-competitive manufacturing capabilities and future technology platforms. Such much-needed investments will speed up the process for successful commercialization and help firms jump through the hurdles associated with the "valley of death" (good ideas flame out before emerging technologies become competitively and commercially successful).

Recommendation 5: Push firms to reach for the high end and do not support competition on low cost for the sake of jobs

Bucking the trend that low-cost manufacturing jobs are migrating to low-cost countries is neither advisable nor realistic. The UK government should encourage firms to reach for the high end, which thrives on high productivity. Focusing on low cost may generate short-run benefits, but will in the long run result in severe stagnation of manufacturing productivity. Thus, the UK should steer away from attempts to compete on lower cost—for example, through policy measures that lower labor cost and lengthen permissible work time. Such policies may encourage manufacturing in sectors where the UK would be competing with countries that have much lower per capita income (such as those in Eastern Europe or East Asia). In the medium term, the UK would be squeezed out of this market segment. In other words, attempts to build such low-cost sectors (such as final assembly of low-end electronics or cars) may generate job growth in the short run, but are not sustainable in the long run—unless the UK is willing to accept a fall in average incomes to the level of, say, Poland or Romania.

Recommendation 6: Strengthen human capital to enable advanced manufacturing

While hardly an original recommendation, this point must be emphasized: UK manufacturing will not (re)gain world-class competitiveness in the absence of high-level human capital. UK firms' endeavors to build high-end, high-productivity-based capabilities are essentially efforts to engage in human capital-intensive manufacturing. Effective government support can help to build human resources that enable such advanced manufacturing. This leads to two ideas. First, the UK has leading-edge universities and technology clusters, yet the gap between the top end and the "average" human capital is rather large. Therefore, the UK ought to foster its elite institutions while at the same time enhancing the diffusion of knowledge and skills from the elite institutions to the second and third tier.

Second, the UK needs to build capabilities in the *workforce* that enable world-class manufacturing. This would entail investing heavily in human capital development. Such investment should in part come from the government. This is because the positive spillovers of skills and capabilities (especially from low to medium levels) from productive individuals to society at large are substantive. Essentially we advocate the raising of skills beyond the elite institutions, because sustaining a high income for an entire nation requires high performance capabilities possessed by a broad segment of the population, and not only by the elites. Three specific priorities can be:

- Providing more resources for primary education in the state system to enable children to enter a path of personal development and human capital formation that is independent of their parents' ability and willingness to invest in their education. This issue is often discussed as a social concern in the UK, yet it has—at least in the long run—major economic and competitiveness implications. Thus, it is relevant to the long run competitiveness of UK manufacturing exports.

- Prioritizing vocational training, which has been severely weakened by past policies such as abolishing traditional apprenticeships and converting polytechs into (too often second or third rate) universities. One stream of actions may extend initiatives to re-introduce vocational training through apprenticeships, which requires multi-year courses in collaboration between industry and educational institutions on a more comprehensive basis and with more resources—far more than what current pilot projects envisage. Germany and other Northern European countries show examples on how this can be done—with a positive impact on export competitiveness. Another stream of action may focus on colleges and universities that provide vocational training, notably providing funding regimes that encourage such training and eliminate the evaluation of third rate universities by the criteria more appropriate for Oxford and Cambridge (which de facto encourages third or fourth rate research of very limited value).

- While the first two actions require much wider efforts and political will, we believe that there is a third action that is smaller in scope and more practically actionable. Given that skilled manufacturing workers are now a scarce resource in the UK but downturns and recessions are inevitable, the UK can take a page from the playbook of Germany's labor market arrangements to reduce employment volatility. Since the 1970s, German firms can apply for subsidies to keep workers on the payroll during downturns. More recently, a "mini-job" program targets younger workers and unemployed but experienced older workers, providing jobs for 15 hours per week at a set pay rate. Such government efforts to reduce labor market volatility, especially during downturns and recessions, enhance employers' willingness to hire and train workers and employees' motivation to invest in and enhance their own human capital. Such government support can also foster the wider spread practice of high commitment work systems. Centered on employee engagement, high commitment work systems can contribute toward innovation and enhance organizational performance.

While our first three recommendations (#4–#6) for policymakers are *resource-based* in nature, aiming at helping UK firms enhance their capabilities, our next six recommendations (#7–#12) for policymakers—the bulk of our advice—are derived primarily from the *institution-based* view.

Recommendation 7: Remove uncertainty by clarifying the UK's commitment to stay within the EU

As rules of the game, institutions serve to reduce uncertainty. Managers hate uncertainty, especially when it comes to long-term commitments such as constructing a new manufacturing plant. Despite the EU's problems, the UK's periodic threats to leave the EU—such as Prime Minister David Cameron's speech in January 2013 (while we were in the middle of doing this research)—heighten uncertainty and undermine UK trade and investment. In view of the large and growing importance of regional integration in supply chains and of the fact that the EU accounts for more than 50% of UK exports, an exit of the UK from full EU integration would be *disastrous* for much of UK manufacturing. Given that emerging economies only collectively purchase less than 8% of UK exports, the loss of exports to the EU will not be compensated by the additional exports to emerging economies.

Uncertainty over the status of the UK's membership in the EU—and hence the specific rules applying to trade between the UK and other EU countries—is in particular likely to depress inward FDI, especially manufacturing investment by non-EU firms in regional platform investment. Historically, the UK has been quite successful in attracting investors looking for a base to serve EU markets—Toyota, Nissan, and Honda come to mind. But such investment in particular will be on hold or go elsewhere if the uncertainty about the future status is not removed. Moreover, participation in regional value chains (and hence intra-regional trades in components) facilitates the exportation of downstream products eventually destined for countries outside the EU. Given the relatively slow growth in the EU, future marginal increases of benefits for the UK to stay within the EU may be less than what they have been in the past. However, we see no reason to put at risk the remaining benefits, which are very substantial (i.e., over half of UK exports).

Recommendation 8: Enhance certainty by negotiating more free trade agreements (FTAs).

Firms from FTA member countries typically increase their trade and investment activities due to the tremendous certainty brought by FTAs. The EU currently has FTAs with 28 countries: Albania, Algeria, Andorra, Bosnia and Herzegovina, Chile, Colombia, Croatia, Egypt, Faroe Islands, Iceland, Israel, Jordan, Lebanon, Liechtenstein, Macedonia, Mexico, Montenegro, Morocco, Norway, Palestinian Authority, Peru, San Marino, Serbia, South Africa, South Korea, Switzerland, Tunisia, and Turkey. The EU recently concluded negotiations with Singapore, and is also currently negotiating with three individual countries (India, Japan, and Russia) and three regional entities (Association of Southeast Asian Nations [ASEAN], Gulf Cooperation Council [GCC], and Mercosur).

Firms clearly prefer multilateral agreements to bilateral FTAs. Bilateral FTAs tend to create different rules applying to different pairs of export/import countries, which greatly increase the bureaucracy that exporters and importers have to deal with and reduce the scope for scale economies. Therefore, we prefer a multilateral FTA between the EU and ASEAN to a bilateral FTA, for example, between the UK and Singapore.

In order to increase more UK manufacturing exports, we recommend that the UK advocate more EU efforts to negotiate the following FTAs:

- Complete the negotiations for the Transatlantic FTA with the United States and Canada. Progress for the Transatlantic FTA has been slow, but may be accelerated following recent initiatives on both sides of the Atlantic.
- Another obvious candidate with which the UK should be interested in having an FTA is the Australia-New Zealand Closer Economic Relations Trade Agreement (ANZCERTA or CER).
- In the long run, the UK (via the EU) should entertain FTA negotiations with China. China already has FTAs with ASEAN, Chile, Costa Rica, New Zealand, Pakistan, Singapore, and Peru, and is negotiating with Australia, Iceland, Japan, Norway, and South Korea as well as two regional bodies: GCC and Southern African Customs Union (SACU). Given the UK's low import market share in China, an FTA will definitely help promote more UK exports there.

Recommendation 9: Create a tax regime that is competitive, stable, and fair

Global competition is also about tax competition. While the UK corporate tax rate of 28% appears to be relatively pro-business, the tax regime has recently given a decidedly *mixed* message to UK firms. Legislation designed to encourage R&D spending in the UK was followed by cutbacks in tax deductions for capital expenditure. Some of the UK's competitors have aggressively used favorable tax as a means to lure investment and jobs. For example, Ireland only levies 10% corporate income tax on manufacturing income between the 1980s and 2002 and 12.5% since 2002, thus attracting many investors to locate in Ireland. In addition, new EU members Hungary and Bulgaria have aggressively reduced their corporate income rates to 16% and 10%, respectively.

A tax system will however only be stable if it is generally accepted by the population (i.e., the electorate in a democracy) to be fair. Some corporate taxation systems de facto do not tax firms at the location where the profit is generated, but (by default or through consciously created loopholes) allow firms to shift profits from high tax locations to low tax locations through practices such as transfer pricing and excessively high licensing fees. This is likely to undermine the legitimacy of an international system of tax competition. In other words, if nations compete on taxes, there also need to be commonly agreed rules (i.e., institutions) by which this competition takes place. Perhaps surprising for most UK observers, the UK may actually benefit from more integration in the EU on this matter because it would prevent incidences such as Google and Starbucks paying virtually no tax in the UK.

Given that the future of UK manufacturing will be mostly high end, high tech, and high R&D, commoditized manufacturing may very well move to low tax jurisdictions. Thus, it is imperative that the UK government create and maintain a tax regime that is competitive, stable, and fair. Otherwise, just like other forms of uncertainties, uncertainties associated with the tax regime will hurt the UK's attractiveness as a manufacturing and R&D location, and undermine future investment and exports. Reducing corporate tax rate from 28% to 23% in 2014/15 will be helpful. But clearly more can be done.

Recommendation 10: Attract more inward FDI and promote more outward FDI

Given that foreign multinationals generate approximately half of UK manufacturing exports, it seems imperative that the UK continue to attract inward FDI in order to increase exports. The most important policies to this end are the same that also promote domestic investment in manufacturing: free trade within the region and valuable, rare, and hard-to-imitate resources that foreign investors can tap into.

Exports are generated by a combination of "push" and "pull" effects. While UK-based firms (including UK-based foreign multinationals) "push" exports, UK multinationals—via outward FDI abroad—"pull" UK exports into their host economies, often in the form of high end products, components, and service exports. Given that the UK has the second largest stock of outward FDI, it seems natural that efforts be strengthened to promote more outward FDI, especially into downstream and service activities. Incorporating the protection of FDI into FTAs (fostering a formal institution)

and promoting the views of businesses "out in the world" as ambassadors and supporters of the British economy (creating an informal institution) are likely to help.

Recommendation 11: Facilitate the mobility of highly qualified individuals into and out of the UK

Mobility of people is an essential precondition for successful international trade, especially in the high end of both manufacturing and services. The UK benefits from being a more multicultural society than most of its EU peers. This attraction enables many knowledge-based, creative industry sectors to thrive, and facilitates the coordination of global operations out of the UK. In this regard, the UK government policy has been confusing to say the least. On the one hand, Deputy Prime Minister Nick Clegg (2013) wrote in the *Economist*: "We will continue to be one of the most open economies on the planet, welcoming trade and investment and welcoming talented individuals who wish to make a contribution to Britain." On the other hand, shrinking immigration quotas, more visa application procedures, abstention from Schengen area free-travel arrangements, and increased requirements in citizenship tests all send a very strong, disconcerting message that—in a complete reversal of UK policies over the past century or more—the UK no longer welcomes skilled immigrants or temporary workers. In summary, if the UK is serious about promoting export competitiveness, it will have to be serious about making it less cumbersome for highly qualified individuals to move into and out of the UK.

Recommendation 12: Lead efforts to lift regulatory trade barriers such as the EU arms embargo on China

Removing regulatory trade barriers can obviously facilitate more UK exports and generate more jobs. Commanding a 6% world share, aerospace and defense represent one of the UK's most globally competitive manufacturing industries. The UK is desperate to expand manufacturing exports to China, where currently the UK only has 0.9% import market share. China has expressed an interest in importing arms from the UK. But the UK has declined, because of an institution-based trade barrier: the EU arms embargo on China since 1989 due to the Tiananmen Square incident.

During the 1980s, the UK, as well as other EU members and the US, did export to China a limited amount of military aerospace products (mostly avionics and engines). Although China was eager to modernize its military with Western help in order to deter the Soviet threat, China's financial means were extremely limited.[3] Yet, since 1989, the US and the EU have imposed arms embargos on China and cancelled all arms contracts. In the 1990s, as China became more wealthy but could not obtain arms from the West, it turned to Russia for advanced weaponry. China has become the number one importer of Russian arms and one of the world's largest arms importers. China now has several hundred high-performance Sukhoi 27 Flanker fighters at the cost of *billions of dollars*, suggesting a missed opportunity of exporting Made-in-UK high performance jets such as Eurofighter Typhoon.

At first glance, our recommendation may appear outside-the-box (or even radical). It is not. From a resource-based perspective, the defense sector—and the aerospace industry in particular—is an area where the UK has cutting-edge capabilities that it can exploit, but needs to continuously renew to remain globally competitive at the high end. From an institution-based view, already in 2004, the EU planned to lift the embargo by 2005. But intense US pressures forced the EU to abandon the plan. In 2009, UK Business Secretary Peter Mandelson stated that the ban should be phased out. China is an officially recognized Strategic Partner of the EU. Not surprisingly, China has called the ban "absurd," "puzzling," and "political discrimination" against a Strategic Partner. In other words, it is time for the UK to quit "lecturing" countries such as China on how their societies should be run (despite their political imperfections).[4]

Moreover, we have to ask: who has benefitted from the EU arms embargo on China? Obviously, Russian aerospace firms such as Sukhoi. Further, US aerospace firms such as Boeing and Northop Grumman also benefit, not by exporting to China (they do not), but by curtailing the economies of scale of UK (and EU) firms that would have been gained by exporting to China. In other words, the arms embargo has helped enhance the competitiveness of UK (and EU) firms' global rivals in Russia and in the United States.

China is likely to be an eager customer for military and aerospace technologies. A simple Porter five forces analysis suggests that China is not likely to be so happy with the bargaining power of its sole high-tech arms supplier, Russia. Fostering more competition, dual sourcing is always better than single sourcing. However, delaying this liberalization further is likely to undermine this demand. With the rapid development of the aerospace industry in China (which started testing two stealth fighters in the last two years and an advanced military transport jet in January 2013), China may no longer be interested in UK (and EU) aerospace and defense products even when the embargo is lifted.

We understand that this recommendation is likely to be controversial because of its potential geopolitical and military ramifications. However, given *our mandate to search for the future markets for UK manufacturing exports with a view to 2050*, we argue that it is important that the issue be discussed free from prejudices.

Conclusion[5]

In global competition, no advantage is forever. As the first industrial nation, the UK enjoyed significant first-mover advantage. In 1900, with 2.2% of the world's population it generated 15% of exports. But it is not realistic to sustain this level of preeminent performance in the face of increasingly strong global competition. However, it is important to note that the UK is still punching *above* its weight: with 0.9% of the world's population, it currently generates approximately 3.3% of the world's exports—including 6.6% of service exports and 2.6% of goods exports.

What does the future hold for UK manufacturing exports? Lacking crystal balls, we have to gain a deeper understanding of the past if we endeavor to engage in the perilous exercise of predicting the future. The data that we have analyzed suggest that the UK's relative decline in manufacturing appears to have accelerated in the last decade, not only vis–à–vis emerging economies but also relative to European peers. In the 1980s and 1990s, there was a widespread belief in the UK that service growth would more than compensate for the relative loss of manufacturing capabilities. Today, in part as a consequence of policies launched two or three decades ago, the UK is indeed a global leader in many service sectors with a service trade surplus. The problem, however, is that the corresponding deficit in the

---

3) In the 1980s, the Chinese military was seriously interested in the British Harrier jump jet and the French Mirage 2000 fighter, and sent test pilots to check them out. Since China at that time could not afford these expensive modern combat aircraft, it did not place any orders.

4) We thank Jim O'Neill (Chairman, Goldman Sachs Asset Management, who coined the term "BRIC" more than a decade ago) for this insight. During our interview for this project, he went on to suggest: "Some policymakers elsewhere think that the UK is both hypocritical and a bit lost in the past, when it does not realize that its time to lecture others passed. I think this is quite an important issue that many British policymakers struggle to grasp."

5) This is the Conclusion section for the entire 55-page report, not merely for this Recommendations part.

trade of goods is so large and growing that it cannot be compensated by the success of service exports. In the future, reviving and strengthening UK manufacturing seem to be a must.

In conclusion, our Review suggests that UK manufacturing firms have good opportunities to compete in both old and new segments within "high end" industries, if they can create and occupy *deep niches* for themselves. To this end, we recommend focusing policy efforts on developing world-class competitiveness of both individuals and firms (and hence of the nation), and to enhance an open and pro-competition trade and investment environment. From the resource-based and institution-based views, the key to winning the future markets for UK manufacturing exports lies in (1) UK firms' possession of valuable, rare, and hard-to-imitate resources and capabilities that can translate into products appreciated by customers, and (2) the UK government's resolve and courage to embrace policy challenges that will ultimately make the nation more competitive and prosperous.

Case Discussion Questions

1. **If you are not studying this book in the UK, ask yourself: How many Made-in-UK products do you use? Then ask your classmates and family members: How many Made-in-UK products do they use? If you were to study this book in the year 1900, how many Made-in-UK products would you, your classmates, or your family members use?**

2. **From a resource-based view, what can UK firms and their managers do to enhance export competitiveness?**

3. **From an institution-based view, what can UK government policymakers do to enhance export competitiveness? Drawing from the list of recommendations, what specific actions do you recommend that they undertake in the short run, medium run, and long run?**

Integrative Case 2.3

Would You Invest in Turkey?[1]

Canan Mutlu (University of Texas at Dallas)

Turkey has tremendous economic dynamism and potential, but also some nontrivial problems. Can Turkey attract investors?

What do countries do to attract investors? The answer to this question usually involves improving infrastructure, increasing standards of living, and ultimately making doing business easier and less costly for investors. However, in today's world, an increasing number of countries are also running campaigns all over the world to attract investors' attention and increase awareness about their countries' business opportunities. Turkey is one of the emerging economies with an impressive campaign with the running title of "Invest in Turkey."

Turkey is the 18th-largest economy in the world with a per capita income that has nearly tripled in less than a decade and now exceeds US$10,000. Turkey is a transcontinental country with land spanning from Southeastern Europe to Western Asia. The majority of Turkey's land is known as Asia Minor or the Anatolian peninsula, which is bounded by the Black Sea to the north, the Mediterranean Sea to the south, and the Aegean Sea to the west. Turkey's location enables the country to have a unique brokerage position between Europe and Asia. In fact, you can see the "Welcome to Europe" and "Welcome to Asia" signs at the two exits of the bridges in Istanbul that unite both continents over the Bosphorus strait. Turkey is not only a geographically but also a historically attractive land, thanks to its roots that date back to the ancient Greece, Rome, the Byzantines, the Ottoman Empire, and Central Asia.

However, all these unique qualities do not guarantee a competitive advantage for Turkey and make it a better country to invest. Well-known management scholar Michael Porter argues that national prosperity is created, not inherited. Accordingly, one of the most comprehensive assessments of national competitiveness, *Global Competitiveness Report*, evaluates the competitiveness of

148 economies, providing insight into the drivers of their productivity and prosperity. In 2013, Turkey ranked 44th among 148 countries (Exhibit 1). During the last decade, due to its vibrant business environment, Turkey has shown stronger economic growth than many European counterparts. This is mostly fueled by a large domestic market (ranked 16th) and intense local competition (ranked 15th). However, in order to sustain the economic growth, the country needs to shift its focus into areas such as education and training to increase its competitiveness in labor market efficiency (ranked 130th). Overall, Turkey shows an increasing trend in terms of economic growth, market size, and market efficiency. However, there are still problematic areas, such as intellectual property protection, judicial independence, educational system, energy costs, and effect of taxation on incentives to invest that raise serious red flags for the sustainability of economic growth.

Economic Growth and Investment

Due to major economic and structural reforms, Turkey has rapidly turned into a major recipient of

Exhibit 1 Turkey's Competitiveness Outlook

Competitiveness Factors	Rank	Score 1–7 (best)
Global Competitiveness Index	**44**	**4.45**
1st pillar: Institutions	56	4.08
2nd pillar: Infrastructure	49	4.45
3rd pillar: Macroeconomic environment	76	4.62
4th pillar: Health and primary education	59	5.86
5th pillar: Higher education and training	65	4.29
6th pillar: Goods market efficiency	43	4.52
7th pillar: Labor market efficiency	130	3.74
8th pillar: Financial market development	51	4.4
9th pillar: Technological readiness	58	4.05
10th pillar: Market size	16	5.3
11th pillar: Business sophistication	43	4.36
12th pillar: Innovation	50	3.47

Source: *The Global Competitiveness Index 2013–2014*

---

1) This case was written by Canan Mutlu (University of Texas at Dallas) under the supervision of Professor Mike Peng. All information used is from the public domain and the author is responsible for any errors. © Canan Mutlu.

foreign direct investment (FDI) and increased its integration with the global economy, accompanied by steady economic growth over the last decade. The goals of the new reforms include increasing the role of private sector and encouraging entrepreneurs to pursue their startups to inject new blood to the economy (Exhibit 2). A solid outcome of these initiatives has been the average gross domestic product (GDP) growth rate of 5.4% between 2002 and 2011, compared to 1.6% in the United States and 1.4% in European Union.

The majority of Turkey's trade is with Europe and the Middle East. In addition to the Customs Union Agreement with the European Union (EU), Turkey also enjoys free trade agreements (FTAs) with Albania, Bosnia and Herzegovina, Chile, Croatia, EFTA member countries (Iceland, Liechtenstein, Norway, and Switzerland), Egypt, Georgia, Israel, Jordan, Macedonia, Montenegro, Morocco, Palestine, Serbia, South Korea, Syria, and Tunisia. Its largest export markets are Germany, Iraq, and Britain. Its import markets are mostly driven by Russia, China, and Germany. Turkey has also shown roaring FDI inflows increasing from US$8.6 billion in 2009 to US$12.9 billion in 2013. The majority of the FDI flows to industrial sectors, manufacturing, and service areas and is dominantly from Europe followed by Near Eastern and Middle Eastern countries. Turkey has especially become an attractive destination for wealthy Middle East investors who search for more secure shores outside of countries riddled with unrest from the Arab Spring.

Given the economic growth, Turkey is now considered a "New Tiger" among foreign investors. One of the leading reasons for this nickname is Turkey's successful weathering of the 2008–2009 global economic crisis driven by modern infrastructure, economic reforms, and also the young and dynamic workforce enabling an attractive investment site. As of 2013, with 76.6 million citizens with a median age of 30, Turkey is the second most populous country after Germany and has the youngest population in Europe. A young and dynamic population fuels the nation's ambition toward becoming a major hub of manufacturing and innovation. Therefore, along with some other emerging economies, such as Argentina, Brazil, Mexico, and Russia, Turkey is now considered in transition from efficiency-driven to innovation-driven countries. Indeed, Jim O'Neill, chairman of Goldman Sachs Asset Management and inventor of the acronym BRIC for the four largest emerging economies (Brazil, Russia, India, and China), has recently come up with a new acronym, MIST. Turkey is the T among the new foursome of fast-track MIST countries that include Mexico, Indonesia, and South Korea.

The EU Agenda and Problematic Borders

Turkey has a complicated relationship with the EU, although the EU is Turkey's largest economic partner, accounting for 46% of Turkish trade in 2011. Becoming a candidate for full membership in the EU in 1999, Turkey has long been at the door of the EU to become a full member. Accession negotiations have led to numerous

Exhibit 2	Turkey's Economic Outlook in 2013
GDP	US$820 billion
GDP per capita	US$10,782
Exports value	US$152 billion
Imports value	US$251 billion
Foreign direct investment	US$12.9 billion
Number of companies with foreign capital	36,450
Inflation rate	7.5%
Major exports markets	Germany (9%); Iraq (7.8%); UK (5.8%); Russia (4.6%); Italy (4.4%); France (4.2%); USA (3.7%); UAE (3.3%); Spain (2.8%); Iran (2.4%)
Major imports sources	Russia (9.9%); China (9.8%); Germany (9.6%); Italy (5.1%); USA (5%); Iran (4.1%); Switzerland (3.8%); France (3.2%); Spain (2.5%); India (2.5%)

Source: Turkey Investment Support and Promotion Agency. www.invest.gov.tr/en-US/turkey/factsandfigures/Pages/TRSnapshot.aspx

institutional reforms benchmarked on the EU standards, yet could not end in full membership because of a number of political obstacles and particularly problematic borders. Surrounded by Armenia, Azerbaijan, Bulgaria, Georgia, Greece, Syria, Iran, and Iraq, Turkey borders potential war zones and, thus, is under the influence of roaring political conflicts. Turkey is not only confronted by problematic borders, but also faces social conflicts within its own borders.

For example, during the Spring of 2013, Turkey witnessed one of the largest social unrests, referred to as Gezi Protests, which included a wide range of complaints such as issues of freedom of the press, increasing authoritarianism, the war in Syria, and concerns over secularism. All these problems lead to ongoing political instability and social tensions within the country, increasing business risks and adding weights on investor confidence on the business environment.

Despite certain problems, Turkey is a stable democratic country in one of the most unstable parts of the globe. Given its growth potential and ongoing concerns, it is viewed as a "high risk, high return" option among investors. Therefore, although the country's economic outlook remains favorable compared to the rest of Europe, there remains ample room for improvement. While Turkey has been resilient to the recent global financial crisis, its challenge is to increase competitiveness and ultimately to sustain economic

growth. To continue to be a safe house in a volatile neighborhood, Turkey needs to speed up institutional reforms in areas such as judiciary system to promote a less-volatile investment environment and also sharpen the educational system to shape the young population into skilled workers. Turkey is not only at the crossroads between East and West, but also sits at the thin line between emerging and advanced economies. Future reforms will determine whether the country will become an economic power house or stay as a forever-emerging economy.

Case Discussion Questions

1. **Discuss the major competitive advantages and disadvantages for Turkey.**

2. **How can emerging economies such as Turkey mitigate certain competitive disadvantages?**

3. **As an executive of a multinational based in Australia that is interested in undertaking FDI in emerging economies, would you be interested in investing in Turkey among many options around the world?**

Sources: Based on (1) *Bloomberg Businessweek*, 2012, Move over, BRICs, here come the MISTs, August 9, www.businessweek.com /articles/2012-08-09/move-over-brics-dot-here-come-the-mists; (2) CNBC, 2012, Investing in Europe's fastest-growing economy, www.cnbc.com/ id/48552347; (3) *Global Competitiveness Report 2013–2014*, www.weforum .org/issues/global-competitiveness; (4) Invest in Turkey, 2014, www.invest. gov.tr/en-US/Pages/Home.aspx.

Integrative Case 2.4

The Myth Behind China's Outward Foreign Direct Investment[1]

Mike W. Peng (University of Texas at Dallas)

The Western media is full of sensational (but often unsubstantiated) reporting on the allegedly huge scale and scope of China's outward foreign direct investment (OFDI). This evidence-based case suggests that as the world's second-largest economy, China is punching below its weight when it comes to OFDI. How should the United States view such FDI from China? In two words: pragmatic nationalism.

As China's economic power grows, it has increased its outward foreign direct investment (OFDI). Western media reporting on China's OFDI has been sensational. For example, popular magazines have had a field day running eye-catching cover stories, such as "China Goes Shopping" (*BusinessWeek*, July 27, 2009), "China Buys the World" (*Fortune*, October 26, 2009), and "Buying Up the World" (*Economist*, November 11, 2009). David Lampton, a leading China scholar in the United States, has summarized this literature as the "China on steroids" literature.[2] This often-unsubstantiated reporting has permeated Western policy discourse, resulting in—as an extreme but provocative expression—a theme of "China threat."[3]

If these sensational headlines are to be believed, three lasting impressions emerge: (1) China is one of the world's largest overseas direct investors. (2) Among emerging economies, it is the largest. (3) China's OFDI extends all over the world. Unfortunately, these impressions cannot be substantiated by hard evidence. The allegedly huge scale and scope of China's OFDI (which can escalate into a "threat") thus become a myth that takes on a life of its own. What exactly are the scale and scope of China's OFDI? How strong is it in the United States? Does it warrant the disproportionate media and political attention? How should the United States view such FDI from China? This case sheds some evidence-based light on this myth behind China's OFDI.[4] (Given our focus on China's foreign *direct* investment, its foreign portfolio investment such as purchasing US Treasury bills is outside the scope of this article)

Hard Data on a Weak Case

A look at the hard evidence points out how weak the case is to believe that China's OFDI is monetarily large, geographically expansive, and politically dangerous. First, take the notion that China is an OFDI powerhouse. According to the United Nations' *World Investment Report 2012*, in 2011, China was merely the ninth largest generator of OFDI flows ($65 billion)—well behind the United States, Japan, Britain, France, Hong Kong, Belgium, Switzerland, and Russia (in that order). *World Investment Report 2014* reported that in 2013 (the most recent year for which data were available), China rose to become the third-largest generator of OFDI flows—but at $101 billion (7% of world total), such OFDI flows were still substantially smaller than those from the United States ($338 billion, 24% of world total) and Japan ($136 billion, 10% of world total). As of 2011, China's OFDI stock (the cumulative OFDI made in all years) ($366 billion) was only 1.7% of the world total ($21 trillion) and 8% of the US OFDI stock ($4.5 trillion). By 2013, China's OFDI stock reached $614 billion (2.3% of world total—$26 trillion) and 10% of the US OFDI stock (24% of world total—$6.5 trillion). In other words, if Chinese companies could buy up the world with that relatively tiny sum, then US companies would have already done that 12 times (in 2011) or ten times (in 2013).

Second, there is also a widespread perception that China must be the largest foreign investor among emerging economies. Again, that is not entirely accurate, according to UN data. Using OFDI stock as a measure, China only became the largest foreign investor among emerging economies *very recently*—since 2011, after China's OFDI stock caught up with Russia's. In 2013, while China's stock of OFDI, at 2.3% of the

1) This research was supported by the Jindal Chair at the Jindal School of Management, University of Texas at Dallas. All views and errors are those of the author. © Mike W. Peng. Reprinted with permission.

2) D. M. Lampton, 2010, Power constrained: Sources of mutual strategic suspicion in U.S.–China relations (p. 7), *NBR Analysis*, June, Seattle: National Bureau of Asian Research.
3) US Congress, 2012, Investigative Report on the US National Security Issues Posed by Chinese Telecommunications Companies Huawei and ZTE, October 8, Washington, DC: US House of Representatives, 112th Congress.
4) M. W. Peng, 2011, The social responsibility of international business scholars: The case of China, *AIB Insights*, 11(4): 8–10; M. W. Peng, S. L. Sun, & D. Blevins, 2011, The social responsibility of international business scholars, *Multinational Business Review*, 19(2): 106–119; M. W. Peng & Z. Xiao, 2011, Busting the China Inc. myth, *Harvard Business Review*, June: blogs.hbr.org.

worldwide total, was six times India's (0.4%) and more than twice Brazil's (1.1%), it was only slightly ahead of Russia's OFDI stock (2%).

Finally, despite media sensations about Chinese multinationals "buying up the world," Chinese OFDI is *not* global. This is because Chinese companies have *not* invested all over the world. Instead, their OFDI is geographically concentrated. Hong Kong commands 67% of China's OFDI stock, while the rest of Asia has received 9%. Significant round tripping of Chinese capital, via Hong Kong, has taken place in order to take advantage of Chinese regulations in favor of "foreign" capital. Of the 12% of China's OFDI stock that Chinese companies have invested in Latin America and the Caribbean, tax havens such as the British Virgin Islands and the Cayman Islands have absorbed 11%. As Beijing's control of Hong Kong intensifies, it is likely that the British Virgin Islands and the Cayman Islands as tax havens increasingly assume the role that Hong Kong has traditionally played—to facilitate significant capital round tripping. By contrast, China's OFDI in Europe (4% of its OFDI stock), North America (2%), and Oceania (3%) is relatively small, while Africa accounts for just 4% of China's OFDI stock.

The world outside Hong Kong accounts for just about one-third of China's stock of OFDI. Doing a little math, we can see that Chinese companies have invested a mere 0.046% of the worldwide stock of OFDI in North America (that is: 2.3% of worldwide total × 2% invested in North America). In dollar terms, that is about US$12.3 billion as of 2013. Note this is the *stock* of China's OFDI in the United States—meaning the accumulation of all such investments over the years (not merely the flows of one year). In comparison, the revenue of the smallest US company on the *Fortune* Global 500, Raytheon (ranked 500th in 2014 based on revenues in 2013), was US$23 billion in just one *year*. Among firms from all countries that hold FDI stock in the United States (with a total stock of US$2.3 trillion), multinationals from China hold approximately 0.1%—a trivial amount compared to firms from Britain (20%), Japan (12%), and Germany (12%). According to an influential Asia Society study, when it comes to FDI in the United States, "the world's second-largest economy still plays in the same league as New Zealand and Austria."[5] A study by the US-China Economic and Security Review Commission reported that until 2009, inward FDI from China had been so tiny that it was recorded in official

US statistics as a *rounding error*.[6] The upshot? China's OFDI, while emerging and increasing, is insignificant in the United States and certainly does not deserve the disproportionate media hoopla and political attention.

Pragmatic Nationalism

To put things in perspective, the United States has little reason to feel threatened by a statistical rounding error.[7] That said, the world's largest economy needs to pay attention to what the world's second-largest economy is doing. Given that the rise of the Chinese economy and the emergence of China's OFDI only started recently, one thing for sure is that China's OFDI will grow and its share in the United States will become higher in the future.

How should the United States view FDI from China? The pros and cons of FDI have been debated for decades around the world. In the United States, the most recent debate prior to the arrival of Chinese FDI took place in the 1980s and the 1990s when Japanese multinationals emerged as a force to be reckoned with. What emerged out of these debates has always been *pragmatic nationalism*—viewing FDI as having both pros and cons and only approving FDI when its benefits outweigh costs. Pragmatic nationalism guided US policy regarding Japan's FDI into the United States, despite some harsh concerns expressed by certain politicians and media outlets at that time. Today, Japanese multinationals, via FDI, employ approximately 700,000 Americans. Not a single American politician or media outlet bothers to worry about the "Japan threat" any more.

Despite the geopolitical rivalry between the United States and China and the uneasy feeling among some Americans that a majority of China's OFDI is undertaken by state-owned enterprises (SOEs), there is no reason to abandon the policy of pragmatic nationalism.[8] Especially considering the tiny scale and scope of China's FDI in the United States, the costs for overhauling the overall regulatory framework governing FDI simply outweigh the benefits.[9] Other than legitimate scrutiny that is sector-specific (such as telecommunications) and issue-specific (such as national security

5) D. Rosen & T. Hanemann, 2011, *An American Open Door? Maximizing the Benefits of Chinese Foreign Direct Investment* (p. 27), New York: Asia Society.

6) A. Szamosszegi, 2012, *An Analysis of Chinese Investments in the US Economy* (p. 1 and p. 80), Washington, DC: US–China Economic and Security Review Commission.
7) M. W. Peng, 2012, Why China's investments aren't a threat, *Harvard Business Review*, February 13, blogs.hbr.org.
8) S. Globerman, 2015, Host governments should not treat state-owned enterprises different than other foreign investors, *Columbia FDI Perspectives*, January, No. 138.
9) S. Globerman & D. Shapiro, 2009, Economic and strategic considerations surrounding Chinese FDI in the United States, *Asia Pacific Journal of Management*, 26: 163–183.

reviews undertaken by the Committee on Foreign Investments in the United States [CFIUS]), a blanket negative, unfriendly, and even hostile attitude toward China's FDI in general will be counter-productive and even self-destructive. In short, the right attitude toward China's FDI should be: "Yes, unless."[10]

Today, China's FDI in the United States supports approximately 20,000 American jobs. While not large, this number is a tangible contribution to the US economy and a clear vote of confidence. This number can grow much higher, as China may generate US$1 *trillion* OFDI to invest around the world by 2020. How much of this OFDI will come to the United States and how many new jobs will be created will depend on the investment decisions made by each and every Chinese multinational.[11] In my executive training and consulting engagements, I have been repeatedly confronted by Chinese executives who are eager to invest in the United States but who are frustrated by negative treatments of Chinese firms in the hands of American politicians and the media (think of CNOOC in 2005 and Huawei in 2012). "Is the United States really hostile to us?" one executive raised a pointed question to me. He then continued: "My company wants to invest abroad. Between America and Africa, where should I go? In Africa, the governments are nice and the terms are friendly. But, in America, politicians make me worry and the media is scary." While I always share with my clients that the United States is *really* open to China's FDI and that the *majority* of China's OFDI deals (never mind CNOOC's and Huawei's) routinely go through, I have a sense that my arguments are not very persuasive, given the negative US political and media sentiments that are widely reported in China.

So far, Africa has indeed absorbed much more of China's OFDI than the United States—the ratio is about 2:1. While there are many economic reasons attracting Chinese multinationals to invest in Africa (think of natural resources), we do not know on the margin how many of them choose to go to Africa because the United States loses out in their investment decision. In other words, we need to be aware that the United States competes with Africa—and with the rest of the world, for that matter—for precious OFDI dollars and for new job creation. After all, Chinese firms are not obligated to invest in the United States. When US unemployment is high, jobs are hard to come by, and state governments are eager to lure Chinese FDI into their jurisdictions,[12] certain US politicians and media outlets' attitude to turn away investors from the second-largest economy in the world due to their alleged "threat" does not make much sense. A case can be made that they are economically and socially irresponsible by destroying US jobs that could have been created by such FDI.

The Myth and the Truth

If not debunked and refuted, myths have a tendency to take on a life of their own. The more myths are reported, the more likely they become self-fulfilling prophecies. The myth behind China's OFDI is one of the crucial but rarely investigated myths of our time. The truth is: as the world's second-largest economy and the largest exporter, China is punching *below* its weight due to its relatively modest sum and limited scope of OFDI. Every Chinese citizen only possesses approximately US$460 in OFDI stock. In comparison, every American citizen enjoys US$13,500 and the global average is US$2,900. Further, a lot of China's OFDI goes back to China due to capital round tripping.[13]

China's OFDI is destined to grow—in 2015, its OFDI is likely to exceed its inward FDI flow for the first time.[14] Overall, a sensible approach is not to view China's expanding OFDI as a fire-breathing "dragon" on the verge of taking over the world—Chinese multinationals are far from being capable of doing that (even if they wanted to). To be sure, host country governments, firms, the media, as well as the public need to be serious in dealing this new phenomenon on the global scene. Therefore, a useful metaphor is to view China's OFDI as a fast and strong "racehorse" unleashed by the forces of globalization in the 21st century.

Case Discussion Questions

1. **Using data from the most recent year, what is the flow of China's FDI into your country? What is the stock of China's in your country? Relative to other countries whose multinationals undertake FDI in your country, what is China's ranking—in both flow and stock—relative to other countries?**

10) R. A. Kapp, 2013, The impending tide of Chinese investment in the United States, *NBR Analysis Brief*, February, Seattle: National Bureau of Asian Research.
11) M. W. Peng, 2012, The global strategy of emerging multinationals from China, *Global Strategy Journal*, 2: 97–107.
12) I was involved in the US–China Investment Week that was kicked off in Dallas on September 21, 2012. To welcome a delegation of 50 investors from China, three governors from Texas, Florida, and Wisconsin came, and former President George W. Bush gave a keynote at the banquet.
13) M. W. Peng & R. C. Parente, 2012, Institution-based weaknesses behind emerging multinationals, *Revista de Administração de Empresas*, 52: 360–364.
14) Economist, 2015, *The World in 2015* (p. 94), London: The Economist Group.

2. **Compare the flow (in the most recent year) and stock of FDI from your country in China versus the flow and stock of FDI from China in your country. Which is bigger? Why?**

3. **Why has China's OFDI received such sensational (but often unsubstantiated) media reporting regarding its scale and scope?**

4. **Identify the largest FDI project (in terms of dollar amount) undertaken by Chinese multinationals in your country. Evaluate its pros and cons, and discuss whether its advantages to the host economy (that is, your country) outweigh the disadvantages.**

Integrative Case 2.5

The Korea-US Free Trade Agreement (KORUS)[1]

Charles M. Byles (Virginia Commonwealth University)

What does the Korea-US Free Trade Agreement cover? Will it deliver its promise?

> "American manufacturers of cars and trucks will gain more access to the Korean market and a level playing field to take advantage of that access. We are strengthening our ability to create and defend manufacturing jobs in the United States; increasing exports of agricultural products for American farmers and ranchers; and opening Korea's services market to American companies. High standards for the protection of workers' rights and the environment make this a model for future trade agreements, which must be both free and fair."
>
> *– Statement by President Barack Obama announcing KORUS on December 3, 2010.*

The Korea-US Free Trade Agreement (KORUS) had its origins on June 5, 2006, when the United States and the Republic of Korea (South Korea—hereafter, "Korea") began negotiations. Although the agreement was signed by both countries on June 30, 2007, it was stalled for a few years because of the expiration of President George W. Bush's fast-track trade authority and disagreements about trade in automobiles and beef. Almost three years later on June 26, 2010, President Barack Obama and President Lee Myung-bak expressed commitment to move ahead with the agreement and address the outstanding disagreements. The United States Congress and the Korean National Assembly approved the agreement on October 12 and November 22, 2011, respectively. The agreement was finally implemented on March 15, 2012.

Importance to the United States of KORUS

According to the Office of the United States Trade Representative (USTR), KORUS is the most commercially significant free trade agreement in almost two decades. Estimates from the US International Trade Commission show an addition of $10 billion to $12 billion to the US annual gross domestic product as a result of Korean tariff reductions on merchandise. In addition, merchandise exports to Korea will increase

by $10 billion. The tariff rates prior to the agreement were 12.1% on average for exports to Korea and 3.5% for Korean exports to the United States Almost 80% of US exports to Korea of consumer and industrial products became duty free on March 15, 2012, and nearly 95% of trade between the two countries will become duty free on March 15, 2017. Within 10 years of the implementation of the agreement, most remaining tariffs will be removed.

The International Trade Commission also estimates the creation of 70,000 jobs as a result of increased merchandise exports. In addition, of particular importance for American companies given their competitive advantage in services is access to Korea's $580 billion services market. There is the potential for additional job creation in a variety of services industries such as telecommunications, education, and health care. In addition, there are opportunities for increases in direct investment in Korea. KORUS will provide an institutional framework to remove previous barriers to investment in Korea and the institutions to make investment easier and more predictable such as dispute settlement mechanisms and intellectual property protections.

Despite the general support in the United States from the government and business community, there have been predictions that KORUS will produce economic losses for the United States. For example, an Economic Policy Institute working paper by Robert E. Scott published in 2010 warned that KORUS could displace up to 159,000 jobs between 2008 and 2015. In addition, the article argues that a major risk of KORUS is surging truck imports from Korea. Scott also notes that one study of the benefits of the agreement ignores currency manipulation by Korea in order to ensure a continued trade surplus.

Bilateral Trade Agreements in the Context of Multilateral Trade

An article in the *Economist* published in 2009 noted that regional and bilateral trade deals were increasing rapidly from 49 in 2001 to 167 in 2009. This increase was a reaction to the failure of the Doha Round of the World Trade Organization (WTO) negotiations. The article,

1) © Charles M. Byles. Reprinted with permission.

however, gave a number of criticisms of regional and bilateral trade deals. First, these deals impose much bureaucracy and paperwork on trade and as a result, many companies do not take advantage of their provisions. Second, the deals favor less efficient companies that gain advantages primarily through lower tariffs. Finally, regional and bilateral deals do not serve as a stepping stone to broader multilateral trade deals but are instead a distraction for governments. Rather than devoting time working on the multilateral process (which could take much time and energy and is less visible to the public), countries instead work on regional and bilateral trade deals such as KORUS and the Colombia and Panama FTAs, which can take less time and are more visible to the public. Will these criticisms apply to KORUS? Can it provide some trade advantages especially to President Obama's National Export Initiative to double exports between 2009 and 2014?

The Essence of KORUS

The KORUS agreement consists of 24 chapters and several annexes, appendices, and confirmation letters. What follows is not a detailed discussion of each chapter, annex, appendix, or confirmation letter, but rather an exposition of the key provisions in order to show the role of institutions (i.e., KORUS) not only on primarily trade (both merchandise and services), but also foreign direct investment (FDI). In addition, the case will show the link between a bilateral trade agreement and the protocols of the WTO agreement of which the United States and Korea are part.

Trade in Goods

KORUS reduces tariff barriers (e.g., customs duties) for goods exported to Korea and imported into the United States. Neither country can increase tariffs on a given item (some exceptions exist such as a safeguard action or as authorized by the WTO's Dispute Settlement Body) and both countries should work to gradually eliminate existing tariffs.

KORUS also addresses nontariff barriers by eliminating existing ones or preventing future ones to be enacted. Examples of prohibited nontariff barriers are export or import price requirements, import licensing conditioned on the fulfillment of a performance requirement, and voluntary export constraints. Administrative fees (charges other than duties applied to imports) must be kept to the approximate cost of the service and cannot be used as a means of protection of domestic industries. Each country must make available

to the other a list of all fees and charges in connection with imports or exports.

The agreement also addresses the so-called "distinctive products" as follows. Korea must recognize Bourbon Whiskey and Tennessee Whiskey as products only of Tennessee. The United States must recognize Andong Soju and Gyeongju Beopju as distinctive products of Korea.

The agreement on trade in goods also has certain institutional provisions. A Committee on Trade in Goods with members from each country will be established for the purposes of ensuring that both parties adhere to the agreement and to handle any disagreements between the parties. This committee may meet at the request of either country or the Joint Committee (described later) to address matters relating to trade in goods, rules of origin (Chapter 6 of the agreement), and customs administration and trade facilitation (Chapter 7 of the agreement). The committee will also resolve any differences between the countries related to the classification of goods under the Harmonized System (a common or "harmonized" method of describing and coding products).

Automobiles

The Korean automobile market presents a major opportunity for US automobile manufacturers. KORUS addresses an important nontariff barrier—Korea's automotive safety standards that have been a major barrier to US automobiles. KORUS also addresses the Korean environmental standards that have in the past been another nontariff barrier. The agreement attempts to articulate standards that address important safety and environmental standards while at the same time minimizes their role as barriers to trade. Some specific aspects of the agreement on automobiles are the following: KORUS reduced the tariff on US automobiles from 8% to 4% with a complete elimination in 2016. The US tariff on Korean imports will be 2.5% until 2016, when the tariffs will be eliminated entirely.

Within the agreement, a dispute settlement panel will hear complaints from either country. If the panel rules in favor of the complaining country, that country may suspend its tariff reductions and assess duties at the previous WTO rate (called a "snapback" as the duties go back to their previous rate).

The agreement also requires amendment to Korea's engine displacement taxes to reduce those taxes over time as these taxes have an adverse effect on US automobile prices. Korea has also agreed to give the United

States up to one year to comply with any new automobile regulations. Additionally, as mentioned earlier, Korea will work at harmonization of automobile safety and environmental standards. For example, KORUS allows some US vehicles that comply with US safety standards to be considered in compliance with Korean standards. The agreement also allows some leniency on meeting Korean environmental standards. Specifically, some US manufacturers (classified according to the number of cars sold) will be considered meeting the standards even if they are below it within certain limits. Finally, the agreement allows a safeguard measure, which allows the United States to impose a duty if there is a surge in Korean imports that cause damage to the US automobile industry.

Agricultural Products

The United States is Korea's main supplier of agricultural products. The agreement requires each party to abide by the Tariff Rate Quotas in the agreement. Tariff Rate Quotas lay out the quantity of agricultural products listed by product type that can enter each country duty free. Typically, the quotas show the quantity in metric tons of a product allowed in duty free for each year of the agreement. At some later year (typically 10, 12, or 15), the duty free amount becomes unlimited.

The agreement also contains an annex of Agricultural Safeguard Measures for Korea. This section includes a schedule by product that gives the year (1, 2, 3, 4), the amount of the import in metric tons that will trigger the safeguard duty, and then the actual duty. A safeguard duty allows the importing country to impose a duty if imports reach a level that would impose damage on a particular sector. For example, if pork imports reach 8,250 metric tons (the trigger level) in year 1, Korea may impose a safeguard duty of 22.5%.

There are certain agricultural items that merit special attention. The first is beef, which in the recent past has been restricted in Korea. In 2003, Korea was the third-largest market for US beef exports (US market share in that year was 76%). A subsequent ban in US beef imports as a result of mad cow disease led some members of the US Congress to condition support of KORUS on a full opening of Korea's market for US beef. Under the KORUS agreement, Korea would eliminate its 40% tariff on US beef imports over a 15-year period. A safeguard system applies to beef as for other agricultural products where Korea can impose safeguard tariffs (temporarily) in response to a surge in imports. The trigger for this tariff was 270,000 metric tons in

2012, and the trigger amount will increase 2% annually until year 16 (2027) when safeguard mechanism will be removed. Since the opening of the Korean market, US exporters have gained market share (38% in 2013 compared to 1% in 2005).

The second agricultural product worth mentioning is rice. Under KORUS, US rice receives no preferential treatment. Korea simply has to abide by its WTO commitment with respect to rice where the United States would receive equal treatment under the WTO's nondiscrimination rule. In the negotiations, Korea would not change its position on rice as a result of the country's desire to maintain self-sufficiency, the cultural identity provided by rice, and the political influence of rice farmers. The United States was faced with the choice of accepting Korea's stand or having no agreement at all.

Geographic Indications for Dairy Products

During the course of negotiations of KORUS, the US dairy sector was concerned that geographic indications (a sort of trademark that restricts the use of certain names such as Champagne or Vidalia onions to products only from that region) negotiated in the EU-Korea FTA might place US dairy products at a disadvantage in the Korean market. For example, if cheese names such as feta, muenster, and parmesan are restricted in the Korean market, US exporters will be at a significant disadvantage. To address these concerns, Korea agreed that use of names such as camembert, mozzarella, emmental, parmesan, and others as applied to US cheeses exported to Korea would be allowed. Other cheeses, however, such as asiago, feta, and gorgonzola can only be sold in Korea by EU exporters.

Textiles and Apparel

Textile and apparel imports into the United States from Korea have been decreasing over the last few years. In 2013, 3% of US textile imports came from Korea compared to 9% in 1990. Similarly, garment imports from Korea in 2013 were less than 1% of all garment imports compared to 10% in 1990. This decrease is partly a result of increases in imports of textiles and apparel from China. US exports to Korea are quite small. In 2013, the US exported $285 million in textiles and $100 million in garments to Korea.

KORUS immediately eliminated tariffs on 52% (of value) of US imports of textiles and apparel from Korea. Tariffs on an additional 19% will be eliminated by 2016, and tariffs on the remaining 29% will be eliminated at the end of 2021. For US textile and apparel exports to Korea, tariffs were eliminated on 77% (in value) in 2012. Tariffs will be eliminated on an additional 13% in 2015, and the remaining 10 % by 2016.

KORUS allows certain "Bilateral Emergency Actions" in response to a surge in imports. Such actions may be in the form of suspension of further tariff reductions or an increase in the tariff rate. The importing country may only take such an action following an investigation. Written notice must be given to the exporting country and the country taking the emergency action must provide concession in the form of tariff reductions on other textile and apparel products or any other products provided both countries agree.

Certain Rules of Origin as laid out in the agreement (Chapter 6 of KORUS) apply to textiles and apparel. In addition, a Committee on Textile and Apparel Trade Matters has been established and will meet at the request of either country to consider any issues relating to trade in textiles and apparel.

Rules of Origin and Origin Procedures

KORUS lays out complex rules of origin and origin procedures that must be met in order for a good to be considered "originating" in either partner country and thus qualifying for a preferential tariff. These rules are stated in Chapters 4 (Textiles and Apparel) and 6 (Rules of Origin and Origin Procedures). The customs office in either country is responsible for applying those procedures to determine whether the relevant country meets the criteria and hence qualifies for the preferential tariff. There has been concern among some US exporters that the Korean Customs Service has undermined the spirit of the FTA by requiring excessive documentation. The United States has questioned a number of decisions issued by the Korean Customs Service on the qualification of certain products for preferential treatment.

Technical Barriers to Trade

KORUS contains a chapter on the rules governing technical barriers to trade. The goal is to allow reasonable technical standards needed for safety and other goals that conform to accepted international standards but that are not barriers to trade. The agreement specifically seeks to have the parties "… seek to identify, develop, and promote trade facilitating initiatives regarding standards, technical regulations, and conformity assessment procedures that are appropriate for particular issues or sectors." In addition, the agreement suggests that "These initiatives may include cooperation on regulatory issues, such as transparency, the promotion of good regulatory practices, alignment with international standards, and the use of accreditation to qualify assessment bodies." The transparency aspect of the agreement requires that each country participate in the development of the standards, technical regulations, and conformity assessment procedures. With respect to automotive standards and technical regulations, the agreement stipulates that technical regulations do not create unnecessary regulations that are impediments to trade. To achieve this goal, KORUS requires that these regulations only be used to achieve legitimate objectives such as national security requirements, the prevention of deceptive practices, the protection of human health or safety, animal or plant life or health, or the environment. The agreement establishes a Committee on Technical Barriers to Trade with the functions of addressing a number of issues relating to problems and questions relating to the implementation of the Chapter on Technical Barriers to Trade.

Trade Remedies

The primary trade remedy in KORUS is the safeguard measure. By definition, a safeguard measure is an allowance to either party to impose a temporary tariff in response to a surge in imports that has the potential to cause damage (loss in sales and/or employment) to a particular industry. The agreement allows either country to respond in one of two ways. First, it may suspend the further reduction of a customs duty in accordance with the agreement. In such a case, the increase in the duty should not exceed the WTO agreed upon Most-Favored-Nation (MFN) duty at about the time the safeguard action is taken. Second, either country may increase the customs duty on the product in question not to exceed the lesser of the MFN duty at the time the action is taken or the MFN duty in effect on the day immediately following the signing of the KORUS agreement.

Foreign Direct Investment

Both countries agree that each country will offer treatment no less favorable than it accords investments in its own country by its own investors. Specifically, the no less favorable rule applies to the establishment, acquisition, expansion, management, conduct, operation, and sale or disposition of investments in either country. In addition, the agreement stipulates that each country provide fair and equitable treatment and full protection and security as customary under international law. Fair and equitable treatment includes agreement not to deny justice in criminal or civil proceedings and adhere to the principles of due process. Full protection and security means that each country should provide police protection as required under international law. KORUS prohibits expropriation of investment property except under certain circumstances (e.g., for a public purpose). Where such expropriation occurs, compensation must be promptly paid.

KORUS requires each country to facilitate transfers relating to investment property (e.g., profits, dividends, and capital gains). The agreement also prohibits the application of performance requirements to any investment (e.g., having a requirement to export at a given level or have a certain level of domestic content). With respect to staffing the investment, the agreement requires that neither country stipulate the nationality of the top management team and board of directors. Finally, KORUS has a dispute settlement process whereby the countries first try to resolve the issue through negotiation before going to arbitration.

Services

A number of chapters in KORUS address services: Chapter 12 (Cross-Border Services), Chapter 13 (Financial Services), and Chapter 15 (Telecommunications). This section deals primarily with Chapter 12, although KORUS broadly seeks to reduce barriers across all service categories. The commitments outlined here generally apply to financial services and telecommunications.

As with investments, the agreement requires that each country provide treatment no less favorable than provided to local service suppliers. The agreement requires that neither country impose limitations on the number of service suppliers, quotas on the value of service transactions, the total number of service operations, or the total number of persons that may be employed in a service sector or in a particular firm providing those services. In addition, no country can restrict or require a particular legal entity through which the service is supplied nor require either country to establish a local office as a condition for trading in services.

As with investments, KORUS requires that transfers (e.g., profits and dividends) be freely permitted without delay. Each country is also required to make available to the other any rules and regulations relating to services.

Institutional Provisions and Dispute Settlement

KORUS establishes a Joint Committee to be co-chaired by the United States Trade Representative and the Korean Minister of Trade. The committee's purpose is to oversee implementation of the agreement, supervise the work of all other committees (which may address specific products such as automobiles), find ways to enhance trade between the countries, and establish panels to resolve disputes.

An important responsibility of the Joint Committee is dispute settlement. KORUS requires that where a dispute arises, the countries first attempt to resolve the dispute through negotiation. The dispute settlement process only applies to issues relating to violations of the agreement as outlined in each chapter, for example where a country fails to execute its obligations as outlined in the agreement. If negotiation fails to resolve the dispute, the Joint Committee will establish a panel of three members to hear the case. The panel will then review the case and present a report within 180 days. The country losing the dispute may make the required changes. If it does not, then the winning country may suspend certain benefits in accordance with recommendations of the panel.

KORUS at its Two Year Anniversary

After two years in force, has KORUS expanded trade and investment between the United States and Korea? Generally, the evidence is in favor of a "yes" answer. According to the Office of the USTR, at the second anniversary of KORUS by March 2014, there have been several benefits. Overall, trade between the two countries has increased to the point that Korea is now the sixth-largest trading partner of the United States. Exports of manufactured goods, services, and agricultural products have increased. US exports of automobiles increased 80% compared to 2011, and service exports to Korea increased 18.5% from 2011 to 2013. According to the USTR, three rounds of tariff cuts or eliminations have taken place since the agreement came into force on March 15, 2012. By January 1, 2016, Korean tariffs on over 95% of US merchandise exports will be eliminated.

For Korea, there have also been gains. Korean investment in the United States has grown considerably and in 2013 exceeded US investment in Korea. Exports of goods to the United States grew by 7% while Korean sales of passenger vehicles grew by 79.5 % and packaged medicines by 98.7% from 2011 to 2013.

Case Discussion Questions

1. Is the WTO becoming less important and are regional and bilateral agreements the wave of the future? Are there advantages of a bilateral agreement such as KORUS over WTO agreements?

2. While trade theories generally support free trade, political realities ensure that trade barriers still exist. How does KORUS address the realities of international trade?

3. Some argue that regional or bilateral trade agreements are building blocks for global trade agreements. Others argue that such "Balkanization" of world trade represents stumbling blocks to international trade. Is KORUS a building block or a stumbling block?

4. How do formal institutions facilitate or impede trade and investment? Give examples from KORUS.

5. Go online and read President Obama's National Export Initiative. To what extent did KORUS contribute to the main goal of this initiative?

Sources: Based on (1) Korea-US Trade Partnership, 2014, The facts about the Korea–US Free Trade Agreement, Embassy of the Republic of Korea, retrieved December 22, 2014, from http://www.uskoreaconnect.org/files/publications/facts-about-the-korea-us-fta.pdf; (2) *Economist*, 2009, Trade agreements: Doing Doha down, September 3, retrieved December 22, 2014 from http://www.economist.com/node/14363297/print; (3) Korea Southeast US Chamber of Commerce, 2014, Happy anniversary KORUS FTA, retrieved January 4, 2015, from http://www.koreaseuschamber.org/kseuscc-news/happy-anniversary-korus-fta; (4) J. Meltzer, 2010, A closer look at the Korea–US Free Trade Agreement, Brookings Institution, December 8, 2010, retrieved December 22, 2014 from http://www.brookings.edu/research/opinions/2010/12/08-us-korea-trade-meltzer; (5) Office of the United States Trade Representative, 2014, US-Korea Free Trade Agreement shows strong results on second anniversary, retrieved December 22, 2014, from http://www.ustr.gov/trade-agreements/free-trade-agreements/korus-fta and http://www.ustr.gov/about-us/press-office/press-releases/2014/March/US-Korea-Free-Trade-Agreement-Shows-Strong-Results-on-Second-Anniversary; (6) R. E. Scott, 2010, Trade policy and job loss: US trade deals with Colombia and South Korea will be costly, EPI Working Paper, February 25, retrieved December 22, 2014, from http://epi.3cdn.net/87da5b7ec4f5677422_o9m6bh6nv.pdf; (7) US Korea Connect, A history of the US-Korea Free Trade Agreement, retrieved December 22, 2014, from http://www.uskoreaconnect.org/about/history.html; (8) US Korea Connect, KORUS FTA trade figures, retrieved December 22, 2014, from http://www.uskoreaconnect.org/facts-figures/issues-answers/korus-trade-figures.html; (9) White House Office of the Press Secretary, 2010, Statement by the President announcing the US-Korea Free Trade Agreement, December 3, retrieved December 22, 2014, from http://www.whitehouse.gov/the-press-office/2010/12/03/statement-president-announcing-us-korea-trade-agreement; (10) B. Williams, M. E. Manyin, R. Jurenas, & M. D. Platzer, 2014, The US–South Korea Free Trade Agreement (KORUS FTA): Provisions and implementation, Congressional Research Service, September 16, 2014, Retrieved December 23, 2014, from https://www.fas.org/sgp/crs/row/RL34330.pdf.

© Lonely/Shutterstock.com

PART 3 Strategizing Around the Globe

iStockphoto.com/Harvepino

Chapters

Jonathan Alcorn/Reuters

CHAPTER 9

Learning Objectives

After studying this chapter, you should be able to

- define entrepreneurship, entrepreneurs, and entrepreneurial firms.

- identify the institutions and resources that affect entrepreneurship.

- discuss three characteristics of a growing entrepreneurial firm.

- understand how international strategies for entering foreign markets are different from those for staying in domestic markets.

- participate in two debates concerning entrepreneurship.

- draw implications for action.

Growing and Internationalizing the Entrepreneurial Firm

Sriracha Spices Up American Food

Named after a seaside city in eastern Thailand, Sriracha is a generic name for a hot sauce made from a paste of chili peppers (jalapeños), garlic, vinegar, sugar, and salt. As a dipping sauce, Sriracha has been used in Thai and Vietnamese cuisine for ages. However, in the United States, most people would associate Sriracha with the specific brand produced by Huy Fong Foods, based in Irwindale (a suburb of Los Angeles), California. It is indeed Huy Fong's Sriracha Hot Chili Sauce—often affectionately called the "rooster sauce" due to the prominent logo of the rooster on its squeeze bottle—that has popularized this once-niche food and spiced up mainstream American taste buds. So what exactly is Sriracha? What does it do? Huy Fong's website has provided an official answer:

> Sriracha is made from sun-ripened chilies which are ground into a smooth paste along with garlic and packaged in a convenient squeeze bottle. It is excellent in soups, sauces, pastas, pizzas, hot dogs, hamburgers, chow mein, or anything else to give it a delicious, spicy taste.

Founded in 1980 by a Vietnamese–Chinese immigrant David Tran, the firm was named after the freighter, *Huy Fong*, that carried him to the land of opportunity. Tran was born and raised in Vietnam. Already an entrepreneur back home, he had a small business making a similar hot sauce there in the 1970s. But the Vietnam War made growth impossible. After the war, the Vietnamese government gave ethnic Chinese businessmen like Tran a hard time. In 1979, he left Vietnam. As a serial entrepreneur, Tran looked for opportunities in his new country. He quickly discovered that (in his view) there was no decent spicy food in the United States. Having identified this gap, he endeavored to fill it by making hot sauce again. By 1983, he came up with the winning recipe that has not changed much since.

Distinguished by a green cap and a clear plastic squeeze bottle, Huy Fong's Sriracha was first sold to Asian supermarkets and restaurants. While popular in the Asian community, Sriracha remained a niche product hardly noticed by mainstream America. Over time, the burgeoning Asian population in the United States made crossover into the mainstream possible. Sriracha created quite a sensation. In 2003, Wal-Mart started selling it in its stores in Los Angeles and Houston. Eventually, Wal-Mart would carry it in its more than 3,000 stores across the nation. Various restaurants, such as Applebee's, P. F. Chang's, Subway, and White Castle, introduced Sriracha-flavored dishes and dipping sauces. Potato chip king Lay's unleased a sriracha-flavored potato chip. In 2010, *Bob Appétit*—an influential foodie magazine—named it Ingredient of the Year. In 2011, its first mainstream kitchen bible, *The Sriracha Cookbook*, was published by Randy Clemens. In 2012, *Cook's Illustrated* claimed Sriracha to be the best-tasting hot sauce, ahead of rivals such as Tobasco, Colula Hot Sauce, and Frank's Red Hot. While focusing on the United States, Sriracha has been exported to many countries around the world.

Sriracha's success has not only inspired a number of imitators and counterfeiters (!), but has also caught the attention of McIlhenny Co., the maker of the standard-bearer of American hot sauce, Tabasco, for the past 160 years. McIlhenny Co. used to dismiss Sriracha as "a West Coast thing." But now Paul McIlhenny, its sixth-generation CEO, can pick up a bottle of rooster sauce at his local Wal-Mart in rural Louisiana. In response, a Tabasco-version of Sriracha will be unleashed soon. Given such strong incumbents and a crowded field, what is Sriracha's secret? Again, Huy Fong's website has provided an official answer: "The secret? Continued high-quality ingredients at low prices and great taste makes it a success in today's trend toward spicy foods."

Sources: Based on (1) *Bloomberg Businessweek*, 2013, Burning sensation: How Sriracha hot sauce won the American kitchen, February 21: 67–69; (2) www.huyfong.com; (3) www.tabasco.com.

How do entrepreneurial firms such as Huy Fong grow? How do they enter international markets? What are the challenges and constraints they face? This chapter deals with these important questions. This is different from many international business (IB) textbooks that typically focus on large firms. To the extent that every large firm today started out small and that some (although not all) of today's small and medium-sized enterprises (SMEs) will become tomorrow's multinational enterprises (MNEs), current and would-be managers will not gain a complete picture of the global business landscape if they focus only on large firms.

SMEs are firms with fewer than 500 employees in the United States, and firms with fewer than 250 employees in the European Union (other countries may have different definitions). Most students will join SMEs for employment. Some will also start up their own SMEs, thus further necessitating our attention to these numerous "Davids" (such as Huy Fong) instead of the smaller number of "Goliaths."

This chapter first defines entrepreneurship. Next, we outline how our two leading perspectives, institution-based and resource-based views, shed light on entrepreneurship. Then we introduce characteristics of a growing entrepreneurial firm and multiple ways to internationalize.

9-1 Entrepreneurship and Entrepreneurial Firms

Although entrepreneurship is often associated with smaller and younger firms, there is no rule banning larger and older firms from being "entrepreneurial." So what exactly is entrepreneurship? Recent research suggests that firm size and age are not defining characteristics of entrepreneurship. Instead, entrepreneurship is defined as "the identification and exploitation of previously unexplored opportunities."[1] Specifically, it is concerned with "the sources of opportunities; the processes of discovery, evaluation, and exploitation of opportunities; and the set of individuals who discover, evaluate, and exploit them."[2] Thus, these individuals are entrepreneurs. French in origin, the word "entrepreneurs" traditionally means intermediaries connecting others.[3] Today, the word mostly refers to founders and owners of new businesses or managers of existing firms. Consequently, international entrepreneurship is defined as "a combination of innovative, proactive, and risk-seeking behavior that crosses national borders and is intended to create wealth in organizations."[4]

Small and medium-sized enterprise (SME)

A firm with fewer than 500 employees in the United States, or with fewer than 250 employees in the European Union.

Entrepreneurship

The identification and exploitation of previously unexplored opportunities.

Learning Objective

Define entrepreneurship, entrepreneurs, and entrepreneurial firms.

Entrepreneur

A founder and/or owner of a new business or a manager of existing firms, who identifies and exploits new opportunities.

International entrepreneurship

A combination of innovative, proactive, and risk-seeking behavior that crosses national borders and is intended to create wealth in organizations.

Although SMEs are not the exclusive domain of entrepreneurship, the convention that many people use is to associate entrepreneurship with SMEs, because, on average, SMEs tend to be more entrepreneurial than are large firms. To minimize confusion, the remainder of this chapter will follow that convention, although it is not totally accurate. In other words, while we acknowledge that some managers at large firms can be very entrepreneurial, we will limit the use of the term "entrepreneurs" to owners, founders, and managers of SMEs. Further, we will use the term "entrepreneurial firms" when referring to SMEs. We will refer to non-SMEs (which are firms with more than 500 employees in the United States, and firms with more than 250 employees in the European Union) as "large firms."

SMEs are important. Worldwide, they account for more than 95% of the number of firms, create approximately 50% of total value added, and generate 60%–90% of employment (depending on the country). Many entrepreneurs will try, and many SMEs will fail. Only a small number of entrepreneurs and SMEs will succeed.

9-2 Institutions, Resources, and Entrepreneurship

Learning Objective
Identify the institutions and resources that affect entrepreneurship.

Shown in Figure 9.1, both institution-based and the resource-based views shed light on entrepreneurship.[5] In this section, we will look at how institutions constrain or facilitate entrepreneurs and how firm-specific (and in many cases, entrepreneur-specific) resources and capabilities determine entrepreneurial success and failure.

9-2a Institutions and Entrepreneurship

First introduced in Chapters 2 and 3, both formal and informal institutional constraints, as rules of the game, affect entrepreneurship (see Figure 9.1). The Opening Case illustrates how Vietnam's entrepreneur-hostile institutional framework drove away David Tran, and how America's entrepreneur-friendly institutional framework has offered rich soil on which his entrepreneurial firm Huy Fong Foods blossoms.

Although entrepreneurship is thriving around the globe in general, its development is uneven (see Emerging Markets 9.1). Whether entrepreneurship is facilitated or retarded significantly depends on formal institutions governing how entrepreneurs start up new firms.[6] A World Bank survey, *Doing Business* (see PengAtlas Map 3.1), reports some striking differences in government regulations

---

Figure 9.1 **Institutions, Resources, and Entrepreneurship**

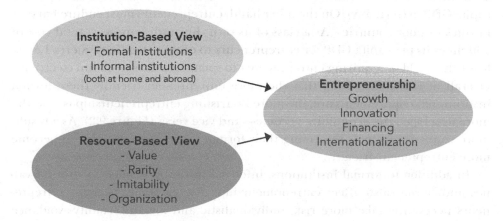

EMERGING MARKETS 9.1

One Rock Formation, Two Countries

North Mexico shares a great deal of similarities with south Texas. They include landscape, weather, people, food, culture . . . and rock formation beneath the land. South Texas has hit the jackpot of sitting on top of Eagle Ford shale, whose rock formation contains significant shale gas deposits. Fueled by hydraulic fracturing—in short, "fracking"—thousands of shale wells have bubbled up throughout Texas. However, the entrepreneurial boom of fracking does not seem to spill over the border. As of May 2014, fewer than 25 shale wells have stood up in all of Mexico. Why has the same rock formation not generated the same entrepreneurial boom in Mexico?

The answer is institution-based. Oil is big business. But Mexicans have a stubborn attachment to smallness in business. Mexico has a higher percentage of small firms with ten or fewer employees as a share of all firms (95.5%) than other Latin American countries

(80%–90% in Argentina, Brazil, and Chile). Known as the Peter Pan syndrome, many firms prefer to stay small than to grow, in an effort to minimize tax and regulatory intrusion. Overall, only 8% of bank loans in Mexico go to SMEs. Of about five million SMEs, only 900,000 are sufficiently formal to be creditworthy. Bank loans they obtain carry much higher interest rate than the interest rate for large firms.

Another reason behind the silence of fracking in Mexico is a lack of incentives. In Texas—as well as the rest of the United States—rights to what is discovered under one's farm or ranch belong to the private owner, whereas in Mexico the government owns what is under your farm or ranch. In other words, private land ownership in Mexico literally only covers the land, but not anything underneath it. As a result, there is hardly any incentive for any Mexican farmer or rancher to be curious about what lies beneath his or her land.

Sources: Based on (1) *Economist*, 2014, Electronic arm-twisting, May 17: 68; (2) *Economist*, 2014, On shaky ground, May 3: 32; (3) *Economist*, 2014, The Peter Pan syndrome, May 17: 63–64.

concerning how easy it is to start up new entrepreneurial firms in terms of registration, licensing, and incorporation. A relatively straightforward (or even "mundane") task of connecting electricity to a newly built commercial building illustrates such tremendous differences. In general, governments in developed economies impose fewer procedures (an average of 4.6 procedures for OECD high-income countries) and a lower total cost (free in Japan and 5.1% of per capita GDP in Germany). On the other hand, entrepreneurs must endure harsher hurdles in poor countries. As a class of its own, Burundi imposes a total cost of 430 times its per capita GDP for entrepreneurs to obtain electricity. Sierra Leone leads the world in requiring entrepreneurs to spend 441 days to obtain electricity. Overall, it is not surprising that the more entrepreneur-friendly these formal institutional requirements are, the more flourishing entrepreneurship is, and the more developed the economies become—and vice versa (Figure 9.2). As a result, more countries are now reforming their formal institutions in order to become more entrepreneur-friendly.

In addition to formal institutions, informal institutions, such as cultural values and norms, also affect entrepreneurship.[7] For example, because entrepreneurs necessarily take more risk, individualistic and low uncertainty-avoidance

Figure 9.2　**Average Ranking on the Ease of Doing Business**

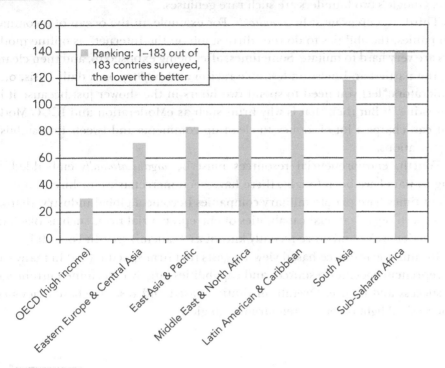

Source: Data extracted from the World Bank, 2010, *Doing Business 2010* (database at www.doingbusiness.org).

societies tend to foster relatively more entrepreneurs, whereas collectivistic and high uncertainty-avoidance societies may result in relatively fewer entrepreneurs. Among developed economies, Japan has the lowest rate of start-ups—one-third of America's rate and half of Europe's.[8] In another example, Russians make heavy use of social networks online, averaging 9.8 hours per month—more than double the world average. While spending that much time online makes sense during the long and cold Russian winter, another important reason is the long-held Russian tradition of relying more on informal information networks for daily life. These informal norms help nurture social network entrepreneurs (such as Russia's VKontakte) and attract foreign entrants (such as Facebook).[9] Overall, the institution-based view suggests that both formal and informal institutions matter.[10] Later sections will discuss *how* they matter.

9-2b Resources and Entrepreneurship

The resource-based view, first introduced in Chapter 4, sheds considerable light on entrepreneurship, with a focus on its value, rarity, imitability, and organizational (VRIO) aspects (see Figure 9.1). First, entrepreneurial resources must create *value*.[11] For example, by offering cheap fares, convenient schedules, Wi-Fi, and a power port on every seat, Megabus offers superb value to travelers for medium-haul trips that are too far for a leisurely drive but too close to justify the expenses and the increasing hassle to fly. On medium-haul routes, Megabus is rapidly changing the way Americans—especially the young—travel.

Second, resources must be *rare*. As the cliché goes, "If everybody has it, you can't make money from it." The best-performing entrepreneurs tend to have the rare knowledge and deeper insights about business opportunities. Math geniuses are few and far between, but the ability to turn a passion for math into profit is truly rare. Google's two founders are such rare geniuses.

Third, resources must be *inimitable*. For example, in the ocean of e-commerce companies, the abilities to do the "dirtiest job on the Internet" as online moderators are very hard to imitate. Sometimes, after being exposed to, and then cleaning up, the nastiest and most undesirable racism and bigotry on a daily basis, online moderators "feel you need to spend two hours in the shower just because it is so disgusting."[12] But then that is why firms such as eModeration and ICUC Moderation can charge a lot of money to clean up comments and tweets for established organizations.

Fourth, entrepreneurial resources must be *organizationally* embedded.[13] As long as wars have been fought, there have been mercenaries for hire. But only in recent times have private military companies become a global industry, thanks to the superb organizational capabilities of entrepreneurial firms such as Blackwater (rebranded as Xe and more recently known as Academi) (see In Focus 9.1).

In sum, the resource-based view suggests that firm-specific (and in many cases, entrepreneur-specific) resources and capabilities largely determine entrepreneurial success and failure. Overall, institution-based and resource-based views combine to shed light on entrepreneurial strategies.

IN FOCUS 9.1

PRIVATE MILITARY COMPANIES

Ethical
Dilemma

Private military companies (PMCs) form a US$100 billion global industry. Although often stereotyped as "mercenaries," modern PMCs are professional firms that offer valuable, unique, and hard-to-imitate organizational capabilities in environments that most individuals, firms, and governments, as well as national militaries, would prefer to avoid. Entrepreneurs thrive on chaos. To PMCs, the war in Iraq and Afghanistan has been a pot of gold. As US forces and allies withdraw, PMCs rush in. Long after the official withdrawal of the US (national) military from Iraq in 2011 and from Afghanistan in 2014, PMCs will remain active in these troubled countries. The State Department alone will employ 5,000 PMC personnel in Iraq. Although not every EMC directly engages in the battlefield, this line of work is certainly dangerous. PMCs reported at least 1,800 dead and 40,000 wounded in Iraq and Afghanistan.

An ethical challenge confronting PMCs is how to *responsively* deploy their lethal capabilities while getting the job done. In 2007, a furious US Congress held hearings on Blackwater, which, according to the Iraqi government, allegedly killed 17 innocent civilians in

Baghdad. Blackwater's staunchest defenders tended to be US officials protected by its private soldiers. US officials preferred PMCs because PMC personnel were regarded as more highly trained than (national) military guards. Blackwater's founder, Erik Prince, told the Congressional committee that "no individual protected by Blackwater has ever been killed or seriously injured," while 30 of its private soldiers died on the job. After the hearing, Blackwater was banned from operating in Iraq. In 2009, Blackwater rebranded itself as Xe (pronounced *zee*), which further changed its name to Academi in 2011.

Continuously looking for new entrepreneurial opportunities, some PMCs have recently branched into maritime security services, thanks to Somali pirates who attack ships off the coast of Africa. Most recently, what countries have commanded a lot of attention from PMCs? Syria, Ukraine, and Yemen.

Sources: Based on (1) *Bloomberg Businessweek*, 2011, As war winds down in Libya, enter the consultants, September 26: 17–18; (2) *Bloomberg Businessweek*, 2011, For sale, cheap, December 19: 32–35; (3) T. Hammes, 2010, Private contractors in conflict zones, *Strategic Forum of National Defense University*, 260: 1–15; (4) M. W. Peng, 2014, Private military companies, in M. W. Peng, *Global Strategy*, 3rd ed., Cincinnati: Cengage Learning.

9-3 Growing the Entrepreneurial Firm

This section discusses three major characteristics associated with a growing entrepreneurial firm: (1) growth, (2) innovation, and (3) financing. A fourth one, internationalization, will be highlighted in the next section.

Learning Objective
Discuss three characteristics of a growing entrepreneurial firm.

9-3a Growth

For many entrepreneurs, such as David Tran (see the Opening Case) and Jack Ma (see the Closing Case), the excitement associated with growing a new company is the very thing that attracts them in the first place.[14] Recall from the resource-based view that a firm can be conceptualized as a bundle of resources and capabilities. The growth of an entrepreneurial firm can, thus, be viewed as an attempt to more fully use currently underutilized resources and capabilities. An entrepreneurial firm can leverage its (intangible) vision, drive, and leadership in order to grow, even though it may be short on (tangible) resources such as financial capital.

One hallmark of entrepreneurial growth is a dynamic, flexible, guerrilla strategy. As underdogs, entrepreneurial SMEs cannot compete against their larger and more-established rivals head-on. "Going for the crumbs" (at least initially), smaller firms often engage in indirect and subtle attacks that large rivals may not immediately recognize as competitive challenges. In the lucrative market of US defense contracts, large firms such as Boeing and Raytheon like "doing the impossible." Meanwhile, smaller firms, such as Alliant Techsystems (known for its stock symbol ATK), focus on the possible and the cheap—upgrading missiles and making mortar munitions more accurate based on proven, off-the-shelf solutions. As a result, ATK is able to consistently beat larger competitors and supply the US military, which has become increasingly concerned about cost overruns.[15]

9-3b Innovation

Innovation is at the heart of an entrepreneurial mindset.[16] Innovation can range from low-tech ones such as Huy Fong's humble Sriracha hot sauce (see the Opening Case) to high-tech ones such as Alibaba's Taobao that can handle millions of online transactions daily (see the Closing Case).

An innovation strategy offers three advantages. First, it allows a potentially more sustainable basis for competitive advantage. Firms that are first to introduce new goods or services are likely to earn (quasi) "monopoly profits" until competitors emerge. If entrepreneurial firms come up with "disruptive technologies," then they may redefine the rules of competition, thus wiping out incumbents' advantages.[17]

Second, innovation should be regarded broadly. Not only are technological breakthroughs innovations, but less-novel and still substantially new ways of doing business are also innovations. Most start-ups reproduce existing organizational routines but *recombine* them to create some novel product/service offerings. Think of FedEx's (re)combination of existing air and ground assets to create a new market.

Entrepreneurial firms are uniquely ready for innovation. Owners, managers, and employees at entrepreneurial firms tend to be more innovative and risk-taking than those at large firms. In fact, many SMEs are founded by former employees of large firms who were frustrated by their inability to translate innovative ideas into realities at those firms. A group of programmers at IBM's German affiliate proposed to IBM that standard programming solutions could

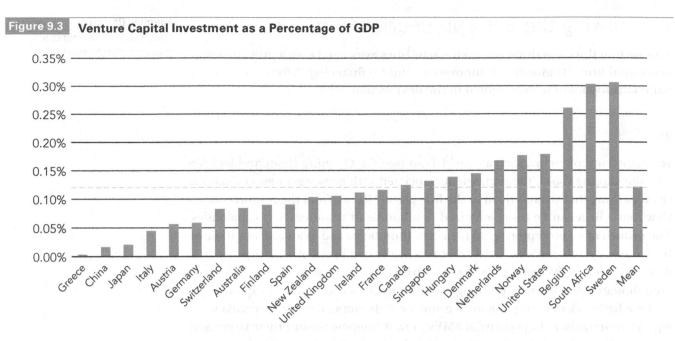

Figure 9.3   **Venture Capital Investment as a Percentage of GDP**

Source: Adapted from M. Minniti, W. Bygrave, & E. Autio, 2006, *Global Entrepreneurship Monitor 2006 Executive Report* (p. 49), Wellesley, MA: Babson College/GEM.

be profitably sold to clients. After their ideas were turned down, they left and founded SAP, now the number-one player in the thriving enterprise resource planning (ERP) market. Innovators at large firms also have limited ability to personally profit from their innovations because property rights usually belong to the corporation. In contrast, innovators at entrepreneurial firms are better able to reap the financial gains associated with innovation, thus fueling their motivation to charge ahead.

9-3c Financing

All start-ups need capital.[18] Here is a quiz (also a joke): Of the "4F" sources of entrepreneurial financing, the first three Fs are founders, family, and friends, but what is the other F source? The answer is … *fools* (!). While this is a joke, it strikes a chord in the entrepreneurial world: Given the well-known failure risks of start-ups (a *majority* of them will fail), why would anyone other than fools be willing to invest in start-ups?[19] In reality, most outside, strategic investors—who can be angels (wealthy individual investors), venture capitalists (VCs), banks, foreign entrants, and government agencies—are *not* fools. They often examine business plans, require a strong management team, and scrutinize financial statements. They also demand some assurance (such as collateral) indicating that entrepreneurs will not simply "take the money and run."[20]

Around the world, the extent to which entrepreneurs draw on resources from outside investors (such as venture capitalists) rather than family and friends varies. Figure 9.3 shows that Sweden, South Africa, Belgium, and the United States lead the world in VC investment as a percentage of GDP. In contrast, Greece and China have the lowest level of VC investment. Figure 9.4 illustrates a different picture: informal investment (mostly by family and friends) as a percentage of GDP. In this case, China leads the world with the highest level of informal investment as a percentage of GDP. In comparison, Brazil and Hungary have the lowest level of informal investment. While there is a lot of "noise" in such worldwide data, the case

Venture capitalist (VC)

An investor who provides risk capital for early stage ventures.

Microfinance

A practice to provide micro loans (US$50–US$300) used to start small businesses with the intention of ultimately lifting the entrepreneurs out of poverty.

Born global firm (international new venture)

A start-up company that attempts to do business abroad from inception.

Figure 9.4 **Informal Investment as a Percentage of GDP**

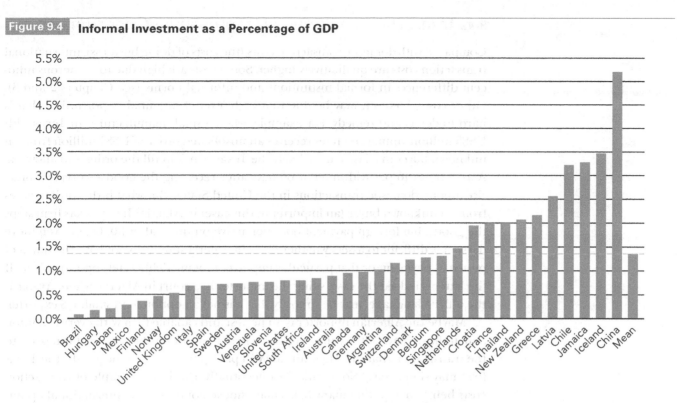

Sources: Adapted from M. Minniti, W. Bygrave, & E. Autio, 2006, *Global Entrepreneurship Monitor 2006 Executive Report* (p. 53), Wellesley, MA: Babson College/GEM.

of China (second-lowest in VC investment and highest in informal investment) is easy to explain: China's lack of formal market-supporting institutions, such as venture capitalists and credit-reporting agencies, requires a high level of informal investment for Chinese entrepreneurs and new ventures, particularly during a time of entrepreneurial boom.[21]

A highly innovative solution, called microfinance, has emerged in response to the lack of financing for entrepreneurial opportunities in many developing countries. Microfinance involves lending small sums (US$50–US$300) used to start small businesses, with the intention of ultimately lifting them out of poverty. Starting in Bangladesh in the 1970s by Muhammad Yunus, microfinance has now become a global movement.[22] Yunus himself won a Nobel Peace Prize in 2006.

epa european pressphoto agency b.v./Alamy

How does the microfinance movement pioneered by Yunus improve entrepreneurial financing?

9-4 Internationalizing the Entrepreneurial Firm

There is a myth that only large MNEs do business abroad and that SMEs mostly operate domestically. This myth, based on historical stereotypes, is being increasingly challenged as more SMEs go international.[23] Further, some start-ups attempt to do business abroad from inception. These are often called born global firms (or international new ventures). This section examines how entrepreneurial firms internationalize.

Learning Objective

Discuss how international strategies for entering foreign markets are different from those for staying in domestic markets.

9-4a Transaction Costs and Entrepreneurial Opportunities

Compared with domestic transaction costs (the costs of doing business), international transaction costs are qualitatively higher. Some costs are high due to numerous innocent differences in formal institutions and informal norms (see Chapters 2 and 3). Other costs, however, may be due to a high level of potential opportunism that is hard to detect and remedy. For example, when a small manufacturer in Texas with US$5 million annual revenues receives an unsolicited order of US$1 million from an unknown buyer in Alaska, most likely the Texas firm will fill the order and allow the Alaska buyer to pay within 30 or 60 days after receiving the goods—a typical practice among domestic transactions in the United States. But what if this order comes from an unknown buyer (an importer in this case) in Algeria? If the Texas firm ships the goods, but foreign payment does not arrive on time (after 30, 60, or even more days), it is difficult to assess whether firms in Algeria simply do not have the norm of punctual payment, or that particular importer is being deliberately opportunistic. If the latter is indeed the case, suing the importer in a court in Algeria, where Arabic is the official language, may be so costly that it is not an option for a small US exporter.

Maybe the Algerian importer is an honest and capable firm with every intention and ability to pay. But because the Texas firm may not be able to ascertain, prior to the transaction, that the Algerian side will pay upon receiving the goods, the Texas firm may simply say, "No, thanks!" Conceptually, this is an example of transaction costs being so high that many firms may choose not to pursue international opportunities. Therefore, entrepreneurial opportunities exist to lower transaction costs and bring distant groups of people, firms, and countries together.[24] Table 9.1 shows that while entrepreneurial firms can internationalize by entering foreign markets, they can also add an international dimension without actually going abroad. Next, we discuss how an SME can undertake some of these strategies.

9-4b International Strategies for Entering Foreign Markets

SMEs can enter foreign markets through three broad modes: (1) direct exports, (2) licensing/franchising, and (3) foreign direct investment (FDI) (see Chapter 10 for more details). First, direct exports entail the sale of products made by entrepreneurial firms in their home country to customers in other countries. This strategy is attractive because entrepreneurial firms are able to reach foreign customers directly. When domestic markets experience some downturns, sales abroad may compensate for such drops. However, one major drawback is that SMEs may not have enough resources to turn overseas opportunities into profits.

Export transactions are complicated. One particular concern is how to overcome the lack of trust between exporters and importers when receiving an export

Direct export

The sale of products made by firms in their home country to customers in other countries.

Table 9.1	**Internationalization Strategies for Entrepreneurial Firms**	

Entering foreign markets	Staying in domestic markets
• Direct exports	• Indirect exports (through export intermediaries)
• Franchising/licensing	• Supplier of foreign firms
• Foreign direct investment (through strategic alliances, greenfield wholly owned subsidiaries, and/or foreign acquisitions)	• Franchisee/licensee of foreign brands
	• Alliance partner of foreign direct investors
	• Harvest and exit (through sell-off to foreign entrants)

Figure 9.5   An Export/Import Transaction

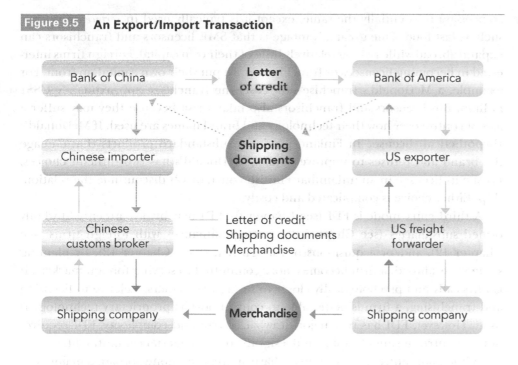

order from unknown importers abroad. For example, while the US exporter in Figure 9.5 does not trust the Chinese importer, banks on both sides can facilitate this transaction by a letter of credit (L/C). An L/C is a financial contract that states that the importer's bank (Bank of China in this case) will pay a specific sum of money to the exporter upon delivery of the merchandise. It has several steps:

- The US exporter may question the unknown Chinese importer's assurance that it will promptly pay for the merchandise. An L/C from the highly reputable Bank of China will assure the US exporter that the importer has good creditworthiness and sufficient funds for this transaction. If the US exporter is not sure whether Bank of China is a credible bank, it can consult its own bank, Bank of America, which will confirm that an L/C from Bank of China is as good as gold.
- With this assurance through the L/C, the US exporter can release the merchandise, which goes through a US freight forwarder, then a shipping company, and then a Chinese customs broker. Finally, the goods will reach the Chinese importer.
- Once the US exporter has shipped the goods, it will present to Bank of America the L/C from Bank of China and shipping documents. On behalf of the US exporter, Bank of America will then collect payment from Bank of China, which, in turn, will collect payment from the Chinese importer.

In short, instead of having unknown exporters and importers deal with each other, transactions are facilitated by banks on both sides that have known each other quite well because of numerous such dealings. In other words, the L/C reduces transaction costs by lowering transaction risks.

A second way to enter international markets is licensing and/or franchising. Usually used in *manufacturing* industries, licensing refers to Firm A's agreement to give Firm B the rights to use A's proprietary technology (such as a patent) or trademark (such as a corporate logo) for a royalty fee paid to A by B. Assume (hypothetically) that a US exporter cannot keep up with demand in Turkey. It may consider granting a Turkish firm the license to use its technology and trademark for a fee.

Letter of credit (L/C)

A financial contract that states that the importer's bank will pay a specific sum of money to the exporter upon delivery of the merchandise.

Franchising is essentially the same, except it is typically used in *service* industries, such as fast food. One great advantage is that SME licensors and franchisors can expand abroad while risking relatively little of their own capital. Foreign firms interested in becoming licensees or franchisees must put their own capital up front. For example, a McDonald's franchise now costs the franchisee approximately US$1 million. But licensors and franchisors also take a risk because they may suffer a loss of control over how their technology and brand names are used. If McDonald's (hypothetical) licensee in Finland produces substandard products that damage the brand and refuses to improve quality, McDonald's has two difficult choices: (1) sue its licensee in an unfamiliar Finnish court, or (2) discontinue the relationship. Either choice is complicated and costly.

A third entry mode is FDI (see Chapter 6). FDI may involve greenfield wholly owned subsidiaries (see Chapter 10), strategic alliances with foreign firms (see Chapter 12), and/or acquisitions of foreign firms (see Chapter 12). By planting some roots abroad, a firm becomes more committed to serving foreign markets. It is physically and psychologically closer to foreign customers. Relative to licensing and franchising, a firm is better able to control how its proprietary technology is used. However, FDI has two major drawbacks: cost and complexity. FDI requires both a nontrivial sum of capital and a significant managerial commitment.

While many entrepreneurial firms have aggressively gone abroad, a majority of SMEs probably will be unable to do so—they already have enough headaches struggling with the domestic market. However, as discussed next, some SMEs can still internationalize by staying at home.

9-4c International Strategies for Staying in Domestic Markets

Table 9.1 also shows a number of strategies for entrepreneurial SMEs to internationalize without leaving their home country. The five main strategies are (1) export indirectly, (2) become suppliers for foreign firms, (3) become licensees or franchisees of foreign brands, (4) become alliance partners of foreign direct investors, or (5) harvest and exit through sell-offs.

First, whereas direct exports may be lucrative, many SMEs simply do not have the resources to handle such work. But they can still reach overseas customers through indirect exports, which involve exporting through domestic-based export intermediaries. Export intermediaries perform an important middleman function by linking domestic sellers and overseas buyers who otherwise would not have been connected. Being entrepreneurs themselves, export intermediaries facilitate the internationalization of many SMEs.[25]

A second strategy is to become a supplier for a foreign firm that enters a domestic market. For example, when Subway came to Northern Ireland, it secured a contract for chilled part-bake bread with a domestic bakery. This relationship was so successful that the bakery now supplies Subway franchisees throughout Europe. Thus, SME suppliers may be able to internationalize by piggybacking on the larger foreign entrants.

Third, an entrepreneurial firm may consider becoming a licensee or franchisee of a foreign brand. Foreign licensors and franchisors provide training and technology transfer—for a fee of course. Consequently, an SME can learn a great deal about how to operate at world-class standards. If enough learning has been accomplished, it is possible to discontinue the relationship and to reap greater entrepreneurial profits. In Thailand, Minor Group, which had held the Pizza Hut franchise

Franchising

Firm A's agreement to give Firm B the rights to use A's proprietary assets for a royalty fee paid to A by B. This is typically done in service industries.

Indirect export

A way to reach overseas customers by exporting through domestic-based export intermediaries.

Export intermediary

A firm that performs an important middleman function by linking domestic sellers and foreign buyers that otherwise would not have been connected.

for 20 years, broke away from the relationship. Its new venture, The Pizza Company, became the market leader in Thailand.

A fourth strategy is to become an alliance partner of a foreign direct investor. Facing an onslaught of aggressive MNEs, many entrepreneurial firms may not be able to successfully defend their market positions. Then it makes great sense to follow the old adage, "If you can't beat them, join them!" While dancing with the giants is tricky, it is better than being crushed by them.

Finally, as a harvest and exit strategy, entrepreneurs may sell an equity stake or the entire firm to foreign entrants. An American couple, originally from Seattle, built a Starbucks-like coffee chain in Britain called Seattle Coffee. When Starbucks entered Britain, the couple sold the chain of 60 stores to Starbucks for a hefty US$84 million. In light of the high failure rates of start-ups, being acquired by foreign entrants may help preserve the business in the long run.

9-5 Debates and Extensions

Entrepreneurship has attracted significant debates. This section discusses two leading debates: (1) traits versus institutions, and (2) slow versus rapid internationalization.

9-5a Traits versus Institutions

This is probably the oldest debate on entrepreneurship. It focuses on the question: "What motivates entrepreneurs to establish new firms, while most others are simply content to work for bosses?" The "traits" school of thought argues that it is personal traits that matter. Compared with non-entrepreneurs, entrepreneurs seem more likely to possess a stronger desire for achievement and are more willing to take risks and tolerate ambiguities. Overall, entrepreneurship inevitably deviates from the norm to work for others, and this deviation may be in the "blood" of entrepreneurs.[26] For example, serial entrepreneurs are people who start, grow, and sell several businesses throughout their career.[27] One example is David Tran, who has founded businesses in both Vietnam and the United States (see the Opening Case).

Critics, however, argue that some of these traits, such as a strong achievement orientation, are not necessarily limited to entrepreneurs, but instead are characteristic of many successful individuals. The diversity among entrepreneurs makes any attempt to develop a standard psychological or personality profile futile. Critics suggest what matters is institutions—namely, the environments that set formal and informal rules of the game (see PengAtlas Map 3.1). Consider the ethnic Chinese, who have exhibited a high degree of entrepreneurship throughout Southeast Asia, whereby as a minority group (usually less than 10% of the population in countries such as Indonesia and Thailand) they control 70%–80% of the wealth. Yet, in mainland China, for three decades (the 1950s to the 1970s), there had been virtually no entrepreneurship, thanks to harsh communist policies. Over the last three decades, however, as government policies became relatively more entrepreneur friendly, the institutional transitions have opened the floodgates of entrepreneurship in China (see the Closing Case).[28]

In Europe, a leading debate focuses on why so few Europeans are interested in entrepreneurship. *Global Entrepreneur Monitor* has reported that in Europe, an alarmingly small percentage of individuals are involved in "early stage entrepreneurship," representing 2.3% of Italy's adult population, 4.2% of Germany's, and 5.8% of France's. These numbers compare unfavorably with 7.6% in

Learning Objective
Participate in two debates concerning entrepreneurship.

Serial entrepreneur
An entrepreneur who starts, grows, and sells several businesses throughout his/her career.

the United States, 14% in China, and 17% of in Brazil. The lack of a risk-taking entrepreneurial culture is one reason. But another reason is a series of formal, institution-based barriers that scare away a lot of would-be entrepreneurs (see In Focus 9.2).

Beyond the macro societal-level institutions, more micro institutions also matter. Family background and educational attainment have been found to correlate with entrepreneurship. Children of wealthy parents, especially those who own businesses, are more likely to start their own firms. So are better-educated people. Taken together, informal norms governing one's socioeconomic group assert some

IN FOCUS 9.2
EUROPE'S ENTREPRENEURSHIP DEFICIT

Ethical Dilemma

Europe has neither shortage of successful large firms nor shortage of entrepreneurial SMEs. But the vast majority of Europe's large firms were born around the turn of the last century. What Europe lacks is successful SMEs that grow quickly and join the ranks of large firms. Of the world's 500 largest publicly listed firms, Europe gave birth to only 12 of them between 1950 and 2007, whereas the United States produced 52 during the same period. One reason that the United States has rocketed ahead of Europe in economic growth and job creation is the ability to produce new, fast-growing SMEs that quickly become giants, such as Amazon, eBay, Google, and Starbucks. Why was Google—one of whose two cofounders was born in Europe—not made in Europe?

In the game of entrepreneurship, nobody knows which SMEs of today will become giants of tomorrow. The key lies in having as many players in the game as possible so that in the end some winners will emerge. If nobody is in the game, then, obviously, no winners will emerge. *Global Entrepreneurship Monitor* has reported that in Europe, an alarmingly small percentage of individuals are involved in "early stage entrepreneurship," representing 2.3% of Italy's adult population, 4.2% of Germany's, and 5.8% of France's. These numbers compare very unfavorably with 7.6% in the United States, 14% in China, and 17% of in Brazil. The lack of a risk-taking entrepreneurial culture is one reason. But another reason is a series of formal, institution-based barriers that scare away a lot of would-be entrepreneurs.

A known fact in entrepreneurship is that risks are high and bankruptcy is likely. However, Europe's personal bankruptcy laws are notoriously unfriendly to bankrupt entrepreneurs. In France, they are responsible for their debts for nine years after the bankruptcy. In Germany, six years. In the United States, failed entrepreneurs can walk away from their debts in less than a year.

Another hurdle is labor law. To remain viable, failed SMEs must reduce staff quickly and cheaply. But in Europe, even very recent hires expect to receive at least six months of severance pay. "In San Francisco and in China, a communist country, I pay one to two months," a frustrated French executive shared with a journalist. Anil de Mello is a Spanish entrepreneur. During the Great Recession of 2008–2009, after his firm went bankrupt and dealt with creditors, Spanish social security pursued him for five *years* to capture funds it had paid to his employees as severance on his behalf. Although eager to start up another firm again, de Mello reasoned that he could not afford another bankruptcy in Spain. Instead, he founded his next new venture in Switzerland, whose labor laws are more entrepreneur friendly.

While de Mello at least stays in Europe, a large army of European entrepreneurs simply leave the continent. There are about 50,000 Germans in Silicon Valley, and approximately 500 start-ups in the San Francisco Bay area are founded by French entrepreneurs. While some will strike it rich and most will fail, one conclusion seems foregone: the next Google will still not be made in Europe.

Sources: Based on (1) *Economist*, 2013, A slow climb, October 5: 65–66; (2) *Economist*, 2012, Les misérable, July 28: 19–22; (3) *Economist*, 2013, Start me up, October 5: 60–61; (4) M. W. Peng, Y. Yamakawa, & S. Lee, 2010, Bankruptcy laws and entrepreneur-friendliness, *Entrepreneurship Theory and Practice*, 34: 517–530.

powerful impact on the propensity to create new ventures. Overall, this debate is an extension of the broader debate on "nature versus nurture." Most scholars now agree that entrepreneurship is the result of both nature *and* nurture.

9-5b Slow Internationalizers versus "Born Global" Start-ups

Two components should be considered here: (1) Can SMEs internationalize faster than what has been suggested by traditional stage models (models that portray SME internationalization as a slow, stage-by-stage process)? (2) Should they rapidly internationalize? The dust has largely settled on the first component: it is possible for some (but not all) SMEs to make very rapid progress in internationalization. Consider Logitech, now a global leader in computer peripherals. It was established by entrepreneurs from Switzerland and the United States, where the firm set up dual headquarters. Research and development (R&D) and manufacturing were initially split between these two countries and then quickly spread to Ireland and Taiwan through FDI. Its first commercial contract was with a Japanese company. Logitech is not alone among such "born global" firms.

What is currently being debated is the second component. On the one hand, advocates argue that every industry has become "global" and that entrepreneurial firms need to go after these opportunities rapidly. On the other hand, stage models suggest that firms need to enter culturally and institutionally close markets first, spend enough time there to accumulate overseas experience, and then gradually move from more primitive modes, such as exports, to more sophisticated strategies, such as FDI in distant markets. Consistent with stage models, Sweden's IKEA, for example, waited 20 years (1943 to 1963) before entering a neighboring country, Norway. Only more recently has it accelerated its internationalization. Stage models caution that inexperienced swimmers may be drowned in unfamiliar foreign waters.

One key issue, therefore, is whether it is better for entrepreneurs to start the internationalization process soon after founding (as Logitech did) or to postpone until the firm has accumulated significant resources (as IKEA did). One view supports rapid internationalization. Specifically, firms following the prescription of stage models, when eventually internationalizing, must overcome substantial inertia because of their domestic orientation.[29] In contrast, firms that internationalize earlier need to overcome fewer of these barriers. Therefore, SMEs without an established domestic orientation (such as Logitech) may outperform their rivals that wait longer to internationalize. In other words, contrary to the inherent disadvantages in internationalization associated with SMEs as suggested by stage models, there may be "inherent advantages" of being small while venturing abroad.

However, some authors argue, "the born-global view, although appealing, is a dangerous half-truth." They maintain, "You must first be successful at home, then move outward in a manner that anticipates and genuinely accommodates local differences."[30] In other words, the teachings of stage models are still relevant. Consequently, indiscriminate advice to "go global" may not be warranted.[31]

Stage model

A model of internationalization that portrays the slow step-by-step (stage-by-stage) process an SME must go through to internationalize its business.

LIU JIN/Stringer/AFP/Getty Images

Although Sweden's IKEA is now active in distant markets such as China, it waited 20 years (1943 to 1963) before first entering a neighboring country, Norway. Did IKEA's slow, cautious approach in initial internationalization—suggested by stage models—make sense?

Table 9.2	**Implications for Action**

- Push for institutions that facilitate entrepreneurship development—both formal and informal

- When internationalizing, be bold, but not too bold

9-6 Management Savvy

Entrepreneurs and their firms are quintessential engines of the "creative destruction" process underpinning global capitalism first described by Joseph Schumpeter. What determines the success and failure of entrepreneurial firms around the globe? The answers boil down to two components. First, the institution-based view argues that institutional frameworks explain a great deal about what is behind the differences in entrepreneurial and economic development around the world. Second, the resource-based view posits that it is largely intangible resources, such as vision, drive, and willingness to take risk, that fuel entrepreneurship around the globe. Overall, the performance of entrepreneurial firms depends on how they take advantage of formal and informal institutional resources and how they leverage their capabilities at home, abroad, or both.

Two clear implications for action emerge (Table 9.2). First, institutions that facilitate entrepreneurship development—both formal and informal—are important.[32] As a result, savvy entrepreneurs have a vested interest in pushing for more entrepreneur-friendly formal institutions in various countries, such as rules governing how to set up new firms (see Figure 9.2, Emerging Markets 9.1, and In Focus 9.2). Entrepreneurs also need to cultivate strong informal norms granting legitimacy to entrepreneurs. Talking to high school and college students, taking on interns, and providing seed money as angels for new ventures are some of the actions that entrepreneurs can undertake.

Second, when internationalizing, entrepreneurs are advised to be bold and venture abroad. Thanks to globalization, the costs of doing business abroad have fallen recently. But being bold does not mean being reckless. One specific managerial insight from this chapter is that it is possible to internationalize without venturing abroad. When the entrepreneurial firm is not ready to take on higher risk abroad, the more limited international involvement at home may be appropriate. In other words, be bold, but not too bold.[33]

CHAPTER SUMMARY/LEARNING OBJECTIVES

9-1 Define entrepreneurship, entrepreneurs, and entrepreneurial firms.

- Entrepreneurship is the identification and exploitation of previously unexplored opportunities.
- Entrepreneurs may be founders and owners of new businesses or managers of existing firms.
- Entrepreneurial firms in this chapter are defined as SMEs.

9-2 Understand how institutions and resources affect entrepreneurship.

- Institutions enable and constrain entrepreneurship around the world.
- Resources and capabilities largely determine entrepreneurial success and failure.

9-3 Discuss the three characteristics associated with a growing entrepreneurial firm.

- (1) Growth, (2) innovation, and (3) financing.

9-4 Distinguish international strategies that enter foreign markets from those that stay in domestic markets.

- Entrepreneurial firms can internationalize by entering foreign markets, through entry modes such as (1) direct exports, (2) licensing/franchising, and (3) FDI.

- Entrepreneurial firms can also internationalize without venturing abroad, by (1) exporting indirectly, (2) supplying foreign firms, (3) becoming licensees/franchisees of foreign firms, (4) joining foreign entrants as alliance partners, and (5) harvesting and exiting through sell-offs to foreign entrants.

9-5 Participate in two leading debates concerning entrepreneurship.

- (1) Traits versus institutions and (2) slow versus rapid internationalization.

9-6 Draw implications for action.

- Push for both formal and informal institutions that facilitate entrepreneurship development.
- When internationalizing, be bold, but not too bold.

KEY TERMS

Born global firm (international new venture), 304

Direct export, 306

Entrepreneur, 298

Entrepreneurship, 298

Export intermediary, 308

Franchising, 308

Indirect export, 308

International entrepreneurship, 298

Letter of credit (L/C), 307

Microfinance, 304

Serial entrepreneur, 309

Small and medium-sized enterprise (SME), 298

Stage model, 311

Venture capitalist (VC), 304

REVIEW QUESTIONS

1. Based on your definition of entrepreneurship, can a firm be truly entrepreneurial if it does not expand globally?

2. How prevalent and important are small entrepreneurial firms in economies around the globe?

3. *ON CULTURE:* Which societal norms tend to encourage entrepreneurship, and which tend to discourage it?

4. How important are an entrepreneur's resources and capabilities in determining his or her success? Why?

5. Name and describe three major characteristics associated with an entrepreneurial firm's growth.

6. What qualities typically compensate for an entrepreneurial firm's lack of tangible resources?

7. Summarize three modes that SMEs can use to enter foreign markets.

8. Name and describe at least three ways that SMEs can internationalize without leaving their home countries.

9. Compare PengAtlas Maps 3.1 and 3.3. Based on that information, which country would be most attractive to you as a place to expand your business? The global economy is subject to constant change. In your opinion, what potential changes in one of the countries shown, including the United States, may make that country less attractive as a place to expand?

10. *ON CULTURE:* In the nature-versus-nurture debate, which do you think carries more power: traits (nature) or institutions (nurture)? Does your response apply equally to all countries around the world? Why or why not?

11. We know that it is possible for an SME to be born global by immediately engaging in FDI, but do you think it is wise? Why?

12. Describe two or three examples of institutions that can be made friendlier and more supportive of entrepreneurs.

13. In comparing PengAtlas Maps 3.1 and 3.3, note that one of the countries that is at the bottom of the list regarding ease of doing business is also among the poorest. Note that the two groups are not identical. However, to what extent can ease of doing business affect the wealth of a country?

14. *ON CULTURE:* Devise your own example of an entrepreneurial action that demonstrates your understanding of the difference between being bold and being reckless. Why may the view of what is bold or reckless vary among countries and cultures?

CRITICAL DISCUSSION QUESTIONS

1. Given that most entrepreneurial start-ups fail, why do entrepreneurs start so many new firms? Why are (most) governments interested in promoting more start-ups?

2. Some suggest that foreign markets are graveyards where entrepreneurial firms overextend themselves. Others argue that foreign markets represent the future for SMEs. If you were the owner of a small, reasonably profitable domestic firm, would you consider expanding overseas? Why or why not?

3. *ON ETHICS:* Your former high-school buddy invites you to join an entrepreneurial start-up that specializes in making counterfeit (generic) drugs to combat HIV/AIDS, which would potentially help millions of patients worldwide who cannot afford the high-priced patented drugs. He has lined up financing and offers you the job of CEO and 10% of the equity of the firm. You are currently unemployed. How would you respond?

GLOBAL ACTION

1. You work for a small foreign-language-services company. You have been asked to present a market assessment of the largest translation companies for competitor evaluation. Your report must include the following attributes for the global industry: company, size, locations, and ownership status. What do your findings suggest about possible worldwide opportunities?

2. **An entrepreneurship research firm has asked you to identify the most entrepreneurial countries in the world. Based on your knowledge of the entrepreneurship field, find a database that may assist in your research. Once the information has been secured, compare the top five countries across the multiple years included in the database. Are there any countries that are included in the database in all years? What is the general percentage of new start-ups in the overall economy for each of the top countries? Is the size of each country similar? Explain these dynamics in your report.**

CLOSING CASE

EMERGING MARKETS: The Rise of Alibaba

Founded in 1999 by a former English teacher Jack Ma, Alibaba has risen to become the largest e-commerce firm not only in China, but also in the world—the value of goods sold on its platforms (US$170 billion in 2013) are more than Amazon and eBay *combined*. Alibaba started as a business-to-business (B2B) portal connecting overseas buyers and small Chinese manufacturers. Inspired by eBay, Alibaba next launched Taobao, a consumer-to-consumer (C2C) portal that now features nearly a billion products and is the one of the 20 most-visited websites worldwide. Finally, with Tmall, Alibaba offers an Amazon-like business-to-consumer (B2C) portal that assists global brands such as Levi's and Disney to reach the middle class in China.

The rise of Alibaba has been breathtaking. As China becomes the largest e-commerce market (already bigger than the United States), Alibaba controls four-fifths of all e-commerce in China. In 2013, on Single's Day (November 11, a marketing invention created to encourage singles to "be nice" to themselves), Alibaba sold more than US$5.7 billion. Preparing to initiate an initial public offering (IPO) in New York, Alibaba had been predicted by the *Economist* to have the potential "to be among the world's most valuable companies." On September 19, 2014, Alibaba's initial public offering (IPO) on the New York Stock Exchange was indeed the world's largest, raising US$25 billion.

Behind the rise of Alibaba is a story of focus and innovation. "eBay may be a shark in the ocean," Ma once said, "but I am a crocodile in the Yangtze River. If we fight in the ocean, I lose; but if we fight in the river, I win." The Crocodile of Yangtze, as Ma became known, has largely focused on China to avoid head-on competition with eBays of the world elsewhere. In China, eBay has been forced to retreat. In a low-trust society such as China, where people generally shy away from buying from strangers online and where people hesitate to use credit cards, Alibaba has pioneered an Alipay system. This is a novel online-payments system that relies an escrow (releasing money to sellers only once their buyers are happy with the goods received). This not only facilitates transactions for Alibaba as well as its buyers and sellers, but also helps build trust at the societal level. Alifinance, Alibaba's financing arm, has become a big microlender to small firms, which are typically underserved by China's state-owned banks. Alifinance now plans to lend to individuals as well. Alibaba is also delivering insurance online. Perhaps its biggest treasure lies in its vast amount of data about the creditworthiness of millions of China's middle class and of thousands of firms that do business via Alibaba—clearly a Big Data gold mine.

From an institution-based standpoint, the fact that Alibaba as a privately owned firm can grow to such an enormous size is remarkable about the Chinese government's tolerance of e-commerce. Ironically the US government placed Alibaba on the list of "notorious markets," because counterfeits could be bought and sold on its websites. Alibaba has endeavored to remove fakes from its websites, and its recent removal from the US government's list of "notorious markets" is indicative of its hard work. However, Western managers of genuine items on Tmall continue to complain that cheap fakes can still be found on Taobao. Evidently the fight is still on.

Formidable as Alibaba is, it is not without challenges. Its business model grows on PC-based e-commerce. Recently, as China becomes the world's largest market for smartphones, it is fast moving to mobile commerce—at a speed faster than any other major economy. The upshot? According to Alibaba's own prospectus, "we face a number of challenges to successfully monetizing our mobile user traffic." In other words, Alibaba is but one of several contenders. Until fairly recently, Alibaba and two other Internet giants in China largely minded their own business as the "three kingdoms," referring to an historical era during which China was divided three ways. While Alibaba dominated e-commerce, Baidu was king of search engines and Tencent made a killing on online games. The truce among the "three kingdoms"

seems to have ended with the arrival of mobile commerce, as all three rush to establish dominance in this new market frontier. Famous for elbowing out Google, Baidu is listed on NASDAQ and is Microsoft's partner in China. In addition to online games, Tencent is more famous for its WeChat social messaging app, which is widely popular. There is no guarantee Alibaba will win in this contest.

In addition to fighting it out in China, the Crocodile of the Yangtze has also been eyeing the wider global ocean. Some 12% of Alibaba's sales are already overseas. Its most attractive overseas markets are likely to be low-trust, underbanked emerging economies in Asia, Africa, and Latin America. But sharks such as eBay and Amazon will not be easy to fight with. Looking forward, whether Alibaba deserves to be one of the world's most valuable companies will depend on how it can defend its e-commerce dominance at home in the mobile era and how it can grow its business abroad.

CASE DISCUSSION QUESTIONS

1. What are the characteristics of Alibaba's growth, innovation, and financing strategies that are typical of successful entrepreneurial firms? What is unusual about Alibaba?

2. Why has Alibaba become globally famous by focusing on its domestic market?

3. Sometimes the IPO of widely successful firms flops—Facebook's disappointing IPO comes to mind. Does Alibaba deserve to be one of the world's most valuable companies?

Sources: Based on (1) *Bloomberg Businessweek*, 2013, Alibaba plays defense against Tencent, August 26: 38–40; (2) *Economist*, 2013, Tencent's worth, September 21: 66–68; (3) *Economist*, 2013, The Alibaba phenomenon, March 23: 15; (4) *Economist*, 2013, The world's greatest bazaar, March 23: 27–30; (5) *Economist*, 2014, From bazaar to bonanza, May 10: 63–65; (6) *Economist*, 2014, After the float, September 6: 66–67; (7) *Economist*, 2014, The world this week, September 27: 9; (8) *South China Morning Post*, 2014, Alibaba expected to be approved for IPO, July 12: B4.

NOTES

[**Journal acronyms**] **AME**—*Academy of Management Executive*; **AMJ**—*Academy of Management Journal*; **AMP**—*Academy of Management Perspectives*; **AMR**—*Academy of Management Review*; **APJM**—*Asia Pacific Journal of Management*; **BW**—*BusinessWeek* (before 2010) or *Bloomberg Businessweek* (since 2010); **ETP**—*Entrepreneurship Theory and Practice*; **HBR**—*Harvard Business Review*; **JBV**—*Journal of Business Venturing*; **JIBS**—*Journal of International Business Studies*; **JMS**—*Journal of Management Studies*; **JWB**—*Journal of World Business*; **SEJ**—*Strategic Entrepreneurship Journal*; **SMJ**—*Strategic Management Journal*; **SMR**—*MIT Sloan Management Review*.

1 M. Hitt, R. D. Ireland, S. M. Camp, & D. Sexton, 2001, Strategic entrepreneurship (p. 480), *SMJ*, 22: 479–491. See also M. Hitt, R. D. Ireland, D. Sirmon, & C. Trahms, 2011, Strategic entrepreneurship, *AMP*, May: 57–75; R. Hoskisson, J. Covin, H. Volberda, & R. Johnson, 2011, Revitalizing entrepreneurship, *JMS*, 48: 1141–1168.

2 S. Shane & S. Venkataraman, 2000, The promise of entrepreneurship as a field of research (p. 218), *AMR*, 25: 217–226.

3 M. W. Peng, S. Lee, & S. Hong, 2014, Entrepreneurs as intermediaries, *JWB*, 49: 21–31.

4 P. McDougall & B. Oviatt, 2000, International entrepreneurship (p. 903), *AMJ*, 43: 902–906. See also Y. Chandra & N. Coviello, 2010, Broadening the concept of international entrepreneurship, *JWB*, 45: 228–236; D. Cumming, H. Sapienza, D. Siegel, & M. Wright, 2009, International entrepreneurship, *SEJ*, 3: 283–296.

5 Y. Yamakawa, M. W. Peng, & D. Deeds, 2008, What drives new ventures to internationalize from emerging to developed economies? *ETP*, 32: 59–82.

6 S. Anokhin & J. Wincent, 2012, Start-up rates and innovation, *JIBS*, 43: 41–60; J. Levie & E. Autio, 2011, Regulatory burden, rule of law, and entry of strategic entrepreneurs, *JMS*, 48: 1392–1419; Y. Zhu, X. Wittman, & M. W. Peng, 2012, Institution-based barriers to innovation in SMEs in China, *APJM*, 29: 1131–1142.

7 D. Kim, E. Morse, R. Mitchell, & K. Seawright 2010 Institutional environment and entrepreneurial cognitions, *ETP*, 34: 491–516.

8 *Economist*, 2011, Son also rises, November 27: 71–72.

9 *BW*, 2011, In Russia, Facebook is more than a social network, January 3: 32–33.

10 S. Lee, Y. Yamakawa, M. W. Peng, & J. Barney, 2011, How do bankruptcy laws affect entrepreneurship development around the world? *JBV*, 26: 505–520.

11 A. Arora & A. Nandkumar, 2012, Insecure advantage? *SMJ*, 33: 231–251; B. Campbell, M. Ganco, A. Franco, & R. Agarwal, 2012, Who leaves, where to, and why worry? *SMJ*, 33: 65–87; D. Hsu & R. Zienonis, 2013, Resources as dual sources of advantage, *SMJ*, 34: 761–781; H. Park & H.K. Steensma, 2012, When does corporate venture capital add value for new ventures? *SMJ*, 33: 1–22; S. Sui & M. Baum, 2014, Internationalization strategy, firm resources, and the survival of SMEs in the export market, *JIBS*, 45: 821–841.

12 *BW*, 2011, The dirtiest job on the Internet, December 5: 95–97.

13 J. Lerner, 2013, Corporate venturing, *HBR*, October: 86–94.

14 M. Cardon, J. Wincent, J. Singh, & M. Drnovsek, 2009, The nature and experience of entrepreneurial passion, *AMR*, 34: 511–532; J. Cerdin, M. Dine, & C. Brewster, 2014, Qualified immigrants' success, *JIBS*, 45: 151–168; D. Souder, Z. Simsek, & S. Johnson, 2012, The differing effects of agent and founder CEOs on the firm's market expansion, *SMJ*, 33: 23–41.

15 *BW*, 2005, The little contractor that could, July 4: 78–79.

16 K. Boudreau & K. Lakhani, 2013, Using the crowd as an innovation partner, *HBR*, April: 62–69; R. Dugan & K. Gabriel, 2013, "Special Forces" innovation, *HBR*, October: 75–84; M. Eisenman, 2013, Understanding aesthetic innovation in the context of technological evolution, *AMR*, 38: 332–351; A. Gaur, D. Mukherjee, S. Gaur, & F. Schmid, 2011, Environmental and firm-level influences on interorganizational trust and SME performance, *JMS*, 48: 1752–1781; B. George, 2011, Entrepreneurial orientation, *JMS*, 48: 1291–1313;

E. Golovko & G. Valentini, 2011, Exploring the complementarity between innovation and export for SMEs' growth, *JIBS*, 42: 362–380; R. Merton, 2013, Innovation risk, *HBR*, April: 48–56; M. Sytch & A. Tatarynowicz, 2014, Exploring the locus of invention, *AMJ*, 57: 249–279; W. Wales, V. Parida, & P. Patel, 2013, Too much of a good thing? *SMJ*, 34: 622–633.

17 C. Christensen, 1997, *The Innovator's Dilemma*, Boston: Harvard Business School Press.

18 P. Vaaler, 2011, Immigrant remittances and the venture investment environment of developing countries, *JIBS*, 42: 1121–1149.

19 R. Koth & G. George, 2012, Friends, family, or fools? *JBV*, 27: 525–543.

20 T. Dalziel, R. White, & J. Arthurs, 2011, Principal costs in initial public offerings, *JMS*, 48: 1346–1364; Y. Li & T. Chi, 2013, Venture capitalists' decision to withdraw, *SMJ*, 34: 1351–1366.

21 M. Humphrey-Jenner & J. Suchard, 2013, Foreign venture capitalists and the internationalization of entrepreneurial companies: Evidence from China, *JIBS*, 44: 607–621.

22 *HBR*, 2012, Muhammad Yunus: Life's work, December: 136.

23 Y. Yamakawa, S. Khavul, M. W. Peng, & D. Deeds, 2013, Venturing from emerging economies, *SEJ*, 7: 181–196.

24 J. Mair, I. Marti, & M. Ventresca, 2012, Building inclusive markets in rural Bangladesh, *AMJ*, 55: 819–850.

25 M. W. Peng & A. York, 2001, Behind intermediary performance in export trade, *JIBS*, 32: 327–346.

26 G. Cassar, 2010, Are individuals entering self-employment overly optimistic? *SMJ*, 31: 822–840.

27 Y. Yamakawa, M. W. Peng, & D. Deeds, 2015, Rising from the ashes, *ETP*, 39: 209–236.

28 D. Ahlstrom, S. Chen, & K. Yeh, 2010, Managing in ethnic Chinese communities, *APJM*, 27: 341–354.

29 S. Nadkarni, P. Herrmann, & P. Perez, 2011, Domestic mindset and early international performance, *SMJ*, 32: 510–531.

30 S. Rangan & R. Adner, 2001, Profits and the Internet (pp. 49–50), *SMR*, summer: 44–53.

31 L. Lopez, S. Kundu, & L. Ciravegna, 2009, Born global or born regional? *JIBS*, 40: 1228–1238.

32 G. Bruton, D. Ahlstrom, & H. Li, 2010, Institutional theory and entrepreneurship, *ETP*, 34: 421–440; S. Puffer, D. McCarthy, & M. Boisot, 2010, Entrepreneurship in Russia and China, *ETP*, 34: 441–467; S. Zahra & M. Wright, 2011, Entrepreneurship's next act, *AMP*, November: 67–83.

33 M. W. Peng, C. Hill, & D. Wang, 2000, Schumpeterian dynamics versus Williamsonian considerations, *JMS*, 37: 167–184.

Marcos Issa/Bloomberg/Getty Images

Learning Objectives

After studying this chapter, you should be able to

- understand how institutions and resources affect the liability of foreignness.

- match the quest for location-specific advantages with strategic goals (*where* to enter).

- compare and contrast first-mover and late-mover advantages (*when* to enter).

- follow the comprehensive model of foreign market entries (*how* to enter).

- participate in three leading debates concerning foreign market entries.

- draw implications for action.

Entering Foreign Markets

EMERGING MARKETS: Wal-Mart's Challenges in Brazil

Ranked as number one on the *Fortune* Global 500 list, Wal-Mart is not only the largest retailer, but also the largest company in the world (measured by sales). Operating more than 6,000 stores in 26 countries outside the United States, Wal-Mart is naturally interested in Brazil—the "B" in BRIC. Yet, two decades after entering Brazil with more than 550 stores in almost 200 cities, Wal-Mart is still struggling. Its everyday prices are evidently not low enough to many shoppers. While there is no shortage of store traffic, most shoppers buy selective items from Wal-Mart—otherwise known as "cherry picking the promotions"—and then go elsewhere to get the bargains. Despite bombardments from TV commercials on Wal-Mart's "everyday low prices," many shoppers are neither convinced that its prices are always the lowest, nor interested in the one-stop shopping convenience. Stretching every real from their average paycheck of about US$900 a month, many shoppers go to different stores to get the best deals on specific items. For example, hypermarket chain Extra, a unit of France's Casino, is known to offer the best deals on cleaning supplies, but only on Wednesdays when they are on sale. Cheapest produce can be found in local street markets. In the land of promotions and bargain hunting, Wal-Mart has not been successful in pushing down its prices on all

(or most) items. This is in part due to its inability to squeeze savings out of its logistics system in a vast country with inefficient infrastructure—back home, its logistics system is one of its legendary secret weapons behind its success. Leadership turmoil is another contributing factor. Its lackluster performance has led to four local CEOs going through the revolving doors of the CEO suite in one decade. In an October 2013 analysts' meeting, Wal-Mart CEO Doug McMillon admitted that "we are not making the most of Brazil."

Despite Wal-Mart's challenges, other foreign entrants have been doing well in Brazil. In the very industry in which Wal-Mart competes, France's Carrefour and Casino are thriving. Beyond this industry, multinationals enjoying Brazil's expanding economy include Coca-Cola, Domino's Pizza, Nestle, Nike, and Procter & Gamble. As for Wal-Mart, Brazil is not the first overseas market in which it has hit a road block. In Germany and South Korea, Wal-Mart shut down its operations after many years of disappointing results. In Russia, Wal-Mart spent six years attempting to acquire a local chain, but closed down its office in Moscow after failing to do so. In India, Wal-Mart cut its ties with its joint venture partner after several years of trying. In China, Wal-Mart had to close down 25 non-performing stores out of a total of 400. While Brazil is not completely hopeless for Wal-Mart, the lessons are very clear: Even the world's most formidable and largest retailer cannot take success in overseas markets for granted.

Sources: Based on (1) *Bloomberg*, 2014, Wal-Mart's everyday low prices fail to stir Brazilians, April 23, www.bloomberg.com; (2) *Bloomberg Businessweek*, 2014, Why Wal-Mart hasn't conquered Brazil, May 12: 24–25; (3) *Business Insider*, 2013, Four countries that Wal-Mart has failed to impress, October 11, www.businessinsider.com; (4) M. W. Peng, 2009, Wal-Mart in Germany, *Global Strategy* (pp. 153–154), Cincinnati: Cengage Learning.

How do firms such as Wal-Mart enter foreign markets? Why do they enter certain countries such as Brazil but not others? Why do some of them succeed while others struggle? These are some of the key questions driving this chapter. Entering foreign markets is crucial for international business (IB). This chapter first draws on the institution-based and resource-based views to discuss ways to overcome the liability of foreignness.[1] Then we focus on three crucial dimensions: *where, when*, and *how*— known as the "2W1H dimensions." Our discussion culminates in a comprehensive model, followed by debates and extensions.

Learning Objective
Understand how institutions and resources affect the liability of foreignness.

10-1 Overcoming the Liability of Foreignness

It is not easy to succeed in an unfamiliar environment. Recall from Chapter 1 that foreign firms such as Wal-Mart have to overcome a liability of foreignness, which is the *inherent* disadvantage that foreign firms experience in host countries because of their non-native status.[2] Such a liability is manifested in at least two dimensions. First, there are numerous differences in formal and informal institutions governing the rules of the game in different countries. While local firms are already well versed in these rules, foreign firms have to invest resources to learn such rules. Some of the rules are in favor of local firms. For example, after working for years to familiarize itself with US defense procurement rules, European Aeronautic Defence and Space (EADS), the maker of Airbus, in 2008 won a major US$35 billion contract to supply the US Air Force with next-generation refueling tankers. Then EADS (along with its US partner, Northrop Grumman) was disappointed to find out that Boeing was able to twist the arms of politicians and change the rules. In 2010, Boeing emerged as the winner of this rich prize, and EADS (which more recently changed its name to the Airbus Group) had to drop out.[3]

Second, although customers in this age of globalization supposedly no longer discriminate against foreign firms, the reality is that foreign firms are often still discriminated against, sometimes formally and other times informally. For years, American rice and beef, suspected (although never proven) to contain long-term health hazards because of genetic modification, have been informally resisted by individual consumers in Japan and Europe, after formal discriminatory policies imposed by their governments were removed. In India, activists singled out both Coca-Cola and Pepsi products as containing pesticides higher than permitted levels and chose not to test any Indian soft drinks that might contain even higher pesticide levels in a country where pesticide residues are present in virtually all groundwater. Although both Coca-Cola and Pepsi denied these charges, their sales suffered.

Against such significant odds, how do foreign firms crack new markets? The answer boils down to our two core perspectives (Figure 10.1). The institution-based view suggests that firms need to take actions deemed legitimate and appropriate by the various formal and informal institutions governing market entries. Differences

Figure 10.1   Institutions, Resources, and Foreign Market Entries

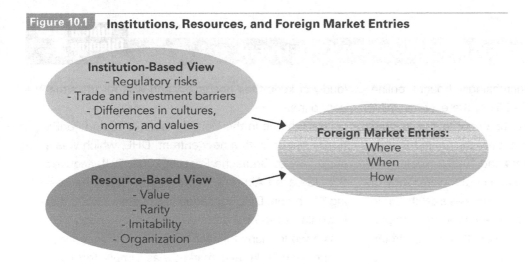

in formal institutions may lead to regulatory risks due to differences in political, economic, and legal systems (see Chapter 2). There may be numerous trade and investment barriers (see Chapters 5, 6, and 8). The existence of multiple currencies—and currency risks as a result—can be viewed as another formal barrier (see Chapter 7). The experience of the euro shows how much more trade and investment can take place when multiple countries remove such a barrier by adopting the same currency (see Chapter 8). Informally, numerous differences in cultures, norms, and values create another source of liability of foreignness (see Chapter 3).

The resource-based view argues that foreign firms need to deploy *overwhelming* resources and capabilities to offset their liability of foreignness.[4] In the absence of overwhelming resources and capabilities, the performance will be mediocre or worse. Applying the VRIO framework introduced in Chapter 4 to our Opening Case, we can suggest that, although formidable, Wal-Mart's resources and capabilities are not overwhelming in Brazil. Offering competitive prices is certainly valuable. But these capabilities are not rare, as other competing stores offer similar (and sometimes better) competitively priced goods. Whatever Wal-Mart does is quickly imitated. Finally, Wal-Mart's organizational capabilities in running ultra-efficient logistics systems back home are not successfully translated into the Brazilian context.

Overall, our two core perspectives shed a lot of light on firms' internationalization. In Focus 10.1 illustrates the liability of foreignness in the express delivery industry. The institution-based view helps explain how FedEx and UPS experienced tremendous institution-based barriers when competing in China, and the resource-based view points out that DHL's lack of overwhelming resources and capabilities torpedoed its ambition to expand in the United States. Next, we investigate the 2W1H dimensions associated with foreign market entries.

10-2 Where to Enter?

Like real estate, the motto for IB is "Location, location, location." In fact, such a *spatial* perspective (that is, doing business outside of one's home country) is a defining feature of IB.[5] Two sets of considerations drive the location of foreign entries: (1) strategic goals and (2) cultural and institutional distances. Each is discussed next.

Learning Objective

Match the quest for location-specific advantages with strategic goals (where to enter).

IN FOCUS 10.1
LIABILITY OF FOREIGNESS IN EXPRESS DELIVERY

As Chinese customers increasingly bought online (spending US$300 billion in 2013), the express delivery industry in China rose to become the second largest in the world—behind only the United States. Having entered China in 1984 and 1988, respectively, United Parcel Service (UPS) and FedEx were ready to benefit from such growth. But here was a catch. Since 2009, the State Post Bureau—a regulator—implemented a new law requiring that all carriers, foreign and local, needed new licenses. Instead of obtaining a license for operations in the entire country, *each* of UPS's 33 branches and FedEx's 58 branches required one license. The slow and arduous processes of getting licenses clipped the wings of UPS and FedEx. Domestic carriers such as Suning Commerce and S.F. Express seemed to be able to get licenses faster, thus rocketing ahead of the global giants. UPS and FedEx thus face the dilemma of whether to protest loudly or keep their heads low and wait for the situation to improve.

Back home in the United States, UPS and FedEx had to put up with a new entrant, DHL, which was a subsidiary of Deutsche Post. In 2003, DHL acquired the US-based Airborne Express. However, after losing $10 billion, DHL conceded in November 2008 that it would exit the US domestic market. Although DHL was a world market leader, its liability of foreignness in the world's largest market was simply too overwhelming. Facing steep sales declines because of the economic crisis, DHL laid off some 10,000 US workers and closed all 18 of its hubs. It would still make international deliveries to and from the United States. Its rivals immediately hustled to grab its customers.

Sources: Based on (1) *Bloomberg Businessweek*, 2014, For FedEx in China: It's hurry up and wait, March 10: 16–17; (2) *BusinessWeek*, 2008, DHL fails to deliver, November 24: 8; (3) *Economist*, 2013, Multinationals in China, August 24: 59.

10-2a Location-Specific Advantages and Strategic Goals

Favorable locations in certain countries may give firms operating there location-specific advantages. These advantages are the benefits a firm reaps from features specific to a particular location. Certain locations simply possess geographical features that are difficult for others to match. For example, Miami, the self-styled "Gateway of the Americas," is an ideal location both for North American firms looking south and Latin American companies coming north. Vienna is an attractive site as multinational enterprise (MNE) regional headquarters for Central and Eastern Europe. Dubai is an ideal stopping point for air traffic between Asia and Europe, and between Asia and Africa (see Emerging Markets 10.1).

Beyond geographic advantages, location-specific advantages also arise from the clustering of economic activities in certain locations, usually referred to as agglomeration (see Chapter 6). The basic idea dates back at least to Alfred Marshall, a British economist who first published it in 1890. Essentially, location-specific advantages stem from (1) knowledge spillovers among closely located firms that attempt to hire individuals from competitors, (2) industry demand that creates a skilled labor force whose members may work for different firms without having to move out of the region, and (3) industry demand that facilitates a pool of specialized suppliers and buyers to also locate in the region. For example, due to agglomeration, Dallas has the world's heaviest concentration of telecom companies. US firms such as AT&T, HP, Raytheon, TI, and Verizon cluster there. Numerous leading foreign telecom firms, such as Alcatel-Lucent, Ericsson, Fujitsu, Huawei, Siemens, STMicroelectronics, and ZTE, have also converged in this region.

Location-specific advantage

The benefits a firm reaps from the features specific to a place.

EMERGING MARKETS 10.1

Dubai Airport Connects the World

As a part of the United Arab Emirates, Dubai has emerged as the undisputed financial, business, and shopping center in the Middle East. Dubai International Airport (DXB) not only positions itself as the aviation center of the region, but also aspires to become the aviation center of the *world*. Geographically, Dubai is indeed the center of the world, known as a natural "pinch point," according to experts. It is the ideal stopping point for air traffic between Europe and Asia and between Africa and Asia. Four billion people live within eight hours of flying time from Dubai. Connecting 220 destinations across six continents with 130 airlines, DXB handles more than 40 million passengers a year. New expansion will allow DXB to serve 60 million passengers a year in the near future. Since Dubai's own population is fewer than four million (most are expatriates), the majority of the passengers are connecting passengers who are not from or going to Dubai. DXB's expansion will have to rely on customers from the rest of the world. Will they come?

DXB's hometown carrier, Emirates Airlines, is betting that connecting passengers will come. Launched in 1985, Emirates is known as a "super-connecting" airline because the majority of its customers are connecting passengers who do not travel to and from Dubai. One of the world's most powerful carriers,

Emirates has an all wide-body fleet of 138 planes and 140 more on firm order (including 50 Airbus A380s). From Dubai, Emirates flies to more than 100 cities in more than 60 countries. Emirates is the largest customer of the ultra-long-range Boeing 777ER (extended range) and one of the largest users of the A380. With these capable jets, any two cities in the world can be linked with just one stop via Dubai. Emirates thus has been directly challenging traditional long-haul carriers such as British Airways (BA), Air France-KLM, and Lufthansa. Emirates has launched services connecting Dubai with secondary (but still very sizable) cities, such as Manchester, Hamburg, and Kolkata. These cities are neglected by BA, Lufthansa, and Air India, respectively, which focus on their own hubs.

Starting in 1950, DXB has been experiencing an astonishing annual growth rate of 15%. Today, it is the world's third-busiest international passenger airport (after London Heathrow and Hong Kong) and the seventh-busiest cargo airport. Yet it will be replaced by an even larger airport, Dubai World Central–Al Maktoum International (DWC), which partially opened in 2010 (with one runway and with cargo flights only). When completed, the new DWC will be the largest airport in the world, with *five* parallel runways and an annual passenger capacity of 160 million (!).

Sources: Based on (1) *Aviation News*, 2011, Dubai International Airport, December: 34–39; (2) *Bloomberg Businessweek*, 2010, Emirates wins with big planes and low costs, July 5: 18–19; (3) *CEO Middle East*, 2013, The waiting game, June: 56–61; (4) *Economist*, 2010, Rulers of the new silk road, June 5: 75–77; (5) *Economist*, 2010, Super-duper-connectors from the Gulf, June 5: 21; (6) *Economist*, 2013, It's bouncing back, November 23: 52.

Given that different locations offer different benefits, it is imperative that a firm match its strategic goals with potential locations. The four strategic goals are shown in Table 10.1.

- *Natural resource-seeking* firms have to go to particular foreign locations where those resources are found. For example, the Middle East, Russia, and Venezuela are all rich in oil. Even when the Venezuelan government became more hostile, Western oil firms had to put up with it.
- *Market-seeking* firms go to countries that have a strong demand for their products and services. For example, China is now the largest car market in the

Table 10.1	Matching Strategic Goals with Locations	
Strategic goals	**Location-specific advantages**	**Examples in the text**
Natural resource seeking	Possession of natural resources and related transport and communication infrastructure	*Oil in the Middle East, Russia, and Venezuela*
Market seeking	Abundance of strong market demand and customers willing to pay	*GM in China*
Efficiency seeking	Economies of scale and abundance of low-cost factors	*Manufacturing in China (especially in Shanghai)*
Innovation seeking	Abundance of innovative individuals, firms, and universities	*IT in Silicon Valley and Bangalore; telecom in Dallas; wind turbines in Denmark*

world, and practically all the automakers in the world are now elbowing into this fast-growing market. General Motors (GM) has emerged as the leader. It now sells more cars in China than in the United States.

- *Efficiency-seeking* firms often single out the most efficient locations featuring a combination of scale economies and cost factors. It is the search for efficiency that induced numerous MNEs to enter China. China now manufactures two-thirds of the world's photocopiers, shoes, toys, and microwave ovens; one-half of the DVD players, digital cameras, and textiles; one-third of the desktop computers; and one-quarter of the mobile phones, television sets, and steel. Shanghai alone reportedly has a cluster of more than 400 of the *Fortune Global 500* firms. Approximately one-quarter of all foreign direct investment (FDI) in China has been absorbed by Shanghai. It is important to note that China does not present the absolutely lowest labor costs in the world, and Shanghai has the *highest* cost in China. However, Shanghai's attractiveness lies in its ability to enhance efficiency for foreign entrants by lowering *total* costs.
- *Innovation-seeking* firms target countries and regions renowned for world-class innovations, such as Silicon Valley and Bangalore (in IT), Dallas (in telecom), and Denmark (in wind turbines). (See Chapter 13 for details.)

It is important to note that location-specific advantages may grow, change, and/or decline, prompting firms to relocate. If policy makers fail to maintain the institutional attractiveness (for example, by raising taxes) and if companies overcrowd and bid up factor costs (such as land and talents), some firms may move out of certain locations previously considered advantageous. For example, the Chinese government has raised minimum wages and tightened environmental regulations. Also, thanks to the "one child" policy that was first implemented in the 1980s, the number of low-skill youth entering the labor market has declined. These changes have eroded the location-specific advantages of coastal China centered on low costs. As a result, many labor-intensive, cost-conscious firms have either moved to inland China (where labor cost has remained relatively low) or Southeast Asian countries such as Indonesia, Malaysia, Thailand, and Vietnam (where labor cost is now lower than coastal China).

Cultural distance

The difference between two cultures along identifiable dimensions such as individualism.

10-2b Cultural/Institutional Distances and Foreign Entry Locations

In addition to strategic goals, another set of considerations centers on cultural/institutional distances (see also Chapters 2 and 3). Cultural distance is the difference between two cultures along some identifiable dimensions (such as individualism).[6] Considering culture as an informal part of institutional frameworks governing a particular country, institutional distance is "the extent of similarity or dissimilarity between the regulatory, normative, and cognitive institutions of two countries."[7] Many Western consumer products firms, such as L'Oreal and Victoria's Secret, have shied away from Saudi Arabia, citing its stricter rules of personal behavior—in essence, the cultural and institutional distances between the West and Saudi Arabia being too large.

Two schools of thought have emerged. The first is associated with stage models, arguing that firms will enter culturally similar countries during their first stage of internationalization, and that they may gain more confidence to enter culturally distant countries in later stages.[8] This idea is intuitively appealing: It makes sense for Belgian firms to first enter France and for Mexican firms to first enter Texas, taking advantage of common cultural, language, and historical ties.[9] Business between countries that share a language is, on average, three times greater than between countries without a common language. Firms from common-law countries (English-speaking countries and Britain's former colonies) are more likely to be interested in other common-law countries. Colony-colonizer links (such as Britain's ties with the Commonwealth and Spain's with Latin America) boost trade significantly. (See PengAtlas maps 1.3, 1.4, and 1.5.)

Citing numerous counterexamples, a second school of thought argues that considerations of strategic goals, such as market and efficiency, are more important than cultural/institutional considerations.[10] For instance, natural resource-seeking firms have compelling reasons to enter culturally and institutionally distant countries, such as Papua New Guinea for bauxite, Venezuela for oil, and Zambia for copper. Because Western firms have few alternatives elsewhere, cultural, institutional, and geographic distance in this case do not seem relevant—they simply have to be there. Overall, in the complex calculus underpinning entry decisions, locations represent but one of several important sets of considerations. As shown next, entry timing and modes are also crucial.

10-3 When to Enter?

Entry timing refers to whether there are compelling reasons to be an early or late entrant in a particular country. Some firms look for first-mover advantages, defined as the benefits that accrue to firms that enter the market first and that later entrants do not enjoy.[11] Speaking of the power of first-mover advantages, "Xerox," "FedEx," and "Google" have now become *verbs*, such as "Google it." In many African countries, "Colgate" is the generic term for toothpaste. Unilever, a late mover, was disappointed to find out that some of its African customers call its own toothpaste "the red Colgate" (!). Table 10.2 outlines such advantages.

- First movers may gain advantage through proprietary technology. Think about Apple's iPod, iPad, and iPhone.
- First movers may also make pre-emptive investments. A number of Japanese MNEs have cherry-picked leading local suppliers and distributors in Southeast Asia as new members of the expanded *keiretsu* networks (alliances of Japanese businesses with interlocking business relationships and shareholdings) and have blocked access to the suppliers and distributors by late entrants from the West.[12]

Learning Objective

Compare and contrast first-mover and late-mover advantages (when to enter).

Institutional distance

The extent of similarity or dissimilarity between the regulatory, normative, and cognitive institutions of two countries.

First-mover advantage

Benefits that accrue to firms that enter the market first and that late entrants do not enjoy.

Table 10.2 **First-Mover Advantages and Late-Mover Advantages**

First-mover advantages	Examples in the text	Late-mover advantages	Examples in the text
Proprietary, technological leadership	*Apple's iPod, iPad, and iPhone*	Opportunity to free ride on first mover investments	*Ericsson won big contracts in Saudi Arabia, free-riding on Cisco's efforts*
Pre-emption of scarce resources	*Japanese MNEs in Southeast Asia*	Resolution of technological and market uncertainty	*BMW, GM, and Toyota have patience to wait until the Nissan Leaf resolves uncertainties about the electric car*
Establishment of entry barriers for late entrants	*Poland's F-16 fighter jet contract*	First mover's difficulty to adapt to market changes	*Greyhound is stuck with the bus depots, whereas Megabus simply uses curbside stops*
Avoidance of clash with dominant firms at home	*Sony, Honda, and Epson go to the US market ahead of their Japanese rivals*		
Relationships with key stake-holders such as governments	*Citigroup, JP Morgan Chase, and Metallurgical Corporation of China enter Afghanistan*		

- First movers may erect significant entry barriers for late entrants, such as high switching costs due to brand loyalty. Buyers of expensive equipment are likely to stick with the same producers for components, training, and services for a long time. That is why American, British, French, German, and Russian aerospace firms competed intensely for Poland's first post–Cold War order of fighters—America's F-16 eventually won.
- Intense domestic competition may drive some nondominant firms abroad to avoid clashing with dominant firms head-on in their home market. Matsushita, Toyota, and NEC were the market leaders in Japan, but Sony, Honda, and Epson all entered the United States in their respective industries ahead of the leading firms.
- First movers may build precious relationships with key stakeholders, such as customers and governments. For example, Citigroup, JP Morgan Chase, and Metallurgical Corporation of China have entered Afghanistan, earning a good deal of goodwill from the Afghan government, which is interested in wooing more FDI.[13]

Late-mover advantage

Benefits that accrue to firms that enter the market later and that early entrants do not enjoy.

© VanderWolf Images/Shutterstock.com

How does winning Poland's first post-Cold War fighter contract help F-16's manufacturer?

The potential advantages of first movers may be counterbalanced by various disadvantages, which result in late-mover advantages (also listed in Table 10.2). Numerous first-mover firms—such as EMI in CT scanners and Netscape in Internet browsers—have lost market dominance in the long run. It is such late-mover firms as GE and Microsoft (Explorer), respectively, that win. Specifically, late-mover advantages are manifested in three ways:

- Late movers can free-ride on first movers' pioneering investments. In Saudi Arabia, Cisco invested millions of dollars to rub shoulders of dignitaries, including the king, in order to help officials grasp the promise of the Internet in fueling economic development. Then Cisco lost out to late movers, such as Ericsson, that offered lower-cost solutions. For instance, the brand new King Abdullah Economic City awarded an US$84 million citywide telecom project to Ericsson, whose bid was more than 20% lower than Cisco's—in part because Ericsson did not have to offer basic education and did not have to entertain that much. "We're very proud to have won against a company that did as much advance work as Cisco did," an elated Ericsson executive noted.[14]

- First movers face greater technological and market uncertainties. Nissan, for example, has launched the world's first all-electric car, the Leaf, which can run without a single drop of gasoline. However, there were tremendous uncertainties. After some of these uncertainties were removed, late movers such as BMW, GM, and Toyota joined the game with their own electric cars.

- As incumbents, first movers may be locked into a given set of fixed assets or reluctant to cannibalize existing product lines in favor of new ones. Late movers may be able to take advantage of the inflexibility of first movers by leapfrogging them. Although Greyhound, the incumbent in intercity bus service in the United States, is struggling financially, it cannot get rid of the expensive bus depots in inner cities that are often ill-maintained and dreadful. Megabus, the new entrant from Britain, simply has not bothered to build and maintain a single bus depot. Instead, Megabus uses curbside stops (like regular city bus stops), which have made travel by bus more appealing to a large number of passengers.

Overall, evidence points out both first-mover advantages and late-mover advantages. Unfortunately, a mountain of research is still unable to recommend conclusively a particular entry-timing strategy.[15] Although first movers may have an opportunity to win, their pioneering status is not a guarantee of success. For example, among the three first movers into the Chinese automobile industry in the 1980s, Volkswagen captured significant advantages, Chrysler had very moderate success, and Peugeot failed and had to exit. Although many of the late movers that entered in the 1990s are struggling, GM, Honda, and Hyundai gained significant market shares. Other late entrants struggled. It is obvious that entry timing cannot be viewed in isolation, and entry timing per se is not the sole determinant of success and failure of foreign entries. It is through interaction with other crucial variables that entry timing has an impact on performance.

10-4 How to Enter?

Learning Objective
Follow the comprehensive model of foreign market entries (how to enter).

This section first focuses on large-scale versus small-scale entries. Then it introduces a comprehensive model. The first step is to determine whether to pursue equity or non-equity modes of entry. Finally, we outline the pros and cons of various equity and non-equity modes.

10-4a Scale of Entry: Commitment and Experience

One key dimension in foreign entry decisions is the scale of entry, which refers to the amount of resources committed to entering a foreign market. The benefits of large-scale entries are a demonstration of strategic commitment to certain markets. This both helps assure local customers and suppliers ("We are here for the long haul!") and deters potential entrants. The drawbacks are (1) limited strategic

Scale of entry
The amount of resources committed to entering a foreign market.

flexibility elsewhere, and (2) huge losses if these large-scale "bets" turn out to be wrong.

Small-scale entries are less costly. They focus on "learning by doing" while limiting the downside risk.[16] For example, to enter the market of Islamic finance whereby no interest can be charged (per teaching of the Koran), Citibank set up a subsidiary Citibank Islamic Bank. Citibank Islamic Bank was designed to experiment with different interpretations of the Koran on how to make money while not committing religious sins. It is simply not possible to acquire such an ability outside the Islamic world. Overall, the longer foreign firms stay in host countries, the less liability of foreignness they experience. The drawbacks of small-scale entries are a lack of strong commitment, which may lead to difficulties in building market share and in capturing first-mover advantages.

10-4b Modes of Entry: The First Step on Equity versus Non-equity Modes

Mode of entry

Method used to enter a foreign market.

Managers are unlikely to consider the numerous modes of entry (methods used to enter a foreign market) at the same time. Given the complexity of entry decisions, it is imperative that managers *prioritize*, by considering only a few manageable, key variables first and then other variables later.[17] Therefore, a comprehensive model shown in Figure 10.2 and explained in Table 10.3 is helpful.

Figure 10.2   **The Choice of Entry Modes: A Comprehensive Model**

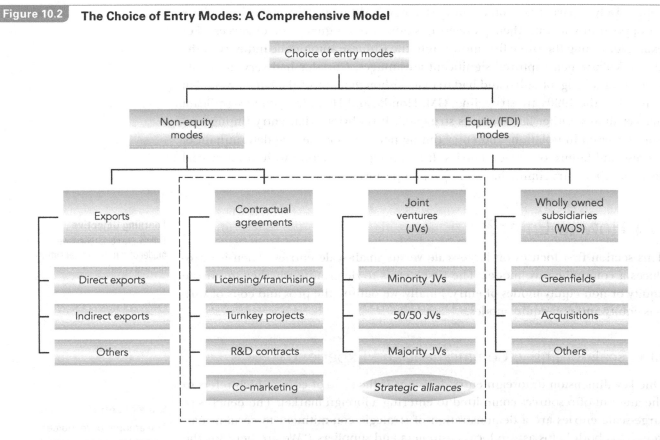

Source: Adapted from Y. Pan & D. Tse, 2000, The hierarchical model of market entry modes (p. 538), *Journal of International Business Studies*, 31: 535–554. The dotted area labeled "strategic alliances" is added by the present author. See Chapter 12 for details.

Table 10.3 **Modes of Entry: Advantages and Disadvantages**

Entry modes (examples in the text)	Advantages	Disadvantages
1. Non-equity modes: Exports		
Direct exports (*Pearl River piano exports to over 80 countries*)	• Economies of scale in production concentrated in home country • Better control over distribution	• High transportation costs for bulky products • Marketing distance from customers • Trade barriers and protectionism
Indirect exports (*Commodities trade in textiles and meats*)	• Focus on production • Avoid export processes	• Less control over distribution • Inability to learn how to compete overseas
2. Non-equity modes: Contractual agreements		
Licensing/franchising (*Pizza Hut in Thailand*)	• Low development costs • Low risk in overseas expansion	• Little control over technology and marketing • May create competitors • Inability to engage in global coordination
Turnkey projects (*Safi Energy's BOT project in Morocco*)	• Ability to earn returns from process technology in countries where FDI is restricted	• May create efficient competitors • Lack of long-term presence
R&D contracts (*wind turbines research in Denmark*)	• Ability to tap into the best locations for certain innovations at low costs	• Difficult to negotiate and enforce contracts • May nurture innovative competitors • May lose core innovation capabilities
Co-marketing (*McDonald's campaigns with movie studios and toy makers; airline alliances*)	• Ability to reach more customers	• Limited coordination
3. Equity modes: Partially owned subsidiaries		
Joint ventures (*Shanghai Volkswagen*)	• Sharing costs, risks, and profits • Access to partners' assets • Politically acceptable	• Divergent goals and interests of partners • Limited equity and operational control • Difficult to coordinate globally
4. Equity modes: Wholly owned subsidiaries		
Greenfield operations (*Microsoft's R&D center in China; TI in Japan; Japanese auto transplants in the United States*)	• Complete equity and operational control • Protection of know-how • Ability to coordinate globally	• Potential political problems and risks • High development costs • Add new capacity to industry • Slow entry speed (relative to acquisitions)
Acquisitions (*Siemens' acquisition of Bonus Energy*)	• Same as greenfield (above) • Do not add new capacity • Fast entry speed	• Same as greenfield (above), except adding new capacity and slow speed • Post-acquisition integration problems

In the first step, considerations for small-scale versus large-scale entries usually boil down to the equity issue. Non-equity modes tend to reflect relatively smaller commitments to overseas markets, whereas equity modes are indicative of relatively larger, harder-to-reverse commitments. Equity modes call for the establishment of independent organizations overseas (partially or wholly controlled). Non-equity modes do not require such independent establishments. Overall, these modes differ significantly in terms of cost, commitment, risk, return, and control.

The distinction between equity and non-equity modes is not trivial. In fact, it is what defines an MNE: An MNE enters foreign markets via equity modes

Non-equity mode

A mode of entry (exports and contractual agreements) that reflects relatively smaller commitments to overseas markets.

Equity mode

A mode of entry (JV and WOS) that indicates a relatively larger, harder-to-reverse commitment.

through FDI. A firm that merely exports or imports with no FDI is usually not regarded as an MNE. As discussed at length in Chapter 6, an MNE, relative to a non-MNE, enjoys the three-pronged advantages along ownership, location, and internalization dimensions—collectively known as the OLI advantages. Overall, the first step in entry mode considerations is crucial. A strategic decision has to be made in terms of whether or not to undertake FDI and to become an MNE by selecting equity modes.

10-4c Modes of Entry: The Second Step on Making Actual Selections

During the second step, managers consider variables within *each* group of non-equity and equity modes. If the decision is to export, then the next consideration is direct exports or indirect exports. Direct exports are the most basic mode of entry, capitalizing on economies of scale in production concentrated in the home country and providing better control over distribution. Shown in Emerging Markets 10.2, the world's largest piano maker, Pearl River, exports its pianos from China to more than 80 countries. This strategy essentially treats foreign demand as an extension of domestic demand, and the firm is geared toward designing and producing first and foremost for the domestic market. While direct exports may work if the export volume is small, it is not optimal when the firm has a large number of foreign buyers. Marketing 101 suggests that the firm needs to be closer, both physically and psychologically, to its customers, prompting the firm to consider more intimate overseas involvement, such as FDI. In addition, direct exports may provoke protectionism, potentially triggering antidumping actions (see Chapters 5 and 11).

E M E R G I N G   M A R K E T S   1 0 . 2

Pearl River's Modes of Foreign Market Entries

For many readers of this book, Pearl River is likely to be the world's largest piano maker you have never heard of. It is also the fastest-growing piano maker in North America, with the largest dealer network in Canada and the United States (more than 300 dealers). Its website proudly announces that Pearl River is "the world's best selling piano." Although some of you may say, "Sorry, I don't play piano, so I don't know anything about leading piano brands," you most likely have heard about Yamaha and Steinway. Therefore, your excuse for not knowing Pearl River would collapse.

The problem is both yours and Pearl River's. Given the relatively low prestige associated with made-in-China goods, you probably would not associate a piece of fine musical instrument such as piano with a Chinese firm. Pearl River Piano Group (PRPG) is China's largest piano maker and has recently dethroned Japan's Yamaha to become the world champion by volume. Despite PRPG's outstanding capabilities, it is difficult for one firm to change the negative country-of-origin image associated with made-in-China goods.

PRPG was founded in 1956 in Guangzhou, China, where the Pearl River flows by. Pearl River (the company) in fact exported its very first piano to Hong Kong. Yet, its center of gravity has remained in China. Pianos have become more affordable with rising income. The one-child policy has made families willing to invest in their only child's education. As a result, the Chinese now buy half of the pianos produced in the world.

If you think life is easy for the leading firm in the largest market in the world, you are wrong. In fact, life is increasingly tough for PRPG. This is because rising demand has attracted numerous new entrants, many of which compete at the low end in China. More than 140 competitors have pushed PRPG's domestic market share from 70% at its peak a decade ago to about 25% now—although it is still the market leader.

Savage domestic competition has pushed PRPG to increasingly look for overseas opportunities. It now exports to more than 80 countries. In North America, PRPG started in the late 1980s by relying on US-based importers. Making its first ever FDI, it set up a US-based sales subsidiary, PRPG America, Ltd., in Ontario, California, in 1999. Acknowledging the importance of the US market and the limited international caliber of his own managerial rank, PRPG's CEO, Tong Zhi Cheng, attracted Al Rich, an American with long experience in the piano industry, to head the subsidiary. In two years, the greenfield subsidiary succeeded in getting Pearl River pianos into about one-third of the specialized US retail dealers. In ten years, the Pearl River brand became the undisputed leader in the low end of the upright piano market in North America. Efforts to penetrate the high-end market, however, were still frustrated.

Despite the enviable progress made by PRPG itself in general and by its US subsidiary in particular, the Pearl River brand suffers from all the usual trappings associated with Chinese brands. "We are very cognizant that our pricing provides a strong incentive to buy," Rich noted in a media interview, "but $6,000 is still a lot of money." In an audacious move to overcome buyers' reservation about purchasing a high-end Chinese product, PRPG made its second major FDI move in 2000 by acquiring Ritmüller of Germany.

Ritmüller was founded in 1795 by Wilhelm Ritmüller, during the lifetimes of composers Beethoven and Haydn. It was one of the first piano makers in Germany and one of the most prominent in the world. Unfortunately, during the post–World War II era, Ritmüller's style of small-scale, handicraft-based piano making had a hard time surviving the disruptive, mass-production technologies first unleashed by Yamaha and, more recently, by Pearl River. Prior to being acquired by Pearl River, Ritmüller ended up being inactive. Today, Ritmüller has entered a new era in its proud history and operated a factory in Germany with full capacity. The entire product line has been re-engineered to reflect a new commitment to a classic heritage and standards of excellence. PRPG has commissioned international master piano designers to marry German precision craftsmanship with the latest piano-making technology.

Sources Based on (1) *Funding Universe*, 2009, Guangzhou Pearl River Piano Group Ltd., www.fundinguniverse.com; (2) Y. Lu, 2009, Pearl River Piano Group's international strategy, in M. W. Peng, *Global Strategy*, 2nd ed. (pp. 437–440), Cincinnati: Cengage Learning; (3) Pearl River Piano Group, 2014, www.pearlriverpiano.com; (4) Pearl River USA, 2014, www.pearlriverusa.com.

Another export strategy is indirect exports—namely, exporting through domestically based export intermediaries. This strategy not only enjoys the economies of scale similar to direct exports, but is also relatively worry free. A significant amount of export trade in commodities such as textiles and meats, which compete primarily on price, is indirect through intermediaries.[18] Indirect exports have some drawbacks. For example, third parties, such as export trading companies, may not share the same objectives as exporters. Exporters choose intermediaries primarily because of information asymmetries concerning foreign markets. Intermediaries with international contacts and knowledge essentially make a living by taking advantage of such information asymmetries.[19] They are not interested in reducing such asymmetries. Intermediaries, for example, may repackage the products under their own brand and insist on monopolizing the communication with overseas customers. If the exporters are interested in knowing more about how their products perform overseas, indirect exports would not provide such knowledge.

The next group of non-equity entry modes involves the following types of contractual agreement: (1) licensing/franchising, (2) turnkey projects, (3) research and development contracts, and (4) co-marketing. In licensing/franchising agreements, the licensor/franchisor sells the rights to intellectual property such as patents and know-how to the licensee/franchisee for a fee. The licensor/franchisor, thus, does not have to bear the full costs and risks associated with expansion. On the other hand, the licensor/franchisor does not have tight control over production and marketing.[20] Pizza Hut, for example, was disappointed when its franchisee in Thailand discontinued the relationship and launched a competing pizza restaurant to eat Pizza Hut's lunch.

In turnkey projects, clients pay contractors to design and construct new facilities and train personnel. At project completion, contractors hand clients the proverbial key to facilities ready for operations, hence the term "turnkey." This mode allows firms to earn returns from process technology (such as construction) in countries where FDI is restricted. The drawbacks, however, are twofold. First, if foreign clients are competitors, turnkey projects may boost their competitiveness. Second, turnkey projects do not allow for a long-term presence after the key is handed to clients. To obtain a longer-term presence, build-operate-transfer agreements are now often used, instead of the traditional build-transfer type of turnkey projects. A build-operate-transfer (BOT) agreement is a non-equity mode of entry used to build a longer-term presence by building and then operating a facility for a period of time before transferring operations to a domestic agency or firm. For example, Safi Energy—a consortium among GDF Suez (France), Mitsui (Japan), and Nareva Holdings (Morocco)—has been awarded a BOT power-generation project in Morocco.[21]

Research and development (R&D) contracts refer to outsourcing agreements in R&D between firms. Firm A agrees to perform certain R&D work for Firm B. Firms thereby tap into the best locations for certain innovations at relatively low costs, such as wind turbines research in Denmark (see In Focus 6.2). However, three drawbacks may emerge. First, given the uncertain and multidimensional nature of R&D, these contracts are often difficult to negotiate and enforce. While delivery time and costs are relatively easy to negotiate, quality is often hard to assess. Second, such contracts may cultivate competitors. Finally, firms that rely on outsiders to perform a lot of R&D may lose some of their core R&D capabilities in the long run.

Co-marketing refers to efforts among a number of firms to jointly market their products and services. Toy makers and movie studios often collaborate in co-marketing campaigns with fast-food chains such as McDonald's to package toys based on movie characters in kids' meals. Airline alliances such as One World, Sky Team, and Star Alliance engage in extensive co-marketing through code sharing (multiple airlines share the code of one flight operated by one partner firm). The advantages are the ability to reach more customers. The drawbacks center on limited control and coordination.

Next are equity modes, all of which entail some FDI and transform the firm to an MNE. A joint venture (JV) is a corporate child, a new entity jointly created and owned by two or more parent companies. It has three principal forms: Minority JV (less than 50% equity), 50/50 JV (equal equity), and majority JV (more than 50% equity). JVs, such as Shanghai Volkswagen, have three advantages. First, an MNE shares costs, risks, and profits with a local partner, so the MNE possesses a certain

Turnkey project

A project in which clients pay contractors to design and construct new facilities and train personnel.

Build-operate-transfer (BOT) agreement

A nonequity mode of entry used to build a longer-term presence by building and then operating a facility for a period of time before transferring operations to a domestic agency or firm.

Research and development (R&D) contract

An outsourcing agreement in R&D between firms.

Co-marketing

Efforts among a number of firms to jointly market their products and services.

Joint venture (JV)

A new corporate entity created and jointly owned by two or more parent companies.

degree of control but limits risk exposure. Second, the MNE gains access to knowledge about the host country, and the local firm, in turn, benefits from the MNE's technology, capital, and management. Third, JVs may be politically more acceptable in host countries.

In terms of disadvantages, JVs often involve partners from different backgrounds and with different goals, so conflicts are natural. Furthermore, effective equity and operational control may be difficult to achieve, since everything has to be negotiated—in some cases, fought over. Finally, the nature of the JV does not give an MNE the tight control over a foreign subsidiary that it may need for global coordination. Overall, all sorts of non-equity-based contractual agreements and equity-based JVs can be broadly considered as strategic alliances (within the *dotted area* in Figure 10.2). Chapter 12 will discuss them in detail.

The last entry mode is to establish a wholly owned subsidiary (WOS), defined as a subsidiary located in a foreign country that is entirely owned by the parent multinational. There are two primary means to set up a WOS.[22] One is to establish greenfield operations, building new factories and offices from scratch (on a proverbial piece of "green field" formerly used for agricultural purposes). For example, Microsoft established a greenfield R&D center in Beijing. There are three advantages. First, a greenfield WOS gives an MNE complete equity and management control, thus eliminating the headaches associated with JVs. Second, this undivided control leads to better protection of proprietary technology. Third, a WOS allows for centrally coordinated global actions. Sometimes, a subsidiary will be ordered to *lose* money. In the semiconductor market, Texas Instruments (TI) faced the low-price Japanese challenge in many countries, whereas rivals such as NEC and Toshiba were able to charge high prices in Japan and use domestic profits to cross-subsidize overseas expansion. By entering Japan via a WOS and slashing prices there, TI retaliated by incurring a loss. However, this forced the Japanese firms to defend their home market, where they had more to lose. Japanese rivals thus had to reduce the ferocity of their price wars outside of Japan. Local licensees/franchisees or JV partners are unlikely to accept such a subservient role—being ordered to lose money.

In terms of drawbacks, a greenfield WOS tends to be expensive and risky, not only financially but also politically. Its conspicuous foreignness may become a target for nationalistic sentiments. Another drawback is that greenfield operations add new capacity to an industry, which will make a competitive industry more crowded. For example, think of all the Japanese automobile plants built in the United States, which have severely squeezed the market share of US automakers. Finally, greenfield operations suffer from a slow entry speed of at least one to several years (relative to acquisitions).

The other way to establish a WOS is an acquisition. Siemens's acquisition of Denmark's Bonus Energy is a case in point. Acquisition shares all the benefits of greenfield WOS but enjoys two additional advantages: (1) adding no new capacity, and (2) faster entry speed. In terms of drawbacks, acquisition shares all of the disadvantages of greenfield WOS except adding new capacity and slow entry speed. But acquisition has a unique disadvantage: post-acquisition integration problems (see Chapter 12 for details).

Overall, while we have focused on one entry mode at a time, firms in practice—as shown by Pearl River (Emerging Markets 10.2)—are not limited by any single entry choice.[23] For example, IKEA stores in China are JVs, and its stores in Hong Kong and Taiwan are separate franchises. Entry modes can also change over time.[24] Starbucks first used franchising. It then switched to JVs and, more recently, to acquisitions.

Wholly owned subsidiary (WOS)

A subsidiary located in a foreign country that is entirely owned by the parent multinational.

Greenfield operation

Building factories and offices from scratch (on a proverbial piece of "greenfield" formerly used for agricultural purposes).

Learning Objective
Participate in three leading debates concerning foreign market entries.

10-5 Debates and Extensions

This chapter has already covered some crucial debates, such as first-mover versus late-mover advantages. Here we discuss three heated *recent* debates: (1) liability versus asset of foreignness, (2) global versus regional geographic diversification, and (3) old-line versus emerging multinationals.

10-5a Liability versus Asset of Foreignness

While we do not need to spill more ink on the term "liability of foreignness," one contrasting view argues that under certain circumstances, being foreign can be an asset (that is, a competitive advantage). German cars are viewed as of higher quality than locally made cars in the United States and Japan. In China, consumers discriminate against Made-in-China luxury goods. Although these Made-in-China luxury goods sport Western brands, they are viewed inferior to Made-in-France handbags and Made-in-Switzerland watches. American cigarettes are "cool" among smokers in Central and Eastern Europe. Anything Korean—ranging from handsets and TV shows to *kimchi* (pickled cabbage)-flavored instant noodles—are considered hip in Southeast Asia.

Conceptually, this is known as the country-of-origin effect, which refers to the positive or negative perception of firms and products from a certain country.[25] Although IKEA is now registered and headquartered in Leiden, the Netherlands (and thus technically a *Dutch* company), it relentlessly displays Swedish flags in front of its stores in an effort to leverage the positive country-of-origin effect of Sweden. Pearl River's promotion of the Ritmüller brand, which highlights its German origin, suggests that the negative country-of-origin effect can be (at least partially) overcome[26] (see Emerging Markets 10.2). Pearl River is not alone in this regard. Here is a quiz: What is the country of origin of Häagen-Dazs ice cream? My students typically answer: Belgium, Denmark, Germany, the Netherlands, Switzerland, Sweden, or some other European countries. Sorry, all wrong. Häagen-Dazs is *American* since its founding.

What is the nationality of this ice cream brand?

Whether foreignness is indeed an asset or a liability remains tricky. Tokyo Disneyland became wildly popular in Japan, because it played up its American image. But Paris Disneyland received relentless negative press coverage in France, because it insisted on its wholesome American look. To play it safe, Hong Kong Disneyland endeavored to strike the elusive balance between American image and Chinese flavor. All eyes are now on the forthcoming Shanghai Disneyland in terms of such balance (see the Closing Case).

10-5b Global versus Regional Geographic Diversification

In this age of globalization, debate continues on the optimal geographic scope for MNEs.[27] Despite the widely held belief that MNEs are expanding "globally," Alan Rugman and colleagues report that, surprisingly, even among the largest *Fortune Global 500* MNEs, few are truly "global."[28] Using some reasonable criteria (at least 20% of sales in *each* of the three regions of the Triad consisting of Asia, Europe, and North America, but less than 50% in any one region), only eight to nine MNEs are found to be really "global" (Table 10.4).

Country-of-origin effect
The positive or negative perception of firms and products from a certain country.

Table 10.4	Only 8–9 "Global" Multinational Enterprises Are Global Measured by Sales								
	1	2	3	4	5	6	7	8	9
2001	Canon	Coca-Cola	Flextronics	IBM	Intel	LVMH	Nokia	Philips	Sony
2008	Accenture	Hochtief	Holcim	Nike	Rio Tinto	Schlumberger	Unilever	Visteon	---

Sources: Adapted from (1) A. Rugman & A. Verbeke, 2004, A perspective on regional and global strategies of multinational enterprises (pp. 8–10), *Journal of International Business Studies*, 35: 3–18; and (2) C. Oh & A. Rugman, 2014, The dynamics of regional and global multinationals, *Multinational Business Review*, 22: 108–117. "Global" MNEs have at least 20% of sales in each of the three regions of the Triad (Asia, Europe, and North America), but less than 50% in any one region.

Should most MNEs further "globalize"? There are two answers. First, most MNEs know what they are doing, and their current geographic scope is the maximum they can manage.[29] Some of them may have already over-diversified and will need to downsize. Second, these data only capture a snapshot (in the 2000s) and some MNEs may become more "globalized" over time. However, more recent data do not show major changes.[30] While the debate goes on, it has at least taught us one lesson: Be careful when using the word "global." The *majority* of the largest MNEs are not necessarily very "global" in their geographic scope.

10-5c Old-Line versus Emerging Multinationals: OLI versus LLL

As discussed extensively in Chapter 6, MNEs presumably possess OLI advantages. The OLI framework is based on the experience of MNEs headquartered in developed economies that typically possess high-caliber technology and management know-how. However, emerging multinationals, such as those from China (see Emerging Markets 10.2), are challenging some of this conventional wisdom.[31] While these emerging multinationals, like their old-line (established) counterparts, hunt for lucrative locations and internalize transactions—conforming to the L and I parts of the OLI framework—they typically do not own world-class technology or management capabilities. In other words, the O part is largely missing. How can we make sense of these emerging multinationals?

One interesting new framework is the "linkage, leverage, and learning" (LLL) framework advocated by John Mathews.[32] Linkage refers to emerging MNEs' ability to identify and bridge gaps. Pearl River has identified the gap between what its pianos can actually offer and what price it can command, given the negative country-of-origin effect it has to confront. Pearl River's answer has been two-pronged: (1) develop the economies of scale to bring down the unit cost of pianos while maintaining high quality, and (2) acquire and revive the Ritmüller brand to reduce some of the negative country-of-origin effect. Thus, Pearl River links China and Germany to propel its global push (see Emerging Markets 10.2).

Leverage refers to emerging multinationals' ability to take advantage of their unique resources and capabilities, which are typically based on a deep understanding of customer needs and wants. For example, Naver enjoys a 76% market share for Internet searches in South Korea. It intends to leverage its deep understanding of Asian languages and cultures by charging into Japan. In the long run, it also aspires to launch other culturally specific search engines, such as "Naver Korean-American" and "Naver Chinese-American." On a global scale, Naver's skills obviously pale in comparison with Google's capabilities. But in certain markets, such as South Korea, emerging multinationals such as Naver have been beating Google.

Learning is probably the most unusual aspect among the motives behind the internationalization push of many emerging multinationals.[33] Instead of the "I-will-tell-you-what-to-do" mentality typical of old-line MNEs from developed economies, many MNEs from emerging economies openly profess that they go abroad to learn. When India's Tata Motors acquired Jaguar and Land Rover and China's Geely acquired Volvo, they expressed a strong interest in learning how to manage world-class brands. Additional skills they need to absorb range from basic English skills (for managers from non-English-speaking countries such as Brazil, China, and Russia) to high-level executive skills in transparent governance, market planning, and management of diverse multicultural workforces.

Of course, there is a great deal of overlap between OLI and LLL frameworks. So, the debate boils down to whether the differences are fundamental, which would justify a new theory (such as LLL advantages) or just a matter of degree, in which case OLI would be just fine to accommodate the new MNEs. Given the rapidly moving progress of these emerging multinationals, one thing for certain is that our learning and debate about them will not stop anytime soon.

Learning Objective
Draw implications for action.

10-6 Management Savvy

Entering foreign markets represents a *foundation* for IB. Without these crucial first steps, firms will remain domestic players. The challenges associated with internationalization are daunting, the complexities enormous, and the stakes high. Recall our fundamental question: What determines the success and failure in foreign market entries? The answers boil down to the two core perspectives, institution-based and resource-based views. Consequently, three implications for action emerge (Table 10.5). First, from an institution-based view, managers need to understand the rules of the game, both formal and informal, governing competition in foreign markets. Failure to understand these rules can be costly. Why did Chinese MNEs' high-profile acquisition attempts in the United States (such as China National Offshore Oil Corporation's [CNOOC] bid for Unocal) and Australia (such as Chinalco's bid for Rio Tinto) often fail? Arabic MNEs' similar attempts (such as DP World's bid for US ports) often fail too, so do Russian MNEs' high-profile acquisitive forays (such as Sherbank's bid for Opel). While there are many reasons, one key reason is these foreign entrants' failure in understanding the informal, unwritten rules of the game that often have protectionist (or even racist) undertones in developed economies. Knowing these rules of the game does not mean these emerging MNEs need to be discouraged. They just need to do

LLL advantages

A firm's quest of linkage (L) advantages, leverage (L) advantages, and learning (L) advantages. These advantages are typically associated with multinationals from emerging economies.

Table 10.5	**Implications for Action**

- Understand the rules of game—both formal and informal—governing competition in foreign markets.
- Develop overwhelming resources and capabilities to offset the liability of foreignness.
- Match efforts in market entry and geographic diversification with strategic goals.

better homework, keep their heads low, and work on *low*-profile acquisitions, which are routinely approved in developed economies.

Second, from a resource-based view, managers need to develop overwhelming capabilities to offset the liability of foreignness. The key word is *overwhelming*. Merely outstanding, but not overwhelming, capabilities cannot ensure success in the face of strong incumbents—a painful lesson that DHL learned when it withdrew from the United States (see In Focus 10.1). In short, being good enough is not good enough.

Finally, managers need to match entries with strategic goals. If the goal is to deter rivals in their home markets by slashing prices there (as TI did when entering Japan), then be prepared to fight a nasty price war and lose money. If the goal is to generate decent returns, then withdrawing from some tough nuts to crack may be necessary (as Best Buy withdrew from China and Wal-Mart withdrew from Germany, India, Russia, and South Korea—see the Opening Case).

In conclusion, entry strategies obviously have something to do with the international success and failure of firms. However, appropriate entry strategies, while certainly important, are only the *beginning*.[34] It takes a lot more to succeed overseas, as we will discuss in later chapters.

CHAPTER SUMMARY/LEARNING OBJECTIVES

10-1 Understand how institutions and resources affect the liability of foreignness.

- When entering foreign markets, firms confront a liability of foreignness.
- Both institution-based and resource-based views advise managers on how to overcome such liability.

10-2 Match the quest for location-specific advantages with strategic goals (where to enter).

- Where to enter depends certain foreign countries' location-specific advantages and firms' strategic goals, such as seeking (1) natural resources, (2) market, (3) efficiency, and (4) innovation.

10-3 Compare and contrast first-mover and late-mover advantages (when to enter).

- Each has pros and cons, and there is no conclusive evidence pointing to one direction.

10-4 Follow the comprehensive model of foreign market entries (how to enter).

- How to enter depends on the scale of entry: large-scale versus small-scale entries.
- A comprehensive model of foreign market entries first focuses on the equity (ownership) issue.
- The second step focuses on making the actual selection, such as exports, contractual agreements, JVs, and WOS.

10-5 Participate in three leading debates concerning foreign market entries.

- (1) Liability versus asset of foreignness, (2) global versus regional geographic diversification, and (3) old-line versus emerging multinationals.

10-6 Draw managerial implications.

- Understand the rules of game governing competition in foreign markets.
- Develop overwhelming resources and capabilities to offset the liability of foreignness.
- Match efforts in market entry with strategic goals.

KEY TERMS

Build-operate-transfer
  (BOT) agreement, 332
Co-marketing, 332
country-of-origin
  effect, 334
Cultural distance, 324
Equity mode, 329
First-mover
  advantage, 325

Greenfield operation, 333
Institutional distance,
  325
Joint venture (JV), 332
Late-mover advantage,
  326
LLL advantages, 336
Location-specific
  advantage, 322

Mode of entry, 328
Non-equity mode, 329
Research and
  development (R&D)
  contract, 332
Scale of entry, 327
Turnkey project, 332
Wholly owned subsidiary
  (WOS), 333

REVIEW QUESTIONS

1. How do foreign firms suffer from liability of foreignness?

2. What does the institution-based view suggest about how a firm should address the liability of foreignness? What does the resource-based view advise?

3. *ON CULTURE:* What risk does a firm take in putting strategic goals ahead of cultural distance?

4. Describe how four strategic goals may affect the decision of where to enter.

5. Summarize the advantages of being a first mover.

6. Regarding PengAtlas Map 3.3, consider emerging economies that are late movers in the economic realm. To what extent do they have some of the same advantages as firms that are late movers?

7. How does a large-scale entry differ from a small-scale entry?

8. What are some of the hallmarks of each type of equity mode?

9. How may the country-of-origin effect change for a firm over time?

10. Devise your own example of how a firm may use its capabilities to overwhelmingly offset the liability of foreignness as it moves into a new foreign market.

11. *ON CULTURE:* If you were a manager charged with choosing a new location for your firm's business, how would you go about matching the location options with your firm's strategic goals?

12. Compare PengAtlas Maps 3.1 and 3.4.

   a. To what extent are the richest countries also among the easiest in which to do business? Are any of the richest countries among the most difficult in which to do business? Indicate whether you think the relationship is coincidental or causal and why you think that way.

   b. If you were thinking of expanding your firm's operations, you would probably wish to go where it is easier to do business and where income is higher. Furthermore, at least some of the poorest countries would like to have your firm expand into them to help lift income. If such is the case, why don't they simply make it easier to do business? What do you think?

   c. Although at present the United States is regarded as one of the easier countries for doing business, do you think that the long-term trend is for it to become even easier or to become more difficult? Why?

CRITICAL DISCUSSION QUESTIONS

1. Pick an industry in which firms from your country are internationally active. What are the top five most favorite foreign markets for firms in that industry? Why?

2. From institution-based and resource-based views, identify the liability of foreignness confronting MNEs from emerging economies interested in expanding overseas. How can such firms overcome them?

3. *ON ETHICS:* Entering foreign markets, by definition, means not investing in a firm's home country. For example, Nissan closed factories in Japan and added a new factory in the United States. GM shut down factories at home but kept them open in Europe. What are the ethical dilemmas here?

GLOBAL ACTION

BUSINESS
INSIGHTS
GLOBAL

1. You work for a mid-sized machinery firm that has never sold anything abroad. Top managers have asked you to identify the top five potential markets that your firm can focus on in its initial efforts to develop export markets. Please prepare a report to present why you have selected those five countries.

2. Your firm has been successfully exporting products to many customers around the world, but has never set up a subsidiary abroad. Top managers want to know whether the firm has reached a point that it would be advantageous to start setting up subsidiaries—and if so, what would be the top three countries where the first batch of subsidiaries can be set up and what would be the ideal mode of entry. Please prepare a report on what your research has uncovered.

CLOSING CASE

EMERGING MARKETS: Mickey Goes to Shanghai

There were signs aplenty that the April 8, 2011, groundbreaking for the US$4.4 billion Shanghai Disney Resort was not aimed at the typical Orlando vacationer. Shanghai school children sang *When You Wish Upon a Star*—in Mandarin. Mickey Mouse showed up clad not in his signature duds but in traditional red Chinese garb to symbolize good fortune. Everything was

Handout/Getty Images

customized to suit the tastes of the world's most-populous nation.

Walt Disney has good reason to sweat the details at its first theme park on the mainland. When it opened Hong Kong Disneyland in 2005, it underestimated how many visitors would show up and how long they would linger. The result: too few rides, inadequate seating and food supplies at restaurants, and angry crowds that had to be turned away. Although the 47% Disney-owned Hong Kong park is expanding, it still lost US$92.3 million in the year ended October 2010, while attendance rose 13%. "We learned a lot from Hong Kong," says Disney Chief Executive Officer Robert A. Iger. "In Shanghai, we're within a three hours' drive of 300 million people. That's a huge opportunity, and we have to be careful about how many will come and their visitation patterns."

For Disney, which will own a 43% stake in the 963-acre resort (three state-owned companies own the rest), Shanghai is a US$1.9 billion wager on a growing Chinese middle class who the company projects will spend US$200 billion annually on leisure travel by 2015. It is also a bet that Disney's characters and 55-year history of running theme parks can be adapted to a culture it may not fully understand. "Disney has too much riding on China to let either Hong Kong or Shanghai fail," says John Gerner, managing director of Leisure Business Advisors, which assessed the potential for theme parks in China for Village Roadshow, an Australian theater and park operator. "Hong Kong was an experiment to see if a smaller park would work, and it didn't. Now they're fixing it."

Shanghai's Disneyland will be almost 85 acres, about 50% larger than the Hong Kong park at its opening, says one executive. There will be traditional Disney rides and others based on Chinese culture, says Iger. The company is adding Chinese nationals to its "Imagineering" team to help develop the park. One staple that will change: Main Street USA,

the turn-of-the-century collection of storefronts and horse-drawn street cars that welcome visitors to most Disney parks. Explains Iger: "We simply believe Main Street USA might not be that interesting to people here."

Disney is not likely to repeat the cultural faux pas it made when it opened Disneyland Resort Paris in 1992, where food sales suffered because the park initially did not serve wine with meals. In Hong Kong, Disney has cut the number of hot dogs in restaurants in order to serve more dim sum and noodle dishes, says a Disney executive, and there is likely to be plenty of local fare in Shanghai. "Disney is paying a lot of attention now to cultural differences," says Evercore Partners analyst Alan Gould. One motivation: The Shanghai park will generate $70 million in management fees for Disney in its first year and $200 million within a decade, Gould estimates.

CASE DISCUSSION QUESTIONS:

1. Why does Disney feel compelled to make significant changes to its theme park when it enters China?

2. Does Disney have any overwhelming resources and capabilities?

3. What are the lessons Disney has learned from operating theme parks outside the United States (in Tokyo, Paris, and Hong Kong)? How applicable are these lessons to the new park in Shanghai?

4. Will Disney's new park in Shanghai be successful?

Source: *Bloomberg Businessweek*, 2011, Disney gets a second chance in China, April 18: 21–22.

NOTES

[**Journal acronyms**] **AMJ**—*Academy of Management Journal;* **AMR**—*Academy of Management Review;* **APJM**—*Asia Pacific Journal of Management;* **BJM**—*British Journal of Management;* **BW**—*BusinessWeek* (before 2010) or *Bloomberg Businessweek* (since 2010); **GSJ**—*Global Strategy Journal;* **HBR**—*Harvard Business Review;* **IBR**—*International Business Review;* **IMR**—*International Marketing Review;* **JIBS**—*Journal of International Business Studies;* **JIM**—*Journal of International Management;* **JM**—*Journal of Management;* **JMS**—*Journal of Management Studies;* **JWB**—*Journal of World Business;* **MIR**—*Management International Review;* **SMJ**—*Strategic Management Journal.*

1 K. Meyer, S. Estrin, S. Bhaumik, & M. W. Peng, 2009, Institutions, resources, and entry strategies in emerging economies, *SMJ,* 30: 61–80.

2 C. Asmussen & A. Goerzen, 2013, Unpacking dimensions of foreignness, *GSJ,* 3: 127–149; B. Baik, J. Kang, J. Kim, & J. Lee, 2013, The liability of foreignness in international equity investments, *JIBS,* 44: 391–411; Z. Bhanji & J. Oxley, 2013, Overcoming the dual liability of foreignness and privateness in international corporate citizenship partnerships, *JIBS,* 44: 290–311; N. Denk, L. Kaufmann, & J. Roesch, 2012, Liabilities of foreignness revisited, *JIM,* 18: 322–334; B. Elango, 2009, Minimizing effects of "liability of foreignness," *JWB,* 44: 51–62; J. Johanson & J. Vahlne, 2009, The Uppsala internationalization process model revisited, *JIBS,* 40: 1411–1431; H. Yildiz & C. Fey, 2012, The liability of foreignness reconsidered, *IBR,* 21: 269–280.

3 *BW,* 2010, Northrop gives up, March 22: 8; *Economist,* 2010, The best plane loses, March 13: 66.

4 M. W. Peng, 2001, The resource-based view and international business, *JM*, 27: 803–829. See also S. Chang, J. Chung, & J. Moon, 2013, When do foreign subsidiaries outperform local firms? *JIBS*, 44: 853–860; A. Kirca, G. T. Hult, S. Deligonul, M. Perryy, & S. T. Cavusgil, 2012, A multilevel examination of the drivers of firm multinationality, *JM*, 38: 502–530; K. S. Powell, 2014, From M-P to MA-P, *JIBS*, 45: 211–226.

5 J. Dunning, 2009, Location and the MNE, *JIBS*, 40: 5–19; A. Goerzen, C. Asmussen, & B. Nielsen, 2013, Global cities and multinational enterprise location strategy, *JIBS*, 44: 427–450; M. Kim, 2013, Many roads lead to Rome, *JIBS*, 44: 898–921.

6 R. Parente, B. Choi, A. Slangen, & S. Ketkar, 2010, Distribution system choice in a service industry, *JIM*, 16: 275–287.

7 D. Xu & O. Shenkar, 2002, Institutional distance and the multinational enterprise (p. 608), *AMR*, 27: 608–618. See also M. Cho & V. Kumar, 2010, The impact of institutional distance on the international diversity-performance relationship, *JWB*, 45: 93–103; G. Delmestri & F. Wezel, 2011, Breaking the wave, *JIBS*, 42: 828–852.

8 T. Hutzschenreuter, J. Voll, & A. Verbeke, 2011, The impact of added cultural distance and cultural diversity on international expansion patterns, *JMS*, 48: 305–329.

9 S. Makino & E. Tsang, 2011, Historical ties and foreign direct investment, *JIBS*, 42: 545–557.

10 J. Steen & P. Liesch, 2007, A note on Penrosian growth, resource bundles, and the Uppsala model of internationalization, *MIR*, 47: 193–206.

11 A. Hawk, G. Pacheci-de-Almeida, & B. Yeung, 2013, First-mover advantages, *SMJ*, 34: 1531–1550.

12 M. W. Peng, S. Lee, & J. Tan, 2001, The *keiretsu* in Asia, *JIM*, 7: 253–276.

13 *BW*, 2011, Land of war and opportunity, January 10: 46–54.

14 *BW*, 2008, Cisco's brave new world (p. 68), November 24: 56–68.

15 S. Dobrev & A. Gotsopoulos, 2010, Legitimacy vacuum, structural imprinting, and the first mover disadvantage, *AMJ*, 53: 1153–1174; J. Gomez & J. Maicas, 2011, Do switching costs mediate the relationship between entry timing and performance? *SMJ*, 32: 1251–1269; M. Semadeni & B. Anderson, 2010, The follower's dilemma, *AMJ*, 53: 1175–1193.

16 G. Gao & Y. Pan, 2010, The pace of MNEs' sequential entries, *JIBS*, 41: 1572–1580; P. Li & K. Meyer, 2009, Contextualizing experience effects in international business, *JWB*, 44: 370–382.

17 C. Bouquet, A. Morrison, & J. Birkinshaw, 2009, International attention and MNE performance, *JIBS*, 40: 108–131; L. Brouthers, S. Mukhopadhyay, T. Wilkinson, & K. Brouthers, 2009, International market selection and subsidiary performance, *JWB*, 44: 262–273.

18 M. W. Peng, Y. Zhou, & A. York, 2006, Behind make or buy decisions in export strategy, *JWB*, 41: 289–300.

19 M. W. Peng, 1998, *Behind the Success and Failure of US Export Intermediaries*, Westport, CT: Quorum.

20 A. Akremi, K. Mignonac, & R. Perrigot, 2011, Opportunistic behaviors in franchise chains, *SMJ*, 32: 930–948; P. Aulakh, M. Jiang, & S. Li, 2013, Licensee technological potential and exclusive rights in international licensing, *JIBS*, 44: 699–718.

21 United Nations (UN), 2014, *World Investment Report 2014* (p. 81), New York and Geneva: UN.

22 A. Slangen, 2013, Greenfield or acquisition entry? *GSJ*, 3: 262–280.

23 T. Jandik & R. Kali, 2009, Legal systems, information asymmetry, and firm boundaries, *JIBS*, 40: 578–599.

24 G. Benito, B. Petersen, & L. Welch, 2009, Towards more realistic conceptualizations of foreign operation modes, *JIBS*, 40: 1455–1470.

25 A. Diamantopoulos, B. Schlegelmilch, & D. Palihawadana, 2011, The relationship between country-of-origin image and brand image as drivers of purchase intentions, *IMR*, 28: 508–524; A. Maher & L. Carter, 2011, The affective and cognitive components of country image, *IMR*, 28: 559–580; S. Samiee, 2011, Resolving the impasse regarding research on the origins of products and brands, *IMR*, 28: 473–485.

26 S. Kabadayi & D. Lerman, 2011, Made in China but sold at FAO Schwarz, *IMR*, 28: 102–126; P. Magnusson, S. Westjohn, & S. Zdravkovic, 2011, "What? I thought Samsung was Japanese," *IMR*, 28: 454–472.

27 E. Banalieva & K. Eddleston, 2011, Home-region focus and performance of family firms, *JIBS*, 42: 1060–1072; L. Cardinal, C. C. Miller, & L. Palich, 2011, Breaking the cycle of iteration, *GSJ*, 1: 175–186; R. Flores, R. Aguilera, A. Mahdian, & P. Vaaler, 2013, How well do supranational regional grouping schemes fit international business research models? *JIBS*, 44: 451–474; T. Osegowitsch & A. Sammartino, 2008, Reassessing (home-)regionalization, *JIBS*, 39: 184–196.

28 S. Collinson & A. Rugman, 2007, The regional character of Asian multinational enterprises, *APJM*, 24: 429–446; A. Rugman & A. Verbeke, 2004, A perspective on regional and global strategies of multinational enterprises, *JIBS*, 35: 3–18.

29 G. Qian, T. Khoury, M. W. Peng, & Z. Qian, 2010, The performance implications of intra- and inter-regional geographic diversification, *SMJ*, 31: 1018–1030; G. Qian, L. Li, & A. Rugman, 2013, Liability of country foreignness and liability of regional foreignness, *JIBS*, 44: 635–647.

30 A. Rugman & C. Oh, 2013, Why the home region matters, *BJM*, 24: 463–479.

31 R. Hoskisson, M. Wright, I. Filatotchev, & M. W. Peng, 2013, Emerging multinationals from mid-range economies, *JMS*, 50: 1295–1321; M. W. Peng, 2012, The global strategy of emerging multinationals from China, *GSJ*, 2: 97–107.

32 J. Mathews, 2006, Dragon multinationals: Emerging players in 21st century globalization, *APJM*, 23: 5–27.

33 Y. Luo & R. Tung, 2007, International expansion of emerging market enterprises, *JIBS*, 38: 481–498.

34 S. Chang & J. Rhee, 2011, Rapid FDI expansion and firm performance, *JIBS*, 42: 979–994; W. Hejazi & E. Santor, 2010, Foreign asset risk exposure, DOI, and performance, *JIBS*, 41: 845–860; R. Jiang, P. Beamish, & S. Makino, 2014, Time compression diseconomies in foreign expansion, *JWB*, 49: 114–121; Y. Kim, J. Lu, & M. Rhee, 2012, Learning from age difference, *JIBS*, 43: 719–745.

Peter Macdiarmid/Getty Images Europe/Getty Images

Learning Objectives

After studying this chapter, you should be able to

- understand the industry conditions conducive to cooperation and collusion.

- outline how formal institutions affect domestic and international competition.

- articulate how resources and capabilities influence competitive dynamics.

- identify the drivers for attacks, counterattacks, and signaling.

- discuss how local firms fight multinational enterprises (MNEs).

- participate in two leading debates concerning competitive dynamics.

- draw implications for action.

Managing Global Competitive Dynamics

OPENING CASE

Ethical Dilemma

Patent Wars and Shark Attacks

The number of worldwide patent applications has shot up from about 800,000 a year in the 1980s to two million a year in the 2000s. The number of patent lawsuits has also skyrocketed. In the hotly contested mobile arena, Apple sued Samsung, Nokia, and HTC for patent violations. In retaliation, Samsung, Nokia, and HTC countersued Apple for patent violations. Kodak also sued Apple and Blackberry. Oracle and Xerox sued Google. Hardly a week goes by without a new lawsuit in "patent wars."

Worldwide, the two tech titans Apple and Samsung fought more than 20 cases in nine countries, which not only include the United States and South Korea, but also Australia, Britain, France, Germany, Italy, Japan, and the Netherlands. In the United States, Apple won a landmark US$1 billion ruling in its favor. But its home court advantage did not go very far. Samsung appealed and was able to reduce the damages to US$290 million. In another US lawsuit Apple filed, it won US$120 million damages. However, Samsung won favorable rulings in South Korea, Japan, and Britain. In South Korea, Apple was found to infringe on two Samsung patents, while Samsung was found to violate one Apple patent. The court awarded small damages to Samsung. In Japan, Samsung was not found to violate Apple's patents and Apple was ordered to

reimburse Samsung's legal costs. In Britain, Samsung won. Apple was required to publish a statement on its own website and in the media that Samsung did not violate Apple's intellectual property. The mess around the world is far from over. In short, these patent wars can be summarized as "iPhone, uCopy, iSue."

In many rapidly developing but patent-choked industries, inadvertently tripping over someone else's patents is a real danger. The open secret, according to the *Economist*, is that "everyone infringes everyone else's patents in some way." This creates an incentive for firms to engage in an "arms race" in filing and hoarding patents. In patent wars, patents are both defensive and offensive weapons.

Contrary to popular thinking, many patents are not truly novel and nonobvious. *BusinessWeek* opined that the United States is now "awash in a sea of junk patents. Some are just plain silly, such as a patent for 'a method of exercising and entertaining cats' (basically teasing them with a laser pointer)." Such "massive overpatenting," according to critics, has resulted in a "patent epidemic." Escalation of patenting obviously costs firms a lot of money: on average, one patent costs half a million dollars. But, firms are rational. Strategically patenting a portfolio of inventions around some core technologies allows them to gain an upper hand in patent lawsuits and negotiations. Patent lawsuits are becoming very predictable. Firm A sues Firm B for patent infringement. B digs through its own patent portfolio and discovers that some of its own patents are infringed by A. So B countersues A. To avoid costly and mutually destructive exchange of endless patent lawsuits, both typically reach cross-licensing deals that, after exchanging small sums of money, give each other the rights to the patents.

But here is a catch: to be a party to such exchange, a firm needs to have a sufficiently large hoard of patents. As a young firm, Google, prior to 2011, only had 307 mobile-related patents. As a result, Google was vulnerable when compared with Blackberry's 3,134 mobile-related patents, Nokia's 2,655, and Microsoft's 2,594. That was a key reason behind Google's colossal US$12.5 billion purchase of Motorola Mobility, a handset maker that was losing money. But Google was not primarily interested in the handset business. Instead, it was buying Motorola's rich hoard of more than 1,000 mobile-related patents. Google recently sold the handset business to Lenovo, but kept all the patents.

Among large firms clashing in emerging industries such as mobile devices, patent fights are normal or even (somewhat) predictable. What are less predictable but no less damaging are attacks by patent "sharks" (or "trolls"). Trolls are patent-holding individuals or (often small) firms that sue manufacturers for patent infringement in order to receive damage awards for the illegitimate use of trolls' patents. While sharks and trolls are colorful labels, the jargon for them is "non-operating entities" (NOEs). In contrast to all the "operating entities" named in the first five paragraphs above, NOEs, by definition, had neither capability nor intention to commercialize their patents.

Traditionally, most NOEs would license their patents to manufacturers that would pay a licensing fee. But many trolls *hope* to be infringed and do everything they can to keep patents as invisible as possible—the jargon is to be a "submarine"—until the patents are illegitimately used by manufacturers. Trolls then pounce in surprise attacks, demanding compensation exceeding what they would reasonably expect from real licensing fees up front. In 1990, individual inventor Jerome Lemelson sued toymaker Mattel for infringing a coupling technology used in toy trucks. Although the court determined that Mattel inadvertently (not willfully) infringed Lemelson's patent, the court nevertheless awarded him US$24 *million*—that was a lot of toy trucks. Most experts agreed that if Lemelson and Mattel had negotiated up front, Lemelson would not have been able to extract a licensing fee close to this astronomical sum. Such cases have motivated a lot of trolls. Although ethically dubious, such a strategy is not only profitable but also perfectly legal. "Operating entities" (manufacturers), especially high-tech ones, are well advised to prepare for shark attacks. Beefing up patent law expertise has become a crucial institution-based capability. One joke in high-tech industries is that firms must spend most of their R&D budgets on patent lawyers.

Sources: Based on (1) *Bloomberg Businessweek*, 2011, Android's dominance is patent pending, August 8: 36–37; (2) *Bloomberg Businessweek*, 2012, Apple vs. Samsung: The longer view, September 3: 32–33; (3) *BusinessWeek*, 2006, The patent epidemic, January 9: 60–62; (4) L. Cohen, U. Gurun, & S. Kominers, 2014, Patent trolls: Evidence from targeted firms, working paper, Jindal School of Management, University of Texas at Dallas and Harvard Business School; (5) *Economist*, 2005, Patent sense, October 22: 5; (6) *Economist*, 2010, The great patent battle, October 23: 75–76; (7) *Economist*, 2011, Inventive warfare, August 20: 57–58; (8) *Economist*, 2011, Patent applications, November 19: 105; (9) *Economist*, 2012, iPhone, uCopy, iSue, September 1: 12–13; (10) M. Reitzig, J. Hendel, & C. Heath, 2007, On sharks, trolls, and their patent prey, *Research Policy*, 36: 134–154.

Competitive dynamics
Actions and responses undertaken by competing firms.

Competitor analysis
The process of anticipating rivals' actions in order to both revise a firm's plan and prepare to deal with rivals' response.

Why do firms such as Apple and Samsung take certain actions such as patent lawsuits? Once one side initiates an action, how does the other respond? These are some of the key questions in this chapter, which focuses on competitive dynamics—actions and responses undertaken by competing firms. Since one firm's actions impact rivals, the initiating firm would naturally like to predict its rivals' responses *before* making its move.[1] This process is called competitor analysis, advocated by the ancient Chinese strategist Sun Tzu, who taught that you must know not only "yourself," but also "your opponents."

As military officers have long known, a good plan never survives the first contact with the enemy because the enemy does not act according to our plan. The key word is *interaction*—how firms interact with rivals. This chapter first discusses competition, cooperation, and collusion. Then, we draw on the institution-based and resource-based views to shed light on competitive dynamics. Attack, counterattack, and signaling are then outlined, with one interesting extension on how local firms fight multinational enterprises (MNEs) in emerging economies. Debates and extensions follow.

11-1 Competition, Cooperation, and Collusion

11-1a War and Peace

While militaries fight over territories, waters, and air space, firms compete over market shares. Note the military tone of such terms as "attack" and "price war."[2] Although it often seems that "business is war," it is obvious that military principles cannot be completely applied in business. The marketplace, after all, is not a battlefield where participants must either "kill or be killed." In business, it is possible to compete and win without destroying the opposition. Business is simultaneously war *and* peace. Alternatively, most competitive dynamics terms can also be explained in terms of sports analogies, such as "offense" and "defense."

11-1b Cooperation and Collusion

In *The Wealth of Nations* (1776), Adam Smith wrote: "People of the same trade seldom meet together, even for merriment and diversion, but their conversation often ends in a conspiracy against the public." In modern jargon, this means that competing firms in an industry may have an incentive to engage in collusion, defined as collective attempts to reduce competition.

Because managers (and students) generally do not like to discuss "collusion," another "C" word, coordination, is now frequently used in preference to collusion.[3] However, given the legal battles centered on collusion, managers (and students) cannot shy away from it. Instead, they need to confront the legal definitions and debates about collusion. Collusion can be tacit or explicit. Firms engage in tacit collusion when they *indirectly* coordinate actions by signaling their intention to reduce output and maintain pricing above competitive levels. Explicit collusion exists when firms *directly* negotiate output and pricing and divide markets. Explicit collusion leads to a cartel—an output-fixing and price-fixing entity involving multiple competitors. A cartel is also known as a trust, whose members have to trust each other in honoring agreements. Since the Sherman Act of 1890, cartels have often been labeled "anticompetitive" and outlawed by antitrust laws in many countries.

In addition to antitrust laws, collusion often suffers from a prisoners' dilemma, which underpins game theory. The term "prisoners' dilemma" derives from a simple game in which two prisoners suspected of a major joint crime (such as burglary) are separately interrogated and told that if either one confesses, the confessor will get a one-year sentence, while the other will go to jail for ten years. Since the police do not have strong incriminating evidence for the more serious burglary charges, if neither confesses, both will be convicted of a lesser charge (such as trespassing), each for two years. If both confess, both will go to jail for ten years. At a first glance, the solution to this problem seems clear enough. The maximum *joint* payoff would be for neither of them to confess. However, even if

Learning Objective
Understand the industry conditions conducive to cooperation and collusion.

Collusion
Collective attempts between competing firms to reduce competition.

Tacit collusion
Firms indirectly coordinate actions by signaling their intention to reduce output and maintain pricing above competitive levels.

Explicit collusion
Firms directly negotiate output and pricing and divide markets.

Cartel (trust)
An output-fixing and price-fixing entity involving multiple competitors.

Antitrust law
Law that makes cartels (trusts) illegal.

Prisoners' dilemma
In game theory, a type of game in which the outcome depends on two parties deciding whether to cooperate or to defect.

Game theory
A theory that studies the interactions between two parties that compete and/or cooperate with each other.

Figure 11.1 A "Prisoners' Dilemma" for Airlines and Payoff Structure (assuming a total of 200 passengers in one market consisting of two cities)

		Airline A	
		Action 1 A keeps price at $500	Action 2 A drops price to $300
Airline B	Action 1 B keeps price at $500	(Cell 1) A: $50,000 B: $50,000	(Cell 2) A: $60,000 B: 0
	Action 2 B drops price to $300	(Cell 3) A: 0 B: $60,000	(Cell 4) A: $30,000 B: $30,000

both parties agree not to confess before they are arrested, there are still tremendous incentives to confess.

Translated to an airline setting, Figure 11.1 illustrates the payoff structure for both airlines A and B in a given market—let's say, between Dubai and Cairo. Assuming a total of 200 passengers, Cell 1 represents the most ideal outcome for both airlines to maintain the price at US$500, and each gets 100 passengers and makes US$50,000—the "industry" revenue reaches US$100,000. In Cell 2, if B maintains its price at US$500 while A drops it to US$300, B is likely to lose all customers. Assuming perfectly transparent pricing information on the Internet, who would want to pay US$500 when you can get a ticket for US$300? Thus, A may make US$60,000 on 200 passengers while B gets nobody. In Cell 3, the situation is reversed. In both Cells 2 and 3, although the industry *decreases* revenue by 40%, the price dropper *increases* its own revenue by 20%. Thus, both A and B have strong incentives to reduce price and hope the other side to become a "sucker." However, neither likes to be a "sucker." Thus, both A and B may want to chop prices, as in Cell 4, whereby each still gets 100 passengers. But both firms, as well as the industry, end up with a 40% reduction of revenue. A key insight of game theory is that even if A and B have a prior agreement to fix the price at US$500, both still have strong incentives to cheat, thus pulling the industry to Cell 4 whereby both are clearly worse off.[4]

11-1c Industry Characteristics and Collusion vis-à-vis Competition

Given the benefits of collusion and the incentives to cheat, what industries are conducive to collusion vis-à-vis competition? Five factors emerge (Table 11.1). The first relevant factor is the number of firms or—more technically—the concentration ratio, defined as the percentage of total industry sales accounted for by the top four, eight, or 20 firms. In general, the higher the concentration, the easier it is to organize collusion. Because the top four concentration in mobile wireless telecommunications services in the United States accounted for more than 90% of market share, the antitrust authorities blocked a merger

Concentration ratio

The percentage of total industry sales accounted for by the top four, eight, or twenty firms.

Table 11.1	**Industry Characteristics and Possibility of Collusion vis-à-vis Competition**	
Collusion possible	**Collusion difficult (competition likely)**
• Few firms (high concentration)	• Many firms (low concentration)
• Existence of an industry price leader	• No industry price leader
• Homogeneous products	• Heterogeneous products
• High barriers to entry	• Low barriers to entry
• High market commonality (mutual forbearance)	• Lack of market commonality (no mutual forbearance)

of the second-largest firm, AT&T, with the fourth-largest firm, T-Mobile. The US Department of Justice argued:

> The substantial increase in concentration that would result from this merger, and the reduction in the number of nationwide providers from four to three, likely will lead to lessened competition due to an enhanced risk of anticompetitive coordination. Certain aspects of mobile wireless communications services markets, including transparent pricing, little buyer-side market power, and high barriers to entry and expansion, make them particularly conductive to coordination.[5]

Second, the existence of a price leader—a firm that has a dominant market share and sets "acceptable" prices and margins in the industry—helps maintain order and stability needed for tacit collusion. The price leader can signal to the entire industry with its own pricing behavior, when it is appropriate to raise or reduce prices, without jeopardizing the overall industry structure. The price leader also possesses the capacity to punish, defined as sufficient resources to deter and combat defection. To combat cheating, the most frequently used punishment entails undercutting the defector by flooding the market with deep discounts, thus making the defection fruitless. Such punishment is costly because it will bring significant financial losses in the short run. However, if small-scale cheating is not addressed, defection may become endemic, and the price leader will have the most to lose if collusion collapses. Thus, a price leader such as De Beers must have both the willingness and the capacity to carry out punishments and bear the costs (see In Focus 11.1).

Third, an industry with homogeneous products, in which rivals are forced to compete on price (rather than differentiation), is likely to lead to collusion. Because price competition is often "cut throat," firms may have stronger incentives to collude. Since the 1990s, many firms in commodity industries around the globe, such as ball bearings, car parts, shipping, and vitamins, have been convicted of price fixing.[6]

Fourth, an industry with high entry barriers for new entrants (such as shipbuilding) is more likely to facilitate collusion than an industry with low entry barriers (such as restaurants). New entrants are likely to ignore the existing industry norms by introducing less homogeneous products with newer technologies (in other words, "disruptive technologies").[7] As "mavericks," new entrants can be loose cannons in otherwise tranquil industries. For example, SpaceX founder Elon Musk, who also founded Tesla, blasted the defense industry and the Pentagon for not using SpaceX's cheaper rockets. He sued the US Air Force in federal court for using

Price leader

A firm that has a dominant market share and sets "acceptable" prices and margins in the industry.

Capacity to punish

Sufficient resources possessed by a price leader to deter and combat defection.

IN FOCUS 11.1

IS A DIAMOND (CARTEL) FOREVER?

Ethical Dilemma

Carl Court/AFP/Getty Images

The longest-running cartel in the modern world is the international diamond cartel headed by De Beers of South Africa. The cartel system underpinning the US$64 billion a year industry is, according to the *Economist*, "curious and anomalous—no other market exists, nor would anything similar be tolerated in a serious industry."

A key reason diamonds were so expensive was because of the deeply ingrained perception of scarcity. If there was an oversupply, prices could plummet. Cecil Rhodes, an English tycoon who founded the De Beers Mines in South Africa in 1875, sought to solve this problem by focusing on two areas. First, Rhodes realized that supply from South Africa, the only significant producer in the world at that time, should be limited. Second, because producers (diggers) had little control over the quality and quantity of their output, they preferred to deal with an indiscriminate buyer willing to purchase both spectacular and mediocre stones. Since most output would be mediocre stones, producers preferred to remove any uncertainty and to be able to sell *all* of their output. On the other hand, buyers (merchants) preferred to secure a steady supply of stones (both high end and low end). Rhodes' solution was to create an ongoing agreement between a single producer and a single buyer in which supply was kept low and prices high.

Putting his idea in action, Rhodes bought out all the major South African mines in the 1890s and formed a diamond merchants' association in the country, called the Diamond Syndicate, to which he would sell his output. In such "single-channel marketing," all members of the syndicate pledged to buy diamonds from Rhodes and sell them in specific quantities and prices. With such an explicit scheme of quantity-fixing and price-fixing, the diamond cartel was born.

Most cartels collapse due to organizational and incentive problems. The longevity of the De Beers cartel, running for more than 100 years, is very unusual. At least three attributes contribute to its longevity. First, the industry has an extraordinarily high concentration. In Rhodes' day, De Beers controlled all of South African (and hence virtually worldwide) production. Today, De Beers still controls approximately 40% of the world's rough diamond production, and its London-based wholly owned subsidiary Diamond Trading Company (DTC) sorts, values, and sells about 70% of the world's rough diamonds by value.

Second, De Beers is the undisputed price leader. Ten times a year, sales of rough diamonds (called "sights") are managed by the DTC to an exclusive group of cherry-picked "sightholders" from cities such as Antwerp, Johannesburg, Mumbai, New York, and Tel Aviv. Sightholders inform the DTC of their preferences, and the DTC then matchs them with inventory. During each sight, the DTC offers each sightholder a preselected parcel. The buyer either takes it or leaves it—no bargaining is permitted. Buyers usually take the parcel. If buyers repeatedly decline to take the parcel, they would not be invited again. This tactic allows De Beers to control, down to the carat, exactly what and how many stones enter the market and at what price. To maintain the exclusivity of the sightholders, their number has been decreased from about 350 in the 1970s to fewer than 100 in the 2000s.

Third, De Beers possesses both the willingness and the capability to enforce cartel arrangements. As in all cartels, the incentives to cheat are tremendous: Both producers and buyers are interested in cutting De Beers out of the process. As a price leader with a significant capacity to punish, De Beers's reactions are typically swift and powerful. In 1981, President

Mobutu Seko of Zaire (now the Democratic Republic of the Congo) announced that his country would break away from De Beers by directly marketing its diamonds. Although only 3% of De Beers' sales were lost, its world order would be at stake if such actions went unpunished. Consequently, De Beers drew on its stockpiles to flood the market, driving the price of Zairian industrial diamonds from US$3 per carat to US$1.8 and wiping out any gains the Zairians hoped to grab. While incurring disproportional losses, De Beers made its point and Zaire crawled back on its knees.

Finally, De Beers faces one major institutional headache. The US government argued that De Beers was in clear violation of US antitrust laws and unsuccessfully tried to prosecute it in 1945, 1974, and 1994. De Beers managed to stay beyond the extraterritorial reach of US laws since it had no legal presence and no (direct) sales in the US. All its diamonds were sold in London, with sightholders then exporting them to the US, which is legal. However, with 50% of the retail diamond buyers in the US, these legal actions had prevented De Beers executives from being able to visit their buyers and retailers in the US for fear of being arrested. In 2008, De Beers settled the US charges for a total of US$295 million and agreed to operate in accordance with competition laws. A question thus looms large on the horizon for De Beers executives and antitrust officials: Has the longest-running cartel really come to an end? This truly is a billion-dollar question.

Sources: Based on (1) *Chicago Tribune*, 2008, Diamond refunds are a consumer's best friend, January 21, www.chicagotribune. com; (2) A. Cockburn, 2002, Diamonds: The real story, *National Geographic*, March: 2–35; (3) *Economist*, 2004, The cartel isn't forever, July 17: 60–62; (4) *Economist*, 2011, Betting on De Beers, November 12: 73; (5) D. Spa, 1994, *The Cooperative Edge: The Internal Politics of International Cartels*, Ithaca, NY: Cornell University Press; (6) www.debeersgroup.com.

a monopoly for rocket launch, United Launch Alliance, which is a joint venture between Boeing and Lockheed Martin.[8] Incumbents naturally have collective interest in resisting such new entrants.

Finally, market commonality—the degree of overlap between two rivals' markets—also has a significant bearing on the intensity of rivalry.[9] A high degree of market commonality may restrain firms from aggressively going after each other. Multimarket competition occurs when firms engage the same rivals in multiple markets.[10] Multimarket firms may respect their rivals' spheres of influence in certain markets and their rivals may reciprocate, leading to tacit collusion—an outcome known as mutual forbearance.[11]

Mutual forbearance, due to a high degree of market commonality, primarily stems from two factors: (1) deterrence and (2) familiarity.[12] Deterrence is important because a high degree of market commonality suggests that if a firm attacks in one market, its rivals may engage in cross-market retaliation, leading to a costly all-out war that nobody can afford. Familiarity is the extent to which tacit collusion is enhanced by a firm's awareness of the actions, intentions, and capabilities of rivals.[13] Repeated interactions lead to such familiarity, resulting in more mutual respect. In the words of GE CEO Jeff Immelt:

> GE has tremendous respect for traditional rivals like Siemens, Philips, and Rolls-Royce. But it knows how to compete with them; they will never destroy GE. By introducing products that create a new price-performance paradigm, however, the emerging giants [such as Mindry, Suzlon, Goldwind, and Haier] very well could.[14]

Overall, the effectiveness of a firm's actions depends significantly on the domestic and international institutions governing competitive dynamics as well as firm-specific resources and capabilities. The next two sections expand on these points, which are illustrated in Figure 11.2.

Market commonality

The overlap between two rivals' markets.

Multimarket competition

Firms engage the same rivals in multiple markets.

Mutual forbearance

Multimarket firms respect their rivals' spheres of influence in certain markets and their rivals reciprocate, leading to tacit collusion.

Cross-market retaliation

Retaliatory attacks on a competitor's other markets if this competitor attacks a firm's original market.

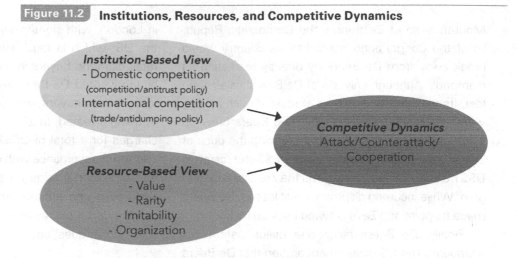

Figure 11.2 **Institutions, Resources, and Competitive Dynamics**

Institution-Based View
- Domestic competition
  (competition/antitrust policy)
- International competition
  (trade/antidumping policy)

Resource-Based View
- Value
- Rarity
- Imitability
- Organization

Competitive Dynamics
Attack/Counterattack/
Cooperation

Learning Objective
Outline how formal institutions affect domestic and international competition.

11-2 Institutions Governing Domestic and International Competition

In a nutshell, the institution-based view advises managers to be well versed in the rules governing domestic and international competition (see the Opening Case). A lack of understanding of these institutions may land otherwise successful firms (such as Microsoft) in deep trouble.

11-2a Formal Institutions Governing Domestic Competition: A Focus on Antitrust

Formal institutions governing domestic competition are broadly guided by competition policy, which "determines the institutional mix of competition and cooperation that gives rise to the market system."[15] Of particular relevance to us is one branch called antitrust policy, which is designed to combat monopolies and cartels. Competition and antitrust policy seeks to balance efficiency and fairness. While efficiency is relatively easy to understand, it is often hard to agree on what is fair. In the United States, fairness means equal opportunities for incumbents and new entrants. It is "unfair" for incumbents to fix prices and raise entry barriers to shut out new entrants. However, in Japan, fairness means the *opposite*—that is, incumbents that have invested in and nurtured an industry for a long time deserve to be protected from new entrants. What Americans approvingly describe as "market dynamism" is negatively labeled by Japanese as "market turbulence." The Japanese ideal is "orderly competition," which may be labeled "collusion" by Americans.

Overall, the American antitrust policy is *pro-competition* and *pro-consumer*, while the Japanese approach is *pro-incumbent* and *pro-producer*. Globally, it is difficult to argue who is right or wrong, but we need to be aware of such crucial differences. In general, because of stronger, pro-consumer antitrust laws, competitive forces have been stronger in the United States than in most other developed economies. As a result, for the same goods, prices on average in the United States are lower than those in Japan.

Competition and antitrust policy focuses on (1) collusive price setting and (2) predatory pricing. Collusive price setting refers to price setting by monopolists

Competition policy
Government policy governing the rules of the game in competition.

Antitrust policy
Government policy designed to combat monopolies and cartels.

Collusive price setting
Price setting by monopolists or collusion parties at a level higher than the competitive level.

or collusion parties at a level higher than the competitive level. The global vitamin cartel convicted in the 2000s artificially jacked up prices by 30% to 40%.

Another area of concern is predatory pricing, which is defined as (1) setting prices below cost *and* (2) intending to raise prices after eliminating rivals to cover its losses in the long run ("an attempt to monopolize"). This is an area of significant contention. First, it is not clear what exactly constitutes "cost." Second, even when firms are found to be selling below cost, US courts have ruled that if rivals are too numerous to eliminate, one firm cannot recoup the losses incurred due charging low prices by later jacking up prices, so its pricing cannot be labeled "predatory." This seems to be the case in most industries. These two legal tests have made it extremely difficult to win a (domestic) predation case in the United States.

11-2b Formal Institutions Governing International Competition: A Focus on Antidumping

In the same spirit of predatory pricing, dumping is defined as (1) an exporter selling below cost abroad and (2) planning to raise prices after eliminating local rivals. While domestic predation is usually labeled "anticompetitive," cross-border dumping is often emotionally accused of being "unfair."

Consider the following two scenarios. First, a steel producer in Indiana enters a new market in Texas, where it offers prices lower than those in Indiana, resulting in a 10% market share in Texas. Texas firms have two choices. The first one is to initiate a lawsuit against the Indiana firm for "predatory pricing." However, it is difficult to prove (1) that the Indiana firm is selling below cost *and* (2) that its pricing is an "attempt to monopolize." Under US antitrust laws, a predation case like this will have no chance of succeeding. In other words, domestic competition/antitrust laws offer no hope for protection. Thus, Texas firms are most likely to opt for their second option—to retaliate in kind by offering lower prices to customers in Indiana, benefitting consumers in both Texas and Indiana.

Now in the second scenario, the "invading" firm is not from Indiana but *India*. Holding everything else constant, Texas firms can argue that the Indian firm is dumping. Under US antidumping laws, Texas producers "would almost certainly obtain legal relief on the very same facts that would not support an antitrust *claim*, let alone antitrust relief."[16] Note that imposing antidumping duties on Indian imports reduces the incentive for Texas firms to counterattack by entering India, resulting in *higher* prices in both Texas and India, where consumers are hurt. These two hypothetical scenarios are highly realistic. A study in Australia, Canada, the EU, and the US reports that 90% of the practices found to be "unfairly" dumping in these countries would never have been

Predatory pricing

An attempt to monopolize a market by setting prices below cost and intending to raise prices to cover losses in the long run after eliminating rivals.

Dumping

An exporter selling goods below cost.

Antidumping law

Law that makes it illegal for an exporter to sell goods below cost abroad with the intent to raise prices after eliminating local rivals.

Pornchai Kittiwongsakul/AFP/Getty Images

Why are these shrimp farmers protesting that "antidumping destroy(s) our livelihood"?

questioned under their own antitrust laws if used between domestic firms.[17] In a nut-shell, foreign firms are discriminated against by the formal rules of the game.

Discrimination is also evident in the actual antidumping investigation. A case is usually filed by a domestic firm with the relevant government authorities. In the United States, the authorities are the International Trade Administration (a unit of the Department of Commerce) and International Trade Commission (an independent government agency). These government agencies then send lengthy questionnaires to the foreign firms accused of dumping and request comprehensive, proprietary data on their cost and pricing, in English, using US generally accepted accounting principles (GAAP), within 30 to 45 days. Many foreign defendants fail to provide such data on time because they are not familiar with US GAAP. The investigation can have one of the four following outcomes:

- If no data are forthcoming from abroad, the estimated data provided by the accusing firm become the evidence, and the complainant can easily win.
- If foreign firms do provide data, the complainant can still argue that these unfair foreigners have lied—"There is no way their costs can be so low!" In the case of Louisiana versus Chinese crawfish suppliers, the authenticity of the US$9 per *week* salary made by Chinese workers was a major point of contention.
- Even if the low-cost data are verified, US (and EU) antidumping laws allow the complainant to argue that these data are not "fair." In the case of China, the argument goes, its cost data reflect "huge distortions" due to government intervention because China is still a "nonmarket" economy. Wages may be low, but workers may also be provided with low-cost housing and government-subsidized benefits. Thus, the crawfish case boiled down to how much it would cost hypothetically to raise crawfish in a market economy. In this particular case, Spain was mysteriously chosen. Because Spanish costs were about the same as Louisiana costs, despite vehement objections, the Chinese were found guilty of dumping in America by selling below *Spanish* costs. Thus, 110% to 123% import duties were levied on Chinese crawfish producers.
- The fourth possible outcome is that the defendant wins the case. But this is rare and happens in only 5% of the antidumping cases in the United States.

One study reports that simply filing an antidumping petition (regardless of the outcome) may result in a nontrivial 1% increase in the stock price for US listed firms (a cool US$46 million increase in market value).[18] Evidently, Wall Street knows that Uncle Sam favors US firms. Globally, this means that governments usually protect their domestic firms in antidumping investigations. Not surprisingly, antidumping cases have proliferated throughout the world. It is ironic that the rising tide of globalization in the last two decades has been accompanied by the rising proliferation of antidumping cases, which are allowed by the World Trade Organization (WTO). The institution-based message to firms defending home markets is clear: Get to know your country's antidumping laws. The institution-based message to firms interested in doing business abroad is also clear: Your degree of freedom in overseas pricing is significantly less than that in domestic pricing. Please drop the "F word" (free) in "free market" competition.

Overall, institutional conditions such as the availability of antidumping protection are not just the "background." They determine directly what weapons a firm has in its arsenal to wage competitive battles. Next, we outline resources and capabilities used in such battles.

11-3 Resources Influencing Competitive Dynamics

Learning Objective
Articulate how resources and capabilities influence competitive dynamics.

A number of resource-based imperatives, informed by the VRIO framework first outlined in Chapter 4, drive decisions and actions associated with competitive dynamics (see Figure 11.2).

11-3a Value

Firm resources must create value when engaging rivals.[19] For example, the ability to attack in multiple markets—of the sort Apple and Samsung possess when launching their smartphones in numerous countries *simultaneously*—throws rivals off balance, thus adding value. Likewise, the ability to respond rapidly to challenges also adds value.[20] Another example is a dominant position in key markets (such as flights in and out of Dallas-Fort Worth for American Airlines). Such a strong sphere of influence poses credible threats to rivals, which understand that the firm will defend its core markets vigorously.

One way to add value is patenting. Firms are rapidly expanding their scale and scope of patenting. Only about 5% of patents end up having any economic value. So, why do firms spend so much money on the "patent race" (on average, half a million dollars in R&D for one patent)? The answer is that the proliferation of patents makes it very easy for one firm to unwittingly infringe on rivals' patents. When being challenged, a firm without a defensive portfolio of patents is at a severe disadvantage: It has to pay its rivals for using their patents. On the other hand, a firm with strong patents can challenge rivals for their infringements, thus making it easier to reach some understanding—or mutual forbearance (see the Opening Case).

11-3b Rarity

Either by nature or nurture (or both), certain assets are very rare, thus generating significant advantage in competitive dynamics. Emirates Airlines, in addition to claiming one of the best locations as its home base, is a well-run organization supported by a supportive government (see Emerging Markets 11.1). Airlines elsewhere, such as British Airways (BA) at London Heathrow airport, cannot run certain flights at night and cannot expand the airport due to complaints from the surrounding community. Emirates is unhindered by airport curfews in Dubai and is able to push through dramatic airport expansion proposals. Also, because Emirates primarily flies long-haul routes, its aircraft are in the air 18 hours a day—making its fleet one of the hardest working and most utilized in the industry. This combination of both geographic advantage and organizational advantage is rare, thus fueling Emirates to soar to become the world's fourth largest airlines in terms of international passengers carried.

11-3c Imitability

Most rivals watch each other and probably have a fairly comprehensive (although not necessarily accurate) picture of how their rivals compete. However, the next hurdle lies in how to imitate successful rivals. Many major airlines have sought to imitate discount carriers such as Southwest and Ryanair but have failed repeatedly. Qatar Airways and Etihad Airlines have realized that Dubai's geographic

EMERGING MARKETS 11.1

Emirates Fights Legacy Airlines

Launched in 1985 in Dubai, United Arab Emirates (UAE), Emirates Airlines has become one of the world's most powerful airlines. Carrying 40 million passengers annually, it is now the fourth largest international airline in the world. It has an all wide-body fleet of 220 planes and more on order (including 50 Airbus A380s). It flies to more than 100 cities in over 60 countries. It is the largest customer of the ultra-long-range Boeing 777 ER and one of the earliest and largest users of the A380. With these capable jets, any two cities in the world can be linked with one stop via Dubai.

Emirates is blessed by its location. Geographically, Dubai International Airport (DXB) may be regarded as the center of the *world*, known as a natural "pinch point." It is the ideal stopping point for air traffic between Europe and Australasia and between Africa and Asia. Four billion people can be reached within seven hours from DXB. Connecting 220 destinations, DXB handles more than 40 million passengers a year. New expansion will allow DXB to serve 60 million a year in the near future. Since Dubai's own population is fewer than four million (most are expatriates), the majority of the passengers are connecting (transit) passengers who are not from or going to Dubai. DXB's expansion will have to rely on customers from the rest of the world. Will they come?

Firmly believing that connecting passengers will come, Emirates positions itself as a "super-connector" airline. It has directly challenged traditional long-haul carriers such as Air France-KLM, British Airways (BA), Lufthansa, Qantas, and Singapore Airlines. These legacy airlines fear that just like no-frills competitors squeeze their short-haul flights, Emirates can threaten their profitable long-haul business. This fear is understandable, as Emirates already has more intercontinental seats than Air France and BA *combined*. Emirates

has launched services connecting Dubai with secondary (but still sizable) cities, such as Manchester, Hamburg, and Kolkata. These cities are, respectively, neglected by BA, Lufthansa, and Air India, which focus on their hubs in London Heathrow, Frankfurt, and Mumbai. In addition, Emirates has made itself more attractive by flying newer and quieter planes, offering cheaper tickets, and providing nicer amenities on board and at DXB. One of Emirates' open secrets of success is to fly super-sized planes—one A380 can carry 500 passengers—to reduce cost per passenger. The savings help it undercut fares of legacy airlines.

While legacy airlines fight back with their own aggressive pricing, they have also complained that Emirates receives "unfair" subsidies ranging from cheaper fuel to lower airport fees. In fact, Emirates pays slightly more for fuel at home (DXB) than abroad, because of the lack of refining capacity in the Gulf. It and 129 other airlines at DXB pay the same airport fees. True, neither Emirates nor its employees pay taxes. But the upshot is that Dubai's social services are poor for expatriates. Emirates ends up spending US$400 million a year to provide accommodation, health care, and schools for its staff—a huge expense none of its rivals has to cough up.

From an institution-based view, Emirates thrives on treaties that permit flights between two countries by an airline from a third country. The model works best on long-haul flights requiring refueling at DXB. As the complaints from its rivals grow, in theory if these rivals mobilize enough political muscle, they can convince European governments to deny route applications from Emirates. But chances are slim, because such a political decision would hurt Airbus and European jobs. So Emirates is in an advantageous position in its dog fights against legacy airlines.

Sources: Based on (1) *Aviation News*, 2011, Dubai International Airport, December: 34–39; (2) *Bloomberg Businessweek*, 2010, Emirates wins with big planes and low costs, July 5: 18–19; (3) *CEO Middle East*, 2013, New world order, June: 36–42; (4) *Economist*, 2010, Rulers of the new silk road, June 5: 75–77; (5) *Economist*, 2010, Super-duper-connectors from the Gulf, June 5: 21.

advantage is not rare and can be imitated once they build up their airports in Doha and Abu Dhabi, respectively. Whether these ambitious regional rivals can successfully imitate Emirates's strong capabilities remains to be seen.

11-3d Organization

Some firms are better organized for competitive actions, such as stealth attacks and answering challenges "tit-for-tat."[21] An intense "warrior-like" culture requires not only top management commitment, but also employee involvement down to the "soldiers in the trenches." It is such a self-styled "wolf" culture that has propelled Huawei to become Cisco and Ericsson's leading challenger. It is difficult for slow-moving firms to suddenly wake up to become more aggressive.[22]

11-3e Resource Similarity

Resource similarity is defined as "the extent to which a given competitor possesses strategic endowment comparable, in terms of both type and amount, to those of the focal firm."[23] Firms with a high degree of resource similarity are likely to have similar competitive actions. For instance, in the 1990s Apple and IBM used to have a lot of resource similarity in personal computers, so they fought a lot. Why did they not fight recently? One reason is that their level of resource similarity decreased. Recently, IBM has to fight Amazon in cloud computing. Why? In the emerging market of cloud computing, both IBM and Amazon have a great deal of resource similarity.

If we put together resource similarity and market commonality (discussed earlier), we can yield a framework of competitor analysis for any pair of rivals (Figure 11.3). In Cell 4, because two firms have a high degree of resource similarity but a low degree of market commonality (little mutual forbearance), the intensity of rivalry is likely to be the highest. Conversely, in Cell 1, since both firms have little resource similarity but a high degree of market commonality, the intensity of their rivalry may be the lowest. Cells 2 and 3 present an intermediate level of competition.

Figure 11.3   **A Framework for Competitor Analysis Between a Pair of Rivals**

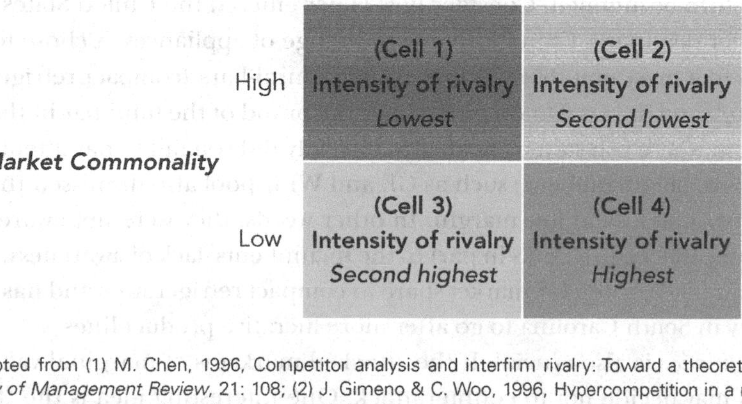

Resource Similarity

	Low	High
High	**(Cell 1)** Intensity of rivalry *Lowest*	**(Cell 2)** Intensity of rivalry *Second lowest*
Low	**(Cell 3)** Intensity of rivalry *Second highest*	**(Cell 4)** Intensity of rivalry *Highest*

Market Commonality

Sources: Adapted from (1) M. Chen, 1996, Competitor analysis and interfirm rivalry: Toward a theoretical integration, *Academy of Management Review*, 21: 108; (2) J. Gimeno & C. Woo, 1996, Hypercompetition in a multimarket environment: The role of strategic similarity and multimarket contact in competitive de-escalation, *Organization Science*, 7: 338.

Resource similarity

The extent to which a given competitor possesses strategic endowment comparable, in terms of both type and amount, to those of the focal firm.

For instance, prior to Fox's entry into the US TV broadcasting industries in the mid 1990s, the three incumbents—ABC, CBS, and NBC—enjoyed relatively tranquil and gentlemanly competition in Cell 2. However, Fox's entry pulled competition down to Cell 4, whose rivalry is the most intense. The primary reason is that Fox is a wholly owned subsidiary of News Corporation, which is not only active in the US, but also in Australia (its original country), Britain, Asia Pacific, and India. In other words, Fox/News Corporation had very little market commonality with the three incumbents, which were US-centric. Not afraid of retaliation elsewhere, Fox unleashed a series of relentless attacks on the incumbents and rocketed ahead to become the leader in the US TV broadcasting industry.

In another example, the high-flying Starbucks and the down-to-earth McDonald's used to have little resource similarity. Both had high market commonality—in the United States, both blanketed the country with chain stores. In other words, they were in Cell 1 with the lowest intensity of rivalry. However, recently, McDonald's aspired to go "up market" and offered products such as iced coffee designed to eat some of Starbucks' lunch (or drink some of Starbucks' coffee). Starbucks, due to profit pressures, had to go "down market" by offering cheaper drinks and instant coffee. We can say that their resource similarity increased. Given that they still maintained high market commonality, their rivalry migrated to Cell 2, whose intensity of rivalry was higher than that in Cell 1. Overall, conscientious mapping along the dimensions outlined in Figure 11.3 can help managers sharpen their analytical focus, allocate resources in proportion to the degree of threat rivals present, and avoid nasty surprises.

Learning Objective

Identify the drivers for attacks, counterattacks, and signaling.

11-4 Attack, Counterattack, and Signaling

11-4a Attack and Counterattack

In the form of price cuts, advertising campaigns, market entries, new product introductions, and lawsuits (see the Opening Case), attack can be defined as an initial set of actions to gain competitive advantage. Consequently, counterattack is defined as a set of actions in response to attack (see the Closing Case). This section focuses on a key question: What kinds of attack are more likely to be successful?

Obviously, unopposed attacks are more likely to be successful. Thus, attackers need to be aware of the three drivers for counterattacks: (1) awareness, (2) motivation, and (3) capability.[24]

Attack

An initial set of actions to gain competitive advantage.

Counterattack

A set of actions in response to attack.

Blue ocean strategy

Strategy that focuses on developing new markets ("blue ocean") and avoids attacking core markets defended by rivals, which is likely to result in a bloody price war ("red ocean").

- If an attack is so subtle that rivals are not *aware* of it, the attacker's objectives are likely to be attained. Consider how Haier entered the United States. Although Haier dominates China with a broad range of appliances, it chose to enter the US in a most non-threatening segment: mini-bars (compact refrigerators) for hotels and dorms. Do you remember the brand of the mini-bar in the last hotel room where you stayed? Evidently, not only did you fail to pay attention to that brand, but incumbents such as GE and Whirlpool also dismissed this segment as peripheral and low margin. In other words, they were not aware they were being attacked. Thanks in part to the incumbents' lack of awareness, Haier now commands a 50% US market share in compact refrigerators and has built a factory in South Carolina to go after more lucrative product lines.
- *Motivation* is also crucial. If the attacked market is of marginal value, managers may decide not to counterattack. One interesting idea is the "blue ocean strategy" that avoids attacking core markets defended by rivals.[25] A thrust on

rivals' core markets is very likely to result in a bloody price war—in other words, a "red ocean." A new airline startup Azul (which means "blue" in Portuguese) has deliberately avoided Brazil's busiest route between São Paulo and Rio de Janeiro. The 45-minute trip between them is already the most-traveled route in the *world*, with an astounding 284 daily flights dominated by two incumbents, Gol and Tam (see Table 11.2). Sticking Azul's nose into such a crowded airspace will immediately attract retaliation, resulting in a "red ocean"—remember Cell 4 in Figure 11.1? Instead, Azul uses its limited slots at São Paulo's and Rio's airports to strengthen its service connecting these two cities and Brazil's vast hinterland. Founded in 2008, Azul has risen to enjoy an 18% market share of Brazil's growing air traffic by positioning itself as a small-town carrier. In three-quarters of the cities it serves, it is the only or dominant airline.[26] Clearly, Brazil's vast, underserved hinterland is the "blue ocean" for the "blue airline." While certainly being aware of Azul's rise, the incumbents are not motivated to counter-attack the markets that they did not bother to enter in the first place.

Paulo Whitaker/Reuters

- Even if an attack is identified and a firm is motivated to respond, it requires strong *capabilities* to carry out counterattacks—as discussed in our earlier section on resources.

Overall, minimizing an opponent's awareness, motivation, and capabilities is more likely to result in successful attacks. Frontal, infrequent, and predictable attacks typically find rivals well prepared. Winning firms excel at making subtle, frequent, but unpredictable moves.

Why does Azul deliberately avoid Brazil's busiest route between São Paulo and Rio de Janeiro?

11-4b Cooperation and Signaling

Some firms choose to compete, and others choose to cooperate. How do firms signal their intention to cooperate in order to *reduce* competitive intensity? Short of illegally talking directly to rivals, firms have to resort to signaling—that is, "While you can't talk to your competitors on pricing, you can always *wink* at them." We outline four means of such winking:

- Firms may enter new markets, not necessarily to challenge incumbents but to seek mutual forbearance by establishing multimarket contact.[27] Thus, MNEs often chase each other, entering one country after another. Airlines that meet in many routes are often less aggressive than airlines that meet in one or a few routes.

Table 11.2 **The World's Busiest Airline Markets (Number of Daily Flights)**

1	2	3	4	5
São Paulo-Rio de Janeiro, Brazil (284)	Seoul-Jeju, South Korea (209)	Sydney-Melbourne, Australia (192)	New York-Chicago, United States (184)	Tokyo-Fukuoka, Japan (136)

Source: Adapted from *Bloomberg Businessweek*, 2014, The carrier that avoids Brazil's No. 1 air route, August 11 : 24.

- Firms can send an open signal for a truce. As GM faced grave financial difficulties in 2005, Toyota's chairman told the media *twice* that Toyota would "help GM" by raising Toyota prices in the United States. Toyota's signal could not have been more unambiguous, short of talking directly to GM, which would have been illegal.

- Sometimes firms can send a signal to rivals by enlisting the help of governments. Although it is illegal to hold direct negotiations with rivals on what constitutes "fair" pricing, holding such discussions is legal under the auspices of government investigations. Thus, filing an antidumping petition or suing a rival does not necessarily indicate a totally hostile intent but rather a signal to talk. When Cisco sued Huawei, Cisco was able to *legally* discuss a number of strategic issues during settlement negotiations, which were mediated by US and Chinese governments. In the end, Cisco dropped its case against Huawei after both firms negotiated a solution.

- Firms can organize strategic alliances with rivals for cost reduction. Although price fixing is illegal, reducing cost by 10% through an alliance, which is legal, has the same impact on the financial bottom line as collusively raising price by 10%.

Overall, because of the sensitive nature of interfirm cooperation designed to reduce competition, we do not know a lot about them. However, to the extent that business is both war and peace, managers need to pay as much attention to making peace with rivals as fighting wars against them.

Learning Objective
Discuss how local firms fight multinational enterprises (MNEs).

11-5 Local Firms versus Multinational Enterprises

While managers, students, and journalists are often fascinated by MNE rivalries, such as those featuring Coca-Cola versus PepsiCo, Mary Kay versus Avon, and Apple versus Samsung (see the Opening Case), much less is known about how local firms cope with MNE attacks. Given the broad choices of competing and/or cooperating, local firms can adopt one of four strategic postures, depending on (1) the industry conditions, and (2) the nature of competitive assets. Shown in Figure 11.4, four strategic actions emerge.

Figure 11.4 **How Local Firms in Emerging Economies Respond to Multinationals**

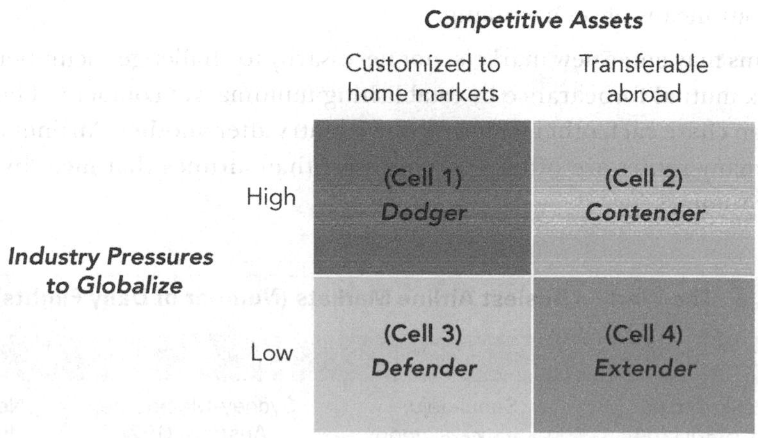

Source: Adapted from N. Dawar & T. Frost, 1999, Competing with giants: Survival strategies for local companies in emerging markets, *Harvard Business Review*, March–April: 122.

Cell 3 shows how in some industries, the pressures to globalize are relatively low, and local firms' strengths lie in a deep understanding of local markets. In this case, local assets where MNEs are weak are leveraged in a defender strategy. For example, facing an onslaught from MNE cosmetics firms, a number of Israeli firms turned to focus on products suited to the Middle Eastern climate and managed to defend their turf. Ahava has been particularly successful, partly because of its highly unique components that are extracted from the Dead Sea that MNEs cannot find elsewhere. In other words, while local firms such as Ahava cede some markets (such as mainstream cosmetics) to MNEs, they build strongholds in narrower, but deeper, product markets (such as the "Dead Sea mud" product that has become popular around the world).

Cell 4 shows industries where pressures for globalization are relatively low, and local firms may possess some skills that are transferable overseas, thus leading to an extender strategy. This strategy centers on leveraging home-grown competencies abroad (see the Closing Case). For example, Asian Paints controls 40% of the house paint market in India. Asian Paints developed strong capabilities tailored to this environment, characterized by thousands of small retailers serving numerous poor consumers who only want small quantities of paint in a single-use sachet (or pouch) that can be diluted to save money. Such capabilities are a winning formula not only in India, but also in much of the developing world. In contrast, MNEs, whose business model typically centers on affluent customers in developed economies who buy paint by the bucket, have had a hard time coming up with profitable low-end products.

Cell 1 depicts local firms that compete in industries with high pressures for globalization. Thus, a dodger strategy is necessary. This is largely centered on cooperating through joint ventures (JVs) with MNEs and sell-offs to MNEs. In the Chinese automobile industry, *all* major domestic automakers have entered JVs with MNEs. In the Czech Republic, the government sold Skoda to Volkswagen. In essence, to the extent that local firms are unable to successfully compete head-on against MNEs, cooperation becomes necessary. In other words, if you can't beat them, join them!

Finally, in Cell 2, some local firms, through a contender strategy, engage in rapid learning and then expand overseas (see the Closing Case). A number of Chinese smartphone makers, such as Lenovo, Huawei, TCL, Xiaomi, and ZTE, rapidly caught up with global heavyweights. Following their success at home, these smartphone makers have now entered foreign markets. Worldwide, Lenovo and Huawei are now the third- and fourth-largest smartphone makers. Xiaomi has dethroned *both* Samsung and Apple to grab the highest market share in *both* China and India, thus enabling it to become the world's fifth-largest smartphone maker.

Particularly in emerging economies, how domestic firms respond is crucial for managers. For example, in China, despite initial dominance, MNEs do not always stay on top. In numerous industries (such as sportswear, smartphones, personal computers, and home appliances), many MNEs have found themselves losing market share to domestic firms. While weak domestic players are washed out, some of the stronger domestic firms not only succeed in the competitive domestic environment, but also now challenge MNEs overseas. In the process, they become a new breed of MNEs themselves. The upshot is that when facing the onslaught of MNEs, local firms are not necessarily "sitting ducks" guaranteed to lose (see the Closing Case).

Defender strategy
Strategy that centers on local assets in areas in which MNEs are weak.

Extender strategy
Strategy that centers on leveraging homegrown competencies abroad.

Dodger strategy
Strategy that centers on cooperating through joint ventures with MNEs and sell-offs to MNEs.

Contender strategy
Strategy that centers on a firm engaging in rapid learning and then expand overseas.

Learning Objective
Participate in two leading debates concerning competitive dynamics.

11-6 Debates and Extensions

Debates abound in this sensitive area. Two of the most significant are discussed: (1) competition versus antidumping, and (2) competitive strategy versus antitrust policy.

11-6a Competition versus Antidumping

Two arguments exist against the practice of imposing antidumping restrictions on foreign firms. First, because dumping centers on selling "below cost," it is often difficult (if not impossible) to prove the case, given the ambiguity concerning "cost." The second argument is that if foreign firms are indeed selling below cost, so what? This is simply a (hyper)competitive action. When entering a new market, virtually all firms lose money on Day 1 (and often in Year 1). Until some point when the firm breaks even, it will lose money because it sells below cost. Domestically, cases abound of such dumping, which is perfectly legal. We all receive numerous coupons in the mail offering free or cheap goods. Coupon items are frequently sold (or given away) below cost. Do consumers complain about such good deals? Probably not. "If the foreigners are kind enough (or dumb enough) to sell their goods to our country below cost, why should we complain?"[28]

One classic response is: What if, through "unfair" dumping, foreign rivals drive out local firms and then jack up prices? Given the competitive nature of most industries, it is often difficult to eliminate all rivals and then recoup losses by charging higher monopoly prices. The fear of foreign monopoly is often exaggerated by special interest groups, who benefit at the expense of consumers in the entire country. Joseph Stiglitz, a Nobel laureate in economics, writes that antidumping duties "are simply naked protectionism" and that one country's "fair trade laws" are often known elsewhere as "unfair trade laws."[29]

One solution is to phase out antidumping laws and use the same standards against domestic predatory pricing. Such a waiver of antidumping charges has been in place between Australia and New Zealand, between Canada and the US, and within the EU. Thus, a Canadian firm, essentially treated as a US firm, can be accused of predatory pricing but cannot be accused of dumping in the United States. Since antidumping is about "us versus them," such harmonization represents essentially an expanded notion of "us." However, domestically, as noted earlier, a predation case is very difficult to make. Thus by legalizing "dumping," competition can be fostered, aggressiveness rewarded, and consumer welfare enhanced.

11-6b Competitive Strategy versus Antitrust Policy

Managers deploy strategy to lead their firms to compete. But antitrust officials sometimes get in the way (see Figure 11.5). Most business school students do not study antitrust policy. When they graduate and become managers, they do not care about it either. Antitrust officials, on the other hand, tend to study economics and law. A background in economics and law, however, does not give antitrust officials an intimate understanding of how firm-level competition and/or cooperation unfolds, which is something that a business school education provides. These officials often believe that in the absence of government intervention (specifically, antitrust action), competitive advantage of large firms will last forever and that monopoly will prevail. Managers know better: given rapid technological changes, ambitious new entrants, and strong global competition, no competitive advantage lasts forever (see Chapter 4). It is possible that none of the antitrust officials has

Figure 11.5 **Confusion Stemming from Antitrust Enforcement**

ever studied a global business textbook like this one. But officials with such a static and unrealistic view of the sustainability of competitive advantage end up enforcing the rules governing competition. Such a disconnect naturally breeds suspicion and frustration on both sides. Business school students and managers will be better off if they arm themselves with knowledge about antitrust concerns and engage in intelligent conversations and debates with officials and policy makers.

Because the United States has the world's oldest antitrust frameworks (dating back to the 1890 Sherman Act), the US debate is the most watched in the world, and so is the focus here. Rather than adopting a US-centric approach, here we treat the US debate as a *case study* that may have global ramifications. In fact, antitrust issues, which originated from a domestic orientation, have been globalized recently.[30]

On behalf of managers, concerned management scholars have made four arguments.[31] First, antitrust laws were often created in response to the old realities of mostly domestic competition—the year 1890 for the Sherman Act is *not* a typo of 1990. However, the largely global competition today means that a large, dominant firm in one country (think of Boeing) does not automatically translate into a dangerous monopoly. The existence of foreign rivals (such as Airbus) forces the large domestic incumbent to be more competitive.

Second, the very actions accused of being "anticompetitive" may actually be highly "competitive" or "hypercompetitive." In the 1990s, the hypercompetitive Microsoft was charged with "anticompetitive" behavior. Its alleged crime? *Not* voluntarily helping its competitors. It is puzzling why Microsoft should have voluntarily helped its competitors. Just imagine: If your managers were to ask you to voluntarily help your firm's competitors, would you just do it or think that your managers were out of their mind?

Third, US antitrust laws create strategic confusion (see Figure 11.5).[32] Because the intention to destroy your firm's rivals is the smoking gun of antitrust cases, managers are forced to use milder language and bland talking points. Don't write an email or say over the smartphone: "We want to beat our competitors!" Otherwise, managers may end up in court or—even worse—go to jail. In contrast, non-US firms often use war-like language: Komatsu is famous for "Encircling Caterpillar!" and Honda for "Annihilate, crush, and destroy Yamaha!" Hiroshi Mikitani, the third-richest man in Japan and founder of Rakuten, the world's third-largest e-commerce marketplace behind Amazon and eBay, makes no secret of his desire to beat Amazon's founder Jeff Bezos. Mikitani has given his subordinates T-shirts emblazoned with the words "Destroy Amazon."[33] In comparison with such a laser-sharp focus embedded in such inspirational (and war-like) language, the inability to talk straight creates confusion among lower-level managers and employees in many US firms. Obviously, confused firms are not likely to be aggressive or successful.

Finally, US antitrust laws may be unfair because these laws discriminate *against* US firms. In 1983, if GM and Ford had proposed to jointly manufacture cars, antitrust officials would have turned them down, citing an (obvious!) intent to collude. The jargon is per se (in and of itself) violation of antitrust laws. Ironically, starting in 1983, GM was allowed to jointly make cars with Toyota. More than 30 years later, Toyota is the number-one automaker in the United States. The upshot? American antitrust laws have helped Toyota but not Ford or GM. One country's (or region's) antitrust laws may be used against other countries' firms. For example, the EU antitrust authorities have been very harsh on US firms and Chinese trust-busters seem eager to punish (certain) foreign firms. While these actions provoked protests, they are at least understandable from a protectionist standpoint (see Emerging Markets 11.2). What is difficult to understand is the reason why US firms are sometimes discriminated against by their own government. The most recent case in point: In 2011, AT&T was forced to abandon its merger of T-Mobile, a wholly owned subsidiary of Deutsche Telekom (DT) and was forced to pay a US$3 billion (!) breakup fee to T-Mobile. A US firm was thus forced by the US government to subsidize a foreign firm, which did not even want to compete in the United States anymore.[34]

EMERGING MARKETS 11.2

From Trade Wars to Antitrust Wars

In the 21st century, traditional trade wars are often threatened but seldom fought. However, a new style of trade wars centered on protectionism is on the rise. These new trade wars are increasingly known as antitrust wars, because antitrust policy, which historically focuses on domestic competition, can be used to score international points.

In 2001, the EU antitrust authorities vetoed the proposed merger of two US firms, GE and Honeywell.

In 2009, the EU fined Intel a record US$1.45 billion for alleged anticompetitive conduct against its smaller US rival, AMD. In 2004, the EU fined Microsoft US$660 million for bundling its own Media Player with Windows and thus excluding market access for RealNetworks, a US-based rival. In 2009, the EU prosecuted Microsoft again for tying Windows with its own Web browser, Internet Explorer, and stifling competition from other browsers—exactly the same alleged crime pursued by US authorities a decade ago. The only viable US competitor from the earlier US case against Microsoft, Netscape, had essentially vanished by 2009, accounting for fewer than 1% of browsers usage. This time, the EU case was triggered by a complaint from Opera Software, an Oslo, Norway–based browser maker. In comparison with Explorer's 86% global browser market share in 1999, in 2009 Microsoft's dominance was weakened. In 2009, Explorer only had 68% of the global market, and its nearest competitor, Firefox (developed by US-based Mozilla), enjoyed 20%. In Europe, Microsoft was even weaker, with Explorer accounting for only 60% of the market, followed by Opera's 5% and Firefox's 3%. In 2013, the EU slapped an additional US$732 million fine on Microsoft for lapsing in its commitment to offer consumers a choice of Internet browers. Overall, the EU antitrust authorities appear to more vigorously pursue leading US firms, suggesting a potential protectionist undertone.

Not to be outdone, the fledgling Chinese antitrust authorities entered the foray by starting to enforce China's new Anti-Monopoly Law, which took effect in 2008. Mergers of firms not headquartered in China, as long as their combined China turnover reached US$120 million in the previous year, had to be cleared by Chinese authorities. For example, the merger between the Belgium-based InBev and the US-based Anheuser-Busch was approved by Chinese authorities, subject to some conditions. Sometimes Chinese antitrust regulators imposed *higher* pro-competition standards than their US and EU colleagues. In 2014, when three of the largest shipping companies—Maersk of Denmark, CMA CGM of France, and Mediterranean Shipping Company (MSC) of Switzerland—proposed to have an alliance called the P3 Alliance, neither US nor EU antitrust authorities would intervene. But the Chinese torpedoed the deal, citing an unhealthy concentration of one-third of global traffic and one-half of all container trade between Asia and Europe in the hands of P3.

Within China, the increasingly assertive Chinese trust-busters routinely round up foreign firms, extract fines, and force price reductions in the name of fostering competition and protecting consumers. The list of prosecuted firms reads like an impressive set of global heavy weights: cars (Fiat Chrysler and Volkswagen), infant formula (Abbott Laboratories, Danone, and Mead Johnson), semiconductor chips (Qualcomm), and software (Microsoft). China's new antitrust activism has attracted a great deal of controversies and protests. Perhaps the Chinese government is targeting foreign firms. Chinese regulators have denied such discriminatory targeting. Many domestic cases are also pursued but have been settled quietly. The media has a tendency to feast on foreign firms being prosecuted. Or perhaps the Chinese are targeting *certain* foreign firms. For example, in one 2014 case ten Japanese auto parts suppliers were found to hold illegal meetings to fix prices. Eight of them (Aisan, Denso, Furukawa, JTEK, Mitsubishi Electric, NSK, NTN, and Sumitomo Electric) were hit with a record US$200 million combined fine (two were not fined because they came forward to offer important evidence). This took place during a time when diplomatic tension between China and Japan was high. Again, denying such motives, Chinese trust-busters pointed out that some of the same Japanese firms were recently found guilty by their trust-busting colleagues in the US, the EU, and Japan itself.

Antitrust wars have now become a part of institution-based competitive dynamics using favorable rules of the game to undermine certain foreign firms' competitive advantage. Is it surprising that after Huawei was labeled a "national security threat" by the US Congress, Apple was announced to be a "national security threat" by the China Central Television due to the iPhone's location-tracking app? As the threat of trade wars goes down, concerned policy makers, managers, and students need to arm themselves with the necessary knowledge, expertise, and steel stomach to deal with the nasty but inevitable institution-based wars.

Sources: Based on (1) *Bloomberg Businessweek*, 2014, Foreign companies cry foul at Chinese probes, September 22: 24; (2) J. Clougherty, 2005, Antitrust holdup source, cross-national institutional variation, and corporate political strategy implications for domestic mergers in a global context, *Strategic Management Journal*, 26: 769–790; (3) *Economist*, 2013, The wrong browsers, March 9: 7; (4) *Economist*, 2013, Microsoft's antitrust fine, March 9: 66; (5) *Economist*, 2014, Boring can still be bad, March 29: 16; (6) *Economist*, 2014, Just one more fix, March 29: 67–70; (7) *Economist*, 2014, Scattering the fleet, June 21: 64; (8) *Economist*, 2014, Trust-busting in China, August 23: 62–63; (9) *Wall Street Journal*, 2009, EU hits Microsoft with new antitrust charges, January 17; (10) *Wall Street Journal*, 2014, China fines Japan auto-parts makers US$200 million, August 20: online.wsj.com.

Learning Objective
Draw implications for action.

11-7 Management Savvy

Let us revisit our fundamental question: What determines the success and failure in managing competitive dynamics around the world? Drawing on the two core perspectives (institution-based and resource-based views), we suggest that to manage competitive dynamics successfully, managers must not only become masters of maneuvers (both confrontation and cooperation), but also experts in government regulations at home and abroad if they aspire to be successful globally.

Consequently, three implications emerge for savvy managers (Table 11.3). First, managers must understand the rules of the game governing competition around the world. Aggressive language such as "Let's beat competitors" may not be allowed in countries such as the United States. Remember, an e-mail or a smartphone conversation—like a diamond—is *forever*, and "deleted" e-mails and smartphone conversations are still stored on servers and can be uncovered. However, carefully crafted ambitions such as Wal-Mart's "We want to be number one in grocery business" are legal, because such wording (at least on paper) shows no illegal intention to destroy rivals. Too bad more than 30 US supermarket chains declared bankruptcy since Wal-Mart charged into groceries in the 1990s—just a tragic coincidence (!).[35]

The necessity to understand the rules of the game is crucial when venturing abroad. What is legal domestically may be illegal elsewhere. Many Chinese managers are surprised that their low-cost strategy is labeled "illegal" dumping in the very countries advocating "free market" competition. In reality, "free markets" are not free. However, managers well versed in the rules of the game may launch subtle attacks without incurring the wrath of antidumping officials. Imports commanding no more than 3% market share or below in a 12-month period are regarded by US antidumping laws as "negligible imports" not worthy of investigation.[36] Thus, foreign firms not crossing such a "red line" would be safe. As an exporter, would you like to maintain a steady 3% of US market share every year over ten years, or a dramatic upsurge to hit 30% in Year 1, which would attract antidumping actions preventing further growth in Year 2 and beyond?

Second, managers need to strengthen capabilities that more effectively compete and/or cooperate. In attacks and counterattacks, subtlety, frequency, complexity, and unpredictability are helpful. In cooperation, market similarity and mutual forbearance may be better. As Sun Tzu advised a long time ago, as a manager you need to "know yourself"—including your unit, your firm, and your industry.

Finally, as a savvy manager, you also need to "know your opponents" by developing skills in competitor analysis (see Figure 11.3). You need to develop skills and instinct to think like your opponents, who are eager to collect competitive intelligence (Table 11.4). Overall, since business is simultaneously war *and* peace, a winning formula, as in war and chess, is "Look ahead, reason back."

Table 11.3	Implications for Action

- Understand the rules of the game governing domestic and international competition around the world.

- Strengthen resources and capabilities to compete and/or cooperate more effectively.

- Develop skills in competitor analysis that guide decision making on attacks, counterattacks, and cooperation.

Table 11.4 **Tips on Competitive Intelligence and Counterintelligence**

- If you are bidding against a major local rival in a foreign country, expect aggressive efforts to gather your information. If you leave your laptop in a hotel room, expect the hard drive to be copied.

- Be careful about cell phones because signals can be intercepted. If you lose your cell phone for 30 seconds, your opponents may be able to put in a look-alike battery with a chip that will record and transmit your calls. This chip can also secretly turn your phone on and use it as a microphone.

- Be careful about the high-speed Internet service at your hotel. Go to the office of your local subsidiary. If there isn't such a safe, local office, a random Wi-Fi spot may be safer than the hotel Internet service.

- If your negotiation counterparts offer to book you into a luxurious suite or hotel, turn it down. Book your own.

Source: Based on text in G. Morse, 2005, H. Keith Melton on corporate espionage, *Harvard Business Review*, November: 26. Note this is an interesting but extremely cautious view.

CHAPTER SUMMARY/LEARNING OBJECTIVES

11-1 Understand the industry conditions conducive to cooperation and collusion.

- Such industries tend to have (1) a smaller number of rivals, (2) a price leader, (3) homogenous products, (4) high entry barriers, and (5) high market commonality (mutual forbearance).

11-2 Outline how formal institutions affect domestic competition and international competition.

- Domestically, antitrust laws focus on collusion and predatory pricing.
- Internationally, antidumping laws discriminate against foreign firms and protect domestic firms.

11-3 Articulate how resources and capabilities influence competitive dynamics.

- Resource similarity and market commonality can yield a powerful framework for competitor analysis.

11-4 Identify the drivers for attacks, counterattacks, and signaling.

- Attackers need to be aware of the three drivers for counterattacks: (1) awareness, (2) motivation, and (3) capability.
- Without talking directly to competitors, firms can use various means to signal rivals.

11-5 Discuss how local firms fight MNEs.

- When confronting MNEs, local firms can choose a variety of strategic choices: (1) defender, (2) extender, (3) dodger, or (4) contender. They may not be as weak as many people believe.

11-6 Participate in two leading debates concerning competitive dynamics.

- (1) Competition versus antidumping and (2) competitive strategy versus antitrust policy.

11-7 Draw implications for action.

- Understand the rules of the game governing domestic and international competition around the world.
- Strengthen resources and capabilities for more effective competitor analysis.
- Develop skills in competitor analysis that guide decision making on attacks, counterattacks, and cooperation.

KEY TERMS

Antidumping law, 351	Competitor	Game theory, 345
Antitrust law, 345	analysis, 344	Market commonality, 349
Antitrust policy, 350	Concentration	Multimarket
Attack, 356	ratio, 346	competition, 349
Blue ocean strategy, 356	Contender strategy, 359	Mutual forbearance, 349
Capacity to punish, 347	Counterattack, 356	Predatory pricing, 351
Cartel (trust), 345	Cross-market	Price leader, 347
Collusion, 345	retaliation, 349	Prisoners'
Collusive price	Defender strategy, 359	dilemma, 345
setting, 350	Dodger strategy, 359	Resource similarity, 355
Competition policy, 350	Dumping, 351	Tacit collusion, 345
Competitive	Explicit collusion, 345	
dynamics, 344	Extender strategy, 359	

REVIEW QUESTIONS

1. Explain the differences between tacit and explicit collusion.

2. Describe the five factors that make an industry particularly conducive to collusion.

3. Some countries' competition and antitrust policies are pro-competition and pro-consumer, whereas other countries' policies are pro-incumbent and pro-producer. How do they differ?

4. Suppose in Country A, a widget firm has absorbed all of its fixed cost (cost that does not change with the level of output such as rent), and now all additional cost is only variable cost (cost that does vary with the level of output such as raw materials). In Country A, the price was enough to cover both its fixed cost of $100 and *variable* cost of $10 and provide an additional profit of $10. It sold only one for a price of $120. Suppose the widget firm received an order from Country B for one widget and indicated that the buyer in Country B would pay $20—enough to cover the variable cost of $10 and provide a $10 profit. If the widget firm agrees, it will have total cost for the two widgets (one sold in Country A and one in Country B) of $100 fixed cost plus $20 variable cost—that is an average total cost for two units of $60. If it sells the widget to Country B for $20, will it be selling it above or below cost? Explain.

5. Use your own examples to identify how resources and capabilities affect competitive dynamics.

6. *ON CULTURE:* How does a firm's corporate culture affect its ability to engage in competitive actions?

7. Name and describe three drivers for counterattacks.

8. *ON ETHICS:* Military terminology and strategy are often used in dealing with global competitors. In your opinion, is there any risk in doing so? Is there a risk in failing to do so? Why?

9. Under what conditions may a firm assume a defender strategy?

10. Under what conditions may a firm adopt an extender strategy?

11. What criteria may induce a firm to choose a dodger strategy over a contender strategy, and vice versa?

12. *ON ETHICS:* Do you support or oppose antidumping restrictions? Why?

13. *ON ETHICS:* Describe four arguments that managers may make regarding antitrust law.

14. Using Peng Atlas Map 3.1, in your option would it be easier or more difficult to apply competitive dynamics in those countries that are at the bottom?

15. As part of your firm's strategy to gain competitive advantage, it wants to cut prices by looking for alternate locations in which to manufacture and market its products. You are part of a committee attempting to select a new manufacturing location. What information in PengAtlas Map 3.3 or 3.4 will be most relevant? Based on your choice, what will your committee recommend and why?

CRITICAL DISCUSSION QUESTIONS

1. *ON ETHICS:* As a CEO, you feel that the price war in your industry is killing profits for all firms. However, you have been warned by corporate lawyers not to openly discuss pricing with rivals, whom you know personally because you went to school with them. How would you signal your intentions?

2. *ON ETHICS:* As a CEO, you are concerned that your firm and the industry in your country are being devastated by foreign imports. Trade lawyers suggest filing an antidumping case against leading foreign rivals and assure you a win. Would you file an antidumping case? Why or why not?

3. *ON ETHICS:* As part of a feint attack, your firm (firm A) announces that in the next year, it intends to enter country X, where the competitor (firm B) is strong. Your firm's real intention is to march into country Y, whereby B is weak. There is actually *no* plan to enter X. However, in the process of trying to "fool" B, customers, suppliers, investors, and the media are also being intentionally misled. What are the ethical dilemmas here? Do the pros of this action outweigh its cons?

GLOBAL ACTION

1. Your home country market (the United States) is being challenged by price wars launched by your top three foreign competitors from three countries that do not share the same US-style antitrust tradition. Prepare a report outlining your top five strategic choices on how to respond to such challenges, discussing the pros and cons of each choice. Then identify, recommend, and defend your top choice.

2. You are an executive assistant for the CEO of Mediterranean Shipping Company (MSC) of Switzerland. Two competitors—Maersk of Denmark and CMA CGM of France—have asked your CEO to jointly discuss the possibility of setting up an alliance that is called the P3 Alliance. Citing the blessing from governments on global airline alliances such as One World, Sky Team,

and Star Alliance, executives from Maersk and CMA CGM believe that the relevant governments for the P3 Alliance are likely to be supportive. Having made up his mind to participate in the negotiations, your CEO has asked you to prepare a report on the do's and don'ts of such discussions. He has also requested that you accompany him to the discussions. What else do you need to prepare in addition to the report?

CLOSING CASE

EMERGING MARKETS: How Firms from Emerging Economies Fight Back

Market opening throughout emerging economies often means the arrival of multinational enterprises (MNEs) from developed economies. While MNEs put an enormous amount of pressure on local firms, MNEs also serve a useful purpose of demonstrating what is possible and motivating local firms to try harder. Since the best defense is offense, trying harder—in addition mounting a rigorous defense—usually means to get out of local firms' increasingly crowded home markets. How do firms from emerging economies fight back? Specifically, how do they enter foreign markets?

At least four strategic patterns have emerged. The first is to follow the well-known Japanese and Korean strategies of first establishing a beachhead by exporting something good enough and then raising quality, perception, and price. By following these steps, Pearl River of China has dethroned Yamaha to become the largest piano maker in the world. It has also significantly improved quality so that the market leader Steinway, after first rejecting Pearl River for an alliance proposal, more recently approached Pearl River to become Steinway's original equipment manufacturer for its low-end models. Likewise, Mahindra & Mahindra of India solidly established itself in the American heartland, and ended up becoming the world's largest tractor maker by volume.

A second path is to follow diasporas. To bring Bollywood hits to the diaspora, Reliance Media of India launched the BIG Cinemas chain in the United States. King of fast food in the Philippines, Jollibee chased the diaspora by expanding to Hong Kong, Dubai, and southern California. But joining the mainstream has

Peter Charlesworth/LightRocket/Getty Images

been hard for companies focusing on the diaspora. More interesting is a "reverse diaspora" strategy: Corona beer of Mexico, after giving American customers a happy time when visiting Mexico, successfully chased such customers back to their home country. Corona is now one of the most frequently served beers in American bars and restaurants that do not have anything to do with Mexico or Mexican food. In short, Corona has "gone native" to become a local beer in the US.

Third, some emerging multinationals simply buy Western companies or brands off the shelf. Before Lenovo purchased the PC division from IBM in 2004, most people in the world, including a lot of gurus, asked: "IBM PC was purchased by *whom*?" Now most readers of this book already knew Lenovo before opening the book. Likewise, Tata Motors of India bought Jaguar Land Rover, and Geely of China acquired Volvo. Such high-profile acquisitions significantly enhanced the global profile and brand awareness of these ambitious firms from emerging economies.

Fourth, firms from emerging economies have to overcome enormous institution-based barriers, some formal and some informal. Although Huawei of China successfully exported telecom equipment to 45 of the world's top 50 telecom operators, it had a hard time penetrating the remaining five, all of which are in the United States. A major reason is blatant discrimination by the US Congress, which labeled Huawei a "national security threat" in the absence of hard evidence. Undeterred, Huawei became an emerging contender in smartphones, in addition to strengthening its excellence in telecom equipment. In addition to formal barriers, how to overcome informal consumer perceptions that typically associate emerging economies with poor quality is another challenge. For example, cosmetics users in the world do not think of Brazil highly—or do not think of Brazil *at all*. Natura of Brazil has no precedents to follow, because no Brazilian consumer products brands have succeeded outside Latin America. Highlighting its natural ingredients from the Amazon rainforest, Natura endeavored to tap into Brazil's positive country-of-origin image of biodiversity. This reigning queen of cosmetics in Brazil was trying hard to show its charm overseas. Sometimes, governments helped. In an effort to help

their firms climb mountains, in the Western media the Indian government ran the "Incredible India" campaign and the Taiwanese government the "innovalue" campaign.

In summary, facing an onslaught of MNEs from developed economies, many firms from emerging economies are determined to fight back by turning up the competitive heat in developed economies as well as numerous other markets. Many will fail, but some will succeed. How rivals from developed economies interact with them by competing with, collaborating with, and/or ignoring them will shape a large part of the future of global competition.

CASE DISCUSSION QUESTIONS:

1. Why are firms from emerging economies so eager to expand from their home markets?

2. What distinguishes firm-specific resources and capabilities of some of the winning firms from emerging economies?

3. ***ON ETHICS:*** Are the institution-based barriers in some developed economies fair or unfair?

4. Pick an established rival of a firm named in this case—for example, Steinway for Pearl River or Avon for Natura. Do some research to understand their resource similarity and market commonality between the pair of rivals (such as Avon versus Natura). Using the competitor analysis framework in Figure 11.3, predict what will happen to their competition in the home country of the established rival, the home country of the emerging challenger, and another third-country market.

Sources: Based on (1) P. Deng, 2009, Why do Chinese firms tend to acquire strategic assets in international expansion? *Journal of World Business*, 44: 74–84; (2) *Economist*, 2013, Looks good, September 28 (special report): 14–15; (3) *Economist*, 2013, The emerging-brand battle, June 22: 70; (4) V. Govindarajan & C. Trimble, 2012, *Reverse Innovation*, Boston: Harvard Business Review Press; (5) S. Lange, 2016, Huawei deals with liability of foreignness, in M. W. Peng, *Global Strategy*, 4th ed., Cincinnati: Cengage Learning; (6) C. Mutlu, Z. Wu, M. W. Peng, & Z. Lin, 2015, Competing in (and out of) transition economies, *Asia Pacific Journal of Management* (in press); (7) M. W. Peng, 2012, The global strategy of emerging multinationals from China, *Global Strategy Journal*, 2: 97–107.

NOTES

[**Journal acronyms**] **AMJ**—*Academy of Management Journal;* **AMR**—*Academy of Management Review;* **BW**—*BusinessWeek* (before 2010) or *Bloomberg Businessweek* (since 2010); **HBR**—*Harvard Business Review;* **JEP**—*Journal of Economic Perspec-tives;* **JIBS**—*Journal of International Business Studies;* **JWB**—*Journal of World Business;* **SMJ**—*Strategic Management Journal*

1 L. Capron & O. Chatain, 2008, Competitors' resource-oriented strategies, *AMR*, 33: 97–121; K. Coyne & J. Horn, 2009, Predicting your competitors' reaction, *HBR*, April: 90–97; W. Tsai, K. Su, & M. Chen, 2011, Seeing through the eyes of a rival, *AMJ*, 54: 761–778.

2 G. Markman, P. Gianiodis, & A. Buchholtz, 2009, Factor-market rivalry, *AMR*, 34: 423–441.

3 J. Baker, 1999, Developments in antitrust economics, *JEP*, 13: 181–194.

4 S. Brenner, 2011, Self-disclosure at international cartels, *JIBS*, 42: 221–234; Y. Zhang & J. Gimeno, 2010, Earnings pressure and competitive behavior, *AMJ*, 53: 743–768.

5 *United States et al. v. AT&T Inc. et al.*, 2011, Second amended complaint (p. 17), September 30, Washington, DC: US District Court for the District of Columbia.

6 *Economist*, 2014, Boring can still be bad, March 29: 16; *Economist*, 2014, Fixed penalty, November 15: 78.

7 M. Benner, 2007, The incumbent discount, *AMR*, 32: 703–720.

8 *BW*, 2014, Fighting for a seat at the grown-ups' table, June 2: 25–27.

9 M. Chen, 1996, Competitor analysis and interfirm rivalry (p. 106), *AMR*, 21: 100–134.

10 J. Anand, L. Mesquita, & R. Vassolo, 2009, The dynamics of multimarket competition in exploration and exploitation activities, *AMJ*, 52: 802–821; H. Greve, 2008, Multimarket contact and sales growth, *SMJ*, 29: 229–249; Z. Guedri & J. McGurie, 2011, Multimarket competition, mobility barriers, and firm performance, *JMS*, 48: 857–890; J. Prince & D. Simon, 2009, Multimarket contact and service quality, *AMJ*, 52: 336–354.

11 A. Bowers, H. Greve, H. Mitsuhashi, & J. Baum, 2014, Competitive parity, status disparity, and mutual forbearance, *AMJ*, 57: 38–62; T. Yu, M. Subramanian, & A. Cannella, 2009, Rivalry deterrence in international markets, *AMJ*, 52: 127–147.

12 G. Clarkson & P. Toh, 2010, "Keep out" signs, *SMJ*, 31: 1202–1225.

13 G. Kilduff, H. Elfenbein, & B. Staw, 2010, The psychology of rivalry, *AMJ*, 53: 943–969; R. S. Livengood & R. Reger, 2010, That's our turf! *AMR*, 35: 48–66.

14 J. Immelt, V. Govindarajan, & C. Trimble, 2009, How GE is disrupting itself, *HBR*, October: 56–65.

15 E. Graham & D. Richardson, 1997, Issue overview (p. 5), in E. Graham & D. Richardson (eds.), *Global Competition Policy*, Washington: Institute for International Economics.

16 R. Lipstein, 1997, Using antitrust principles to reform antidumping law (p. 408, original italics), in E. Graham & D. Richardson (eds.), *Global Competition Policy*, Washington: Institute for International Economics.

17 OECD, 1996, *Trade and Competition: Frictions After the Uruguay Round* (p. 18), Paris: OECD.

18 S. Marsh, 1998, Creating barriers for foreign competitors, *SMJ*, 19: 25–37.

19 D. Sirmon, S. Gove, & M. Hitt, 2009, Resource management in dynamic competitive rivalry, *AMJ*, 51: 919–935.

20 H. Ndofor, D. Sirmon, & X. He, 2011, Firm resources, competitive actions, and performance, *SMJ*, 32: 640–657.

21 M. Chen, H. Lin, & J. Michel, 2010, Navigating in a hypercompetitive environment, *SMJ*, 31: 1410–1430; G. Vroom & J. Gimeno, 2007, Ownership form, managerial incentives, and the intensity of rivalry, *AMJ*, 50: 901–922.

22 J. Boyd & R. Bresser, 2008, Performance implications of delayed competitive responses, *SMJ*, 29: 1077–1096; B. Connelly, L. Tihanyi, S. T. Certo, & M. Hitt, 2010, Marching to the beat of different drummers, *AMJ*, 53: 723–742; V. Rindova, W. Ferrier, & R. Wiltbank, 2010, Value from gestalt, *SMJ*, 31: 1474–1497.

23 Chen, 1996, Competitor analysis and interfirm rivalry (p. 107). See also W. Desarbo, R. Grewal, & J. Wind, 2006, Who competes with whom? *SMJ*, 27: 101–129; L. Fuentelsaz & J. Gomez, 2006, Multipoint competition, strategic similarity, and entry into geographic markets, *SMJ*, 27: 477–499.

24 M. Chen, K. Su, & W. Tsai, 2007, Competitive tension, *AMJ*, 50: 101–118.

25 W. C. Kim & R. Mauborgne, 2005, *Blue Ocean Strategy*, Boston: Harvard Business School Press.

26 *BW*, 2014, The carrier that avoids Brazil's No. 1 air route, August 11: 24–25

27 E. Rose & K. Ito, 2008, Competitive interactions, *JIBS*, 39: 864–879.

28 R. Griffin & M. Pustay, 2003, *International Business*, 3rd ed. (p. 241), Upper Saddle River, NJ: Prentice Hall.

29 J. Stiglitz, 2002, *Globalization and Its Discontent* (pp. 172–173), New York: Norton.

30 J. Clougherty, 2005, Antitrust holdup source, cross-national institutional variation, and corporate political strategy implications for domestic mergers in a global context, *SMJ*, 26: 769–790.

31 R. D'Aveni, 1994, *Hypercompetition*, New York: Free Press; M. W. Peng, 2016, *Global Strategy*, 4th ed., Cincinnati: Cengage Learning.

32 E. Rockefeller, 2007, *The Antitrust Religion*, Washington, DC: Cato Institute.

33 *BW*, 2013, Japan's billionaire brawl, October 21: 42–43; H. Mikitani, 2013, Rakuten's CEO on humanizing e-commerce, *HBR*, November: 47–50.

34 M. W. Peng, 2014, The antitrust case on the AT&T-T-Mobile merger (pp. 456–459), in M. W. Peng, *Global Strategy*, 3rd ed., Cincinnati: Cengage Learning.

35 C. Fishman, 2006, *The Wal-Mart Effect*, New York: Penguin.

36 M. Czinkota & M. Kotabe, 1997, A marketing perspective of the US International Trade Commission's antidumping actions (p. 183), *JWB*, 32: 169–187.

© Lonely/Shutterstock.com

Bill Pugliano/Getty Images News/Getty Images

Learning Objectives

After studying this chapter, you should be able to

- define alliances and acquisitions.

- articulate how institutions and resources influence alliances and acquisitions.

- describe how alliances are formed.

- outline how alliances are evolved and dissolved.

- discuss how alliances perform.

- explain why firms undertake acquisitions.

- understand why acquisitions often fail.

- participate in two leading debates concerning alliances and acquisitions.

- draw implications for action.

Making Alliances and Acquisitions Work

OPENING CASE

Fiat Chrysler: From Alliance to Acquisition

The year 2009 was one of the most tragic and the most unforgettable years in the history of the US automobile industry: two of the Big Three automakers, GM and Chrysler, went bankrupt in April. However, there was one glimmer of hope: Fiat came to rescue Chrysler was a "white knight." Chrysler had recently gone through a traumatic divorce with Daimler in 2007. By 2009, nobody wanted Chrysler, which was pulled down by deteriorating products, hopeless finances, and the Great Recession. Its desperate call asking GM, Honda, Nissan-Renault, Toyota, and Volkswagen to help went nowhere. Only Fiat answered the call with US$5 billion. As the "new Chrysler"—Chrysler Group LLC, which is different from the pre-bankruptcy "old Chrysler," formerly called Chrysler LLC—emerged out of bankruptcy in June 2009, the US government (which spent US$8 billion in total to bail out Chrysler) had 10% of shares. The Canadian government had 2%. The United Auto Workers (union) had 68%. Although Fiat only had 20%, clearly as the senior partner in this new alliance it was calling all the shots.

While Chrysler got itself another European partner, Fiat itself was a weak automaker. Would the relationship work? The DaimlerChrysler marriage consisted of a luxury automaker and a working-class truck and SUV maker, which had a hard time working together. The

Fiat-Chrysler alliance at least consisted of two similar mass market operations. Each offered the other a set of complementary skills and capabilities. In addition to cash, Chrysler needed attractive small cars. Fiat supplied Chrysler with its award-winning Alfa Romeo Giulietta small car and its excellent small-engine technology that would comply with the increasingly strict fuel-economy standards in the United States. In 2013, while Chrysler's US factories were running at nearly full capacity, only 40% of the capacity of Fiat's Italian factories was being utilized. Thanks to Italian politics, Fiat could not close any major factories. Therefore, Fiat needed novel models from Chrysler and made them in Italy. Fiat recently assigned Chrysler's brand-new Jeep Renegade SUV to be built in Italy. In third-country markets, while each of these relatively smaller players was weak, their odds would be better by working together. In Brazil, which is Fiat's number-one market (where Fiat sold more cars than in Italy), Fiat faced major challenges from GM and Renault. Assistance from Chrysler in the form of newer models and technologies would certainly be valuable. In Asia (especially China), neither of them was very strong, although Chrysler's Jeep models did better. Combining forces allowed them to scale new heights in the tough but important Asian markets.

After several years of experimentation, both sides seemed satisfied with the alliance. Sergio Marchionne, who served as chairman and CEO for both Fiat and Chrysler, was instrumental in making sure both sides worked together. Many American managers at Chrysler used to resent European dominance, thanks to their DaimlerChrysler days. This time as Chrysler owed its existence to Marchionne, its managers tended to give him the benefit of the doubt as he turned Chrysler around. Instead of the more centralized German style, Marchionne practiced a more decentralized management style. He also hired third-country (non-US and non-Italian) executives to help reduce the binational cultural barriers. By 2011, Chrysler had repaid US$7.6 billion loans to the US and Canadian governments and bought out the shares both governments held. Overall, Fiat gradually increased its Chrysler shares, reaching 59% by 2013. In 2014, Fiat acquired the remaining shares and owned 100% of Chrysler.

Set up in 2014, the combined entity is called Fiat Chrysler Automobiles (FCA), which interestingly is headquartered neither in Turin, Italy (Fiat's home), nor Auburn Hills (a Detroit suburb), Michigan (Chrysler's

base). Instead, it is registered in the Netherlands, which has emerged as "Europe's Delaware." Many famous firms that you normally would not think of as "Dutch," such as Airbus Group and IKEA, are in fact registered there. But FCA's CEO and the top management team will be based in London—operational headquarters. Cross-listed in both the Borasa Italiana and New York Stock Exchange, FCA is the world's seventh-largest automaker. With combined annual output of 4.5 million cars, FCA would be behind Toyota, GM, Volkswagen, Hyundai, Ford, and Nissan-Renault, but ahead of Honda and Peugeot. This is not bad for the 11th-ranked Chrysler (2.4 million vehicles prior to the full merger) and 13th-ranked Fiat (2.1 million vehicles). FCA has a broad portfolio of brands, such as Alfa Romeo, Chrysler, Dodge, Ferrari, Fiat, Fiat Professional, Jeep, Maserati, and Ram Trucks. Whether tighter integration would enable FCA to challenge the global heavyweights remains to be seen.

Sources: Based on (1) *Bloomberg Businessweek*, 2014, This "baby Jeep" has an Italian accent, March 7: 23–24; (2) *Economist*, 2013, Hoping it will hold together, August 24: 57; (3) *Economist*, 2014, Here, there, and everywhere, February 22: 56–57; (4) www.fcagroup.com.

Learning Objective

Define alliances and acquisitions.

Strategic alliance

A voluntary agreement of cooperation between firms.

Contractual (non-equity-based) alliance

Alliance between firms that is based on contracts and does not involve the sharing of ownership.

Equity-based alliance

Alliance based on ownership or financial interest between the firms.

Strategic investment

One firm investing in another as a strategic investor.

Cross-shareholding

Both firms investing in each other to become cross-shareholders.

Why did Fiat and Chrysler enter into an alliance relationship? How did they use the alliance to help each other in challenging markets? Why then did Fiat decide to completely acquire Chrysler? These are some of the key questions driving this chapter. Alliances and acquisitions are two major strategies for growth used by firms around the world, thus necessitating our attention.[1] This chapter first defines alliances and acquisitions, followed by a discussion of how institution-based and resource-based views shed light on these topics. We then discuss the formation, evolution, and performance of alliances and acquisitions. Finally, we introduce two leading debates and discuss some tips on managing alliances and acquisitions.

12-1 Defining Alliances and Acquisitions

Strategic alliances are voluntary agreements of cooperation between firms.[2] Figure 12.1 illustrates alliances as degrees of *compromise* between pure market transactions and acquisitions. Contractual (non-equity-based) alliances are associations between firms that are based on contracts and do not involve the sharing of ownership. They include co-marketing, research and development (R&D) contracts, turnkey projects, strategic suppliers, strategic distributors, and licensing/franchising. Equity-based alliances, on the other hand, are based on ownership or financial interest between the firms. They include strategic investment (one partner invests in another) and cross-shareholding (each partner invests in the other). Equity-based alliances also include joint ventures (JVs), which involve the establishment of a new

Figure 12.1 **The Variety of Strategic Alliances**

legally independent entity (in other words, a new firm) whose equity is provided by two or more partners.

An acquisition is a transfer of the control of operations and management from one firm (target) to another (acquirer), the former becoming a unit of the latter. For example, Volvo is now a unit of Geely. A merger is the combination of operations and management of two firms to establish a new legal entity. Shown in the Opening Case, the merger between Fiat and Chrysler resulted in Fiat Chrysler Automobiles (FAC).

Although the phrase "mergers and acquisitions" (M&As) is often used, in reality, acquisitions dominate the scene. In the 2010s, approximately 40% of M&As are cross-border deals. Twenty years ago, only about one-sixth were cross-border deals.[3] Of all cross-border M&As, only 3% are mergers. Even many so-called "mergers of equals" turn out to be one firm taking over another (such as DaimlerChrysler, 1998–2007). Because the number of "real" mergers is very low, for practical purposes, we can use the two terms, "M&As" and "acquisitions," interchangeably. Specifically, we focus on cross-border (international) M&As, whose various types are illustrated in Figure 12.2.

Acquisition

A transfer of the control of operations and management from one firm (target) to another (acquirer), the former becoming a unit of the latter.

Merger

The combination of operations and management of two firms to establish a new legal entity.

Figure 12.2 **The Variety of Cross-Border Mergers and Acquisitions**

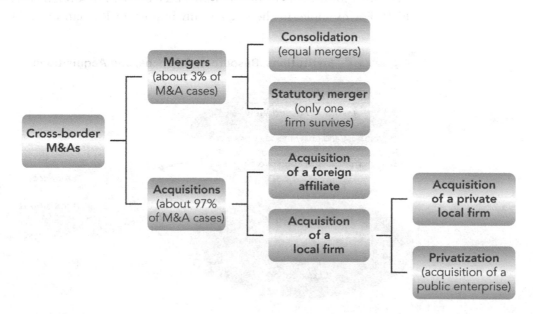

Learning Objective
Articulate how institutions and resources influence alliances and acquisitions.

12-2 Institutions, Resources, Alliances, and Acquisitions

What drives alliances and acquisitions? The institution-based and resource-based views shed considerable light on this question (see Figure 12.3). The institution-based view suggests that, as rules of the game, institutions affect how a firm chooses between alliances and acquisitions in terms of its strategy. However, rules are not made just for one firm. The resource-based view argues that, although a number of firms may be governed by the same set of rules, some firms, such as Fiat (see the Opening Case), excel more than others because of the differences in firm-specific capabilities that make alliances and acquisitions work.

12-2a Institutions, Alliances, and Acquisitions

Formal Institutions. Alliances and acquisitions function within formal legal and regulatory frameworks.[4] The impact of these formal institutions can be found along two dimensions: (1) antitrust concerns and (2) entry mode requirements. First, many firms establish alliances with competitors. Cooperation between competitors is usually suspected of at least some tacit collusion by antitrust authorities (see Chapter 11). However, because integration within alliances is usually not as tight as acquisitions (which would eliminate one competitor), antitrust authorities are more likely to approve alliances than they are acquisitions.[5] For instance, the proposed merger between American Airlines and British Airways was blocked by both US and UK antitrust authorities. However, the two airlines were allowed to form an alliance that eventually grew to become the multipartner One World. In another example, the proposed merger between AT&T and T-Mobile (a wholly owned subsidiary of Deutsche Telekom in the United States) was torpedoed by the US antitrust authorities. But the US government *blessed* AT&T and T-Mobile's collaboration in roaming.

Second, formal requirements on market entry modes affect alliances and acquisitions. In many countries, governments discourage or simply ban acquisitions to establish wholly owned subsidiaries (WOS), thereby leaving some sort of alliances with local firms to be the only entry choice for foreign direct investment (FDI). For example, in the strategically important Russian oil industry, Chinese

Figure 12.3   **Institutions, Resources, Alliances, and Acquisitions**

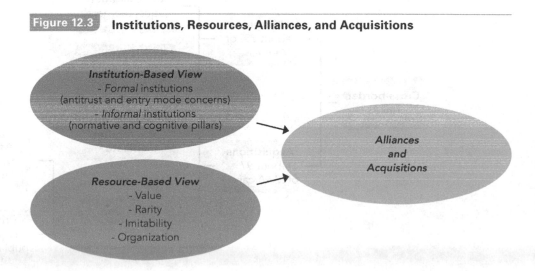

automobile industry, and Indian retail industry, the governments do not allow WOS—regardless of greenfields or acquisitions. Therefore, foreign entrants are often restricted to using an alliance mode (especially JV).

Recently, two trends have emerged concerning formal government policies on entry mode requirements. First is the general trend toward more liberal policies. Many governments (such as those in Mexico and South Korea) that historically only approved JVs have now allowed WOS as an entry mode. As a result, there is now a noticeable decline of JVs and a corresponding rise of acquisitions in emerging economies.[6] A second characteristic is that many governments still impose considerable requirements, especially when foreign firms acquire domestic assets. US regulations only permit up to 25% of the equity of any US airline to be held by foreign carriers, and EU regulations limit non-EU ownership to 49% of EU-based airlines.

Informal Institutions. The first set of informal institutions centers on collective norms, supported by a normative pillar. One core idea of the institution-based view is that because firms act to enhance or protect their legitimacy, copying other reputable organizations—even without knowing the direct performance benefits of doing so—may be a low-cost way to gain legitimacy. Therefore, when competitors have a variety of alliances, jumping on the alliance "bandwagon" may be perceived as a cool way to join the norm, as opposed to ignoring industry trends. When M&As are "in the air," even managers with doubts about the wisdom of M&As may nevertheless be tempted to hunt for acquisition targets. Although not every alliance or acquisition decision is driven by imitation, this motivation seems to explain a lot of these activities. Otherwise, how can we explain the "waves" of M&As? The flipside is that many firms rush into alliances and acquisitions without adequate due diligence (investigation prior to signing contracts) and then get burned big time.

A second set of informal institutions stresses the cognitive pillar, which centers on the internalized taken-for-granted values and beliefs that guide firm behavior. BAE Systems (formerly British Aerospace) announced in the 1990s that *all* its future aircraft development programs would involve alliances, evidently believing that an alliance strategy was the right thing to do. Likewise, in the area of acquisitions, Spain's Santander is a firm believer. It has undertaken a total of US$70 billion in acquisitions throughout Europe, Latin America, and North America. Clearly, managers at BAE Systems and Santander believe that such alliances and acquisitions, respectively, are the right (and sometimes the only) thing to do, which have become part of their informal norms and beliefs.

12-2b Resources and Alliances

How does the resource-based view, embodied in the VRIO framework, enhance our understanding of strategic alliances? (See Figure 12.3.)

Value. Alliances must create value.[7] The three global airline alliances—One World, Sky Team, and Star Alliance—create value by reducing 18%–28% of the ticket costs booked on two-stage flights, compared with separate flights on the same route if these airlines were not allied.[8] Table 12.1 identifies three broad categories of value creation in terms of how advantages outweigh disadvantages. First, alliances can reduce costs, risks, and uncertainties.[9] As Emirates Airlines from Dubai rises to preeminence, Etihad Airways from Abu Dhabi, a fellow emirate in the United Arab

Due diligence
Investigation prior to signing contracts.

Table 12.1	Strategic Alliances: Advantages and Disadvantages	
Advantages	**Disadvantages**
Reducing costs, risks, and uncertainties	Choosing wrong partners
Accessing complementary assets and learning opportunities	Potential partner opportunism
Possibilities to use alliances as real options	Risks of helping nurture competitors (learning race)

Emirates, has set up a number of alliances with smaller airlines around the world in an effort to eat some of Emirates' lunch (see Emerging Markets 12.1). Second, alliances allow firms such as Fiat and Chrysler to tap into complementary assets of partners and facilitate learning (see the Opening Case).[10]

Finally, one important advantage of alliances lies in their value as real options.[11] Conceptually, an option is the right, but not the obligation, to take some action in the future. Technically, a financial option is an investment instrument permitting its holder, having paid for a small fraction of an asset (often known as a deposit), the right to increase investment to eventually acquire it if necessary. A real option is an investment in real operations as distinguished from financial capital.[12] Two steps are involved:

- In the first phase, an investor makes a relatively small, initial investment to buy an option, which leads to the right to make a future investment without being obligated to do so.
- The investor then holds the option until a decision point arrives in the second phase, and then decides between exercising the option or abandoning it.

For firms interested in eventually acquiring other companies, but not sure about such moves, working together in alliances thus affords an insider view to evaluate the capabilities of partners. This is similar to trying on new shoes to see if they fit before buying them.[13] Since acquisitions are not only costly but also very likely to fail, alliances permit firms to *sequentially* increase their investment should they decide to pursue acquisitions (see the Opening Case). After working together as partners, if firms find that acquisitions are not a good idea, there is no obligation to pursue them. Overall, alliances have emerged as real options because of their flexibility to sequentially scale *up* or scale *down* the investment.

Alliances also have a number of nontrivial drawbacks. First, there is always a possibility of being stuck with the wrong partner(s).[14] Firms are advised to choose a prospective mate with caution. Yet, the mate should also be sufficiently differentiated to provide some complementary (nonoverlapping) capabilities.[15] Just like many individuals who have a hard time figuring out the true colors of their spouses before they get married, many firms find it difficult to evaluate the true intentions and capabilities of their prospective partners until it is too late.

Another disadvantage is potential partner opportunism. While opportunism is likely in any kind of economic relationship, the alliance setting may provide especially strong incentives for some (but not all) partners to be opportunistic. This is because cooperative relationships always entail some elements of trust, which may be easily abused.[16] Finally, alliances, especially those between rivals, can be dangerous, because they may help competitors. By opening "doors" to outsiders, alliances

Real option

An investment in real operations as opposed to financial capital.

EMERGING MARKETS 12.1

Etihad Airways' Alliance Network

Founded in 2003 and based in Abu Dhabi, Etihad Airways is both inspired by Emirates Airlines and a direct competitor of Emirates, which is based in Dubai, a fellow emirate in the United Arab Emirates (UAE). Etihad, which means "union" in Arabic, quickly became the fastest growing airline in the history of commercial aviation. Now with 101 aircraft, Etihad serves 11 million passengers to nearly 100 destinations around the world. Now the fourth-largest airline in the world, Emirates is a mammoth that has 220 aircraft and carries 40 million passengers to more than 100 cities.

Etihad imitates the highly successful Emirates by (1) equipping itself with modern long-haul jets (such as Airbus A380 and Boeing 777 Extended Range [ER]), and (2) leveraging the enviable location of the Abu Dhabi International Airport, which is only 45 minutes away by car from Dubai's storied airport. Given the small local population (three million in Abu Dhabi vis-à-vis four million in Dubai), Etihad—like Emirates—can only grow by being a "super-connector" airline. In other words, most of the passengers travel neither from nor to Abu Dhabi. Blessed by its Middle East location, Abu Dhabi, just like Dubai, is an ideal stopping point for air traffic between Europe and Australasia and between Asia and Africa.

One area that Etihad has decisively deviated from its role model Emirates is an interest in weaving an alliance network. Other than a single alliance with Qantas, Emirates either has been very shy or does not care about collaboration. However, in the industry with three major multipartner networks—One World, Sky Team, and Star Alliance—airlines are no strangers to alliances. But Etihad's alliances are not what you think. Its talks to join these three mega networks did not go anywhere, because none of them was interested in admitting an ambitious new airline determined to eat their lunch. Instead, Etihad has built its own alliance network consisting of eight smaller airlines. In 2011, Etihad took a 29% equity in Air Berlin, Europe's sixth-largest airline. Since then, through a series of equity-based strategic investments, Etihad acquired stakes in Dublin, Ireland-based Aer Lingus (4%); Rome, Italy-based Alitalia (49%)—the largest airline in Italy; Belgrade, Serbia-based Air Serbia (49%)—the largest airline in Serbia, formerly known as Jat Airways; Mahe, Seychelles-based Air Seychelles (40%); Lugano, Switzerland-based Darwin Airline (34%)—recently rebranded as Etihad Regional; Mumbai, India-based Jet Airways (24%); and Brisbane, Australia-based Virgin Australia (20%).

Etihad CEO James Hogan, who is an Australian, is viewed as a white knight who bailed out a bunch of money-losing or cash-poor airlines, including the struggling flag carriers of Ireland, Italy, Serbia, and Seychelles. Hogan has argued that his multibillion-dollar investments in airlines that serve smaller markets made economic sense by increasing Etihad's passenger tally and securing economies of scale when competing with Emirates. But can Etihad turn such an alliance network profitable? The most broken member is Alitalia, which lost €1.1 trillion (US$1.5 billion) in five years, and Etihad spent €560 million to breathe some new life into it.

Always known for using nasty language, Michael O'Leary, CEO of Ireland's and Europe's largest airline Ryanair, bluntly told journalists that Etihad "bought a lot of rubbish, and increasing their stake in Aer Lingus is consistent with that." Indeed, no other airline in the world is doing what Etihad is doing at this scale. Does Etihad, despite its deep pockets, have what it takes to turn around a whole bunch of also-rans? Stay tuned . . .

Sources: Based on (1) *Bloomberg Businessweek*, 2014? Will Etihad's flock of also-rans fly? April 14: 22–24; (2) *CEO Middle East*, 2013, Airline alliances: New world order, June: 36–42.

Etienne DE MALGLAVE/Gamma-Rapho/Getty Images

What factors or behaviors do you think have contributed to GE and Snecma's successful JV CFM International?

make it *easier* to observe and imitate firm-specific capabilities. In alliances between competitors, there is a potential "learning race," in which partners aim to outrun each other by learning the "tricks" from the other side as fast as possible. For example, when Danone of France and Wahaha of China had an alliance relationship, both engaged in a "learning race." Danone attempted to learn the tricks of how to operate in China, and Wahaha soaked up the knowledge of how to run world-class operations. Then in a nasty, high-profile divorce, both accused each other of being opportunistic.

Rarity. The abilities to successfully manage interfirm relationships—often called relational (or collaborative) capabilities—may be rare. Managers involved in alliances require relationship skills rarely covered in the traditional business school curriculum that emphasizes competition as opposed to collaboration.[17] To truly derive benefits from alliances, managers need to foster trust with partners, while at the same time being on guard against opportunism.[18]

As much as alliances represent a strategic and economic arrangement, they also constitute a social, psychological, and emotional phenomenon: words such as "courtship," "marriage," and "divorce" often surface. Given that the interests of partner firms do not fully overlap and are often in conflict, managers involved in alliances live a precarious existence, trying to represent the interests of their respective firms while attempting to make the complex relationship work. Given the general shortage of good relationship skills in the human population (remember, 50% of human marriages in the United States fail), it is not surprising that sound relational capabilities to manage alliances successfully are in short supply.

Imitablility. The issue of imitability pertains to two levels: (1) the firm level and (2) the alliance level. First, as noted earlier, one firm's resources and capabilities may be imitated by partners. Another imitability issue refers to the trust and understanding among partners in successful alliances. Firms without such "chemistry" may have a hard time imitating such activities. CFM International, a JV set up by GE and Snecma to produce jet engines in France, has successfully operated for more than 40 years. Rivals would have a hard time imitating such a successful relationship.

Organization. Some successful alliance relationships are organized in a way that makes it difficult for others to replicate. There is much truth behind Tolstoy's opening statement in *Anna Karenina*: "All happy families are like one another; each unhappy family is unhappy in its own way." Given the difficulty for individuals in unhappy marriages to improve their relationship (despite an army of professional marriage counselors, social workers, friends, and family members), it is not

Learning race

In which partners aim to outrun each other by learning the "tricks" from the other side as fast as possible.

Relational (or collaborative) capability

Ability to manage interfirm relationships.

surprising that firms in unsuccessful alliances (for whatever reason) often find it exceedingly challenging, if not impossible, to organize and manage their interfirm relationships better.

12-2c Resources and Acquisitions

We now consider how the VRIO framework affects acquisitions.

Value. Do acquisitions create *value*?[19] Overall, their performance record is sobering. As many as 70% of acquisitions reportedly fail. On average, the performance of acquiring firms does not improve after acquisitions.[20] Target firms, after being acquired and becoming internal units, often perform worse than when they were independent, stand-alone firms. The only identifiable group of winners is the shareholders of target firms, who may experience on average a 25% increase in their stock value.[21] This is due to acquisition premium, which is the difference between the acquisition price and the market value of target firms.[22]

Acquirers of US firms pay, on average, a 20% to 30% premium, and acquirers of EU firms pay a slightly lower premium (about 18%).[23] Shareholders of acquiring firms experience a 4% loss in their stock value during the same period. The combined wealth of shareholders of both acquiring and target firms is only marginally positive, less than 2%.[24] Unfortunately, many M&As destroy value.

Rarity. For acquisitions to add value, one or all of the firms involved must have rare and unique skills that enhance the overall strategy. Although acquirers from emerging economies generally have a hard time delivering value from their acquisitions, Lenovo, according to *Bloomberg Businessweek*, was able to "find treasure in the PC industry's trash" by turning around the former IBM PC division and using it to propel itself to become the biggest PC maker in the world (see the Closing Case).[25] Such skills are not only rare among emerging acquirers, but also rare among established acquirers—think of DaimlerChrysler.

Imitability. While many firms undertake acquisitions, a much smaller number of them have mastered the art of post-acquisition integration. Consequently, firms that excel in integration possess *hard-to-imitate* capabilities that are advantages in acquisitions. For example, each of Northrop Grumman's acquisitions must conform to a carefully orchestrated plan of nearly 400 items, from how to issue press releases to which accounting software to use. Unlike its bigger defense rivals such as Boeing and Raytheon, Northrop Grumman thus far has not stumbled with any of its acquisitions.

Organization. Fundamentally, whether acquisitions add value boils down to how merged firms are *organized* to take advantage of the benefits while minimizing the costs. Pre-acquisition analysis often focuses on strategic fit, which is the effective matching of complementary strategic capabilities.[26] Yet, many firms do not pay adequate attention to organizational fit, which is the similarity in cultures, systems, and structures. On paper, Nomura and Lehman Brothers' Asia and Europe operations seemed to have a great deal of strategic fit: Nomura was strong in Asia and weak in Europe. Lehman was strong in Europe and weak in Asia. (Lehman was also strong in its home region, North America, but its North American assets were sold to another firm and, thus, were not relevant to Nomura.) Why was the integration between the two such a mess? Mostly because of the almost total lack of organizational fit (see In Focus 12.1).

Acquisition premium
The difference between the acquisition price and the market value of target firms.

Strategic fit
The effective matching of complementary strategic capabilities.

Organizational fit
The similarity in cultures, systems, and structures.

IN FOCUS 12.1

NOMURA INTEGRATES LEHMAN BROTHERS IN ASIA AND EUROPE

Ethical Dilemma

In September 2008, Lehman Brothers went bankrupt. Britain's Barclay Capital bought its North America operations for US$3.75 billion. Lehman's assets in Asia and Europe were purchased by Nomura for the bargain-basement price of US$200 million. Founded in 1925, Nomura is the oldest and largest securities brokerage and investment banking firm in Japan. Although Nomura had operated in 30 countries prior to the Lehman deal in 2008, it had always been known as a significant, but still primarily regional (Asian), player in the big league of the global financial services industry. In addition to Lehman, the list of elite investment banking firms in early 2008 would include Bear Stearns, Citigroup, Goldman Sachs, JP Morgan, and Morgan Stanley of the United States; Credit Suisse and UBS of Switzerland; and Deutsche Bank of Germany. No one would include Nomura in this group. Nomura viewed itself primarily as an Asian version of Merrill Lynch.

The tumultuous 2008 left Bear Stearns dead first and Lehman second, and all of the firms in the big league named above in deep financial trouble. For Nomura, this became the opportunity of a lifetime. Within a lightning 24 hours, CEO Kenichi Watanabe decided to acquire Lehman's remnants in Asia and Europe. Some of the Lehman assets were dirt cheap. For example, its French investment banking operations were sold to Nomura for only €1. Overall, by cherry-picking Lehman's Asia and Europe operations and adding 8,000 employees, who tripled Nomura's size outside Japan, Nomura transformed itself into a global heavyweight overnight. The question was: "Does Nomura have what it takes to make this acquisition a success?"

The answer was a decisive "No!" from Nomura's investors, who drove its shares down by 70% by 2012. Since there was little evidence that Nomura had overpaid, the biggest challenge was post-acquisition integration, merging a hard-charging New York investment bank with a hierarchical Japanese firm that practiced lifetime employment.

Clearly, Lehman's most valuable, rare, and hard-to-imitate assets were its talents. To ensure that Nomura retained most of the ex-Lehman talents, Nomura set aside a compensation pool of US$1 billion and guaranteed all ex-Lehman employees who chose to stay with Nomura not only their jobs but also their 2007 pay level (including bonuses) for three years. About 95% of them accepted Nomura's offer. Given the ferociousness of the financial meltdown in 2008 and 2009 (which, if you remember, was triggered by Lehman's collapse), many employees at other firms that were not bankrupt lost their jobs. The fact that Nomura guaranteed both jobs and pay levels was widely appreciated by ex-Lehman employees who otherwise would have been devastated.

Instead, acquiring Lehman introduced significant stress to Nomura's long-held traditions. One leading challenge was pay level. Most senior executives at Lehman made, on average, over US$1 million in 2007. On average, Nomura employees only received *half* the pay of their Lehman counterparts. Not surprisingly, guaranteeing ex-Lehman employees such an astronomical pay level (viewed from a Nomura perspective) created a major problem among Nomura's Japanese employees. In response, Nomura in 2009 offered its employees in Japan higher pay and bonuses that would start to approach the level ex-Lehman employees were commanding, in exchange for less job security—in other words, they could be fired more easily if they underperformed. About 2,000 Japanese employees accepted the offer, which would link pay to individual and departmental performance rather than to the firm as a whole.

Another challenge was the personnel rotation system. Like many leading Japanese firms, Nomura periodically rotated managers to different positions. For example, Yoshihiro Fukuta, who served as head of Nomura International Hong Kong Ltd. in 2008, was rotated back to Tokyo as head of the Internal Audit Division in 2009. While these practices produced well-rounded generalist managers, they generated a rigid hierarchy: a manager in a later cohort year, no matter how superb his (always a male) performance was, was unlikely to supervise a manager in an earlier cohort year. These Nomura practices directly clashed with Western norms: (1) work was increasingly done by specialists who developed deep expertise, and (2) superstars were typically on a fast track rocketing ahead. Although the personnel rotation system largely did not apply to Nomura's overseas employees, it resulted in a top echelon that entirely consisted of Japanese executives who went through the rotations. In an effort to globalize, Nomura's top echelon needed to attract diverse talents, especially those from Lehman. Could the rotation system accommodate the arrival of ex-Lehman employees who had neither experience nor stomach in such rotations?

Four years after the acquisition, the performance was disappointing. In 2009, Nomura moved its investment banking headquarters to London to demonstrate its commitment to break into the top tier. In 2011, in Europe Nomura was number 13 in underwriting equities and number 15 in advising on mergers. In Asia outside of Japan and in the United States, it was a distant number 24 and number 22, respectively, in underwriting equity offerings. Its dominance in Japan was indeed strengthened by the Lehman deal. Nomura's market share in advising Japanese acquirers that made deals overseas shot up from 10% in 2007 to 25% in 2011.

Integration continued to be Nomura's headache number one. Outside Japan, the deal turned out to be a "reverse" takeover with *gaijin* (foreigners) running most of the show. Nomura undertook a campaign to expunge the long shadows of the Lehman hangover. Both symbolically and comically, mentioning the "L" word (such as "This is how we did it at Lehman") during senior executive meetings in London would cost executives £5 every time—they had to toss the money into a box as a penalty. In 2012, Jesse Bhattal, who was the former Asia Pacific CEO of Lehman, deputy president of Nomura group, and CEO of Nomura's investment banking group (the highest-ranked non-Japanese executive at Nomura), resigned amid heavy losses. Bhattal failed to see eye to eye with the board and was frustrated by his inability to undertake much-needed cost-cutting. His departure was regarded as "the culmination of a clash with Nomura's old guard," according to Bloomberg. The dark clouds over Nomura thickened. . . .

Sources: Based on (1) Bloomberg, 2012, Nomura reeling from Lehman hangover, February 28, www.bloomberg.com; (2) *BusinessWeek*, 2009, Nomura is starting to flex its Lehman muscles, September 28; (3) E. Choi, H. Leung, J. Chan, S. Tse, & W. Chu, 2009, How can Nomura be a true global financial company? case study, University of Hong Kong; (4) *Economist*, 2009, Numura's integration of Lehman, July 11; (5) A. Huo, E. Liu, R. Gampa, & R, Liew, 2009, Nomura's bet on Lehman, case study, University of Hong Kong; (6) Reuters, 2012, Ex-Lehman's Bhattal quits Nomura amid deep losses, January 10: www.reuters.com.

12-3 Formation of Alliances

Learning Objective
Describe how alliances are formed.

How are alliances formed? Figure 12.4 illustrates a three-stage model to address this question.[27] In Stage One, a firm must decide whether growth can be achieved strictly through market transactions, acquisitions, or alliances.[28] To grow by pure market transactions, the firm has to confront competitive challenges independently. This is demanding, even for resource-rich multinationals. As noted earlier in the chapter, acquisitions have some unique drawbacks, leading many managers to conclude that alliances are the way to go. For example, Dallas-based Sabre Travel Network has used alliances to enter Australia, Bahrain, India, Israel, Japan, and Singapore.

In Stage Two, a firm must decide whether to take a contract or an equity approach. As noted in Chapters 6 and 10, the choice between contract and equity is crucial. Table 12.2 identifies four driving forces. The first driving force is shared capabilities. The more tacit (that is, hard to describe and codify) the capabilities, the greater the preference for equity involvement. Although not the only way, the most effective way to learn *complex* processes is through learning by doing. One good

Learning by doing

A way of learning, not by reading books but by engaging in hands-on activities.

Figure 12.4   **Alliance Formation**

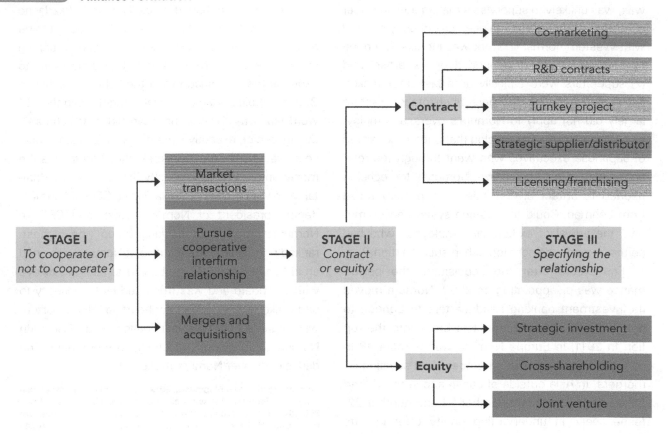

Source: Adapted from S. Tallman & O. Shenkar, 1994, A managerial decision model of international cooperative venture formation (p. 101), *Journal of International Business Studies*, 25 (1): 91–113

example is learning to cook by actually cooking and not by simply reading cookbooks. Many business processes are the same way. A firm that wants to produce cars will find that codified knowledge found in books or reports is not enough. Tacit knowledge can only be acquired via learning by doing, preferably with experts (such as Toyota) as alliance partners.

A second driving force is the importance of direct monitoring and control. Equity relationships allow firms to have some direct control over joint activities on a continuing basis, whereas contractual relationships usually do not. In general,

Table 12.2   **Equity-Based versus Non-Equity-Based Alliances**

Driving forces	Equity-based alliances	Non-equity-based alliances
Nature of shared resources and capabilities (degree of tacitness)	High	Low
Importance of direct organizational monitoring and control	High	Low
Potential as real options	High (for possible upgrading to M&As)	High (for possible upgrading to equity-based relationships
Influence of formal institutions	High (when required or encouraged by regulations)	High (when required or encouraged by regulations)

firms that fear their intellectual property may be expropriated prefer equity alliances (and a higher level of equity).

A third driver is real options thinking. Some firms prefer to first establish contractual relationships, which can be viewed as real options (or stepping stones) for possible upgrading into equity alliances should the interactions turn out to be mutually satisfactory (see the Opening Case).

Finally, the choice between contract and equity also boils down to institutional constraints. As noted earlier, some governments eager to help domestic firms climb the technology ladder either require or encourage JVs between foreign and domestic firms. The Chinese auto industry is a case in point.

Eventually, in Stage Three, firms choose a specific format. Figure 12.4 lists the different format options. Since Chapter 10 has already covered this topic when discussing entry modes, we will not repeat it here.

12-4 Evolution and Dissolution of Alliances

Learning Objective
Outline how alliances are evolved and dissolved.

All relationships evolve—some grow, others fail.[29] This section deals with two aspects of such evolution: (1) combating opportunism and (2) evolving from corporate marriage to divorce.

12-4a Combating Opportunism

The threat of opportunism looms large on the horizon. Most firms want to make their relationship work, but also want to protect themselves in case the other side is opportunistic. While it is difficult to completely eliminate opportunism, it is possible to minimize its threat by (1) walling off critical capabilities, or (2) swapping critical capabilities through credible commitments.

First, both sides can contractually agree to wall off critical skills and technologies not meant to be shared. For example, GE and Snecma cooperated to build jet engines, yet GE was not willing to share its proprietary technology fully with Snecma. GE thus presented sealed "black box" components (the inside of which Snecma had no access to), while permitting Snecma access to final assembly. This type of relationship, in human marriage terms, is like couples whose premarital assets are protected by prenuptial agreements. As long as both sides are willing to live with these deals, these relationships can prosper.

The second approach, swapping skills and technologies, is the exact *opposite* of the first approach. Both sides not only agree not to hold critical skills and technologies back, but also make credible commitments to hold each other as a "hostage." Motorola, for instance, licensed its microprocessor technology to Toshiba, which, in turn, licensed its memory chip technology to Motorola. Setting up such a reciprocal relationship may increase the incentives for both partners to cooperate.

In human marriage terms, mutual "hostage taking" is similar to the following commitment: "Honey, I will love you forever. If I betray you, feel free to kill me. But if you dare to betray me, I'll cut your head off!" To think slightly outside the box, the precarious peace during the Cold War can be regarded as a case of mutual "hostage taking" that worked. Because both the United States and Soviet Union held each other as a "hostage," neither dared to launch a first nuclear strike. As long as the victim of the first strike had only *one* nuclear ballistic missile submarine left (such as the American Ohio class or the Soviet Typhoon class), this single submarine would have enough retaliatory firepower to wipe the top 20 Soviet or US cities off the surface of earth, an outcome that neither of the two superpowers found acceptable. (See the movie *The Hunt for Red October.*) The Cold War did not turn hot, in part because of such a "mutually assured destruction" (MAD) strategy—a real military jargon.

Both of these approaches help minimize the threat of opportunism in alliances. Unfortunately, sometimes none of these approaches works and the relationship deteriorates, as shown next.

12-4b From Corporate Marriage to Divorce[30]

Alliances are often described as corporate marriages and, when terminated, as corporate divorces. Figure 12.5 portrays a dissolution model. To apply the metaphor of divorce, we focus on the two-partner alliance such as the Danone-Wahaha case (and ignore multi-partner alliances such as One World). Following the convention in research on human divorce, the party who begins the process of ending the alliance is labeled the "initiator," and the other party is termed the "partner"—for lack of a better word.

The first phase is initiation. The process begins when the initiator starts feeling uncomfortable with the alliance (for whatever reason). Wavering begins as a quiet, unilateral process by the initiator. In the Danone-Wahaha case, Danone seemed to be the initiator. After repeated requests to modify Wahaha's behavior failed, Danone began to escalate its demands. At that point, its display of discontent became bolder. Initially, Wahaha, the partner, might simply not "get it." The initiator's "sudden" dissatisfaction may confuse the partner. As a result, initiation tends to escalate.

The second phase is going public. The party that breaks the news first has a first-mover advantage. By presenting a socially acceptable reason in favor of its cause, this party is able to win sympathy from key stakeholders, such as parent company executives, investors, and journalists. Not surprisingly, the initiator is

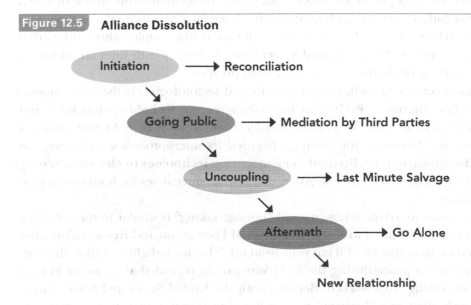

Figure 12.5   Alliance Dissolution

Initiation ⟶ Reconciliation

Going Public ⟶ Mediation by Third Parties

Uncoupling ⟶ Last Minute Salvage

Aftermath ⟶ Go Alone

New Relationship

Source: M. W. Peng & O. Shenkar, 2002, Joint venture dissolution as corporate divorce (p. 95), *Academy of Management Executive,* 16 (2): 92–105.

likely to go public first. Alternatively, the partner may preempt by blaming the initiator and establishing the righteousness of its position—this was exactly what Wahaha did. Eventually, both Danone and Wahaha were eager to air their grievances publicly.

The third phase is uncoupling. Like human divorce, alliance dissolution can be friendly or hostile. In uncontested divorces, both sides attribute the separation more to, say, a change in circumstances. For example, Eli Lilly and Ranbaxy phased out their JV in India and remained friendly with each other. In contrast, contested divorces involve a party that accuses another. The worst scenario is the "death by a thousand cuts" inflicted by one party at every turn. A case in point is the numerous lawsuits and arbitrations against each other filed in many countries by Danone and Wahaha, not only in France and China, but also in the British Virgin Islands, Italy, Sweden, and the United States.

In your opinion, should Danone and/or Wahaha have behaved differently to bring a better resolution to their troubled relationship?

The last phase is aftermath. Like most divorced individuals, most (but not all) "divorced" firms, such as Chrysler (see the Opening Case), are likely to search for new partners. Understandably, the new alliance is often negotiated more extensively.[31] However, excessive formalization may signal a lack of trust—in the same way that prenuptials may scare away some prospective human marriage partners.

12-5 Performance of Alliances

Learning Objective
Discuss how alliances perform.

Alliance performance is important.[32] Figure 12.6 illustrates four factors that may influence alliance performance: (1) equity, (2) learning and experience, (3) nationality, and (4) relational capabilities.

First, the level of equity may be crucial in how an alliance performs. A greater equity stake may signal that a firm is more committed, which is likely to result in higher performance. Second, whether firms have successfully learned from partners is important when assessing alliance performance. Since learning is abstract,

Figure 12.6 **What Is Behind Alliance Performance?**

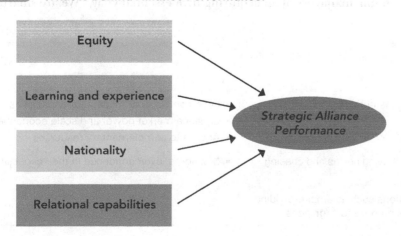

experience is often used as a proxy because it is relatively easy to measure.[33] While experience certainly helps, its impact on performance is not linear. There is a limit beyond which further increase in experience may not enhance performance.[34] Third, nationality may affect performance. For the same reason that marriages are more stable when both parties have similar backgrounds, dissimilarities in national culture may create strains in alliances. Not surprisingly, international alliances tend to have more problems than domestic ones. Finally, alliance performance may fundamentally boil down to soft, hard-to-measure relational capabilities. The art of relational capabilities, which are firm-specific and difficult to codify and transfer, may make or break alliances.

However, none of these factors asserts an unambiguous, direct impact on performance.[35] Research has found that they may have some *correlations* with performance. It would be naïve to think that any of these factors would guarantee success. It is their *combination* that jointly increases the odds for alliance success.

Learning Objective

Explain why firms undertake acquisitions.

12-6 Motives for Acquisitions

What drives acquisitions? Table 12.3 shows three potential motives for acquisition: (1) synergistic, (2) hubristic, and (3) managerial motives. All three can be explained by the institution-based and resource-based views. From an institution-based view, synergistic motives for acquisitions are often responses to formal institutional constraints and transitions that affect a company's search for synergy.[36] It is not a coincidence that the number of cross-border acquisitions has skyrocketed in the last two decades. This is the same period during which trade and investment barriers have gone down and FDI has risen (see the Closing Case).

From a resource-based view, the most important synergistic rationale is to leverage superior resources. Indian firms' cross-border acquisitions have primarily targeted high-tech and computer services in order to leverage their superior resources in these industries (see the Closing Case). Another motive is to access complementary resources, as evidenced by Nomura's interest in Lehman Brothers' worldwide client base.[37]

While all the synergistic motives, in theory, add value, hubristic and managerial motives reduce value. Hubris refers to overconfidence in one's capabilities. Managers of acquiring firms make two strong statements. The first is "We can manage *your* assets better than you [target firm managers] can!" The second statement is even bolder. Given that purchasing a publicly listed firm requires paying an acquisition premium, managers of an acquiring firm essentially say, "We are smarter than

Hubris

Overconfidence in one's capabilities.

Table 12.3   **Motives for Acquisitions**

	Institution-based issues	Resource-based issues
Synergistic motives	• Respond to formal institutional constraints and transitions	• Leverage superior managerial capabilities • Enhance market power and scale economies • Access to complementary resources
Hubristic motives	• Herd behavior—following norms and chasing fads of M&As	• Managers' overconfidence in their capabilities
Managerial motives	• Self-interested actions such as empire-building guided by informal norms and cognitions	

the market!" Acquiring firm managers can quantitatively state exactly how much smarter they are relative to the market—as evidenced by the specific acquisition premium they are willing to pay. In other words, a 10% acquisition premium, by definition, is the acquiring firms' announcement "We are 10% smarter than the market."

To the extent that the capital market is efficient and that the market price of target firms reflects their intrinsic value,[38] there is simply no hope to profit from such acquisitions. Even when we assume the capital market to be inefficient, it is still apparent that when the premium is too high, acquiring firms must have overpaid. This attitude is especially dangerous when multiple firms are bidding for the same target. The winning acquirer may suffer from what is called the "winner's curse" in auctions—the winner has overpaid. From an institution-based view, hubristic motives are at play when managers join the acquisition bandwagon. The fact that M&As come in waves speaks volumes about such herd behavior. After a few first-mover firms start making some deals in the industry, waves of late movers, eager to catch up, may rush in, prompted by a "Wow! Get it!" mentality. Not surprisingly, many of those deals turn out to be busts.

While the hubristic motives suggest that some managers may *unknowingly* overpay for targets, some managers may *knowingly* overpay for targets. Such self-interested actions are fueled by managerial motives, defined as managers' desire for power, prestige, and money, which may lead to decisions that do not benefit the firm overall in the long run. As a result, some managers may deliberately overdiversify their firms through M&As for such personal gains. These are known as agency problems (see Chapter 16 for details).

Overall, synergistic motives add value, and hubristic and managerial motives destroy value. They may *simultaneously* coexist. The Closing Case uses emerging multinationals as a new breed of cross-border acquirers to illustrate these dynamics. Next, we discuss the performance of M&As.

Managerial motive
Managers' desire for power, prestige, and money, which may lead to decisions that do not benefit the firm overall in the long run.

12-7 Performance of Acquisitions

Learning Objective
Understand why acquisitions often fail.

Why do as many as 70% of acquisitions reportedly fail?[39] Problems can be identified in both pre-acquisition and post-acquisition phases (Table 12.4). During the pre-acquisition phase, because of executive hubris and/or managerial motives, acquiring firms may overpay targets—in other words, they fall into a "synergy trap." For example, in 1998, when Chrysler was profitable, Daimler-Benz paid US$40 billion, a 40% premium over its market value, to acquire it. Given that Chrysler's

Table 12.4 **Symptoms of Acquisition Failures**

	Problems for All M&As	Particular problems for cross-border M&As
Pre-acquisition: Overpayment for targets	• Managers overestimate their ability to create value • Inadequate pre-acquisition screening • Poor strategic fit	• Lack of familiarity with foreign cultures, institutions, and business systems • Inadequate number of worthy targets • Nationalistic concerns against foreign takeovers (political and media levels)
Post-acquisition: Failure in integration	• Poor organizational fit • Failure to address multiple stakeholder groups' concerns	• Clashes of organizational cultures compounded by clashes of national cultures • Nationalistic concerns against foreign takeovers (firm and employee levels)

expected performance was already built into its existing share price, at a *zero* premium, Daimler-Benz's willingness to pay for such a high premium was indicative of (1) strong managerial capabilities to derive synergy, (2) high levels of hubris, (3) significant managerial self-interests, or (4) *all of the above.* As it turned out, by the time Chrysler was sold in 2007, it only fetched US$7.4 billion, destroying four-fifths of the value. In another case, in 2010, Microsoft paid US$8.5 billion to buy Skype, which was 400 times greater than Skype's income. Although many readers of this book use Skype, Skype has remained an underachieving Internet icon—how many people have paid money to Skype each other? As a result, this acquisition, Microsoft's biggest, raised a lot of eyebrows.

Another primary pre-acquisition problem is inadequate screening and failure to achieve strategic fit. In September 2008, Bank of America, in a hurry to make a deal, spent only 48 hours before agreeing to acquire Merrill Lynch for US$50 billion. Not surprisingly, failure to do adequate homework (technically, due diligence) led to numerous problems centered on the lack of strategic fit. Consequently, this acquisition was labeled by the *Wall Street Journal* as "a deal from hell."[40]

Acquiring international assets can be even more problematic, because institutional and cultural distances can be even large and nationalistic concerns over foreign acquisitions may erupt (see the Closing Case). When Japanese firms acquired Rockefeller Center and movie studios in the 1980s and 1990s, the US media reacted with indignation. In the 2000s, when DP World of the United Arab Emirates and CNOOC of China attempted to acquire US assets, they had to back off due to political backlash.

Numerous integration problems may surface during the post-acquisition phase.[41] Although "mergers of equals" sound nice, their integration tends to be awful (see In Focus 2.2). Organizational fit is just as important as strategic fit. Many acquiring firms (such as Nomura) do *not* analyze organizational fit with targets (such as Lehman Brothers' assets in Asia and Europe). The result was a mess (see In Focus 12.1). Firms often fail to address the concerns of multiple stakeholders, including job losses and diminished power (see Figure 12.7). Most firms focus on

---

Figure 12.7   Stakeholder Concerns During Mergers and Acquisitions

Investors	Will synergy benefits be downscaled?	Optimistic view of return on investment?	Will efficiency and short-term revenues fall?
Top management	Synergies difficult to attain	Internal conflicts: fractious management groups, key staff leave	Unrealistic euphoria
Middle management	Concern over job security	Expected to do M&A + day jobs at the same time	Overwhelmed by scale and scope
Frontline employees	What should I tell my customers?	When do lay-offs begin?	Who is setting my priorities and objectives?
Customers	So what?	Service quality dips, relationship suffers	No one is listening to me. Do I still matter?

IN FOCUS 12.2
CAN MERGERS OF EQUALS WORK?

Ethical
Dilemma

Romanticized by the ideal of human marriages, mergers of equals between firms sound nice. But can they work? The answer is hardly. In 1998, Daimler and Chrysler announced their "merger of equals" (their own words). Very soon, it was clear who called the shots at DaimlerChrsyler AG. After two years, Chrysler's former boss Robert Eaton left. Jürgen Schrempp, Daimler's boss, shared with the media that the term "merger of equals" had been used only for "psychological reasons." Not surprisingly the two sides divorced each other later (in 2007).

In case you think the DaimlerChrysler tragedy was caused in part by the cross-cultural difficulties (which undoubtedly added to the challenges), mergers of equals between two firms from the same country may still be unworkable. In 1998, two US firms Citibank and Travelers merged with great fanfare to become Citigroup. Within two years only one boss survived. Within five years, Citigroup had a divorce by spinning off Travelers, suggesting that the celebrated merger should not have taken place in the first place. In 2000, AOL Time Warner was born of a merger between an "old economy" media firm Time Warner and a "new economy" Internet firm American Online. The burst of the dotcom bubble in 2001 quickly revealed the shaky economics and the shaky power-sharing arrangements. In late 2001, Time Warner's former boss announced retirement. In 2009, AOL was spun off. The new boss of Time Warner called the merger "the biggest mistake in corporate history."

Why are mergers of equals so hard? Because both firms are not willing to let the other have an upper hand and both bosses, whose egos are typically huge, are not willing to let the other to be in charge. It is possible at least one of the two bosses is opportunistic in the beginning and determined to drive away another—as evidenced in the case of Schrempp at Daimler. But even in the absence of opportunism, when both bosses believe they can share power, a merger of equals can "effectively translate into rudderless behemoth," according to one expert. *Economist* put it more bluntly: "Forget the romance of power sharing. When it comes to the tricky business of making a merger work, someone must be in charge."

Sources: Based on (1) A. Cowen, 2012, An expanded model of status dynamics, *Academy of Management Journal*, 55: 1169–1186; (2) *Economist*, 2013, Riding the wave, November 5: 71; (3) *Economist*, 2013, Shall we? February 9: 65; (4) *Economist*, 2014, Love on the rocks, May 17: 65; (5) *Economist*, 2014, Return of the big deal, May 3: 55–57; (6) *Economist*, 2014, The new rules of attraction, November 15: 66–67; (7) J. Krug, P. Wright, & M. Kroll, 2014, Top management turnover following mergers and acquisitions, *Academy of Management Perspectives*, 28: 147–163.

task issues such as standardizing reporting, and pay inadequate attention to people issues, which typically results in low morale and high turnover.[42]

In cross-border M&As, integration difficulties may be much worse because clashes of organizational cultures are compounded by clashes of national cultures.[43] Due to cultural differences, Chinese acquirers such as Geely often have a hard time integrating Western firms such as Volvo (see the Closing Case). But even when both sides are from the West, cultural conflicts may still erupt. After Alcatel acquired Lucent, the situation, in the words of *Bloomberg Businessweek*, became "almost comically dysfunctional."[44] At an all-hands gathering at an Alcatel-Lucent European facility, employees threw fruits and vegetables at executives announcing another round of restructuring.

Although acquisitions are often the largest capital expenditures most firms ever make, they frequently are the worst planned and executed activities of all.[45] Unfortunately, while merging firms are sorting out the mess, rivals are likely to launch aggressive attacks. When Daimler-Benz struggled first with the chaos associated with the marriage with Chrysler and then was engulfed in the divorce with Chrysler, BMW overtook Mercedes-Benz to become the world's number-one luxury carmaker. Adding all of the above together, it is hardly surprising that most M&As fail.

Learning Objective
Participate in two leading debates concerning alliances and acquisitions.

12-8 Debates and Extensions

While this chapter has introduced a number of debates (such as the merits of acquisitions), this section discusses two leading debates: (1) alliances versus acquisitions and (2) majority JVs versus minority JVs.

12-8a Alliances versus Acquisitions

Although alliances and acquisitions are alternatives, many firms seem to plunge straight into "merger mania." HP, IBM, Microsoft, and Oracle are known as "rapid-fire" acquirers, often swallowing a dozen firms in any given year. In many firms, an M&A group reports to the CFO, while a separate unit, headed by the VP or director for business development, deals with alliances. M&As and alliances are thus often undertaken in isolation. A smaller number of firms, such as Eli Lilly, have a separate office of alliance management. Few firms have established a combined "mergers, acquisitions, *and* alliance" function. In practice, it may be advisable to explicitly compare acquisitions vis-à-vis alliances.

Compared with acquisitions, alliances cost less and allow for opportunities to learn from working with each other before engaging in full-blown acquisitions. While alliances do not preclude acquisitions and may indeed lead to acquisitions, acquisitions are often one-off deals swallowing both the excellent capabilities and mediocre units of target firms, leading to "indigestion" problems. Many acquisitions (such as DaimlerChrysler) probably would have been better off had firms pursued alliances first. For this reason, FCA, which was set up after Fiat and Chrysler collaborated for a few years in an alliance, would probably have better odds for success (see the Opening Case).

12-8b Majority JVs as Control Mechanisms versus Minority JVs as Real Options

A longstanding debate focuses on the appropriate level of equity in JVs. While the logic of having a higher level of equity control in majority JVs is straightforward, its actual implementation is often problematic. Asserting one party's control rights, even when justified based on a majority equity position and stronger bargaining power, may irritate the other party. This is especially likely in international JVs in emerging economies, whereby local partners often resent the dominance of Western MNEs. However, a 50/50 JV has its own headaches—everything must be negotiated or fought over.

In addition to the usual benefits associated with being a minority partner in JVs (such as low cost and less demand on managerial resources and attention), an additional benefit alluded to earlier is exercising real options. In general, the more uncertain the conditions, the higher the value of real options. In highly uncertain, but potentially promising, industries and countries, M&As or majority JVs may be inadvisable, because the cost of failure may be tremendous. Therefore, minority JVs are recommended *toehold* investments, seen as possible stepping stones for future scaling up—if necessary—while not exposing partners too heavily to the risks involved.

Since the real options thinking is relatively new, its applicability is still being debated.[46] While the real options logic is straightforward, its practice—when applied to acquisitions of JVs—is messy. This is because most JV contracts do not specify a previously agreed-upon price for one party to acquire the other's assets. Most contracts only give the rights of first refusal to the parties, which agree to negotiate in "good faith." It is understandable that "neither party will be willing to buy the JV for more than or sell the JV for less than its own expectation of the venture's wealth generating potential."[47] As a result, how to reach an agreement on a "fair" price is tricky.

12-9 Management Savvy

Learning Objective
Draw implications for action.

What determines the success and failure in alliances and acquisitions? Our two core perspectives shed considerable light on this big question. The institution-based view argues that alliances and acquisitions depend on a thorough understanding and skillful manipulation of the rules of the game governing alliances and acquisitions. The resource-based view calls for the development of firm-specific capabilities to make alliances and acquisitions work.

Consequently, three clear implications for action emerge (Tables 12.5, 12.6, and 12.7). First, managers need to understand and master the rules of the game—both formal and informal—governing alliances and acquisitions around the world.[48]

Table 12.5 | **Implications for Action**

- Understand and master the rules of the game governing alliances and acquisitions around the world.

- When managing alliances, pay attention to the "soft" relationship aspects.

- When managing acquisitions, do not overpay, focus on both strategic and organizational fit, and thoroughly address integration concerns.

Table 12.6 | **Improving the Odds for Alliance Success**

Areas	Do's and don'ts
Contract versus "chemistry"	No contract can cover all elements of the relationship. Relying on a detailed contract does not guarantee a successful relationship. It may indicate a lack of trust.
Warning signs	Identify symptoms of frequent criticism, defensiveness (always blaming others for problems), and stonewalling (withdrawal during a fight).
Invest in the relationship	Like married individuals working hard to strengthen their ties, alliances require continuous nurturing. Once a party starts to waver, it is difficult to turn back the dissolution process.
Conflict resolution mechanisms	"Good" married couples also argue. Their secret weapon is to find mechanisms to avoid unwarranted escalation of conflicts. Managers need to handle conflicts—inevitable in any alliance—in a credible and controlled fashion.

Source: Based on text in M. W. Peng & O. Shenkar, 2002, Joint venture dissolution as corporate divorce (pp. 101–102), *Academy of Management Executive*, 16 (2): 92–105.

Table 12.7	Improving the Odds for Acquisition Success
Areas	**Do's and don'ts**
Pre-acquisition	• Do not overpay for targets, and avoid a bidding war when premiums are too high.
	• Engage in thorough due diligence concerning both strategic and organizational fit.
Post-acquisition	• Address the concerns of multiple stakeholders, and try to keep the best talents.
	• Be prepared to deal with roadblocks thrown up by people whose jobs and power may be jeopardized.

When negotiating its acquisition of IBM's PC assets, Lenovo clearly understood and tapped into the Chinese government's support for home-grown multinationals. IBM likewise understood the necessity for the new Lenovo to maintain an American image when it persuaded Lenovo to set up a second headquarters in the United States. This highly symbolic action made it easier to win approval from the US government. In contrast, GE and Honeywell proposed to merge and cleared US antitrust scrutiny, but failed to anticipate the EU antitrust authorities' incentive to kill the deal. In the end, the EU torpedoed the deal. The upshot is that, in addition to the economics of alliances and acquisitions, managers need to pay attention to the politics behind such high-stakes strategic moves.

Second, when managing alliances, managers must pay attention to the soft relational capabilities that often make or break relationships (see Table 12.6). To the extent that business schools usually provide a good training on hard number-crunching skills, it is time for all of us to beef up on soft, but equally important (and perhaps more important), relational capabilities.

Finally, when managing acquisitions, managers are advised not to overpay for targets and to focus on both strategic and organizational fit (see Table 12.7). Refusing to let the bidding war go out of hand and admitting failure in proposed deals by walking away are painful but courageous. Around the world between 10% and 20% of the proposed deals collapse.[49] Despite the media hoopla about the "power" of emerging multinationals from China, in reality more than half of their announced deals end in tears. Indian multinationals do better, but still one-third of their deals cannot close (see the Closing Case). This is not a problem that only affects emerging acquirers. Experienced acquirers such as AT&T, News Corporation, and Pfizer, respectively, withdrew from their multi-billion-dollar deals to acquire T-Mobile, Time Warner, and AstraZeneca recently. Given that 70% of acquisitions fail and that integration challenges loom large down the road even if deals close, acquisitions that fail to close may sometimes be a blessing in disguise.

CHAPTER SUMMARY/LEARNING OBJECTIVES

12-1 Define alliances and acquisitions.

- A strategic alliance is a voluntary agreement of cooperation between firms.
- An acquisition is a transfer of the control of operations and management from one firm (target) to another (acquirer), the former becoming a unit of the latter.

12-2 Articulate how institutions and resources influence alliances and acquisitions.

- Formal institutions influence alliances and acquisitions through antitrust and entry mode concerns.
- Informal institutions affect alliances and acquisitions through normative and cognitive pillars.
- The impact of resources on alliances and acquisitions is illustrated by the VRIO framework.

12-3 Describe how alliances are formed.

- Alliances are typically formed when managers go through a three-stage decision process.

12-4 Outline how alliances are evolved and dissolved.

- Managers need to combat opportunism and, if necessary, manage the dissolution process.

12-5 Discuss how alliances perform.

- (1) Equity, (2) learning, (3) nationality, and (4) relational capabilities may affect alliance performance.

12-6 Explain why firms undertake acquisitions.

- Acquisitions are often driven by synergistic, hubristic, and managerial motives.

12-7 Understand why acquisitions often fail.

- Many acquisitions fail because managers fail to address pre-acquisition and post-acquisition problems.

12-8 Participate in two leading debates concerning alliances and acquisitions.

- (1) Alliances versus acquisitions and (2) majority JVs versus minority JVs.

12-9 Draw implications for action.

- Understand and master the rules of the game governing alliances and acquisitions around the world.
- When managing alliances, pay attention to the soft relationship aspects.
- When managing acquisitions, do not overpay, and focus on both strategic and organizational fit.

KEY TERMS

Acquisition, 375

Acquisition premium, 381

Contractual (non-equity-based) alliance, 374

Cross-shareholding, 374

Due diligence, 377

Equity-based alliance, 374

Hubris, 388

Learning by doing, 383

Learning race, 380

Managerial motive, 389

Merger, 375

Organizational fit, 381

Real option, 378

Relational (collaborative) capability, 380

Strategic alliance, 374

Strategic fit, 381

Strategic investment, 374

REVIEW QUESTIONS

1. **List several examples of contractual and equity-based alliances.**

2. **Are mergers or acquisitions more common? Why?**

3. In what two primary areas do formal institutions affect alliances?

4. Describe at least one norm (or collective assumption) and how it would affect a firm's perspective on creating an alliance.

5. Explain the three stages in the formation of an alliance.

6. Of the two methods allied firms can use to combat opportunism, which one do you think is better? Why?

7. What happens when an alliance fails and must be terminated? Summarize the process.

8. Of the four factors that may influence alliance performance shown in Figure 12.6, which do you think is the most important, and which the least important? Why?

9. *ON CULTURE:* How do dissimilarities in national culture affect the performance of alliances?

10. Describe the three most common motives for acquisition.

11. How does hubris affect value in a different way than the other two motives for acquisition?

12. What are some criteria managers should consider to avoid pre-acquisition and post-acquisition problems?

13. *ON CULTURE:* What impact does the combination of organizational culture and national culture have on cross-border M&As?

14. If you were part of a firm's leadership team, under what conditions would you choose an acquisition over an alliance and vice versa?

15. When does a majority JV seem more appropriate, and when is a minority JV more appealing?

16. Identify a country or region on PengAtlas Map 3.1 in which it is relatively difficult to do business. In spite of any difficulty, suppose you wish to expand into that country. Would you expand through an acquisition or an alliance? Why?

17. In reference to PengAtlas Map 1.1, firms in which group of countries are most likely to overpay for acquisitions in the other group of countries?

CRITICAL DISCUSSION QUESTIONS

1. Pick any recent announcement of a cross-border strategic alliance or acquisition. Predict its likelihood of success or failure.

2. *ON ETHICS:* During the courtship and negotiation stages, managers often emphasize "equal partnerships" and do not reveal (or even try to hide) their true intentions. What are the ethical dilemmas here?

3. *ON ETHICS:* As a CEO, you are trying to acquire a foreign firm. The size of your firm will double, and it will become the largest in your industry. On the one hand, you are excited about the opportunity to be a leading captain of industry and to attain the associated power, prestige, and income. (You expect your salary, bonus, and stock option to double next year.) On the other hand, you have just read this chapter and are troubled by the finding that 70% of M&As reportedly fail. How would you proceed?

GLOBAL ACTION

1. You are an entrepreneur in the cyber security industry seeking to develop alliances in India. India has diverse regions with many different peoples, traditions, and levels of economic development. Which two regions of India may be most conducive to developing your entrepreneurial alliances? Why?

2. Identifying new sources of energy has been an important business opportunity for quite some time. Your firm is interested in acquiring geothermal and solar energy firms around the world that can offer the best growth potential. What are the top three countries with strong firms in the geothermal and solar energy industry that you would recommend your firm to look into?

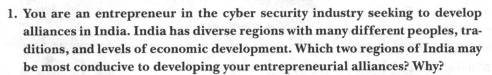

CLOSING CASE

EMERGING MARKETS: Emerging Acquirers from China and India

Multinational enterprises (MNEs) from emerging economies, especially those from China and India, have emerged as a new breed of acquirers around the world. Causing "oohs" and "ahhs," they have grabbed media headlines and caused controversies. Anecdotes aside, are the patterns of these new global acquirers similar? How do they differ? Only recently has rigorous academic research been conducted to allow for systematic comparison (Table 12.8).

Overall, China's stock of outward foreign direct investment (OFDI) (1.5% of the worldwide total) is about three times India's (0.5%). One visible similarity is that both Chinese and Indian MNEs seem to use M&As as their primary mode of OFDI. Throughout the 2000s, Chinese firms spent US$130 billion to engage in M&As overseas, whereas Indian firms made M&A deals worth US$60 billion.

MNEs from China and India target different industries to support and strengthen their own most competitive industries at home. Given China's prowess in manufacturing, Chinese firms' overseas M&As primarily target energy, minerals, and mining—crucial supply industries that feed their manufacturing operations at home. Indian MNEs' world-class position in high-tech and software services is reflected in their interest in acquiring firms in these industries.

The geographic spread of these MNEs is indicative of the level of their capabilities. Chinese firms have undertaken most of their deals in Asia, with Hong Kong being their most favorable location. In other

Table 12.8 **Comparing Cross-Border M&As Undertaken by Chinese and Indian MNEs**

	Chinese MNEs	Indian MNEs
Top target industries	Energy, minerals, and mining	High-tech and software services
Top target countries	Hong Kong	United Kingdom
Top target regions	Asia	Europe
Top acquiring companies involved	State-owned enterprises	Private business groups
% of successfully closed deals	47%	67%

Source: Extracted from S. Sun, M. W. Peng, B. Ren, & D. Yan, 2012, A comparative ownership advantage framework for cross-border M&As: The rise of Chinese and Indian MNEs, *Journal of World Business*, 47: 4–16.

words, the geographic distribution of Chinese M&As is not global; rather, it is quite regional. This reflects a relative lack of capabilities to engage in managerial challenges in regions distant from China, especially in more developed economies. Indian MNEs have primarily made deals in Europe, with the UK as the leading target country. For example, acquisitions made by Tata Motors (Jaguar Land Rover [JLR]) and Tata Steel (Corus Group) propelled Tata Group to become the number-one private-sector employer in the UK. Overall, Indian firms display a more global spread in their M&As, and demonstrate a higher level of confidence and sophistication in making deals in developed economies.

From an institution-based view, the contrasts between the leading Chinese and Indian acquirers are significant. The primary M&A players from China are state-owned enterprises (SOEs), which have their own advantages (such as strong support from the Chinese government) and trappings (such as resentment and suspicion from host-country governments). The movers and shakers of cross-border M&As from India are private business groups, which generally are not viewed with strong suspicion. The limited evidence suggests that M&As by Indian firms tend to create value for their shareholders. On the other hand, M&As by Chinese firms tend to destroy value for their shareholders—indicative of potential hubristic and managerial motives evidenced by empire building and agency problems.

Announcing high-profile deals is one thing, but completing them is another matter. Chinese MNEs have particularly poor records in completing the overseas acquisition deals they announce. Fewer than half (47%) of their announced acquisitions were completed, which compares unfavorably to Indian MNEs' 67% completion rate and to a global average of 80% to 90% completion rate. Chinese MNEs' lack of ability and experience in due diligence and financing is one reason, but another reason is the political backlash and resistance they encounter, especially in developed economies. The 2005 failure of CNOOC's bid for Unocal in the United States and the 2009 failure of Chinalco's bid for Rio Tinto's assets in Australia are but two high-profile examples.

Even assuming successful completion, integration is a leading challenge during the post-acquisition phase. Acquirers from China and India have often taken the "high road" to acquisitions, in which acquirers deliberately allow acquired target companies to retain autonomy, keep the top management intact, and then gradually encourage interaction between the two sides. In contrast, the "low road" to acquisitions would be for acquirers to act quickly to impose their systems and rules on acquired target companies. Although the "high road" sounds noble, this is a reflection of these acquirers' lack of international management experience and capabilities.

From a resource-based view, examples of emerging acquirers that can do a good job in integration and deliver value are far and few. According to the *Economist*, Tata "worked wonders" at JLR by increasing 30% sales and keeping the factory at full capacity. This took place during a recession when European automakers were suffering. Fiat, for example, could only utilize 40% of its factory capacity in Italy. According to *Bloomberg Businessweek*, Lenovo was able to "find treasure in the PC industry's trash" by turning around the former IBM PC division and using it to propel itself to become the biggest PC maker in the world. In ten years it grew from a US$3 billion company to a US$40 billion one. However, Lenovo knew that worldwide PC sales were going down, thanks to the rise of mobile devices. In response, Lenovo recently bought "the mobile phone industry's trash"—Motorola Mobility division—from Google and endeavored to leverage the Motorola brand to become a top player in the smartphone world. This deal quickly made Lenovo the world's third best-selling smartphone maker after Samsung and Apple.

CASE DISCUSSION QUESTIONS:

1. Why have M&As emerged as the primary mode of foreign market entry for Chinese and Indian MNEs?

2. Drawing on the industry-based and resource-based views, outline the similarities and differences between Chinese and Indian multinational acquirers.

3. ***ON ETHICS:*** As CEO of a firm from either China or India engaging in a high-profile acquisition overseas, shareholders at home are criticizing you of "squandering" their money, and target firm management and unions—as well as host country government and the media—are resisting. Should you proceed with the acquisition or consider abandoning the deal? If you are considering abandoning the deal, under what conditions would you abandon it?

Sources: Based on (1) BBC News, 2014, Lenovo completes Motorola takeover after Google sale, October 30: *www.bbc.co.uk*; (2) *Bloomberg Businessweek*, 2014, Jackpot! How Lenovo found treasure in the PC industry's trash, May 12: 46–51; (3) Y. Chen & M. Young, 2010, Cross-border M&As by Chinese listed companies, *Asia Pacific Journal of Management*, 27: 523–539; (4) *Economist*, 2012, The cat returns, September 29: 63; (5) S. Gubbi, P. Aulakh, S. Ray, M. Sarkar, & R. Chittoor, 2010, Do international acquisitions by emerging economy firms create shareholder value? *Journal of International Business Studies*, 41: 397–418; (6) O. Hope, W. Thomas, & D. Vyas, 2011, The cost of pride, *Journal of International Business Studies*, 42: 128–151; (7) S. Lebedev, M. W. Peng, E. Xie, & C. Stevens, 2015, Mergers and acquisitions in and out of emerging economies, *Journal of World Business* (in press); (8) S. Sun, M. W. Peng, B. Ren, & D. Yan, 2012, A comparative ownership advantage framework for cross-border M&As: The rise of Chinese and Indian MNEs, *Journal of World Business*, 47: 4–16; (9) Y. Yang, 2014, "I came back because the company needed me," *Harvard Business Review*, July: 104–108.

NOTES

[**Journal acronyms**] **AME**—*Academy of Management Executive;* **AMJ**—*Academy of Management Journal;* **AMP**—*Academy of Management Perspectives;* **AMR**—*Academy of Management Review;* **APJM**—*Asia Pacific Journal of Management;* **BW**—*BusinessWeek* (prior to 2010) *or Bloomberg Businessweek* (since 2010); **HBR**—*Harvard Business Review;* **JEP**—*Journal of Economic Perspectives;* **JIBS**—*Journal of International Business Studies;* **JIM**—*Journal of International Management;* **JM**—*Journal of Management;* **JMS**—*Journal of Management Studies;* **JWB**—*Journal of World Business;* **OSc**—*Organization Science;* **SMJ**—*Strategic Management Journal;* **WSJ**—*Wall Street Journal*

1 J. Reuer & R. Ragozzino, 2012, The choice between JVs and acquisitions, *OSc,* 23: 1175–1190; J. Reuer, T. Tong, B. Tyler, & A. Arino, 2013, Executive preferences for governance modes and exchange partners, *SMJ,* 34: 1104–1122.

2 P. Beamish & N. Lupton, 2009, Managing JVs, *AMP,* May, 75–94; P. Kale & H. Singh, 2009, Managing strategic alliances, *AMP,* August: 45–62; A. Shipilov, R. Gulati, M. Kilduff, S. Li, & W. Tsai, 2014, Relational pluralism within and between organizations, *AMJ,* 57: 449–459.

3 *Economist,* 2014, The new rules of attraction (p. 66), November 15: 66–67.

4 P. Brockman, O. Rui, & H. Zhou, 2013, Institutions and the performance of politically connected M&As, *JIBS,* 44: 833–852; D. Chen, Y. Paik, & S. Park, 2010, Host-country policies and MNE management control in IJVs, *JIBS,* 41: 526–537; W. Shi, S. Sun, & M. W. Peng, 2012, Sub-national institutional contingencies, network positions, and IJV partner selection, *JMS,* 49: 1221–1245.

5 Federal Trade Commission, 2000, *Antitrust Guidelines for Collaborations among Competitors,* Washington: FTC; T. Tong & J. Reuer, 2010, Competitive consequences of interfirm collaboration, *JIBS,* 41: 1056–1073.

6 M. W. Peng, 2006, Making M&As fly in China, *HBR,* March: 26–27.

7 J. Adegbesan & M. Higgins, 2010, The intra-alliance division of value created through collaboration, *SMJ,* 32: 187–211; R. Agarwal, R. Croson, & J. Mahoney, 2010, The role of incentives and communication in strategic alliances, *SMJ,* 31: 413–437; F. Castellucci & G. Ertug, 2010, What's in it for them? *AMJ,* 53: 149–166; E. Fang, 2011, The effect of strategic alliance knowledge complementarity on new product innovativeness in China, *OSc,* 22: 158–172; A. Joshi & A. Nerkar, 2011, When do strategic alliances inhibit innovation by firms? *SMJ,* 32: 1139–1160; E. Klijn, J. Reuer, F. Van den Bosch, & H. Volberda, 2013, Performance implications of IJV boards, *JMS,* 50: 1245–1266; M. Schreiner, P. Kale, & D. Corsten, 2009, What really is alliance management capability and how does it impact alliance outcomes and success? *SMJ,* 30: 1395–1419; M. Srivastava & D. Gnyawali, 2011, When do relational resources matter? *AMJ,* 54: 797–810.

8 *Economist,* 2003, Open skies and flights of fancy (p. 67), October 4: 65–67.

9 C. Wang, S. Rodan, M. Fruin, & X. Xu, 2014, Knowledge networks, collaboration networks, and exploratory innovation, *AMJ,* 57: 484–514.

10 H. Mitsuhashi & H. Greve, 2009, A matching theory of alliance formation and organizational success, *AMJ,* 52: 975–995.

11 A. Chintakananda & D. McIntyre, 2014, Market entry in the presence of network effects, *JM,* 40: 1535–1557; I. Cuypers & X. Martin, 2010, What makes and what does not make a real option? *JIBS,* 41: 47–69; T. Tong & S. Li, 2013, The assignment of call option rights between partners in IJVs, *SMJ,* 34: 1232–1243.

12 T. Tong, J. Reuer, & M. W. Peng, 2008, International joint ventures and the value of growth options, *AMJ,* 51: 1014–1029.

13 M. McCarter, J. Mahoney, & G. Northcraft, 2011, Testing the waters, *AMR*, 36: 621–640.

14 L. Hsieh, S. Rodrigues, & J. Child, 2010, Risk perception and post-formation governance in IJVs in Taiwan, *JIM*, 16: 288–303; M. Meuleman, A. Lockett, S. Manigart, & M. Wright, 2010, Partner selection decisions in interfirm collaborations, *JMS*, 47: 995–1018.

15 X. Luo & L. Deng, 2009, Do birds of a feather flock higher? *JMS*, 46: 1005–1030; W. Shi, S. Sun, B. Pinkham, & M. W. Peng, 2014, Domestic alliance network to attract foreign partners, *JIBS*, 45: 338–362.

16 A. Arino & P. Ring, 2010, The role of fairness in alliance formation, *SMJ*, 31: 1054–1087.

17 D. Zoogah & M. W. Peng, 2011, What determines the performance of strategic alliance managers? *APJM*, 28: 483–508.

18 G. Ertug, I. Cuypers, N. Nooderhaven, & B. Bensaou, 2013, Trust between IJV partners, *JIBS*, 44: 263–282; C. Jiang, R. Chua, M. Kotabe, & J, Murray, 2011, Effects of cultural ethnicity, firm size, and firm age on senior executives' trust in their overseas business partners, *JIBS*, 42: 1150–1173; Y. Luo, 2009, Are we on the same page? *JWB*, 44: 383–396; F. Molina-Morales & M. Martinez-Fernandez, 2009, Too much love in the neighborhood can hurt, *SMJ*, 30: 1013–1023; A. Phene & S. Tallman, 2012, Complexity, context, and governance in biotechnology alliances, *JIBS*, 43: 61–83.

19 N. Lahiri & S. Narayanan, 2013, Vertical integration, innovation, and alliance portfolio size, *SMJ*, 34: 1042–1064; A. Phene, S. Tallman, & P. Almeida, 2012, When do acquisitions facilitate technological exploration and exploitation? *JM*, 38: 753–783; A. Sleptsov, J. Anand, & G. Vasudeva, 2013, Relational configurations with information intermediaries, *SMJ*, 34: 957–977; C. Zhou & J. Li, 2008, Product innovation in emerging market-based IJVs, *JIBS*, 39: 1114–1132.

20 D. King, D. Dalton, C. Daily, & J. Covin, 2004, Meta-analyses of post-acquisition performance, *SMJ*, 25: 187–200.

21 *Economist*, 2014, Mergers and acquisitions: The new rules of attraction (p. 67), November 15: 66–67.

22 S. Malhotra & P. Zhu, 2013, Paying for cross-border acquisitions, *JWB*, 48: 271–281.

23 C. Moschieri & J. Campa, 2009, The European M&A industry (p. 82), *AMP*, 23: 71–87.

24 G. Andrade, M. Mitchell, & E. Stafford, 2001, New evidence and perspectives on mergers, *JEP*, 15: 103–120.

25 *BW*, 2014, Jackpot! How Lenovo found treasure in the PC industry's trash, May 12: 46–51.

26 J. Kim & S. Finkelstein, 2009, The effects of strategic and market complementarity on acquisition performance, *SMJ*, 30: 617–646.

27 This section draws heavily from S. Tallman & O. Shenkar, 1994, A managerial decision model of international cooperative venture formation, *JIBS*, 25: 91–113.

28 G. Lee & M. Lieberman, 2010, Acquisition versus internal development, *SMJ*, 31: 140–158.

29 H. Ness, 2009, Governance, negotiations, and alliance dynamics, *JMS*, 46: 451–480; H. K. Steensma, J. Barden, C. Dhanaraj, M. Lyles, & L. Tihanyi, 2008, The evolution and internalization of IJVs in a transitioning economy, *JIBS*, 39: 491–507.

30 This section draws heavily from M. W. Peng & O. Shenkar, 2002, JV dissolution as corporate divorce, *AME*, 16: 92–105.

31 N. Pangarkar, 2009, Do firms learn from alliance terminations? *JMS*, 46: 982–1004.

32 R. Kaplan, D. Norton, & B. Rugelsjoen, 2010, Managing alliances with the balanced scorecard, *HBR*, January: 114–120; J. Li, C. Zhou, & E. Zajac, 2009, Control, collaboration, and productivity, *SMJ*, 30: 865–884.

33 M. Cheung, M. Myers, & J. Mentzer, 2011, The value of relational learning in global buyer–supplier exchanges, *SMJ*, 32: 1061–1082; F. Evangelista & L. Hau, 2009, Organizational context and knowledge acquisition in IJVs, *JWB*, 44: 63–73; E. Fang & S. Zou, 2010, The effects of absorptive and joint learning on the instability of IJVs in emerging economies, *JIBS*, 41: 906–924; R. Gulati, D. Lavie, & H. Singh, 2009, The nature of partnering experience and the gains from alliances, *SMJ*, 30: 1213–1233; J. Lai, S. Chang, & S. Chen, 2010, Is experience valuable in international strategic alliances? *JIM*, 16: 247–261; C. Liu, P. Ghauri, & R. Sinkovics, 2010, Understanding the impact of relational capital and organizational learning on alliance outcomes, *JWB*, 45: 237–249; B. Nielsen & S. Nielsen, 2009, Learning and innovation in international strategic alliances, *JMS*, 46: 1031–1058; S. Tallman & A. Chacar, 2011, Communities, alliances, networks, and knowledge in multinational firms, *JIM*, 17: 201–210; G. Vasudeva & J. Anand, 2011, Unpacking absorptive capacity, *AMJ*, 54: 611–623; M. Zollo & J. Reuer, 2010, Experience spillovers across corporate development activities, *OSc*, 21: 1195–1212.

34 Y. Luo & M. W. Peng, 1999, Learning to compete in a transition economy, *JIBS*, 30: 269–296.

35 C. Chung & P. Beamish, 2010, The trap of continual ownership change in international equity JVs, *OSc*, 21: 995–1015; J. Xia, 2011, Mutual dependence, partner substitutability, and repeated partnership, *SMJ*, 32: 229–253.

36 Z. Lin, M. W. Peng, H. Yang, & S. Sun, 2009, How do networks and learning drive M&As? *SMJ*, 30: 1113–1132; H. Yang, S. Sun, Z. Lin, & M. W. Peng, 2011, Behind M&As in China and the United States, *APJM*, 28: 239–255.

37 H. Yang, Z. Lin, & M. W. Peng, 2011, Behind acquisitions of alliance partners, *AMJ*, 54: 1069–1080.

38 A. Gaur, S. Malhotra, & P. Zhu, 2013, Acquisition announcements and stock market valuations of acquiring firms' rivals, *SMJ*, 34: 215–232.

39 D. Siegel & K. Simons, 2010, Assessing the effects of M&As on firm performance, *SMJ*, 31: 903–916; G. Valentini, 2012, Measuring the effect of M&A on patenting quantity and quality, *SMJ*, 33: 336–346.

40 *WSJ*, 2009, Bank of America–Merrill Lynch: A US$50 billion deal from hell, January 22: blogs.wsj.com.

41 J. Allatta & H. Singh, 2011, Evolving communication patterns in response to an acquisition event, *SMJ*, 32: 1099–1118; M. Brannen & M. Peterson, 2009, Merging without alienating, *JIBS*, 40: 468–489; R. Chakrabarti, S. Gupta-Mukherjee, & N. Jayaraman, 2009, Mars-Venus marriages, *JIBS*, 40: 216–236; G. Chung, J. Du, & J. Choi, 2014, How do employees adapt to organizational change driven by cross-border M&As? *JWB*, 49: 78–86; P. Monin, N. Noorderhaven E. Vaara & D. Kroon, 2013, Giving sense to and making sense of justice in postmerger integration, *AMJ*, 56: 256–284; J. Xia & S. Li, 2013, The divestiture of acquired subunits, *SMJ*, 34: 131–148.

42 M. Cording, J. Harrison, R. Hoskisson, & K. Jonsen, 2014, Walking the talk, *AMP*, 28: 38–56

43 S. Malhotra & A. Gaur, 2014, Spatial geography and control in foreign acquisitions, *JIBS*, 45: 191–210; T. Reus & B. Lamont, 2009, The double-edged sword of cultural distance in international acquisitions, *JIBS*, 40: 1298–1316; R. Sarala & E. Vaara, 2010, Cultural differences, convergence, and crossvergence as explanations

of knowledge transfer in international acquisitions, *JIBS*, 41: 1365–1390.

44 *BW*, 2011, Hi-yah! Alcatel–Lucent chops away at years of failure (p. 29), May 2: 29–31.

45 M. Cording, P. Christmann, & D. King, 2010, Reducing causal ambiguity in acquisition integration, *AMJ*, 51: 744–767.

46 R. Ragozzino & C. Moschieri, 2014, When theory doesn't meet practice, *AMP*, 28: 22–37.

47 T. Chi, 2000, Option to acquire or divest a JV, *SMJ* (p. 671), 21: 665–687.

48 J. Clougherty, K. Gugler, L. Sorgard, & F. Szucs, 2014, Cross-border mergers and domestic firm wages, *JIBS*, 45: 450–470; D. Li, S. Miller, L. Eden, & M. Hitt, 2012, The impact of rule of law on market value creation for local alliance partners in BRIC countries, *JIM*, 18: 305–321.

49 *Economist*, 2014, Coming unstuck, August 9: 53–54.

AP Images/McDonald's

Learning Objectives

After studying this chapter, you should be able to

- describe the relationship between multinational strategy and structure.

- explain how institutions and resources affect strategy, structure, and learning.

- outline the challenges associated with learning, innovation, and knowledge management.

- participate in two leading debates concerning multinational strategy, structure, and learning.

- draw implications for action.

Strategizing, Structuring, and Learning Around the World

Launching the McWrap

It is hard to believe, but McDonald's is no longer the world's largest fast food chain—at least measured by the number of restaurants. Subway has rocketed ahead, with close to 42,000 restaurants worldwide vis-à-vis McDonald's' 34,000. While McDonald's still sells more than Subway (US$28 billion versus US$18 billion in 2013), McDonald's seems to have lost momentum, with US sales slowing down noticeably. McDonald's, of course, does not only compete with Subway, but also with the likes of Five Guys and Chipotle. In all three competitors, customers can see their food being prepared and feel that it is fresher and seemingly healthier. In the Fresh Wars, Subway has elevated its food preparers to become "sandwich artists." Chipotle has bragged about its "food with integrity," and released a short film critical of industrial farming—with a finger pointing at you know what.

In response, McDonald's has unleashed the McWrap, a high-profile salvo in the Fresh Wars in an effort to grab customer attention. At $3.99 in the United States, the McWrap is a ten-inch, white-flour tortilla wrapped around three ounces of chicken (grilled or crispy), lettuce, spring greens, sliced cucumbers, tomatoes, and cheddar jack cheese. Customers can choose their preferred dressing: ranch, sweet chili,

or creamy garlic. Only made to order (not pre-made), the McWrap can be prepared under 60 seconds. When served, it comes with a cool cardboard wrapper whose top can be zipped open. The whole thing can fit vertically in a cup holder in a car. The two-year, nine-ingredient, focus-grouped efforts to fix McDonald's freshness problem are an amazing case study of how a multinational changes its strategy, taps into its global organization, and leverages its knowledge—all under the pressures of cost reduction and local responsiveness. Dissecting what is behind the launch of McWrap, we can see at least three things.

First, the idea did not come from the United States. It came from three operations in Europe. In 2004, McDonald's in the Czech Republic started selling the Chicken Roll Up. In 2005, McDonald's in Poland introduced a tortilla sandwich, inspired by the kebab, a popular street food. In 2009, Austria pioneered the nifty cardboard container that can be unzipped. Thanks to a European food studio (which would be called an R&D lab in many other firms), these local innovations were noticed and diffused to the rest of the McDonald's organization.

Second, the attention the McWrap idea attracted from the headquarters was driven by a strategic interest in search of fresher and healthier items to outcompete rivals in the Fresh Wars. Specifically, it was the search for local responsiveness—in this case primarily in McDonald's home country, the United States—that identified the wrap to be a potential good fit. Americans are eating more chicken and prefer more fresh food, and the wrap might enable McDonald's to respond to such changing tastes.

Third, significant experimentation, learning, and innovation went into the process. While the idea seemed appealing, McDonald's did not operate on gut feelings. Led by Dan Courfreaut, executive chef and vice president of culinary innovation (whose nick name is Chef Dan), McDonald's menu innovation team undertook intense research and numerous experiments that ultimately took two years (2011–2013) to finish. To introduce new items to a restaurant chain as large as McDonald's was mind boggling. The food had to be tasty, the cost low, and the time to serve short—without compromising quality. "My job," according to Chef Dan, "is pushing ourselves without breaking the system." To enhance freshness, two slices of English cucumber were added for the first time to McDonald's offerings. While adding a tiny bit of cucumber did not sound like a big deal, it actually was quite a challenge to McDonald's supply chain structure. About a decade ago McDonald's introduced sliced apples to its menu, and it quickly became one of the largest buyers of apples in the United States. Initially, a half-breast of

chicken was used. But focus groups thought the wrap was a salad—with too much vegetable. Despite the rising health awareness, customers actually wanted more meat—as long as it was chicken. So the final version of the wrap had a full breast of chicken. The wrap's name also went through intense testing. In the first trial in Chicago, it was called the Grande Wrap. But customers could not figure out what "grande" was. Then the name Fresh Garden Wrap was tested in Orlando, and it flopped too. Eventually, McWrap was chosen.

In a leaked, internal memo obtained by the media, McDonald's admitted that it was not even in the top ten of the Millennial Generation's list of favorite restaurant chains. Calling the McWrap a "Subway buster," the memo suggested that "McWrap offers us the perfect food offering to address the needs of this very important customer to McDonald's." When asked to elaborate, a McDonald's spokesperson noted: "We don't think we have a problem with Millennials, but we want to remain relevant to all of our customers." Whether McWrap will prove to be relevant to customers remains to be seen—or tasted.

Sources: Based on (1) the author's interviews, (2) *Bloomberg Businessweek*, 2013, McFresh, July 8: 44–49; (3) *Bloomberg Businessweek*, 2014, Have we reached peak burger? September 8: 21–22; (4) *Wall Street Cheat Sheet*, 2013, 8 reasons McDonald's is praying the McWrap is a smash hit, July 10, wallstcheatsheet.com; (5) www.mcdonalds.com; (5) www.subway.com.

How can multinational enterprises (MNEs) such as McDonald's strategically manage growth around the world so that they can be successful both locally and internationally? How can they learn country tastes and global trends? How can they improve the odds for better innovation? These are some of the key questions we address in this chapter, which focuses on relatively large MNEs. We start by discussing the crucial relationship between four strategies and four structures. Next, we consider how the institution-based and resource-based views shed light on these issues. Then, we discuss worldwide learning, innovation, and knowledge management and look at two debates. Finally, we go over some tips for savvy managers.

Learning Objective
Describe the relationship between multinational strategy and structure.

13-1 Multinational Strategies and Structures

This section first introduces an integration-responsiveness framework centered on the pressures for cost reductions and local responsiveness. We then outline the four strategic choices and the four corresponding organizational structures that MNEs typically adopt.

13-1a Pressures for Cost Reduction and Local Responsiveness

MNEs confront primarily two sets of pressures: cost reduction and local responsiveness. These two sets of pressures are captured in the integration-responsiveness framework, which allows managers to deal with the pressures for both global integration and local responsiveness. Cost pressures often call for global integration, while local responsiveness pushes MNEs to adapt locally. In both domestic and international competition, pressures to reduce costs are universal. What is unique in international competition is the pressures for local responsiveness, which means reacting to different consumer preferences and host-country demands (see the Opening Case and the Closing Case). Consumer preferences vary tremendously around the world. For example, McDonald's beef-based hamburgers would obviously find few customers in India, a land where cows are held sacred by the Hindu majority. Thus, changing its menu is a must in India. Host-country demands and expectations add to the pressures for local responsiveness. In Europe, Canadian firm Bombardier manufactures an Austrian version of railcars in Austria, a Belgian version in Belgium, and other versions in other countries. Bombardier believes that such local responsiveness, although not required, is essential for making sales to railway operators in Europe, which tend to be state-owned.

Taken together, being locally responsive certainly makes local customers and governments happy but unfortunately increases costs. Given the universal interest in lowering cost, one natural tendency is to downplay or ignore the different needs and wants of various local markets and instead market a global version of products and services. The movement to globalize offerings can be traced to a 1983 article by Theodore Levitt: "The Globalization of Markets."[1] Levitt argued that worldwide consumer tastes are converging. As evidence, Levitt pointed to the worldwide success of Coke Classic, Levi Strauss jeans, and Sony TV. Levitt predicted that such convergence would characterize most product markets in the future.

Levitt's idea has often become the intellectual force propelling many MNEs to integrate their offerings globally while minimizing local adaptation. Ford experimented with "world car" designs. MTV pushed ahead with the belief that viewers would flock to global (essentially American) programming. Unfortunately, most of these experiments are not successful. Ford found that consumer tastes ranged widely around the globe. MTV eventually realized that there is no "global song." In a nutshell, one size does not fit all. This leads us to look at how MNEs can pay attention to *both* dimensions: cost reduction and local responsiveness.

13-1b Four Strategic Choices

Based on the integration-responsiveness framework, Figure 13.1 plots the four strategic choices: (1) home replication, (2) localization, (3) global standardization, and (4) transnational. Each strategy has a set of pros and cons outlined in Table 13.1. (Their corresponding structures are discussed in the next section.)

Home replication strategy, often known as "international strategy," duplicates home-country-based competencies in foreign countries. Such competencies include production scales, distribution efficiencies, and brand power. In manufacturing, this is usually manifested in an export strategy. In services, this is often done through licensing and franchising. This strategy is relatively easy to implement and usually the first one adopted when firms venture abroad.

On the disadvantage side, home replication strategy often lacks local responsiveness because it focuses on the home country. This strategy makes sense when

Integration-responsiveness framework

A framework of MNE management on how to simultaneously deal with the pressures for both global integration and local responsiveness.

Local responsiveness

The necessity to be responsive to different customer preferences around the world.

Home replication strategy

A strategy that emphasizes the duplication of home country-based competencies in foreign countries.

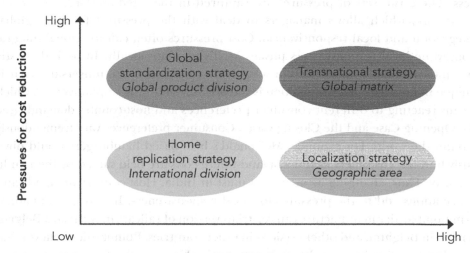

Figure 13.1 **Multinational Strategies and Structures: The Integration-Responsive Framework**

Note: In some other textbooks, "home replication" may be referred to as "international" or "export" strategy, "localization" as "multidomestic" strategy, and "global standardization" as "global" strategy. Some of these labels are confusing, because one can argue that all four strategies here are "international" or "global," thus resulting in some confusion if we label one of these strategies as "international" and another as "global." The present set of labels is more descriptive and less confusing.

Table 13.1 **Four Strategic Choices for Multinational Enterprises**

	Advantages	Disadvantages
Home replication	• Leverages home country-based advantages • Relatively easy to implement	• Lack of local responsiveness • May result in foreign customer alienation
Localization	• Maximizes local responsiveness	• High costs due to duplication of efforts in multiple countries • Too much local autonomy
Global standardization	• Leverages low-cost advantages	• Lack of local responsiveness • Too much centralized control
Transnational	• Cost efficient while being locally responsive • Engages in global learning and diffusion of innovations	• Organizationally complex • Difficult to implement

Localization (multidomestic) strategy

A strategy that focuses on a number of foreign countries/regions, each of which is regarded as a standalone local (domestic) market worthy of significant attention and adaptation.

the majority of a firm's customers are domestic. However, when a firm aspires to broaden its international scope, failing to be mindful of foreign customers' needs and wants may alienate them. When Wal-Mart entered Brazil, the stores had exactly the same inventory as the US stores, including a large number of *American* footballs. Considering that Brazil is the land of soccer and has won the World Cup five times, more wins than any other country, nobody (except a few homesick American expatriates in their spare time) plays American football there.

Localization strategy is an extension of the home replication strategy.[2] Localization (multidomestic) strategy focuses on a number of foreign countries/regions, each of which is regarded as a standalone local (domestic) market worthy of significant attention and adaptation (see Emerging Markets 13.1). While sacrificing

EMERGING MARKETS 13.1

Otis Rides on China's Growth

Founded in 1853, Otis is the world's leading manufacturer of elevators and escalators that are used in more than 200 countries. Since 1976, it has been a wholly owned subsidiary of United Technologies. Otis elevators and escalators reportedly carry the equivalent of the *entire* world's population every nine days. It is possible that *every* reader of this book has taken at least one elevator or escalator ride on an Otis. As China grows to become the second-largest economy, China has also become Otis's second-largest market, measured by the number of installed elevators—only behind the United States. In terms of the number of new elevators sold, China is by far the world market leader, with a demand of 500,000 to 600,000 per year. While India is currently the world's second-largest market for new elevators, its annual demand is only approximately 25,000. Therefore, without a doubt, Otis's growth rides on China's growth.

Initially operating a home replication strategy with a great deal of centralized control, Otis has found that it has to become more responsive to the unique needs and wants of its number-one growth market. For example, in North America and Europe, the mainstream elevator goes to the fifth floor and carries about five to six individuals. Such an elevator would be too small for China. The number-one best-selling elevator in China would go to the 15th floor, with a capacity to carry 11–13 individuals. Therefore, pushing a "global mainstream product," which is really based on the preferences of North American and European customers, would not go very far in China. Also, due to the much higher population density in China, elevators and escalators in China are

used more frequently by a lot more people, resulting in faster depreciation of machinery. As a result, designs catering to other markets need to be significantly strengthened and adapted to Chinese realities. Over time, given the importance of the China market, Otis has moved its global R&D center for high-speed elevators and escalators from Germany to China. The center's mandate is to not only serve China, but also Otis's worldwide markets. More broadly, the China subsidiary has been given more resources, power, and autonomy, which have underpinned its success.

In addition to products, services in China are also distinct from those elsewhere. In developed economies, more than 60% of Otis's revenues come from repair and maintenance. However, in China, the ratio is less than 10%. In other words, more than 90% of Otis's revenues in China come from selling and installing new elevators. This would not be a problem if China's economic growth—and the corresponding construction boom—continues. But this would become a huge problem when China's growth slows down. After all, there are only so many skyscrapers a city (or a country) can build. For example, anyone going to Shanghai in the 1990s and the 2000s would be very impressed by the rapid shooting up of high rises throughout the city. While still very impressive, the Shanghai skyline has not changed much in the 2010s. To Otis, this means the days of selling a lot of new elevators are over—in Shanghai at least. Whether Otis can transform the Chinese elevator market from new sales-driven to service-and-maintenance-driven remains a key to its future growth in China—and beyond.

Sources: Based on (1) *Business Management Review*, 2014, Otis in China, June: 29–30; (2) www.otis.com; (3) www.otisworldwide.com; (4) www.xiziotis.com.

global efficiencies, this strategy is effective when differences among national and regional markets are clear, and pressures for cost reductions are low. For example, Disney has attempted to localize some of its offerings in its five theme parks in Anaheim, California; Orlando, Florida; Hong Kong; Paris; and Tokyo. Its newest park in Shanghai will feature traditional Disney rides and those based on Chinese culture. It will drop a standard feature common in Disney parks: Main Street USA.

In terms of disadvantages, the localization strategy has high costs due to duplication of efforts in multiple countries. The costs of producing a variety of programming for MTV are obviously greater than the costs of producing one set of programming. As a result, this strategy is only appropriate in industries where the pressures for cost reductions are not significant. Another potential drawback is too much local autonomy, which happens when each subsidiary regards its country as so unique that it is difficult to introduce corporate-wide changes. In the 1980s, Unilever had 17 country subsidiaries in Europe. It took four *years* to persuade all 17 subsidiaries to introduce a single new detergent across Europe.

As the opposite of the localization strategy, global standardization strategy is sometimes referred to simply as "global strategy." Its hallmark is the development and distribution of standardized products worldwide in order to reap the maximum benefits from low-cost advantages. While both the home replication and global standardization strategies minimize local responsiveness, one crucial difference is that an MNE pursuing a global standardization strategy is not limited to its major operations at home. In a number of countries, the MNE may designate centers of excellence, defined as subsidiaries explicitly recognized as a source of important capabilities, with the intention that these capabilities be leveraged by, and/or disseminated to, other subsidiaries. Centers of excellence are often given a worldwide (or global) mandate—a charter to be responsible for one MNE function throughout the world. For example, Otis's China subsidiary has a worldwide mandate to develop and produce all of Otis's high-speed elevators for high-rises (see Emerging Markets 13.1). Huawei's Sweden subsidiary has a worldwide mandate in network consulting.

In terms of disadvantages, a global standardization strategy obviously sacrifices local responsiveness. This strategy makes great sense in industries where pressures for cost reductions are paramount and pressures for local responsiveness are relatively minor (particularly in commodity industries such as tires). However, as noted earlier, in industries ranging from automobiles to consumer products, a one-size-fits-all strategy may be inappropriate. Consequently, arguments such as "all industries are becoming global" and "all firms need to pursue a global (standardization) strategy" are potentially misleading.

Transnational strategy aims to capture the best of both worlds by endeavoring to be both cost efficient and locally responsive. In addition to cost efficiency and local responsiveness, a third hallmark of this strategy is global learning and diffusion of innovations. Traditionally, the diffusion of innovations in MNEs is a one-way flow from the home country to various host countries—the label "home replication" says it all. Underpinning the traditional one-way flow is the assumption that the home country is the best location for generating innovations. However, given that innovations are inherently risky and uncertain, there is no guarantee that the home country will generate the highest-quality innovations.

MNEs that engage in a transnational strategy promote global learning and diffusion of innovations in multiple ways. Innovations not only flow from the home country to host countries (which is the traditional flow), but also flow from host countries to the home country, and flow among subsidiaries in multiple host

Global standardization strategy

A strategy that focuses on development and distribution of standardized products worldwide in order to reap the maximum benefits from low-cost advantages.

Center of excellence

An MNE subsidiary explicitly recognized as a source of important capabilities, with the intention that these capabilities be leveraged by, and/or disseminated to, other subsidiaries.

Worldwide (global) mandate

A charter to be responsible for one MNE function throughout the world.

Transnational strategy

A strategy that endeavors to be simultaneously cost efficient, locally responsive, and learning-driven around the world.

countries (see the Closing Case). Kia Motors, for example, designs cars not only in Seoul, but also in Los Angeles and Frankfurt, tapping into automotive innovations generated in North America and Europe.

On the disadvantage side, a transnational strategy is organizationally complex and difficult to implement. The large amount of knowledge sharing and coordination may slow down decision making. Trying to achieve cost efficiencies, local responsiveness, and global learning simultaneously places contradictory demands on MNEs (to be discussed in the next section).

Overall, it is important to note that given the various pros and cons, there is no optimal strategy. The new trend in favor of a transnational strategy must be qualified with an understanding of its significant organizational challenges. This point leads to our next topic.

13-1c Four Organizational Structures

Figure 13.1 also shows four organizational structures that are appropriate for each strategic choice: (1) international division, (2) geographic area, (3) global product division, and (4) global matrix.

International division is typically used when firms initially expand abroad, often engaging in a home replication strategy. Figure 13.2 shows Starbucks's international division in addition to the four US-centric divisions. Although this structure is intuitively appealing, it often leads to two problems. First, foreign subsidiary managers, whose input is channeled through the international division, are not given sufficient voice relative to the heads of domestic divisions. Second, by design, the international division serves as a silo whose activities are not coordinated with the rest of the firm, which focuses on domestic activities. Consequently, many firms phase out this structure after their initial stage of overseas expansion.

Geographic area structure organizes the MNE according to different geographic areas (countries and regions). It is appropriate for a localization strategy. Figure 13.3 illustrates such a structure for Avon. A geographic area can be a country or a region, led by a country (or regional) manager. Each area is largely stand alone. In contrast to the limited voice of subsidiary managers in the international division structure, country (and regional) managers carry a great deal of weight in a geographic area structure. Interestingly and paradoxically, *both* the strengths and weaknesses of this structure lie in its local responsiveness. While being locally responsive can be a virtue, it also encourages the fragmentation of the MNE into fiefdoms.

International division

An organizational structure that is typically set up when firms initially expand abroad, often engaging in a home replication strategy.

Geographic area structure

An organizational structure that organizes the MNE according to different geographic areas (countries and regions).

Country (regional) manager

Manager of a geographic area, either a country or a region.

Figure 13.2 **International Division Structure at Starbucks**

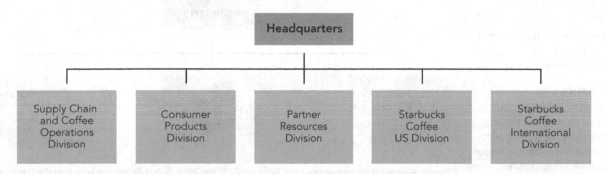

Sources: Adapted from (1) www.cogmap.com and (2) www.starbucks.com. Headquartered in Seattle, Starbucks is a leading international coffee and coffeehouse company.

| Figure 13.3 | **Geographic Area Structure at Avon Products** |

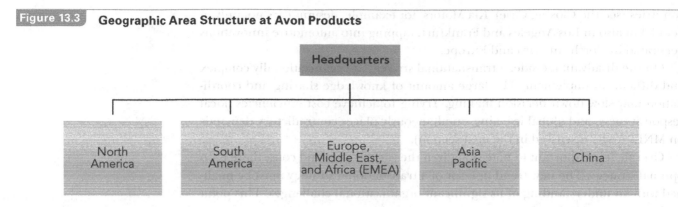

Source: Adapted from www.avoncompany.com. Headquartered in New York, Avon is a leading global beauty products company.

Global product division structure, which is the opposite of the geographic area structure, supports the global standardization strategy by assigning global responsibilities to each product division. Figure 13.4 shows an example from Airbus Group. This structure treats each product division as a stand-alone entity with full worldwide responsibilities. This structure is highly responsive to pressures for cost efficiencies, because it allows for consolidation on a worldwide (or at least regional) basis and reduces inefficient duplication in multiple countries. For example, Unilever reduced the number of soap-producing factories in Europe from ten to two after adopting this structure. Recently, because of the popularity of the global standardization strategy, the global product division structure is on the rise. Its main drawback is that local responsiveness suffers, as Ford discovered when it phased out the geographic area structure.

A global matrix alleviates the disadvantages associated with both geographic area and global product division structures, especially for MNEs adopting a transnational strategy. Shown in Figure 13.5, its hallmark is the coordination of responsibilities between product divisions and geographic areas.[3] In this hypothetical example, the country manager in charge of Japan—in short, the Japan manager—reports to Product Division 1 and Asia Division, both of which have equal power.

In theory, this structure supports the goals of the transnational strategy, but in practice it is often difficult to deliver. The reason is simple: While managers (such as the Japan manager in Figure 13.5) usually find dealing with one boss to

| Figure 13.4 | **Global Product Division Structure at Airbus Group** |

Global product division structure

An organizational structure that assigns global responsibilities to each product division.

Global matrix

An organizational structure often used to alleviate the disadvantages associated with both geographic area and global product division structures, especially for MNEs adopting a transnational strategy.

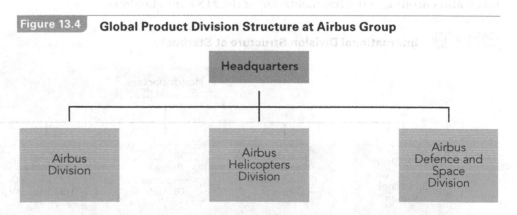

Source: Adapted from www.airbus.com. Between 2000 and 2014, Airbus Group was known as the European Aeronautic Defence and Space Company (EADS). Headquartered in Toulouse, France, Airbus Group is the largest commercial aircraft maker and the largest defense contractor in Europe.

Figure 13.5   **A Hypothetical Global Matrix Structure**

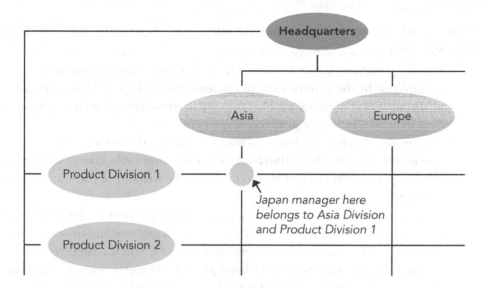

be headache enough, they do not appreciate having two bosses who are often in conflict (!). For example, Product Division 1 may decide that Japan is too tough a nut to crack and that there are more promising markets elsewhere, thus ordering the Japan manager to *curtail* his investment and channel resources elsewhere. This makes sense because Product Division 1 cares about its global market position and is not wedded to any particular country. However, Asia Division, which is evaluated by how well it does in Asia, begs to differ. Asia Division argues that it cannot afford to be a laggard in Japan if it expects to be a leading player in Asia. Therefore, Asia Division demands that the Japan manager *increase* his investment in the country. Facing these conflicting demands, the Japan manager, who prefers to be politically correct, does not want to make any move before consulting corporate headquarters. Eventually, headquarters may provide a resolution. But crucial time may be lost in the process, and important windows of opportunity for competitive actions may be missed.

Despite its merits on paper, the matrix structure may add layers of management, slow down decision speed, and increase costs while not showing significant performance improvement. There is no conclusive evidence for the superiority of the matrix structure. The following quote from the CEO of Dow Chemical, an early adopter of the matrix structure, is sobering:

> We were an organization that was matrixed and depended on teamwork, but there was no one in charge. When things went well, we didn't know whom to reward; and when things went poorly, we didn't know whom to blame. So we created a global product division structure, and cut out layers of management. There used to be 11 layers of management between me and the lowest-level employees; now there are five.[4]

Overall, the positioning of the four structures in Figure 13.1 is not random. They develop from the relatively simple international division through either geographic area or global product division structures and may finally reach the more complex global matrix stage. Not every MNE experiences all of these structural stages, and the movement is not necessarily in one direction. For example, the matrix structure's poster child, the Swedish–Swiss conglomerate ABB, recently withdrew from this structure.

13-1d The Reciprocal Relationship between Multinational Strategy and Structure

In one word, the relationship between strategy and structure is *reciprocal*. Three ideas stand out.

- Strategy usually drives structure.[5] The fit between strategy and structure, as exemplified by the *pairs* in each of the four cells in Figure 13.1, is crucial.[6] A misfit, such as combining a global standardization strategy with a geographic area structure, may have grave consequences.

- The relationship is not one way. As much as strategy drives structure, structure also drives strategy. The withdrawal from the unworkable matrix structure at MNEs such as ABB has called into question the wisdom of the transnational strategy.

- Neither strategy nor structure is static. It is often necessary to change strategy, structure, or both. In an effort to move toward a global standardization strategy, many MNEs have adopted a global product division structure while de-emphasizing the role of country headquarters. However, unique challenges in certain countries, especially China, have now pushed some MNEs to revive the country headquarters to coordinate numerous activities within a large, complex, and important host country.[7] Panasonic, for example, set up Panasonic Corporation of China to manage its 40-plus operations in China. A further experimentation is to have an emerging economies division, which is not dedicated to any single country but dedicated to pursuing opportunities in a series of emerging economies ranging from Brazil to Saudi Arabia. Cisco pioneered this structure, which has been followed by rivals such as IBM.[8]

Learning Objective
Explain how institutions and resources affect strategy, structure, and learning.

13-2 How Institutions and Resources Affect Multinational Strategies, Structures, and Learning

Having outlined the basic strategy/structure configurations, let us introduce how the institution-based and resource-based views shed light on these issues (see Figure 13.6).

Figure 13.6   **How Institutions and Resources Affect Multinational Strategy, Structure, and Learning**

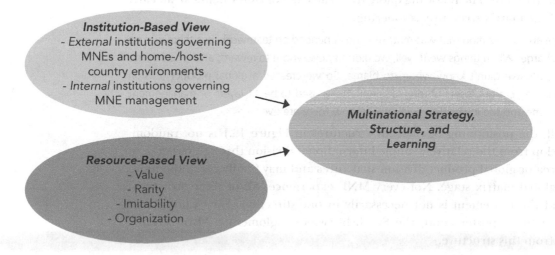

Institution-Based View
- *External* institutions governing MNEs and home-/host-country environments
- *Internal* institutions governing MNE management

Resource-Based View
- Value
- Rarity
- Imitability
- Organization

Multinational Strategy, Structure, and Learning

13-2a Institution-Based Considerations

MNEs face two sets of the rules of the game: Formal and informal institutions governing (1) *external* relationships and (2) *internal* relationships. Each is discussed in turn.

Externally, MNEs are subject to the formal institutional frameworks erected by various home-country and host-country governments.[9] In order to protect domestic employment, the British government taxes the foreign earnings of British MNEs at a higher rate than their domestic earnings.

Host-country governments, on the other hand, often attract, encourage, or coerce MNEs into undertaking activities that they otherwise would not. For example, basic manufacturing generates low-paying jobs, does not provide sufficient technology spillovers, and carries little prestige. Advanced manufacturing, R&D, and regional headquarters, on the other hand, generate better and higher-paying jobs, provide more technology spillovers, and lead to better prestige. Therefore, host-country governments (such as those in China, Hungary, and Singapore) often use a combination of carrots (such as tax incentives and free infrastructure upgrades) and sticks (such as threats to block market access) to attract MNE investments in higher value-added areas (see In Focus 13.1).

IN FOCUS 13.1
MOVING HEADQUARTERS OVERSEAS

Ethical Dilemma

A number of MNEs have moved headquarters (HQ) overseas (see Table 13.2). In general, there are two levels of HQ: *business unit* HQ and *corporate* HQ. The question is: Why?

If you have moved from one house to another in the same city, you can easily appreciate the logistical challenges (and nightmares!) associated with relocating HQ overseas. One simple answer is that the benefits must significantly outweigh the drawbacks. At the business unit level, the answer is straightforward: the "center of gravity" of the activities of a business unit may pull its HQ toward a host country. See the following letter to suppliers from IBM's chief procurement officer informing them of the move to China:

> IBM Global Procurement is taking a major step toward developing a more geographically distributed executive structure. . . By anchoring the organization in this location, we will be better positioned to continue developing the skills and talents of our internal organization in the region . . . Clearly, this places us closer to the core of the technology supply chain which is important, not only for IBM's own internal needs, but increasingly for the needs

of external clients whose supply chains we are managing via our Procurement Services offerings. As IBM's business offerings continue to grow, we must develop a deeper supply chain in the region to provide services and human resource skills to clients both within Asia and around the world.

At the corporate level, there are at least five strategic rationales. First, a leading symbolic value is an unambiguous statement to various stakeholders that the firm is a global player. News Corporation's new corporate HQ in New York is indicative of its global status, as opposed to being a relatively parochial firm from "down under." Lenovo's coming of age is undoubtedly underpinned by the establishment of its second HQ in the United States.

Second, there may be significant efficiency gains. If the new corporate HQ is in a major financial center, such as New York or London, the MNE can have more efficient and more frequent communication with institutional shareholders, financial analysts, and investment banks. The MNE also increases its visibility in a financial market, resulting in a broader shareholder base and greater market capitalization. Three

IN FOCUS 13.1 (continued)

Table 13.2 **Examples of Moving Headquarters Overseas**

Corporate headquarters	From	To
HSBC	Hong Kong	London, UK
IKEA	Stockholm, Sweden	Leiden, Netherlands
Lenovo	Beijing, China*	Raleigh (suburb), North Carolina, USA
News Corporation	Melbourne, Australia	New York, USA
Old Mutual	Cape Town, South Africa	London, UK
Tetra Pak	Lund, Sweden	Lausanne (suburb), Switzerland
Business unit headquarters		
Chevron Asia Pacific Division	San Francisco (suburb), California, USA	Singapore
IBM Global Procurement Division	Armonk, New York, USA	Shenzhen, China
P&G Global Cosmetics and Personal Care	Cincinnati, Ohio, USA	Singapore
Nokia Finance Division	Helsinki, Finland	New York, USA
Nomura Investment Banking Division	Tokyo, Japan	London, UK

*Lenovo maintains dual headquarters in both Beijing and North Carolina.

leading (former) South African firms, Anglo American, Old Mutual, and SABMiller, have now joined the FTSE 100—the top 100 UK firms by capitalization.

Third, firms may benefit from their visible commitment to the laws of the new host country. They can also benefit from the higher-quality legal and regulatory regime they now operate under. These benefits are especially crucial for firms from emerging economies where local rules are not world class. A lack of confidence about South Africa's political stability drove Anglo American, Old Mutual, and SABMiller to London. By moving to London in 1992, HSBC likewise deviated from its Hong Kong roots at a time when the political future of Hong Kong was uncertain.

Fourth, moving corporate HQ to a new country clearly indicates a commitment to that country. In addition to political motivation, HSBC's move to London signaled its determination to become a more global player, instead of being a regional player centered on Asia. HSBC indeed carried out this more global strategy since the 1990s. However, in an interesting twist of events, HSBC's CEO relocated back to Hong Kong in 2010. Technically, HSBC's corporate HQ is still in London, and its chairman remains in London. However, the symbolism of the CEO's return to Hong Kong is clear. As China becomes more economically powerful, HSBC is interested in demonstrating its commitment to that important part of the world, which was where HSBC started. (HSBC was set up in Hong Kong in 1865 as Hongkong and Shanghai Banking Corporation.)

Finally, by moving (or threatening to move) HQ, firms enhance their bargaining power vis-à-vis that of their (original) home-country governments. Tetra Pak's move of its HQ to Switzerland was driven primarily by the owners' tax disputes with the Swedish government. Likewise, as three of Britain's large banks—Barclays, HSBC, and Standard Chartered, the three best-run ones that did not need bailouts during the Great Recession of 2008–2009—now face higher taxes and more government intervention, they, too, have threatened to move their HQ out of London. The message is clear: If the home-country government treats us harshly, we will pack our bags.

The last point, of course, is where the ethical and social responsibility controversies erupt. In 2014, Fiat announced its plan to merge itself and Chrysler into a new Netherlands-based holding company Fiat Chrysler Automobiles NV. So Fiat will in the end leave Italy—on paper at least. Although the absolute number of jobs lost is not great, these are high-quality (and high-paying) jobs that every government would prefer to see. For MNEs' home countries, if a sufficient number of HQ move overseas, there is a serious ramification that other high-quality service providers, such as lawyers, bankers, and accountants, will follow them. In response, proposals are floating to offer tax incentives for these "footloose" MNEs to keep HQ at home. However, critics question why these wealthy MNEs (and executives) need to be subsidized (or bribed), while many other sectors and individuals are struggling.

Sources: Based on (1) M. Baaij & A. Slangen, 2013, The role of headquarters-subsidiary geographic distance in strategic decisions by spatially disaggregated headquarters, *Journal of International Business Studies*, 44: 941–952; (2) G. Benito, R. Lunnan, & S. Tomassen, 2011, Distant encounters of the third kind: Multinational companies locating divisional headquarters abroad, *Journal of Management Studies*, 48: 373–394; (3) *Economist*, 2011, HSBC: Gulliver's travels, April 16: 75–77; (4) *Economist*, 2014, Here, there and everywhere, February 22: 56–57; (5) IBM, 2006, IBM Procurement headquarters moves to Shenzhen, China, May 22, www-03.ibm.com; (6) T. Laamanen, T. Simula, & S. Torstila, 2012, Cross-border relocations of headquarters in Europe, *Journal of International Business Studies*, 43: 187–210; (7) P. Nell & B. Ambos, 2013, Parenting advantage in the MNC, *Strategic Management Journal*, 34: 1086–1103; (8) M. W. Peng & W. Su, 2014, Cross-listing and the scope of the firm, *Journal of World Business*, 49: 42–50; (9) *Wall Street Journal*, 2009, HSBC re-emphasizes its "H," September 26, www.wsj.com; (10) *Wall Street Journal*, 2013, Chevron is placing big bets on Australia, July 8, www.wsj.com.

In addition to formal institutions, MNEs also confront a series of informal institutions governing their relationships with *home* countries (see In Focus 13.1). In the United States, few laws ban MNEs from aggressively setting up overseas subsidiaries, although the issue is a hot button in public debate. Therefore, managers contemplating such moves must consider the informal but vocal backlash against such activities due to the associated losses in domestic jobs.

Dealing with *host* countries also involves numerous informal institutions. Airbus spends 40% of its procurement budget with US suppliers in 40 states. While there is no formal requirement for Airbus to farm out supply contracts, its sourcing is guided by the informal norm of reciprocity: If one country's suppliers are involved with Airbus, airlines based in that country are more likely to buy Airbus aircraft.

Institutional factors affecting MNEs are not only external. How MNEs are governed *internally* is also determined by various formal and informal rules of the game. Formally, organizational charts, such as those in Figures 13.2 to 13.5, specify the scope of responsibilities for various parties. Most MNEs have systems of evaluation, reward, and punishment in place based on these formal rules.

What the formal organizational charts do not reveal are the informal rules of the game, such as organizational norms, values, and networks. The nationality of the head of foreign subsidiaries is an example. Given the lack of formal regulations, MNEs essentially have three choices:

- a home-country national as the head of a subsidiary (such as an American for a subsidiary of a US-headquartered MNE in India).
- a host-country national (such as an Indian for the same subsidiary above).
- a third-country national (such as an Australian for the same subsidiary above).

MNEs from different countries have different norms when making these appointments. Most Japanese MNEs follow an informal rule: Heads of foreign subsidiaries, at least initially, must be Japanese nationals. In comparison, European MNEs are more likely to appoint host-country and third-country nationals to lead subsidiaries. As a group, US MNEs are somewhere between Japanese and European practices. These staffing approaches may reflect strategic differences.

Home-country nationals, especially long-time employees of the same MNE at home, are more likely to have developed a better understanding of the informal workings of the firm and to be better socialized into its dominant norms and values. Consequently, the Japanese propensity to appoint home-country nationals is conducive to their preferred global standardization strategy, which values globally coordinated and controlled actions. Conversely, the European comfort in appointing host-country and third-country nationals is indicative of European MNEs' (traditional) preference for a localization strategy.

Beyond the nationality of subsidiary heads, the nationality of top executives at the highest level (such as chairman, CEO, and board members) seems to follow another informal rule: They are almost always home-country nationals. To the extent that top executives are ambassadors of the firm and that the MNE's country of origin is a source of differentiation (for example, a German MNE is often perceived to be different from an Italian MNE), home-country nationals would seem to be the most natural candidates for top positions.

In the eyes of stakeholders such as employees and governments around the world, however, a top echelon consisting of largely one nationality does not bode well for an MNE aspiring to globalize everything it does. Some critics argue that this "glass ceiling" reflects "corporate imperialism."[10] Consequently, BP, Citigroup, Coca-Cola, Electrolux, GSK, HP, Lenovo, Microsoft, Nissan, Nokia, PepsiCo, and Sony have appointed foreign-born executives to top posts. Nestlé boasts executive board members from eight countries other than Switzerland. Such foreign-born executives bring substantial diversity to the firm, which may be a plus.

What are the challenges associated with non-native top executives at multinationals?

However, such diversity puts an enormous burden on these non-native top executives to clearly articulate the values and exhibit behaviors expected of senior managers of an MNE associated with a particular country. In 2010, HP appointed Léo Apotheker, a native of Germany, to be its CEO. Unfortunately, HP lost US$30 billion in market capitalization during his short tenure (over ten months), thanks to his numerous change initiatives. He was quickly fired in 2011. Since then, the old rule is back: HP is again led by an American executive.

Overall, while formal internal rules on how the MNE is governed may reflect conscientious strategic choices, informal internal rules are often taken for granted and deeply embedded in administrative heritages, thus making them difficult to change.

13-2b Resource-Based Considerations

Shown in Figure 10.6, the resource-based view—exemplified by the value, rarity, imitability, and organization (VRIO) framework—adds a number of insights.[11] First, when looking at structural changes, it is critical to consider whether a new structure (such as a matrix) adds concrete *value*. The value of innovation must also be considered. A vast majority of innovations simply fail to reach market, and most new products that do reach market end up being financial failures. The difference between an innovator and a *profitable* innovator is that the latter not only has plenty of good ideas, but also lots of complementary assets (such as appropriate organizational structures and marketing muscles) to add value to innovation. Philips, for example, is a great innovator. It invented rotary shavers, video cassettes, and CDs. Still, its ability to profit from these innovations lags behind that of Matsushita, Samsung, and Sony.

A second question is *rarity*. Certain strategies or structures may be in vogue at a given point in time. So, for example, when a company's rivals all move toward a global standardization strategy, this strategy cannot be a source of differentiation. To improve global coordination, many MNEs spend millions of dollars to equip themselves with enterprise resource planning (ERP) packages provided by SAP and Oracle. However, such packages are designed to be implemented widely and appeal to a broad range of firms, thus providing no firm-specific advantage for any particular adopting firm.

Even when capabilities are valuable and rare, they have to pass a third hurdle—*imitability*. Formal structures are easier to observe and imitate than are informal structures. This is one of the reasons why the informal, flexible matrix is in vogue now. The informal, flexible matrix "is less a structural classification than a broad organizational concept or philosophy, manifested in organizational capability and management mentality."[12] Obviously, imitating an intangible mentality is much harder than imitating a tangible structure.

The last hurdle is *organization*—namely, how MNEs are organized, both formally and informally, around the world.[13] One elusive, but important, concept is organizational culture. Recall from Chapter 3 that culture is defined by Hofstede as "the collective programming of the mind which distinguishes the members of one group or category of people from another." We can extend this concept to define organizational culture as the collective programming of the mind that distinguishes members of one organization from another. Huawei, for example, is known to have a distinctive "wolf" culture, which centers on "continuous hunting" and "relentless pursuit" with highly motivated employees who routinely work overtime and sleep in their offices. Although rivals can imitate everything Huawei does technologically, their biggest hurdle lies in their inability to wrap their arms around its "wolf" culture.

Organizational culture
The collective programming of the mind that distinguishes the members of one organization from another.

13-3 Worldwide Learning, Innovation, and Knowledge Management

13-3a Knowledge Management

Learning Objective
Outline the challenges associated with learning, innovation, and knowledge management.

Underpinning the recent emphasis on worldwide learning and innovation is the emerging interest in knowledge management.[14] Knowledge management can be defined as the structures, processes, and systems that actively develop, leverage, and transfer knowledge.

Many managers regard knowledge management as simply information management. Taken to an extreme, "such a perspective can result in a profoundly mistaken belief that the installation of sophisticated information technology (IT) infrastructure is the be-all and end-all of knowledge management."[15] Knowledge management

Knowledge management
The structures, processes, and systems that actively develop, leverage, and transfer knowledge.

depends not only on IT, but also on informal social relationships within the MNE.[16] This is because there are two categories of knowledge: (1) explicit knowledge and (2) tacit knowledge. Explicit knowledge is codifiable—it can be written down and transferred with little loss of richness. Virtually all of the knowledge captured, stored, and transmitted by IT is explicit. Tacit knowledge is non-codifiable, and its acquisition and transfer require hands-on practice. For example, reading a driver's manual (a ton of explicit knowledge) without any road practice does not make you a good driver. Tacit knowledge is evidently more important and harder to transfer and learn. It can only be acquired through learning by doing (driving in this case). Consequently, from a resource-based view, explicit knowledge captured by IT may be strategically *less* important. What counts is the hard-to-codify and hard-to-transfer tacit knowledge.

13-3b Knowledge Management in Four Types of Multinational Enterprises

Explicit knowledge

Knowledge that is codifiable (can be written down and transferred with little loss of richness).

Tacit knowledge

Knowledge that is non-codifiable, whose acquisition and transfer require hands-on practice.

Shown in Table 13.3, differences in knowledge management among four types of MNEs in Figure 13.1 fundamentally stem from the interdependence (1) between the headquarters and subsidiaries, and (2) among various subsidiaries.[17] In MNEs pursuing a home replication strategy, such interdependence is moderate, and the role of subsidiaries is largely to adapt and leverage parent-company competencies (see Figure 13.7 on Mary Kay around 2005). Thus, knowledge on new products and technologies is mostly developed at the center and flown to subsidiaries, representing the traditional one-way flow. Starbucks, for example, insists on replicating its US coffee shop concept around the world, down to the elusive "atmosphere."

Table 13.3 **Knowledge Management in Four Types of Multinational Enterprises**

Strategy	Home replication	Localization	Global standardization	Transnational
Examples	Apple, Baidu, Carrefour, Google, Harley Davison, Kraft, P&G, Starbucks, Wal-Mart	Heinz, Johnson & Johnson, KFC, McDonald's, Nestlé, Pfizer, Unilever	Canon, Caterpillar, Haier, HP, Huawei, LVMH, Otis, Texas Instruments, Toyota	GE, Häagen-Dazs, IBM, Kikkoman, Panasonic, Tata, Zara
Interdependence	Moderate	Low	Moderate	High
Role of foreign subsidiaries	Adapting and leveraging parent company competencies	Sensing and exploiting local opportunities	Implementing parent company initiatives	Differentiated contributions by subsidiaries to integrate worldwide operations
Development and diffusion of knowledge	Knowledge developed at the center and transferred to subsidiaries	Knowledge developed and retained within each subsidiary	Knowledge mostly developed and retained at the center and key locations	Knowledge developed jointly and shared worldwide
Flow of knowledge	Extensive flow of knowledge and people from headquarters to subsidiaries	Limited flow of knowledge and people in both directions (to and from the center)	Extensive flow of knowledge and people from center and key locations to subsidiaries	Extensive flow of knowledge and people in multiple directions

Sources: Adapted from (1) C. Bartlett & S. Ghoshal, 1989, *Managing Across Borders: The Transnational Solution* (p. 65), Boston: Harvard Business School Press; (2) T. Kostova & K. Roth, 2003, Social capital in multinational corporations and a micro-macro model of its formation (p. 299), *Academy of Management Review*, 28: 297–317. Examples are added by M. W. Peng.

Figure 13.7 **Mary Kay in 2005**

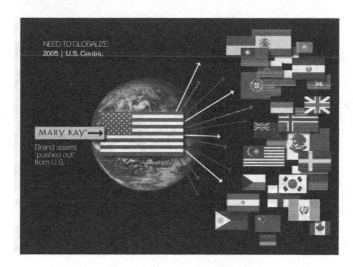

Source: © Mary Kay Inc.

When MNEs adopt a localization strategy, the interdependence is low. Knowledge management centers on developing insights that can best serve local markets. Ford of Europe used to develop cars for Europe, with a limited flow of knowledge to and from headquarters. In MNEs pursuing a global standardization strategy, on the other hand, the interdependence is increased. Knowledge is developed and retained at the headquarters and a few centers of excellence. Consequently, knowledge and people typically flow from headquarters and these centers to other subsidiaries. For example, Yokogawa Hewlett-Packard, HP's subsidiary in Japan, won a coveted Japanese Deming Award for quality. The subsidiary was then charged with transferring such knowledge to the rest of HP, which resulted in a tenfold improvement in corporate-wide quality in ten years.

A hallmark of transnational MNEs is a high degree of interdependence, and extensive and bi-directional flows of knowledge (see the Closing Case). Kikkoman first developed teriyaki sauce specifically for the US market as a barbecue glaze. It was then marketed to Japan and the rest of the world. Similarly, Häagen-Dazs developed a popular ice cream in Argentina based on a locally popular caramelized milk dessert. The company then took the new flavor and sold it as Dulce De Leche throughout the United States and Europe. Within one year, it became the second-most-popular Häagen-Dazs ice cream (next only to vanilla). Particularly fundamental to transnational MNEs is knowledge flows among dispersed subsidiaries. Instead of a top-down hierarchy, the MNE thus can be conceptualized as an integrated network of subsidiaries. Each subsidiary not only develops locally relevant knowledge but also aspires to contribute knowledge to benefit the MNE as a whole (see Figure 13.8 on Mary Kay today).

13-3c Globalizing Research and Development (R&D)

R&D represents a crucial arena for knowledge management. Relative to production and marketing, only more recently has R&D emerged as an important function to be internationalized—often known as innovation-seeking investment.[18] The intensification of competition for innovation drives the globalization of R&D. Such

Figure 13.8   Mary Kay Today

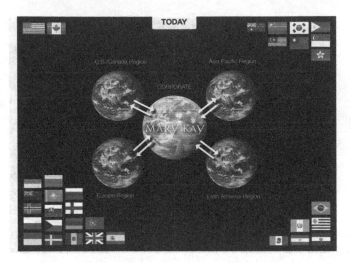

Source: © Mary Kay Inc.

R&D provides a vehicle to access a foreign country's talents and expertise.[19] Recall earlier discussions in Chapters 6 and 10 on the importance of *agglomeration* of high-caliber innovative firms within a country. For foreign firms, a most effective way to access such a cluster is to be there through foreign direct investment (FDI)—as Shiseido did in France by setting up a perfume lab there.

From a resource-based standpoint, a fundamental basis for competitive advantage is innovation-based firm heterogeneity (being different). Decentralized R&D performed by different locations and teams around the world virtually guarantees that there will be persistent heterogeneity in the solutions generated.[20] GSK, for example, has aggressively spun off R&D units, because it realizes that adding more researchers in centralized R&D units does not necessarily enhance global learning and innovation.[21] GE's China units have developed low-cost, portable ultrasound machines at a fraction of the cost of existing machines developed in the United States. GE has not only been selling the developed-in-China machines throughout emerging economies, but has also brought them back to the United States and other developed economies.

Open innovation

The use of purposive inflows and outflows of knowledge to accelerate internal innovation and expand the markets for external use of innovation.

13-3d Problems and Solutions in Knowledge Management

Institutionally, how MNEs employ the formal and informal rules of the game has a significant bearing behind the success or failure of knowledge management.[22] Shown in Table 13.4, a number of informal "rules" can become problems in knowledge management. In knowledge acquisition, many MNEs prefer to invent everything internally. However, for large firms, R&D actually offers *diminishing* returns. Consequently, a new model, open innovation, is emerging.[23] Open innovation is "the use of purposive inflows and outflows of knowledge to accelerate internal

What are some of the ways that global virtual team members can effectively communicate knowledge among themselves?

Triangle Images/Photodisc/Getty Images

Table 13.4	Problems in Knowledge Management
Areas	**Common problems**
Knowledge acquisition	Failure to share and integrate external knowledge
Knowledge retention	Employee turnover and knowledge leakage
Knowledge outflow	"How does it help me?" syndrome and "knowledge is power" mentality
Knowledge transmission	Inappropriate channels
Knowledge inflow	"Not invented here" syndrome and absorptive capacity

Source: Adapted from A. Gupta & V. Govindarajan, 2004, *Global Strategy and Organization* (p. 109), New York: Wiley.

innovation and expand the markets for external use of innovation."[24] It relies on more collaborative research, among various internal units, external firms, and university labs. Firms that skillfully share research outperform those that fail to do so.

In knowledge retention, the usual problems of employee turnover are compounded when such employees are key R&D personnel, whose departure will lead to knowledge leakage.[25] In knowledge outflow, there is the "How does it help me?" syndrome. Specifically, managers of the source subsidiary may view the outbound sharing of knowledge as a diversion of scarce time and resources. Further, some managers may believe that "knowledge is power"—monopolizing certain knowledge may be viewed as the currency to acquire and retain power within the MNE.

Even when certain subsidiaries are willing to share knowledge, inappropriate transmission channels may still torpedo effective sharing.[26] It is tempting to establish global virtual teams, which do not meet face to face, to transfer knowledge. Unfortunately, such teams often have to confront tremendous communication and relationship barriers.[27] Videoconferences can hardly show body language, and Skype often breaks down. Thus, face-to-face meetings are often still necessary. Finally, recipient subsidiaries may block successful knowledge inflows. First, the "not invented here" syndrome creates a resistance to ideas from other units. Second, recipients may have limited absorptive capacity—the "ability to recognize the value of new information, assimilate it, and apply it."[28]

As solutions to combat these problems, headquarters can manipulate the formal "rules of the game," such as (1) tying bonuses to measurable knowledge outflows and inflows, (2) using high-powered corporate-based or unit-based incentives (as opposed to individual-based and single-subsidiary-based incentives), and (3) investing in codifying tacit knowledge (such as the codification of the Toyota Way). However, these formal policies fundamentally boil down to the very challenging (if not impossible) task of how to accurately measure inflows and outflows of tacit knowledge. The nature of tacit knowledge simply resists such formal bureaucratic practices. Consequently, MNEs often have to rely on a great deal of informal integrating mechanisms, such as (1) facilitating management and R&D personnel networks among various subsidiaries through joint teamwork, training, and conferences; and (2) promoting strong organizational (i.e., MNE-specific) cultures and shared values and norms for cooperation among subsidiaries (see the Closing Case).

Global virtual team

Team whose members are physically dispersed in multiple locations in the world and often operate on a virtual basis.

Absorptive capacity

The ability to recognize the value of new information, assimilate it, and apply it.

Instead of using traditional formal command-and-control structures that are often ineffective, knowledge management is best facilitated by informal social capital, which refers to the informal benefits that individuals and organizations derive from their social structures and networks.[29] Because of the existence of social capital, individuals are more likely to go out of their way to help friends and acquaintances. Consequently, managers of the Canada subsidiary are more likely to help managers of the China subsidiary with needed knowledge if they know each other and have some social relationship. Otherwise, managers of the Canada subsidiary may not be as enthusiastic to provide such help if the call for help comes from managers of the Chile subsidiary, with whom there is no social relationship. Overall, the micro informal interpersonal relationships among managers of various units may greatly facilitate macro intersubsidiary cooperation among various units—in short, a micro-macro link.[30]

Learning Objective
Participate in three leading debates concerning multinational strategy, structure, and learning.

13-4 Debates and Extensions

The question of how to manage complex MNEs has led to numerous debates, some of which have been discussed earlier (such as the debate on the matrix structure). Here we outline two leading debates not previously discussed: (1) corporate controls versus subsidiary initiatives; and (2) customer-focused dimensions versus integration, responsiveness, and learning.

13-4a Corporate Controls versus Subsidiary Initiatives

One of the leading debates on how to manage large firms is centralization versus decentralization.[31] Within an MNE, the debate boils down to central controls versus subsidiary initiatives. A starting point is that subsidiaries are not necessarily at the receiving end of commands from headquarters. When headquarters promote certain practices (such as ethics training), some subsidiaries may be in full compliance, others may pay lip service to them, and still others may simply refuse to adopt them, citing local differences.[32]

In addition to reacting to headquarters' demands differently, some subsidiaries may actively pursue their own *subsidiary*-level strategies and agendas.[33] These activities are known as subsidiary initiatives, defined as the proactive and deliberate pursuit of new opportunities by a subsidiary (see In Focus 13.2). Advocates argue that such initiatives may inject a much-needed spirit of entrepreneurship throughout the larger bureaucratic MNE (see the Closing Case).

However, from the perspective of corporate headquarters, it is hard to distinguish between good-faith subsidiary initiative and opportunistic "empire building."[34] A lot is at stake when determining which subsidiary initiatives are supported.[35] Subsidiaries whose initiatives fail to receive support may see their roles marginalized and, in the worst case, their facilities closed. Subsidiary managers are often host-country nationals, who would naturally prefer to strengthen their subsidiary. However, these tendencies, although very understandable, are not necessarily consistent with the MNE's *corporate*-wide goals. These tendencies, if not checked and controlled, can surely lead to chaos. According to the title of an influential article authored by Andy Grove, former chairman and CEO of Intel, the challenge for MNE management is:

"Let chaos reign, then reign in chaos—repeatedly."[36]

Social capital

The informal benefits individuals and organizations derive from their social structures and networks.

Micro-macro link

The micro, informal interpersonal relationships among managers of various units may greatly facilitate macro, intersubsidiary cooperation among these units.

Subsidiary initiative

The proactive and deliberate pursuit of new opportunities by a subsidiary.

IN FOCUS 13.1

A SUBSIDIARY INITIATIVE AT BAYER MATERIALSCIENCE NORTH AMERICA

Bayer Group is a US$50 billion chemical and health care giant based in Germany. Its three main product divisions are Bayer MaterialScience (BMS), Bayer CropScience, and Bayer HealthCare. In this matrix organization, each of these product divisions has country/regional subsidiaries in major markets. Between 2004 and 2011, the CEO for Bayer MaterialScience North America (BMS NA) was Greg Babe. Contributing 25% of BMS's global revenues, BMS NA delivered highly respected performance. It had strong sales growth in 2005 (US$3.5 billion, increasing from US$2.7 billion in 2004) and suffered a modest flattening in 2006 (US$3.3 billion). However, in early 2007, BMS made a radical decision: to dismantle BMS NA—in other words, to shut down the North America regional headquarters in Pittsburgh. Allegedly undermining cost competitiveness, the regional structure was viewed as too bloated.

Shocked, Babe asked for time to propose another solution. In his own words: "The stakes couldn't have been higher: not only the future of my position but the credibility of the entire regional operation was in question." Cost cutting was nothing unusual in this cyclical industry, and the norm was usually to shave off a certain percentage of overhead (such as 10%). A month into the analysis, Babe and his team had an "aha" moment. The cost structure, they realized, should be dictated by how they grew the business, not by an arbitrary target. With that insight, they looked at the overall picture through a strategic-growth lens rather than a tactical cost-reduction lens. They set two specific goals: (1) to grow at 1% to 2% above GDP; and (2) to save 25% on selling, general, and administrative (SG&A) costs. To deliver that, Babe not only needed to completely reshape his unit, but also needed additional investment of US$70 million.

In late 2007, when Babe presented to BMS's global leadership team, everyone expected him to come up with a cost-cutting exercise. Instead, he presented a subsidiary growth initiative. BMS's global leadership team challenged key concepts of the proposal, many of which deviated from Bayer's global norms. For example, transportation was historically deemed by Bayer as a core competence. Babe proposed to outsource it, which would allow customers to give 12 (rather than 72) hours' notice for shipping. Overall, Babe promised to turn BMS NA into a lean-growth engine. In the end, the bold proposal paid off. Babe left the meeting with US$70 million in hand. In his own words:

I was excited, but also scared to death, because delivering on it was by no means going to be easy. It would require laying off hundreds of employees and retraining more than 1,000 others, outsourcing many operations, rolling out new IT systems, and modifying our product offerings, all within 18 months—not much time for a project of that scale.

To make the matters worse, the chemical industry soon entered a severe downturn worldwide, and BMS suffered eight consecutive quarters of declining sales starting in 2008. In such a bleak environment, BMS NA's efforts became more strategically important. By early 2009, BMS NA delivered on everything Babe had promised: it reduced SG&A costs by 25% (US$100 million) and head count by 30%. It actually overdelivered: only US$60 million of the US$70 million allotted for growth was spent. By 2010, BMS NA's sales turned around and enjoyed double-digit quarterly growth (2010 sales went up to US$2.7 billion from the bottom of US$2.1 billion in 2009). What was more valuable was that some of the reorganized processes (such as outsourcing transportation), so foreign at the time to BMS, now became implemented by BMS around the world. Overall, by endorsing the regional subsidiary's initiative, BMS's global leadership team took some significant risk. But in the end, the payoff was handsome.

Sources: Based on (1) G. Babe, 2011, The CEO of Bayer Corp. on creating a lean growth engine, *Harvard Business Review*, July: 41–45; (2) Bayer AG, 2014, www.bayerus.com.

13-4b Customer-Focused Dimensions versus Integration, Responsiveness, and Learning

As discussed earlier, juggling the three dimensions of integration, responsiveness, and learning has often made the global matrix structure so complex that it is unworkable. However, instead of simplifying, many MNEs have added new dimensions. Often, new customer-focused dimensions of structure are placed on top of an existing structure, resulting in a four- or five-dimension matrix.[37]

Of the two primary customer-focused dimensions, the first is a global account structure to supply customers (which often are other MNEs) in a coordinated and consistent way across various countries.[38] Most original equipment manufacturers (OEMs)—namely, contract manufacturers that produce goods *not* carrying their own brands (such as the makers of Nike shoes and Microsoft Xbox)—use this structure. The second customer-focused dimension is the oft-used solutions-based structure. For instance, as a "customer solution" provider, IBM will sell whatever combination of hardware, software, and services that customers prefer, whether that means selling IBM's or rivals' products.

The typical starting point is to put in place temporary solutions rather than create new layers or units. However, this ad hoc approach can quickly get out of control, resulting in subsidiary managers' additional duties of reporting to three or four "informal bosses" (acting as global account managers) on top of their "day jobs." Eventually, new formal structures may be called for, resulting in more bureaucracy. So what is the solution when confronting the value-added potential of customer-focused dimensions and their associated complexity and cost? One solution is to *simplify*. For instance, ABB, when facing performance problems, transformed its sprawling "Byzantine" matrix structure to a mere two product divisions.

Learning Objective
Draw implications for action.

13-5 Management Savvy

MNEs are the ultimate large, complex, and geographically dispersed business organizations. What determines the success or failure of multinational strategies, structures, and learning? The answer boils down to the institution-based and resource-based dimensions. The institution-based view calls for thorough understanding and skillful manipulation of the rules of the game, both at home and abroad. The resource-based view focuses on the development of firm-specific capabilities to enhance the odds for success.

Shown in Table 13.5, three clear implications emerge for savvy managers. First, understanding and mastering the external rules of the game governing MNEs and home-country/host-country environments become a must.[39] For

Global account structure
A customer-focused dimension that supplies customers (often other MNEs) in a coordinated and consistent way across various countries.

Solution-based structure
A customer-focused solution in which a provider sells whatever combination of goods and services the customers prefer, including rivals' offerings.

Table 13.5   **Implications for Action**
• Understand and master the external rules of the game governing MNEs and home-country/host-country environments
• Understand and be prepared to change the internal rules of the game governing MNE management
• Develop learning and innovation capabilities to leverage multinational presence as an asset—"think global, act local"

example, some MNEs take advantage of the rules that subsidiaries in different countries must be registered as independent legal entities in these countries, and claim that other subsidiaries do not have to be responsible for the wrongdoing of one subsidiary in one country. Other MNEs abandon their original countries of origin and move their headquarters to be governed by more market-friendly laws and regulations in their new countries of domicile (see In Focus 13.1). Despite the Swedish flags in front of its stores, IKEA is now a *Dutch* company, having set up its headquarters in Leiden, the Netherlands, and enjoyed lower (and, thus, more friendly) taxes there.

Second, managers need to understand and be prepared to change the internal rules of the game governing MNE management. Different strategies and structures call for different internal rules. Some facilitate, and others constrain, MNE actions. A firm using a home replication strategy should not look to hire a foreign-born executive as its CEO. Yet, as operations become more global, an MNE's managerial outlook must be broadened as well.

Finally, managers must actively develop learning and innovation capabilities to leverage multinational presence. One winning formula is "*think global, act local.*"[40] The Opening Case illustrates how McDonald's leverages its global presence and learns from its European operations in order to solve a local problem—back home in the United States customers do not find McDonald's food to be as fresh, healthy, and cool as those offered by rivals. The Closing Case illustrates how LEGO overcame its initial resistance to a new idea that came from its North America subsidiary.

CHAPTER SUMMARY/LEARNING OBJECTIVES

13-1 Describe the relationship between multinational strategy and structure.

- Governing multinational strategy and structure is an integration-responsiveness framework.
- There are four strategy/structure pairs: (1) home replication strategy/international division structure, (2) localization strategy/geographic area structure, (3) global standardization strategy/global product division structure, and (4) transnational strategy/global matrix structure.

13-2 Explain how institutions and resources affect strategy, structure, and learning.

- MNEs are governed by external and internal rules of the game around the world.
- Management of MNE structure, learning, and innovation needs to take into account of VRIO.

13-3 Outline the challenges associated with learning, innovation, and knowledge management.

- Knowledge management primarily focuses on tacit knowledge.
- Globalization of R&D calls for capabilities to combat a number of problems associated with knowledge creation, retention, outflow, transmission, and inflow.

13-4 Participate in two leading debates on multinational structure, learning, and innovation.

- (1) Corporate controls versus subsidiary initiatives; and (2) customer-focused dimensions versus integration, responsiveness, and learning

13-5 Draw implications for action.

- Understand and master the external rules of the game governing MNEs and home-country/host-country environments.
- Understand and be prepared to change the internal rules of the game governing MNEs.
- Develop learning and innovation capabilities to leverage multinational presence as an asset—"think global, act local."

KEY TERMS

Absorptive capacity, 421
Center of excellence, 408
Country (regional)
  manager, 409
Explicit knowledge, 418
Geographic area
  structure, 409
Global account
  structure, 424
Global matrix, 410
Global product division
  structure, 410
Global standardization
  strategy, 408

Global virtual team, 421
Home replication
  strategy, 405
Integration-
  responsiveness
  framework, 405
International division, 409
Knowledge
  management, 417
Local responsiveness, 405
Localization (multi-
  domestic) strategy, 406
Micro-macro link, 422
Open innovation, 420

Organizational
  culture, 417
Social capital, 422
Solution-based
  structure, 424
Subsidiary initiative, 422
Tacit knowledge, 418
Transnational
  strategy, 408
Worldwide (global)
  mandate, 408

REVIEW QUESTIONS

1. The pressure to reduce costs is common to both domestic and international competition, but what additional kind of pressure is unique to international competition?
2. Referring to Figure 13.1, describe the four strategic choices and the four corresponding organizational structures in the integration-responsiveness framework.
3. List three examples of how formal and informal external institutions affect MNEs.
4. Describe some of the informal rules of the game that govern what type of individual an MNE can appoint to be the head of a foreign subsidiary.
5. Summarize the insights revealed by using a VRIO framework to analyze a potential structural change.
6. In your opinion, what type of knowledge is more important to an MNE—explicit or tacit? Why?
7. How is knowledge developed and disseminated in each of the four types of MNEs?
8. *ON CULTURE:* Name one problem with a global virtual team and how you would solve the problem? How would cultural differences make the problem worse?

9. What are some of the actions that MNEs can take to combat common problems in knowledge management?

10. Which do you think would be more integral to a firm's success: corporate controls or subsidiary-level strategies and agendas?

11. Describe the two primary customer-focused dimensions that many MNEs add to their global matrix structures.

12. From time to time, a manager may be faced with the need to change the internal rules of the game within his or her MNE. What skills and capabilities may be useful in achieving this?

13. What is your interpretation of the phrase "Think global, act local"?

14. After reviewing PengAtlas Map 2.1, in your opinion, how do you explain why most of the top ten exporters are also among the top ten importers?

15. After comparing PengAtlas Map 2.1 and 2.2, in your opinion, why are most of the top ten on 2.1 also on 2.2?

CRITICAL DISCUSSION QUESTIONS

1. In this age of globalization, some gurus argue that all industries are becoming global and that all firms need to adopt a global standardization strategy. Do you agree? Why or why not?

2. *ON ETHICS:* You are the head of the best-performing subsidiary in an MNE. Because bonuses are tied to subsidiary performance, your bonus is the highest among managers of all subsidiaries. Now headquarters is organizing managers from other subsidiaries to visit and learn from your subsidiary. You are worried that if performance at other subsidiaries improves, then your subsidiary will no longer be a star unit and your bonus will go down. What are you going to do?

3. *ON ETHICS:* You are a Peruvian national who serves as head of the Brazilian subsidiary of a large US multinational. While Brazil is theoretically attractive, the going has been tough and chances for becoming profitable in the next five years are not great. Headquarters has asked for your recommendation on whether to increase or decrease investment in Brazil. If a decision to cut investment in Brazil is indeed made, it is possible to focus on other Latin American countries, such as Peru. Since your parents are aging, you personally would be interested in leading operations in Peru so that you can be closer to them. What would be your recommendation?

GLOBAL ACTION

1. Currently, considerable growth has been documented in Latin American and Caribbean economies. Based on the specific regulations in each country, part of your company's strategy in the Western Hemisphere is to ensure that contracts made by the firm are agreed to and abided by in all business dealings. Since your company has sales offices in every Latin American and Caribbean economy, where should your company focus first? Provide detailed justification for your choices.

2. **To remain competitive, a multinational steel company needs to reconfigure its operations to align with worldwide production. As a consultant on world steel production, provide a report that indicates appropriate personnel and resource allocation to each region of the world. As a part of your analysis, be sure to include your analysis for specific countries in which your client should maintain regional headquarters.**

CLOSING CASE

Subsidiary Initiative at LEGO North America

In 1997, Peter Eio, head of LEGO North America, proposed to LEGO Group senior management at its headquarters in Denmark, the idea of licensing *Star Wars* characters for LEGO toys. This would enable LEGO to capitalize on the anticipated release of the new *Star Wars* trilogy starting with *The Phantom Menace* in 1999. From his North America headquarters in Enfield, Connecticut, Eio was convinced that the US toy market had become a license-driven market. Licensed toys such as Disney characters from Disney movies and Buzz Lightyear from *Toy Story* accounted for half of all toys sold in the United States. Despite its success, LEGO's go-it-alone culture had prevented it from leveraging any licensed products up to this point.

Northern Exposure Photography/Alamy

Encouraged by Lucasfilm executives who were LEGO fans and who wanted to partner with LEGO, Eio thought he had proposed a winning product that would enable LEGO to get into the world of licensing. Unfortunately, LEGO senior executives' initial reaction, according to Eio himself, "was one of shock and horror. It wasn't the LEGO way." Specifically, LEGO executives felt LEGO did not need to license intellectual property from another player. Further, the specific characters centered on war and violence would violate one of LEGO founder Ole Kirk Christiansen's core values: never let war seem like child's play. According to critics, the very name, *Star Wars*, would violate the essence of the LEGO identity. Heated debate took place. One executive even claimed, "Over my dead body will LEGO ever introduce *Star Wars*."

During the next round, Eio and his team surveyed parents in the United States to gauge their opinion on

the marriage between LEGO and *Star Wars*. He also convinced his colleague in charge of Germany, which was LEGO's largest and by far its most conservative market, to conduct a similar survey. While US parents strongly supported the idea, German parents were also enthusiastic. Armed with such supportive consumer data, Eio pushed this subsidiary-driven initiative further and continued to meet resistance and push-back from senior executives at headquarters. Eventually, the founder's grandson and the president and CEO of LEGO Group at that time, Kjeld Kirk Kristiansen, who was a *Star Wars* fan himself, overruled his conservative executives and gave the licensing deal his blessing. In 1999, LEGO *Star Wars* products were released on the wings of the blockbuster *The Phantom Menace*, becoming one of the most successful product launches not only for LEGO, but also for the global toy industry. In the end, more than one-sixth of LEGO Groups' earnings in the early 2000s came from the *Star Wars* line.

CASE DISCUSSION QUESTIONS

1. What did LEGO North America do when corporate headquarters rejected its initial ideas?

2. Why do most multinational headquarters not pay sufficient attention to ideas from subsidiaries?

3. What are the lessons we can draw from the successful pushing of one subsidiary initiative in this case? What are the do's and don'ts?

Sources: Based on (1) the author's interviews; (2) *Economist*, 2014, Unpacking Lego, March 8: 71; (3) D. Robertson, 2013, *Brick by Brick: How LEGO Rewrote the Rules of Innovation and Conquered the Global Toy Industry*, New York: Crown.

NOTES

[**Journal acronyms**] **AME**—*Academy of Management Executive;* **AMJ**—*Academy of Management Journal;* **AMP**—*Academy of Management Perspectives;* **APJM**—*Asia Pacific Journal of Management;* **AMR**—*Academy of Management Review;* **ASQ**—*Administrative Science Quarterly;* **BW**—*BusinessWeek* (before 2010) or *Bloomberg Businessweek* (since 2010); **GSJ**—*Global Strategy Journal;* **HBR**—*Harvard Business Review;* **JIBS**—*Journal of International Business Studies;* **JIM**—*Journal of International Management;* **JMS**—*Journal of Management Studies;* **JWB**—*Journal of World Business;* **MIR**—*Management International Review;* **OSc**—*Organization Science;* **SMJ**—*Strategic Management Journal*

1 T. Levitt, 1983, The globalization of markets, *HBR,* May: 92–102.

2 J. Arregle, P. Beamish, & L. Hebert, 2009, The regional dimension of MNEs' foreign subsidiary localization, *JIBS*, 40: 86–107; C. Asmussen, 2009, Local, regional, or global? *JIBS*, 40: 1192–1205.

3 W. Egelhoff, J. Wolf, & M. Adzic, 2013, Designing matrix structures to fit MNC strategy, *GSJ*, 3: 205–226.

4 R. Hodgetts, 1999, Dow Chemical CEO William Stavropoulos on structure, *AME,* 13: 30.

5 A. Chandler, 1962, *Strategy and Structure*, Cambridge, MA: MIT Press. See also W. C. Kim & R. Mauborgne, 2009, How strategy shapes structure, *HBR*, September: 73–80; J. Galan & M. Sanchez-Bueno, 2009, The continuing validity of the strategy–structure nexus, *SMJ*, 30: 1234–1243.

6 J. Garbe & N. Richter, 2009, Causal analysis of the internationalization and performance relationship based on neural networks, *JIM*, 15: 413–431.

7 X. Ma, A. Delios, & C. Lau, 2013, Beijing or Shanghai? *JIBS,* 44: 953–961.

8 *BW*, 2008, Cisco's brave new world, November 24: 56–66.

9 E. Clark & M. Geppert, 2011, Subsidiary integration as identity construction and institution building, *JMS*, 48: 395–416; P. Regner & J. Edman, 2014, MNE institutional advantage, *JIBS*, 45: 275–302.

10 C. K. Prahalad & K. Lieberthal, 1998, The end of corporate imperialism, *HBR,* August: 68–79.

11 S. Morris, R. Hammond, & S. Snell, 2014, A microfoundations approach to transnational capabilities, *JIBS*, 45: 405–427; J. Vahlne & I. Ivarsson, 2014, The globalization of Swedish MNEs, *JIBS,* 45: 227–247.

12 C. Bartlett & S. Ghoshal, 1989, *Managing Across Borders* (p. 209), Boston: Harvard Business School Press.

13 M. Hada, R. Grewal, & M. Chandrashekaran, 2013, MNC subsidiary channel relationships as extended links, *JIBS*, 44: 787–812; L. Nachum & S. Song, 2011, The MNE as a portfolio, *JIBS*, 42: 381–405; G. McDermott, R. Mudambi, & R. Parente, 2013, Strategic modularity and the architecture of multinational firm, *GSJ*, 3: 1–7;

J. MacDuffie, 2013, Modularity-as-property, modularization-as-process, and 'modularity'-as-frame, *GSJ*, 3: 8–40.

14 N. Driffield, J. Love, & S. Menghinello, 2010, The MNE as a source of international knowledge flows, *JIBS*, 41: 350–359; N. Foss, K. Husted, & S. Michailova, 2010, Governing knowledge sharing in organizations, *JMS*, 47: 455–482; A. Fransson, L. Hakanson, & P. Liesch, 2011, The underdetermined knowledge-based theory of the MNC, *JIBS*, 42: 427–435; J. Martin & K. Eisenhardt, 2010, Rewiring, *AMJ*, 53: 265–301; S. Tallman & A. Chacar, 2011, Knowledge accumulation and dissemination in MNEs, *JMS*, 48: 278–304; H. Yang, C. Phelps, & H. K. Steensma, 2010, Learning from what others have learned from you, *AMJ*, 53: 371–389; J. Zhang & C. Baden–Fuller, 2010, The influence of technological knowledge base and organizational structure on technology collaboration, *JMS*, 47: 679–704.

15 A. Gupta & V. Govindarajan, 2004, *Global Strategy and Organization* (p. 104), New York: Wiley.

16 P. Gooderham, D. Minbaeva, & T. Pedersen, 2011, Governance mechanisms for the promotion of social capital for knowledge transfer in MNCs, *JMS*, 48: 123–150.

17 T. Ambos, P. Nell, & T. Pedersen, 2013, Combining stocks and flows of knowledge, *GSJ*, 3: 283–299.

18 K. Asakawa & A. Som, 2008, Internationalizing R&D in China and India, *APJM*, 25: 375–394; R. Belderbos, B. Leten, & S. Suzuki, 2013, How global is R&D, *JIBS*, 44: 765–786; D. Castellani, A. Jimenez, & A. Zanfei, 2013, How remote are R&D labs? *JIBS*, 44: 649–675; N. Lahiri, 2010, Geographic distribution of R&D activity, *AMJ*, 53: 1194–1209; A. Minin & M. Bianchi, 2011, Safe nests in global nets, *JIBS*, 42: 910–934; M. Nieto & A. Rodriguez, 2011, Offshoring of R&D, *JIBS*, 42: 345–361.

19 N. Foss, J. Lyngsie, & S. Zahra, 2013, The role of external knowledge sources and organizational design in the process of opportunity exploitation, *SMJ*, 34: 1453–1471; M. W. Peng & D. Wang, 2000, Innovation capability and foreign direct investment, *MIR*, 40: 79–83.

20 I. Guler & A. Nerkar, 2012, The impact of global and local cohesion on innovation in the pharmaceutical industry, *SMJ*, 33: 535–549; E. Tippmann, P. Scott, & V. Mangematin, 2012, Problem solving in MNCs, *JIBS*, 43: 746–771.

21 A. Witty, 2011, Research and develop (p. 140), *The World in 2011*, London: The Economist Group. Witty is CEO of GSK.

22 Y. Yanadori & V. Cui, 2013, Creating incentives for innovation? *SMJ*, 34: 1502–1511.

23 H. Hoang & F. Rothaermel, 2010, Leveraging internal and external experience, *SMJ*, 31: 734–758.

24 H. Chesbrough, W. Vanhaverbeke, & J. West (eds.), 2006, *Open Innovation* (p. 1), Oxford, UK: Oxford University Press. See also

P. Gianiodis, J. Ettlie, & J. Urbina, 2014, Open service innovation in the global banking industry, *AMP*, 28: 76–91.

25 Q. Yang & C. Jiang, 2007, Location advantages and subsidiaries' R&D activities, *APJM*, 24: 341–358.

26 A. Dinur, R. Hamilton, & A. Inkpen, 2009, Critical context and international intrafirm best-practice transfers, *JIM*, 15: 432–446; H. Gardner, F. Gino, & B. Staats, 2012, Dynamically integrating knowledge in teams, *AMJ*, 55: 998–1022; D. Gnyawali, M. Singal, & S. Mu, 2009, Knowledge ties among subsidiaries in MNCs, *JIM*, 15: 387–400; A, Pieterse, D. van Knippenberg, & D. van Dierendonck, 2013, Cultural diversity and team performance, *AMJ*, 56: 782–804.

27 M. Haas, 2010, The double-edged swords of autonomy and external knowledge, *AMJ*, 53: 989–1008; K. Raab, B. Ambos, & S. Tallman, 2014, Strong or invisible hands? *JWB*, 49: 32–41; Z. Sharp, 2010, From unilateral transfer to bilateral transition, *JIM*, 16: 304–313.

28 W. Cohen & D. Levinthal, 1990, Absorptive capacity, *ASQ*, 35: 128–152. See also Y. Chang, Y. Gong, & M. W. Peng, 2012, Expatriate knowledge transfer, subsidiary absorptive capacity, and subsidiary performance, *AMJ*, 55: 927–948; A. Cuervo-Cazurra & C. A. Un, 2010, Why some firms never invest in formal R&D, *SMJ*, 31: 759–779; L. Perez-Nordtvedt, E. Babakus, & B. Kedia, 2010, Learning from international business affiliates, *JIM*, 16: 262–274.

29 N. Noorderhaven & A. Harzing, 2009, Knowledge-sharing and social interaction within MNEs, *JIBS*, 40: 719–741; S. Schleimer & T. Pedersen, 2014, The effects of MNC parent effort and social structure on subsidiary absorptive capacity, *JIBS*, 45: 303–320.

30 M. W. Peng & Y. Luo, 2000, Managerial ties and firm performance in a transition economy, *AMJ*, 43: 486–501. See also D. Levin & H. Barnard, 2013, Connections to distant knowledge, *JIBS*, 44: 676–698; M. Mors, 2010, Innovation in a global consulting firm, *SMJ*, 31: 841–872; M. Reinholt, T. Pedersen, & N. Foss, 2011, Why a central network position isn't enough, *AMJ*, 54: 1277–1297; Z. Zhao & J. Anand, 2013, Beyond boundary spanners, *SMJ*, 34: 1513–1530.

31 S. Wang, Y. Luo, X. Lu, J. Sun, & V. Maksimov, 2014, Autonomy delegation to foreign subsidiaries, *JIBS*, 45: 111–130.

32 F. Ciabuschi, M. Forsgren, & O. Martin, 2011, Rationality versus ignorance, *JIBS*, 42: 958–970.

33 C. Garcia–Pont, I. Canales, & F. Noboa, 2009, Subsidiary strategy, *JMS*, 46: 182–214; X. Tian & J. Slocum, 2014, What determines MNC subsidiary performance? *JWB*, 49: 421–430.

34 T. Ambos, U. Andersson, & J. Birkinshaw, 2010, What are the consequences of initiative-taking in multinational subsidiaries? *JIBS*, 41: 1099–1118; F. Ciabuschi, H. Dellestrand, & O. Martin, 2011, Internal embeddedness, headquarters involvement, and innovation importance in MNEs, *JMS*, 48: 1612–1638; I. Filatotchev & M. Wright, 2011, Agency perspectives on corporate governance of multinational enterprises, *JMS*, 48: 471–486.

35 J. Balogun, P. Jarzabkowski, & E. Vaara, 2011, Selling, resistance, and reconciliation, *JIBS*, 42: 765–786; H. Dellestrand, 2011, Subsidiary embeddedness as a determinate of divisional headquarters involvement in innovation transfer processes, *JIM*, 17: 229–242; C. Dorrenbacher & J. Gammelgaard, 2010, MNCs, inter-organizational networks, and subsidiary charter removals, *JWB*, 45: 206–216; P. Scott, P. Gibbons, & J. Coughlan, 2010, Developing subsidiary contribution to the MNC-subsidiary entrepreneurship and strategy creativity, *JIM*, 16: 328–339; A. Schotter & P. Beamish, 2011, Performance effects of MNC headquarters-subsidiary conflict and the role of boundary spanners, *JIM*, 17: 243–259.

36 R. Burgelman & A. Grove, 2007, Let chaos reign, then reign in chaos—repeatedly, *SMJ*, 28: 965–979.

37 S. Segal–Horn & A. Dean, 2009, Delivering "effortless" experience across borders, *JWB*, 44: 41–50.

38 L. Shi, C. White, S. Zou, & S. T. Cavusgil, 2010, Global account management strategies, *JIBS*, 41: 620–638.

39 K. Meyer, R. Mudambi, & R. Narula, 2011, Multinational enterprises and local contexts, *JMS*, 48: 235–252.

40 S. Gould & A. Grein, 2009, Think glocally, act glocally, *JIBS*, 40: 237–254.

© Lonely/Shutterstock.com

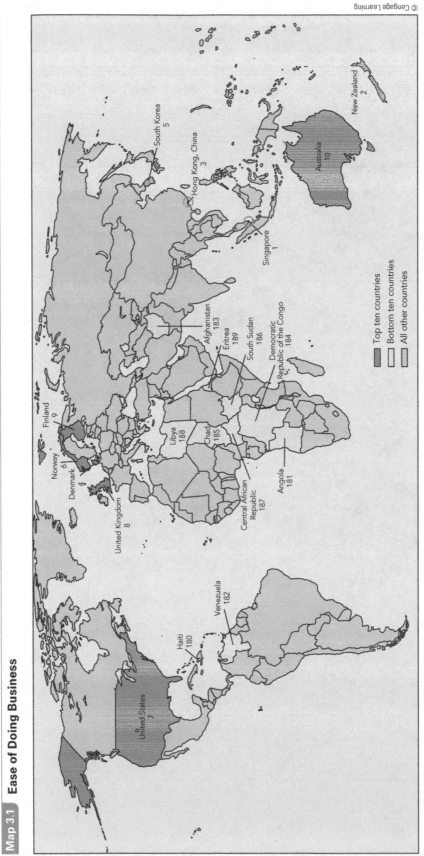

Map 3.1 Ease of Doing Business

© Cengage Learning

Top ten countries

Bottom ten countries

All other countries

New Zealand 2

Australia 10

South Korea 5

Hong Kong, China 3

Singapore 1

Afghanistan 183

Eritrea 189

South Sudan 186

Democratic Republic of the Congo 184

Angola 181

Central African Republic 187

Chad 185

Libya 188

Finland 9

Norway 6

Denmark 4

United Kingdom 8

United States 7

Haiti 180

Venezuela 182

Source: Data extracted from www.doingbusiness.org/rankings. *Doing Business 2014.*

Map 3.2 **Top Reformers in Doing Business**

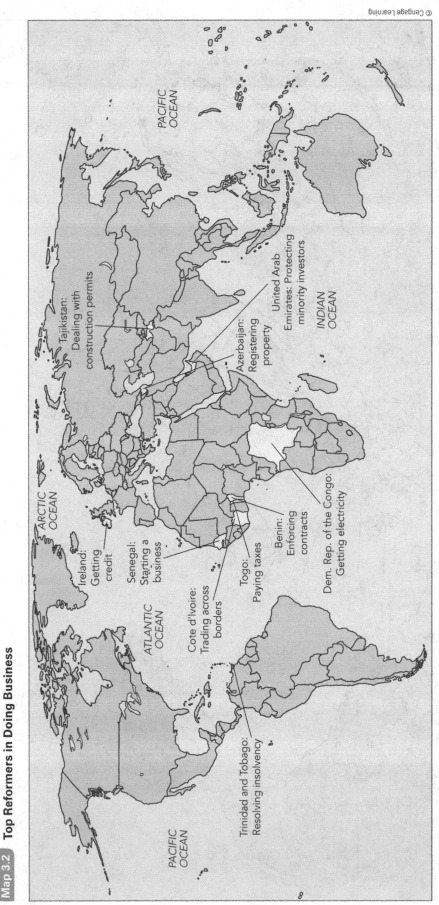

© Cengage Learning

Tajikistan:
Dealing with
construction permits

Ireland:
Getting
credit

Senegal:
Starting a
business

Cote d'Ivoire:
Trading across
borders

Togo:
Paying taxes

Trinidad and Tobago:
Resolving insolvency

Azerbaijan:
Registering
property

United Arab
Emirates: Protecting
minority investors

Benin:
Enforcing
contracts

Dem. Rep. of the Congo:
Getting electricity

ARCTIC
OCEAN

ATLANTIC
OCEAN

PACIFIC
OCEAN

PACIFIC
OCEAN

INDIAN
OCEAN

Source: Data extracted from http://www.doingbusiness.org/reforms/top-reformers-2015.

Map 3.3 Top 20 Countries by GDP

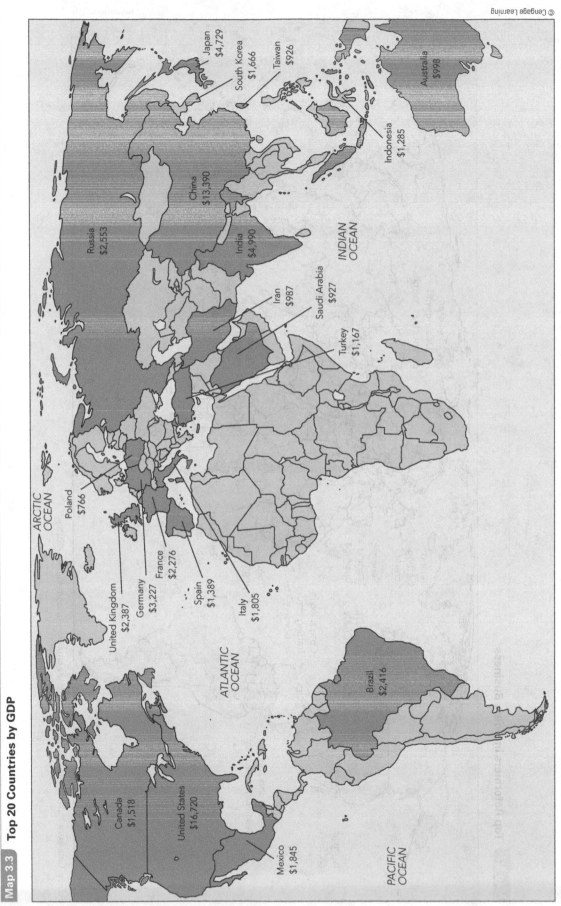

© Cengage Learning

Source: Adapted from Country Comparison: GDP CIA World Factbook, 2013. Amounts in billions of US dollars.

© Cengage Learning

Map 3.4 Top Ten and Bottom Ten Countries by Per Capita Income

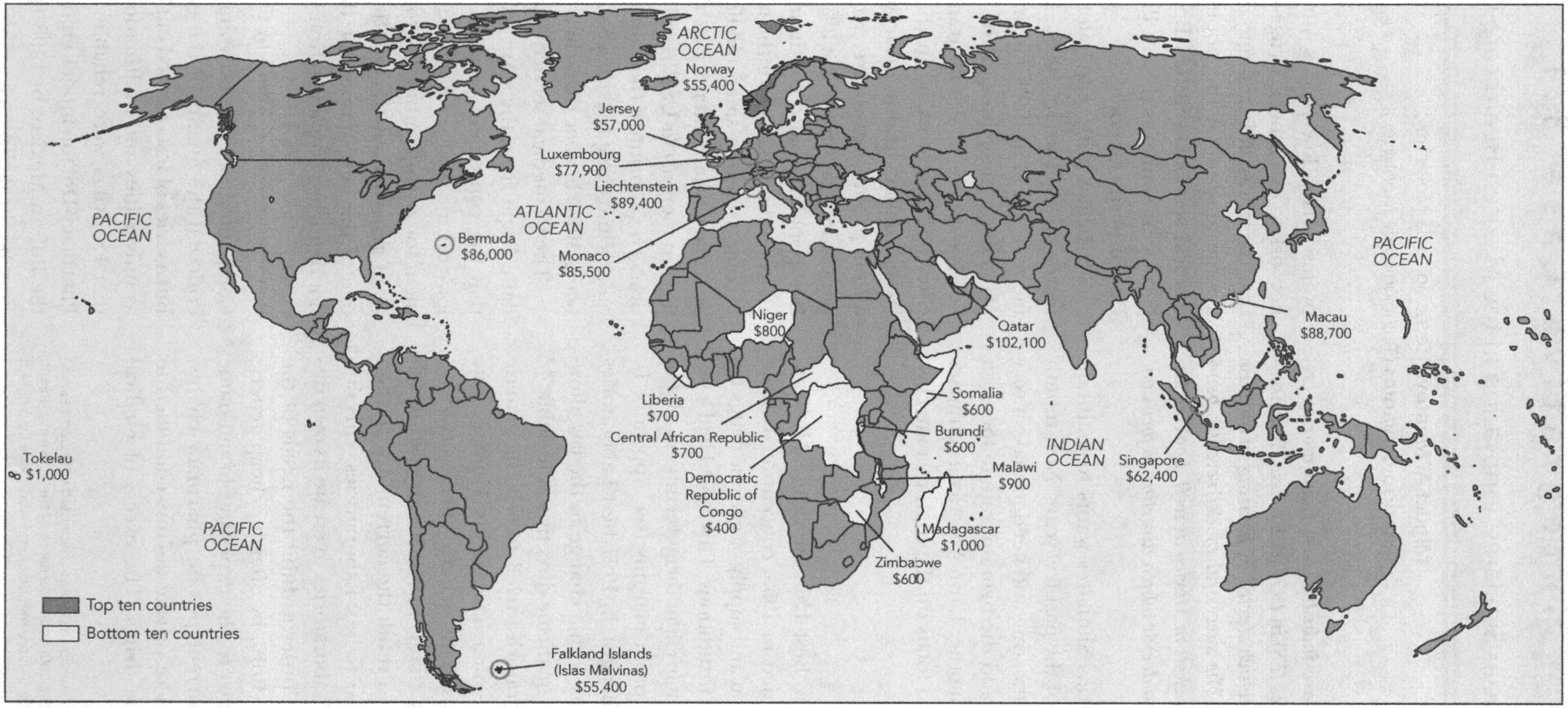

PACIFIC OCEAN

Macau $88,700

Singapore $62,400

INDIAN OCEAN

Qatar $102,100

Somalia $600

Burundi $600

Malawi $900

Madagascar $1,000

Zimbabwe $600

Niger $800

Liberia $700

Central African Republic $700

Democratic Republic of Congo $400

ARCTIC OCEAN

Norway $55,400

Jersey $57,000

Luxembourg $77,900

Liechtenstein $89,400

Monaco $85,500

ATLANTIC OCEAN

Bermuda $86,000

Falkland Islands (Islas Malvinas) $55,400

PACIFIC OCEAN

Tokelau $1,000

Top ten countries

Bottom ten countries

Source: Adapted from Central Intelligence Agency, 2013, *The World Factbook 2013*. Amounts in US dollars.

Integrative Case 3.1

Farmacias Similares: Innovating in the Mexican Healthcare Industry[1]

Miguel A. Montoya (Tecnológico de Monterrey)

Mauricio Cervantes (Tecnológico de Monterrey)

In the Mexican healthcare industry, Best Laboratories created Farmacias Similares (FS) in 1997 with a new Pharmacy-Doctor business model, which started by focusing on the base of the pyramid (BoP). The successful model recently penetrated higher-income markets in Mexico as well. Looking forward, the Board needs to decide which direction to focus on.

The Board of Farmacias Similares wants to maintain the firm growth rate of the past few years. Next month it will have its annual meeting and need to make a very strategic decision: should the firm migrate to focus on the low-income class in other Latin American countries or should it migrate to focus on the high-income class in Mexico.

Introduction

For over four decades, Best Laboratories, a Mexican-owned company founded in 1953, concentrated exclusively on the production and supply of generic drugs for Mexican public health institutions. This model had a significant weakness: a single client the government, a lot of competition, and low profit margins (see Appendix 1). Faced with these challenges, in 1997 Best Laboratories saw a huge opportunity with a change in the law allowing the sale of generic medicine directly to the public.[2]

At first Best Laboratories tried to sell the generic drugs through private pharmacy chains. However, due to a campaign to discredit generic medicine, existing private pharmacy chains in Mexico refused to sell the generic drugs. As a result the current distribution channels were of no use to Best Laboratories. This situation motivated Best Laboratories to create its own distribution channels in order to fulfil the needs of the base of the pyramid (BoP), by offering cheap generic drugs in direct contrast to the expensive brand-name drugs sold by the current private pharmacy chains. However, the majority of private doctors continued to prescribe brand-name drugs. The excess of medical

professionals, low profits, and refusal of the private network to use generic drugs—combined with the fact that there was only a single client and that there was a large amount of the population without access to medical services—pushed Best Laboratories to create Farmacias Similares (FS) in 1997 with a new Pharmacy-Doctor business model.

FS began with one pilot model in 1997, which increased to two in 1998. There was then a large increase to 144 in 1999. The initial objective was to supply generic medicines to the BoP population without access to public health insurance (59% in 1997), mainly covering those working in the informal economy who lacked public health insurance and who could not afford private healthcare. At that time the Mexican population was growing at 2% annually, with the urban BoP population also continuing to expand, signifying an expanding market for the new service. The FS model is comprised of a small medical clinic attached to the pharmacy where clients visit the doctor for a nominal fee (no more than US$2) and receive a quick prescription. The consumer then purchases the generic drugs quickly and cheaply at the FS pharmacy, with most drugs being 50% cheaper than their brand-name equivalents.

The FS medical service is available for over 12 hours daily. Right from the start, users interviewed reported that the convenient location of the pharmacies, the low-cost medical service, and the lack of the requirement for an appointment—together with the availability of generic medicine at affordable prices—made FS one of the best options for the treatment of illnesses not requiring hospitalization.

Increasing Market Share in the Low-Cost Segment

Competitors of FS (mostly multinational drug makers) criticized the quality of the generic drugs sold by FS. But a series of tests carried out by the authorities, as well as universities and multinational laboratories, showed that FS drugs were reliable. The innovative low-cost Pharmacy-Doctor model enjoyed rapid growth within the BoP in Mexico: in 1998 the company had two in-store medical clinics, a number that expanded to 1,215

1) © Miguel A. Montoya and Mauricio Cervantes. Reprinted with permission.
2) Generic medications are those sold under the name of the active ingredient, in contrast to brand-name drugs that are manufactured worldwide by different pharmaceutical companies for brand-name owners.

in 2003, 3,630 in 2008, and 4,053 in 2011. More than 5 million visits a month were recorded in 2011, with the cost of the medical consultation being approximately US$2. FS only sold generic drugs, and over 220 million generic units were sold in 2013, achieving a market penetration of 60% of units sold. The Pharmacy-Doctor business model immediately began to spread within the industry. GI Pharmacies began operations in 1999, simultaneously piloting the low-cost Pharmacy-Doctor model for the BoP population and purchasing generic drugs from several laboratories. GI is only a distributor: it has no dedicated laboratories and no plans to integrate the entire process in the same manner as FS.

The successful Pharmacy-Doctor business model for those lacking health insurance pioneered by FS gradually became threatened by new legislation. At the beginning of 2003, the government launched the Seguro Popular (universal public health insurance), offering medical coverage to all Mexicans with no formal employment and therefore without access to IMSS or ISSSTE. Seguro Popular coverage grew rapidly, and by 2011 more than 49 million Mexicans were affiliated (43% of the population). As a result, when adding 52 million Social Security system users and users of other public health systems, the country's public health coverage reached over 89% of the population. The market segment of the BoP for FS was therefore reduced from 59% in 1997 to 11% in 2011. As the innovation grew in acceptance, an unforeseen factor came into play: the ability of the system to save service-users time. Although IMSS, ISSSTE, and Seguro Popular are totally free, they have a long waiting list for their services, including emergencies. The BoP population is mostly employed in the informal sector, meaning if people lose time waiting for medical services they lose their daily wage. It is also difficult for employees to obtain permission to visit the doctor's office. BoP clients prefer to spend an average between US$7 and US$10 on a doctor's prescription and medicine than to lose their daily wage waiting in line for free public services.

Despite the increase in public health coverage, the new Pharmacy-Doctor model continued to grow. The perception of poor quality of public health services (such as significant waiting time before being seen by a doctor and a lack of medicine in public health institutions) provided an opportunity for the consolidation of the new model. An interview with a lower middle-class user of state-run medical services revealed that: "even with an advance appointment, the waiting time for a consultation is about *three* hours." The interviewee

further stated that visiting the doctor with no appointment involved an average wait of more than *five* hours, despite the average consultation not exceeding ten minutes. Finally, the interviewee claimed that "in most cases, four out of five, the drug is not free".

As the Pharmacy-Doctor model started to become more established, positive discussions on the quality of generic medicines and brand-name rights between FS and international drug makers began to take place, resulting in collaboration between the various actors. An example of this would be Sandoz de Mexico, the generic division of the Novartis Group, which began to work towards becoming the supplier for FS. Regardless of the efficiency of implementation and the increasing healthcare coverage resulting from Seguro Popular, the FS Pharmacy-Doctor model continued to grow. The emergence of the model and its nationwide diffusion in the BoP by FS was a huge success.

Imitators in the High-Income Level Segment

Up until 2011, FS and GI focused on servicing the BoP and had no plans to enter the healthcare field for the middle or upper class in Mexico. In 2009, external events once again affected the dynamics of the model. Mexico was affected by a pandemic (the H1N1 influenza virus), leading to increased regulations of drug sales and making a prescription mandatory for the sale of antibiotics. This became a strong contributing factor to the diffusion of the business model. The treatment of H1N1 was complicated because the Mexican population was accustomed to self-medication without the necessity of a prescription. The lack of national regulations preventing the sale of antibiotics without a prescription and the prevalence of self-medication led to the deaths of several people affected by H1N1. In order to address this problem, in May 2010 the government tightened the regulations governing the sale of drugs, particularly the sale of antibiotics. These legislative changes, combined with an ever-increasing time-poor middle and upper classes, helped the Pharmacy-Doctor model to diffuse to large segments of the population.

In 2011, the majority of the national pharmacy chains had adopted the Pharmacy-Doctor model in most of their branches, not just in areas populated by the BoP, but also in mainly middle and upper-class neighborhoods. Initially pharmacies sold brand-name drugs. But by 2011, many adopted the new model, making space within the pharmacy for a doctor's office. Today many pharmacies offer an almost identical model: a physician who can be seen quickly (10 to 15 minutes waiting time) and economically (up to US$2.50 per consultation), attached to a pharmacy offering brand-name (normally-priced) drugs and generic (economically-priced) drugs.

Therefore, the model initially conceived for the BoP in effect migrated upwards to serve middle and upper-income market segments, a process described as trickle-up innovation. Just as with the BoP, the middle and upper classes also go to the pharmacy to consult a doctor in order to treat symptoms not requiring hospitalization. They are able to purchase not only generic drugs, but also brand-name drugs.

The great difference between the BoP and the middle and upper-classes is in the reason why they go to the new Pharmacy-Doctor clinics: the latter group has access to public medical services as well as private insurance (the majority have both) and can easily afford to pay the fees charged by private doctors. The main reason both groups use the service is that they are short on time. Time is extremely valuable for urban populations in general, and the quick service has become the main success factor in the new model. In addition, the requirement for a medical prescription, the proximity of the service to the patient's home and work, and low prices are the main contributory factors behind their decision to use the service.

The middle and upper classes believe that significant time is wasted in waiting to obtain private appointments, and that such appointments, once obtained, are liable to significant delay. In addition, they frequently cost up to US$50 or more. Private health insurance in the country generally has a high deductible, usually more than US$300, and so is not used for common or minor ailments. Pharmacies located in middle or upper-class neighborhoods are spacious, comfortable (with parking and air conditioning) with a large range of medicines and related items. The first pharmacies to offer an onsite medical consultation service, FS, were small stores, with the doctor's office immediately adjacent to the pharmacy, being separated from it by a thin wall. Doctor's offices in Farmacias Guadalajara or Del Ahorro are generally larger in size overall and always have a street-door. In supermarkets such as Walmart the consulting room is usually located inside the store and always next to the pharmacy (see Exhibit 1).

Exhibit 1   **Examples of Pharmacy-Doctor Model Layouts**

Farmacias Similares

Farmacias del Ahorro

Farmacias Guadalajara (Fragua)

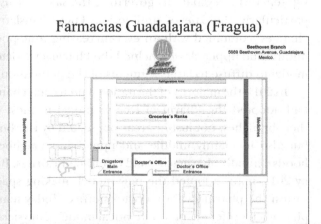

Walmart Pharmacy

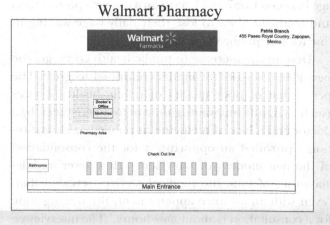

| Exhibit 2 | Growth of the Pharmacy-Doctor Model in the Base of the Pyramid in Mexico, 1997–2011 |

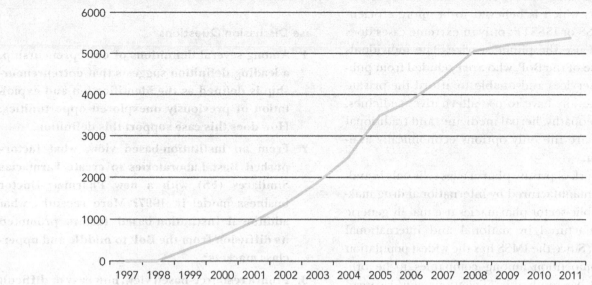

Number of Pharmacies of FS and GI combined.

In the beginning, the legislative change making drug prescriptions mandatory negatively affected sales of medicines in drugstores that did not offer low-cost physician consultations. This in turn led to pharmacy chains for all social strata (BoP, middle class, and upper class) seeking to implement the Pharmacy-Doctor business model. As a result, the model diffused upwards socially bringing the Pharmacy-Doctor pairing to middle and upper-class clients. Consumers are willing to pay out-of-pocket for Pharmacy-Doctor clinics to receive care more quickly. Many are willing to use a Pharmacy-Doctor clinic for a minor condition if it means being seen immediately. Pharmacy chains that offer their products to wealthy social classes have thus adopted a model originally designed for the BoP, realizing that there is an opportunity to increase sales due to the fact that even the middle or upper classes do not go to their private doctor for a prescription for minor ailments. As one FS patient commented: "The wait was 10 minutes and the consultation was 15 minutes. The doctor's professional qualification was from a highly-regarded private school in the area. The attention was good and I paid US$1.5 for the consultation and US$2 for the medicine. My eye infection disappeared in two days." Doctors consulting inside the pharmacies also viewed this avenue as a useful way of obtaining experience after graduation and helping them to decide on a future specialization.

Overall, the new Pharmacy-Doctor model is a win-win-win for consumers (patients), drug makers, and doctors. It is a successful innovation that has proliferated throughout the Mexican healthcare industry (Exhibit 2). Looking forward, the Board of Farmacias Similares, which pioneered this model, needs to make a strategic decision: should the firm go international and export the model to focus on the low-income class in other Latin American countries or should it stay domestic and further penetrate the higher-income (middle and upper-class) markets in Mexico.

Appendix 1. The Healthcare Industry in Mexico

In 1997 the healthcare industry was mainly made up of the following: the Mexican Public Health Service (IMSS) founded in 1943 and covering 35% of the population; the Government Workers Social Security Scheme (ISSSTE) founded in 1960 and covering 5% of the population; and other social security systems founded between 1940 and 1950 and covering 1% of the population. In 1997, Mexico had approximately 59% of the population without medical coverage, the majority of whom belonging to the BoP. In addition, there is a private network of insurance companies, hospitals, pharmacies, and doctors that charge expensive fees for their medical services and medicines. This private network is used by the middle and upper classes as they can afford to take out private health insurance, and this private network covers 19% of the population. This 19% is already covered by the IMSS or ISSSTE, since these individuals are most likely employees and all employers must provide public service benefits. However, this segment takes out private insurance in order to avail itself of the private network, which is believed to be more efficient than the IMSS or ISSSTE: only in extreme cases does this segment use the public service. The individuals who comprise of the BoP, who are excluded from public medical services and unable to afford the private services, generally have to use alternative medicines, such as homeopathy, herbal medicine, and traditional healers that are the only options economically available to them.

The network of private pharmacies sells only brand-name drugs manufactured by international drug makers, while public-sector pharmacies use mainly generic drugs manufactured by national and international drug makers. Since the IMSS has the widest population coverage, competition among companies to be official suppliers has resulted in allegations of widespread corruption. Another noteworthy characteristic of the medical industry is the excellent social status that doctors have, along with the excellent wages they can earn in private hospitals or consultancies. Annually more doctors graduate from Mexican universities than are required in large urban areas. There is a scarcity of doctors in rural areas, but the majority prefer urban to rural environments as low-income people are often unable to pay for medical services. As a result, many medical graduates swell the ranks of the urban underemployed, filling temporary positions. This is a general picture of the conditions prevailing in the medical industry in Mexico in 1997.

Case Discussion Questions

1. **Among several definitions of entrepreneurship, a leading definition suggests that entrepreneurship is defined as the identification and exploitation of previously unexplored opportunities. How does this case support this definition?**

2. **From an institution-based view, what factors pushed Best Laboratories to create Farmacias Similares (FS) with a new Pharmacy-Doctor business model in 1997? More recently, what additional institution-based factors promoted its diffusion from the BoP to middle and upper-class markets?**

3. **From a resource-based view, how easy or difficult it is for competitors to offer a similar Pharmacy-Doctor business model? Given your answer, how sustainable is FS's competitive advantage?**

4. **If you were a member of the FS Board, of the two directions being entertained, which one would you recommend?**

Sources: Extracted from (1) company web pages; (2) Euromonitor International, 2012, *Consumer Health–Mexico*, Retrieved February 12, 2012, www.euromonitor.com/mexico; (3) P. Keckley, S. Coughlin, L. Korenda, & G. Moreno, 2011, *Survey of Health Care Consumers in Mexico: Key Findings, Strategic Implications*, Deloitte Center for Health Solutions.

Integrative Case 3.2

Wikimart: Building a Russian Version of Amazon[1]

Daniel J. McCarthy (Northeastern University)

Sheila M. Puffer (Northeastern University)

How does a Russian Internet startup grow? How does it line up financing? How promising are its prospects?

Wikimart was founded in 2008 by Stanford MBA students Maxim Faldin and Kamil Kurmakayev as an online marketplace for Russia and Russian-speaking countries. Its focus was a B2C platform for Russian retailers who listed goods at no charge but initially paid a minimum 3% fee to Wikimart on each transaction, later reduced to 1.5%. Wikimart also provided services to these retailers, including order fulfillment, accounting and legal support, and ecommerce marketing tools. The company's objective was to become a dominant ecommerce marketplace in Russia and other countries of the former Soviet Union.

Time Line of Financing and Growth

In the first half of 2009, financing of $700,000 was secured from a number of sophisticated angel investors including Michael van Swaaij who had invested in Skype and eBay Europe; Mark Zaleski and Robert Dighero who had invested in QXL ricardo; Alec Oxenford, founder of OLX, DineroMail.com, and DeRemate; Jose Marin, founder of DeRemate; and Kerim Baran, founder of Yonja.com. By mid 2009, Wikimart's website was attracting 5,000 daily visitors and had more than 1,000 online merchants offering over 370,000 products.

In early 2010, Series A financing was secured from Tiger Global Management, a successful US-based private equity investor specializing in technology start-ups, often in emerging economies. The deal raised $5 million for Wikimart, and resulted in 50% ownership for Tiger, according to a filing with the US Securities and Exchange Commission. In August 2010, Wikimart secured Series B financing of $7 million, again from Tiger Global.

1) This case was written by Daniel J. McCarthy (McKim d'Amore Distinguished Professor of Global Management and Innovation, Northeastern University) and Sheila M. Puffer (University Distinguished Professor and Cherry Family Senior Fellow of International Business, Northeastern University). The authors would like to acknowledge the excellent research assistance provided by Northeastern University College of Business student Maxim Russkikh. © Daniel J. McCarthy and Sheila M. Puffer. Reprinted with permission.

By mid 2010, the company website had 2,000 online merchants generating $1.5 million in monthly revenues for Wikimart. By 2011, it had increased to 2,500 merchants and $3 million in monthly revenues. Of course, online sales were of a significant larger order of magnitude. Company revenues would have been greater if the order completion rates could be improved beyond the 68% level prevailing in 2011. Achieving such an increase, however, would remain a major challenge to implementing the company's strategy since retailers often had insufficient inventories to fulfill customer orders.

By March 2011 the company had signed up 2,200 retailers that listed more than 528,000 products through Wikimart's website. The company reported that the site was attracting 2 million visitors per month, although one of the founders stated that the number could be as large as 3 million. Among the products prominent on its website were home goods and appliances, consumer electronics, wine and tobacco, and virtually any product that could be found on Amazon's website, with the best-selling categories being clothing, sporting goods, and children's products. The vast majority of the products were familiar, internationally known brands.

Why Tiger?

One of Wikimart's founders, Kurmakayev, explained in 2011 why the company had chosen Tiger Global from among various potential core investors: "We chose Tiger because they did not impose their views and did not seek to participate in the business management, but are ready for the long-term partnership." Other potential core investors included Accel Partners, a firm based primarily in the United States, with offices in Palo Alto, California, and New York, that had invested in companies like Groupon and Veritas. Accel also had offices in Britain, China, and India. Another potential core investor was Index Ventures, a US investor with successful investments in technology startups such as Skype and Dropbox. It seemed that all of these investment firms might have been looking for the next Google, the hugely successful Internet giant cofounded a decade earlier by Russian-born University of Maryland and Stanford University graduate Sergei Brin.

Business Model

Wikimart's business model centered around creating an Amazon-like online retail platform in the Russian-speaking countries of the former Soviet Union. Similar models had been developed in Korea by Gmarket and in Japan by Rakuten Ichiba. The company's business model offered free space online to merchants while collecting a minimum of 1.5% of each transaction once sales began.

Company Strategy and Organization

The company's strategy included reaching a younger, tech-savvy segment of customers in the Russian-speaking world. The company was headquartered in Moscow, and merchants selling on its site delivered goods only within Russia as of early 2011. One of the partners stressed that Wikimart's objective was to continue developing the Russian market even after they moved to new markets. The company planned to expand overall services to other Russian-speaking countries of the former Soviet Union such as Ukraine and Kazakstan. The partner reasoned that Russia was the tenth largest European country in terms of GDP but had even greater promise in terms of Internet users. Although Wikimart seemed to have vast potential, the company had not turned a profit by early 2012. However, the cofounders believed that 2013 could be a profitable year. With an objective of eventually attaining 20% to 30% share of the fast-growing online retail market, company executives saw the possibility of annual revenues reaching as high as $15 billion by 2018.

The two cofounders initially assumed separate responsibilities, with Kurmakayev being in charge of maintaining relations with retailers and developing the company's technology and Faldin being responsible for sales, marketing, and business development. As the company grew, they recognized early that they had to change to a more corporate-like structure. Faldin became CEO responsible for the operational aspects of the business, such as developing metrics and achieving goals. Kurmakayev took on a strategic role incorporating forecasting and budgeting, as well as developing the company's competitive strategy.

One of the cofounders claimed that a significant percentage of company costs stemmed from intensive development efforts. Wikimart, although an online retail business, was basically a technology company. The vast majority of the 260 employees in 2011 were programmers who wrote software code to support the company's online business. They were guided in their development work with Silicon Valley expertise provided by their investors and consultants.

Russia's Internet Industry and Wikimart's Competition

The overall Russian ecommerce market was estimated at $7 billion to $9 billion in 2011, a substantial increase over the $6 billion in 2010, growth that attracted many competitors. Exponential future growth, with forecasts of 40% annually, saw estimates of up to a $50 billion market by 2018. Such forecasts added luster to the already attractive Russian online retail market. Wikimart's largest competitor was Ozon.ru, the oldest ecommerce giant of the Russian Internet. Sites like Groupon and KupiVip offering group discounts on products and services were also substantial competitors, and both had attracted relatively large investments from US firms. The order fulfillment challenge for Wikimart noted earlier was due to retailers relying on relatively poor IT technologies. One of Wikimart's founders noted that the online retail industry in Russia required huge investments in IT and supply chain. In 2012, only 1.5% of all Russian retail purchases took place online, but the cofounders believed that the number would grow to 10% to 20% within five to ten years.

Some Russian companies, such as mail.ru, had already become powerful Internet players within Russia. That firm's parent, the mail.ru Group, was formerly known as Digital Sky Technologies and was an early-stage investor in Facebook, owning between 5% to 10% of that company by 2011 according to various reports. It had invested $200 million in 2009 and an additional $500 million in 2011. This is another example of the globalization of private investments, this time, however, the participants were a Russian investment group taking a stake in a US online venture. Mail.ru itself was an extremely successful publicly traded Internet company. Other successful Russian online companies included Vkontakte and Rambler. Vkontakte was a private company that offered social network services and was notable for design and functionality that mimicked Facebook. As of February 2012, Vkontakte reportedly had 116.6 million user accounts and was the fourth most popular Russian Internet website.

Rambler was a search engine that offered Web 2.0 services such as e-mail aggregation and e-commerce, with its main competitors being mail.ru and Yandex. Yandex had a reported 64% market share of the Russian search provider space and was the fifth largest search engine worldwide with 1.7% of global searches as of September 2011. The company had enjoyed a decade of success before going public in 2011 on NASDAQ in the United States. Its IPO raised $1.3 billion and its stock price soon traded up by 55%. The price of $1.3 billion valued the company at about $8 billion.

Wikimart's Future

Analysts noted that startups like Wikimart had become attractive for strategic investors as the Internet expansion in Russia accelerated. In 2012, the number of Internet users in Russia was not large but was expected to grow by approximately 10% per year. Some analysts expected that if Wikimart continued to increase revenues and profits, it could soon be targeted by strategic investors such as Amazon or eBay. Having US investors like Tiger Global that were very familiar with the Russian Internet market could be very positive in attracting other investors including strategic investors who might invest funds with the intention of acquiring Wikimart at some point. Wikimart's cofounders and other major shareholders, such as Tiger Global, might eventually have to decide between selling the company to a strategic investor, or continuing to maintain control while

growing the company to its full potential. As is typical in such cases, timing would be a key factor.

Case Discussion Questions

1. **Given the fragmented, rapidly growing nature of online retail space in the Russian-speaking world, how would you characterize the competition in this industry?**

2. **Why was Wikimart able to secure financing during its early stages of growth? Put it differently, if you were an angel investor or private equity investor, what special qualities of Wikimart would attract you?**

3. **While Wikimart's objective is to become a dominant ecommerce marketplace in Russia and other countries of the former Soviet Union, given the existing competition (such as Ozon.ru), is such ambition realistic?**

4. **What are some of the viable exit strategies for the two cofounders?**

Sources: Based on (1) DST smenila nazvanie (DST changes its name), 2010, www.vedomosti.ru/companies/news/1103680/dst_smenila_nazvanie; (2) A. Hesseldahl, 2012. Zuckerberg is the billion-share man: Who owns what, who makes what in the Facebook IPO, *AllThingsD*, February 1, http://allthingsd .com/20120201/facebooks-ipo-filing-who-owns-what-who-makes-what/; (3) *Forbes*, 2011, My stroim Amazon in Russia (We are building Amazon in Russia), July 20, www.forbes.ru/tehno-opinion/internet-i-telekommunikatsii/70954-my -stroim-amazon-v-rossii; (4) *RT*, 2011, Tiger Global ups the ante on Wikimart, March 2, http://rt.com/business; (5) http://bloomberg.com/news/2011-05-24 /yandex-jumps-after-raising-1-3-billion-in-biggest-technology-ipo-of-the-year.html; (6) http://en.wikipedia.org/wiki/Yandex.

Integrative Case 3.3

Business Jet Makers Eye China[1]

Mike W. Peng (University of Texas at Dallas)

Business jet makers of all stripes are elbowing their way into China's virgin skies. Will China's institutions facilitate or prohibit their flights? Do they have the necessary resources and capabilities to soar?

"The Chinese economy slows down" is one of the leading themes in global business news. Foreign firms interested in the legendary "one billion customers" are advised to adjust their high-flying expectations down to earth. Defying this trend, business jet makers continue to have sky-high expectations for China—for a good reason. Arriving in China as recently as in 2003, this industry is literally just "taking off." Business jets (also known as corporate jets or private jets) are ideal for China, which has a vast territory (the third largest in the world, behind Russia and Canada) good for flying. China has also amassed the world's second-largest number of billionaires (behind the United States) and is rapidly churning out new ones who can afford to buy jets. Yet, only fewer than 400 business jets currently fly in China, a number that is not only smaller than the number in Brazil and Mexico, but also smaller than what can be found in *one* single airport—Orange County airport outside Los Angeles—in the United States.

Institutions

The rise of China for business aviation also coincides with the aftermath of the 2008 global financial crisis, during which many buyers cancelled their orders. Not surprisingly, anybody who is somebody in business aviation is eager to elbow its way into essentially the virgin skies of China. But here is an institution-based catch. The skies in China are formally controlled by the military, and flight plans have to be submitted via a cumbersome process. Beijing's airport only gives two take-off slots an hour to business jets. Buyers importing jets are hit by onerous duties and taxes, and officials have talked about slapping a new luxury tax on top of those. Further, an anti-corruption (and anti-conspicuous

MARK HALSTON/Getty Images

consumption) campaign unleashed by President Xi Jinping has scared away a lot of large state-owned enterprises (SOEs), which used to make up approximately 15% of the business jet market in China—now down to about 5%.

While institution-based barriers persist, the government has offered a glimmer of hope. It seems to have realized the value of business aviation. The latest Five-Year Plan explicitly calls for the development of *non-airline aviation*, and the military is instructed to give up some chunks of air space to leave room for business jets. The industry, of course, has been marketing and lobbying intensely, claiming that business aviation is not merely a luxury, but also a productivity booster that can propel firms' (and China's) growth to new heights.

Resources and Capabilities

Leveraging resources and capabilities, each business jet maker is endeavoring to outshine the other. Beech Hawker, Cessna, and Gulfstream of the United States, Dassault Falcon of France, and Learjet of Canada (owned by Bombardier) are the traditional competitors. Each carrying 8–12 passengers, they offer privacy, luxury, and often very long range. Salivating at the growth potential, the top three larger jet makers—Boeing, Airbus, and Embraer (of Brazil)—have also entered the fray. Boeing adapted its 737 to offer the Boeing Business Jet (up to 60 passengers). Airbus

1) This research was supported by the Jindal Chair at the Jindal School of Management, University of Texas at Dallas. All views and errors are those of the author. © Mike W. Peng. Reprinted with permission.

modified its A320 to launch the Airbus Corporate Jet (up to 40 passengers). Embraer turned its ERJ 190 regional jet into Lineage 1000 (up to 20 passengers). These ultra-large business jets offer more spacious interiors, better-circulated air (due to their larger cabin), and longer range—at price ranges competitive to those of the traditional business jets.

In China, the current market leader is Gulfstream, which has sold more than 100 jets and holds the biggest market share. Gulfstream does whatever it takes to win orders, including changing the model number instead of offending potential buyers with an unintended meaning. Specifically, in July 2011, Gulfstream renamed its G250 introduced in 2008 to G280. Its website explained: "As demand for Gulfstream business jets grows around the world, the move was prompted by the company's sensitivity to the varied cultures of its international customer base." While it never explained exactly why, it was because "250" means "stupid" or "useless" in some parts of China. One senior executive explained to the press that "we determined that G280 is a more amenable number sequence in certain cultures." Such market-oriented efforts have been handsomely rewarded by eager Chinese customers. In April 2014 at the Asian Business Aviation Conference and Exhibition (ABACE) in Shanghai—a major industry gathering—Gulfstream signed a 60-plane deal with Minsheng Financial Leasing, the aviation-finance arm of a major private bank in China. This is not only one of the largest deals for Gulfstream, but also one of the largest worldwide.

As the industry takes off, rising signs of sophistication emerge. A decade ago, the first Chinese buyers tended to pay cash and flew rarely—only to impress friends. Today's buyers often take advantage of financing or leasing (as evidenced by the Gulfstream–Minsheng deal). They fly more and endeavor to get more bang out of their bucks (or yuans). Some of them cannot wait for 1–2 years, so they have done something *unthinkable* for the super rich: buying *used* jets. Experts estimate that in the next 20 years, demand in China will be the third largest in the world, resulting in 1,500 business jets—behind 9,500 in the United States and 4,000 in Europe.

Case Discussion Questions

1. **Why are corporate jet makers so eager to enter China?**

2. **From an institution-based view, what needs to be done to enhance the prospects of this industry in China?**

3. **From a resource-based view, what does it take to win in China?**

Sources: Based on (1) *Airport Journal*, 2013, Business jet player plans to spreads its wings in China, June: 17–49; (2) *Airport Journal*, 2015, Focus on ABACE 2015, May: 20-23; (3) *Economist*, 2014, Business aviation: Fasten seat belts, April 19; (4) *South China Morning Post*, 2012, Bargain hunting takes flight, July 10: A4; (5) www.abace.aero; (6) www.gulfstreamnews.com.

Integrative Case 3.4

The Antitrust Case on the AT&T–T-Mobile Merger[1]

Mike W. Peng (University of Texas at Dallas)

In 2011, the second-largest US mobile wireless carrier AT&T (with a 25% market share) proposed to merge with the fourth-largest carrier T-Mobile, which had a 15% market share and was a wholly owned subsidiary of Deutsch Telekom. Antitrust authorities blocked this merger. Why?

The Merger

In March 2011, Dallas-based AT&T announced that it had reached an agreement with Deutsch Telekom (DT) to purchase DT's wholly owned US subsidiary, T-Mobile USA, for $39 billion. The top four concentrations in mobile wireless telecommunications services in the United States accounted for more than 90% of market share. Of the Big Four, the second-ranked AT&T had about 25% market share, and the fourth-ranked T-Mobile had 15%. The largest player was Verizon (31%), and the third was Sprint Nextel (20%). Although some small carriers competed in certain regions, no carriers other than the Big Four competed nationally. After the proposed merger, the combined AT&T–T-Mobile would become the nation's largest wireless carrier, commanding more than 40% of market share, with 132 million customers and $72 billion in revenues. The scale and scope of the merger would require regulatory approval. AT&T indicated its willingness to sell off certain assets if necessary, and planned to complete the merger in one year.

AT&T argued that the merger would allow AT&T to expand 4G LTE broadband to another 55 million Americans, reaching a total of 97% of the population and especially benefitting rural areas currently without broadband coverage. Because T-Mobile was losing money and suffered from its poor economies of scale, it (and its parent company DT) had been unable to upgrade its networks and invest in 4G broadband. While AT&T was booming and adding customers, T-Mobile was losing customers—it was the only major carrier that did not offer the iPhone. But T-Mobile possessed some hard-to-substitute resources: spectrum.

Spectrum represented finite resources auctioned by the Federal Communications Commission (FCC). Exhausting its own spectrum, AT&T could benefit from tapping into T-Mobile's underutilized spectrum. Accelerating 4G wireless deployment would not only generate new jobs due to AT&T's own investment, but would also stimulate broader job creation and civil engagement due to better access to more affordable and more widespread wireless broadband services.

A variety of labor, environmental, and business groups supported the merger. These groups pointed to AT&T's record and commitments to labor and environmental standards, and appreciated the investment and the jobs the merger would bring. Also, civil rights groups applauded the additional boost in civil engagement that could be facilitated by more widespread broadband. Governors of 26 states wrote letters to support the merger.

However, other diverse groups were opposed to this merger. Not surprisingly, Verizon and Sprint did not like this deal, because it would make them weaker. Sprint would become a distant third, so clearly it would not appreciate the outcome. Verizon would lose its top position, but it would still be a strong player in a new duopoly. Internet companies did not like the merger either, because the merger would leave them with fewer service providers to negotiate with for getting their content and applications to customers. The Computer and Communication Industry Association—which included eBay, Google, Microsoft, and Yahoo as its members—was opposed to the merger. Consumer groups argued that the merger would raise prices and stifle innovation by consolidating so much of the wireless industry in one firm.

On the core issue of whether increasing AT&T's market power would hurt consumers, AT&T pointed out that the average inflation-adjusted price for wireless services in the United States *fell* by 50% from 1999 to 2009, according to the Government Accountability Office. AT&T also argued that in many local markets AT&T would still be competing with four or more rivals, so taking T-Mobile (which was losing customers

1) This research was supported by the Jindal Chair at the Jindal School of Management, University of Texas at Dallas. All views and errors are those of the author. © Mike W. Peng. Reprinted with permission.

anyway) out of the mix would not dent competition. If AT&T could not acquire T-Mobile (which had sizable infrastructure, such as cellular towers and significant spectrum), then AT&T might be forced to build its own infrastructure, which would be an unnecessarily costly undertaking and social waste, especially in crowded urban areas such as San Francisco. But even if AT&T went head-to-head with infrastructure building, it would still suffer from a shortage of spectrum, while T-Mobile, at the same time, could not fully utilize its spectrum—clearly a waste of finite resources.

The Antitrust Case

In August 2011, the US Department of Justice (DOJ) filed a lawsuit alleging that this merger would reduce competition and violate antitrust law. DOJ alleged that the "anticompetitive harm" of this merger would include:

(a) actual and potential competition between AT&T and T-Mobile will be eliminated; (b) competition in general likely will be lessened substantially; (c) prices are likely to be higher than they otherwise would; (d) the quality and quantity of services are likely to be less than they otherwise would due to reduced incentives to invest in capacity and technology improvements; and (e) innovation and product variety likely will be reduced.

In particular, given T-Mobile's positioning as a self-styled "Disruptive Pricing" provider, "AT&T's acquisition of T-Mobile," alleged DOJ, "would eliminate the important price, quality, product variety, and innovation competition that an independent T-Mobile brings to the marketplace." In addition, DOJ argued:

The substantial increase in concentration that would result from this merger, and the reduction in the number of nationwide providers from four to three, likely will lead to lessened competition due to an enhanced risk of anticompetitive coordination. Certain aspects of mobile wireless communications services markets, including transparent pricing, little buyer-side market power, and high barriers to entry and expansion, make them particularly conductive to coordination.

In conclusion, DOJ argued that the proposed merger would violate Section 7 of the Clayton Act and that it should be stopped. In the lawsuit, DOJ also sued T-Mobile and DT as co-defendants. On behalf of the US government, DOJ was the sole plaintiff in its first complaint filed on August 31, 2011. In its first amended complaint filed on September 16, DOJ was joined by the states of New York, Washington, California, Illinois,

Massachusetts, Ohio, and Pennsylvania as co-plaintiffs. In its second amended complaint filed on September 30, Puerto Rico joined as a co-plaintiff. The case was officially the *United States et al. v. AT&T Inc. et al.*

AT&T was not a stranger to antitrust lawsuits. Today's AT&T is the direct result of the first *United States v. AT&T* antitrust lawsuit. Because of its monopoly in long distance (land-line) telephone, the *original* AT&T ("Ma Bell") was forced by DOJ to break up into seven regional Bell operating companies (known as "Baby Bells") in 1983. Between 1983 and 2005, today's AT&T was one of these Baby Bells—named Southwestern Bell Corporation between 1983 and 1995, and shortened to SBC between 1995 and 2005. Due to its successful market performance, SBC emerged as a leading offspring of the original AT&T (Verizon was another leading offspring). In 2005, SBC spent $16 billion to purchase its former parent company, AT&T Corporation—a Baby Bell acquiring Ma Bell. Quitting the SBC name, the merged entity named itself AT&T Inc. and took on the iconic AT&T branding (including its logo and its stock ticker "T," which simply stands for "telephone"). Before the filing of the second *United States v. AT&T* case, the *Economist* asked: "Could the bid for T-Mobile be a sign that monopoly Ma is trying to return from her grave?"

The Outcome

In November 2011, the FCC issued its opinion and joined DOJ in opposing the merger. In December 2011 (before the antitrust case went on trial), AT&T gave up the merger and DOJ dismissed the case. A triumphant DOJ announced:

Consumers won today . . . Had AT&T acquired T-Mobile, consumers in the wireless market place would have faced higher prices and reduced innovation. We sued to protect consumers who rely on competition in this important industry. With the parties' abandonment, we achieved that result.

A frustrated AT&T noted in its press release:

[Dallas, Texas, December 19, 2011] AT&T Inc. (NYSE: T) said today that after a thorough review of options it has agreed with Deutsch Telekom AG to end its bid to acquire T-Mobile USA, which began in March of this year.

The actions by the Federal Communications Commission and the Department of Justice to block this transaction do not change the realities of the US wireless industry. It is one of the most fiercely competitive industries in the world, with a mounting need for more spectrum that has not diminished and must be addressed immediately. The AT&T and T-Mobile USA combination would have offered an interim solution to this spectrum shortage. In the absence of such steps, customers will be harmed and needed investment will be stifled.

"AT&T will continue to be aggressive in leading the mobile Internet revolution," said Randall Stephenson, AT&T chairman and CEO. "Over the past four years we have invested more in our networks than any other US company. As a result, today we deliver best-in-class mobile broadband speeds—connecting smartphones, tablets, and emerging devices at a record pace—and we are well underway with our nationwide 4G LTE deployment.

"To meet the needs of our customers, we will continue to invest," Stephenson said. "However, adding capacity to meet these needs will require policymakers to do two things. First, in the near term, they should allow the free markets to work so that additional spectrum is available to meet the immediate needs of the US wireless industry, including expeditiously approving our acquisition of unused Qualcomm spectrum currently pending before the FCC. Second, policymakers should enact legislation to meet our nation's longer-term spectrum needs.

"The mobile Internet is a dynamic industry that can be a critical driver in restoring American economic growth and job creation, but only if companies are allowed to react quickly to customer needs and market forces," Stephenson said.

The fine prints in the deal included DOJ's *blessing* of AT&T and T-Mobile's collaboration in roaming. The more significant (or, if you will, the more bizarre) outcome was that as per AT&T's original deal with DT, in the event of merger failure, AT&T would pay T-Mobile $3 billion as a break-up fee and give T-Mobile $1 billion worth of AT&T-held wireless spectrum. In short, the US government reduced the competitiveness of a US firm by forcing a US firm to subsidize the wholly owned subsidiary of a foreign firm.

In the name of preserving (domestic) competition, the US government preserved a (foreign) competitor. "The problem is," noted one expert at *Slate*, "T-Mobile doesn't want to be a competitor anymore. Its parent company DT wants out of the US market." As the weakest among the Big Four, T-Mobile only added 89,000 new customers between 2009 and 2011, while the industry took in 33 million new customers. By essentially giving up since March 2011, T-Mobile lost 467,000 lucrative contract customers during the merger process. By focusing on its terms of exit, T-Mobile turned its attention away from network upgrades and improvements.

DOJ and FCC cannot force T-Mobile to be in business, just like no one can force customers to sign up for plans they do not want. By breathing a new lease on life into T-Mobile, that was exactly what DOJ and FCC did: forcing T-Mobile to be in business against its (and its parent company's) own wishes. The same expert at *Slate* continued:

> Sure, companies like T-Mobile and Sprint can offer cheaper plans, but the success of Verizon and AT&T shows price is not our primary concern when it comes to wireless service. We want shiny smartphones and big, powerful, reliable networks... Rather than stifle competition, the merger would have intensified the war between the two giants, AT&T and Verizon. And for those people for whom price is paramount, there would remain not only Sprint, but a slew of smaller, regional providers like Leap and MetroPCS.

Case Discussion Questions

1. **Defend AT&T's position as its CEO.**

2. **Defend this merger as T-Mobile's or Deutsch Telekom's CEO (both firms were co-defendants in this case).**

3. **Provide an expert testimonial as Verizon's or Spring Nextel's CEO.**

4. **Challenge AT&T's position as an antitrust lawyer working for the government.**

5. *ON ETHICS:* **As a party not directly involved in the case (such as a manager at another firm not in this industry or a student), what do you think is right about antitrust policy? What is wrong about antitrust policy? Why?**

Sources: Based on (1) the author's interviews of AT&T executives in Dallas, Texas, 2011; (2) AT&T, 2011, AT&T ends bid to add network capacity through T-Mobile USA purchase, December 19, www.att.com; (3) AT&T, 2011, AT&T statement on Department of Justice action, August 31, www.att.com; (4) *Bloomberg Businessweek*, 2011, Behind AT&T's epic lobbying failure, December 12: 40–42; (5) *Bloomberg Businessweek*, 2011, For wireless giants, reception may get spotty, July 18: 35–36; (6) CBS News, 2011, What the AT&T-T-Mobile breakup means for you, December 20, www.cbsnews.com; (7) *Economist*, 2011, An audacious merger with a poor reception, March 26: 71–72; (8) *Economist*, Tripped at the altar, September 3: 62; (9) W. Oremus, 2011, Truth, justice, and terrible mobile service, *Slate*, December 21, www.slate.com; (10) *United States of America v. AT&T, T-Mobile USA, Inc., and Deutsch Telecom AG*, 2011, Complaint, Case 1:11-cv-01560, August 31, Washington, DC: US District Court for the District of Columbia; (11) *United States of America et al. v. AT&T Inc, et al.*, 2011, Amended complaint, Civil Action No. 11-01560 (ESH), September 16, Washington, DC: US District Court for the District of Columbia; (12) *United States of America et al. v. AT&T Inc. et al.*, 2011, Second amended complaint, Civil Action No. 11-01560 (ESH), September 30, Washington, DC: US District Court for the District of Columbia; (13) *United States of America et al. v. AT&T Inc. et al.*, 2011, Stipulation of dismissal, Civil Action No. 11-01560 (ESH), December 20, Washington, DC: US District Court for the District of Columbia; (14) *Wall Street Journal*, 2012, T-Mobile will focus on network quality in wake of deal failure, January 11, online.wsj.com.

Integrative Case 3.5

Teliasonera's Alliances and Acquisitions in Eurasia[1]

Canan Mutlu (University of Texas at Dallas)

How did TeliaSonera leverage alliances and acquisitions to grow in Eurasia markets, which are not known to be "easy" markets?

Today, climbers can have 3G access on Mount Everest to brag about their experience on top of the world. However, not many people know that it is a Nordic company providing this service in such an alien environment. The company is TeliaSonera, which provides telecommunications services in a wide geographic area, from Nordic countries to Nepal, which includes the emerging and highly valued Eurasian markets. TeliaSonera is the fifth-largest telecom operator in Europe. It has operations in Azerbaijan, Belarus, Denmark, Estonia, Finland, Georgia, Kazakhstan, Latvia, Lithuania, Moldova, Nepal, Norway, Russia, Spain, Sweden, Tajikistan, Turkey, Ukraine, and Uzbekistan.

How could a Nordic company with roots in highly developed markets in Europe expand in such politically risky and institutionally ambiguous settings? Savvy use of alliances and acquisitions throughout Eurasia appeared to be a key. Itself the result of the merger between Telia of Sweden and Sonera of Finland in 2002, TeliaSonera certainly understood the importance of alliances and

acquisitions. Its alliances and acquisitions throughout Eurasia resulted in enviable performance in many host countries, often commanding either the number-one or number-two position shown in Exhibit 1.

To overcome its liability of foreignness, TeliaSonera leveraged its decades of telecom expertise developed in Nordic countries in Eurasia. It was the world's first operator of 4G networks first deployed in Europe. Although it did not offer 4G in Eurasia, the generally better-quality network investments provided TeliaSonera a leading edge in Eurasia, compared to local competitors. This high investment cost turned into a larger and more satisfied customer base, upgrading TeliaSonera into leading positions in most countries.

TeliaSonera faced certain challenges due to weak institutional settings, especially in former Soviet Union countries in Eurasia. Although each country was in a different phase of transition to become a market economy, the economic, legal, and regulatory systems were still highly bureaucratic and risky. The ambiguity in the institutional frameworks brings additional risks for businesses, significantly increasing the costs of investments. The telecom industry has further liabilities in

Exhibit 1 **TeliaSonera's Operations in Eurasia**

COUNTRY	POPULATION	GDP GROWTH	BRAND NAME	TELIASONERA OWNERSHIP	MARKET POSITION	SUBSCRIPTION RATE	MARKET SHARE
Azerbaijan	9 million	2.8%	Azercell	51%	1	4 million	55%
Georgia	4.4 million	5.5%	Geocell	100%	1	2 million	44%
Kazakhstan	16.5 million	5.9%	Kcell	51%	1	9 million	50%
Moldova	3.6 million	4.5%	Moldcell	100%	2	907,000	32%
Nepal	28.5 million	4.5%	Ncell	80%	2	4.1 million	42%
Russia	141.9 million	4.8%	MegaFon	44%	2	57 million	26%
Tajikistan	7.1 million	5.8%	Tcell	60%	1	1.7 million	36%
Turkey	73.7 million	4.6%	Turkcell	38%	1	34 million	55%
Uzbekistan	27.8 million	7%	Ucell	94%	2	7 million	32%

Source: www.teliasonera.com.

1) This case was written by Canan Mutlu (University of Texas at Dallas) under the supervision of Professor Mike Peng. All information used is from public domain and the author is responsible for any errors. © Canan Mutlu.

terms of heavy infrastructure spending and related fix costs. TeliaSonera's success in its Eurasia expansion was largely due to its utilization of strong business and government ties that had been developed in decades throughout the company's (and its predecessors') history in the region.

In addition to the challenges, the markets in emerging economies in Eurasia presented many opportunities. In contrast to Europe, fixed landlines were not as developed in Eurasia. This, in turn, made these countries rely more on mobile networks. This, in fact, meant a jump into a higher technology for consumers in Eurasia. Moreover, mobile network penetration was lower in Eurasia than in TeliaSonera's mature markets, thus offering a great deal of potential for TeliaSonera. There were fewer competitors, which enabled TeliaSonera to attain higher margins.

Another significant aspect of market conditions is the expanding and younger population in Eurasia, in contrast to the stagnant and older population in Europe. Eurasia thus provides enormous growth opportunities for TeliaSonera. Moreover, improved macroeconomic situations and economic growth led to strong subscription intake, which increased revenues by 16% in 2010.

Nepal is an interesting case study for TeliaSonera's challenges in Eurasia. After TeliaSonera's 2008 acquisition of 80% equity of Nepalese youth brand MeroMobile, the start-up company, which was now called Ncell, grew into a GSM leader in the whole country. However, the road to success had serious difficulties. There was an ongoing political and security crisis involving terrorist attacks and union strikes, which negatively affected multinationals. TeliaSonera contributed to the efforts to overcome such host-country difficulties by offering world-class technologies to this country traditionally suffering from poor telecommunications, and by generating local jobs and employment opportunities. The base stations (cell transmission towers) increased from 300 to 1,500 in three years. As a result, the percentage of the population covered by mobile TeliaSonera networks increased from 44% to 80%. Another significant contributor was the hiring of local employees. Other than employing 25 expatriates, Ncell created 500 solid jobs for locals in a variety of positions.

TeliaSonera's operations in Eurasia aimed to be the trendsetter in these highly dynamic and low-penetration markets. For example, its alliance with a local player, Kcell (in which TeliaSonera held a 51% share), was the first company to launch GPRS technologies that provided the people of Kazakhstan the opportunity to access mobile Internet, WAP, and MMS services. Kcell owed its reputation to providing the best network coverage and also distribution systems in the whole country. There was also a great potential for mobile data in Kazakhstan, due to the young and dynamic population. Already 8% of total Kcell revenues in Kazakhstan came from mobile data in Kcell.

Case Discussion Questions

1. **Many multinational companies fail in their expansion in emerging economies. What are the main capabilities and resources that drive TeliaSonera's successful growth in Eurasia markets?**

2. **Given the institutional differences between European and Eurasia markets, what are the main challenges faced by TeliaSonera in Eurasia? Which strategies enable TeliaSonera to minimize the risks of these challenges?**

3. **How does TeliaSonera differentiate itself from its competitors in Eurasia?**

Sources: Based on publicly available information and press releases of TeliaSonera. The following sources were especially helpful: (1) TeliaSonera CEO's speech, Annual General Shareholders Meeting, April 6, 2011; (2) TeliaSonera Annual Report 2010.

Integrative Case 3.6

China Merchants Group's Acquisition of the Newcastle Port[1]

Hao Tan (University of Newcastle, Australia)

Why was China Merchants Group, a state-owned enterprise, able to successfully close the deal to acquire the Newcastle Port of Australia?

On April 30, 2014, the world's largest coal export port, the Newcastle Port of Australia, changed hands. The owner of the Australian port, the New South Wales state government, agreed to lease the port for 98 years to a consortium formed by the China Merchants Group (hereafter "Merchants") and Australia's Hastings Funds Management, for A$1.7 billion (US$1.57 billion). Over the lease period, the consortium will exercise control over the port, as well as the land, roads, railways, and other infrastructure within the wharf area, and will be entitled to earnings derived from the port's operations.

In the 2012–2013 financial year, the Newcastle Port exported 140 million tonnes of coal, worth A$15 billion (US$13.8 billion). The spot price of coal at the Newcastle Port is a benchmark for the international coal market. Given the significance of the port, the lease had attracted bidders from all over the world. These included Cheung Kong Infrastructure, owned by the Hong Kong tycoon Li Ka-shing; China State Construction; Deutsche Bank; and Macquarie Bank. The short-term and long-term financial benefits of this acquisition for Merchants remain to be seen. However, its successful bid will certainly create opportunities to further internationalize its infrastructure business, and synergises well with its existing shipping and port operations. Control of the Newcastle port will further help the company—a large state-owned enterprise (SOE) from China—to play a more significant part in the global energy transport market.

Mergers and acquisitions (M&A) in Western countries by China's large SOEs have faced considerable political difficulties for a long time, especially for those M&As that concerned "strategic" assets in host countries. In 2009, an acquisition bid by the Aluminium

Corporation of China (Chinalco) for Rio Tinto, one of the top three global mining companies, failed. This was largely because of strong objections in Australia over concerns related to Chinalco's state ownership. However, the acquisition of the Newcastle Port by Merchants appeared to generate much less criticism in Australia. After the announcement of the bidding outcome, the Australian media has been largely positive about the deal. For other Chinese companies that are considering to "go abroad," there seem to be at least three lessons they can learn from the success of Merchants.

First, the acquisition came at a beneficial time, making it a win-win-win situation for the government, the local community, and the foreign investor. The acquisition came as a result of governmental changes in Australia, both at the state and the federal levels, from Labour Party control to that of the Liberal Party. The new Liberal government appealed to the public with plans to invest in new infrastructure. Many of those infrastructure projects had been long overdue in New South Wales and elsewhere in Australia. The Newcastle Port acquisition will provide capital for some of those much needed projects in the local area of Newcastle. Thus it is widely welcome by the government and the community. This is quite different from the bid of Rio Tinto by Chinalco a few years ago, where the Chinese company was perceived by many as a potential monopolist in the Australian resource sector seeking to take advantage of that period's industry downturn.

Second, it appears that Merchants had convinced the owner of the port and the Australian public that the motivation for its acquisition was a commercial rather than a political one. State ownership may be a winning factor for SOEs in China. However, it is often seen as a negative factor in foreign markets. Fully aware of this difference, Merchants, in its bid efforts, had highlighted a range of commercial advantages of the company, such as (1) its long experience in the shipping and port industries over the past 140 years; (2) its current investments and management portfolio, with a number of large ports across continents; (3) the related businesses of the company enabling operational

1) © Hao Tan. Reprinted with permission. A longer, Chinese version of the case originally appeared in the author's column at Caixin.com, a financial and business news and information media website in China, available at http://energy.caixin.com/?p=2003.

synergies, including a super tanker fleet and the world's largest container manufacturing business; and (4) the governance of the company, as a Hong Kong-based and Hong Kong-listed company. As a result, the company's industry expertise was well received and its state ownership less of a concern.

Finally, the bid of Merchants had been greatly helped by its track record in developed countries, especially in Australia. Merchants has been operating in Australia for more than 20 years. Its track record included acquisitions of Loscam Ltd. in 2010 and of Terminal Link in 2013. A majority of the foreign investments made by Merchants had proved successful, which had enhanced the positive image of the company as a responsible multinational corporate citizen. In other words, Merchants was not a total stranger to Australia, which significantly reduced its liability of foreignness.

Of course, the confidence of the owner and the public in the host country not only relies on the good story the company tells, but also on its fundamentals, including its financial capabilities, as well as the conditions and terms of its bid. However, it is certainly important for the management of a multinational company to be able to frame and communicate effectively to various stakeholders the motivations and the consequences of its international M&As. As the philosopher Terence McKenna used to say, "the world is made of words." The stories we receive affect how we understand and participate in the world. The stories a company can tell also affect whether it can reduce resistance in the host country, gain support from stakeholders, and eventually succeed in its internationalisation endeavours.

Case Discussion Questions

1. **Who are the main stakeholders in China Merchants Group's acquisition of the Newcastle Port and what are their key interests and concerns in this acquisition?**

2. **What are the challenges facing large state-owned enterprises (SOEs) in their efforts to acquire strategic assets in foreign countries in comparison with those by private firms? What can SOEs do to deal with those challenges?**

3. **What are your recommendations for China Merchants Group to effectively manage and operate the Newcastle Port after its acquisition?**

Integrative Case 3.7

Japanese Multinationals in Emerging Economies[1]

Mike W. Peng (University of Texas at Dallas)

What is behind the success and failure of Japanese multinationals competing in emerging economies?

How Do Japanese Multinationals Compete?

Generally speaking, Japanese multinationals have struggled in emerging economies. In five major economies (Brazil, China, India, Indonesia, and Russia), Boston Consulting Group (BCG) studied seven industries in which Japanese multinationals are traditionally excellent: automobiles, beauty and personal care, beverages, home appliances, packaged food, retail hygiene, and TVs. BCG identified a market share leader in every industry in every economy studied. Of the total of 35 industry leaders (seven industries × five economies), only four were found to be Japanese. Western multinationals were identified to be leaders 20 times, and local firms from emerging economies 11 times.

Clearly, given the sluggish economic growth in Japan and other developed economies, emerging economies represent the future for the growth of Japanese multinationals. However, most Japanese multinationals have failed to appreciate the scale, scope, and speed of the transitions in these rapidly moving economies, while their Western and local rivals have rocketed ahead. Intense soul searching has identified three common problems:

- *A distaste for low-end markets.* For example, inexpensive but bulky cathode-ray-tube TVs still account for 65% of the sets sold in India. But Japanese electronics firms focus on more expensive flat-screen TVs, leaving LG, Samsung, and India's own Videocon to have the entire low-end market for themselves. Of the entire Indian TV market (high-end and low-end combined), each of the two Korean rivals has a 25% market share, followed by Videocon's 19%. The top three Japanese players—Sony, Panasonic, and Toshiba—only manage to grab a combined total of 13%.
- *A lack of commitment.* Still focusing on Japan as well as other developed markets, most Japanese

multinationals are not as aggressive as some of their rivals in channeling resources to emerging economies. Honda's CR-V SUV sells very well in Europe and North America, but very poorly in India—only about 13,000 cars in ten years (2003–2013). A major reason is that most Indians prefer diesel, but Honda has refused to commit resources to develop a diesel-powered CR-V, claiming that its diesel engines would not work with Indian fuel quality. The upshot? Very poor sales (a mere 100 CR-Vs per month) for a very capable car.
- *A lack of talent, which results in a lack of localization.* The traditional norm of sending a large number of expats to staff overseas positions has created a shortage of capable local managers. But Japanese firms are reluctant to send high-caliber executives to emerging economies, and these individuals are also reluctant to go even when asked. The net result is a large number of relatively mediocre expats. At one leading Japanese electronics firm, 20 expats—due to their compensation—eat up a large chunk of the budget for the 350-person workforce in India. In contrast, LG only has 15 expats to manage its 5,500-person workforce in India.

Panasonic in China and Beyond

Of course, not all Japanese multinationals are hopeless. Some are aggressively adapting to the new realities by rapidly learning and transforming themselves. Panasonic's experience in China serves as a case in point. Although Panasonic started having manufacturing operations in China in 1987, most product development and engineering had been done in Japan, and local adaptation had been minimal. In a radical departure from its traditional practice, in 2005 it set up the Shanghai-based China Lifestyle Research Center, which was its first serious effort to gain a deep understanding of consumer lifestyles anywhere outside of Japan. Led by a high-caliber executive, center staff undertook a series of meticulous research. For example, visits to Chinese households uncovered that the kitchen space for a refrigerator was small, typically only

1) This research was supported by the Jindal Chair at the Jindal School of Management, University of Texas at Dallas. All views and errors are those of the author. © Mike W. Peng. Reprinted with permission.

55 centimeters wide. Panasonic's standard refrigerator was 65 centimeters wide. In response, Panasonic's engineers in Kusatsu, Japan, and Hangzhou, China, worked together to downsize refrigerators—especially low-end ones—for China. The market reaction was swift. In one year, its most popular model of refrigerators increased its sales *ten* times compared with the sales in the previous year.

In another example, the Shanghai-based center found that in more than 90% of Chinese households with washing machines consumers still washed their underwear by hand. Consumer interviews revealed a fear that bacteria picked up by other clothing would spread to underwear during the wash, resulting in infections. Although the fear was never proven, the solution clearly was to sterilize the clothing in the wash. Close collaboration between China-based and Japan-based teams led to the 2007 launch of Panasonic's sterilizing washing machines in China. In less than a year, its market share for front-loading machines rose from 3% to 15% in China. In a departure from the conventional flow of innovation from Japan to emerging economies, Panasonic brought the sterilization concept from China back to Japan.

While these two examples are high-profile successes, they have been enabled by numerous efforts to foster formal and informal relationships among the Shanghai-based market researchers, engineers, and managers throughout the over 40 operations in China, and engineers and managers throughout Panasonic units in Japan and beyond. Overall, knowledge flew in both directions: from the rest of Panasonic to China and from China to the rest of Panasonic. To better manage the extensive flows of knowledge, Panasonic set up a China headquarters: Beijing-based Panasonic Corporation of China. China operations were gradually given more autonomy—rare among multinationals in general and among Japanese firms in particular. Since 2008, the China subsidiary, which has a high level of localization in staff, has had almost complete autonomy in new product decisions for China.

Going beyond China, Panasonic has leveraged its learning from the China experience by transforming its organization on a global basis. Encouraged by the fruits from paying close attention to local consumer needs in China, Panasonic also developed air conditioners in India and refrigerators in Vietnam. In 2009, Panasonic established a lifestyle research center for Europe (in Wiesbaden, Germany) and in 2010 it set up a similar center for India (in Delhi). In 2012, Panasonic created the Global Consumer Marketing organization to facilitate the diffusion of learning from the most insightful research and best practices outside Japan, especially in emerging economies. While the outcomes of these tremendous efforts are encouraging, they are far from reaching their full potential. In China, although Panasonic is the top Japanese (and foreign) brand of washing machines, it still trails behind Haier and White Swan, the two domestic market share leaders. Therefore, the BCG study has not identified Panasonic as an "industry winner." Whether Panasonic will emerge as a true winner in China and other emerging economies remains to be seen.

Case Discussion Questions

1. **Why do Japanese multinationals generally fall behind in emerging economies?**

2. **What contributions have Panasonic's China operations made to the rest of Panasonic?**

3. **Given the traditional flow of knowledge and innovation from headquarters to subsidiaries, what are the challenges of transferring knowledge and innovation from China to Japan and beyond?**

4. **How does Panasonic as a whole benefit from its commitment and success in China?**

Sources: Based on (1) S. Ichii, S. Hattori, & D. Michael, 2012, How to win in emerging markets, *Harvard Business Review*, May: 126–130; (2) T. Wakayama, J. Shintaku, & T. Amano, 2012, What Panasonic learned in China, *Harvard Business Review*, December: 109–113; (3) www.panasonic.co.jp; (4) www.panasonic.com.cn; (5) www.panasonic.net.

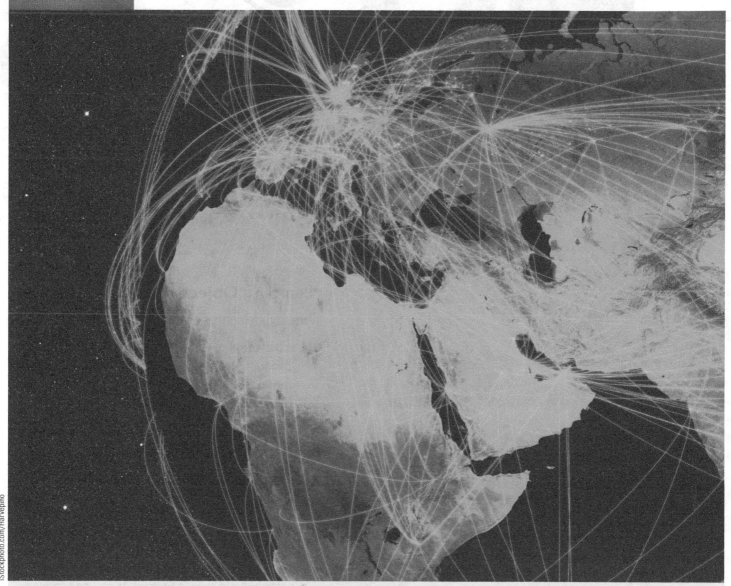

PART 4

Building Functional Excellence

iStockphoto.com/Harvepino

Chapters

Everett Kennedy Brown/epa/Corbis Wire/Corbis

CHAPTER 14

Learning Objectives

After studying this chapter, you should be able to

- articulate three of the four Ps in marketing (product, price, and promotion) in a global context.

- explain how the fourth P in marketing (place) has evolved to be labeled supply chain management.

- outline the triple A's in supply chain management (agility, adaptability, and alignment).

- discuss how institutions and resources affect marketing and supply chain management.

- participate in two leading debates concerning marketing and supply chain management.

- draw implications for action.

Competing on Marketing and Supply Chain Management

Marketing Aflac in the United States and Japan

Founded in 1955 and based in Columbus, Georgia, Aflac is the largest provider of supplemental insurance in the United States. It also operates in one other country—Japan. In fact, it sells more insurance in Japan than at home. It insures one of four Japanese households and is the largest life insurer in Japan in terms of individual insurance policies in force. In 1999, approximately four-fifths of its US$8.6 billion revenues came from Japan.

Although Aflac's business has been successful, its name has been problematic from the beginning. It first started as American Family Life Insurance Company. But a Wisconsin insurance company had an *identical* name (!). As a result of a gentlemen's coin toss between the two owners, "Assurance" was used instead of "Insurance." But the company still had difficulty differentiating itself from numerous other insurance and non-insurance companies whose names start with "American." In the 1990s, the company decided to go with the acronym only: Aflac. But Aflac still struggled with its unnatural (and "weird") name.

In 1999, in an effort to market itself better, Aflac engaged Kaplan Thaler Group, an advertising agency based in New York. But the agency had a hard time coming up with an idea that would make the relatively obscure insurance company's name memorable. During one lunch break, one of the agency's frustrated directors took a walk around Central Park and still scratched his head, uttering "Aflac, Aflac." As he walked around the duck pond, in a moment of inspiration he realized how much "Aflac" sounded like a duck's quack. In the absence of other more effective ideas, Kaplan Thaler Group pitched the duck to Aflac, hoping Aflac would not be offended by the commercial's making fun of its name. While this idea convinced CEO Daniel Amos, he had a hard time selling the idea to his colleagues and board members. In his own words:

> When I tried explaining to people what we were thinking about, no one got it. "Well, there's this duck," I'd say. "And he quacks Aflac." The response was always the same: a silent stare. So I stopped telling people. I didn't even tell our board; I just said we're trying to do something very bold and creative for our advertising campaign.

The Aflac Duck debut was aired on CNN on New Year's Day, 2000, with the Duck quacking "Aflac" to prospective policyholders. It ran four times an hour. The world watched CNN to see if the Y2K bug would wreak havoc, thus giving the Duck the maximum exposure. The response was overwhelming. After the first day on the air, Aflac had more visits to its website than in the entire year 1999. In the first year, Aflac sales in the United States went up by 29% and in three years they doubled. Thanks to the Duck, Aflac's name recognition was up to 67% after two years of running the commercial and is now higher than 90%. The Aflac Duck went on to be enshrined on Madison Avenue's Walk of Fame as one of America's Favorite Advertising Icons.

The famous American duck, however, had a hard time making itself heard in Japan. In Japan, a duck does not yell "quack-quack," it says "ga-ga." In Japan since 1973, Aflac did not suffer from being in the middle of a crowd of firms named "American." Instead, in Japan it was known for its full name: American Family Life Assurance Company. While the Japan subsidiary was not wholehearted in its support for the new ad, the Aflac Duck debuted in Japan in 2003. After some mild adaptation (such as toning down the yelling voice to a softer, more courteous tone), the Duck became a rock star in Japan and sales increased by 12% in 2003. Encouraged by the Duck's success, the

The Maneki Neko cat.

Japanese marketing team introduced a new incarnation: a mix of the Duck and the traditional Asian good luck white cat Maneki Neko—simply known as the Maneki Neko Duck or the cat duck. The cat duck became so popular that it was voted number-one commercial in Japan. The jingle from the commercial became the number-one downloaded mobile-phone ringtone in Japan, and the Maneki Neko Duck attracted thousands of followers on Facebook, Twitter, and YouTube. Aflac rocketed ahead to become the number-one insurance company in Japan, an honor held by Nippon Life for more than 100 years. Now when people come to visit Aflac's headquarters in Georgia, they want to see the Aflac Duck. So the company has added a duck pond to its headquarters—probably the first and only duck pond among all American (and Japanese) company headquarters.

Sources: Based on (1) D. Amos, 2010, Aflac's CEO explains how he fell for the duck, *Harvard Business Review*, January: 131–134; (2) *BuzzFeed*, 2014, Aflac Duck in Japan, www.buzzfeed.com; (3) www.aflac.com; (4) www.japanprobe.com.

Marketing

Efforts to create, develop, and defend markets that satisfy the needs and wants of individual and business customers.

Supply chain

Flow of products, services, finances, and information that passes through a set of entities from a source to the customer.

Supply chain management

Activities to plan, organize, lead, and control the supply chain.

How can firms such as Aflac market themselves to attract customers around the world? How can they tailor and adapt their messages to capture the hearts, minds, and wallets of different customers who have different tastes and preferences? Having attracted customers, how can firms ensure a steady supply of products and services? This chapter deals with these and other important questions associated with marketing and supply chain management. Marketing refers to efforts to create, develop, and defend markets that satisfy individual and business customers. Supply chain is the flow of products, services, finances, and information that passes through a set of entities from a source to the customer.[1] Supply chain management refers to activities to plan, organize, lead, and control the supply chain.[2] In this chapter, instead of viewing marketing and supply chain as two stand-alone, separate functions, we view them as one crucial, integrated function.

We first outline major marketing and supply chain activities in global business. Then we discuss how the institution-based and resource-based views enhance our understanding of the drivers behind marketing and supply chain management success. Finally, debates and implications follow.

14-1 Three of the Four Ps in Marketing

Learning Objective
Articulate three of the four Ps in marketing (product, price, and promotion) in a global context.

Shown in Figure 14.1, marketing is crucial for firm performance. Figure 14.2 shows the four Ps that collectively consist of the marketing mix: (1) product, (2) price, (3) promotion, and (4) place.[3] We start with the first three Ps. The last P—place (where the product is sourced, produced, and distributed)—will be discussed in the next section.

14-1a Product

Product refers to offerings that customers purchase. Although the word "product" originally referred to a physical product, its modern use has included services (such as maintenance and upgrades).[4] Even for a single category (such as women's dress or sports car), product attributes vary tremendously. For multinational enterprises (MNEs) doing business around the world, a leading concern is standardization

---

Figure 14.1 **Marketing and Firm Performance**

"What's your marketing plan?"

Bill Abbott

Source: *Harvard Business Review*, December 2012: 32.

Figure 14.2 **The Four Ps of Marketing Mix**

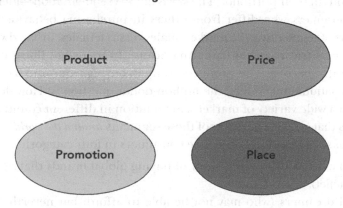

Marketing mix

The four underlying components of marketing: (1) product, (2) price, (3) promotion, and (4) place.

Product

Offering that customers purchase.

versus localization.[5] Localization is natural. McDonald's, for example, sells wine in France, beer in Germany, mutton pot pies in Australia, and Maharaja Mac and McCurry Pan in India. In China, KFC features menus items that would not be recognizable to its customers in the United States. Alongside the Colonel's "secret recipe" fried chicken, KFC in China also markets congee, a chicken wrap in a Peking duck-type sauce, and spicy tofu chicken rice. In Japan, Wendy's sells a US$16 *Foie Gras Rossini* (goose-liver pâté) hamburger.[6]

What is interesting is the rise of standardization, which is often attributed to Theodore Levitt's 1983 article, "The Globalization of Markets"[7] (first discussed in Chapter 13). This article advocated globally standardized products and services, as evidenced by Hollywood movies and Coke Classic. However, numerous subsequent experiments such as Ford's world car and MTV's global (essentially American) programming backfired. Marketers thus face a dilemma: while one size does not fit all, most firms cannot afford to create products and services for just one group of customers. Shown in the Opening Case, how much to standardize and how much to localize remain challenges.[8]

As first noted in Chapter 13, localization is appealing (in the eyes of local consumers and governments) but expensive. One sensible solution is to have a product that *appears* to be locally adapted while deriving as much synergy (commonality) as possible in ways that customers cannot easily recognize. Consider the two global business weekly magazines, the US-based *Bloomberg Businessweek* and the UK-based *Economist*. In addition to its US edition, *Bloomberg Businessweek* publishes two English (language) editions for Asia and Europe and a Chinese edition for China. While these four editions share certain content, there is a lot of local edition-only material that is expensive to produce. In comparison, each issue of the *Economist* has the following regional sections (in alphabetical order): (1) the Americas (excluding the United States), (2) Asia (excluding China), (3) Britain, (4) China, (5) Europe (excluding Britain), (6) the Middle East and Africa, and (7) the United States. While the content for each issue is identical, the order of appearance of the regional sections is different. For US subscribers, their *Economist* would start with the US section. For Chinese subscribers, their magazine would start with the China section. By doing that, the *Economist* appears to be responsive to readers with different regional interests without incurring the costs of running multiple editions for different regions, as *Bloomberg Businessweek* does. Therefore, how many editions does one issue of the *Economist* have? We can say one—or seven if we count the seven different ways of stapling regional sections together.

One of the major concerns for MNEs is to decide whether to market global brands or local brands in their portfolio.[9] The key is market segmentation—identifying segments of consumers who differ from others in purchasing behavior.[10] There are limitless ways of segmenting the market (males versus females, urban dwellers versus rural residents, Africans versus Latin Americans). In Focus 14.1 illustrates a surprising segment that becomes the strongest group in buying cars—the Baby Boomers.

For international marketers, the million-dollar question is: How does one generalize from a wide variety of market segmentation in different countries to generate products that can cater to a few of these segments *around the world*? One globally useful way of segmentation is to divide consumers in four categories:[11]

- Global citizens (who are in favor of buying global brands that signal prestige and cachet).
- Global dreamers (who may not be able to afford, but nevertheless admire, global brands).

Market segmentation
Identifying segments of consumers who differ from others in purchasing behavior.

IN FOCUS 14.1

WHICH MARKET SEGMENT BUYS MORE NEW CARS?

Young, energetic, and sexy drivers are among the most frequently featured models in car commercials. Too bad, young people—the 35- to 44-year-old group (Generation X) and the 18- to 34-year-old group (Generation Y)—are not the strongest segment of car buyers in the United States. Instead, American consumers aged 55 to 64 have the *highest* rate of new vehicle purchases in the last five years. Even consumers aged 75 and above have bought cars at a higher rate than 18- to 34-year olds. In other words, a lot of advertising targeting Generation Y misses the mark. Instead, their Baby Boomer *parents* over take them as car buyers. New car registration data suggest that in 2002, people 50 years and older registered 40% new cars, those between 35 and 49 purchased 36%, and those between 18 and 24 bought 24%. In 2012, the three groups, respectively, had 62%, 24%, and 14% new car registrations.

Such purchasing behavior deviates from the conventional wisdom, which alleges that as people get older, they become less active and thus less interested in cars. Further digging reveals two interesting observations. First, as a segment Baby Boomers—specifically, people who were born between the end of World War II and the 1960s—grew up in an era during which their cars defined them. "A 20-year-old doesn't see the car this way," according to an expert. In 2011, only 79% of people between 20 and 24 had a driver's license; in 1983, 92% of them had a driver's license. On the other hand, in 2011, 93% of those between 60 and 64 maintained a driver's license, up from 84% in 1983. These data suggest that Baby Boomers refuse to follow the earlier trend: they want to stay young and stay active longer, go to more places, and—if they cannot afford to retire

thanks to the Great Recession of 2008–2009—need comfortable and flexible transportation. Second, Baby Boomers simply have more money to spend on new wheels than younger generations, who suffered more unemployment during the Great Recession and its aftermath. The upshot? A lot of youth-oriented models and features, such as Toyota's Scion and Honda's Element, end up selling better to Baby Boomers. In response, automakers have endeavored to come up with models and features that cater to Boomers. For example, Toyota has been embracing Boomers with the US$27,850 Venza sport wagon. Relative to a high-riding SUV, the down-to-earth Venza is easier to climb into—a crucial feature for aging drivers, some of whom may have knee problems. Other automakers such as GM, Ford, and Chrysler have also been turning toward buyers in their golden years.

Sources: Based on (1) P. Allison, 2012, US car industry: Who is buying domestic vs. imported? www.pamallison.com; (2) *Bloomberg Businessweek*, 2013, The Boomer car boom, September 2: 23–24; (3) *New Media and Marketing*, 2014, Guess which demographic segment rules car sales? www.newmediaandmarketing.com.

- Anti-globals (who are skeptical about whether global brands deliver higher-quality goods).
- Global agnostics (who are most likely to lead anti-globalization demonstrations, such as smashing McDonald's windows).

The implications are clear. For the first two categories of global citizens and global dreamers, firms are advised to leverage the global brands and their relatively more standardized products and services. "Global brands make us feel like citizens of the world," an Argentine consumer observed. However, MNEs do not necessarily have to write off the anti-globals and global agnostics as lost customers, because they can market localized products and services under local brands. Nestlé, for example, owns 8,000 (!) brands around the world, most of which are local, country-specific (or region-specific) brands not marketed elsewhere.

Overall, Levitt may be *both* right and wrong. A large percentage of consumers around the world indeed have converging interests and preferences centered on global brands. However, a substantial percentage of them also resist globally standardized brands, products, and services. Armed with this knowledge, both MNEs and local firms can better craft their products and services.[12]

14-1b Price

Price refers to the expenditures that customers are willing to pay for a product. Most consumers are "price sensitive." The jargon is price elasticity—how demand changes when price changes. Basic economic theory of supply and demand suggests that when price drops, consumers will buy more and generate stronger demand, which in turn will motivate firms to expand production to meet this demand. This theory, of course, underpins numerous firms' relentless drive around the world to cut costs and then prices. The question is *how* "price sensitive" consumers are. Holding the product (such as shampoo) constant, in general the lower income level the consumers are, the more price sensitive they are. While American, European, and Japanese consumers take it for granted that shampoo is sold by the bottle, in India shampoo is often sold in single-use sachets, each costing about one to ten cents. Many consumers there find the cost for a bottle of shampoo to be prohibitive. Some African telecommunications operators charge customers by the *second*—a big deal for those making pennies a day.[13]

In addition to the price at the point of purchase, another dimension of price is the total cost of ownership. One example in consumer products is the ubiquitous HP laser printer. Owners typically spend two to three times more on HP print cartridges than on the printer itself. While many individual consumers (such as buyers of HP printers) do not pay explicit attention to the total cost of ownership, it is obviously more important in business-to-business marketing and is often explicitly evaluated prior to purchase decisions. Aircraft makers (such as Airbus) can reap additional revenues for as long as 20 to 30 years after the initial sale. More importantly, after-sales (spare) products and services are less price sensitive and thus have higher margins. Consequently, many firms compete on winning the initial sale with a lower price, with the aim of capturing more revenue through after-sales products and services.

Finally, in international marketing, it is important to note that aggressively low prices abroad may be accused of dumping, thus triggering protectionist measures. Because Chapter 11 has already discussed the antidumping issue at length, we will not repeat it here other than stressing its importance.

14-1c Promotion

Promotion refers to all the communications that marketers insert into the marketplace. Promotion includes TV, radio, print, and online advertising, as well as coupons, direct mail, billboards, direct marketing (personal selling), and public relations.

Price

The expenditures that customers are willing to pay for a product.

Price elasticity

How demand changes when price changes.

Total cost of ownership

Total cost needed to own a product, consisting of initial purchase cost and follow-up maintenance/service cost.

Promotion

Communicatons that marketers insert into the marketplace.

As Aflac's experience in both the United States and Japan (see the Opening Case) shows, marketers face a strategic choice of whether to standardize or localize promotional efforts. Standardized promotion not only projects a globally consistent message (crucial for global brands), but can also save a lot of money.

However, there is a limit to the effectiveness of standardized promotion.[14] In the 1990s, Coca-Cola ran a worldwide campaign featuring a cute polar bear cartoon character. Research later showed that viewers in warmer-weather countries had a hard time relating to this ice-bound animal with which they had no direct experience. In response, Coca-Cola switched to more costly, but more effective, country-specific advertisements. For instance, the Indian subsidiary launched a campaign that equated Coke with *thanda*, the Hindi word for "cold." The German subsidiary developed commercials that showed a "hidden" kind of eroticism (!). While this is merely one example, it does suggest that even some of the most global brands (such as Coca-Cola) can benefit from localized promotion.

Many firms promote products and services overseas without doing their "homework" and end up with blunders (huge mistakes). GM marketed its Chevrolet Nova in Latin America without realizing that "*no va*" means "no go" in Spanish. Coors Beer translated its successful slogan "Turn it loose" from English to Spanish as "Drink Coors, get diarrhea."[15] Table 14.1 outlines some blunders that are hilarious to readers but *painful* to marketers, some of whom were fired because of these blunders.

In international marketing, country-of-origin effect refers to the positive or negative perception of firms and products from a certain country (first discussed in Chapter 10).[16] Marketers have to decide whether to enhance or downplay such an effect. This can be very tricky. Disneyland Tokyo became popular in Japan because it played up its American image. But Disneyland Paris received relentless negative press coverage in France, because it insisted on its "wholesome American look." Singapore Airlines projects a "Singapore girl" image around the world. In contrast, Li Ning downplays its Chinese origin by using American NBA players in

Table 14.1 Some Blunders in International Marketing

- One US toymaker received numerous complaints from American mothers, because a talking doll told their children, "Kill mommy!" Made in Hong Kong, the dolls were shipped around the world. They carried messages in the language of the country of destination. A packing error sent some Spanish-speaking dolls to the United States. The message in Spanish "Quiero mommy!" means "I love mommy!" (This is also a supply chain blunder.)

- AT&T submitted a proposal to sell phone equipment in Thailand. Despite its excellent technology, the proposal was rejected out of hand by telecom authorities. This was because Thailand required a 10-year warranty but AT&T only offered a five-year warranty—thanks to standardization on warranty imposed by US headquarters.

- Japan's Olympia tried to market a photocopier to Latin America under the name "Roto." Sales were minimal. Why? *Roto* means "broken" in Spanish.

- Chinese exporters have marketed the following products overseas: White Elephant brand batteries, Sea Cucumber brand shirts, and Maxipuke brand poker cards (the two Chinese characters, *pu ke*, mean poker, and it should have been translated as Maxi brand poker cards—but its package said "Maxipuke").

Sources: Based on text in (1) T. Dalgic & R. Heijblom, 1996, International marketing blunders revisited—some lessons for managers, *Journal of International Marketing*, 4 (1): 81–91; (2) D. Ricks, 1999, *Blunders in International Business*, 3rd ed., Oxford, UK: Blackwell.

its commercials. What is the nationality of Häagen-Dazs ice cream? If you thought Häagen-Dazs was a German, Austrian, or Belgium brand and had been happily paying a premium price for "European" ice cream, you were fooled. Häagen-Dazs is a US brand. Sometimes, multiple countries of origin are disclosed. For example, Apple stamped on the back of every iPhone: "Designed by Apple in California. Assembled in China." Some Toyota cars' dealer stickers disclose: "Made in the USA. Engine made in Japan."

In addition to the traditional domestic versus international challenge, a new challenge lies in the pursuit of online versus offline (traditional) advertising.[17] As the first cohort to grow up Internet savvy, today's teens and twenty-somethings in many countries flock to social networks such as Facebook, Twitter, and their equivalents around the world. These young people "do not buy stuff because they see a magazine ad," according to one expert, "they buy stuff because other kids tell them to online."[18] What is challenging is how marketers can reach such youth.[19] A basic threat to such social networks is the whim of their users, whose interest in certain topics and networks themselves may change or even evaporate overnight.

Overall, marketers need to experiment with a variety of configurations of the three Ps (product, price, and promotion) around the world in order to optimize the marketing mix. Next, we discuss the fourth P, place.

14-2 From Distribution Channel to Supply Chain Management

Learning Objective
Explain how the fourth P in marketing (place) has evolved to be labeled supply chain management.

As the fourth P in the marketing mix, place refers to the location where products and services are provided (which now, of course, includes the online marketplace). Technically, place is also often referred to as the distribution channel—the set of firms that facilitates the movement of goods from producers to consumers. Until the 1980s, many producers made most goods in-house and one of the key concerns was distribution. Since then, production outsourcing has grown significantly. Many producers (such as Apple) do not physically produce their branded products at all; they rely on contract manufacturers (such as Foxconn) to get the job done. Other producers that still produce in-house (such as Dell) rely on their suppliers to provide an increasingly higher percentage of the value-added. Therefore, the new challenge is how to manage the longer distribution channel—more specifically, the distribution from suppliers (and contract manufacturers) all the way to consumers (see Figure 14.3).

Place
The location where products and services are provided.

Distribution channel
The set of firms that facilitates the movement of goods from producers to consumers.

Consequently, a new term, "supply chain," has been coined, and it has now almost replaced the old-fashioned "distribution channel." To be sure, the focal firm has always dealt with suppliers. Strategy guru Michael Porter labels this

---

Figure 14.3   **Supply Chain Management**

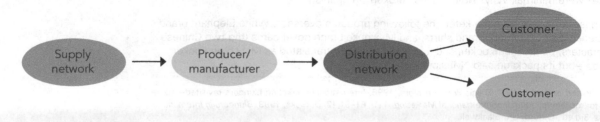

function as "inbound logistics" (and the traditional distribution channel as "outbound logistics").[20] In a broad sense, the new term "supply chain" is almost synonymous with "value chain," encompassing both inbound and outbound logistics (see Chapter 4). In the military, logistics is widely acknowledged as a contributor to wartime success. But no army recruitment material would brag about a glamorous career in logistics in the military to attract new soldiers. Similarly, business logistics tends to be tactical and lacks prestige. However, if supply chain is value chain, then supply chain management essentially handles the *entire* process of value creation, which is the core mission of the firm. Consequently, supply chain management has now taken on new strategic importance and gained tremendous prestige.

One indication that supply chain management has gained traction is that instead of being obscure players, leading supply chain management firms, such as DHL, FedEx, and UPS, have now become household names. On any given day, 2% of the world's GDP can be found in UPS trucks and planes. "FedEx" has become a verb, and even live *whales* have reportedly been "FedExed." Modern supply chains aim to "get the right product to the right place at the right time—all the time."[21] Next, we discuss the triple As underpinning supply chains: (1) agility, (2) adaptability, and (3) alignment.[22]

14-3 Triple As in Supply Chain Management

14-3a Agility

Agility refers to the ability to quickly react to unexpected shifts in supply and demand.[23] To reduce inventory, many firms now use the trucks, ships, and planes of their suppliers and carriers as their warehouse. In their quest for supply chain speed, cost, and efficiency, many firms fail to realize the cost they have to pay for disregarding agility. On the other hand, firms such as Zara thrive in large part because of the agility of their supply chain (see the Closing Case). Zara's agility permeates throughout its entire operations, starting with design processes. As soon as designers spot certain trends, they create sketches and go ahead to order fabrics without finalizing designs. This speeds things up because fabric suppliers require a long lead time. Designs are finalized when reliable data from stores come. Production commences as soon as designs are complete. In addition, Zara's factories only run one shift, easily allowing for overtime production if demand calls for it. Its distribution centers are also highly efficient, allowing it to handle demand fluctuation without creating bottlenecks.

Agility may become more important in the 21st century because shocks to supply chains are now more frequent. Recently, notable disruptions have included terrorist attacks (such as "9/11" and Islamic State), civil wars (such as Syria and Ukraine), political unrest (such as Arab Spring, Hong Kong, Iraq, and Libya), and natural disasters (such as Ebola, H1N1 swine flu, Icelandic volcano eruption, Indian Ocean tsunami, and Japanese earthquake). Under shocks, an agile supply chain can rise to the challenge, while a static supply chain can pull a firm down.[24]

In 2000, Nokia and Ericsson fought in the mobile handset market. Consider how Nokia and Ericsson

Learning Objective
Outline the triple As in supply chain management (agility, adaptability, and alignment).

Agility

The ability to react quickly to unexpected shifts in supply and demand.

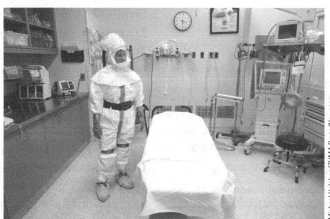

How do outbreaks such as Ebola affect the supply chain and what steps can firms take to ensure adequate agility for such disasters?

reacted differently to a fire induced by thunderstorm at a New Mexico factory of their handset chip supplier, Philips. The damage was minor, and Philips expected to resume production within a week. However, Nokia took no chances, and it quickly carried out design changes so that two other suppliers, one in Japan and another in the United States, could manufacture similar chips for Nokia. (These were the only two suppliers in the world other than Philips that were capable of delivering similar chips.) Nokia then quickly placed orders from these two suppliers. In contrast, Ericsson's supply chain had no such agility: It was set up to function exclusively with the damaged Philips plant in New Mexico—there was no plan B. Unfortunately, Philips later found out that the damage was larger than first reported, and production would be delayed for months. By that time Ericsson scrambled to contact the other two suppliers, only to find out that Nokia had locked up all of their output for the next few months. The upshot? By 2001, Ericsson was driven out of the handset market as an independent player.[25] (In 2001, Ericsson reentered the market with a joint venture with Sony called Sony Ericsson. In 2012, it sold its shares to Sony.)

14-3b Adaptability

While agility focuses on flexibility that can overcome short-term fluctuation in the supply chain, adaptability refers to the ability to change supply chain configurations in response to longer-term changes in the environment and technology. Enhancing adaptability often entails making a series of make-or-buy decisions.[26] This requires firms to *continuously* monitor major geopolitical, social, and technological trends, make sense of them, and reconfigure the supply chain accordingly.[27] The damage for failing to do so may not be visible immediately, but across a number of years firms failing to do so may be selected out of market.

Consider Lucent, the American telecommunications equipment giant. In the mid-1990s, in response to competitive pressures from its rivals Siemens and Alcatel that benefited from low-cost, Asia-based production, Lucent successfully adapted its supply chain by phasing out more production in high-cost developed economies and setting up plants in China and Taiwan. However, Lucent then failed to adapt continuously. It concentrated its production in its own Asia-based plants, whereas rivals outsourced such manufacturing to Asian suppliers that became more capable of taking on more complex work. In other words, Lucent used foreign direct investment (FDI) to "make," whereas rivals adopted outsourcing to "buy." Ultimately, Lucent was stuck with its own relatively higher cost (although Asia-based) plants and was overwhelmed by rivals. By 2006, Lucent lost its independence and was acquired by its archrival Alcatel.

14-3c Alignment

Alignment refers to the alignment of interests of various players in the supply chain. In a broad sense, every supply chain is a strategic alliance involving a variety of players, each of which is a profit-maximizing, stand-alone firm.[28] As a result, conflicts are natural. However, players associated with one supply chain must effectively coordinate to achieve desirable outcomes. Therefore, this is a crucial dilemma. Supply chains that can better solve this dilemma may outperform other supply chains. For example, for Boeing's 787 Dreamliner, some 70% of the US$8 billion development cost is outsourced to suppliers: Mitsubishi makes the wings, Messier-Dowty

Adaptability
The ability to change supply chain configurations in response to longer-term changes in the environment and technology.

Make-or-buy decision
Decision about whether to produce inhouse ("make") or to outsource ("buy").

Alignment
Alignment of interests of various players.

provides the landing gear, and so forth. Many suppliers are responsible for end-to-end design of whole subsections. Headed by a vice president for global partnerships, Boeing treats its suppliers as partners, has "partner councils" with regular meetings, and fosters long-term collaboration.

Conceptually, there are two key elements to achieve alignment: (1) power and (2) trust.[29] Not all players in a supply chain are equal, and more powerful players such as Boeing naturally exercise greater bargaining power.[30] Having a recognized leader exercising power, such as De Beers in diamonds, facilitates legitimacy and efficiency of the whole supply chain. Otherwise, excessive bargaining will have to be conducted among supply chain members of more or less equal standing.

Trust stems from perceived fairness and justice from all supply chain members. While supply chains have become ever more complex, modern practices—such as low (or zero) inventory, frequent just-in-time (JIT) deliveries, and more geographic dispersion of production—have made all parties more vulnerable if the *weakest* link breaks down.[31] This happened during the Japanese earthquake in 2011. Therefore, it is in the best interest of all parties to invest in trust-building mechanisms in order to foster more collaboration.

For instance, 7-Eleven Japan exercises a great deal of power by dictating that vendors resupply its 9,000 stores at three *specific* times a day. If a truck is late by more than 30 minutes, the vendor has to pay a penalty equal to the gross margin of the products carried to the store. This may seem harsh, but is necessary. This is because 7-Eleven Japan staff reconfigure store shelves three times a day to cater to different consumers at different *hours*, such as commuters in the morning and school kids in the afternoon—time, literally, means money. However, 7-Eleven Japan softens the blow by trusting its vendors. It does not verify the contents of deliveries. This allows vendors to save time and money, because after deliveries, truck drivers do not have to wait for verification and can immediately move on to make other trips. The alignment of interest of such a supply chain is legendary. Hours after the earthquake in March 2011, when relief trucks moved at two miles per hour (if they moved at all) on the damaged roads, 7-Eleven Japan's vendors went the extra mile by deploying helicopters and motorcycles to deliver much-needed food and supplies to the devastated region.

Sometimes, introducing neutral intermediaries (middlemen)—more specifically, third-party logistics (3PL) providers—may more effectively align the interests in the supply chain. In the case of outsourcing in Asia, buyers (importers) tend to be large Western MNEs such as Gap, Nike, and Marks & Spencer, and suppliers (exporters) are often smaller Asian manufacturers. Despite best intentions, both sides may still distrust each other. MNE buyers are not sure of the quality and timeliness of delivery. Further, MNE buyers are unable to control labor practices in supplier factories, some of which may be dubious (such as running "sweatshops"). In the 1990s, Nike's reputation took a severe hit due to alleged questionable labor practices at its supplier factories. However, suppliers may also be suspicious. Since most contracts for shoes, clothing, toys, and electronics are written several months ahead, suppliers are not confident about MNE buyers' ability to forecast demand correctly. Suppliers thus worry that in case of lower-than-anticipated demand, buyers may reject shipments to reduce excess inventory, by opportunistically citing excuses such as labor practices or quality issues. One solution lies in the involvement of 3PL intermediaries, such as Hong Kong-based Li & Fung. Overall, 3PL firms may add value by aligning the interests of all parties.

Third-party logistics (3PL) provider

A neutral, third-party intermediary in the supply chain that provides logistics and other support services.

Learning Objective
Discuss how institutions and resources affect marketing and supply chain management.

14-4 How Institutions and Resources Affect Marketing and Supply Chain Management

Having outlined the basic features of marketing and supply chain management, let us now use the institution-based and resource-based views to shed additional light on these topics (Figure 14.4).

14-4a Institutions, Marketing, and Supply Chain Management

As an important form of institutions, formal rules of the game obviously have a significant impact.[32] Most countries impose restrictions, ranging from taboos in advertising to constraints on the equity level held by foreign retailers and 3PL providers. Germany bans advertising that portrays another product as inferior. Goodyear Tire exported a successful commercial used in the United States to Germany, by showing that its tire cord could break a steel chain. Because the commercial was viewed as insulting the German steel chain manufacturers, the German government banned it. In India, FDI had not been allowed in the mass retail sector. Likewise, China forbids foreign retailers from operating wholly owned stores and only approves joint-venture stores. In China, France's Carrefour is the most aggressive foreign retailer, with sales ahead of Wal-Mart. In some cities, Carrefour struck sweetheart deals with officials and operated wholly owned stores, which provoked Beijing's wrath. The upshot? Carrefour was forced to sell a portion of its equity to Chinese partners and convert its wholly owned stores to joint-venture stores to be in compliance with regulations.

Informal rules also place significant constraints on marketing and supply chain management. In marketing, most of the blunders documented in Table 14.1 happen due to firms' failure to appreciate the deep underlying differences in cultures, languages, and norms—all part of the informal institutions. In supply chains, leading firms headquartered in developed economies may be able to diffuse leading-edge practices. In the 1990s, as a new norm, large numbers of European firms adopted the ISO 9000 series of quality management systems. They then imposed the standard on their suppliers and partners throughout the world. Over time, these suppliers and partners spread ISO 9000 to other domestic firms. At present,

Figure 14.4   **Institutions, Resources, Marketing, and Supply Chain Management**

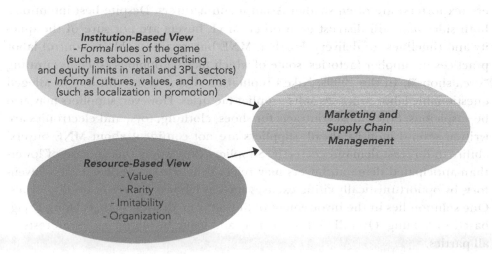

more than 560,000 sites in more than 150 countries have been ISO 9000 certified. In other words, due to the normative influence, suppliers and partners that export goods and services to a particular country in a supply chain may be simultaneously *importing* that country's norms and practices.[33]

14-4b Resources, Marketing, and Supply Chain Management

As before, we can evaluate marketing and supply chain management activities based on the VRIO criteria (see Figure 14.4). First, do these activities add *value*?[34] Marketers now increasingly scratch their heads, as traditional media are losing viewers, readers, and thus effectiveness, but marketers do not have a good handle of how advertising in the new online media adds value. Firms combating the recession have tried hard to add value to their increasingly frugal customers.[35] One interesting idea is to focus on the *disloyal*, not loyal, customers. For example, Starbucks already has 90% of the coffee dollars of its most loyal customers, leaving little room for further growth for that group. However, it is the sizable group of "switchers"—those who go to both Starbucks and other coffee houses—that may represent the largest potential for growth. The challenge is: How can Starbucks add value to these "switchers"?

Second, managers need to assess the *rarity* of marketing and supply chain activities. If all rival firms use FedEx to manage logistics (which does add value), these activities, in themselves, are not rare. In supply chain management, first movers in radio frequency identification (RFID) tags may derive benefits, because they are rare. However, as RFID becomes more available, its rarity (novelty value) will drop. In Focus 14.2 illustrates how the world's largest shipping line, Maersk, has launched the mightiest ships ever built, the Triple-E class, to enhance the value and rarity of its container shipping services.

IN FOCUS 14.2

GIANTS OF THE SEA

Compared with the high-flying DHL, FedEx, and UPS jets, it is the slow-moving ships that are the backbone of modern supply chains. Every day, container ships carry 90% of the world's traded cargo by value, and such ocean shipping is known as "box trade." Taking off since the 1970s, container shipping has significantly reduced shipping cost so that China's location in the *Far* East does not seem to be too far away from major markets in North America and Europe. Yet, this industry is far from smooth sailing. Just as numerous new ships joined the fleet in the late 2000s, the Great Recession of 2008–2009 reduced trade volume, causing pricing levels to collapse.

As various shipping lines struggle and look for solutions, Maersk Line, the Copenhagen, Denmark-based largest shipping line in the world, has come up

Made in South Korea, the first ship of the Triple-E class, the *Maersk Mc-Kinney Møller*, passes the Suez Canal on its maiden journey from Asia to Europe in August 2013.

Stefan Hofecker/Alamy

IN FOCUS 14.2 (continued)

with some of the biggest splashes. In 2001, Maersk awarded Daewoo Shipbuilding of South Korea a US$3.8 billion contract to build 20 of the world's largest ships: The Maersk Triple-E Class. The maiden journey of the first ship, the *Maersk Mc-Kinney Møller*, sailed in August 2013.

The name "Triple-E" is derived from the class' three design principles: economy, energy, and environment. With a dead weight of 165,000 tons, the colossal ship is 59 meters (194 feet) wide and 400 meters (1,312 feet) long—in other words, its length is longer than the Eiffel Tower (324 meters or 1,070 feet). The first E, economy of scale, is achieved not only by such dimensions, but also by fundamental design changes. Instead of a V-shaped hull, the ship's hull is much rectangular and closer to U-shaped. The upshot? A whopping 18,000 twenty-foot-equivalent unit (TEU) containers—2,500 more than the next biggest ships (the Maersk E class), which were launched in 2006. A new Triple-E ship is also packed with a lot of new automation technologies, so that it only requires a crew between 22 (standard) and 34 (maximum) members.

Energy efficiency is achieved by deliberate slow steaming. Slower than earlier generations, the Triple-E ships' design speed is 19 knots (35 kilometers or 22 miles per hour), which reduces fuel consumption by 20% compared to the E class. The final E, environmental friendliness, is also enabled by such low fuel burn. For each ton of cargo transported one kilometer, a Maersk Triple-E ship only emits three grams of CO_2. This is a far smaller environmental footprint than other modes of transportation: 18 grams of CO_2 for rail, 47 grams for truck, and 560 grams for air freight.

The last but nontrivial component of environmental friendliness is that each ship is designed and built for recycling. All components are traced and listed so that when the ship is scrapped, the useful materials can be efficiently channeled to various recycling categories, tremendously reducing the lifetime (and post-lifetime) environmental footprint of the colossal giant. Winner of the "Sustainable Ship Operator of the Year" Award in 2011 (before the launch of the Triple-E class), Maersk believes that environmental friendliness will increasingly be a competitive differentiation factor and that the Triple-E class will help strengthen its edge.

At a cost of US$190 million each, the Maersk Triple-E class ships are certainly valuable, rare, hard-to-imitate, and supported by the strong organizational capabilities of the world's largest shipping line. But they are too big. No port in the Americas (either North and South) can handle them. Specifically, no crane is wide enough to reach its containers on the far side. With a draft of 14.5 meters (48 feet), they are too deep to cross the Panama Canal anyway. They can transit the Suez Canal when sailing between Europe and Asia. They will be limited to serving routes between Europe and Asia. The Europe–Asia trade represents Maersk's largest market, already with more than 100 ships plying the waves. Maersk hopes to strengthen its leading position of the Europe–Asia trade with the addition of the new giants of the sea.

Sources: Based on (1) *Bloomberg Businessweek*, 2013, An ill-timed bet on the world's largest ship, April 29: 21; (2) *BusinessWeek*, 2009, Hedging bets on the high seas, April 27: 10; (3) *Economist*, 2007, Container ships, March 3: 71; (4) *Economist*, 2009, Sea of troubles, August 1: 55–56; (5) *Focus Denmark*, 2014, A slow steaming giant, Summer-Autumn: 68–71.

Third, having identified valuable and rare capabilities, managers need to assess how likely it is for rivals and partners to *imitate*. While there is no need to waste more ink on the necessity to watch out for rivals, firms also need to be careful about partners in the supply chain. As more Western MNEs outsource production to suppliers (or, using new jargon, contract manufacturers), it is always possible that some of the aggressive contract manufacturers may bite the hand that feeds them by directly imitating and competing with Western MNEs. This is not necessarily "opportunism." It is natural for ambitious contract manufacturers such as Foxconn and Flextronics to flex their muscle. While it is possible to imitate and acquire world-class manufacturing capabilities, marketing prowess and brand power are more intangible and, thus, harder-to-imitate. Thus, Western MNEs often cope by (1) being careful about what they outsource, and (2) strengthening customer loyalty to their brands (such as Apple) to fend off contract manufacturers.

Finally, managers need to ask: Is our firm *organizationally* ready to accomplish our objectives?[36] Oddly, in many firms, Marketing and Sales functions do not get along well—to avoid confusion, here we use the two terms with capital letters, "Marketing" and "Sales," to refer to these functions. When revenues are disappointing, the blame game begins: Marketing blames Sales for failing to execute a brilliant plan, and Sales blames Marketing for setting the price too high and burning too much cash in high-flying but useless promotion. Marketing staff tend to be better educated, more analytical, and disappointed when certain initiatives fail. Sales people are often "street smart," persuasive, and used to rejections all the time. It is not surprising that Marketing and Sales have a hard time working together.[37] Yet, work together they must. Some leading firms have disbanded Marketing and Sales as separate functions and have created an integrated function—called Channel Enablement at IBM.

14-5 Debates and Extensions

Learning Objective
Participate in two leading debates concerning marketing and supply chain management.

There are some long-standing debates in this field, such as the debate on standardization versus localization (discussed earlier). Here, we focus on two important debates that are not previously discussed: (1) manufacturing versus services and (2) market orientation versus relationship orientation.

14-5a Manufacturing versus Services

This debate deals with the nature of economic activities. Consider contract manufacturing service. Is it manufacturing? Service? Both? Our vocabulary evolves with—and is also trapped by—the history of economic development. As the first sector for organized economic activities, agriculture was usually seen as *primary*. Emerging in the Industrial Revolution, manufacturing was often the *secondary* sector (after agriculture). Consequently, the residual service activities were typically viewed as *tertiary* (third sector).

Throughout the first-half of the 20th century, agriculture declined in importance, and "economic development" often meant industrialization centered on manufacturing. However, in the second-half of the 20th century, it was services that occupied the commanding height.[38] In the 21st century, manufacturing only contributes 10% of the British and French GDP, and 11% to 12% of the Canadian and US GDP. Besides the small contributions to GDP made by agriculture (generally lower than 3% in the four countries named above), the rest is all services.

Despite the recent prominence of the service sector, it historically lacks prestige. Service has a much longer history than manufacturing. The word "service" originated from the Latin word *servus*, which means slave or servant. Nothing could be lower than that. To "add salt to injury," Adam Smith in *The Wealth of Nations* (1776) labeled service "non-productive activities." Believing that "real man makes stuff," the Soviet Union and China during the heyday of socialism had highly developed heavy manufacturing industries but a severely underdeveloped service sector. Thus, they were able to launch rockets to outer space but did not have enough decent mechanics to fix toilets (!).

Toward the end of the 20th century, as Russia and China "woke up" and looked at developed economies for inspiration, they found a highly developed service sector. In fact, it is innovations in services that drive much of economic growth now.[39] Consider McDonald's. In the 1950s, McDonald's drew on the principle of the assembly line, a core manufacturing principle dating back to Henry Ford in the 1910s, to develop high-volume, fast, and standardized food services—and the rest is history.

While marketing and supply chain management would be regarded as services historically, this classification may not matter that much. Half-jokingly, we can ask: Does McDonald's manufacture hamburgers? Seriously, how much difference is there between McDonald's and Airbus? Both market new products, both make-to-order (finalize a product based on an order), and both extensively rely on powerful supply chain management systems around the world. As alluded to earlier, in the "black-and-white" world separating manufacturing and services, "contract manufacturing service" would be an oxymoron. Yet, today, *integrating* manufacturing and services is both a reality and a necessity.[40]

14-5b Market Orientation versus Relationship Orientation

Market orientation refers to a philosophy or way of thinking that places the highest priority on the creation of superior customer value in the marketplace.[41] A market-oriented firm genuinely listens to customer feedback and allocates resources accordingly to meet customer expectation. For example, Boeing used to be an engineering-driven firm that believed its engineers would do airlines a favor by sharing technological wonders with them. Since the development of the 777 in the 1990s, Boeing has transformed itself by involving not only its customers (airlines), but also its suppliers in the conceptualization and design processes. Many firms around the world have similarly enjoyed better performance by being more market oriented. The debate centers on how firms benefit from market orientation *differently* around the world.

Another concept is relationship orientation, defined as a focus to establish, maintain, and enhance relationships with customers.[42] Like market orientation, relationship orientation has more recently been expanded to touch many functions beyond marketing. Given the necessity for building trust and coordinating operations, supply chains certainly can benefit from a relationship orientation. Instead of selling engines and then waiting for customers to order spare parts, Rolls-Royce now builds deeper relationships with airlines. Specifically, Rolls-Royce rents engines to airlines, provides 24/7 monitoring, carries out full maintenance, and gets paid for every hour the engine is in flight. Thus, Rolls-Royce can fix problems before they create damage, thus offering superior value for airlines. More than half the engines manufactured by Rolls-Royce are now sold with such a service contract.

Marketers have heavily debated whether a market orientation or a relationship orientation is more effective in global markets. Key to the debate is how firms benefit from market or relationship orientation *differently* around the world. Consider competition in China, where *guanxi* (relationship) reportedly is crucial.[43] Firms have to allocate resources between building market-oriented capabilities (such as quality, pricing, and delivery) and relationship-oriented assets (such as wining and dining). Researchers find two interesting results. First, relationship-oriented assets do add value. Second, for truly outstanding performance, relationships are

Market orientation

A philosophy or way of thinking that places the highest priority on the creation of superior customer value in the marketplace

Relationship orientation

A focus to establish, maintain, and enhance relationships with customers.

necessary but not sufficient. Market-oriented capabilities contribute *more* toward performance.[44] These results make sense, in light of China's increasingly market-driven competition that gradually reduces (but does not eliminate) the importance of *guanxi*.

Viewed globally, the strongest effect of market orientation on performance has been found in US firms, which operate in arguably the most-developed market economy.[45] In weak market economies, such as Russia and Ukraine, the returns from being market oriented are very limited. In other words, firms there can "get away" from a minimal amount of market orientation. Viewed collectively, these findings support the *institution-based* view: By definition, market orientation functions more effectively in a market economy.[46]

14-6 Management Savvy

Learning Objective
Draw implications for action.

What determines the success and failure in marketing and supply chain management? The institution-based view points out the impact of formal and informal rules of the game. In a nonmarket economy (think of North Korea), marketing would be irrelevant. In a world with high trade and investment barriers, globe-trotting DHL, FedEx, and UPS jets would be unimaginable. The resource-based view argues that holding institutions constant, firms such as Aflac and Zara that develop the best capabilities in marketing and supply chain management will emerge as winners (see the Opening and Closing Cases).[47] Emerging Markets 14.1 illustrates how tour destinations can leverage both the institution-based and resource-based views to better market themselves to Chinese tourists, who are currently the world's largest group of international tourists.

EMERGING MARKETS 14.1

Marketing to Chinese Tourists

Representing one out of every ten international tourists in the world, the Chinese have recently emerged to become the largest group of tourists from any country. Countries ranging from Australia to Zimbabwe are eager to market their destinations to these new tourists, thus necessitating an eagerness to know more about them. Three observations have emerged.

First, Chinese tourists spend more, and focus more on shopping. As a group they spent US$129 billion in 2013, followed by American tourists who spent US$86 billion. In a decade, thanks to the inflow of Chinese tourists, Macau has dethroned Las Vegas

Source: *Economist*, 2014, Coming to a beach near you, April 19: 53.

as the undisputed gambling capital of the world. In 2012, Macau's casino takings were US$38 billion vis-à-vis Las Vegas' US$6 billion. Per-visitor spending is even more striking: US$1,354 for Macau (the majority of its gambling visitors are Chinese) versus US$156 for Las Vegas. More than 80% of Chinese tourists indicate that shopping is crucial for their travel plans, compared with 56% of Middle Eastern tourists and 48% of Russian tourists. The average Chinese tourist indulges him/herself with US$1,130 tax-free purchases vis-à-vis US$494 by the average Russian tourist. Interestingly, the Chinese spend more on luxury goods abroad than at home. Luxury goods purchased abroad have more value—not only the perceived value from Made-in-France perfume purchased in France, but also, literally, the lower cost. Chinese consumption taxes of 20% to 30% on luxury goods mean such goods often end up costing 50% more in China than in Europe, thus motivating tourists to haul home some of these high-priced goods as "bargains." Second, they like to come as groups, often partaking in exhausting group bus tours of "20 cities in 10 days." A most unusual format is "6+1," which is a young couple with one (the only!) child and two sets of (grand)parents. Third, many tourists do not speak English and are outside of China for the first time. They are often uncomfortable with Western food with butter, cheese, and cream—ingredients that Chinese never use in their cuisine.

In response, tourist destinations have vigorously competed for a growing share of Chinese tourists. From an institution-based view, removing or minimizing visa hassles will be a booster. In 2014, Chinese citizens can only visit 44 countries visa-free, while Taiwanese can visit 130 countries and Americans and British over 170. A quarter of would-be Chinese tourists had to abandon their plans for visiting Europe, thanks to visa delays. Outside the EU Schengen area (a visa issued by one Schengen member country can be used to enter all other 25 Schengen member countries), Britain requires its own visa. The upshot? Britain only receives one-ninth of the Chinese tourists that France entertains. When the United States no longer required all Chinese visa applicants to be interviewed, 22% more Chinese visitors showed up the next year. When tiny Maldives waived its requirements for a visa, 45% more Chinese tourists came, contributing one-third of the 1.1 million total.

From a resource-based view, enhancing the value proposition is a must. For relatively obscure destinations, how to get on the tour itinerary is challenging. Abilities to successfully tap into the group and collectivistic mentality are rare, but—if developed well—can generate a lot of buzz. In 2012, Tourism New Zealand hosted the fairy-tale wedding of Yao Chen, an actress with 66 million followers on Weibo, China's equivalent of Twitter. It generated 7,000 news pieces, 40 million posts on discussion boards, and a significant number of Chinese honeymooners to follow the actress to check out the "100% Pure New Zealand" (Tourism New Zealand's campaign line). To make Chinese tourists feel comfortable, not only are Chinese-speaking tour guides necessary, but Chinese-speaking store personnel can also add value by gently nudging shoppers to commit to big-ticket luxury items in their native tongue. Harrods of London has positioned 100 Union Pay terminals throughout its store to cater to Chinese credit card and ATM cardholders. Having store signs and restaurant menus in Chinese helps. In Copenhagen, the sign for its landmark, the Little Mermaid, sports three languages: Danish, English, and Chinese. Hilton Hotels greet Chinese guests by a Chinese-speaking service member, outfit guest rooms with amenities such as tea kettles and slippers (two items traditionally missing even in high-end Western hotels), and serve such traditional Chinese breakfast items as dim sum, congee, and fried noodles.

While the growing Chinese middle class has already changed the global tourism industry, it is important to know that only about 5% of the population possesses passports and that most go to Hong Kong or Macau. Therefore, their impact as well as our learning about them are not likely to stop anytime soon.

Sources: Based on (1) the author's interviews; (2) *China Business Review*, 2012, Hilton welcomes Chinese travelers at home and abroad, January: 16–19; (3) *Economist*, 2013, The rise of the low-rollers, September 7: 63–64; (4) *Economist*, 2014, Coming to a beach near you, April 19: 53–54.

Table 14.2   **Implications for Action**

- Know the formal and informal rules of the game on marketing and supply chain management inside and out.

- In marketing, focus on product, price, promotion, and place (the four Ps) and do all it takes to avoid blunders.

- In supply chain management, focus on agility, adaptability, and alignment (the triple A's).

Consequently, three implications for action emerge (Table 14.2). First, marketers and supply chain managers need to know the rules of the game inside and out in order to craft savvy responses. For instance, given the limitations of formal regulatory frameworks in prosecuting cross-border credit card crimes, some US e-commerce firms refuse to ship to overseas addresses. Legitimate overseas purchasers are, in turn, denied business. As online shopping became a more widespread informal norm, FedEx acquired Kinkos (which was turned into FedEx Office stores), and UPS took over Mail Boxes stores (which turned into UPS Stores). E-commerce firms can now ship to the US addresses of FedEx Offices and UPS Stores, and FedEx and UPS can then forward products to the overseas purchasers from these stores. This is but one example of superb problem solving in the face of cumbersome formal rules and changing informal norms.

Second, in marketing, focus on the four Ps. This obviously is a cliché. However, in international marketing, managers need to do all it takes to avoid costly and embarrassing blunders (see Table 14.3). Remember: despite their magnitude, blunders are *avoidable* mistakes. At the very least, international marketers should try very hard to avoid being written up as blunders in a new edition of this textbook.

Finally, in supply chain management, focus on the triple As. This is not a cliché, as the idea was just published a few years ago. Not aware of the importance of the triple A's, many firms would only deliver container loads to minimize the number

Table 14.3   **Do's and Don'ts to Avoid Blunders in International Marketing**

Do's	Don'ts
• Avoid ethnocentrism. Be sensitive to nationalistic feelings of local consumers and governments.	• Don't be overconfident about the potential of your products or services.
• Do your homework about the new market. Pay attention to details and nuances, especially those related to cultures, values, and norms.	• Don't cut corners and save back-translation cost—always back-translate (after translating from English to Russian, get someone else to translate it from Russian to English to check accuracy).
• Avoid the pushy salesman approach. Impatience does not bring sales.	• Don't use jokes in international advertising. Humor is usually impossible to translate.
• Act like a diplomat—build relationships.	

Sources: Based on text in (1) T. Dalgic & R. Heijblom, 1996, International marketing blunders revisited—some lessons for managers, *Journal of International Marketing*, 4 (1): 81–91; (2) D. Ricks, 1999, *Blunders in International Business*, 3rd ed., Oxford, UK: Blackwell.

of deliveries and freight costs. When demand for a particular product suddenly rises, these firms often fail to react quickly—they have to wait until the container (or sometimes even the whole container *ship*) is full. Such a "best" practice typically delays shipment by a week or more, forcing stock-outs in stores that disappoint consumers. When firms eventually ship container loads, they often result in excess inventory, because most buyers do not need a full container load. To get rid of such inventory, as much as a third of the merchandise carried by department stores ends up in sales. Such discounts not only destroy profits for every firm in the supply chain, but also undermine brand equity by upsetting consumers who recently bought the discounted items at full price. In contrast, the triple A's urge savvy supply chain managers to focus on agility, adaptability, and alignment of interests of the entire chain.

CHAPTER SUMMARY/LEARNING OBJECTIVES

14-1 Articulate three of the four Ps in marketing (product, price, and promotion) in a global context.

- In international marketing, the leading concern about product is standardization versus localization.
- Marketers care about price elasticity—how responsive purchasing behavior is when prices change.
- In promotion, marketers need to decide whether to enhance or downplay the country-of-origin effect.

14-2 Explain how the fourth P (place) has evolved to be labeled supply chain management.

- Technically, "place" used to refer to distribution channel—the location where products are provided.
- More recently, the term "distribution channel" has been replaced by "supply chain management," in response to more outsourcing to suppliers, contract manufacturers, and 3PL providers.

14-3 Outline the triple As in supply chain management.

- Agility involves the ability to react quickly to unexpected shifts in supply and demand.
- Adaptability refers to the ability to reconfigure supply chain in response to longer-term external changes.
- Alignment focuses on the alignment of interests of various players in the supply chain.

14-4 Discuss how institutions and resources affect marketing and supply chain management.

- Formal and informal rules of the game around the world significantly impact these two areas.
- Managers need to assess marketing and supply chain management based on the VRIO criteria.

14-5 Participate in two leading debates concerning marketing and supply chain management.

- (1) Manufacturing versus service and (2) market orientation versus relationship orientation.

14-6 Draw implications for action.

- Know the formal and informal rules of the game inside and out.
- In marketing, focus on product, price, promotion, and place (the four Ps).
- In supply chain management, focus on agility, adaptability, and alignment (the triple A's).

KEY TERMS

Adaptability, 466	Marketing mix, 459	Supply chain, 458
Agility, 465	Place, 464	Supply chain
Alignment, 466	Price, 462	management, 458
Distribution channel, 464	Price elasticity, 462	Third-party logistics
Make-or-buy decision, 466	Product, 459	(3PL) provider, 467
Market orientation, 472	Promotion, 462	Total cost of
Market segmentation, 460	Relationship	ownership, 462
Marketing, 458	orientation, 472	

REVIEW QUESTIONS

1. *ON CULTURE:* What cultural issue could be involved in product decisions in terms of localization versus standardization?

2. If global warming persists, how would it affect shipping and transportation routes? You can probably list some of the dangers of global warming, but how may it actually benefit the economies of some countries or regions?

3. Refer to PengAtlas Map 4.2 (World Labor Force) and to Maps 2.1 and 2.2 that cover the top exporters and importers. To what extent is the size of the labor force an indicator of the size of markets, and to what extent is it not? Why?

peng
atlas

4. If marketing efforts can help produce an inelastic demand for a product, a firm would have much more upward pricing flexibility. Explain why that is true.

5. Which of the four P's has come to be known by a new term? Why the change?

6. What marketing risks are taken by outsourcing? How would you minimize those risks?

7. In supply chain management, what are the differences between agility and adaptability?

8. In aligning the interests of various players in the supply chain, what is the role of power and trust?

9. What are examples of how formal institutions affect marketing and supply chain management—i.e., examples of government-imposed rules of the game?

10. How is the issue of the "value" of some traditional marketing resources being affected by recent changes in technology?

11. In your opinion, are manufacturing and service separate issues, and can one of the two be considered more important than the other? Explain.

12. What is the difference between market orientation and relationship orientation?

13. Select one of the four Ps, and make the case that it is more important than the other three. Then make the case that all are equally important.

14. Select one of the Triple As, and make the case that it is more important than the other two. Then make the case that all are equally important.

CRITICAL DISCUSSION QUESTIONS

1. *ON CULTURE:* Canada has an official animal: the beaver. In 2007, the Canadian prime minister suggested replacing it with the wolverine, and stirred up a national debate. Does your country have an official animal? If you were hired as a marketing expert by the Government of Canada (or of whatever country), how would you best market the country using an animal?

2. *ON ETHICS:* In Hollywood movies, it is common to have product placement (having products from sponsor companies, such as cars, appear in movies without telling viewers that these are commercials). As a marketer, you are concerned about the ethical implications of product placement via Hollywood, yet you know the effectiveness of traditional advertising is declining. How do you proceed?

3. *ON ETHICS:* You are a supply chain manager at a UK firm. In 2014, Ebola broke out in Africa and the United States, potentially affecting your suppliers in these regions. On the one hand, you are considering switching to a new supplier in Asia. On the other hand, at this difficult moment you feel bad about abandoning your African and American suppliers, with whom you have built a pleasant personal and business relationship. Yet, your tightly coordinated production cannot afford to miss one supply shipment. How do you proceed?

GLOBAL ACTION

1. Your company has developed an extensive global supply network that has contact with nearly every country in the world. However, recent internal initiatives have encouraged managers to reconfigure your company's supply network to increase efficiency. As a part of this process, you must use established logistics performance metrics to identify the country that has the highest logistics competence on each continent (Africa, Asia, Europe, North America, and South America). Prepare a report that indicates your recommendations and rationale for each continent. What can explain the results of your analysis?

2. You are conducting an international survey concerning possible acceptance of a new leisure activity: space tourism. One issue that can influence whether individuals in a country find this new concept interesting is culture. Discuss what cultural traits can be used to measure general acceptance of space tourism by country. Then, determine which countries are ideal to target for initial commercialization. Explain why.

CLOSING CASE

Zara Excels in Marketing and Supply Chain Management

© TonyV3112/Shutterstock.com

Zara is one of the hottest fashion chains. Founded in 1975, Zara's parent, Inditex, has become a leading global apparel retailer. Since its initial public offering (IPO) in 2001, Inditex quadrupled its profits and its sales (to US$19.1 billion or €13.8 billion). It doubled the number of its stores of eight brands, of which Zara contributes two-thirds of total sales. In this intensely competitive industry, Zara excels in both marketing and supply chain management. Zara succeeds by first breaking and then rewriting industry rules—also known as industry norms.

Rule number one: The origin of a fashion house usually carries some cachet. However, Zara does not hail from Italy or France—it is from Spain. Even within Spain, Zara is not based in a cosmopolitan city like Barcelona or Madrid. It is headquartered in Arteixo, a town of only 25,000 people in a remote corner of northwestern Spain that a majority of this book's readers would have never heard of. Yet, Zara is active not only throughout Europe, but also in Asia and North America. Currently, the total number of stores is more than 2,000 in 88 countries. Zara stores occupy some of the priciest top locations: Champs-Elysées in Paris, Fifth Avenue in New York, Galleria in Dallas, Ginza in Tokyo, Queen's Road Central in Hong Kong, and Huaihai Road in Shanghai.

Rule number two: Avoid stock-outs (a store running out of items in demand). Zara's answer? Occasional shortages contribute to an urge to buy now. With new items arriving at stores *twice* a week, experienced Zara shoppers know that "If you see something and don't buy it, you can forget about coming back for it because it will be gone." The small batch of merchandise during a short window of opportunity for purchasing motivates shoppers to visit Zara stores more frequently. In London, shoppers visit the average store four times a year, but frequent Zara 17 times. There is a good reason to do so: Zara makes about 20,000 items per year, about triple what Gap does. "At Gap, everything is the same," according to a Zara fan, "and buying from Zara, you'll never end up looking like someone else."

Rule number three: Bombarding shoppers with ads is a must. Gap and H&M spend on average 3% to 4% of their sales on ads. Zara begs to differ: It devotes just 0.3% of its sales to ads. The high traffic in the stores alleviates some need for advertising in the media, most of which only serves as a reminder to visit the stores.

Rule number four: Outsource. Gap and H&M do not own any production facilities. However, outsourcing production (mostly to Asia) requires a long lead time, usually several months. Again, Zara has decisively deviated from the norm. By concentrating (more than half of) its production in-house (in Spain, Portugal, and Morocco), Zara has developed a super-responsive supply chain. It designs, produces, and delivers a new garment to its stores worldwide in a mere 15 *days*, a pace that is unheard of in the industry. The best speed the rivals can achieve is two *months*. Outsourcing may not necessarily be "low cost," because errors in prediction can easily lead to unsold inventory, forcing retailers to offer steep discounts. The industry average is to offer 40% discounts across all merchandise. In contrast, Zara sells more at full price and, when it discounts, it averages only 15%.

Rule number five: Strive for efficiency through large batches. In contrast, Zara intentionally deals with small batches. Because of its flexibility, Zara does not worry about "missing the boat" for a season. When new trends emerge, Zara can react quickly. It runs its supply chain like clockwork with a fast but predictable rhythm: Every store places orders on Tuesday/Wednesday and Friday/Saturday. Trucks and cargo flights run on established schedules—like a bus service. From Spain, shipments reach most European stores in 24 hours, US stores in 48 hours, and Asian stores in 72 hours. Not only do store staff know exactly when shipments will arrive, but regular customers also know that too, thus motivating them to check out the new merchandise more frequently on those days, which are known as "Z days" in some cities.

Zara has no shortage of competitors. Why has no one successfully copied its business model of "fast fashion"? "I would love to organize our business like Inditex [Zara's parent]," noted an executive from Gap, "but I would have to knock my company down and rebuild it from scratch." This does not mean Gap and other rivals are not trying to copy Zara. The question is how long it takes for rivals to out-Zara Zara.

CASE DISCUSSION QUESTIONS

1. Using the four Ps of marketing, explain what is behind Zara's marketing.

2. From a VRIO standpoint, identify the features of Zara's supply chain management that contribute to its performance.

3. Visit a Zara store in (or near) your city. Does it meet your expectations for a successful firm?

Sources: Based on (1) *BusinessWeek*, 2006, Fashion conquistador, September 4: 38–39; (2) *Economist*, 2012, Fashion forward, March 24: 63–64; (3) Inditex, 2014, Presencia internacional, www.inditex.com; (4) K. Ferdows, M. Lewis, & J. Machuca, 2004, Rapid-fire fulfillment, *Harvard Business Review*, November: 104–110; (5) www.zara.com.

NOTES

[Journal acronyms] AMJ—*Academy of Management Journal;* BW—*BusinessWeek* (before 2010) or *Bloomberg Businessweek* (since 2010); HBR—*Harvard Business Review;* JIBS—*Journal of International Business Studies;* JIMktg—*Journal of International Marketing;* JMktg—*Journal of Marketing;* JMS—*Journal of Management Studies;* JOM—*Journal of Operations Management;* JSCM—*Journal of Supply Chain Management;* JWB—*Journal of World Business;* MSOM—*Manufacturing and Service Operations Management*

1 M. Lejeune & N. Yakova, 2005, On characterizing the 4 C's in supply chain management, *JOM*, 23: 81–100.

2 T. Choi & D. Krause, 2006, The supply base and its complexity, *JOM*, 24: 637–652.

3 P. Kotler & K. Keller, 2005, *Marketing Management*, 12th ed., Upper Saddle River, NJ: Prentice Hall; R. Rust, C. Moorman, & G. Bhalla, 2010, Rethinking marketing, *HBR*, January: 94–101.

4 V. Shankar, L. Berry, & T. Dotzel, 2009, A practical guide to combining products and services, *HBR*, November: 95–99.

5 L. Li, G. Qian, & Z. Qian, 2014, Inconsistencies in international product strategies and performance in high-tech firms, *JIMktg*, 22: 94–113.

6 *BW*, 2012, Wendy's goes beyond the dollar menu in Japan, January 9: 25–26.

7 T. Levitt, 1983, The globalization of markets, *HBR*, May–June: 92–102.

8 G. Walsh, E. Shiu, & L. Hassan, 2014, Cross-national advertising and behavioral intentions, *JIMktg*, 22: 77–97.

9 D. Alden, J. Kelley, P. Riefler, J. Lee, & G. Soutar, 2013, The effect of global company animosity on local brand attitudes in emerging and developed markets, *JIMktg*, 21: 17–38; X. Guo, 2013, Living in a global world, *JIMktg*, 21: 1–22; J. Townsend, S. Yeniyurt, & M. Talay, 2009, Getting to global, *JIBS*, 40: 539–558.

10 D. Griffith, 2010, Understanding multi-institutional convergence effects on international market segments and global marketing strategy, *JWB*, 45: 59–67; T. Schlager & P. Maas, 2013, Fitting international segmentation for emerging markets, *JIMktg*, 21: 39–61.

11 D. Holt, J. Quelch, & E. Taylor, 2004, How global brands compete, *HBR*, September: 68–75.

12 M. Fletcher, S. Harris, & R. Richey, 2013, Internationalization knowledge, *JIMktg*, 21: 47–71; O. Kravets & O. Sandikci, 2014, Competently ordinary, *JMktg*, 78: 125–140; V. Kumar, A. Sharma, R. Shah, & B. Rajan, 2013, Establishing profitable customer loyalty for multinational companies in the emerging economies, *JIMktg*, 21: 57–80; B. Swoboda & S. Elsner, 2013, Transferring the retail format successfully into foreign countries, *JIMktg*, 21: 81–109.

13 *Economist*, 2008, Africa calling, June 7: 78.

14 C. Nye, M. Roth, & T. Shimp, 2008, Comparative advertising in markets where brands and comparative advertising are novel, *JIBS*, 39: 851–863; A. Navarro, F. Losada, E. Ruzo, & J. Diez, 2010, Implications of perceived competitive advantages, adaptation of marketing tactics, and export commitment on export performance, *JWB*, 45: 49–58; S. Speck & A. Roy, 2008, The interrelationships between television viewing, values, and perceived well-being, *JIBS*, 39: 1197–1219.

15 D. Ricks, 1999, *Blunders in International Business*, 3rd ed. (p. 88), Oxford: Blackwell.

16 C. Funk, J. Arthurs, L. Trevino, & J. Joireman, 2010, Consumer animosity in the global value chain, *JIBS*, 41: 439–651; P. Sharma, 2011, Country of origin effects in developed and emerging markets, *JIBS*, 42: 285–306.

17 C. Schulze & B. Skiera, 2014, Not all fun and games, *JMktg*, 78: 1–19; J. Xu, C. Forman, J. Kim, & K. Van Ittersum, 2014, News media channels, *JMktg*, 78: 97–112.

18 *BW*, 2005, The MySpace generation (p. 92), December 12: 86–96.

19 M. Yadav & P. Pavlou, 2014, Marketing in computer-mediated environments, *JMktg*, 78: 20–40; J. Schumann, F. von Wangenheim, & N. Groene, 2014, Targeted online advertising, *JMktg*, 78: 59–75.

20 M. Porter, 1985, *Competitive Advantage*, New York: Free Press.

21 R. Slone, 2004, Leading a supply chain turnaround (p. 116), *HBR*, October: 114–121.

22 The following discussion draws heavily from H. Lee, 2004, The triple-A supply chain, *HBR*, October: 102–112.

23 L. Cheng, D. Cantor, C. Grimm, & M. Dresner, 2014, Supply chain drivers of organizational flexibility, *JSCM*, 50: 62–76; B. Williams, J. Roh, T. Tokar, & M. Swink, 2013, Leveraging supply chain visibility for responsiveness, *JOM*, 31: 543–554.

24 C. Bode, S. Wagner, K. Petersen, & L. Ellram, 2011, Understanding responses to supply chain disruptions, *AMJ*, 54: 833–856.

25 *Economist*, 2006, When the chain breaks, June 17: 18–19.

26 M. W. Peng, Y. Zhou, & A. York, 2006, Behind make or buy decisions in export strategy, *JWB*, 41: 289–300.

27 B. Brewer, B. Ashenbaum, & J. Carter, 2013, Understanding the supply chain outsourcing cascade, *JSCM*, 49: 90–110; M. Casson, 2013, Economic analysis of international supply chains, *JSCM*, 49: 8–13; L. Ellram, W. Tate, & K. Petersen, 2013, Offshoring and reshoring, *JSCM*, 49: 14–22; J. Gray, K. Skowronski, G. Esenduran, & M. J. Rungtusanatham, 2013, The reshoring phenomenon, *JSCM*, 49: 27–33.

28 L. Mesquita & T. Brush, 2008, Untangling safeguard and production coordination effects in long-term buyer-supplier relationships, *AMJ*, 51: 785–807; M. Ju, J. Murray, M. Kotabe, & G. Gao, 2011, Reducing distributor opportunism in the export market, *JWB*, 46: 487–496.

29 Y. Li, E. Xie, H. Teo, & M. W. Peng, 2010, Formal control and social control in domestic and international buyer-supplier relationships, *JOM*, 28: 333–344.

30 S. Handley & W. C. Benton, 2013, The influence of task- and location-specific complexity on the control and coordination costs in global outsourcing relationships, *JOM*, 31: 109–128; E. Katok & V. Pavlov, 2013, Fairness in supply chain contracts, *JOM*, 31: 129–137; R. Narasimhan, S. Narayanan, & R. Srinivasan, 2013, An investigation of justice in supply chain relationships and their performance impact, *JOM*, 31: 236–247; G. Nyaga, D. Lynch, D. Marshall, & E. Ambrose, 2013, Power asymmetry, adaptation, and collaboration in dyadic relationships involving a powerful partner, *JSCM*, 49: 42–65; S. Pathak, Z. Wu, & D. Johnston, 2014, Toward a structural view of co-opetition in supply networks, *JOM*, 32: 254–267; N. Pulles, J. Veldman, H. Schiele, & H. Sierksma, 2014, Pressure or pamper? *JSCM*, 50: 16–36; Q. Wang, C. Craighead, & J. Li, 2014, Justice served, *JOM*, 32: 374–386.

31 C. Bode, D. Hubner, & S. Wagner, 2014, Managing financially distressed suppliers, *JSCM*, 50: 24–43; J. Hartman & S. Moeller, 2014, Chain liability in multitier supply chains? *JOM*, 32: 281–294; A. Steven, Y. Dong, & T. Corsi, 2014, Global sourcing and quality recalls, *JOM*, 32: 241–253.

32 V. Bhako & T. Choi, 2013, The iron cage exposed, *JOM*, 31: 432–449.

33 C. Corbett, 2006, Global diffusion of ISO 9000 certification through supply chains, *MSOM*, 8: 330–350.

34 E. Brandon-Jones, B. Squire, C. Autry, & K. Petersen, 2014, A contingent resource-based perspective of supply chain resilience and robustness, *JSCM*, 50: 55–73; M. Dixon, K. Freeman, & N. Toman, 2010, Stop trying to delight your customers, *HBR*, July: 116–122; T. Esper & R. Crook, 2014, Supply chain resources, *JSCM*, 50: 3–5; D. Ketchen, K. Wowak, & C. Craighead, 2014, Resource gaps and resource orchestration shortfalls in supply chain management,

JSCM, 50: 6–15; A. Meckelprang & A. Nair, 2010, Relationship between just-in-time manufacturing practices and performance, *JOM*, 28: 283–302; S. Mishra, S. Modi, & A. Animesh, 2013, The relationship between information technology capability, inventory efficiency, and shareholder wealth, *JOM*, 31: 298–312; P. Skilton, 2014, Value creation, value capture, and supply chain structure, *JSCM*, 50: 74–93; S. Sun & R. Lee, 2013, Enhancing innovation through international joint venture portfolios, *JIMktg*, 21: 1–21.

35 K. Dooley, T. Yan, S. Mohan, & M. Gopalakrishnan, 2010, Inventory management and the bullwhip effect during the 2007–2009 recession, *JSCM*, 46: 12–18; L. Sprague & T. Callarman, 2010, Supply management is not a beer game, *JSCM*, 46: 9–11.

36 T. Kull, S. Ellis, & R. Narasimhan, 2013, Reducing behavioral constraints to supplier integration, *JSCM*, 49: 64–86; F. Salvador & V. Villena, 2013, Supplier integration and NPD outcomes, *JSCM*, 49: 87–113.

37 P. Kotler, N. Rackham, & S. Krishnaswamy, 2006, Ending the war between sales and marketing, *HBR*, July: 68–78.

38 R. Chase & U. Apte, 2007, A history of research in service operations, *JOM*, 25: 375–386.

39 K. Sivakumar, M. Li, & B. Dong, 2014, Service quality, *JMktg*, 78: 41–58.

40 I. Kastalli & B. Looy, 2013, Servitization, *JOM*, 31: 169–180.

41 G. Challagalla, B. Murtha, & B. Jaworski, 2014, Marketing doctrine, *JMktg*, 78: 4–20; J. Murray, G. Gao, M. Kotabe, & N. Zhou, 2007, Assessing measurement invariance of export market orientation, *JIMktg*, 15: 41–62.

42 W. Dou, H. Li, N. Zhou, & C. Su, 2010, Exploring relationship satisfaction between global professional service firms and local clients in emerging markets, *JIBS*, 41: 1198–1217; G. Gonzalez, D. Claro, & R. Palmatier, 2014, Synergistic effects of relationship managers' social networks on sales performance, *JMktg*, 78: 76–84; R. Jean, R. Sinkovics, & S. T. Cavusgil, 2010, Enhancing international customer-supplier relationships through IT resources, *JIBS*, 41: 1218–1239; L. Leonidous, S. Samiee, B. Aykol, & M. Talias, 2014, Antecedents and outcomes of exporter-importer relationship quality, *JIMktg*, 22: 21–46; S. Samaha, J. Beck, & R. Palmatier, 2014, The role of culture in international relationship marketing, *JIMktg*, 78: 78–98; C. Wallenburg & T. Schaffler, 2014, The interplay of relational governance and formal control in horizontal alliances, *JSCM*, 50: 41–58.

43 S. Cai & Z. Yang, 2014, The role of the *guanxi* institution in skill acquisition between firms, *JSCM*, 50: 3–23; F. Gu, K. Hung, & D. Tse, 2008, When does *guanxi* matter? *JMktg*, 72: 12–28.

44 M. W. Peng & Y. Luo, 2000, Managerial ties and firm performance in a transition economy, *AMJ*, 43: 486–501. See also M. Dong, C. Li, & D. Tse, 2013, Do business and political ties differ in cultivating channels for foreign and local firms in China? *JIMktg*, 21: 39–56; M. Ju, H. Zhao, & T. Wang, 2014, The boundary conditions of export relational governance: A "strategy tripod" perspective, *JIMktg*, 22: 89–106; K. Zhou, Q. Zhang, S. Sheng, E. Xie, & Y. Bao, 2014, Are relational ties always good for knowledge acquisition? *JOM*, 32: 88–98.

45 P. Ellis, 2006, Market orientation and performance, *JMS*, 43: 1089–1107.

46 F. Wiengarten, M. Pagell, M. Ahmed, & C. Gimenez, 2014, Do a country's logistical capabilities moderate the external integration performance relationship? *JOM*, 32: 51–63.

47 S. Golicic & C. Smith, 2013, A meta-analysis of environmentally sustainable supply chain management practices and firm performance, *JSCM*, 49: 78–95; R. Leuschner, D. Rogers, & F. Charvet, 2013, A meta-analysis of supply chain integration and form performance, *JSCM*, 49: 34–57.

© Avava/Shutterstock.com

CHAPTER 15

Learning Objectives

After studying this chapter, you should be able to

- explain staffing decisions with a focus on expatriates.

- identify training and development needs for expatriates and host-country nationals.

- discuss compensation and performance appraisal issues.

- understand labor relations in both home and host countries.

- discuss how the institution-based and resource-based views shed additional light on HRM.

- participate in three leading debates concerning HRM.

- draw implications for action.

Managing Human Resources Globally

EMERGING MARKETS: Samsung's Global Strategy Group

Founded in 1938, Samsung Group is South Korea's leading conglomerate. In the mid 2010s, it has approximately 480,000 employees in 500 units in 80 countries, with more than $300 billion in annual revenues. The flagship company within Samsung Group is Samsung Electronics Corporation (SEC). With more than $200 billion revenues, SEC is the largest information technology (IT) firm in the world. In addition to SEC, other major Samsung Group companies include Samsung Life Insurance (the 13th largest life insurer in the world), Samsung C&T Corporation (one of the world's largest developers of skyscrapers and solar/wind power plants), and Samsung Heavy Industries (the world's largest shipbuilder). Samsung's performance has been impressive. Despite the Great Recession of 2008–2009, SEC's profits have been higher than those of its five largest Japanese rivals (Sony, Panasonic, Toshiba, Hitachi, and Sharp) combined.

Clearly, Samsung has done something right. However, it has not been easy. To increasingly compete outside Korea, Samsung needs to attract more non-Korean talents. But given its traditionally rigid hierarchical structure and the language barrier, its efforts to attract and retain non-Korean talents had often been disappointing. In response, Samsung Group headquarters in 1997 set up a unique internal consulting unit, the Global Strategy Group, which reports directly to the CEO. Members of the Global Strategy Group are non-Korean MBA graduates of top Western business schools who have worked for leading multinationals such as Goldman Sachs, Intel, and McKinsey. They are required to spend two years in Seoul and study basic Korean. The group's mission, according to its website, is to "(1) develop a pool of global managers, (2) enhance Samsung's business performance, and (3) globalize Samsung." By 2013, Samsung's global strategists have come from 18 countries, with 19 native languages, six years of average work experience, and an average age of 30 years.

Global Strategy teams work on various internal strategy projects for different Samsung companies. Each team has a project leader, which gives the individual an opportunity to take on a leadership role in a high-level consulting project much earlier than a typical consulting career provides. Each team has one to two global strategists. It also has a project coordinator, who is a senior Korean manager acting as a liaison between the team and the management of the (internal) client company. On average, projects last three months and typically involve some overseas travel. Starting with 20 global strategists in the class of 1997, more than 400 projects have been completed. These projects help global strategists form informal ties and expose them to the organizational culture. After two years, global strategists would "graduate" and be assigned to Samsung subsidiaries, many of which are in their home countries.

Despite good-faith efforts by both Korean and non-Korean sides, the success of the Global Strategy Group is anything but assured. Overall, cultural integration is a tough nut to crack. Of the 208 non-Korean MBAs who joined the group since its inception, 135 were still with Samsung as of 2011. The most successful ones are those who have taken the greatest pains to fit into the Korean culture, such as eating kimchi and drinking Korean wine at dinner parties. Before the establishment of the Global Strategy Group, not a single non-Korean MBA lasted more than three years at SEC. With the Global Strategy Group as a cohort group, one-third of the non-Korean MBAs in the first class of 1997 were still with SEC three years later (in 2000). Over the next decade,

the retention rate went up to two-thirds. Three experts noted how the non-Korean members of the Global Strategy Group have slowly, but surely, globalized Samsung's corporate DNA:

The effects of these employees on the organization have been something like that of a steady trickle of water on stone. As more people from the Global Strategy Group are assigned to SEC, their Korean colleagues have had to change their work styles and mindsets to accommodate Westernized practices, slowly and steadily making the environment more friendly to ideas from abroad. Today, SEC goes out of its way to ask the Global Strategy Group for more newly hired employees.

Sources: Based on (1) S. Chang, 2008, *Sony vs. Samsung*, Singapore: Wiley; (2) T. Khanna, J. Song, & K. Lee, 2011, The paradox of Samsung's rise, *Harvard Business Review*, July: 142–147; (3) Samsung Global Strategy Group, 2015, gsg.samsung.com.

Human resource management (HRM)

Activities that attract, select, and manage employees.

Staffing

HRM activities associated with hiring employees and filling positions.

Host-country national (HCN)

Individual from the host country who works for an MNE.

Parent-country national (PCN)

Individual who comes from the parent country of the MNE and works at its local subsidiary.

How can firms such as Samsung select, retain, reward, and motivate the best employees that they can attract? How can they link the management of people from diverse cultural and professional backgrounds with firm performance? These are some of the crucial questions driving this chapter. This chapter is devoted to human resource management (HRM)—activities that attract, select, and manage employees.[1] As a function, HRM used to be called "personnel" and before that "records management." Few of you are HRM experts, but everyone can appreciate HRM's rising importance just by looking at the evolution of the terminology. The term "HRM" clearly indicates that people are key resources of the firm to be actively managed and developed (see PengAtlas Maps 4.2). In the last two decades, HRM has become more important, and it often sports the word "strategic" to make it "strategic HRM." From a lowly administrative support function, HRM is increasingly recognized as a strategic function that, together with other crucial functions, such as finance and marketing, helps accomplish organizational effectiveness and financial performance.[2]

This chapter first reviews the four main areas of HRM: (1) staffing, (2) training and development, (3) compensation and performance appraisal, and (4) labor relations. Then, we use the institution-based and resource-based views to shed light on these issues. Debates and extensions follow.

Learning Objective

Explain staffing decisions with a focus on expatriates.

15-1 Staffing

Staffing refers to HRM activities associated with hiring employees and filling positions. In multinational enterprises (MNEs), there are two types of employees: host-country nationals (HCNs) (often known as "locals") and expatriates (expats) (nonnative employees who work in a foreign country). Among expatriates, there are two types: (1) Parent-country nationals (PCNs) come from the parent country of the MNE and work at its local subsidiary. (2) Third-country nationals (TCNs) come from neither the parent country nor the host country.

The majority of an MNE's employees are HCNs. For example, of Siemens's 400,000 employees worldwide, only a small cadre of 300 executives are expatriates, and another 2,000 executives are short-term assignees abroad. Of these 2,300 executives, about 60% are PCNs (Germans) and 40% are TCNs (from countries other than Germany and the host country). In international HRM, one leading concern is how to staff the *top* executive positions abroad, such as the subsidiary CEO, country manager, and key functional heads (such as CFO and CIO). Of the three choices for top positions, PCNs, TCNs, and HCNs all have their pros and cons (Table 15.1). The staffing choices are not random and are often a reflection of the strategic posture of the MNE—as discussed next.

15-1a Ethnocentric, Polycentric, and Geocentric Approaches in Staffing

There are three primary staffing approaches when making staffing decisions for top positions at subsidiaries. An ethnocentric approach emphasizes the norms and practices of the parent company (and the parent country of the MNE) by relying on PCNs. PCNs can not only ensure and facilitate control and coordination by headquarters, but they may also be the best-qualified people for the job because of special skills and experience. A perceived lack of talent and skills of HCNs often necessitates an ethnocentric approach. In addition, a cadre of internationally mobile and experienced managers, who are often PCNs, can emerge to spearhead further expansion around the world.

A polycentric approach is the opposite of an ethnocentric approach. A polycentric approach focuses on the norms and practices of the host country. In short, "when in Rome, do as the Romans do." Who will be the best managers if we have an operation in Rome? Naturally Roman (or Italian) managers—technically, HCNs. HCNs have no language and cultural barriers. Unlike PCNs who often pack their bags and move after several years, HCNs stay in their positions longer, thus providing more continuity of management. Further, placing HCNs in top subsidiary positions sends a morale-boosting signal to other HCNs who may feel that they can reach the top as well (at least in that subsidiary).

Third-country national (TCN)
Individual who is from neither the parent country nor the host country of the MNE.

Ethnocentric approach
An emphasis on the norms and practices of the parent company (and the parent country of the MNE) by relying on PCNs.

Polycentric approach
An emphasis on the norms and practices of the host country.

Table 15.1	**Parent-, Third-, and Host-Country Nationals**	
	Advantages	**Disadvantages**
Parent-country nationals (PCNs)	• Control by headquarters is facilitated • PCNs may be the most qualified people • Managers are given international experience	• Opportunities for HCNs are limited • Adaptation may take a long time • PCNs are usually very expensive
Third-country nationals (TCNs)	• TCNs may bridge the gap between headquarters and the subsidiary (and between PCNs and HCNs) • TCNs may be less expensive than PCNs	• Host government and employees may resent TCNs • Similar to disadvantages for PCNs
Host-country nationals (HCNs)	• Language and cultural barriers are eliminated • Continuity of management improves, since • Usually cheaper	• Control and coordination by headquarters may be impeded • HCNs may have limited career opportunity • International experience for PCNs are limited

Source: Adapted from P. Dowling & D. Welch, 2005, *International Human Resource Management*, 4th ed. (p. 63), Cincinnati: Cengage Learning.

Table 15.2	Multinational Strategies and Staffing Approaches	
MNE strategies	**Typical staffing approaches**	**Typical top managers at local subsidiaries**
Home replication	Ethnocentric	Parent-country nationals
Localization	Polycentric	Host-country nationals
Global standardization	Geocentric	A mix of parent-, host-, and third-country nationals
Transnational	Geocentric	A mix of parent-, host-, and third-country nationals

Disregarding nationality, a geocentric approach focuses on finding the most suitable managers, who can be PCNs, HCNs, or TCNs. In other words, a geocentric approach is "color blind"—the color of a manager's passport does not matter. For a geographically dispersed MNE, a geocentric approach can facilitate the emergence of a corporate-wide culture and identity. This can reduce the typical "us versus them" feeling in firms that use either ethnocentric or polycentric approaches. On the other hand, molding managers from a variety of nationalities is a lot more complex than integrating individuals from two (parent and host) countries (see the Opening Case).

Overall, there is a systematic link between MNEs' strategic postures (see Chapter 13) and staffing approaches (Table 15.2). MNEs pursuing a home replication strategy usually pursue an ethnocentric approach, staffing subsidiaries with PCNs. MNEs interested in a localization strategy is typically polycentric in nature, placing HCNs to head subsidiaries. Global standardization or transnational strategies often necessitate a geocentric approach, resulting in a mix of HCNs, PCNs, and TCNs.[3] As more firms, such as Samsung, become more global in their operations, they increasingly have to look beyond the pool of their PCNs and attract and nurture talented HCNs and TCNs (see the Opening Case).

15-1b The Role of Expatriates

Expatriation is the process of selecting, managing, and motivating expatriates to work abroad. Shown in Figure 15.1 and exemplified in the Opening and Closing Cases, expatriates play four important roles:

- Expatriates are *strategists* representing the interests of the MNE's headquarters.[4] Expatriates, especially PCNs who have a long tenure with a particular MNE, may have internalized the parent firm's values and norms. They may not only enable headquarters to control subsidiaries, but also facilitate the socialization process to bring subsidiaries into an MNE's global orbit.

Geocentric approach

A focus on finding the most suitable managers, who can be PCNs, HCNs, or TCNs.

Expatriation

The process of selecting, managing, and motivating expatriates to work abroad.

Figure 15.1	The Roles of Expatriates

- Expatriates act as *daily managers* to run operations and to build local capabilities, where local management talent is lacking.[5]
- Expatriates are also *ambassadors*.[6] Representing headquarters, they build relationships with host-country stakeholders such as local managers, employees, suppliers, customers, and officials. Importantly, expatriates also represent the interests of the *subsidiaries* when interacting with headquarters.
- Finally, expatriates are *trainers* for their replacements.[7] Over time, some localization in staffing is inevitable, calling for expatriates to train local employees.

15-1c Expatriate Failure and Selection

Few expatriates can simultaneously play the challenging multidimensional roles effectively.[8] Not surprisingly, expatriate failure rates are high. "Expatriate failure" can be defined differently, such as (1) premature (earlier-than-expected) return, (2) unmet business objectives, and (3) unfulfilled career-development objectives. Using the easiest-to-observe measure of "premature return," studies in the 1980s reported that 76% of US MNEs have more than 10% of expatriates failing, and that 41% and 24% of European and Japanese MNEs, respectively, have comparable numbers of failure cases.[9] More recent studies find failure rates to have declined a little.[10] However, given the much larger number of expatriates now (at present, more than one million from the United States alone), expatriate failure rates are still high enough to justify attention.

A variety of reasons can cause expatriate failure. Surveys of US and European MNEs find that the inability of the spouse and the family to adjust is the leading cause. In the case of Japanese MNEs, the leading cause is the inability to cope with the larger scope of responsibilities overseas. It usually is a *combination* of work-related and family-related problems that leads to expatriate failures.

Given the importance of expatriates and their reported high failure rates, how can firms enhance the odds for expatriate success? Figure 15.2 outlines a model

Figure 15.2 **Factors in Expatriate Selection**

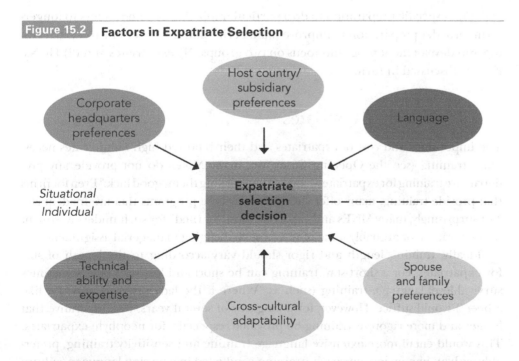

Source: Adapted from P. Dowling & D. Welch, 2005, *International Human Resource Management*, 4th ed. (p. 98), Cincinnati: Cengage Learning.

for expatriate selection, with six underlying factors grouped along situational and individual dimensions. In terms of situation dimensions, both headquarters' and subsidiary's preferences are important (Table 15.2). The subsidiary may also have specific requests, such as "Send a strong IT person." It is preferable for expatriates to have some command (or, better yet, mastery) of the local language.

In terms of individual dimensions, both technical ability and cross-cultural adaptability are a must. Desirable attributes include a positive attitude, emotional stability, and previous international experience. Last (but certainly not the least), spouse and family preferences must enter the equation.[11] The accompanying spouse may have left behind a career and a social network. He or she has to find meaningful endeavors abroad. (To protect local jobs, many countries do not permit the spouse to work.) It is not surprising that frustration permeates many families, thus leading to expatriate failure.

Expatriates are expensive, and failure rates are high in general. But middle-aged expatriates (forty-something) are the most expensive, because the employer often has to provide heavy allowance for children's education. High-quality schools are expensive—in places such as Manila, Mexico City, Moscow, and Sao Paulo, international or American schools cost $15,000 to $45,000 per year. Unfortunately, these expatriates also have the highest percentage of failure rates in part because of their family baggage. In response, many MNEs choose to (1) select expatriates in their fifties, whose children may have left the home, and/or (2) promote younger expatriates in their late twenties and early thirties, who may not yet have a family (or children). The younger expatriates typically have no need for a large home and no school-age kids. The second preference has strong implications for students studying this book now: these overseas opportunities may come sooner than you expect—are *you* ready?

15-2 Training and Development

Learning Objective
Identify training and development needs for expatriates and host-country nationals.

Training is specific preparation to do a particular job. Development refers to longer-term, broader preparation to improve managerial skills for a better career.[12] Training and development programs focus on two groups: (1) expatriates and (2) HCNs. Each is discussed in turn.

15-2a Training for Expatriates

The importance and cost of expatriates and their reported high failure rates necessitate training (see the Opening Case). Yet, many MNEs do not provide any pre-departure training for expatriates—other than wishing them "good luck." Even for firms that provide training, many offer short, one-day-type programs that are inadequate. Not surprisingly, many MNEs and expatriates are "burned" for such underinvestment in preparation for arguably some of the most challenging managerial assignments.

Ideally, training length and rigor should vary according to the length of stay for expatriates. For a short stay, training can be short and less rigorous. Sometimes survival-level language training (such as "Where is the lady's room?" and "I'd like a beer") would suffice. However, for a long stay of several years, it is imperative that longer and more rigorous training be provided, especially for neophyte expatriates. This would entail more extensive language training and sensitivity training, preferably with an immersion approach (training conducted in a foreign language/culture environment). More enlightened firms now involve the spouse in expatriate training.

Training
Specific preparation to do a particular job.

Development
Long-term, broader preparation to improve managerial skills for a better career.

15-2b Development for Returning Expatriates (Repatriates)

Many expatriate assignments are not "one shot" deals. Instead, they are viewed as part of the accumulation of a manager's experience and expertise for their long-term career development in the firm (see the Opening Case and the Closing Case).[13] While in theory this idea sounds good, in practice, many MNEs do a lousy job managing repatriation—the process of facilitating the return of expatriates (see Table 15.3).

Chief among the problems is career anxiety experienced by repatriates (returning expatriates). One leading concern is: "What kind of position will I have when I return?" Prior to departure, many expatriates are encouraged by their boss: "You should take (or volunteer for) this overseas assignment. It's a smart move for your career." Theoretically, this is known as a psychological contract—an informal understanding of expected delivery of benefits in the future for current services. However, a psychological contract is easy to violate. Bosses may have changed their mind, or they may have been replaced by new bosses. Violated psychological contracts naturally lead to disappointments.

Many returning expatriates experience painful adjustment in the workplace. Ethnocentrism continues to characterize many MNEs: knowledge transfer is typically one way—from headquarters to subsidiaries via expatriates. However, few (or none) at headquarters seem interested in learning from expatriates' overseas experience and knowledge.[14] Having been "big fish in a small pond" in subsidiaries, they often feel like being "small fish in a big pond" at headquarters. Instead of being promoted, many end up taking a comparable (or lower-level) position.

Returning expatriates may also experience a loss of status. Overseas, they are "big shots," rubbing shoulders with local politicians and visiting dignitaries. They often command lavish expatriate premiums, with chauffeured cars and maids. However, most of these perks disappear once they return.

Lastly, the spouse and the children may also find it difficult to adjust back home. The feeling of being a part of a relatively high-class, close-knit expatriate community is gone. Instead, life at home may now seem lonely and dull. Children, being out of touch with current slang, sports, and fashion, may struggle to regain acceptance into peer groups. Having been brought up overseas, (re)adjusting back to the home country educational system may be especially problematic. Some of the returning Japanese teenagers committed suicide after failing to make the grade back home.

Repatriation, if not managed well, can be traumatic not only for expatriates and their families, but also for the firm. Unhappy returning expatriates do not last very long. Approximately one in four or one in three exits the firm within one year.[15] Since a US MNE spends, on average, around $1 million on each expatriate over the duration of a foreign assignment, losing that individual can wipe out any return on

Repatriation
The process of facilitating the return of expatriates.

Repatriate
Returning expatriate.

Psychological contract
An informal understanding of expected delivery of benefits in the future for current services.

Table 15.3	**Problems Associated with Repatriation**

- Career anxiety—what kind of position will I have when I return (if I will have a position)?

- Work adjustment—from a big fish in a small pond (at the subsidiary) to a small fish in a big pond (at headquarters)

- Loss of status and pay—expatriate premiums are gone, chauffeured cars and maids are probably unavailable

- Difficult for the spouse and children to adjust—"going home" is not that easy

How did Carlos Ghosn's experience as an expatriate running Nissan help secure his appointment as CEO of the parent company, Renault?

investment. Worse yet, the returnee may end up working for a rival firm.

The best way to reduce expatriate turnover is a career-development plan. A good plan also comes with a mentor (also known as a champion, sponsor, or god-father).[16] The mentor helps alleviate the "out-of-sight, out-of-mind" feeling by ensuring that the expatriate is not forgotten at headquarters and by helping secure a challenging position for the expatriate upon return.

Overall, despite numerous "horror stories," many expatriates do succeed.[17] Carlos Ghosn, after successfully turning around Nissan as a PCN, went on to become CEO of the parent company, Renault. To reach the top at most MNEs today, international experience is a must. Therefore, despite the drawbacks, aspiring managers should not be deterred—who said being a manager was easy?

15-2c Training and Development for Host-Country Nationals

While most international HRM practice and research focus on expatriates, it is important to note that HCNs deserve significant attention for their training and development needs. In the ongoing "war for talent" in Brazil, Russia, India, China (BRIC), and other emerging economies, a key factor in retaining or losing top talent is which employer can provide better training and development opportunities.[18] To stem the tide of turnover, many MNEs now have formal career-development plans and processes for hot-shot HCNs in these countries. GE, for example, has endeavored to make promising managers in China stimulated, energized, and recognized. This has resulted in a managerial turnover rate of "only" 7% per year, substantially lower than the nationwide average of 40% for HCNs at the managerial rank working at multinationals in China.

Learning Objective

Discuss compensation and performance appraisal issues.

15-3 Compensation and Performance Appraisal

As an HRM area, compensation refers to the determination of salary and benefits. Performance appraisal entails the evaluation of employee performance for promotion, retention, or termination purposes. We discuss three related issues here: (1) compensation for expatriates, (2) compensation for HCNs, and (3) performance appraisal.

Compensation

The determination of salary and benefits.

15-3a Compensation for Expatriates

A leading issue in international HRM is how to properly compensate, motivate, and retain expatriates. Table 15.4 shows two primary approaches: (1) going rate and (2) balance sheet. The going rate approach pays expatriates the going rate for comparable positions in a host country. When Lenovo sends Chinese expatriates to New York, it pays them the going rate for comparable positions for HCNs and other expatriates in New York. This approach fosters equality among PCNs, TCNs, and HCNs in the same subsidiary. This would be attractive for PCNs and TCNs to work in a location where pay is higher than in their home countries. This approach excels in its simplicity. Expatriates also develop strong identification with the host country.

Performance appraisal

The evaluation of employee performance for promotion, retention, or termination purposes.

Going rate approach

A compensation approach that pays expatriates the prevailing (going) rate for comparable positions in a host country.

Table 15.4	**Going Rate versus Balance Sheet Approach in Expatriate Compensation**	
	Advantages	**Disadvantages**
Going rate	• Equality among parent-, third-, and host-country nationals in the same location • Simplicity • Identification with host country	• Variation between assignments in different locations for the same employee • Reentry problem if the going rate of parent country is less than that of host country
Balance sheet	• Equity between assignments for the same employee • Facilitates expatriate re-entry	• Costly and complex to administer • Great disparities between expatriates and host-country nationals

However, the going rate, for the same position, differs around the world, with the United States leading in managerial compensation. For example, the typical US CEO commands a total compensation package of more than $2 million, whereas the British CEO fetches less than $1 million, the Japanese CEO $500,000, and the Chinese CEO $200,000. According to the going-rate approach, returning Lenovo expatriates, having been used to New York-level high salaries, will have a hard time accepting relatively lower Beijing-level salaries, thus triggering repatriation problems.

A second approach is the balance sheet approach, which balances the cost-of-living differences based on parent-country levels and adds a financial inducement to make the package attractive. This is the most widely used method in expatriate compensation. There is a historical reason for this preference, because until recently, a majority of expatriates went from higher-pay developed economies to lower-pay locations. In this case, the going-rate approach would not work because no expatriate from New York would accept the going rate in Beijing. The balance sheet approach offers "New York Plus" for Beijing-bound expatriates. The "Plus" is nontrivial: additional financial inducement (premium), cost-of-living allowance (such as housing and children's education), and hardship allowance. (Although fewer companies now pay a hardship allowance for Beijing, many MNEs used to.) Table 15.5 shows one hypothetical example. Adding housing and taxation that the MNE pays (not shown in the table), the total cost to the firm may reach $300,000.

The balance sheet approach has two advantages (see Table 15.4). First, there is equity between assignments for the same employee, whose compensation is always anchored to the going rate in the parent country. Second, it also facilitates repatriation, with relatively little fluctuation between overseas and parent country pay despite the cost-of-living differences around the world.

Table 15.5	**A Hypothetical Expatriate Compensation Package Using the Balance Sheet Approach**

Items for a hypothetical US expatriate	Amount (US$)
Base salary	$150,000
Cost-of-living allowance (25%)	$37,500
Overseas premium (20%)	$30,000
Hardship allowance (20%)	$30,000
Housing deduction (−7%)	−$10,500
TOTAL (pretax)	$237,000

Note: The host country has a cost-of-living index of 150 relative to the United States. *Not* shown here are (1) the full cost of housing, and (2) the cost to pay the difference between a higher income tax in a host country and a lower income tax in the parent country. Adding housing and taxation, the net cost on the MNE can reach $300,000 in this case.

Balance sheet approach

A compensation approach that balances the cost of living differences relative to parent country levels and adds a financial inducement to make the package attractive.

However, there are three disadvantages. The first is cost. Using the example in Table 15.5, the cost can add to $1 million for a three-year tour of duty. The second disadvantage is the great disparities in pay between expatriates (especially PCNs) and HCNs, causing resentment among HCNs.

Lastly, the balance sheet approach is organizationally complex to administer. For a US firm operating in South Africa, both the American PCNs and Australian TCNs are likely to be compensated more than the South African HCNs. The situation becomes more complicated when the US firm recruits South African MBAs before they finish business school training in the United States. Should they be paid as locally hired HCNs in South Africa or as expatriates from the United States? What about TCNs from Kenya, Morocco, and Nigeria who also finish US MBA training and are interested in going to work for the US MNE in South Africa? Ideally, firms pay for a position regardless of colors of their passports. However, the market for expatriate compensation is not quite there yet.

15-3b Compensation for Host-Country Nationals

At the bottom end of the compensation scale, low-level HCNs, especially those in developing countries, have relatively little bargaining power. The very reason that they have a job at the MNE subsidiaries is often their low labor cost—that is, they are willing to accept wage levels substantially lower than those in developed countries (see Table 15.6). Low-level HCNs compare their pay to the farmhands sweating in the fields and making much less, or to the army of unemployed who make nothing but still have a family to feed (see PengAtlas Maps 4.2 and 4.3. Despite some social activist groups' accusations of "exploitation" by MNEs, MNEs typically pay *higher* wages relative to similar positions in developing countries.

On the other hand, HCNs in management and professional positions have increasing bargaining power. MNEs are rushing into emerging economies, whereby local supply of top talent is limited. This may be hard to believe, but the most populous country in the world has a shortage of people—executives. To fuel their growth, Chinese and foreign firms need 75,000 globally competitive executives in China. At present, approximately 5,000 to 8,000 Chinese executives fit the profile. Some executives in China reportedly receive calls from headhunters *every day*.[19] Likewise, in India—until the 2008–2009 recession—wage inflation in its hot IT sector was at 16% a year, with a 40% turnover. Although such increase has slowed down, the "war for talent" (specifically, the bidding war for top-notch HCNs) is real. It is not surprising that high-caliber HCNs, because of their scarcity, will fetch more pay.[20] The question is: How much more? Most MNEs aim to eventually replace even top-level expatriates with HCNs, in part to save cost. However, if HCNs occupying the same top-level positions are paid the same as expatriates, then there will be no cost savings. However, MNEs unwilling to pay top local talent top dollar may end up losing such high-caliber HCNs to competitors that are willing to do so. The war for talent is essentially a bidding war for top HCNs. MNEs may eventually have to pay international rates, regardless of nationality.

Table 15.6 **Compensation for Host-Country Nationals in Asia (Average Monthly Pay in US$)**

Dhaka, Bangladesh	Ho Chi Minh City, Vietnam	Jakarta, Indonesia	Shenyang, (north) China	Shenzhen, (south) China	Taipei, Taiwan	Seoul, South Korea	Yokohama, Japan
$47	$100	$148	$197	$235	$888	$1,220	$3,099

Source: Extracted from data in *Bloomberg BusinessWeek*, 2011, Global inflation starts with Chinese workers, March 7: 10.

15-3c Performance Appraisal

Although initial compensation is determined upon entering a firm, follow-up compensation usually depends on performance appraisal. It focuses on decision making (to determine pay and promotion), development, documentation, and subordinate expression. In our case, performance appraisal entails (1) how expatriates provide performance appraisal to HCNs, and (2) how expatriates are evaluated.

When expatriates evaluate HCNs, cultural differences may create problems.[21] Typically from low-power distance countries, Western MNEs emphasize an opportunity for subordinates to express themselves. However, high-power distance countries in Asia and Latin America would not foster such an expression, which would potentially undermine the power and status of supervisors. Employees themselves do not place a lot of importance on such an expression. Thus, Western expatriates pushing HCNs in these cultures to express themselves in performance-appraisal meetings may be viewed as indecisive and lacking integrity.

Expatriates need to be evaluated by their own supervisors. However, in some cases, expatriates are the top manager in a subsidiary (such as country manager), and their supervisors are more senior executives based at headquarters. Some of these offsite managers have no experience as expatriates themselves. They often evaluate expatriates based on hard numbers, such as productivity and market growth, some of which are beyond the control of expatriates. (What about a currency crisis?) This is one of the reasons why many expatriates feel that they are not evaluated fairly. The solution lies in (1) fostering more visits and exchange of views between onsite expatriates and offsite supervisors, and (2) relying on former expatriates now based at headquarters to serve as offsite supervisors.

Always sensitive, compensation and performance evaluation are even more important during tough economic times. Facing grave financial situations, should the firm impose across-the-board pay cuts or engage in reduction in force, which is massive layoffs? If someone has to go, according to what criteria based on performance evaluation should the firm decide who will receive the pink slip first? These are crucial questions that HR managers must be prepared for (see In Focus 15.1).

IN FOCUS 15.1

ACROSS-THE-BOARD PAY CUTS VERSUS MASS LAYOFFS

Ethical Dilemma

Both HR and line managers often have to make tough decisions. One of the most challenging decisions is how to cope with an economic downturn such as the financial market meltdown during 2008 and 2009. Reduction in force (RIF), a euphemism for mass layoffs, is often used in the United States and the United Kingdom. Outside the Anglo-American world, however, mass layoffs are often viewed as unethical. Some critics label mass layoffs as "corporate cannibalism." One alternative is for the entire firm to have across-the-board pay cuts while preserving all current jobs. Which approach is better?

Earlier experiences with across-the-board pay cuts may provide some clue. In 2003, SARS hit Asia. The Portman Ritz-Carlton in Shanghai, a five-star hotel, implemented across-the-board pay cuts. A majority of Chinese HCNs supported this practice, as evidenced by the 99.9% employee satisfaction in

IN FOCUS 15.1 (continued)

that year. However, when US firms experiment with across-the-board pay cuts, the results tend to be very *negative*. To avoid RIF in its US facilities during the post–2001 downturn, Applied Materials implemented across-the-board pay cuts: Executives took a 10% hit, managers and professionals 5%, and hourly production workers 3%. The pay cuts lasted for 18 months. An HR executive at Applied Materials commented:

> These across-the-board pay cuts have a longer-lasting and far greater negative impact on morale than RIFs would have. RIFs are very hard on the impacted employees as well as the survivors. However, when managed correctly, impacted employees are able to separate from the company with dignity and in the case of Applied Materials, with a very generous financial package . . . I don't know of any surviving employees that appreciated having their paycheck impacted every two weeks for 18 months . . . Ultimately, pay levels were restored. However, employee memories are very long and this particular event was pointed to over and over again throughout multiple employee surveys as an indicator of poor leadership and a major cause of employee dissatisfaction.

Applied Materials and other US firms that implemented across-the-board pay cuts lost numerous star performers who found greener pastures elsewhere. This raises serious concerns as to whether such large-scale sacrifice is worth it, at least in an individualistic culture. In the 2008–2009 recession, a small but increasing number of US firms, such as FedEx, HP, and The New York Times Company, trimmed base pay for all employees—more for senior executives than for the rank and file. While President Obama praised such practices in his inaugural speech in January 2009, some HRM experts complained that these managers were "chicken managers" who did not have the guts to make tough choices and, therefore, in their cowardice, chose to inflict equal pain on everybody.

Sources: Based on (1) *BusinessWeek*, 2009, Cutting salaries instead of jobs, June 8: 48; (2) S. Parker, EMBA student in the author's class, individual assignment 1, Jindal School of Management, University of Texas at Dallas, January 2007; (3) A. Yeung, 2006, Setting the people up for success, *Human Resource Management*, 45: 267–275.

Learning Objective
Understand labor relations in both home and host countries.

15-4 Labor Relations

Labor relations refer to firms' relations with organized labor (unions) in both home and host countries. Each is discussed in turn.

15-4a Managing Labor Relations at Home

In developed economies, firms' key concern is to enhance competitiveness to fight off low-cost rivals from emerging economies. Labor unions' declared interest is to help workers earn higher wages and obtain more benefits through collective bargaining. In the United States, unionized employees earn 30% more than non-unionized employees. As a result, disagreements and conflicts between managers and unions are natural.

Labor unions' bargaining chip is their credible threat to strike, slow down, refuse to work overtime, or some other forms of disruption. Managers' bargaining chip lies in their threat to shut down operations and move jobs overseas. It is clear which side is winning. In the United States, union membership dropped from 20% of the workforce in 1983 to 11% now (just 7% in the private sector and 36% in the public sector). Membership of United Auto Workers (UAW), for example, fell from 1.5 million to fewer than 400,000 at present.[22] The trend is similar in other developed economies exposed to globalization, such as Britain, France, Germany, and Japan.[23]

Labor relation
A firm's relation with organized labor (unions) in both home and host countries.

Unlike MNEs, which can move operations around the world, unions are organized on a country-by-country basis. Efforts to establish multinational labor organizations have not been effective. In the 1990s, in the face of US MNEs' aggressive efforts to move operations to Mexico to take advantage of NAFTA, the AFL-CIO, the leading US union, contacted the Mexican government, requesting that it be permitted to recruit members in Mexico. It was flatly rejected.

15-4b Managing Labor Relations Abroad

If given a choice, MNEs would prefer to employ nonunionized workforces. When Japanese and German automakers came to the United States, they avoided the Midwest, a union stronghold. Instead, these MNEs went to the rural South and set up nonunion plants in small towns in Alabama (Daimler-Benz and Hyundai), Kentucky (Toyota), and South Carolina (BMW). When MNEs have to deal with unions abroad, they often rely on experienced HCNs, instead of locally inexperienced PCNs or TCNs.

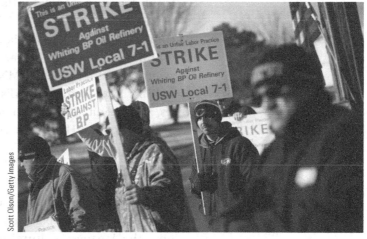

Throughout many developing countries, governments typically welcome MNEs and at the same time silence unions. However, things are changing. In 2010, a series of high-profile strikes took place at plants run by Taiwan's Foxconn and Japan's Honda in China. Instead of cracking down, the Chinese government chose to look the other way. Emboldened workers ended up forcing these MNEs to accept 30% to 40% pay increases. The media widely reported that "the days of cheap labor [in China] are gone."[24]

How does the organization of a union affect both the domestic and foreign companies doing business in that industry and country?

15-5 Institutions, Resources, and Human Resource Management

Learning Objective
Discuss how the institution-based and resource-based views shed additional light on HRM.

Having outlined the four basic areas of HRM, let us now turn to the institution-based and resource-based views to see how they shed additional light (see Figure 15.3).

Figure 15.3 **Institutions, Resources, and Human Resource Management**

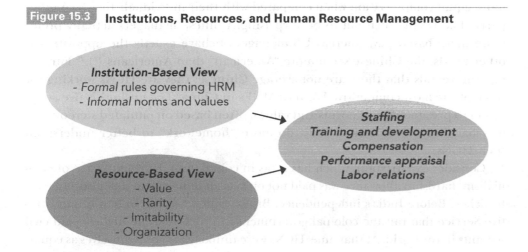

Institution-Based View
- *Formal* rules governing HRM
- *Informal* norms and values

Resource-Based View
- Value
- Rarity
- Imitability
- Organization

Staffing
Training and development
Compensation
Performance appraisal
Labor relations

15-5a Institutions and Human Resource Management

HRM is significantly shaped by formal and informal rules of the game—both at home and abroad.[25] Every country has formal rules, laws, and regulations governing the do's and don'ts of HRM. Foreign firms ignoring such rules do so at their own peril. For instance, in Japan, firms routinely discriminate against women and minorities. However, when Japanese MNEs engage in such "usual" practices in the United States, they are often legally challenged.

On the other hand, foreign firms well versed in local regulations may take advantage of them. In France, legal hurdles for firing full-time workers are legendary—HP got a phone call from then-president Jacques Chirac, who complained after HP had announced a plan to lay off 1,200 employees.[26] Interestingly, France is a highly lucrative market for the US-based Manpower. Manpower's expertise in providing part-time workers is highly valued by French firms unwilling to hire full-time employees. France is now Manpower's *largest* market ahead of the United States.

Informal rules of the game—embodied in cultures, norms, and values—also assert powerful influence. MNEs from different countries have different norms in staffing. Most Japanese MNEs follow an informal rule: Heads of foreign subsidiaries, at least initially, need to be PCNs.[27] In comparison, European MNEs are more likely to appoint HCNs and TCNs to lead subsidiaries. There is a historical reason for such differences: Most European MNEs expanded globally before low-cost telephones, faxes, e-mails, and Skype were available. Thus, a localization strategy relying on HCNs and TCNs was necessary.

Most Japanese MNEs went abroad in the 1980s, when modern communication technology enabled more centralized control from headquarters. In addition, the Japanese cultural preference for low uncertainty also translated into higher interest in headquarters control. Thus, Japanese MNEs often implemented a home replication strategy that relied on PCNs who constantly communicated with headquarters.

Interestingly, the emerging Chinese MNEs are more likely to appoint HCNs as managers. This may be due to the lack of international talents among their ranks or due to the more open-minded nature of some Chinese MNEs. Regardless of the reason, the upshot is the same: More managerial jobs for locals.[28]

While informal cultures, norms, and values are important, HR managers must avoid stereotyping and consider changes. In the area of compensation, one study hypothesizes that presumably collectivistic Chinese managers would prefer more equal compensation when compared with their individualistic US counterparts. The results turn out to be surprising: Chinese managers actually prefer more merit-based pay, whereas US managers behave exactly the opposite—in other words, the Chinese seem more "American" than Americans (!).[29] Further digging reveals that these are not average Chinese; they are HCNs working for some of the most competitive Western MNEs in China. The upshot? Naïve adaptation to presumed local norms and values, often based on outdated stereotypes, may backfire. HR managers must do more "homework" to better understand their HCNs.

Consider expatriation, which has roots in colonialism. During the age of colonialism, hardship allowance was paid not only as an inducement, but also as a path to riches. Before India's independence, British officers in the Indian Administrative Service that ran the colonial government in India were the highest paid civil servants in the world. At that time, HCNs were unlikely to view themselves as equals of PCNs. In the 21st century, many well-educated Indians—often armed with degrees from Western universities—are as qualified as some Western expatriates. Such HCNs naturally resent being treated as second-class citizens.

One norm that is changing is the necessity to pay extra compensation to attract higher-caliber and more senior expatriates. Since overseas experience, especially in major emerging economies such as China, is now viewed as a necessary step to advance one's career, demand is outstripping supply of such opportunities.[30] Therefore, many firms do not feel compelled to offer financial inducements, because, according to Siemens's HRM chief, "We don't want people to take the job merely for the money."[31] Many Western managers are willing to accept a "local plus" package instead of the traditional expatriate package full of perks. Further, more expatriates are now younger. They may be sent abroad to gain experience—often with more down-to-earth titles such as "assignees" or "secondees." In addition, more expatriates are now sent on short-term, commuter-type assignments for which they do not need to uproot their family—a major source of stress for the family and a cost item for the firm. Overall, the norms and images associated with the stereotypical expatriate, a more senior executive leading a life of luxury to compensate for hardship overseas, are changing rapidly.

15-5b Resources and Human Resource Management

From a resource-based view, employees, by definition, are crucial resources. As HRM becomes more "strategic," the VRIO dimensions are increasingly at the center stage.[32] To start, managers must ask: Does a particular HR activity add *value*?[33] Consider two examples. First, labor-intensive chores, such as administering payroll, benefits, and basic training, may not add value. They can often be outsourced. Second, training is expensive. Does it really add value? Results pooled from 397 studies find that, on average, training adds value by leading to approximately 20% performance improvement for that individual.[34] Thus, training is often justified.

Next, are particular HR activities *rare*? The relentless drive to learn, share, and adopt "best practices" may reduce their rarity and thus usefulness. If every MNE in Turkey provides training to high-caliber HCNs, such training, which is valuable, will be taken for granted but not be viewed as rare.

Further, how *imitable* are certain HR activities? It is relatively easy to imitate a single practice, but it is much more difficult to imitate a complex HR *system* (or *architecture*) consisting of multiple, mutually reinforcing practices that work together.[35] Consider the Portman Ritz-Carlton hotel in Shanghai, which has been repeatedly voted the Best Employer in Asia. Its expatriate general manager personally interviews *every* new hire. It selects HCNs genuinely interested in helping guests. It deeply cares about employee satisfaction, which has led to superb guest satisfaction. Each single practice here may be imitable, and the Portman Ritz-Carlton has been meticulously studied by rivals (and non-rivals) in China and around the world. Yet, none has been able to imitate its system successfully. On the surface, every firm says, "We care about our people." But the reality at many firms is increasing underinvestment by both employers and employees, with declining loyalty and commitment. A mutual investment approach is likely to result in excellent performance, as exemplified by Whole Foods (see In Focus 15.2). However, it is very difficult to imitate a mutual investment approach that comes together as a system (or architecture).

IN FOCUS 15.2

HUMAN RESOURCE SYSTEM AT WHOLE FOODS

Headquartered in Austin, Texas, Whole Foods is the leading retailer of natural and organic foods and an iconic brand in the United States. It has more than 300 locations in the United States, Canada, and Britain, with sales of $11 billion. Advocated by its founder John Mackey, its strategy focuses on conscious capitalism, which is a more conscious way of thinking about business and its relationships with various stakeholders. What is the role of HR in all this? Mackey shared his thoughts with *Harvard Business Review*:

> Management's job at Whole Foods is to make sure that we hire good people, that they are well trained, and that they flourish in the workplace, because we found that when people are really happy in their jobs, they provide much higher degrees of service to the customers. Happy team members result in happy customers. Happy customers do more business with you. They become advocates for your enterprise, which results in happy investors. That is a win-win-win-win strategy. You can expand it to include your suppliers and the communities where you do business, which are tied in to this prosperity circle.

Underpinning this strategy is its HR system. Starting with *staffing*. Each of its 70,000 employees is hired into a particular team. Each store has ten teams. New hires are on a probationary basis for 30–90 days. After that, they need to earn two-thirds of votes from team members in order to be accepted as a full member. Employees who do not fit the Whole Foods conscious capitalism culture, even though their performance may be satisfactory, are asked to leave. Teams look for people who are "inclusive" and value diversity. Since teams have a great deal of autonomy in making decisions and are responsible for their performance, being a contributing, productive team member is crucial.

Whole Foods's *performance appraisal* processes are team-oriented. Members are evaluated by their peers on the team. Its *compensation* program is very different from that in other firms. Reflecting the firm's philosophy of egalitarianism, everyone knows what everybody else makes. This transparency enables team members to provide feedback to management on what they deem unfair. The entire team shares one bonus pool. A bonus is divided among team members if above-target performance is achieved. If the team fails to hit performance targets, bonus is not paid out. Whole Foods also imposes a cap on CEO pay. While in many US publicly listed firms the CEO is paid several hundred times what the average rank-and-file employees are paid, at Whole Foods the ratio of CEO pay vis-à-vis team member pay is only 19-to-1.

Finally, Whole Foods's *training and development* programs are also reflective of the tenets of conscious capitalism. Every team member is cross-trained to ensure everyone can perform multiple tasks. When a manager fails, instead of firing this individual—which is typical of many firms—Whole Foods removes him/her from the current job, but gives the manager six months at full pay to find another position within the firm. In this way, development truly becomes "longer-term, broader preparation to improve managerial skills for a better career" (which is our textbook definition on page 490). Whole Foods is not totally altruistic. It is doing this because each manager represents a significant investment that the firm has made into his/her career. Firing a failed manager would simply wipe out that investment. Keeping the failed manager and encouraging him/her to find a new job that has a better fit is part of the win-win strategy that Mackey has emphasized.

Sources: Based on (1) J. Mackey, 2011, What is it that only I can do? *Harvard Business Review*, January: 119–123; (2) J. Slocum, D. Lei, & P. Buller, 2014, Executing business strategies through human resource management practices, *Organizational Dynamics*, 43: 73–87; (3) www .wholefoodsmarket.com.

Finally, do HR practices support *organizational capabilities* to help the firm accomplish its performance goals? Consider teamwork and diversity, especially multinational teams consisting of members from different subsidiaries.[36] While most firms promote some sort of teamwork and diversity, it is challenging to organizationally leverage such teamwork and diversity to enhance performance.[37] Too little or too much diversity may hurt performance. In teamwork, certain disagreements may be helpful to promote learning. But obviously, too many disagreements may be too much, lead to conflicts, and torpedo team effectiveness. However, few managers (and few firms) master the art of drawing the line before disagreements within a team get out of control.

15-6 Debates and Extensions

Learning Objective
Participate in two leading debates concerning HRM.

This chapter has already alluded to a number of HR debates, such as the value of expatriates. Here we focus on two previously untouched debates: (1) best fit versus best practice and (2) expatriation versus inpatriation.

15-6a Best Fit versus Best Practice

The "best fit" school argues that a firm needs to search for the best external and internal fit. Externally, HRM is shaped by national and industry contexts. Internally, HRM is driven by firm strategy. On the product dimension, a firm pursuing a differentiation strategy needs to reinforce the passion for higher quality, better service, and more sustained learning. On the international dimension, a firm using a localization strategy must deploy more HCNs (Table 15.2). Moreover, the quest for the best fit is *continuous*. Even for the same MNE in the same country, a good fit now may not be good enough ten years later. In two words, the "best fit" school argues: it depends.[38]

The "best practice" school begs to differ. Proponents argue that firms should adopt "best practices" regardless of context. Such "best practices" often include extensive training, high pay for high performance, and self-managed teams (emphasizing teamwork). While the list of "best practices" may vary, the underlying spirit seems to be the same around the world.[39]

Critics of the "best practice" school make two points. First, they point out that "there is overwhelming evidence against a universal set of HR practices based on national variations."[40] Second, they argue that from a resource-based view, if all firms adopt universal "best practices," such practices lose their value. To reconcile the debate, experts note that "it is not a question of either/or but a question of the appropriate balance."[41] They argue that most firms may still benefit from adopting some "best practices," because most firms are not yet at that frontier.

15-6b Expatriation versus Inpatriation

Addressing the expatriation problem, one solution is inpatriation—relocating employees of a foreign subsidiary to the MNE's headquarters for the purposes of (1) filling skill shortages at headquarters, and (2) developing a global mindset for such inpatriates. The term "inpatriation," of course, is derived from "expatriation," and most inpatriates are expected to eventually return to their home country to replace expatriates. Examples would include IT inpatriates from India to work at IBM in the United States and telecom inpatriates from China to work at Alcatel-Lucent in France. Technically, these inpatriates are expatriates from India and China, who will experience some of the problems associated with expatriation discussed earlier in this chapter.

In addition, some inpatriates, being paid by the going rate of their home (typically developing) countries, are upset after finding out the compensation level of colleagues at headquarters doing equivalent work—the cost of an Indian IT professional is approximately 10% to 20% of that of an American one. Some inpatriates

Inpatriation
Relocating employees of a foreign subsidiary to the MNE's headquarters for the purposes of filling skill shortages at headquarters and developing a global mindset for such inpatriates.

thus refuse to go back and find work in their host countries. Other inpatriates go back to their home countries but quit their sponsoring MNEs—they jump ship to rival MNEs willing to pay more.

Even for inpatriates who return to assume leadership positions in subsidiaries in their home countries (as planned), unfortunately, many are ineffective. In China, inpatriated ethnic Chinese often struggle with an ambiguous identity: Western headquarters views them as "us," whereas HCNs also expect them to be "us." When these managers favor headquarters on issues where headquarters and locals conflict (such as refusing to pay HCNs more), HCNs view them as traitors of sorts. These problems erupt in spite of these inpatriates' Chinese roots—or, perhaps, *because* of their Chinese roots.[42] Overall, one lesson is that there will be no panacea in international staffing. Inpatriates, just like expatriates, have their fair share of headaches.

Learning Objective
Draw implications for action.

15-7 Management Savvy

What determines the success and failure of HRM around the world? A simple answer is effectiveness of HR activities in areas such as staffing, training and development, compensation, and labor relations. A more interesting question is: "How much is the impact of effective HRM on firm performance?"[43] Results from 3,200 firms find that change of one standard deviation in the HR system affects 10% to 20% of a firm's market value.[44] Findings from 92 studies suggest that an increase of one standard deviation in the use of effective HR system is associated with a 4.6% increase in return on assets (ROA).[45] These recent findings validate a long-held belief among HRM practitioners and scholars: HRM is indeed *strategic*, as it has become a direct answer to the fundamental question of our field: What determines the success and failure of firms around the world?[46]

Consequently, we identify implications for actions, listed in Table 15.7, that center on the four Cs developed by Susan Meisinger, president of the Society for Human Resource Management.[47] These insights have important implications for HR managers.

First, savvy HR managers need to be *curious*. They need to be well versed in the numerous formal and informal rules of the game governing HRM worldwide. They must be curious about emerging trends in the world and be prepared to respond to these trends.[48] Second, HR managers must be *competent*. Far from its lowly roots as a lackluster administrative support function, HRM is now acknowledged as a strategic function. Many HR managers may have been trained more narrowly and with a more micro (non-strategic) focus. Now, HR managers must be able to not only contribute to the strategy conversation, but also take things off the CEO's desk as full-fledged business partners (see In Focus 15.3).

Finally, HR managers must be *courageous* and *caring*. As guardians of talent, HR managers need to nurture and develop employees (see the Opening Case).[49] This

Table 15.7 Implications for Action

For HR managers: The four Cs
- Be *curious*.
- Be *competent*.
- Be *courageous*.
- Be *caring*.

For non-HR managers: The fifth C
- Be proactive in managing your (international) *career*

IN FOCUS 15.3
A RADICAL PROPOSAL

Ram Charan is one of the most influential consultants in the world. He finds most HR executives to have expertise in compensation, benefits, and labor relations. They tend to focus on internal matters, such as engagement, empowerment, and cultural sensitivity. But they do not seem to do well as advisors to CEOs on the talent implications of the firm's strategy. Therefore, Charan has proposed a radical solution in *Harvard Business Review*. In his own words:

It is radical, but it is grounded in practicality. My proposal is to eliminate the position of chief human resource officer (CHRO) and split HR into two strands. One—we might call it HR-A (for administration)—would primarily manage compensation and benefits. It would report to the CFO, who would have to see compensation as a talent magnet, not just a major cost. The other, HR-LO

Jasjeet Plaha/Hindustan Times/Getty Images

(for leadership and organization), would focus on improving the people capabilities of the business and would report to the CEO.

The ideal candidates to serve as HR-LO would not be traditional HR managers. Instead, HR-LO positions ideally would be better served by high-potential line managers from operations or finance. They can develop people skills and link the HR system with operational or financial performance. After a few years, these executives may move to horizontal or higher-level line management positions. Although Charan expects "plenty of opposition" to his proposal, he is convinced that it is time to split HR. What do you think?

Source: Based on R. Charan, 2014, It's time to split HR, *Harvard Business Review*, July: 34. See also R. Charan, D. Barton, & D. Carey, 2015, People before strategy: A new role for the CHRO, *Harvard Business Review*, July-August: 63–71.

often means that as employee advocates, HR managers sometimes need to be courageous enough to disagree with the CEO and other line managers if necessary. GE's recently retired head of HR, William Conaty, is such an example. "If you just get closer to the CEO, you're dead," Conaty shared with a reporter. "I need to be independent. I need to be credible." GE's CEO Jeff Immelt called Conaty "the first friend, the guy that could walk in my office and kick my butt when it needed to be"—exactly how a full-fledged business partner should behave.[50]

In addition, there is a fifth "C" for non-HR managers: Proactively manage your *career* in order to develop a global mindset. LEGO, for example, encourages managers to build a "T-shaped" career. The vertical leg represents one particular area, while the horizontal bar signals a breadth of knowledge across multiple disciplines.[51] Since international experience is a prerequisite for reaching the top at many firms, managers must prepare by investing in their own technical expertise and cross-cultural adaptability. Some of these investments (such as language) are long-term in nature. This point thus has strategic implications for students who are studying this book *now*: Have you learned a foreign language? Have you spent one semester or year abroad? Have you made any friends from abroad, perhaps fellow students who are taking this class with you now? Have you put this course on your resume? Arm yourself with the knowledge now, make proper investments, and advance your career. Remember: your career is in your hands.[52]

CHAPTER SUMMARY/LEARNING OBJECTIVES

15-1 Explain staffing decisions with a focus on expatriates.

- International staffing primarily relies on ethnocentric, polycentric, and geocentric approaches.
- Expatriates (primarily PCNs and, to a lesser extent, TCNs) play multiple challenging roles and often have high failure rates. They need to be carefully selected, taking into account a variety of factors.

15-2 Identify training and development needs for expatriates and HCNs.

- Expatriates need to be properly trained and cared for during expatriation and repatriation.
- Training and development of HCNs are now an area of differentiation among many MNEs.

15-3 Discuss compensation and performance appraisal issues.

- Expatriates are compensated using the going rate and balance sheet approaches.
- Top-talent HCNs now increasingly command higher compensation.
- Performance appraisal needs to be carefully provided to achieve its intended purposes.

15-4 Understand labor relations in both home and host countries.

- Despite efforts to revive unions, the power of unions has been declining in developed countries.
- The power of unions in most developing countries requires some attention but is mostly limited.

15-5 Discuss how the institution-based and resource-based views shed additional light on HRM.

- HRM is significantly shaped by formal and informal rules of the game—both at home and abroad.
- As HRM becomes more strategic, VRIO dimensions are now more important.

15-6 Participate in two leading debates concerning HRM.

- (1) Best fit versus best practice and (2) expatriation versus inpatriation.

15-7 Draw implications for action.

- HR managers need to have the four Cs: being curious, competent, courageous, and caring about people.
- Non-HR managers need to proactively develop their career by developing a global mindset.

KEY TERMS

Balance sheet approach, 491	Geocentric approach, 486	Inpatriation, 499
Compensation, 490	Going rate approach, 490	Labor relation, 494
Development, 488	Host-country national (HCN), 484	Parent-country national (PCN), 484
Ethnocentric approach, 485	Human resource management (HRM), 484	Performance appraisal, 490
Expatriation, 486		Polycentric approach, 485

REVIEW QUESTIONS

1. Name and describe three staffing approaches.

2. *ON CULTURE:* What factors often lead to an expatriate experiencing difficulties or even failure on an overseas assignment?

3. *ON CULTURE:* How would you use training for spouses of expatriate employees to improve employee performance and the duration of service overseas?

4. *ON CULTURE:* Describe some of the problems experienced by repatriates. How may training and development alleviate those problems?

5. In relation to expatriate compensation, what is the difference between the going rate approach and the balance sheet approach?

6. What are some of the problems inherent in evaluating an expatriate's job performance?

7. Why has union power declined in developed countries?

8. If you were trying to establish a multinational labor organization, what barriers would you need to overcome?

9. In HR use of VRIO, why is it more difficult to imitate an HR system than a practice?

10. Look at the countries on PengAtlas Map 4.2. Suppose your multinational team consists of people from these countries. In your opinion, is it possible to have too much diversity?

11. Regarding the two countries with the largest labor force shown on PengAtlas Map 4.2, what advantage does the large size provide? What is the disadvantage?

12. What concept can be used to reconcile the best fit versus best practice debate, and how does it work?

13. What are the benefits of inpatriation?

14. What are the four Cs that can benefit HR managers?

15. What can you do to develop a global mindset and help your career?

CRITICAL DISCUSSION QUESTIONS

1. You have been offered a reasonably lucrative opportunity for an expatriate assignment for the next three years, and your boss will have a meeting with you next week. How would you discuss this opportunity with your boss?

2. *ON ETHICS:* If you were a HCN, do you think pay should be equal between HCNs and expatriates in equivalent positions? If you were president of your subsidiary in a host country who has profit/loss (P/L) responsibilities, as a PCN your pay is ten times higher than the pay for the highest paid HCN (your vice president, who is the third highest-paid employee). The second highest-paid employee is another vice president, a fellow PCN like you, who does

essentially the same work as the HCN vice president and is paid five times more than the PCN. What do you think?

3. *ON ETHICS:* As HR director for an oil company, you are responsible for selecting 15 expatriates to go to work in Iraq. However, you are personally concerned about the safety there. How do you proceed?

BUSINESS INSIGHTS GLOBAL

GLOBAL ACTION

1. You work at a large MNE that operates in every one of the top 100 metropolitan areas worldwide. One of the most pressing concerns in your firm at the moment is to control costs. Therefore, you have been asked to develop a forecast for the coming year that identifies the markets in which the firm can expect an increase in the cost of living and, as a result, general salary expenditures. After the report needed for your evaluation is secured, classify the cities that have experienced cost increases into their respective countries. Which countries have more than one city that meets the criteria for your forecast? What are the salary-increase traits associated with each city identified?

2. Currently, your European company is evaluating its standing in the fast-growing emerging economies known as BRIC (Brazil, Russia, India, and China). Based on your evaluation of the cost of living in each country, the company may reconfigure some of its operations to increase profitability. Your company's manufacturing facilities are located in Shanghai, China; Mumbai, India; São Paulo, Brazil; and St. Petersburg, Russia. How much could be saved if the company were to consolidate into one BRIC location that has the lowest cost of living?

CLOSING CASE

EMERGING MARKETS: Dallas versus Delhi

Prashant Sarkar is director for corporate development for the New Delhi, India, subsidiary of the US-based Dallas Instruments. Sarkar has an engineering degree from the Indian Institute of Technology and an MBA from the University of Texas at Dallas. After obtaining his MBA in 1995, Sarkar worked at a Dallas Instruments facility in Richardson, Texas (a suburb of Dallas in which UT Dallas is located), and picked up a green card (US permanent residency) while maintaining his Indian passport. In 2005, when Dallas Instruments opened its first Indian subsidiary in New Delhi, Sarkar was tapped to be one of the first managers sent from the United States. India of the 21st century is certainly different from the India of the 1990s that Sarkar had left behind. Reform is now in the air, multinationals are coming left and right, and an exhilarating self-confidence permeates the country.

As a manager, Sarkar has shined in his native New Delhi. His wife and two children (born in 2001 and 2003 in Dallas) are also happy. After all, curry in New Delhi is a lot more authentic and fresher than that in Indian grocery stores in Dallas. Grandparents, relatives, and friends are all happy to see the family back. In Dallas, Prashant's wife, Neeli, a teacher by training, taught on a part-time basis, but could not secure a full-time teaching position because she did not have a US degree. Now she is principal of a great school. The two children are enrolled in the elite New Delhi American School, the cost of which is paid for by the company. New Delhi is not perfect, but the Sarkars feel good about coming back.

At the end of 2016, the American CEO of the subsidiary has a conversation with Sarkar:

Prashant, I have great news for you! Headquarters wants you to move back to Dallas. Your pay will jump quite a bit. You'll be in charge of strategy development for *global* expansion, working directly under the Group Vice President. Isn't that exciting?! They want someone with proven success. You are my best candidate. I don't know what design they have for you after this assignment, but I suspect it'll be highly promising. Don't quote me, but I'd say you may have a shot to eventually replace me or the next subsidiary CEO here. As you know, while I personally enjoy working here, my family sometimes still complains a bit about the curry smell. Or, folks in Dallas may eventually want you to go somewhere else like China or Brazil as a third-country national—frankly, I don't know but I'm just trying to help you speculate. I know it's a big decision. Talk to Neeli and the kids. But they lived in Dallas before, so they should be fine going back. Of course, I'll put you in touch with the folks in Dallas directly so that you can ask them all kinds of questions. Let me know what you think in a week.

Instead of calling his wife immediately, Sarkar has decided to wait till he gets home in the evening so that he can have a few hours to think about this. Going from Dallas to New Delhi, Sarkar, with his Indian passport, is a host-country national (HCN). However, with his green card, he is also considered a US national and thus an expatriate. He wonders whether he would accept the new assignment and whether he would be an expatriate or inpatriate if he decides to go to Dallas from New Delhi. He thinks this will be a career move for him, but he is not sure if his family will like it.

CASE DISCUSSION QUESTIONS

1. What questions should Sarkar ask the people at headquarters in Dallas? Please help him prepare a list.
2. Will Neeli and the children be happy about this move? Why?
3. What differences does Sarkar's status as an expatriate or inpatriate make?
4. Should Sarkar accept or decline this opportunity? Why?

Sources: Based on the author's interviews in Dallas and New Delhi. All individual and corporate names are fictitious.

NOTES

[**Journal acronyms**] **AME**—*Academy of Management Executive;* **AMJ**—*Academy of Management Journal;* **AMR**—*Academy of Management Review;* **ASR**—*American Sociological Review;* **BW**—*BusinessWeek* (before 2010) or *Bloomberg Businessweek* (since 2010); **CMR**—*California Management Review;* **GSJ**—*Global Strategy Journal;* **HBR**—*Harvard Business Review;* **HRM**—*Human Resource Management;* **HRMR**—*Human Resource Management Review;* **IJHRM**—*International Journal of Human Resource Management;* **IJMR**—*International Journal of Management Reviews;* **JAP**—*Journal of Applied Psychology;* **JIBS**—*Journal of International Business Studies;* **JIM**—*Journal of International Management;* **JM**—*Journal of Management;* **JMS**—*Journal of Management Studies;* **JOB**—*Journal of Organizational Behavior;* **JWB**—*Journal of World Business;* **OD**—*Organizational Dynamics;* **PP**—*Personnel Psychology;* **SMJ**—*Strategic Management Journal.*

1 P. Cappelli, 2013, HR for neophytes, *HBR*, October: 25–27.

2 C. Fey, S. Morgulis-Yukushev, H. Park, & I. Bjorkman, 2009, Opening the black box of the relationship between HRM practices and firm performance, *JIBS*, 40: 690–712; K. Jiang, R. Takeuchi, & D. Lepak, 2013, Where do we go from here? *JMS*, 50: 1448–1480; J. Paauwe, 2009, HRM and performance, *JMS*, 46: 129–142.

3 E. Farndale et al., 2010, Context-bound configurations of corporate HR functions in MNCs, *HRM*, 49: 45–66.

4 G. Peng & P. Beamish, 2014, MNC subsidiary size and expatriate control, *JWB*, 49: 51–62; S. Riaz, W. G. Rowe, & P. Beamish, 2014, Expatriate-deployment levels and subsidiary growth, *JWB*, 49: 1–11.

5 D. Elenkov & I. Manev, 2009, Senior expatriate leadership's effects on innovation and the role of cultural intelligence, *JWB*, 44: 357–369.

6 B. Reiche, A. Harzing, & M. Kraimer, 2009, The role of international assignees' social capital in creating inter-unit intellectual capital, *JIBS*, 40: 509–526; D. Vora & T. Kostova, 2007, A model of dual organizational identification in the context of the MNE, *JOB*, 28: 327–350.

7 Y. Chang, Y. Gong, & M. W. Peng, 2012, Expatriate knowledge transfer, subsidiary absorptive capacity, and subsidiary performance, *AMJ*, 55: 927–948.

8 B. Firth, G. Chen, B. Kirkman, & K. Kim, 2014, New comers abroad, *AMJ*, 57: 280–300.

9 R. L. Tung, 1982, Selection and training procedures for US, European, and Japanese multinationals, *CMR*, 25: 57–71. See also A. Harzing, 2002, Are our referencing errors undermining our scholarship and credibility? *JOB*, 23: 127–148.

10 P. Dowling & D. Welch, 2005, *International Human Resource Management*, 4th ed. (p. 87), Cincinnati: Cengage Learning.

11 M. Lazarova, M. Westman, & M. Shaffer, 2010, Elucidating the positive side of the work-family interface on international assignments, *AMR*, 35: 93–117.

12 L. Dragoni, P. Tesluk, J. Russell, & I. Oh, 2009, Understanding managerial development, *AMJ*, 52: 731–743; C. Mabey, 2008, Management development and firm performance in Germany, Norway, Spain, and the UK, *JIBS*, 39: 1327–1342.

13 J. Cerdin & C. Brewster, 2014, Talent management and expatriation, *JWB*, 49: 245–252.

14 N. Furuya, M. Stevens, A. Bird, G. Oddou, & M. Mendenhall, 2009, Managing the learning and transfer of global management competence, *JIBS*, 40: 200–215; G. Oddou, J. Osland, & R. Blakeney, 2009, Repatriating knowledge, *JIBS*, 40: 181–199.

15 M. Kraimer, M. Shaffer, D. Harrison, & H. Ren, 2012, No place like home? *AMJ*, 55: 399–420.

16 S. Carraher, S. Sullivan, & M. Crocitto, 2009, Mentoring across global boundaries, *JIBS*, 39: 1310–1326.

17 B. S. Reiche, 2012, Knowledge benefits of social capital upon repatriation, *JMS*, 49: 1052–1077.

18 F. Cooke, D. Saini, & J. Wang, 2014, Talent management in China and India, *JWB*, 49: 225–235.

19 C. Schmidt, 2011, The battle for China's talent, *HBR*, March: 25–27.

20 M. W. Peng, S. Sun, & L. Markoczy, 2015, Human capital and CEO compensation during institutional transitions, *JMS*, 52: 117–147.

21 F. Chiang & T. Birtch, 2010, Appraising performance across borders, *JMS*, 47: 1365–1392.

22 *Economist*, 2014, Chattanooga shoo-shoo, February 22: 57.

23 *Economist*, 2013, Unions, Inc., April 6: 68.

24 *BW*, 2010, A new labor movement is born in China, June 14: 8.

25 I. Bjorkman, C. Fey, & H. Park, 2007, Institutional theory and MNC subsidiary HRM practices, *JIBS*, 38: 430–446.

26 *BW*, 2005, HP's French twist, October 10: 52–53.

27 D. Brock, O. Shenkar, A. Shoham, & I. Siscovick, 2008, National culture and expatriate deployment, *JIBS*, 39: 1293–1309.

28 M. W. Peng, 2012, The global strategy of emerging multinationals from China, *GSJ*, 2: 97–107.

29 C. Chen, 1995, New trends in allocation preferences, *AMJ*, 38: 408–428.

30 Economist Intelligence Unit, 2010, *Up or Out: Next Moves for the Modern Expatriate*, London: The Economist.

31 *HBR*, 2011, Developing your global know-how, March: 72.

32 D. Holtbrugge, C. Friedmann, & J. Puck, 2010, Recruitment and retention in foreign firms in India, *HRM*, 49: 439–455; K. Makela, I. Bjorkman, M. Ehrnrooth, A. Smale, & J. Sumelius, 2013, Explaining stakeholder evaluations of HRM capabilities in MNC subsidiaries, *JIBS*, 44: 813–832; K. Mossholder, H. Richardson, & R. Settoon, 2011, HR systems and helping in organizations, *AMR*, 36: 33–52; G. Reilly, A. Nyberg, M. Maltarich, & I. Weller, 2014, Human capital flows, *AMJ*, 57: 766–790; W. Sofka, M. Preto, & P. Faria, 2014, MNC subsidiary closures, *JIBS*, 45: 723–750.

33 S. Kang, S. Morris, & S. Snell, 2007, Relational archetypes, organizational learning, and value creation, *AMR*, 32: 236–256; J. Shaw, T. Park, & E. Kim, 2013, A resource-based perspective on human capital losses, HRM investments, and organizational performance, *SMJ*, 34: 572–589.

34 W. Arthur, W. Bennett, P. Edens, & S. Bell, 2003, Effectiveness of training in organizations, *JAP*, 88: 234–245; P. Patel, J. Messersmith, & D. Lepak, 2013, Walking the tightrope, *AMJ*, 56: 1420–1442.

35 J. Slocum, D. Lei, & P. Buller, 2014, Executing business strategies through human resource management practices, *OD*, 43: 73–87.

36 S. Fitzsimmons, 2013, Multicultural employees, *AMR*, 38: 525–549; D. Zoogah, D. Vora, O. Richard, & M. W. Peng, 2011, Strategic alliance team diversity, coordination, and effectiveness, *IJHRM*, 22: 510–529.

37 L. Jia, J. Shaw, A. Tsui, & T. Park, 2014, A social-structural perspective on employee-organizational relationships and team creativity, *AMJ*, 57: 869–891; A. Joshi & H. Roh, 2009, The role of context in work team diversity research, *AMJ*, 52: 599–627.

38 J. Delery & D. Doty, 1996, Modes of theorizing in strategic HRM, *AMJ*, 39: 80–835.

39 J. M. Geringer, C. Frayne, & J. Milliman, 2002, In search of "best practices" in international HRM, *HRM*, 41: 5–30; M. von Glinow, E. Drost, & M. Teagarden, 2002, Converging on IHRM best practices, *HRM*, 41: 123–140.

40 P. Boxall & J. Purcell, 2000, Strategic HRM (p. 190), *IJMR*, 2: 183–203.

41 B. Becker & M. Huselid, 2006, Strategic HRM (p. 905), *JM*, 32: 898–925.

42 M. W. Peng, 2006, Making M&As fly in China, *HBR*, March: 26–27.

43 S. Colakoglu, D. Lepak, & Y. Hong, 2006, Measuring HRM effectiveness, *HRMR*, 16: 209–218.

44 Becker & Huselid, 2006, Strategic HRM (p. 907).

45 J. Combs, D. Ketchen, A. Hall, & Y. Liu, 2006, Do high performance work practices matter? *PP*, 59: 501–528.

46 K. Jiang, D. Lepak, J. Hu, & J. Baer, 2012, How does human resource management influence organizational outcomes? *AMJ*, 55: 1264–1294.

47 S. Meisinger, 2005, The four Cs of the HR profession, *HRM*, 44: 189–194.

48 P. Cappelli & J. Keller, 2013, Classifying work in the new economy, *AMR*, 38: 575–596; A. Kalleberg, 2009, Precarious work, insecure workers, *ASR*, 74: 1–22; Y. Xie, Y. Zhu, & M. Warner, 2013, Exploring the reality of educated middle managers' capability and involvement in human resource management in China, *IJHRM*, 24: 3478–3495.

49 A. Ariss, W. Cascio, & J. Paauwe, 2014, Talent management, *JWB*, 49: 173–179; E. Farndale, A. Pai, P. Sparrow, & H. Scullion, 2014,

Balancing individual and organizational goals in global talent management, *JWB*, 49: 204–214; M. Festing & L. Schafer, 2014, Generational challenges to talent management, *JWB*, 49: 262–271; S. Nijs, E. Gallardo-Gallardo, N. Dries, & L. Sels, 2014, A multidisciplinary review into the definition, operationalization, and measurement of talent, *JWB*, 49: 180–191; M. Meyers & M. van Woerkom, 2014, The influence of underlying philosophies on talent management, *JWB*, 49: 192–203; Y. Sidani & A. Ariss, 2014, Institutional and corporate drivers of global talent management, *JWB*, 49: 215–224; M. Sonnenberg, V. van Zijderveld, & M. Brinks, 2014, The role of talent-perception incongruence in effective talent management, *JWB*, 49: 272–280.

50 *BW*, 2007, Secrets of an HR superstar, April 19: 66.

51 D. C. Robertson, 2013, *Brick by Brick: How LEGO Rewrote the Rules of Innovation and Conquered the Global Toy Industry*, New York: Crown Business.

52 J. Claussen, T. Grohsjean, J. Luger, & G. Probst, 2014, Talent management and career development, *JWB*, 49: 236–244; D. Collings, 2014, Integrating global mobility and global talent management, *JWB*, 49: 253–261; D. Leonard, G. Barton, & M. Barton, 2013, Make yourself an expert, *HBR*, April: 127–130; N. Lovegrove & M. Thomas, 2013, Triple-strength leadership, *HBR*, September: 46–56.

ChinaFotoPress/Getty Images

Learning Objectives

After studying this chapter, you should be able to

- outline the two means of financing decisions, equity and debt.

- differentiate various ownership patterns around the world.

- articulate the role of managers in both principal–agent and principal–principal conflicts.

- explain the role of the board of directors.

- identify voice-based and exit-based governance mechanisms and their combination as a package.

- acquire a global perspective on how governance mechanisms vary around the world.

- articulate how institutions and resources affect corporate finance and governance.

- participate in two leading debates concerning corporate finance and governance.

- draw implications for action.

Financing and Governing the Corporation Globally

OPENING CASE

High Drama at Hewlett-Packard (HP)

Starting in a legendary garage in 1939, Hewlett-Packard (HP) is the founding company of Silicon Valley. In the first 15 years of the 21st century, the firm went through four top leaders, with a ton of drama in the highest places. In 1999, Carly Fiorina was the first outsider in HP's history hired for the CEO job. She became chairman in 2000. In an effort to acquire computer maker Compaq, she spent her first two years fighting a high-profile battle with dissenting shareholders led by co-founder Bill Hewlett's son Walter Hewlett. Fiorina won the battle but lost the war. Under her watch, HP repeatedly missed Wall Street's revenue numbers and unfolded the high-level intrigue that has plagued its leadership since. In 2005, Fiorina was fired in a boardroom coup after HP lost half its value. But, for her lackluster performance, she was paid more than $20 million to leave—hardly a bad punishment.

In 2005, Mark Hurd, former CEO of NCR, became the new CEO of HP. He assumed the chairman position in 2006. In short order, Hurd turned around loss-making businesses such as PCs and servers. A ruthless cost cutter, he discontinued the use of all consultants and slashed more than 48,000 jobs. He prepared the ground for further growth by putting together a series of multibillion-dollar deals, snapping up Electronic Data Systems (EDS), 3Com, and Palm. Under Hurd's

watch, HP sped past IBM to grab the title of being the world's largest information technology (IT) company by revenues. It also became the first IT company to have sales exceeding $100 billion. Shareholders were happy, because Hurd hit Wall Street's revenue numbers in 21 out of 22 quarters and increased profits 22 quarters in a row. HP share prices more than doubled, reaching $54 in 2009.

Unfortunately, in August 2010, Hurd suddenly resigned amid stories of sexual harassment and iffy expense reports—with a golden parachute of $12 million. In short order, HP saw $10 billion wiped off its stock market value. In the absence of strong evidence presented by the complainant (on alleged sexual misconduct) or the board (on expenses), why did HP get rid of a star CEO? The answer remains a mystery. Larry Ellison, chairman and CEO of Oracle (an HP rival in data processing), called it "the worst personnel decision since the idiots on the Apple board fired Steve Jobs many years ago." Within one month after Hurd's departure from HP, Ellison named Hurd co-president of Oracle, which was determined to eat some of HP's lunch.

HP's high drama did not end after Hurd's resignation. In November 2010, its board hired a new CEO Léo Apotheker, former CEO of SAP who had been ousted. Apotheker returned HP to its free-spending days. He dished out companywide raises, brought back consultants, and bought a software maker, Autonomy, with a lavish price of $10 billion—ten times its annual revenue. Apotheker first announced all HP devices would be equipped with Palm software, and then after a few months announced that Palm would be abandoned. During his short tenure as CEO, HP lost $30 billion in market capitalization. In September 2011, the board fired him. But for his fewer than 11 months of hard work (during which he sometimes nodded off in business review meetings), Apotheker walked away with $13 million: severance payment of $7.2 million, HP shares worth $3.4 million, and performance *bonus* of $2.4 million.

In September 2011, Meg Whitman, an HP board member and eBay's former CEO, was named HP's newest CEO—the fourth since 2005 and the seventh since 1999 (between CEO regime changes there were several interim CEOs). Whitman became chairman in mid-2014. While no boardroom or executive suite intrigues were reported lately, HP faced brutal product market competition. Revenue fell from $127 billion in 2011 to $120 billion in 2012 and then to $112 billion in 2013. Although printers—especially the cartridges—continued to be cash cows, customers were simply not printing as much as before. In PCs, HP lost its champion status to Lenovo. In servers and cloud computing, HP was a laggard. Despite its breadth (or perhaps because

of its breadth), HP did a poor job in coordinating among its various divisions. Further, HP ended up having to write off close to $9 billion of the $10 billion acquisition of Autonomy mostly due to accounting irregularities. From a high of $54 during Hurd's tenure, HP's share price went down to a low of $14 in mid 2012. "Are you kidding me? That's all it's worth?" an expert who served on the board of ExxonMobil, Goldman Sachs, and Mayo Clinic noted in a *Bloomberg Businessweek* interview. He went on to suggest: "This is one of the great corporate destructions of all time."

Fortunately, HP's share price went back to above $30 in early 2014. In late 2014, Whitman announced plans to split HP into two publicly traded companies: Hewlett-Packard Enterprise (for software and services) and HP, Inc. (for PCs and printers). Each (hopefully) would be more nimble in going after opportunities. Originally entertained by Apotheker, the deal was expected to close by October 2015. Whitman remained committed to both, by serving as chairman for Hewlett-Packard Enterprise and CEO for HP, Inc. According to the *Economist*, it seemed that Whitman managed to keep the iconic Silicon Valley legend "out of the scrapyard." But can she steer it back onto the "highway"?

Sources: Based on (1) *Bloomberg Businessweek*, 2013, Free fall: Inside Meg Whitman's plan to keep Hewlett-Packard's from going…splat, January 14: 44–50; (2) CNN Money, 2014, HP to split into two companies, report says, October 5: money.cnn.com; (3) *Economist*, 2010, The curse of HP, August 14: 54; (4) *Economist*, 2015, Still in the garage, June 14: 57–58.

Financing

The management of a firm's money, banking, investments, and credit.

Corporate governance

The relationship among various participants in determining the direction and performance of corporations.

While HP's high drama is an extreme case, it raises a series of questions affecting many firms: What is the optimal way to govern corporations so that investors will be willing to finance the operations and reap the returns? What is the proper role of the board of directors? How should CEOs be properly motivated and compensated? These are some of the key questions addressed in this chapter, which focuses on how to finance and govern corporations around the world. Financing refers to how a firm's money, banking, investments, and credit are managed. Corporate governance is "the relationship among various participants in determining the direction and performance of corporations."[1] The primary participants are (1) owners, (2) managers, and (3) boards of directors—collectively known as the "tripod" (Figure 16.1).

We start by outlining the two means of financing decisions, issue equity or bonds. Then we discuss each of the three legs of the governance "tripod." Next, we introduce internal and external governance mechanisms from a global perspective. Then, institution-based and resource-based views on corporate finance and governance are outlined. As before, debates and extensions follow.

Figure 16.1 **The Tripod of Corporate Governance**

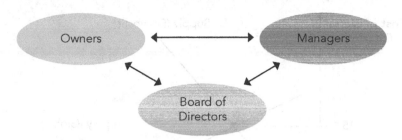

16-1 Financing Decisions

Learning Objective
Outline the two means of financing decisions, equity and debt.

Finance is the lifeblood of firms. Firms, of course, can finance their operations using their own money. But beyond firms' own money, what are the *external* sources of financing? Broadly, firms' external sources of financing can be classified as (1) equity and (2) debt.[2] The decision on which way to go boils down to the cost of financing.

16-1a Equity and Debt

Equity refers to the stock (usually expressed in shares) in a firm, which is an embodiment of equity holders' rights as firm owners. Firm owners are often known as shareholders. Ranging from entrepreneurial start-ups to multinational enterprises (MNEs), all firms need to raise capital. Shareholders, by definition, share the firm's income generated by its operations, and the firm honors this claim by paying dividends. However, the amount of dividends is not fixed and is determined by management. Shareholders purchase stock both for dividends and for the growth potential of the stock.[3] Firms issue equity to attract investors to become shareholders so that firms can access a larger pool of capital that is at management's discretion.

Debt refers to a loan that the firm needs to pay back at a given time with interest. The loan is called a bond and is issued by the firm and held by debtors known as bondholders. Management has little discretion over a bond. Unlike dividends, which can be curtailed or cancelled, the firm has to pay back its bondholders on time. Otherwise, it will be in default—failure to satisfy the terms of a loan obligation. Short of a default, bondholders will get their money back with interest.[4] In other words, relative to shareholders, bondholders face a lower level of uncertainty.

16-1b Reducing the Cost of Capital

Financing decisions are primarily driven by the cost of capital, which is the rate of return that the firm needs to pay to capital providers.[5] For equity, the cost of capital is the dividend. For bonds, the cost of capital is the interest. Basic laws in supply and demand suggest that, in general, the larger the pool of capital providers, the lower the cost of capital. This is because risk can be spread over a larger pool. This is illustrated in Figure 16.2, using basic supply-and-demand curves. Hypothetically, if HP (in the Opening Case) could only borrow from the United States, to sell a $10 million bond, it would have to pay a 15% interest rate (point A). However, if HP could tap into a global pool (and a larger supply) of capital providers, which by

Equity

The stock in a firm (usually expressed in shares), which represents the owners' rights.

Shareholder

Firm owner.

Debt

A loan that the firm needs to pay back at a given time with an interest.

Bond

Loan issued by the firm and held by creditors.

Bondholder

Buyer of bonds.

Default

A firm's failure to satisfy the terms of a loan obligation.

Cost of capital

The rate of return that a firm needs to pay to capital providers.

Figure 16.2   **Cost of Capital Is Lower Globally Than Domestically**

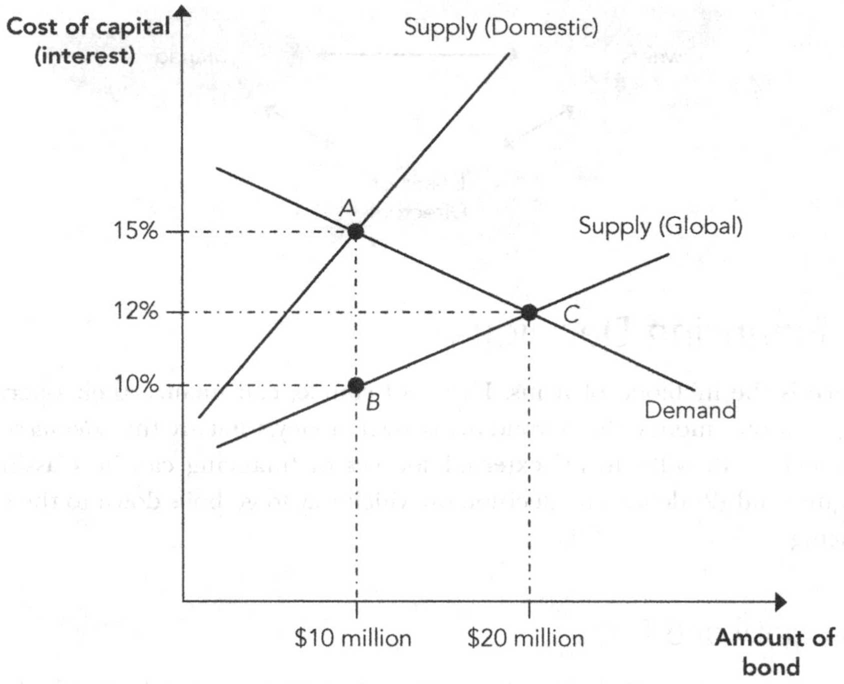

definition is larger than the domestic pool, it could sell a $10 million bond for only a 10% interest rate (point B). Further, HP may be able to raise $20 million at a 12% interest rate (point C).

This analysis has major ramifications both for firms' appetite to tap into global capital markets and for financial services providers' interest to serve this demand on a worldwide basis. Many firms have listed their stocks not only on their domestic stock exchanges, but also on many foreign stock exchanges. Listing shares on foreign stock exchanges is known as cross-listing.[6] The New York Stock Exchange (NYSE) and the National Association of Securities Dealers Automated Quotations (NASDAQ) have a lot of non-US firms listed. The London Stock Exchange (LSE) attracts numerous non-UK firms. The Hong Kong Stock Exchange (HKSE) benefits from the gush of mainland Chinese listings. Cross-listing has numerous costs, especially the more expensive preparation to meet the reporting and compliance requirements of foreign securities authorities. Despite the costs, numerous firms have cross-listed their shares overseas because the benefits, which are primarily derived from a lower cost of capital, outweigh the costs. Likewise, about 30% of the bonds are now international bonds, which can be sold at a lower interest rate than domestically.

Obviously, financing decisions—whether to issue stocks or bonds—are crucial, because they can make or break a firm. Overall, how firms safeguard and advance the interest of owners as providers of capital is at the heart of corporate governance, a topic to which we turn next.

Cross-listing

Listing shares on a foreign stock exchange.

Learning Objective

Differentiate various ownership patterns around the world.

16-2 Owners

Owners provide capital, bear risks, and own the firm.[7] Three broad patterns exist: (1) concentrated versus diffused ownership, (2) family ownership, and (3) state ownership.

16-2a Concentrated versus Diffused Ownership

Founders usually start up firms and completely own and control them. This is referred to as concentrated ownership and control. However, at some point, if the firm aspires to grow and needs more capital, the owners' desire to keep the firm in family hands will have to accommodate the arrival of other shareholders. Approximately 80% of listed US firms and 90% of listed UK firms are now characterized by diffused ownership, with numerous small shareholders but none with a dominant level of control.[8] In such firms, there is a separation of ownership and control, in that ownership is dispersed among many small shareholders and control is largely concentrated in the hands of salaried professional managers who own little (or no) equity. In short, this refers to separation of ownership (by dispersed shareholders) and day-to-day control (by managers).

If majority or dominant owners (such as founders) do not personally run the firm, they are naturally interested in keeping a close eye on how the firm is run. However, dispersed owners, each with a small stake, have neither incentives nor resources to do so. Most small shareholders do not bother to show up at annual shareholder meetings. They prefer to free-ride and hope that other shareholders will properly monitor and discipline managers. If small shareholders are not happy, they will simply sell the stock and invest elsewhere. However, if all shareholders were to behave in this manner, then no shareholder would care, and managers would end up acquiring significant *de facto* control power.

The rise of institutional investors, such as professionally managed mutual funds and pension pools, has significantly changed this picture.[9] Institutional investors have both incentives and resources to closely monitor and control managerial actions. However, the increased size of institutional holdings limits the ability of institutional investors to dump the stock. This is because when one's stake is large enough, selling out depresses the share price and harms the seller.

While the image of widely held corporations is a reasonably accurate description of most modern large US and UK firms, it is *not* the case in other parts of the world. Outside the Anglo-American world, there is relatively little separation of ownership and control. Most large firms are typically owned and controlled by families or the state.[10] Next, we turn our attention to such firms.

16-2b Family Ownership

The vast majority of large firms throughout continental Europe, Asia, Latin America, and Africa feature concentrated family ownership and control.[11] On the positive side, family ownership and control may provide better incentives to focus on long-term performance. It may also minimize the conflicts between owners and professional managers typically encountered in widely owned firms. However, on the negative side, family ownership and control may lead to the selection of less-qualified managers (who happen to be the sons, daughters, and relatives of founders), the destruction of value because of family conflicts, and the expropriation of minority shareholders (discussed later). At present, there is no conclusive evidence on the positive or negative role of family ownership and control on the performance of large firms.[12]

16-2c State Ownership

Other than families, the state is another major owner of firms around the world. Since the 1980s, many countries—ranging from Britain to Brazil to Belarus—have

Concentrated ownership and control

Founders start up firms and completely own and control them on an individual or family basis.

Diffused ownership

Publicly traded corporations owned by numerous small shareholders but none with a dominant level of control.

Separation of ownership and control

The dispersal of ownership among many small shareholders, in which control is largely concentrated in the hands of salaried, professional managers who own little (or no) equity.

realized that their state-owned enterprises (SOEs) often perform poorly. SOEs typically suffer from an incentive problem. Although in theory, all citizens (including employees) are owners, in practice, they have neither the rights to enjoy dividends generated from SOEs (as shareholders would) nor the rights to transfer or sell "their" property. SOEs are *de facto* owned and controlled by government agencies, far removed from ordinary citizens and employees. Thus, SOE managers and employees have little motivation to improve performance, which they can hardly benefit from personally. In a most cynical fashion, SOE employees in the former Soviet Union summed it up well: "They pretend to pay us, and we pretend to work." A wave of privatization has hit the world since the 1980s. However, SOEs have staged a spectacular comeback recently.[13] In 2008, many governments in developed economies nationalized major firms, ranging from General Motors (GM, which has been nicknamed "Government Motors") to Royal Bank of Scotland (RBS), in order to prevent massive bankruptcies and job losses. Like the swing of a pendulum (see Chapters 1 and 2), the upsurge of state ownership has wiped out a substantial chunk of the gains of privatization.

16-3 Managers

Learning Objective

Articulate the role of managers in both principal-agent and principal-principal conflicts.

Top management team (TMT)

The team consisting of the highest level of executives of a firm led by the CEO.

Chief executive officer (CEO)

The main executive manager in charge of the firm.

Agency relationship

The relationship between principals (such as shareholders) and agents (such as professional managers).

Principal

Individual (such as owner) delegating authority.

Agent

Individual (such as manager) to whom authority is delegated.

Agency theory

A theory that focuses on principal-agent relationships (or in short, agency relationships).

Principal–agent conflict

Conflict between principals and agents.

Agency cost

The cost associated with principal-agent relationships.

Managers, especially executives on the top management team (TMT) led by the chief executive officer (CEO), represent another crucial leg of the corporate governance "tripod."

16-3a Principal-Agent Conflicts

The relationship between shareholders and professional managers is a relationship between principals and agents—in short, an agency relationship. Principals are persons (such as owners) delegating authority, and agents are persons (such as managers) to whom authority is delegated. Agency theory suggests a simple, yet profound, insight: To the extent that the interests of principals and agents do not completely overlap, there will *inherently* be principal–agent conflicts. These conflicts result in agency costs, including (1) the principals' costs of monitoring and controlling the agents and (2) the agents' costs of bonding (signaling their trustworthiness).[14]

In a corporate setting, when shareholders (principals) are interested in maximizing the long-term value of their stock, managers (agents) may be more interested in maximizing their own power, income, and perks. For example, in 2001 HP's chairman and CEO Carly Fiorina, in an effort to acquire a PC maker Compaq, clashed with dissenting shareholders led by co-founder Bill Hewlett's son Walter Hewlett. Fiorina won the battle, but shareholders ended up footing the bill for the performance mess afterwards (see the Opening Case). Overall, manifestations of agency problems include:

- Excessive executive compensation.
- On-the-job consumption (such as corporate jets).
- Low-risk short-term investments (such as maximizing current earnings while cutting long-term R&D).
- Empire-building (such as value-destroying acquisitions).
- Excess CEO returns (CEO financial returns in excess of shareholder returns).[15]

Consider executive compensation. In 1980, the average US CEO earned 40 times what the average worker earned. Today, the ratio is 400 times. Despite some performance improvement, it seems difficult to argue that the average firm CEO improved performance ten times faster than the average worker since 1980, and thus deserved the salary of 400 workers today. In other words, one can "smell" some agency costs.

Directly measuring agency costs, however, is difficult. In two most innovative (and hair-raising) studies to measure agency costs directly, scholars find that some sudden CEO *deaths* (plane crashes or heart attacks) are accompanied by an increase in share prices of their firms.[16] These CEOs reduced agency costs that shareholders had to shoulder by dropping dead (!). Conversely, we could infer how much value these CEOs destroyed when they had been alive. The capital market, sadly, was pleased with such human tragedies.

Do you think top executives deserve high-end benefits such as private transportation?

The primary reason agency problems persist is because of information asymmetries between principals and agents—that is, agents such as managers almost always know more about the property they manage than principals do.[17] While it is possible to reduce information asymmetries through governance mechanisms, it is not realistic to completely eliminate agency problems.

16-3b Principal–Principal Conflicts

Since concentrated ownership and control by families is the norm in many parts of the world, different kinds of conflicts are at play. One of the leading indicators of concentrated family ownership and control is the appointment of family members as board chairman, CEO, and other TMT members. In East Asia, approximately 57% of the corporations have board chairmen and CEOs from the controlling families.[18] In continental Europe, the number is 68%.[19] The families are able to do so, because they are controlling (although not necessarily majority) shareholders (see the Closing Case). For example, at News Corporation, neither the board nor angry shareholders can get rid of the Murdochs, who are controlling shareholders (In Focus 16.1).

Information asymmetry
Asymmetric distribution and possession of information between two sides.

IN FOCUS 16.1
THE MURDOCHS VERSUS MINORITY SHAREHOLDERS

Ethical Dilemma

Founded in Adelaide, Australia, News Corporation (in short, News Corp.) is now headquartered in New York and listed on NASDAQ with secondary listings on the Australian Securities Exchange. While the unethical conduct of its British tabloid operations rocked the world in 2011, this was not the first time News Corp., which enjoys reporting controversies of others, stirred up controversies itself. One consistent theme of controversies is how controlling shareholders Rupert Murdoch and his family treat minority shareholders.

Exhibit A: In 2003, the 30-year-old James Murdoch became CEO of BSkyB, Europe's largest satellite broadcaster, in the face of loud minority shareholder resistance. The reason? James's father Rupert controlled 35% of BSkyB equity and controlled the board.

Exhibit B: In 2007, Rupert Murdoch pursued a pet project by paying a rich US$5.6 billion price to buy Dow Jones, publisher of the *Wall Street Journal*—against the wishes of numerous minority shareholders and the advice of Peter Chernin, News Corp.

IN FOCUS 16.1 (continued)

president and a non-family member. The upshot? After four months, News Corp. wrote down its value by US$2.8 billion. In 2009, Chernin left.

Exhibit C: In 2011, in a related transaction, News Corp. announced that it would pay US$673 million to buy Shine Group, a London–based media studio owned by Rupert's daughter Elisabeth Murdoch. While Shine produced some hit shows such as NBC's *The Office* and The *Biggest Loser*, minority shareholders alleged that News Corp. had overpaid for Shine with 13.1 times Shine's US$45.6 million in earnings before interest, taxes, depreciation, and amortization (EBITDA). In contrast, Apollo Global Management, a leading private equity firm, paid US$510 million to purchase *American Idol* owner CKx, a deal valued at 8.5 times CKx's US$60.23 million in EBITDA. Frustrated minority shareholders, such as Amalgamated Bank and other pension funds, filed a lawsuit in Delaware (where News Corp. is registered) to block the sale. The complaint alleged that:

Murdoch did not even pretend there was a valid strategic purpose for News Corp. to buy Shine . . . The transaction is a naked and selfish endeavor by Murdoch to further infuse the upper ranks of News Corp. with his offspring.

Rupert Murdoch has been named by the *Economist* as the "last of the moguls." The problem is that "no one could say no to Rupert Murdoch," according to Michael Wolff, author of Murdoch's biography *The Man Who Owns the News.* As a result, News Corp.'s stock performance has trailed behind that of its largest rivals such as Time Warner, Walt Disney, and Viacom. "There's just this sort of generic Murdoch discount, which encompasses the concern that he will make decisions that are not consistent with other shareholder interests," noted one analyst.

Sources: Based on (1) *Bloomberg Businessweek*, 2011, Will the scandal tame Murdoch? July 25: 18–20; (2) *Economist*, 2011, How to lose friends and alienate people, July 16: 25–27; (3) *Economist*, 2011, Last of the moguls, July 23: 9.

Principal–principal conflict

Conflict between two classes of principals: controlling shareholders and minority shareholders.

Expropriation

Activities that enrich controlling shareholders at the expense of minority shareholders.

Tunneling

A form of corporate theft that diverts resources from the firm for personal or family use.

Related transaction

Controlling shareholders sell firm assets to another firm they own at below-market prices or spin off the most profitable part of a public firm and merge it with another private firm they own.

The Murdochs case is a classic example of the conflicts in family-owned and family-controlled firms. Instead of between principals (shareholders) and agents (professional managers), the primary conflicts are between two classes of principals: controlling shareholders and minority shareholders—in other words, principal–principal conflicts[20] (Figure 16.3 and Table 16.1). Family managers such as the Murdochs, who represent (or are) controlling shareholders, may advance family interests at the expense of minority shareholders. Controlling shareholders' dominant positions as *both* principals and agents (managers) may allow them to override traditional governance mechanisms designed to curtail principal–agent conflicts, such as the board of directors (see the Closing Case).

One manifestation of principal–principal conflicts is that family managers may have the potential to engage in expropriation of minority shareholders, defined as activities that enrich controlling shareholders at the expense of minority shareholders (see the Closing Case). For example, managers from the controlling family may simply divert resources from the firm for personal or family use. This activity is vividly nicknamed "tunneling"—digging a tunnel to sneak resources out. While such "tunneling" (often known as "corporate theft") is illegal, expropriation can be legally done through related transactions, whereby controlling owners buy firm assets from another firm they own at above-market prices or spin-off the most profitable part of a public firm and merge it with another private firm of theirs (see In Focus 16.1).

Overall, while corporate governance practice and research traditionally focus on how to control professional managers because of the separation of ownership

Figure 16.3 **Principal–Agent Conflicts and Principal–Principal Conflicts**

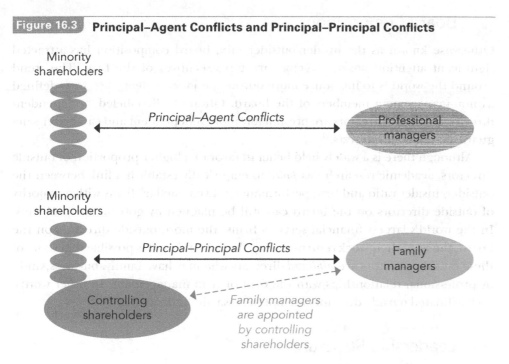

Source: M. Young, M. W. Peng, D. Ahlstrom, G. Bruton, & Y. Jiang, 2008, Corporate governance in emerging economies: A review of the principal-principal perspective (p. 200), *Journal of Management Studies*, 45: 196–220.

Table 16.1 **Principal–Agent versus Principal–Principal Conflicts**

	Principal–Agent conflicts	Principal–Principal conflicts
Ownership pattern	Dispersed—shareholders holding 5% of equity are regarded as "blockholders."	Dominant—often greater than 50% of equity is controlled by the largest shareholders.
Manifestations	Strategies that benefit entrenched managers at the expense of shareholders (such as shirking, excessive compensation, and empire building).	Strategies that benefit controlling shareholders at the expense of minority shareholders (such as minority shareholder expropriation, and cronyism).
Protection of minority shareholders	Courts are more protective of minority shareholder rights. Informal norms support this view.	Formal institutional protection is often lacking. Informal norms favor controlling shareholders.
Market for corporate control	Active, at least in principle as the "governance mechanism of last resort."	Inactive even in principle. Concentrated ownership thwarts notions of takeover.

Source: Adapted from M. Young, M. W. Peng, D. Ahlstrom, G. Bruton, & Y. Jiang, 2008, Corporate governance in emerging economies: A review of the principal-principal perspective (p. 202), *Journal of Management Studies*, 45: 196–220.

and control in a majority of US and UK firms, how to govern family managers in firms with concentrated ownership and control is of equal or higher importance around the world (including in certain US and UK firms, such as News Corporation).

16-4 Board of Directors

As an intermediary between owners and managers, the board of directors oversees and ratifies strategic decisions. It evaluates, rewards, and, if necessary, penalizes top managers.

Learning Objective
Explain the role of the board of directors.

16-4a Board Composition

Otherwise known as the insider/outsider mix, board composition has attracted significant attention. Inside directors are top executives of the firm. The trend around the world is to introduce more outside (or independent) directors, defined as non-management members of the board. Often ideally labeled "independent directors," outside directors are presumably more independent and can better safeguard shareholder interests.[21]

Although there is a widely held belief in favor of a higher proportion of outside directors, academic research has *failed* to empirically establish a link between the outsider/insider ratio and firm performance.[22] Even "stellar" firms with a majority of outside directors on the board can still be plagued by governance problems. In the world's largest financial services firms, the more outside directors on the board, the *worse* their stock returns during the 2008 crisis. It is possible that some of these outside directors are *affiliated* directors who may have family, business, and/or professional relationships with the firm or firm management. In other words, such affiliated outside directors are not necessarily "independent."

16-4b Leadership Structure

Whether the board is led by a separate chairman or by the CEO who doubles as a chairman—a situation known as CEO duality—is also important. From an agency theory standpoint, if the board is to supervise agents such as the CEO, it seems imperative that the board be chaired by a separate individual. Otherwise, how can the CEO be evaluated by the body that he/she chairs? In other words, can a schoolboy grade his own papers? However, a corporation led by two top leaders (a chairman and a CEO) may lack a unity of command and experience top-level conflicts. As a powerful executive, a CEO obviously does not appreciate being constantly second-guessed by a chairman. Not surprisingly, there is significant divergence across countries. For instance, while a majority of the large UK firms separate the two top jobs, many large US firms combine them (see the Opening Case). One practical difficulty often cited by US boards is that it is hard to recruit a capable CEO without the board chairman title.

Academic research is inconclusive on whether CEO duality (or non-duality) is more effective.[23] However, pressures have arisen around the world for firms to split the two jobs to at least show that they are serious about controlling the CEO.

16-4c The Role of Boards of Directors

In a nutshell, boards of directors perform (1) control, (2) service, and (3) resource acquisition functions. Boards' effectiveness in serving the control function stems from their independence, deterrence, and norms. Specifically:

- The ability to effectively control managers boils down to how *independent* directors are. Outside directors who are personally friendly and loyal to the CEO are unlikely to challenge managerial decisions. Exactly for this reason, CEOs often nominate family members, personal friends, and other passive directors.[24]
- There is a lack of *deterrence* on the part of directors should they fail to protect shareholder interests. Courts usually will not second-guess board decisions in the absence of bad faith or insider dealing.

Inside director

Member of the board who is a top executives of the firm.

Outside (independent) director

Nonmanagement member of the board.

CEO duality

The CEO doubles as a chairman of the board.

- When challenging management, directors have few *norms* to draw on. Directors who "stick their necks out" by confronting the CEO in meetings tend to be frozen out of board deliberations.

In addition to control, another important function of the board is service—primarily advising the CEO.[25] Finally, another crucial board function is resource acquisition for the focal firm.

Overall, until recently, many boards of directors simply "rubber stamp" (approve without scrutiny) managerial actions. Prior to the 1997 economic crisis, many South Korean boards did not bother to hold meetings, and so board decisions were literally "rubber stamped"—not even by directors themselves, but by corporate secretaries who stamped the seals of all the directors, which were kept in the corporate office. However, change is in the air throughout the world. In South Korea, board meetings are now regularly held, and seals are personally stamped by the directors themselves.[26]

16-5 Governance Mechanisms As a Package

Learning Objective

Identify voice-based and exit-based governance mechanisms and their combination as a package.

Governance mechanisms can be classified as internal and external ones—otherwise known as voice-based and exit-based mechanisms, respectively. Voice-based mechanisms refer to shareholders' willingness to work with managers, usually through the board, by "voicing" their concerns. Exit-based mechanisms indicate that shareholders no longer have patience and are willing to "exit" by selling their shares. This section outlines these mechanisms.

Voice-based mechanism

Corporate governance mechanism that focus on shareholders' willingness to work with managers, usually through the board, by "voicing" their concerns.

16-5a Internal (Voice-Based) Governance Mechanisms

The two internal governance mechanisms typically employed by boards can be characterized as "carrots" and "sticks." In order to better motivate managers, increasing executive compensation as "carrots" is often a must. Stock options that help align the interests of managers and shareholders have become increasingly popular.[27] The underlying idea is pay for performance, which seeks to link executive compensation with firm performance.[28] While in principle this idea is sound, in practice it has a

Exit-based mechanism

Corporate governance mechanism that focuses on exit, indicating that shareholders no longer have patience and are willing to "exit" by selling their shares.

number of drawbacks. If accounting-based measures (such as return on sales) are used, managers are often able to manipulate numbers to make them look better. If market-based measures (such as stock prices) are adopted, stock prices obviously are subject to too many forces beyond managers' control. Consequently, the pay-for-performance link in executive compensation is usually not very strong.[29]

In general, boards are likely to use "carrots" before considering "sticks." However, when facing continued performance failures, boards may have to dismiss the CEO.[30] Among the world's 2,500 largest listed firms, CEO tenure has decreased from 8.1 years in 2000 to 6.3 years in 2012 (see the Closing Case).[31] In brief, boards seem to be more "trigger happy"

Sullivan/PhotoLibrary/Getty Images

What are some of the "carrots" and "sticks" that boards use as internal governance mechanisms?

recently.[32] Léo Apotheker only served *ten months* as CEO of HP before the board fired him (see the Opening Case).

Because top managers must shoulder substantial firm-specific employment risk (a fired CEO is unlikely to run another publicly traded company), they naturally demand more generous compensation—a premium on the order of 30% or more—before taking on new CEO jobs. This in part explains the rapidly rising levels of executive compensation.[33]

16-5b External (Exit-Based) Governance Mechanisms

There are three external governance mechanisms: (1) market for product competition, (2) market for corporate control, and (3) market for private equity. Product market competition is a powerful force compelling managers to maximize profits and, in turn, shareholder value. However, from a corporate governance perspective, product market competition *complements* the market for corporate control and the market for private equity, each of which is outlined next.

The Market for Corporate Control. This is the main external governance mechanism, otherwise known as the takeover market or the mergers and acquisitions (M&A) market (see Chapter 12). It is essentially an arena where different management teams contest for the control rights of corporate assets. As an external governance mechanism, the market for corporate control serves as a disciplining mechanism of last resort when internal governance mechanisms fail. The underlying logic is spelled out by agency theory, which suggests that when managers engage in self-interested actions and internal governance mechanisms fail, firm stock will be undervalued by investors. Under these circumstances, other management teams, which recognize an opportunity to create new value, bid for the rights to manage the firm (see Chapter 12). How effective is the market for corporate control? Three findings emerge:

- On average, shareholders of target firms earn sizable acquisition premiums.
- Shareholders of acquiring firms experience slight but insignificant losses.
- A substantially higher level of top management turnover occurs following M&As.

In summary, while internal mechanisms aim at "fine-tuning," the market for corporate control enables the "wholesale" removal of entrenched managers. As a radical approach, the market for corporate control has its own limitations. It is very costly to wage such financial battles because acquirers must pay an acquisition premium. In addition, a large number of M&As are driven by acquirers' sheer hubris or empire building,[34] and the long-term profitability of post-merger firms is not particularly impressive (see Chapter 12).

Nevertheless, the net impact, at least in the short run, seems to be positive, because the threat of takeovers does limit managers' divergence from shareholder wealth maximization. For example, in Japan, an increasingly credible threat of takeovers has been constraining managerial behavior.[35]

The Market for Private Equity. Instead of being taken over, a large number of publicly listed firms have gone private by tapping into private equity—equity capital invested in private (non-public) companies. Private equity is primarily invested through leveraged buyouts (LBOs). In an LBO, private investors, often in partnership with incumbent managers, issue bonds and use the cash raised to buy the firm's stock—in essence, replacing shareholders with bondholders and transforming the

Private equity

Equity capital invested in private companies that, by definition, are not publicly traded.

Leveraged buyout (LBO)

Means by which investors, often in partnership with incumbent managers, issue bonds and use the cash raised to buy the firm's stock.

firm from a public to a private entity.[36] As another external governance mechanism, private equity utilizes the bond market, as opposed to the stock market, to discipline managers. LBO-based private equity transactions are associated with three major changes in corporate governance:[37]

- LBOs change the incentives of managers by providing them with substantial equity stakes (typically 5% for the CEO and 16% for the whole top management team).
- The high amount of debt imposes strong financial discipline.
- LBO sponsors closely monitor the firms they have invested in.

Overall, evidence suggests that private equity results in relatively small job losses (about 1% to 2%) and improves efficiency by about 2%, at least in the short run.[38] The picture is less clear regarding the long run because LBOs may have forced managers to reduce investments in long-term R&D. However, recent research reports that private equity-backed firms do not suffer from a reduction of R&D in the long run.[39]

16-5c Internal Mechanisms + External Mechanisms = Governance Package

Taken together, the internal and external mechanisms can be considered a "package."[40] Michael Jensen, a leading agency theorist, argues that in the United States, failures of internal governance mechanisms in the 1970s activated the market for corporate control in the 1980s. Managers initially resisted (see In Focus 16.2). However, over time, many firms that are not takeover targets or that have successfully defended themselves

---

IN FOCUS 16.2

PROFESSOR MICHAEL JENSEN AS AN OUTSIDE DIRECTOR

Ethical Dilemma

Harvard professor Michael Jensen, a leading agency theorist, served on the board of Armstrong World Industries as an outside director between 1990 and 1996. He described this experience at a conference:

> Let me say that there were very good people on that board. But what was true at Armstrong is that even the outside directors basically see themselves as employees of the CEO. That's just the way it is. And the outside directors in this case seemed even more deferential and beholden to the CEO than the managers who actually reported to him.
>
> I was put on the compensation committee. And at the first meeting of that committee, there was a proposal to give the management a substantial bonus for the excellent performance they'd had that year. The problem, however, was that the equity value of the company had fallen by roughly 50% over that period. So I was listening to this discussion—and, by the way, the CEO was there running the meeting whose main focus was his own compensation. And when I pointed

out that it was really hard to argue that management had done a good job when the value of the company had fallen by 50%, my fellow members of the compensation committee acted as if they were shocked. The response I got was, "How did you calculate that?"

> My own experience suggests that one person on a board can make a difference. It took a couple of years, but we did fire the CEO for poor performance. I would show up at every board meeting and say, "We've destroyed US$50 million since the last meeting." And finally things moved.
>
> After we eventually fired the CEO, I kept asking hard questions. And then the next CEO fired me from the board because, as he put it, I had a tendency to ask "trick questions." And that, apparently, was inappropriate behavior. A trick question, as I gathered from this experience, is one that the CEO either can't answer or finds it uncomfortable to do so.

Source: Excerpts from *Journal of Applied Corporate Finance*, 2008, US corporate governance accomplishments and failings: A discussion with Michael Jensen and Robert Monks (p. 34), 20(1): 28–46.

against such attempts end up restructuring and downsizing—doing exactly what "raiders" would have done had these firms been taken over. In other words, the strengthened external mechanisms force firms to improve their internal mechanisms.

Overall, since the 1980s, American managers have become much more focused on stock prices, resulting in a new term, "shareholder capitalism," which has been spreading around the world. In Europe, executive stock options become popular and M&As more frequent. In China and Russia, some traces of modern corporate governance have emerged.[41]

Learning Objective
Acquire a global perspective on how governance mechanisms vary around the world.

16-6 A Global Perspective

Figure 16.4 illustrates how different corporate ownership and control patterns around the world lead to a different mix of internal and external mechanisms. The most familiar type is Cell 4, exemplified by most large US and UK firms. While external governance mechanisms (M&As and private equity) are active, internal mechanisms are relatively weak due to the separation of ownership and control that gives managers significant *de facto* control power.

The opposite can be found in Cell 1, namely, firms in continental Europe and Japan where the market for corporate control is relatively inactive (although there is more activity recently). Consequently, the primary governance mechanisms remain concentrated ownership and control.

Overall, the Anglo–American and continental European–Japanese (otherwise known as German–Japanese) systems represent the two primary corporate governance families in the world, with a variety of labels (see Table 16.2). Given that both the United States and United Kingdom as a group and continental Europe and Japan as another group are highly developed and successful economies, it is difficult (and probably not meaningful) to argue whether the Anglo–American or German–Japanese system is better.

Some other systems do not easily fit into such a dichotomous world. Placed in Cell 2, Canada has *both* a relatively active market for corporate control and a large

Shareholder capitalism

A view of capitalism that suggests that the most fundamental purpose for firms to exist is to serve the economic interests of shareholders (also known as capitalists).

| Figure 16.4 | **Internal and External Governance Mechanisms: A Global Perspective** |

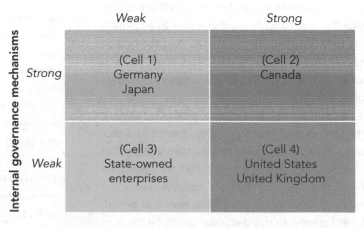

Source: Cells 1, 2, and 4 are adapted from E. Gedajlovic & D. Shapiro, 1998, Management and ownership effects: Evidence from five countries (p. 539), *Strategic Management Journal*, 19: 533–553. The label of Cell 3 is suggested by M. W. Peng.

Table 16.2	Two Primary Families of Corporate Governance Systems
Corporations in the United States and United Kingdom	**Corporations in Continental Europe and Japan**
Anglo-American corporate governance models	German-Japanese corporate governance models
Market-oriented, high-tension systems	Bank-oriented, network-based systems
Rely mostly on exit-based, external mechanisms	Rely mostly on voice-based, internal mechanisms
Shareholder capitalism	Stakeholder capitalism

number of firms with concentrated ownership and control—more than 380 of the 400 largest Canadian firms are controlled by a single shareholder. Canadian managers thus face powerful internal and external constraints.

Finally, SOEs (of all nationalities) are in an unfortunate position of both weak external and internal governance mechanisms (Cell 3). Externally, effective market for corporate control hardly exists. Internally, managers are supervised by officials who act as *de facto* "owners" with little control.

Overall, firms around the world are governed by a combination of internal and external mechanisms. For firms in Cells 1, 2, and 4, there is some partial substitution between internal and external mechanisms (for example, weak boards may be partially substituted by a strong market for corporate control).

16-7 Institutions, Resources, and Corporate Finance and Governance

Learning Objective
Articulate how institutions and resources affect corporate finance and governance.

The institution-based view posits that differences around the world are affected on the one hand by *formal* securities laws, corporate charters, and codes, and on the other hand by *informal* conventions, norms, and values—collectively known as "institutions."[42] The resource-based view argues that among a number of firms financed in the same way and governed by the same set of rules, some outperform others because of differences in firm-specific capabilities (Figure 16.5). This section examines these views.

Figure 16.5	Institutions, Resources, and Corporate Finance and Governance

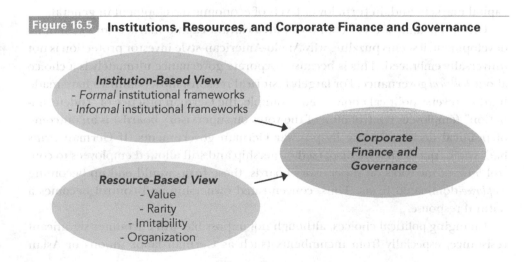

16-7a Institutions and Corporate Finance and Governance

Formal Institutional Frameworks. A fundamental difference is between the separation of ownership and control in (most) Anglo-American firms and the concentration of ownership and control in the rest of the world. Why is there such a difference? While explanations abound, one leading answer is an institutional one. In brief, better formal legal protection of shareholder rights, especially those held by *minority* shareholders, in the United States and the United Kingdom encourages founding families to dilute their equity to attract minority shareholders and delegate day-to-day management to professional managers.[43] Given reasonable investor protection, founding families themselves (such as the Rockefellers) may, over time, feel comfortable becoming minority shareholders of the firms they founded. On the other hand, when formal legal and regulatory institutions are dysfunctional, founding families *must* run their firms directly. In the absence of investor protection, inviting outside professional managers may invite abuse and theft.

Strong evidence exists that the weaker the formal legal and regulatory institutions protecting shareholders, the more concentrated the ownership and control rights become—in other words, there is some substitution between the two. Common-law countries generally have the strongest legal protection of investors and the lowest concentration of corporate ownership.[44] Among common-law countries, such ownership concentration is higher for firms in emerging economies (such as Hong Kong, India, and Israel) than in developed economies (such as Australia, Canada, Ireland, and New Zealand). In short, concentrated ownership and control is an answer to potentially rampant principal–agent conflicts in the absence of sufficient legal protection of shareholder rights.

However, what is good for controlling shareholders is not necessarily good for minority shareholders and for an economy (see the Closing Case). As noted earlier, the minimization of principal–agent conflicts through concentration of ownership and control, unfortunately, introduces more principal–principal conflicts (see In Focus 16.1). Consequently, many potential minority shareholders may refuse to invest. "How does one avoid being expropriated as a minority shareholder?" One popular saying suggests, "Don't be one!" If minority shareholders are informed enough to be aware of these principal–principal conflicts and still decide to invest, they are likely to discount the shares floated by family owners, such as the Murdoch discount for News Corporation (see In Focus 16.1). In the aggregate, such a discount results in lower valuations, fewer publicly traded firms, inactive and smaller capital markets, and, in turn, lower levels of economic development in general.

Given that almost every country desires vibrant capital markets and economic development, it seems puzzling why Anglo-American-style investor protection is not universally embraced. This is because corporate governance ultimately is a choice about *political* governance. For largely historical reasons, most countries have made hard-to-reverse political choices. For example, the German practice of "codetermination" (employees control 50% of the votes on supervisory boards) is an outcome of political decisions made by postwar German governments. If German firms had Angle-American-style dispersed ownership and still allowed employees to control 50% of the votes on supervisory boards, these firms would end up becoming *employee*-dominated firms. Thus, concentrated ownership and control becomes a natural response.

Changing political choices, although not impossible, will encounter significant resistance, especially from incumbents (such as German labor unions or Asian families) who benefit from the present system. Some of the leading business families not only have great connections with the government, sometimes, they *are* the government. For example, three recent prime ministers of Italy and Thailand—Silvio Berlusconi, Thaksin Shinawatra, and Yingluck Shinawatra—came from leading business families and were the richest individuals in these countries.

Only when extraordinary events erupt would some politicians muster sufficient political will to initiate major reforms. The spectacular corporate governance scandals in the United States (such as Enron) are examples of such extraordinary events prompting more serious political reforms, such as the Sarbanes-Oxley Act (SOX). The 2008 financial crisis resulted in the enactment of the Dodd-Frank Act in 2010, which for the first time allows shareholders to cast proxy votes on executive compensation—in short, "say on pay."

Informal Institutional Frameworks. In the last three decades around the world, why and how have informal norms and values concerning corporate governance changed to such a great extent?[45] As the idea of shareholder capitalism rapidly spreads, three sources of these changes can be identified: (1) the rise of capitalism, (2) the impact of globalization, and (3) the global diffusion of "best practices."

First, recent changes in corporate governance around the world are part of the greater political, economic, and social movement embracing capitalism. The triumph of capitalism naturally boils down to the triumph of *capitalists* (otherwise known as shareholders). However, "free markets" are not necessarily free. Even some of the most developed countries have experienced significant governance failures, calling for a sharper focus on shareholder value.

Second, at least three aspects of recent globalization have a bearing on corporate governance:

- Thanks to more trade and investment, firms with different governance norms increasingly come into contact and expose their differences. Being aware of alternatives, shareholders as well as managers and policymakers are no longer easily persuaded that "our way" is the best way of corporate governance.
- Foreign portfolio investment (FPI)—foreigners purchasing stocks and bonds—has scaled new heights. These investors naturally demand better shareholder protection before committing their funds.
- The global thirst for capital has prompted many firms to pay attention to corporate governance. Foreign firms cross-listed in New York and London have to be in compliance with US and UK listing requirements.

Third, the changing norms and values are also directly promoted by the global diffusion of "best practices" in the form of corporate governance codes.[46] A lot of codes are advisory and not legally binding. However, strong pressures exist for firms to adopt these codes "voluntarily." For example, in Russia, although adopting the Code of Corporate Conduct is voluntary, firms not adopting it must publicly explain why, essentially naming and shaming themselves. In addition, the Organization for Economic Cooperation and Development (OECD)—a club of rich countries—has spearheaded efforts to globally diffuse "best practices" through the *OECD Principles of Corporate Governance* (1999). The *Principles* are non-binding, even for the 34 OECD member countries. Nevertheless, the global norms seem to be moving toward the *Principles*. For example, China and Taiwan, both non-OECD members, have recently taken a page from the *Principles* and allowed for class action lawsuits brought by shareholders.

Slowly but surely, change is in the air. But such change is not necessarily in one direction. The ferociousness of the 2008 global financial crisis has caused tremendous resentment toward fat executive pay packages, income inequality, and the financial services industry in general. Movements such as Occupy Wall Street and Occupy London are tangible indications of the changing informal sentiments as the swing of the pendulum, which have triggered or intensified formal regulatory changes.

16-7b Resources and Corporate Finance and Governance

From a corporate finance and governance standpoint, the abilities to successfully list on a high-profile exchange such as NYSE and LSE are valuable, rare, and hard to imitate. In 1997, the valuations of foreign firms listed in New York were 17% higher than their domestic counterparts in the same country that were either unable or unwilling to list abroad.[47] Now, despite hurdles such as SOX, the select few that are able to list in New York are rewarded more handsomely: Their valuations are now 37% higher than comparable groups of domestic firms in the same country.[48] London-listed foreign firms do not enjoy such high valuations.[49] This is classic resource-based logic at work: Precisely because it is much more challenging to list in New York in the SOX era, the small number of foreign firms that are able to do this are truly exceptional. Thus, they deserve much higher valuations.

Some of the most valuable, rare, and hard-to-imitate firm-specific resources are top managers and directors—often regarded as managerial human capital.[50] Some of these resources, such as the social networks of these executives, are highly unique and likely to add value.[51] Also, top managerial talents are hard to imitate—unless they are hired away by competitor firms.

The last crucial component in the VRIO framework is O: organizational. It is within an organizational setting (in TMTs and boards) that managers and directors function.[52] Overall, the few people at the top of an organization can make a world of difference—Steve Jobs at Apple was a great example. Governance mechanisms need to motivate and discipline them properly to ensure that they make a positive impact.

Learning Objective
Participate in two leading debates concerning corporate finance and governance.

16-8 Debates and Extensions

Corporate finance and governance often generate significant debates.[53] This section discusses two: (1) opportunistic agents versus managerial stewards and (2) global convergence versus divergence.

16-8a Opportunistic Agents versus Managerial Stewards

Managerial human capital
The skills and abilities acquired by top managers.

Stewardship theory
A "pro-management" theory that suggests that most managers can be viewed as owners' stewards interested in safeguarding shareholders' interests.

Agency theory assumes managers to be agents who may engage in self-serving opportunistic activities if left to their own devices. However, critics contend that most managers are likely to be honest and trustworthy. Managerial mistakes may be due to a lack of competence, information, or luck, and not necessarily due to self-serving motives. Thus, it may not be fair to characterize all managers as opportunistic agents. Although very influential, agency theory has been criticized as an "anti-management theory of management."[54] A "pro-management" theory, stewardship theory, has emerged recently. It suggests that most managers can be viewed as owners' stewards. Safeguarding shareholders' interests and advancing organizational goals will maximize (most) managers' own utility functions.[55]

If all principals view all managers as self-serving agents with control mechanisms to put managers on a "tight leash," some managers, who initially view themselves as stewards, may be so frustrated that they end up engaging in the very self-serving behavior that agency theory seeks to minimize. In other words, as a self-fulfilling prophecy, agency theory may *induce* such behavior.

16-8b Global Convergence versus Divergence

Another leading debate is whether corporate governance is converging or diverging globally. Convergence advocates argue that globalization unleashes a "survival-of-the-fittest" process by which firms will be forced to adopt global best (essentially Anglo-American) practices. Global investors are willing to pay a premium for stock in firms with Anglo-American-style governance, prompting other firms to follow.

One interesting phenomenon often cited by convergence advocates is cross-listing. Cross-listing is primarily driven by the desire to tap into larger pools of capital. Foreign firms thus must comply with US and UK securities laws and adopt Anglo-American corporate governance norms. For instance, Japanese firms listed in New York and London, compared with those listed at home, are more concerned about shareholder value. A US or UK listing can be viewed as a signal of the firm's commitment to strengthen shareholder value, resulting in higher valuations.

Critics contend that governance practices will continue to diverge throughout the world.[56] For example, promoting more concentrated ownership and control is often recommended as a solution to combat principal-agent conflicts in US and UK firms. However, making the same recommendation to reform firms in the rest of the world may be counterproductive or even disastrous.[57] This is because the main problem there is that controlling shareholders typically already have too much ownership and control. Finally, some US and UK practices differ significantly. In addition to the split on CEO duality (the UK against, the US for) discussed earlier, none of the US anti-takeover defenses (such as "poison pills") is legal in the UK.

In the case of cross-listed firms, divergence advocates make two points. First, despite some convergence on paper (such as having more outside directors), cross-listed foreign firms do not necessarily adopt US governance norms before or after listing.[58] Second, despite the popular belief that US and UK securities laws would apply to cross-listed foreign firms, in practice, these laws have rarely been effectively enforced against foreign firms' "tunneling."[59]

At present, complete divergence is probably unrealistic, especially for large firms in search of capital from global investors. Complete convergence also seems unlikely. What is more likely is "cross-vergence," balancing the expectations of global investors and those of local stakeholders.[60]

16-9 Management Savvy

Learning Objective
Draw implications for action.

From the institution-based and resource-based views, two straightforward implications for action emerge (Table 16.3). First, savvy managers need to understand both the formal and informal rules, anticipate changes, and be aware of differences when addressing financing and governance issues.[61] Consider executive compensation. In 2008, a year during which Wall Street had to be bailed out by billions of

EMERGING MARKETS 16.1

Satyam versus Infosys: A Corporate Governance Tale of Two Indian Firms

Satyam, which means "truth" in Sanskrit, an ancient Indian language, once belonged to the top tier of India's most celebrated industry: information technology (IT). During its heyday, Satyam was proudly listed on the National Stock Exchange and Bombay Stock Exchange. But it ended up becoming India's largest corporate fraud—"India's Enron," according to some critics. In 2009, Satyam's founder and chairman, B. Ramalinga Raju, confessed to falsifying books

for years, inflating revenues, and fabricating cash of about US$1 billion that did not really exist. Instead of having 53,000 employees, there were only 40,000. Every month, Raju engaged in "tunneling" by stealing US$3 million to pay such nonexistent employees. PricewaterhouseCoopers auditors endorsed Satyam's books even as hundreds of millions of rupees were unaccounted for. Immediately following the news, Merrill Lynch (now part of Bank of America) and

taxpayer dollars, Wall Street executives paid themselves US$18 billion in bonuses. In 2011, the first year that shareholders were granted a "say on pay" in US firms, median pay for CEOs at S&P 500 firms *jumped* 35% to US$8.4 million.[62] While these practices did not break any formal laws, what the executives failed to read was the informal, but very tangible, normative pressures coming from an angry public fanned by the media and fueled by politicians who wanted to show they were "tough." As a result, formal efforts to limit executive compensation have been initiated in most countries. While critics may argue that governments have no business in limiting executive compensation at private-sector firms, unfortunately, the rules have changed. As controlling shareholders of many formerly private-sector firms that have now become SOEs financed by public funds, governments do have legitimate ownership rights to intervene.

Second, managers must develop firm-specific capabilities to differentiate on governance dimensions. Shown in Emerging Markets 16.1, in India, while Satyam has emerged as a "bad apple," Infosys has served as an exemplar in corporate governance. The primary reason for such practices, according to Infosys executives, is to gain credibility with Western customers in the rough-and-tumble software market. In other words, excellent financing and governance practices make Infosys stand out in the product market. Conversely, corporate governance drama at HP not only undermines investors' confidence in the firm, but also consumers' confidence in its products, thus chipping away its competitive advantage in the product marketplace (see the Opening Case).

Table 16.3   **Implications for Action**

- Understand the rules affecting corporate finance and governance, anticipate changes, and be aware of differences.

- Develop firm-specific capabilities to differentiate a firm on corporate finance and governance dimensions.

State Farm Insurance terminated engagement with Satyam. Unable to go on, Satyam in 2009 was partially acquired by Tech Mahindra, a part of the Mahindra & Mahindra group, which was interested in diversifying into IT. The firm was rebranded "Mahindra Satyam" lately, and the merger was completed in 2013.

On the other hand, another leading Indian IT firm, Infosys, is a shining example of how excellent corporate governance can strengthen product market success. Infosys led the pack by being the first Indian firm to follow US generally accepted accounting principles (GAAP) and one of the first to introduce outside directors. Since its listings in Bombay in 1993 and on NASDAQ in 1999, it went far beyond disclosure requirements mandated by both Indian and US standards. On NASDAQ, Infosys *voluntarily* behaved like a US domestic issuer, rather than subjecting itself to the less-stringent standards of a foreign issuer. The primary reason for such practices, according to Infosys executives, was to gain credibility with Western clients in the rough-and-tumble software market. In other words, excellent financing and governance practices made Infosys stand out in the product market. In 2012, Infosys transferred its listing from NASDAQ to NYSE. By 2014, it had 160,000 employees working in 32 countries and its market capitalization reached US$31 billion.

Sources: Based on (1) *Business Week*, 2009, Corporate India's governance crisis, February 2: 78; (2) *Economist*, 2009, Salvaging the truth, April 18: 68–69. (3) *The Hindu*, 2013, 1:8.5 swap for Tech Mahindra, Mahindra Satyam merger, June 25: www.thehindu.com; (4) T. Khanna & K. Palepu, 2004, Globalization and convergence in corporate governance, *Journal of International Business Studies*, 35: 484–507; (5) *Wall Street Journal*, 2012, NYSE snags Infosys listing from NASDAQ, November 30: online.wsj.com; (6) www.infosys.com; (7) www.techmahindra.com.

CHAPTER SUMMARY/LEARNING OBJECTIVES

16-1 Outline the two means of financing decisions, equity and debt, that center on the cost of capital.

- Equity refers to the stock (usually expressed in shares) in a firm, and debt refers to the loan that the firm needs to pay back at a given time with a prespecified interest.
- Tapping into a larger pool of capital globally allows firms to lower their cost of capital.

16-2 Differentiate various ownership patterns (concentrated/diffused, family, and state ownership).

- In the US and UK, firms with separation of ownership and control dominate.
- Elsewhere, firms with concentrated ownership and control in the hands of families or governments are predominant.

16-3 Articulate the role of managers in both principal–agent and principal–principal conflicts.

- In firms with separation of ownership and control, the primary conflicts are principal–agent conflicts.
- In firms with concentrated ownership, principal–principal conflicts prevail.

16-4 Explain the role of the board of directors.

- The board of directors performs (1) control, (2) service, and (3) resource-acquisition functions.
- Around the world, boards differ in composition and leadership structure.

16-5 Identify voice-based and exit-based governance mechanisms and their combination as a package.

- Internal, voice-based mechanisms and external, exit-based mechanisms combine as a package to determine corporate governance effectiveness.

The market for corporate control and the market for private equity are two primary means of external mechanisms.

16-6 Acquire a global perspective on how governance mechanisms vary around the world.

- Different combinations of internal and external governance mechanisms lead to four main groups.

16-7 Articulate how institutions and resources affect corporate finance and governance.

- Institution-based and resource-based views shed light on finance and governance issues.

16-8 Participate in two leading debates on corporate finance and governance.

- (1) Opportunistic agents versus managerial stewards and (2) global convergence versus divergence.

16-9 Draw implications for action.

- Understand the rules, anticipate changes, and be aware of differences.
- Develop firm-specific capabilities to differentiate a firm on corporate finance and governance dimensions.

KEY TERMS

Agency cost, 514

Agency relationship, 514

Agency theory, 514

Agent, 514

Bond, 511

Bondholder, 511

Chief executive officer (CEO), 514

CEO duality, 518

Concentrated ownership and control, 513

Corporate governance, 510

Cost of capital, 511

Cross-listing, 512

Debt, 511

Default, 511

Diffused ownership, 513

Equity, 511

Exit-based mechanism, 519

Expropriation, 516

Financing, 510

Information asymmetry, 515

Inside director, 518

Leveraged buyout (LBO), 520

Managerial human capital, 526

Outside (independent) director, 518

Principal, 514

Principal–agent conflict, 514

Principal–principal conflict, 516

Private equity, 520

Related transaction, 516

Separation of ownership and control, 513

Shareholder, 511

Shareholder capitalism, 522

Stewardship theory, 526

Top management team (TMT), 514

Tunneling, 516

Voice-based mechanism, 519

REVIEW QUESTIONS

1. What are the two primary means of financing? How do they differ?

2. Why can tapping into a global pool of capital providers result in a lower cost of capital?

3. How would you characterize a corporation with diffused ownership?

4. *ON CULTURE:* What are some of the pros and cons of family ownership?

5. Describe the differences between principal–agent conflicts and principal–principal conflicts.

6. Define the concept of expropriation of minority shareholders.

7. What do inside directors bring to a board of directors? What do outside directors have to offer?

8. What are the advantages and disadvantages of having two different individuals hold the positions of board chair and CEO rather than combining these two positions?

9. Name and describe the two internal governance mechanisms typically employed by boards.

10. Briefly summarize the three external governance mechanisms.

11. Under what conditions are the primary governance mechanisms likely to involve concentration of ownership and control?

12. Why do most SOEs suffer from weak external and internal governance mechanisms?

13. What are some of the formal institutions that affect corporate governance?

14. Explain how three aspects of recent globalization have influenced corporate governance.

15. Where does managerial human capital fit into a VRIO framework?

16. Explain stewardship theory, and compare it to agency theory.

17. Given the arguments for converging versus diverging corporate governance around the world, which do you think is more likely to occur and why?

18. Compare PengAtlas Map 1.1 with Map 3.4. Countries that have low levels of development often benefit from outsourcing due to their low wages. Assume that a firm's board of directors is truly independent and makes decisions based only on economic considerations. Why would it not also outsource the top executive jobs? To the extent that such a thing might be possible, how might it be done?

19. See PengAtlas Map 3.4's "Poorest Ten." Other than low wages, why might a firm outsource its activities to one of these countries?

CRITICAL DISCUSSION QUESTIONS

1. Some argue that the Anglo-American-style separation of ownership and control is an inevitable outcome. Others contend that this is one variant (among several) of how large firms can be effectively governed and that it is not necessarily the most efficient form. What do you think?

2. Recent corporate governance reforms in various countries urge (and often require) firms to add more outside directors to their boards and to separate the jobs of board chairman and CEO. Yet, academic research has not been able to conclusively support the merits of both practices. Why?

3. *ON ETHICS:* As a chairman/CEO, you are choosing between two candidates for one outside (independent) director position on your board. One is another CEO, a longtime friend on whose board you have served for many years. The other is a known shareholder activist whose tag line is "No need to make fat cats fatter." Placing him on the board will earn you kudos among analysts and journalists for inviting a leading critic to scrutinize your work. But he may try

to prove his theory that CEOs are overpaid—in other words, your compensation can be on the line. Whom would you choose?

4. *ON ETHICS:* Suppose you were CEO of a firm that lost US$50 million, but you were given a bonus of US$10 million. You were vilified in the media and brought before a Congressional committee that accused you of financial outrage. However, you pointed out that the most optimistic forecast for your firm had been that it would lose over US$6 billion. There was no significant change in markets, the economy, or anything else during the year other than the new strategy that you implemented—a strategy that reduced losses by US$5,950,000,000 to only US$50,000,000, and thus you felt that you were actually underpaid. But the politicians felt that it still looked bad and that if you had been socially responsible, you would have refused the bonus. How do you respond?

BUSINESS
INSIGHTS
GLOBAL

GLOBAL ACTION

1. Your privately owned company consistently balances the interests of business freedom and labor freedom in its operations. As such, it has become an example for other firms worldwide to emulate. Since the tension between wages and prices at both the labor and business levels must be constantly reevaluated and improved, evaluate the leading countries that your firm can use as a model for continued commitment to the freedoms of business as well as labor.

2. As CEO of a large multinational firm, the financial globalization level of a country can present different problems and solutions for success. Using a well-known index of financial globalization, evaluate and discuss specific countries in which the concerns of a high and low level of globalization must be addressed.

CLOSING CASE

Ethical
Dilemma

What Makes Analysts Say Buy?

A research study conducted by Harvard Business School professors regarding analyst ratings of companies which provide buy, sell, or hold ratings for those companies sought to answer whether there were differences between analysts in different parts of the world. This synopsis of their findings appeared in the Harvard Business Review. *Read about their findings and answer the questions at the end of the case.*

Wall Street analysts' recommendations can move markets. But even though leaders of public companies spend significant amounts of time interacting with this constituency, there's little information about how analysts arrive at their recommendations. What factors most influence their thinking?

We set out to answer that question through a global study of analyst forecasts and stock performance over two consecutive years in the mid-2000s. We surveyed nearly 1,000 analysts in Asia, Europe, Latin America, and in the U.S., asking them to rate almost 1,000 large companies on 12 factors, using a scale of one to five, and to forecast revenue growth, earnings growth, and gross margin on the basis of those ratings. We also estimated how important each factor was to their ultimate recommendations.

The strongest determinant of a buy or sell recommendation, we learned, is projected industry growth, followed by the quality of the top management team. Analysts in different regions often weighed factors

Factors That Drive Buy Recommendations	Importance to Analysts			
	Low	Moderate	High	Very High
Clear, well-communicated strategy	A L U			E
Ability to execute strategy	A L	U	E	
Governance strength	A L		E	U
Quality of top management	L			A E U
Innovativeness	A	U	E	L
Low-price strategy	A L		E	U
Superior products or services strategy	A E L		U	
Balance sheet strength	A E L U			
Culture	A E L		U	
High performance compensation	A E L	U		
Projected industry growth			E	A L U
Industry competitiveness	L	A E U		

A Asia   E Europe   L Latin America   U USA

quite differently, though. For example, having a clear, well-communicated strategy was of "very high" importance to analysts in Europe but of "low" importance to those in other regions. One of the most interesting findings was the uneven importance of governance: It's much more significant to U.S. and European analysts than to analysts in Latin America and Asia. Why? Our best guess is that increased governance disclosure and regulation in the U.S. and Europe have made governance an area of focus for many analysts in those regions.

Some of the factors that affect analysts' views lie beyond a company's or an executive's power-a manager has little sway over industry growth, for example. But many are well within executive control. For instance, it's the job of the CEO and the Management team to communicate the team's strengths to the market.

Leaders can use this research to shape what they emphasize in managing their companies and when sharing information about them with the outsiders who drive market cap. The rewards, though also variable by region, can be significant. Consider this finding: A new buy recommendation for large firms that analysts viewed as having high-quality top management increased market cap, on average, by $2.4 billion in Asia, $1.4 billion in Europe, and $40 million in Latin America. And if the buy recommendation is contrarian-that is, if the consensus recommendation is hold or sell- the effect is even greater.

CASE DISCUSSION QUESTIONS

1. Why do analysts in the US and Europe pay more attention to corporate governance?

2. How do analysts in different regions rate the importance of the quality of top management? Why are there such differences?

3. If you were CEO of a listed company in Asia, what are the top three areas that you would focus on in order to attract analysts to make a buy recommendation?

Source: B. Groysberg, P. Healy, N. Nohria, & G. Serafeim What Makes Analysts Say "Buy"? *Harvard Business Review*, November, 2012.

NOTES

[Journal acronyms] AER—*American Economic Review;* AMJ—*Academy of Management Journal;* AMP—*Academy of Management Perspectives;* AMR—*Academy of Management Review;* APJM—*Asia Pacific Journal of Management;* BW—*BusinessWeek* (before 2010) or *Bloomberg Businessweek* (since 2010); EMR—*Emerging Markets Review;* JAE—*Journal of Accounting and Economics;* JBE—*Journal of Business Ethics;* JEP—*Journal of Economic Perspectives;* JF—*Journal of Finance;* JFE—*Journal of Financial Economics;* JIBS—*Journal of International Business Studies;* JM—*Journal of Management;* JMS—*Journal of Management Studies;* JWB—*Journal of World Business;* MIR—*Management International Review;* MOR—*Management and Organization Review;* OSc—*Organization Science;* OSt—*Organization Studies;* RFS—*Review of Financial Studies;* SMJ—*Strategic Management Journal.*

1 R. Monks & N. Minow, 2001, *Corporate Governance* (p. 1), Oxford, UK: Blackwell. See also S. Globerman, M. W. Peng, & D. Shapiro, 2011, Corporate governance and Asian companies, *APJM*, 28: 1–14.

2 E. Lim, S. Das, & A. Das, 2009, Diversification strategy, capital structure, and the Asian financial crisis, *SMJ*, 30: 577–594.

3 X. Zhao, 2009, Determinants of flows into retail international equity finds, *JIBS*, 39: 1169–1177.

4 G. Dissanaike & I. Markar, 2009, Corporate financing in East Asia before the 1997 crash, *JIBS*, 40: 990–1004.

5 V. Bruno & H. Shin, 2014, Globalization of corporate risk taking, *JIBS*, 45: 800–820; L. Hail & C. Leuz, 2009, Cost of capital effects and changes in growth expectations around US cross-listings, *JFE*, 93: 428–454.

6 M. W. Peng & W. Su, 2014, Cross-listing and the scope of the firm, *JWB*, 49: 42–50.

7 B. Connelly, R. Hoskisson, L. Tihanyi, & S. T. Certo, 2010, Ownership as a form of corporate governance, *JMS*, 47: 1561–1589.

8 R. Stulz, 2005, The limits of financial globalization (p. 1618), *JF*, 60: 1595–1638.

9 K. Schnatterly, K. Shaw, & W. Jennings, 2008, Information advantages of large institutional owners, *SMJ*, 29: 219–227.

10 R. La Porta, F. Lopez-de-Silanes, & A. Shleifer, 1999, Corporate ownership around the world, *JF*, 54: 471–517.

11 Y. Lu, K. Au, M. W. Peng, & E. Xu, 2013, Strategic management in private and family business, *APJM*, 30: 633–639.

12 Y. Jiang & M. W. Peng, 2011, Are family ownership and control in large firms good, bad, or irrelevant? *APJM*, 28: 15–39; M. W. Peng & Y. Jiang, 2010, Institutions behind family ownership and control in large firms, *JMS*, 47: 253–273.

13 *Economist*, 2012, The rise of state capitalism, January 21: 11.

14 M. Jensen & W. Meckling, 1976, Theory of the firm, *JFE*, 3: 305–360.

15 A. Nyberg, I. Fulmer, B. Gerhart, & M. Carpenter, 2010, Agency theory revisited, *AMJ*, 53: 1029–1042; S. Sauerwald, Z. Lin, & M. W. Peng, 2015, Board social capital and excess CEO returns, *SMJ* (in press).

16 J. Combs, D. Ketchen, A. Perryman, & M. Donahue, 2007, The moderating effect of CEO power on the board composition-firm performance relationship, *JMS*, 44: 1309–1322; W. Johnson, R. Magee, N. Nagarajan, & H. Newman, 1985, An analysis of the stock price reaction to sudden executive deaths, *JAE*, 7: 151–174.

17 S. Graffin, M. Carpenter, & S. Boivie, 2011, What's all that (strategic) intent? *SMJ*, 32: 748–770; Y. Zhang, 2008, Information asymmetry and the dismissal of newly appointed CEOs, *SMJ*, 29: 859–872.

18 S. Claessens, S. Djankov, & L. Lang, 2000, The separation of ownership and control in East Asian corporations, *JFE*, 58: 81–112.

19 M. Faccio & L. Lang, 2002, The ultimate ownership of Western European corporations, *JFE*, 65: 365–395.

20 S. Sauerwald & M. W. Peng, 2013, Informal institutions, shareholder coalitions, and principal-principal conflicts, *APJM*, 30: 853–870; M. Young, M. W. Peng, D. Ahlstrom, G. Bruton, & Y. Jiang, 2008, Corporate governance in emerging economies, *JMS*, 45: 196–220.

21 J. Campbell, T. C. Campbell, D. Sirmon, L. Bierman, & C. Tuggle, 2012, Shareholder influence over director nomination via proxy access, *SMJ*, 33: 1431–1451.

22 M. W. Peng, 2004, Outside directors and firm performance during institutional transitions, *SMJ*, 25: 453–471.

23 V. Chen, J. Li, & D. Shapiro, 2011, Are OECD-prescribed "good corporate governance practices" really good in an emerging economy? *APJM*, 28: 115–138; M. W. Peng, S. Zhang, & X. Li, 2007, CEO duality and firm performance during China's institutional transitions, *MOR*, 3: 205–225; T. Quigley & D. Hambrick, 2012, When the former CEO stays on as board chair, *SMJ*, 33: 834–859.

24 J. Tang, M. Crossan, & W. G. Rowe, 2011, Dominant CEO, deviant strategy, and extreme performance, *JMS*, 48: 1479–1502.

25 A. Gore, S. Matsunaga, & P. E. Yeung, 2011, The role of technical expertise in firm governance structure, *SMJ*, 32: 771–786; M. McDonald, J. Westphal, & M. Graebner, 2008, What do they know? *SMJ*, 29: 1155–1177.

26 A. Chizema & J. Kim, 2010, Outside directors on Korean boards, *JMS*, 47: 109–129.

27 G. Pandher & R. Currie, 2013, CEO compensation, *SMJ*, 34: 22–41; A. Wowak & D. Hambrick, 2010, A model of person-pay interaction, *SMJ*, 31: 803–821.

28 T. Cho & W. Shen, 2007, Changes in executive compensation following an environmental shift, *SMJ*, 28: 747–754.

29 L. Bebchuk & J. Fried, 2004, *Pay without Performance*, Cambridge, MA: Harvard University Press.

30 A. Cowen & J. Marcel, 2011, Damaged goods, *AMJ*, 54: 509–527.

31 *Economist*, 2012, The shackled boss, January 21: 76.

32 M. Wiersema & Y. Zhang, 2013, Executive turnover in the stock option backdating wave, *SMJ*, 34: 590–609.

33 R. Hoskisson, M. Castleton, & M. Withers, 2009, Complementarity in monitoring and bonding, *AMP*, May: 57–74.

34 V. Bodolica & M. Spraggon, 2009, The implementation of special attributes of CEO compensation contracts around M&A transactions, *SMJ*, 30: 985–1011.

35 M. Nakamura, 2011, Adoption and policy implications of Japan's new corporate governance practices after the reform, *APJM*, 28: 187–213; T. Yoshikawa & J. McGuire, 2008, Change and continuity in Japanese corporate governance, *APJM*, 25: 5–24.

36 R. Hoskisson, W. Shi, X. Yi, & J. Jin, 2013, The evolution and strategic positioning of private equity firms, *AMP*, 27: 22–38; M. Wright, 2013, Private equity, *AMP*, 27: 1–6.

37 P. Klein, J. Chapman, & M. Mondelli, 2013, Private equity and entrepreneurial governance, *AMP*, 27: 39–51.

38 N. Bacon, M. Wright, R. Ball, & M. Meuleman, 2013, Private equity, HRM, and employment, *AMP*, 27: 7–21.

39 J. Lerner, P. Stromberg, & M. Sorensen, 2008, Private equity and long-run investment, in J. Lerner & A, Gurung (eds), *The Global*

Economic Impact of Private Equity Report 2008 (pp. 27–42), Geneva, Switzerland: World Economic Forum.

40 R. Aguilera, I. Filatotchev, H. Gospel, & G. Jackson, 2008, An organizational approach to comparative corporate governance, *OSc*, 19: 475–492; B. Boyd, K. Haynes, & F. Zona, 2011, Dimensions of CEO-board relations, *JMS*, 48: 1892–1923; G. Dowell, M. Shackell, & N. Stuart, 2011, Boards, CEOs, and surviving a financial crisis, *SMJ*, 32: 1025–1045.

41 D. McCarthy & S. Puffer, 2008, Interpreting the ethicality of corporate governance decisions in Russia, *AMR*, 33: 11–31.

42 K. Bae, L. Purda, M. Welker, & L. Zhong, 2013, Credit rating initiation and accounting quality for emerging-market firms, *JIBS*, 44: 216–234; B. Baik, J. Kang, J. Kim, & J. Lee, 2013, The liability of foreignness in international equity markets, *JIBS*, 44: 391–411; N. Boubakri, S. Mansi, & W. Saffar, 2013, Political institutions, connectedness, and corporate risk-taking, *JIBS*, 44: 195–215; I. Filatotchev & D. Allcock, 2010, Corporate governance and executive remuneration, *AMP*, 24: 20–33; L. Markoczy, S. Sun, M. W. Peng, W. Shi, & B. Ren, 2013, Social network contingency, symbolic management, and boundary stretching, *SMJ*, 34: 1367–1387; L. Shao, C. Kwok, & R. Zhang, 2013, National culture and corporate investment, *JIBS*, 44: 745–763; J. Siegel, 2009, Is there a better commitment mechanism than cross-listings for emerging-economy firms? *JIBS*, 40: 1171–1191; M. Van Essen, P. Heugens, J. Otten, & J. van Oosterhout, 2012, An institution-based view of executive compensation, *JIBS*, 43: 396–423; K. Weber, G. Davis, & M. Lounsbury, 2009, Policy as myth and ceremony? *AMJ*, 52: 1319–1347.

43 R. D. McLean, T. Zhang, & M. Zhao, 2012, Why does the law matter? *JF*, 67: 313–350.

44 A. Bris & C. Cabolis, 2008, The value of investor protection, *RFS*, 21: 605–648.

45 S. Estrin & M. Prevezer, 2011, The role of informal institutions in corporate governance, *APJM*, 28: 41–67.

46 I. Haxhi & H. van Ees, 2010, Explaining diversity in the worldwide diffusion of codes of good governance, *JIBS*, 41: 710–726.

47 C. Doidge, A. Karolyi, & R. Stulz, 2004, Why are foreign firms listed in the US worth more? *JFE*, 71: 205–238.

48 A. Karolyi, 2012, Corporate governance, agency problems, and international cross-listings, *EMR*, 13: 516–547.

49 C. Doidge, A. Karolyi, & R. Stulz, 2009, Has New York become less competitive than London in global markets? *JFE*, 91: 253–277; N. Fernandes, U. Lel, & D. Miller, 2010, Escape from New York, *JFE*, 95: 129–147.

50 M. W. Peng, S. Sun, & L. Markoczy, 2015, Human capital and CEO compensation during institutional transitions, *JMS*, 52: 117–147. See also C. Crossland, J. Zyung, N. Hiller, & D. Hambrick, 2014, CEO career variety, *AMJ*, 57: 652–674; C. Fracassi & G. Tate, 2012,

External networking and internal firm governance, *JF*, 67: 153–194; M. McDonald & J. Westphal, 2011, My brother's keeper? *AMJ*, 54: 661–693; L. Oxelheim, A. Gregoric, T. Randoy, & S. Thomsen, 2013, On the internationalization of corporate boards, *JIBS*, 44: 173–194; J. Tian, J. Haleblian, & N. Rajagopalan, 2011, The effects of board human and social capital on investor reactions to new CEO selection, *SMJ*, 32: 731–747.

51 D. Hambrick & T. Quigley, 2014, Toward more accurate contextualization of the CEO effect on firm performance, *SMJ*, 35: 473–491; A. Mackey, 2008, The effects of CEOs on firm performance, *SMJ*, 29: 1357–1367.

52 S. Boivie, D. Lange, M. McDonald, & J. Westphal, 2011, Me or we, *AMJ*, 54: 551–576; C. Devers, G. McNamara, J. Haleblian, & M. Yoder, 2013, Do they walk the talk? *AMJ*, 56: 1679–1702; J. He & Z. Huang, 2011, Board informal hierarchy and firm financial performance, *AMJ*, 54: 1119–1139; A. Karaevli & E. Zajac, 2013, When do outside CEOs generate strategic change? *JMS*, 50: 1267–1294; S. Nadkarni & P. Herrmann, 2010, CEO personality, strategic flexibility, and firm performance, *AMJ*, 53: 1050–1073; A. Raes, M. Heijltjes, U. Glunk, & R. Roe, 2011, The interface of the top management team and middle managers, *AMR*, 36: 102–126; C. Tuggle, K. Schnatterly, & R. Johnson, 2010, Attention patterns in the boardroom, *AMJ*, 53: 550–571; A. Wowak, D. Hambrick, & A. Henderson, 2011, Do CEOs encounter within-tenure settling up? *AMJ*, 54: 719–739.

53 M. Bednar, 2012, Watchdog or lapdog? *AMJ*, 55: 131–150; T. Donaldson, 2012, The epitemic fault line in corporate governance, *AMR*, 37: 256–271.

54 L. Donaldson, 1995, *American Anti-management Theories of Management*, Cambridge, UK: Cambridge University Press.

55 M. Hernandez, 2012, Toward an understanding of the psychology of stewardship, *AMR*, 37: 172–193.

56 Y. Shi, M. Magnan, & J. Kim, 2012, Do countries matter for voluntary disclosure? *JIBS*, 43: 143–165.

57 M. Van Essen, J. van Oosterhout, & P. Heugens, 2013, Competition and cooperation in corporate governance, *OSc*, 24: 530–551.

58 P. Rejchrt & M. Higgs, 2015, When in Rome, *JBE* (in press).

59 J. Siegel, 2003, Can foreign firms bond themselves effectively by renting US securities laws? *JFE*, 75: 319–359.

60 A. Chizema & Y. Shinozawa, 2012, The "company with committees," *JMS*, 49: 77–101.

61 G. Davis, 2009, The rise and fall of finance and the end of the society of organizations, *AMP*, 23: 27–44; M. Goranova & L. Ryan, 2014, Shareholder activism, *JM*, 40: 1230–1268; I. Larkin, L. Pierce, & F. Gino, 2012, The psychological costs of pay-for-performance, *SMJ*, 33: 1194–1214.

62 *BW*, 2011, After much hoopla, investor "say on pay" is a bust, June 20: 23–24.

epa european pressphoto agency b.v./Alamy

Learning Objectives

After studying this chapter, you should be able to

- articulate what is a stakeholder view of the firm.

- apply the institution-based and resource-based views to analyze corporate social responsibility (CSR).

- participate in two leading debates concerning CSR.

- draw implications for action.

Managing Corporate Social Responsibility Globally

Ethical Dilemma

OPENING CASE

EMERGING MARKETS: Foxconn

Until 2010, the vast majority of the end users of Apple iPhones and iPads, Hewlett-Packard laptops, Amazon Kindles, and Microsoft Xboxes around the world had no clue about the firm that manufactured their beloved gadgets. The firm is Foxconn, which is headquartered in Taipei, Taiwan. Foxconn's shares (under the name of Hon Hai) are not only listed in Taipei in the Taiwan World Stock Exchange (TWSE: 2317), but also in Hong Kong (SEHK: 2038), London (LSE: HHPD), and NASDAQ (HNHPF). With US$132 billion in annual revenue, Foxconn is the global leader in contract manufacturing services. In other words, everybody has heard that leading firms such as Cisco, Dell, Ericsson, Intel, Motorola, Nintendo, Nokia, and Sony—in addition to those named in the first three lines of this box above—have outsourced a large chunk of their manufacturing to "low-cost producers." But to *whom*? Prior to 2010, only a small number of people knew the answer: Foxconn has been scooping up a tremendous number of outsourcing orders.

Starting in 1975 in Taipei with a meager US$7,500, Foxconn was founded by Taiwanese entrepreneur Terry Gou, who still serves as its chairman. As Foxconn became a giant, industry insiders knew and respected it. But outside the industry, Foxconn lived in relative obscurity. It is likely to be the largest firm many people around the world never heard of. Just how big is

Foxconn? Worldwide, it has 1.3 million employees. In China alone, it employs over 900,000 workers (300,000 on one factory campus in Shenzhen). To put these mind-boggling numbers in perspective, its worldwide headcount is as large as the entire US military, and its headcount in China is three times the size of the Taiwanese military. In addition to China, Foxconn has factories in 11 countries: Brazil, the Czech Republic, Hungary, India, Japan, Malaysia, Mexico, Pakistan, Slovakia, South Korea, and the United States. Foxconn is the largest private employer and the largest exporter in China and the second-largest exporter in the Czech Republic.

In 2010, Foxconn stumbled into media spotlight, not because of its accomplishments, but because of a dozen suicides committed by employees in Shenzhen, China, in a span of several months. Most of them died by jumping from high-rise Foxconn dormitories. This was one of the biggest paradoxes associated with Foxconn. What were Foxconn's secrets for being so successful? Just as when 100 years ago Henry Ford created the mass assembly line by standardizing each worker's job, Foxconn pioneered a business model that it called e-enabled Components, Modules, Moves, and Services (eCMMS) that helped its clients save a ton of money. But why were there so many worker suicides that shocked the world? The business model was certainly a culprit. Working at Foxconn demands a great deal of concentration and repetition that breed enormous stress. *Bloomberg Businessweek* described Gou as "a ruthless taskmaster." Although the media and corporate social responsibility (CSR) gurus criticized Foxconn for treating workers like machines and exploiting cheap labor, there was no evidence—according to audits run by Apple and other clients—that Foxconn mistreated or abused employees. Instead, in China, labor watchdogs gave Foxconn credit for exceeding the norms, by paying workers (relatively) higher salaries, on time, and for overtime. In both 2005 and 2006, it was among the Best Employers in China, according to a ChinaHR.com poll. In response to the suicides, Foxconn in 2010 installed nets outside dormitories to prevent suicides and increased Shenzhen factory workers' pay by 30% to US$176 a month. Such raises cut earnings per share by about 5% in 2010 and by 12% in 2011. As a result, Gou recently scaled back his annual growth target from 30% to 15%.

Given Apple's "green" image, it reportedly entertained the notion of dropping Foxconn as a supplier, which had spilled some "blood" on pristine iPhones and iPads. But Apple quickly and quietly dropped this idea, which would be suicidal—thanks to Foxconn's unrivaled bargaining power. Foxconn, for its part, promised to beef up CSR. Virtually all workers in Shenzhen were away from their families and friends. Just across the border from Hong Kong, Shenzhen itself was a "new" city that became a boom town since the 1980s. Although Shenzhen now has more than ten million people, it had a trivial population before the economic reforms took off. Practically no twentysomethings or thirtysomethings were raised in Shenzhen. They all came to Shenzhen in search of jobs. A majority of such migrant workers (who were known as "low-cost"

laborers in the West) came from poor inland provinces. Thanks to the loneliness and boredom, some of the most depressed employees ended up killing themselves. Wouldn't it be better if Foxconn could set up factories in inland provinces so that workers would stay close to their families and friends, instead of migrating over a long distance to work in Shenzhen? Hopefully, not many of them would commit suicide, which would be very embarrassing to Foxconn and Apple. Since cost of living in Shenzhen rose sharply, it recently became a high-cost city in China. So moving some production inland would also help Foxconn reduce labor costs.

As a result, Foxconn recently constructed a huge new factory in Zhengzhou, Henan province, which is one of the poorest provinces south of Beijing and a major source of migrant workers. This major undertaking also earned CSR kudos from the Chinese government, which encouraged more multinationals to invest in inland, underdeveloped regions such as Henan. Now with 120,000 employees, Foxconn's Zhengzhou factory made your iPhone 6. In 2014, if you were among the first customers who ordered iPhone 6 from the United States, that iPhone package in the mail actually had a Zhengzhou address—it was *not* from an Apple factory; it was from the Foxconn factory. While no worker suicide or other incidents were reported in Zhengzhou, Foxconn for the first time also installed a large number of robots—known as Foxbots—to handle repetitive work. Robots can break down but they will never commit suicide.

Sources: Based on (1) *Bloomberg Businessweek*, 2010, Chairman Gou, September 13: 58–69; (2) *Bloomberg Businessweek*, 2011, How to beat the high cost of happy workers, May 9: 39–40; (3) W. Su, 2014, Foxconn, in M. W. Peng, *Global Business*, 3rd ed. (pp. 595–597), Cincinnati: Cengage Learning; (4) W. Su, M. W. Peng, W. Tan, & Y. Cheung, 2015, The signaling effect of corporate social responsibility in emerging economies, *Journal of Business Ethics* (in press); (5) www.foxconn.com.

Corporate social responsibility (CSR)

Consideration of, and response to, issues beyond the narrow economic, technical, and legal requirements of the firm to accomplish social benefits along with the traditional economic gains which the firm seeks.

Why were Foxconn and Apple so embarrassed by worker suicides? Why having designed and produced highly popular products such as iPhones and iPads was not enough? What else were Foxconn and Apple expected to do? This chapter helps you answer these and other questions concerning corporate social responsibility (CSR), which refers to "consideration of, and response to, issues beyond the narrow economic, technical, and legal requirements of the firm to accomplish social benefits along with the traditional economic gains which the firm seeks."[1] Although historically, issues concerning CSR have been on the "back burner" of global business discussions, these issues are increasingly brought to the forefront of corporate agendas.[2] While this chapter is positioned as the

Figure 17.1　**A Stakeholder View of the Firm**

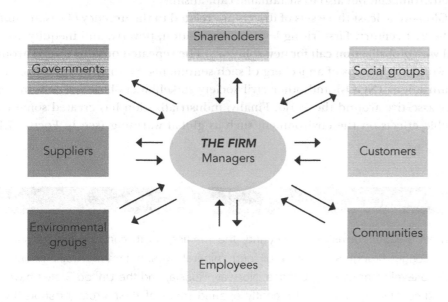

Source: Adapted from T. Donaldson & L. Preston, 1995, The stakeholder theory of the corporation: Concepts, evidence, and implications (p. 69), *Academy of Management Review*, 20: 65–91.

last in this book, by no means do we suggest that CSR is the least important topic. Instead, this chapter is one of the best ways to *integrate* previous chapters concerning international trade, investment, strategy, supply chain, and human resources.[3]

At the heart of CSR is the concept of stakeholder, which is "any group or individual who can affect or is affected by the achievement of the organization's objectives."[4] Shown in Figure 17.1, while shareholders certainly are an important group of stakeholders, other stakeholders include managers, nonmanagerial employees (hereafter "employees"), suppliers, customers, communities, governments, and social and environmental groups. Since Chapter 16 has already discussed shareholders at length, this chapter focuses on *non-shareholder stakeholders*, whom we term "stakeholders" here for compositional simplicity. One leading debate on CSR is whether managers' efforts to promote the interests of these stakeholders are at odds with their fiduciary duty (required by law) to safeguard shareholder interests.[5] To the extent that firms are *not* social agencies and that their primary function is to serve as economic enterprises, it is certainly true that firms should not (and are unable to) take on all the social problems of the world. However, failing to heed to certain CSR imperatives may be self-defeating in the long run (see the Opening Case).

The remainder of this chapter first introduces a stakeholder view of the firm. Then we discuss how the institution-based and resource-based views inform the CSR discussion. Debates and extensions follow.

17-1 A Stakeholder View of the Firm

17-1a A Big Picture Perspective

A stakeholder view of the firm, with a quest for global sustainability, represents a "big picture." One key goal for CSR is global sustainability, which is defined as the ability "to meet the needs of the present without compromising the ability of future

Stakeholder

Any group or individual who can affect or is affected by the achievement of the organization's objectives.

Global sustainability

The ability to meet the needs of the present without compromising the ability of future generations to meet their needs around the world.

Learning Objective

Articulate what is a stakeholder view of the firm.

generations to meet their needs."[6] It refers not only to a sustainable social and natural environment, but also to sustainable capitalism.[7]

Globally, at least three sets of drivers are related to the urgency of sustainability in the 21st century. First, rising levels of population, poverty, and inequity associated with globalization call for new solutions. The repeated protests staged around the world are but tips of an iceberg of such sentiments. Second, nongovernmental organizations (NGOs) and other civil society stakeholders have become increasingly assertive around the world. Finally, industrialization has created some irreversible effects on the environment such as global warming (see In Focus 17.1).[8]

IN FOCUS 17.1

GLOBAL WARMING AND ARCTIC BOOM

"Global warming" is one of the most dreadful terms in recent times. Hotter summers. Longer droughts. More-frequent hurricanes. Rising sea levels that may wash away many island nations and coastal regions. Can anyone like global warming? Can any firms profit from it? It turns out: Plenty.

As a stunning illustration of global warming, Arctic sea ice has lost half of its area since record keeping began in 1979. The Intergovernmental Panel on Climate Change (IPCC) predicted that Arctic summers would become ice free beginning in 2070. Other estimates moved the date to around 2035. Instead of being terrified by such warming, many people, firms, and governments in the Arctic region are excited about it.

Two sources of excitements stand out. First, ships sailing between the Pacific Ocean and the Atlantic Ocean can go through the Arctic Ocean. The distance between Shanghai and Rotterdam can be shortened by 15% if ships use the Northwest Passage going through the Canadian Arctic Archipelago and by 22% if ships sail through the Northeast Passage, which the Russians call the Northern Sea Route (NSR), by hugging the northern Siberian coast (see Figure 17.2). An expert noted that "the Arctic stands to become a central passageway for global maritime transportation, just as it already is for aviation." It is likely to become "an emerging epicenter of industry and trade akin to the Mediterranean Sea." While Canada and Russia look forward to profiting from maritime services such as refueling and pilotage, "such cities as Anchorage and Reykjavik could someday become major shipping centers and financial capitals—the high-latitude equivalents of Singapore and Dubai."

Second, the melting north can unearth tremendous oil and mineral wealth in the Arctic region. Canada, Norway, Russia, and the United States have all recently opened more of their Arctic offshore to oil exploration. Although Greenland only has 60,000 people, it is the world's largest island and its area is larger than all of Western Europe. Global warming not only means mining riches, but also Greenland's ultimate freedom: independence.

Colonized by Denmark in the 1700s, Greenland in 2009 gained more autonomy assuming self-government in all affairs except foreign affairs and defense. Denmark provided Greenland an annual grant of 3.6 billion Danish kroner (US$660 million), which is roughly a quarter of Greenland's GDP and close to half of the government budget. Both sides agreed to split revenue from oil, gas, and minerals until Greenland could earn enough so that it would not need the subsidy, which meant US$12,000 for every Greenlander. Then Greenland can gain its full independence. The Greenlandic government thus has been eager to grant permissions for energy and mining companies to explore the underground and offshore riches. For example, an Australian company called Greenland Minerals and Energy has been developing Greenland's first open pit uranium and rare earth mine. However, some environmentalists and traditionalists are not happy with such development. Overall, how to strike the right balance between exploitation and environmentalism is not only a challenge for Greenland, but also for all the communities, firms, and governments that aspire to take advantage of the coming Arctic boom.

Climate change, air and water pollution, deforestation, soil erosion, and overfishing have become problems demanding solutions (see PengAtlas Map 4.4). Because firms contribute to many of these problems, many citizens believe that firms should also take on some responsibility for solving them.

Drivers underpinning global sustainability are complex and multidimensional. For multinational enterprises (MNEs) with operations spanning the globe, their CSR areas, shown in Table 17.1, seem mind-boggling. This bewilderingly complex "big picture" forces managers to *prioritize*.[9] To be able to do that, primary and secondary stakeholders must be identified.[10]

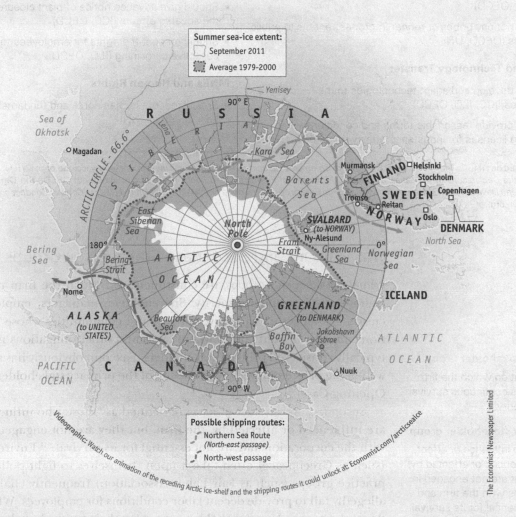

Figure 17.2 The Artic Region

Sources: *Economist*, 2012, The melting north, June 16 (special report): 4.

Source: Based on (1) *Bloomberg Businessweek*, 2014, Drill sergeant, May 5: 62–67; (2) S. Borgerson, 2013, The coming Arctic boom, *Foreign Affairs*, July: 76–89; (3) *Economist*, 2012, The melting north, June 16 (special report): 3–5; (4) *Economist*, 2012, Short and sharp, June 16 (special report): 14–15.

Table 17.1	Corporate Social Responsibilities for Multinational Enterprises (MNEs) Recommended by International Organizations

MNEs and Host Governments

- Should not interfere in the internal political affairs of the host country (OECD, UN)
- Should consult governmental authorities and national employers' and workers' organizations to ensure that their investments conform to the economic and social development policies of the host country (ICC, ILO, OECD, UN)
- Should reinvest some profits in the host country (ICC)

MNEs and Laws, Regulations, and Politics

- Should respect the right of every country to exercise control over its natural resources (UN)
- Should refrain from improper or illegal involvement in local politics (OECD)
- Should not pay bribes or render improper benefits to public servants (OECD, UN)

MNEs and Technology Transfer

- Should develop and adapt technologies to the needs of host countries (ICC, ILO, OECD)
- Should provide reasonable terms and conditions when granting licenses for industrial property rights (ICC, OECD)

MNEs and Environmental Protection

- Should respect the host country laws and regulations concerning environmental protection (OECD, UN)
- Should supply to host governments information concerning the environmental impact of MNE activities (ICC, UN)

MNEs and Consumer Protection

- Should preserve the safety and health of consumers by disclosing appropriate information, labeling correctly, and advertising accurately (UN)

MNEs and Employment Practices

- Should cooperate with host governments to create jobs in certain locations (ICC)
- Should give advance notice of plant closures and mitigate the adverse effects (ICC, OECD)
- Should respect the rights for employees to engage in collective bargaining (ILO, OECD)

MNEs and Human Rights

- Should respect human rights and fundamental freedoms in host countries (UN)

Sources: Based on (1) ICC: *The International Chamber of Commerce Guidelines for International Investment* (www.iccwbo.org); (2) ILO: *The International Labor Office Tripartite Declarations of Principles Concerning Multinational Enterprises and Social Policy* (www.ilo.org); (3) OECD: *The Organization for Economic Cooperation and Development Guidelines for Multinational Enterprises* (www.oecd.org); (4) UN: *The United Nations Code of Conduct on Transnational Corporations* (www.un.org).

17-1b Primary and Secondary Stakeholder Groups

Primary stakeholder group

Constituent on which the firm relies for its continuous survival and prosperity.

Secondary stakeholder group

Those who influence or affect, or are influenced or affected by, the firm but are not engaged in transactions with the firm and are not essential for its survival.

Triple bottom line

Economic, social, and environmental performance that simultaneously satisfies the demands of all stakeholder groups.

Primary stakeholder groups are constituents on which the firm relies for its continuous survival and prosperity. Shareholders, managers, employees, suppliers, customers—together with governments and communities whose laws and regulations must be obeyed and to whom taxes and other obligations may be due—are typically considered primary stakeholders. Foxconn obviously has to care about the well-being of its employees, who are one of the primary stakeholder groups (see the Opening Case).

Secondary stakeholder groups are defined as "those who influence or affect, or are influenced or affected by, the firm, but they are not engaged in transactions with the corporation and are not essential for its survival."[11] Environmental groups (such as Greenpeace) often take it upon themselves to fight pollution. Fair labor practice groups (such as Fair Labor Association) frequently challenge firms that allegedly fail to provide decent labor conditions for employees. While firms do not depend on secondary stakeholder groups for their survival, such groups may have the potential to cause significant embarrassment and damage—think of Nike in the 1990s.

One key proposition of the stakeholder view of the firm is that instead of only pursuing economic bottom line such as profits and shareholder returns, firms should pursue a more balanced set of triple bottom line, consisting of *economic, social,* and *environmental* performance, by simultaneously satisfying the demands of all stakeholder groups. Since competing demands obviously exist, it seems evident that the CSR proposition represents a dilemma (see the Closing Case). In fact, it has provoked a fundamental debate introduced next.

17-1c A Fundamental Debate

The CSR debate centers on the nature of the firm in society. Why does the firm exist? Most people would intuitively answer, "To make money." Milton Friedman, a former University of Chicago economist and Nobel laureate, eloquently argued: "The business of business is business."[12] The idea that the firm is an economic enterprise seems uncontroversial. At issue is whether the firm is *only* an economic enterprise.[13]

One side of the debate argues that "the social responsibility of business is to increase its profits," which is the title of Friedman's influential article mentioned earlier, published in 1970. This free market school of thought draws upon Adam Smith's idea that pursuit of economic self-interest (within legal and ethical bounds) leads to efficient markets. Free market advocates believe that the first and foremost stakeholder group is shareholders, whose interests managers have a fiduciary duty to look after. To the extent that the hallmark of our economic system remains capitalism, the providers of capital—namely, capitalists or shareholders—deserve utmost managerial attention. Since the 1980s, a term that explicitly places shareholders as the single most important stakeholder group, *shareholder capitalism,* has become increasingly influential around the world (see Chapter 16).

Free market advocates argue that if firms attempt to attain social goals, such as providing employment and social welfare, managers will lose their focus on profit maximization (and its derivative, shareholder value maximization). Consequently, firms may lose their character as capitalistic enterprises and become *socialist* organizations. This perception of socialist organization is not a pure argumentative point, but an accurate characterization of numerous state-owned enterprises (SOEs) throughout the pre-reform Soviet Union, Eastern Europe, and China, as well as other developing countries in Africa, Asia, and Latin America. To privatize, in essence, is to remove the social function of these firms and restore their economic focus through private ownership (see Chapter 16). Overall, the free market school is influential around the world. It has also provided much of the intellectual underpinning for globalization spearheaded by MNEs.

It is against such a formidable and influential school of thought that the CSR movement has emerged.[14] CSR advocates argue that a free market system that takes the pursuit of self-interest and profit as its guiding light—although in theory constrained by rules, contracts, and property rights—may in practice fail to constrain itself, thus often breeding greed, excesses, and abuses. Firms and managers, if left to their own devices, may choose self-interest over public interest. The financial meltdown in 2008 and 2009 is often fingered as a case in point. While not denying that shareholders are important stakeholders, CSR advocates argue that all stakeholders have an *equal* right to bargain for a "fair deal." Given the often-conflicting demands of stakeholders, the very purpose of the firm, instead of being a profit-maximizing entity, is argued to serve as a vehicle for coordinating their interests. Of course, one very thorny issue in the debate is whether all stakeholders indeed have an equal right and how to manage their (sometimes inevitable) conflicts.[15]

Starting in the 1970s as a peripheral voice in an ocean of free market believers, the CSR school of thought has slowly but surely made progress in becoming a more central part of global business discussions. Recently even competitiveness guru Michael Porter has been vehemently advocating the importance of creating shared value, "which involves creating economic value in a way that also creates value for society by addressing its needs and challenges" (see In Focus 17.2).

The CSR school has two driving forces. First, even as free markets march around the world, the gap between the haves and have-nots has *widened*. Although many emerging economies have been growing by leaps and bounds, the per capita income gap between developed economies and much of the developing world has widened.[16] While 2% of the world's children living in America enjoy 50% of the world's toys, one-quarter of the children in Bangladesh and Nigeria are in their countries' work force. Within developed economies such as the United States, the income gap between the upper and lower echelons of society has widened. In 1980, the average American CEO was paid 40 times more than the average worker. The ratio is now above 400. Although American society accepts greater income inequality than many others do, aggregate data of such

IN FOCUS 17.2
MICHAEL PORTER ON CREATING SHARED VALUE

Ethical Dilemma

The capitalist system is under siege. In recent years, business increasingly has been viewed as a major cause of social, environmental, and economic problems. Companies are widely perceived to be prospering at the expense of the broader community.

Even worse, the more business has begun to embrace CSR, the more it has been blamed for society's failures. The legitimacy of business has fallen to levels not seen in recent history. This diminished trust in business leads political leaders to set policies that undermine competitiveness and sap economic growth. Business is caught in a vicious circle.

A big part of the problem lies with companies themselves, which remain trapped in an outdated approach to value creation that has emerged over the past few decades. They continue to view value creation narrowly, optimizing short-term financial performance in a bubble while missing the most important customer needs and ignoring the broader influences that determine their long-term success. How else could companies overlook the well-being of customers, the depletion of natural resources vital to their businesses,

the viability of key suppliers, or the economic distress of the communities in which they produce and sell? How else could companies think that simply shifting activities to locations with even lower wages was a sustainable "solution" to competitive challenge? Government and civil society have often exacerbated the problem by attempting to address social weaknesses at the expense of business. The presumed trade-offs between economic efficiency and social progress have been institutionalized in decades of policy choices.

Companies must take the lead in bringing business and society back together. The recognition is there among sophisticated business and thought leaders, and promising elements of a new model are emerging. Yet, we still lack an overall framework for guiding these efforts, and most companies remain stuck in a "CSR" mindset in which societal issues are at the periphery, not the core.

The solution lies in the principles of shared value, which involves creating economic value in a way that *also* creates value for society by addressing its needs and challenges. Businesses must reconnect company widening inequality, which both inform and numb, often serve as a stimulus for reforming the "leaner and meaner" capitalism. Participants in the Occupy Wall Street movement in 2011 argued that the 1% have gained at the expense of the 99%.[17] However, the response from free market advocates is that to the extent there is competition, there will always be *both* winners and losers. What CSR critics describe as "greed" is often translated as "incentive" in the vocabulary of free market advocates.

A second reason behind the rise of CSR seems to be waves of disasters and scandals.[18] In 1989, the oil tanker *Exxon Valdez* spilled its cargo of oil in the pristine waters of Alaska. In 2002, scandals of Enron, WorldCom, Royal Ahold, and Parmalat rocked the world. In 2009, excessive amounts of Wall Street bonuses distributed by financial services firms receiving government bailout funds were criticized as being socially insensitive and irresponsible. In 2010, BP made a huge mess in the Gulf of Mexico. In 2011, a Japanese earthquake triggered the meltdown of the Fukushima nuclear power station. Not surprisingly, new disasters and scandals often propel CSR to the forefront of public policy and management discussions.

Gamma-Rapho/Getty Images

In what ways do manmade accidents and natural disasters, like the 2011 earthquake in Japan, affect people, businesses, communities, and the environment?

success with social progress. Shared value is not CSR, philanthropy, or even sustainability, but a new way to achieve economic success. It is not on the margin of what companies do but at the center. We believe that it can give rise to the next major transformation of business thinking.

A growing number of companies known for their hard-nosed approach to business—such as GE, Google, IBM, Intel, Johnson & Johnson, Nestlé, Unilever, and Wal-Mart—have already embarked on important efforts to create shared value by reconceiving the intersection between society and corporate performance. Yet, our recognition of the transformative power of shared value is still in its genesis. Realizing it will require leaders and managers to develop new skills and knowledge—such as a far deeper appreciation of societal needs, a greater understanding of the true bases of company productivity, and the ability to collaborate across profit/nonprofit boundaries. Government must learn how to regulate in ways that enable shared value rather than work against it.

Capitalism is an unparalleled vehicle for meeting human needs, improving efficiency, creating jobs, and building wealth. But a narrow conception of capitalism has prevented business from harnessing its full potential to meet society's broader challenges. The opportunities have been there all along but have been overlooked. Businesses acting as businesses, not as charitable donors, are the most powerful force for addressing the pressing issues we face. The moment for a new conception of capitalism is now; society's needs are large and growing, while customers, employees, and a new generation of young people are asking business to step up.

The purpose of the corporation must be redefined as creating shared value, not just profit per se. This will drive the next wave of innovation and productivity growth in the global economy. It will also reshape capitalism and its relationship to society. Perhaps most important of all, learning how to create shared value is our best chance to legitimate business again.

Source: Excerpts from M. E. Porter & M.R. Kramer, 2011, Creating shared value, *Harvard Business Review*, January–February: 62–77. Michael Porter is a professor at Harvard Business School, and Mark Kramer is managing director of FSG, a global social impact consulting firm that he cofounded with Porter.

Overall, managers as a stakeholder group are unique in that they are the only group positioned at the center of all these relationships.[19] It is important to understand how they make decisions concerning CSR, as illustrated next.

Learning Objective
Apply the institution-based and resource-based views to analyze corporate social responsibility (CSR).

17-2 Institutions, Resources, and Corporate Social Responsibility

While some people do not view CSR as an integral part of global business, Figure 17.3 shows that the two traditional perspectives that we have used throughout the book thus far can inform CSR discussions with relatively little adaptation. This section articulates why this is the case.

17-2a Institutions and CSR

The institution-based view sheds considerable light on the gradual diffusion of the CSR movement and the strategic responses of firms.[20] At the most fundamental level, regulatory pressures underpin *formal* institutions, whereas normative and cognitive pressures support *informal* institutions.[21] The strategic response framework consists of (1) reactive, (2) defensive, (3) accommodative, and (4) proactive strategies, as first introduced in Chapter 3 (see Table 3.5). This framework can be extended to explore how firms make CSR decisions, as outlined in Table 17.2.

A reactive strategy is indicated by relatively little or no support by top management of CSR causes. Firms do not feel compelled to act in the absence of disasters and outcries. Even when problems arise, denial is usually the first line of defense. Put another way, the need to accept some CSR is neither internalized through cognitive beliefs, nor does it result in any norms in practice. That leaves only formal regulatory pressures to compel firms to comply. For example, in the United States, food and drug safety standards that we take for granted today were fought by food and drug companies in the early half of the 20th century. The basic idea that food and drugs should be tested before being sold to customers and patients was bitterly contested, even as unsafe foods and drugs killed thousands of people. As a result,

---

Figure 17.3 **Institutions, Resources, and Corporate Social Responsibility**

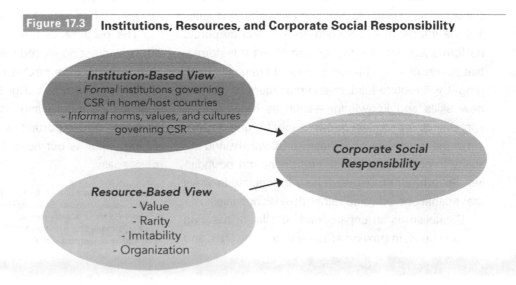

Reactive strategy
A strategy that would only respond to CSR causes when required by disasters and outcries.

Table 17.2	The US Chemical Industry Responds to Environmental Pressures	
Phase	**Strategic response**	**Representative statements from the industry's trade journal, *Chemical Week***
1962–70	Reactive	Denied the severity of environmental problems and argued that these problems could be solved independently through the industry's technological prowess.
1971–82	Defensive	"Congress seems determined to add one more regulation to the already 27 health and safety regulations we must answer to. This will make the EPA [Environmental Protection Agency] a chemical czar. No agency in a democracy should have that authority" (1975).
1983–88	Accommodative	"The EPA has been criticized for going too slow. . . . Still, we think that it is doing a good job" (1982). "Critics expect an overnight fix. The EPA deserves credit for its pace and accomplishments" (1982).
1989–present	Proactive	"Green line equals bottom line—The Clean Air Act (CAA) equals efficiency. Everything you hear about the 'costs' of complying with the CAA is probably wrong ... Wiser competitors will rush to exploit the Green Revolution" (1990).

Sources: Extracted from text from A. Hoffman, 1999, Institutional evolution and change: Environmentalism and the US chemical industry, *Academy of Management Journal*, 42: 351–371. Hoffman's last phase ended in 1993. Its extension to the present is done by the present author.

the Food and Drug Administration (FDA) was progressively granted more powers. That era is not necessarily over. Today, many dietary supplement makers, which are beyond the FDA's regulatory reach, continue to sell untested supplements and deny responsibility.

A defensive strategy focuses on regulatory compliance. Top management involvement is piecemeal at best, and the general attitude is that CSR is an added cost or nuisance. Firms admit responsibility but often fight it. After the establishment of the Environmental Protection Agency (EPA) in 1970, the US chemical industry resisted the EPA's intrusion (see Table 17.2). The regulatory requirements were at significant odds with the norms and cognitive beliefs held by the industry at that time.

How do various institutional pressures change firm behavior? In the absence of informal normative and cognitive beliefs, formal regulatory pressures are the only feasible way to push firms ahead.[22] One key insight of the institution-based view is that individuals and organizations make *rational* choices given the right kind of incentives. For example, one efficient way to control pollution is to make polluters pay some "green" taxes—ranging from gasoline retail taxes to landfill charges. But how demanding these regulatory pressures should be remains controversial. One side of the debate argues that tough environmental regulation may lead to higher costs and reduced competitiveness, especially when competing with foreign rivals that are not subject to such demanding regulations. Others argue, however, that "green" taxes simply force firms to pay real costs that they otherwise place on others. If a firm pollutes, it is imposing a cost on the surrounding community that must either live with the pollution or pay to clean it up. By imposing a pollution tax that roughly equals the cost to the community, the firm has to account for pollution as a real cost. Economists refer to this as "internalizing an externality."

CSR advocates, endorsed by former vice president and Nobel laureate Al Gore, further argue that stringent environmental regulation may force firms to innovate, however reluctantly, thus benefiting the competitiveness of both the industry and country.[23] For example, a Japanese law set standards to make

Defensive strategy

A strategy that focuses on regulatory compliance but with little actual commitment to CSR by top management.

products easier to disassemble. Although Hitachi initially resisted the law, it responded by redesigning products to simplify disassembly. The firm reduced the parts in its washing machines by 16% and in vacuum cleaners by 30%. The products became not only easier to disassemble, but also easier and cheaper to *assemble* in the first place, thus providing Hitachi with a significant cost advantage.

The accommodative strategy is characterized by some support from top managers, who may increasingly view CSR as a worthwhile endeavor. Since formal regulations may be in place and informal social and environmental pressures may be increasing, a number of firms themselves may be concerned about CSR, leading to the emergence of some new industry norms. Further, new managers who are passionate about, or sympathetic toward, CSR causes may join the organization, or some traditional managers may change their outlook, leading to increasingly strong cognitive beliefs that CSR is the right thing to do.[24] In other words, from both normative and cognitive standpoints, it becomes legitimate or a matter of social obligation to accept responsibility and do all that is required.[25] For example, in the US chemical industry, such a transformation probably took place in the early 1980s (see Table 17.2). More recently, Burger King, Kraft, Nestlé, and Unilever were pressured by Greenpeace to be concerned about the deforestation practices undertaken by their major palm oil supplier, Sinar Mas, in Indonesia. Eventually, the food giants accommodated Greenpeace's demands and dumped Sinar Mas as a supplier, leading to a new industry norm that is more earth friendly.[26]

Adopting a code of conduct is a tangible indication of a firm's willingness to accept CSR. A code of conduct (sometimes called a code of ethics) is a set of written policies and standards outlining the proper practices for a firm. The global diffusion of codes of conduct is subject to intense debate. First, some argue that firms adopting these codes are not necessarily sincere. This *negative* view suggests that an apparent interest in CSR may simply be window dressing. Some firms feel compelled to appear sensitive to CSR, following what others are doing, but have not truly and genuinely internalized CSR concerns.[27] For example, in 2009, BP implemented a new safety-oriented operating management system.[28] But after the 2010 oil spill, it became apparent that this system had not been seriously implemented, and the result was a huge catastrophe.

Second, an *instrumental* view suggests that CSR activities simply represent a useful instrument to make good profits.[29] Firms are not necessarily becoming more ethical. For example, after the 2010 oil spill, BP reshuffled management and created a new worldwide safety division. The instrumental view would argue that these actions did not really mean that BP became more ethical.

Finally, a *positive* view believes that (at least some) firms and managers may be self-motivated to do it right regardless of social pressures.[30] Codes of conduct tangibly express values that organizational members view as central and enduring.

The institution-based view suggests that all three perspectives are probably valid. This is to be expected, given how institutional pressures work to instill value.[31]

Accommodative strategy

A strategy characterized by some support from top managers, who may increasingly view CSR as a worthwhile endeavor.

Tom Atkeson/U.S. Coast Guard/MCT /Getty Images

Is a written code of conduct enough to ensure that a firm has truly become ethical?

Regardless of actual motive, the fact that firms are practicing CSR is indicative of the rising *legitimacy* of CSR on the management agenda.[32] Even firms that adopt a code of conduct simply as window dressing open doors for more scrutiny by concerned stakeholders, because they have publicized a set of CSR criteria against which they can be judged. Such pressures are likely to transform the firms internally into more self-motivated, better corporate citizens. Thus, it probably is fair to say that Nike is a more responsible corporate citizen in 2014 than it was in 1994.

From a CSR perspective, the best firms embrace a proactive strategy when engaging in CSR, constantly anticipating responsibility and endeavoring to do more than is required.[33] Top management at a proactive firm not only supports and champions CSR activities, but also views CSR as a source of differentiation that permeates the corporate DNA. Whole Foods' co-founder and co-CEO John Mackey commented:

> When people are really happy in their jobs, they provide much higher degrees of service to the customers. Happy team members result in happy customers. Happy customers do more business with you. They become advocates for your enterprise, which results in happy investors. That is a win-win-win-win strategy. You can expand it to include your suppliers and the communities where you do business, which are tied in to this prosperity circle.[34]

Similarly, since 2001 Starbucks has voluntarily published an annual report on CSR, which embodies its founder, chairman, and CEO Howard Schultz's vision that "we must balance our responsibility to create value for shareholders with a social conscience."[35]

Proactive firms often engage in three areas of activity. First, some firms, such as Swiss Re and Duke Energy, actively participate in regional, national, and international policy and standards discussions.[36] To the extent that policy and standards discussions today may become regulations in the future, it seems better to get involved early and (hopefully) steer the course in a favorable direction. Otherwise—as the saying goes—if you're not at the table, you're on the menu. For example, Duke Energy operates 20 coal-fired power plants in five states. It is the third-largest US emitter of CO_2 and the 12th largest in the world. But its CEO, Jim Rogers, has proactively worked with green technology producers, activists, and politicians to engage in policy and legislative discussions. These are not merely defensive moves to protect his firm and the power utility industry. Unlike his industry peers, Rogers has been "bitten by the climate bug" and is genuinely interested in reducing greenhouse gas emissions.[37]

Second, proactive firms build alliances with stakeholder groups. For example, many firms collaborate with NGOs.[38] Because of the historical tension and distrust, these "sleeping with the enemy" alliances are not easy to handle. The key lies in identifying relatively short-term, manageable projects of mutual interests. For instance, Starbucks collaborated with Conservation International to help reduce deforestation practices.

Third, proactive firms often engage in *voluntary* activities that go beyond what is required by regulations.[39] While examples of industry-specific self-regulation abound, an area of intense global interest is the pursuit of the International Standards Organization (ISO) 14001 certification of the environment management system (EMS). Headquartered in Geneva, Switzerland, the ISO is an influential NGO consisting of national standards bodies in 111 countries. Launched in 1996, the ISO 14001 EMS has become the gold standard for CSR-conscious firms. Although not required by law, many MNEs, such as Ford and IBM, have adopted ISO 14001 standards in all

Proactive strategy

A strategy that endeavors to do more than is required in CSR.

their facilities worldwide. Firms such as General Motors, Siemens, and Toyota have demanded that all of their top-tier suppliers be ISO 14001 certified.

From an institutional perspective, these proactive activities are indicative of the normative and cognitive beliefs held by many managers on the importance of doing the right thing.[40] While there is probably a certain element of window dressing and a quest for better profits, it is obvious that these efforts provide some tangible social and environmental benefits.

Overall, the typology of (1) reactive, (2) defensive, (3) accommodative, and (4) proactive strategies is an interesting menu provided for different firms to choose. At present, the number of proactive firms is still a minority. While many firms are compelled to do something, a lot of CSR activities probably are still window dressing. Only sustained pressures along regulatory, normative, and cognitive dimensions may push and pull more firms to do more. Since CSR cannot be embarked upon in a vacuum, a firm's particular strategy needs to have some alignment with the CSR

IN FOCUS 17.3

MARKS & SPENCER'S PLAN A

Founded in 1884, Marks & Spencer (M&S) is a leading UK retailer specializing in clothing and luxury food products. It is the UK's largest clothing retailer with a 12% market share. It also has 4% of the UK food market. Listed on the London Stock Exchange, M&S is a constituent member of the FTSE 100 Index. In the mid 2010s, it had 86,000 employees, more than 700 stores in the UK, and 300-plus stores in more than 40 other countries, serving approximately 21 million customers every week.

In 2007, M&S launched an ambitious corporate-wide Plan A—a five-year plan that addressed some of the biggest social and environmental challenges with 100 concrete commitments that it aspired to achieve by 2012. In 2010, following three years of successful implementation of Plan A, M&S added 80 commitments. Every store had a dedicated Plan A champion. Plan A was divided into five areas (with leading examples):

- Climate change (such as becoming carbon neutral for all its UK and Irish operations).
- Waste reduction (such as sending no waste to landfills).
- Sustainable raw materials (such as tripling sales of organic food).
- Fair partnership with suppliers (such as introducing random checking of suppliers to ensure that M&S's Global Sourcing Principles are being adhered to at all times).

- A healthy lifestyle for customers and employees (such as introducing more nutritionally balanced food).

In Plan A's first year (2007), M&S reduced energy-related CO_2 emissions from its stores and offices by 55,000 tons, opened three pilot "eco-stores," and completed a carbon footprint assessment for its food business. Among its numerous actions was an effort to reduce plastic shopping bags, which were always given away free of charge. M&S argued that from an environmental standpoint, plastic bags are not "free" because they are not biodegradable and will be stuck in landfills forever. Starting in 2007, its 50 stores in Southwest England and Northern Ireland gave customers a free cloth Bag for Life. After four weeks, these trial stores started charging 10 pence (US$0.16) for each Bag for Life (which would be replaced free of charge when worn out), and five pence (US$0.08) for each plastic food carrier bag. The effect was immediate: in trial stores, the customer use of food carrier bags dropped by more than 70%, and M&S also sold eight times more Bags for Life than it did in 2006. Overall, in 2007, M&S reduced its use of plastic bags by 11% across all its stores—a total of 37 million *fewer* bags given out. All profits from the sale of bags in 2007, more than US$125,000, went to an environmental charity, Groundwork. Based on these successful trials, M&S rolled out its program to

propensity of its consumers, employees, and other stakeholders. After implementing its Plan A, Marks & Spencer (M&S) reported interesting data on the distribution of its consumers and employees along the four dimensions (In Focus 17.3). In other words, it is not realistic to implement a proactive strategy when the firm has numerous reactive employees and consumers.

17-2b Resources and CSR

CSR-related resources can include *tangible* technologies and processes as well as *intangible* skills and attitudes.[41] The VRIO framework can shed considerable light on CSR.

Value. Do CSR-related resources and capabilities add *value*?[42] This is the litmus test for CSR work (see the Closing Case). Many large firms, especially MNEs, can apply their financial, technological, and human resources toward a variety of CSR causes. For example, firms can choose to appease environmental groups by purchasing energy only from "green" power sources. Or firms can respond to human

---

Table 17.3 **Distribution of Marks & Spencer's Consumers and Employees**

Conceptual category	M&S's label	Percentage of consumers	Percentage of employees
Reactive	"Not my problem"	24%	1%
Defensive	"What's the point"	38%	21%
Accommodative	"If it's easy"	27%	54%
Proactive	"Green crusaders"	11%	24%

Source: Based on text in Marks & Spencer, 2008, *Plan A: Year 1 Review* (p. 16), January 15, plana.marksandspencer.com.

---

charge for shopping bags in all its UK and Irish stores in 2008.

Although clearly motivated by considerations for corporate social responsibility (CSR), M&S was careful *not* to label this program a "CSR" plan. The committee in charge of Plan A was called the "How We Do Business" (HWDB) Committee, which was headed by the CEO. Where did the term "Plan A" come from? According to Plan A's website: "We're calling it Plan A because we believe it's now the only way to do business. There is no Plan B."

CSR efforts obviously cannot be embarked upon in a vacuum. Of course neither all M&S's employees are true believers, nor are all its consumers. However, using the typology of four categories—reactive, defensive, accommodative, and proactive—M&S has a higher percentage of employees in the accommodative and proactive categories (see Table 17.3).

"Backed by a strong business case," said Richard Gillies, director of Plan A, CSR, and sustainable business, "Plan A is at the heart of the exciting new growth plan for M&S, both in the UK and internationally." Starting in its first year, Plan A earned numerous kudos from various CSR groups. M&S led the global retail sector in the Dow Jones Sustainability Index. It was awarded the World Environment Center Gold Medal for Sustainable Business. In the UK, it received recognition from Greenpeace, Compassion in World Farming, and National Consumer Council. In 2014, M&S launched Plan A 2020 with a new set of ambitious challenges in an effort to scale new heights.

Sources: Based on (1) *Economist*, 2008, Just good business, January 19: 3–6; (2) M&S, 2007, *Plan A News*, plana. marksandspencer.com; (3) M&S, 2008, *Plan A: Year 1 Review*, January 15, plana.marksandspencer.com; (4) M&S, 2011, *How We Do Business Report 2011*, plana.marksandspencer.com; (5) M&S, 2014, Introducing Plan A 2020, planareport.marksandspencer.com.

rights groups by not doing business with countries accused of human rights violations. These activities can be categorized as social issue participation, which refers to a firm's participation in social causes not directly related to the management of its primary stakeholders. Such activities may actually *reduce* shareholder value.[43] Although social issue participation may create some remote social and environmental benefits, it does not satisfy the economic leg of the triple bottom line, so these abilities do not qualify as value-adding firm resources.

Rarity. CSR-related resources are not always *rare*. Even a valuable resource is not likely to provide a significant advantage if competitors also possess it. For example, both Home Depot and Lowe's have NGOs such as the Forest Stewardship Council certify that suppliers in Brazil, Indonesia, and Malaysia use only material from renewable forests. These complex processes require strong management capabilities, such as negotiating with local suppliers, undertaking internal verification, coordinating with NGOs for external verification, and disseminating such information to stakeholders. Such capabilities are valuable. But since both competitors possess capabilities to manage these processes, they are common (but not rare) resources.

Imitability. Although valuable and rare resources may provide some competitive advantage, the advantage will only be temporary if competitors can *imitate* it. Resources must be not only valuable and rare, but also hard to imitate in order to give firms a sustainable (not merely temporary) competitive advantage. At some firms, CSR-related capabilities are deeply embedded in idiosyncratic managerial and employee skills, attitudes, and interpretations. The socially complex way of channeling organizational energy and conviction toward CSR at M&S cannot be easily imitated (see In Focus 17.3).

Organization. Does the firm have *organizational* capabilities to do a good job on CSR? Numerous components within a firm, such as formal management control systems and informal social relationships, may be relevant. These components are often called complementary assets (see Chapter 4), because, by themselves, they typically do not generate advantage. However, complementary assets, when combined with valuable, rare, and hard-to-imitate capabilities, may enable a firm to fully utilize its CSR potential.

For example, assume that Firm A is able to overcome the three hurdles mentioned above (V, R, I) by achieving a comprehensive understanding of some competitors' best practices in pollution prevention. Although Firm A has every intention to implement such best practices, chances are that they will not work unless Firm A also possesses a number of complementary assets. Process-focused best practices of pollution prevention are not in isolation and are often difficult to separate from a firm's other activities. These best practices require a number of complementary assets, such as a continuous emphasis on process innovation and a dedicated workforce. These complementary assets are not developed as part of new environmental strategies; rather, they are grown from more general business strategies such as differentiation. If such complementary assets are already in place, they can be leveraged in the new pursuit of best environmental practices. Otherwise, single-minded imitation is not likely to be effective.

Social issue participation

Firms' participation in social causes not directly related to the management of primary stakeholders.

The CSR-Economic Performance Puzzle. The resource-based view helps solve a major puzzle in the CSR debate: the CSR-economic performance puzzle. The puzzle—a source of frustration to CSR advocates—is why there is no conclusive evidence on a direct, positive link between CSR and *economic* performance such as profits and shareholder returns. Although some studies do indeed report a *positive* relationship,[44] others find a *negative* relationship[45] or *no* relationship.[46] Viewed together, "CSR does not hurt [economic] performance, but there is no concrete support to believe that it leads to supranormal [economic] returns."[47]

While there can be a number of explanations for this intriguing mess, a resource-based explanation suggests that because of the capability constraints discussed above, many firms are not cut out for a CSR-intensive (differentiation) strategy.[48] Since all studies have some sampling bias (no study is perfect), studies that oversample firms not yet ready for a high level of CSR activities are likely to report a negative relationship between CSR and economic performance. Likewise, studies that oversample firms ready for CSR may find a positive relationship. Also, studies with more balanced (more random) samples may fail to find any statistically significant relationship. In summary, since each firm is different (a basic assumption of the resource-based view), not every firm's economic performance is likely to benefit from CSR.

17-3 Debates and Extensions

Learning Objective
Participate in two leading debates concerning CSR.

CSR has no shortage of debates. Here, we discuss two previously unexplored debates particularly relevant for international operations: (1) race to the bottom versus race to the top, and (2) active versus inactive CSR engagement overseas.

17-3a Race to the Bottom ("Pollution Haven") versus Race to the Top

One side of the debate argues that because of heavier environmental regulation in developed economies, MNEs may have an incentive to shift pollution-intensive production to developing countries with lower environmental standards. To attract investment, developing countries may enter a "race to the bottom" by lowering (or at least not tightening) environmental standards, and some may become "pollution havens" (see PengAtlas Map 4.4).

The other side argues that globalization does not necessarily have negative effects on the environment in developing countries to the extent suggested by the "pollution haven" hypothesis. This is largely due to the *voluntary* adherence of many MNEs to environmental standards higher than those required by host countries.[49] Most MNEs reportedly outperform local firms in environmental management. The underlying motivations behind MNEs' voluntary "green practices" can be attributed to (1) worldwide CSR pressures in general, (2) CSR demands made by customers in developed economies, and (3) requirements of MNE headquarters for worldwide compliance of higher CSR standards (such as ISO 14001). Although it is difficult to suggest that the "race to the bottom" does not exist, MNEs as a group do not necessarily add to the environmental burden in developing countries.[50] Some MNEs, such as Dow Chemical, have actively facilitated the diffusion of better environmental technologies to these countries.

17-3b Active versus Inactive CSR Engagement Overseas

Active CSR engagement is now increasingly expected of MNEs.[51] MNEs that fail to engage are often criticized by NGOs. In the 1990s, Shell was harshly criticized for "not lifting a finger" when the Nigerian government brutally cracked down on rebels in the Ogoni region where Shell operated. In 2009, Shell settled a long-running case brought by Ogoni activists for US$16 million.[52] However, such well-intentioned calls for greater CSR engagement are in direct conflict with a longstanding principle governing the relationship between MNEs and host countries: *non*-intervention in local affairs (see the *first* principle in Table 17.1).

The non-intervention principle originated from concerns that MNEs may engage in political activities against the national interests of the host country. Chile in the 1970s serves as a case in point. After the democratically elected socialist President Salvador Allende had threatened to expropriate the assets of MNEs, ITT (a US-based MNE), allegedly in connection with the Central Intelligence Agency (CIA), promoted a coup that killed President Allende. Consequently, the idea that MNEs should not interfere in the domestic political affairs of the host country has been enshrined in a number of codes of MNE conduct sponsored by international organizations such as the United Nations (UN).

However, CSR advocates have been emboldened by some MNEs' actions during the apartheid era in South Africa, when local laws required racial segregation of the workforce. While many MNEs withdrew, those that remained (such as BP) challenged the apartheid system, by desegregating their employees and thus undermining the government's base of power. Emboldened by the successful removal of the apartheid regime in South Africa in 1994, CSR advocates have unleashed a new campaign, stressing the necessity for MNEs to engage in actions that often constitute political activity, in particular in the human rights area. Shell, after its widely criticized (lack of) action in Nigeria, has explicitly endorsed the UN Declaration on Human Rights and supported the exercise of such rights "within the legitimate role of business."

But what exactly is the "legitimate role" of CSR initiatives in host countries? In almost every country, there are local laws and norms that some foreign MNEs may find objectionable. In Estonia, ethnic Russians are being discriminated against. In many Arab countries, women do not have the same legal rights as men. In the United States, a number of groups (ranging from Native Americans to homosexuals) claim to be discriminated against. At the heart of this debate is whether foreign MNEs should spearhead efforts to remove some of these discriminatory practices or should remain politically neutral by conforming to current host country laws and norms. This obviously is a nontrivial challenge.

Learning Objective
Draw implications for action.

17-4 Management Savvy

Concerning CSR, the institution-based and resource-based views suggest three clear implications for action (Table 17.4). First, savvy managers need to understand the formal and informal rules of the game, anticipate changes, and seek to shape such changes. In the area of climate change, although the US government refused to ratify the 1997 Kyoto Protocol and did not agree to any binding target in the 2009 Copenhagen Accord, many farsighted US managers realize that competitors based in countries whose governments support serious efforts in greenhouse gas reduction may gain a strong "green" advantage. Therefore, many US firms such as Chevron, Dow Chemical, DuPont, ExxonMobil, Google, and Microsoft voluntarily participate in CSR activities (such as being prepared to pay "green" taxes for carbon emissions—known as carbon pricing) not (yet) mandated by law, in anticipation of more stringent environmental requirements down the road.[53]

Table 17.4	**Implications for Action**

- Understand the rules of the game, anticipate changes, and seek to shape and influence such changes.

- Pick your CSR battles carefully—don't blindly imitate other firms' CSR activities.

- Integrate CSR as part of the core activities and processes of the firm—faking it doesn't last very long.

Second, savvy managers need to pick CSR battles carefully.[54] The resource-based view suggests an important lesson captured by Sun Tzu's timeless teaching: "Know yourself, know your opponents." While your opponents may engage in high-profile CSR activities, allowing them to earn a lot of bragging rights while contributing to their triple bottom line, blindly imitating these practices, while not knowing enough about "yourself" (you as a manager and the firm/unit you lead) may lead to some disappointment. Instead of always chasing the newest best practices, firms are advised to select CSR practices that fit with their *existing* resources and capabilities. For example, in a recession, launching expensive new CSR initiatives may be inadvisable. Managers have to put profitability first and be more selective about CSR involvement.

Third, given the increasingly inescapable responsibility to be good corporate citizens, managers may want to integrate CSR as part of the core activities of the firm—instead of "faking it," making cosmetic changes, or just giving away some money.[55] For example, instead of treating NGOs as threats, Dow Chemical, Home Depot, Lowe's, and Unilever work with them. The attitude viewing CSR as a nuisance may underestimate potential business opportunities brought by CSR (see In Focus 17.2).

What determines the success and failure of firms around the world? No doubt, CSR will increasingly be an important part of the answer. The best-performing firms are likely to be those that can integrate CSR activities into their core economic functions while addressing social and environmental concerns. We live in a dangerous period of global capitalism devastated by financial meltdown, economic crisis, and climate change. In the post–Great Recession and post–Occupy Wall Street world, managers, as a unique group of stakeholders, have an important and challenging responsibility to safeguard and advance capitalism. From a CSR standpoint, this means building more humane, more inclusive, and fairer firms that not only generate wealth and develop economies, but also respond to changing societal expectations concerning the social and environmental role of the firm around the world (see the Closing Case).[56]

CHAPTER SUMMARY/LEARNING OBJECTIVES

17-1 Articulate what is a stakeholder view of the firm.

- A stakeholder view of the firm urges companies to pursue a more balanced set of triple bottom line, consisting of economic, social, and environmental performance.
- Despite the fierce defense of the free market school, especially its shareholder capitalism variant, the CSR movement has now become a more central part of management discussions around the globe.

17-2 Apply the institution-based and resource-based views to analyze CSR.

- The institution-based view suggests that when confronting CSR pressures, firms may employ (1) reactive, (2) defensive, (3) accommodative, and (4) proactive strategies.
- The resource-based view suggests that not all CSR activities satisfy the VRIO requirements.

17-3 Participate in two leading debates concerning CSR.

- (1) Race to the bottom versus race to the top, and (2) active versus inactive CSR engagement overseas.

17-4 Draw implications for action.

- Understand the rules of the game, anticipate changes, and seek to influence such changes.
- Pick your CSR battles carefully—don't blindly imitate other firms' CSR activities.
- Integrate CSR as part of the core activities and processes of the firm.

KEY TERMS

Accommodative strategy, 548

Corporate social responsibility (CSR), 538

Defensive strategy, 547

Global sustainability, 539

Primary stakeholder group, 542

Proactive strategy, 549

Reactive strategy, 546

Secondary stakeholder group, 542

Social issue participation, 552

Stakeholder, 539

Triple bottom line, 542

REVIEW QUESTIONS

1. How do you define global sustainability?

2. How do the concerns of a primary stakeholder differ from those of a secondary stakeholder?

3. What does it mean for a corporation to have a triple bottom line?

4. Using Table 17.2, summarize the four types of strategies that can be used to make CSR decisions.

5. Devise two examples: one in which a firm's participation in a social issue adds value to the shareholders and one in which it decreases value in the eyes of the shareholders.

6. Using a resource-based view, explain why some firms improve their economic performance by adopting a CSR strategy, whereas others achieve either no results or damaging results.

7. Do you think "green practices" should be voluntary or mandatory for businesses? Explain your answer.

8. *ON ETHICS:* In your opinion, do you think an MNE should remain politically neutral and adopt practices and laws of the host country?

9. As a manager, what are some of the considerations you would take into account before adopting any CSR-related policy?

10. How does the concept of "picking your battles carefully" apply to CSR?

11. Using PengAtlas Map 4.2, which country, from a labor perspective, would present the biggest CSR challenge if your firm had operations in that country?

12. Using PengAtlas Map 4.3, which country, from a profit perspective, would be at the greatest risk if your firm aggressively pursued in CSR values regarding human rights?

13. Compare PengAtlas Map. 4.4 with Map 1.1. Suppose your firm is located in a developed economy that is considering curbing carbon emissions, which could create severe problems for your firm and threaten its existence. Would you recommend relocating operations to an emerging economy that still has many people in desperate need of employment and where the government is defiantly resisting any restrictions to curb such emissions because its scientists have different views of the risks than many in the United States? What are the pros and cons of relocating?

CRITICAL DISCUSSION QUESTIONS

1. *ON ETHICS:* In a landmark case in 1919, *Dodge v. Ford*, the Michigan State Supreme Court determined whether or not Henry Ford could withhold dividends from the Dodge brothers (and other shareholders of the Ford Motor Company) to engage in what today would be called CSR activities. With a resounding "No," the court opined, "A business organization is organized and carried on primarily for the profits of the stockholders." If the court in your country were to decide on this case this year (or in 2019), what do you think would be the likely outcome?

2. *ON ETHICS:* Your employer encourages you to contribute to CSR causes using your personal time. Is your employer being ethical or unethical? Why?

3. *ON ETHICS:* Your CPA firm is organizing a one-day-long CSR activity using company time, such as cleaning up a dirty road or picking up trash on the beach. A colleague tells you: "This is so stupid! I already have so much unfinished work. Now to take a *whole* day away from work? Come on! I don't mind CSR. If the company is serious, why don't they donate one day of my earnings, which I am sure will be more than the value I can generate by cleaning up the road or picking up trash for one day? With that money, they can just hire someone to do a better job than I would." What are you going to say to her? (Your colleague makes US$73,000 a year and on a per-day basis she makes US$200.)

4. *ON ETHICS:* Hypothetically, your MNE is the largest foreign investor in Vietnam, where dissidents and religious leaders are reportedly being persecuted. As the country manager there, you understand that the MNE is being pressured by NGOs to help the oppressed groups in Vietnam. But you also understand that the host government would be upset if your firm were found to engage in local political activities deemed inappropriate. These alleged activities, which you personally find distasteful, are not directly related to your operations. How would you proceed?

BUSINESS
INSIGHTS
GLOBAL

GLOBAL ACTION

1. **China has been a recipient of considerable investment recently. However, little research has been conducted by the green technologies company for which you work concerning the exact nature of socially responsible technology investment. Since your firm's goal is to operate in China that promotes social responsibility, you must identify the sectors of green technology that receive the most investment. Develop a report that addresses this issue and adds to the development of your company's strategy in China. Based on your analysis, be sure to include possible new products that may be introduced in the Chinese market.**

2. **Microfinance is an emerging area of individualized financial investment in developing countries that is based on social responsibility principles. However, since it involves the investment of resources with the expectation that a profit will be made, microfinance investors tend to search for regions and portfolios that have the highest profitability. Analyze information in a global data set to determine which areas of the world seem to have the most profitable microfinance activities. What conclusions can you draw from this information?**

CLOSING CASE

Ethical Dilemma

EMERGING MARKETS: The Ebola Challenge

First reported in 1976 in Sudan and Zaire (now called the Democratic Republic of the Congo [DRC]), Ebola has been a known virus for four decades. Yet, there is still no effective vaccine or medicine. Between 1976 and 2013, there were 24 outbreaks in Sub-Saharan Africa, with 1,716 cases. What really put Ebola on the center stage of global media—and on the pages of this book—was the 2014 outbreak, which was the most devastating outbreak with 15,000 reported cases and 6,000 deaths. Starting in Guinea, Liberia, and Sierra Leone, the disease quickly diffused to other West African countries, such as the DRC, Nigeria, and Senegal. By September 2014, a Liberian man who traveled to Dallas, Texas, was diagnosed to have Ebola. He died in early October. Two American nurses who treated the patient became the first confirmed cases to be infected by Ebola in the United States, triggering panic and chaos not only in Texas but also in other parts of the country. State governments in Connecticut, Illinois, New Jersey, and New York demanded that

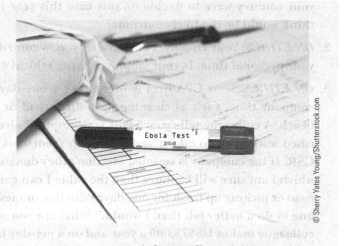

anyone who traveled from affected West African countries be subject to 21 days of quarantine—the longest period the Ebola virus was thought to need to incubate. In mid October 2014, President Obama appointed a national Ebola response coordinator. All passengers arriving from affected African countries now had to go through screening, and all patients showing up at a US health care establishment had to

© Sherry Yates Young/Shutterstock.com

answer a questionnaire regarding whether they traveled from these countries.

In the absence of effective vaccine or medicine, treatment was indirect. It centered on early supportive care with rehydration and symptomatic treatment. The measures would include management of pain, nausea, fever, and anxiety, as well as rehydration via the oral or by intravenous (IV) route. Blood products such as packed red blood cells, platelets or fresh frozen plasma might also be used. Intensive care was often used in the developed world. This might include maintaining blood volume and electrolytes (salts) balance as well as treating any bacterial infections. Thankfully, the two American nurses recovered after several weeks of treatment, as did the other six American health care workers who went to Africa and came home with Ebola. By December 2014, there had been ten Ebola cases in the United States, and only two resulted in death—the second case of death was an African doctor who was contaminated by his patients in an Ebola-infested country.

Throughout the crisis, the initial silence of the pharmaceutical industry was conspicuous. Dr. Margaret Chan, Director-General of the World Health Organization (WHO), criticized the industry for failing to develop a vaccine for Ebola over the four decades during which the virus threatened poor African countries. She complained that "a profit-driven industry does not invest in products for markets that cannot pay." Initially reluctant, some pharmaceutical firms jumped in. In October 2014, British drugmaker GlaxoSmithKline (GSK) announced that it had expedited its R&D in search of a vaccine. In 2010, the Canadian government developed an experimental vaccine VSV-EBOV and licensed it to a small, virtually unknown biotech firm NewLink Genetics in Ames, Iowa, for clinical trials. However, progress was slow and funding tight. In November 2014, a US giant, Merck, paid NewLink US$50 million to buy the rights to the vaccine and to expedite R&D. Also in November 2014, a French Big Pharma player, Sanofi, announced its intention to work with industry partners to combat Ebola. Another experimental drug ZMapp, developed by a small San Diego, California-based biopharmaceutical firm, Mapp, showed encouraging results on primates, and had been used on at least seven (human) patients in Africa in 2014. But ZMapp

had not received FDA approval. In the absence of the financial, technological, and production capabilities of Big Pharma, ZMapp's stocks quickly ran out. The US government had to provide US$25 million to scale up production.

The reason that until recently, pharmaceutical firms—especially Big Pharma firms—had been reluctant to apply their significant resources to find a cure for Ebola was simple. Even if successful, these efforts, which would mostly benefit African countries, would not be profitable. In other words, there was "no compelling business case." Now that the disease came to the United States (and a few Western European countries), firms felt compelled to move. Debates continued to rage. One side argued that pharmaceutical firms only focused on markets and products from which they could profit—with "Botox, baldness, and bonus" as their guiding light. Tropical diseases such as malaria and Ebola naturally would receive little (or no) attention. Another side argued that given limited resources, pharmaceutical firms rightly and strategically ignored (relatively) smaller-scale diseases such as Ebola, because there were other diseases such as HIV/AIDS that impact a lot more people than Ebola. A number of pharmaceutical firms jumped onto the "Ebola bandwagon" simply to earn CSR kudos, knowing that they would be unlikely to make any profits for their efforts. Or they were simply driven to do so due to public pressure— the series of eager announcements made in October and November 2014 were defensive in nature. Given the long lead time to develop any effective vaccine and the urgency to have a vaccine at hand when confronting an outbreak of Ebola (and other contagious diseases), how pharmaceutical firms manage their quest for the triple bottom line remains one of the leading strategic challenges they have to overcome.

CASE DISCUSSION QUESTIONS

1. **ON ETHICS:** Dr. Margaret Chan, Director-General of the WHO, criticized the pharmaceutical industry for being "profit-driven" and for failing to invest in the development of a vaccine or cure for Ebola. As CEO of a leading pharmaceutical firm, how do you respond to these criticisms?

2. **ON ETHICS:** As a shareholder of a pharmaceutical firm that announced its new investment to

develop an Ebola vaccine and that as a result, your dividend would be reduced, would you support or not support the firm's decision to spend your money to combat Ebola?

3. ***ON ETHICS:*** As a US government official, what would be your recommendations to incentivize pharmaceutical firms to develop an Ebola vaccine?

Sources: Based on (1) C. Campos, C. Cole, & J. Steele, 2014, Ebola and corporate social responsibility, EMBA strategy class term project, November, Jindal School of Management, University of Texas at Dallas; (2) CBC, 2014, Canada should cancel NewLink Ebola vaccine contract, November 19: www.cbc.ca; (3) *Independent*, 2014, Ebola outbreak: Why has 'Big Pharma' failed deadly virus's victims? September 7: www.independent.co.uk; (4) National Public Radio, 2014, Merck partners with NewLink to speed up work on Ebola vaccine, November 24: www.npr.org; (5) *Time*, 2014, WHO pillories drug industry for failure to develop Ebola vaccine, November 4: time.com; (5) World Health Organization, 2014, Ebola virus disease fact sheet, November: www.who.int.

NOTES

[Journal acronyms] AMJ—*Academy of Management Journal;* AMP—*Academy of Management Perspectives;* AMR—*Academy of Management Review;* BW—*BusinessWeek* (before 2010) or *Bloomberg Businessweek* (since 2010); GSJ—*Global Strategy Journal;* HBR—*Harvard Business Review;* JBE—*Journal of Business Ethics;* JIBS—*Journal of International Business Studies;* JIM—*Journal of International Management;* JMS—*Journal of Management Studies;* JWB—*Journal of World Business;* NYTM—*New York Times Magazine;* OSc—*Organization Science;* OSt—*Organization Studies;* SMJ—*Strategic Management Journal.*

1 K. Davis, 1973, The case for and against business assumption of social responsibilities (p. 312), *AMJ*, 16: 312–322. See also J. Campbell, L. Eden, & S. Miller, 2012, Multinationals and CSR in host countries, *JIBS*, 43: 84–106; D. Matten & J. Moon, 2008, "Implicit" and "explicit" CSR, *AMR*, 33: 404–424.

2 T. Devinney, A. McGahan, & M. Zollo, 2013, A research agenda for global stakeholder strategy, *GSJ*, 3: 325–337; C. Egri & D. Ralston, 2008, Corporate responsibility, *JIM*, 14: 319–339; T. London, 2009, Making better investments at the base of the pyramid, *HBR*, May: 106–113.

3 A. Scherer & G. Palazzo, 2011, The new political role of business in a globalized world, *JMS*, 48: 899–931.

4 E. Freeman, 1984, *Strategic Management: A Stakeholder Approach* (p. 46), Boston: Pitman. See also D. Crilly, 2011, Predicting stakeholder orientation in the MNE, *JIBS*, 42: 694–717; T. Jensen & J. Sandstrom, 2011, Stakeholder theory and globalization, *OSt*, 32: 473–488; A. Kacperczyk, 2009, With greater power comes greater responsibility? *SMJ*, 30: 261–285.

5 P. David, M. Bloom, & A. Hillman, 2007, Investor activism, managerial responsiveness, and corporate social performance, *SMJ*, 28: 91–100; J. Harrison, D. Bosse, & R. Phillips, 2010, Managing for stakeholders, stakeholder utility functions, and competitive advantage, *SMJ*, 31: 58–74.

6 World Commission on Environment and Development, 1987, *Our Common Future* (p. 8), Oxford: Oxford University Press.

7 S. Hart, 2005, *Capitalism at the Crossroads*, Philadelphia: Wharton School Publishing; R. Rajan, 2010, *Fault Lines*, Princeton, NJ: Princeton University Press.

8 J. Howard-Grenville, S. Buckle, B. Hoskins, & G. George, 2014, Climate change and management, *AMJ*, 57: 615–623.

9 J. Surroca, J. Tribo, & S. Zahra, 2013, Stakeholder pressure on MNEs and the transfer of socially irresponsible practices to subsidiaries, *AMJ*, 56: 549–572.

10 J. Bundy, C. Shropshire, & A. Buchholtz, 2013, Strategic cognition and issue salience, *AMR*, 38: 352–376.; J. Vergne, 2012,

Stigmatized categories and public disapproval of organizations, *AMJ*, 55: 1027–1052.

11 M. Clarkson, 1995, A stakeholder framework for analyzing and evaluating corporate social performance (p. 107), *AMR*, 20: 92–117. See also S. Waddock, 2008, Building a new institutional infrastructure for corporate responsibility, *AMP*, August: 87–109.

12 M. Friedman, 1970, The social responsibility of business is to increase its profits, *NYTM*, September 13: 32–33.

13 D. Ahlstrom, 2010, Innovation and growth, *AMP*, August: 11–24.

14 M. Hollerer, 2013, From taken-for-granted to explicit commitment, *JMS*, 50: 573–606.

15 A. Delios, 2010, How can organizations be competitive but dare to care? *AMP*, August: 25–36.

16 G. Bruton, 2010, Business and the world's poorest billion, *AMP*, August: 6–10.

17 *Economist*, 2011, Rage against the machine, October 22: 13.

18 Y. Mishina, B. Dykes, E. Block, & T. Pollock, 2010, Why "good" firms do bad things, *AMJ*, 53: 701–722; A. Muller & R. Kraussl, 2011, Doing good deeds in times of need, *SMJ*, 32: 911–929; C. Oh & J. Oetzel, 2011, Multinationals' response to major disasters, *SMJ*, 32: 658–681.

19 K. Basu & G. Palazzo, 2008, CSR, *AMR*, 33: 122–136; L. Christensen, A. Mackey, & D. Whetten, 2014, Taking responsibility for CSR, *AMP*, 28: 164–178; B. King, T. Fellin, & D. Whetten, 2010, Finding the organization in organization theory, *OSc*, 21: 290–305.

20 J. Murillo-Luna, C. Garces-Ayerbe, & P. Rivera-Torres, 2008, Why do patterns of environmental response differ? *SMJ*, 29: 1225–1240; F. Wijen, 2014, Means versus ends in opaque institutional fields, *AMJ*, 39: 302–323; S. Young & M. Makhija, 2014, Firms' CSR behavior, *JIBS*, 45: 670–698.

21 B. Gifford, A. Kestler, & S. Anand, 2010, Building local legitimacy into CSR, *JWB*, 45: 304–311.

22 A. Doshi, G. Dowell, & M. Toffel, 2013, How firms respond to mandatory information disclosure, *SMJ*, 34: 1209–1231.

23 A. Gore, 2006, *An Inconvenient Truth*, Emmaus, PA: Rodale Press.

24 D. Jones, C. Willness, & S. Madey, 2014, Why are job seekers attracted by corporate social performance? *AMJ*, 57: 383–404.

25 P. M. Bal, D. Kooij, & S. Jong, 2013, How do developmental and accommodative HRM enhance employee engagement and commitment? *JMS*, 50: 545–572; A. Muller & A. Kolk, 2010, Extrinsic and intrinsic drivers of corporate social performance, *JMS*, 47: 1–26.

26 *Economist*, 2010, The other oil spill, June 26: 71–73.

27 J. Janney & S. Gove, 2011, Reputation and CSR aberrations, trends, and hypocrisy, *JMS*, 48: 1562–1584.

28 *BW*, 2010, Nine questions (and provisional answers) about the spill, June 14: 62.

29 D. Siegel, 2009, Green management matters only if it yields more green, *AMP*, August: 5–16.

30 A. Marcus & A. Fremeth, 2009, Green management matters regardless, *AMP*, August: 17–26.

31 P. Berrone, A. Fosfuri, L. Gelabert, & L. Gomez-Mejia, 2013, Necessity as the mother of "green" inventions, *SMJ*, 34: 891–909.

32 V. Hoffmann, T. Trautmann, & J. Hemprecht, 2009, Regulatory uncertainty, *JMS*, 46: 1227–1253.

33 N. Darnall, I. Henriques, & P. Sadorsky, 2010, Adopting proactive environmental strategy, *JMS*, 47: 1072–1094.

34 J. Mackey, 2011, What is it that only I can do? (p. 121), *HBR*, January: 119–123.

35 *Starbucks Global Responsibility Report 2010*, 2011, Message from Howard Schultz, www.starbucks.com.

36 G. Unruh & R. Ettenson, 2010, Winning in the green frenzy, *HBR*, November: 110–116.

37 *BW*, 2010, The smooth-talking king of coal—and climate change, June 7: 65.

38 A. Kourula, 2010, Corporate engagement with NGOs in different institutional contexts, *JWB*, 45: 395–404; J. Nebus & C. Rufin, 2010, Extending the bargaining power model, *JIBS*, 41: 996–1015.

39 M. Barnett & A. King, 2008, Good fences make good neighbors, *AMJ*, 51: 1150–1170; M. Delmas & M. Montes-Sancho, 2010, Voluntary agreements to improve environmental quality, *SMJ*, 31: 575–601.

40 B. Arya & G. Zhang, 2009, Institutional reforms and investor reactions to CSR announcements, *JMS*, 46: 1089–1112; M. Delmas & M. Toffel, 2008, Organizational responses to environmental demands, *SMJ*, 29: 1027–1055; E. Reid & M. Toffel, 2009, Responding to public and private politics, *SMJ*, 30: 1157–1178; E. Wong, M. Ormiston, & P. Tetlock, 2011, The effects of top management team integratige complexity and decentralized decision making on corporate social performance, *AMJ*, 54: 1207–1228.

41 A. Kolk & J. Pinkse, 2008, A perspective on MNEs and climate change, *JIBS*, 39: 1359–1378.

42 C. Flammer, 2013, CSR and shareholder reaction, *AMJ*, 56: 758–781; W. Su, M. W. Peng, W. Tan, & Y. Cheung, 2015, The signaling effect of CSR in emerging economies, *JBE* (in press);

43 A. Hillman & G. Keim, 2001, Shareholder value, stakeholder management, and social issues, *SMJ*, 22: 125–139.

44 R. Chan, 2010, Corporate environmentalism pursuit by foreign firms competing in China, *JWB*, 45: 80–92; Y. Eiadat, A. Kelly, F. Roche, & H. Eyadat, 2008, Green and competitive? *JWB*, 43: 131–145; P. Godfrey, C. Merrill, & J. Hansen, 2009, The relationship between CSR and shareholder value, *SMJ*, 30: 425–445; B. Lev, C. Petrovits, & S. Radhakrishnan, 2010, Is doing good good for you? *SMJ*, 31: 182–200; S. Ramchander, R. Schwebach, & K. Staking, 2012, The informational relevance of CSR, *SMJ*, 33: 303–314; M. Sharfman & C. Fernando, 2008, Environmental risk management and the cost of capital, *SMJ*, 29: 569–592; H. Wang & C. Qian, 2011, Corporate philanthropy and corporate financial performance, *AMJ*, 54: 1159–1181.

45 S. Ambec & P. Lanoie, 2008, Does it pay to be green? *AMP*, November: 45–62; D. Vogel, 2005, The low value of virtue, *HBR*, June: 26.

46 S. Brammer & A. Millington, 2008, Does it pay to be different? *SMJ*, 29: 1325–1343; J. Surroca, J. Tribo, & S. Waddock, 2010, Corporate responsibility and financial performance, *SMJ*, 31: 463–490.

47 T. Devinney, 2009, Is the socially responsible corporation a myth? *AMP*, May: 53.

48 J. Choi & H. Wang, 2009, Stakeholder relations and the persistence of corporate financial performance, *SMJ*, 30: 895–907; C. Hull & S. Rothenberg, 2008, Firm performance, *SMJ*, 29: 781–789.

49 P. Christmann & G. Taylor, 2006, Firm self-regulation through international certifiable standards, *JIBS*, 37: 863–878.

50 P. Madsen, 2009, Does corporate investment drive a "race to the bottom" in environmental protection? *AMJ*, 52: 1297–1318.

51 S. Brammer, S. Pavelin, & L. Porter, 2009, Corporate charitable giving, MNCs, and countries of concern, *JMS*, 46: 575–596; B. Scholtens, 2009, CSR in the international banking industry, *JBE*, 86: 159–175.

52 *Economist*, 2009, Spilling forever, June 13: 51.

53 *BW*, 2014, If it's good enough for Big Oil ..., November 17: 10–11.

54 T. Waldron, C. Navis, & G. Fisher, 2013, Explaining differences in firms' responses to activism, *AMJ*, 38: 397–417; M. Zhao, S. Park, & N. Zhou, 2014, MNC strategy and social adaptation in emerging markets, *JIBS*, 45: 842–861.

55 D. Crilly, M. Zollo, & M. Hansen, 2012, Faking it or muddling through? *AMJ*, 55: 1429–1448.

56 I. Filatotchev & C. Nakajima, 2014, Corporate governance, responsible managerial behavior, and CSR, *AMP*, 28: 289–306; C. Kock, J. Santalo, & L. Diestre, 2012, Corporate governance and the environment, *JMS*, 49: 492–514.

Map 4.1 World's Busiest Airports

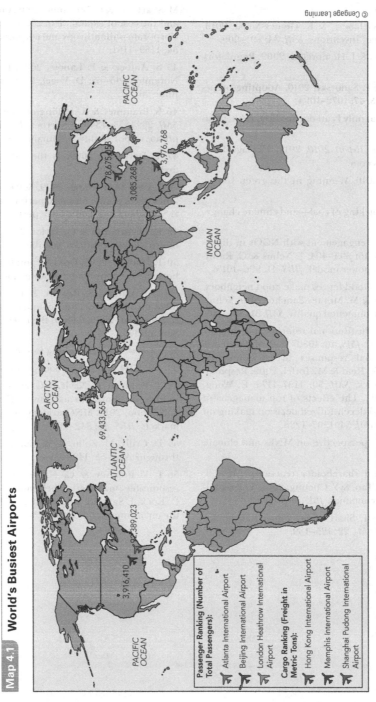

© Cengage Learning

Source: Adapted from Airports Council International (ACI), 2013 data.

© Cengage Learning

Map 4.2 **Countries with the Largest Labor Forces**

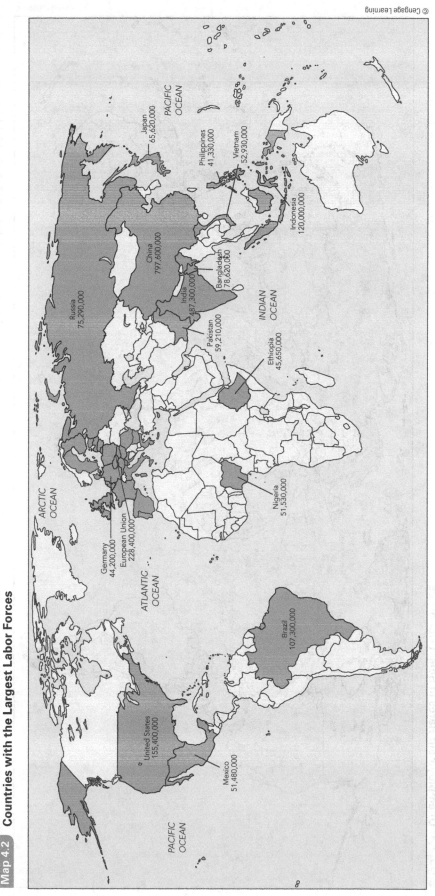

PACIFIC
OCEAN

Japan
65,620,000

Philippines
41,330,000

Vietnam
52,930,000

Indonesia
120,000,000

China
797,600,000

Bangladesh
78,620,000

INDIAN
OCEAN

Russia
75,290,000

India
487,300,000

Pakistan
59,210,000

Ethiopia
45,650,000

ARCTIC
OCEAN

Germany
44,200,000

European Union
228,400,000

Nigeria
51,530,000

ATLANTIC
OCEAN

Brazil
107,300,000

United States
155,400,000

Mexico
51,480,000

PACIFIC
OCEAN

Source: Adapted from Country Comparison: Labor Force, *World Factbook*, 2013.

Map 4.3   Unemployment Rates in Select Countries

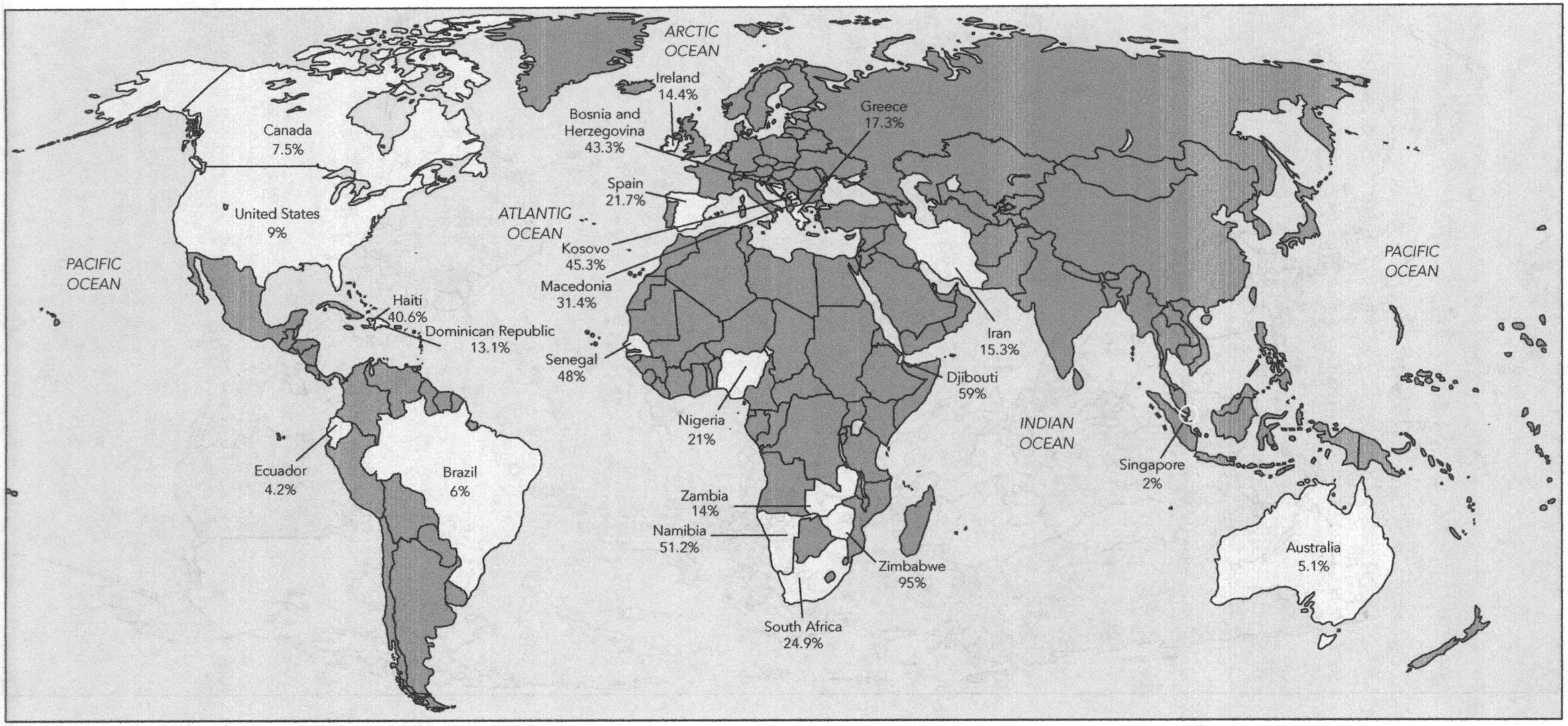

© Cengage Learning

PACIFIC
OCEAN

Australia
5.1%

Singapore
2%

INDIAN
OCEAN

Iran
15.3%

Djibouti
59%

Zimbabwe
95%

Greece
17.3%

South Africa
24.9%

ARCTIC
OCEAN

Ireland
14.4%

Nigeria
21%

Zambia
14%

Bosnia and
Herzegovina
43.3%

Spain
21.7%

Namibia
51.2%

ATLANTIC
OCEAN

Kosovo
45.3%

Macedonia
31.4%

Senegal
48%

Dominican Republic
13.1%

Haiti
40.6%

Brazil
6%

Canada
7.5%

United States
9%

Ecuador
4.2%

PACIFIC
OCEAN

Sources: IndexMundi: http://www.indexmundi.com/g/r.aspx?v=74, Central Intelligence Agency, 2014, *The World Factbook 2014*: https://www.cia.gov/library/publications/the-world-factbook/

© Cengage Learning

Map 4.4 Top CO$_2$ Emissions in Metric Tons Per Person

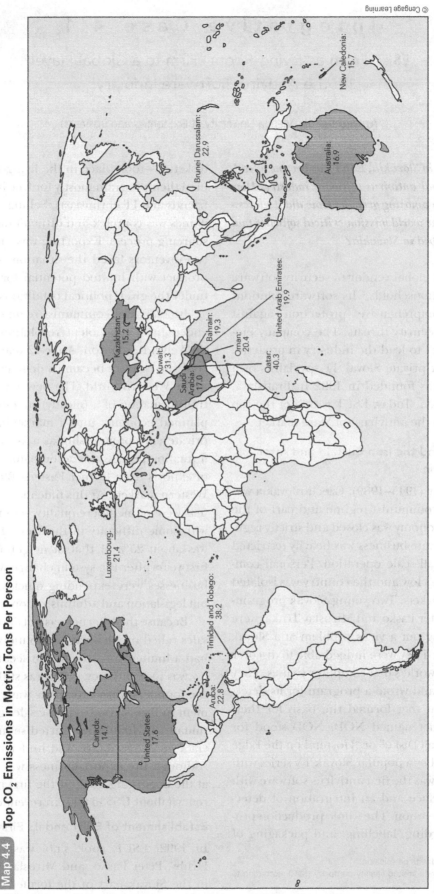

New Caledonia: 15.7

Brunei Darussalam: 22.9

Australia: 16.9

Kazakhstan: 15.2

United Arab Emirates: 19.9

Bahrain: 19.3

Kuwait: 31.3

Oman: 20.4

Qatar: 40.3

Saudi Arabia: 17.0

Luxembourg: 21.4

Trinidad and Tobago: 38.2

Aruba: 22.8

Canada: 14.7

United States: 17.6

Source: Adapted from World Bank data, 2014, http://data.worldbank.org/indicator/EN.ATM.CO2E.PC?order=wbapi_data_value_2010+wbapi_data_value+wbapi_data_value-first&sort=desc

Integrative Case 4.1

ESET: From a "Living-Room" Firm to a Global Player in the Antivirus Software Industry[1]

Arnold Schuh (Vienna University of Economics and Business)

From its humble roots in Slovakia, ESET has become a leading player in the global antivirus software industry. How did it accomplish such amazing growth? How did it successfully market around the world mission-critical software that was originally developed in Slovakia?

ESET, spol. s.r.o. is a global vendor of security software for companies and households.[2] Its software solutions deliver instant, comprehensive protection against evolving computer security threats. The company pioneered and continues to lead the industry in proactive threat detection. Six private Slovak IT specialists own the company that was founded in 1992 in Bratislava, the capital of Slovakia. Today, ESET is one of the top five global players in the antivirus software market.

The Beginning Behind the Iron Curtain and After the Velvet Revolution

During the Cold War (1945–1989), Czechoslovakia was a country run by a communist regime and part of the Eastern Bloc. The economy was closed and strictly regulated. Running a private business was heavily restricted but allowed as a small scale operation. Personal computer penetration was low and the country was isolated from Western IT markets. Two young Slovak programming enthusiasts, Peter Pasko and Miroslav Trnka, were asked to help sorting out a virus problem at a Slovak nuclear power plant. They were indeed able to discover the virus, one of the world's first computer viruses. They dubbed it "Vienna" and wrote a program for its detection and elimination that formed the basis for their first antivirus product named NOD. NOD stood for "Nemocnica Na Okraji Disku" or "Hospital on the Edge of the Disk." Inspired by a popular Slovak TV series with the same title, NOD was the first antivirus software with graphical user interface and an integration of detection, fixing, and prevention. The whole production process of NOD—recording, labelling, and packaging of

diskettes—took place in the living room. They distributed their program mostly for free in a small network of friends and IT enthusiasts. Selling to state-owned companies was complex and difficult due to a bureaucratic sourcing process. Exporting was impossible. Thus, the two inventors faced the situation of having a brilliant product with limited potential for commercialization under the given political conditions.

In 1989, the communist regime in Czechoslovakia ended in a non-violent revolution, which was called the Velvet Revolution. After 42 years under communist rule, the country became a democracy and opened up to the Western world. The new government started the transformation of a (mostly) state-owned and centrally planned economy into a market-based economy with private entrepreneurship as a key element. The transformation process was accompanied by a re-orientation of exports from former Eastern Bloc countries toward Western markets. At this time many Czechoslovak products were of mediocre quality, selling at a discount and with some difficulty in the West. The GDP per capita was about 25% of that of neighbouring Austria. The first years after the system change were chaotic. Private businesses were expanding quickly in Czechoslovakia, but legislation and administration were lagging behind.

Because the Internet was not developed yet, software sales relied on physical distribution. Computer viruses had a limited spread and the security software industry was in its infancy. NOD was still a side business for the founders whose company was run out of an apartment in Bratislava. Domestic sales grew slowly but continually. In 1990, they started selling NOD in Austria via a local distributor and under the name "Stopvir." Although the export business was not very successful at the beginning, in 1991 the first million in local currency (about US$36,000) in revenues was earned.

Establishment of ESET and its First Year

In 1992, ESET, spol. s.r.o. was founded by Rudolf Hruby, Peter Pasko, and Miroslav Trnka in Bratislava in the Slovak part of the former Czechoslovakia as a

1) © Arnold Schuh. Reprinted with permission.
2) "spol. s.r.o." refers to private limited liability company (LLC), according to Slovak law.

privately owned limited liability company (LLC). At this time, the founders did not focus on antivirus software alone. They also saw a good business opportunity in developing book keeping software. In the early years of the transition process, thanks to the enormous pent-up demand, almost any business was offering attractive growth to entrepreneurs. Although computer usage was still in its infancy, the demand for applications in all types of functional and sectoral areas was growing. Then came the break-up of Czechoslovakia in 1993 into two independent countries, the Czech Republic and the Slovak Republic.

Suddenly, ESET lost a large part of the former home market, which forced the founders to look for new export markets. In the same year, Trnka began contributing to the column "Virus Radar" in the leading Slovak periodical *PC Revue*, what helped building ESET's reputation as an antivirus specialist. In the following years improved versions of NOD were launched. A turning point was winning the first *Virus Bulletin* award in 1998. *Virus Bulletin* is a British magazine dedicated to providing PC users with regular information about the prevention, detection, and removal of computer malware. When this renowned magazine praised ESET for its quality, international users became aware of the company and foreign distributors started to ask for sales agreements.

However, the Slovak origin of the company still posed a psychological barrier to prospective foreign buyers and, as a consequence, restrained the growth of sales in foreign markets. Software originating from a relatively unknown, former Eastern bloc country was not perceived as a reliable high-performance product. Management discussed how they could counter this negative country-of-origin effect. In 1999 ESET LLC was established in San Diego, California, in the United States, with the help of Anton Zajac. This subsidiary was upgraded to be the international business center for ESET being responsible for all foreign markets. By selling its software through the US subsidiary, ESET got rid of the negative country-of-origin associations and international revenues began to rise. This dual structure was terminated in 2008 through a merger of the US subsidiary with its parent ESET, spol. s.r.o. In the meantime, ESET had itself established as a leading player in the industry and was valued above all for its competence and not its country of origin anymore. The choice of the United States as a location for the international business center was also driven by the

fact that it was the largest and leading IT market of the world, with a progressive IT industry and demanding customers who would stimulate ESET's innovation efforts.

Era of Rapid International Expansion and Growth

From the year 2000 on, the company showed remarkable growth. In 2002, the global auditing and consulting company Deloitte added ESET to its rankings of fastest growing companies, namely "Deloitte Technology Fast 50 in Central Europe" and "Fast 500 in EMEA" (Europe, Middle East, and Africa). This growth of sales was driven, on the one hand, by demand as viruses became a widespread threat through the fast evolution of the Internet and, on the other hand, by the improved international presence. In 1990, estimates of new and different computer viruses ranged from 200 to 500 per year. In 2000, the number was 50,000 viruses In 2010, the estimate was 2 million. Today, in 2015, ESET records more than 300,000 new pieces of malware per *day*. All statistics show that the number is exponentially growing. A higher penetration of computers, new devices such as smartphones and tablets, widely available mobile broadband technology, cloud computing, and intensified usage have increased the exposure of computer users to malware. The need to protect against these cyber threats has fuelled the sales of ESET: sales volume in local currency grew from 2000 to 2014 by a factor of 480 (!). While foreign sales accounted for less than 30% of overall sales in 2003, this share grew to 97% in 2014.

In the first 15 years the company grew organically. That changed in the last few years. In 2008 and 2010, two companies in the field of information security services and antispam systems were acquired. In 2008, ESET bought the Czech security company Setnet in order to expand its offering to information security services. Two years later, ESET acquired Comdom Software, a Slovak software company acclaimed for antispam solutions. By acquiring Comdom, ESET increased its capacity for developing advanced security solutions. "ESET is a research and development-oriented company that is going to benefit from this merger by tapping into the potential of this manufacturer of advanced antispam solutions. Building on the team of skilled programmers and researchers, we envision introducing new activities, along with injecting new potential into the development of security software," noted Trnka, ESET's then CEO.

People and Culture as a Basis of Success

Highly talented and motivated employees are central to ESET's success. Andrew Lee, CEO of ESET North America, emphasizes this aspect:

> Great software is the product of great people. ESET seeks to recruit people who are not only some of the brightest and best at what they do, but who also fit the positive culture of trust, integrity, innovation, effectiveness, and cheerfulness that drives everything that we do as a company. Throughout our organization, each employee is a carefully selected fit for the role, and as such is a key to our success.

This attitude is also expressed in the mission statement: "Intelligent people develop intelligent products for intelligent customers". In order to attract and retain this type of employees ESET has to pay salaries according to West European standards. Team building events, skill trainings, language courses, pension schemes, and health insurance contribute to a high level of employee satisfaction and low employee turnover. Owners and management cultivate an informal and personal style in the interaction with their employees and try to not only know their professional skills and strengths, but also their personal life.

Due to the fast growth of the company it became more difficult to find excellent software programmers in Slovakia alone, a country of five million inhabitants. Therefore, ESET opened a new R&D center in Krakow, Poland, in 2008. The purpose was to strengthen its research base and to be better able to deliver innovation in countering the growing volumes and sophistication of cyber threats. Krakow is a major center of education in Poland and Central Europe with around 210,000 students and well-known technical universities. It is a place where the IT community is very strong and well organized (with about 320 IT firms). Krakow is even dubbed by some folks as "Europe's Silicon Valley."

Today, ESET offers a portfolio of products for all types of users—home users, small and medium-sized companies, and large corporate and institutional customers. NOD32 Antivirus is the basic product for homes and businesses. ESET Mobile Security protects smartphones. ESET Smart Security, the flagship consumer product, provides a comprehensive protection combining antivirus, firewall, and antispam. Cybersecurity for Macs was developed for Apple users. The superior antivirus performance of ESET is documented in several tests by industry magazines. The NOD32 Antivirus program holds the world record for the largest consecutive number of the Virus Bulletin "VB100%"

Award since 1998 and has never missed a single "In-the-Wild" worm or virus since the launch of the test. A vast distribution network of partners and resellers parallel to sales offices in all major markets guarantee a presence in more than 180 countries worldwide. More than 100 million people use ESET security software today. Almost one thousand employees generated a turnover of 328 million euros in 2014, nearly all of it outside of Slovakia. The company grew by close to 139% in the last five years (2010–2014). According to IDC, a global market intelligence firm in the IT sector, ESET held a market share of 4.5%, the 5th rank in the global antivirus market in 2013 (Exhibit 1). With an annual growth rate of 23% ESET has grown six times faster than the whole market since 2013, according to IDC in its report titled *Worldwide Endpoint Security 2014–2018 Forecast and 2013 Vendor Shares* in August 2014.

The foundations of ESET's strategy have not changed markedly since the inception. Despite its growth from a "living-room" company to a global player, this firm is still driven by an entrepreneurial spirit and built on excellent technological competence. The goal is to develop high-performance, mission-critical security solutions for private and business users to keep out all known and emerging forms of malware. The focus on research and continuous product development is crucial for the superior performance of its NOD product. Top management and employees are living these values, creating a culture that is characterized by responsibility, reliability, and innovativeness.

Exhibit 1	Worldwide Antivirus Vendor Market Shares (2013)	

Vendor	Market Share
1. Symantec	31.5%
2. McAfee (an Intel company)	15.6%
3. Trend Micro	9.7%
4. Kaspersky Lab	7.6%
5. ESET	4.5%
6. Sophos	3.5%
7. AVG Technologies	2.9%
8. IBM	2.2%
9. F-Secure	2.0%
10. Panda Security	1.7%

Note: Market shares are based on revenue.

Source: C. J. Kolodgy, 2014, *Worldwide Endpoint Security 2014–2018 Forecast and 2013 Vendor Shares*, IDC, August, p. 4.

Antivirus business is built on the users' trust and this is mirrored in the culture of ESET. What changed over the last 23 years is the scope of operations. A broader range of solutions is offered today to home users, companies of all sizes, and mobile phone users worldwide. In February 2015, ESET launched an all-new range of next-generation business security products that offers maximum proactive protection with enhanced usability for all sizes of companies, highlighting the new strategy focus on business customers.

The higher degree of internationalization of its business today is not only reflected in a larger volume and share of foreign sales but also in the presence of its R&D centers on all continents. ESET currently runs malware research and R&D centers in Europe (Bratislava, Kosice, Krakow, and Prague), the Americas (Buenos Aires, Montreal, and San Diego), and Asia (Singapore). Spreading its malware research centers over many time zones allows ESET to respond effectively to the rise of cyber threats and technological challenges. This is the only way to learn quickly about new cyber threats and monitor trends. It also gives access to programming talent and knowledge hubs that are located all over the world.

Case Discussion Questions

1. **How could a company from Slovakia become a leading global player in the antivirus software industry?**

2. **From a resource-based view, what are ESET's sources of competitive advantage?**

3. **When companies from emerging economies market their products abroad, what do they typically encounter?**

4. **From an institution-based view, country-of-origin images reflect the informal rules and perceptions of the game that customers (especially those in developed economies) accept. How can companies from emerging economies overcome negative country-of-origin images?**

Sources: Based on (1) Company Report of ESET, spol. s.r.o., Amadeus (Bureau van Dijk) database, March 2015, and personal interviews with M. Trnka and B. Ondrasik in February and March 2015; (2) K. Dyba & J. Svejnar, 1992, Stabilization and transition in Czechoslovakia, in O. Blanchard, K. Froot, & J. Sachs (eds), *The Transition in Eastern Europe*, Volume 1 (pp. 93–122), Chicago: University of Chicago Press; (3) ESET website, March 2015, www.eset.com/int/about/history/ and http://www.eset.com/us/; (4) C. J. Kolodgy, 2014, *Worldwide Endpoint Security 2014–2018 Forecast and 2013 Vendor Shares*, IDC, August. (5) M. Trnka on the History of ESET, 2012, Presentation at the 4th Grow East Congress, March 7, Vienna, Austria.

Integrative Case 4.2

Employee Retention and Institutional Change at PIGAMU[1]

David B. Zoogah (Morgan State University)

The President of PIGAMU, an academic institution in Ghana, has sought to initiate institutional change toward an employee retention system based on performance. However, employees who were dismissed brought legal action, triggering a series of disputes that ended up with the President's resignation.

PIGAMU is an academic institution in Ghana, an emerging economy located in Africa and bordered by the Atlantic Ocean in the south, Cote d'Ivoire in the West, Togo in the East, and Burkina Faso in the North. As a former colony of Britain, Ghana's name was changed from the Gold Coast to Ghana after independence in 1957. Even though the period after independence was marred by a series of military coup d'etats, the country has been democratic since the late 1980s.

Ghana has a population of 23 million, 58% of which are between the ages of 15 and 64 years, and 48% female.[2] Life expectancy at birth is 57 years. Economic activity measured by industrial productivity is $13.31 billion (2000 US dollars). Manufacturing contributes about 7% of GDP. GNI per capita is US$670. The human development index (HDI), a comparative measure of life expectancy, literacy, education, and standard of living for countries worldwide, indexes the well-being and the impact of economic policies on quality of life. It shows where each country stands in relation to specific goalposts, expressed as a value between 0 and 1. Ghana has an HDI of 0.526, which is relatively higher than other sub-Saharan countries, but far lower than Western and some Asian economies.[3] It has an education index of 0.622. Adult and youth literacy rates are 60% and 71%, respectively.

1) This case was first published as D. B. Zoogah, 2012, Employee retention during institutional transition: A case study of PIGAMU, in J. C. Hayton, L. C. Christiansen, & B. Kuvaas (eds.), *Global Human Resource Management Casebook* (pp. 203–216), New York: Routledge. © Taylor & Francis. Reprinted with permission. This case was based on the institutional transition of a real organization in Ghana. However, for confidentiality reasons, the actors were disguised. Data from interviews with employees, internet sources, newspaper archives, TV news, conference participation, and visit of the author to the institution were used to develop the case. It was not sponsored by the institution.
2) http://databank.worldbank.org.
3) http://hdrstats.undp.org/en/countries/country_fact_sheets/cty_fs_GHA.html.

Organizational Setting

Located in Ghana's capital city Accra, PIGAMU was established in 1961 as a joint Ghana Government/United Nations Special Fund Project. Originally it was an Institute of Public Administration with the objective of developing the public administrative system and producing civil servants with administrative and professional competence to plan and administer national, regional, and local services. PIGAMU's activities over the last 47 years have been guided by a series of mandates beginning with the first Legislative Instrument of 1961 to the current Act of 2004 (Act 676). It is one of several public sector organizations in the country that depended on government subventions, and until 2000 was in need of drastic reform. Consequently, it was selected, as part of the World Bank-funded Public Sector Reform Program in 1999/2000, to be taken off government subvention. Its status as an institution of higher learning was converted to that of a university. It was also given privileges to extend its services to the private sector. Thus, the institution's clientele and stakeholders now range from politicians and bureaucrats to mid-level personnel from the public and private sectors and civil society as well as local and international (African) organizations. All these stakeholders attend a variety of courses in leadership, management, business and public administration.

Vision and Mission of the Institution

PIGAMU's vision is to be a world class center of excellence for training, consultancy and research in leadership, management and administration consistent with the economic and development objectives of Ghana. As a result, it sought to use competent and motivated staff along with state-of-the-art facilities to fulfill its mission of continuous enhancement of the capabilities of middle and top level executives in public and private sectors as well as nongovernmental organizations in Ghana, Africa, and other parts of the world. Its objective is to facilitate human capital development in Ghana. This is to be achieved through the training, research and consultancy expertise of the institution in line with its core values of academic excellence, superior professional standards, speedy response to clientele and stakeholders, purposefulness in national character, conformity to global organizational standards, honesty, hard work, integrity, transparency, innovation, and accountability.

PIGAMU has undergraduate degree programs for working adults in public and business administration including marketing, human resources, accounting and finance, banking and finance, hospitality management, economics, entrepreneurship, and information technology. It is structured into four semi-autonomous units: (i) Public Services unit focusing on training of civil and other public servants; (ii) Governance, Leadership and Public Management, which is a graduate school; (iii) Business School modeled modelled after the US business school system; and (iv) Technology School. The Business School has Executive Masters Programs in Business Administration (EMBA), Public Administration (EMPA) and Governance and Leadership (EMGL). As of 2005, there were about 1,300 students enrolled in its programs. It also has a Center for IT Professional Development (CIPD), a Center for Management Development (CMD), a Consultancy unit, and a Distance Learning Center.

As shown in Exhibit 1, Schools and Centers are headed by Deans, who reports to the President (Rector). The President reports to the Governing Council. Even though the institution is semi-public, governmental influence seems very limited. A new Parliamentary Act in 2004 (Act 676) granted academic and financial autonomy to PIGAMU under an 11-member Governing Council. The autonomy enables PIGAMU to function consistent with the demands of tertiary institutions.

All Schools and Centers are staffed by well-qualified faculty (n = 100) and interconnected with a network of international faculty. Through the progressive orientation, PIGAMU performed better financially than the other six public universities in Ghana. According to the former President, PIGAMU's improved performance resulted from maintenance of a clean environment that is conducive to teaching and learning; introduction of performance-based incentive packages for staff; continuous faculty development (e.g., ten faculty members pursuing PhD degrees; nine middle/junior staff pursuing undergraduate degrees; and three faculty members on International Faculty Fellows Program); improved infrastructure and facilities (e.g., from five lecture halls in 2001 to 30 in 2006; from two office blocks to nine; from zero to four computer laboratories; a new

---

Exhibit 1   **Structure of Leadership in PIGAMU**

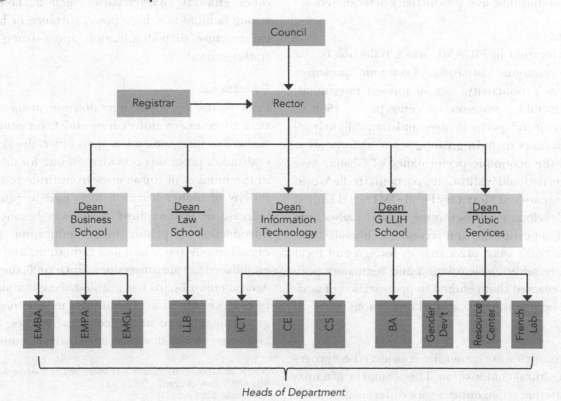

Heads of Department

auditorium with 640-seating capacity; and a 131-bedroom executive hostel with conference facilities); and an increased budget from 8.6 billion Ghanaian cedis in 2001 to 67.5 billion in 2006 (representing a growth of about 785% in five years). The reforms also included a changed work ethic and collaborative affiliation with international institutions and agencies (e.g., Africa Virtual University; Public Sector Management Master's Training Program funded by the African Capacity Building Foundation) for Anglophone West Africa.

Pressures Necessitating Organizational Change

Prior to the impressive outcomes above, a number of macro and micro forces compelled the government to demand changes. The macro factors relate to educational, cultural, economic, and political reforms.

Political

From the year of independence to the early 1980s, Ghana had been predominantly run by military juntas. The last military coup d'etat in 1980 stabilized the country until its return to constitutional democracy. With frequent changes in military regimes, little attention was paid to educational institutions and human capital development. Consequently, institutions such as PIGAMU that were established to contribute to economic growth through human capital development centered on business and productivity deteriorated.

Economic

The deterioration in PIGAMU was a reflection of the national economic situation. Economic pressures such as low productivity, lack of foreign investment, underperforming state-owned enterprises (SOEs), poor agricultural performance, and natural environmental disasters including drought and deforestation worsened the economic performance of Ghana. As a result, international institutions, particularly the World Bank, International Monetary Fund (IMF), and United Nations Development Programme (UNDP), advocated structural adjustments and economic liberalization programs. SOEs were privatized to foreign and local investors. In addition, legislation and regulatory policies were enacted that resulted in privatization of agricultural, service, and educational institutions.

Cultural

African countries are generally considered heterogeneous in cultural composition. They comprise of a mixture of different tribal entities with different linguistic, belief, value, and normative systems.[4] Nevertheless, there are similarities among different African countries and ethnic cultures that suggest the existence of "Africanity"—namely, the "special configuration of various features and cultural patterns that may be encountered in the study of African modes of livelihood, beliefs, attitudes, behaviors, even in languages, and artistic expression."[5] The same is true of Ghana. There are over 200 tribes in Ghana, most of which have distinct languages (e.g., Dagbane, Twi, Ewe, Ga, and Fante), dialects, lineages, and traditions. These cultural characteristics of tribes are so strong and deeply engrained in the minds of Ghanaians that they are often characterized by thinking tribe first and nation second. The tribalistic tendencies manifest in political, economic, social, and educational institutions such that jobs, school admissions, marriages, and career advancements are often based on tribal networks. It is not uncommon for one president or executive of an institution to be sacked and his position given to another person who is a kinsman or tribesman of the boss. In fact, it is common for a subordinate to undermine a supervisor because of differences in tribal origins. Despite the Ghanaian culture or Ghanaian mentality that seeks to transcend ethnic divisions, tribalism has permeated every institution in Ghana. When a new president assumed leadership, tribalism dominated other cultural characteristics such as collectivism, strong familial ties, high power distance or hierarchical structure, male domination, and a strong focus on traditional values.

Educational

Prior to the economic liberalization programs there were three major universities and five institutions of higher learning (i.e., other than universities). The liberalization programs provided avenue for an increase in the number of universities from three to ten; institutions of higher learning increased to fifteen. The increase in tertiary institutions was because of the introduction of private higher education. Religious organizations (i.e., Catholic, Protestant, and Muslim) established private universities. Since 2000, the National Accreditation Board has granted accreditation to over fifteen private tertiary institutions to offer degree programs in religious and theological studies, business, and other social disciplines. As private entities, they

4) A. K. Awedoba, 2007, *Culture and Development in Africa*, Accra, Ghana: Historical Society of Ghana.
5) Awedoba, 2007, p. 21.

can introduce innovations in course design and delivery and also respond to changes in the labor market more quickly because they do not have the institutional history of the traditional and public universities.[6]

Micro Factors

Internal factors in PIGAMU also contributed to the need for change. The deterioration of physical facilities discouraged young professionals with business qualifications from joining the institution. As a result, aged professors and instructors ran the institution. Because the institution was regarded as a training or competence-enhancement center, knowledge exploration was not emphasized. Another reason is that staff compensation was guaranteed because PIGAMU depended on government subvention. The leadership prior to the change focused on maintenance rather than growth of the institution. The increased number of individuals—some minimally qualified, others not qualified at all—were employed sometimes due to nepotistic reasons or political influence. Changes that could transform the institution never materialized because of previous leaders were perceived as feeble at the time or encountered constraints from government. As a result, the deterioration continued for several years and became so pronounced that individuals who received certificate training from the institute were perceived as inferior or sub-standard.

Consistent with the initial objective for the establishment of PIGAMU—assistance with human capital development initiatives—the government decided to partially privatize the institution. PIGAMU was upgraded to a university and a law enacted to support it. The law proposed that PIGAMU could combine a private objective and a public mandate by charging fees. It also granted PIGAMU authority to focus on its core competence—development of public employees. As a result, PIGAMU now functions as a semi public institution. It charges fees but attends predominantly to public institutions.

Institutional Transition

Leadership Change

In order to help PIGAMU achieve its objectives and to function effectively, the government appointed a new President (Rector). He had studied in Ghana and abroad, earning BSc, MSc, and PhD degrees. Prior to his appointment he had worked at diplomatic and foreign institutions in Europe, Africa, and Australia. His academic credentials suggested strong capabilities. Further, his cross-cultural experience from sojourning in Europe, America, and other African countries, and work with both private and public international institutions (e.g., Commonwealth Secretariat) suggested the new President had strong leadership abilities and competencies. His appointment was therefore viewed positively by several stakeholders including the government and employees. There seemed to be support or commendation of his appointment especially when the initiatives he introduced began to transform the organization.[7]

Expectations and Challenges

A number of expectations and challenges awaited the new President. The stakeholders expected him to transform PIGAMU, not only because it was now a university, but also because they wanted the institution to contribute to business productivity. PIGAMU's explicit focus on administrative and productivity enhancement expertise seemed to make it more qualified than the other tertiary institutions in Ghana. The government in particular expected the new President to transform the institution financially so that the government would no longer need to subsidize it. Employees, regardless of their performance orientation, expected him to develop the institution in a way that ensured job security. The faculty also expected the new President to develop the institution to function as a university. "It was a burden, you would imagine, to be a savior to several people," he mused in a speech. "These expectations seemed to be the least of my worries," he added, "I had numerous challenges." "If I wanted to achieve my objective—make the institution a center of excellence—I had to find a way to overcome those challenges," he continued. [8]

First, the human capital essential for building a center of excellence for knowledge exploration was lacking. Some faculty lacked the requisite qualifications, specifically doctoral degrees required by the Association for the Advancement of Colleges and Schools of Business (AACSB). The second challenge was how to implement whatever changes he envisioned. As an outsider, the new President was likely to meet employee resistance to his initiatives. Previous change initiatives were unsuccessful

6) http://nab.gov.gh/nabsite/

7) Comment by TV interviewer during interview with the new President (Rector), accessed on July 7, 2010.
8) Keynote speech at IAABD conference, Metropolitan University, London, UK, July 2007.

mainly due to employee resistance. The third challenge was adoption of a leadership style that could not only encourage a culture of excellence, but also transform the institution. Even though he was conscientious with regard to his duties, he was sometimes perceived as brash and disrespectful, particularly toward individuals who were perceived as less qualified. His leadership and personality was also perceived as incongruent with the consensual leadership attributes of Ghanaians. The new President knew that an aggressive leadership style was likely to lead to resistance, but a consensual style was also not going to yield the transformation he envisioned. Previous leaders who adopted that approach did not achieve their transformation goals.

The final and biggest challenge was employee retention. He knew that retaining human resources (HR) were vital to his transformation agenda and that amongst the multitude of employees was a few gems that could be harnessed to improve the institution. How to sift the wheat from the chaff caused nightmares for him. This challenge was aggravated by the lack of an HR department. Had there been one, he could have used it as a medium that would help minimize resistance to his initiatives; after all most of the changes centered on HR development.

Changes

After several weeks of critical reflection the new President (hereafter "the President") decided to initiate his changes. Even though his ultimate goal was to implement the HR initiatives, he knew that those initiatives had to be preceded by structural changes and supplemented with academic initiatives.

Structural Changes

The President began by advocating for legislative changes that would enable the institution to support itself financially. In 2004, Parliament enacted a new law (Act 676), which gave PIGAMU (1) autonomy to charge fees, (2) power to train public servants, and (3) authority under an 11-member Governing Council to develop programs and services consistent with its university status (i.e., leadership, management and administration) for both the public and private sectors. The Governing Council provided new leadership infrastructure that was consistent with the President's vision.

Academic Changes

The President initiated programs that would enable the institution to achieve its objective as a center of excellence. First, he brought in foreign faculty from all regions of the globe (e.g., Africa, Asia, Europe, North America, and South America) to teach. Second, he set up new schools—business, technology, governance—and hired qualified faculty to help run them. Professors from the USA and Europe were appointed as Deans of those schools. They in turn marketed the University at local, regional, and international conferences. They also succeeded in gaining international accreditation from the prestigious AACSB. The accreditation enhanced PIGAMU's image and motivated foreign faculty to visit the institution. In addition, the President insisted on continuous development; encouraged faculty members who had graduate (i.e., master's) degrees to pursue doctoral degrees before they were qualified to teach. Employees who did not have college degrees were required to obtain undergraduate degrees. For example, in-service programs were established for staff. With these programs, the institution improved its image from one of low quality to a center of excellence. Press reports suggested PIGAMU was being transformed.[9]

Human Resource Changes

The third set of changes focused on HR. Prior to the appointment of the new President, PIGAMU did not have an HR department; it had a personnel department that performed such operational functions as recruiting and selecting (often through familiar and friendship networks, and operative workers); distribution of wage and salary checks; and dismissal, albeit rarely, of employees for egregious offences. The lack of an HR department suggests that strategic and efficient human capital functions—skill acquisition, allocation, maintenance, and development, as well as performance management, communication, employee involvement, and compensation—were nonexistent. The President recognized that his principal objective—making PIGAMU a center of excellence—required HR initiatives, which could be effectively and efficiently implemented by the HR department. So, he initiated programs to enhance HR within the institution. First, he focused on improving working conditions. Although peripheral, working conditions fulfill attitudinal, behavioral, and financial benefits. He believed good working conditions can stimulate involvement, commitment, identification, and engagement of employees and external stakeholders. He also believed that maintenance of a clean teaching and learning environment was essential to knowledge generation and distribution. Such

9) http://sakyi-addo.com/pages/posts/, accessed on July 7, 2010.

an environment could attract consulting opportunities and induce potential students to enroll in its programs.

The second initiative centered on performance management. As mentioned, performance of staff and faculty were not managed prior to the appointment of the President. Attendance and punctuality were arbitrary and capricious. Staff reported to work when they wanted, spent more time for lunch breaks, and closed earlier than the scheduled work day. Further, productivity was not measured. In fact, some workers did not even have work to do. They merely reported to work in order to get a pay check at the end of the month. With regard to faculty, knowledge generation through research and publication, an index of academic productivity, was not emphasized. Due to the seniority culture, the faculty (especially senior faculty) could not be dismissed for poor performance. Knowledge dissemination through teaching was also not evaluated. Consequently, the faculty relied on old and disproven theories and models.

Consequently, the President instituted performance management for staff and faculty. Staff was evaluated for attendance, punctuality, and productivity. In fact, extra-role behaviors such as supporting and helping coworkers, staying beyond the work day, loyalty, and obedience were included in the performance indicators. In order to observe staff for such behaviors, the President sometimes visited departments unannounced and outside of work hours (e.g., before 8 am and after 5 pm or 6 pm). Employee performance was measured through a recording system. Expected behaviors were tallied and aggregated at the end of the month. Wages were determined based on that record. With regard to academic performance, the faculty were expected to develop themselves through participation in national, regional, and international conferences; to produce and publish research; and to improve teaching. In addition to evaluating every faculty member's teaching at the end of the teaching period, annual reports were required. Those who were found deficient were warned for a number of times. If no improvement was observed, they could be terminated (if they were not tenured). Tenured faculty could also be dismissed for very poor performance. Foreign faculty who received poor evaluations were not invited in future as visiting professors.

The third HR change was instituting a reward system that was tied to performance. The incentive package was intended for staff and faculty conditioned on productivity and profitability. This initiative was particularly unappealing to many employees because it linked remuneration to performance. Prior to the President's appointment, faculty and staff were rewarded by seniority, a compensation system that did not link performance to the strategic objectives of the organization. The President believed that the return on investment under such conditions was very low. As a result, he changed it to performance-based compensation.

The fourth initiative was employee involvement. In contrast to the past, durbars were held every Friday to facilitate congeniality, collegiality, socialization, bonding, and shared identity. A durbar is an event in which members of a community gather for ceremonial purposes. Traditionally, it was an occasion when the African chiefs met their subjects to celebrate, share information, and strategize on the future of the community. The President used durbars to not only celebrate accomplishments, but also to engage in collective strategy development. Further, durbars were avenues for staff and faculty to interact, thereby minimizing the divide between academics and non-academics. Employees, particularly the staff, seemed to anticipate the durbars for a number of reasons. First, they enabled the staff to solicit advancement advice from faculty. They also afforded opportunities to develop external social networks (i.e., outside of the employees' departments). Third, employees obtained updated information about the performance of the institution through which they could infer job security. Above all, the durbars provided opportunity for employees to demonstrate engagement; staff and faculty could provide suggestions to the President. Overall, the President believed the durbars were mechanisms by which he could cultivate a high performance work environment. Durbars enabled groups that shared a common identity to promote and support one another.

In addition, the President mandated communication initiatives. He communicated daily with staff and faculty through notices. Department heads were not only informed of the policies in advance, but they were also instructed to inform all employees within their purview. Even though employees appreciated dissemination of the information, they did not seem to to like the unidirectional or top-down approach. Further, some employees perceived that he did not tolerate excuses for inability to distribute the information. In fact, some employees seemed to resent the fact that some policies were not discussed at executive or academic council meetings. Nevertheless, the President perceived that policies that required speedy actions could be slowed down at Council meetings, thereby hindering the progress of PIGAMU.

The final initiative focused on retention. It proved contentious and as discussed below very consequential. This initiative involved retrenchment of several employees. "How do I get people who are not contributing to the objectives of the institution but rather are draining it off the payroll?" he wondered in a speech. "Of course, it is Africa and you cannot ask them to leave like that," he continued.[10] Given the tribalistic and superstitious Ghanaian culture, the New President first devised a retention criteria based on performance of employees. Unqualified employees were retrenched. "I decided to retrench them with pay," he added. "Why?" asked the moderator.[11] "Because I did not want to create chaos; the transition had to be smooth and that was the only way of doing it, I thought," he responded. The retrenched employees were on payroll for two years at the end of which they were terminated. All other employees were informed of new policies and standards of excellence.

Problems

Shortly after the changes were initiated problems began to emerge. The style of leadership of the New President, though results-laden, was disapproved by some employees. First, he was perceived as dictatorial. The grapevine indicated that any employee who dared to question a policy, initiative, or program was summarily dismissed, punished, or disparaged publicly. Several faculty members were victimized as a consequence. This style seemed to invalidate the transformation initiatives. Staff and faculty began to question the value of suggestions if they could be victimized as a consequence. It seemed conflicts could not be amicably resolved. As a result, dissatisfied employees explored alternative mechanisms of conflict resolution: legal action.

Although a number of legal actions challenged the initiatives, one action was prominent and eventually proved damaging. A retrenched employee brought action against the President for illegal dismissal. The proceedings lasted several years but was eventually dismissed. However, before that case was dismissed, it was revealed that the President was not academically qualified as a professor. First, a newspaper revealed that an institution in a southern African country—not

PIGAMU—conferred the professorship to the President. However, the President later admitted that "he's not a prof."[12] That seemed contrary to the rules and regulations of the institution. By PIGAMU's convention, "nobody could use any foreign title unless it was verified by its Academic Board."[13] To rectify the situation, the President then applied for Full Professorship. He submitted a letter to the Deputy President and Dean of Academic Affairs of the Institute in which he sought PIGAMU's appointment as a professor. The letter was circulated to members of the PIGAMU Governing Council and was leaked to the press. Based on that, a relative of a former employee who was dismissed as part of the new President's HR initiatives took legal action challenging the qualifications of the President. The lawsuit requested the court to order the PIGAMU Governing Council to declare the position of President vacant and to take all necessary steps to appoint a *new* President, because the latter's application showed inconsistency with the rules and regulations that the current President had insisted should be adhered to without exemptions. The current President who always insisted that the rules and regulations that existed before he came into office should be followed was perceived as subverting them. Legal actions and press reports that uncovered unsavory and unethical academic practices negatively affected the image of the institute. The bad image was seemingly affecting the functioning and growth of PIGAMU.

Compounding the situation was the concern other executives of the institution (e.g., Governing Council members) had about the bad publicity. Maybe this concern influenced the Chairman of the Board not to sign the appointment letter for the President's second term.[14] The court dismissed an application by the editor of the newspaper who filed the case seeking the court's order to restrain the President as a professor.[15] Nevertheless, the effect was damaging. Concerned about his position, the President filed a counter suit, alleging that PIGAMU should confirm his appointment for the second term. In response, the PIGAMU Governing Council challenged the competence and leadership of the President. It produced some evidence of plagiarism misconduct of the President to support its case. PIGAMU also alleged that the President was not leading by the rules and regulations of the institution.

10) Keynote speech to IAABD conference at Metropolitan University, London, UK, July 2007.

11) http://sakyi-addo.com/kwaku-one-on-one-on-sunday/, accessed on July 7, 2010.

12) GYE NYAME CONCORD, 2007, General News of Monday, October 1.

13) Ghana News Agency, 2008, General News, April 21.

14) Ghana News Agency, 2008, General News, April 21.

15) Myjoyonline.com, 2008, Social affairs, November 2.

Specifically, representatives of PIGAMU argued that the President seemed dishonest for dismissing students for intolerable behaviors—plagiarism—when he exhibited the same behaviors. By that standard, he was also to be dismissed. In fact, one newspaper magazine reproduced the article from which the President had plagiarized. Other accusations included naming a building complex at the institute after his hometown without approval from the Governing Council.[16] The President was perceived to be running the institution in a way that had contravened its rules.

Obviously, the climate was perceived as very hostile. In fact, many employees seemed to work in fear of being victimized, since the alleged misconduct of the President (e.g., plagiarism) was leaked by employees of the institution. The psychological effects of these legal actions seemed to have had an effect on the President. His attitude toward staff and faculty (including visiting professors) as well as students was very abrasive, insensitive, and condescending. His distrust intensified. As a result, he resorted to threats of arbitrary dismissal of

16) Ghana News Agency, 2008, General news, March 19.

staff. Staff and faculty were uncertain about the future of the institution and their own careers. The climate was so toxic that productivity was diminishing. Given that environment, the President could only resign. He did so in 2008. Although the government appointed a new successor, PIGAMU no longer enjoys the enormous goodwill it once enjoyed.

Case Discussion Questions

1. **How would the presence of an HR department have made a difference in the implementation?**

2. **If you were the President, how would you have implemented the changes differently?**

3. **What conflict resolution systems would you have instituted during the implementation phase?**

4. **How would you have minimized resistance to the changes?**

5. **What is the role of societal culture in the case?**

6. **If you were invited by the Governing Council as a consultant, what would you recommend to the Governing Council and to the new President?**

Integrative Case 4.3

Sino Iron: Engaging Stakeholders in Australia[1]

Sunny Li Sun (University of Missouri – Kansas City)
Yanli Zhang (Montclair State University)
Zhu Chen (SIA Energy, Beijing)

Confronting significant liabilities of foreignness, the Sino Iron project in Australia experienced a great deal of delays and cost overruns. What could the management team do to better engage stakeholders in the host country?

In January 2010, Hua Dongyi rushed to his Sino Iron chairman's office in Perth the largest city in Western Australia. The parent company of Sino Iron, China International Trust and Investment Corporation (CITIC), just moved his position from CITIC Construction Co., a subsidiary focused on infrastructural projects in Africa and Asia to Sino Iron Australia.

Hua had an urgent meeting with his management team. Sino Iron faced tremendous challenges: Spotting the high potential demand for iron ores in China, CITIC had purchased the mining license of Australian magnetite iron ores, and started the project in 2007. After investing A\$1.6 billion, the project had suffered significant delays and overruns, pushing back the planned date of operation from the first half of 2009 to early 2011, and now even that date was not likely. The challenge for Hua and his team was to push the project forward and launch operations soon.

The global price of iron ores changed dramatically. In 2010, the negotiation broke down between China Steel Association and the three biggest mining companies in the world—BHP Billiton, Rio Tinto, and Vale of Brazil. Some Chinese steel companies had to accept nearly 100% price increase of iron ore imports from these three mining companies and quarterly price adjustment. After the recent price hike, a correction could be due any time and price could fall drastically later, which would be bad timing for Sino Iron if production was further delayed. Furthermore, magnetite iron ores due to its nature had a 40% higher production cost than other premium resources (which are

mainly under the control of BHP Billiton and Rio Tinto, and they are never interested in joint investment with Chinese companies). This could put Sino Iron in a very disadvantaged position if it found price dropping after its mine started operating.

CEO Barry Fitzgerald was a local guy with 30 years of experience in iron ore operations. Although he reported to Hua, he was not responsible for the delay of progress and cost overruns. The main reason was the unexpectedly long time of approval procedure from the government. Delay meant higher labor cost, and meant that the cost of prospecting would increase another US\$350 million on top of the original plan of US\$3.5 billion.

However, Hua did not trust the local managers very well, because they were still leaving work on regular time, taking vacations, and expecting bonuses at the end of the year. Sometimes engineers were in the middle of processing concrete and as soon as it was time to go home, they would leave work without worrying about whether it would cause problems. When there were problems, they would try to blame each other, and the sense of belonging and loyalty in Chinese firms at home were nowhere to be found here.

At the end of 2009, during the wave of acquisitions in Australia by Chinese steel companies, Australian people's resistance of and hostility to Chinese companies increased suddenly. Once, an Australian employee blurted out that after all this investment was the Chinese government's money, so why should they care. Hua got upset: "Our parent company, CITIC Pacific, is a publicly listed company in Hong Kong. The Chinese government is only one of the shareholders, and there are also other investors. I represent all of the investors!" (see Exhibit 1).

In order to control the progress of the project, Hua had to have some capable Chinese expatriates working for him. From the end of 2009 to January 2010, four of his old subordinates from CITIC Construction came to his rescue in Perth. However, Hua and his management team still faced significant challenges to deal with different stakeholders in Australia.

1) Research for this case was supported in part by the Bloch Summer Research Grants, University of Missour—Kansas City. We thank Professors Mike Peng and John Cantwell for their constructive guidance. The views expressed are those of the authors and not those of the sponsor. © Sunny Li Sun, Yanli Zhang, and Zhu Chen. Reprinted with permission.

Exhibit 1 **Ownership Structure of Sino Iron Project**

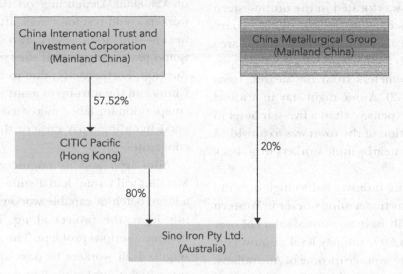

Government Relationship

In recent years, many Chinese companies began to invest in Australian mines. For example, Yanzhou Coal Enterprise acquired Australia Felix; Sichuan Hanlong invested US$200 million into Molybdenum mine, Chongqing Iron & Steel Group acquired the Asian Iron and Steel Holding Company, which was in control of Australian iron ore in Istanbul Xin; and China Minmetals Corporation acquired some assets of Australia OZ Minerals with US$1.4 billion. Overall, the Australian government was open to these acquisitions, yet was also on the alert regarding the acquirers, which mostly had some government background. It was concerned that these companies would try to reduce tax to the Australian government through internal transfer pricing, diminish local employment opportunities, and affect the local environment. Thus the Australian government increased regulation. For example, the Australian Foreign Investment Review Board (FIRB) required China Nonferrous Metal Mining Group to reduce its stake during its acquisition of Lynas, which led to the failure of the acquisition. China Alumni Corporation's acquisition of Rio Tinto also failed due to the extended review of FIRB, which led to the opposition of other stakeholders.

At the same time, since Australia's premium iron ore resources were mainly under the control of BHP Billiton and Rio Tinto, foreign companies—being late comers—could only invest in those magnetite iron ores that had a 40% higher production cost. For example, Australia's third largest iron ore producer FMG never

allowed joint investment with Chinese companies, thinking that it would not be worthwhile to give the foreign side shares. At the same time, the Australian side would seek Chinese investment in magnetite iron ore projects. The reason that CITIC and Chongqing Iron & Steel Group's acquisitions obtained the approval of FIRB and they were able to achieve 100% acquisitions were exactly due to the fact that the production cost and risk of magnetite iron ores were too high and local Australian firms did not want to touch it.

Hua's interactions with the Australian government were forceful but did not have much effect. In Africa, CITIC could leverage its state ownership background and obtain much support from the local government and many preferential treatments. However, in Australia, the state ownership background of CITIC had not brought any benefits. On the contrary, state-owned enterprises and their subsidiaries could easily be regarded as agents of foreign governments, and therefore viewed as threats to national security.

In May 2010, the Australian government announced that it would impose a 40% Resource Super Profits Tax (RSPT) on mining firms starting from July 2012, in order to pay for the increasingly higher cost of infrastructure investment and pensions. The new tax encouraged more exploration and mergers and acquisitions (M&As) within policy constraints. Sino Iron could gain some competitive advantage over BHP Billiton and Rio Tinto for the resource tax, because the new tax would allow companies to deduct the book value of inventory assets during the first five years of the new tax.

Labor Relations and Contractor Relationship

The Sino Iron project was located in the northwestern corner of Australia, occupying an area of 25 square kilometers. Looking from the airplane, it was an area of flat brown earth with few trees and not many people. The mine was 85 kilometers from the nearest town Karratha (see Exhibit 2). A one-night stay in a motel there was even more expensive than a five-star hotel in Sydney. The only function of the town was to provide a point of transit for the nearby mine workers to go back to Perth.

A prosperous mining industry led to high demand for labor. The result was that a mine worker in Western Australia would typically have an annual salary of over A\$100,000— approximately the pay level of university professors and twice the average income of Australians. A regular excavator driver could make A\$160,000 a

year. Even cleaners could command an annual income of A\$80,000. Depending on the type of work, some workers could rest for a week after working every three weeks—and some every two weeks. The company would pay their airfare if they went back home during vacation. Furthermore, due to the high demand from China and the start-up of many large resource projects, competition for labor increased with many mine workers demanding a pay raise or threatening to switching companies.

Sino Iron and its engineering contractor China Metallugical Group had assumed that they could move a large batch of capable workers from China and rapidly move the project along. However, worker visas became a serious problem. The Australian government required all workers to pass an English certification test, which almost made it impossible for all the workers

---

Exhibit 2   **The Location of Sino Iron Project**

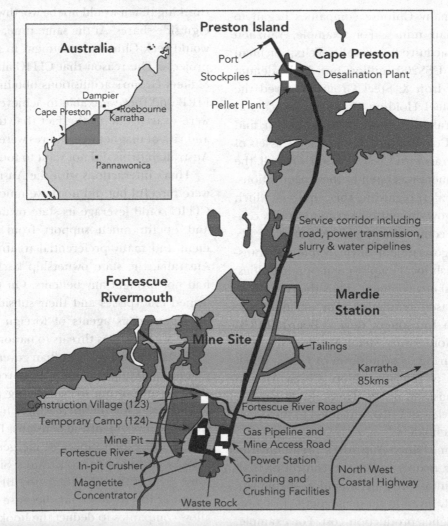

Source: CITIC Pacific Annual Report 2011.

ready to be exported. Despite the lobbying of both the Chinese companies and the Chinese government, only several hundred visas were issued.

"If our workers can score a 7 in IELTS (International English Language Testing System), they would not be coming here," Hua sighed helplessly. Chinese workers were not the only group who could not come to work, the chefs that CITIC found to cater to the Chinese stomach of their executives could not get visas either. "We have found three chefs, but none of them can get a visa." Now the executives could only cook for themselves after work in the apartment that Hua rented.

In order to save labor cost, the project used the world's biggest and most powerful rod mill, the world's largest wheel loader, and the world's largest excavator—with a price tag of US$19 million and a capacity of 1,000 tons each time. This also promoted the development of China's domestic equipment industry. For example, CITIC Pacific's sister company CITIC Heavy Industries developed a large-scale mining rod mill, which increased mining abilities by 40%, reduced resource consumption by 20%, and thus can fully utilize low-grade iron ores.

Community Relations

"Even though this is a developed country, it is the countryside, in many areas it is not even as good as Africa." This was Hua's first impression after arriving in the project site. CITIC Pacific had invested a great deal in infrastructure. Since the project started in August 2006, billions of dollars had already been invested in the mineral processing plant, pellet plant, slurry pipeline, port facilities, power plant, and desalination plant (see Exhibit 3). The Chinese side secretary joked, "Usually you would be more accomplished when you construct things and be able to see the effect, but here it seems that even though you have invested hundreds of thousands of dollars, still not much difference." What was more, these infrastructure investments could not be taken away, so after the end of the 25-year mining period, they would be given to the locals for free.

Sino Iron also established a team to deal with historical remains, and did a series of exploration in the project site (see Exhibit 4). In 2009, it obtained the various permits on land development and utilization. With these permits and proper care of historical remains, Sino Iron was able to enter the whole area in the project site, which enabled the smooth operation of construction work. The historical remains team also abided by the obligations as listed in the Agreement on Utilizing the Aboriginals' Land, and ensured the close relationship between the project and the aboriginals living in the area.

Sino Iron also obtained various environmental permits critical to the progress of the project and its future expansion. In one year, team members monitored the underground water, animals in caves, sea turtles and birds on land, and audited the environment performance of Sino Iron's contractor, in order to make sure the protection of the natural environment.

By March 2010, Hua had obtained all the key government permits and approvals regarding the environment and historical remains, yet also began to worry about the cost increases they would bring. A two-hole bridge, which would cost about 5 million RMB (approximately A$1 million) in China, ended up costing over

---

Exhibit 3 **Magnetite Mining and Process Flowchart**

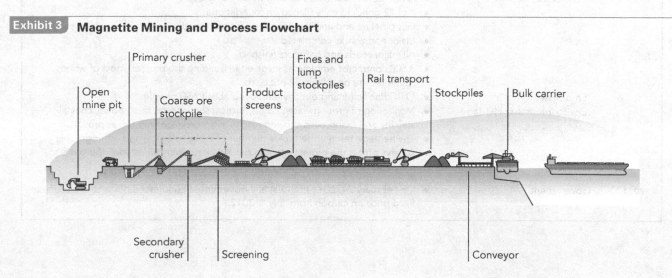

Source: CITIC Pacific Annual Report 2010.

| Exhibit 4 | Project Milestones and Stakeholder Relationships |

	Stakeholder Categories	Milestones
2008	Main Mine Business	• A bulk sample of iron ore was extracted from the mine pit in August, and testing was conducted successfully to refine and optimize the process plant design.
	Government	• Australian Government approval to commence construction in May. • Amendments to the State Agreement Act under which the project operates were passed by the Western Australian Parliament in December. • Indigenous Land Use Agreements were signed with three Native Title claimant groups covering the Cape Preston area.
	Contractors	• 500 contractors on site. • Bulk earthworks for the concentrator and power plant were completed and civil works commenced.
	Employees	• 530 employees in Western Australia. • The business was also certified as a registered training organization.
	Environment and Heritage	• CITIC Pacific Mining's heritage team successfully managed obligations under Australian Native Title and cultural heritage legislation to allow ground disturbance over the project area. • Completed the transfer of approximately 2,500 hectares of land to Western Australia's Conservation Estate.
2009	Main Mine Business	• Over 50 million tons of material removed from the mine pit.
	Government	• Obtained approval under the Western Australian Government's Environmental Protection Act and Iron Ore Processing (Mineralogy Pty Ltd) Agreement Act to build port and expand the project to export 28 mtpa of concentrate product.
	Contractors	• Close to 3,000 contractors on site. • The contractors completed the installation of the gas and steam turbine generators, heat recovery steam generators, and cooling towers. • More than 7.8 million tons of material was removed, much of it used to build the port breakwater.
	Employees	• Directly employed approximately 800 people.
	Environment and Heritage	• The heritage team fulfilled obligations under Indigenous Land Use Agreements (ILUAs) to ensure relationships remain strong with the indigenous people where the project operates.
2010	Main Mine Business	• More than 87 million tons of waste removed from the mine pit. • About 830,000 tons of magnetite stockpiled.
	Government	• Australian Government announced it would introduce a Resource Super Profits Tax (RSPT).
	Contractor	• About 80% of concentrator civil works completed. • 4 of 12 grinding mills placed on foundations. • Gas pipeline and ancillary facilities commissioned. • Major earthworks completed. • All major roads and corridors finished. • 3,500 contractor employees involved in building the project, most of whom reside on site on a fly-in fly-out basis.
	Employees	• CITIC Pacific Mining directly employed about 650 people.
	Environment and Heritage	• Monitoring of ground water, corals, turtles, shore birds, dust, noise, coastal stability and mangroves showed results in accordance with the approvals. • The heritage team undertook a number of archaeological and ethnographic surveys across the project site and gained all relevant Ministerial approvals to clear and develop the land.
2011	Government	• On February 24, 2011 the Australia government announced plans to introduce a fixed price on carbon from July 1, 2012.

Exhibit 5   **Iron Ore Monthly Price in US Dollars per Dry Metric Ton**

Iron Ore Monthly Price – US Dollars per Dry Metric Ton

Source: IndexMundi.

A\$50 million since it used steel pipe pile to protect the ecology. The cost difference was in tens of times. Moreover, there were many other things that drove him crazy. During the EPC department meetings, usually the first two hours would be spent discussing issues not about the project, but about environment protection. For example, if a hole was left in the mining area, would the team need to build a ladder in case animals fall into it and cannot climb up? If they built a two-hole bridge near the dock, would that affect the ecological environment of crabs near the seawall?

All of these certainly increased the various costs on the project, and were unforeseen before the investment. It was clear that during overseas acquisitions and investments, Chinese managers needed to put different priorities on different issues and stakeholders. Things that were easy to deal with in China were often difficult here, and vice versa.

Epilogue

Sino Iron finally began to operate the first production line and ship the iron ore at the end of 2013. However, the cost of the project ballooned to US\$7.8 billion, five times of its initial budget. Only by the end of 2016 would all six production lines open. With iron ore price falling since 2013 (see Exhibit 5), CITIC had to write down up to US\$1.8 billion in 2014 for the loss of this long delayed project.

Case Discussion Questions

1. **If you were Hua Dongyi, Chairman of Sino Iron in Australia, how would you deal with the Australian government given its negative attitude on Chinese investment?**

2. **Compare CITIC's overseas project investments and operations in Africa and Australia. What are the institutional differences? How do these differences affect firm performance?**

3. **What liabilities of foreignness did CITIC encounter in Australia? How could these be overcome?**

4. **Who were the stakeholders in the Sino Iron project? How can the Chinese company best engage them?**

© Lonely/Shutterstock.com

Glossary

A

Absolute advantage. The economic advantage one nation enjoys that is absolutely superior to other nations.

Absorptive capacity. The ability to recognize the value of new information, assimilate it, and apply it.

Accommodative strategy. A strategy characterized by some support from top managers, who may increasingly view CSR as a worthwhile endeavor.

Acquisition. A transfer of the control of operations and management from one firm (target) to another (acquirer), the former becoming a unit of the latter.

Acquisition premium. The difference between the acquisition price and the market value of target firms.

Adaptability. The ability to change supply chain configurations in response to longer-term changes in the environment and technology.

Administrative policy. Bureaucratic rules that make it harder to import foreign goods.

Agency cost. The cost associated with principal-agent relationships.

Agency relationship. The relationship between principals (such as shareholders) and agents (such as professional managers).

Agency theory. A theory that focuses on principal-agent relationships (or in short, agency relationships).

Agent. Individual (such as manager) to whom authority is delegated.

Agglomeration. Clustering of economic activities in certain locations.

Agility. The ability to react quickly to unexpected shifts in supply and demand.

Alignment. Alignment of interests of various players.

Andean Community. A customs union in South America that was launched in 1969.

Antidumping duty. Tariff levied on imports that have been "dumped" (selling below costs to "unfairly" drive domestic firms out of business).

Antidumping law. Law that makes it illegal for an exporter to sell goods below cost abroad with the intent to raise prices after eliminating local rivals.

Antitrust law. Law that makes cartels (trusts) illegal.

Antitrust policy. Government policy designed to combat monopolies and cartels.

Appreciation. An increase in the value of the currency.

Asia-Pacific Economic Cooperation (APEC). The official title for regional economic integration involving 21 member economies around the Pacific.

Association of Southeast Asian Nations (ASEAN). The organization underpinning regional economic integration in Southeast Asia.

Attack. An initial set of actions to gain competitive advantage.

B

Balance of payment (BoP). A country's international transaction statement, which includes merchandise trade, service trade, and capital movement.

Balance of trade. The aggregation of importing and exporting that leads to the country-level trade surplus or deficit.

Balance sheet approach. A compensation approach that balances the cost of living differences relative to parent country levels and adds a financial inducement to make the package attractive.

Bandwagon effect. The effect of investors moving in the same direction at the same time, like a herd.

Bargaining power. Ability to extract favorable outcome from negotiations due to one party's strengths.

Base of the pyramid (BoP). Economies where people make less than $2,000 per capita per year.

Beijing Consensus. A view that questions Washington Consensus' belief in the superiority of private ownership over state ownership in economic policy making, which is often associated with the position held by the Chinese government.

Benchmarking. Examining whether a firm has resources and capabilities to perform a particular activity in a manner superior to competitors.

Bid rate. The price to buy a currency.

Blue ocean strategy. Strategy that focuses on developing new markets ("blue ocean") and avoids attacking core markets defended by rivals, which is likely to result in a bloody price war or a "red ocean."

Bond. Loan issued by the firm and held by creditors.

Bondholder. Buyer of bonds.

Born global firm (international new venture). A start-up company that attempts to do business abroad from inception.

Bounded rationality. The necessity of making rational decisions in the absence of complete information.

Bretton Woods system. A system in which all currencies were pegged at a fixed rate to the US dollar.

BRIC. Brazil, Russia, India, and China.

BRICS. Brazil, Russia, India, China, and South Africa.

Build-operate-transfer (BOT) agreement. A nonequity mode of entry used to build a longer-term presence by building and then operating a facility for a period of time before transferring operations to a domestic agency or firm.

Business process outsourcing (BPO). Outsourcing business processes to third-party providers.

C

Capability. The tangible and intangible assets a firm uses to choose and implement its strategies.

Capacity to punish. Sufficient resources possessed by a price leader to deter and combat defection.

Capital flight. A phenomenon in which a large number of individuals and companies exchange domestic currency for a foreign currency.

Captive sourcing. Setting up subsidiaries abroad so that the work done is in-house but the location is foreign. Also known as foreign direct investment (FDI).

Cartel (trust). An output-fixing and price-fixing entity involving multiple competitors.

Causal ambiguity. The difficulty of identifying the actual cause of a firm's successful performance.

Center of excellence. An MNE subsidiary explicitly recognized as a source of important capabilities, with the intention that these capabilities be leveraged by, and/or disseminated to, other subsidiaries.

CEO duality. The CEO doubles as a chairman of the board.

Chief executive officer (CEO). The main executive manager in charge of the firm

Civil law. A legal tradition that uses comprehensive statutes and codes as a primary means to form legal judgments.

Civilization. The highest cultural grouping of people and the broadest level of cultural identity people have.

Classical trade theories. The major theories of international trade that were advanced before the 20th century, which consist of (1) mercantilism, (2) absolute advantage, and (3) comparative advantage.

Clean (free) float. A pure market solution to determine exchange rates.

Cluster. Countries that share similar cultures.

Code of conduct. A set of guidelines for making ethical decisions.

Cognitive pillar. The internalized (or taken-for-granted) values and beliefs that guide individual and firm behavior.

Collectivism. The idea that an individual's identity is fundamentally tied to the identity of his or her collective group.

Collusion. Collective attempts between competing firms to reduce competition.

Collusive price setting. Price setting by monopolists or collusion parties at a level higher than the competitive level.

Co-marketing. Efforts among a number of firms to jointly market their products and services.

Command economy. An economy that is characterized by government ownership and control of factors of production.

Commoditization. A process of market competition through which unique products that command high prices and high margins gradually lose their ability to do so, thus becoming commodities.

Common denominator. A currency or commodity to which the value of all currencies are pegged.

Common law. A legal tradition that is shaped by precedents and traditions from previous judicial decisions.

Common market. Combining everything a customs union has, a common market, in addition, permits the free movement of goods and people.

Comparative advantage. Relative (not absolute) advantage in one economic activity that one nation enjoys in comparison with other nations.

Compensation. The determination of salary and benefits.

Competition policy. Government policy governing the rules of the game in competition.

Competitive dynamics. Actions and responses undertaken by competing firms.

Competitor analysis. The process of anticipating rivals' actions in order to both revise a firm's plan and prepare to deal with rivals' response.

Complementary asset. The combination of numerous resources and assets that enable a firm to gain a competitive advantage.

Concentrated ownership and control. Founders start up firms and completely own and control them on an individual or family basis.

Concentration ratio. The percentage of total industry sales accounted for by the top four, eight, or twenty firms.

Contagion (imitation) effect. The reaction of local firms to rise to the challenge demonstrated by MNEs through learning and imitation.

Contender strategy. Strategy that centers on a firm engaging in rapid learning and then expand overseas.

Context. The underlying background upon which social interaction takes place.

Contractual (non-equity-based) alliance. Association between firms that is based on contracts and does not involve the sharing of ownership.

Copyright. Exclusive legal right of authors and publishers to publish and disseminate their work.

Corporate governance. The relationship among various participants in determining the direction and performance of corporations.

Corporate social responsibility (CSR). Consideration of, and response to, issues beyond the narrow economic, technical, and legal requirements of the firm to accomplish social benefits along with the traditional economic gains which the firm seeks.

Corruption. The abuse of public power for private benefits, usually in the form of bribery.

Cost of capital. The rate of return that a firm needs to pay to capital providers.

Counterattack. A set of actions in response to attack.

Country-of-origin effect. The positive or negative perception of firms and products from a certain country.

Country (regional) manager. Manager of a geographic area, either a country or a region.

Cross-listing. Listing shares on a foreign stock exchange.

Cross-market retaliation. Retaliatory attacks on a competitor's other markets if this competitor attacks a firm's original market.

Cross-shareholding. Both firms investing in each other to become cross-shareholders.

Cultural distance. The difference between two cultures along identifiable dimensions such as individualism.

Cultural intelligence. An individual's ability to understand and adjust to new cultures.

Culture. The collective programming of the mind that distinguishes the members of one group or category of people from another.

Currency board. A monetary authority that issues notes and coins convertible into a key foreign currency at a fixed exchange rate.

Currency hedging. A transaction that protects traders and investors from exposure to the fluctuations of the spot rate.

Currency risk. The potential for loss associated with fluctuations in the foreign exchange market.

Currency swap. A foreign exchange transaction between two firms in which one currency is converted into another at Time 1, with an agreement to revert it to the original currency at a specified Time 2 in the future.

Customs union. One step beyond a free trade area (FTA), a customs union imposes common external policies on nonparticipating countries.

D

Deadweight cost. Net losses that occur in an economy as a result of tariffs.

Debt. A loan that the firm needs to pay back at a given time with an interest.

Default. A firm's failure to satisfy the terms of a loan obligation.

Defender strategy. Strategy that centers on local assets in areas in which MNEs are weak.

Defensive strategy. Strategy that focuses on regulatory compliance but with little actual commitment to CSR by top management.

Democracy. A political system in which citizens elect representatives to govern the country on their behalf.

Demonstration effect. The reaction of local firms to rise to the challenge demonstrated by MNEs through learning and imitation.

Depreciation. A loss in the value of the currency.

Development. Long-term, broader preparation to improve managerial skills for a better career.

"Diamond" theory. A theory that suggests that the competitive advantage of certain industries in different nations depends on four aspects that form a "diamond."

Dictatorship (totalitarianism). A political system in which one person or party exercises absolute political control over the population.

Diffused ownership. Publicly traded corporations owned by numerous small shareholders but none with a dominant level of control.

Direct export. The sale of products made by firms in their home country to customers in other countries.

Dirty (managed) float. Using selective government intervention to determine exchange rates.

Dissemination risk. The risk associated with unauthorized diffusion of firm-specific know-how.

Distribution channel. The set of firms that facilitates the movement of goods from producers to consumers.

Dodger strategy. Strategy that centers on cooperating through joint ventures with MNEs and sell-offs to MNEs.

Doha Round. A round of WTO negotiations to reduce agricultural subsidies, slash tariffs, and strengthen intellectual property protection that started in Doha, Qatar, in 2001. Officially known as the "Doha Development Agenda," it was suspended in 2006 due to disagreements.

Downstream vertical FDI. A type of vertical FDI in which a firm engages in a downstream stage of the value chain in a host country.

Due diligence. Investigation prior to signing contracts.

Dumping. An exporter selling goods below cost.

E

Economic system. Rules of the game on how a country is governed economically.

Economic union. Having all the features of a common market, members also coordinate and harmonize economic policies (in areas such as monetary, fiscal, and taxation) to blend their economies into a single economic entity.

Emerging economies. A term that has gradually replaced the term "developing countries" since the 1990s.

Emerging market. A term that is often used interchangeably with "emerging economies."

Entrepreneur. A founder and/or owner of new businesses or managers of existing firms who identifies and exploits new opportunities.

Entrepreneurship. The identification and exploitation of previously unexplored opportunities.

Equity. The stock in a firm (usually expressed in shares), which represents the owners' rights.

Equity-based alliance. Alliance based on ownership or financial interest between the firms.

Equity mode. Mode of entry (JV and WOS) that indicates a relatively larger, harder-to-reverse commitment.

Ethical imperialism. A perspective that suggests that "there is one set of Ethics (with a capital E) and we have it."

Ethical relativism. A perspective that suggests that all ethical standards are relative.

Ethics. The principles, standards, and norms of conduct that govern individual and firm behavior.

Ethnocentric approach. An emphasis on the norms and practices of the parent company (and the parent country of the MNE) by relying on PCNs.

Ethnocentrism. A self-centered mentality by a group of people who perceive their own culture, ethics, and norms as natural, rational, and morally right.

Euro. The currency currently used in 18 EU countries.

Euro zone. The 18 EU countries that currently use the euro as the official currency.

European Union (EU). The official title of European economic integration since 1993.

Exit-based mechanism. Corporate governance mechanism that focuses on exit, indicating that shareholders no longer have patience and are willing to "exit" by selling their shares.

Expatriate manager (expat). A manager who works abroad, or "expat" for short.

Expatriation. The process of selecting, managing, and motivating expatriates to work abroad.

Explicit collusion. Firms directly negotiate output and pricing and divide markets.

Explicit knowledge. Knowledge that is codifiable (can be written down and transferred with little loss of richness).

Export. Selling abroad.

Export intermediary. A firm that performs an important middleman function by linking domestic sellers and foreign buyers that otherwise would not have been connected.

Expropriation. (1) Government's confiscation of foreign assets; (2) Activities that enrich controlling shareholders at the expense of minority shareholders.

Extender strategy. Strategy that centers on leveraging home-grown competencies abroad.

F

Factor endowment. The extent to which different countries possess various factors of production such as labor, land, and technology.

Factor endowment theory (Heckscher-Ohlin theory). A theory that suggests that nations will develop comparative advantages based on their locally abundant factors.

FDI flow. The amount of FDI moving in a given period (usually a year) in a certain direction.

FDI inflow. Inbound FDI moving into a country in a year.

FDI outflow. Outbound FDI moving out of a country in a year.

FDI stock. Total accumulation of inbound FDI in a country or outbound FDI from a country during a given period (usually several years).

Femininity. A relatively weak form of societal-level sex role differentiation whereby more women occupy positions that reward assertiveness and more men work in caring professions.

Financing. How a firm's money, banking, investments, and credit are managed.

First-mover advantage. Benefits that accrue to firms that enter the market first and that late entrants do not enjoy.

Fixed exchange rate policy. A government policy to set the exchange rate of a currency relative to other currencies.

Floating (flexible) exchange rate policy. A government policy to let supply-and-demand conditions determine exchange rates.

Foreign Corrupt Practices Act (FCPA). A US law enacted in 1977 that bans bribery of foreign officials.

Foreign direct investment (FDI). Investing in, controlling, and managing value-added activities in other countries.

Foreign exchange market. The market where individuals, firms, governments, and banks buy and sell foreign currencies.

Foreign exchange rate. The price of one currency in terms of another.

Foreign portfolio investment (FPI). Investment in a portfolio of foreign securities such as stocks and bonds.

Formal institution. Institution represented by laws, regulations, and rules.

Forward discount. A condition under which the forward rate of one currency relative to another currency is higher than the spot rate.

Forward premium. A condition under which the forward rate of one currency relative to another currency is lower than the spot rate.

Forward transaction. Foreign exchange transaction in which participants buy and sell currencies now for future delivery.

Franchising. Firm A's agreement to give Firm B the rights to use A's proprietary assets for a royalty fee paid to A by B. This is typically done in service industries.

Free market view. A political view that suggests that FDI unrestricted by government intervention is the best.

Free trade. The idea that free market forces should determine how much to trade with little or no government intervention.

Free trade area (FTA). A group of countries that remove trade barriers among themselves.

G

Game theory. A theory that studies the interactions between two parties that compete and/or cooperate with each other.

General Agreement on Tariffs and Trade (GATT). A multilateral agreement governing the international trade of goods (merchandise).

General Agreement on Trade in Services (GATS). A WTO agreement governing the international trade of services.

Geocentric approach. A focus on finding the most suitable managers, who can be PCNs, HCNs, or TCNs.

Geographic area structure. An organizational structure that organizes the MNE according to different geographic areas (countries and regions).

Global account structure. A customer-focused dimension that supplies customers (often other MNEs) in a coordinated and consistent way across various countries.

Global business. Business around the globe.

Global economic integration. Efforts to reduce trade and investment barriers around the globe.

Global matrix. An organizational structure often used to alleviate the disadvantages associated with both geographic area and global product division structures, especially for MNEs adopting a transnational strategy.

Global product division structure. An organizational structure that assigns global responsibilities to each product division.

Global standardization strategy. A strategy that focuses on development and distribution of standardized products worldwide in order to reap the maximum benefits from low-cost advantages.

Global sustainability. The ability to meet the needs of the present without compromising the ability of future generations to meet their needs around the world.

Global virtual team. Team whose members are physically dispersed in multiple locations in the world and often operate on a virtual basis.

Globalization. The close integration of countries and peoples of the world.

Going rate approach. A compensation approach that pays expatriates the prevailing (going) rate for comparable positions in a host country.

Gold standard. A system in which the value of most major currencies was maintained by fixing their prices in terms of gold.

Great Transformation. Transformation of the global economy embodied embodied by the tremendous shift in economic weight and engines of growth toward emerging economies in general and BRIC(S) in particular.

Greenfield operation. Building factories and offices from scratch (on a proverbial piece of "green field" formerly used for agricultural purposes).

Gross domestic product (GDP). The sum of value added by resident firms, households, and governments operating in an economy.

Gross national income (GNI). GDP plus income from non-resident sources abroad. GNI is the term used by the World Bank and other international organizations to supersede the term GNP.

Gross national product (GNP). GDP plus income from non-resident sources abroad.

Group of 20 (G-20). The group of 19 major countries plus the European Union (EU) whose leaders meet on a biannual basis to solve global economic problems.

H

High-context culture. Culture (such as that in Arab and Asian countries) where communication relies a lot on the underlying unspoken context, which is as important as the words used.

Home replication strategy. A strategy that emphasizes the duplication of home country-based competencies in foreign countries.

Horizontal FDI. A type of FDI in which a firm duplicates its home country-based activities at the same value chain stage in a host country.

Host-country national (HCN). Individual from the host country who works for an MNE.

Hubris. Overconfidence in one's capabilities.

Human resource management (HRM). Activities that attract, select, and manage employees.

I

Import. Buying from abroad.

Import quota. Restrictions on the quantity of imports.

Import tariff. A tax imposed on imports.

Indirect export. A way to reach overseas customers by exporting through domestic-based export intermediaries.

Individualism. The idea that an individual's identity is fundamentally his or her own.

Infant industry argument. The argument that if domestic firms are as young as "infants," in the absence of government intervention, they stand no chances of surviving and will be crushed by mature foreign rivals.

Informal institution. Institution represented by cultures, ethics, and norms.

Information asymmetry. Asymmetric distribution and possession of information between two sides.

In-group. Individuals and firms regarded as a part of "us."

Initiator. The party who begins the process of ending the alliance.

Inpatriation. Relocating employees of a foreign subsidiary to the MNE's headquarters for the purposes of filling skill shortages at headquarters and developing a global mindset for such inpatriates.

Inside director. Member of the board who is a top executive of the firm.

Institution-based view. A leading perspective in global business that suggests that the success and failure of firms are enabled and constrained by institutions.

Institutional distance. The extent of similarity or dissimilarity between the regulatory, normative, and cognitive institutions of two countries.

Institutional framework. Formal and informal institutions that govern individual and firm behavior.

Institutional transition. Fundamental and comprehensive changes introduced to the formal and informal rules of the game that affect firms as players.

Institution. Formal and informal rules of the game.

Intangible resource and capability. Assets that are hard to observe and difficult (if not impossible) to quantify.

Integration-responsiveness framework. A framework of MNE management on how to simultaneously deal with the pressures for both global integration and local responsiveness.

Intellectual property (IP). Intangible property that is the result of intellectual activity.

Intellectual property right (IPR). Right associated with the ownership of intellectual property.

Internalization. The replacement of cross-border markets (such as exporting and importing) with one firm (the MNE) locating and operating in two or more countries.

International business (IB). (1) A business (or firm) that engages in international (cross-border) economic activities and/or (2) the action of doing business abroad.

International division. An organizational structure that is typically set up when firms initially expand abroad, often engaging in a home replication strategy.

International entrepreneurship. A combination of innovative, proactive, and risk-seeking behavior that crosses national borders and is intended to create wealth in organizations.

International Monetary Fund (IMF). An international organization that was established to promote international monetary cooperation, exchange stability, and orderly exchange arrangements.

International new venture. Start-up company that attempts to do business abroad from inception.

International premium. A significant pay raise when working overseas.

Intrafirm trade. International transactions between two subsidiaries in two countries controlled by the same MNE.

J

Joint venture (JV). A new corporate entity created and jointly owned by two or more parent companies.

K

Knowledge management. The structures, processes, and systems that actively develop, leverage, and transfer knowledge.

Knowledge spillover. Knowledge diffused from one firm to others among closely located firms.

L

Labor relation. A firm's relation with organized labor (unions) in both home and host countries.

Late-mover advantage. Benefits that accrue to firms that enter the market later and that early entrants do not enjoy.

Learning by doing. A way of learning, not by reading books but by engaging in hands-on activities.

Learning race. Alliance partners aim to outrun each other by learning the "tricks" from the other side as fast as possible.

Legal system. The rules of the game on how a country's laws are enacted and enforced.

Letter of credit (L/C). A financial contract that states that the importer's bank will pay a specific sum of money to the exporter upon delivery of the merchandise.

Leveraged buyout (LBO). Means by which investors, often in partnership with incumbent managers, issue bonds and use the cash raised to buy the firm's stock.

Liability of foreignness. The inherent disadvantage that foreign firms experience in host countries because of their non-native status.

Licensing. Firm A's agreement to give Firm B the rights to use A's proprietary technology (such as a patent) or trademark (such as a corporate logo) for a royalty fee paid to A by B. This is typically done in manufacturing industries.

Lingua franca. A global business language.

LLL advantages. A firm's quest of linkage (L) advantages, leverage (L) advantages, and learning (L) advantages. These advantages are typically associated with multinationals from emerging economies.

Local content requirement. Requirement stipulating that a certain proportion of the value of the goods made in one country must originate from that country.

Local responsiveness. The necessity to be responsive to different customer preferences around the world.

Localization (multidomestic) strategy. A strategy that focuses on a number of foreign countries/regions, each of which is regarded as a stand-alone local (domestic) market worthy of significant attention and adaptation.

Location. Advantages enjoyed by firms operating in a certain location.

Location-specific advantage. The benefits a firm reaps from the features specific to a place.

Long-term orientation. Dimension of how much emphasis is placed on perseverance and savings for future betterment.

Low-context culture. Culture (such as that in North American and Western European countries) where communication is usually taken at face value without much reliance on unspoken context. In other words, "no" means "no."

M

Make-or-buy decision. Decision about whether to produce inhouse ("make") or to outsource ("buy").

Management control right. The right to appoint key managers and establish control mechanisms.

Managerial human capital. The skills and abilities acquired by top managers.

Managerial motive. Managers' desire for power, prestige, and money, which may lead to decisions that do not benefit the firm overall in the long run.

Market commonality. The overlap between two rivals' markets.

Market economy. An economy that is characterized by the "invisible hand" of market forces

Market imperfection (market failure). The imperfect rules governing international transactions.

Market orientation. A philosophy or way of thinking that places the highest priority on the creation of superior customer value in the marketplace

Market segmentation. Identifying segments of consumers who differ from others in purchasing behavior.

Marketing. Efforts to create, develop, and defend markets that satisfy the needs and wants of individual and business customers.

Marketing mix. The four underlying components of marketing: (1) product, (2) price, (3) promotion, and (4) place.

Masculinity. A relatively strong form of societal-level sex role differentiation whereby men tend to have occupations that reward assertiveness and women tend to work in caring professions.

Merchandise (goods). Tangible products being traded.

Mercosur. A customs union in South America that was launched in 1991.

Merger. The combination of operations and management of two firms to establish a new legal entity.

Microfinance. A practice to provide micro loans ($50–$300) used to start small businesses with the intention of ultimately lifting the entrepreneurs out of poverty.

Micro-macro link. The micro, informal interpersonal relationships among managers of various units may greatly facilitate macro, intersubsidiary cooperation among these units.

Mixed economy. An economy that has elements of both a market economy and a command economy.

Modern trade theory. The major theory of international trade that was advanced in the 20th century, which consist of (1) product life cycle, (2) strategic trade, and (3) national competitive advantage of industries.

Mode of entry. Method used to enter a foreign market.

Monetary union. A group of countries that use a common currency.

Moral hazard. Recklessness when people and organizations (including firms and governments) do not have to face the full consequences of their actions.

Multilateral trading system. The global system that governs international trade among countries—otherwise known as the GATT/WTO system.

Multimarket competition. Firms engage the same rivals in multiple markets.

Multinational enterprise (MNE). A firm that engages in foreign direct investment (FDI).

Mutual forbearance. Multimarket firms respect their rivals' spheres of influence in certain markets and their rivals reciprocate, leading to tacit collusion.

N

Nondiscrimination. A principle that a country cannot discriminate among its trading partners.

Nonequity mode. A mode of entry (exports and contractual agreements) that tends to reflect relatively smaller commitments to overseas markets.

Nongovernmental organization (NGO). An organization that is not affiliated with governments.

Nontariff barrier (NTB). Trade barrier that relies on nontariff means to discourage imports.

Normative pillar. The mechanism through which norms influence individual and firm behavior.

Norm. Values, beliefs, and actions of relevant players that influence the focal individuals and firms.

North American Free Trade Agreement (NAFTA). A free trade agreement among Canada, Mexico, and the United States.

O

Obsolescing bargain. The deal struck by MNEs and host governments, which change their requirements after the initial FDI entry.

Offer rate. The price to sell a currency.

Offshoring. Outsourcing to an international or foreign firm.

OLI advantages. A firm's quest for ownership (O) advantages, location (L) advantages, and internalization (I) advantages via FDI.

Oligopoly. Industry dominated by a small number of players.

Onshoring. Outsourcing to a domestic firm.

Open innovation. The use of purposive inflows and outflows of knowledge to accelerate internal innovation and expand the markets for external use of innovation.

Opportunism. The act of seeking self-interest with guile.

Opportunity cost. Cost of pursuing one activity at the expense of another activity, given the alternatives (other opportunities).

Organizational culture. The collective programming of the mind that distinguishes the members of one organization from another.

Organizational fit. The similarity in cultures, systems, and structures.

Original brand manufacturer (OBM). Firm that designs, manufactures, and markets branded products.

Original design manufacturer (ODM). Firm that both designs and manufactures products.

Original equipment manufacturer (OEM). Firm that executes design blueprints provided by other firms and manufactures such products.

Out-group. Individuals and firms not regarded as a part of "us."

Outside (independent) director. Nonmanagement member of the board.

Outsourcing. Turning over an activity to an outside supplier that will perform it on behalf of the focal firm.

Ownership. An MNE's possession and leveraging of certain valuable, rare, hard-to-imitate, and organizationally embedded (VRIO) assets overseas in the context of FDI.

P

Parent-country national (PCN). Individual who comes from the parent country of the MNE and works at its local subsidiary.

Patent. Exclusive legal rights of inventors of new products or processes to derive income from such inventions.

Peg. A stabilizing policy of linking a developing contry's currency to a key currency.

Performance appraisal. The evaluation of employee performance for promotion, retention, or termination purposes.

Place. The location where products and services are provided.

Political risk. Risk associated with political changes that may negatively impact domestic and foreign firms.

Political system. The rules of the game on how a country is governed politically.

Political union. The integration of political and economic affairs of a region.

Polycentric approach. An emphasis on the norms and practices of the host country.

Post-Bretton Woods system. A system of flexible exchange rate regimes with no official common denominator.

Power distance. The extent to which less powerful members within a country expect and accept that power is distributed unequally.

Pragmatic nationalism. A political view that only approves FDI when its benefits outweigh its costs.

Predatory pricing. An attempt to monopolize a market by setting prices below cost and intending to raise prices to cover losses in the long run after eliminating rivals.

Price. The expenditures that customers are willing to pay for a product.

Price elasticity. How demand changes when price changes.

Price leader. A firm that has a dominant market share and sets "acceptable" prices and margins in the industry.

Primary stakeholder group. Constituent on which the firm relies for its continuous survival and prosperity.

Principal. Individual (such as owner) delegating authority.

Principal–agent conflict. Conflict between principals and agents.

Principal–principal conflict. Conflict between two classes of principals: controlling shareholders and minority shareholders.

Prisoners' dilemma. In game theory, a type of game in which the outcome depends on two parties deciding whether to cooperate or to defect.

Private equity. Equity capital invested in private companies that, by definition, are not publicly traded.

Proactive strategy. A strategy that endeavors to do more than is required in CSR.

Product. Offering that customers purchase.

Product life cycle theory. A theory that accounts for changes in the patterns of trade over time by focusing on product life cycles.

Promotion. Communicatons that marketers insert into the marketplace.

Property right. The legal right to use an economic property (resource) and to derive income and benefits from it.

Protectionism. The idea that governments should actively protect domestic industries from imports and vigorously promote exports.

Psychological contract. An informal understanding of expected delivery of benefits in the future for current services.

Purchasing power parity (PPP). A conversion that determines the equivalent amount of goods and services that different currencies can purchase.

Q

Quota. The weight a member country carries within the IMF, which determines the amount of its financial contribution (technically known as its "subscription"), its capacity to borrow from the IMF, and its voting power.

R

Radical view. A political view that is hostile to FDI.

Reactive strategy. A strategy that would only respond to CSR causes when required by disasters and outcries.

Real option. An investment in real operations as opposed to financial capital.

Regional economic integration. Efforts to reduce trade and investment barriers within one region.

Regulatory pillar. The coercive power of governments.

Related transaction. Controlling shareholders sell firm assets to another firm they own at below-market prices or spin off the most profitable part of a public firm and merge it with another private firm they own.

Relational (collaborative) capability. Ability to manage interfirm relationships.

Relationship orientation. A focus to establish, maintain, and enhance relationships with customers.

Repatriate. Returning expatriate.

Repatriation. The process of facilitating the return of expatriates.

Research and development (R&D) contract. Outsourcing agreement in R&D between firms.

Reshoring. Moving formerly offshored activities back to the home country of the focal firm.

Resource. The tangible and intangible assets a firm uses to choose and implement its strategies.

Resource mobility. Assumption that a resource used in producing a product for one industry can be shifted and put to use in another industry.

Resource similarity. The extent to which a given competitor possesses strategic endowment comparable, in terms of both type and amount, to those of the focal firm.

Reverse innovation. An innovation that is adopted first in emerging economies and is then diffused around the world.

Risk management. The identification and assessment of risks and the preparation to minimize the impact of high-risk, unfortunate events.

S

Scale of entry. The amount of resources committed to entering a foreign market.

Scenario planning. A technique to prepare and plan for multiple scenarios (either high- or low-risk).

Schengen. A passport-free travel zone within the EU.

Secondary stakeholder group. Those who influence or affect, or are influenced or affected by, the firm but are not engaged in transactions with the firm and are not essential for its survival.

Semiglobalization. A perspective that suggests that barriers to market integration at borders are high, but not high enough to insulate countries from each other completely.

Separation of ownership and control. The dispersal of ownership among many small shareholders, in which control is largely concentrated in the hands of salaried, professional managers who own little (or no) equity.

Serial entrepreneur. An entrepreneur who starts, grows, and sells several businesses throughout a career.

Service. Intangible offering being traded.

Shareholder. Firm owner.

Shareholder capitalism. A view of capitalism that suggests that the most fundamental purpose for firms to exist is to serve the economic interests of shareholders (also known as capitalists).

Small and medium-sized enterprise (SME). A firm with fewer than 500 employees in the United States and with fewer than 250 employees in the European Union.

Social capital. The informal benefits individuals and organizations derive from their social structures and networks.

Social complexity. The socially intricate and interdependent ways firms are typically organized.

Social issue participation. Firms' participation in social causes not directly related to the management of primary stakeholders.

Social mobility. The degree to which members from a lower social category can rise to a higher status.

Social stratification. The hierarchical arrangement of individuals into social categories (strata) such as classes, castes, and divisions within a society.

Social structure. The way a society broadly organizes its members.

Solutions-based structure. A customer-focused solution in which a provider sells whatever combination of goods and services the customers prefer, including rivals' offerings.

Sovereign wealth fund (SWF). A state-owned investment fund composed of financial assets such as stocks, bonds, real estate, or other financial instruments funded by foreign exchange assets.

Spot transaction. The classic single-shot exchange of one currency for another.

Spread. The difference between the offer rate and the bid rate.

Staffing. HRM activities associated with hiring employees and filling positions.

Stage model. A model of internationalization that portrays the slow step-by-step (stage-by-stage) process an SME must go through to internationalize its business.

Stakeholder. Any group or individual who can affect or is affected by the achievement of the organization's objectives.

State-owned enterprise (SOE). A firm owned and controlled by the state (government).

Stewardship theory. A "pro-management" theory that suggests that most managers can be viewed as owners' stewards interested in safeguarding shareholders' interests.

Strategic alliance. A voluntary agreement of cooperation between firms.

Strategic fit. The effective matching of complementary strategic capabilities.

Strategic hedging. Spreading out activities in a number of countries in different currency zones to offset any currency losses in one region through gains in other regions.

Strategic investment. One firm investing in another as a strategic investor.

Strategic trade policy. Government policy that provides companies a strategic advantage in international trade through subsidies and other supports.

Strategic trade theory. A theory that suggests that strategic intervention by governments in certain industries can enhance their odds for international success.

Subsidiary initiative. The proactive and deliberate pursuit of new opportunities by a subsidiary.

Subsidy. Government payments to domestic firms.

Sunk cost. Cost that a firm has to endure even when its investment turns out to be unsatisfactory.

Supply chain. Flow of products, services, finances, and information that passes through a set of entities from a source to the customer.

Supply chain management. Activities to plan, organize, lead, and control the supply chain.

SWOT analysis. A tool for determining a firm's strengths (S), weaknesses (W), opportunities (O), and threats (T).

T

Tacit collusion. Firms indirectly coordinate actions by signaling their intention to reduce output and maintain pricing above competitive levels.

Tacit knowledge. Knowledge that is noncodifiable, whose acquisition and transfer require hands-on practice.

Tangible resource and capability. Assets that are observable and easily quantified.

Target exchange rate (crawling band). Specified upper or lower bounds within which an exchange rate is allowed to fluctuate.

Tariff barrier. Trade barrier that relies on tariffs to discourage imports.

Technology spillover. Technology diffused from foreign firms to domestic firms.

Theocratic law. A legal system based on religious teachings.

Theory of absolute advantage. A theory that suggests that under free trade, a nation gains by specializing in economic activities in which it has an absolute advantage.

Theory of comparative advantage. A theory that focuses on the relative (not absolute) advantage in one economic activity that one nation enjoys in comparison with other nations.

Theory of mercantilism. A theory that suggests that the wealth of the world is fixed and that a nation that exports more and imports less will be richer.

Theory of national competitive advantage of industries. A theory that suggests that the competitive advantage of certain industries in different nations depends on four aspects that form a "diamond."

Third-country national (TCN). Individual who is from neither the parent country nor the host country of the MNE.

Third-party logistics (3PL) provider. A neutral, third-party intermediary in the supply chain that provides logistics and other support services.

Top management team (TMT). The team consisting of the highest level of executives of a firm led by the CEO.

Total cost of ownership. Total cost needed to own a product, consisting of initial purchase cost and follow-up maintenance/service cost.

Totalitarianism (dictatorship). A political system in which one person or party exercises absolute political control over the population.

Trade deficit. An economic condition in which a nation imports more than it exports.

Trade embargo. Politically motivated trade sanctions against foreign countries to signal displeasure.

Trade-Related Aspects of Intellectual Property Rights (TRIPS). A WTO agreement governing intellectual property rights.

Trade surplus. An economic condition in which a nation exports more than it imports.

Trademark. Exclusive legal rights of firms to use specific names, brands, and designs to differentiate their products from others.

Training. Specific preparation to do a particular job.

Transaction cost. The cost associated with economic transactions or, more broadly, the cost of doing business.

Transition economies. A subset of "emerging economies," particularly those moving from central planning to market competition (such as China, Poland, Russia, and Vietnam).

Transnational strategy. A strategy that endeavors to be simultaneously cost efficient, locally responsive, and learning-driven around the world.

Trans-Pacific Partnership (TPP). A multilateral free trade agreement being negotiated by 12 Asia Pacific countries.

Triad. North America, Western Europe, and Japan.

Triple bottom line. Economic, social, and environmental performance that simultaneously satisfies the demands of all stakeholder groups.

Trust (cartel). An output-fixing and price-fixing entity involving multiple competitors.

Tunneling. A form of corporate theft that diverts resources from the firm for personal or family use.

Turnkey project. Project in which clients pay contractors to design and construct new facilities and train personnel.

U

Uncertainty avoidance. The extent to which members in a culture accept or avoid ambiguous situations and uncertainty.

Union of South American States (USAN/UNASUR). A regional integration mechanism integrating two existing customs unions (Andean Community and Mercosur) in South America.

United States-Dominican Republic-Central America Free Trade Agreement (CAFTA). A free trade agreement between the United States and five Central American countries and the Dominican Republic.

Upstream vertical FDI. A type of vertical FDI in which a firm engages in an upstream stage of the value chain in a host country.

V

Value chain. A series of activities used in the production of goods and services that make a product or service more valuable.

Venture capitalist (VC). An investor who provides risk capital for early stage ventures.

Vertical FDI. A type of FDI in which a firm moves upstream or downstream at different value chain stages in a host country.

Voice-based mechanism. Corporate governance mechanism that focuses on shareholders' willingness to work with managers, usually through the board, by "voicing" their concerns.

Voluntary export restraint (VER). International agreements that show that exporting countries voluntarily agree to restrict their exports.

VRIO framework. The resource-based framework that focuses on the value (V), rarity (R), imitability (I), and organizational (O) aspects of resources and capabilities.

W

Washington Consensus. A view centered on the unquestioned belief in the superiority of private ownership over state ownership in economic policy making, which is often spearheaded by the U.S. government and two Washington-based international organizations: the International Monetary Fund and the World Bank.

Wholly owned subsidiary (WOS). A subsidiary located in a foreign country that is entirely owned by the parent multinational.

World Trade Organization (WTO). The official title of the multilateral trading system and the organization underpinning this system since 2005.

Worldwide (global) mandate. A charter to be responsible for one MNE function throughout the world.

© Lonely/Shutterstock.com

Name Index

Organization Index

Subject Index

ISBN-13: 978-1-305-64246-1
ISBN-10: 1-305-64246-5

90000

9 781305 642461